The Official Visitor's Guide of the National Park Foundation

Comprehensive Information on all 375 of America's National Park areas

The Complete Guide to

America's National Parks

1988–1989 Edition

Distributed by:
Prentice Hall
1 Gulf + Western Plaza
New York, New York 10023

Acknowledgements

DEAR VISITOR:

I hope the National Park Foundation's *Complete Guide To America's National Parks* will be a useful companion on many visits to the areas of the National Park System— the world's first and most envied park system. You can imagine the task of obtaining and verifying the quantity of information needed for the *Guide* from the more than 370 National Park areas. This would not have been possible without the unstinting cooperation of the superintendents and staffs of each area, and Elizabeth Nealon, Roma Slobodian, and Robert Pierce of the National Park Foundation staff who compiled, proofread, reviewed and edited this 5th Edition of the *Guide*. The excellent text design and typesetting was provided by Dovecote Studio of Warrenton, Virginia. The weather information which is a new feature of the *Guide* was compiled by Climadate Corporation of Philadelphia, Pennsylvania.

Our National Park System, with its diversity, beauty, and breadth of visitor activities has become an integral part of our way of life. It has evolved through the hard work, the vision, the tenacity and the generosity of the people of the United States. It is unique and embodies the commitment that we as a nation have made to preserve the best of our natural, scenic, recreational and historic heritage for the use and enjoyment of all.

For our National Parks to flourish, our commitment to them must be on-going. The National Park Foundation was chartered by the United States Congress in 1967 as a non-profit organization to provide a means for all people to directly support the improvement and enhancement of the National Parks. If you would like to contribute for the benefit of the National Parks, please write to me at the National Park Foundation, Department CG, P.O. Box 57473, Washington, D.C. 20037.

Have safe and enjoyable visits to your National parks—they belong to you!

John L. Bryant, Jr.
President
National Park Foundation

Library of Congress Catalog Card No. 87-063170

ISBN: 0-13-159815-5

©Copyright 1988 National Park Foundation. Printed in the United States of America.

Introduction

USING THE GUIDE

The 1988-1989 Fifth Edition of *The Complete Guide To America's National Parks* has been made as accurate as possible. The entry for each park has been prepared by the park's superintendent and staff, resubmitted to each park for review, and checked again for accuracy by the staff of the National Park Foundation. **Although every effort has been made to provide accurate and authoritative information in the 5th Edition of the *Guide*, the National Park Foundation can assume no responsibility for any inconvenience, delay or damage which may arise from any inaccuracy or omission. You should verify the accuracy and completeness of important details before beginning a trip. While information on accommodations, campgrounds and other facilities has been included for the convenience of our readers, no attempt has been made to evaluate these facilities, and no endorsement of any of them should be inferred from their inclusion.**

You will find information in the *Guide* on more than 370 areas of the National Park System, including those areas which, while not part of the System, receive administrative, technical or financial support from the National Park Service.

WEATHER INFORMATION

The Climatables™

For the first time, the 5th Edition of the *Guide* contains weather information on each park area in the form of "Climatables™" beginning at page 000. These are referenced in each park area entry in the book. The Climatables™ presented are compilations of official National Oceanic and Atmospheric Administration (NOAA) data from individual National Weather Service Offices, cooperative observation stations, and from several publications on the National Climatic Data Center. A complete bibliography of weather information used in compiling the Climatables™ follows in this Introduction.

Each Climatable™ is intended to represent or characterize the normal and extreme weather conditions that might be expected to be encountered in the specified National Park area. **The Climatables™ do not in any way represent a forecast of weather conditions, but simply indicate to the Park visitor the type and range of weather conditions that have occurred in the past. The Climatables™ should not be read as predictions of the weather you will actually encounter in your park visit.**

In some National Parks, where the area represented is quite large and there are extensive variations in topography and elevation, a single table of values cannot possibly characterize the weather at every location in the park. **The Climatables™ are not a definitive and detailed climatology of the entire park area, but they present the park visitor with a good understanding of the general types and intensity of weather conditions that have occurred in the past in each area and a reasonable indication of the possible range of weather conditions that could occur throughout the year.** The weather information in the *Guide* ought to be considered when planning a visit to park areas, recognizing that during any particular visit, near-normal weather conditions could be encountered or new weather records could be set.

The weather normals and extremes given in the Climatables™ are not, for the most part, taken from any one observation site. Since each Climatable™ is intended to typify or characterize the weather and climate over the entire area represented, in almost all cases the data have been assembled from a number of observation sites applicable to the designated area. In only a few cases, the area represented was sufficiently limited to permit the data record from a single major National Weather Service office to be used for the Climatable™.

Using The Climatables™

Each Climatable™ contains information in tabular form typifying the temperature, precipitation, and sunshine/cloudiness for all of the National Park sites listed at the top of the table. Two graphs to assist in visualization of some of the temperature and cloudiness information are also included. Other climate or weather information, important or unique to the area covered, is inserted in the box entitled *"ETC . . ."*

TEMPERATURE: The values for *Normal Daily Maximum* and *Normal Daily Minimum* together indicate the normal daily range of temperature that might be expected to occur during each month of the year. Of course, on any given day, temperatures may be warmer or colder than normal. The values given for *Extreme High* and *Extreme Low* Temperature indicate the full range of temperatures that have occurred in the past. In planning your visit, it would be advisable to consider the possibility of encountering temperatures anywhere between these monthly extremes. Once again, remember, the given values are generally typical or characteristic of the entire area and do not necessarily reflect the absolute record high or low temperature that may have been recorded at any specific location within the area covered.

The number of days each month on which it can normally be expected that the temperature will reach or exceed 90°F or will fall to or below freezing are the last two parameters given under the temperature section. In any given year, these numbers can be exceeded or many fewer days with temperatures reaching these levels might occur. The values presented simply indicate over what portion of each month these temperatures might normally be expected.

PRECIPITATION: The *Normal* and *Maximum* monthly precipitation values together are an indication of how much total precipitation, that is rain and snow combined, is apt to be encountered under normal and extremely wet conditions. At the opposite extreme, it should be noted that at some time in the past, every part of the country has experienced very dry or drought conditions in all months of the year. The values given for *Maximum 24-Hour Precipitation* suggests the wettest day that could be expected to be encountered.

The occurrence of snow can be a delight to the eye and at the same time an incon-venience or even a hazard to the park visitor. In those areas and times of year when the precipitation is primarily in the form of snow, as evidenced by normal daily maximum temperatures being near or below freezing, multiplying the normal precipitation by 10 provides a fairly good estimate of the normal monthly snowfall in inches. The values for *Maximum Snowfall* shown in the Climatable™ indicate how much snow has fallen in the past; but remember these are extreme values.

How often it can be expected to rain or snow is also of importance to the traveler. *Days With Measurable Precipitation* indicates the normal number of days each month on which a measurable amount of precipitation (one-one hundredth inch) can be expected to fall. Of course, a day is counted as a "precipitation day" whether it rains all day or the precipitation is recorded in just one brief shower. To further indicate the nature of the precipitation in each area, the *Average Number of Thunderstorms* that occur each month is given. Those months when the average number of thunderstorms is relatively high are the times of year when the precipitation, even in the absence of thunderstorms, might be expected to be showery or intermittent in nature. It should always be remembered that any thunderstorm can bring with it locally heavy rain, hail, high winds and electrical activity; treat them with respect.

SUNSHINE/CLOUDINESS: This section of the Climatable™ presents a simple tabulation of the average number of days each month when the period between sunrise and sunset can be characterized as being, *Clear, Partly Cloudy* or *Cloudy. The normal Percentage of Possible Sunshine* that can be expected each month expresses the number of daytime hours each month during which sunshine will be seen. This entire section of the Climatables™ together with the number of precipitation days is also helpful in further understanding whether the precipitation indicated for the area is most likely to be in the form of intermittent showers or extended periods of rain.

GRAPHS: The two graphs that are part of each Climatable™ are included to help visualize the temperature and cloudiness information that are in the accompanying table. The bars in the upper graph indicate the extremes in temperature for each month. The two curves through the center of the graph show the normal daily range of temperature. In the lower graph, the number of clear, partly cloudy and cloudy days are expressed as a percentage. Thus, it is relatively easy to see the proportion of each month throughout the year when these sky cover conditions may be expected to be encountered.

"*ETC*...": The information included as "ETC ..." is intended to both emphasize important weather information and to highlight unique and interesting weather and climate information not brought out by the accompanying tabulation. Where relevant, some cautionary notes are included relative to severe or extreme weather typical of the area.

Climatable™ Bibliography

Great care has been taken in the compilation of historical weather information on the National Park areas included in the *Guide* as Climatables™. The following is a complete listing of the sources of that information:

1. NOAA/National Climatic Data Center, "Divisional Normals and Standard Deviations of Temperature and Precipitation, 1931-1980," *Climatography of the United States No. 85*, Asheville, NC, September, 1981.

2. Changery, M.J., "National Thunderstorm Frequencies for the Contiguous United States," Prepared for U.S. Nuclear Regulatory Commission, NOAA/NCC, Asheville, NC, November, 1981.

3. ESSA/Environmental Data Service, "Climatic Atlas of the United States," Asheville, NC, June, 1968.

4. NOAA/National Climatic Data Center, "Ninety-One Years of Weather Records at Yellowstone National Park, Wyoming, 1887-1977," Compiled & Edited by Henry F. Diaz, Asheville, NC, March, 1979.

5. Dightman, R.A., "Climate of Glacier National Park," Published by Glacier Natural History Association in cooperation with the National Park Service, Bulletin No. 7, March, 1961.

6. NOAA/National Climatic Data Center, *Local Climatological Data, Annual Summaries for 1986*, Asheville, NC. [169 reporting stations*]

7. NOAA/National Climatic Data Center, *Local Climatological Data, Annual Summaries for 1978*, Asheville, NC. [3 reporting stations*]

8. NOAA/National Climatic Data Center, *Local Climatological Data, Annual Summaries for 1964*, Asheville, NC. [1 reporting station*]

9. NOAA/National Climatic Data Center, "Climatic Summaries for Selected Sites, 1951-1980," *Climatography of the United States No. 20*, Asheville, NC. [208 reporting stations*]

10. NOAA/National Climatic Data Center, "Climatic Summaries for Selected Sites, Group II," *Climatography of the United States No. 20*, Asheville, NC. [selected years, 1951-1975, 57 reporting stations*]

11. NOAA/National Climatic Data Center, "Climatic Summaries for Selected Sites, Group III," *Climatography of the United States No. 20*, Asheville, NC. [selected years, 1855-1972, 106 reporting stations*]

12. NOAA/National Climatic Data Center, "Climatic Summaries of Resort Areas," *Climatography of the United States No. 21*, Asheville, NC. [19 reporting stations*]

13. USAF/Air Weather Service, Environmental Technical Applications Center (ETAC), *Worldwide Airfield Summaries*, Asheville, NC. [3 reporting stations*]

14. NOAA/National Climatic Data Center, "Climates of the States," *Climatography of the United States No. 60*, Asheville, NC, Reprinted June, 1982. [48 states reported*]

*For information concerning the location(s) of the reporting station(s) for a particular Climatable™, write to the National Park Foundation, P.O. Box 57473, Washington, D.C. 20037.

BEFORE YOU START YOUR TRIP

When you are planning your trip, consult the *Guide* to find out what parks are near your primary destination. You may be close to a fascinating site that you haven't heard about, and may be able to plan a side trip for a day or an afternoon.

To orient you with the locations of park sites, we have included state maps marking the major roads and relative positions of park areas. **These maps are meant only to show you what parks are located in the immediate vicinity of your destination. In order to keep the maps simple we have not made them to exact scale, and have eliminated some smaller roads which might be necessary to reach the parks. So,** the maps in this book cannot subsitute for detailed road maps. Additional location information is given in the *DIRECTIONS* section of each park listing.

We have included as much specific information as possible, such as hours, fees, holiday closings and weather information to help you plan your park visit. We have made every attempt to be accurate, however, **you should verify in advance any details of importance to you.** Likewise, every effort has been made to obtain accurate information on hospital and first aid facilities. **Persons traveling who are concerned about possible health problems, or who have been advised to restrict their activities because of known health problems, should investigate the specific nature of the hospital and first aid facilities available in the area of planned travel.** You should also carry a first aid kit with you while you travel.

ENTRANCE FEES

Legislation passed in the United States Congress mandated entrance fees for several areas within the National Park System starting in 1987. The fees vary at each park, while most remain free to those under 16 and over 62 years of age. Please be aware that fees may change from those quoted in the *Guide* as decisions concerning entrance fees were still being made at the time of printing of this 5th Edition. Call ahead to the park if fees are a concern to you.

An annual entrance permit, the *Golden Eagle Pass,* is issued for $25 at all parks charging entrance fees and other park related locations. Persons 62 years of age and older are entitled to a free lifetime entrance permit, the *Golden Age Passport.* Handicapped persons who are eligible for Federal benefits as a result of disability may obtain the *Golden Access Passport.* Admission fees at all areas collecting fees are waived to holders of the Golden Eagle Pass and the Golden Age and Golden Access Passports and those persons accompanying the holder in a non-commercial vehicle. You can obtain more information on these annual passports by contacting the National Park Service in Washington, D.C. (202) 343-4747 or any of the National Park Service regional offices: Alaska (907) 271-2737 (Alaska Public Lands Informa-

tion Center); Mid-Atlantic (215) 597-7018; Midwest (402) 221-3431; National Capital (202) 485-9880; North Atlantic (617) 565-8888; Pacific Northwest (206) 442-4830; Rocky Mountain (303) 969-2000; Southeast (404) 331-4998; Southwest (505) 988-6375; and Western (415) 556-0560. Campsite fees are not waived for holders of any of the Pass/Passport series, although holders of the Golden Age Passport are generally given a reduced rate.

RESERVATION INFORMATION

Generally, most campgrounds in National Parks are on a "first come-first served" basis. However, campsites in the following National Park areas can be reserved through the "Ticketron" system: Acadia National Park, Maine; Cape Hatteras National Seashore, North Carolina; Grand Canyon National Park, Arizona; Great Smoky Mountains National Park, Tennessee; Joshua Tree National Monument, California; Rocky Mountain National Park, Colorado; Sequoia-Kings Canyon National Parks, California; Shenandoah National Park, Virginia; and Yosemite National Park, California. In addition, admission tickets to Mammoth Cave National Park, Kentucky can also be obtained through Ticketron.

Concessioner operated lodges are also to be found in the National Park System's more visited parks. These hotels and lodges are extremely popular and usually require advanced reservations. You are advised to call the particular park you intend to visit to obtain the name and number of the concessioner or reservation system in use in that park. We also suggest that you obtain official government brochures on the areas you intend to visit since they contain detailed maps of the parks themselves. They are generally available without charge by writing to: National Park Service, Office of Public Information, Department of Interior, Washington, D.C. 20240.

Officers and Board Members of the National Park Foundation

Table of Contents

Alabama

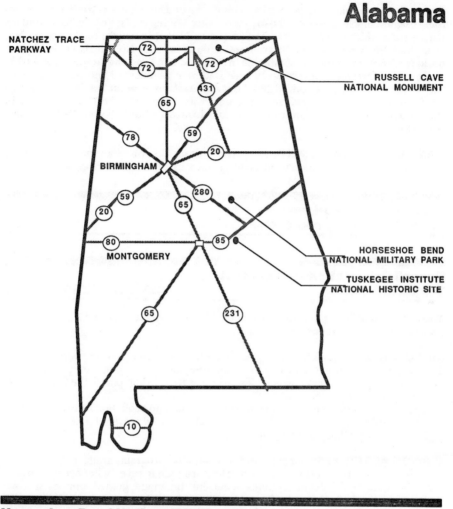

NATCHEZ TRACE PARKWAY

RUSSELL CAVE NATIONAL MONUMENT

BIRMINGHAM

MONTGOMERY

HORSESHOE BEND NATIONAL MILITARY PARK

TUSKEGEE INSTITUTE NATIONAL HISTORIC SITE

Horseshoe Bend National Military Park
Daviston, Alabama   **SEE CLIMATABLE NO. 1**

MAILING ADDRESS: Superintendent, Horseshoe Bend National Military Park, Route 1, Box 103, Daviston, Alabama 36256 **Telephone:** 205-234-7111

DIRECTIONS: The Park, on AL-49, is 12 miles (19 km) north of Dadeville and 18 miles (29 km) east of Alexander City via New Site.

General Andrew Jackson's forces broke the power of the Creek Indian Confederacy and opened Alabama and other parts of the Old Southwest to settlement after fierce fighting here on Mar. 27, 1814, on the "horseshoe bend" of the Tallapoosa River. Authorized for addition to the National Park System on July 25, 1956. Established Aug. 11, 1959.

VISITOR ACTIVITIES: Interpretive and audiovisual exhibits, auto and walking tours, picnicking, boating, hiking, fishing, flintlock rifle demonstrations given when staffing permits; **Permits:** No;**Fees:** Only for special uses; **Visitor facilities:** Visitor

Center, museum, hiking trails, boat launching ramp, picnic area; **Any limitations on vehicle usage:** Vehicles are restricted to paved roads; **Hiking trails:** Yes, the park contains nature trails which vary from 3 to 7 miles (4.5 to 11 km) in length; **Backcountry:** No; **Camping:** No; **Other overnight accommodations on site:** No; **Meals served in the park:** No; **Food and supplies obtainable in the park:** No; **Food and supplies obtainable nearby:** Yes; **Overnight accommodations:** Dadeville 12 miles (19 km), and Alexander City 18 miles, (29 km), both on US 280; **First Aid available in park:** Yes; **Nearest Hospital:** Dadeville, 12 miles (19 km) and Alexander City, 18 miles (29 km), both on US 280; **Days/Hours:** Museum and grounds open daily from 8 a.m. to 4:30 p.m; **Holiday Closings:** Dec 25; Jan. 1.

GENERAL INFORMATION: Be alert to hazards such as poisonous snakes, poison ivy, and fire ants. Exercise caution while boating and walking along the river bank.

Natchez Trace Parkway
For details see listing in Mississippi

Russell Cave National Monument
Bridgeport, Alabama   **SEE CLIMATABLE NO. 2**

MAILING ADDRESS: Russell Cave National Monument, Rte. 1, Box 175, Bridgeport, Alabama 35740 **Telephone:** 205-495-2672

DIRECTIONS: The park is best approached by US 72 leading to Bridgeport, Alabama. Turn north on County Road 91 to the community of Mt. Carmel, then turn right on County Road 75 to the Park entrance. The distance from Bridgeport to the Park is about 8 miles (12 km) over paved road.

An almost continuous archaeological record of human habitation from at least 7000 B.C. to about 1650 A.D. is revealed in this cave, which was "discovered" in 1953. Created by Presidential Proclamation on May 11, 1961.

VISITOR ACTIVITIES: Interpretive films and slide programs available for showing upon request in park's audiovisual room. Slide program in cave shelter area. Interpretive exhibits and talks, demonstrations of ancient Indian life, guided tours of the cave shelter for groups; **Permits:** No; **Fees:** No; **Visitor facilities:** Picnic area, hiking trails, restrooms; **Any limitations on vehicle usage:** No; **Hiking trails:** Yes, a 1.2 mile (.8 km) hiking trail; nature trail extends to a hiking trail; **Backcountry:** No; **Camping:** No; **Other overnight accommodations on site:** No; **Meals served in the park:** No; **Food and supplies obtainable in the park:** No; **Food and supplies obtainable nearby:** Yes, in Bridgeport, South Pittsburg, Stevenson; **Overnight accommodations:** Kimball, TN, Junction of US 72 and I-24, 18 miles (29 km) Stevenson, Alabama, on U.S. 72, approximately 13 miles from the park; **First Aid available in park:** Yes; **Nearest Hospital:** Bridgeport, County 75 to 91 to US 72, 10 miles (16 km); **Days/Hours:** Open daily from 8 a.m. to 5 p.m., C.S.T.; **Holiday Closings:** Dec. 25; **Visitor attractions closed for seasons:** None; **Weather:** Summers are hot and humid, winters are relatively mild, with occasional near-zero temperatures and snow.

GENERAL INFORMATION: You are advised not to run on the trails and not to wander from them or to take short cuts. The hiking trail is steep and arduous and you are urged to walk it with care.

Tuskegee Institute National Historic Site
Tuskegee Institute, Alabama   **SEE CLIMATABLE NO. 1**

MAILING ADDRESS: Superintendent, Tuskegee Institute National Historic Site, P.O. Drawer 10, Tuskegee Institute, Alabama 36088 **Telephone:** 205-727-6390

DIRECTIONS: The site is located on Old Montgomery Road (126) and is adjacent to the city of Tuskegee, AL. When approaching via Interstate 85, exit onto AL 81 South. Turn right at the intersection of 81 and Old Montgomery Road. Follow signs to Visitor Center located in Carver Museum.

Booker T. Washington founded this college for black Americans in 1881. Preserved here are the student-made brick buildings, Washington's home, and the George Washington Carver Museum. Authorized for addition to the National Park System on Oct. 26, 1974.

VISITOR ACTIVITIES: informal interpretive talks at Carver Museum, 30 minute docu-drama on BTW, formal tours at The Oaks, special activities intermittently throughout the year; **Permits:** No; **Fees:** No; **Visitor facilities:** museum, restored home; **Any limitations on vehicle usage:** No; **Hiking trails:** No; **Backcountry:** No; **Camping:** No; **Other overnight accommodations on site:** Yes, for reservations at Dorothy Hall Guest House, contact Tuskegee Institute, Tuskegee Institute, AL 36088, phone 205-727-8753; **Meals served in the park:** No; **Food and supplies obtainable in the park:** No; **Food and supplies obtainable nearby:** Yes, Tuskegee Institute campus or downtown Tuskegee; **Overnight accommodations:** I-85 and Notasulga Highway, 5 miles (8 km); **First Aid available in park:** Yes; **Nearest Hospital:** John Andrew Hospital on Tuskegee Institute campus; **Days/Hours:** Open daily from 9 a.m.-5 p.m.; **Holiday Closings:** Dec. 25 & Jan. 1; **Visitor attractions closed for seasons:** No; **Weather:** Summer is humid, with high temperatures in mid-90's from July-Sept.; winter is cold, with lows in the 20's from Dec.-Feb.; spring and fall have moderate rainfall, with temperatures from 75-85°.

GENERAL INFORMATION: *For your safety*—Be especially careful on old walkways and steps. Natural areas have steep slopes, poisonous or spiny vegetation, and animals that sting or bite. Pedestrians have the right-of-way on campus roads.

TRAVEL ACCESS: Bus: Greyhound offers daily service to downtown Tuskegee, AL; **Rail:** No; **Air:** Delta, Southeastern service Montgomery/Auburn, AL.

NEARBY FACILITIES & POINTS OF INTEREST: Hotel/Motel: Tuskegee Inn, I-85 & Notasulga Hwy, 205-727-5400 5 miles; **Campgrounds:** Tuskegee National Forest; **Parks, other points of interest:** Tuskegee National Forest, Chewacla State Park.

Alaska

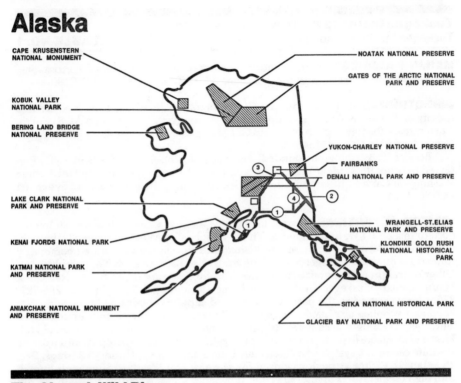

CAPE KRUSENSTERN
NATIONAL MONUMENT

NOATAK NATIONAL PRESERVE

GATES OF THE ARCTIC NATIONAL
PARK AND PRESERVE

KOBUK VALLEY
NATIONAL PARK

BERING LAND BRIDGE
NATIONAL PRESERVE

YUKON-CHARLEY NATIONAL PRESERVE

FAIRBANKS

DENALI NATIONAL PARK AND PRESERVE

LAKE CLARK NATIONAL
PARK AND PRESERVE

WRANGELL-ST.ELIAS
NATIONAL PARK AND PRESERVE

KENAI FJORDS NATIONAL PARK

KLONDIKE GOLD RUSH
NATIONAL HISTORICAL
PARK

KATMAI NATIONAL PARK
AND PRESERVE

ANIAKCHAK NATIONAL MONUMENT
AND PRESERVE

SITKA NATIONAL HISTORICAL PARK

GLACIER BAY NATIONAL PARK AND PRESERVE

The Alagnak Wild River
Alaska   **SEE CLIMATABLE NO. 3**

MAILING ADDRESS: Superintendent, Katmai National Park & Preserve, P.O. Box 7, King Salmon, AK 99613-0007 **Telephone:** 907-246-3305

DIRECTIONS: Accessible by scheduled airlines to King Salmon, charter flights available to Kukaklek Lake, the source of the Alagnak.

VISITOR ACTIVITIES: fishing and recreational river floating; **Permits:** Yes, backcountry permits are available from the Superintendent, Katmai N.P. at the above address; **Fees:** None; **Visitor facilities:** None; **Any limitations on vehicle usage:** N.A. (no roads); **Hiking trails:** No; **Backcountry:** cross country hiking only; **Camping:** wilderness camping only; **Other overnight accommodations on site:** None; **Meals served in the park:** None; **Food and supplies obtainable in the park:** None; **Food and supplies obtainable nearby:** King Salmon; **Overnight accommodations:** None; **First Aid available in park:** None; **Nearest Hospital:** Dillingham, AK; **Days/Hours:** N.A. **Holiday Closings:** N.A. **Visitor attractions closed for seasons:** N.A. **Weather:** Be prepared for cool, rainy weather in summer; for snow, wind and freezing temperatures in other seasons. Good rain gear and wool clothing is advised.

GENERAL INFORMATION: This is a wilderness area used primarily by recreational river floaters and fishermen. There are several allotments (private property) along the river. These are marked with orange marker stakes.

TRAVEL ACCESS: Bus: No; **Rail:** No; **Air:** charter aircraft from King Salmon, AK.

Aniakchak National Monument and Preserve
Alaska   **SEE CLIMATABLE NO. 4**

MAILING ADDRESS: Aniakchak National Monument and Preserve, Box 7, King Salmon, AK 99613-0007 **Telephone:** 907-246-3305

DIRECTIONS: To visit Aniakchak is no simple task. Reeve Aleutian Airways, Inc. has scheduled flights between Anchorage and Port Heiden Airfield. The cost of a round trip ticket is around $400. From Port Heiden Airfield a person could walk to the monument, which is a distance of about 10 miles (16 km), and quite a difficult job. The terrain is tundra meadow, interspersed with scattered thickets of willow, alder, and birch. Very few people have tried to make this walk. A person can also charter an aircraft and fly into the monument. This cost is about $200 per hour. Mark Air, Sea Air, & Air Pac all have twice daily flights from Anchorage to King Salmon for $292 round trip. From King Salmon, one can charter an airplane for approximately $200 per hour. As evidenced by the methods available, this is quite an expensive place to visit.

Thirty square-mile Aniakchak Crater, one of the world's largest, contains a lake and a river, and a volcano which erupted in 1931. Aniakchak River flows through the caldera wall to the Pacific. Established as a national monument and preserve through the Alaska National Interest Lands Conservation Act, Dec. 2, 1980.

VISITOR ACTIVITIES: wildlife-watching, float trips, primitive camping, fishing; **Permits:** Alaska fishing license, available in Anchorage and King Salmon, is required; **Fees:** No; **Visitor facilities:** No; **Any limitations on vehicle usage:** No roads; **Hiking trails:** No; **Backcountry trails:** Yes, information can be obtained from Alaska Regional Office of the National Park Service or Superintendent, Katmai National Park/Preserve in King Salmon; **Camping:** Yes, primitive camping available; **Other overnight accommodations on site:** No; **Meals served in the park:** No; **Food and supplies obtainable in the park:** No; **Food and supplies obtainable nearby:** No, should be obtained in Anchorage or King Salmon; **Overnight accommodations:** King Salmon, about 150 miles (240 km); **First Aid available in the park:** No; **Nearest Hospital:** Kodiak, Dillingham; **Days/Hours:** Monument never closes; **Holiday Closings:** No; **Visitor attractions closed for seasons:** No; **Weather:** The weather will vary a great deal. For winter, the maximum may be in the low 30°s F to -30° below zero. Summer temperatures range from the mid and upper 40°s to a high of 70°. The caldera is subject to violent wind storms which can make camping inside the caldera very difficult. In June and July, 1973, an individual had his camp destroyed twice during a six-week period and his boat blown away. Local pilots who have flown into the caldera have reported bad experiences with strong turbulent winds.

GENERAL INFORMATION: Visitors in the area should have wool clothing, rubber boots and good rain gear. Bring your own food if camping and be sure that the tent can withstand bad weather conditions. One of the most experienced air taxi services for this area is Peninsula Airways, Inc., P.O. Box 36, King Salmon, AK 99613, phone 907-246-3372. Other charter aircraft are available in Anchorage, Port Heiden Airfield, and King Salmon.

Bering Land Bridge National Preserve
Alaska   **SEE CLIMATABLE NO. 5**

MAILING ADDRESS: Box 220, Nome, AK 99762-0220 **Telephone:** 907-443-2522

DIRECTIONS: The Preserve is quite isolated. No roads lead to the area, and airports at

Nome and Kotzebue that handle jets are rather distant from the Preserve's boundaries. Nonetheless, Nome and Kotzebue are for most visitors the intermediate points from which to fly into the Preserve or to Native villages in close proximity to the boundaries. Round trip air fare from Anchorage to either Kotzebue or Nome is $426.00. It is possible to charter flights out of Nome and Kotzebue into Serpentine Hot Springs and onto beaches of the Preserve. Charter fares run about $200 per hour.

This area on the north side of Seward Peninsula 50 miles (80 km) from Siberia contains remains of land bridge once connecting Asia and North America. The promising archaeological site is also the habitat of polar bear, grizzly bear, wolves, 21 other mammals and 112 bird species. Established by Alaska National Interest Lands Conservation Act, Dec. 2, 1980.

VISITOR ACTIVITIES: wilderness hiking and camping, photography, fishing, river floating, boating, canoeing, walking, wildlife- and wildflower-watching. Part of the attraction of the Preserve is to see Eskimos from the neighboring villages pursue subsistence lifestyles, manage reindeer herds, and produce pieces of arts and crafts.; **Permits:** Alaska fishing license, available locally, is required; **Fees:** No; **Visitor facilities:** No; **Any limitations on vehicle usage:** No roads; **Hiking trails:** No; **Backcountry:** Yes, information available from Superintendent; **Camping:** Only primitive camping—no reservations; **Other overnight accommodations on site:** No; **Meals served in the park:** No.; **Food and supplies obtainable in the park:** No; **Food and supplies obtainable nearby:** Yes, certain items—food, clothing, beverages, and some gear—may be purchased from merchants in Nome and Kotzebue, but supplies in village stores are generally limited; **Overnight accommodations:** Lodging and eating facilities are available at the intermediate points of Nome and Kotzebue. Room reservations are suggested because touring groups book much of the touring space. Rooms average about $85 per day, and meals are proportionately as expensive. Transportation costs for goods and services in "bush" Alaska raise prices considerably in such places as Nome and Kotzebue. Visitors planning to stay in the Preserve should plan to arrive self-sufficient. **First Aid available in park:** No; **Nearest Hospital:** Nome and Kotzebue; **Days/Hours:** Preserve never closes; **Holiday Closings:** None; **Visitor attractions closed for seasons:** None; **Weather:** Most visitors come into the area between mid-June and mid-September when the temperatures average in the mid-40's F along the coast and mid-60's F inland. During the ice-free periods along the coasts (late May to late October), cloudy skies prevail, fog occurs, daily temperatures remain fairly constant in the long hours of daylight, and the relative humidity is high.

GENERAL INFORMATION: Visitors to the Preserve must arrive self-sufficient with their food, clothing, and shelter, and in some cases with fuel. There is some driftwood along the beaches, but inland wood is scarce and should be used chiefly for cooking. You should possess skills, talents, and stamina to survive some difficult conditions. In other words, you should have hiking, backpacking, and camping experience; and be knowledgeable about food, clothing, and gear. Since visitors carry everything on their backs once they've arrived in the Preserve, they bring only the *essentials*: good tents with rain flies, sleeping bags and pads, insect repellents and head nets, cooking and eating utensils, first aid items, maps, knife, food, warm clothing and rain gear, calf-high boots with waterproof lowers, fishing tackle, extra socks, and possibly some camera equipment. In parties of two or more—it is advisable to always travel with others in the Preserve—many of the above items can be shared, reducing the weight one must carry.

Cape Krusenstern National Monument
Alaska **SEE CLIMATABLE NO. 5**

MAILING ADDRESS: National Park Service, Cape Krusenstern National Monument, P.O. Box 1029, Kotzebue, Alaska 99752 **Telephone:** 907-442-3890

DIRECTIONS: The Monument is in northwestern Alaska. Access is from Kotzebue via charter airplane.

The 114 beach ridges on this Chukchi Sea area, 600 miles (966 km) northwest of Anchorage, tell of successive Eskimo communities living here for 400 years. Created by Act of Congress Dec. 2, 1980.

VISITOR ACTIVITIES: wildlife-watching, beach walking, fishing, primitive camping; **Permits:** Alaska fishing license, available locally, is required; **Fees:** No; **Visitor facilities:** information can be obtained from Superintendent Cape Krusenstern National Monument Kotzebue, Alaska 99752; **Camping:** Yes, primitive camping only; **Other overnight accommodations on site:** No; **Meals served in the park:** No; **Food and supplies obtainable in the park:** No; **Food and supplies obtainable nearby:** Yes, at Kotzebue; **Overnight accommodations:** Kotzebue; **First Aid available in park:** No; **Nearest Hospital:** Kotzebue; **Days/Hours:** Monument never closes; **Holiday Closings:** No; **Visitor attractions closed for seasons:** No.

TRAVEL ACCESS: Bus: No; **Rail:** No; **Air:** Alaska Airlines provides daily service to Kotzebue; **Other:** Air charter available in Kotzebue. A few charter boats available intermittently in Kotzebue.

NEARBY FACILITIES & POINTS OF INTEREST: Hotel/Motel: Nul-Luk-Vik, Kotzebue, AK 99752, 907-442-3331 20 miles by air or boat to the Monument; **Parks, other points of interest:** Noatak National Preserve, Kobuk Valley National Park, Bering Land Bridge National Preserve, Nana Museum of the Arctic; **Reservation systems in use for campsites, other facilities:** None; **New information:** Because of rugged terrain and harsh climate visitors should contact NPS visitor information office in Kotzebue prior to visiting the area.

Denali National Park & Preserve
McKinley Park, Alaska **SEE CLIMATABLE NO. 6**

MAILING ADDRESS: Superintendent, Denali National Park & Preserve P.O. Box 9, McKinley Park, Alaska 99755-0009 **Telephone:** 907-683-2294

DIRECTIONS: The park is 238 miles (386 km) north of Anchorage and 126 miles (193 km) south of Fairbanks, on Alaska Highway 3. Buses run regularly from both cities. The Alaska Railroad provides passenger and freight service to the park; 8 hours from Anchorage and 4 hours from Fairbanks. For information write to Alaska Railroad, Traffic Division, P.O. Box 7-2111, Anchorage, AK 99510

Mount McKinley, at 20,320 feet, is the highest mountain in North America. Large glaciers of the Alaska Range, caribou, sheep, moose, grizzly bears, wolves, and other wildlife are highlights of this national park. Originally established as Mount McKinley National Park in 1917, and expanded and renamed Denali National Park & Preserve in 1980. Established by act of Congress on Feb. 26, 1917.

VISITOR ACTIVITIES: camping, wildlife-watching, interpretive talks and walks, hiking, backcountry use, fishing, dog sledding, cross-country skiing; **Permits:** for backcountry, required all year, at Visitor Centers and Ranger Stations, in Winter, at Park Headquarters; **Fees:** for wildlife scenic tours, $35 per person. Campground fees vary from free to $10 per night, depending on facilities; **Visitor facilities:** campsites, lodging, food service, groceries, supplies, gas. Minor auto repairs are available in Healy, 12 miles north. After you leave the entrance area for the park interior, gasoline and food service are not available. **Any limitations on vehicle usage:** Maximum speed limit is 35 mph. During the visitor season, private vehicles are not permitted beyond the Savage River except to proceed to several registered campgrounds. Other campgrounds are accessed by camper bus only. Trail bikes and motorcycles must not leave the park road. Snowmobiles are prohibited. Pickup campers, motor homes and trailers, if they are not excessive size, may travel only as far as Teklanika campground.

Since private vehicles are not allowed, there is *free transportation.* Buses regularly run from the Information Center to Eielson Visitor Center and on to Wonder Lake. The buses make regularly scheduled stops at key points along the park road for your convenience, but you should feel free to get on and off *at any point* and to change buses as many times as you please. Bring all the food you will need, because there is no food service beyond the entrance area; **Hiking trails:** Yes, most hiking is cross-country. Both long- and short-range trips are available. Take extra caution in crossing streams; they are swifter than they seem; **Backcountry:** Yes, a permit is required for backcountry use. Obtain information from the Information Center upon arrival or by contacting the Park in advance; **Camping:** Yes, if you plan to camp in the park you must first register for it at the Information Center in the Headquarters-entrace area. All campsites are available on first-come first-served basis. Register at Riley Creek Information Center for sites in all campgrounds. After you have registered in some instances, you will be allowed to drive your own vehicle just to the campsite. Once there you must hike or use the free public transportation system to get to other points of interest in the park. There is a privately-owned campground 10 miles (16 km) north and 6 miles (10 km) south of the McKinley Park entrance, and Byer's Lake campground is in the Denali State Park 90 miles (145 km) to the south of the park entrance. **Other overnight accommodations on site:** Yes, for information and reservations at Denali National Park Hotel contact Denali National Park Company, McKinley Park, AK 99755, or you may call (numbers noted below). Also contact Camp Denali, c/o Wally Cole, Box 67, McKinley Park, AK 99755; **Meals served in the park:** Yes, at Denali National Park Hotel; **Food and supplies obtainable in the park:** Yes, near Denali National Park Hotel. For detailed information on this concessioner's services, contact ARA Outdoor World Ltd., P.O. Box 87, Denali National Park, AK 99755, phone 907-683-2215, from May 22 thru September 12. In off season, contact ARA Outdoor World, Ltd., 825 W. 8th Ave., #240, Anchorage, AK 99501, phone 907-276-7234.

Gates of the Arctic National Park & Preserve
Alaska   **SEE CLIMATABLE NO. 5**

MAILING ADDRESS: Gates of the Arctic National Park & Preserve, P.O. Box 74680 Fairbanks, Alaska, 99707-4680 **Telephone:** 907-456-0281

DIRECTIONS: Most visitors to the central Brooks Range fly via scheduled flights from Fairbanks to Bettles (about $78 one-way), and then charter small aircraft in Bettles for flights into the Park ($125-$185 per hour). Charter flights into the Brooks Range can also begin in Fairbanks (air-time is generally paid to and from the desination). Additionally, scheduled flights from Fairbanks and Bettles to Anaktuvuk Pass (in the center of the Park) are available several times a week.

It is best for the visitor to write directly to the park for a list of scheduled airline and charter prices.

This vast tundra wilderness contains six designated wild rivers and many lakes and rivers yet unnamed. Broad valleys contrast with razor-like Arrigetch Peaks and turreted Mt. Igikpak, high point of the central and western Brooks Range. Here, 200 miles (324 km) northwest of Fairbanks, is habitat vital to the arctic caribou, grizzly bear, sheep, moose, wolves and raptors. Created by U.S. Congress on Dec. 2, 1980.

VISITOR ACTIVITIES: hiking, backcountry, rock and mountain climbing, fishing, wildlife-watching, canoeing; **Permits:** Alaska fishing and hunting licenses, available in Fairbanks, are required. Hunting is allowed only in the Preserve; **Fees:** No; **Visitor facilities:** No; **Any limitations on vehicle usage:** No roads or off road vehicles; **Hiking trails:** No; **Backcountry:** Yes, information can be obtained from Park Office in Fairbanks; U.S.G.S. quadrangle maps available in Fairbanks and Bettles; **Camping:** Allowed, but there are no designated campsites; **Other overnight accommodations on site:** Yes, camping sites are available throughout the area. A few private lodges are located within or adjacent to the Park. **Meals served in the park:** No; **Food and supplies obtainable in the park:** No; **Food and supplies obtainable nearby:** Yes, Bettles, Fairbanks; **Overnight accommodations:** Bettles, 20 miles (32 km) south; **First Aid available in park:** No; **Nearest Hospital:** Fairbanks; **Days/Hours:** Park never closes; **Holiday Closings:** None; **Visitor attractions closed for seasons:** None; **Weather:** Long cold winters and short, mild summers are the rule. Along the south slopes of the Brooks Range, particularly in the lowlands, mid-summer temperatures may occasionally rise into the 80's and rarely into the 90's. Temperatures in the highlands are generally cooler, and on the northern slopes temperatures range from 30°F to 60°F. In the highlands and on the north slopes freezing temperatures may occur in mid-August and definitely occur in early September. August is often a rainy month. Frost may occur in any month, especially at higher elevations.

GENERAL INFORMATION: This Park/Preserve is extremely remote. Visitors must come prepared to be totally self-sufficient. Because nearly all visitors to the Park will be backpacking for extended periods, it is essential that clothing, camping gear and food are of good quality and are light in weight. Clothing should include enough "layers", even during the summer months to provide warmth in sub-freezing temperatures; and rain gear is essential. Tents should be strong, light and have a rainfly. Food will have to consist primarily of dried and freeze-dried items, and should be in greater quantities than what is expected to be consumed during the planned trip since Air Charter delays often occur in bad weather. Visitors should be well familiar with their gear before starting a backpacking trip in this area, and should additionally be competent at hiking, camping, and survival skills. Winter travel requires special skills and hardiness, and should only be undertaken after careful planning.

Mosquitoes usually come out in mid-June and begin to disappear in early or mid-August. Gnats and whitesocks hatch in August. Insects are most bothersome in wet lowlands and areas of heavy vegetation, and are not as numerous on dry highlands where breezes are frequent. Carry good mosquito repellent and a headnet.

Sport Hunting is permitted in preserve areas with Alaska State License. Not permitted in Park areas.

Glacier Bay National Park and Preserve
Gustavus, Alaska   **SEE CLIMATABLE NO. 7**

MAILING ADDRESS: Superintendent, Glacier Bay National Park and Preserve, Gustavus, Alaska 99826 **Telephone:** 907-697-2230

DIRECTIONS: The Park is located at the northwest end of the Alexander Archipelago in southeastern Alaska. There are no roads to the Park, and access is by various types of commercial transport, including regularly scheduled and charter air services, cruise ships and charter boats, private boats, and tours via kayak. By boat, the distance from Juneau is about 100 miles (161 km). Flying time from Juneau is about 30 minutes. An airfield is at Gustavus, just outside the park.

Great tidewater glaciers, a dramatic range of plant communities, and rare species of wildlife can be found in this unit of the National Park System. Created by Presidential Proclamation on Feb. 25, 1925.

VISITOR ACTIVITIES: glacier-viewing, boating, camping, hiking, fishing, wildlife- and bird-watching, evening programs; **Permits:** required for fishing; **Fees:** only for concession-operated and commercial transportation to tidewater glaciers; **Visitor facilities:** restrooms, lodge, interpretive programs and hikes, hiking trails, food service, campground. Boaters may obtain gasoline, diesel fuel, and water, permits required for boating and use limited during humpback whale season, June 1-August 30. No other public facilities for boats are available at the Park. **Any limitations on vehicle usage:** No; **Hiking trails:** Yes, the Park's several hundred miles of shoreline, numerous islands and alpine meadows offer nearly unlimited camping and hiking opportunities; **Backcountry:** Yes, a hikers' guide with many suggestions for backcountry use and topographical maps covering the Park can be obtained at Bartlett Cove; **Camping:** Yes, campers should bring food and supplies to Glacier Bay. There are no camping services locally. **Other overnight accommodations on site:** Yes, concessioner-operated Glacier Bay Lodge at Bartlett Cove is open from about mid-May to mid-Sept. Rooms and meals are available. For reservations, write to Glacier Bay Lodge, Glacier Bay National Park, Gustavus, AK 99826, during the operating season, and Glacier Bay Lodge, Inc., 1500 Metropolitan Park Bldg., Olive Way at Boren Ave., Seattle, WA 98101, phone 206-625-9600 the remainder of the year. A tour boat makes daily cruises from the lodge to the glaciers. For campers and hikers, rain gear, a tent fly, and water-resistant boots are often essential items for a successful trip. **Meals served in the park:** Yes, at Glacier Bay Lodge, in season; **Food and supplies obtainable in the park:** A limited amount of food and supplies is available at Gustavus general store; **Food and supplies obtainable nearby:** No, at Juneau, AK, 100 miles (161 km) distant; **Overnight accommodations:** Gustavus, 10 miles (16 km) distant. Otherwise Juneau, 100 miles (161 km); **First Aid available in park:** Yes, at Park Headquarters; **Nearest Hospital:** Juneau, 100 miles (161 km) by air; **Days/Hours:** Park always open, concession facilities are open from late May to mid-September; **Holiday Closings:** No; **Visitor attractions closed for season:** Only concession facilities are closed from mid-Sept. to mid-May; **Weather:** Warm clothing and rain gear are essential when visiting the Park. Summer temperatures seldom exceed 24°C (72°F) and extended periods of wet weather are to be expected. The ground is usually moist and footwear should be selected accordingly.

Katmai National Park & Preserve
Alaska   **SEE CLIMATABLE NO. 3**

MAILING ADDRESS: Superintendent, Katmai National Park & Preserve, P.O. Box 7, King Salmon, Alaska 99613-0007 **Telephone:** 907-246-3305

DIRECTIONS: Katmai is 290 air miles (467 km) southwest of Anchorage. Daily commercial jet flights connect Anchorage with King Salmon. Travel from King Salmon to Brooks Camp is by amphibious bush aircraft. Visitor information is available at the Brooks Camp Ranger Station and at Park Headquarters in King Salmon.

Variety marks this vast land: lakes, forests, mountains, and marshlands all abound in wildlife—including the Alaska brown bear, the world's largest carnivore. Here, in one of the largest areas in the National Park System, Novarupta Volcano erupted violently in 1912, forming the ash-filled "Valley of Ten Thousand Smokes." Today, only a few active vents remain. Created by Presidential Proclamation on Sept. 24, 1918. Katmai National Monument was greatly enlarged in 1978 and became the 4,093,214 acre Katmai National Park and Preserve by Congressional Action on December 2, 1980.

VISITOR ACTIVITIES: hiking, walking, wildlife-watching, fishing, camping, backcountry travel, bird-watching, boating, mountain climbing; **Permits:** Fishing licenses can be obtained at Brooks Lodge; backcountry permits available without charge at Brooks Camp Ranger Station or at Headquarters in King Salmon; **Fees:** Yes, for Alaska State fishing licenses; **Visitor facilities:** concession boats, van tours, interpretive talks, charter aircraft, cabins, lodge, dining room, campgrounds, rental tents and stoves, fuel, fishing equipment rental, concession boats are available with guide, canoes can be rented; **Any limitations on vehicle usage:** 80% of Katmai's visitors are recorded at lake camp (just inside boundary), which is 10 miles (16 km) from King Salmon by dirt road. Brooks camp and other areas are not accessible by any road system—access is by aircraft or boat; **Hiking trails:** Yes, detailed information on hiking is provided in a free publication, available by mail or at Brooks Camp Ranger Station or from Headquarters in King Salmon; **Backcountry:** Yes, permit required; check at Brooks Camp Ranger Station or at Headquarters in King Salmon; **Camping:** Yes; **Other overnight accommodations on site:** Yes, a lodge is at Brooks Camp. Katmailand Inc. 4700 Aircraft Dr. Suite 2 Anchorage, AK 99502 907-243-5448, provides accommodations and services at Brooks Camp and Grosvenor Lake. Katmailand also operates Kulik Lodge—a 16 bed lodge on private land within the Park extensions, Katmailand also operates wilderness camps at Nonvianuk and Battle Lakes. All serve meals, provide guide service and beds; **Meals served in the park:** Yes, at Brooks Camp and Grosvenor Lake Camp; **Food and supplies obtainable in the park:** Yes, camping supplies and groceries should be obtained before visiting the park. Limited freeze-dried food items and stove fuel available at the park. **Food and supplies obtainable nearby:** Yes, a small general store in King Salmon; **Overnight accommodations:** motel in King Salmon; **First Aid available in park:** Yes, or nearby medical facilities in Naknak, Dr. on duty in summer; **Nearest Hospital:** Anchorage, 290 miles (467 km) by air; **Days/Hours:** It is accessible by private aircraft or charter anytime; but is accessible by commercial aircraft only June-Sept. The Park is never actually closed; **Visitor attractions closed for season:** Lodge and concession facilities closed from Sept 11 to June 1. **Weather:** Summer high temperatures average 63°F and low temperatures average 44°F. Strong winds and sudden, gusty rainstorms known as williwawes periodically sweep the area. The sky is clear about 20% of the summer.

GENERAL INFORMATION: Day hikers should have sturdy hiking boots with good support, good gear, and warm clothing. Come prepared for some sunshine and some stormy weather. Clothing that may be useful includes comfortable sport clothes, a warm sweater or windbreaker, walking shoes or boots with thick soles and good support, wool socks and a rain coat or hat. You will need insect repellent.

Katmai is a wildlife sanctuary. Keep your distance from and do not feed the animals. Keep all food sealed to reduce odors; use food caches. Make lots of noise when you walk.

NEARBY FACILITIES & POINTS OF INTEREST: Hotel/Motel: King Ko Inn, King Salmon, 907-246-3377; Quinnet Landing Hotel, King Salmon, 907-246-3000. **Food/Supplies:** King Salmon Commercial, King Salmon, 907-246-3411; **Other points of interest:** Salmon fishing activities in Naknek in July; **New information:** The Park, as expanded, now includes three other lodges (operated by Katmailand) in the northern extension.

Kenai Fjords National Park
Alaska   **SEE CLIMATABLE NO. 4**

MAILING ADDRESS: Kenai Fjords National Park Box 1727, Seward, Alaska 99664-1727 **Telephone:** 907-224-3874

DIRECTIONS: The gateway community of Seward, Alaska is within a few hours' drive from Anchorage. Air transportation from Anchorage is available via commercial and charter flights. In addition, Seward has bus service. Exit Glacier is the most accessible area of the park and can be reached by a 9-mile (14.5 km) road and short walk. Scheduled boat services provide opportunities to see and enjoy the coast. Air charters are also available for access to the Fjords as well as the icefield.

Within a few miles of Seward, this 580,000 acre National Park is a portion of the southern Kenai Mountains, two interrelated icefields and a coastal Fjord system where abundant marine mammals, seabirds and mountain goats are found. Created by Congressional Action on Dec. 2, 1980.

VISITOR ACTIVITIES: fishing, sailing, hiking, skiing, snowmachining, dog sledding, snowshoeing, visiting a glacier, wildlife-watching, flightseeing, and charter boats; **Permits:** Alaska fishing licenses required, available in Seward or Anchorage; **Fees:** None; **Visitor facilities:** Visitor Center in Seward, open 8-5, 7 days a week May-Sept. and 8-5 M-F rest of the year. Ranger Station at Exit Glacier. A State Ferry System links Seward with Prince William Sound, Homer, and Kodiak Island. Flightseeing chartered tours leave from Seward and Homer. Hotels, motels, and campgrounds, food and services are available in Seward. **Any limitations on vehicle usage:** One 9-mile (14.5 km) gravel road to Exit Glacier; **Hiking trails:** Yes, trails to Exit Glacier, Harding Icefield and other areas in the park as well as on adjacent federal and state lands; **Backcountry:** Yes, information can be obtained from the Park Service Office in Seward; **Camping:** Yes, 10-site walk in campground at Exit Glacier; **Other overnight accommodations on site:** Public use cabin in Aialik Bay, Fee and reservations required. No reservations required for campgrounds in Seward and within adjacent national forest land. Contact the Chamber of Commerce in either Seward, AK, 99664, phone 907-244-3046, or Homer, AK 99603 for information on other facilities; **Meals served in the park:** No; **Food and supplies obtainable in the park:** No; **Food and supplies obtainable nearby:** Yes, at Seward; **Overnight accommodations:** Seward; **First Aid available in park:** Yes; **Nearest Hospital:** Seward; **Days/Hours:** Park always open; **Holiday Closings:** No; **Visitor attractions closed for season:** Exit Glacier may be closed to vehicles during the winter due to snow. Charterboats operate from late May to Labor Day; **Weather:** A coastal maritime climate influences the area.

GENERAL INFORMATION: Nights are cool along the coast and high humidity and rainfall can be expected. Comfortable wool clothing and appropriate rain gear are important considerations.

Klondike Gold Rush National Historical Park
Skagway, Alaska and Seattle, Washington   **SEE CLIMATABLE NO. 7**

MAILING ADDRESS: Superintendent, Klondike Gold Rush National Historical Park, P.O. Box 517, Skagway, Alaska 99840 *OR* Superintendent, Klondike Gold Rush National Historical Park, 117 S. Main St., Seattle, Washington 98104 **Telephone:** AK: 907-983-2921 WA: 206-442-7220

DIRECTIONS: Access to Skagway is by auto, plane, bus, cruise ship, or by State of Alaska ferry. For further information, contact your travel agent or the City of Skagway, Box 415, Skagway, AK 99840. Visitor center is located at 2nd and Broadway. The Seattle Visitor Center is at 117 S. Main Street in the Pioneer Square area.

The Park is a memorial to the thousands of miners who followed trails from Skagway, AK to the Yukon Territory of Canada during the 1898 gold rush. It preserves historic structures in Skagway, Chilkoot Trail, (from Dyea to the Canadian Border), and part of the White Pass Trail. Authorized for addition to the National Park System on June 30, 1976. Established May 14, 1980.

VISITOR ACTIVITIES: Skagway: wildlife-watching, camping, foot, bus, and chartered aircraft tours. Information on films, displays, interpretive programs and guided walks available at the Skagway Visitor Center, Alaska; Seattle: interpretive displays, films, special tours and other events; **Permits:** No; **Fees:** No; **Visitor facilities:** Seattle: Visitor Center, restrooms, exhibits; Alaska: Visitor Center, campground, groceries and other limited supplies, and restrooms; **Any limitations on vehicle usage:** Vehicles are restricted to designated roadways; **Hiking trails:** In Alaska, the 40 mile (64 km) Chilkoot Trail is accessible only on foot. You must be properly outfitted before embarking on a hike over the Chilkoot Trail. Weather conditions may change rapidly from hour to hour, especially in the summit area. You must be prepared for cold temperatures, snow or rain, fog and travel through swampy areas and snow fields. Proper equipment includes warm clothing (preferably wool), sturdy rain gear (not plastic), a tent with waterproof fly, campstove, and adequate fuel (there is no wood in the summit area and campfires are not allowed at all in the Canadian portion), good hiking boots, adequate food plus emergency rations and first-aid kit. Current trail information available at the visitor center in Skagway or the Environment Canada, Parks Office, Yukon National Historic Sites, P.O. Box 5540, Whitehorse, Yukon, YIA5H4 Canada. Hiking the trail north from Dyea is recommended because it is the historic route. Traveling the trail in reverse is not recommended because descending the steep summit scree, the "Gold Stairs" of the gold rush days is dangerous.

For Your Safety—Be alert for symptoms of hypothermia—a lowering of the body temperature that results in uncontrollable shivering, disorientation, weariness, and possibly death. Never feed wild animals. Make noise when you hike, announcing your presence, since bears are most dangerous when startled or cornered. Never approach a potentially dangerous animal. Keep your campsite and equipment clean. Food should be sealed in airtight containers and hung from trees so that animals will not be attracted by the food odors. You are advised not to take pets on the Chilkoot Trail. It is a difficult hike. **Backcountry:** Yes; **Camping:** In Alaska, no reservations available for primitive campsites; **Other overnight accommodations on site:** Yes; **Meals served in the park:** Not within either section of the park, but meals are available nearby; **Food and supplies obtainable in the park:** Yes, groceries and limited supplies in Alaska; **Food and supplies obtainable nearby:** Yes, Seattle: 2 blocks north, Alaska: Skagway Historic District; **Overnight accommodations:** Seattle and Skagway; **First Aid available in park:** Yes; **Nearest Hospital:** Seattle 1 mile (1.6 km) away for Skagway; Whitehorse 112, Juneau 90 airm.; **Days/Hours:** Seattle: 9 a.m. to 7 p.m. in Summer; shorter hours during the off-season, Skagway: Visitor Center open from 8 a.m. to 8 p.m., only in summer; **Holiday Closings:** Seattle Visitor Center holiday closings have not yet been determined. **Visitor attractions closed for season:** Skagway Visitor Center open only in summer.

GENERAL INFORMATION: International Regulations: Customs and Immigration laws require that anyone travelling to Canada must report to Canadian Customs. Canadian Customs Offices are located in Fraser, B.C. and Whitehorse, YT. Anyone proceeding to Skagway from Canada must report to U.S. Customs and Immigration authorities in Skagway.

TRAVEL ACCESS: Bus: Gray Line of Alaska, White Pass & Yukon motorcoaches have scheduled bus service in the region, phone 1-800-544-2206; (Alaska Sightseeing Company) from Skagway to Dyea. Weekly service from Skagway to Anchorage; **Air:** Scheduled & charter small aircraft (single engine) operate daily service.

Kobuk Valley National Park
Alaska   **SEE CLIMATABLE NO. 5**

MAILING ADDRESS: National Park Service, Kobuk Valley National Park, Box 1029, Kotzebue, Alaska 99752. **Telephone:** 907-442-3890

DIRECTIONS: Access is via charter aircraft from Kotzebue.
    The Kobuk River, flowing west across this area to the Chukchi Sea, has been a major transportation route for centuries. Archaeological resources are extensive. Other features in this area between the Baird Mountains on the north and Waring Mountains are the Salmon River, caribou migrating routes of moose, grizzly bear, black bear and wolves; and the Great Kobuk Sand Dunes. Created by Act of Congress, Dec. 2, 1980.

VISITOR ACTIVITIES: float trips, fishing, hiking, photography, primitive camping; **Permits:** Alaska fishing license, available in Anchorage, or Kotzebue is required; **Fees:** No; **Visitor facilities:** No; **Any limitations on vehicle usage:** No roads; **Hiking trails:** No; **Backcountry:** Yes, information can be obtained from The National Park Service Information Office in Kotzebue; **Camping:** Yes, primitive camping only; **Other overnight accommodations on site:** No; **Meals served in the park:** No; **Food and supplies obtainable in the park:** No; **Food and supplies obtainable nearby:** Yes, in Kotzebue, Ambler or Kiana; **Overnight accommodations:** No; **First Aid available in park:** No; **Nearest Hospital:** Kotzebue; **Days/Hours:** Park never closes.

TRAVEL ACCESS Bus: No; **Rail:** No; **Air:** Alaska Airlines provides daily service to Kotzebue; scheduled flights also serve nearby villages of Ambler and Kiana; **Other:** Air charter available in Kotzebue. A few charter boats available intermittently in Kotzebue or other nearby villages.

NEARBY FACILITIES & POINTS OF INTEREST: Hotel/Motel: Nul-Luk-Vik, Kotzebue, AK 99752, 907-442-3331, 120 miles (193 km) from the park by air; **Parks, other points of interest:** Cape Krusenstern National Monument, Noatak National Preserve, Bering Bridge National Preserve, NANA Museum of the Arctic. **New Information:** Visitor Contact facility now available in Kotzebue. Because of rugged terrain & harsh climate visitors should contact NPS office prior to visiting the area.

Lake Clark National Park & Preserve
Alaska   **SEE CLIMATABLE NO. 3**

MAILING ADDRESS: Lake Clark National Park and Preserve, 701 C Street, Box 61 Room E-561, Anchorage, AK 99513-0001 **Telephone:** 907-271-3751

DIRECTIONS: Most visitors charter an aircraft from Anchorage to the Lake Clark area at a cost of $180 an hour depending on the weight load, number of passengers and type of aircraft. Most places in the Park & Preserve are within one and a half hours flight time from Anchorage. There is commercial air service available from Anchorage to Iliamna, costing about $160-$210 round trip. Points within the Park & Preserve from Iliamna are visited via air charter, at the same cost per hour as Anchorage's air charter services.
    Already popular with summer hikers and fishermen, this 3.7 million acre area across Cook Inlet from Anchorage provides major recreational potential. Among the

wildlife to be viewed in this rugged country are caribou, grizzly bear, black bear, sheep at the southern limit of its range, wolves, wolverine, mink, marten, lynxes, and other fur bearers. The coastal mountains contain two steaming volcanoes. The Park & Preserve preserves major red salmon spawning waters. This area was set aside by Presidential Proclamation on December 1, 1978. Later on December 2, 1980, the Park and Preserve was set aside by Congress.

VISITOR ACTIVITIES: hiking, wildlife, birdwatching, fishing, hunting in Preserve, boating, river trips, primitive camping; **Permits:** Alaska fishing licenses are required and are available in Anchorage; **Fees:** No; **Visitor facilities:** boat rental, fishing tackle, guide services on the coast shores of Lake Clark, Fishtrap Lake, and Lake Iliamna, lodging and Guide Services at Silver Salmon Coast and Crescent Lake; **Any limitations on vehicle usage:** No roads; aircraft landing permitted. **Hiking trails:** Yes, several primitive and unmarked trails; **Backcountry:** Yes, information can be obtained from Park Headquarters; **Camping:** Yes, primitive camping only; **Other overnight accommodations on site:** Yes, One Lodge is located within the Park, while 4 other lodges are located within the boundaries of the Preserve along the shores of Lake Clark. Other lodging is available through commercial and air charter services in Anchorage to points on the periphery of the area. Lodging ranges from primitive cabins to modern lodges with plumbing; **Meals served in the park:** Yes, but generally for guests at lodging facilities; **Food and supplies obtainable in the park:** Yes, limited food and supplies at nearby Nondalton and Iliamna; **Overnight accommodations:** No; **First Aid available in park:** Yes, limited. Clinic in Iliamna; **Nearest Hospital:** Kenai, Anchorage; **Days/Hours:** Park and preserve never close; **Holiday Closings:** None; **Visitor attractions closed for season:** None; **Weather:** Most vistors arrive between mid-June and early September, when high temperatures average between 60° and 75°, with an occasional 80° day in the interior. Coastline areas are cooler with temperatures between 50° and 65°. Wind and rainfall are present on the coastal areas, with mostly sunny and milder temperatures in the interior.

GENERAL INFORMATION: Insects are numerous and precautions should be made by obtaining adequate tents for camping on open river and lake bars. Having an ample supply of insect repellent is a must. One should plan on wearing clothing that will ward off the extremes of possible freezing temperatures, wet weather, and warm sunny days. Extra socks and tennis shoes are practical for river running travel, plus a rainsuit, wool shirts and pants. Campers should travel light by carrying freeze-dried and high energy foods, dried fruit, powdered milk and packaged soups. Ordinary camping gear such as a warm sleeping bag, tent with rain fly and mosquito-proof webbing, knife, small hatchet or saw, insect repellent, sturdy hat, matches in waterproof container, and maps with protective casing are suggested.

TRAVEL ACCESS: Bus: No; **Rail:** No; **Air:** Yes, unscheduled air service to Anchorage, Kenai/Soldotna, Homer, Iliamna.

NEARBY FACILITIES & POINTS OF INTEREST: Parks, other points of interest: Lake Iliamna, Katmai, Denali.

Noatak National Preserve
Alaska   **SEE CLIMATABLE NO. 5**

MAILING ADDRESS: National Park Service Noatak National Preserve, Box 1029, Kotzebue, Alaska 99752 **Telephone:** 907-442-3890

DIRECTIONS: Access is via charter aircraft from Kotzebue.

The Noatak River has the country's largest mountain-ringed basin unaffected by man's technology, a 65-mile (105 km) Grand Canyon of the Noatak, a transition zone for diverse plant and animal life and a vital caribou migration route. Some of its 200 archaeological sites date back 5000 years. Created by Act of Congress on Dec. 2, 1980.

VISITOR ACTIVITIES: float trips, fishing, primitive camping; **Permits:** Alaska fishing license, available in Anchorage or Kotzebue is required; **Fees:** No; **Visitor facilities:** No; **Any limitations on vehicle usage:** No roads; **Hiking trails:** No; **Backcountry:** Yes, information can be obtained from The National Park Service Information Office in Kotzebue; **Camping:** Yes, primitive camping only; **Other overnight accommodations on site:** No; **Meals served in the park:** No; **Food and supplies obtainable in the park:** No; **Food and supplies obtainable nearby:** Yes, at Kotzebue; **Overnight accommodations:** None; **First Aid available in park:** No; **Nearest Hospital:** Kotzebue; **Days/Hours:** Preserve never closes; **Holiday Closings:** None; **Visitor attractions closed for season:** No.

TRAVEL ACCESS: Bus: No; **Rail:** No; **Air:** Alaska Airlines offers regular service to Kotzebue; **Other:** Air charter available in Kotzebue. A few charter boats available intermittently in Kotzebue or other nearby villages.

NEARBY FACILITIES & POINTS OF INTEREST: Hotel/Motel: Nul-Luk-Vik, Kotzebue, AK 99752, 907-442-3331, 70 miles from the Preserve by air; **Parks, other points of interest:** Cape Krusenstern National Monument, Kobuk Valley National Park, Bering Land Bridge National Preserve, NANA Museum of the Arctic; **New information:** Visitor contact facility available in Kotzebue. Because of rugged terrain & harsh climate visitors should contact NPS office prior to visiting the area.

Sitka National Historical Park
Sitka, Alaska   **SEE CLIMATABLE NO. 7**

MAILING ADDRESS: Sitka National Historical Park, Box 738, Sitka, AK 99835 **Telephone:** 907-747-6281

DIRECTIONS: Sitka is in Alaska's southeastern panhandle. It can be reached by commerical airline direct from Seattle, Juneau, and Anchorage, and is port of call for cruise ships and ferries on the Alaska Marine Highway System.
     The site of the 1804 fort and battle which marked the last major Tlingit Indian resistance to Russian colonization is preserved here. Native artists demonstrate crafts and discuss their culture. The Park features totem pole exhibits and the restoration of one of the oldest Russian buildings in Alaska. Created March 23, 1910.

VISITOR ACTIVITIES: interpretive talks, audiovisual exhibits, and craft demonstrations at the Visitor Center, picnicking, walking tours; **Permits:** No; **Fees:** No; **Visitor facilities:** parking and restrooms, picnic tables, fireplaces, Indian Cultural Center, trails, beach; **Any limitations on vehicle usage:** No; **Hiking trails:** Yes, almost 2 miles (3 km) of walkways thread the park; **Backcountry:** No; **Camping:** No; **Other overnight accommodations on site:** No; **Meals served in the park:** No; **Food and supplies obtainable in the park:** No; **Food and supplies obtainable nearby:** Yes, in Sitka, 1/2 mile (.8 km); **Overnight accommodations:** Sitka, 1/2 mile (.8 km); **First Aid available in park:** Yes; **Nearest Hospital:** Sitka, 1/2 mile (.8 km); **Days/Hours:** Open daily from 8 a.m. to 5 p.m. with extended hours in Summer, closed Sundays in winter; **Holiday Closings:** Thanksgiving, Dec. 25 and Jan. 1; **Visitor attractions closed for seasons:** None; **Weather:** Summer has frequent rain, temperatures range from the high 50's-mid 60's. Winter is rainy and snowy; temperatures from high teens to the 30's.

GENERAL INFORMATION: Visitors should also see nearby landmarks: St. Michael's Cathedral, Castle Hill, the Russian Memorial, and Old Sitka.

TRAVEL ACCESS: Bus: No; **Rail:** No; **Air:** Yes, Alaska Airlines provides daily service to Sitka Airport; **Other:** Alaska Marine Highway Ferry System.

NEARBY FACILITIES & POINTS OF INTEREST: Parks, other points of interest: Castle Hill, St. Michael's Cathedral, Sheldon Jackson Museum.

Wrangell-St. Elias National Park & Preserve
Alaska **SEE CLIMATABLE NO. 4**

MAILING ADDRESS: P.O. Box 29, Glennallen, AK 99588 **Telephone:** 909-822-5234

DIRECTIONS: Access into the central portion of the park by road is available from the community of Chitina via the state maintained Chitina-McCarthy road, passable by conventional vehicle with good clearance, which is generally passable during the summer months, and extends some 61 miles (98 km) up the Chitina River Valley following the historic route of the Copper River and Northwestern Railroad to the Kennicott River. Regularly scheduled van service is available from Glennallen and Chitina to McCarthy during the summer season. Road access into the northern section of the Park/Preserve is from Slana (on the Tok cutoff) along a state maintained route passable by conventional vehicle which extends some 45 miles into the abandoned mining community of Nabesna. (Nabesna is private land.) Access to the remaining interior portions of the Park/Preserve is by air. Charter air service is available from the Gulkana and Tok airports to a number of interior landing strips. Costs vary but an average round trip cost from Gulkana to McCarthy with pick up at a later point in time would cost about $700/plane with 3 people and gear for a Cessna 185. The community of Gulkana is some 200 miles (322 km) by paved highway from Anchorage and is reached by regularly scheduled bus service. Air access to the southern coastal sections including the beaches is available from Yakutat, Cordova & Valdez. Costs are about the same as above. At present there are no charter boats available out of Yakutat.

A day's drive east of Anchorage, this Park/Preserve contains a vast mountain wilderness that receives only light visitation. Here is the country's largest collection of glaciers and of peaks over 16,000 feet, including the 18,008-foot Mount St. Elias, the continent's third highest. Caribou, dall sheep, and grizzly and black bears, wolves, wolverine, moose and mountain goats are among the wildlife. Created by the Alaska National Interest Lands Conservation Act P.L. 96-487, December 2, 1980.

VISITOR ACTIVITIES: backpacking, lake fishing, camping, river rafting, cross-country skiing, mountain climbing, hiking, rafting, air tours; **Permits:** Alaska fishing licenses required, available in communities surrounding the park; **Fees:** No; **Visitor facilities:** lodging and meals available in McCarthy and Kennecott and along the Nabesna Road; Surface transportation available between McCarthy and Kennecott, 5 miles; **Any limitations on vehicle usage:** Both roads are passable to conventional vehicle with good ground clearance; **Hiking trails:** Yes, trails are primitive. Contact the Park Office for further information; **Backcountry:** Yes; **Camping:** Yes; **Other overnight accommodations on site:** Yes; There are scattered remote cabins located throughout the region which will accommodate backcountry parties. Standard accommodations are available in motels and cabins in and around the communities of Chitina and Glennallen, on the Glenn and Richardson highways, and along the Tok cutoff. State campgrounds are found at Liberty Creek near Chitina and along the major highways. **Food and supplies obtainable near the park:** Yes, Glennallen has a good supermarket, and limited supplies available in McCarthy, but all visitors to the backcountry must of necessity be self-sufficient and carry sufficient food to cover unexpected delays in getting picked up; **First Aid available in park:** No; **Nearest Clinic:** Glennallen; **Days/Hours:** Park/Preserve never closes; **Holiday Closings:** None; **Visitor attractions closed for season:** Check locally for conditions and services; **Weather:** Summer weather can be cool, but warm, sunny days are not uncommon in July and August. Weather conditions can interfere with scheduled air pickups, resulting in trips longer than scheduled. Clear, hot days are not uncommon, particularly in July which has the best weather. August is cooler and wetter but generally more mosquito free. The fall is excellent but of short duration. Winters are cold and dark, but clear weather is common. Average snow cover is about two feet.

GENERAL INFORMATION: Good rain gear and wool clothing are a must. Road conditions can change on very short notice making the road impassable to all but 4-wheel drive vehicles.

TRAVEL ACCESS: Air: No scheduled Airline, Charters available to Park from fixed base operators. Charges for charter fares vary. Yakutat, Cordova, Valdez, Anchorage, Gulkana, Northway, Tok & Fairbanks.

NEARBY FACILITIES & POINTS OF INTEREST: Campgrounds: Liberty Creek (near Chitina), Sour Dough (North of Gulkana).

Yukon-Charley Rivers National Preserve
Alaska   **SEE CLIMATABLE NO. 6**

MAILING ADDRESS: Superintendent, Yukon-Charley Rivers National Preserve, P.O. Box 64, Eagle, Alaska 99738 **Telephone:** 907-547-2233

DIRECTIONS: Eagle and Circle are the gateway cities to the Preserve. Take either the Taylor Highway to Eagle (the highway connects with the Alaska Highway at Tetlin Junction near Tok, Alaska.) or the Steese Highway from Fairbanks to Circle. There are scheduled flights from Fairbanks to both Eagle and Circle. Round trip fare to Eagle is $172 and to Circle $108. (1987 prices)
    This Preserve encompasses a 130-mile (209 km) stretch of the 1800-mile (2900 km) Yukon river and the 118 mile (190 km) scenic Charley River which drains a million-acre watershed near the Canadian border. Also protected are one of the largest nesting concentrations of the endangered peregrine falcon, and historic resources of the gold rush days. Created by Alaska National Interest Lands Conservation Act, December 2, 1980.

VISITOR ACTIVITIES: Walking and guided tours of historic towns, wildlife- and bird-watching, river floating, hiking, camping, photography, backcountry, picnicking, kayaking, canoeing; **Permits:** Alaska fishing and hunting licenses, available at local sporting goods stores, are required; **Fees:** None; **Visitor facilities:** Campground at Eagle, stores, 2 small restaurants at Eagle; 2 motels; Trading Post, cafe bar, liquor store, and campground at Circle; **Any limitations on vehicle usage:** no roads within preserve; **Hiking trails:** No; **Backcountry:** Information can be obtained from the Superintendent's office in Eagle; topographic maps are available from the Alaska National History Association outlet at the park headquarters, and there is also a small reference library for visitor use. **Camping:** Yes; no reservations needed at Eagle or Circle campgrounds; **Other overnight accommodations on site:** No; **Meals served in the park:** No; **Food and supplies obtainable in the park:** No **Food and supplies obtainable nearby:** Yes, Eagle and Circle; **Overnight accommodations:** Circle Hot Springs or along the Alaska Highway and Eagle, Circle; **First Aid available in park:** No; **Nearest Hospital:** Fairbanks (180 air-miles); **Days/Hours:** Preserve never closes; **Holiday Closings:** None; **Visitor attractions closed for season:** Many highways closed in winter; **Weather:** Most visitors come into the Preserve between mid-June and mid-September when the temperatures average between 40° and 70°F and water conditions are most conducive to travel. Thunderstorms with strong winds can arise suddenly. They can become violent, pose dangers, and raise whitecaps on the wider stretches on the Yukon. Water may also rise on the Charley River.

GENERAL INFORMATION: If you intend to be out among the elements in Alaska for a few days or longer in summer, you had best carry clothing for *all* seasons. Within a span of a few hours on the Yukon River you can be very warm and very cold, so you should prepare accordingly. You can always shed garments when temperatures rise, but you can't make a hasty purchase of a jacket when temperatures fall. Tennis shoes are practical for river travel because they dry easily, but you'll need additional footwear. Extra socks and a rain suit or poncho are essential. Your choice of *food* items will depend upon a number of variables: length of planned visit, activities planned, weight you can carry, and kinds of meals planned. If weight is no problem and you want to go "first class" from Eagle to Circle or vice versa, you can carry fresh meat and produce in a cooler packed with *chunk* ice. Local merchants rarely carry these items so make your purchases elsewhere. The weight-conscious traveller such as the backpacker or kayaker or the person wishing to abandon some of the amenities of civilization for a while will travel lightly and simply: freeze-dried and high-energy foods, packaged soups, dried fruit, powdered milk, etc. Ordinary *camping gear* is sufficient for summer visitors: a good sleeping bag that will dry, a tent with rain fly, knife, hatchet, insect repellent and head net, matches in waterproof container, cooking and eating utensils, water container, good maps, fishing tackle, and photographic equipment. *Insects* are numerous and irritating from early Summer to early August when they diminish. To avoid some of the irritation from insects, most travellers camp on bars and open shorelines where winds are most likely to prevail. Yukon river currents are strong and swift and deceptive in that they may not be readily apparent. The Charley River, and other floatable side streams are subject to rapid rise in water levels due to up-river thunderstorms.

Arizona

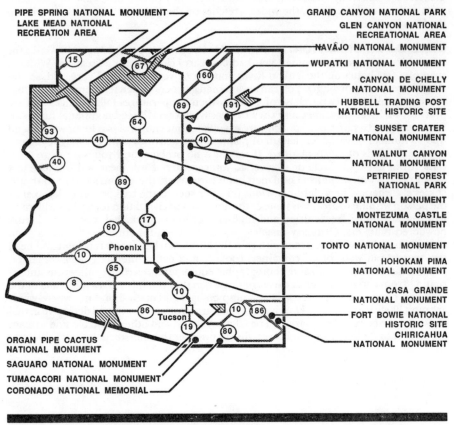

PIPE SPRING NATIONAL MONUMENT
LAKE MEAD NATIONAL
RECREATION AREA

GRAND CANYON NATIONAL PARK
GLEN CANYON NATIONAL
RECREATIONAL AREA
NAVÂJO NATIONAL MONUMENT
WUPATKI NATIONAL MONUMENT
CANYON DE CHELLY
NATIONAL MONUMENT
HUBBELL TRADING POST
NATIONAL HISTORIC SITE
SUNSET CRATER
NATIONAL MONUMENT
WALNUT CANYON
NATIONAL MONUMENT
PETRIFIED FOREST
NATIONAL PARK
TUZIGOOT NATIONAL MONUMENT
MONTEZUMA CASTLE
NATIONAL MONUMENT
TONTO NATIONAL MONUMENT
HOHOKAM PIMA
NATIONAL MONUMENT
CASA GRANDE
NATIONAL MONUMENT
FORT BOWIE NATIONAL
HISTORIC SITE
CHIRICAHUA
NATIONAL MONUMENT

Phoenix
Tucson

ORGAN PIPE CACTUS
NATIONAL MONUMENT
SAGUARO NATIONAL MONUMENT
TUMACACORI NATIONAL MONUMENT
CORONADO NATIONAL MEMORIAL

Canyon de Chelly National Monument
Chinle, Arizona   **SEE CLIMATABLE NO. 8**

MAILING ADDRESS: Superintendent, Canyon De Chelly National Monument, P.O. Box 588, Chinle, Arizona 86503 **Telephone:** 602-674-5436

DIRECTIONS: The Visitor Center is 3 miles (4.8 km) from Route 191 in Chinle. From Gallup, NM follow Routes 666, 264 to 191, 99 miles (159 km) to Chinle. From Grand Canyon, AZ, Routes 64, 89, 160, 264 to 191, 270 miles (370 km). From Holbrook-Petrified Forest, I-40, to 191. From Kayenta, Routes 160, 59 to 191, (82 miles). From Mesa Verde, Routes 789, 160 to 191, 158 miles (254 km). From Monument Valley, Routes 163, 160 to 191, 128 miles (206 km). From Page-Lake Powell, Routes 98, 160, 59 to 191, 208 miles (334.7 km). From Tuba City, Route 160, 59 to 191, 176 miles (283 km).
    Ruins of Indian villages built between A.D. 350 and 1300 are at the base of sheer red cliffs and in caves in canyon walls. Modern Navajo Indians live and farm here. Authorized for addition to the National Park System on Feb. 14, 1931.

VISITOR ACTIVITIES: auto tours, hiking, pictograph-viewing, ruin tours, interpretive exhibits and talks, horseback riding (by prior arrangement with the monument), picnicking, photography; **Permits:** Yes, you must have a tribal permit to fish on the reservation. Concession jeep tours available from Thunderbird Lodge, P.O. Box 548,

Chinle, AZ 86503. Phone 602-674-5443 or -5265. Hiking within the canyon, requires a Park Service permit plus an authorized Navajo guide, except along the White House Ruins Trail. A $6.50 per hour fee for up to 6 people is paid directly to the guide. To drive on the canyon bottom, you must obtain a Park Service permit and be accompanied by an authorized Navajo guide. Fee is $6.00 per hour for 1 to 5 vehicles, with a 5 vehicle maximum per guide; **Fees:** For concession jeep tours and guided tours; **Visitor facilities:** hiking and auto trails, parking, restrooms, exhibits, concession canyon trips, rental horses (by prior arrangement), campgrounds; **Any limitations on vehicle usage:** Autos should use paved highways only, jeeps or 4-wheel drive vehicles must be used to travel to the bottom of the canyon; **Hiking trails:** Yes, a 2½ mile (4 km) hiking trail leads to White House Ruin; **Backcountry:** No; **Camping:** Yes, no reservations for individual campsites, which are free of charge and are open year-round. Reservations for group sites, of 14 or more people, may be made by contacting the park. **Other overnight accommodations on site:** Yes, lodging is available at Thunderbird Lodge. Make reservations in advance by writing Thunderbird Lodge, Box 548, Chinle, AZ 86503, phone 602-674-5443 or -5265; **Meals served in the park:** Yes, at Thunderbird Lodge; **Food and supplies obtainable in the park:** No; **Food and supplies obtainable nearby:** Yes; **Overnight accommodations:** Window Rock, AZ 66 miles (106.2 km) away, Monument Valley, Hwy 191 and 160 to 163, 128 miles (206 km); and Gallup, NM Hwy 191 and 264 to 666, 99 miles (159 km), which has over 50 motels; **First Aid available in park:** Yes; **Nearest Hospital:** Chinle Hospital, 3 miles (4.8 km), 602-674-5281. Other hospitals in Gallup, NM, 99 miles (159 km), Ganado, AZ 36 miles (56 km) 607-753-3411; **Days/Hours:** Visitor Center open daily 8 a.m. to 5 p.m. **Holiday Closings:** Thanksgiving; Dec. 25 and Jan.1; **Visitor attractions closed for seasons:** The inner canyons become impassable in Winter and at certain other times of the year; **Weather:** Hot summers and cold winters, with little precipitation all year

GENERAL INFORMATION: Quicksand, deep dry sand, cliffs, loose rocks and flash floods make the canyons hazardous.

NEARBY FACILITIES & POINTS OF INTEREST: Parks, other points of interest: Hubbell Trading Post National Historic Site

Casa Grande Ruins National Monument
Coolidge, Arizona **SEE CLIMATABLE NO. 9**

MAILING ADDRESS: Superintendent, Casa Grande Ruins National Monument, P.O. Box 518, Coolidge, Arizona 85228 **Telephone:** 602-723-3172

DIRECTIONS: The monument is located in North Coolidge on AZ 87, about halfway between Phoenix and Tucson.

Perplexing ruins of a massive four-story building, constructed of high-lime desert soil by Indians who farmed the Gila Valley 600 years ago, raise many unanswered questions for modern man. The Casa Grande Ruin Reservation was authorized by Congress on Mar. 8, 1889 and proclaimed a national monument on Aug. 3, 1918 at which time the National Park Service assumed administration of the area.

VISITOR ACTIVITIES: interpretive talks and exhibits, walking tours, picnicking; **Permits:** No; **Fees:** entrance fee is $3 per vehicle. Golden Eagle, Golden Age and Golden Access Passports accepted and available; **Visitor facilities:** parking and restrooms at Visitor Center, drinking water, picnic area; **Any limitations on vehicle usage:** No; **Hiking trails:** Yes, a 400-yard round trip self-guiding walking trail leads through the ruins area; **Backcountry:** No; **Camping:** No; **Other overnight accommodations on site:** No; **Meals served in the park:** No; **Food and supplies obtainable in the park:** No; **Food and supplies obtainable nearby:** Yes, in Coolidge; **Overnight accommodations:** Coolidge,

AZ 87, Florence, AZ 287, 12 miles (19 km) east; Casa Grande, AZ 287, 22 miles (33 km) southwest; **First Aid available in park:** Yes, or nearby in Coolidge, AZ 87; **Nearest Hospital:** Florence, AZ 287, 12 miles (19 km) east; **Days/Hours:** Open from 7 a.m. to 6 p.m., 365 days a year; **Holiday Closings:** None; **Weather:** The most comfortable time for visiting is between early October and early May, because summer temperatures approach 120°F.

GENERAL INFORMATION: WARNING: You are in harsh desert area. Beware of the cactus. Intense heat can cause varying degrees of discomfort. Be cautious of poisonous snakes, centipedes, and scorpions.

Chiricahua National Monument
Willcox, Arizona   **SEE CLIMATABLE NO. 10**

MAILING ADDRESS: Superintendent, Chiricahua National Monument, Dos Cabezas Route, Box 6500, Willcox, Arizona 85643 **Telephone:** 602-824-3560

DIRECTIONS: The Visitor Center is 36 miles (61 km) south of Willcox on AZ 186 and 181.
    The varied rock formations here were created millions of years ago by volcanic activity, aided by erosion. Established by Presidential Proclamation on April 18, 1924.

VISITOR ACTIVITIES: camping, hiking, auto tours, interpretive exhibits, campfire programs in Spring and Summer, picnicking; **Permits:** No; **Fees:** $3 per car entrance fee; $5 per night per site camping fee, with Golden Eagle Passport, free admission, camping $5; Golden Age Passport, free admission, camping $2.50. Camping and entrance fees are subject to change. **Visitor facilities:** parking and restrooms at Visitor Center, campgrounds, drinking water, fireplaces, tables, picnic area; **Any limitations on vehicle usage:** No wheeled vehicles are permitted on the trails; **Hiking trails:** Yes, more than 17 miles (27 km) of trails provide views of all the park's features; **Backcountry:** No; **Camping:** Yes, no reservations for campsites maximum trailer length of 26 feet; **Other overnight accommodations on site:** No; **Meals served in the park:** No; **Food and supplies obtainable in the park:** No; **Food and supplies obtainable nearby:** Yes, in Willcox; **Overnight accommodations:** Willcox, AZ 186, 36 miles (61 km) north, has motels, restaurants, commercial campgrounds and trailer parks; **First Aid available in park:** Generally; **Nearest Hospital:** Willcox, AZ 186, 36 miles (61 km); **Days/Hours:** Open daily year-round 8 a.m. to 5 p.m.; **Holiday Closings:** Dec. 25; **Visitor attractions closed for seasons:** Road occasionally closed in Winter; **Weather:** Temperatures are generally moderate. The mean daily temperature in January is 4°C (40°F) and in July, 23°C (74°F). Most of the precipitation occurs in July and August. Except for Winter, the rest of the year is relatively dry.

GENERAL INFORMATION: *For Your Safety*-Be alert for an occasional rattlesnake during warm weather. The scenic drive is winding and mountainous; watch for fallen rocks on the road, and ice in the Winter.

TRAVEL ACCESS: Bus: several buses from Tucson - 120 miles from park.

NEARBY FACILITIES & POINTS OF INTEREST: Hotel/Motel: Willcox, AZ, 36 miles from park; **Food/Supplies:** Willcox, AZ, 36 miles from park; **Campgrounds:** Willcox, AZ, 40 miles from park and U.S. Forest Service, Coronado Nat'l Forest; **Parks, other points of interest:** Cochise Visitor Center; Chiricahua Wilderness area, and nearby Fort Bowie NHS; tremendous birding opportunities; **New park programs:** addition of the FARAWAY RANCH in the monument a historic structure depicting ranch life on the early frontier in the southwest.

Coronado National Memorial
Hereford, Arizona   **SEE CLIMATABLE NO. 10**

MAILING ADDRESS: Superintendent, Coronado National Memorial, Rural Route 2, Box 126, Hereford, Arizona 85615 **Telephone:** 602-366-5515 - 458-9333

DIRECTIONS: The Memorial is about 22 miles (35 km) south of Sierra Vista, AZ, and 30 miles (48 km) west of Bisbee, AZ. Memorial headquarters is 5 miles (8 km) off of AZ 92 in Montezuma Canyon.

Our Hispanic heritage and the first European exploration of the southwest, by Francisco Vasquez de Coronado in 1540-42, are commemorated here, near the point where Coronado's expedition entered what is now the United States. Established by act of Congress on Nov. 5, 1952.

VISITOR ACTIVITIES: interpretive exhibits, picnicking, self-guided walking tours, hiking, climbing, Hispanic, Indian, Anglo cultural borderlands festival in April each year; **Permits:** No; **Fees:** No; **Visitor facilities:** parking, restrooms, wayside exhibits, picnic area, foot trails, trailside benches; **Any limitations on vehicle usage:** No off road travel, no motorized vehicles on trails; **Hiking trails:** Yes, scenic foot trails begin at the parking area and Visitor Center, and at Montezuma Pass area; **Backcountry:** No; **Camping:** No; **Other overnight accommodations on site:** No, a U.S. Forest Service campground is at Parker Lake 18 miles (29 km) west of the Memorial; **Meals served in the park:** No; **Food and supplies obtainable in the park:** No; **Food and supplies obtainable nearby:** Yes, at Sierra Vista, Bisbee; **Overnight accommodations:** Sierra Vista, AZ 92 North, 22 miles (35 km); Bisbee, AZ 92 East, 30 miles (48 km); **First Aid available in park:** Yes; **Nearest Hospital:** Sierra Vista, AZ 92 North, 22 miles (35 km), Bisbee, AZ 92 East, 30 miles (48 km); **Days/Hours:** Park open daily from dawn to dusk, Visitor Center open daily from 8 a.m. to 5 p.m.; **Holiday Closings:** Dec. 25; **Visitor attractions closed for seasons:** No; **Weather:** Rainy periods are July through Oct. and Dec. through March. Temperatures are generally in the 70's to 90's in Summer and into the 20's in Winter. There are light snowfalls in Winter.

GENERAL INFORMATION: *For Your Safety*—Watch out for unexpected steps, low branches, cactus, poison ivy, black widow spiders, scorpions and rattlesnakes.

Fort Bowie National Historic Site
Bowie, Arizona   **SEE CLIMATABLE NO. 10**

MAILING ADDRESS: Superintendent, Fort Bowie National Historic Site, P.O. Box 158, Bowie, Arizona 85605 **Telephone:** 602-847-2500

DIRECTIONS: There is no road to the ruins proper. They can be reached only by a 1½ mile (2.4 km) foot trail that begins midway in Apache Pass. The trailhead may be reached from two directions: from the town of Willcox, located on Int. 10, drive 22 miles (35.4 km) south on AZ 186 to the graded road leading east into Apache Pass; from the town of Bowie, also on Int. 10, drive southerly 12 miles (19.3 km) on a graded dirt road that then bears westerly into Apache Pass.

Established in 1862, this fort was the focal point of military operations against Geronimo, Cochise and their band of Chiricachua Apaches. Authorized for addition to the National Park System on Aug. 30, 1964.

VISITOR ACTIVITIES: walking tours, exhibits, wildflower- and wildlife-watching, hiking; **Permits:** No; **Fees:** No; **Visitor facilities:** small museum in the ranger station, parking area, pit toilets. Limited Handicap access is available to Fort ruins, but requires advance notice. To make arrangements or obtain further information, write or call Fort Bowie National Historic Site, P.O. Box 158, Bowie, Arizona 85605, 602-847-2500; **Any limitations on vehicle usage:** No vehicle access beyond the parking lot at the trail head; **Hiking trails:** Yes, 1½ miles (2.4 km) foot trail to ruins 1½ mile alternate return trail via Overlook Ridge to main trail & parking area; **Backcountry:** Yes, write the Site for information; **Camping:** No; **Other overnight accommodations on site:** No; **Meals served in the park:** No; **Food and supplies obtainable in the park:** No; **Food and supplies obtainable nearby:** Yes, at Willcox and Bowie; **Overnight accommodations:** Willcox and Bowie, Int. 10, 22 miles (35.4 km) and 12 miles (19.3 km); **First Aid available in park:** Yes, at the contact station in the ruins; **Nearest Hospital:** Willcox, 12 miles (19.2 km) to Bowie & 25 miles (40 km) more by I-10; **Days/Hours:** A ranger is on duty at the contact station from 8 a.m. to 5 p.m. daily; **Holiday Closings:** Dec. 25; **Visitor attractions closed for seasons:** No; **Weather:** Drizzling rain in Winter, heavy rains in July and August, with flash flood warnings. Beware of muddy roads for short period of time after major storms.

GENERAL INFORMATION: Water is available at the fort. However, the summer hiker should consider a canteen since temperatures may climb above 100°. Summer storms may suddenly and briefly flood the washes. Simply wait out high water. Be alert for an occasional rattlesnake or Gila monster.

Glen Canyon National Recreation Area
Page, Arizona (also in Utah)   **SEE CLIMATABLE NO. 11**

MAILING ADDRESS: Superintendent, Glen Canyon National Recreation Area, P.O. Box 1507, Page, Arizona 86040 **Telephone:** 602-645-2471

DIRECTIONS: Park Headquarters is at 337 North Navajo Drive in Page, Arizona, off US 89. There is a Visitor Center by Glen Canyon Dam, about 2 miles (3.2 km) from Page on US 89.
　　Glen Canyon NRA includes Lake Powell which is formed by the Colorado River, and stretches for 186 miles (299 km) behind one of the highest dams in the world. Established by act of Congress on Oct. 27, 1972.

VISITOR ACTIVITIES: camping, swimming, boating, fishing, water skiing, hunting, driving, hiking, dam tours, photography, interpretive exhibits, picnicking; **Permits:** fishing permits are available at sporting goods stores in Page or at the park's marina. Licenses vary in length of validity and cost; **Fees:** Camping fee is $6.00 per night per site; **Visitor facilities:** restrooms, marinas, launching ramps, beaches, campgrounds, trailer villages, restaurants, lodging, boat rentals and tours, picnic areas; **Any limitations on vehicle usage:** Drive only on designated roads. Boaters should be familiar with boating regulations; see pamphlet available at the Visitor Center; **Hiking trails:** Yes, Rangers can suggest good routes; **Backcountry:** Yes, nearly 90 percent of the area is wilderness proposed backcountry. Write for information; **Camping:** Yes, no reservations; **Other overnight accommodations on site:** Yes, lodging at Wahweap, Bullfrog, Hite and Halls Crossing. R.V. Hookups available Wahweap, Bullfrog, Halls Crossing. Houseboats available at Wahweap, Bullfrog, Halls Crossing, San Juan and Hite. Write: Reservations, Del Webb Recreational Properties, Box 29040, Phoenix, AZ 85038 or call 1-800-528-6154 (In AZ 1-800-352-6508) or San Juan Marina, 356 South Main Street, Blanding, Utah 84511, 801-678-2217; **Meals served in the park:** Yes, Wahweap, and Bullfrog; **Food and supplies obtainable in the park:** Yes, Wahweap, Bullfrog, Halls Crossing, Dangling Rope, Hite and San Juan; **Overnight accommodations:** Page, 2 miles (3.2 km) from the Park on US 89; **First Aid available in park:** Yes, at Dangling Rope Marina and

Ranger Stations at Wahweap, Bullfrog, Halls Crossing, and Hite; **Nearest Hospital:** Page, about 6.5 miles from Wahweap, Samaritan Health Clinic at Bullfrog; Clinic in Green River, Hospital in Grand Junction, CO; **Days/Hours:** Park never closes; **Holiday Closings:** Visitor Center closes on Dec. 25 and Jan. 1; **Visitor attractions closed for seasons:** None; **Weather:** July and August are the hottest months, but the weather is mild through the middle of November. Winters are short with spring arriving in March.

GENERAL INFORMATION: An all day and 1/2 day cruise takes boaters to Rainbow Bridge National Monument (see listing in this book). If you are camping, be sure to pick a campsite on flat or gently sloping terrain, not on talus slopes or underneath ledges where you can see that rock has fallen.

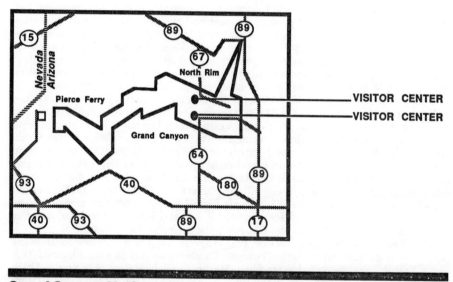

Grand Canyon National Park
Grand Canyon, Arizona   **SEE CLIMATABLE NO. 11**

MAILING ADDRESS: Suprintendent, Grand Canyon National Park, P.O. Box 129, Grand Canyon, Arizona 86023 **Telephone:** 602-638-7888

DIRECTIONS: There are three separate areas in the park-the South Rim, the North Rim, (open approximately mid-May to late October only) and the Inner Canyon. Each has different facilities, different activities, and even different climates. The South Rim Visitor Center is 3.5 miles (6 km) north of the South Entrance Station, in Grand Canyon Village, 60 miles (96.6 km) north of Williams and 57 miles (92 km) west of Cameron, both on AZ 64. The North Rim Ranger Station and developed area is on State Hwy 67, 45 miles (72 km) south of Jacob Lake (at intersection with Hwy 89).

The park, focusing on the world-famous Grand Canyon of the Colorado River, encompasses the entire course of the river and adjacent uplands from the southern terminus of Glen Canyon National Recreation Area to the eastern boundary of Lake Mead National Recreation Area. The forces of erosion have exposed an immense variety of formations which illustrate vast periods of geological history. National Park established by act of Congress on Feb. 26, 1919.

VISITOR ACTIVITIES: Interpretive exhibits, guided and self-guiding tours, picnicking, camping, backcountry hiking, horseback riding, white water rafting, kayaking, fishing, biking, bus tours, mule trips, river tours, horses available from outside park. Some trails open to stock use in park; **Permits:** Required for backcountry camping, stock use and river running. For fishing, licenses and trout stamps are available at Babbitt's Store in Grand Canyon Village; **Fees:** $5 entrance fee; $6 camping fee at Desert View, $8 at Mather and $6 at North Rim Campgrounds. Golden Eagle, Golden Age and Golden Access Passports accepted and available; **Visitor facilities:** Picnic areas, campgrounds, hiking trails, bus, taxi, guided hikes, river float trips, religious services, post office, bank, backpacking equipment rentals, food and lodging facilities, air tours from outside the park; **Any limitations on vehicle usage:** No vehicles may be operated outside of established public roads and designated areas (includes cars, pickups, trucks, motorcycles, trail bikes, etc.); **Hiking trails:** Yes, 38 maintained trails of nearly 400 miles (644 km), 400 non-maintained trails. Check at Information Centers for details; **Backcountry:** Yes, backcountry reservations and permits are required and issued by mail or in person. Contact Backcountry Reservations Office, Grand Canyon National Park, Grand Canyon, AZ 86023, phone 602-638-2474 for recorded information; **Camping:** Desert View and North Rim, no reservations required; both closed in winter; Trailer Village (hookups available—open year round) is operated by concessioner on South Rim, phone 602-638-2401; Reservations are taken for Mather Campground (South Rim) sites for the period between May 15-Sept. 30: Contact Ticketron Reservation Office, P.O. Box 2715, San Francisco, CA 94126. Any unreserved campsites will be assigned on a first-come, first-served basis. Most in-park campsites fill by noon, May through Sept. No reservations are available for other campsites at Grand Canyon. Other sites are available near the Park; contact Grand Canyon for further information; **Other overnight accommodations on site:** On South Rim: Bright Angel Lodge, El Tovar Hotel, Kachina Lodge, Thunderbird Lodge, Maswick Lodge, Yavapai Lodge for reservations phone 602-638-2401, Grand Canyon Youth Hostel, phone 602-638-9018; On the North Rim: Grand Lodge, phone 801-586-7686; **Meals served in the park:** Yes, at North Rim, Grand Canyon Village, Desert View, Phantom Ranch and Tusayan; **Food and supplies obtainable in the park:** Yes, Grand Canyon Village, Desert View, and the North Rim; **Food and supplies obtainable nearby:** Yes, Tusayan, AZ, 1 mile (1.6 km) south of the park; **Overnight accommodations:** Tusayan, Cameron, Gray Mountain, Flagstaff, Williams, Kaibab Lake, Jacob Lake, Fredonia, Marble Canyon, & Page, AZ; Kanab, Utah; **First Aid available in park:** Yes, at the Information Desk in Grand Lodge (North Rim) or at Grand Canyon Clinic, Center Road between South Entrance Station and Grand Canyon Village. In case of emergency, telephone 602-638-2477; **Nearest Hospital:** For South Rim, Flagstaff, I-40 & AZ 180, 80 miles (129 km)—Williams has daytime clinic only. For North Rim, Kanab, UT via UT 89, 81 miles (130 km); **Days/Hours:** South Rim never closes; North Rim open 24 hours a day from mid-May to late-Oct.; **Holiday Closings:** None; **Visitor attractions closed for seasons:** North Rim closed in winter, from about late Oct. to mid-May; **Weather:** Temperature ranges—South Rim, 51°-82°F in Summer, 20°-43°F in Winter; North Rim, 43°-75°F in Summer, 18°-39°F in Winter; Inner Canyon, 76°-115°F in Summer, 39°-59°F in Winter.

GENERAL INFORMATION: For up-to-date recorded information about weather, road conditions, phone 602-638-2245, 24 hours a day. For information (recorded daily) about interpretive activities phone 602-638-9304. *For Your Safety*—Do not climb in the canyon; most of the rock is too crumbly for safety. Avoid overexertion. The South Rim averages 7000 feet and the North Rim over 8000 feet in elevation. Cardiac and respiratory patients should take care. Temperatures within the Inner Canyon can reach extremes. Take enough water and food, dress for the weather, and know your own physical limitations. If you are hiking, carry plenty of water. Be careful near the canyon rim.

TRAVEL ACCESS: Bus: Nava-Hopi provides regular service between Flagstaff, AZ and Bright Angel Lodge in the park; **Rail:** Amtrak to Flagstaff (AZ), 80 miles south of

Park. **Air:** Scenic Airlines, Las Vegas Airlines, Air Nevada and others provide service to Grand Canyon National Park Airport Tusayan, Arizona (8 miles south of Grand Canyon Village) **Other:** Taxi available in park and from airport to Grand Canyon Village.

NEARBY FACILITIES & POINTS OF INTEREST: Hotel/Motel: South Rim: Red Feather Lodge (602) 638-2673 and Canyon Squire Motel (602) 638-2681 Tusayan, AZ, 8 miles south of Grand Canyon Village. For North Rim: Kaibab Lodge, (602) 638-2389; Jacob Lake Lodge, (602) 643-7232; **Food/Supplies:** Canyon Food Mart in Tusayan, AZ; **Camping:** Grand Canyon Camper Village (Private) Tusayan, AZ, (602) 638-2887, and Ten X (U.S.F.S.—closed in winter), 5 miles south of Tusayan, AZ, (602) 638-2443.

Hohokam Pima National Monument
Sacaton, Arizona   **SEE CLIMATABLE NO. 9**

MAILING ADDRESS: Superintendent, Hohokam Pima National Monument, c/o Casa Grande Ruins National Monument, P.O. Box 518, Coolidge, Arizona 85228 **Telephone:** 602-723-3172

DIRECTIONS: NOT OPEN TO THE PUBLIC.
   The Monument will preserve the Snaketown archeological site, which contains the remains of a large Hohokam Indian village occupied between 300 A.D. and 1100 A.D. Although the Monument was authorized by Congress for addition to the National Park System on Oct. 21, 1972, it has not yet been established. The area remains closed to the public pending completion of land exchanges necessary to bring the site under National Park Service administration.

Hubbell Trading Post National Historic Site
Ganado, Arizona   **SEE CLIMATABLE NO. 8**

MAILING ADDRESS: Superintendent, Hubbell Trading Post National Historic Site, P.O. Box 150, Ganado, Arizona 86505 **Telephone:** 602-755-3475/3477

DIRECTIONS: The site is on the Navajo Indian Reservation, 1 mile (1.6 km) west of Ganado and 55 miles (89 km) northwest of Gallup, New Mexico. It can be reached by AZ 264 (Navajo Route 3) from the east and west by US 191 from the north and south.
   This still-active 100 year-old trading post illustrates the influence of reservation traders on the Indians' way of life. Authorized for addition to the National Park System on August 28, 1965.

VISITOR ACTIVITIES: walking tours, exhibits, weaving and silversmithing demonstrations, picnicking, tours of the Hubbell Farmstead, watching the ongoing trading operation and craft demonstrations; **Fees:** No; **Visitor facilities:** parking and restrooms at Visitor Center, picnic area; **Any limitations on vehicle usage:** Off-road vehicle travel is prohibited; **Hiking trails:** No; **Backcountry:** No; **Camping:** No; **Other overnight accommodations on site:** No; **Meals served in the park:** No, restaurant in Ganado; **Food and supplies obtainable in the park:** Yes, groceries; **Food and supplies obtainable nearby:** Yes, at Chinle or Window Rock; **Overnight accommodations:** Chinle, 35 miles (56 km) north on US 191; Window Rock, 30 miles (48 km) east on AZ 264; Chambers, 38 miles (61 km) south on US 191; Second Mesa, 67 miles (92 km) west on AZ 264; **First Aid available in park:** Yes; **Nearest Hospital:** Ganado, 1 mile (1.6 km) east; **Days/Hours:** Open daily from 8 a.m. to 5 p.m., until 6 p.m. in Summer; **Holiday Closings:** Thanksgiving, Dec. 25 and Jan. 1; **Visitor attractions closed for seasons:** None; **Wea-**

ther: Elevation is 6300 feet. Climate is mild. Record extremes are -50°F and 100°F. High winds blow the sand in Spring. Fall and early Spring may bring snow flurries.

GENERAL INFORMATION: You will find Hubbell Trading Post on the way to Grand Canyon National Park, Canyon de Chelly National Monument (see listings in this book) and the Hopi Mesas. *For your safety,* be cautious when walking around the grounds as burrs and bits of metal and glass have been left over the years. In many cases the floors are uneven in the buildings, and there is usually a step between rooms. Portable wheelchair ramps are available.

Montezuma Castle National Monument
Camp Verde, Arizona   **SEE CLIMATABLE NO. 12**

MAILING ADDRESS: Superintendent, Montezuma Castle National Monument, P.O. Box 219, Camp Verde, Arizona 86322 **Telephone:** 602-567-3322

DIRECTIONS: The Visitor Center is 2½ miles (3.8 km) off Interstate 17, 5 miles (8 km) north of Camp Verde.

One of the best-preserved cliff dwellings in the United States, this 5-story, 20-room pueblo was built by prehistoric farmers over 700 years ago. Montezuma Well, a separate section of the Monument, is 10½ miles (17 km) north of the Castle. This natural sinkhole is continually fed by spring water at the rate of 1½ million gallons a day. Archaeological sites include pueblo ruins, cliff dwellings, and an excavated pithouse. Created by Presidential Proclamation on Dec. 8, 1906.

VISITOR ACTIVITIES: picnicking, photography, self-guiding walking tours, exhibits; **Permits:** No; **Fees:** Yes, entrance fee is $3 per carload. No charge to US residents age 62 and older. Golden Eagle and Golden Age Passports accepted and available; **Visitor facilities:** restrooms, picnic areas, interpretive trails, museum; **Any limitations on vehicle usage:** Visitors should arrive before 10 a.m. or after 3 p.m. during the summer months because of limited parking; **Hiking trails:** Yes, a ⅓ mile (.6 km) self-guiding trail leads to the ruins; **Backcountry:** No; **Camping:** No; **Other overnight accommodations on site:** No; **Meals served in the park:** No; **Food and supplies obtainable in the park:** No; **Food and supplies obtainable nearby:** Yes, at Camp Verde; **Overnight accommodations:** Camp Verde, 5 miles (8 km) south; **First Aid available in park:** Yes, or nearby at Camp Verde; **Nearest Hospital:** Cottonwood, Int. 17 to AZ 279 to by pass road to Jerome, 20 miles (32.2 km); **Days/Hours:** Open daily from 8 a.m. to 5 p.m., and from 7 a.m. through 7 p.m. from June to September.

GENERAL INFORMATION: Visitors may wish to explore other nearby monuments, including Tuzigoot, Walnut Canyon, Wupatki & Sunset Crater (see listings in this book). Nearby points of interest include Fort Verde and Jerome State Historical Parks.

Navajo National Monument
Tonalea, Arizona   **SEE CLIMATABLE NO. 8**

MAILING ADDRESS: Superintendent, Navajo National Monument, HC 71 Box 5, Tonalea, Arizona 86044-9704 **elephone:** 602-672-2366/2367

DIRECTIONS: The monument is in north-eastern Arizona, south to southeast of Lake Powell and the Glen Canyon Recreation Area. It is reached from US 160 which diagonals through the Navajo Reservation. At Black Mesa 50 miles (80.5 km) northeast of Tuba City, 22 miles (35.4 km) southwest of Kayenta-you turn north onto Route 564. Route

564 dead-ends at the Monument Headquarters, 9 miles (14.5 km) from US 160.

Betatakin, Keet Seel, and Inscription House are three of the best-preserved and most elaborate cliff dwellings known. Created by Presidential Proclamation Mar. 20, 1909.

VISITOR ACTIVITIES: hiking, interpretive exhibits and trails, guided tours during visitor season, evening campfire programs in summer, camping, picnicking, horseback riding; **Permits:** required for tours to Keet Seel only, apply by mail, phone, or in person; **Fees:** No; **Visitor facilities:** Visitor Center, exhibits, craft shop in summer, hiking trails, picnic area, campgrounds; **Any limitations on vehicle usage:** Vehicles are limited to paved roads; **Hiking trails:** Yes, Sandal Trail is 1 mile (1.6 km) long roundtrip and leads to the Betatakin Point Overlook. May-October, weather permitting, tours of not more than 24 people leave from the Visitor Center to Betatakin Ruin down into the canyon. It is only about 3 miles (5 km), roundtrip but it's not easy. You climb down and back up a 700 feet steep incline, equivalent to a 70-story building! The tour takes about 3-4 hours and is Ranger-led. You cannot go into the canyon or the ruin without a Ranger!

Keet Seel, the largest cliff dwelling in Arizona, is about eight miles north of the Visitor Center. It can be reached only on foot or horseback; the trail is rugged and the elevation change is over a thousand feet. You cannot enter Keet Seel without a Park Ranger. All travel is by reservation and there is a limit of 25 people per day. So write or phone ahead up to 2 months in advance if you want to make this trip; **Backcountry:** Yes, for information write or phone Headquarters; **Camping:** Yes, no reservations available for campsites. The Monument maintains a campground of 30 sites at the Headquarters area. Trailers up to 25 feet in length can be accommodated. The campground is closed from October 15 to May 1. There is a group campground and overflow camping about ¼ mile from the Visitor Center, open when weather permits; **Other overnight accommodations on site:** No; **Meals served in the park:** No; **Food and supplies obtainable in the park:** No; **Food and supplies obtainable nearby:** Yes, at the shopping center at Black Mesa, where you turn off US 160 to get to the Monument; **Overnight accommodations:** Kayenta, US 160, 31 miles (50 km) northeast of the Monument; Tuba City, US 160, 59 miles (95 km) southwest; Tsegi, 20 miles (32 km) east; **First Aid available in park:** Yes; **Nearest Hospital:** Flagstaff, AZ, 150 miles (241.4 km) or Tuba City, AZ. **Days/Hours:** The Visitor Center is open year-round from 8 a.m. to 5 p.m. daily, until 6 p.m. in Summer; **Holiday Closings:** Thanksgiving, Dec. 25, Jan. 1; **Visitor attractions closed for seasons:** Sandal Trail to the overlook is closed when snow and ice are severe, Betatakin Cliff dwelling approx. Nov. - Apr., Keet Seel from Labor Day to Memorial Day weekend, Inscription House is closed indefinitely to the public; **Weather:** The Monument is at an elevation of over 7,280 feet. Winter comes early and stays late. Snow accumulation is heavy, especially in the small canyons which provide access to the cliff dwellings. Trails into the canyon are closed after the first snowfall and remain closed until all snow melts in Spring.

GENERAL INFORMATION: While you hike, remember that the altitude is 7280 feet. The air is thin. You may find that walking can tire you out faster than you might expect if you are not used to the elevation. Pace yourself, eat well and don't try to rush. None of the more strenuous trips are recommended for anyone who has heart or respiratory ailments. The formations are sandstone and natural rockfalls are common. When traveling the Navajo Reservation you should always watch out for livestock wandering on or about the highway, and respect the privacy and land of the Navajo People.

Organ Pipe Cactus National Monument
Ajo, Arizona   **SEE CLIMATABLE NO. 13**

MAILING ADDRESS: Superintendent, Organ Pipe Cactus National Monument, Route 1, Box 100, Ajo, Arizona 85321 **Telephone:** 602-387-6849

DIRECTIONS: The monument lies on the border of the United States and Mexico, 140 miles (225 km) south of Phoenix via Arizona 85, and 142 miles (229 km) west of Tucson via AZ 86 and AZ 85. Access to the park from Mexico is via Mexico Route 2 from the west and Mexico Routes 2 and 8 from the South. The Visitor Center is 17 miles (28 km) south of the park entrance.

Sonoran Desert plants and animals found nowhere else in the United States are protected here, alongside traces of a historic trail, Camino del Diablo. Established by Presidential Proclamation on Apr. 13, 1937.

VISITOR ACTIVITIES: Interpretive talks and walks, scenic drives, hiking, backpacking, photography, wildlife- and bird-watching, camping, picnicking; **Permits:** for backcountry, available at Visitor Center; **Fees:** $3.00 entrance fee; Camping Fee is $6 per night per site; **Visitor facilities:** Visitor Center, museum, campgrounds, picnic areas, mail drop, trails, restrooms, general store, snack bar, and gas station in Lukeville; **Any limitations on vehicle usage:** Drive only on established roads and turnouts, large recreational vehicles not recommended on graded dirt roads. Visitors should be prepared for driving on desert roads. In summer carry a gallon of water per person in the car. If water is flowing across the road, do not try to drive through it. Wait until the water goes down-usually this takes about an hour. During the summer storm season (July and August), check at the Visitor Center for possible park road closures. When driving at night, be alert for wildlife on the road; **Hiking trails:** Yes, check at Visitor Center for information on the trails; **Backcountry:** Yes, permit is required, check at Visitor Center. Most backpacking is cross-country (no trails); **Camping:** Yes, no reservations for the 208-site campground except for organized groups using the group campsites, Recreational Vehicles not to exceed 35' in length; **Other overnight accommodations on site:** No; **Meals served in the park:** No; **Food and supplies obtainable in the park:** No; **Food and supplies obtainable nearby:** Yes, at Lukeville; **Overnight accommodations:** Lukeville, 5 miles (8 km) south, Why, 22 miles (35 km) north, and Ajo, 35 miles (56 km) north; **First Aid available in park:** Yes; **Nearest Hospital:** Tucson or Phoenix 145 miles (241 km); **Days/Hours:** Visitor Center is open 7 days a week from 8 a.m. to 5 p.m., year round; **Holiday Closings:** None; **Visitor attractions closed for seasons:** Interpretive programs during winter months only; **Weather:** November-April is mild and usually sunny, May-October is hot, with daytime temperatures over 100°F.

GENERAL INFORMATION: The Monument is a good stopoff while travelling to Mexico via Tucson or Phoenix. *Beware of the cactus!* The spines of these plants and many other trees and shrubs can cause you painful injury . Visitors should be prepared for desert walking. For protection from the sun, rough terrain and the weather, you should have a hat and wear clothing and shoes that are comfortable and sturdy. Carry enough drinking water (4 liters or 1 gallon per day per person when hiking). At night, walk carefully and use a flashlight to look for rattlesnakes in your path; five species are found in the monument. Snakes play an important role in the ecology of the desert and should not be harmed. Poisonous creatures such as rattlesnakes are common.

Travelling in Mexico. There is free access into Sonoyta and westward on Mexico Route 2. However, if you continue into the interior or go to Puerto Peñasco, you must have a tourist permit. A car entry permit is required for trips into the interior. Permits may be obtained from Mexican officials at the border. To get a tourist permit, you must have proof of citizenship (birth certificate, voters registration card or passport), and to get a car permit, you will need your automobile registration. To re-enter the United States with pets, you must carry proof of valid pet vaccinations. Transportation of firearms into Mexico is a violation of Mexican law.

Petrified Forest National Park
Petrified Forest National Park, Arizona   **SEE CLIMATABLE NO. 14**

MAILING ADDRESS: Superintendent, Petrified Forest National Park, Petrified Forest National Park, Arizona 86028 **Telephone:** 602-524-6228

DIRECTIONS: The Painted Desert Visitor Center is 26 miles (42 km) east of Holbrook on Interstate 40. The Rainbow Forest Entrance Station is 19 miles (30.6 km) east of Holbrook on US 180.

Features of the park include a large section of the colorful Painted Desert, Indian ruins and petroglyphs, trees that have been petrified, or changed to multicolored stone, and remains of prehistoric animals. Created by Presidential Proclamation on Dec. 8, 1906. Established as a National Park, December 9, 1962.

VISITOR ACTIVITIES: paved trails and wilderness hiking, interpretive walks and talks in Summer, film, picknicking, self-guiding auto tours; **Permits:** required for overnight backcountry, can be obtained at Rainbow Forest Museum and Painted Desert Visitor Center; **Fees:** $5 entrance fee, Golden Eagle, Golden Age and Golden Access Passports accepted and available; **Visitor facilities:** picnic areas, restrooms, film about the Park at Painted Desert Visitor Center, interpretive exhibits including specimens of petrified wood. A guide map of the 28 mile (48 km) park road is available at the entrance stations; **Any limitations on vehicle usage:** No off-road vehicular use permitted. Park only in designated parking areas; **Hiking trails:** Yes, walking trails at Giant Logs (behind Rainbow Forest Museum), Long Logs, Agate House, Crystal Forest, Blue Mesa, and Kachina Point to Tawa Point. Trails vary in length from 1/2-3/4 mile (.8 km-1.2 km); **Backcountry:** Yes, approximately 50,000 acres of wilderness area are open for camping and hiking; **Camping:** Yes, camping is limited to the wilderness area, required permits available at either the museum or Visitor Center; **Other overnight accommodations on site:** No; **Meals served in the park:** Yes, at Painted Desert Oasis; **Food and supplies obtainable in the park:** No; **Food and supplies obtainable nearby:** Yes, at Holbrook, AZ, 26 miles (42 km) west on I-40; Sanders, AZ, 30 miles (48.3 km) east; Gallup, NM, 70 miles (113 km) east; **Overnight accommodations:** Sun Valley, AZ, 18 miles (29 km) west on I-40; Holbrook, 26 miles (42 km) west on I-40; Chambers, Arizona, 20 miles (33 km) east on I-40; Gallup, NM 70 miles (113 km) east; **First Aid available in park:** Yes; **Nearest Hospital:** Holbrook, AZ, just off I-40, 26 miles (42 km) from the Park; **Days/ Hours:** The Park is open during daylight hours all year, with occasional closings due to heavy snow and icy roads.; **Holiday Closings:** Park closed on Christmas day; **Weather:** Summer days may be quite warm, and clear weather may be broken by sudden thundershowers. In Winter, cold and snowy days are not uncommon. High winds may be expected in any season.

GENERAL INFORMATION: Have sufficient water and notify park personnel if you plan an extended hike. Park elevations range from 5100 to 6235 feet; beware of overexertion in the high altitude. Do not climb on petrified logs; petrified wood can be extremely sharp. Federal law prohibits removal of any petrified wood or any other object from this park.

TRAVEL ACCESS: Bus: No, Closest bus service by Trailways and Greyhound to Holbrook, AZ; **Rail:** No, closest rail service by Amtrak to Winslow, AZ: Service may be cut back; **Air:** No, closest air service to Winslow or Flagstaff, Arizona.

NEARBY FACILITIES & POINTS OF INTEREST: Campgrounds: KOA: Holbrook Hilltop KOA, 102 Hermosa Drive, Holbrook, AZ (602) 524-6689 , 26 miles west; OK RV Park, Roadrunner Lane, Holbrook, AZ (602) 524-3226, 26 miles west.

Pipe Spring National Monument
Moccasin, Arizona   **SEE CLIMATABLE NO. 15**

MAILING ADDRESS: Superintendent, Pipe Spring National Monument, Moccasin, Arizona 86022 **Telephone:** 602-643-7105

DIRECTIONS: Pipe Spring is 14 miles (22.5 km) west of Fredonia, AZ, and can be reached from US 89A via AZ 389; from I-15, UT 9 and 17 connect with UT 59 at Hurricane, UT, from which a paved road leads to the Monument.

This historic fort and other structures, built here by Mormon pioneers in the 1860's and 1870's, commemorate the struggle for exploration and settlement of the Southwest. Created by Presidential Proclamation on May 31, 1923.

VISITOR ACTIVITIES: walking tours; **Permits:** No; **Fees:** $1.00 per person 13 through 62. Golden Age, Access and Eagle Passports accepted and available; **Visitor facilities:** self-guiding tours around the fort; conducted tours, exhibits, and visual interpretation within; **Any limitations on vehicle usage:** Vehicles must park in the lot at the Visitor Center; **Hiking trails:** Yes, self-guiding 1/2 mile (.8 km) loop trail; **Backcountry:** No; **Camping:** No; **Other overnight accommodations on site:** No; **Meals served in the park:** No; **Food and supplies obtainable in the park:** No; **Food and supplies obtainable nearby:** Yes, at Kanab or Fredonia; **Overnight accommodations:** Kanab, 21 miles (33.8 km) east on US 89 or Fredonia, 14 miles (22.5 km) east on AZ 389; **First Aid available in park:** Yes, or nearby in Fredonia, 14 miles (22.5 km) east on AZ 389; **Nearest Hospital:** Kanab via AZ 389 & US 89; **Days/Hours:** Monument open daily from 8 a.m. to 4:30 p.m. until 6 p.m. in Summer; tours closed off at 4:00 p.m, 5:30 p.m. in Summer. Park operates on Mountain Standard Time year-round; **Holiday Closings:** Thanksgiving, Dec. 25 and Jan. 1; **Weather:** Dry and sunny with some summer storms; temperatures range from 85° to 100°F.

GENERAL INFORMATION: Be especially careful of the steep, narrow stairways and low doorways in the buildings. Watch children around ponds.

NEARBY FACILITIES & POINTS OF INTEREST: Campgrounds: Kaibab Campground 1/4 mile north of Monument entrance. 47 RV spaces, 15 tent spaces, hot showers, hiking trails on the Kaibab-Paiute Indian Reservation, laundramat. RV & electricity $8.00, RV site only $6.00, tent $5.00, firewood $2.00 a bundle.

Saguaro National Monument
Tucson, Arizona   **SEE CLIMATABLE NO. 13**

MAILING ADDRESS: Superintendent, 3693 South Old Spanish Trail, Saguaro National Monument, Tucson, Arizona 85730-5699 **Telephone:** 602-296-8576

DIRECTIONS: The Visitor Center and Park Headquarters in the Rincon Mountain District are located on Old Spanish Trail at Freeman Road, 2 miles (3.2 km) east of Tucson City limit. The Visitor Information Center in the Tucson Mountain District is on Kinney Road, 2 miles (3.2 km) west of the Arizona-Sonora Desert Museum.

Giant Saguaro cactus, unique to the Sonoran Desert of southern Arizona and northwestern Mexico, sometimes reach a height of 10 m (40 feet) in this cactus forest. Created by Presidential Proclamation on Mar. 1, 1933.

VISITOR ACTIVITIES: wildlife- and bird-watching, hiking, picnicking, photography, wilderness backcountry, overnight hiking (Rincon Mtn. District Only), horseback riding, scenic pleasure driving; Tucson Mtn. & Rincon Mtn. Districts; **Permits:** required for overnight backcountry, can be obtained at Visitor Center; **Fees:** Rincon Mtn. District $3 per car entrance fee; $1 walk-in fee per person; $1 per bicyclist; $1 per person, backcountry; No fees TMU. Golden Eagle, Golden Age and Golden Access Passports accepted and available; **Visitor facilities:** Rincon Mtn. District audiovisual program and exhibits in the Visitor Center. Naturalist walks both units, self-guiding walks and picnic areas in both units; **Any limitations on vehicle usage:** Drive only on established roadways; **Hiking trails:** Yes, in backcountry. Also in Cactus Forest; **Backcountry:** Yes, information from Visitor Center in the Rincon Mtn. District and Information Center in the Tucson Mtn. District; **Camping:** Backcountry only, Rincon Mtn. District; **Other overnight accommodations on site:** No; **Meals served in the park:** No, but meals are available nearby (1-3 miles) **Food and supplies obtainable in the park:** No; **Food and supplies obtainable nearby:** Yes, at Tucson; **Overnight accommodations:** Downtown Tucson, 16 miles (26 km) east of the Rincon Mtn. District and 15 miles (24 km) est of the Tucson Mtn. District along Int. 10 and at Gilbert Ray Campground 2 miles from TMU information center. **First Aid available in park:** Yes; **Nearest Hospital:** 10 miles (16 km) west of the park via Broadway Blvd., at Wilmot and 5th Streets; St. Mary's Hospital XX miles east of Tucson Mtn. District, Corner of St. Mary's and Silverbell. **Days/Hours:** Rincon Mtn. District is open from 7:00 a.m. to 7:00 p.m. April 1-Oct., 8:00 a.m. to 5:00 p.m. Nov.-March, Visitor Center 8 a.m.-5 p.m. Tucson Mtn. District open all year, Information Center from 8:00 a.m. to 5:00 p.m.; **Holiday Closings:** Christmas Day both units; **Visitor attractions closed for seasons:** no; **Weather:** Winter and summer have rainy periods. Spring and fall are dry. Annual rainfall is 11". Temperatures at Tucson Mtn. District may reach 115°F in summer.

GENERAL INFORMATION: On the way to Tucson Mtn. District, visit the adjacent Arizona-Sonora Desert Museum to see a presentation of living plants and animals of the desert in simulated natural habitats.

TRAVEL ACCESS: Bus: Greyhound and Trailways provide regular service into Tucson; **Rail:** No; **Air:** Major airlines service Tucson; **Other:** Taxi service from Tucson, Bicycle trail from Tucson to Rincon Mountain District along side Old Spanish Trail (road).

NEARBY FACILITIES & POINTS OF INTEREST: Campgrounds: Gilbert Ray Campground, Pima County Parks and Recreation, 602-883-4200, 2 miles south of Tucson Mt. District; **Parks, other points of interest:** Sabino Canyon-Coronado National Forest, N. Sabino Rd., 602-749-3223, 13 miles from Rincon Mt. District; Arizona-Sonoran Desert Museum - Kinney Rd., 602-883-1380, 2 miles from Tucson Mt. District.

Sunset Crater National Monument
Flagstaff, Arizona   **SEE CLIMATABLE NO. 14**

MAILING ADDRESS: Superintendent, Sunset Crater National Monument, Route 3, Box 149, Flagstaff, Arizona 86004 **Telephone:** 602-527-7042

DIRECTIONS: Drive north of Flagstaff on US Hwy 89 approximately 13 miles. Turn right on the Sunset Crater-Wupatki Loop Road and continue two miles to the visitor center.
    This colorful volcanic cinder cone with summit crater was formed just before 1100 A.D., and looks as if it has barely cooled. Created by Presidential Proclamation on May 26, 1930.

VISITOR ACTIVITIES: naturalist activities, campfire programs in Summer, exhibits, picnicking; **Permits:** No; **Fees:** Yes; **Visitor facilities:** information and drinking water at the Visitor Center, picnic areas, restrooms; **Any limitations on vehicle usage:** You should stay strictly on the road, due to soft shoulders; **Hiking trails:** Yes, one foottrail, self-guiding Lava Flow Nature Trail; **Backcountry:** No; **Camping:** Yes, first-come basis located in U.S. Forest Service campground next to Sunset Crater Visitor Center and managed by N.P.S. Fee charged per night. Camping season: May 15 to Sept. 15th; **Other overnight accommodations on site:** No; **Meals served in the park:** No; **Food and supplies obtainable in the park:** No; **Food and supplies obtainable nearby:** Yes, in Flagstaff; **Overnight accommodations:** Flagstaff, Hwy 89, 15 miles (24 km); **First Aid available in park:** Yes; **Nearest Hospital:** Flagstaff, 15 miles (24 km) south on Hwy 89; **Days/Hours:** Open daily from 8 a.m. to 5 p.m.; **Holiday Closings:** Dec. 25 & Jan. 1; **Visitor attractions closed for seasons:** At times, roads are icy and snowy during the winter, but rarely closed.

GENERAL INFORMATION: Sunset Crater is an interesting stopoff while driving to the Grand Canyon. Wupatki National Monument (see listing in this book), containing pre-historic Indian ruins, is located twenty miles distant. Both Monuments are located on a scenic 36-mile loop drive. The most prominent hazards in the parks are deep, narrow earth cracks and razor-sharp lava, and unstable backcountry ruins. Watch for sheep and cattle during the winter months, when the area is open range. Do not walk on pre-historic walls or disturb plants, animals, and geological and archeological features. Sunset Crater is closed to hiking.

Tonto National Monument
Roosevelt, Arizona   **SEE CLIMATABLE NO. 9**

MAILING ADDRESS: Superintendent, Tonto National Monument, P.O. Box 707, Roosevelt, Arizona 85545 **Telephone:** 602-467-2241

DIRECTIONS: The park is located near Roosevelt Lake, two miles east of the town of Roosevelt. From Phoenix, take U.S. Highway 60 to Apache Junction. For the scenic route, turn left on Arizona Highway 88 and proceed along the "Apache Trail"—22 miles of which is unpaved mountain road—to the park entrance. Average driving time one way from Phoenix is three hours. To stay on paved highway, continue on U.S. Highway 60 to the Globe-Miami area. From there, take Arizona Highway 88 to the park entrance, a distance of 28 miles (45 minutes).

These well-preserved cliff dwellings were occupied during the 14th century by Salado Indians, who farmed in the Salt River Valley. Created by Presidential Proclamation on December 19, 1907.

VISITOR ACTIVITIES: interpretive exhibits, guided tours, slide program; **Fees:** Entrance fee is $3 per vehicle; Golden Eagle and Golden Age Passports accepted and available.; **Visitor facilities:** museum, observation deck, parking, restrooms, picnic area; **Any limitations on vehicle usage:** Vehicles must stay on the paved road; 30 ft. limit on vehicles traveling the Apache Trail or crossing Roosevelt Dam on Highway 188; **Hiking trails:** Yes, A self-guiding (.5 mile) trail leads to the Lower Ruin. Tours of the 40-room Upper Ruin are available from mid-September to mid-May on a reservation only basis at least 24 hours in advance. This trail climbs 600 vertical feet in one and one-half miles and requires three hours to complete. This conducted tour departs from the visitor center at 9:00 a.m. and returns at noon.; **Backcountry:** No; **Camping:** No, Numerous primitive non-reserved campsites can be found in the surrounding Tonto National Forest. For further information contact the forest at P.O. Box 648, Rooseelt, AZ, phone 602-467-2236; **Other overnight accommodations on site:** No; **Meals served in the park:** No; **Food and supplies obtainable in the park:** No; **Food and supplies obtainable**

nearby: Yes, immediate area and in the Globe-Miami area; **Overnight accommodations:** Roosevelt Lake Resort, 8 miles (14.5 km) and at Globe, 28 miles (45 km); **First Aid available in park:** Yes, aid station located at Roosevelt; **Nearest Hospital:** Globe-Miami area, 28 miles (45 km); **Days/Hours:** Open year-round from 8 a.m. to 5 p.m. The trail to the Lower Ruin closes at 4 p.m. each day; **Holiday Closings:** Dec. 25; **Visitor attractions closed for seasons:** None; **Weather:** The most comfortable weather occurs between late October and early June.

GENERAL INFORMATION: *For Your Safety*—Natural features here could be hazardous. Be on the lookout for steep slopes, falling rocks, spiny vegetation, rattlesnakes and Gila monsters. Stay on the trails.

TRAVEL ACCESS: Bus: Grayline/Sun Valley Bus provides a weekly tour from Phoenix, Arizona Bus Lines provides charter service from Phoenix; **Rail:** No; **Air:** No.

NEARBY FACILITIES & POINTS OF INTEREST: Hotel/Motel: Roosevelt Lake Resort, Box 485 Payson Star Rt., Globe, AZ 85501, 602-467-2276, 9 miles from Monument; **Food/Supplies:** Spring Creek Store, Payson Star Route Globe, AZ 85501, 602-467-2468, 8 miles from Monument & Roosevelt Lake Marina, Roosevelt, AZ, 602-467-2245, 3 miles; **Parks, other points of interest:** Roosevelt Dam (Highest Masonry; 1st Bureau of Reclamation Dam), 5 miles.

Tumacacori National Monument
Tumacacori, Arizona   **SEE CLIMATABLE NO. 13**

MAILING ADDRESS: Superintendent, Tumacacori National Monument, P.O. Box 67, Tumacacori, Arizona 85640 **Telephone:** 602-398-2341

DIRECTIONS: Tumacacori is 45 miles (72.4 km) south of Tucson on I-19, 18 miles (28.97 km) north of Nogales and the Mexican border.
　　This historic Spanish Catholic mission building stands near the site first visited by Jesuit Father Kino in 1691. Created by Presidential Proclamation on Sept. 15, 1908.

VISITOR ACTIVITIES: interpretive exhibits, self-guiding walks, living history demonstrations, picnicking; **Permits:** No; **Fees:** Entrance fee is $3 per carload or $1 per person on bus tours. Golden Eagle and Golden Age Passports accepted and available; **Visitor facilities:** parking, picnic area; **Any limitations on vehicle usage:** No; **Hiking trails:** No; **Backcountry:** No; **Camping:** No; **Other overnight accommodations on site:** No; **Meals served in the park:** No; **Food and supplies obtainable in the park:** No; **Food and supplies obtainable nearby:** Yes, in Tucson or Nogales; **Overnight accommodations:** Tucson, 45 miles (72.42 km) north and Nogales, 18 miles (29 km) south; **First Aid available in park:** Yes; **Nearest Hospital:** Nogales, 18 miles (29 km) south; **Days/Hours:** Open year-round from 8 a.m. to 5 p.m.; **Holiday Closings:** Dec. 25; **Weather:** Summers are very hot.

GENERAL INFORMATION: A fiesta is held the first Sunday in December, featuring an outdoor Mariachi Mass, continuous entertainment, and craft and native food sales.

TRAVEL ACCESS: Bus: Citizen Auto Stage provides regular service to Nogales, AZ; **Rail:** No; **Air:** No;

NEARBY FACILITIES & POINTS OF INTEREST: Hotel/Motel: Rio Rico Resort, Rio Rico AZ 85621, (602) 281-1901, 8 miles; **Food/Supplies:** Carmen Store, Carmen, AZ, 1 mile; **Campgrounds:** Rio Rico Campground, Rio Rico, AZ 85621, 8 miles; **Parks, other points of interest:** Tubac State Historic Park, 3 miles Pena Blanca Lake, 30 miles.

Tuzigoot National Monument
Clarkdale, Arizona
SEE CLIMATABLE NO. 12

MAILING ADDRESS: Superintendent, Tuzigoot National Monument, P.O. Box 68, Clarkdale, Arizona 86324 **Telephone:** 602-634-5564

DIRECTIONS: The Visitor Center is 2 miles (3 km) east of Clarkdale.
Ruins of a large Indian pueblo which flourished in the Verde Valley between A.D. 1100 and 1450 have been excavated here. Created by Presidential Proclamation on July 25, 1939.

VISITOR ACTIVITIES: interpretive exhibits in the museum, walking tours; **Permits:** No; **Fees:** Entrance fee is $3 per vehicle, Golden Eagle and Golden Age Passports accepted and available; **Visitor facilities:** parking and restrooms at Visitor Center; **Any limitations on vehicle usage:** No; **Hiking trails:** Yes, from the Visitor Center to the ruin and overlook; **Backcountry:** No; **Camping:** No; **Other overnight accommodations on site:** No; **Meals served in the park:** No; **Food and supplies obtainable in the park:** No; **Food and supplies obtainable nearby:** Yes, in Cottonwood, AZ, 3 miles (4.8 km); **Overnight accommodations:** Cottonwood, AZ, 3 miles (4.8 km); **First Aid available in park:** Yes; **Nearest Hospital:** Cottonwood, AZ, 3 miles (4.8 km); **Days/Hours:** Open daily from 8 a.m. to 5 p.m. year-round; **Holiday Closings:** None; **Weather:** Summer is very hot. Spring and Fall are pleasant, Winter is mild.

GENERAL INFORMATION: 27 miles (40 km) from Tuzigoot is Montezuma Castle National Monument, one of the best preserved cliff dwellings in the United States. It can be reached from a good road branching from US 89A. If you plan to continue north on US 89A to Flagstaff, you can easily reach other national monuments: Walnut Canyon, Wupatki, and Sunset Crater (see listings in this book).

NEARBY FACILITIES & POINTS OF INTEREST: Parks, other points of interest: Jerome State Park, Dead Horse Ranch State Park.

Walnut Canyon National Monument
Flagstaff, Arizona
SEE CLIMATABLE NO. 14

MAILING ADDRESS: Superintendent, Walnut Canyon National Monument, Walnut Canyon Road, Flagstaff, Arizona 86004-9705 **Telephone:** 602-526-3367

DIRECTIONS: The entrance road to Walnut Canyon is a 3 mile (4.5 km) highway connecting with Int. 40 at a point 7.5 miles (12 km) east of Flagstaff.
These cliff dwellings were built in shallow caves under ledges of limestone by Sinagua Indians about 800 years ago. Created by Presidential Proclamation on Nov. 30, 1915.

VISITOR ACTIVITIES: interpretive exhibits, hiking, picnicking, interpretive walks in summer; **Permits:** No; **Fees:** Entrance fee is $3 per carload in private, noncommercial vehicles, $1.00 per person entering by bus or foot; Golden Eagle, Golden Age, or Golden Access Passports accepted and available; **Visitor facilities:** parking, museum, picnic area, hiking trails; **Any limitations on vehicle usage:** Vehicles are restricted to designated roadways; **Hiking trails:** Yes, a paved foot trail leads to 25 of the cliff dwelling rooms; you can see several others from the trail. There is also a short rim trail; **Backcountry:** No; **Camping:** No; **Other overnight accommodations on site:** No; **Meals served in the park:** No, meals and lodging may be obtained at Flagstaff, Sedona, and Winslow, and along major highways: I-40, I-17, 89N & 89S **Food and supplies obtaina-**

ble in the park: No; **Food and supplies obtainable nearby:** Yes, at Flagstaff, 10 miles (16 km); **Overnight accommodations:** Flagstaff, 10 miles (16 km) west of the Monument; **First Aid available in park:** Yes; **Nearest Hospital:** Flagstaff, 12 miles (19 km); **Days/ Hours:** Open all year, from 7 a.m. to 6 p.m. Memorial Day through Labor Day; 8 a.m. to 5 p.m. the rest of the year; **Holiday Closings:** Dec. 25 and Thanksgiving; **Visitor attractions closed for seasons:** No.

GENERAL INFORMATION: *For Your Safety*—It is prohibited to walk off designated trails. Those with heart ailments or other infirmities should realize that the ISLAND trail includes a 55-meter (185-foot) climb at an altitude of nearly 2134 meters (7000 feet). These conditions can tax the heart.

NEARBY FACILITIES & POINTS OF INTEREST: Campgrounds: USFS Campground 18 miles north at Sunset Crater, KOA and other private campgrounds in Flagstaff area; **Parks, other points of interest:** North Sunset Crater NM (18 miles), Wupatki NM (35 miles), Grand Canyon NP (90 miles), East Petrified Forest NP (110 miles), South Montezuma Well NM (50 miles), Montezuma Castle NM (56 miles), Tuzigoot NM (64 miles), Oak Creek Canyon USFS (27 miles).

Wupatki National Monument
Flagstaff, Arizona   **SEE CLIMATABLE NO. 14**

MAILING ADDRESS: Superintendent, Wupatki National Monument, 2717 N. Steves Blvd., Suite #3, Flagstaff, Arizona 86001 **Telephone:** Headquarters 602-527-7134, Monument 602-527-7040

DIRECTIONS: The Visitor Center is on the 18 mile (30 km) loop road which connects Wupatki with Sunset Crater National Monument. Drive 15 miles (24 km) north of Flagstaff on Highway 89, then east on the loop road (22 miles) 35 km to Wupatki Visitor Center.

Ruins of red sandstone pueblos built by farming Indians about A.D. 1065 are preserved here. The modern Hopi Indians are believed by some to be descendants of these people. Created by Presidential Proclamation on Dec. 9, 1924.

VISITOR ACTIVITIES: interpretive exhibits, hiking, walking, auto tours; **Permits:** No; **Fees:** No, but subject to change; **Visitor facilities:** parking and restrooms at Visitor Center, hiking trails; **Any limitations on vehicle usage:** Due to soft shoulders, drivers should stay strictly on the road; **Hiking trails:** Yes, self-guiding trails to Nalakihu-Citadel Ruins, to Wupatki Ruin; Doney Crater Trail; **Backcountry:** No; **Camping:** No; **Other overnight accommodations on site:** No, no reservations are accepted for U.S. Forest Service campsites which are located across from Sunset Crater Visitor Center. For further information, contact Sunset Crater at 2717 N. Steves Blvd., Suite #3, Flagstaff, AZ 86001, phone 602-527-7042; **Meals served in the park:** No; **Food and supplies obtainable in the park:** No; **Food and supplies obtainable nearby:** Yes, at Flagstaff, 37 miles (59 km) south on Hwy 89; **Overnight accommodations:** Flagstaff, 37 miles (59 km) south on Hwy 89; **First Aid available in park:** Yes; **Nearest Hospital:** Flagstaff, 37 miles (59 km) south on Hwy 89; **Days/Hours:** Visitor Centers open from 8 a.m. to 5 p.m. daily; 7 a.m. to 7 p.m. in Summer; **Holiday Closings:** Dec. 25 and Jan. 1; **Visitor attractions closed for seasons:** No. The campground Sunset Crater is open from April 15 to Nov. 15; **Weather:** Summer is moderate to hot; Winter is cold, with snow common a. Sunset Crater.

GENERAL INFORMATION: The most common hazards in the park are aeep, narrow earth cracks, razor-sharp lava, unstable backcountry ruins, and wild animals. Drinking water is available at Headquarters of Wupatki and Sunset Crater.

Arkansas

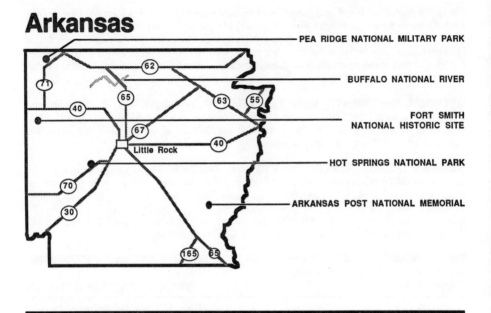

PEA RIDGE NATIONAL MILITARY PARK

BUFFALO NATIONAL RIVER

FORT SMITH
NATIONAL HISTORIC SITE

HOT SPRINGS NATIONAL PARK

ARKANSAS POST NATIONAL MEMORIAL

Arkansas Post National Memorial
Gillett, Arkansas   **SEE CLIMATABLE NO. 16**

MAILING ADDRESS: Superintendent, Arkansas Post National Memorial, Route 1, Box 16, Gillett, Arkansas 72055 **Telephone:** 501-548-2432

DIRECTIONS: The memorial is on AR 169, 7 miles (11 km) south of Gillett via U.S. 165 (The Great River Road) and about 32 km (20 miles) northeast of Dumas via U.S. 165.

The first permanent French settlement in the lower Mississippi Valley was founded on this site in 1686. Authorized for addition to the National Park System on July 6, 1960.

VISITOR ACTIVITIES: exhibits, audiovisual programs, walking tour, picnicking, fishing, biking; **Permits:** an Arkansas fishing license required, available locally; **Fees:** No; **Visitor facilities:** walking trails, picnic area, restrooms; **Any limitations on vehicle usage:** off-road vehicle use is prohibited; **Hiking trails:** Yes, a 1 mile (1.6 km) nature-history trail; **Backcountry:** No; **Camping:** No; **Other overnight accommodations on site:** No; No reservations are available for campsites at Moore's Bayou, 1/2 mile (.8 km) away. This is a developed Corps of Engineers recreation area, with no extra accommodations for trailers. Contact Arkansas Post for further information. **Meals served in the park:** No; **Food and supplies obtainable in the park:** No; **Food and supplies obtainable nearby:** Yes, in Gillett, AR, 7 miles (11 km) north on U.S. 165; **Overnight accommodations:** Dewitt, 20 miles (32 km) north or Dumas 20 miles (32 km) southwest on U.S. 165; **First Aid available in park:** Yes, or nearby in Gillett; **Nearest Hospital:** Dewitt, 20 miles (32 km) north or Dumas, 20 miles (32 km) southwest; **Days/Hours:** Visitor Center open daily from 8 a.m. to 5 p.m., park open until dark; **Holiday Closings:** Dec. 25; **Visitor attractions closed for seasons:** None.

GENERAL INFORMATION: Be on the lookout for snakes and poison ivy as you walk through the area. Watch your step and stay on the trails. The best time to visit the area is Sept. through May because of the extreme heat, humidity and insects in Summer.

Buffalo National River
Harrison, Arkansas   **SEE CLIMATABLE NO. 17**

MAILING ADDRESS: Superintendent, Buffalo National River, P.O. Box 1173, Harrison, Arkansas 72602-1173 **Telephone:** 501-741-5443

DIRECTIONS: Buffalo Point, off AR 14, 17 miles (27.4 km) south of Yellville, is the major center for visitor activities at the river. Information centers are operated at the Buffalo Point, Silver Hill, and Pruitt District Ranger Stations. Information can also be secured at Buffalo National River Headquarters, Federal Building, Walnut and Erie Streets, Harrison 72601.

Offering both swift-running and placid stretches, the Buffalo is one of the few remaining unpolluted, free-flowing rivers in the lower 48 states. It courses through multicolored bluffs and past numerous caves and springs along its 132 mile (213 km) length. Authorized for addition to the National Park System on Mar. 1, 1972.

VISITOR ACTIVITIES: interpretive exhibits, camping, picnicking, canoeing, swimming, hiking, fishing, campfire programs, guided walks, guided canoe trips; **Permits:** an Arkansas fishing or hunting license is required, available locally for a nominal fee; **Fees:** $8 ($5 for walk in tent sites) per site per night camping fee at Buffalo Point Campground. Twelve less developed campgrounds are free of charge; **Visitor facilities:** year-round campground, picnic areas, day-use pavilions, canoe launch areas, hiking trails, food service, boat and canoe rentals, restrooms, cabin rentals; **Any limitations on vehicle usage:** motor vehicles are restricted to open roadways; **Hiking trails:** Yes, self-guiding hiking trails; **Backcountry:** Yes, information can be obtained by writing Park Headquarters in Harrison; **Camping:** Yes, arrive early in the day in summer, since all campgrounds are available on a first-come, first-served basis; **Other overnight accommodations on site:** Yes, for cabin information and reservations write to Buffalo Point Concessions, HCR#66, Box 388, Yellville, AR 72687; **Meals served in the park:** Yes, at Buffalo Point; **Food and supplies obtainable in the park:** No; **Food and supplies obtainable nearby:** Yes, in Yellville, Harrison, Jasper, Marshall, Mountain Home and Gilbert; **Overnight accommodations:** Yellville, Harrison, Jasper, Marshall and Mountain Home; **First Aid available in park:** Yes, at Buffalo Point Ranger Station; **Nearest Hospital:** Harrison, Hwy 62, approx. 50 miles (80 km); Yellville, Hwy 14, 17 miles (27 km) north of Hwy #14; **Days/Hours:** open 24 hours a day, 7 days a week; **Holiday Closings:** None; **Visitor attractions closed for seasons:** No; **Weather:** Summer is hot and humid; Fall and Winter are pleasant.

GENERAL INFORMATION: *For Your Safety*—Stay off the bluffs. Don't dive into the river!! Keep alert to river conditions and avoid the river during high water.

Fort Smith National Historic Site
Fort Smith, Arkansas   **SEE CLIMATABLE NO. 18**

MAILING ADDRESS: Superintendent, Fort Smith National Historic Site, P.O. Box 1406, Fort Smith, Arkansas 72902 **Telephone:** 501-783-3961

DIRECTIONS: The site is on Rogers Avenue between Second and Third Streets in downtown Fort Smith. It can be reached from Garrison Ave. (US 64) by turning one block south to Rogers Avenue. A Visitor Center is in the old Barracks Building.

One of the first U.S. military posts in the Louisiana Territory, the Fort was a center of authority for the untamed region to the West from 1817 to 1896. Authorized for addition to the National Park System on Sept. 13, 1961.

VISITOR ACTIVITIES: interpretive exhibits and walks; **Permits:** No; **Fees:** $1.00 for adults, children 12 and under are free; **Visitor facilities:** parking and restrooms at Visitor Center; **Any limitations on vehicle usage:** No; **Hiking trails:** No; **Backcountry:** No; **Camping:** No; **Other overnight accommodations on site:** No; **Meals served in the park:** No; **Food and supplies obtainable in the park:** No; **Food and supplies obtainable nearby:** Yes, in Fort Smith; **Overnight accommodations:** Fort Smith; **First Aid available in park:** Yes; **Nearest Hospital:** Fort Smith, South I Street, 1 mile (1.6 km) from the park; **Days/Hours:** Open daily from 9:00 a.m. to 5 p.m.; **Holiday Closings:** Dec. 25; **Visitor attractions closed for seasons:** No; **Weather:** Summer is hot and humid, winter is generally mild and humid, strong winds occur often in the spring.

TRAVEL ACCESS: Bus: Trailways, Greyhound, and Jefferson provide frequent service into Fort Smith; **Rail:** Passenger service is at Little Rock, AR; **Air:** American Eagle, Air Midwest, Atlantic Southeast Airlines provide service to Fort Smith.

NEARBY FACILITIES & POINTS OF INTEREST: Parks, other points of interest: Old Fort Museum; **New park programs:** Exhibit of rare documents from the Federal Court period (1875-1896).

Hot Springs National Park
Hot Springs, Arkansas   **SEE CLIMATABLE NO. 19**

MAILING ADDRESS: Superintendent, Hot Springs National Park, P.O. Box 1860, Hot Springs, Arkansas 71902 **Telephone:** 501-624-3383

DIRECTIONS: The park can be reached by auto via US 70 and 270, and AR 7. The Visitor Center is on the corner of Central and Reserve Avenues.

Approximately one million gallons of water a day flow from 47 hot springs here, unaffected by climate or seasonal temperatures. Persons suffering from illness or injury often seek relief in the ancient tradition of thermal bathing. Also used by persons who simply want to soak and relax in the soothing, naturally heated water. Set aside as Hot Springs Reservation on Apr. 20, 1832; designated a national park on Mar. 4, 1921.

VISITOR ACTIVITIES: Thermal water baths & Swedish massages, audiovisual and interpretive exhibits at Visitor Center, campfire programs and exhibits at campground Ranger Station, hiking, auto tours, picnicking, scenic overlooks. **Permits:** No; **Fees:** Campground: $6 per night; Observation Tower, Hot Springs MT: Adults-$2.25, Children $1.75. Fees are charged by bathhouses. Rate schedules available from the Superintendent; **Visitor facilities:** The 6 bathing establishments-2 in the park (including the Hot Springs Health Spa) and 4 in the hotels in the city-use thermal waters of the park. All are concessions or permittees of the Federal Government, subject to regulation and inspection. The baths (full immersion type) may be taken by direct application to the bathhouses. Bathing in the thermal water is not recommended for persons who suffer from certain ailments. When in doubt, consult a Registered Physician. All bathhouses have facilities for whirlpool baths, showers, massages, and alcohol rubs. The Libbey Memorial Physical Medicine Center offers hydrotherapy treatments by registered physical therapists under physician prescriptions; **Any limitations on vehicle usage:** Bicycles, motorcycles, and similar vehicles are not allowed on the park trails; **Hiking trails:** Yes, many wooded trails; **Backcountry:** Yes; **Camping:** Yes, the campground is at Gulpha Gorge, 2 miles (3.2 km) northeast of the center of the city. Campers must first register at the campground ranger station; Camping is on a first come basis. Contact the park for further information; **Other overnight accommodations on site:** No; **Meals served in the park:** No; **Food and supplies obtainable in the park:** No; **Food and supplies obtainable nearby:** Yes, in city of Hot Springs, adjacent to the Park; **Overnight accommoda-**

tions: Yes, the city of Hot Springs, a separate municipality not under National Park Service jurisdiction, nearly surrounds the park. The city has many large hotels offering a choice of American or European plans, smaller hotels, motels, boardinghouses, housekeeping quarters, and furnished or unfurnished cottages. Lists of accommodations and general information are available from the Hot Springs Chamber of Commerce, P.O. Box 1500, Hot Springs, AR 71902, phone 501-321-1700; **First Aid available in park:** Yes; **Nearest Hospital:** Hot Springs, AR, adjacent to the park; **Days/Hours:** Park open 24 hours daily. Visitor Center; Open daily 8:00 a.m. to 5:00 p.m.; **Holiday Closings:** Dec. 25 and Jan. 1; **Visitor attractions closed for seasons:** Bathhouse tours closed from December thru March; **Weather:** Hot Springs enjoys a favorable climate all year. The Winters are mild and, except for infrequent short intervals, are conducive to outdoor recreation. The mild weather and sunshine are often decided aids to the bath treatments. Summers are usually hot and humid.

GENERAL INFORMATION: *Fires* are one of the park's greatest perils. Campfires are permitted only in designated sites. Cigars and cigarettes should be completely extinguished.

Pea Ridge National Military Park
Pea Ridge, Arkansas **SEE CLIMATABLE NO. 17**

MAILING ADDRESS: Superintendent, Pea Ridge National Military Park, Pea Ridge, Arkansas 72751 **Telephone:** 501-451-8122

DIRECTIONS: The Visitor Center is 10 miles (16 km) north of Rogers off US Hwy 62.
The Union victory here on March 7-8, 1862 led to the Union's total control of Missouri. The battle was one of the major engagements of the Civil War west of the Mississippi. Authorized for addition to the National Park System on July 20, 1956.

VISITOR ACTIVITIES: interpretive exhibits, biking, self-guiding auto tours; **Permits:** Yes; Entrance Permit required. Entrance fee $1.00 per person (under 13 and over 62 free.) $3.50 maximum charge for family; **Fees:** Yes; **Visitor facilities:** parking, restrooms, drinking water, picnic area, fireplaces, observation deck, bicycle and nature trails, 7 mile (11 km) self-guiding auto tours; **Any limitations on vehicle usage:** Drive only on paved roads; **Hiking trails:** Yes, 1/2 mile (.8 km) nature trail and 10 mile (16 km) Boy Scout trail; **Backcountry:** No; **Camping:** No; **Other overnight accommodations on site:** No, camping is permitted at Beaver Lake, 10 miles (16 km) away, on the north edge of Rogers. **Meals served in the park:** No; **Food and supplies obtainable in the park:** No; **Food and supplies obtainable nearby:** Yes, in Pea Ridge and Rogers; **Overnight accommodations:** Rogers, US 71S, 10 miles (16 km) from the park; **First Aid available in park:** Yes; **Nearest Hospital:** Rogers, US 62, 10 miles (16 km); Bentonville, US 62 to AR 102, 15 miles (24 km); **Days/Hours:** Open daily from 8 a.m. to 5 p.m.; **Holiday Closings:** Thanksgiving Day, Dec. 25 and Jan. 1; **Weather:** Relatively mild Winters and warm, humid Summers.

TRAVEL ACCESS: Bus: Trailways provides daily service to Rogers, 11 miles; **Air:** Nearest service into Joplin, MO, 80 miles, Fayetteville, AR 35 miles.

NEARBY FACILITIES & POINTS OF INTEREST: Hotel/Motel: Battle Field Inn, Garfield, 501-451-1188, 2 miles; **Parks, other points of interest:** Prairie Grove State Park, 42 miles.

California

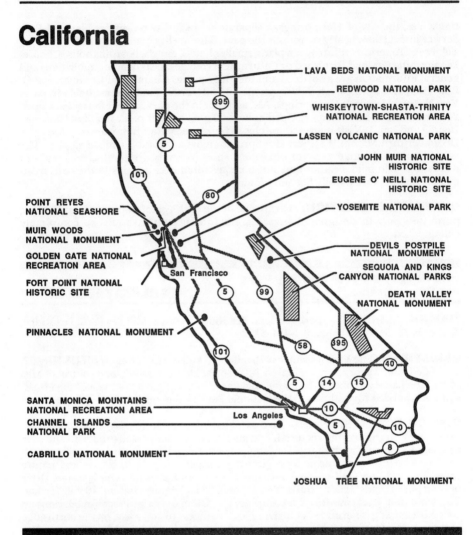

LAVA BEDS NATIONAL MONUMENT

REDWOOD NATIONAL PARK

WHISKEYTOWN-SHASTA-TRINITY
NATIONAL RECREATION AREA

LASSEN VOLCANIC NATIONAL PARK

JOHN MUIR NATIONAL
HISTORIC SITE

EUGENE O' NEILL NATIONAL
HISTORIC SITE

YOSEMITE NATIONAL PARK

POINT REYES
NATIONAL SEASHORE

MUIR WOODS
NATIONAL MONUMENT

GOLDEN GATE NATIONAL
RECREATION AREA

FORT POINT NATIONAL
HISTORIC SITE

San Francisco

DEVILS POSTPILE
NATIONAL MONUMENT

SEQUOIA AND KINGS
CANYON NATIONAL PARKS

DEATH VALLEY
NATIONAL MONUMENT

PINNACLES NATIONAL MONUMENT

SANTA MONICA MOUNTAINS
NATIONAL RECREATION AREA

CHANNEL ISLANDS
NATIONAL PARK

Los Angeles

CABRILLO NATIONAL MONUMENT

JOSHUA TREE NATIONAL MONUMENT

Cabrillo National Monument
San Diego, California   **SEE CLIMATABLE NO. 20**

MAILING ADDRESS: Superintendent, Cabrillo National Monument, P.O. Box 6670,
San Diego, California 92106 **Telephone:** 619-557-5450

DIRECTIONS: To reach the Monument, follow Rosecrans Street to Cañon Street
(State Route 209), merge into Catalina Boulevard, then go through the gates at the
Naval Oceans Systems Center and continue to the tip of Point Loma. Stop first at the
Visitor Center.
    Juan Rodriquez Cabrillo, who claimed the west coast of the United States for Spain
in 1542, is memorialized here. Gray whales migrate offshore during the Winter.
Created by Presidential Proclamation on Oct. 14, 1913.

VISITOR ACTIVITIES: interpretive exhibits, self-guided walking and lighthouse
tours, audio-visual programs, tidepools, whale-watching (Dec. through Feb.); **Permits:**

No; **Fees:** $3.00/vehicle; **Visitor facilities:** Visitor Center, parking, restrooms, museum, auditorium, benches, water fountain, walkways, overlooks, lighthouse, wayside exhibits; **Any limitations on vehicle usage:** Vehicles are not allowed in the historic lighthouse complex; **Hiking trails:** Yes, the Monument features a self-guiding ethno-botanical trail through historical coastal defense and chapparal and tide pool walks; **Backcountry:** No; **Camping:** No; **Other overnight accommodations on site:** No; **Meals served in the park:** No; **Food and supplies obtainable in the park:** Vending machines for drinks and snacks are available; **Food and supplies obtainable nearby:** Yes, ten minutes by auto in the Point Loma-San Diego area; **Overnight accommodations:** San Diego, 5 miles (8 km); **First Aid available in park:** Yes; **Nearest Hospital:** Cabrillo Medical Center, 5 miles (8 km); **Days/Hours:** Open 9:00 a.m. to 5:15 p.m. throughout the year (may be open 9:00 a.m. to sunset. May through August subject to change without notice.) **Holiday Closings:** None; **Visitor attractions closed for seasons:** No; **Weather:** Mediterranean-type climate: cooler weather in Winter, night and morning fog and clouds in early Summer.

GENERAL INFORMATION: *For Your Safety*—Stay back from the edge of cliffs and off unpaved trails. Barnacle-encrusted rocks can cut bare feet. Wear rubber-soled shoes if you visit the tide pool areas. Leather soles slip on the wet rocks.

TRAVEL ACCESS: Bus: San Diego Transit provides daily service to the Park approximately hourly; **Rail:** To San Diego; **Air:** To San Diego.

NEARBY FACILITIES & POINTS OF INTEREST: Parks, other points of interest: San Diego Zoo, Sea World, many museums.

Channel Islands National Park
Ventura, California   **SEE CLIMATABLE NO. 20**

MAILING ADDRESS: Superintendent, Channel Islands National Park, 1901 Spinnaker Drive, Ventura, CA 93001 **Telephone:** 805-644-8262

DIRECTIONS: Southbound on U.S. Highway 101-take Seaward offramp in Ventura, take Harbor Blvd. south to Spinnaker Drive, right turn and proceeding to Visitor's Center at the end of the drive. Northbound on U.S. Highway 101 take Victoria offramp in Ventura, follow Channel Islands signs.
 The Park includes Anacapa, Santa Barbara, San Miguel, Santa Rosa and Santa Cruz Islands although the latter one is still privately owned. Each island hosts a variety of cultural and natural resources including Indian middens, large rookeries of sea lions, nesting sea birds and unique plants and animals. Created by an Act of Congress March 5, 1980.

VISITOR ACTIVITIES: hiking, camping, exhibits and audiovisual programs, scuba diving, picnicking, wildlife- and bird-watching, fishing, snorkeling, swimming, boating; **Permits:** for camping and island landing permits, call or write Park Superintendent; **Fees:** for concession-operated boat trips. Inquire with The Island Packers (see below); **Visitor facilities:** Visitor Center, boat service to and from the islands, campgrounds, comfort facilities, picnic area. For public transportation and tour information write or call: The Island Packers, 1867 Spinnaker Drive, Ventura, CA 93001, phone 805-642-1393; **Any limitations on vehicle usage:** No vehicles are allowed on the islands; **Hiking trails:** Yes, self-guiding trails; **Backcountry:** Yes, call or write Park Superintendent; **Camping:** Yes, but only on Anacapa and Santa Barbara Islands. Write or call Park Headquarters. You will need to bring water, camping gear, food, cooking equipment, and fuel for campfires. Bring warm clothing, for the nights are cool. You will want a tent as shelter from the ever-present winds. If you are camping on Anacapa, keep in mind that everything must be carried up a steep stairway (152 steps) and then ¼ mile (.4 km) to the camping area; **Other overnight accommodations on site:** No; **Meals served in the park:** No; **Food and supplies obtainable in the park:** No; **Food and supplies obtainable nearby:** Yes, in Ventura, Oxnard; **Overnight accommodations:** Ventura, Oxnard have hotels and motels; **First Aid available in park:** Yes; **Nearest Hospital:** Ventura, 4 miles (6.4 km) from Headquarters, 18 miles (28.8 km) from Anacapa; **Days/Hours:** Islands: daylight hours & overnight camping available on Anacapa and Santa Barbara Islands. Visitor Center—8:00 a.m. - 5 p.m. with extended hours in summer, 7 days a week; **Holiday Closings:** Visitor Center closed Thanksgiving, Dec. 25 and Jan. 1; **Visitor attractions closed for seasons:** No.

GENERAL INFORMATION: *For Your Safety*—hike only on beaches and established trails when on Anacapa and Santa Barbara Islands. Landing permit required for San Miguel, Santa Rosa Islands.

TRAVEL ACCESS: Bus: Greyhound Bus Service to Ventura, CA, several times a day, also Southcoast Area Transit (city bus) goes from Ventura to Pierpont Bus Terminal, near the park headquarters several times a day; **Rail:** Amtrak provides daily service to Oxnard; **Air:** several daily flights to Oxnard Airport. Area airports include Los Angeles International 70 miles south and Santa Barbara 40 miles north.

NEARBY FACILITIES & POINTS OF INTEREST: Hotel/Motel: Several in nearby area; **Campgrounds:** McGrath State Beach Park, about 3 miles south off Harbor Blvd. **Reservation systems in use for campsites, other Facilities;** Camping on Anacapa, Santa Barbara Islands by permit only; Day use on San Miguel and Santa Rosa Islands by permit only; **New park programs:** New Visitor Center with "hands-on" exhibits, films, videotape programs and regularly scheduled evening programs. The Ventura Visitors and Convention Bureau (785 S. Seaward Avenue, Ventura, CA 93001) offers more extensive details on accommodations and activities in "Recreation Guide" and "Motel and Restaurant Guide."

Death Valley National Monument
Death Valley, California and Nevada   **SEE CLIMATABLE NO. 21**

MAILING ADDRESS: Superintendent, Death Valley National Monument, Death Valley, California 92328 **Telephone:** 619-786-2331

DIRECTIONS: US 395 passes west of Death Valley and connects with State Routes 190 and 136 or by an unnumbered county road from Trona, CA to the park. US 95 passes east of the Park and connects with NV 267, 374, and 373 to the park. Interstate 15 passes southeast of the park and connects with State Route 127 to the park.

This large desert, nearly surrounded by high mountains, contains the lowest point in the Western Hemisphere. The area includes Scotty's Castle, the palatial home of a famous prospector, and other remnants of gold and borax mining activity. Created by Presidential Proclamation on Feb. 11, 1933.

VISITOR ACTIVITIES: driving, hiking, jeep riding, camping, photography, biking, interpretive exhibits, guided tours, picnicking, backcountry, horseback riding; **Permits:** backcountry permits are encouraged, available at Ranger Stations; **Fees:** Yes, $5 entrance fee, campground fees at major campgrounds, Guided Castle tours are $4 per person and $2 for Golden Age passport holders; **Visitor facilities:** Visitor Center, campgrounds, hiking trails, parking, restrooms, lodging, picnic areas, interpretive programs, post office, bicycle rentals; **Any limitations on vehicle usage:** Drive only on existing roads, only on main roads in Summer and always carry water for your car. In case of breakdown, remain with your car until help arrives; **Hiking trails:** Yes, self-guiding walking trails; **Backcountry:** Yes, contact the park for further information; **Camping:** Yes, no reservations for campsites. For further information, write for a copy of the folder *Camping in Death Valley* or pick up a copy at the Visitor Center or any Ranger Station; **Other overnight accommodations on site:** Yes, resorts provide lodging and other commercial services at two locations within the Monument. Facilities at Furnace Creek and Stove Pipe Wells are operated by Fred Harvey, Inc. P.O. Box 187, Death Valley, CA 92328 phone 619-786-2345. Services at these locations are limited from May through Oct. Call or write for details; **Meals served in the park:** Yes, at Furnace Creek, Stove Pipe Wells, Scotty's Castle; **Food and supplies obtainable in the park:** Yes, at Stove Pipe Wells, Furnace Creek & Scotty's Castle; **Food and supplies obtainable nearby:** Yes, in Beatty, Shoshone; **Overnight accommodations:** Beatty, 45 miles from park HQ or Furnace Creek; Shoshone, 60 miles from park HQ or Furnace Creek; Trona, 40 miles from Wildrose; **First Aid available in park:** Yes, or nearby in Beatty, US 95; Trona, State Route 178; Shoshone, CA 127; **Nearest Hospital:** Lone Pine, 100 miles (61 km) west; Las Vegas, 140 miles (225 km) east, Tonopah, 90 miles Northeast (145 km); **Days/Hours:** Park never closes. Visitor Center open 8 a.m. to 8 p.m. from Nov. 1 to Easter; 8-5 the rest of the year. **Holiday Closings:** None; **Visitor attractions closed for seasons:** No; **Weather:** Summer has extreme heat and low humidity; winter is cooler with snow at high elevations.

GENERAL INFORMATION: *For Your Safety—the desert can be dangerously hot in summer.* Always carry water for you and your car. *Never enter mines or tunnels;* abandoned shafts are often deep and old timbers rotten. *Forgotten caches of explosives* are occasionally found in mine areas. Do not touch them, but report them to a park ranger as soon as possible. Be alert for *flash floods* when it looks stormy. Do not ford low places when water is running. Flood waters can undercut pavement or sweep a car from the road. *All animals in the park are wild.* They can bite and/or carry diseases. Never feed or touch them. *Never travel alone.* Always tell someone where you are going and when you expect to return. Be extremely cautious in this wild area. If you travel in Death Valley in Summer, pick up a copy of the folder, *Hot Weather Hints*, at distribution boxes at any entrance to the Monument, at the Visitor Center, or any Ranger Station.

TRAVEL ACCESS: Bus: None; **Rail:** None; **Air:** Service available; **Other:** Bicycle rental available at Furnace Creek.

Devils Postpile National Monument
Mammoth Lakes, California   **SEE CLIMATABLE NO. 22**

MAILING ADDRESS: Park Manager, Devils Postpile National Monument, P.O. Box 50, Mammoth Lakes, CA 93546. **Telephone:** 619-934-2289 summer and fall, 209-565-3341 winter and spring.

DIRECTIONS: The Monument is reached by a 10-mile (16 km) drive to Minaret Summit on a paved road from US 395, then by 7 miles (11.2 km) of mountain road.

Hot lava cooled and cracked some 100,000 years ago to form basalt columns 12 to 18 m (40 to 60 feet) high resembling a giant pipe organ. The John Muir Trail between Yosemite and Kings Canyon National Parks crosses the Monument. Created by Presidential Proclamation on July 6, 1911.

VISITOR ACTIVITIES: guided walks, picnicking, evening campfire programs, fishing, camping; **Permits:** California fishing license, available locally for a nominal fee is required; **Fees:** $5.00 camping fee; **Visitor facilities:** restrooms near Ranger Station, picnic area, campground, shuttle bus; **Any limitations on vehicle usage:** Restricted use mid-day during heavy use season, visitors will be required to use a shuttle bus to reach the Monument. Contact the park for further information; **Hiking trails:** Yes, trips may be made north or south along the John Muir Trail and west on the King Creek Trail. Devils Postpile also has several short trails; **Backcountry:** No; **Camping:** Yes, no reservations are available for the campground, which is open from about June 20 to Oct. 1, depending on the weather; **Other overnight accommodations on site:** No; **Meals served in the park:** No; **Food and supplies obtainable in the park:** No; **Food and supplies obtainable nearby:** Yes, at Mammoth Lakes or Reds Meadow; **Overnight accommodations:** Mammoth Lakes, 14 miles (22.5 km), Reds Meadow, 1.5 miles (2.4 km); **First Aid available in park:** Yes; **Nearest Hospital:** Complete 24 hours a day emergency services at Centinela Mammoth Hospital, 14 miles (22.5 km); **Days/Hours:** Open 24 hours a day, 7 days a week in season; **Holiday Closings:** None; **Visitor attractions closed for seasons:** The Monument is open from approximately July through Oct.; **Weather:** Summer thundershowers occur frequently in the afternoon.

GENERAL INFORMATION: Warning: Bears inhabit the Monument; proper food storage is required by Federal law. Stay on the regular designated trails since these are the safest places to hike. Stay back when viewing features from near the edge of a cliff or gorge. Footing is hazardous.

Eugene O'Neill National Historic Site
Danville, California   **SEE CLIMATABLE NO. 23**

MAILING ADDRESS: Superintendent, John Muir National Historic Site, 4202 Alhambra Avenue, Martinez, California 94553 **Telephone:** 415-838-0249

DIRECTIONS: Limited public access is available for Ranger guided tours of the site via a national park service operated van. Reservations are required and can be arranged by contacting the address above or by phoning (415) 838-0249. Tours are offered twice daily, seven days a week.

Tao House, near Danville, CA, was built for Eugene O'Neill, who lived here from 1937 to 1944. Several of his best-known plays, including "The Iceman Cometh" and "Long Day's Journey Into Night" were written here—now a memorial to the playwright. Authorized for addition to the National Park System on October 12, 1976. Title transferred to the National Park Service on July 29, 1980.

VISITOR ACTIVITIES: Park Ranger guided tours.

Fort Point National Historic Site
Presidio of San Francisco, California   **SEE CLIMATABLE NO. 23**

MAILING ADDRESS: Site Manager, Fort Point National Historic Site, P.O. Box 29333, Presidio of San Francisco, California 94129 **Telephone:** 415-556-1693 or 556-2857

DIRECTIONS: Fort Point is located under the south end of the Golden Gate Bridge. Turn off Hwy 101 at the bridge to reach the fort.

This classic brick and granite mid-19th Century coastal fortification is the only one of its type on the west coast of North America. Established by Act of Congress on Oct. 16, 1970.

VISITOR ACTIVITIES: interpretive exhibits and guided tours, cannon drills, picnicking, fishing; **Permits:** No; **Fees:** No; **Visitor facilities:** parking and restrooms; **Any**

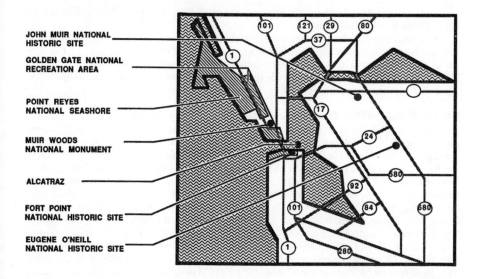

limitations on vehicle usage: All motor vehicles are restricted to developed, paved roadways and parking areas; **Hiking trails:** Yes, short scenic trails through the area; **Backcountry:** No; **Camping:** No; **Other overnight accommodations on site:** No; **Meals served in the park:** No; **Food and supplies obtainable in the park:** No; **Food and supplies obtainable nearby:** Yes, in the immediate area; **Overnight accommodations:** San Francisco—reservations are advisable; **First Aid available in park:** Yes; **Nearest Hospital:** in Letterman Army Medical Center, Lincoln Blvd., 1 mile (1.6 km); **Days/ Hours:** Park open sunrise to sunset. Fort open daily from 10 a.m. to 5 p.m.; **Holiday Closings:** Thanksgiving, Dec. 25 & Jan. 1; **Weather:** Average temperature is 58°F with winds 5-10 mph. Wear warm clothes when you visit the area.

GENERAL INFORMATION: Use caution while climbing or descending stairs, which are steep and narrow. Stay on established roadways and off walls, which can be dangerous if climbed.

TRAVEL ACCESS: Bus: Municipal buses from San Francisco provide access to park area; **Rail:** Amtrak and Southern Pacific Railroads provide service to the Oakland/San Francisco area; **Air:** Major airlines serve San Francisco and Oakland airports.

Golden Gate National Recreation Area
San Francisco, California   **SEE CLIMATABLE NO. 24**

MAILING ADDRESS: General Superintendent, Golden Gate National Recreation Area, Fort Mason, San Francisco, California 94123 **Telephone:** 415-556-0560

DIRECTIONS: In San Francisco, Golden Gate National Recreation Area follows the city's northern and western shoreline. These areas are accessible by the Municipal Railway (MUNI) bus system and can easily be reached by car. Ferries provide access to Alcatraz. Across the Golden Gate Bridge in Marin County, the park is reached by various access roads off Hwy 101: Alexander Avenue, Shoreline Highway, and Sir Francis Drake Boulevard. MUNI serves Rodeo Beach in Marin on Sundays. Visitor information is available at Fort Mason, the Cliff House, Ft. Point, The National Maritime Museum, Rodeo Beach, and Muir Woods.

Golden Gate National Recreation Area offers a variety of recreational, scenic, natural, and historic areas on the doorstep of San Francisco. The beauty of the city, the Bay, the ocean, and coastal landscape are brought together in one park which contains about 26,000 acres of open space on both sides of the Golden Gate. The park was established in 1972 and represents an effort to bring parks closer to people in urban areas.

VISITOR ACTIVITIES: An endless variety of recreational, cultural, and educational activities are available here, including tours of Alcatraz, the National Maritime Museum, picnicking, fishing, camping, swimming, short walks and sightseeing, hiking, and cultural programs at Fort Mason Center; **Permits:** Needed for special use only; **Fees:** Balclutha, $3.00, Alcatraz audio tour, $2.00; **Visitor facilities:** picnic sites, fishing piers, beaches, tours of historic areas, campgrounds, snack bars, restrooms, parking, recreational equipment is not available; **Any limitations on vehicle usage:** No off road vehicles; **Hiking trails:** Yes, trails vary in length and difficulty. Major trailheads are in the Marin Headlands, Muir Woods, and Tennessee Valley; **Backcountry:** No; **Camping:** Yes, American Youth Hostels offer overnight accommodations in the Marin Headlands Area of the park and at Fort Mason. Hike-in and group camping available in the Marin Headlands; **Other overnight accommodations on site:** No; **Meals served in the park:** Yes, food service facilities are available at the Fort Mason Center, The Cliff House, and Muir Woods. In addition, food is easily obtained in the nearby urban community; **Food and supplies obtainable in the park:** No; **Food and supplies obtainable nearby:** Yes, in the nearby urban community; **Overnight accommodations:** The San Francisco Area offers a wide variety of overnight accommodations, many within walking distance of the park; **First Aid available in park:** Yes, at most Visitor Centers and in the surrounding community; **Nearest Hospital:** Letterman, San Francisco General Hospital, and many others in the vicinity; **Days/Hours:** Most of the park is open all day, all year. Hours for individual facilities vary, but 10 a.m.-5 p.m. are the most common hours of operation; **Holiday Closings:** Alcatraz, Hyde Street Pier, Maritime Museum, and Fort Point are closed on Dec. 25 and Jan. 1; **Visitor attractions closed for seasons:** No; **Weather:** Weather at the park is variable. Wind and fog are common from June to September, especially near the Golden Gate. Fall generally brings the warmest weather. Most rainfall occurs from November to April. Bring a sweater or light jacket that you can carry easily if it warms up.

TRAVEL ACCESS: Bus: MUNI System in San Francisco, Greyhound provides services to San Francisco; **Rail:** Amtrak service Oakland, and Southern Pacific has passenger service into San Francisco; **Air:** Major airlines service San Francisco International Airport and Oakland International Airport.

John Muir National Historic Site
Martinez, California   **SEE CLIMATABLE NO. 23**

MAILING ADDRESS: Superintendent, John Muir National Historic Site, 4202 Alhambra Ave., Martinez, California 94553 **Telephone:** 415-228-8860

DIRECTIONS: The site is located at the foot of the off ramp of the Alhambra Ave. exit of State Route 4, 10 miles (16 km) east of Interstate 80, 5 miles (8 km) west of State Route 680. Access is also available via Bay Area Rapid Transit (BART). Call 415-933-2278 for information on connecting schedules between BART trains and bus service to Martinez.

This 9-acre site preserves the 17 room Victorian home and orchard fragment of the great American writer, naturalist, and defender of the national parks, John Muir. Authorized for addition to the National Park System on Aug. 31, 1964.

VISITOR ACTIVITIES: Guided and self-guiding tours are available. A film about Muir's life and philosophy is shown hourly. Picnicking is available. Guided tours are available for groups over 10 by reservation. Please notify park 2 weeks in advance. Self guided tours are available daily between 10 a.m.-4:30 p.m.; **Permits:** No; **Fees:** $1 adults 12-62, seniors free. Golden Eagle and Golden Age Passports are available; **Visitor facilities:** Visitor Center, parking, restrooms, picnic area; **Any limitations on vehicle usage:** No vehicles are allowed in the park, access cart available for handicapped visitors; **Hiking trails:** Yes, short trails around the grounds; **Backcountry:** No; **Camping:** No; **Other overnight accommodations on site:** No; **Meals served in the park:** No; **Food and supplies obtainable in the park:** No; **Food and supplies obtainable nearby:** Yes, in Martinez; **Overnight accommodations:** Yes, overnight accommodations are available a few blocks away and also in Martinez, 1/2 mile (.8 km); **First Aid available in park:** Yes; **Nearest Hospital:** Martinez, 1 mile (1.6 km); **Days/Hours:** Open daily from 10:00 a.m.-4:30 p.m.; **Holiday Closings:** Thanksgiving, Dec. 25 & Jan. 1; **Visitor attractions closed for seasons:** No; **Weather:** Moderate climate; warm Summers.

Joshua Tree National Monument
Twentynine Palms, California   **SEE CLIMATABLE NO. 25**

MAILING ADDRESS: Superintendent, Joshua Tree National Monument, 74485 National Monument Drive, Twentynine Palms, California 92277 **Telephone:** 619-367-7511

DIRECTIONS: The Monument is 140 miles (225 km) east of Los Angeles; from the West it is approached via I-10 (US 60) and Twentynine Palms Hwy (Hwy 62) to the North entrances at the town of Joshua Tree and Twentynine Palms. The Cottonwood Spring (South) entrance is 25 miles (40 km) east of Indio, CA, via I-10 (US 60).

The Monument is a desert area of great diversity encompassing the unique ecosystems of both the Joshua Tree-defined Mojave and lower Colorado deserts. Rich in ecological, historical and recreational resources, the Monument was established Aug. 10, 1936.

VISITOR ACTIVITIES: hiking, interpretive walks and talks, picnicking, wildlife-watching, camping; **Permits:** For backcountry; **Fees:** Not for backcountry use. General entrance fee is $5.00 for 1-7 day; $15.00 for year pass; $25.00 Golden Eagle (all park pass)—campground use fee at two campgrounds is $6 and $8 per night; **Visitor facilities:** campgrounds, tables, fireplaces, toilets, picnic area; **Any limitations on vehicle usage:** Vehicles must be operated only on established roads; **Hiking trails:** Yes, trails vary in length and difficulty; **Backcountry:** Yes, there is a self registration system used throughout the monument. Contact the park or inquire at the Visitor Center; **Camping:** Yes, first-come, first-served. Campers must bring their own water and firewood and be prepared for wide fluctuations in temperature. Three group camping sites available, reservations required through Ticketron. **Other overnight accommodations on site:** No; **Meals served in the park:** No; **Food and supplies obtainable in the park:** No; **Food and supplies obtainable nearby:** Yes, in Twentynine Palms, Yucca Valley, Joshua Tree; **Overnight accommodations:** Twentynine Palms, 3 miles (5 km) from North Park Entrance; in Joshua Tree, 5 miles (8 km) from West Park Entrance; Yucca Valley, 11 miles (17.7 km) from West Park entrance; **First Aid available in park:** Yes; **Nearest Hospital:** Joshua Tree, 8 miles (13 km) from West Park entrance; **Days/Hours:** Open all year, 24 hours a day. Visitor Center open daily from 8 a.m. to 5 p.m.; **Holiday Closings:** Visitor Center closed Dec. 25; **Visitor attractions closed for seasons:** Guided walks and talks in Spring and Fall only; **Weather:** It is cold from Dec. through mid-Feb., July and Aug. temperatures range from 100°F to 115°F.

GENERAL INFORMATION: When hiking, biking, or driving in Joshua Tree, during hot weather drink two liters (at least one-half gallon) of water per day. Stay clear of mine shafts. Beware of rattlesnakes.

Lassen Volcanic National Park
Mineral, California   **SEE CLIMATABLE NO. 26**

MAILING ADDRESS: Superintendent, Lassen Volcanic National Park, P.O. Box 100, Mineral, California 96063-0100 **Telephone:** 916-595-4444

DIRECTIONS: From the north and south, the park is reached via CA 89. From the east and west, via State Route 36 and 44. Redding is 48 miles (77.2 km) west of the Park on State Route 44.

The park contains examples of volcanic phenomena, including Lassen Peak, a recently active volcano which erupted intermittently from 1914 to 1921. Created by an Act of Congress on August 9, 1916.

VISITOR ACTIVITIES: interpretive programs, nature walks, hiking, self-guiding auto tours, camping, cross-country and downhill skiing, picnicking, boating, backpacking, swimming, winter sports; **Permits:** Wilderness permits are required for overnight stays in the backcountry. Permits are available at Park Headquarters and all Ranger Stations. They may be requested by mail or telephone, but they should be requested at least 2 weeks in advance; **Fees:** Yes, entrance fee is $5 per car; campground fee is $3 to $6 per campsite, depending on facilities. Golden Eagle, Golden Access, and Golden Age Passports are accepted and available; **Visitor facilities:** campgrounds, hiking trails, fast food service, picnic areas, boat ramp, supplies, and ski trails, tows, and equipment rental; **Any limitations on vehicle usage:** motor (electric, etc.) are not allowed on any park waters; **Hiking trails:** Yes, there are 150 miles (240 km) of foot trails in the park; **Backcountry:** Yes, permit is required for overnight stays check at Park Headquarters, any Ranger Station, or send for information; **Camping:** Yes, three campgrounds are located along Lassen Park Road. The campgrounds at Manzanita Lake, Summit Lake, and Butte Lake have sanitary facilities and spaces for trailers (no hookups for electricity, water, or sewage). The Southwest Campground also has modern facilities. The Juniper Lake and Warner Valley Campgrounds have primitive facilities. The Juniper Lake and Warner Valley Campgrounds have primitive facilities and are not recommended for trailers due to the rough road. Campgrounds are open from June to October, depending on the weather and the location of the campground. Group campgrounds are also available, and reservations must be made in advance. Complete campground information is provided on request. Call 916-595-4444 for information on lodging facilities; **Other overnight accommodations on site:** Yes, at Drakesbad Guest Ranch, call 916-595-3306; **Meals served in the park:** Yes, fast food services are available at the Manzanita Lake Camper Service Store and Chalet; **Food and supplies obtainable in the park:** Yes, Manzanita Lake Campground; **Food and supplies obtainable nearby:** Yes, in Mineral, 10 miles (16 km) south; Hat Creek, 16 miles (20 km) north; **Overnight accommodations:** Mineral, 10 miles (16 km) south; Hat Creek, 14 miles (20 km) north; **First Aid available in park:** Yes; **Nearest Hospital:** Burney, State Route 44, 45 miles (77 km) west of the north end; Chester, State Route 36, 35 miles (56 km) from the south end; **Days/Hours:** Park is always open; **Holiday Closings:** None; **Visitor attractions closed for seasons:** Trans-park Road is closed during winter; **Weather:** Most of the 30-mile (48 km) Lassen Park Road is closed by snow from the end of October until early June, although the park is open all year. Winter sports are centered in an area near the southwest entrance.

GENERAL INFORMATION: *For Your Safety*—Stay on established trails at all times in hot springs or steaming areas. Keep small children under strict physical control to avoid burns or accidents. Ground crusts which appear to be safe may be dangerously thin. Hot lunches, and ski-rental equipment and accessories are available on weekends and holidays. Ski lifts are operated three days a week. Overnight accommodations are available at Mineral and Chester.

The terrain and snow conditions are usually excellent for cross-country skiing. For safety reasons, Park Rangers should be notified of all trips. Wilderness permits are required for all overnight stays.

The road is kept open from the northwest entrance to the Manzanita Lake District Office. Many people visit this section of the Park to enjoy the scenery and winter sports.

TRAVEL ACCESS: Bus: Mt. Lassen Motor Transit stops at Mineral, CA and Red Bluff daily, except Sundays and holidays.

NEARBY FACILITIES & POINTS OF INTEREST: Hotel/Motel: South of park; Mineral, Mill Creek, Paynes Creek and Chester, CA; North of park; Old Station and Shingletown, CA; **Food/Supplies:** Chalet, Mineral, Manzanita, Old Station and Shingletown, CA.

Lava Beds National Monument
Tulelake, California   **SEE CLIMATABLE NO. 27**

MAILING ADDRESS: Superintendent, Lava Beds National Monument, P.O. Box 867, Tulelake, California 96134 **Telephone:** 916-667-2282

DIRECTIONS: Park Headquarters is 30 miles (48 km) from Tulelake, CA, and 58 miles (93 km) from Klamath Falls, OR, off State Route 139, 5 miles (8 km) south of Tulelake and 26 miles (42 km) north of Canby. 1.3 miles (2 km) of the road between Tulelake and the park are not paved.

Volcanic activity spewed forth molten rock and lava here creating an incredibly rugged landscape—a natural fortress used by the Indians in the Modoc Indian War, 1872-73. Created by Presidential Proclamation on Nov. 1, 1925.

VISITOR ACTIVITIES: camping, walking, picnicking, interpretive talks, campfire programs, cave exploration, bird- and animal-watching; **Permits:** No; **Fees:** Entrance fees $3, campground fees are $5 per day per site from Memorial Day through Sept. 30; **Visitor facilities:** picnic areas, campgrounds, drinking water, toilets; **Any limitations on vehicle usage:** Vehicles are restricted to maintained roads; **Hiking trails:** Yes, moderate to rugged both in and outside of the wilderness areas; **Backcountry:** Yes, information available by writing or calling the park, or from Park Headquarters; **Camping:** Yes, no reservations for campsites, which are near Monument Headquarters and are open all year. The 40-unit campground has sites suitable for tents, pickup campers, and small trailers and has water and toilets. From Sept. 15 through May 15 water must be carried from Headquarters. Fleener Chimneys picnic area has no water, and fires may not be built there; **Other overnight accommodations on site:** No; **Meals served in the park:** No; **Food and supplies obtainable in the park:** No; **Food and supplies obtainable nearby:** Yes, at Tulelake and Klamath Falls; **Overnight accommodations:** Tulelake, State Route 139, 30 miles (48 km); Klamath Falls, OR, State Route 139, 58 miles (93 km), and Merrill, OR; **First Aid available in park:** Yes, or nearby in Tulelake, State Route 139, 30 miles (48 km); **Nearest Hospital:** Klamath Falls, OR, State Route 139, 58 miles (93 km); **Days/Hours:** Park never closes, Visitor Center open daily from 8 a.m. to 5 p.m.; until 6 p.m. in Summer; **Holiday Closings:** Thanksgiving and Christmas days; **Visitor attractions closed for seasons:** None; **Weather:** At these elevations, cold weather is possible anytime; snow has been recorded in nearly all months. Winter daily high temperatures average around 5°C (40'sF); lows are only a few degrees below 0°C (in the 20's F). Fog is frequent. Summers are moderate; with daytime highs averaging from 24° to 27°C (75 to 80°F), lows are about 10°C (40's and 50's F). Precipitation in this area averages 3.18 cm (1.25 inches) or less per month.

GENERAL INFORMATION: Hunting, gathering specimens, and collecting souvenirs is prohibited. Among the potential hazards you may encounter in the lava tubes are low ceilings, steep trails and stairways, and uneven footing. Take more than one light source. Wear protective headgear. Wear adequate clothing—cave temperatures are cool. Notify a Park Ranger before exploring caves other than those listed in the park's brochure, or if you plan to use your own lighting equipment. Be aware that rattlesnakes are found throughout the park; children should be cautioned never to put their hands and feet in places they cannot see.

TRAVEL ACCESS: Bus: Greyhound provides daily service to Tulelake, CA; **Rail:** Amtrak provides daily service into Klamath Falls, Oregon; **Air:** Horizon Air, American Eagle provide daily services to Klamath Falls, OR.

Muir Woods National Monument
Mill Valley, California   **SEE CLIMATABLE NO. 24**

MAILING ADDRESS: Site Manager, Muir Woods National Monument, Mill Valley, California 94941 **Telephone:** 415-388-2595

DIRECTIONS: The Monument is 17 miles (27 km) north of San Francisco and is reached by US 101 and CA 1. Tour bus service is available from downtown San Francisco.
    This virgin stand of coastal redwoods was named for John Muir, conservationist and co-founder of the Sierra Club. Created by Presidential Proclamation on Jan. 9, 1908.

VISITOR ACTIVITIES: walking, hiking; **Permits:** No; **Fees:** No; **Visitor facilities:** Visitor Center, parking, restrooms, souvenir stand, group interpretive talks by advance arrangement, trailside markers, signs, and exhibits; **Any limitations on vehicle usage:** No motorized equipment, horses, or bicycles are permitted; **Hiking trails:** Yes, 6 miles (10 km) of trails join those of other public lands. Bridges along Redwood Creek make short loops possible; **Backcountry:** No; **Camping:** No; **Other overnight accommodations on site:** No; **Meals served in the park:** Yes, snacks are available at the concession shop near the Visitor Center; **Food and supplies obtainable in the park:** No; **Food and supplies obtainable nearby:** Yes; **Overnight accommodations:** Mill Valley, 4 miles (6.4 km); **First Aid available in park:** Yes; **Nearest Hospital:** San Rafael, 12 miles (19.3 km); **Days/Hours:** Open daily from 8 a.m. to sunset; **Holiday Closings:** None; **Visitor attractions closed for seasons:** No; **Weather:** 40 inches of rain per year, mostly between November and May.

GENERAL INFORMATION: Weather is often cool and wet, so jackets are advisable. Stay on trails, which can become slippery when wet. Poison oak and nettles are common. Do not pick berries, roots or mushrooms. Several plants found in Muir Woods are poisonous. No picnicking or dogs allowed at the Monument.

Pinnacles National Monument
Paicines, California
SEE CLIMATABLE NO. 28

MAILING ADDRESS: Superintendent, Pinnacles National Monument, Paicines, California 95043 **Telephone:** 408-389-4578

DIRECTIONS: The Monument is separated into an east and west district with Visitor Service facilities located in both districts. Park Headquarters and the Bear Gulch Visitor Center are on the east side of the Monument and are reached via CA 25, and Highway 146, from Hollister. The Chaparral Ranger Station and campground are on the west side and can be reached via CA 146 from Soledad. The road from Soledad to West Pinnacles is steep and narrow. Visitors driving large campers and towing trailers should use extreme caution. There is no road connecting the east and west sides of the Monument.

Spirelike rock formations 1200 to 3300 feet high, with caves and a variety of organic features, rise above the smooth contours of the surrounding countryside. Created by Presidential Proclamation on Jan. 16, 1908.

VISITOR ACTIVITIES: hiking, climbing, picnicking, camping, evening talks on spring and fall weekends, wildlife-, wildflower-, and bird-watching; **Permits:** none required, but climbers are advised to register with a Park Ranger before and after a climb; **Fees:** $3 per vehicle entrance fee. Golden Eagle and Golden Age Passports accepted and available. $5 per night per site camping fee; **Visitor facilities:** picnic areas, campsites, drinking water, comfort stations, self-guiding trails, hiking trails, **Any limitations on vehicle usage:** Motor vehicles and mountain bikes are not allowed on any of the trails; **Hiking trails:** Yes, trails vary in length and difficulty. Pets are not allowed on the trails. For further information, inquire at Visitor Center; **Backcountry:** No; **Camping:** Yes, West Side Chapparal campground is reached from Highway 101, 11 miles (17.7 km) east from the turnoff at Soledad with sites available on a first come, first served basis for *individuals* only. Organized groups are permitted from June 1st to January 31st. Requests for reservations must be received by mail or telephone seven days prior to arrival date. Reservations *for group sites only* can be made by calling (408) 389-4526. Picnic tables, fireplaces, water, and chemical toilets are provided. No gasoline, food or supplies are available. Pinnacles Campground Inc., a private campground, is adjacent to the park's east boundary on CA 146. It offers individual and group campsites with tables and grills and modern restrooms. It has showers, a camper store, gas pump, swimming pool, recreation vehicle utility hookups and an amphitheater. Call for fee information. The campground operates on a first come, first served basis. Reservations are required for groups of ten or more. For further information call 408-389-4462, or write 2400 Highway 146, Paicines, CA 95043; **Other overnight accommodations on site:** No; **Meals served in the park:** No; **Food and supplies obtainable in the park:** No; **Food and supplies obtainable nearby:** Yes, stores at Pinnacles Campground and in Paicines, 23 miles (37 km) to the north; **Overnight accommodations:** Soledad, Hollister and King City; **First Aid available in park:** Yes; **Nearest Hospital:** Hollister and King City; **Days/Hours:** Park never closes; **Holiday Closings:** None; **Visitor attractions closed for seasons:** None; **Weather:** Fall and Spring are the Park's busiest seasons. Spring is one of the best times to enjoy the Park. Summer daytime temperatures can exceed 38°C (100°F).

GENERAL INFORMATION: *For Your Safety*—Caves have low ceilings and very slippery rocks. Use flashlights. Only experienced climbers and persons under competent leadership should attempt rock climbs in the park. *Stay on regular designated trails.* Rock faces off the trails are unstable and likely to flake off beneath you. *Poison oak* abounds; stay on the trails and in developed areas which are kept reasonably free of this plant. *Rattlesnakes* may be on the trails in the Spring and Fall. *Water* is not always as pure as it seems, so drink only from hydrants and fountains on the Park's water supply. Be sure to *wear stout, comfortable shoes*, loose fitting clothing, and in the summer, a hat.

TRAVEL ACCESS: Bus: Greyhound provides daily service to Gilroy or King City; **Rail:** No; **Air:** No.

Point Reyes National Seashore
Point Reyes Station, California   **SEE CLIMATABLE NO. 29**

MAILING ADDRESS: Superintendent, Point Reyes National Seashore, Point Reyes, California 94956 **Telephone:** 415-663-1092

DIRECTIONS: The Seashore is one hour or 40miles (65-70 km) north of San Francisco via US 101 and Sir Francis Drake Blvd., or via US 1 near Mill Valley.

This peninsula, near San Francisco, is noted for its long beaches backed by tall cliffs, lagoons and esteros, forested ridges and offshore bird and sea lion colonies. Part of the area remains in pastoral use. Authorized for addition to the National Park System on Sept. 13, 1962.

VISITOR ACTIVITIES: hiking, biking, picnicking, surfing, wading, guided tours, surf fishing, horseback riding, bird watching, backcountry; **Permits:** required for camping, obtained by registering at the Bear Valley Visitor Center. **Fees:** No; **Visitor facilities:** beaches, campgrounds, hiking trails, horse trails, picnic areas, three Visitor Centers, self-guiding trails, four hike-in campgrounds with 50 sites total; **Any limitations on vehicle usage:** all motor vehicles are restricted to developed, paved roadways and parking areas; **Hiking trails:** Yes, Bear Valley Trailhead is a gateway to more than 140 miles (273.6 km) of trails. The 4.4 mile (7 km) Bear Valley Trail is the most popular route, winding through grassy meadows and forests to the sea. Other trails branch from it and ascend steeply into the high country of the Inverness Ridge and the southern portion of the Seashore. Stay on designated trails; wandering off may result in losing your way or being exposed to poison oak, which abounds here. Carry a canteen—stream water is not potable; **Backcountry:** Yes, information can be obtained from the Superintendent; **Camping:** Yes, to obtain a permit, register at Bear Valley Visitor Center; **Other overnight accommodations on site:** No; **Meals served in the park:** Yes, at Drakes Beach; **Food and supplies obtainable in the park:** No; **Food and supplies obtainable nearby:** Yes, at Point Reyes Station, Inverness, Olema; **Overnight accommodations:** Olema, US 1, 1 mile (1.6 km); Inverness, Sir Francis Drake Highway, 5 miles (8 km); **First Aid available in park:** Yes, or nearby in Point Reyes Station, Inverness, Olema; **Nearest Hospital:** San Rafael and Petaluma, both 20 miles (32 km) away; **Days/Hours:** Park is always open; Visitor Center is generally open from 9 a.m. to 5:00 p.m.; **Holiday Closings:** some facilities close on Dec. 25; **Visitor attractions closed for seasons:** None; **Weather:** The ocean strongly influences the weather at Point Reyes. The ocean beaches are frequently foggy and windy enough to make warm clothing welcome. Throughout the Summer these beaches experience more days of fog than sunshine, but Spring and Autumn can be mild and pleasant. The country east of Inverness Ridge, accessible by hiking trails, is free of Summer fog, but it has heavy rains in Winter and Spring.

GENERAL INFORMATION: A privately operated tent and trailer campground is 1/2 mile (0.8 km) from seashore Headquarters. Horses can be rented nearby. *Caution!* Pounding surf and rip currents make some Point Reyes beaches too dangerous for swimming, surfing and wading. Steep cliffs are dangerous; walking near the edge or below invites catastrophe.

TRAVEL ACCESS: Bus: Golden Gate Transit provides regular service to Inverness and Point Reyes, CA; **Rail:** Amtrak provides service into Oakland, CA; **Air:** Major Airlines offer service into San Mateo Co. CA; **Other:** Taxi service available in San Rafael, CA 20 miles (32 km) distant. Bicycling is possible, but not recommended because of hazardous road conditions.

NEARBY FACILITIES & POINTS OF INTEREST: Hotel/Motel: Inverness Valley Inn, Inverness, CA 415-669-7250 about 6 miles (10 km); Golden Hinde Boatel, Inverness, CA 415-699-1389 about 6 miles (10 km); **Campgrounds:** Olema Ranch Campground, Olema, CA 415-663-1363, 0.6 mile (1 km); Samuel P. Taylor State Park, Lagunitas, CA 415-448-9897, 6 miles (10 km); **Parks, other points of interest:** Muir Woods National Monument, Audubon Canyon Ranch, Golden Gate NRA, Samuel P. Taylor State Park, Tomales Bay, & Mt. Tamalpais State Parks.

Redwood National Park
Crescent City, California   **SEE CLIMATABLE NO. 27**

MAILING ADDRESS: Superintendent, Redwood National Park, 1111 Second St., Crescent City, California 95531 **Telephone:** 707-464-6101

DIRECTIONS: The Park can be reached by private auto and scheduled bus lines on US 101 south from the Oregon coast, north from Eureka and Arcata, and from east via US 199 from Grants Pass and Medford, OR and East via US 299 from Redding. Ranger stations are in Hiouchi, Crescent City and Orick.

The park contains coastal redwood forests with virgin groves of ancient trees, including the world's tallest. It includes 40 miles (64 km) of scenic Pacific coastline. Established by Act of Congress on Oct. 2, 1968.

VISITOR ACTIVITIES: driving, hiking, shoreline walks, photography, fishing, picnicking, bird- and wildflower-watching, interpretive services, camping; **Permits:** for fishing and backcountry; backcountry permits issued without charge at trailhead, fishing license may be purchased at hardware and tackle shops. Licenses vary in length of validity and cost; **Fees:** $10 per night at campgrounds, $3.00 per vehicle for day-use picnic areas in State Parks; **Visitor facilities:** hiking trails, exhibits, campgrounds, picnicking facilities are at a number of locations, including Enderts Beach Road, Lagoon Creek, and the State parks; **Any limitations on vehicle usage:** Trailers should not be taken off main roads because of weather, general road conditions and steep grades; **Hiking trails:** Yes, on the shore and through redwood forests; **Backcountry:** Yes, inquire any Ranger Station or write the above address. Redwood National Park has 3 primitive campsites located at Enderts Beach, DeMartin and Flint Ridge (see map and guide) all are located along Coastal Trail; **Camping:** No, the National Park does not have developed campgrounds, but camping is available in the state parks and national forests. Each state park has a developed campground suitable for tents, campers, and small trailers up to 6 feet (8 m) long. There are 349 campsites in the 3 state parks. Sites may be reserved through MISTIX, P.O. Box 85705, San Diego, CA 92138-5705, or call (800) 446-7275. A reservation fee of $3.75 is charged. Information and forms are available at any California State Park Office. Reservations are helpful from July 1 to after Labor Day. Campsites not filled by reservation are assigned on a first-come, first-served basis. State Parks have fees for camping and day-use picnic areas. Interpretive programs are presented daily in the Summer. National forests: Four campgrounds are off US 199 in Six Rivers National Forest. They contain 87 campsites, developed for tents, campers, and small trailers, and are about a 30-minute drive from US 101. Other campgrounds are also on CA 299 and 96 in Six Rivers, Klamath, and Trinity National Forests. These are 1- to 4-hour drives from US 101; **Other overnight accommodations on site:** No; **Meals served in the park:** No; **Food and supplies obtainable in the park:** No; **Food and supplies obtainable nearby:** Yes, at Crescent City, Eureka, Klamath, Orick; **Overnight accommodations:** A number of motels, private trailer parks, and campgrounds are along US 101 from Eureka, CA to the Oregon line, and on CA 299 and 96 and US 199 to the east; **First Aid available in park:** Yes; **Nearest Hospital:** Nearest hospital from Orick is Mad River Hospital, 300 Janes Road, Arcata 30 miles south of Orick on US 101. Hospital in Crescent City is Sutter Coast Hospital, 100A Crescent City; **Days/Hours:**

Open 24 hours a day year-round; **Holiday Closings:** Ranger Stations closed on Dec. 25, Jan. 1 and Jan. 18; **Visitor attractions closed for seasons:** Mill Creek Campground closes in Winter; **Weather:** Summer, Spring and Fall visits are recommended. Winter is windy and rainy.

GENERAL INFORMATION: For current information on access to park lands, inquire at a Ranger Station or ask a Park Ranger. Shuttle bus service June - Sept. from Orick to Tall Trees Grove Trail (1½ miles). Grove includes tallest known tree in world. Fee: Adult: $3.00, children (15 and under) $1.00, Senior (62 and over) $1.50. See map & guide info on the new Redwood Information Center.

TRAVEL ACCESS: Bus: Greyhound provides daily service to Crescent City, Arcata; **Rail:** None; **Air:** Commuter & scheduled air lines to Crescent City and Arcata/Eureka. Rental cars available Medford, Oregon and Arcata/Eureka CA.

Santa Monica Mountains National Recreation Area
California   **SEE CLIMATABLE NO. 20**

MAILING ADDRESS: Superintendent, Santa Monica Mountains National Recreation Area, Suite 140, 22900 Ventura Blvd., Woodland Hills, California 91364 **Telephone:** 818-888-3770

DIRECTIONS: The Santa Monica Mountains National Recreation Area is bordered by Griffith Park on the east and Los Posas Road on the west; with Pacific Coast Hwy. to the south and the 101 Frwy to the north. The area has many roads which allow accessibility. Some of the roads which run north-south are Topanga Canyon Blvd., Malibu Canyon Road, and Kanan-Dune Road. The main east-west roadway is Mulholland Highway. Set among 50,000 acres of federal, state and local parks, the Santa Monica Mountains National Recreation Area encompasses rolling hills, oak forests, canyons, streams, and beaches. The recreation area preserves Mediterranean chapparal ecosystems through cooperative land management between government agencies and the private sector. Birdwatching, hiking, riding trails, picnicking, festivals, nature centers, evening programs, and fishing are available year round. Some of the parks are minutes away from Los Angeles, while others are more remote, providing isolated habitat for hawks, eagles, cougars and bobcats. March and April are the best months to enjoy the colorful displays of wildflowers.

Sequoia and Kings Canyon National Parks
Three Rivers, California   **SEE CLIMATABLE NO. 30**

MAILING ADDRESS: Superintendent, Sequoia and Kings Canyon National Parks, Three Rivers, California 93271 **Telephone:** 209-565-3341

DIRECTIONS: Proceed east on CA 198 from US 99 to the south entrance of Sequoia Park. To reach Kings Canyon Park, go east on CA 180 from US 99 to the entrance. Generals Highway connects CA 198 and 180, and passes through Sequoia Park to the Grant Grove area, Kings Canyon Park, a 2-hour drive.

    Two enormous canyons of the Kings River and the summit peaks of the High Sierra dominate Kings Canyon. Grant Grove, with its giant sequoias, is a detached section of the Park. Attractions at Sequoia include Mount Whitney, the highest mountain in the U.S. outside of Alaska, and giant sequoia groves. Kings Canyon established by act of Congress on Mar. 4, 1940; Sequoia established on Sept. 25, 1890.

VISITOR ACTIVITIES: sightseeing, photography, camping, hiking, fishing, Nordic and downhill skiing, horseback riding, exhibits, campfire programs, guided nature walks; **Permits:** For wilderness use, camping (including wilderness camping): obtain permit at Park Headquarters and Visitor Center. Fishing licenses from local stores; **Fees:** $5 entrance fee per car. Camping is $6.00 per night. Golden Eagle and Golden Age Passports accepted and available; **Visitor facilities:** campgrounds, lodges and cabins, cafeteria, dining rooms, camper supply stores, post offices, rental pack and saddle stock, ski trails; **Any limitations on vehicle usage:** All vehicles are restricted to developed roadways. No vehicles are permitted on trails. Park roads are paved and steep with many turns; drive slowly, keep to the right, and use lower gears to avoid overheating the brakes and transmissions. Trailers are limited to specific campgrounds; **Hiking trails:** Yes, 700 miles (1190 km) of hiking from relatively easy to steep mountain trails. Elevations range from 2,000 to 14,495 feet; **Backcountry:** Yes, information available by contacting the Superintendent; **Camping:** Yes, campground reservations are required, at Lodgepole campground only; other campgrounds are operated on a first-come, first-served basis. Reservations can be made in person at over 150 Ticketron outlets in California or by mail from throughout the United States to: Ticketron, Dept. R, 401 Hackensack Ave., Hackensack, NJ 07601. Reservations at Lodgepole available Memorial Day to Labor Day. They can be made no more than 8 weeks in advance of day of visit. Most campgrounds and picnic areas have at least one campsite accessible to physically disabled; **Other overnight accommodations on site:** Yes, for reservations at cabins, contact: Sequoia and Kings Canyon Guest Services, Sequoia National Park, CA 93262, phone 209-561-3314; and Wilsonia Lodge, Kings Canyon National Park, CA 93633, phone 209-335-2310; **Meals served in the park:** Yes, at Giant Forest, Grant Grove, Cedar Grove, Stony Creek, and Wilsonia; **Food and supplies obtainable in the park:** Yes, at Giant Forest, Lodgepole, Grant Grove, Cedar Grove, Stony Creek, Wilsonia; **Food and supplies obtainable nearby:** Yes, in Three Rivers, Visalia, Fresno; **Overnight accommodations:** Kings Canyon: Fresno, CA 180, 55 miles (88.5 km) from Grant Grove. Sequoia: Three Rivers, CA 198, 7 miles (11.3 km) from Headquarters: Visalia, CA 198, 55 miles (88.5 km) from Giant Forest; **First Aid available in park:** Yes; **Nearest Hospital:** Kings Canyon: Fresno, CA, CA 180, 55 miles (88.5 km) from Grant Grove. Sequoia: Exeter, CA, CA 198, 30 miles (48.3 km) from Headquarters; **Days/Hours:** Parks open all year; **Holiday Closings:** None; **Visitor attractions closed for seasons:** Some activities are closed during the winter snow period. The Generals Highway between Lodgepole & Grant Grove is open year-round, but may be closed during winter months for several days at a time due to heavy snow; **Weather:** Warm mountain climate with cool nights in Summer; snow and relatively severe mountain Winters.

GENERAL INFORMATION: *For Your Safety—Drowning* is the leading cause of fatalities. Extreme caution is advised around rivers, especially in the Spring and early Summer when they are swift, deep, and very cold. *Lightning* is dangerous on exposed peaks. *Injuries from falling* are best prevented by staying away from steep places, wearing proper footgear, and hiking in the company of others. *Respiratory or circulatory problems* may be aggravated at higher elevations. *Bears and other wildlife*, though sometimes tame in appearance, are wild and could be dangerous. Regulations that prohibit feeding or aggravating animals are enforced for your safety, as well as for the benefit of the animals.

TRAVEL ACCESS: Bus: Tulare County Transit operates twice-weekly service between Three Rivers and Visalia (Does not enter the park); **Rail:** Amtrak service into Hanford; **Air:** Nearest access to Fresno and Visalia.

Whiskeytown-Shasta-Trinity National Recreation Area
Whiskeytown, California   **SEE CLIMATABLE NO. 26**

MAILING ADDRESS: Superintendent, Whiskeytown-Shasta-Trinity National Recreation Area, P.O. Box 188, Whiskeytown, California 96095 **Telephone:** 916-241-6584

DIRECTIONS: The main Visitor Center is Overlook Information Station, located at the intersection of CA 299 and Kennedy Memorial Drive.

Whiskeytown Lake, formed by a dam on Clear Lake in a scenic mountain region, is an excellent resource for water-related recreation. The other two units are administered by the U.S. Forest Service. Created by an act of Congress on Nov. 8, 1965.

VISITOR ACTIVITIES: Whiskeytown Lake is excellent for most water-related activities, including swimming, scuba diving, water skiing, boating and fishing. Picnicking, camping backcountry, hunting, interpretive programs, and horseback riding are also popular; **Permits:** Free backcountry permits are available at headquarters; **Fees:** camping fee at Oak Bottom for tent sites or recreational vehicles, year round; **Visitor facilities:** historical museum at Shasta, self-guiding trail, picnic area, campground, bathhouse, boat ramp and rentals, food and supplies, hiking and horse trails; **Any limitations on vehicle usage:** Vehicles are restricted to designated roadways; **Hiking trails:** Yes, 3.7 miles (5.9 km) of frontcountry hiking trails; **Backcountry:** Yes, information can be obtained from Visitor Center and headquarters; **Camping:** Yes, reservations available for campsites through Ticketron (Fees vary according to seasons and vehicles); **Other overnight accommodations on site:** No; **Meals served in the park:** Yes, snack bars at Oak Bottom and Brandy Creek during summer season; **Food and supplies obtainable in the park:** Yes, Snack Bars at Oak Bottom Marina and Whiskeytown Store, ¼ mile (.4 km) off CA 299 during summer season; **Food and supplies obtainable nearby:** Yes, at Redding, CA, 8 miles (12.9 km) east of Overlook Information Station; **Overnight accommodations:** Redding, CA 299, 8 miles (12.9 km) east of Overlook Information Station; **First Aid available in park:** Yes; **Nearest Hospital:** Redding, CA 299, 8 miles (12.9 km) east; **Days/Hours:** Open all year, camping and boating hours are unlimited, swimming beaches close at 11 p.m. **Holiday Closings:** None; **Visitor attractions closed for seasons:** None.

GENERAL INFORMATION: Visitors should inquire at Overlook Information Station or Headquarters for information about the recreation area and programs. Most of the Park is accessible to the handicapped. The most prominent landmark of the region is 6,209 foot Shasta Bally, rising in the midst of rolling woodlands and clear-flowing streams. The summit may be reached on foot and by four-wheel drive auto.

NEARBY FACILITIES & POINTS OF INTEREST: Parks, other points of interest: Redwoods National Park, Lassen Volcanic National Park, Lava Beds National Monument, Shasta State Historic Park.

Yosemite National Park
Yosemite National Park, California   **SEE CLIMATABLE NO. 22**

MAILING ADDRESS: Superintendent, P.O. Box 577, Yosemite National Park, California 95389 **Telephone:** 209-372-0200

DIRECTIONS: Access to Yosemite is via State Route 140 and 120 eastbound from Merced and Manteca; State Route 41 northbound from Fresno; State Route 120 westbound from Lee Vining (closed in Winter).

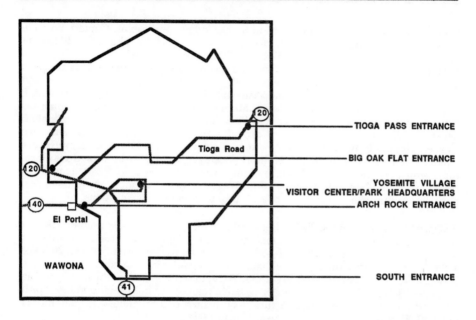

Granite peaks and domes rise high above broad meadows in the heart of the Sierra Nevada Mountains; groves of giant sequoias dwarf other trees and wildflowers; and mountains, lakes, and waterfalls, including the Nation's highest, are found here. Established by act of Congress on Oct. 1, 1890.

VISITOR ACTIVITIES: camping, hiking, climbing, horseback riding, fishing, swimming, rafting, boating (no motors), alpine and cross-country skiing, rock climbing, backpacking, bus tours, walks, talks, cultural demonstrations, self-guiding tours, interpretive exhibits, natural history seminars; **Permits:** Backcountry wilderness permits can be obtained by written application to Backcountry Office between February 1 and May 31, or in person at Wawona, Yosemite Valley, Big Oak Flat Entrance or Tuolomne Meadows; fishing licenses available in person only; **Fees:** Daily vehicle entrance fee is $5; daily campground use fee varies from $2 to $10, depending on facilities; Golden Eagle and Golden Age Passports accepted and available; **Visitor facilities:** individual and group campgrounds, picnic areas, Visitor Centers, showers, laundromat, repair garage, service stations, food service, accommodations, alpine and nordic ski schools, mountaineering school, recreational equipment rental, scheduled transportation and interpretive bus tours; **Any limitations on vehicle usage:** All vehicles are required to stay on surfaced roads. Commercial vehicles are allowed only on Park business; commercial buses require written permission (trip-lease agreement) with the concessioner plus fee; **Hiking trails:** Yes, 750 miles (1,207 km) of trails; **Backcountry:** Yes, information can be obtained at all Ranger Stations, Visitor Centers, and wilderness permit kiosks. Visitors planning trips during Summer holiday weekends should reserve wilderness permits in advance. Contact the Park's Backcountry Office well in advance; **Camping:** Yes, camping is available year-round on a first-come, first-served basis. The five Yosemite Valley Campgrounds are on the Ticketron reservation system year-round. Reservations can be made eight weeks in advance at Ticketron outlets nationwide, or by writing to: Ticketron Reservations Offices. Group campsites are available during the summer season and must be reserved in advance; the Yosemite Valley Group Camp is reservable through Ticketron up to 12 weeks in advance. Campsite reservations cannot be made by telephone. **Other overnight accommodations on site:** Yes, at Yosemite Valley, White Wolf, Wawona, Tuolumne Meadows and the five High Sierra Camps. Reservations are advised at all times for accommodations in hotels, lodges, and cabins. Contact Yosemite Park and Curry Company, 5410 E. Home, Fresno, CA 93727, phone 209-252-4848; **Meals served in the park:** Yes, at Yosemite Valley, Wawona, White Wolf, Tuolumne Meadows, and the five High Sierra Camps; **Food and supplies obtainable in the park:** Yes, Yosemite Valley, Wawona, White Wolf, Tuolumne Meadows and the five High Sierra Camps; **Food and supplies obtainable nearby:** Yes, in Lee Vining, Groveland, El Portal, Wawona, Oakhurst, Fish Camp, Mariposa; **Overnight accommodations:** Lee Vining, Groveland, El Portal, Oakhurst, Fish Camp, Mariposa; **First Aid available in park:** Yes, Yosemite Medical Group provides 24 hour emergency outpatient care; **Nearest Hospital:** Merced, Fresno, Sonora, Bridgeport and Mariposa; **Days/Hours:** Open 24 hours a day year-round; **Holiday Closings:** None; **Visitor attractions closed for seasons:** Mariposa Grove Road, Tuolumne Grove, Glacier Point Road, Tioga Road closed from mid-November to late May; **Weather:** Cool Summers above 5000 feet, periodic late Summer thunderstorms and snow flurries in high elevations.

GENERAL INFORMATION: Facilities and activities available to and usable by the disabled upon request. Life and death emergency only telephone 9-1-1. For weather and road conditions, telephone 209-372-4605. For general park information, call 209-372-0624. To report structural and wildland fires, telephone: Yosemite Valley—9-1-1; Wawona—9-1-1; El Portal—209-379-2333. To report emergencies within the Park, Dial Toll Free "9-1-1." Shuttlebus service is available year-round in Yosemite Valley. For illustrated publications describing natural features write to Yosemite Association, P.O. Box 230, El Portal, CA 95318, or stop at a Visitor Center.

TRAVEL ACCESS: **Bus:** VIA and California Yosemite Tours provides daily service from Merced; **Rail:** Amtrak provides daily service to Merced, Fresno and Madera. Connecting bus service by California Yosemite Tours, Parlor Car, and Yosemite Express and Greyhound to Merced (all year); **Air:** West Air Commuter, United, Pacific Southwest Airlines (PSA), Western provide daily service to Fresno. West Air Merced. Connecting bus service by VIA and California Yosemite Tours; **Other:** Rental Cars are available in Fresno & Merced.

Colorado

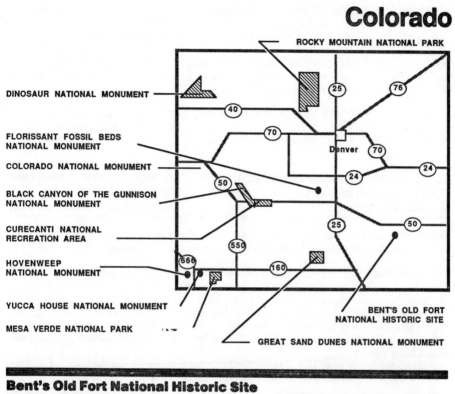

ROCKY MOUNTAIN NATIONAL PARK

DINOSAUR NATIONAL MONUMENT

FLORISSANT FOSSIL BEDS
NATIONAL MONUMENT

COLORADO NATIONAL MONUMENT

BLACK CANYON OF THE GUNNISON
NATIONAL MONUMENT

CURECANTI NATIONAL
RECREATION AREA

HOVENWEEP
NATIONAL MONUMENT

YUCCA HOUSE NATIONAL MONUMENT

MESA VERDE NATIONAL PARK

Denver

BENT'S OLD FORT
NATIONAL HISTORIC SITE

GREAT SAND DUNES NATIONAL MONUMENT

Bent's Old Fort National Historic Site
La Junta, Colorado   **SEE CLIMATABLE NO. 31**

MAILING ADDRESS: Superintendent, Bent's Old Fort National Historic Site, 35110 Highway 194 East, La Junta, Colorado 81050 **Telephone:** 303-384-2596

DIRECTIONS: The site is 8 miles (13 km) east of La Junta and 15 miles (24 km) west of Las Animas on CO 194.

As a principal crossroads of civilization on the Santa Fe Trail in the early 1800's and a trading post for Indians, the Fort became the center of a vast fur-trading empire in the West. Authorized for addition to the National Park System on June 3, 1960. Fort reconstructed in 1975-76.

VISITOR ACTIVITIES: interpretive and audiovisual program, guided tours, living history program; **Permits:** No; **Fees:** Yes; Visitor entrance fee $3.00 per vehicle; pedestrian, bicycle, and commercial bus passengers $1.00; **Visitor facilities:** Parking area is 600 yards from the fort. Transportation available for the elderly and handicapped— 8.00 a.m. to 4:30 p.m. daily. Restrooms are available, picnic area (reservations for groups over 15); **Any limitations on vehicle usage:** Visitor vehicles are restricted to the parking lot; **Hiking trails:** No; **Backcountry:** No; **Camping:** No; **Other overnight accommodations on site:** No; **Meals served in the park:** No; **Food and supplies obtainable in the park:** No; **Food and supplies obtainable nearby:** Yes, in La Junta; **Overnight accommodations:** La Junta, CO 194, 8 miles (13 km) west; **First Aid available in park:** Yes; **Nearest Hospital:** La Junta, CO 194, 8 miles (13 km) west; **Days/Hours:** Open daily 8 a.m. to 4:30 p.m. from Sept. through May; 8 a.m. to 6 p.m. Memorial Day through Labor Day; **Holiday Closings:** All federal holidays except for Memorial Day, Fourth of July and Labor Day; **Visitor attractions closed for seasons:** No.

GENERAL INFORMATION: *For Your Safety*—Remain on the stairs and walks, and watch your step on the steep stairways. Don't let children climb on the walls or run on the upper gallery; there are no handrails. Please do not annoy the animals.

TRAVEL ACCESS: Bus: Trailways provides daily service to La Junta, CO; Daily East & West; **Rail:** Amtrak provides daily service to La Junta, CO; **Air:** Charter and Private aircraft accommodated at La Junta, CO.

NEARBY FACILITIES & POINTS OF INTEREST: Campgrounds: KOA, 26680 Highway 50 W. La Junta, CO (303) 384-9817, 10 miles from Park; **Parks, other points of interest:** Koshare Indian Museum, 18th & Santa Fe, La Junta, CO, (303) 384-4801, 8 miles from Park.

Black Canyon of the Gunnison National Monument
Montrose, Colorado   **SEE CLIMATABLE NO. 32**

MAILING ADDRESS: Superintendent, Black Canyon of the Gunnison National Monument, P.O. Box 1648, Montrose, Colorado 81402 **Telephone:** 303-249-7036

DIRECTIONS: You can drive both rims of the Canyon. The South Rim is open to traffic all year; the North is closed to traffic in Winter. From Montrose, CO, the distance to the South Rim entrance is 11 miles (18 km)-6 miles (9.7 km) east via US 50 and 5 miles (8 km) north over a hard-surfaced road. You can reach the North Rim from CO 92, just east of Crawford over a 14 mile (22.5 km) graded road. Information is available at Park Headquarters on Highway 50 East at 2233 East Main, or during the season, at the South Rim Visitor Center.

Shadowed depths of this sheer-walled canyon accentuate the darkness of ancient rocks of obscure origin. Created by President Proclamation on Mar. 2, 1933.

VISITOR ACTIVITIES: camping, fishing, hiking, wildlife- and bird-watching, interpretive exhibits; **Permits:** State fishing license, free backcountry permit are required. Fishing license available from any sporting goods store in Montrose, backcountry permit from a Park Ranger no more than 24 hours in advance of the trip; **Fees:** Yes, camping fee is $4 per site, 7 people per site. Golden Eagle and Golden Age Passports accepted and available. $3 per car entrance fee; **Visitor facilities:** campgrounds, snack bar, souvenir stand, picnic areas, restrooms and overlooks (all closed in Winter); **Any limitations on vehicle usage:** All vehicles must stay on established roadways; **Hiking trails:** Yes, trails to overlooks and nature trails; **Backcountry:** Yes, you should register at the Ranger Station before starting any inner canyon activity; **Camping:** Yes, no reservations for the two campgrounds/one on each rim; **Other overnight accommodations on site:** No; **Meals served in the park:** No, but snacks are available on the South Rim; **Food and supplies obtainable in the park:** No; **Food and supplies obtainable nearby:** Yes, in Montrose, US 50, 11 miles (18 km); **Overnight accommodations:** US 50, 11 miles (18 km); **First Aid available in park:** Yes, but only in season; **Nearest Hospital:** Montrose, US 50 11 miles (18 km); **Days/Hours:** Open 24 hours a day, but occasionally closed in Winter due to heavy snow; **Visitor attractions closed for season:** Gunnison Point Visitor Center open intermittently in Winter. Rim House open only from mid-May through Sept.; **Weather:** Extremely low temperatures and heavy snows in Winter; travel not advised.

GENERAL INFORMATION: *For Your Safety*—Stay on the trails! View the canyon from behind the railings at the designated overlooks. *Fire* is Black Canyon's greatest peril. Fires are permitted only in the fireplaces in the campground. Be sure your fire is out. All pets must be kept on a leash. No pets are permitted in the inner canyon or in the wilderness areas.

TRAVEL ACCESS: Bus: No bus service of any kind to the monument but regular service to Montrose from other Colorado towns; **Rail:** No; **Air:** Aspen Airways and Trans-Colorado Airlines provide daily service to town of Montrose—12 miles from Park.

Colorado National Monument
Fruita, Colorado   **SEE CLIMATABLE NO. 32**

MAILING ADDRESS: Superintendent, Colorado National Monument, Fruita, Colorado 81521 **Telephone:** 303-858-3617

DIRECTIONS: The monument is easily accessible by highway: US 6, 50, and I-70 to Grand Junction; and US 6, 50, and I-70 to Fruita. The monument is 4 miles (6.4 km) west of Grand Junction and 2.5 miles (4 km) south of Fruita, CO. Both entrances directly accessible via Colorado Hwy 340.

Sheer-walled canyons, towering monoliths, and strange formations reflect the action of time and weather on colorful sandstone. Created by Presidential Proclamation on May 24, 1911.

VISITOR ACTIVITIES: exhibits, audiovisual programs, auto tours, interpretive talks, nature walks, campfire programs, camping, picnicking, backcountry, hiking, climbing, cross-country skiing; **Permits:** suggested for backcountry, can be obtained at Ranger Stations; **Fees:** $3 entrance fee per single-visit carload, $1.00 per person for commercial tours. Golden Age, Golden Access and Golden Eagle Passports accepted and available. Camping is $6 per night per site, or $3 for Golden Age and Golden Access; **Visitor facilities:** Visitor Center, parking, handicapped restrooms, campground, picnic areas, hiking trails; **Any limitations on vehicle usage:** No off-road use; **Hiking trails:** Yes, 21 miles (34 km) of constructed trails, self-guiding nature-walks; **Backcountry:** Yes, write or call for more information; **Camping:** Yes, no reservations for campgrounds; **Other overnight accommodations on site:** No; **Meals served in the park:** No; **Food and supplies obtainable in the park:** No; **Food and supplies obtainable nearby:** Yes, Grand Junction, Fruita, and Glade Park Store; **Overnight accommodations:** Grand Junction 4 miles (6.4 km) east; Fruita, 3 miles (5.6 km) north; **First Aid available in park:** Yes; **Nearest Hospitals:** Fruita, 2.5 miles (4 km) north; Grand Junction, 4 miles (6.4 km) east; **Days/Hours:** Park is open 24 hours a day. Visitor Center open from 8 a.m. to 4:30 p.m., with extended hours in Summer; **Holiday Closings:** Reduced hours at the Visitor Center on Dec. 25; **Visitor attractions closed for seasons;** No, but snow may hamper access; **Weather:** Summers are hot and dry; Winters are generally cool and snowy.

GENERAL INFORMATION: *For Your Safety*—Do not touch, feed, or harm the animals. Do not hike or climb alone. Register for difficult and technical climbs.

TRAVEL ACCESS: Bus: Continental Trailways and Greyhound provide daily service to Grand Junction/Fruita; **Rail:** Amtrak provides service to Grand Junction every other day; **Air:** American West, Continental, Frontier, and Sky West Airlines have daily service to Grand Junction.

NEARBY FACILITIES & POINTS OF INTEREST: Campgrounds: Fruita Junction RV Park, 607 Highway 340, Fruita, Colorado (303) 858-3155.

Curecanti National Recreation Area
Gunnison, Colorado   **SEE CLIMATABLE NO. 32**

MAILING ADDRESS: Superintendent, Curecanti National Recreation Area, 102 Elk Creek, Gunnison, Colorado 81230 **Telephone:** 303-641-2337

DIRECTIONS: The Elk Creek Visitor Center is 16 miles (25 km) west of Gunnison via US 50, on Blue Mesa Lake. A Visitor Center and Narrow Gauge Railroad exhibit is also available at the Cimarron Area, 20 miles E of Montrose.
Beautiful fiord like Crystal Lake and Morrow Point Lake are encompassed by this 42,000 acre Colorado High Country recreation area as well as Blue Mesa Lake—the largest lake in Colorado. Eleven miles of the Gunnison River and numerous tributary streams provide many additional recreational opportunities.

VISITOR ACTIVITIES: boating, fishing, swimming, water skiing, campfire programs, camping, picknicking, hunting, snowmobiling, naturalist activities, backcountry camping, ice fishing, interpretive exhibits, boat tours of Morrow Point Lake (call 303-641-0402 for information, fees and schedules); **Permits:** Fishing requires a Colorado license available from the Colorado Division of Wildlife Office or local sporting goods stores. Licenses vary in length of validity and cost; **Fees:** Elk Creek, Lake Fork, Cimarron $6.00 night/site; Red Creek, Dry Gulch, Ponderosa, East Portal & Stevens Creek $5.00 night/site; **Visitor facilities:** parking, campgrounds, launching ramps, scenic overlooks, two marinas, restaurant, showers, boat and slip rentals, grocery store, fish observation pond, restrooms, hiking trails, cross-country ski routes, amphitheater, telephones, snowmobile route; **Any limitations on vehicle usage:** Vehicles are restricted to designated roadways; **Hiking trails:** Yes; **Backcountry:** Yes, boat in campsites on Blue Mesa, Morrow Pt. and Crystal Lakes; **Camping:** Yes, no reservations available for campgrounds except for East Elk Creek group camping area. **Other overnight accommodations on site:** No; **Meals served in the park:** Yes, restaurant at Elk Creek Marina; **Food and supplies obtainable in the park:** Yes, some groceries available at the Elk Creek and Lake Fork Marinas; **Food and supplies obtainable nearby:** Yes, in Gunnison and Montrose; **Overnight accommodations:** Gunnison and Montrose area; **First Aid available in park:** Yes; **Nearest Hospital:** Gunnison, US 50, 16 miles (25.7 km) east of the Elk Creek Headquarters Area; Montrose, US 50, 20 miles (32.2 km) west of Cimarron; **Days/Hours:** Open 24 hours a day, year-round; **Holiday Closings:** None; **Visitor attractions closed for seasons:** Campgrounds with limited facilities are kept open until closed by snow; **Weather:** Winter temperatures drop as low as − 35°F at night. Summer daytime highs may reach the mid 20sC (90°F), (average temperature 83°F) with around upper 30's to 40°F at night.

GENERAL INFORMATION: There are no designated areas for swimming and no lifeguards. Watch out for precipitous shorelines, submerged rocks, and cold water.

TRAVEL ACCESS: Bus: Continental Trailways stops in Gunnison 16 miles easy of Park Headquarters - No bus service to Park; **Rail:** No; **Air:** Airport is in Gunnison. Trans Colorado airline—Charter service is available to other areas.

NEARBY FACILITIES & POINTS OF INTEREST: Parks, other points of interest: Black Canyon of the Gunnison National Monument; Rocky Mountain National Park; Dinosaur National Monument; Mesa Verde National Park; Great Sand Dunes National Monument; Florissant Fossil Beds National Monument.

Dinosaur National Monument
Dinosaur, Colorado   **SEE CLIMATABLE NO. 33**

MAILING ADDRESS: Superintendent, Dinosaur National Monument, P.O. Box 210, Dinosaur, Colorado 81610 **Telephone:** 303-374-2216

DIRECTIONS: The Dinosaur Quarry Visitor Center: 13 miles (21 km) east of Vernal, UT, to Jensen, UT on US 40; then 7 miles (11.3 km) north to Quarry on UT 149. Headquarters is 2 miles (3 km) east of Dinosaur, CO on US 40 37 miles (60 km) east of Vernal, UT on US 40.

The quarry contains fossil remains of dinosaurs and other ancient animals. Spectacular canyons were cut by the Green and Yampa Rivers through upfolded mountains. Created by Presidential Proclamation on Oct. 4, 1915.

VISITOR ACTIVITIES: Dinosaur fossil displays, talks, programs (summers only), walking, hiking, picnicking, camping, backcountry driving, fishing, white-water boating, wildflower-watching; **Permits:** for fishing, white-water boating, and backcountry hiking. For boating apply between Dec. 1 and Jan. 15 for the following season; **Fees:** $5 entrance fee to enter park on Quarry road; $5 per night camping fee; **Visitor facilities:** Campgrounds, nature walks and trails, concession-operated boat trips, interpretive programs, parking and restrooms at Visitor Center, telephones, boat ramp, **Any limitations on vehicle usage:** Some backcountry roads require a high clearance vehicle and are impassable when wet, inquire at the Visitor Center. All visitors use a shuttlebus to the quarry from Memorial Day to Labor Day; **Hiking trails:** Yes, short nature walks at Plug Hat and Harpers Corner and self-guided nature trails at Split Mountain Campground and Lodore; **Backcountry:** Yes, write Park Superintendent in advance, or see any Ranger on arrival. Drinking water in the backcountry is scarce; **Camping:** Yes, no reservations available for campsites; **Other overnight accommodations on site:** No; **Meals served in the park:** No; **Food and supplies obtainable in the park:** No; **Food and supplies obtainable nearby:** Yes, in Dinosaur, Rangely, and Craig, CO; Vernal and Jensen, UT; **Overnight accommodations:** Dinosaur, Rangely, and Craig, CO; Vernal and Jensen, UT; **First Aid available in park:** in Emergency; **Nearest Hospital:** Vernal, US 40, 21 miles (33.8 km); Rangely, CO via CO 64; **Days/Hours:** Visitor Center open 8 a.m.-4:30 p.m. Oct. through May, 8 a.m.-7 p.m. Memorial Day through Labor Day; **Holiday Closings:** Thanksgiving, Dec. 25 and Jan. 1; **Visitor attractions closed for seasons:** Backcountry and canyon road closed by snow; **Weather:** Summer days 90°, nights 60°; Spring and Fall are mild with cool nights. Winters are cold with 60 days of snow on ground. Low humidity all year.

GENERAL INFORMATION: *For Your Safety*—Most of the accidents at Dinosaur occur while people are boating the rivers or while climbing or hiking in the rugged canyon areas. For your benefit, it is suggested that you check with a Park Ranger about your plans and about local road conditions. Annual Discovery Day program held on the weekend closest to August 17.

TRAVEL ACCESS: Bus: Continental Trailways provides service to Dinosaur, CO and to Jensen and Vernal, UT; **Rail:** None; **Air:** Sky West from Salt Lake City (UT); **Other:** Hertz Rent-A-Car available in Vernal, UT.

NEARBY FACILITIES & POINTS OF INTEREST: Parks, other points of interest: Ashley National Forest/Flaming Gorge National Recreation Area 50 miles north of Vernal on UT 44. Utah Field House of Natural History State Park in Vernal, UT.

Florissant Fossil Beds National Monument
Florissant, Colorado   **SEE CLIMATABLE NO. 34**

MAILING ADDRESS: Superintendent, Florissant Fossil Beds National Monument, P.O. Box 185, Florissant, Colorado 80816 **Telephone:** 303-748-3253 or 748-3051

DIRECTIONS: The Park can be reached by taking US 24 west from Colorado Springs to the small village of Florissant, 35 miles (56 km) away. At the Village Center, turn south toward Cripple Creek on the unpaved Teller County Road #1. The Visitor Center is 2½ miles (4 km) from Florissant.

The finest of fossil insects, seeds, and leaves of the Oligocene Period are preserved here in remarkable detail. An unusual display of standing petrified sequoia stumps is also here. Authorized for addition to the National Park System on Aug. 20, 1969.

VISITOR ACTIVITIES: interpretive exhibits and walks, hiking, picnicking, horseback riding, cross-country skiing; **Permits:** No; **Fees:** $1 per person; **Visitor facilities:** Parking and restrooms at Visitor Center, picnic areas, trails, exhibits; **Any limitations on vehicle usage:** Motor vehicles are restricted to designated roadways; **Hiking trails:** Yes, a one-half mile and one mile self guided nature walk around some of the largest petrified Sequoia stumps in the world, plus 10 additional miles of backcountry trails; **Camping:** No; **Other overnight accommodations on site:** No, there are several well-marked public campgrounds in the surrounding Pike National Forest; **Meals served in the park:** No; **Food and supplies obtainable in the park:** No; **Food and supplies obtainable nearby:** Yes, in Woodland Park, Divide, Florissant, Lake George, and Cripple Creek; **Overnight accommodations:** Woodland Park, Divide, Florissant, Lake George, and Cripple Creek; **First Aid available in park:** Yes; **Nearest Hospital:** Colorado Springs, 35 miles (56 km) east on US 24; **Days/Hours:** Open daily from 8 a.m. to 4:30 p.m., until 7 p.m. in Summer; **Holiday Closings:** Thanksgiving, Dec. 25 and Jan. 1; **Weather:** Heavy snow in Winter may occasionally cause hazardous driving.

GENERAL INFORMATION: *WARNING:* Ticks spreading Colorado tick fever and Rocky Mountain spotted fever are here in Spring and early Summer. If you are hiking, tuck your pant legs inside your socks and check yourself for ticks periodically. If you have any imbedded ticks, contact a ranger or physician.

TRAVEL ACCESS: Bus: No; **Rail:** No; **Air:** Major airlines provide daily service through Colo. Springs Municipal Airport.

NEARBY FACILITIES & POINTS OF INTEREST: Campgrounds: Lake George, Pikes Peak National Forest; **Parks, other points of interest:** Cripple Creek, Pikes Peak, Air Force Academy, Garden of the Gods, Bear Creek Nature Center, White House Ranch.

Great Sand Dunes National Monument
Mosca, Colorado   **SEE CLIMATABLE NO. 35**

MAILING ADDRESS: Superintendent, Great Sand Dunes National Monument, Mosca, Colo. 81146 **Telephone:** 303-378-2312

DIRECTIONS: The Visitor Center is on Hwy 150, 37 miles (60 km) northeast of Alamosa, Colorado. Write or phone ahead for detailed information on facilities and activities.

The tallest dunes in the United States, these dunes were deposited over thousands of years by southwesterly winds blowing toward the passes of the lofty Sangre de Cristo Mountains. Established by Executive Proclamation on Mar. 17, 1932.

VISITOR ACTIVITIES: hiking, nature walks, dune climbing, camping, picnicking, fishing, 4-wheel drive auto tours, snowshoeing, cross-country skiing, interpretive exhibits, naturalist activities from June through August; **Permits:** Yes, free backcountry permits available at the Visitor Center. Colorado fishing licenses, available locally, are required; **Fees:** $3 per vehicle entrance fee: hikers, bikers, and bus passengers are admitted for $1 per day. Golden Age and Golden Eagle Passports are accepted and available. $5 per vehicle per night charge for developed campsites in the summer. Campground open April 1st through October 31st. Entrance fees are collected from May through September; **Visitor facilities:** Visitor Center, air pump, drinking water, picnic area, campground with restrooms, fire grates & picnic tables, 4-wheel drive road, group campsites; **Any limitations on vehicle usage:** All motor vehicles and their operators must be licensed on all roads within the Monument. The Medano Pass Primitive Road is restricted to 4-wheel drive vehicles and licensed trail bikes. Off road travel or driving on the dunes is prohibited; **Hiking trails:** Yes, trails vary in length and degree of difficulty; **Backcountry:** Yes, contact the Park for information. Permits and maps are available at the Visitor Center; **Camping:** Yes, no reservations available for individual campsites. Group camping may be arranged in advance by writing the Superintendent; **Other overnight accommodations on site:** No; **Meals served in the park:** No; **Food and supplies obtainable in the park:** No; **Food and supplies obtainable nearby:** Yes, groceries, snacks, gasoline, showers, campground, gifts, and hookups are located four miles south of the entrance station, food and supplies open year-round with reduced winter services; **Overnight accommodations:** Alamosa, 37 miles (60 km); Salida, 90 miles (145 km); and Ft. Garland, 29 miles (46.7 km); **First Aid available in park:** Yes; **Nearest Hospital:** Alamosa, Hwy 160, 37 miles (60 km); **Days/Hours:** Open 24 hours a day year-round; **Holiday Closings:** Visitor Center closed Federal Holidays in December, January and February.

GENERAL INFORMATION: Hiking on the dunes is most pleasant early and late in the day. Surface temperatures in the Summer can reach 140°F at midday-hot enough to blister your feet. Shoes should be worn or carried. Most visitors begin their walk on the dunes from the picnic area, choosing their own routes because there are no trails on the dunes. A walk to the top and back requires about 3 hours.

Hovenweep National Monument
(near) Cortez, Colorado   **SEE CLIMATABLE NO. 36**

MAILING ADDRESS: Area Manager, Hovenweep National Monument, c/o Mesa Verde National Park, Mesa Verde National Park, Colorado 81330 **Telephone:** 303-529-4465

DIRECTIONS: Travel 18 miles (29 km) north of Cortez on Highway 666, and then west at Pleasant View, following a graded dirt road for 25 miles (40 km) to Square Tower Group, Utah.

Pre-Columbian Indians built these pueblos, remarkable for the numerous standing towers and preserved in six separate units in Colorado and Utah as a national monument. Authorized for addition to the National Park System on Mar. 2, 1923.

VISITOR ACTIVITIES: walking tours, camping, picnicking, hiking; **Permits:** No; **Fees:** $3 per night camping fee; **Visitor facilities:** picnic area, campground, trails, comfort station; **Any limitations on vehicle usage:** Vehicles are restricted to roadways. The graded dirt roads can become muddy and sometimes impassable during or following storms. Inquire locally during stormy weather regarding road conditions; **Hiking trails:** Yes, a self-guiding trail leads through the prehistoric ruins of Square Tower Group; **Backcountry:** No; **Camping:** Yes, no reservations available for the modern campground near the Ranger Station which is open all year. Camping supplies, firewood and gasoline are not available at the Monument; **Other overnight accommodations on site:** No; **Meals served in the park:** No; **Food and supplies obtainable in the park:** No; **Food and supplies obtainable nearby:** Yes, Hatch Trading Post, 16 miles (26 km) west, and Ismay Trading Post, 14 miles (22.5 km) southeast; **Overnight accommodations:** Cortez, CO, 43 miles (69 km); **First Aid available in park:** Yes; **Nearest Hospital:** Cortez, CO, 43 miles (69 km); **Days/Hours:** The Monument is open from 8 a.m. to 5 p.m. year-round; **Holiday Closings:** None.

GENERAL INFORMATION: Visitors to Hovenweep can also see nearby Mesa Verde National Park (see listing in this book).

TRAVEL ACCESS: Bus: None; **Rail:** None; **Air:** Trans Colorado Airline provides daily service to Cortez from Denver.

Mesa Verde National Park
Mesa Verde National Park, Colorado   **SEE CLIMATABLE NO. 36**

MAILING ADDRESS: Superintendent, Mesa Verda National Park, Mesa Verde National Park, Colorado 81330 **Telephone:** 303-529-4465

DIRECTIONS: To get the most out of your visit, you should go first to either the Far View Visitor Center (open only in Summer from 8 a.m. to 5 p.m.) or the Chapin Mesa Museum (open from 8 a.m. to 6:30 p.m. in Summer and 8 a.m. to 5 p.m. the rest of the year). The Park entrance is midway between Cortez and Mancos on US 160. It is 21 miles (34 km) from the entrance to the museum and the Chapin Mesa ruins area. The Morefield campground is 4 miles (6 km) from the entrance. The Far View Visitor Center is 15 miles (25 km) away. The narrow, mountainous road has sharp curves and steep grades. Depending on traffic and weather conditions, allow at least 45 minutes to make this drive. Park roads are generally designed as scenic drives with reduced speed limits. The average speed limit in the Park is 35 miles (55 km) per hour.

These pre-Columbian cliff dwellings and other works of early man are among the most notable and best preserved in the United States. Established by act of Congress on June 29, 1906.

VISITOR ACTIVITIES: photography, interpretive exhibits and talks, camping, picnicking, auto tours, guided tours, biking, (limited) hiking, campfire and religious programs in Summer. **Permits:** Yes, for hiking only, available at Chief Ranger's Office; **Fees:** $5 per vehicle entrance fee, $2 for bus passengers. Golden Access, Golden Age & Golden Eagle Passports are accepted and available. Camping fee is $6 per night, $3 with Golden Age. Organized groups are $10 or $1 per person, whichever is greater. Full hookup fee is $11 per day plus $2 per person for three or more in party, (camping rates are subject to changes); **Visitor facilities:** campground, gas stations, stores, showers, picnic areas, post office, laundry, hiking trails, restaurants, telephones, lodging; **Any limitations on vehicle usage:** Motor vehicles are allowed only on roadways, turnouts, or parking areas. Weight and length restrictions for vehicles using Wetherill Mesa Road. Check with rangers; **Hiking trails:** Hiking is restricted to only five trails within the Park. Register at the Chief Ranger's Office; **Backcountry:** No; **Camping:** Yes, Morefield campground is open from mid-April through mid-Oct. for tents and trailers. It has restrooms and single and group campsites. Reservations cannot be made. Each campsite has a table, benches, and grills for which fuel can be bought at the store. There are 15 sites with utility hookups, and the campground has a disposal system for dumping trailer holding tanks. Groceries, souvenirs, carry-out food, a gasoline station, showers, and laundry facilities are also available. All services and facilities are closed from approximately mid-Oct. to early-May; **Other overnight accommodations on site:** Yes, at Far View, which has lodging, dining room, cafeteria, gift shops, and gas station. Concessioner-operated commercial bus tours of Chapin Mesa leave from this point. *Lodging* is available from mid-May to mid-Oct. From June 1 to Labor Day it is advisable to make reservations with the Mesa Verde Co., P.O. Box 227, Mancos, CO 81328, phone 303-529-4421; **Meals served in the park:** Yes, at Morefield, Far View, and Chapin Mesa, and snacks at Wetherill Mesa; **Food and supplies obtainable in the park:** Yes, at Morefield and Chapin Mesa; **Food and supplies obtainable nearby:** Yes, at Cortez and Mancos, CO; **Overnight accommodations:** Cortez, Hwy 160, 7 miles (11.2 km) west; Mancos, Hwy 160, 8 miles (13 km) east; **First Aid available in park:** Yes, emergency first aid is provided at the Chief Ranger's Office and the Morefield Campground Ranger Station; **Nearest Hospital:** Cortez, 7 miles (11.2 km) west of the Park entrance; **Days/Hours:** Accommodations, facilities, and services are available from mid-May to mid-Oct. Maximum interpretive services begin mid-June and last until Labor Day; **Holiday Closings:** None; **Visitor attractions closed for seasons:** The Museum and Spruce Tree House cliff dwelling are open all year. Ruins Road may be closed in Winter by snowfall. Cliff Palace and Balcony House ruins are closed from approx. mid Oct. to mid-April. Wetherill Mesa ruins (Long House, Step House and Badger House Community complex) open from early June through Labor Day only, closed the rest of the year. From mid-Oct. to mid-Apr. all concession facilities, including gasoline, food, and lodging are closed; **Weather:** In Summer, daytime temperatures are comfortably warm with highs ranging from 29°C (85°F) to 38°C (100°F). Evening temperatures are cool with lows ranging from 13°C (55°F) to 18°C (65°F). Winter highs range from 4°C (40°F) to 10°C (50°F) with lows of −32°C (25°F) to −10°C (15°F). Snow covered ground is predominant.

GENERAL INFORMATION: *For Your Safety*—Visits to cliff dwellings, whether on a Ranger-guided tour or a self-guided walk, tend to be quite strenuous. Adequate footwear, such as hiking boots or sturdy shoes, is recommended for these trips. Strenuous activity at the high elevations (7,000-8,500 ft.) of the Park may adversely affect those persons who experience heart or respiratory ailments. You may wish to reconsider climbing into and out of the cliff dwellings. With the exception of Balcony House, all major cliff dwellings can be viewed from overlooks on the canyon rims. Parents should be especially alert for their childrens' safety when nearing the canyon rim cliff areas. Do not throw rocks or other objects, for other visitors may be below. Be on the lookout for bicycles on the narrow roads. Contact a Ranger if you are involved in an accident or are injured.

TRAVEL ACCESS: Bus: Mesa Verde bus service, Cortez, Colo. 6:45 a.m. and 4:30 p.m.; **Rail:** None; **Air:** Trans-Colorado Airlines serve Cortez, Colo. from Denver. Rental cars available at airport.

NEARBY FACILITIES & POINTS OF INTEREST: Hotel/Motel: Cortez or Mancos 7 and 8 miles from Park; **Food/Supplies:** Cortez or Mancos; **Campgrounds:** Cortez or Mancos, and within 1 mile of the park. McPhee Reservoir (boating and fishing), second largest lake in Colorado, 10 miles north of Cortez.

Rocky Mountain National Park
Estes Park, Colorado   **SEE CLIMATABLE NO. 37**

MAILING ADDRESS: Superintendent, Rocky Mountain National Park, Estes Park, Colorado 80517 **Telephone:** 303-586-2371; TDD 303-586-8506

DIRECTIONS: The Park is accessible by Trail Ridge Road, which crosses the Continental Divide. Access from the east is by US 34/36 to Estes Park, from the southwest by US 34 to Grand Lake. Trail Ridge Road is usually closed from mid-October until Memorial Day. Opening and closing dates vary depending on weather conditions.

The Park's rich scenery typifies the grandeur of the Rocky Mountains. Peaks towering over 13,000 feet shadow wildlife and wildflowers in 414 square miles of the Rockies' Front Range. Established by act of Congress on Jan. 26, 1915.

VISITOR ACTIVITIES: interpretive programs, auto touring, camping, picnicking, hiking, mountain climbing, fishing, horseback riding, downhill and cross-country skiing, snowshoeing, snowmobiling (west side only), bird and animal watching; **Permits:** a Colorado fishing license, available locally, is required. Backcountry use permits for overnight stays available from Park Headquarters or the Kawuneeche Visitor Center; **Fees:** Entrance fees, subject to change, are $5 per noncommercial vehicle and $2 per person for commercial vehicles or bus passengers. Golden Age, Golden Access and Golden Eagle Passports are accepted and available. Entrance fees are waived for persons under 13 years of age. Campground fees are $6 per night per site. Holders of Golden Age and Golden Access Passports will be given a 50% discount; **Visitor facilities:** Schedules for guided walks, campfire programs, and other activities are available at Information Centers in Summer. Be sure to see the orientation program at Headquarters. Interpretive programs offered daily in summer. Contact the Park for a detailed list of camping facilities and picnic areas; **Any limitations on vehicle usage:** Vehicles must remain on established roads and parking areas; No vehicles or combination rigs (i.e. trailers, RV's mobile homes) over 50 ft. maximum length over Trail Ridge Road. No trailers allowed up Old Fall River Road maximum length 25 ft. **Hiking trails:** Yes, more than 355.6 miles (572.5 km) of trails provide access to remote sections of the Park; **Backcountry:** Day use requires no permit. A permit for bivouac and overnight stays is required, and can be obtained without charge on a first-come basis at Park Headquarters or the Kawuneeche Visitor Center or by writing no earlier than 30 days ahead of the visit. The number of permits issued is limited. Contact the Park for detailed information on backcountry; **Camping:** Yes, Rocky Mountain has five roadside campgrounds: Moraine Park, Glacier Basin, Aspenglen, Longs Peak, and Timber Creek. Camping is limited to 3 days at Longs Peak and 7 days parkwide at the other sites, in Summer. Campgrounds usually fill to capacity early each day. Group sites at Glacier Basin can be reserved. Longs Peak is restricted to tent camping. There are no showers, electrical, water, or sewage connections at any campground. Three campgrounds are kept open all year. Reservations for the Moraine Park and Glacier Basin Campgrounds are available through Ticketron during the summer months. Wood fires are permitted in fire grates at campgrounds and picnic areas. A written permit is required for fires outside of those areas. Wood gathering is prohibited parkwide except in designated backcountry campsites with valid permit. Warm clothing and rain gear are advised. Contact the Park for detailed information on camping and campsites. Privately owned facilities are available in the vicinity. For information about facilities adjacent to the Park, write to the Chamber of Commerce at either Estes Park, Co 80517 or Grand Lake, CO 80447; **Other overnight accommodations on site:** No; **Meals served in the park:** No, but light lunches at Train Ridge Store (Fall River Pass) in Summer and at Hidden Valley Winter Use Area in Winter; **Food and supplies obtainable in the park:** No; **Food and supplies obtainable nearby:** Yes, at Estes Park and Grand Lake; **Overnight accommodations:** Estes Park, US 34 or 36, 2-4 miles (3.2-6.4 km) from the Park & Grand Lake, US 34, 1 mile (1.6 km);

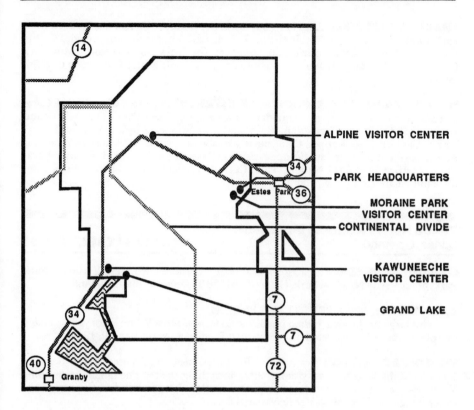

First Aid available in park: Yes, or nearby in Estes Park and Grand Lake; **Nearest Hospital:** Granby, 14 miles (22.5 km) southwest of the Grand Lake Entrance, just beyond the junction of US 40 with US 34; & Estes Park, US 34 or 36, 2- 4 miles (3.2-6.4 km) from the Park; **Days/Hours:** Open 24 hours a day year-round; **Holiday Closings:** Park Headquarters-Visitor Center closed Dec. 25; **Visitor attractions closed for seasons:** Trail Ridge Road and Old Fall River Road usually close in October. **Weather:** The high country produces a variable weather pattern primarily due to differences in altitude, slope and exposure. Elevation plays a most important role. Contact the Park for detailed seasonal and monthly weather information.

GENERAL INFORMATION: There are several hazards which you should be aware of. Many serious accidents have occurred on *snow and ice fields* in the Summer. Stay away from the edge of steep snow slopes and avoid sliding on snow and/or ice. Know and obey park regulations.

Remember, *mountain climbing* is a technical sport requiring extensive training, skill, conditioning and proper equipment. Registration with a Park Ranger is required for all Bivouac climbs.

Although they appear small, *streams and waterfalls* can be deceptively dangerous, especially in the spring when they are high and turbulent from melting snow. During *thunderstorms*, stay off ridges and peaks and avoid exposed lone objects such as large rocks, trees, or telephone lines. If you are riding horseback, dismount and get away from your horse.

Trail Ridge Road reaches elevations (max. 12,183') and could be dangerous to persons with heart conditions and respiratory ailments. Even healthy persons are normally winded by the slightest exertion at these levels.

TRAVEL ACCESS: Bus: Estes Park Bus Co. & Grayline, provide service between Estes Park and Denver Airport. Within the park, Bear Lake Shuttle System provides shuttle service to main attractions during the Summer; Estes Park Bus Co., Rocky Mtn. Park Co., and Grayline provide tour service into the park. **Rail:** None; **Air:** Access through Denver.

NEARBY FACILITIES & POINTS OF INTEREST: Contact Chamber of Commerce, for information on accommodations & camping; Estes Park CO 80517, Grand Lake, CO 80447. **New information:** Braille and cassette tapes of publications available at Visitor Centers. Handicapped Campsite is available for backcountry type camping for wheelchaired and other handicapped visitors. Reservations required. Contact Backcountry Office, Rocky MT National Park, CO 80517, telephone 303-586-4459 for complete information on these programs.

Yucca House National Monument
Cortez, Colorado   **SEE CLIMATABLE NO. 36**

MAILING ADDRESS: Yucca House National Monument, c/o Mesa Verde National Park, Mesa Verde National Park, Colorado 81330 **Telephone:** 303-529-4465

DIRECTIONS: NOT OPEN TO THE PUBLIC
    This large prehistoric Indian pueblos ruin west of Mesa Verde is not yet excavated or open to the public. Created by Presidential Proclamation on Dec. 19, 1919.

VISITOR ACTIVITIES: No activities for public visitors to Yucca House National Monument, because to most visitors, there is nothing to see. The lands surrounding Yucca House are in private ownership, and visitors should seek directions from the Chief Rangers Office, Mesa Verde National Park.

TRAVEL ACCESS: Bus: No; **Rail:** No; **Air:** Continental Airlines provides daily service to Cortez from Denver.

NEARBY FACILITIES & POINTS OF INTEREST: Parks, other points of interest: Mesa Verde National Park, Hovenweep National Monument.

District of Columbia

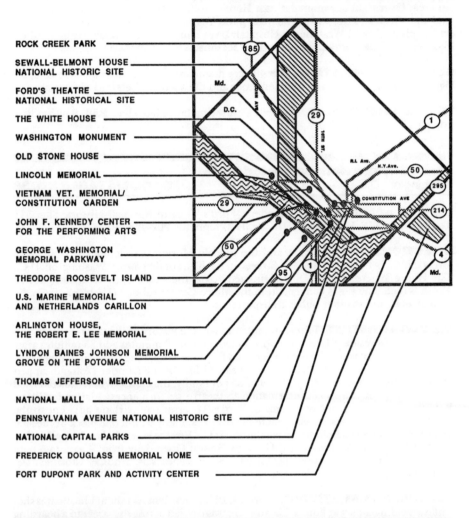

ROCK CREEK PARK

SEWALL-BELMONT HOUSE
NATIONAL HISTORIC SITE

FORD'S THEATRE
NATIONAL HISTORICAL SITE

THE WHITE HOUSE

WASHINGTON MONUMENT

OLD STONE HOUSE

LINCOLN MEMORIAL

VIETNAM VET. MEMORIAL/
CONSTITUTION GARDEN

JOHN F. KENNEDY CENTER
FOR THE PERFORMING ARTS

GEORGE WASHINGTON
MEMORIAL PARKWAY

THEODORE ROOSEVELT ISLAND

U.S. MARINE MEMORIAL
AND NETHERLANDS CARILLON

ARLINGTON HOUSE,
THE ROBERT E. LEE MEMORIAL

LYNDON BAINES JOHNSON MEMORIAL
GROVE ON THE POTOMAC

THOMAS JEFFERSON MEMORIAL

NATIONAL MALL

PENNSYLVANIA AVENUE NATIONAL HISTORIC SITE

NATIONAL CAPITAL PARKS

FREDERICK DOUGLASS MEMORIAL HOME

FORT DUPONT PARK AND ACTIVITY CENTER

Constitution Gardens
Washington, D.C. **SEE CLIMATABLE NO. 38**

MAILING ADDRESS: Superintendent, National Capital Parks-Central, 900 Ohio Drive, S.W., Washington, D.C. 20242 **Telephone:** 202-485-9880

DIRECTIONS: Located between Washington Monument and the Lincoln Memorial, bordered by Constitution Ave., 17th St. and the Reflecting Pool.

VISITOR ACTIVITIES: Sightseeing and to be enjoyed for scenic beauty; **Permits:** Needed for special events, First Amendment Activities; **Fees:** None; **Visitor facilities:** Food Kiosk, restrooms; **Any limitations on vehicle usage:** Yes, bikes only; **Hiking trails:** No; **Backcountry:** No; **Camping:** No; **Other overnight accommodations on site:**

No; **Meals served in the park:** Snack bar open approximately April-Oct.; **Food and supplies obtainable in the park:** No; **Food and supplies obtainable nearby:** Metropolitan area; **Overnight accommodations:** Hotels in Washington, D.C. and nearby Maryland and Virginia; **First Aid available in park:** Yes, at nearby Lincoln Memorial; **Nearest Hospital:** George Washington Hospital; **Days/Hours:** dawn to dusk; **Holiday Closings:** None; **Visitor attractions closed for seasons:** None; **Weather:** Seasonal.

GENERAL INFORMATION: This 40-acre manmade park includes a 7-acre lake, 56 Signers of the Declaration of Independence and the Vietnam Veterans Memorials.

TRAVEL ACCESS: Bus: Tourmobile sightseeing bus, Metro bus; **Rail:** Smithsonian stop plus 5 blocks; **Air:** No.

Ford's Theatre National Historic Site
Washington, D.C.   **SEE CLIMATABLE NO. 38**

MAILING ADDRESS: Superintendent, Ford's Theatre National Historic Site, 511 Tenth Street, NW, Washington, DC 20004 **Telephone:** 202-426-6924

DIRECTIONS: Ford's Theatre and the Lincoln Museum are located at 511 Tenth Street, N.W., between "E" and "F" Streets, in the heart of downtown Washington, D.C.. The House Where Lincoln Died is situated across the street from the theatre at 516 Tenth Street. The site is convenient to the Metro Center subway (1½ blocks from the 11th St. exit) and to other public transportation.

VISITOR ACTIVITIES: Fifteen-minute talks on the history of the theatre and the assassination of President Lincoln are presented daily at 10 minutes and 35 minutes after each hour., except when the theatre is closed for stage work, rehearsals, or matinee performances. Call for details. **Permits:** No; **Fees:** $1 fee. Over 62, under 12, handicapped and educational groups exempt. Limit of $3 per family; the House Where Lincoln Died is free. See below for ticket information to theatre performances; **Visitor facilities:** Bookstore, museum, and restrooms at Ford's Theatre; pay parking adjacent to the theatre; **Food and supplies obtainable nearby:** Yes, many within one block of the site; **Overnight accommodations:** Washington, D.C.; **First Aid available in park:** Yes; **Nearest Hospital:** Washington, D.C.; **Days/Hours:** Open daily from 9 a.m. to 5 p.m. The theatre closes for matinee performances and rehearsals; **Holiday Closings:** December 25.

GENERAL INFORMATION: On April 14, 1865, President Abraham Lincoln was shot while attending a play at Ford's Theatre. He was carried across the street to a boarding house where he died nine hours later. The Lincoln Museum, located downstairs in the theatre, contains an exhibit on the assassination and depicts various phases of Lincoln's life. Ford's Theatre operates as a legitimate theatre with productions throughout the year. *For information on performances,* call 202/347-4833.

TRAVEL ACCESS: Bus: Local subway and Metrobus information, 202/637-2437; **Rail:** Amtrak provides regular service to Washington's Union Station; **Air:** Major airlines service National Airport, Dulles International Airport, and the Baltimore-Washington International Airport.

NEARBY FACILITIES & POINTS OF INTEREST: Washington Convention Center, National Archives, Smithsonian Museums, F.B.I., and many shops and restaurants.

Fort Dupont Park and Activity Center
Washington, D.C.   **SEE CLIMATABLE NO. 38**

MAILING ADDRESS: Site Manager, Fort Dupont Park and Activity Center, Minnesota Avenue and Randle Circle, S.E., Washington, D.C. 20019 **Telephone:** 202-426-7723

DIRECTIONS: The Park is located just north of Alabama Ave. between Massachusetts Ave Extension and Ridge Rd., S.W., at Randle Circle. It may be reached by heading east on Pennsylvania Avenue, crossing the Anacostia River and proceeding to the 2nd traffic light, Minnesota Ave. Turn left onto Minnesota; go 10 blocks to Randle Circle and follow signs.

The 375-acre Park is designed for many types of recreational and community activities. Authorized for addition to the National Park System in 1949.

VISITOR ACTIVITIES: basketball, arts and crafts programs, day camp, football, baseball, tennis, walking, ice skating, picnicking, guided talks, nature walks, film programs. Free summer concerts; **Permits:** Yes, for picnic areas, call 673-7647; **Fees:** None; **Visitor facilities:** basketball courts and football, baseball and soccer fields, year-round ice skating rink, picnic areas, Visitor Center, tennis courts, nature trails; **Any limitations on vehicle usage:** No; **Hiking trails:** Yes; **Backcountry:** No; **Camping:** No; **Other overnight accommodations on site:** No; **Meals served in the park:** No; **Food and supplies obtainable in the park:** No; **Food and supplies obtainable nearby:** Yes, in Washington; **Overnight accommodations:** Washington, D.C. or suburban Maryland; **Nearest Hospital:** Greater Southeast Community Hospital; **Days/Hours:** Park open from dawn to dusk; Activity Center open Mon.-Fri. from 7:45 a.m. to 4:15 p.m.; **Holiday Closings:** Visitor Center closed on all holidays.

Frederick Douglass Memorial Home
Washington, D.C.   **SEE CLIMATABLE NO. 38**

MAILING ADDRESS: Site Manager, Frederick Douglass Memorial Home, 1411 W Street, SE, Washington, D.C. 20020 **Telephone:** 202-426-5961

DIRECTIONS: The Home can be best reached by crossing the 11th Street (Anacostia) Bridge to Good Hope Road, turning left on Good Hope Road to 14th Street, and right on 14th Street to W Street. The Home is on top of the hill at 14th and W Streets, SE. Visitors arriving from the north or south on Int. 295 (Anacostia Freeway) should use the "Pennsylvania Avenue East" exit. Proceed east on Pennsylvania Avenue 2 blocks to Minnesota Avenue. Turn right on Minnesota to Good Hope Road. Turn right on Good Hope Road, proceed one-half block, and turn left on 14th Street. Public transportation is available within a short distance of the site.

This was the home of the Nation's leading 19th-century Black spokesman from 1877 to 1895. He was U.S. minister to Haiti, 1889. Authorized for addition to the National Park System on Sept. 5, 1962.

VISITOR ACTIVITIES: guided house tours, interpretive talks; **Permits:** No; **Fees:** No; **Visitor facilities:** parking area; **Any limitations on vehicle usage:** No; **Hiking trails:** No; **Meals served in the park:** No; **Food and supplies obtainable in the park:** No; **Food and supplies obtainable nearby:** Yes, in Washington, D.C.; **Overnight accommodations:** Washington D.C. or vicinity; **First Aid available in park:** Yes; **Nearest Hospital:** Washington (Southeast Community), Martin Luther King Jr. Ave. to South Capitol Street to Southern Ave., 5 miles (8 km); **Days/Hours:** Open daily from 9 a.m. to 4 p.m., until 5 p.m. Apr. 14 through Sept. 28; **Holiday Closings:** Dec. 25 and Jan. 1.

GENERAL INFORMATION: *For Your Safety*—Be extra careful when climbing steps and walking on the hilly grounds. Visitor Center and off street parking are available.

John F. Kennedy Center for the Performing Arts
Washington, D.C.   **SEE CLIMATABLE NO. 38**

MAILING ADDRESS: General Manager, National Park Service, John F. Kennedy Center for the Performing Arts, Washington, D.C. 20566 **Telephone:** 202-254-3760

DIRECTIONS: The Center is at New Hampshire Ave. and F Street, N.W. overlooking the Potomac River.
    The marble structure, designed by Edward Durell Stone, is the sole official memorial in Washington, DC to the 35th President. It culminates an interest in a National Cultural Center dating back to George Washington. The Center houses five auditoriums—the Opera House, the Concert Hall, the Eisenhower Theatre, the rooftop Terrace Theatre and the American Film Institute Theatre. Authorized for addition to the National Park System on Sept. 3, 1972.

VISITOR ACTIVITIES: interpretive tours, exhibits, cultural events; **Permits:** No; **Fees:** Tickets are required for many of the cultural events held at the Center; **Visitor facilities:** restrooms, exhibits, restaurants, telephones; **Any limitations on vehicle usage:** Parking is available in a garage underneath the Center; **Meals served in the park:** Yes, restaurants are on the rooftop level; **Food and supplies obtainable in the park:** No; **Food and supplies obtainable nearby:** Yes, in Washington, DC; **Overnight accommodations:** Washington, DC or vicinity; **First Aid available in park:** Yes; **Nearest Hospital:** George Washington Hospital within ¼ mile (.4 km); **Days/Hours:** The building is open daily from 10 a.m. to midnight. Tours are given every day from 10:00 a.m. to 1:00 p.m.; **Holiday Closings:** No; **Visitor attractions closed for seasons:** No.

GENERAL INFORMATION: The Center is furnished with gifts from 30 foreign governments. Visitors should consult the Center's calendar of events for specific offerings or call Friends of the Kennedy Center at (202) 254-8700.

TRAVEL ACCESS: Bus: D.C. Metrobus provides services to Kennedy Center, subway stops nearby at Foggy Bottom; **Rail:** Amtrak and others provide daily service into Union Station, Washington, DC; **Air:** Major Airlines service National Airport, Dulles Airport and Baltimore-Washington International, Washington, DC.

Lincoln Memorial
Washington, D.C.   **SEE CLIMATABLE NO. 38**

MAILING ADDRESS: Superintendent, National Capital Parks—Central, 900 Ohio Drive SW, Washington, DC 20242 **Telephone:** 202-485-9880

DIRECTIONS: The Memorial is in downtown Washington at the beginning of 23rd St., NW., between Constitution and Independence Avenues. From Virginia, follow Rte. 50 west to Washington and turn right on 23rd St. or take George Washington Parkway to Memorial Bridge.
    This classical structure contains Daniel Chester French's monumental sculpture of the 16th President of the United States. Lincoln's Gettysburg Address and Second Inaugural Address are carved on the marble walls. Authorized for addition to the National Park System on Feb. 9, 1911.

VISITOR ACTIVITIES: Interpretive talks are given upon request daily from 8 a.m. to 11:30 p.m.; **Permits:** Yes, for special events and First Amendment activities; **Fees:** No; **Visitor facilities:** telephones and restrooms, parking on nearby Ohio Drive, handicapped elevator, drinking water, snack bar, bookstore, souvenir stand; **Any limitations on vehicle usage:** Lincoln Memorial Circle is closed to vehicles; **Meals served in the park:** Yes, concessioner snack bar on Lincoln Memorial Circle; **Food and supplies obtainable in the park:** No; **Food and supplies obtainable nearby:** Yes, in Washington, DC; **Overnight accommodations:** Washington, DC or vicinity; **First Aid available in park:** Yes; **Nearest Hospital:** George Washington University Hospital, 6 blocks from the Memorial; **Days/Hours:** Open daily from 8 a.m. to midnight all year; **Holiday Closings:** No interpretive talks on Dec. 25; **Weather:** Summer is hot and humid, with an average temperature of 88° and occasional thundershowers. Winter can be cold, average temperature is 30°.

Lyndon Baines Johnson Memorial Grove on the Potomac
Washington, D.C.   **SEE CLIMATABLE NO. 38**

MAILING ADDRESS: Superintendent, George Washington Memorial Parkway, % Turkey Run Park, McLean, Virginia 22101 **Telephone:** 703-285-2598

DIRECTIONS: The Grove is in Lady Bird Johnson Park on the George Washington Memorial Parkway, west of I-95 and the 14th Street Bridge. Parking is at nearby Columbia Island Marina.

A living memorial to the 36th President, the Park overlooks the Potomac River, providing a vista of the Capitol. The design features 500 white pines and engravings on Texas granite. Authorized for addition to the National Park System on Dec. 28, 1973.

VISITOR ACTIVITIES: picnicking, strolling, fishing; **Permits:** No; **Fees:** No; **Visitor facilities:** restrooms, water, picnic tables, parking area; **Any limitations on vehicle usage:** Vehicles are restricted to parking lots; **Trails:** Yes, 1 mile (1.6 km) of woodland walkways; **Meals served in the park:** No, but nearby at Columbia Island Marina; **Food and supplies obtainable in the park:** No; **Food and supplies obtainable nearby:** Yes, in Washington, DC area; **Overnight accommodations:** Washington, DC and vicinity; **First Aid available in park:** No; **Nearest Hospital:** Arlington, VA; **Days/Hours:** Open during daylight hours year-round; **Visitor attractions closed for seasons:** No; **Weather:** Hot, humid Summers; cold winters.

National Capital Region
Washington, D.C. (also in Maryland, Virginia and West Virginia)

MAILING ADDRESS: National Capital Region, 1100 Ohio Drive SW, Washington, DC 20242 **Telephone:** 202-485-9666

DIRECTIONS: For information about or directions to any of the more than 300 park units in the Washington metropolitan area, call 202-485-9666. For a recorded message of daily events in metropolitan Washington park areas, call 202-485-PARK.

This park system in the Nation's Capital includes parks, parkways and reservations in the Washington metropolitan area, including such properties as the National Mall, Vietnam Memorial, Old Post Office tower, the President's Parks (Lafayette Park north of the White House and the Ellipse south of the White House), the parks flanking the Great Falls of the Potomac, and a variety of military fortifications and greenswards. Authorized for addition to the National Park System on Aug. 10, 1933.

National Mall
Washington, D.C.   **SEE CLIMATABLE NO. 38**

MAILING ADDRESS: Superintendent, National Capital Parks-Central, 900 Ohio Drive SW, Washington, DC 20242 **Telephone:** 202-485-9880

DIRECTIONS: For general information on the Mall, call the management office at 202-426-6841.

Rows of stately elms mark the sweep of the greensward from the U.S. Capitol to the Washington Monument, a key feature of Pierre Charles L'Enfant's plan for the city of Washington in 1790. The Mall today includes many buildings of the Smithsonian Institution. For further information on the Smithsonian, contact: Information and Reception Center, Smithsonian Institution, Washington, D.C. 20560, phone 202-381-6264.

TRAVEL ACCESS: Bus: Trailways, Greyhound, Tourmobile Service provide regular services to terminal three blocks from Mall; **Rail:** Amtrak offers inter-city service into Union Station two blocks from Mall, local transportation via Metro (subway) stops in the Mall; **Air:** Major Airlines service Washington, D.C. airports.

Old Stone House
Washington, D.C.   **SEE CLIMATABLE NO. 38**

MAILING ADDRESS: Old Stone House, 3051 M Street N.W., Washington, D.C. 20007 **Telephone:** 202-426-6851 voice or TDD (TDD is a phone device for the hearing impaired.)

DIRECTIONS: The house is located at 3051 M Street, N.W. in Georgetown.

Built in 1765, Old Stone House is a fine example of pre-Revolutionary architecture, and the oldest existing house in the Nation's Capital. Administered by the National Park Service since 1953.

VISITOR ACTIVITIES: guided and self-guiding tours, living history demonstrations, interpretive exhibits, walking through the garden, candlelight evening program with 18th century music on the second Wednesday of each month 7-9:30 p.m. Oct-June, Christmas Program Friday of the 3rd week in Dec. 7-9:30 p.m.; **Permits:** No; **Fees:** No; **Handicapped accessible:** There is a sign language interpreter for the hearing-impaired. The first floor is accessible for the physically impaired. We have a slide projector of the upper floors for those who cannot go upstairs. **Any limitations on vehicle usage:** Only commercial or on-street parking is available; **Hiking trails:** No; **Meals served in the park:** No; **Food and supplies obtainable in the park:** No; **Food and supplies obtainable nearby:** Yes, Georgetown or Washington, DC; **Overnight accommodations:** within several blocks or anywhere in metropolitan Washington; **First Aid available in park:** Yes; **Nearest Hospital:** Washington, D.C., Pennsylvania Ave., 8 blocks; **Days/Hours:** Open from 9:30 a.m. to 5 p.m. Wednesday through Sunday. Closed Monday and Tuesday; **Holiday Closings:** Thanksgiving, Dec. 25 & Jan. 1.

Pennsylvania Avenue National Historic Site
Washington, D.C.   **SEE CLIMATABLE NO. 38**

MAILING ADDRESS: Pennsylvania Avenue Development Corporation, 331 Pennsylvania Ave., N.W., Suite 1220 North, Washington, D.C. 20004-1703 **Telephone:** 202-724-9091

DIRECTIONS: The Site includes the architecturally and historically significant area between the Capitol and The White House in Washington, D.C.

The Site includes a portion of Pennsylvania Avenue and the area adjacent to it between the Capitol and the White House encompassing Ford's Theatre National Historic Site, several blocks of the Washington commercial district, and a number of Federal structures. Existing park areas are listed separately in this book. Designated Sept. 30, 1965.

VISITOR ACTIVITIES: walking tours, theatrical performances, shopping, ice skating & cafe in Pershing Park, 14th & Pa.; Noon time activities in Western Plaza, 13th & Pa., tours of the National Archives, FBI, and National Museum of American Art and National Gallery of Arts buildings; **Permits:** No; **Fees:** Only for admission to performances at the National Theatre and Ford's Theatre; **Visitor facilities:** museums, theatres, stores, restaurants, lodging; **Any limitations on vehicle usage:** No trucks; **Meals served in the park:** Yes, there are numerous restaurants in the downtown area; **Food and supplies obtainable in the park:** Yes, a grocery store at 12th and F Streets, N.W.; **Food and supplies obtainable nearby:** Yes, Washington and vicinity; **Overnight accommodations:** Washington and vicinity; **First Aid available in park:** Yes, at museums and theatres within the Historic Site; **Nearest Hospital:** George Washington University Hospital, 23rd and Pennsylvania Ave., N.W.; **Days/Hours:** Site always open; **Visitor attractions closed for seasons:** No.

GENERAL INFORMATION: Architour, a non-profit educational organization, is offering regularly scheduled architectural tours of the Pennsylvania Avenue National Historic Site. For information, call 202-265-6454.

TRAVEL ACCESS: Bus: DC Metro (subway) stops at Federal Triangle and Metro Center.

NEARBY FACILITIES & POINTS OF INTEREST: Hotel/Motel: Harrington Hotel, E. St. & 1st Street N.W.; Hotel Washington, 15th Street and Pennsylvania Ave., N.W., JW Marriott Hotel 14th & Pa. Ave., Willard Hotel. Numerous hotels are located in this vicinity.

Potomac Heritage National Scenic Trail
Washington, D.C.   **SEE CLIMATABLE MAP**

MAILING ADDRESS: National Park Service, National Capital Regional Office, 1100 Ohio Drive, S.W., Washington, D.C. 20242 **Telephone:** 202-485-9666

DIRECTIONS: The Potomac Heritage National Scenic Trail was authorized to be included in the National Park System on March 28, 1983. The trail route has not yet been formally designated and, therefore, is not generally available for public use. A planning effort is underway which will result in a comprehensive management plan leading to ultimate designation of trail segments. The trail segments can only be designated upon application to the Secretary of the Interior by state or local governments.

The 700-mile-long trail will extend through the Potomac River Valley linking sites that commemorate a rich blend of historical events, natural scenes, and recreational opportunities. The general trail corridor will extend from the Chesapeake Bay at Smith Point, Virginia, and Point Lookout, Maryland, through tidewater Virginia and Maryland to Washington, D.C., and west through Virginia hunt country to Harpers Ferry where it crosses to Maryland and joins the Chesapeake and Ohio Canal towpath to Cumberland. The entire 184-mile length of the Cheaspeake and Ohio Canal is included as a segment of the trail from Georgetown in the District of Columbia to Cumberland, Maryland. From Cumberland, the trail would continue through Maryland into Pennsylvania to Conemaugh Gorge, just west of Johnstown.

VISITOR ACTIVITIES: For activities within the Chesapeake and Ohio Canal National Historical Park, see that listing for details or write to Superintendent, C&O Canal National Historical Park, P.O. Box 4, Sharpsburg, Maryland 21782.

GENERAL INFORMATION: The Chesapeake and Ohio Canal towpath, 184 miles long, is included as a principle segment of the trail. In addition, the 17-mile Mount Vernon Trail for pedestrians and cyclists along the George Washington Memorial Parkway from Mount Vernon to Memorial Bridge is scheduled for inclusion as a segment of the trail.

Rock Creek Park
Washington, D.C.   **SEE CLIMATABLE NO. 38**

MAILING ADDRESS: Superintendent, Rock Creek Park, 5000 Glover Road, N.W., Washington, D.C. 20015 **Telephone:** 202-426-6832

DIRECTIONS: The Nature (Visitor) Center is located south of Military Road and Oregon Avenue at 5200 Glover Road, N.W., Washington, D.C. Telephone: 202-426-6829.
   Rock Creek Park is the largest Natural Park in an urban area. The wooded preserve contains a wide range of natural, historical, cultural, and recreational resources in the midst of metropolitan Washington, D.C. Authorized for addition to the National Park System on Sept. 27, 1890.

VISITOR ACTIVITIES: Nature walks and hikes, horseback riding, picnicking, planetarium, golf, tennis, recreation fields, exercise trails, running and jogging; **Permits:** Required for large picnic areas. To reserve call D.C. Recreation Dept.: 202-673-7647; **Fees:** For rental horses, Rock Creek Horse Centre, near the Nature Center on Glover Road, offers rental horses and riding instruction. Telephone: 202-362-0117. There is an 18 hole public golf course with a greens fee, golf cart and golf club rental, entrance 16th & Rittenhouse Streets, NW. Telephone: 202-723-9832. Tennis: 17 soft and 5 hard surface tennis courts at 16th & Kennedy Streets, NW., six soft surface courts located off Park Road, east of Peirce Mill. Reservations. Telephone: 723-2669. **Visitor facilities:** Nature Center and planetarium, operating grist mill, Peirce Mill; Art Barn, Old Stone House, Carter Barron Amphitheatre for summer events, 1 able-bodied and 1 handicapped-able-bodied exercise trail; **Any limitations on vehicle usage:** Vehicles must stay on road and park in designated areas; **Bike trails:** 7.5 miles (12 km) bike trails. 2.5 mile section of Beach Drive between Joyce Road and Broad Branch Roads and a one-mile section of Beach Drive at Picnic Grove #10, located just north of Sherill Drive, to Wise Drive, is closed from 7 a.m. Saturdays thru 7 p.m. Sundays and holidays for recreation activities; **Hiking Trails:** Yes, there are about 20 miles (35 km) of trails, with footbridges across Rock Creek. Hikers may also use 11 miles of bridle trails; **Backcountry:** No; **Camping:** No; **Other overnight accommodations on site:** No; **Meals served in the park:** Yes, snacks are available at the golf and tennis courts; **Food and supplies obtainable in the park:** No; **Food and supplies obtainable nearby:** Yes, in Washington, D.C.; **Overnight accommodations:** Washington and vicinity; **First Aid available in park:** No, obtain local assistance by telephoning 911; **Nearest Hospital:** Washington-George Washington University Hospital; **Days/Hours:** Open dawn to dusk. Parking areas closed at dark. No overnight camping or parking allowed. Peirce Mill and Art Barn & Old Stone House are closed on Monday and Tuesday; **Holiday Closings:** Nature Center, Peirce Mill, and Art Barn & Old Stone House are closed on Christmas, New Years and Thanksgiving; **Visitor attractions closed for seasons:** None.

GENERAL INFORMATION: Wading, swimming, and fishing are not recommended in Rock Creek Park or its tributaries because of polluted water. Trails can be slippery.

Sewall-Belmont House National Historic Site
Washington, D.C.   **SEE CLIMATABLE NO. 38**

MAILING ADDRESS: Superintendent, Sewall-Belmont House National Historic Site, 144 Constitution Ave., N.E., Washington, D.C. 20002 **Telephone:** 202-546-3989 or 546-1210

DIRECTIONS: The house is located near the U.S. Capitol at 144 Constitution Ave., N.E. (corner of 2nd St. N.E.)
Rebuilt after fire damage from the War of 1812, this red brick house is one of the oldest on Capitol Hill. It has been the National Woman's Party headquarters since 1929 and commemorates the party's founder and suffrage leader, Alice Paul, and associates. Authorized for addition to the National Park System on Oct. 26, 1974.

VISITOR ACTIVITIES: guided tours, exhibits; **Permits:** No; **Fees:** No; **Visitor facilities:** memorabilia of suffrage and equal rights campaigns including busts and portraits of suffrage and equal rights leaders and valuable antique furniture, garden; **Any limitations on vehicle usage:** On-street parking can be scarce during the week, plentiful spaces on weekends and holidays; **Meals served in the park:** No; **Food and supplies obtainable in the park:** No; **Food and supplies obtainable nearby:** Yes; **Overnight accommodations:** Washington, D.C.; **First Aid available in park:** No; **Nearest Hospital:** Capitol Hill Hospital, 7 blocks; **Days/Hours:** Guided tours offered from 10 a.m. to 3:00 p.m. on weekdays (closed Mondays) and from noon to 4 p.m. on weekends and holidays; **Holiday Closings:** Thanksgiving, Dec. 25 & Jan. 1; **Visitor attractions closed for seasons:** None.

Theodore Roosevelt Island
Washington, D.C.   **SEE CLIMATABLE NO. 38**

MAILING ADDRESS: Superintendent, George Washington Memorial Parkway, c/o Turkey Run Park, McLean, Virginia 22101. **Telephone:** 703-285-2598

DIRECTIONS: The parking area is accessible from the northbound lane of the George Washington Memorial Parkway, Virginia side of the Potomac River. A footbridge connects the Island to the Virginia shore.
Wooded trails lead to an imposing statue and memorial to Roosevelt, the 26th President, on this island sanctuary in the Potomac River. Authorized for addition to the National Park System on May 21, 1932.

VISITOR ACTIVITIES: guided tours, hiking, fishing, wayside exhibits; **Permits:** No; **Fees:** No; **Visitor facilities:** restrooms, first aid, drinking water, hiking trails; **Any limitations on vehicle usage:** No vehicles are permitted on the Island; **Hiking trails:** Yes, 2 1/2 miles (4 km) of wooded trails; **Backcountry:** No; **Camping:** No; **Other overnight accommodations on site:** No; **Meals served in the park:** No; **Food and supplies obtainable in the park:** No; **Food and supplies obtainable nearby:** Yes, Arlington, VA or the Washington area; **Overnight accommodations:** Arlington, VA or the Washington metropolitan area; **First Aid available in park:** Yes; **Nearest Hospital:** Arlington, VA or Washington, D.C.; **Days/Hours:** Open year round during daylight hours; **Holiday Closings:** None; **Visitor attractions closed for seasons:** None; **Weather:** Hot, humid

Summers. **Note:** In 1988 a footbridge will be completed connecting Rosslyn with the Virginia shoreline allowing easy pedestrian access to the island. **Closest Metro stop:** Rosslyn.

Thomas Jefferson Memorial
Washington, D.C.   **SEE CLIMATABLE NO. 38**

MAILING ADDRESS: Superintendent, National Capital Parks—Central, 900 Ohio Drive SW, Washington, D.C. 20242 **Telephone:** 202-485-9880

DIRECTIONS: The Memorial is on the south bank of the Tidal Basin, near downtown Washington. From Virginia, take the George Washington Parkway to Memorial Bridge, cross the bridge and follow Ohio Drive to the Memorial.

The circular, colonnaded Memorial to the 3rd President of the United States contains a bronze statue and is surrounded by Japanese cherry trees. Dedicated April 13, 1943.

VISITOR ACTIVITIES: interpretive talks given upon request by Park Rangers, paddle boating on the Tidal Basin, Cherry Blossom Festival about the first week of April; **Permits:** for special events and First Amendment activities; **Fees:** Only for paddle boat rentals; **Visitor facilities:** parking, handicapped parking, paddle boat rentals, telephones, restrooms, drinking water; **Any limitations on vehicle usage:** No; **Meals served in the Park:** No; **Food and supplies obtainable in the park:** No; **Food and supplies obtainable nearby:** Yes, in Washington, D.C. and vicinity; **Overnight accommodations:** Washington and vicinity; **First Aid available in park:** Yes; **Nearest Hospital:** George Washington Hospital, 8 blocks from the Memorial; **Days/Hours:** Open 7 days a week from 8 a.m. to Midnight year-round; **Holiday Closings:** No interpretive talks offered on Dec. 25; **Visitor attractions closed for seasons:** No.

Vietnam Veterans Memorial
Washington, D.C.   **SEE CLIMATABLE NO. 38**

MAILING ADDRESS: Superintendent, National Capital Parks-Central, 900 Ohio Dr., SW, Washington, D.C. 20242 **Telephone:** 202-485-9880

DIRECTIONS: Constitution Avenue and 23rd Street, NW., Washington, D.C. Constitution Gardens, a part of West Potomac Park, built in 1982.

The memorial is composed of two black granite walls 250 feet long which intersect at a 130° angle. Inscribed on these tablets are the names of over 58,000 men and women who were killed or remain missing as a result of the Vietnam conflict. A bronze statue of three servicemen is located near the wall.

VISITOR ACTIVITIES: **Permits:** For First Amendment activities, Yes, contact Office of Public Affairs, NRC, 1100 Ohio Drive SW., Washington, D.C. 20242; **Fees:** No; **Visitor facilities:** restrooms, bookstores located in nearby park areas and memorials; **Any limitations on vehicle usage:** No vehicles or bikes are permitted; **Hiking trails:** No; **Backcountry:** No; **Camping:** No; **Other overnight accommodations on site:** No; **Meals served in the park:** No; **Food and supplies obtainable in the park:** No; **Food and supplies obtainable nearby:** Yes, Washington, D.C.; **Overnight accommodations:** Numerous hotels in the Washington area; **First Aid available in park:** Yes; **Days/Hours:** Open daily; **Holiday Closings:** No; **Visitor attractions closed for seasons:** No.

TRAVEL ACCESS: All major transportation available; **Rail:** Union Station, Washington, D.C.; **Air:** National Airport/Dulles Airport, Baltimore-Washington.

NEARBY FACILITIES & POINTS OF INTEREST: Contact Washington Convention & Visitor Association, 1575 Eye Street, NW., Washington, D.C. 20005, for general information; **Parks, other points of interest:** Contact Office of Public Affairs address above or telephone weekdays (202) 485-9666.

Washington Monument
Washington, D.C.   **SEE CLIMATABLE NO. 38**

MAILING ADDRESS: Superintendent, National Capital Parks-Central, 900 Ohio Drive SW, Washington, DC 20242 **Telephone:** 202-485-9880

DIRECTIONS: The Monument is located on the National Mall between 15th and 17th Streets and Independence and Constitution Avenues. From Virginia follow Rte. 50 east or Int. 395 north to Washington.

    This 555-foot (169 m) obelisk honors the country's first President and is a dominant feature of the Nation's Capital. Construction began in 1848, and the monument was dedicated on Feb. 21, 1885.

VISITOR ACTIVITIES: Visitors can ascend to the top by elevator and view the city through eight windows; **Permits:** No; **Fees:** No; **Visitor facilities:** restrooms, snack bar, parking lot, handicapped parking spaces, information booths; **Any limitations on vehicle usage:** Parking is limited to 1 hour, but there is limited free parking along nearby Ohio Drive; **Hiking trails:** No, but the Mall is suitable for short and long walks; **Meals served in the park:** Snacks at Kiosk on 15th Street; **Food and supplies obtainable in the park:** No; **Food and supplies obtainable nearby:** Yes, in downtown Washington or the metropolitan area; **Overnight accommodations:** Washington or the metropolitan area; **First Aid available in park:** Yes, or nearby in Washington; **Nearest Hospital:** George Washington University Hospital 6 blocks from the Monument; **Days/Hours:** Open daily from 9 a.m. to 5 p.m. from Oct.-Mar. and 8 a.m. to Midnight from Apr. through Labor Day; **Holiday Closings:** Dec. 25; **Visitor attractions closed for seasons:** No; **Weather:** Summers are hot; average temperature 88°F, with very high humidity and occasional thunderstorms. Winter is mild, with average temperatures of 30° and some snow.

GENERAL INFORMATION: Tickets are not required for entry to monument. In Spring and Summer, waiting lines often exceed one hour.

The White House
Washington, D.C.   **SEE CLIMATABLE NO. 38**

MAILING ADDRESS: The White House, c/o National Park Service, 1100 Ohio Drive, S.W., Washington, D.C. 20242 **Telephone:** 202-755-7798. For current tour schedules, telephone 202-456-7041 (recorded message).

DIRECTIONS: The White House is at 1600 Pennsylvania Ave., NW in downtown Washington, D.C. Visitors should use the East Gate, on East Executive Park to enter for tours.

    The White House has been the official residence of every American President since November of 1800. The cornerstone was laid on Oct. 13, 1792, on the site selected by George Washington and included in the L'Enfant Plan. The building was renovated between 1949-52. Administration transferred to the National Park Service on Aug. 10, 1943.

VISITOR ACTIVITIES: Free public tours year-round Tuesdays through Saturdays, 10:00 a.m. until 12:00 p.m. **Labor Day to Memorial Day**—no tickets required. Tickets may be picked up on the Ellipse, the park area south of the White House grounds, beginning at 8:00 a.m. on the day of the tour. Each person wishing to tour the White House must pick up his or her own ticket that gives the designated tour time! **Special Events Open to the Public:** Easter Egg Roll on Easter Monday; Spring and Fall Garden Tours, one weekend in April and October, respectively; Candlelight Tours in late December; **Permits:** No; **Fees:** No admission is ever charged; beware of people attempting to sell White House Tours; **Meals served in the park:** No; **Food obtainable in the park:** On the Ellipse; **Food and supplies obtainable nearby:** Yes, in Washington, within several blocks; **Overnight accommodations:** Washington, D.C.; **First Aid available in park:** On the Ellipse; **Nearest Hospital:** George Washington University Hospital, 23rd Street, N.W.; **Visitor attractions closed for seasons:** No. The White House is closed for tours on Thanksgiving, Christmas and New Year's Day, and for official functions.

GENERAL INFORMATION: More detailed information about The White House may be found in "The President's House," "The White House, An Historic Guide," "The Living White House," "The Presidents," and "First Ladies of The White House," published by The White House Historical Association, 740 Jackson Place, N.W., Washington, D.C. 20506, phone 202-737-8292.

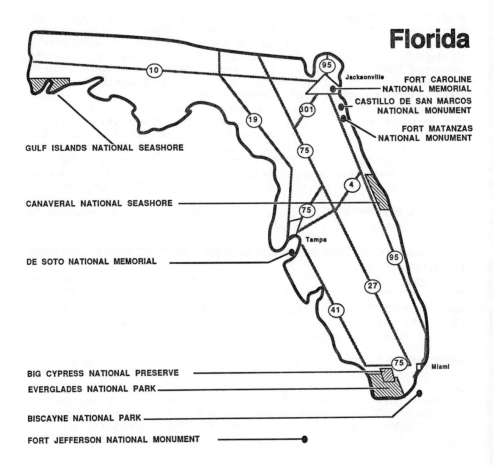

Florida

FORT CAROLINE NATIONAL MEMORIAL

CASTILLO DE SAN MARCOS NATIONAL MONUMENT

FORT MATANZAS NATIONAL MONUMENT

GULF ISLANDS NATIONAL SEASHORE

CANAVERAL NATIONAL SEASHORE

DE SOTO NATIONAL MEMORIAL

BIG CYPRESS NATIONAL PRESERVE

EVERGLADES NATIONAL PARK

BISCAYNE NATIONAL PARK

FORT JEFFERSON NATIONAL MONUMENT

Big Cypress National Preserve
Ochopee, Florida   **SEE CLIMATABLE NO. 39**

MAILING ADDRESS: Superintendent, Big Cypress National Preserve, S. R. Box 110, Ochopee, Florida 33943 **Telephone:** 813-695-2000 or 813-262-1066

DIRECTIONS: The Superintendent's Office (Preserve Headquarters) is approximately 35 miles east of Naples, Florida on U.S. 41, Satinwood Drive. The west boundary of the Preserve is 30 miles (48 km) from Naples, via US 41 and Alligator Alley. The east boundary is 30 miles (48 km) from Miami, FL.

The Preserve comprises 570,000 acres of watershed which provide a natural freshwater supply to the northwest portion of Everglades National Park. It is the ancestral home of the Seminole and Miccosukee Indians, and contains abundant subtropical plant and animal life. Authorized for addition to the National Park System on Oct. 11, 1974.

VISITOR ACTIVITIES: camping, hiking, backpacking, swimming, picnicking, sightseeing, canoeing, boating (small watercraft), fishing, hunting; **Permits:** for hunting and fishing from the Florida Game and Fresh Water Fish Comm., Tallahassee, FL 32301, phone 904-488-1960; **Fees:** for fresh water fishing; for more information, write: Florida Game and Fish Commission, Tallahassee, FL 32301. Licenses vary in cost and in length of validity; **Visitor facilities:** The only facility is Oasis Ranger Station, the field operational base. Staff is available from 8 a.m.-4:30 p.m. daily; **Any limitations on vehicle usage:** Permits required; Off-road vehicle use is restricted; **Hiking trails:** Yes, developed hiking trails are located on private lands; **Backcountry:** Yes, information available from Florida Trail Association, P.O. Box 13708, Gainesville, FL 32604; **Camping:** No, camping facilities are at Collier Seminole State Park and Everglades National Park, and at privately owned campgrounds in the vicinity; **Other overnight accommodations on site:** No; **Food and supplies obtainable in the park:** Yes, along US 41; **Food and supplies obtainable nearby:** Yes, in Miami and Naples; **Overnight accommodations:** Miami and Naples, approx. 50 miles (80 km) from Oasis Ranger Station; All nearby areas are on US 41; **First Aid available in park:** Yes, at Oasis Ranger Station; **Nearest Hospital:** Naples Community Hospital, US 41 west, approx. 58 miles (93 km) from the Oasis Ranger Station; **Days/Hours:** Open year-round; **Holiday Closings:** Oasis Ranger Station closed Christmas Day; **Visitor attractions closed for seasons:** No.

Biscayne National Park
Homestead, Florida   **SEE CLIMATABLE NO. 40**

MAILING ADDRESS: Superintendent, Biscayne National Park, P.O. Box 1369, Homestead, Florida 33090-1369 **Telephone:** 305-247-PARK.

DIRECTIONS: Public boat transportation is available by concession. For information, call 305-247-2400. Otherwise you must have your own boat or a hired boat to explore the keys and to swim and dive. You should stop at Park Headquarters on Convoy Point, 9 miles (14.5 km) east of Homestead, or at the Ranger Station on Elliott Key. Park personnel can answer your questions and help you plan your visit.

Most of the Park is reef and water, but within its boundaries about 44 keys, or islands, form a north-south chain, with Biscayne Bay on the west and the Atlantic Ocean on the east. The Park contains a significant example of living coral reef. Most of the shoreline on both mainland and keys is exposed, rough coral rock. Authorized for addition to the National Park System on Oct. 18, 1968.

VISITOR ACTIVITIES: boating, fishing, swimming, snorkeling, scuba diving, camping, picnicking, hiking, interpretive exhibits, bird-watching; **Permits:** backcountry permits can be obtained from a Park Ranger; **Fees:** No; **Visitor facilities:** At Elliott Key Harbor Ranger Station: 64 slip harbor, primitive campground, picnic area, interpretive trail, restrooms, and cold water showers. At Convoy Point: Picnic area, restrooms, ranger-led activities, and visitor center. At Boca Chita Key: Docking facilities, primitive campground, restrooms, picnic tables, grills. At Adams Key: Day-use only, docking facilities, picnic tables, grills, restrooms. Gasoline is not available at the Park but it can be obtained near the Headquarters at Homestead Bayfront Park. Meals, lodging, campgrounds, gasoline, and other supplies are available in Homestead. Many well-supplied marinas are located along the mainland coast and in the Florida Keys. Check your charts or ask a Park Ranger; **Any limitations on vehicle usage:** Be familiar with boating rules. Obtain a copy of them at Headquarters or the Ranger Station; **Hiking trails:** Yes; **Backcountry:** Yes; **Camping:** Yes, no reservations for campsites; **Other overnight accommodations on site:** No; **Meals served in the park:** No; **Food and supplies obtainable in the park:** No; **Food and supplies obtainable nearby:** Yes, limited food and supplies at Homestead Bayfront Park; **Overnight accommodations:** Homestead, US 1, 10 miles (16 km); **First Aid available in park:** Yes, at Elliott Key and Convoy Pt. Visitor Centers; **Nearest Hospital:** Homestead, US 1, 15 miles (24 km); **Days/Hours:** Open 24 hours a day, 365 days per year. Headquarters: Convoy Point Visitor Center, open 8:00 a.m. to sunset—year-round. Elliott Key Visitor Center open only on weekends, year-round; **Holiday Closings:** None; **Visitor attractions closed for seasons:** None; **Weather:** Summers are humid with frequent rain, Winters are cool and clear.

GENERAL INFORMATION: Be sure to read the safety precautions published in the pamphlet on Biscayne available from Headquarters or the Ranger Station. Nearby points of interest include Everglades National Park (see listing in this book) and John Pennekamp Coral Reef State Park.

Canaveral National Seashore
Titusville, Florida   **SEE CLIMATABLE NO. 41**

MAILING ADDRESS: Superintendent, Canaveral National Seashore, P.O. Box 6447, Titusville, Florida 32782 **Telephone:** 305-267-1110

DIRECTIONS: Located midway down the Florida east coast between Jacksonville and West Palm Beach, the Seashore is readily accessible via such major arteries as US 1 and Int. I-95, I-4, and I-75. New Smyrna Beach provides access via FL A1A into the Seashore in the vicinity of Turtle Mound, a shell midden made by pre-Hispanic Indians. Titusville, the southern Gateway City, provides access via FL 402. Playalinda Beach on the Seashore's southern end is now the principal visitor use area. It is accessible via FL 402 from Titusvile and FL 3, which cuts off to the south from U.S. 1 between Titusville and Oak Hill. In addition, the Intercoastal Waterway linking Florida with the north skirts the western edge of Mosquito Lagoon before entering the Indian River via the Haulover Canal.

The Seashore offers a great variety of wildlife, including many species of birds, on a segment of largely undeveloped lands. The area includes a portion of the 140,393-acre Merritt Island National Wildlife Refuge, administered by Fish and Wildlife Service, U.S. Dept. of the Interior. Established by act of Congress Jan 3, 1975.

VISITOR ACTIVITIES: bird-watching, boating, swimming, surfing, sun bathing, shell collecting, surf fishing, wildlife observation, photography, wildland hiking, waterfowl hunting, picnicking, walking; **Permits:** Backcountry camping, horse use; no others except hunting, but hunting in season is subject to U.S. Fish and Wildlife Service and state regulations; **Fees:** Yes; **Visitor facilities:** portable toilets at beaches, picnic tables; **Any limitations on vehicle usage:** Vehicles are restricted to established roads and are prohibited on the beach; **Hiking trails:** Yes, Turtle Mound, ¼ mile (.4 km), Castle Windy Trail (½ mile), Eldora Hammock (½ mile), and Old Eldora (¼ mile) all self-guiding; **Backcountry:** Yes, camping is permitted on the north beach and islands in the north end of Mosquito Lagoon; **Camping:** Beach backcountry camping closed during period (October 1-May 15); **Other overnight accommodations on site:** No, there are private campgrounds in nearby communities; **Meals served in the park:** No; **Food and supplies obtainable in the park:** No; **Food and supplies obtainable nearby:** Yes, at Titusville, 12 miles (20 km); New Smyrna Beach 10 miles (16 km); **Overnight accommodations:** Titusville, 12 miles (20 km); New Smyrna Beach, 10 miles (16 km); **First Aid available in park:** limited; **Nearest Hospital:** Titusville, 12 miles (20 km); New Smyrna Beach, 10 miles (16 km); **Days/Hours:** Open 6:30 a.m.-8:00 p.m. (Eastern Standard) to 6:00 p.m. (Daylight Savings) 7 days a week; **Holiday Closings:** None; **Visitor attractions closed for seasons:** No; **Weather:** The climate is sub-tropical, with short, mild Winters and hot, humid Summers. Ocean temperatures remain relatively warm all year.

GENERAL INFORMATION: Exhibits and slide program. Handicapped facilities: Handicapped accessible restrooms and beach access at designated areas, and handicapped designated parking places. Swimming can be dangerous due to strong ocean currents. Life guards are not provided. Visitors to inland areas away from the influence of off-shore breezes should carry a repellent to protect themselves from mosquitoes and other biting insects. Space operations at Kennedy Space Center require closing of Playalinda Beach for safety and security prior to and during launch of the space shuttle. Pets and glass containers are not allowed on the beaches.

TRAVEL ACCESS: Bus: Greyhound provides daily service to Titusville and New Smyrna Beach, FL; **Rail:** No; **Air:** Daily commuter air service into Tico Airport, Titusville, FL, Daytona Beach, FL.

NEARBY FACILITIES & POINTS OF INTEREST: Campgrounds: KOA campgrounds in Mims and New Smyrna Beach, FL, Jetty Park, Cape Canaveral, Fl.-campground; **Parks, other points of interest:** Kennedy Space Center, Merritt Island National Wildlife Refuge.

Castillo de San Marcos National Monument
St. Augustine, Florida   **SEE CLIMATABLE NO. 42**

MAILING ADDRESS: Superintendent, Castillo de San Marcos National Monument, 1 Castillo Drive, St. Augustine, Florida 32084 **Telephone:** 904-829-6506

DIRECTIONS: The Monument is at 1 Castillo Drive in downtown St. Augustine.
    This oldest masonry fortification in the continental United States, constructed in 1672-95 and "modernized" by 1756, replaced the last one of the wooden forts built in succession since the founding of St. Augustine in 1565. These structures affirmed the Spanish title to Florida, and Castillo eventually became the principal fortification in a regional defense system that preserved Spanish dominion during 235 years.

VISITOR ACTIVITIES: interpretive exhibits, guided tours, living history demonstration, self-guiding tours; **Permits:** No; **Fees:** $1 per person fee for those 12 and older. Golden Age and Golden Eagle Passports accepted and available; **Visitor facilities:** parking, restrooms; **Any limitations on vehicle usage:** No; **Hiking trails:** No; **Meals served in the park:** No; **Food and supplies obtainable in the park:** No; **Food and supplies obtainable nearby:** Yes, adjacent to the Park in St. Augustine; **Overnight accommoda-**

tions: St. Augustine; **First Aid available in park:** Yes; **Nearest Hospital:** 2 major hospitals in St. Augustine; **Days/Hours:** 8:30 a.m.-5:15 p.m. Winters; 9:00 a.m.-5:45 p.m. Summer; **Holiday Closings:** Dec. 25.

GENERAL INFORMATION: *For Your Safety*—Watch out for rough and uneven floors, fragile walls, and steep drops.

TRAVEL ACCESS: Bus: Greyhound/Trailways provides daily service to within 1/2 mile of Park; **Rail:** No; **Air:** Not direct; **Other:** Two "tour" trains operate in St. Augustine stopping at the Park.

NEARBY FACILITIES & POINTS OF INTEREST: Campgrounds: Anastasia St. Park, Anastasia Island St. Augustine FLA, 904-829-2668, 3 miles from Park.

DeSoto National Memorial
Bradenton, Florida   **SEE CLIMATABLE NO. 43**

MAILING ADDRESS: Superintendent, DeSoto National Memorial, 75th Street NW, Bradenton, Florida 34209-9656 **Telephone:** 813-792-0458

DIRECTIONS: The Park is on Tampa Bay 5 miles (8 km) west of Brandenton, FL, on 75th Street, NW.
   The landing of Spanish explorer Hernando de Soto in Florida in 1539 and the first extensive organized exploration of what is now the southern United States by Europeans are commemorated here. Authorized for addition to the National Park System on Mar. 11, 1948.

VISITOR ACTIVITIES: interpretive film, exhibit, trail, fishing, living history demonstration in season; **Permits:** No; **Fees:** No; **Visitor facilities:** parking and restrooms at Visitor Center; **Any limitations on vehicle usage:** No vehicles allowed on the trails or outside the parking area; **Hiking trails:** Yes, an ½ mile (.8 km) nature trail; **Backcountry:** No; **Camping:** No; **Other overnight accommodations on site:** No; **Meals served in the park:** No; **Food and supplies obtainable in the park:** No; **Food and supplies obtainable nearby:** Yes, in Bradenton; **Overnight accommodations:** Bradenton; Palmetto 10 miles (16 km); **First Aid available in park:** Yes; **Nearest Hospital:** Bradenton, 59th Street, 5 miles (8 km); **Days/Hours:** Open daily from 8 a.m. to 5:30 p.m.; **Holiday Closings:** None; **Visitor attractions closed for seasons:** Living history program closed from Apr. through Nov.; **Weather:** Temperatures are in the low 90°s F in Summer, with high humidity. Winter highs range from the 70°s to the mid 50°s with moderate humidity. Winter days are characterized by strong breezes and blue skies.

TRAVEL ACCESS: Bus: Greyhound, Trailways provide daily service to Bradenton; **Rail:** No; **Air:** Delta, Eastern, National, Republic, United and others provide daily service to Sarasota/Bradenton.

NEARBY FACILITIES & POINTS OF INTEREST: Hotel/Motel: Found in Bradenton; **Food/Supplies:** Found in Bradenton; **Campgrounds:** Found in Bradenton; **Parks, other points of interest:** Benjamin Memorial, Lake Manatee, Myakka River State Park.

Everglades National Park
Homestead, Florida   **SEE CLIMATABLE NO. 39**

MAILING ADDRESS: Superintendent, Everglades National Park, P.O. Box 279, Homestead, Florida 33030 **Telephone:** 305-247-6211

DIRECTIONS: The main Visitor Center is near the Park entrance, 12 miles (20 km) southwest of Homestead on Route 9336. Other Visitor Centers are at Royal Palm, Shark Valley, Flamingo, and Everglades City.

This largest remaining subtropical wilderness in the conterminous United States has extensive fresh- and salt-water areas, open prairies, and mangrove forests. Abundant wildlife includes rare birds. Park dedicated on Dec. 6, 1947.

VISITOR ACTIVITIES: boating, camping, picnicking, wildlife- and bird-watching, photography, hiking, interpretive talks and exhibits, fishing, backcountry, canoeing, open-air tram and sightseeing boat rides; **Permits:** Florida fishing license, available at local bait and tackle shops, is required for fresh water fishing. In the near future the state of Florida will require a salt water fishing license. Licenses vary in length of validity and cost. Free backcountry permits available at Everglades City and Flaming ranger stations. The May-Oct. off season has a self-registration system; **Fees:** $5 per vehicle or $3 per person at main entrance; $3 per vehicle or $2 per person at Shark Valley entrance. Overnight camping in developed sites is $7 per night and $4 for walk-in tent sites, from Nov. 1-Apr. 30; free the remainder of the year. Shark Valley tram tours are concession fee-operated. Golden Age, Golden Eagle & Golden Access Passports available. It is suggested that frequent visitors to the park purchase the Everglades National Pass for $15, good for unlimited entrances on a calendar year basis; **Visitor facilities:** bookstore, parking, restrooms, and telephones at Visitor Center, boat rentals and ramp, marina, nature trails, campgrounds, picnic areas, environmental study area, restaurant, house boat rentals; **Any limitations on vehicle usage:** No off-road vehicles are permitted in the park. No private vehicles permitted on Shark Valley Road; all vehicles restricted to designated roadways; **Hiking trails:** Yes, many short trails lead off the main park road; **Backcountry:** Yes, required permit available from Ranger Stations at Everglades City and Flamingo. Insect repellent is needed on all backcountry trails throughout the year; **Camping:** Yes, individual campsites cannot be reserved. Group campsites can be reserved by contacting Chief Ranger, ENP, P.O. Box 279, Homestead, FL 33030; **Other overnight accommodations on site:** Yes, there is a motor lodge at Flamingo. Reservations should be made well in advance to Flamingo Lodge, Marina & Outpost, Flamingo, FL 33030; 24-hour phone 813-695-3101. Additional camping near Everglades City can be found at Copeland, 7 miles (11 km) north on FL 29, and at Collier-Seminole State Park, 19 miles (30.5 km) west on US 41; **Meals served in the park:** Yes, at Flamingo; **Food and supplies obtainable in the park:** Yes, at Flamingo marina; **Food and supplies obtainable nearby:** Yes, at Homestead, Key Largo, Everglades City; **Overnight accommodations:** Homestead, Florida City, 12 miles (19.3 km); Florida Keys, 40 miles (64.4 km); Everglades City, 90 miles (144.8 km); **First Aid available in park:** Yes, at Ranger Stations; **Nearest Hospital:** Homestead, 48 miles (77 km) from Flamingo; **Days/Hours:** Open 24 hours a day year-round; **Holiday Closings:** None; **Visitor attractions closed for seasons:** Services reduced at Flamingo during the Summer; **Weather:** Winters are dry and clear; Summers are rainy with torrential local downpours and lightning storms. Temperatures range in the 80's and 90's during the Summer and on rare occasions drop to the 30's in Winter.

GENERAL INFORMATION: Rates for overnight accommodations are considerably higher throughout South Florida during the winter season (Dec. 15-Apr. 15.) Mosquitoes and other biting insects make camping and backcountry use during the rainy season virtually unbearable by all but the most dedicated outdoorsperson.

NEARBY FACILITIES & POINTS OF INTEREST: Hotel/Motel: All services available in Homestead, FL, 12 miles from main entrance; **Parks, other points of interest:** Biscayne National Park; Big Cypress National Preserve.

Fort Caroline National Memorial
Jacksonville, Florida   **SEE CLIMATABLE NO. 42**

MAILING ADDRESS: Superintendent, Fort Caroline National Memorial, 12713 Fort Caroline Road, Jacksonville, Florida 32225 **Telephone:** 904-641-7155

DIRECTIONS: The Memorial is about 10 miles (16 km) east of Jacksonville, and 5 miles (8 km) west of Mayport. It can be reached by FL 10: turn off on the St. Johns Bluff Road or Monument Road, then proceed east on Fort Caroline Road.
 A replica fort overlooks the Site of a French Huguenot colony of 1564-65, the second French attempt at settlement within the present United States. The French and Spanish began two centuries of European colonial rivalry in North America here. Authorized for addition to the National Park System on Sept. 21, 1950.

VISITOR ACTIVITIES: interpretive exhibits, walking tours; **Permits:** No; **Fees:** No; **Visitor facilities:** Visitor Center, museum, sales outlet, walking trails, picnic area (no fires); **Any limitations on vehicle usage:** No; **Hiking trails:** Yes, three trails; the longest is 1 mile (1.6 km); **Backcountry:** No; **Camping:** No; **Other overnight accommodations on site:** No; **Meals served in the park:** No; **Food and supplies obtainable in the park:** No; **Food and supplies obtainable nearby:** Yes, in Jacksonville and Jax Beaches; **Overnight accommodations:** Jacksonville, FL 10, 9 miles (14.4 km) and Jax Beaches, 12 miles (19 km); **First Aid available in park:** Yes; **Nearest Hospital:** Jacksonville, 12 miles (19 km); **Days/Hours:** 9:00 a.m.-5:00 p.m., year around; **Holiday Closings:** Dec. 25 and Jan. 1.

GENERAL INFORMATION: The proximity of the river to the Fort requires additional caution. Visitors are advised to bring mosquito repellent.

Fort Jefferson National Monument
70 miles (112 km) west of Key West, Florida   **SEE CLIMATABLE NO. 44**

MAILING ADDRESS: Superintendent, Everglades National Park, P.O. Box 279, Homestead, Florida 33030 **Telephone:** 305-247-6211

DIRECTIONS: The Monument can only be reached by boat or seaplane. Several operators of charter boat and air taxi services offer trips to the Dry Tortugas from Key West, Sugar Loaf Key, Marathon, and Naples. Specific information regarding these services may be obtained from the Chambers of Commerce located at: 3330 Overseas Highway, Marathon, FL 33052, phone 305-743-5417; Old Mallory Square, Key West, FL 33040, phone 305-294-2587; and 1700 N. Tamiami Trail, Naples, FL 33940, 813-262-6141.
 Built in 1856 to help control the Florida Straits, this is the largest all-masonry fortification in the Western world. It is the central feature of the seven Dry Tortugas Islands and the surrounding shoals and waters of the Gulf of Mexico, some 100 square miles that make up the National Monument. It is famous for its birds and marine life. Created by Presidential Proclamation on Jan 4, 1935.

VISITOR ACTIVITIES: interpretive exhibits, self-guiding tours, bird and wildlife-watching, picnicking, salt-water sport fishing, snorkeling, swimming, and scuba diving;

Permits: No; **Fees:** No; **Visitor facilities:** exhibit area, picnic area, restrooms; **Any limitations on vehicle usage:** the island is roadless; **Hiking trails:** No; **Backcountry:** No; **Camping:** Yes, no reservations are available for the 10 group sites, which are at Garden Key at Fort Jefferson; **Other overnight accommodations on site:** No; **Meals served in the park:** No; **Food and supplies obtainable in the park:** No; **Food and supplies obtainable nearby:** obtain supplies at Key West, 70 miles (112 km) by water; **Overnight accommodations:** Key West, 70 miles (112 km) by water; **First Aid available in park:** Yes; **Nearest Hospital:** Key West, 70 miles (112 km) by water; **Days/Hours:** Open daily from 8:00 a.m. to sunset year-round; **Holiday Closings:** None; **Visitor attractions closed for seasons:** Bush Key is closed to visitors from April to the last part of September to protect nesting Sooty and Noddy Terns. **Weather:** Weather is generally sunny and warm. Occasional squalls are common, however, so visitors should be prepared for inclement weather, particularly during the Winter months. Hurricane season is from May 1 to Nov. 30.

GENERAL INFORMATION: Since the Site is isolated, visitors must provide for their own independent existence. All food, water, and supplies must be brought from the mainland. Visitors must remove all refuse brought into or generated within the Monument. *For Your Safety*—Do not stand near wall edges. Mortar in historic structures may be loose or softened. Watch for uneven walking surfaces, spiral stairways, sudden dropoffs, and darkened areas. Never swim alone. Be cautious in areas with strong currents. Cuts from coral and punctures from the spiny sea urchins may be painful and slow to heal.

Fort Matanzas National Monument
Saint Augustine, Florida   **SEE CLIMATABLE NO. 42**

MAILING ADDRESS: Superintendent, Castillo de San Marcos National Monument, 1 Castillo Drive, St. Augustine, Florida 32084 **Telephone:** 904-471-0116

DIRECTIONS: The Park is 14 miles (22 km) south of St. Augustine and can be reached by FL A1A on Anastasia Island. The Park consists of 298 acres on Rattlesnake Island, where the fort is located, and on Anastasia Island, where the Visitor Center is. The Fort is accessible only by boat. A ferry crosses to Rattlesnake Island daily between 9:00 a.m. and 4:30 p.m. daily year-round, weather permitting.
    This Spanish fort was built between 1740-42 to protect St. Augustine from attack via Matanzas Inlet. Created by Presidential Proclamation on Oct. 15, 1924.

VISITOR ACTIVITIES: interpretive walks and talks, ferry boat rides, fishing; **Permits:** No; **Fees:** No; **Visitor facilities:** restrooms and parking at Visitor Center; **Any limitations on vehicle usage:** Vehicles are restricted to designated roadways; **Hiking trails:** No; **Backcountry:** No; **Camping:** No; **Other overnight accommodations on site:** No; **Meals served in the park:** No; **Food and supplies obtainable in the park:** No; **Food and supplies obtainable nearby:** Yes, in St. Augustine Beach, 10 miles (16 km); **Overnight accommodations:** St. Augustine Beach, 10 miles (16 km), St. Augustine, 15 miles (24 km); **First Aid available in park:** Yes; **Nearest Hospital:** St. Augustine, 15 miles (24 km); **Days/Hours:** Open daily from 8:30 a.m. to 5:30 p.m.; **Holiday Closings:** Dec. 25; **Visitor attractions closed for seasons:** No; **Weather:** a wide variety of weather conditions.

GENERAL INFORMATION: *For Your Safety*—Do not swim in the treacherous waters near the inlet or climb on the fort walls. Be wary of sharp oyster shells.

NEARBY FACILITIES & POINTS OF INTEREST: **Campgrounds:** KOA, Anastasia St. Park; **Parks, other points of interest:** Marineland-5 miles from park.

Gulf Islands National Seashore
Florida and Mississippi   SEE CLIMATABLE NO. 45

MAILING ADDRESS: Superintendent, Gulf Islands National Seashore, 1801 Gulf Breeze Parkway, Gulf Breeze, Florida 32561. **Telephone:** FL: 904-934-2600, MS: 601-875-0821

DIRECTIONS: Access to Ship Island in the Mississippi District is provided by concession boats from Gulfport and Biloxi, MS, Spring through Fall. Consult the concessioners' printed schedules for frequency and times. Private boats may dock at Fort Massachusetts in the daytime. Horn and Petit Bois Islands are reached by chartered or private boats. Davis Bayou can be reached by following the signs on U.S. 90 for Gulf Islands National Seashore. Recommended routes for reaching the major visitor areas within the Florida District are: Johnson Beach (Perdido Key)-take FL 292 southwest from Pensacola; historic mainland forts and Naval Aviation Museum-use the main entrance of Pensacola Naval Air Station off Barrancas Ave. (FL 295); Naval Live Oaks and the Fort Pickens and Santa Rosa Areas-take US 98 from downtown Pensacola across the Pensacola Bay Bridge.

This series of offshore islands and mainland areas has both historic forts and sparkling white sand beaches near Pensacola, FL, and Pascagoula and Biloxi, MS, with mainland facilities in Ocean Springs, Mississippi. Authorized for addition to the National Park System on Jan. 8, 1971.

VISITOR ACTIVITIES: interpretive exhibits and programs, picnicking, camping, hiking, sunbathing, swimming, boating, fishing, auto tours, scuba diving, guided fort tours; **Permits:** No; **Fees:** $8 fee for campgrounds without electricity, $10 with; **Visitor facilities:** picnic areas, campgrounds, bathhouses, boat dock and ramp, laundry, boat charters, campground store, restrooms, snack shops, visitor contact stations, visitor centers, guarded beaches, souvenir and bookstore, fishing pier, hiking and bicycle trails, playground, ball field, ball court, wilderness area; **Any limitations on vehicle usage:** Motor vehicles are not allowed on sand dunes and beaches. **Hiking trails:** Yes, interpretive trails are in each state; **Backcountry:** Yes, Horn & Petit Bois Islands are wilderness areas, and can be reached by private or charter boat. **Camping:** Yes, no reservations available for campsites. Long tent stakes for use in the sand and mosquito netting are a must; **Other overnight accommodations on site:** No; **Meals served in the park:** Yes, snacks at Santa Rosa Area, Perdido Key Area, Fort Pickens Area, Ship Island; **Food and supplies obtainable in the park:** Yes, at Ft. Pickens Area-campground store; **Food and supplies obtainable nearby:** Yes, in major urban centers along the entire 150 mile (241 km) route from Ship Island, MS to Santa Rosa Island, FL; **Overnight accommodations:** In urban centers: Gulfport, Biloxi, Ocean Springs, & Pascagoula, MS; Pensacola & Ft. Walton Beach, FL; **First Aid available in park:** Yes; **Nearest Hospital:** Ocean Springs, MS, Highway 90, 5 miles (8 km); Pensacola, FL, Baptist Hosp., 12 miles (20 km); **Days/Hours:** Open 24 hours a day, except Santa Rosa, Perdido Key, Ship Island, and Okaloosa Areas; **Holiday Closings:** None; **Visitor attractions closed for seasons:** Guarded beaches closed from Sept.-May, Redoubt closed from Sept.-May; **Weather:** Hot, humid Summer; cool, moderate Winter; comfortable Spring and Fall.

GENERAL INFORMATION: *For Your Safety*—Be extremely careful of strong currents in heavy surf, and avoid stinging jellyfish and Portuguese man-of-war. Do not swim alone in unguarded waters. Watch your step while exploring the forts and batteries. You should carry a flashlight since the passageways are dimly lighted.

TRAVEL ACCESS: **Bus:** Greyhound, Trailways provides service to Biloxi, and Pensacola; **Rail:** None; **Air:** Eastern and Delta services into Pensacola, Republic service into Gulfport.

NEARBY FACILITIES & POINTS OF INTEREST: Parks, other points of interest: Naval Air Museum (Pensacola), Home of Jefferson Davis (Biloxi).

Georgia

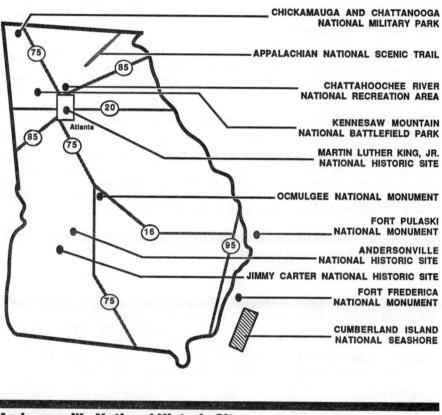

CHICKAMAUGA AND CHATTANOOGA NATIONAL MILITARY PARK

APPALACHIAN NATIONAL SCENIC TRAIL

CHATTAHOOCHEE RIVER NATIONAL RECREATION AREA

KENNESAW MOUNTAIN NATIONAL BATTLEFIELD PARK

MARTIN LUTHER KING, JR. NATIONAL HISTORIC SITE

OCMULGEE NATIONAL MONUMENT

FORT PULASKI NATIONAL MONUMENT

ANDERSONVILLE NATIONAL HISTORIC SITE

JIMMY CARTER NATIONAL HISTORIC SITE

FORT FREDERICA NATIONAL MONUMENT

CUMBERLAND ISLAND NATIONAL SEASHORE

Andersonville National Historic Site
Andersonville, Georgia   **SEE CLIMATABLE NO. 46**

MAILING ADDRESS: Superintendent, Andersonville National Historic Site, Rt. 1, Box 85, Andersonville, Georgia 31711 **Telephone:** 912-924-0343

DIRECTIONS: The Site is southwest of Macon and southeast of Columbus on Route 49, in Macon County, Georgia. Interstate 75 south of Macon intersects Route 49, and further south Routes 224 and 27 connect I-75 with Route 49. From south I-75 exit at Cordele on U.S. 280.

Established by act of Congress on July 1, 1971, this 470-acre Site consists of a national cemetery and preserves the Civil War prison camp where more than 12,000 union soldiers died and were interred nearby. Andersonville was mandated by Congress on October 16, 1970 to commemorate the sacrifices of American POW's throughout the history of our country.

VISITOR ACTIVITIES: picnicking, auto tours, walking, commemorative Monuments, interpretive exhibits; **Permits:** No; **Fees:** Yes, $1 per person ages 13-61; **Visitor facilities:** parking and restrooms at Visitor Center; **Any limitations on vehicle usage:** Vehicles are confined to parking area and auto tour roads; **Hiking trails:** No; **Backcountry:** No; **Camping:** No; **Other overnight accommodations on site:** No; **Meals served in the park:** No; **Food and supplies obtainable in the park:** No; **Food and supplies obtainable nearby:** Yes, Andersonville, ½ mile (.8 km), Americus, 10 miles (16 km), Montezuma, 10 miles (16 km); **Overnight accommodations:** Americus, Highway 49, 10 miles (16 km), Montezuma, 10 miles (16 km); **First Aid available in park:** Yes; **Nearest Hospital:** Americus, Hwy 49, 10 miles (16 km); **Days/Hours:** Open 7 days a week: 8 a.m. to 5 p.m., until 7 p.m. on Memorial Day; **Holiday Closings:** No; **Visitor attractions closed for season:** No.

GENERAL INFORMATION: *For Your Safety*—Wear shoes to protect yourself from sandspurs which grow wild in the grass. Also be aware of snakes, poison ivy, and fire ants (characterized by red sandy mounds) which have a painful sting. Do not climb on Monuments, fences, or earthworks.

TRAVEL ACCESS: Bus: Continental Trailways will stop at Americus upon request to Bus Driver.

NEARBY FACILITIES & POINTS OF INTEREST: Campgrounds: Perry, Ga. 30 miles, Andersonville ½ mile, and Plains, Ga. 20 miles; **Parks, other points of interest:** American Camelia Society, State-owned River Ferry, Antebellum Homes, GA Veterans State Park, Plains, Georgia—Home of the 39th President, Jimmy Carter. **New park programs:** Old prison carriage house converted as a POW exhibit for all wars.

Appalachian National Scenic Trail
For details see listing in Maine

Chattahoochee River National Recreation Area
Atlanta, Georgia   SEE CLIMATABLE NO. 47

MAILING ADDRESS: Chattachoochee River National Recreation Area, 1978 Island Ford Parkway, Dunwoody, Georgia 30350 **Telephone:** 404-394-7912

DIRECTIONS: Sixteen separate land units along a 48 mile (77 km) stretch of the Chattahoochee River, extending into northwest Atlanta, are preseved "for public enjoyment" for their scenic, recreational, natural and cultural features. Authorized for addition to the National Park System on August 15, 1978. Land units and river access points are readily accessible via the Interstate and major road systems.

VISITOR ACTIVITIES: fishing, picnicking, jogging, hiking, birdwatching, photography, horseback riding and various river paddling (floating) activities; **Permits:** No; **Fees:** No; **Visitor facilities:** Watercraft rentals and bus shuttling service (mid-May through September), limited picnic areas, parking and restroom facilities; **Any limitations on vehicle usage:** All vehicle use is restricted to park-established roadways and designated parking areas; **Hiking trails:** Yes, most are unimproved trails; Some facilities and trails (improved) are handicapped accessible. **Backcountry:** No; **Camping:** No; **Other overnight accommodations on site:** No; **Meals served in the park:** No; **Food and supplies obtainable in the park:** No; **Food and supplies obtainable nearby:** Yes, within the nearby communities; **Overnight accommodations:** Metro-Atlanta area; **First Aid available in park:** Yes; **Nearest Hospital:** Hospitals are located in close proximities to most park units; **Days/Hours:** Open seven days a week, closing hours posted; **Holiday Closings:** Christmas; **Visitor attractions closed for seasons:** No.

GENERAL INFORMATION: *For Your Safety*—Please respect the river corridor and private property rights. Only self-contained fires are permitted.

Chickamauga & Chattanooga National Military Park
Fort Oglethorpe, Georgia   **SEE CLIMATABLE NO. 48**

MAILING ADDRESS: Superintendent, Chickamauga and Chattanooga National Military Park, P.O. Box 2128, Fort Oglethorpe, Georgia 30742 **Telephone:** 404-866-9241

DIRECTIONS: The Chickamauga Visitor Center is on U.S. 27 off I-75, south of Chattanooga, TN. The Lookout Mountain Visitor Center is at entrance to Point Park.
   The Park includes the Civil War Battlefields of Chickamauga, Orchard Knob, Lookout Mountain, Signal Point and Missionary Ridge. Established by act of Congress on Aug. 19, 1890.

VISITOR ACTIVITIES: interpretive exhibits, auto tours, living history demonstrations, hiking, horseback riding; **Permits:** No; **Fees:** Yes, admission fee for Cravens House in the Lookout Mountain Unit is $1.00, not to exceed $3.00 per family. Golden Age and Golden Eagle Passports accepted and available; **Visitor facilities:** Parking and restrooms at Visitor Center, museum, hiking trails; **Any limitations on vehicle usage:** No overnight parking is allowed; **Hiking trails:** Yes, self-guiding trails; **Backcountry:** No; **Camping:** Group sites only BSA/GSA etc. $8.00 per site per night Chickamauga Battlefield only; **Other overnight accommodations on site:** No; **Meals served in the park:** No; **Food and supplies obtainable in the park:** No; **Food and supplies obtainable nearby:** Yes, Fort Oglethorpe and Chattanooga; **Overnight accommodations:** Fort Oglethorpe, Ga, US 27, continues to Chickamauga Battlefield; Chattanooga, TN (surrounds park areas); **First Aid available in park:** Yes; **Nearest Hospital:** Fort Oglethorpe, GA, US 27, several blocks from the Visitor Center; **Days/Hours:** Park open 24 hours a day, except Lookout Mountain Unit, which is closed at night; **Holiday Closings:** Dec. 25; **Visitor attractions closed for seasons:** None; **Weather:** Summer is hot and humid; Winter is cold, with a few days below freezing; early Spring is rainy.

NEARBY FACILITIES & POINTS OF INTEREST: **Hotels/Motels:** Cluster of motels located within 10 miles of area; Ramada Inn, Holiday Inn, Howard Johnson, Days Inn, Quality Inn, Scottish Inn, etc.; **Campgrounds:** Cloudland Canyon, GA; Harrison Bay, TN, KOA-Chattanooga, TN; **Parks, other points of interest:** Fort Mountain, Chatsworth, GA; Russell Cave, Bridgeport, AL; Rock City, Ruby Falls, Lookout Mountain, TN.

Cumberland Island National Seashore
Saint Marys, Georgia   **SEE CLIMATABLE NO. 49**

MAILING ADDRESS: Superintendent, Cumberland Island National Seashore, P.O. Box 806, Saint Marys, Georgia 31558 **Telephone:** 912-882-4335—Reservations only, and 912-882-4337—Information.

DIRECTIONS: The temporary Park Headquarters and Visitor Center are on US 40, which ends at the St. Marys River. To reach St. Marys, take GA 40 east from I-95 near Kingsland. A National Park Service concession passenger ferry provides access to the Seashore from St. Marys, GA daily except Tuesday and Wednesday, 7 days a week in

June, July and August. A 7 day/week coverage between Apr.-Oct. is projected. Mainland departure times are 9:00 a.m. and 11:45 p.m. Island departure times are 10:15 a.m. and 4:45 p.m. The trip takes 45 minutes. Ferry reservations are advisable and can be made by calling 912-882-4335. No written reservations. *Don't miss the ferry from the island.* It leaves as scheduled. If you miss the boat, you must camp or charter a boat to take you to the mainland. The ferry does not transport cars, bicycles, or pets.

Magnificent beaches and dunes, marshes, maritime forest and freshwater lakes make up this largest of Georgia's Golden Isles, one of the finest remaining natural areas on the East Coast. Established by act of Congress on Oct. 23, 1972.

VISITOR ACTIVITIES: naturalist programs, walking tours, bird- and wildlife-watching, swimming, fishing, photography, hiking, camping, backcountry; **Permits:** required for backcountry, available at Island debarkation point; **Fees:** fee for foundtrip ferry tickets, $7.80 adults 13 to 65, $6.50 - 65 and older, $4.25 - 12 and under; **Visitor facilities:** restrooms, campgrounds, bath house, beaches, hiking trails; **Any limitations on vehicle usage:** No transportation on the island; **Hiking trails:** Yes, a 2 mile (3 km) nature trail leads to the Dungeness Ruins complex, plus another 30 miles (48.0 km) of nature trails. Maps for other trails are available; **Backcountry:** Yes, backpackers should make reservations with headquarters. Campfires are prohibited so a portable stove is necessary; **Camping:** Yes, campers should make reservations with Headquarters and be sure to carry adequate equipment and supplies. All camping equipment must be hand carried ½ mile from the boat dock to campground; **Other overnight accommodations on site:** No; **Meals served in the park:** No; **Food and supplies obtainable in the park:** No; **Food and supplies obtainable nearby:** Yes, at St. Marys; **Overnight accommodations:** Motel accommodations are available in nearby communities. Camping facilities may be found at private commercial campgrounds and 10 miles (16 km) away at Crooked River State Park, Route 1, Box 207, Kingsland, GA 31548, phone 912-882-5256; **First Aid available in park:** Yes; **Nearest Hospital:** St. Marys, GA via emergency boat from the Island; **Days/Hours:** Seashore closed to public for managed hunts. Check with Headquarters for dates. Sea Camp Visitor Center is open from 8 a.m. to 4:30 p.m. daily; **Holiday Closings:** Dec. 25; **Visitor attractions closed for seasons:** No; **Weather:** Cumberland's climate is moderate with short, mild Winters. Summer temperatures range from about 27°C to 35°C (80s to low 90sF) with some humidity.

GENERAL INFORMATION: Before leaving St. Marys, day and overnight visitors should carefully consider what supplies-food, drinks, suntan lotion, film, sunglasses, and insect repellent-they will need, for there are no stores on the Island. Casual dress, comfortable walking shoes, and rain gear are also recommended.

For Your Safety—Dungeness ruins and most of its outbuildings are unstable. For your protection, these structures are closed. The Island is home to several species of poisonous snakes. Visitors are advised to take normal precautions when venturing into areas where vegetation is thick. Lifeguards are not provided; be careful while swimming. Be alert for possible hunting activity on adjacent private lands.

TRAVEL ACCESS: **Bus:** Greyhound provides daily service to Kingsland, GA; **Rail:** Seaboard Coast line provides service to Jacksonville, FL; **Air:** Major airlines service Jacksonville International Airport; **Other:** Yellow Taxi Co., Kingsland, GA, Blue & White Taxi, St. Marys, GA.

NEARBY FACILITIES & POINTS OF INTEREST: **Hotel/Motel:** Riverview Hotel, St. Marys, GA, 912-882-3242, Across St. from Visitor Center; **Food/Supplies:** Downtown St. Marys; **Campgrounds:** Crooken River St. Park - St. Marys, 912-882-5256, 10 miles from visitor center; **Parks, other points of interest:** Okefenokee Swamp, Fort Frederica, Jekyll Island; **Reservation system in use for campsites:** Reservations only 2 months in advance 8 weeks to the day).

Fort Frederica National Monument
St. Simons Island, Georgia   **SEE CLIMATABLE NO. 49**

MAILING ADDRESS: Superintendent, Fort Frederica National Monument, Route 9, Box 286-C, St. Simons Island, Georgia 31522 **Telephone:** 912-638-3639

DIRECTIONS: The Monument is 12 miles (19.3 km) from Brunswick, GA on St. Simons Island. It can be reached by taking the Brunswick-St. Simons toll causeway which connects with US 17 at Brunswick.

Gen. James E. Oglethorpe built this British fort in 1736-48, during the Anglo-Spanish struggle for control of what is now southeastern United States. Authorized for addition to the National Park System on May 26, 1936.

VISITOR ACTIVITIES: interpretive exhibits and film, walking tours, living history demonstrations in Summer; **Permits:** No; **Fees:** $1.00 adults and children over 12; **Visitor facilities:** parking and restrooms at Visitor Center, interpretive publications and sales items. Picnicking is available at several points on St. Simons Island; **Any limitations on vehicle usage:** Vehicles are restricted to the entrance road and parking lot; **Hiking trails:** No; **Backcountry:** No; **Camping:** No; **Other overnight accommodations on site:** No; **Meals served in the park:** No; **Food and supplies obtainable in the park:** No; **Food and supplies obtainable nearby:** Yes, St. Simons Island has restaurants, grocery stores, and convenience stores; **Overnight accommodations:** Several motels are on St. Simons Island; **First Aid available in park:** Yes, there is an emergency squad on St. Simons Island; **Nearest Hospital:** Brunswick, GA, 12.5 miles (20 km); **Days/Hours:** Open daily from 8 a.m. to 5 p.m. Hours may be extended in Summer. Contact the Superintendent for further information; **Holiday Closings:** Dec. 25; **Visitor attractions closed for seasons:** None; **Weather:** Spring and Fall are mild; Winter has occasional cold temperatures. Summers are hot & humid with numerous afternoon thundershowers.

GENERAL INFORMATION: Do not touch the ruins, which are old and fragile and can easily by destroyed. The water is deep and the banks are slippery at the fort. Do not take shelter under the trees during high winds and thunderstorms. Bring an insect repellent in Summer.

TRAVEL ACCESS: Bus: Greyhound provides daily service to Brunswick, GA 12.5 miles from park; **Rail:** Amtrak provides daily service to Jessup, GA, 52 miles from Park; **Air:** Major airlines provide daily service to Jacksonville, FLA 75 miles from Park. Atlantic SE Airlines provides daily service to Brunswick; **Other:** Bicycles and mopeds available for rent on St. Simon's Island.

NEARBY FACILITIES & POINTS OF INTEREST: Parks, other points of interest: Jekyll Island Resort Area (10 miles south of Brunswick).

Fort Pulaski National Monument
Tybee Island, Georgia   **SEE CLIMATABLE NO. 49**

MAILING ADDRESS: Superintendent, Fort Pulaski National Monument, P.O. Box 98, Tybee Island, Georgia 31328 **Telephone:** 912-786-5787

DIRECTIONS: The Visitor Center is in the delta area of the Savannah River, 15 miles (24 km) east of Savannah on US 80.

Bombardment of this early 19th-century fort by Federal rifled cannon in 1862 first demonstrated the ineffectiveness of old-style masonry fortifications. Created by Presidential Proclamation on Oct. 15, 1924.

VISITOR ACTIVITIES: interpretive talks, walks, tours (guided and self-guided), exhibits, wildlife- and bird-watching, picnicking, fishing; **Permits:** No; **Fees:** Entrance fee is $1 per person. Golden Age, Golden Access and Golden Eagle Passports accepted and available; **Visitor facilities:** Parking and restrooms at Visitor Center, picnic area; **Any limitations on vehicle usage:** Vehicles are confined to designated roadways; **Hiking trails:** Yes, hiking and nature trails lead around the fort 1/4 mile to 2 miles in length; **Backcountry:** No; **Camping:** No; **Other overnight accommodations on site:** No; **Meals served in the park:** No; **Food and supplies obtainable in the park:** No; **Food and supplies obtainable nearby:** Yes, Tybee Island 4 miles (6 km); Savannah 15 miles (24 km); **Overnight accommodations:** Tybee Island, 4 miles (6 km) east of Park, Savannah, 15 miles (24 km) west of the Monument on US 80; **First Aid available in park:** Yes; **Nearest Hospital:** Savannah, Abercorn, Waters, and Reynolds, about 20 miles (32 km); **Days/Hours:** Open daily from 8:30 a.m. to 5:30 p.m. with extended hours in late spring and summer; **Holiday Closings:** Dec. 25, Jan. 1; **Weather:** Temperatures range from 7°C (20°F) in Winter to 37°C (100°) in Summer.

GENERAL INFORMATION: *For Your Safety*—Stay off mounds and top-most walls of the fort. Don't run on the terreplein (upper level) of the fort. Come down when there is lightning. Mosquitoes and horseflies are present in Spring and Summer; use a repellent and wear protective clothing. Watch your step in the Fort, and stay on the trails when walking or hiking. Beware of poisonous snakes.

TRAVEL ACCESS: Bus: C & H Bus Lines, Inc. provides service from Savannah, 8:15 a.m. & 3:35 p.m. daily to Highway 80 within one mile of Fort; **Rail:** Amtrak provides service to Savannah; **Air:** Delta, Eastern and American Airlines.

NEARBY FACILITIES & POINTS OF INTEREST: Parks, other points of interest: Savannah National Historic Landmark District, Old Fort Jackson, Wormsloe State Historic Site, Fort McAllister and Richmond Hill State Park, Tybee Island: public beach, museum, lighthouse, historic Fort Screven area.

Jimmy Carter National Historic Site
Plains, Georgia

MAILING ADDRESS: Office of Public Affairs, Southeast Regional Office, National Park Service, 75 Spring Street, SW, Atlanta, Georgia 30303 **Telephone:** 404-331-4998

DIRECTIONS: NOT YET OPEN TO PUBLIC. NO VISITOR FACILITIES. The site will interpret President Jimmy Carter's birthplace, home and campaign headquarters. Established by Act of Congress, December 23, 1987.

Kennesaw Mountain National Battlefield Park
Marietta, Georgia   **SEE CLIMATABLE NO. 47**

MAILING ADDRESS: Superintendent, Kennesaw Mountain National Battlefield Park, P.O. Box 1167, Marietta, Georgia 30061 **Telephone:** 404-427-4686

DIRECTIONS: The Park is 3 miles (5 km) north of Marietta, Georgia, a short distance off US 41, and 20 miles (33 km) northwest of Atlanta, off I-75.

Two engagements took place here between Union and Confederate forces during the Atlanta Campaign, June 20-July 2, 1864. Authorized for addition to the National Park System on Feb. 8, 1917.

VISITOR ACTIVITIES: exhibits and audiovisual programs at Visitor Center, walking and auto tours of the Park, hiking; **Permits:** No; **Fees:** No; **Visitor facilities:** picnic areas, restrooms, and hiking trails; **Any limitations on vehicle usage:** All vehicles are restricted to designated roadways; **Hiking trails:** Yes, the Park trails, which start at the Visitor Center, can be used for short walks or long hikes. **Backcountry:** No; **Camping:** No; **Other overnight accommodations on site:** No; **Meals served in the park:** No; **Food and supplies obtainable in the park:** No; **Food and supplies obtainable nearby:** Yes, in Marietta or Atlanta; **Overnight accommodations:** Marietta, 2 miles (3.2 km) south; or Atlanta, 15 miles (24 km) southeast; **First Aid available in park:** Yes; **Nearest Hospital:** Marietta, 2 miles (3.2 km); **Days/Hours:** Open daily from 8:30 a.m. to 5 p.m. year-round; **Holiday Closings:** Dec. 25 and Jan 1; **Weather:** Moderate temperatures year round. Daytime temperatures are usually in the 40° range in Winter and 80° range in Summer.

Martin Luther King, Jr., National Historic Site and Preservation District
Atlanta, Georgia   **SEE CLIMATABLE NO. 47**

MAILING ADDRESS: Superintendent, Martin Luther King, Jr., National Historic Site and Preservation District, 522 Auburn Avenue, N.E., Atlanta, Georgia 30312

DIRECTIONS: East at I-75 and I-85 in downtown Atlanta.

Established October 10, 1980, located in downtown Atlanta, the site (23.5 acres) includes the birthplace, church, and gravesite of Dr. Martin Luther King, Jr., leader of the Civil Rights Movement. This neighborhood also includes The Martin Luther King Jr. Center for Nonviolent Social Change, Inc., Victorian row houses, an 1895 fire station and a Catholic mission. The surrounding preservation district (80.1 acres) includes the Sweet Auburn District, the economic and cultural center of Atlanta's black community during most of the 20th century, and the larger residential areas surrounding the Birth Home.

VISITOR ACTIVITIES: At present the federal government owns one historic structure used for administrative offices and twelve additional historic structures, several of which have been rehabilitated, while the remaining structures are undergoing rehabilitation. Two information stations and walking tours are open to visitors seven days a week. Tours of the King Birth Home are given daily by the Park Service free of charge. Additional visitor activities are provided by other organizations and key sites are opened periodically by their owners, including the King Birth Home and Ebenezer Baptist Church. An exhibit entitled "King: Images of a Drum Major" is open to visitors in the King Center; **Permits:** No; **Fees:** No; **Visitor facilities:** Information Station; **Any limitations on vehicle usage:** No; **Hiking trails:** No; **Backcountry:** No; **Camping:** No; **Other overnight accommodations on site:** No; **Meals served in the park:** No; **Food and supplies obtainable in the park:** No; **Food and supplies obtainable nearby:** Yes, downtown Atlanta; **Overnight accommodations:** Atlanta, immediately adjacent to Sweet Auburn; **First Aid available in park:** No; **Nearest Hospital:** Hospital adjacent to preservation district; covered by city emergency services; **Park open to visitors:** Yes; **Holiday Closings:** Christmas Day and New Years Day; **Visitor attractions closed for seasons:** No.

TRAVEL ACCESS: Bus: Marta Bus Company, stops in park, frequent schedule; **Rail:** Amtrak, stops in Atlanta; **Air:** Most major air carriers, nearest terminal Atlanta-Hartsfield.

NEARBY FACILITIES & POINTS OF INTEREST: Hotel/Motel: Most major chains—numerous other hotels/motels in Atlanta area; **Campgrounds:** No; **Parks, other points of interest:** Chattahoochee River NRA, Kennesaw Mountain National Battlefield Park, Stone Mountain, Atlanta Historical Soc. and Martin Luther King Jr. Center for Nonviolent Social Change.

Ocmulgee National Monument
Macon, Georgia   SEE CLIMATABLE NO. 46

MAILING ADDRESS: Superintendent, Ocmulgee National Monument, 1207 Emery Highway, Macon, Georgia 31201 **Telephone:** 912-752-8257

DIRECTIONS: The Monument is on the east edge of Macon, Georgia on US 80 east. Main access is from Int. 75 to Int. 16 east, at the north end of Macon. Take either the first or second exit from Int. 16 and follow the signs 1 mile (1.6 km) to the Park entrance.

The cultural evolution of the Indian civilizations in the southern United States are represented in the remains of mounds and villages here. Authorized for addition to the National Park System on June 14, 1934.

VISITOR ACTIVITIES: auto tours, interpretive exhibits, picnicking, nature walks, hiking, fishing; **Permits:** none; **Fees:** $1 for ages 13-61, or $10 annual park pass, or $25 Golden Eagle National Park Pass; **Visitor facilities:** parking and restrooms at Visitor Center, picnic area, craft demonstrations in Summer, nature trail; **Any limitations on vehicle usage:** Vehicles must be parked only in designated parking areas; **Hiking trails:** Yes, 3 1/2 miles (5.5 km) of nature and historical trails; **Backcountry:** No; **Camping:** No; **Other overnight accommodations on site:** No, the closest camping area is Lake To-besofkee Recreation Area, 8 miles (13 km) west of Macon. No reservations available for campsites. For further information, contact the lake at 6600 Mosley-Dixon Road, Macon, GA 31210, phone 912-474-8770; **Meals served in the park:** No; **Food and supplies obtainable in the park:** No; **Food and supplies obtainable nearby:** Yes, at Macon; **Overnight accommodations:** Macon; **First Aid available in park:** Yes; **Nearest Hospital:** Macon, Highway 80, 1/2 mile (.8 km); **Days/Hours:** Open daily from 9 a.m. to 5 p.m.; **Holiday Closings:** Dec. 25 and Jan. 1; **Visitor attractions closed for seasons:** None; **Weather:** Summers are hot & humid, Winters are mostly mild.

GENERAL INFORMATION: *For Your Safety*—Mound slopes and steep banks are dangerous. Please use the marked trails. Drivers of camping vehicles and school buses should be aware of the 9'9" clearance of the tunnel leading to Greater Temple Mound.

TRAVEL ACCESS: Bus: Greyhound provides service to Macon; **Air:** ASA Airlines (Delta connector) provides service to Lewis B. Wilson Airport.

NEARBY FACILITIES & POINTS OF INTEREST: Campgrounds: Lake Tobesofkee Recreation Area, 8 miles west of Macon; **Tours:** Macon Historic District.

Hawaii

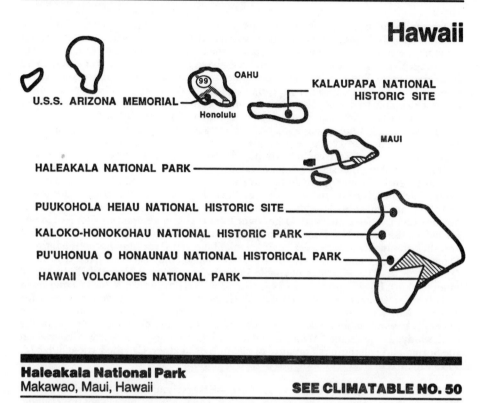

U.S.S. ARIZONA MEMORIAL

OAHU

Honolulu

KALAUPAPA NATIONAL HISTORIC SITE

MAUI

HALEAKALA NATIONAL PARK

PUUKOHOLA HEIAU NATIONAL HISTORIC SITE

KALOKO-HONOKOHAU NATIONAL HISTORIC PARK

PU'UHONUA O HONAUNAU NATIONAL HISTORICAL PARK

HAWAII VOLCANOES NATIONAL PARK

Haleakala National Park
Makawao, Maui, Hawaii **SEE CLIMATABLE NO. 50**

MAILING ADDRESS: Superintendent, Haleakala National Park, P.O. Box 369, Makawao, Maui, Hawaii 96768 **Telephone:** 808-572-9177

DIRECTIONS: The Park extends from the 3055 meter (10,023-foot) summit of Mt. Haleakala down the southeast flank to the Kipahulu coast near Hana. These two sections of the Park are not directly connected by road, but can be reached by auto from Kahului, as follows: Haleakala Crater is a 3 hour round trip drive from Kahului via HI 36, 37, 377, and 378. The Kipahulu District of the Park is an 8-to-10 hour round trip drive from Kahului via HI 36 to Hana, then via HI 31 towards Kipahulu. The road around East Maui, which is narrow, winding and slow, is for the adventurous only; it offers roadside state parks, frequent overlooks, and views of rain forests, black lava shores, and rugged coastal cliffs. West of Kipahulu, HI 31 becomes an unpaved road.

The Park preserves the outstanding features of Haleakala Crater on the Island of Maui and protects the unique and fragile ecosystems of Kipahulu Valley, the scenic pools along 'Ohe'o Gulch, and many rare and endangered species. Authorized for addition to the National Park System on Aug. 1, 1916.

VISITOR ACTIVITIES: Kipahulu: hiking, camping, walking, picnicking, swimming. Haleakala Crater: interpretive exhibits and talks, walking, hiking, camping, picnicking. Park Headquarters, where information, permits, and publications are furnished, is 1 mile (1.5 km) from the entrance to the Park. The Visitor Center, which contains exhibits and is where interpretive talks are held, is about 10 miles (17.5 km) from the park entrance. For detailed information on both areas, contact the Superintendent; **Permits:** For backcountry camping at Haleakala Crater. Permits available from Headquarters or from a Park Ranger; **Fees:** Yes, for backcountry cabin rental; Park entrance fee $3; **Visitor facilities:** Picnic areas, campgrounds, scenic overlooks, interpretive observatory programs, backcountry cabins; **Any limitations on vehicle usage:** Watch out for traffic on narrow roads; **Hiking trails:** Yes, trails vary in difficulty and length; there are several short nature trails; **Backcountry:** Yes, contact the Superintendent for a free brochure; **Camping:** Yes, campsites cannot be reserved ahead and are operated on a first come first served basis. These are primitive campsites with only pit toilets and drinking water. Campers should have equipment appropriate for possible cold, wet weather, and must bring a sleeping bag, tent, and cooking stove with fuel (because of the prohibition against open fires). Three crater cabins are maintained by the National Park Service for visitor use on an advance reservation basis only. Each cabin is allocated to one party at a time, with a capacity of 12 people per night; at least one member of the group must be 18 years of age or older. Each cabin has bunks, limited water and firewood, cookstove, and eating and cooking utensils. To reserve cabins, write to the Superintendent at least 90 days in advance of your trip. Include your first and alternate choices of dates and cabins preferred. The less restrictive your choices, the better your chance of confirmation. Reservations are limited to 3 nights per month, with no more than 2 consecutive nights at any one cabin. A fee is charged; **Other overnight accommodations on site:** No; **Meals served in the park:** No; **Food and supplies obtainable in the park:** No; **Food and supplies obtainable nearby:** Yes, at Pukalani, Maui, HI; **Overnight accommodations:** From Kipahulu, 10 miles (16 km) on Rt. 31 to Hana. From Haleakala Crater, 12 miles (19 km) on Rt. 377; **First Aid available in park:** Yes; **Nearest Hospital:** Kahului, 30 miles (48 km); **Days/Hours:** Open 24 hours a day, 365 days a year, Visitor Center open daily from 8:30 a.m. to 3 p.m.; **Holiday Closings:** None; **Visitor attractions closed for seasons:** No; **Weather:** Weather near the summit varies considerably; Summers are generally dry and moderately warm, but you should come prepared for occasionally cold, windy, damp weather. Winters tend to be cold, wet, foggy, and windy. Generally in the Spring and Fall there is a mixture of all kinds of weather. Call the Park at 808-572-7749 for current weather conditions before beginning your trip.

GENERAL INFORMATION: *For Your Safety*—Hikers should bring comfortable, durable hiking shoes, canteen, light raincoat, sun hat, and suntan lotion. Do not travel alone. Swimmers should never swim during high water. If you notice the water rising, GET OUT FAST! 'Ohe'o stream can become a raging torrent in minutes. Be careful on wet rocks; they are slippery. Check before diving or jumping. In some places there are submerged ledges near the pool's edge.

Hawaii Volcanoes National Park
Hawaii Volcanoes National Park, Hawaii   **SEE CLIMATABLE NO. 51**

MAILING ADDRESS: Superintendent, Hawaii Volcanoes National Park, Hawaii 96718 **Telephone:** 808-967-7311

DIRECTIONS: Visitor Centers are at Kilauea and Wahaula. Park Headquarters area, including Kilauea Visitor Center, is located 29 miles southwest of Hilo, off HI 11. The coastal section of the park presently is not accessible from Keaau and Hwy. 130. Lava flows have blocked road since Feb. 1987 and flows continue to this date with no anticipated reopening date. Accessible from the Chain of Craters Road from Park Headquarters. A new visitor facility was dedicated in January, 1987—located on the rim of Kilauea Caldera—adjacent to the new Hawaiian Volcano Observatory. The new facility is known as 'Jaggar Museum'. New Visitor Center interpreting volcanic story of park.

Active volcanism continues here on the Island of Hawaii. Rare and luxuriant vegetation provides food and shelter for a variety of native birds. Established by act of Congress on Aug. 1, 1916.

VISITOR ACTIVITIES: auto tours, walking, hiking, camping, backcountry, picnicking, fishing, interpretive programs. Schedule of events available from either Visitor

Center or by contacting the park; **Permits:** for backcountry use can be obtained at Headquarters; **Fees:** Entrance fee of $5 per car or $2 per person on foot, bike, or bus; **Visitor facilities:** parking, restrooms and museums at Visitor Centers, lodging, cabins, picnic areas; **Any limitations on vehicle usage:** All vehicles are restricted to designated roadways; **Hiking trails:** Yes, check at Visitor Center or write for information on the 150 miles (241 km) of trails; **Backcountry:** Yes, hiker shelters and cabins are available, but you must register at Park Headquarters for overnight stays. Detailed maps are available at Park Headquarters and are highly recommended. Check on trail conditions and water supplies before you start; **Camping:** Yes, no reservations available for individual campsites; **Other overnight accommodations on site:** Yes, Volcano House on the rim of Kilauea Crater is open all year. Reservations are advised year round. Cabins with the use of showers are operated at Namakani Paio by the Volcano House. For reservations contact: The Volcano House, Hawaii Volcanoes National Park, HI 96718, phone 808-967-7321. Kilauea Military Camp, a rest and recreation camp for active and retired military personnel, is 1 mile (1.6 km) west of Park Headquarters; **Meals served in the park:** Yes, at Volcano House Restaurant; **Food and supplies obtainable in the park:** No; **Food and supplies obtainable nearby:** Yes, groceries, gasoline, and camping supplies are available in the community of Volcano, 1 mile (1.6 km) north of the park on HI 11. Stores there are open all year. Groceries and meals are also available in the village of Kalapana, 4 miles (6 km) east of the coastal section of the park but are not accessible at this time from the park; **Overnight accommodations:** Hilo, Highway 11, 29 miles (47 km) from the park; **First Aid available in park:** Yes; **Nearest Hospital:** Hilo, Highway 11, 29 miles (47 km); **Days/Hours:** Park open 24 hours a day year-round; **Holiday Closings:** None; **Visitor attractions closed for seasons:** None; **Weather:** The northern side of Kilauea's summit is 4000 feet (1200 meters) above sea level, so the climate can be cool and rain can fall at any time of year. At the same time, Kilauea's leeward side is usually dry and warm. There are few records of freezing at Kilauea, but in Winter the snow can extend down to 10,000 feet (3000 meters) on Mauna Loa.

GENERAL INFORMATION: *For Your Safety*—Stay on trails. The surface of Kilauea is laced with deep cracks, and many of these are hidden by vegetation. Recent lava flows are shelly and collapse easily. Fumes from volcanoes can compound respiratory and heart problems. If in doubt, heed the warning signs. A number of trails lie along the edges of cliff tops, so be sure of your footing.

Eruption Bulletins: You can get up-to-date information about on-going eruptions or potential activity by calling 808-967-7977 anytime. The automatic answering service is updated whenever Kilauea or Mauna Loa shows signs of change. Because eruptions are the most exciting events at Hawaii Volcanoes, temporary road signs will direct you to access or vantage points where you can confront the power of these events when conditions are safe.

Special publications on the geology, human history, and natural history of Hawaii Volcanoes are published by the Hawaii Natural History Association to help you enjoy the park. For a price list write to the Association, Hawaii Volcanoes National Park, HI 96718. An award winning video tape on the Mauna Loa eruption of 1984 is now available. Funded entirely by the Hawaii Natural History Association 'River of Fire' was presented the 'Eastman Kodak Award' and an 'Indy' Award from the Industrial Film and Video Competition in New York City, 1985 Awards.

Kalaupapa National Historic Park
Hawaii   **SEE CLIMATABLE NO. 52**

MAILING ADDRESS: Kalaupapa National Historical Park, Kalaupapa, Hawaii 96742

DIRECTIONS: On the windward coast of the Island of Molokai this Historic Park is open to the public on a limited basis. All visitors are required to first obtain permission from the State of Hawaii, Department of Health.

Kalaupapa, unlike many other National Park areas, has a living community as one of the prime resources of the Park. The residents of Kalaupapa are those people that were banished here for committing no crime, but for contracting a much misunderstood and greatly feared disease. The disease, now called Hansen's Disease, is more widely known throughout the world as leprosy. These people with Hansen's Disease were banished here to protect the health and safety of the public. Today this once dreaded disease is curable with treatment, and there is no longer any medical reason to isolate people with leprosy. Those people who remain here, do so out of choice.

Kalaupapa is jointly managed by the State of Hawaii, Department of Health, and the National Park Service. To protect the privacy of the community, access to Kalaupapa is still quite limited. You must obtain a visitor permit from the Department of Health to enter the settlement. This may be done through one of two tour companies that are owned, and operated by patients. You may write for information to DAMIEN TOURS or IKE'S SCENIC TOURS, c/o Kalaupapa Settlement, Kalaupapa, Hawaii 96742. There are no public facilities (camping, restaurants, or stores). Overnight stays are limited to invited guests of residents.

Kaloko-Honokohau National Historical Park
On the Kona coast of the Island of Hawaii   **SEE CLIMATABLE NO. 53**

MAILING ADDRESS: P.O. Box 129, Honaunau, Hawaii 96726.

DIRECTIONS: *Newly opened to the public. Printed fact sheets available;* Pacific Area Office, National Park Service, 300 Ala Moana Blvd., Honolulu, Hawaii 96850.

The Park contains a great number of Hawaiian archaeological sites and features. According to legend, the first Hawaiian King, Kamehameha I is buried somewhere in the park. The park also provides important habitat for three endangered species of Hawaiian waterbirds.

Pu'uhonua o Honaunau National Historical Park
Honaunau, Kona, Hawaii   **SEE CLIMATABLE NO. 53**

MAILING ADDRESS: Superintendent, Pu'uhonua o Honaunau National Historical Park, P.O. Box 129, Honaunau, Kona, Hawaii 96726 **Telephone:** 808-328-2326

DIRECTIONS: The Park is located 30 miles (48 km) south of Keahole Airport on HI 160. Take HI 19 to Kailua, thence HI 11 to Honaunau, thence HI 160 to the park.

Until 1819, vanquished Hawaiian warriors, noncombatants and taboo breakers could escape death by reaching this sacred ground. Prehistoric house sites, royal fishponds, coconut groves and spectacular shore scenery comprise the park. Authorized for addition to the National Park System on June 26, 1955.

VISITOR ACTIVITIES: picnicking, snorkeling, swimming, walking tours, craft demonstrations, interpretive exhibits, hiking, fishing; **Permits:** Yes, for picnicking by groups of over 30 people; **Fees:** Yes; **Visitor facilities:** parking and restrooms at Visitor Center, picnic area; **Any limitations on vehicle usage:** Vehicles are restricted to designated roadways; **Hiking trails:** Yes, self-guiding walking trail through the park; **Backcountry:** No; **Camping:** No; **Other overnight accommodations on site:** No; **Meals served in the park:** No, the nearest restaurant is 10 miles (16 km) away; **Food and supplies obtainable in the park:** No; **Food and supplies obtainable nearby:** No, limited supplies on HI 11, grocery stores at Captain Cook; **Overnight accommodations:** Captain Cook, HI 11, 10 miles (16 km) away; **First Aid available in park:** Yes; **Nearest Hospital:** Kona, 12 miles (19 km); **Days/Hours:** Open daily from 6 a.m. to midnight; **Holi-**

day Closings: None; Visitor attractions closed for seasons: No; Weather: The Park is sunny 95% of the time. Summer is the rainy season; average rainfall is 25 inches per year.

GENERAL INFORMATION: *For Your Safety*—Be alert for unexpected high waves when you are on the shore; don't turn your back on the ocean. Do not climb on the Stone Walls or on the framework of the house models. If you leave the trail, watch for falling coconuts and coconut fronds. Do not climb the coconut trees. Visitors to the area can also see Puukohola Heiau National Historic Site (see listing in this book), at Kawaihae Bay, on the island's northwestern shore.

TRAVEL ACCESS: Bus: 1/2 day bus tours operate from Kailu, Kona (20 miles); Rail: No; Air: No.

NEARBY FACILITIES & POINTS OF INTEREST: Hotel/Motel: Manago Hotel, Capt. Cook, HI 96704, 808-323-2642, 12 miles; Food/Supplies: Morihara Grocery Store on Intersection of 11 and 160 (3 miles); Campgrounds: None nearby; Parks, other points of interest: Kealakekua Bay (4 miles south) Site of Cooks Landing, painted church (3 miles east).

Puukohola Heiau National Historic Site
Kawaihae, Hawaii   SEE CLIMATABLE NO. 53

MAILING ADDRESS: Superintendent, Puukohola Heiau National Historic Site, P.O. Box 4963, Kawaihae, HI 96743 Telephone: 808-882-7218

DIRECTIONS: Puukohola Heiau is on the northwestern shore of the Island of Hawaii. Airlines make scheduled flights several times daily from Honolulu to airports at Hilo, Keahole, and Waimea-Kohala, which is about 12 miles (19 km) from the park. Taxis and car rentals are available at all airports, except Waimea-Kohala Airport.

Ruins of Puukohola Heiau ("Temple on the Hill of the Whale"), built by King Kamehameha the Great (1753-1819) in 1791, during his rise to power are preserved here. Authorized for addition to the National Park System on Aug. 17, 1972.

VISITOR ACTIVITIES: hiking, guided and self-guiding tours. Swimming and picnicking are permitted at nearby Spencer Beach Park; Permits: No; Fees: No; Visitor facilities: Informal interpretive talks are given at the Visitor Center; Any limitations on vehicle usage: If you park in front of Puukohola Heiau on the Spencer Beach Road, use caution while entering and leaving the road, due to heavy traffic; Hiking trails: Yes, all points of interest in the park can be visited on foot; Backcountry: No; the Hawaii Visitors Bureau, a non-profit organization with offices in Honolulu, Hilo, Kona, Waikiki, Lihu, and 209 Post Street, San Francisco, CA 94108, phone 415-392-8273, will supply information on trips to and through the Hawaiian Islands; Camping: No, information on camping at nearby Spencer Beach Park may be obtained from Hawaii Visitors Bureau, 209 Post Street, San Francisco, CA 94108, phone 415-392-8173; Other overnight accommodations on site: No; Meals served in the park: No; Food and supplies obtainable in the park: No; Food and supplies obtainable nearby: Yes, at Kawaihae, 1 mile (1.5 km) away; Overnight accommodations: Waimea, 12 miles (19.3 km) southeast; First Aid available in park: Yes; Nearest Hospital: Honokaa, 29 miles (46.5 km); Days/Hours: Visitor Center open from 7:30 a.m. to 4 p.m.; Holiday Closings: No; Visitor attractions closed for seasons: No; Weather: Nine inches of rainfall per year; occasional 90°F temperatures.

GENERAL INFORMATION: *For Your Safety*—Stay on the designated trails, and do not climb on the walls of the temple. The trail from the Visitor Center is long, hot, & rugged. If you are not physically fit and attired in proper clothing or footwear, do not attempt the hike. You may view the area from the Spencer Beach Park road. To prevent grass fires, do not smoke. The beach fronting Puukohola is unsuitable for swimming, due to silt and coral collections.

TRAVEL ACCESS: Bus: No; **Rail:** No; **Air:** Nearest airport is Waimea-Kohala, 12 miles (19 km).

NEARBY FACILITIES & POINTS OF INTEREST: Hotel/Motel: Mauna Kea Beach Hotel, P.O. Box 218, Kamuela, H 96743, (808) 882-7222, 1.5 miles; **Food/Supplies:** Jin Ho's & Doi Store, 7/11 Complex and Harbor Hut .5-1 miles; **Campgrounds:** Spencer Beach Park (County facility) adjoining the Park; **Parks, other points of interest:** Puako Petroglyphs, (6 miles); **Reservation system in use for campsites, other facilities:** Information may be obtained by calling or writing to the following: Superintendent, Puukohola Heiau NHS (see above for address). Permits are necessary for camping in most Parks. **New Information:** A Cultural Festival for two days is held annually in August to celebrate the establishment of Puukohola Heiau as a National Historic Site.

U.S.S. Arizona Memorial
Honolulu, Hawaii   **SEE CLIMATABLE NO. 55**

MAILING ADDRESS: USS Arizona Memorial, National Park Service, 1 Arizona Memorial Place, Honolulu, Hawaii 96818. **Telephone:** (808) 422-2771. Recorded Information (808) 422-0561 or 422-0562

DIRECTIONS: The Memorial is a ½ hour drive from Waikiki. From Waikiki take H-1 west pass the airport to the "Stadium-Arizona" exit. Take "Stadium-Arizona" exit off freeway. Turn left at 4th traffic light at sign to USS Arizona Memorial. Public transportation is available from Waikiki (2 hours) and downtown Honolulu to USS Arizona Memorial Visitor Center. For information, call 808-531-1611.

The Memorial is supported by pilings on either side of the Battleship USS *Arizona*, sunk in Pearl Harbor on Dec. 7, 1941. Owned by U.S. Navy, administered by National Park Service.

VISITOR ACTIVITIES: free tour with Park Ranger, (includes Ranger talk, movie and shuttle boat, ½ mile, to and from Memorial). Periodic audiovisual Programs, Ranger and Pearl Harbor Survivor talks. Museum with permanent and temporary exhibits; **Permits:** No; **Fees:** No; **Visitor facilities:** Restrooms and limited parking available at the Visitor Center. Museum bookshop, (film, slides, videotapes, books and photos.) **Meals served in the park:** No, snacks only; **Food and supplies obtainable in the park:** No; **Food and supplies obtainable nearby:** Yes, at Pearl Ridge Shopping Center; **Overnight accommodations:** at the Airport or Waikiki; **First Aid available in park:** Yes; **Nearest Hospital:** Fronk Clinic, Aiea. **Days/Hours:** Visitor Center open daily 7:30 a.m.-5:00 p.m., Boat tours 8:00 a.m. to 3:00 p.m. daily; **Holiday Closings:** Closed Christmas, New Years, Thanksgiving, open all others; **Visitor attractions closed for seasons:** None.

TRAVEL ACCESS: Bus: The Bus (City/County of Honolulu) provides frequent service #20 from Waikiki to Kamehameha Highway; Private, Shuttle Bus Co. and organized tours serve Memorial from Waikiki; **Rail:** No; **Air:** Major airlines service to Honolulu.

NEARBY FACILITIES & POINTS OF INTEREST: Hotel/Motel: at Airport; Pearlridge Shopping Center, Kamehameha Highway, 1½ miles West; **Campgrounds:** No; **Parks, other points of interest:** USS Bowfin Museum, World War II Fleet Submarine— 150 yards west, fee area; U.S. Navy open ship at Pearl Harbor Naval Station first Saturday of each month.

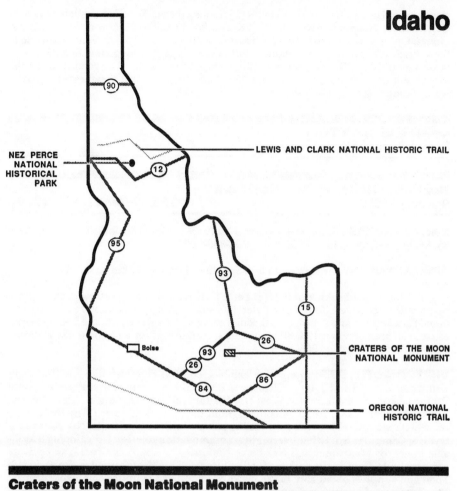

Idaho

NEZ PERCE
NATIONAL
HISTORICAL
PARK

LEWIS AND CLARK NATIONAL HISTORIC TRAIL

Boise

CRATERS OF THE MOON
NATIONAL MONUMENT

OREGON NATIONAL
HISTORIC TRAIL

Craters of the Moon National Monument
Arco, Idaho   **SEE CLIMATABLE NO. 56**

MAILING ADDRESS: Superintendent, Craters of the Moon National Monument, P.O. Box 29, Arco, Idaho 83213 **Telephone:** 208-527-3257

DIRECTIONS: The Monument is 18 miles (29 km) west of Arco on US 20, 26, and 93.
Volcanic cones, craters, lava flows, and caves make this an astonishing landscape. Established by act of Congress on May 2, 1924.

VISITOR ACTIVITIES: interpretive exhibits, audiovisual programs, naturalist trips, camping, cross-country skiing; **Permits:** required for backcountry, available at Visitor Center; **Fees:** $3 entrance fee; $5 camping fee; **Visitor facilities:** restrooms, campground, drinking water, nature trails, picnic area, amphitheater, scenic overlooks; **Any limitations on vehicle usage:** Vehicles must remain on paved roads; **Hiking trails:** Yes, self-guided trails lead to points of interest; **Backcountry:** Yes, write to Superintendent for information; **Camping:** Yes, no reservations for campsites, which have charcoal grills, tables, drinking water, and flush toilets; **Other overnight accommodations on site:** No; **Meals served in the park:** No; **Food and supplies obtainable in the park:** No; **Food and supplies obtainable nearby:** Yes, in Arco, Idaho; **Overnight accommoda-**

tions: Arco, US 20, 26, and 93, 18 miles (29 km) northeast; **First Aid available in park:** Yes; **Nearest Hospital:** Arco, US 93, 26, and 20, 18 miles (29 km) northeast; **Days/ Hours:** Open Sept. to mid-June from 8 a.m. to 4:30 p.m., until 6 p.m. from mid-June to Sept. Visitor Center open year-round; **Holiday Closings:** Thanksgiving, Dec. 25, Jan. 1, Washington's Birthday; **Visitor attractions closed for season:** The road through the Monument is closed by snow from late November to mid-April; **Weather:** Dry, warm, windy Summers; cold snowy Winters.

Lewis and Clark Trail
For details see listing in Illinois

Nez Perce National Historical Park
Spalding, Idaho   **SEE CLIMATABLE NO. 54**

MAILING ADDRESS: Superintendent, Nez Perce National Historical Park, P.O. Box 93, Spalding, Idaho 83551 **Telephone:** 208-843-2261

DIRECTIONS: The Visitor Center is in Spalding, 11 miles (17 km) east of Lewiston on US 95.

The history and culture of the Nez Perce Indian country are preserved, commemorated, and interpreted here. Four federally-owned Sites are administered by the National Park Service, and twenty sites through cooperative agreements; the 24 Sites are located in an area of about 12,000 square miles. Authorized for addition to the National Park System on May 15, 1965.

VISITOR ACTIVITIES: intepretive exhibits, cultural demonstrations, self-guiding walks, picnicking, fishing in the Clearwater River adjacent to the park; **Permits:** Idaho fishing license, available locally; **Fees:** No; **Visitor facilities:** parking at Visitor Center, restrooms, overlooks, and pullouts throughout the park, picnic area; **Any limitations on vehicle usage:** Vehicles are restricted to paved roads; **Hiking trails:** No; **Backcountry:** No; **Camping:** No; **Other overnight accommodations on site:** No, camping is available in nearby Clearwater and Nez Perce National Forests, 3 state parks, and private campgrounds. Contact the park for further information; **Meals served in the park:** No; **Food and supplies obtainable in the park:** No; **Food and supplies obtainable nearby:** Yes, Lewiston, Lapwai, Orofino, Kamiah, and Grangeville; **Overnight accommodations:** Lewiston, Orofino, Kamiah, and Grangeville; **First Aid available in park:** Yes; **Nearest Hospital:** Lewiston, US 95, 12 miles (19.3 km); **Days/Hours:** Visitor Center at Spalding is open 8 a.m.-4:30 p.m. Sept. 1-May 31; until 6 p.m. Memorial Day-Labor Day; **Holiday Closings:** Thanksgiving, Dec. 25, Jan. 1; **Visitor attractions closed for season:** Cultural demonstrations offered only in Summer.

TRAVEL ACCESS: Bus: Greyhound provides daily service into Lewiston; **Air:** Horizon offers daily service to Lewiston; **Other:** A bicycle path extends along the Clearwater River to within 6 miles of the Spalding Site from Lewiston.

NEARBY FACILITIES & POINTS OF INTEREST: Campgrounds: Hellsgate, Winchester & Chief Timothy State Parks; National Forest Campgrounds area also nearby; **Parks, other points of interest:** Dworshak Dam, Hell's Canyon, River of No Return Wilderness.

Oregon National Scenic Trail
For details see listing in Missouri

Illinois

CHICAGO PORTAGE
NATIONAL HISTORIC SITE

MORMON PIONEER
NATIONAL HISTORIC TRAIL

LINCOLN HOME
NATIONAL HISTORIC SITE

LEWIS AND CLARK
NATIONAL HISTORIC TRAIL

Chicago Portage National Historic Site
River Forest, Illinois   **SEE CLIMATABLE NO. 57**

MAILING ADDRESS: Superintendent, Chicago Portage National Historic Site, c/o Cook County Forest Preserve, Cummings Square, River Forest, Illinois 60305 **Telephone:** 312-366-9420

DIRECTIONS: Site is located on the west side of Harlem Ave. (IL 42A), approx. ½ mile (.8 km) North of Stevenson Expressway (I-55).

A portion of the portage discovered by French explorers Jacques Marquette and Louis Joliet is preserved here. Used by pioneers as a link between the Great Lakes and the Mississippi, the portage was one of the economic foundations of Chicago. Designated Jan. 3, 1952. Owned and administered by Cook County Forest Preserve District.

VISITOR ACTIVITIES: interpretive story board, picnicking; **Permits:** No; **Fees:** No; **Visitor facilities:** parking, water, picnic area. Formal development has been delayed; **Any limitations on vehicle usage:** Vehicles are restricted to the parking area; **Hiking trails:** No; **Backcountry:** No; **Camping:** No; **Other overnight accommodations on site:** No; **Meals served in the park:** No; **Food and supplies obtainable in the park:** No; **Food and supplies obtainable nearby:** Yes, Lyons, IL; **Overnight accommodations:** Lyons, Highway 34 (Ogden Ave.), 2 miles (3 km); **First Aid available in park:** No; **Nearest Hospital:** LaGrange, Willow Springs Road, approx. 4 miles (9.7 km); **Days/Hours:** 9 a.m. to sunset; **Visitor attractions closed for season:** Site closed in Winter.

Lewis and Clark National Historic Trail
Illinois (also in Missouri, Kansas, Nebraska, Iowa, South Dakota, North Dakota, Montana, Idaho, Oregon, Washington)   **SEE CLIMATABLE MAP**

MAILING ADDRESS: c/o Midwest Regional Office, National Park Service, 1709 Jackson Street, Omaha, Nebraska 68102 **Telephone:** 402-221-3481

DIRECTIONS: The designation of the 4500 mile Lewis and Clark National Historic Trail by Congress on November 10, 1978, included both the outbound and inbound routes of the 1804-06 expedition. A comprehensive management plan, completed in January 1982, calls for the development of water-based trails (along the Missouri and Columbia Rivers and tributaries), land-based trails (for travel on foot), and marked motor routes for public retracement of the Trail.

Over 500 recreation and historic sites provide or have potential to provide access to the route and interpretation of the expedition. These sites are or will be owned and managed as part of the trail by cooperating Federal, State, and local agencies and private organizations. Efforts have begun to officially certify and mark these sites as part of the national historic trail. NPS areas which provide interpretation of the expedition are: Jefferson National Expansion Memorial Historic Site (MO), Knife River Indian Villages National Historic Site (ND), Nez Perce National Historical Park (ID), and Fort Clatsop National Memorial (OR). The Lewis and Clark Trail highways marked and maintained by State highway departments are not part of the national historic trail, but complementary to it.

Lincoln Home National Historic Site
Springfield, Illinois   **SEE CLIMATABLE NO. 58**

MAILING ADDRESS: Superintendent, Lincoln Home National Historic Site, 426 S. 7th Street, Springfield, Illinois 62701 **Telephone:** 217-492-4150

DIRECTIONS: The Site is in downtown Springfield. The Visitor Center is 426 7th Street, one block west of the Lincoln Home.

While living in this home—now the focal point of this historic area—Abraham Lincoln rose from the practice of a small-town lawyer to become the 16th President of the United States, 1861-65. The two-story structure, built in 1839, was the only home he ever owned and his residence for 17 years. Authorized for addition to the National Park System on Aug. 18, 1971.

VISITOR ACTIVITIES: interpretive exhibits and film, house tours; **Permits:** No; **Fees:** Parking fee is $1.00 per hour; **Visitor facilities:** Visitor Center, restrooms; **Any limitations on vehicle usage:** No vehicle traffic is allowed within the park; **Hiking trails:** No; **Backcountry:** No; **Camping:** No; **Other overnight accommodations on site:** No; **Meals served in the park:** No; **Food and supplies obtainable in the park:** No; **Food and supplies obtainable nearby:** Yes, in Springfield; **Overnight accommodations:** Springfield, surrounding the Site; **First Aid available in park:** Yes; **Nearest Hospital:** 7 blocks north of the Home; **Days/Hours:** Open daily from 8:30 a.m. to 5 p.m.; **Holiday Closings:** Thanksgiving, Dec. 25 and Jan. 1 (home closed for restoration until June, 1988); **Weather:** Winters are cold and snowy; Summers are hot and humid.

GENERAL INFORMATION: Watch out for uneven, slippery boardwalks and steep, narrow staircases.

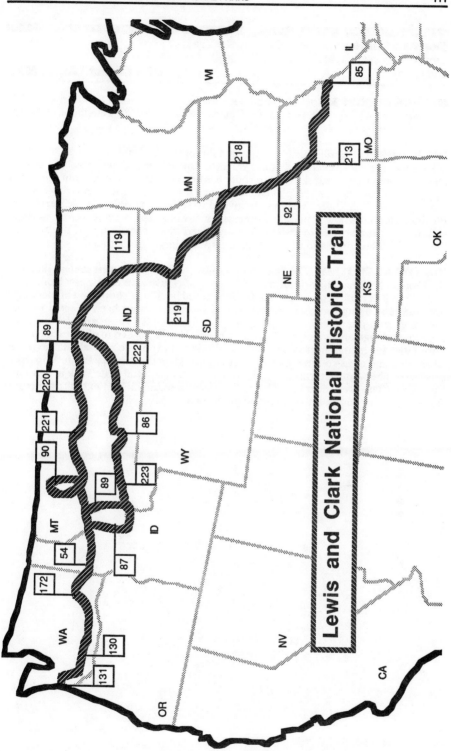

Lewis and Clark National Historic Trail

Mormon Pioneer National Historic Trail
Illinois (also in Iowa, Nebraska, Wyoming,
and Utah)   **SEE CLIMATABLE MAP**

MAILING ADDRESS: Rocky Mountain Regional Office, National Park Service, 12795 W. Alameda Parkway, P.O. Box 25287, Denver, Colorado 80225 **Telephone:** 303-969-2828

DIRECTIONS: It is still possible to closely follow this 1,300-mile-long trail of history. Where wagons once rolled and teams traveled now highways, railroads, and bridges allow for modern day travel. An auto route has been designated to go from the Mississippi River across the midwest plains and through the Rocky Mountains to descend into the Great Salt Lake Basin. Visitors are invited to retrace the route. While nearly two-thirds of the trail is now in private ownership, many of the places and events associated with the trail can be seen or visited. It is suggested that visitors send for the Mormon Pioneer Trail brochure and use the Primary Route Map to guide them.

VISITOR ACTIVITIES: The eastern end of the trail begins in west central Illinois at the Nauvoo National Historic District. The town of Nauvoo sits on the east bank of the Mississippi River and contains authentically restored buildings, shops, and homes of historic interest. Along the trail, seventy-three historic sites have been selected to commemorate and interpret important events and landmarks. There are also six cross-country trail segments totaling 47 miles on Federal lands, chosen to offer excellent opportunities for hiking, horseback riding, and other appropriate recreational activities. These sites and cross-country segments are identified on the Primary Route Map in the brochure. The western terminus of the trail is at Pioneer Trail State Park in Salt Lake City, Utah. The area includes "This is the Place" monument and exhibits structures from temporary dug-outs to substantial public buildings.

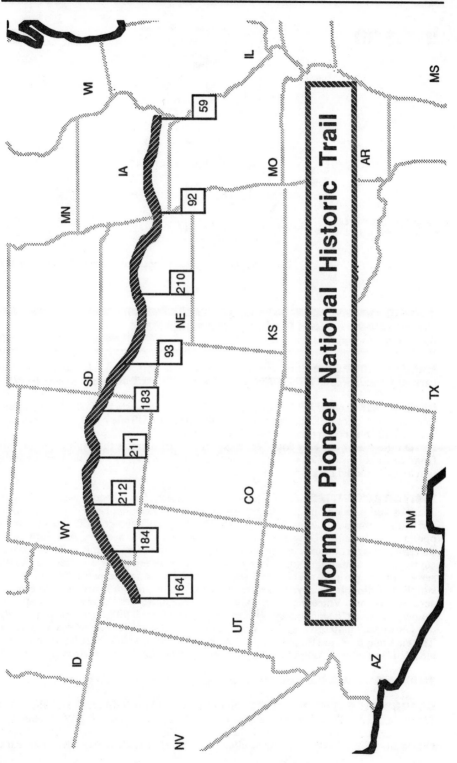

Mormon Pioneer National Historic Trail

Indiana

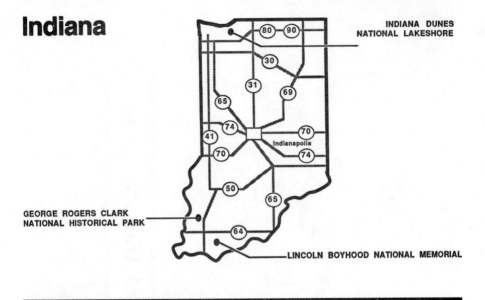

INDIANA DUNES
NATIONAL LAKESHORE

Indianapolis

GEORGE ROGERS CLARK
NATIONAL HISTORICAL PARK

LINCOLN BOYHOOD NATIONAL MEMORIAL

George Rogers Clark National Historical Park
Vincennes, Indiana   **SEE CLIMATABLE NO. 60**

MAILING ADDRESS: Superintendent, George Rogers Clark National Historical Park, 401 South Second Street, Vincennes, Indiana 47591 **Telephone:** 812-882-1776

DIRECTIONS: Follow US 50 (east and west) which intersects with US 41 (north and south) at Vincennes, park can be reached by 6th Street on US 50 or Willow Street exit on US 41. The entrance to the Park is on Second Street.

On the site of old Fort Sackville, the park commemorates the capture of the fort from the British by Lt. Col. George Rogers Clark on Feb. 25, 1779. Authorized for addition to the National Park System on July 23, 1966.

VISITOR ACTIVITIES: interpretive exhibits and film, living history weapon demonstrations and talks on Sunday afternoons in Summer; **Permits:** No; **Fees:** No; **Visitor facilities:** Memorial building, Visitor Center, parking. In Summer, a "Trailblazer" train operated by Vincennes University tours points of interest in Vincennes; **Any limitations on vehicle usage:** Motorcycles are not permitted on sidewalks; **Hiking trails:** No; **Backcountry:** No; **Camping:** No; **Other overnight accommodations on site:** No; **Meals served in the park:** No; **Food and supplies obtainable in the park:** No; **Food and supplies obtainable nearby:** Yes, close to the Park in downtown Vincennes; **Overnight accommodations:** Vincennes; **First Aid available in park:** Yes; **Nearest Hospital:** Vincennes, 7th Street, 6 blocks; **Days/Hours:** Open daily from 9:00 a.m. to 5:00 p.m.; **Holiday Closings:** Thanksgiving, Dec. 25 and Jan. 1; **Visitor attractions closed for season:** The Park may be closed for a day or two in severe Winter weather; **Weather:** snow possible from December through March; the annual temperature range is from -10 to 100°F.

TRAVEL ACCESS: Bus: Greyhound provides daily service to Vincennes.

NEARBY FACILITIES & POINTS OF INTEREST: Hotel/Motel: Travelodge, 1411 Willow St., 812-882-1282, (1 mile); Holiday Inn, 600 Wheatland Rd., 812-886-9900, (3 miles); Executive Inn, 1 Executive Blvd., 812-886-5000, (3 miles); **Campgrounds:** Ouabache Trails Park, Fort Knox Road (6 miles), 812-882-4316; Kimmel Park,

Oliphant Street, 812-882-1140, (2 miles); **Parks, other points of interest;** William Henry Harrison Home, Old Cathedral, Old French House, Fort Knox II, Indiana Territory Capitol State Historic Site, Western Sun Print Shop, Maurice Thompson Birthplace, and Old State Bank and Art Gallery.

Indiana Dunes National Lakeshore
Porter, Indiana   **SEE CLIMATABLE NO. 61**

MAILING ADDRESS: Superintendent, Indiana Dunes National Lakeshore, 1100 N. Mineral Springs Road, Porter, Indiana 46304 **Telephone:** 219-926-7561

DIRECTIONS: The lakeshore runs between Gary and Michigan City along the southern shore of Lake Michigan, about 60 miles (100 km) east of Chicago. US 12 and 20, Interstate 94, IN 49, and Indiana Toll Road (I-80 and I-90) pass through the area and connect with roads which lead directly to the lakeshore. The Visitor Center is 3 miles (5 km) east of Indiana 49 on US 12 at the Intersection of US 12 and Kemil Road.

Along the southern shore of Lake Michigan between Gary and Michigan City are several sections of clean, sandy beaches backed by huge sand dunes. Many dunes are covered with dense forests, others are continually reshaped by the wind. The parkland, totaling about 13,000 acres, preserves some of these remaining dunes and their associated bogs and marshes and provides recreational opportunities along the beaches and interior lands. Authorized for addition to the National Park System on Nov. 5, 1966.

VISITOR ACTIVITIES: biking, hiking, horseback riding, cross-country skiing, auto tours, swimming, fishing, photography, interpretive talks, films and programs; **Permits:** an Indiana fishing license available locally; **Fees:** Parking fee at West Beach area, $2.50 per vehicle ($1.25 with Golden Age or Golden Access Passport); **Visitor facilities:** first aid, horse trail, handicapped facilities, parking lots, restrooms, drinking water, food service, bathhouse, interpretive hikes, trails, talks and films; **Any limitations on vehicle usage:** Dune buggies, motor bikes, and other motorized vehicles must remain on public roadways; **Hiking trails:** Yes, check at Visitor Center for information on hiking trails in each area; **Backcountry:** No; **Camping:** None available in the National Lakeshore. Private and state campgrounds are nearby. Reservations are accepted for campsites at Indiana Dunes State Park, Chesterton, IN 46304, phone (219) 926-4520; **Other overnight accommodations on site:** No; **Meals served in the park:** Yes, West Beach area (summer only); **Food and supplies obtainable in the park:** Yes, food at West Beach area (summer); **Food and supplies obtainable nearby:** Yes, Porter, Chesterton, Pines, Michigan City, Gary, Portage; **Overnight accommodations:** Many motels available in neighboring communitites; Michigan City, 6 miles (9.7 km); Pines, 3 miles (4.8 km); Portage, 8 miles (13 km); Gary, 12 miles (19 km) from the park; **First Aid available in park:** Yes; **Nearest Hospital:** Michigan City, 6 miles (9.7 km), Gary, 12 miles (19 km); **Days/Hours:** Visitor Center is open from 8 a.m. to 5 p.m. daily, and until 6 p.m. in Summer; **Holiday Closings:** Thanksgiving, Dec. 25 and Jan. 1; **Weather:** 75°-90° temperatures in Summer, 0°-35° and snowy in Winter.

GENERAL INFORMATION: Hunting and open fires are prohibited. Grills and portable stoves using charcoal, gas or liquid fuels are permitted. Private property rights must be respected.

TRAVEL ACCESS: Bus: No; **Rail:** South Shore Line runs regularly to the nearby Dune Park Terminal; **Air:** No.

NEARBY FACILITIES & POINTS OF INTEREST: Parks, other points of interest: Indiana Dunes State Park, Chesterton, IN 46304 (219) 926-4520; **New information:** Maple Sugar Festival held in March. Duneland Harvest Festival held in September.

Lewis and Clark Trail
For details see listing in Illinois

Lincoln Boyhood National Memorial
Lincoln City, Indiana   **SEE CLIMATABLE NO. 60**

MAILING ADDRESS: Superintendent, Lincoln Boyhood National Memorial, Lincoln City, Indiana 47552 **Telephone:** 812-937-4541

DIRECTIONS: The Park is on IN 162, 2 miles (3.2 km) east of Gentryville, 4 miles (6.5 km) south of Dale, IN, and 4 miles (6.5 km) west of Santa Claus, IN. Exit I-64 at Dale (exit 57) South on US 231 to IN 162 east, or Santa Claus (exit 63) to IN 162 west.

On this southern Indiana farm Abraham Lincoln grew from youth to manhood. His mother is buried here. Authorized for addition to the National Park System on Feb. 19, 1962.

VISITOR ACTIVITIES: Visitor Center with memorial halls, museum, and film: burial site of Nancy Hanks Lincoln: Lincoln Living Historical Farm, a working pioneer farm with costumed interpretation; walking trails; group tours available by reservation; **Permits:** No; **Fees:** Yes, $1.00 per person, maximum of $3.00 per family, no charge for children age 12 and under, or for senior citizens age 62 or over; **Visitor facilities:** Memorial Visitor Center (handicapped accessible) with parking, information services, book sales, restrooms, telephone; **Any limitations on vehicle usage:** Parking is at the Visitor Center and Living Historical Farm parking area. Drivers should be alert for hikers, bikers, and the handicapped; **Hiking trails:** Yes, 2 miles (3.2 km) self-guiding trails, including Memorial Trail, Trail of Twelve Stones, and Lincoln Historical Trail; **Backcountry:** No, but adjacent is the 1747-acre Lincoln State Park with 12 miles (19.2 km) of connecting hiking trails; **Camping:** No, but available at adjacent Lincoln State Park; facilities for picnicking, swimming, boating and fishing; **Other overnight accommodations on site:** No; **Meals served in the park:** No; **Food and supplies obtainable in the park:** No; **Food and supplies obtainable nearby:** Yes, in Dale and Santa Claus, IN; **Overnight accommodations:** Dale, 4 miles (6.4 km) north on US 231, Huntingburg, 15 miles (24 km) north and Jasper, 20 miles (32 km) north on US 231; **First Aid available in park:** Yes; **Nearest Hospital:** Huntingburg, 15 miles (24 km) north on US 231; **Days/Hours:** Grounds open daily during daylight hours, year-round; **Holiday Closings:** Thanksgiving, Dec.25 and Jan. 1; **Visitor attractions closed for season:** Farm cabin is open on a limited basis in Winter; **Weather:** Summer is humid with temperatures to 95°; Winter is moderate, but snow and ice storms occur in Jan. & Feb., and roads can be slippery.

GENERAL INFORMATION: The Memorial is on the "Lincoln Heritage Trail," an auto tour route which connects sites relating to Lincoln's life in Kentucky, Indiana and Illinois.

For Your Safety—Stay on established trails. Beware of insects, poison ivy, snakes and farm animals that bite. Pets must be leashed or carried.

NEARBY FACILITIES & POINTS OF INTEREST: Hotel/Motel/Restaurants/ **Campgrounds:** Available nearby, contact park for list; **Parks, other points of interest:** Lincoln State Park (Lincoln-related sites), Col. William Jones House, St. Meinrad Archabbey, Ferdinand State Forest, Hoosier National Forest, Patoka Lake.

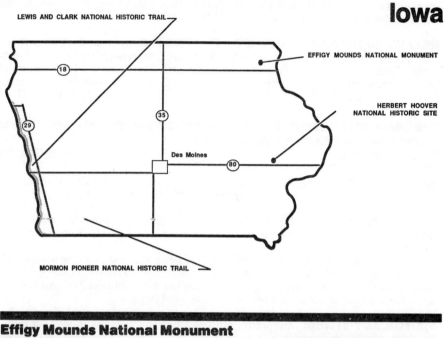

Iowa

LEWIS AND CLARK NATIONAL HISTORIC TRAIL

EFFIGY MOUNDS NATIONAL MONUMENT

HERBERT HOOVER
NATIONAL HISTORIC SITE

Des Moines

MORMON PIONEER NATIONAL HISTORIC TRAIL

Effigy Mounds National Monument
McGregor, Iowa   **SEE CLIMATABLE NO. 62**

MAILING ADDRESS: Superintendent, Effigy Mounds National Monument, Rural Route 1, Box 25A, Harpers Ferry, Iowa 52146 **Telephone:** 319-873-3491

DIRECTIONS: The Monument is 3 miles (5 km) north of Marquette on IA 76.
    The Monument contains outstanding examples of prehistoric burial mounds, some in the shapes of birds and bears. Created by Presidential Proclamation on Oct. 25, 1949.

VISITOR ACTIVITIES: interpretive exhibits, self-guiding and guided walks; **Permits:** No; **Fees:** Federal Entrance Fee Area $1.00 per visit, 12 years and under free; **Visitor facilities:** parking and restrooms at Visitor Center, walking trail, exhibits and markers, guided walks 4 times daily from Memorial Day through Labor Day; **Any limitations on vehicle usage:** There are no roads; **Hiking trails:** Yes, 1-3 hour self-guiding trail; **Backcountry:** No; **Camping:** No; **Other overnight accommodations on site:** No; **Meals served in the park:** No; **Food and supplies obtainable in the park:** No; **Food and supplies obtainable nearby:** Yes, in Waukon and McGregor and Prairie du Chien; **Overnight accommodations:** Waukon, 20 miles (30 km), McGregor, 4 miles (7 km), and Prairie du Chien, WI, 4 miles (7 km); **First Aid available in park:** Yes; **Nearest Hospital:** Prairie du Chien, WI, 4 miles (7 km); **Days/Hours:** Visitor Center open daily from 8 a.m. until 5 p.m. and remains open until 7 p.m. in Summer; **Holiday Closings:** Dec. 25; **Weather:** Summers are warm to hot with moderate-to-high humidity; Winters are cold and snowy with temperatures in the 15°-30° range.

GENERAL INFORMATION: When hiking, stay on trails and do not venture too close to cliff edges. Hikers should remain on the trail and be alert for poison ivy and stinging nettles.

TRAVEL ACCESS: Bus: None; **Air:** Northwest, United, American Eagle, and Mississippi Valley provide daily service to Dubuque, IA; and Mid State Airlines provide daily service to LaCross, WI; **Other:** Taxi available from Prairie du Chien, WI to park. Rental cars available at Dubuque, IA and LaCross, WI airports.

NEARBY FACILITIES & POINTS OF INTEREST: Campgrounds: Yellow River State Forest; Pikes Peak State Park (within 10 miles); **Parks, other points of interest:** Yellow River State Forest, IA; Pikes Peak State Park, IA; Villa Louis, WI (State Historical Society); Stonefield Village, Wisconsin State Historical Society; Governor Dewey State Park, WI; Montauk House, Iowa State Historical Society; Wyalusing State Park, WI.

Herbert Hoover National Historic Site
West Branch, Iowa   **SEE CLIMATABLE NO. 59**

MAILING ADDRESS: Superintendent, Herbert Hoover National Historic Site, P.O. Box 607, West Branch, Iowa 52358 **Telephone:** 319-643-2541

DIRECTIONS: West Branch is 10 miles (16 km) east of Iowa City on I-80 and 40 miles (65 km) west of Davenport on I-80. The Visitor Center is on Parkside Drive at the intersection with Main Street.

The birthplace home, and 19th century (1874-84) boyhood neighborhood of the 31st President, 1929-33, the gravesites of President and Mrs. Hoover, a restored native prairie, and the Hoover Presidential Library-Museum, are within the Park. Authorized for addition to the National Park System on Aug. 12, 1965.

VISITOR ACTIVITIES: Interpretive talks and exhibits, picnicking, walking tours, cross-country skiing; **Permits:** No; **Fees:** National Park Service fee $1.00 adults. National Park Service Passports accepted. The Hoover Presidential Library-Museum is administered by the National Archives and Records Administration, and a $1.00 entrance fee is charged; **Visitor facilities:** parking and restrooms at Visitor Center, picnic areas, walking trails, interpretive exhibits, operating blacksmith in summer; **Any limitations on vehicle usage:** vehicles are restricted to designated roadways; **Hiking trails:** Yes, self-guiding trails; **Backcountry:** No; **Camping:** No; **Other overnight accommodations on site:** No; **Meals served in the park:** No; **Food and supplies obtainable in the park:** No; **Food and supplies obtainable nearby:** Yes, at West Branch; **Overnight accommodations:** West Branch, ½ mile (.8 km); **First Aid available in park:** Yes; **Nearest Hospital:** Iowa City, Iowa, 10 miles (16 km) via I-80; **Days/Hours:** Open 24 hours a day every day, with exception of Thanksgiving, Dec. 25 and Jan. 1. Visitor Center and Birthplace Cottage are open daily from 8 a.m. to 5 p.m., and until 6 p.m. during the summer. The Hoover Presidential Library-Museum is open daily from 9 a.m. to 5 p.m. with the exception of Thanksgiving, Christmas and New Years Day. **Holiday Closings:** Thanksgiving, Dec. 25 & Jan. 1.

GENERAL INFORMATION: Please note the historic walkway surfaces. Boardwalks are especially slippery in frost or wet weather.

Lewis and Clark Trail
For details see listing in Illinois

Kansas

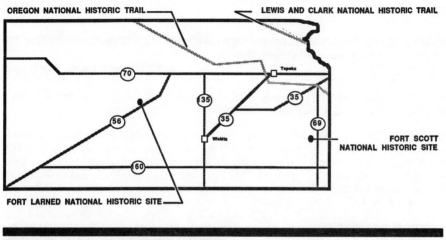

OREGON NATIONAL HISTORIC TRAIL

LEWIS AND CLARK NATIONAL HISTORIC TRAIL

FORT SCOTT NATIONAL HISTORIC SITE

FORT LARNED NATIONAL HISTORIC SITE

Fort Larned National Historic Site
Larned, Kansas   **SEE CLIMATABLE NO. 63**

MAILING ADDRESS: Superintendent, Fort Larned National Historic Site, Route 3, Larned, Kansas 67550 **Telephone:** 316-285-6911

DIRECTIONS: The Site is 6 miles (9.5 km) west of the city of Larned, KS, on KS 156.
A military fort from 1859 to 1878, Fort Larned was used for protection of mail and travellers on the eastern leg of the Santa Fe Trail. It served as an Indian Agency from 1861 to 1868 and a base for military operations against the Southern Plains Indians. Authorized for addition to the National Park System on Aug. 31, 1964; established in 1966.

VISITOR ACTIVITIES: guided tours upon request and daily during Summer, Living history programs on weekends during Summer; **Permits:** No; **Fees:** Scheduled for fees in 1988, pending legislation. $1.00 per adult; 16 and under, free; **Visitor facilities:** parking, restrooms, exhibits, sales area, and audiovisual facilities at Visitor Center; historic military buildings; interpretive signs; **Any limitations on vehicle usage:** Vehicles are only allowed in the parking area, separate picnic area; **Hiking trails:** Yes—1; **Backcountry:** No; **Camping:** No; **Other overnight accommodations on site: No.** Commercial campgrounds are available in Larned. Contact Fort Larned for further information; **Meals served in the park:** No; **Food and supplies obtainable in the park:** No; **Food and supplies obtainable nearby:** Yes, at Larned; **Overnight accommodations:** Larned, 7 miles (11.3 km) on KS 156; **First Aid available in park:** No; **Nearest Hospital:** Larned, 7 miles (11.3 km) East on KS 156; **Days/Hours:** Open year-round. From early June through Labor Day from 8 a.m. to 6 p.m.; the rest of the year from 9 a.m. to 5 p.m.; **Holiday Closings:** Thanksgiving, Dec. 25, Jan. 1; **Visitor attractions closed for season:** Living history programs are offered regularly in Summer, irregularly the remainder of the year; **Weather:** Summer is warm to hot and often windy. Winter is moderately cold; snow possible between late Dec. and early March.

TRAVEL ACCESS: Rail: Amtrak provides daily service to Dodge City; **Air:** Regular service connects Great Bend to Denver, Kansas City, and Wichita and Oklahoma City.

NEARBY FACILITIES & POINTS OF INTEREST: Hotel/Motel: Townsman Inn, 123 E. 14th Larned, KS, 285-3216, 7 miles from park; Country Inn-Motel, 135 E. 14th

Larned KS, 285-3216, 7 miles from park; **Food/Supplies:** Dillon's Family Center, 423 Main, Larned, KS, 285-3171, 7 miles from park; Several other stores available (some 24 hrs); **Parks, other points of interest:** Santa Fe Trail Center, KS 156, 285-2054, 4 miles from park.

Fort Scott National Historic Site
Fort Scott, Kansas   **SEE CLIMATABLE NO. 64**

MAILING ADDRESS: Superintendent, Fort Scott National Historic Site, Old Fort Boulevard, Fort Scott, Kansas 66701 **Telephone:** 316-223-0310

DIRECTIONS: The fort is near the intersection of US 69 and US 54 in Fort Scott, which is 90 miles (144 km) south of Kansas City and 60 miles (97 km) northwest of Joplin, MO.
    The fort commemorates the national significance of the "Permanent Indian Frontier" of 1842-1853; Bleeding Kansas 1853-1861; the Civil War 1861-1865; and the Railroad Years of 1869-1873. This area was authorized for addition to the National Park System on October 19, 1978.

VISITOR ACTIVITIES: tours of reconstructed and restored historic buildings, including 33 furnished rooms, interpretive exhibits, living interpretive demonstrations and special events as scheduled; **Permits:** No; **Fees:** Yes, $1.00 admission for ages 13 through 61, others free; **Visitor facilities:** restrooms, book store, museum; **Any limitations on vehicle usage:** No vehicles are allowed on historic grounds; **Hiking trails:** No; **Backcountry:** No; **Camping:** No; **Other overnight accommodations on site:** No, KOA campground is 2 miles (3 km) from the Site; **Meals served in the park:** No; **Food and supplies obtainable in the park:** No; **Food and supplies obtainable nearby:** Yes, at Fort Scott; **Overnight accommodations:** Fort Scott, 2 blocks to 1 mile (1.6 km) from the Site; **First Aid available in park:** Yes; **Nearest Hospital:** Fort Scott, 1 mile (1.6 km); **Days/ Hours:** Open daily from 8 a.m. to 5 p.m. extended hours of operation 8:00 a.m.-6:00 p.m. June through Labor Day; **Holiday Closings:** Thanksgiving and Dec. 25, and New Years Day; **Visitor attractions closed for seasons:** None; **Weather:** Summers are hot and humid with an average temperature of 80°. Winters are cold; average temperature is 25°.

GENERAL INFORMATION: Restored and furnished buildings open to public include post headquarters, barracks, post hospital, bakery, guardhouse, officer's quarters, dragoon stables, quartermaster storehouse and powder magazine. Introductory audio visual program available at visitor center. A wide range of interpretive activities and special events is scheduled from May through October. Write for details.

TRAVEL ACCESS: **Bus:** Trailways Bus System provides daily service to/from Kansas City, Missouri; **Rail:** None; **Air:** None; **Other:** Independent Taxi Service in Fort Scott— City Cab Company (223-5720) and Dee's Cab (223-3270).

NEARBY FACILITIES & POINTS OF INTEREST: **Hotel/Motel:** Best Western-Fort Scott Inn, 101 State Street 316-223-0100, 1/4 mile from park; Downtowner Motor Hotel, 2 South National, 316-223-3500, 1/8 mile from park; **Parks, other points of interest:** National Cemetery, Ralph Richards Museum, Gunn Park City recreational facility, picnic areas and fishing, Victorian homes tour.

Oregon National Scenic Trail
For details see listing in Missouri

Kentucky

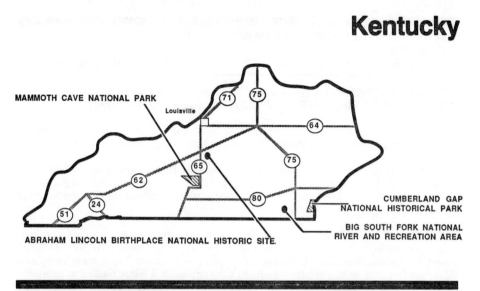

MAMMOTH CAVE NATIONAL PARK

Louisville

CUMBERLAND GAP
NATIONAL HISTORICAL PARK

BIG SOUTH FORK NATIONAL
RIVER AND RECREATION AREA

ABRAHAM LINCOLN BIRTHPLACE NATIONAL HISTORIC SITE.

Abraham Lincoln Birthplace National Historic Site
Hodgenville, Kentucky   **SEE CLIMATABLE NO. 65**

MAILING ADDRESS: Superintendent, Abraham Lincoln Birthplace National Historic Site, Route 1, Hodgenville, Kentucky 42748 **Telephone:** 502-358-3874

DIRECTIONS: The Site is 3 miles (4.8 km) south of Hodgenville on US 31E and KY 61, 60 miles (96 km) south of Louisville.

Established by act of Congress on July 17, 1916, this 116.50-acre historic site preserves in its Memorial Building an early 19th-century Kentucky cabin, symbolic of the one in which Lincoln was born.

VISITOR ACTIVITIES: interpretive talks, exhibits and films, hiking, picnicking; **Permits:** No; **Fees:** No; **Visitor facilities:** parking at Visitor Center, parking and restrooms at picnic area, environmental study area; **Any limitations on vehicle usage:** Restricted to designated roadways & parking areas; **Hiking trails:** Yes, through forest land; **Backcountry:** No; **Camping:** No; **Other overnight accommodations on site:** No; **Meals served in the park:** No, but available in Hodgenville; **Food and supplies obtainable in the park:** No; **Food and supplies obtainable nearby:** Yes, in Hodgenville; **Overnight accommodations:** Motels are adjacent to the park; **First Aid available in park:** Yes, and nearby in Hodgenville, US 31E; **Nearest Hospital:** Elizabethtown, KY 61, 12 miles (20 km); **Days/Hours:** Open daily from 8 a.m. to 6:45 p.m. from Early June-Labor Day, September, October, April, May, 8 a.m.-5:45 p.m.; 8 a.m. to 4:45 p.m. remainder of the year; Schedule subject to change. **Holiday Closings:** Christmas Day; **Visitor attractions closed for season:** None; **Weather:** Warm Summers with frequent rain; moderate Winters with light snow.

GENERAL INFORMATION: *For Your Safety*—Watch for exposed roots and uneven ground along trails. Poison ivy and briars are abundant in woodland. Handicap Access.

Big South Fork National River and Recreation Area
For details see listing in Tennessee

Cumberland Gap National Historical Park
Middlesboro, Kentucky
(also in Tennessee and Virginia)   **SEE CLIMATABLE NO. 66**

MAILING ADDRESS: Superintendent, Cumberland Gap National Historical Park, P.O. Box 1848, Middlesboro, Kentucky 40965 **Telephone:** 606-248-2817

DIRECTIONS: The Park can be reached by taking US 25E from Kentucky and Tennessee or US 58 from Virginia. The Visitor Center is ½ mile (.8 km) south of Middlesboro on US 25E.
　　The mountain pass in the wilderness, explored by Daniel Boone, developed into a main artery of the great trans-Allegheny migration for settlement of "the Old West" and an important military objective in the Civil War. Authorized for addition to the National Park System on June 11, 1940.

VISITOR ACTIVITIES: interpretive and audiovisual exhibits, hiking, camping, picnicking, campfire programs, walking, music and craft demonstrations, living history programs, fishing; **Permits:** for backcountry, available from the Superintendent; **Fees:** $7.00 for camping in the Wilderness Road Campground; **Visitor facilities:** primitive and developed campgrounds, hiking trails, restrooms, picnic areas, drinking water, museum; **Any limitations on vehicle usage:** Off-road vehicle use is not permitted; 20-foot maximum vehicle length on Pinnacle road; **Hiking trails:** Yes, there are about 50 miles (80 km) of hiking trails in the Park. Trail guides and information are available at the Visitor Center; **Backcountry:** Yes, get information from the Superintendent; **Camping:** Yes, organized group camping area and primitive campsites are reserved by contacting the Superintendent. No other reservations are available; **Other overnight accommodations on site:** No; **Meals served in the park:** No; **Food and supplies obtainable in the park:** No; **Food and supplies obtainable nearby:** Yes, in Middlesboro, KY, Cumberland Gap, TN, Gibson Station and Ewing, VA; **Overnight accommodations:** Middlesboro, KY, US 25E, several blocks; Cumberland Gap, TN, US 25E 2½ miles (4 km); Harrogate, TN, US 25E, 4 miles (6.4 km); **First Aid available in park:** Yes; **Nearest Hospital:** Middlesboro, KY, US 25E to Hwy 74, 1 mile (1.6 km); **Days/Hours:** Park gates are open from 8 a.m. to dusk year-round. The Visitor Center is open from 8 a.m. to 5 p.m.; **Holiday Closings:** Dec. 25; **Visitor attractions closed for season:** Pinnacle can be closed temporarily due to snow; **Weather:** Summer is hot and humid; Winter is cold to moderate.

GENERAL INFORMATION: *For Your Safety*—Never hike alone. Beware of snakes, poison ivy and poison oak. Nearby points of interest include Cudjo's Cave; the June Tolliver House at Big Stone Gap, VA; Lincoln Memorial University in Harrogate, TN; Pine Mountain State Park, KY; and Dr. Thomas Walker State Park, near Barbourville, KY. Directions and further information on these sites are available at the Middlesboro Visitor Center.

TRAVEL ACCESS: Bus: Greyhound provides daily service within 2 miles of park; **Rail:** No; **Air:** Airport at Knoxville, Tennessee 60 miles south.

NEARBY FACILITIES & POINTS OF INTEREST: Hotel/Motel: Holiday Inn, Cumberland Gap Tennessee 615-869-3631 3 miles from Park; **Campgrounds:** Pine Mountain State Park Campground; **Parks, other points of interest:** Pine Mountain State Park.

Mammoth Cave National Park
Mammoth Cave, Kentucky   **SEE CLIMATABLE NO. 65**

MAILING ADDRESS: Superintendent, Mammoth Cave National Park, Mammoth Cave, Kentucky 42259 **Telephone:** 502-758-2251

DIRECTIONS: Visitor Center (which includes cave tour information and ticket sales) is 9 miles (14.5 km) northwest of Park City off Interstate 65 via KY 255 or 70, and 10 miles (16 km) west of Cave City off Interstate 65 via Highway 70.

Mammoth Cave is a series of underground passageways containing travertine and gypsum formations, deep pits and high domes and an underground river. Over 300 miles (480 km) of interconnected passageways have been surveyed and mapped, making it the longest recorded cave system in the world. Authorized for addition to the National Park System on May 25, 1926. Selected as a world heritage site Oct. 27, 1981.

VISITOR ACTIVITIES: guided cave tours, guided nature walks and evening programs in Summer, self-guiding walking trails, camping, picnicking, boating, fishing, backcountry hiking, and Green River boat trip; **Permits:** for backcountry camping, available at Park Headquarters or campground station; **Fees:** for cave tours, Green River boat trip, and camping in the main campground. Cave tours vary in length (1¼ to 6 hours), season offered and time of departure. Green River boat trip available April through Oct. For a description of tours available, current tour schedule and prices, contact the Superintendent or Ticketron agent; **Visitor facilities:** Visitor Center, hiking trails, picnic area, boat ramps, post office, service station, campgrounds, groceries and camping supplies, coin-operated laundry, showers, lodging, dining room and coffee shop, souvenirs and Green River boat trip; **Any limitations on vehicle usage:** Off road vehicles prohibited, trail bikes permitted only on public roads; **Hiking trails:** Yes, Variety of hiking trails available ranging from short self-guiding nature trails to several miles of hiking trails. Trail information at Visitor Center; **Backcountry:** Yes, information available at Visitor Center or by contacting the Superintendent. Backcountry camping permit required and may be obtained at the Park Headquarters or campground station; **Camping:** Yes, no reservations accepted for the 108 individual campsites (2 sites modified to accommodate handicapped). Camping fee is $6 per night per site. A free campground with 12 sites is at Hounchins Ferry. A group campsite available by reservation through chief ranger's office; **Other overnight accommodations on site:** Yes, Mammoth Cave Hotel is open all year. For reservations, contact National Park Concessions, Inc., Mammoth Cave, KY 42259, phone 502-758-2225; **Meals served in the park:** Yes, at Mammoth Cave Hotel; **Food and supplies obtainable in the park:** Yes, at the service center located next to the main campground. The store is closed from Thanksgiving to Easter Week and is only open on weekends, including Fridays in the Spring and Fall; **Food and supplies obtainable nearby:** Yes, at Bowling Green, Glasgow, Horse Cave, Park City, Brownsville, and Cave City; **Overnight accommodations:** Numerous overnight accommodations are available within a 15-45 minute drive of the park which includes the communities of Bowling Green, Glasgow, Horse Cave, Park City and Cave City. For information on areas outside the park write the Department of Public Information, Capitol Annex Building, Frankfort, KY 40601; **First Aid available in park:** Yes; **Nearest Hospital:** Caverna Hospital at Horse Cave, US 31W, 15 miles (24 km); **Days/Hours:** Open year-round; Visitor Center open 7:30 a.m.-7 p.m. in Summer; 8 a.m.-5:20 p.m. the rest of the year; **Holiday Closings:** Cave tours available year-round except Dec. 25; **Visitor attractions closed for season:** Main campground open year-round.

GENERAL INFORMATION: In the caves the temperature remains at 12°C (54°F) and the humidity is a high 87%. Bring along a sweater or light jacket. Some cave tours are strenuous, requiring stooping, ascending and descending steps and walking over unlevel terrain. Be sure to select the tour that best meets your physical ability. Portions of cave and surface trails are uneven and wet and slippery, so wear sturdy walking shoes—not sandals. Children under 16 years of age must be accompanied by an adult. Tours are available for the disabled. While driving, be on the alert for deer crossing the roadway, particularly at night. Poisonous snakes and poison ivy are common, even around the most heavily visited areas.

TRAVEL ACCESS: Bus: Greyhound provides service to Cave City, KY, 10 miles away; **Rail:** None: **Air:** Access to Nashville and Louisville, both about 90 miles away. Local airports at Glasgow 18 miles; Bowling Green 35 miles—private aircraft.

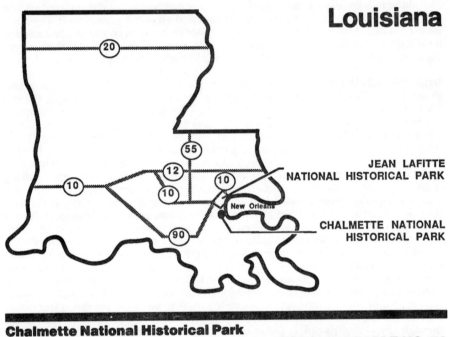

Louisiana

JEAN LAFITTE
NATIONAL HISTORICAL PARK

CHALMETTE NATIONAL
HISTORICAL PARK

Chalmette National Historical Park
Chalmette, Louisiana   **SEE CLIMATABLE NO. 70**

MAILING ADDRESS: Unit Manager, Chalmette National Historical Park, 8606 West St. Bernard Highway, Chalmette, LA 70043 **Telephone:** 504-589-4428

DIRECTIONS: The Park is in St. Bernard Parish on the east bank of the Mississippi River, 6 miles (9.7 km) from the heart of New Orleans. From Canal Street follow the main thoroughfare that begins at Rampart Street and merges into St. Claude Avenue, then into St. Bernard Hwy., which passes directly in front of the Park. The riverboats 'Creole Queen' and 'Voyageur' offer daily cruises to the battlefield from downtown New Orleans.

America won a brilliant victory here in the Battle of New Orleans in the War of 1812. The Park includes Chalmette National Cemetery. Established by act of Congress on Mar. 4, 1907. Administered by Jean Lafitte National Historical Park.

VISITOR ACTIVITIES: audiovisual and interpretive exhibits, auto tours, walking and self-guiding tours. Living History—War of 1812 soldiers, June-Aug., weekends—Spring and Fall; **Permits:** No; **Fees:** No; **Visitor facilities:** exhibits, parking, restrooms; **Any limitations on vehicle usage:** Vehicles are restricted to designated roadways; **Hiking trails:** No; **Backcountry:** No; **Camping:** No; **Other overnight accommodations on**

site: No; **Meals served in the park:** No; **Food and supplies obtainable in the park:** No; **Food and supplies obtainable nearby:** Yes, in the town of Chalmette, within a 1/2 mile; **Overnight accommodations:** New Orleans and vicinity, approx. 5 miles (8 km); **First Aid available in park:** Yes: **Nearest Hospital:** Chalmette, LA, LA 46, 3 miles (4.8 km); **Days/Hours:** Open daily 8 a.m. to 5 p.m., open 8:00 a.m. to 6:00 p.m. from Memorial Day to Labor Day; **Holiday Closings:** Dec. 25, and Mardi Gras; **Visitor attractions closed for seasons:** None; **Weather:** Hot humid Summers, mild Winters.

Jean Lafitte National Historical Park
New Orleans, Louisiana   **SEE CLIMATABLE NO. 70**

MAILING ADDRESS: Jean Lafitte National Historical Park, U.S. Customs House, 423 Canal Street, Room 210, New Orleans, Louisiana 70130-2341

DIRECTIONS: Please note that the park consists of 3 different units located in separate sectors of the Greater New Orleans area.

French Quarter Unit: Visitor and Folklife Center is located in the French Market on Decatur Street.

Chalmette Unit: Located 6 miles from downtown; follow N. Rampart Street east until it merges with St. Claude Avenue. Continue until St. Claude merges with the St. Bernard Highway (LA 46), which passes directly in front of the park.

Barataria Unit: Located on the West Bank of the Mississippi River, 40 minutes from downtown. Take Route 90 across the Greater New Orleans Bridge, then continue on 90 (which becomes the West Bank Expressway) to Barataria Boulevard (LA highway 45). Turn left (south) on 45, and continue 7.5 miles until you see signs for Barataria.

The Park was established to preserve and interpret the cultural diversity of the Mississippi Delta region. Authorized for addition to the National Park Service on November 10, 1978.

VISITOR ACTIVITIES: *French Quarter Unit:* Ranger-guided walking tours, audiovisual and interpretive exhibits. New Visitor and Folklife Center features performances and demonstrations by traditional artists, craftspeople, and musicians of the Mississippi Delta region. *Chalmette Unit:* Interpretive talks presented by rangers, audiovisual and interpretive exhibits, 1 self-guiding tour road. *Barataria Unit:* Visitor Center containing audiovisual and interpretive exhibits. Guided and self-guided walking tours, canoeing, fishing. **Permits:** Barataria Unit requires Park permit and State License for hunting and State License for fishing. **Fees:** No; **Visitor facilities:** French Quarter: exhibits and audiovisual programs. Chalmette: Exhibits and audiovisual programs, parking, restrooms, and picnic tables. Barataria: Parking, restroom, and picnic tables; **Any limitations on vehicle usage:** Vehicles are restricted to designated roadways; **Hiking trails:** Yes, Bayou Coquille Trail and Ring Levee Trail are open in the Barataria Unit; **Backcountry:** No; **Camping:** No; **Other overnight accommodations on site:** No; **Meals served in the park:** No; **Food and supplies obtainable nearby:** Yes, there are many excellent restaurants in the French Quarter and throughout New Orleans; **Overnight accommodations:** Yes, throughout the Greater New Orleans area; **First Aid available in park:** Yes; **Nearest Hospitals:** French Quarter Unit: Charity, Hotel Dieu, Touro. Chalmette Unit: De La Ronde and Chalmette General. Barataria Unit: West Jefferson Medical Center, in Marrero; **Days/Hours:** French Quarter Unit is open from 9:00 a.m. to 5:00 p.m. daily, closed Christmas and Mardi Gras days. Chalmette Unit is open daily. with extended summer hours. Barataria Unit is open daily with extended summer hours; **Holiday Closings:** French Quarter and Chalmette Units only, Dec. 25, Jan 1, and Mardi Gras; **Visitor attractions closed for seasons:** No.

GENERAL INFORMATION: Summers are hot and humid, winters are mild. Heavy rain showers can occur through the year.

Maine

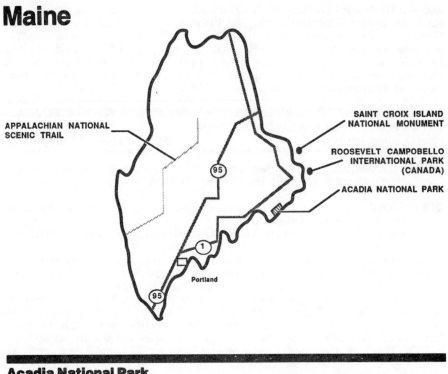

SAINT CROIX ISLAND
NATIONAL MONUMENT

APPALACHIAN NATIONAL
SCENIC TRAIL

ROOSEVELT CAMPOBELLO
INTERNATIONAL PARK
(CANADA)

ACADIA NATIONAL PARK

Portland

Acadia National Park
Bar Harbor, Maine   **SEE CLIMATABLE NO. 71**

MAILING ADDRESS: Superintendent, Acadia National Park, Box 177, Bar Harbor, Maine 04069 **Telephone:** 207-288-3338

DIRECTIONS: The Park is located on ME 3, 47 miles (75 km) southeast of Bangor, ME. Schoodic Penninsula, the only part of the Park on the mainland, is accessible via ME 186.
     Set aside in 1916 and declared a national park in 1919, it combines unusual ocean and mountain scenery over 40 square miles of Mount Desert Island, the mainland Schoodic Peninsula, Isle au Haut, and several smaller islands.

VISITOR ACTIVITIES: 27-mile scenic drive connects lakes, mountains, and seashore; carriage paths open to hikers, bicycles and horses; foot trails; museums on mainland and Little Cranberry Island; frequent showing of a film at the Visitor Center; naturalist programs; boat cruises; **Permits:** No; **Fees:** Park entrance fee collected approx. May 1-Nov. 1, $5/car/week, for boat cruises, the fee ranges from $5.00- $9.00 for adults and $4.00-$5.00 for children under 12. Prices are subject to change; **Visitor facilities:** beaches, campgrounds, museums, nature walks, campfire programs, audiovisual and interpretive programs, cassette tape tours, rental horses, picnic areas, bathhouse; **Any limitations on vehicle usage:** Vehicles are confined to established roadways; no motorized vehicles on carriage roads; **Hiking trails:** Yes, there are more than 120 miles (192 km) of hiking trails; **Backcountry:** no backcountry camping; day use only; **Camping:** Yes, two campgrounds are available in the Park, and there are numerous private campgrounds in the area. Camping at park campgrounds is limited to 14 days; **Other overnight accommodations on site:** No; **Meals served in the park:** Yes; **Food and supplies obtainable in the park:** No; **Food and supplies obtainable nearby:** Yes, Bar Harbor, Northeast Harbor, Southwest Habor, Ellsworth; **Overnight accommodations:** Bar Harbor, ME, 3 miles (4.8 km); Northeast Harbor, ME 3, 14 miles (22.5 km); Ellsworth, ME 3, 20 miles (32 km); Southwest Harbor, ME 3, 18 miles (29 km); **First Aid available in park:** Yes; **Nearest Hospital:** Bar Harbor, ME 3, 3 miles (4.8 km); **Days/Hours:** Open year-round. Visitor Center is open from May 1-Oct. 31, 7 days; 8 a.m. to 4:30 p.m. and 8 a.m. to 6 p.m. in Spring/Fall; 8 a.m. to 8 p.m. in Summer. Visitor Center hours subject to change; **Holiday Closings:** The park is always open, but the Park Headquarters building closes on Thanksgiving, Christmas & New Years Day; **Visitor attractions closed for seasons:** Visitor Center, Nature Center, Museum, major portions of Park Loop Road is not plowed in winter; **Weather:** Cool Summers and fog are common, low temperature 55°-60°, high temperature 68°-75°.

GENERAL INFORMATION: *For Your Safety*—Be particularly careful on the rugged shores of Acadia. Ledges and rocks below high tide are slippery with algae, so walk carefully. Watch out for storm waves, particulary in spring and autumn. Occasionally an unusually large wave reaches far up on the ledge or beach—it could knock you down and sweep you into the sea. Watch the trail when hiking, to avoid poison ivy or falling loose stones. If you find one trail too steep or precarious, choose another.

TRAVEL ACCESS: Bus: Greyhound may operate between Bangar & Bar Harbor during the summer months. Call 617-423-5810 for current information; **Rail:** None; **Air:** Bar Harbor Airlines daily service to Bar Harbor Airport 10 miles from Bar Harbor; **Other:** Downeast Transportation, Inc. operates local public transportation, Gooch's Taxi Service of Bar Harbor, and Ralph Savage, Summer Taxi of Northeast Harbor also service the Park. Bike rentals in Bar Harbor & Southwest Harbor. Bus tours from Bar Harbor.

NEARBY FACILITIES & POINTS OF INTEREST: Hotel/Motel: Contact Chamber of Commerce, Bar Harbor, 04069; Southwest Harbor, 04679; Northeast Harbor, 04662; **Campgrounds:** Eleven private campgrounds outside the park. **Reservation system in use for campsites, other facilities:** Seawall open from late May to late Sept. on a first come basis. Blackwoods open year-round. Operates on a Ticketron reservation system from mid-June to mid-September (subject to change). Contact headquarters for reservation changes.

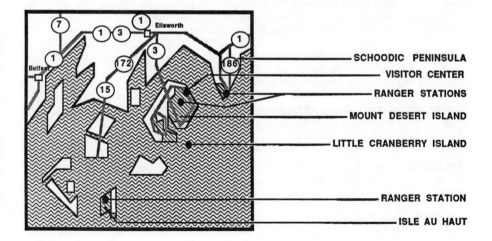

Appalachian National Scenic Trail

Maine, New Hampshire, Vermont, Massachusetts, Connecticut, New York, New Jersey, Pennsylvania, Maryland, West Virginia, Virginia, Tennessee, North Carolina, and Georgia   **SEE CLIMATABLE MAP**

MAILING ADDRESS: Appalachian Trail Conference, P.O. Box 807, Harpers Ferry, West Virginia 25425 **Telephone:** 304-535-6331

DIRECTIONS: Contact the Appalachian Trail Conference for detailed information on directions to the Trail.

Approximately 2,099 miles (3,358 km) of this scenic trail follow the Appalachian Mountains from Mount Katahdin, ME through to Springer Mountain, GA. The trail is one of the two initial units of the National Trail System. Designated by act of Congress on Oct. 2, 1968; completed by volunteers, Aug. 14, 1937.

VISITOR ACTIVITIES: short- and long-term hiking, camping, bird- and wildlife-watching, backcountry; **Permits:** A permit is not required to hike the Trail, but camping permits are necessary in the Shenandoah National Park and Great Smoky Mountains National Park. These permits are available at ranger stations upon arrival. See listings on these parks in this book for information on facilities and reservations. Camping facilities are also available at Green Mountain National Forest, VT; White Mountain National Forest, NH; and Baxter State Park, ME; **Fees:** At certain Northeast campsites, a $2 fee per site for 98 miles (158 km) through Long Trail Area, VT; **Visitor facilities:** lean-to shelters, fire pits, picnic tables; **Any limitations on vehicle usage:** Motor vehicles are prohibited on hiking trails; **Hiking trails:** Yes, some circuit hikes (blue blazed). Guide books with maps may be ordered from address above; **Backcountry:** Yes, Contact the Appalachian Trail Conference, P.O. Box 807, Harpers Ferry, WV 25425, phone 304-535-6331; **Camping:** Yes, no reservations available for campsites; **Other overnight accommodations on site:** There are youth hostels, church- related hostels, and other sleeping accommodations along certain sections of the Appalachian Trail. Guidebooks describe. **Meals served in the park:** Only in some national parks along the trail. Hikers have regular food drop points at post offices near the trail; **Food and supplies obtainable in the park:** No; **Food and supplies obtainable nearby:** Yes, stores are often located near major road crossings. Hut system operates in White Mountains, providing shelter and food at higher fee; **Overnight accommodations:** Accommodations are generally available at nearby towns; **First Aid available in park:** No; **Nearest Hospital:** In most of the larger nearby towns; **Days/Hours:** Park never closes.

GENERAL INFORMATION: Most long-distance hikers start in March or April and take 4 to 5 months to hike the entire trail, mostly from south to north. Primary use of trail is by weekend or short-distance hikers.

Saint Croix Island International Historic Site

Red Beach, Maine   **SEE CLIMATABLE NO. 71**

MAILING ADDRESS: Superintendent, Saint Croix Island International Historic Site, c/o Acadia National Park, Box 177, Bar Harbor, Maine 04609 **Telephone:** 207-288-3338.

DIRECTIONS: The site is 120 miles (193 km) north of Bar Harbor. It is 12 miles (19 km) south of Calais, Maine along US 1. There is currently no ferry service to the island.

The attempted French settlement of 1604, which led to the founding of New

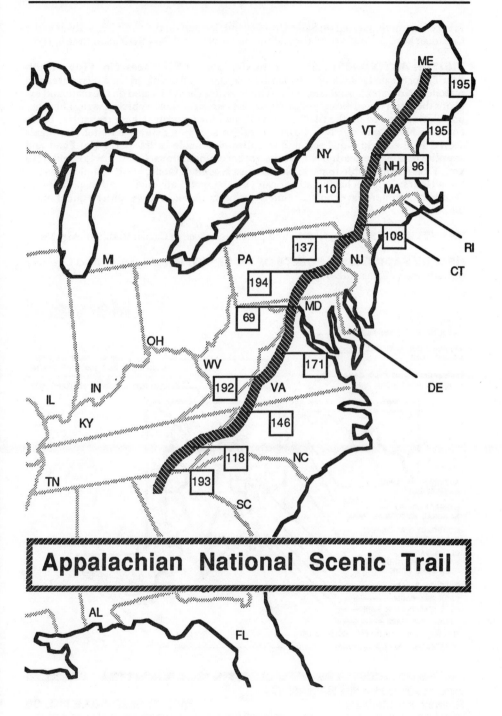

Appalachian National Scenic Trail

France is commemorated on Saint Croix Island, located on the Saint Croix River at the Canadian border. Authorized for addition to the National Park System on June 8, 1949.

VISITOR ACTIVITIES: walking, picnicking; **Permits:** No; **Fees:** No; **Visitor facilities:** There are no facilities on the island at this time. The mainland has a picnic area and pit toilets. No water is available. A small interpretive shelter located on the mainland explains the historic significance of St. Croix; **Any limitations on vehicle usage:** There are no vehicles allowed on the island. It is reached only by boat; **Hiking trails:** No; **Backcountry:** No; **Camping:** No; **Other overnight accommodations on site:** No; **Meals served in the park:** No; **Food and supplies obtainable in the park:** No; **Food and supplies obtainable nearby:** No; **Overnight accommodations:** Calais, US 1, 12 miles (19 km); **First Aid available in park:** No; **Nearest Hospital:** Calais, US 1, 12 miles (19 km); **Days/Hours:** Persons having a boat can visit the island anytime, weather permitting; **Weather:** Summers have cool maritime air, winters are cold and wet with frequent snowfall.

TRAVEL ACCESS: Bus: Greyhound provides service to Calais; **Rail:** No; **Air:** No.

NEARBY FACILITIES & POINTS OF INTEREST: Hotel/Motel: Contact Chamber of Commerce, Calais, ME 04619.

Maryland

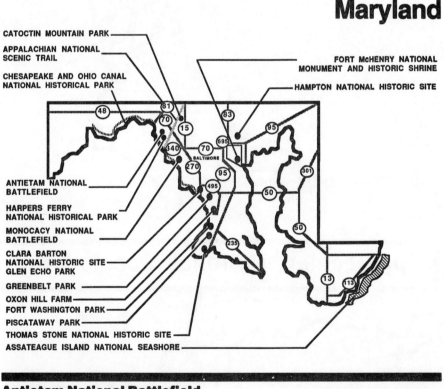

Antietam National Battlefield
Sharpsburg, Maryland   **SEE CLIMATABLE NO. 68**

MAILING ADDRESS: Superintendent, Antietam National Battlefield, P.O. Box 158, Sharpsburg, Maryland 21782 **Telephone:** 301-432-5124

DIRECTIONS: The Site is 11 miles south of Hagerstown off MD 65.

Established by Act of Congress on Aug. 30, 1890, this site marks the end of General Robert E. Lee's first invasion of the North in Sept. 1862, a battle which claimed over 23,000 casualties in one single day, Sept. 17, 1862.

VISITOR ACTIVITIES: 26-minute film shown on the hour, Civil War exhibits, self-conducted auto tours (rental taped tours available), hike or bike the 8-1/2 mile (13.6 km) tour road; **Permits:** No; **Fees:** $1.00 per person (No fee under age 13 or 62 and over); **Visitor facilities:** Visitor Center with observation deck, exhibit and display room, audiovisual orientation programs, taped tour or self-guiding auto tours (in your vehicle); historic & nature trail; **Any limitations on vehicle usage:** Vehicles are confined to parking area and park roads; **Hiking trails:** nature and historic; **Backcountry:** No; **Camping:** No; **Other overnight accommodations on site:** Bed & Breakfast (commercial) nearby; **Meals served in the park:** No; **Food and supplies obtainable in the park:** No; **Food and supplies obtainable nearby:** Yes, in Sharpsburg, 1 mile (1.6 km); **Nearest Hospital:** Hagerstown, MD, 12 miles (19 km); **Days/Hours:** Open daily 8:30 a.m. to 5 p.m.; Summer hours are 8 a.m. to 6 p.m.; **Holiday Closings:** Thanksgiving, Dec. 25, Jan. 1; **Visitor attractions closed for season:** Historic church and wayside audio stations not open in Winter (Nov.-Mar.).

GENERAL INFORMATION: *For your Safety*—Motorists should be aware of speed limits, one-way roads, pedestrians, and bicyclists. Motor vehicle drivers. . .stop and pull to road shoulder or designated parking area while reading interpretive signs along the tour road.

Appalachian National Scenic Trail
For details see listing in Maine

Assateague Island National Seashore
Maryland and Virginia   **SEE CLIMATABLE NO. 72**

MAILING ADDRESS: Superintendent, Assateague Island National Seashore, Route 2, Box 294, Berlin, Maryland 21811 **Telephone:** 301-641-1441 (MD) or 804-336-6577 (VA District Office).

DIRECTIONS: Via US 50, the Seashore is about 150 miles (241 km) from Baltimore or Washington. Via US 13 and 113, it is about 140 miles (224 km) from Philadelphia and 90 miles (145 km) from Norfolk. Visitor facilities are located at the extreme ends of Assateague Island—on the north end near Ocean City, MD and on the south opposite Chincoteague, VA. More than 22 miles (35 km) of roadless barrier island beach and marsh lie between these developed areas. To get from one end of the island to the other, visitors must drive back onto the mainland.

This 37 mile (60 km) barrier island has a sandy beach, pine forests, salt marsh, many kinds of waterfowl and other birds, and a variety of mammals including wild ponies. Most of the Virginia portion consists of the Chincoteague Island National Wildlife Refuge which was established in 1943. Most of the Maryland section was authorized for addition to the National Park System on Sept. 21, 1965.

VISITOR ACTIVITIES: surf fishing, clamming, crabbing, canoeing, hiking, bird-watching, camping, swimming, interpretive programs in Summer, shell collecting, hunting, pony round-up and auction on the last Wednesday and Thursday of July; **Permits:** Oversand vehicle permits required for oversand use. Backcountry permits required; permits for night surf fishing required in Virginia; **Fees:** For camping, entrance and oversand vehicle permits. Camping is $5.00 per night. (Now charged the year-round.) Entrance fee in Maryland is $3 per vehicle, good for 7 days. Entrance fee in Virginia is $3 per vehicle, 7 days. Golden Eagle/Age/Access passports apply in both states. Oversand vehicle permits are $30 each year. Assateague State Park camping fees are $15, but the facilities are more modern; **Visitor facilities:** campgrounds and canoe launch in Maryland, picnic areas, bathhouses, lifeguarded beaches in Summer, wildlife refuge, self-guided nature trails, crabbing, Visitor Centers with exhibits; **Any limitations on vehicle usage:** Vehicles must be registered and licensed; all vehicles must stay on marked routes; motorcycles are restricted to hard surfaced roads. Oversand vehicles must have a permit before using the oversand routes. Potential users of oversand routes should contact the park for information on required equipment; **Hiking trails:** Yes, short self-guiding nature trails in both state sections; **Backcountry:** Yes, both hike-in and canoe-in are available. Contact the park or the Visitor Center; **Camping:** Yes, primitive campsites only in Maryland. No reservations for most campsites. Some state park campsites may be reserved in Summer for a full week only; **Other overnight accommodations on site:** No; **Meals served in the park:** No, but at Assateague State Park, only in Summer; **Food and supplies obtainable in the park:** No; **Food and supplies obtainable nearby:** Yes, Berlin, MD and Chincoteague, VA; **Overnight accommodations:** Chincoteague, VA, 5 miles (8 km); Ocean City, MD, Rte 611, 7 miles (11.3 km); **First Aid available in park:** Yes, or nearby in Chincoteague, VA, Berlin & Ocean City, MD; **Nearest Hospital:** Salisbury, MD, Rte 50 or US 13, approximately 35 miles (72 km) from each end of the island; **Days/Hours:** Virginia section open from 4 a.m.-10 p.m. with shorter hours in Winter. Maryland section open 24 hours with certain exceptions. Contact the seashore for details on hours of operation; **Holiday Closings:** Visitor Center closed Thanksgiving, Dec. 25 & Jan. 1; **Visitor attractions closed for seasons:** Maryland National Park Service family campgrounds limited from Nov. to mid-Apr.; **Weather:** Summers can be hot & humid with many biting insects. Spring and Autumn offer brisk nights and placid days, allowing a chance to avoid the crowds.

GENERAL INFORMATION: *For Your Safety*—Swim where there are lifeguards; avoid swimming in heavy surf and do not use air mattresses or flotation devices. Seek shelter during lightning. Beware of sunburn and wear shoes in the campgrounds; do not approach ponies; guard against mosquitoes, ticks, and poison ivy. Backcountry canoeing and hiking has its own set of hazards; review the backcountry folders.

Visitors are discouraged from bringing pets, which are prohibited in most areas of the Seashore. The hot, blowing sand and saltwater are hard on dog's feet and eyes.

TRAVEL ACCESS: Bus: Trailways provides daily service to Ocean City, MD and T's Corner, VA; **Rail:** None; **Air:** Piedmont Commuter service daily to Salisbury, MD. **Other:** bicycles may be rented in Chincoteague, VA and Ocean City, MD.

NEARBY FACILITIES & POINTS OF INTEREST: For commercial information on hotels and campgrounds contact: Ocean City Chamber of Commerce, Rt. 2, Box 310A, Ocean City, MD 21842 (301) 289-8559; Chincoteague Chamber of Commerce, Chincoteague, VA 23336 (804) 336-6161; **Parks, other points of interest:** Pocomoke River State Park, MD; Trap Pond State Park, Del.; **Reservations system in use for campsites, other facilities:** Reserve sites for 7-day periods only in Assateague State Park, Rt. 2, Box 293, Berlin, MD 21811; **New park programs:** Canoeing, surf-fishing, clamming and crabbing interpretive demonstrations done during summer.

Catoctin Mountain Park
Thurmont, Maryland   **SEE CLIMATABLE NO. 69**

MAILING ADDRESS: Superintendent, Catoctin Mountain Park, Thurmont, Maryland 21788 **Telephone:** 301-663-9330

DIRECTIONS: Catoctin is located in the foothills of the Blue Ridge Mountains. From Rte 15 take Rte 77 west for approximately 3 miles (4.8 km). The Visitor Center is on the right.

In 1936 more than 10,000 acres were acquired by the Federal Government and developed to demonstrate the possibilities of creating parks from wornout land. In 1954 the area was divided into two parts, separated by Rte 77. The Federal Government retained the area to the north (Catoctin Mountain Park) and the remaining acreage was deeded to the State of Maryland to be managed for recreational use (Cunningham Falls State Park).

VISITOR ACTIVITIES: hiking, auto tour, camping, picnicking, exhibits, Spring wildflower walks, campfire programs, family walks, children walks, fishing, horseback riding, rock climbing, cross-country skiing, demonstration of whiskey-making; **Permits:** for the use of Adirondack (hike-in) shelters and for rock-climbing. Both permits available free of charge at the Visitor Center; **Fees:** $6.00 per night camping fee at Owens Creek campground; **Visitor facilities:** self-guiding trails, picnic areas, bridle trail, craft center, hike-in camp shelters; **Any limitations on vehicle usage:** Motorized vehicles and bicycles are restricted to roads; **Hiking trails:** Yes, hiking is permitted on over 30 miles (48 km) of trails; **Backcountry:** Yes, information can be obtained from the Visitor Center; **Camping:** Yes, no reservations accepted for individual campsites; **Other overnight accommodations on site:** Yes, two large Environmental Education Cabin Camps are rented to groups of 60 or more people. They are reserved through applications taken between Dec. 1 and Dec. 15 for Long Term Groups, between Jan. 1 and Jan. 30 for Spring Weekend Groups, and between May 1 and May 30 for Fall Weekend Groups. Individual family cabins are also for rent at Camp Misty Mount April-October; **Meals served in the park:** No; **Food and supplies obtainable in the park:** No; **Food and supplies obtainable nearby:** Yes, Cunningham Falls State Park has a concession at the William Houck Lake Area which is open Memorial Day through Labor Day and also in nearby Thurmont; **Overnight accommodations:** Motels in Thurmont. Camping is also available in Cunningham Falls State Park and in four privately-owned campgrounds within a 15 mile (24 km) radius of the Visitor Center; **First Aid available in park:** Yes, or nearby in Thurmont; **Nearest Hospital:** Frederick and Hagerstown Hospitals are within 20 miles (32 km); **Days/Hours:** The park is open from dawn to dusk. No overnight parking is permitted. **Holiday Closings:** Visitor Center closed Thanksgiving, Dec. 25 and Jan. 1; **Visitor attractions closed for seasons:** Owens Creek Campground is open Apr. 15 through the third Sunday in Nov.

GENERAL INFORMATION: Activities at Cunningham Falls State Park include camping, picnicking, hiking, swimming, boating and fishing. Big Hunting Creek offers the opportunity to fly fish for trout; regulations require a Maryland license, trout stamp, and "Catch and Return" of all trout.

Chesapeake and Ohio Canal National Historical Park
Maryland, District of Columbia   **SEE CLIMATABLE MAP**

MAILING ADDRESS: Superintendent, C&O Canal National Historical Park, P.O.

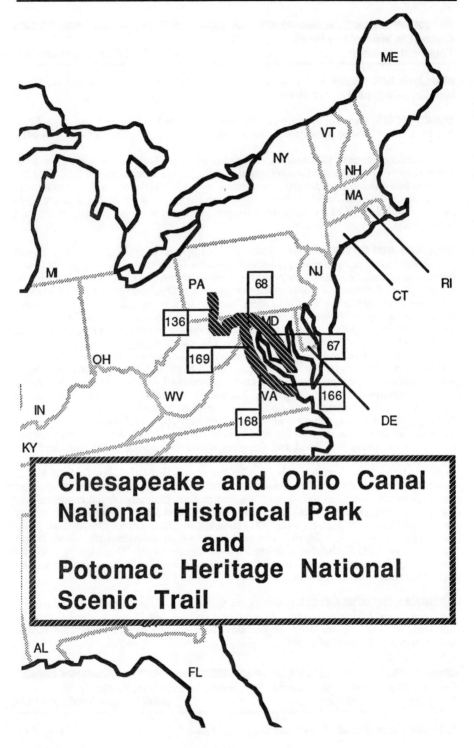

Chesapeake and Ohio Canal
National Historical Park
and
Potomac Heritage National
Scenic Trail

Box 4, Sharpsburg, Maryland 21782 **Telephone:** 301-739-4200; **Park Emergency:** 301-739-4206

DIRECTIONS: Park Headquarters Ferry Hill House 8:00 a.m. to 4:30 p.m. Mon.-Fri. is 4 miles (6.4 km) west of Sharpsburg, MD on MD 34. Visitor Centers are: Georgetown Visitors Center, The Foundry Mall, 1055 Thomas Jefferson St., N.W., Washington, DC; Great Falls Canal Tavern Museum, 11710 MacArthur Blvd., Potomac, Maryland 20854 301-299-3613; Hancock, Maryland, 180 West Main St. 301-678-5463; Western Maryland Railroad Station Center, Canal Street, Cumberland, MD 301-722-8226.

The Park follows the route of the 184 miles (295 km) canal along the Potomac River between Washington, DC and Cumberland, MD. The canal was built between 1828 and 1850, ceased operation in 1924, transferred to the National Park Service in 1938, became a National Park in 1971.

VISITOR ACTIVITIES: hiking, biking, camping, limited horseback riding, canoeing, boating, fishing, picnicking, conducted walks, canal museum at Great Falls, MD, mule drawn boat ride at Georgetown and Great Falls Tavern mid-April through mid-October weather permitting: phone in advance 301-299-2026 (Great Falls) or 202-472-4376 (Georgetown); **Permits:** for camping at Marsden Tract 11 1/2 miles from Georgetown; (Washington, D.C.) Permit may be obtained from the Park Ranger at Great Falls Tavern, 11710 MacArthur Boulevard, Potomac, MD 20854 9 a.m. to 5 p.m., 301-299-3613; **Fees:** No; **Visitor facilities:** picnic areas, campgrounds, museum, boat rentals, boat ramps, bicycles: hiking/biking on towpath; **Any limitations on vehicle usage:** parking available in designated areas along canal; **Hiking trails:** Yes, the towpath follows the canal's entire length; **Backcountry:** No; **Camping:** Yes, no reservations for "Hiker-Biker" campsites. A Campsite 11 1/2 miles from Georgetown, (Washington, D.C.) Marsden Tract, primitive, permit only (see permits above); **Other overnight accommodations on site:** No; **Meals served in the park:** No; **Food and supplies obtainable in the park:** Yes, fast food and drink available from concessioners spring through fall at Great Falls, MD., Swains Lock and Fletchers Boat House. Fishing supplies available from Swains Boat House and Fletchers Boat House; **Food and supplies obtainable nearby:** Yes, in stores along the various adjacent access routes; **Overnight accommodations:** In major urban areas, near I-70; **First Aid available in park:** Yes, at all Visitor Centers and Park Headquarters; **Nearest Hospital:** Along the route of the canal, in or near Potomac, Seneca, Poolesville, Brunswick, Sharpsburg, Williamsport, Hancock, Oldtown, and Cumberland; **Days/Hours:** Towpath open year around—museum and visitor centers closed Christmas Day; **Holiday Closings:** Selected closings. Call in advance; **Visitor attractions closed for seasons:** Boat ride operations closed from mid-Oct.-Apr. Mule drawn canal boats operate mid-April through mid-October weather permitting.

GENERAL INFORMATION: *For Your Safety* —Help prevent drownings by keeping your family or group together. Stay on the trail and out of the water. Be prepared to deal with such annoyances as insects, polluted river water, and adverse weather conditions.

Clara Barton National Historic Site
Glen Echo, Maryland   **SEE CLIMATABLE NO. 67**

MAILING ADDRESS: Superintendent, George Washington Memorial Parkway, Turkey Run Park, McLean, Virginia 22101 **Telephone:** 301-492-6246

DIRECTIONS: The Park is just north of Washington, D.C. Take MacArthur Boulevard from Washington or Exit 40 or 41 from the Capital Beltway (I-495) to Glen Echo, MD. Turn left at Oxford Road just past Glen Echo Park.

This 38-room home of the founder of the American Red Cross was for 7 years the headquarters of that organization. Authorized for addition to the National Park System on Oct. 26, 1974.

VISITOR ACTIVITIES: guided tours and exhibits; "interpretive programs and demonstrations on turn-of-the-century lifestyles." **Permits:** No; **Fees:** No; **Visitor facilities:** restrooms, parking; **Any limitations on vehicle usage:** Vehicles are restricted to the parking lot; **Hiking trails:** No, but hiking is available on the nearby C&O Canal towpath; **Backcountry:** No; **Camping:** No; **Other overnight accommodations on site:** No; **Meals served in the park:** No; **Food and supplies obtainable in the park:** No; **Food and supplies obtainable nearby:** Yes, limited food and supplies in Glen Echo, MD; wider range in Bethesda, MD and Washington, D.C.; **Overnight accommodations:** Washington, D.C. or vicinity; **First Aid available in park:** Yes, or nearby at Glen Echo Fire Dept., Massachusetts Ave.; **Nearest Hospital:** Sibley Hospital, Washington, D.C., 4 miles (6.4 km); **Days/Hours:** Open daily 10-5; **Holiday Closings:** Thanksgiving, Dec. 25, Jan. 1; **Visitor attractions closed for seasons:** Site is open year-round; **Weather:** Hot, humid Summer.

GENERAL INFORMATION: Visitors can see the adjacent Glen Echo Park (see listing in this book). Group tours (10 or more), by reservation.

TRAVEL ACCESS: Bus: Washington Metro bus runs limited schedule from downtown Washington to about 2 blocks from Park; **Rail:** Amtrak provides service to Washington D.C.; **Air:** Major airlines provide service to Washington D.C.

Fort McHenry National Monument and Historic Shrine
Baltimore, Maryland   **SEE CLIMATABLE NO. 73**

MAILING ADDRESS: Superintendent, Fort McHenry National Monument and Historic Shrine, Baltimore, Maryland 21230 **Telephone:** 301-962-4290

DIRECTIONS: From Interstate 95 Northbound or Southbound, take Exit 55 Key Highway/Fort McHenry National Monument and follow the BLUE and GREEN signs on Key Highway to Lawrence St. Turn left on Lawrence St. and left on Fort Ave. Proceed to Fort McHenry National Monument. From the Inner Harbor take Light St. south to Key Highway. Turn left and follow the BLUE and GREEN signs to Lawrence St. Turn right on Lawrence St. and left on Fort Ave. Proceed to Fort McHenry National Monument.
   Successful defense of this fort in the War of 1812, Sept. 13-14, 1814, inspired Francis Scott Key to write "The Star-Spangled Banner" Authorized for addition to the National Park System on Mar. 3, 1925.

VISITOR ACTIVITIES: interpretive exhibits and film, walking tours, picnicking, guided tours during summer months and by reservation to groups; **Permits:** No; **Fees:** Yes, $1 persons age 12 through 61; all others free; **Visitor facilities:** parking and restrooms at Visitor Center, picnic area, seawall walking-jogging path; **Any limitations on vehicle usage:** Vehicles must stay on designated roadways; **Hiking trails:** Yes, a 1 mile (1.6 km) paved foot trail leads around the seawall; **Backcountry:** No; **Camping:** No; **Other overnight accommodations on site:** No; **Meals served in the park:** No; **Food and supplies obtainable in the park:** No; **Food and supplies obtainable nearby:** Yes, in Baltimore; **Overnight accommodations:** Baltimore **First Aid available in park:** Yes, paramedic ambulance service on call; **Nearest Hospital:** South Baltimore General Hosp., Hanover St., 2 miles (3 km); **Days/Hours:** Open 7 days a week, 8 a.m. to 5 p.m. Please call regarding extended hours from Mid-June through Labor Day; **Holiday**

Closings: Dec. 25 and Jan. 1; **Weather:** Summer is hot and humid; air quality is often poor. Winter is cold, damp and windy; Spring and Autumn are mild.

GENERAL INFORMATION: *For Your Safety*—do not climb on monuments, trees, cannons, or the seawall. Stay away from the edge of the fort walls.

TRAVEL ACCESS: **Bus:** Greyhound, Trailways provide daily service to Baltimore City, local transportation runs to park entrance every 1/2 hour; **Rail:** Regular Amtrak service to Pennsylvania Station; **Air:** Major airlines provide service into Baltimore/Washington International Airport.

NEARBY FACILITIES & POINTS OF INTEREST: **Hotel/Motel:** Baltimore; **Campgrounds:** Patapsco State Park, Route 40, West of Baltimore 301-461-5005, (20 miles).

Fort Washington Park
Fort Washington, Maryland   **SEE CLIMATABLE NO. 67**

MAILING ADDRESS: Superintendent, National Capital Parks East, 1900 Anacostia Drive S.E. Washington D.C. 20020 **Telephone:** 202-433-1185 or 301-763-4600

DIRECTIONS: The Park is on the Maryland side of the Potomac River. To reach the Park from the Capital Beltway, take MD 210 (Indian Head Hwy) south approx. 4 miles (6.4 km). Turn right on to Fort Washington Road, go 3 miles (4.8 km) to park entrance. The old fort is 1/2 mile (.8 km) inside the Park.

This fort, situated across the Potomac from Mount Vernon and built to protect Washington, D.C., was begun in 1814 to replace an earlier fort destroyed that same year. Recreational facilities are included in the Park. Authorized for addition to the National Park System on May 29, 1930.

VISITOR ACTIVITIES: interpretive tours and living history demonstrations, auto tours, picnicking, hiking; **Permits:** Yes, reserved picnic areas available for groups of 50 or more; **Fees:** Yes; **Visitor facilities:** picnic areas, parking, restrooms, museum; **Any limitations on vehicle usage:** No trucks are allowed in the Park; **Hiking trails:** Yes, a short trail along the Potomac River and Piscataway Bay; **Backcountry:** No; **Camping:** No; **Other overnight accommodations on site:** No; **Meals served in the park:** No; **Food and supplies obtainable in the park:** No; **Food and supplies obtainable nearby:** Yes, 3.5 miles (5.6 km) from the Park on Fort Washington Road; **Overnight accommodations:** in the Washington metropolitan area; **First Aid available in park:** Yes, or nearby in Oxon Hill, 12 miles (19.3 km), on Oxon Hill Road; **Nearest Hospital:** Washington, D.C., Southern Avenue, 20 miles (32 km); **Days/Hours:** Fort open from 7:30 a.m. to 5:00 p.m. Sept. 1 through April 30 open from 7:30 a.m. to 8:00 p.m. May 1 through August 30. Park open from 7:30 a.m. to dark every day; **Holiday Closings:** None; **Weather:** Winters are cool & wet, with light snow; Summers are hot and humid. This is a fee area.

George Washington Memorial Parkway
For details see listing in Virginia

Glen Echo Park
Glen Echo, Maryland   **SEE CLIMATABLE NO. 67**

MAILING ADDRESS: Site Manager, Glen Echo Park, MacArthur Blvd., Glen Echo, Maryland 20812 **Telephone:** 301-492-6282

DIRECTIONS: The Park is just north of Washington, DC at MacArthur Boulevard and Oxford Road. Take MacArthur Boulevard from Washington, Capital Beltway Exit 40 or 41, or George Washington Memorial Parkway from Maryland. Information on facilities and activities may be obtained at Glen Echo Gallery.

Located on Maryland's Potomac Palisades, the Park was formerly a 19th century Chautauqua assembly center and then an amusement park. It is now a cultural and arts center. Authorized for addition to the National Park System in 1976.

VISITOR ACTIVITIES: walking tours, carousel rides on Summer weekends, arts and crafts courses, special programs, free concerts and festivals, picnicking; **Permits:** No; **Fees:** Carousel rides are 25¢, tuition fees are charged for courses and admission fees for some performances; **Visitor facilities:** restrooms, parking, gallery, picnic areas; **Any limitations on vehicle usage:** Vehicles are restricted to the parking lot; **Hiking trails:** No; **Backcountry:** No; **Camping:** No; **Other overnight accommodations on site:** No; **Meals served in the park:** Yes, food service on weekends only, from May-Sept.; **Food and supplies obtainable in the park:** No; **Food and supplies obtainable nearby:** Yes, in town of Glen Echo; **Overnight accommodations:** suburban Maryland or Washington, DC; **First Aid available in park:** Yes; **Nearest Hospital:** Sibley Hospital, MacArthur Blvd. and Loughboro Rd., Washington, DC; **Days/Hours:** Grounds open 24 hours a day 7 days a week; **Holiday Closings:** Thanksgiving, Dec. 25, Jan. 1; **Visitor attractions closed for seasons:** Most festivals are held between May and Oct.; **Weather:** Hot, humid Summers; cold, snowy Winters.

GENERAL INFORMATION: Visitors can also see the adjacent Clara Barton National Historic Site (see listing in this book).

Greenbelt Park
Greenbelt, Maryland   **SEE CLIMATABLE NO. 67**

MAILING ADDRESS: Superintendent, Greenbelt Park, 6565 Greenbelt Road, Greenbelt, Maryland 20770 **Telephone:** 301-344-3948

DIRECTIONS: From the Capital Beltway (Int. 95), take Exit 23 at Kenilworth Avenue (MD 201) proceed south toward Bladensburg and follow the signs into the Park. From the Baltimore-Washington Parkway, exit at Greenbelt Road (MD 193) and follow signs.

Just 12 miles (19 km) from Washington, D.C., this woodland Park offers urban dwellers access to many forms of outdoor recreation. Established by Act of Congress in 1950.

VISITOR ACTIVITIES: picnicking, camping, nature walks, horse trails, biking, hiking; **Permits:** No; **Fees:** Camping fee is $4 per night, $2 if camper has a Golden Age Passport; **Visitor facilities:** picnic areas, campgrounds, nature trails, interpretive walks, and evening programs, fireplaces (charcoal and wood is permitted), restrooms; **Any limitations on vehicle usage:** Park only in designated areas. All vehicles, including bicycles, are restricted to paved roads. Their use on any trail is strictly prohibited; **Hiking trails:** Yes, nearly 12 miles (19 km) of well-marked trails lead through the Park. A 6 mile (9.6 km) loop, also designated a bridle trail, circles the Park's western half; **Backcountry:**

No; **Camping:** Yes, no reservations for the 174-site family campground, which is open all year. In Summer, the campground is usually filled by nightfall. Visitors should plan to arrive by mid-afternoon to be assured of a site. There are no showers or hookups; **Other overnight accommodations on site:** No; **Meals served in the park:** No; **Food and supplies obtainable in the park:** No; **Food and supplies obtainable nearby:** Yes, Greenbelt or vicinity; **Overnight accommodations:** Greenbelt; **First Aid available in park:** Yes, but only for emergencies, or nearby in Lanham, MD; **Nearest Hospital:** Doctors Hospital, New Carrollton, Good Luck Road, 4 miles (6.4 km); **Days/Hours:** Open dawn until dark. Campers have access at all times; **Holiday Closings:** Thanksgiving, Christmas and New Year's Day; **Visitor attractions closed for seasons:** Bike trail is closed for Winter; **Weather:** High heat and humidity in Summer, cold in Winter with some snow.

Hampton National Historic Site
Towson, Maryland   **SEE CLIMATABLE NO. 73**

MAILING ADDRESS: Site Manager, Hampton National Historic Site, 535 Hampton Lane, Towson, Maryland 21204 **Telephone:** 301-823-7054

DIRECTIONS: To reach Hampton from Baltimore, follow the Jones Falls Expressway, the York Road (MD 45), or Charles Street north to Towson. In Towson, take Dulaney Valley Road (MD 146) across the Beltway (I-695) and immediately thereafter turn right into Hampton Lane which leads to the Site. This is a dangerous intersection; make sure that you do not enter the Beltway exit ramp. The Site can also be reached from Beltway exit 27, Providence Road.

This is a fine example of one of the great Georgian architecture mansions built in America during the latter part of the 18th century. 60 acre site includes landscaped formal gardens and countryside grounds with exotic and specimen trees. 23 historic structures/dependencies remain from a once vast agricultural/industrial farm-plantation complex. Designated June 22, 1948.

VISITOR ACTIVITIES: Regularly scheduled guided tours of mansion with tour group size limit of 10 people max., self-guiding grounds tours, stable and garden exhibits; **Permits:** No; **Fees:** None; **Visitor facilities:** parking, restrooms, tea room, gift shop (gift shop open Mon-Sat, 11 a.m.-4 p.m., Sun, 1-4 p.m.); **Any limitations on vehicle usage:** No; **Hiking trails:** Yes, a 1 mile (1.6 km) walking tour of the grounds; **Meals served in the park:** Yes, lunch is available at the tea room in the east wing; **Food and supplies obtainable in the park:** No; **Food and supplies obtainable nearby:** Yes, in Towson; **Overnight accommodations:** In Towson, MD. approx. 1 mile (1.6 km) south; **First Aid available in park:** Yes, **Nearest Hospital:** Towson, MD, approx. 2 miles (3 km); **Days/Hours:** Grounds open daily 9 a.m. to 5 p.m.; Mansion open Mon. thru Sat. 11 a.m. to 4:00 p.m. Sundays 1 p.m. to 4:00 p.m.; **Holiday Closings:** Thanksgiving, Jan. 1 & Dec. 25; **Visitor attractions closed for seasons:** No.

GENERAL INFORMATION: Be especially careful on the earthen ramps leading into the gardens; they are steeper than they appear. The cobblestone walks are slippery when wet.

Harpers Ferry National Historical Park
For details see listing in West Virginia

Monocacy National Battlefield Park
Frederick County, Maryland   **SEE CLIMATABLE NO. 68**

MAILING ADDRESS: Superintendent, Antietam National Battlefield, P.O. Box 158, Sharpsburg, Maryland 21782 **Telephone:** 301-432-5124

DIRECTIONS: NOT YET OPEN TO THE PUBLIC
On July 9, 1864, Confederate Gen. Jubal T. Early and his troops met the Union Forces of Major General Lew Wallace south of Frederick, along the banks of the Monocacy River. Early's forces defeated the Union but Wallace was able to delay confederate forces long enough for reinforcements to arrive in Washington to defend the Capital against Southern troops. Battlefield was established on June 21, 1934. Will open when sufficient land is available for public use and development. Write address above.

Oxon Hill Farm
Oxon Hill, Maryland   **SEE CLIMATABLE NO. 67**

MAILING ADDRESS: Superintendent, National Capital Parks East, 1900 Anacostia Drive, S.E., Washington, D.C. 20020 **Telephone:** 301-839-1177

DIRECTIONS: From southbound Indian Head Highway, (MD 210) at the Capital Beltway (Interstate Rt. 95) exit 3-A bear right onto Oxon Hill Road. Turn right approx. 200 yards down Oxon Hill Road to the farm parking lot.
The Farm is like many of those found in the Maryland and Virginia countryside around Washington at the end of the 19th Century. It includes pasture lands, woodland, typical farm buildings, animals, and equipment. In operation as a Park since 1967, the Farm is especially attractive for children.

VISITOR ACTIVITIES: picnicking, machinery and equipment displays, live animal exhibits, daily demonstrations of 1900 era farm chores, educational programs for children, seasonal farming and craft demonstrations, recreational activities; **Permits:** No, but large groups should make advance arrangments; **Fees:** No; **Visitor facilities:** picnic areas, nature trail, restrooms, Visitor Center, exhibits, farm buildings; **Any limitations on vehicle usage:** All vehicles must use the designated parking area; **Hiking trails:** Yes, 1/2 mile (.8 km) self-guiding woodlot nature trail; **Backcountry:** No; **Camping:** No; **Other overnight accommodations on site:** No; **Meals served in the park:** No, many fast-food facilities are 1/2 mile (.8 km) east on Oxon Hill Road; **Food and supplies obtainable in the park:** No; **Food and supplies obtainable nearby:** Yes, 1/2 mile (.8 km) east on Oxon Hill Road; **Overnight accommodations:** in the Washington metropolitan area; **First Aid available in park:** Yes; **Nearest Hospital:** Washington, D.C.-Southeast Community Hosp.—take Indian Head Highway (MD 201) North 1 mile (1.6 km) to Southern Ave., Turn right on Southern Ave. 2 miles (3 km) to hospital on left; **Days/ Hours:** Open daily all year from 8:30 a.m.-5 p.m.; **Holiday Closings:** Thanksgiving, Dec. 25 & Jan. 1; **Visitor attractions closed for seasons:** Activities, programs and demonstrations are curtailed from Dec. to Mar. due to weather; **Weather:** Spring and Fall are temperate, pleasant (60°F) and usually sunny. Summer is warm to hot (70-95°F) and humid. Winter is moderately cold and windy.

GENERAL INFORMATION: *For Your Safety* —Do not smoke in any of the buildings. Be cautious around animals and all machines, which can be dangerous and have heavy moving parts and sharp edges. Be alert for moving equipment such as wagons and tractors. Large groups should call in advance to arrange for visits.

TRAVEL ACCESS: Bus: Washington Metro buses (Routes D-12 and W-12) stop at Oxon Hill & Livingston Roads.

Appalachian National Scenic Trail
For details see listing in Maine

Piscataway Park
Accokeek, Maryland   **SEE CLIMATABLE NO. 67**

MAILING ADDRESS: Piscataway Park, Superintendent, National Capital Parks East, 1900 Anacostia Drive S.E., Washington D.C. 20020 **Telephone:** 202-433-1190 **Park Telephone:** 301-292-2112

DIRECTIONS: Take Exit 37S from the Capital Beltway (Int. 495) to Route 210S (Indian Head Highway) 10 miles (16 km) to the intersection in Accokeek. Turn right onto Bryan's Point Road and go 4 miles (6.7 km) to the Potomac River.

The tranquil view of the Maryland shore of the Potomac from Mount Vernon is preserved as a pilot project in the use of easements to protect Parklands from obtrusive urban expansion. Authorized for addition to the National Park System on Oct. 4, 1961.

VISITOR ACTIVITIES: picnicking, fishing, bird-watching, farm tours; **Permits:** No; **Fees:** A fee is charged for tours of the National Colonial Farm, which is located at Piscataway; **Visitor facilities:** picnic area, boat dock, National Colonial Farm; **Any limitations on vehicle usage:** No; **Hiking trails:** No; **Backcountry:** No; **Camping:** No; **Other overnight accommodations on site:** No; **Meals served in the park:** No; **Food and supplies obtainable in the park:** No; **Food and supplies obtainable nearby:** Yes, Shopping Centers are along Route 210; **Overnight accommodations:** Suburban Maryland or metropolitan Washington, D.C.; **First Aid available in park:** No; **Nearest Hospital:** Washington, D.C., Route 210 to Southern Ave. 20 miles (32 km); **Days/Hours:** Open daily during daylight hours; **Holiday Closings:** None; **Weather:** Hot, humid Summers, and cold, wet Winters.

Thomas Stone National Historic Site
Port Tobacco, Maryland   **SEE CLIMATABLE NO. 67**

MAILING ADDRESS: Superintendent, George Washington Birthplace National Monument, RR #1, P.O. Box 717, Washington's Birthplace, Virginia 22443 **Telephone:** 804-224-1732

DIRECTIONS: NOT YET OPEN TO THE PUBLIC.

The Georgian home of Thomas Stone, a signer of the Declaration of Independence, was built by him in 1771. Authorized for addition to the National Park System on Nov. 10, 1978.

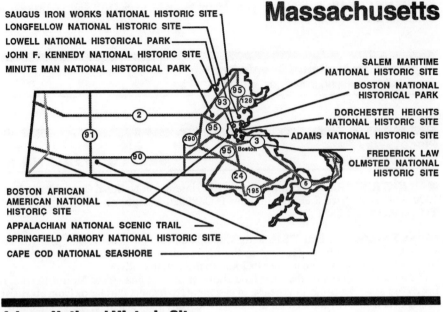

SAUGUS IRON WORKS NATIONAL HISTORIC SITE
LONGFELLOW NATIONAL HISTORIC SITE
LOWELL NATIONAL HISTORICAL PARK
JOHN F. KENNEDY NATIONAL HISTORIC SITE
MINUTE MAN NATIONAL HISTORICAL PARK

Massachusetts

SALEM MARITIME
NATIONAL HISTORIC SITE
BOSTON NATIONAL
HISTORICAL PARK
DORCHESTER HEIGHTS
NATIONAL HISTORIC SITE
ADAMS NATIONAL HISTORIC SITE
FREDERICK LAW
OLMSTED NATIONAL
HISTORIC SITE

BOSTON AFRICAN
AMERICAN NATIONAL
HISTORIC SITE
APPALACHIAN NATIONAL SCENIC TRAIL
SPRINGFIELD ARMORY NATIONAL HISTORIC SITE
CAPE COD NATIONAL SEASHORE

Adams National Historic Site
Quincy, Massachusetts   **SEE CLIMATABLE NO. 74**

MAILING ADDRESS: Superintendent, Adams National Historic Site, P.O. Box 531, Quincy, Massachusetts 02269 **Telephone:** 617-773-1177

DIRECTIONS: 8 miles (12.9 km) south of Boston. Take Route 93 South (Southeast Expressway) to Exit 8 (formerly Exit 24) (Furnace Brook Parkway). Once on Furnace Brook Pkwy. at third set of traffic lights take a right onto Adams Street. Site is one mile ahead on left at the corner of Adams St. and Newport Ave.

Established by act of Congress on Dec. 9, 1946, the Site contains 8.45 acres and includes the house, library, garden and stables of Presidents John Adams and John Quincy Adams, and statesman Ambassador Charles Francis Adams and his four illustrious sons.

The John Adams and John Quincy Adams Birthplaces: Approximately 9 miles south of Boston, Take Exit 8 (formerly Exit 24) (Furnace Brook Parkway interchange) of the Southeast Expressway (Route 3) to Adams Street East to Hancock Street through Quincy Center to School Street. Turn right onto School Street then left on Franklin Street. The Adams Birthplaces are on your right at 133 and 141 Franklin Street.

VISITOR ACTIVITIES: Historic Site tours; **Permits:** No; **Fees:** $2.00 admission fee for adults, children under 12 admitted free when accompanied by an adult. Entrance fee includes all three homes. Golden Eagle, Golden Age, and Golden Access Passports accepted and available; **Visitor facilities:** None; **Any limitations on vehicle usage:** Parking for visitors is available on the public street in front of the house; **Other overnight accommodations on site:** No; **Meals served in the park:** No; **Food and supplies obtainable in the park:** No; **Food and supplies obtainable nearby:** Yes, Quincy, about ¼ mile (.4 km) south of the Site; **Overnight accommodations:** Boston area along Route 3; **First Aid available in park:** No; **Nearest Hospital:** Quincy City Hospital, less than ¼ mile (.4 km) from the site; **Days/Hours:** Open 9 a.m.-5.p.m. daily April 19 through Nov. 10, Adams Birthplaces are open daily April 19 through Nov. 10 only; **Holiday Closings:** None; **Visitor attractions closed for seasons:** Closed Nov. 11 through April 18.

TRAVEL ACCESS: Bus: Mass Bay Trans. Authority service to nearby Quincy Center; **Rail:** Mass Bay Trans. Authority hourly service to nearby Quincy Center; **Air:** All major airlines provide daily service to Logan Airport.

NEARBY FACILITIES & POINTS OF INTEREST: Hotel/Motel: President's City Motel, Hancock Street, about ½ mile; **Food/Supplies:** Many stores in Quincy Center ¼ mile from Site; **Campgrounds:** None nearby; **Parks, other points of interest:** First Parish Church and other historic Sites in Quincy.

Appalachian National Scenic Trail
For details see listing in Maine

Boston African American National Historic Site
Boston, Massachusetts   **SEE CLIMATABLE NO. 74**

MAILING ADDRESS: Site Manager, Boston African American National Historic Site, National Park Service, 46 Joy Street, Boston, Massachusetts 02114 **Telephone:** 617-742-5415.

DIRECTIONS: As parking is difficult in downtown Boston, visitors are advised to park and take mass transit (MBTA Green or Red Lines to Park Street Station). Parking is available at the Boston Common. If driving from the Massachusetts Turnpike, take the Prudential-Copley Square Exit to Stuart Street, then left onto Route 28 to the Boston Common. From Route 93, take Storrow Drive to Copley Square Exit. Turn left onto Beacon, right onto Arlington, left onto Boylston, left onto Charles Street (Route 28).

Established in 1980, Boston African American comprises the largest concentration of pre-Civil War black history sites in the U.S.

VISITOR ACTIVITIES: Self-guided walking tours. Guided tours are offered daily Memorial Day to Labor Day, and by special request at other times. **Permits:** required for special use and obtained by contacting the site manager; **Fees:** No; **Visitor facilities:** Restrooms and information are located at the Boston African American NH Site's Office, 46 Joy St., Boston, MA 02114; **Any limitations on vehicle usage:** No; one-way streets make driving on Beacon Hill difficult; **Hiking trails:** Yes, the 1.6 mile Black Heritage Trail connects the 16 sites; **Backcountry:** No; **Camping:** No; **Other overnight accommodations on site:** No; **Food and supplies obtainable in the park:** No; **Food and supplies obtainable nearby:** Yes, on Charles and Cambridge Streets; **Overnight accommodations:** Boston. List available at Site Office, 46 Joy Street, Boston, MA 02114; **First Aid available in park:** No; **Nearest Hospital:** Boston Hospitals—Massachusetts General, Tufts University Clinic; **Days/Hours:** 5 days a week in the Winter, Spring and Fall 9 a.m.-4 p.m., Summer 9 a.m.-5 p.m.; **Holiday Closings:** Thanksgiving, Christmas and New Year's Day; **Visitor attractions closed for seasons:** No; **Weather:** Spring, Summer are best times to visit. Winter is icy.

GENERAL INFORMATION: The visitor experience here is an outdoor walking tour. The African Meeting House is open to the public on weekdays during the winter, spring and fall, and daily during the summer.

TRAVEL ACCESS: Bus: Major companies, daily; **Rail:** Amtrak, Boston, North and South Stations, daily; **Air:** Major Airlines serve Boston (Logan), daily; **Other:** Bay State Lines (Boats from Provincetown) Boston, daily.

NEARBY FACILITIES & POINTS OF INTEREST: Boston Harbor Islands State Park offers primitive camping. Contact (617) 727-5250 for information.

Boston National Historical Park
Boston, Massachusetts   **SEE CLIMATABLE NO. 74**

MAILING ADDRESS: Superintendent, Boston National Historical Park, Charlestown Navy Yard, Boston, Massachusetts 02129 **Telephone:** 617-242-5644

DIRECTIONS: We recommend that you don't drive in downtown Boston; mass transit provides a good option. If you do drive, from Route 1 south and Route 93 north or south, follow the signs to the Charlestown Navy Yard (berth of USS Constitution). Further directions into downtown Boston can be obtained here.

The Park consists of 7 historic sites and a Visitor Center along Boston's Freedom Trail plus Dorchester Heights and the Boston African American National Historic Site. The Park was founded in 1974. The Freedom Trail is a red line painted on the sidewalks of Boston.

VISITOR ACTIVITIES: During the peak season (Summer), the Sites provide historic information in a variety of ways: tours, lectures, living history. Park Service Rangers are at Faneuil Hall, Charlestown Navy Yard, Bunker Hill Monument, and the Visitor Center. **Permits:** only for special use; **Fees:** Yes, entrance fees are collected at the privately owned and operated Sites, by self-supporting associations working cooperatively with the Park; **Visitor facilities:** rest rooms at the Visitor Center, Navy Yard and Faneuil Hall; **Any limitations on vehicle usage:** parking is not available in the Navy Yard, but very limited parking is available just outside the facility. Commercial parking lots at fairly high cost are available in the City convenient to the Freedom Trail and public transportion; **Hiking trails:** Yes, the Freedom Trail follows an urban route; **Camping:** No; **Other overnight accommodations on site:** Yes, hostel available by pre-arrangement for organized groups; **Meals served in the park:** No; **Food and supplies obtainable in the park:** Yes, snack bar serves light food; **Food and supplies obtainable nearby:** Yes, in Quincy Market, North End, and Charlestown. There are many restaurants in the vicinity; **Overnight accommodations:** Hotels and motels throughout the city; **First Aid available in park:** Yes; **Nearest Hospital:** Hospitals near Sites include Mass. General, Bunker Hill Community Health Center, Tufts University, and University Hospital; **Days/Hours:** Summer: 7 days per week, 9:00 a.m.-6:00 p.m. Winter: 7 days per week, 9:00 a.m.-5:00 p.m. or 10:00 a.m.-5:00 p.m., depending on Site; **Holiday Closings:** Thanksgiving, December 25 and January 1; **Visitor attractions closed for seasons:** No; **Weather:** Summer is usually hot and humid with a sea breeze; Winter is windy and usually cold.

TRAVEL ACCESS: Bus: Major bus companies; **Rail:** daily service into Boston's South Station and North Station; **Air:** Major airlines service into Boston Logan Airport.

NEARBY FACILITIES & POINTS OF INTEREST: Parks, other points of interest: Lowell NHP, Adams NHS, Saugus Ironworks NHS, Minuteman NHP; Kennedy Birthplace NHS, Longfellow NHS, Frederick Law Olmsted NHS, Salem Maritime NHS.

Bunker Hill Monument
Boston National Historical Park, Boston, MA   **SEE CLIMATABLE NO. 74**

MAILING ADDRESS: Superintendent, Boston National Historical Park, Charlestown Navy Yard, Boston, MA 02129 **Telephone:** 617-242-5644

DIRECTIONS: The Monument is located in residential Charlestown where street parking is limited. We recommend Mass transit. It is a 10 minute walk to the Monument from the Community College subway station (orange subway line).

The Bunker Hill Monument is constructed on the site of the famous Battle of Bunker Hill fought on June 17, 1775. Though the British won the battle, the colonials gained new found respect by their determined resistance to the Redcoats.

VISITOR ACTIVITIES: Bunker Hill Monument is a unit of Boston National Historical Park. The Bunker Hill Lodge is open daily and features exhibits on the battle. A climb to the top of the Monument will provide a spectacular view of Boston and the surrounding area. Park Rangers on duty provide 15 minute talks on the battle every hour; **Permits:** Only for special usage. Special programs for children or visiting groups can be arranged by contacting the site in advance; **Fees:** None; **Visitor facilities:** Restrooms are available at the lodge. The restrooms and exhibits in the lodge are accessible by wheelchair; **Any limitations on vehicle usage:** There is limited street parking in Charlestown near the Monument; **Hiking trails:** Bunker Hill Monument is located along Boston's historic Freedom Trail; **Camping:** None; **Food Service:** There are restaurants located along Main Street in Charlestown and throughout Boston; **Overnight accommodations:** Hotels and motels are located throughout Boston; **First Aid available in park:** Yes; **Nearest Hospitals:** Massachusetts General, Bunker Hill Community Clinic; **Days/Hours:** Open daily from 9:00 a.m. until 5:00 p.m. Visitors may climb the Monument until 4:30 p.m; **Holiday Closings:** Thanksgiving, Christmas and New Years Day; **Visitor attractions closed for seasons:** None; **Weather:** Summer temperatures generally in the 80's; Winter is windy with temperatures down to the teens.

NEARBY FACILITIES & POINTS OF INTEREST: Lowell NHP, Adams NHS, Saugus Iron Works NHS, Minute Man NHP, John Fitzgerald Kennedy NHS, Longfellow NHS, Frederick Law Olmsted NHS, and Salem Maritime NHS.

Cape Cod National Seashore
South Wellfleet, Massachusetts   **SEE CLIMATABLE NO. 75**

MAILING ADDRESS: Superintendent, Cape Cod National Seashore, South Wellfleet, Massachusetts 02663 **Telephone:** 617-349-3785

DIRECTIONS: Visitor Centers are at Salt Pond (in Eastham on Route 6) and Province Lands (in Provincetown on Race Point Road). Headquarters is at the Marconi Station Area in Wellfleet.

Ocean and bay beaches, dunes, woodlands, freshwater ponds, and marshes make up this Park on outer Cape Cod. The area preserves notable examples of Cape Cod houses, an architectural style founded in America. Authorized for addition to the National Park System on Aug. 7, 1961.

VISITOR ACTIVITIES: Interpretive exhibits and talks, swimming, surfing, driving, horseback riding, camping, picnicking, fishing, hiking, shellfishing, biking; **Permits:** shellfishing from local towns fresh water fishing, state license applicable; oversand vehicles from Race Point Ranger Station, subject to inspection and annual fee; **Fees:** Beach parking lot $3 per carload entrance fee late June through Labor Day. Golden Eagle, Golden Age and Golden Access Passports accepted and available. Annual oversand vehicle fees are $30 for regular ORV's and $50 for self-contained; **Visitor facilities:** bicycle trails, nature trails, bridle paths and beaches, lifeguard services and other swimming facilities, picnic areas; bicycle rentals in adjoining communities, horse rentals, restaurants, lodging, gift stores; **Any limitations on vehicle usage:** Summer traffic is very heavy-roads are narrow. Motorized vehicles including mopeds are not allowed on paved bicycle trails; **Hiking trails:** Yes, day use only; outer beach is also good for day hiking;

Camping: Camping not permitted on National Seashore property, however, various private campgrounds are available locally. Reservations are essential for Summer season. A large state-owned campground is in Nickerson State Park in nearby Brewster. Reservations cannot be made for this campground. Sleeping and campground accommodations, restaurants, gift shops, grocery and other stores, and gas stations are in towns adjoining the seashore. For information and reservations, write to: Cape Cod Chamber of Commerce, Hyannis, MA 02601; **Other overnight accommodations on site:** No; **Meals served in the park:** No; **Food and supplies obtainable in the park:** No; **Food and supplies obtainable nearby:** Yes, along Route 6 and in local towns; **Overnight accommodations:** Available in areas serving the seashore. Contact Chamber of Commerce as noted above; **First Aid available in park:** Yes, emergency only; all towns have rescue squads; **Nearest Hospital:** Hyannis, 30 miles (48 km) away; **Days/Hours:** Open from 6 a.m. to midnight year-round; **Holiday Closings:** Salt Pond Visitor Center closed January and February. Province Lands Visitor Center closed December to mid-April; **Visitor attractions closed for seasons:** Interpretive services, walks, talks etc. are offered from April-Nov.; **Weather:** Summer and Fall are the best times to visit; Spring is often damp; Winter is mild and potentially stormy.

GENERAL INFORMATION: *Caution*—Swim only where lifeguards are on duty. Sand collapses easily. Climbing slopes or digging deep holes is hazardous. The ocean can be dangerous. Be alert for riptides and underwater obstacles. For your safety, do not take glass containers, rafts, rubber tubes, snorkels, or masks to any beach. Watch out for painful sunburn. Do not leave valuables in vehicles.

TRAVEL ACCESS: Bus: Plymouth & Brockton Bus Lines Boston to Hyannis. Bonanza Bus Lines, Providence to Hyannis, Cape Cod Bus Co., Via Route 6, Hyannis-Provincetown; **Rail:** Amtrak, Providence and Boston; **Air:** New York Air; Continental Express, Hyannis, Provincetown. **Other:** Paved bicycle trail from Nickerson State Park in Brewster to Salt Pond Visitor Center, Eastham.

Charlestown Navy Yard
Boston National Historical Park, Boston, MA   **SEE CLIMATABLE NO. 74**

MAILING ADDRESS: Superintendent, Boston National Historical Park, Charlestown Navy Yard, Boston, MA 02129 **Telephone:** 617-242-5644

DIRECTIONS: The Charlestown Navy Yard can be reached by following the signs from Route 1 south and Route 93 north or south. Limited parking is available outside the Yard. The site is a 15 minute walk from either the Bunker Hill Community College subway station (orange subway line) or North Station (orange or green subway lines). Water transportation including a harbor cruise is available from Long Wharf near the Aquarium.
   The Charlestown Navy Yard is a unit of Boston National Historical Park. The Navy Yard, established in 1800, continued in operation until 1974. It is best known as home port of USS CONSTITUTION, and for the developments in shipbuilding and repair technology that took place there.

VISITOR ACTIVITIES: Park Rangers operate an information center and lead tours of the Navy Yard, the Commandant's House, and the World War II destroyer, CASSIN YOUNG. Other cooperative attractions in the Navy Yard include USS CONSTITUTION, operated by the U.S. Navy, the Constitution Museum and the Museum of the Boston Marine Society, which features exhibits on Boston's maritime past. Special programs for school and other visiting groups can be arranged by contacting the site in advance; **Permits:** For special usage and commercial photography; **Fees:** Admission to the

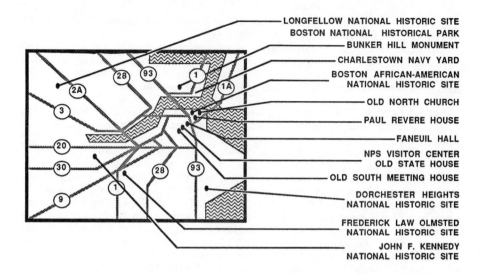

LONGFELLOW NATIONAL HISTORIC SITE
BOSTON NATIONAL HISTORICAL PARK
BUNKER HILL MONUMENT
CHARLESTOWN NAVY YARD
BOSTON AFRICAN-AMERICAN NATIONAL HISTORIC SITE
OLD NORTH CHURCH
PAUL REVERE HOUSE
FANEUIL HALL
NPS VISITOR CENTER
OLD STATE HOUSE
OLD SOUTH MEETING HOUSE
DORCHESTER HEIGHTS NATIONAL HISTORIC SITE
FREDERICK LAW OLMSTED NATIONAL HISTORIC SITE
JOHN F. KENNEDY NATIONAL HISTORIC SITE

Constitution Museum is $2.00 adults, $1.50 for seniors, and $1 for children 6 to 16, those under 6 are free. All other sites in the Navy Yard are free; **Visitor facilities:** Restrooms are available and accessible to the disabled; **Any limitations on vehicle usage:** Parking at the Navy Yard is limited, particularly for trailers or large vehicles; **Hiking trails:** The Charlestown Navy Yard is located along Boston's historic Freedom Trail; **Camping:** None; **Overnight accommodations:** Hotels and motels are located throughout Boston; **First Aid available in park:** Yes; **Nearest Hospitals:** Massachusetts General, Bunker Hill Clinic; **Days/Hours:** The Navy Yard is open every day from 8:00 a.m. until 5:00 p.m. USS CONSTITUTION is open daily 9:30 a.m. until 3:50 p.m. The Constitution Museum is open daily 9:00 a.m. until 5:00 p.m. (until 6:00 p.m. in summer). The Boston Marine Society is open on weekdays from 9:00 a.m. until 3:00 p.m. The Commandant's House is open daily in the summer and on weekends in Spring and Fall; **Holiday Closings:** The USS CONSTITUTION is open every day. Other sites in the Navy Yard are closed on Thanksgiving, Christmas and New Years Day; **Visitor attractions closed for seasons:** The main deck of CASSIN YOUNG is open for casual visitation in Spring, Summer and Fall. In winter the ship is open by guided tour only; **Weather:** Summer temperatures generally in the 80's; Winter is windy with temperatures down to the teens.

NEARBY FACILITIES & POINTS OF INTEREST: Lowell NHP, Adams NHS, Saugus Iron Works NHS, Minute Man NHP, John Fitzgerald Kennedy NHS, Longfellow NHS, Frederick Law Olmsted NHS, and Salem Maritime NHS.

Dorchester Heights
Boston National Historical Park, Boston, MA   **SEE CLIMATABLE NO. 74**

MAILING ADDRESS: Superintendent, Boston National Historical Park, Charlestown Navy Yard, Boston, MA 02129

DIRECTIONS: Dorchester Heights is located in South Boston, approximately 2 miles from downtown. By public transit take the subway (Red Line) to Broadway Station. From here board MBTA Bus #9 (City Point) and get off at "G" Street. It is a short walk to the Heights. By car from downtown Boston, cross into South Boston on the Congress

Street Bridge. Turn right onto "A" Street, then left onto West Broadway. Follow Broadway to "G" Street and turn right to the monument.

The colonial revival monument and small park mark the site of George Washington's 1776 fortifications. By placing men and artillery here the Americans forced the British evacuation of Boston on March 17, 1776. This bloodless victory was Washington's first military action as Commander-in-Chief of the new Continental Army.

VISITOR ACTIVITIES: The monument offers a magnificent view of Boston and her harbor. The surrounding park is a pleasant place for rest and passive recreation. Park Rangers are on duty during warmer weather to explain the significance of the site. Special tours of the monument and grounds for school or adult groups can be arranged by contacting the Park in advance; **Permits:** Only for special usage and commercial photography; **Fees:** None; **Visitor facilities:** There are no restrooms at the site; **Any limitations on vehicle usage:** Dorchester Heights is in a residential area of South Boston, street parking around the monument is usually available; **Hiking trails:** None; **Camping:** None; **Food service:** There are restaurants on nearby Broadway and in downtown Boston; **Overnight accommodations:** Hotels and motels are located throughout Boston; **First Aid available in park:** Only when personnel are on duty; **Nearest Hospitals:** Massachusetts General, Tufts New England Medical Center; **Days/Hours:** Monument grounds are open daily until sunset; **Holiday Closings:** The grounds are open every day until sunset; **Visitor attractions closed for seasons:** The monument is open on a limited basis during the summer; **Weather:** Summer temperatures generally in the 80's; Winter is windy with temperatures down to the teens.

NEARBY FACILITIES & POINTS OF INTEREST: Lowell NHP, Adams NHS, Saugus Iron Works NHS, Minute Man NHP, John Fitzgerald Kennedy NHS, Longfellow NHS, Frederick Law Olmsted NHS, and Salem Maritime NHS.

Faneuil Hall
Boston National Historical Park, Boston, MA   **SEE CLIMATABLE NO. 74**

MAILING ADDRESS: Superintendent, Boston National Historical Park, Charlestown Navy Yard, Boston, MA 02129 **Telephone:** 242-5644

DIRECTIONS: We recommend that you do not drive in downtown Boston; mass transit provides a good alternative. Faneuil Hall is located at Dock Square next to Quincy Market. The nearest subway stops are Government Center (green and blue subway lines) or State Street (blue and orange subway lines). From either station, it is a five minute walk to Faneuil Hall.

Faneuil Hall was built in 1742 to serve as the town meeting hall and as a public marketplace for colonial Boston. In the years before the American Revolution, meetings held here rallied public opposition to British rule. The "Cradle of Liberty" continues today to serve as a popular meeting place and assembly hall for Bostonians.

VISITOR ACTIVITIES: Faneuil Hall is owned by the City of Boston and is part of Boston National Historical Park. The National Park Service maintains the Hall and provides visitor services and interpretation of the site. The first floor of Faneuil Hall still serves as a marketplace. The meeting hall, located on the second floor, is open daily and staffed by Rangers who provide information and regularly scheduled talks throughout the day. A military musuem and armory, maintained by the Ancient and Honorable Artillery Company, is located on the third floor; **Permits:** Faneuil Hall is still regularly used for gatherings and functions. Contact the Superintendent, Faneuil Hall, 1 Merchants Row, Boston, MA 02109. Telephone: 617-725-3105; **Fees:** None; **Visitor facilities:** Restrooms are available. The second floor meeting hall is accessible to the disabled; **Any limitations on vehicle usage:** Faneuil Hall is located in downtown Boston. Parking is very limited. Commercial parking lots are located on nearby Congress Street; **Hiking trails:** Yes. Faneuil Hall is located along Boston's historic Freedom Trail; **Camping:** None; **Food service:** Numerous restaurants are located in the vicinity; **Overnight accommodations:** Hotels and motels are located throughout Boston; **First Aid available in park:** Yes; **Nearest Hospital:** Massachusetts General; **Days/Hours:** Faneuil Hall is open daily from 9:00 a.m. until 5:00 p.m. The Museum and Armory of the Ancient and Honorable Artillery Company is open on weekdays from 10:00 a.m. until 4:00 p.m. Faneuil Hall is still frequently used as a meeting hall for various groups and organizations and may, at times, be closed to the public in preparation for or during these functions. For more information call the National Park Service Visitor Center at 617-242-5642; **Holiday Closings:** Thanksgiving, Christmas and New Years Day; **Visitor attractions closed for seasons:** None; **Weather:** Summer temperatures generally in the 80's; Winter is windy with temperatures down to the teens.

NEARBY FACILITIES & POINTS OF INTEREST: Lowell NHP, Adams NHS, Saugus Iron Works NHS, Minute Man NHP, John Fitzgerald Kennedy NHS, Longfellow NHS, Frederick Law Olmsted NHS, and Salem Maritime NHS.

Frederick Law Olmsted National Historic Site
Brookline, Massachusetts **SEE CLIMATABLE NO. 74**

MAILING ADDRESS: 99 Warren Street, Brookline, Massachusetts 02146 **Telephone:** 617-566-1689

DIRECTIONS: From Rt. 128 (I-95), take exit for Rt. 9 East (toward Boston), follow past Brookline Reservoir, turn right on Warren Street to Site (two blocks) to corner of Dudley and Warren Streets. From Southeast Expressway (I-93), go to Massachusetts Turnpike West and follow to Brighton-Harvard Street exit, stay on Harvard Street to Rt. 9 (Boylston Street), take right, go two traffic lights west to Warren Street and turn left and follow to site.

Historic home and office of the Founder of American landscape architecture, used by Frederick Law Olmsted, Sr. and his sons. Established December, 1979.

VISITOR ACTIVITIES: Guided tour of home with exhibits, guided tour of office & restored grounds, slide presentation; **Permits:** No; **Fees:** No; **Visitor facilities:** restrooms & bookstore; **Any limitations on vehicle usage:** Very limited parking; **Hiking trails:** No; **Backcountry:** No; **Camping:** No; **Other overnight accommodations on site:** No; **Meals served in the park:** No; **Food and supplies obtainable in the park:** No; **Food and supplies obtainable nearby:** Yes, available in Brookline (1½ miles) and Boston (3 miles); **Overnight accommodations:** Available in Brookline and Boston; **First Aid available in park:** No; **Nearest Hospital:** Hospital within ½ mile; **Days/Hours:** Friday-Sunday 10 a.m.-4:30 p.m.—Groups at other times by reservation; **Holiday Closings:** Thanksgiving, Christmas, and New Year's; **Visitor attractions closed for seasons:** No.

TRAVEL ACCESS: Bus: MBTA; **Rail:** MBTA (Riverside) Rail, nearest terminal-Brookline Hills Stop; **Air:** Boston Terminals.

NEARBY FACILITIES & POINTS OF INTEREST: Hotel/Motel: nearby in Boston; **Campgrounds:** Nearby; **Parks, other points of interest:** Boston Park System designed by Olmsted; Longfellow National Historic Site; Boston National Historical Park; John F. Kennedy National Historic Site; and John F. Kennedy Library.

John F. Kennedy National Historic Site
Brookline, Massachusetts   **SEE CLIMATABLE NO. 74**

MAILING ADDRESS: Superintendent, John F. Kennedy National Historic Site, 83 Beals Street, Brookline, Massachusetts 02146 **Telephone:** 617-566-7937

DIRECTIONS: Take exit #18 from Mass. Turnpike Extension. Proceed towards Allston along Cambridge Street, turn left onto Harvard Street. Turn left from Harvard Street onto Beals Street. Directional signs are posted at nearby intersections. The Site is easily reached by public transportation.

This nine-room, three-story structure is the birthplace and early childhood home (1917-1921) of the 35th President of the United States. Authorized for addition to the National Park System on May 26, 1967.

VISITOR ACTIVITIES: ranger-guided with tape-recorded tour narrated by the President's mother; **Permits:** No; **Fees:** $1.00 for adults. Those under 12 and over 62-free. Golden Eagle and Golden Age Passports accepted and available; **Visitor facilities:** small visitor reception area with exhibits and sales center; **Any limitations on vehicle usage:** Parking is available only on the street, which may be congested. Buses must not idle motors for more than five minutes; **Meals served in the park:** No; **Food and supplies obtainable in the park:** No; **Food and supplies obtainable nearby:** Yes, about two-four blocks away; **Overnight accommodations:** Brookline, 1/2 mile (.8 km). Boston is 3 miles (4.5 km) distant; **First Aid available in park:** Yes; **Nearest Hospital:** Brookline, 1 mile (1.6 km); **Days/Hours:** Open daily from 10:00 a.m. to 4:30 p.m.; **Holiday Closings:** Thanksgiving, Dec. 25 and Jan. 1.

Longfellow National Historic Site
Cambridge, Massachusetts   **SEE CLIMATABLE NO. 74**

MAILING ADDRESS: Superintendent, Longfellow National Historic Site, 105 Brattle Street, Cambridge, Massachusetts 02138 **Telephone:** 617-876-4491

DIRECTIONS: Cambridge is a historic city with both old and new buildings of interest. For visitors unfamiliar with the area the easiest way to see some of Cambridge's sights including the Longfellow House is to park in Boston under the Common, and take the Red Line subway to Harvard Square. From there walk to Brattle Street and continue down Brattle about .6 mile (1 km) to Longfellow House. On your way you will pass two colonial mansions, the William Brattle House and the John Vassall, Sr. House. On your return to Harvard Square, you may wish to go via Mason Street and Cambridge Common. On the Common a bronze plaque marks the Site of the "Washington Elm" under whose branches George Washington took command of the Continental Army.

Poet Henry Wadsworth Longfellow lived here from 1837 to 1882. The house had been George Washington's headquarters during the siege of Boston, 1775-76. Authorized for addition to the National Park System on Oct. 9, 1972.

VISITOR ACTIVITIES: guided tours, garden concerts on alternate Sundays during the Summer beginning in mid-June; **Permits:** No; **Fees:** Entrance fee is $2 for adults. No charge for persons 12 and under or 62 and over. Golden Eagle and Golden Age Passports accepted and available; **Visitor facilities:** None on Site. A free brochure is available on request; **Any limitations on vehicle usage:** No parking is available at the Site. Limited parking is .6 mile (1 km) distant; **Hiking trails:** No; **Meals served in the park:** No; **Food and supplies obtainable in the park:** No; **Food and supplies obtainable nearby:** Yes, in Cambridge (Harvard Square); **Overnight accommodations:** Cambridge, within walking distance, or Boston, 7 miles (11 km); **First Aid available in park:** No; **Nearest Hospital:** Mt. Auburn, .6 mile (1 km); **Days/Hours:** Open daily from 10 a.m. to 4:30 p.m.; **Holiday Closings:** Thanksgiving, Dec. 25 and Jan. 1; **Weather:** Moderately warm and humid Summer, occasional inconvenience from snow and ice in Winter.

GENERAL INFORMATION: Group tours are required to make reservations. On Site parking for handicapped people may be arranged in advance. Telephone 617-876-4491.

TRAVEL ACCESS: Bus: Trailways/Greyhound provide daily service to Boston; MBTA stops at Harvard Square; **Rail:** Amtrak provides daily service to Boston; **Air:** Major Airlines offer regular service into Boston; **Other:** Taxi service to the House is available from Harvard Square.

NEARBY FACILITIES & POINTS OF INTEREST: Hotel/Motel: Sheraton Commander, 16 Garden Street, Cambridge 617-547-4800; **Parks, other points of interest:** Tory Row Houses; Harvard and Radcliffe Universities in Cambridge.

Lowell National Historical Park
Lowell, Massachusetts **SEE CLIMATABLE NO. 77**

MAILING ADDRESS: Superintendent, Lowell National Historical Park, 169 Merrimack St., Lowell, Massachusetts 01852 **Telephone:** 617-459-1000

DIRECTIONS: Take the Lowell Connector from either Int. 495 or US 3. Exit on Thorndike Street North, and proceed approx. .5 mile (.8 km) to Dutton Street. Take a right turn on Dutton Street. Follow Dutton to the marked parking lot. There is train access to Lowell from the Boston North Station. The Visitor Center is at 246 Market Street.

The park includes seven original mill complexes, a power canal system and other early 19th Century structures of this planned city of the Industrial Revolution. Authorized for addition to the National Park System on June 5, 1978.

VISITOR ACTIVITIES: Free guided tours by barge, trolley and on foot are conducted 14 times daily from Memorial Day to Columbus Day. For reservations, call 617-459-1000. Self-guided tours and downtown walking tours offered daily, year round; **Permits:** No, but tour reservations are required; **Fees:** No admission fees for National Park Service facilities; **Visitor facilities:** Visitor Center, 246 Marker St., open daily 8:30 a.m.-5:00 p.m. The Patrick J. Mogan Cultural Center will open in the spring of 1988; the Boott Mills Museum is scheduled to open in late 1989, parking, restrooms. Lowell Heritage State Park Waterpower Exhibit, open daily, 9:00-4:30; **Any limitations on vehicle usage:** Use of public transportation is recommended; **Hiking trails:** No; **Backcountry:** No; **Camping:** No; **Other overnight accommodations on site:** Lowell Hilton, 50 Warren Ave.; **Meals served in the park:** Yes; **Food and supplies obtainable in the park:** Yes; **Food and supplies obtainable nearby:** Yes; **Overnight accommodations:** On the periphery of Lowell, 2 miles (3 km); **First Aid available in park:** Yes; **Nearest Hospital:** St. John's, 1/4 mile (.4 km); **Days/Hours:** Visitor Center open from 8:30 a.m. to 5 p.m. year-round; **Holiday Closings:** Thanksgiving, Christmas, and New Years Day; **Visitor attractions closed for seasons:** Mill and canal tour from Memorial Day through Columbus Day only, walking tours year round.

TRAVEL ACCESS: Bus: Trailways provides daily service into Lowell's New Industrial Ave. terminal; Lowell Regional Transit has regular service downtown; **Rail:** Boston & Maine RR provides regular service; **Air:** Access through Boston-Logan airport.

NEARBY FACILITIES & POINTS OF INTEREST: Hotel/Motel: Town House Motor Inn, 850 Chelmsford St., Lowell, 617-454-5606, 2 miles; Howard Johnson Motor Lodge, 187 Chelmsford St., Chelmsford MA, 617-256-7511, 3 miles; Quality Inn, Rt. I-495 (Exit 34) & Rt. 110, Chelmsford, 617-256-0800, 3 miles; Holiday Inn, 95 Main St., Tewksbury, 617-851-7301, 3 miles; Appleton Inn, 30 Industrial Ave., Lowell, 617-458-7575, 2 miles; **Campgrounds:** KOA Minuteman Campground (617-772-0042); **Parks, other points of interest:** Lowell Heritage State Park, Whistler House, Museum of American Textile History, Lowell-Dracut-Tyngsboro State Forest, Lawrence Heritage State Park.

Minute Man National Historical Park
Concord, Massachusetts   **SEE CLIMATABLE NO. 74**

MAILING ADDRESS: Superintendent, Minute Man National Historical Park, P.O. Box 160, Concord, Massachusetts 01742 **Telephone:** 617-369-6993

DIRECTIONS: The North Bridge Visitor Center is located off Liberty Street in Concord. The Battle Road Visitor Center is located off Route 2A in Lexington. Information is available at both places.

This is the scene of the fighting on the opening day of the Revolutionary War, April 19, 1775. It includes The North Bridge, the Minute Man Statue, 4 miles (6.4 km) of Battle Road between Lexington and Concord, and "The Wayside," Nathaniel Hawthorne's Home. Authorized by act of Congress, September 21, 1959.

VISITOR ACTIVITIES: interpretive exhibits and film, walking tours, interpretive talks. Sales and informational material are available; **Permits:** No; **Fees:** $1 admission fee at "The Wayside" for persons 16 and over. Golden Eagle and Golden Age Passports accepted and available; **Visitor facilities:** The North Bridge Unit (includes the famous Minute Man statue by Daniel Chester French), The Battle Road Visitor Center, the Wayside, Fiske Hill, parking, restrooms; **Any limitations on vehicle usage:** Use the parking facilities provided. State Route 2A is a heavily travelled road and slowing down for sightseeing could be a hazard; **Hiking trails:** Yes, a 1 mile (1.6 km) self-guiding trail is available at Fiske Hill on Route 2A in Lexington. The restored battle road from the North Bridge leads to the North Bridge Visitor Center; **Backcountry:** No; **Camping:** No; **Other overnight accommodations on site:** No; **Meals served in the park:** No; **Food and supplies obtainable in the park:** No; **Food and supplies obtainable nearby:** Yes, in nearby towns: Concord, Lexington, Acton, & Bedford; **Overnight accommodations:** Concord, Lexington, Acton & Bedford; **First Aid available in park:** Yes; **Nearest Hospital:** Emerson Hospital, Concord, 2 miles (3.2 km) from the Park; **Days/Hours:** North Bridge Visitor Center is open the year-round 8:30 a.m. - 5:00 p.m. except Dec. 25 & Jan. 1. Call 617-369-6993 for hours and days of other facilities; **Weather:** New England climate: cold Winters; warm Summers.

GENERAL INFORMATION: Please respect the rights of private families living within the Park boundary. Visitors to the area can also see historic Sites relating to the lives of Henry David Thoreau, Louisa May Alcott and Ralph Waldo Emerson.

Old North Church
Boston National Historical Park, Boston, MA   **SEE CLIMATABLE NO. 74**

MAILING ADDRESS: Old North Church, 193 Salem Street, Boston, MA 02113 **Telephone:** 617-523-6676

DIRECTIONS: We recommend that you do not drive in downtown Boston; mass transit provides a good alternative. The closest subway stop is Haymarket Station (orange or green subway lines). From here cross under the elevated expressway into Boston's North End. At the tunnel entering the North End begin to follow the red line of the Freedom Trail. It is a fifteen minute walk to the Old North Church.

The Old North Church, also known as Christ's Church, was built in 1723 and remains an active Episcopal church today. It was from the steeple of Old North that two lanterns were hung on April 18th, 1775 warning colonials in Charlestown that the British were marching from Boston to Lexington and Concord to destroy colonial military supplies. On this night, Paul Revere made his famous "midnight ride" to warn the countryside that "the British are coming."

VISITOR ACTIVITIES: The Old North Church is a cooperative site of Boston National Historical Park. It remains an active Episcopal Church. Sunday services at 9:30 and 11:30 a.m. and 4:00 p.m. Old North Church is open every day. The site is maintained by the Church through donations. Staff are available to give historic talks on the Church throughout the day. A museum and gift shop are located on the grounds; **Permits:** Permits are required for special activities and commercial photography; **Fees:** Free, donations welcome; **Any limitations on vehicle usage:** The Old North Church is in Boston's crowded North End. Street parking is limited to neighborhood residents; **Hiking trails:** Yes, Old North Church is located along Boston's historic Freedom Trail; **Camping:** None; **Food service:** There are numerous restaurants in the vicinity; **Overnight accommodations:** Hotels and motels are located throughout Boston; **First Aid available in park:** Yes, limited; **Nearest Hospital:** Massachusetts General; **Days/Hours:** Open every day from 9:00 a.m. until 5:00 p.m.; **Holiday Closings:** None; **Visitor attractions closed for season:** None; **Weather:** Summer temperatures generally in the 80's; Winter is windy with temperatures down to the teens.

NEARBY FACILITIES & POINTS OF INTEREST: Lowell NHP, Adams NHS, Saugus Iron Works NHS, Minute Man NHP, John Fitzgerald Kennedy NHS, Longfellow NHS, Frederick Law Olmsted NHS, and Salem Maritime NHS.

Old South Meeting House
Boston National Historical Park, Boston, MA   **SEE CLIMATABLE NO. 74**

MAILING ADDRESS: The Old South Meeting House, 310 Washington Street, Boston, MA 02108 **Telephone:** 6179

DIRECTIONS: We recommend that you do not drive in downtown Boston. Mass transit provides a good alternative. The closest subway stop is at State Street (orange and blue subway lines).

The Old South Meeting House, built as a Congregational place of meeting and worship in 1729, was the site of many meetings protesting British policies in the 1760's and 1770's most notably the meeting preceding the Boston Tea Party. In 1876 the Old South Association was founded to save the property from demolition, one of the first instances of historic preservation in the nation.

VISITOR ACTIVITIES: The Old South Meeting House is a cooperative site in Boston National Historical Park. It is owned and operated by the Old South Association in Boston. Visitors are invited to tour this beautifully restored meeting hall that contains multimedia exhibits on the history of the site and life in 18th century Boston. "Middays the Meeting House," a lecture and concert series, presents the issues, individuals, and music of America's past, every Tuesday at 12:15 p.m. from October to March. "Town Meetings" pit Loyalists against Patriots in debates on "What's to be done with the obnoxious tea?" every Saturday at 2:00 p.m., mid-June through Labor Day. Old South is still used as a hall for concerts, meetings and school activities throughout the year; **Permits:** Contact Old South Association Marketing Coordinator. Programs for school groups and others can be arranged in advance by contacting the site. A featured program is "Tea is Brewing," where school groups trace the events of the Boston Tea Party at Faneuil Hall, Old South and the Boston Tea Party Ship. "Tea is Brewing" is available by reservation from September through June; **Fees:** Admission $1.25 for adults, $.75 for seniors, $.50 for children 6-18, free for those under 6; **Visitor facilities:** There are no restrooms at the site. Old South is accessible by wheelchair; **Any limitations on vehicle usage:** Old South is located in downtown Boston. Parking is very limited. Commercial parking lots are located on nearby Washington Street and the Boston Common; **Hiking trails:** Old South Meeting House is located along Boston's historic Freedom Trail; **Camping:** None; **Food Service:** Numerous restaurants are located in the vicinity; **Overnight accommodations:** Hotels and motels are located throughout Boston; **First Aid available in park;** Yes, limited; **Nearest Hospital:** Massachusetts General, Tufts New England Medical Center; **Days/Hours:** April 1 through October 31, 9:30 a.m.-4:45 p.m. daily. November 1 through March 31, weekends 10:00 a.m.-4:00 p.m. weekends 10:00 a.m.-5:00 p.m.; **Holiday Closings:** Thanksgiving, December 24, Christmas, and New Years Day; **Vistor attractions closed for seasons:** None; **Weather:** Summer temperatures generally in the 80's; Winter is windy with temperatures down to the teens.

NEARBY FACILITIES & POINTS OF INTEREST: Lowell NHP, Adams NHS, Saugus Iron Works NHS, Minute Man NHP, John Fitzgerald Kennedy NHS, Longfellow NHS, Frederick Law Olmsted NHS, and Salem Maritime NHS.

Old State House
Boston National Historical Park, Boston, MA   **SEE CLIMATABLE NO. 74**

MAILING ADDRESS: The Old State House, 206 Washington Street, Boston, MA 02109 **Telephone:** 617-242-5655

DIRECTIONS: We recommend that you do not drive in downtown Boston; mass transit provides a good alternative. The Old State House is located at the State Street stop on the subway (blue or orange subway lines).

The Old State House was built in 1712/13 and served as the seat of government for both colonial, and later state government. The Boston Massacre took place outside the building on March 5, 1770. James Otis eloquently argued against the Writs of Assistance within its chambers in 1761. Because of the speech, John Adams later remarked, "Here the child independence was born."

VISITOR ACTIVITIES: The Old State House is owned by the City of Boston and is a part of Boston National Historical Park. It is managed by the Bostonian Society (the historical society for the city of Boston). The Old State House contains a gift ship and exhibits of Boston's colonial, revolutionary and maritime history. Historical talks are offered hourly during summer months. Special activities are held throughout the year and announced in Boston newspapers; **Permits:** Required for special activities. Programs for school groups can be arranged by contatcting the site in advance; **Fees:** Admission fee $1.25 for adults, 75¢ for students and seniors, 50¢ for children under 16, children under 6 and Massachusetts school children admitted free; **Visitor facilities:** There are no restrooms on the site (restrooms are available at the National Park Service Visitor Center directly across from the site); **Any limitations on vehicle usage:** The Old State House is located in downtown Boston. Parking is limited. Commercial parking lots are located on nearby Congress and Washington Streets; **Hiking trails:** Yes. The Old State House is located on Boston's historic Freedom Trail; **Camping:** None; **Food service:** There are numerous restaurants in the vicinity; **Overnight accommodations:**

Hotels and motels are located throughout Boston; **First Aid available in park:** Yes, at the National Park Service Visitor Center across from the Old State House; **Nearest Hospitals:** Massachusetts General, Tufts New England Medical Center; **Days/Hours:** April 1 through October 31 open daily from 9:30 a.m. until 5:00 p.m. November 1 through March 31 open Monday through Friday 10:00 a.m. until 4:00 p.m. Saturdays 9:30 a.m. until 5:00 p.m. and Sundays 11:00 a.m. until 5:00 p.m.; **Holiday Closings:** Thanksgiving, Christmas, New Years Day and Easter Sunday; **Visitor attractions closed for seasons:** None; **Weather:** Summer temperatures generally in the 80's; Winter is windy with temperatures down to the teens.

NEARBY FACILITIES & POINTS OF INTEREST: Lowell NHP, Adams NHS, Saugus Iron Works NHS, Minute Man NHP, John Fitzgerald Kennedy NHS, Longfellow NHS, Frederick Law Olmsted NHS, and Salem Maritime NHS.

Paul Revere House
Boston National Historical Park, Boston, MA   **SEE CLIMATABLE NO. 74**

MAILING ADDRESS: Paul Revere House, 19 North Square, Boston, MA 02113 **Telephone:** 617-523-1676

DIRECTIONS: We recommend that you do not drive in downtown Boston; mass transit provides a good alternative. The closest subway stop is at Haymarket Station (orange or green subway lines). From here cross under the elevated expressway into Boston's North End. At the tunnel entering the North End begin to follow the red line of the Freedom Trail. It is a ten minute walk from Haymarket to the Paul Revere House.
    The Paul Revere House was built around 1680 and is the oldest surviving house in Boston. Paul Revere owned the house from 1770 until 1800. It was from here that he departed on his famous "midnight ride" to warn the colonials in Lexington and Concord of the approaching British.

VISITOR ACTIVITIES: The Paul Revere House is a cooperative site of Boston National Historical Park. It is managed by the Paul Revere Memorial Association. Visitors may tour the two story colonial house throughout the year. Staff and exhibits tell the story of Paul Revere and life in colonial Boston; **Permits:** Only for special uses. Programs for school groups or other visiting organizations can be arranged by contatcting the site in advance; **Fees:** Admission fee $2.00 for adults, $1.50 for senior citizens and students, 50¢ for children under 17. Group rates are available by reservation only; **Visitor facilities:** There are no restrooms on the site. The first floor of the house is accessible by wheelchair. Foreign language folders are available in Japanese, French, German, Italian, and Spanish; **Any limitations on vehicle usage:** The Paul Revere House is located in Boston's crowded North End. Street parking is limited to neighborhood residents; **Hiking trails:** Yes, the Paul Revere House is located along Boston's historic Freedom Trail; **Camping:** None; **Food service:** There are numerous restaurants in the vicinity; **Overnight accommodations:** Hotels and motels are located throughout Boston; **First Aid available in park:** Yes, limited; **Nearest Hospitals:** The closest hospital is Massachusetts General; **Days/Hours:** Mid-April through October 31, 9:30 a.m. until 5:15 p.m. November 1 through mid-April, 9:30 a.m. until 4:15 p.m. The site is closed on Mondays in January, February and March; **Holiday Closings:** Thanksgiving, Christmas, New Years Day; **Visitor attractions closed for seasons:** Closed on Mondays in January, February and March; **Weather:** Summer temperatures generally in the 80's; Winter is windy with temperatures down to the teens.

NEARBY FACILITIES & POINTS OF INTEREST: Lowell NHP, Adams NHS, Saugus Iron Works NHS, Minute Man NHP, John Fitzgerald Kennedy NHS, Longfellow NHS, Frederick Law Olmsted NHS, and Salem Maritime NSH.

Salem Maritime National Historic Site
Salem, Massachusetts   **SEE CLIMATABLE NO. 74**

MAILING ADDRESS: Superintendent, Salem Maritime National Historic Site, Custom House, Derby Street, Salem, Massachusetts 01970 **Telephone:** 617-744-4323

DIRECTIONS: Site headquarters is at Custom House, 178 Derby Street, Salem, 20 miles (32 km) northeast of Boston.

This waterfront Site is a cross-section of the Port of Salem from the years when Salem ships were opening American trade with ports of the Far East. Nine acres of wharves and grounds provide public open space on the harbor, and ten historic buildings associated with port activities complete the historic scene. Area authorized for addition to the National Park System on Mar. 17, 1938.

VISITOR ACTIVITIES: Derby Wharf, Central Wharf, Hatch's Wharf, plus yards and gardens are normally open all day, as are the 1819 Custom House and c. 1800 West India Goods Store and Bonded Warehouse. Costumed interpretation, demonstrations, or ranger-guided tours to additional historic buildings are scheduled on a seasonal basis. School programs available by reservation. **Permits:** No; **Fees:** None except for concessioner services. Golden Age and Golden Eagle Passports available. **Visitor facilities:** limited parking, restrooms, visitor information, interpretive exhibits, slide show; **Any limitations on vehicle usage:** Autos are prohibited on the historic roadway; **Hiking trails:** 1-mile (round trip) Derby Wharf Historic Trail. **Backcountry:** No; **Camping:** No; **Other overnight accommodations on site:** No; **Meals served in the park:** No; **Food and supplies obtainable in the park:** No; **Food and supplies obtainable nearby:** Yes, in downtown Salem, within ½ mile (.8 km); **Overnight accommodations:** Downtown Salem, within ½ mile (.8 km); **First Aid available in park:** Yes; **Nearest Hospital:** Salem, 1½ mile (2.4 km); **Days/Hours:** Custom House open daily, 8:30 a.m.-5 p.m. Check here for hours of other structures; **Holiday Closings:** Thanksgiving, Dec. 25 & Jan. 1; **Visitor attractions closed for seasons:** Tour routes and structures visited may vary with season; **Weather:** There is a great weather and temperature range. Weather can be windy or snowy in Winter, with temperatures from 0°F; with sunny or rainy summer days and temperatures ranging as high as 90°F.

TRAVEL ACCESS: Bus: Mass. Bay Transit Authority provides service approximately hourly from Haymarket Square, Boston, to New Derby St., ¼ mi. West of Site; **Rail:** Mass. Bay Transit Authority provides service from North Station, Boston to Salem Depot, ½ mile East of Site; **Air:** Airlines serving Boston; **Other:** Taxis, available within city. Also rental cars within city. Private car: Traffic can be heavy and parking limited in City. Walking is best way to get around City. Bicycle travel is convenient, but traffic is heavy.

NEARBY FACILITIES & POINTS OF INTEREST: Hotel/Motel: Hawthorne Inn, 18 Washington Square, Salem, 617-744-4080, ¼ mile from Site; **Campgrounds:** Nearest State campgrounds: Harold Parker State Forest, North Reading, MA (617) 686-3391 (approx. 10 miles); **New information:** Special events for Summer and school vacation include visitor participation.

Saugus Iron Works National Historic Site
Saugus, Massachusetts   **SEE CLIMATABLE NO. 74**

MAILING ADDRESS: Superintendent, Saugus Iron Works National Historic Site, 244 Central Street, Saugus, Massachusetts 01906 **Telephone:** 617-233-0050

DIRECTIONS: Take the "Main Street Saugus" exit from Route 1, which brings you into Saugus Center. Park 2 blocks from Saugus Center—244 Central Street.

This reconstruction of the first integrated iron works in North America, begun in 1646, includes the Iron Works House, furnace, forge and rolling and slitting mill. Authorized for addition to the National Park System on April 5, 1968.

VISITOR ACTIVITIES: photography, walking tours, exhibits, film; **Permits:** No; **Fees:** No; **Visitor facilities:** Visitors can tour the Site and museum and watch demonstrations of iron workings; **Any limitations on vehicle usage:** No; **Meals served in the park:** No; **Food and supplies obtainable in the park:** No; **Food and supplies obtainable nearby:** Yes, at Saugus Center—2 blocks; **Overnight accommodations:** On Route 1, 1 mile (1.6 km) from the Site; **First Aid available in park:** Yes; **Nearest Hospital:** Wakefield, Lynn; **Days/Hours:** Open daily from 9 a.m. to 4 p.m. from Nov. 1 through March 31 and from 9 a.m. to 5 p.m. from April 1 to Oct. 31; **Holiday Closings:** Thanksgiving, Dec. 25 and Jan. 1; **Visitor attractions closed for season:** None; **Weather:** Humid in Summer, cold in Winter. This is an outdoor facility so visitors should dress for inclement weather.

GENERAL INFORMATION: *For Your Safety*—Be careful around the waterwheel pits and do not climb on the waterwheels or other historic structures. The slag can cause severe cuts.

Springfield Armory National Historic Site
Springfield, Massachusetts   **SEE CLIMATABLE NO. 78**

MAILING ADDRESS: Superintendent, Springfield Armory National Historic Site, One Armory Square, Springfield, Massachusetts 01105 **Telephone:** 413-734-8551

DIRECTIONS: The Site is in downtown Springfield, MA just off State Street. To reach the site from the Massachusetts Turnpike take exit 6 to Route I-291, then exit 3 to Armory Street south to Federal Street. From I-91, exit on I-291 eastbound (follow signs to Boston); take Armory St. exit; thereafter, same directions as above. The Site is entered through the gate on Federal Street.

Over a span of 200 years this small-arms manufacturing center produced weapons ranging from the 1795 flintlock to the 1903, M-1 and M-14 rifles. A large collection of small arms is maintained here. Authorized for addition to the National Park System on Oct. 26, 1974.

VISITOR ACTIVITIES: self-guiding museum tours, guided tours by advance arrangement. Museum will be closed for renovation September, 1987 to Spring, 1989; **Permits:** No; **Fees:** No; **Visitor facilities:** museum, restrooms; **Any limitations on vehicle usage:** No; **Hiking trails:** No; **Backcountry:** No; **Camping:** No; **Other overnight accommodations on site:** No; **Meals served in the park:** No; **Food and supplies obtainable in the park:** No; **Food and supplies obtainable nearby:** Yes, in Springfield; **Overnight accommodations:** Springfield, within walking distance; **First Aid available in park:** No; **Nearest Hospital:** Springfield, directly across from the museum; **Days/Hours:** Open daily from 8:30 a.m. to 4:30 p.m. year-round; **Holiday Closings:** Thanksgiving, Dec. 25 & Jan. 1; **Weather:** Typical New England conditions prevail.

USS Constitution
Boston National Historical Park, Boston, MA   **SEE CLIMATABLE NO. 74**

See Charlestown Navy Yard.

Visitor Center
Boston National Historical Park, Boston, MA   **SEE CLIMATABLE NO. 74**

MAILING ADDRESS: Superintendent, Boston National Historical Park, Charlestown Navy Yard, Boston, MA 02129 **Telephone:** 617-242-5644

DIRECTIONS: The Visitor Center is located at 15 State Street in downtown Boston across from the Old State House. We recommend that you don't drive in downtown Boston; mass transit provides a good alternative. The Visitor Center is located at the State Street stop on the subway, (blue or orange subway lines).

The Visitor Center provides information on the Boston area and beyond, as well as an orientation to the historic sites and services of Boston National Historical Park. The Park includes the Old South Meeting House, the Old State House, Faneuil Hall, the Paul Revere House, Old North Church, the Bunker Hill Monument, the Charlestown Navy Yard and Dorchester Heights. The Center also provides information on Boston African American National Historic Site.

VISITOR ACTIVITIES: Park Rangers provide information on the park and facilities in the Boston area. A bookstore carries titles on Boston history, the American Revolution, U.S. maritime history, Black History, and travel in New England. A 7-minute slide program on Boston's historic Freedom Trail is available throughout the day. Ranger led walks along the Freedom Trail originate from the Visitor Center. Walks, that last 90 minutes, depart daily from mid-April through November; **Permits:** Only for special usage. Special services for school or other visiting groups can be arranged by contacting the site in advance; **Fees:** None; **Visitor facilities:** Restrooms are available. The site is completely accessible by wheelchair; **Any limitations on vehicle usage:** The Visitor Center is located in downtown Boston. Street parking is limited. Commercial parking lots are located on nearby Congress and Washington Streets; **Hiking trails:** The Visitor Center is located along Boston's historic Freedom Trail; **Camping:** None; **Food service:** There are numerous restaurants in the vicinity; **Overnight accommodations:** Hotels and motels are located throughout Boston; **First Aid available in park:** Yes; **Nearest Hospitals:** Massachusetts General, Tufts New England Medical Center; **Days/Hours:** Open daily from 9:00 a.m. until 5:00 p.m. on weekends, 8:00 a.m. until 5:00 p.m. on weekdays; **Holiday Closings:** Thanksgiving, Christmas and New Year's Day; **Visitor attractions closed for seasons:** None; **Weather:** Summer temperatures generally in the 80's; Winter is windy with temperatures down to the teens.

NEARBY FACILITIES & POINTS OF INTEREST: Lowell NHP, Adams NHS, Saugus Iron Works NHS, Minute Man NHP, John Fitzgerald Kennedy NHS, Longfellow NHS, Frederick Law Olmsted NHS, and Salem Maritime NHS.

Michigan

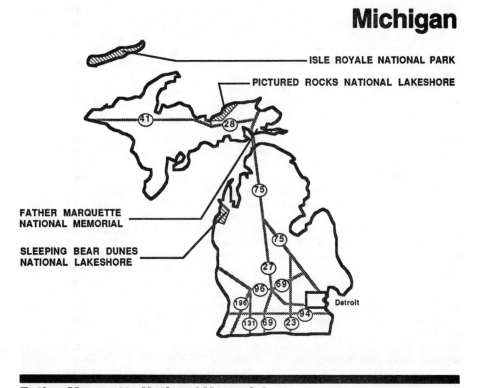

ISLE ROYALE NATIONAL PARK

PICTURED ROCKS NATIONAL LAKESHORE

FATHER MARQUETTE
NATIONAL MEMORIAL

SLEEPING BEAR DUNES
NATIONAL LAKESHORE

Detroit

Father Marquette National Memorial
St. Ignace, Michigan   **SEE CLIMATABLE NO. 76**

MAILING ADDRESS: Straits State Park, 720 Church Street, St. Ignace, Michigan 49781 **Telephone:** 906-643-9394

DIRECTIONS: The Memorial to Father Jacques Marquette, French priest and explorer, is in Straits State Park near St. Ignace, Mich., where he founded a Jesuit mission in 1671 and was buried in 1678. A Memorial structure, restrooms, picnic area, parking lots, foot-trails, overlook, and kiosks have been completed. The museum-theatre building and an amphitheatre are now completed and in use. This affiliated area was authorized for addition to the National Park System on Dec. 20, 1975.

Isle Royale National Park
Houghton, Michigan   **SEE CLIMATABLE NO. 80**

MAILING ADDRESS: Superintendent, Isle Royale National Park, 87 North Ripley St., Houghton, Michigan 49931 **Telephone:** 906-482-0984

DIRECTIONS: Transportation from the mainland to Isle Royale is by boat or float-plane. Reservations are recommended. Boats go from Houghton to Rock Harbor from June to Sept. For schedules, rates and reservations for the National Park Service boat, Ranger III, contact the Superintendent, Isle Royale National Park, Houghton MI 49931, phone 906-482-0984. From Copper Harbor to Rock Harbor (late June to late September), contact Isle Royale Queen II, Copper Harbor, MI 49918, phone 906-289-

4437 (mid-June to Aug.) and 906-482-4950 (Sept. to mid-June). From Grand Portage to Windigo (late June to Labor Day) and Grand Portage to Rock Harbor via Windigo (May to Oct.), contact GPIR Transportation Lines, 1332 London Rd., Duluth, MN 55801, phone 218-728-1237 year-round. One boat circumnavigates Isle Royale and will discharge and pick up passengers at various points. Isle Royale Seaplane Service operates from Houghton; Phone 906-482-8850 (summer).

The largest in Lake Superior, this forested island is also distinguished for its wilderness character, timber wolves and moose, and pre-Columbian copper mines. Authorized for addition to the National Park System on Mar. 3, 1931.

VISITOR ACTIVITIES: boating (rentals at Windigo and Rock Harbor Lodge), boat tours, hiking, scuba diving, camping, fishing, wildlife-watching, canoeing, interpretive programs; **Permits:** for camping; Permits available at Rock Harbor and Windigo; **Fees:** Entrance fee $2 per person; **Visitor facilities:** boat tours, rental boats and motors, water taxi service, hiking trails, campgrounds, guided fishing trips, self-guiding trails, interpretive programs, full services and facilities available mid-June to August 31, limited services and facilities at other times; **Any limitations on vehicle usage:** No vehicles of any type are allowed on the island and there are no roads; **Hiking trails:** 165 miles of foot trails; **Backcountry:** 99% Federal Wilderness. A number of combination trips—boat one way and hike the other—can be arranged with commercial boat operators (note phone numbers above); **Camping:** Yes, campsites cannot be reserved. All campers must obtain a camping permit, available at Rock Harbor or Windigo; **Other overnight accommodations on site:** Yes, lodge and housekeeping facilities are available from late June through Labor Day. For reservations and rates during the seasons, contact Rock Harbor Lodge, P.O. Box 405, Houghton, MI 49931, phone 906-337-4993; out of season, contact National Park Concessions, Inc. Mammoth Cave, KY 42259, phone 502-773-2191; **Meals served in the park:** Yes, restaurant service is available at Rock Harbor; **Food and supplies obtainable in the park:** Yes, (limited) at Rock Harbor & Windigo; **Food and supplies obtainable nearby:** Yes, in Houghton, MI and Grand Portage, MN; **Overnight accommodations:** Houghton, MI 60 miles (96.6 km) & Grand Portage, MN, 20 miles (32.2 km); **First Aid available in park:** Yes, at Ranger Stations; **Nearest Hospital:** Houghton, MI. Note: evacuation from the island is done at the cost of the visitor; **Days/ Hours:** The Park is open to visitors from April 16 to Oct. 31, with full services offered mid June to Aug. 31. Call or write for current information prior to your visit; **Visitor attractions closed for seasons:** Park is closed Nov. 1-April 15; **Weather:** Mid-summer temperatures rarely exceed 80°; evenings are usually cool. Rain is frequent throughout the season.

GENERAL INFORMATION: Because the waters of Lake Superior are often rough, it is not safe to use boats of 20 feet or less to go to the island. However, such boats can be transported to Isle Royale on the Ranger III. The concession boat operators mentioned in the directions above will transport small runabouts and canoes. Fuel may be purchased at Rock Harbor and Windigo. Firearms, pets and wheeled vehicles are prohibited in the Park.

Lake Survey Chart 14976, "Isle Royale" is recommended for anyone navigating the Park's waters. This chart and others can be purchased from the Park. A topographic map of Isle Royale can be purchased at the Park.

North Country National Scenic Trail
For details see listing in New York

Pictured Rocks National Lakeshore
Munising, Michigan   **SEE CLIMATABLE NO. 76**

MAILING ADDRESS: Superintendent, Pictured Rocks National Lakeshore, P.O. Box 40, Munising, Michigan 49862 **Telephone:** 906-387-2607

DIRECTIONS: Pictured Rocks Cliffs are accessible by car at Miner's Castle, 7 miles (11.3 km) east of Munising off County Road H-58. The Interpretive Center is at Munising Falls, 2.5 miles (4 km) east of Munising. The Munising Falls Interpretive Center is open daily in summer. The Munising Information Center, located at the intersection of M-28 and H-58 in Munising, is operated jointly by the National Park Service and the U.S. Forest Service and is open year-round. The headquarters building is at Sand Point, 2 miles (3 km) further and is open Monday through Friday, year-round. Grand Sable Visitor Center, one mile east of Grand Marais, is open daily in summer. The Grand Marais Maritime Museum, located in Grand Marais on Coast Guard Point, is open daily in the summer, and on an intermittent basis during the remainder of the year.

Multicolored sandstone cliffs, broad beaches, sand dunes, waterfalls, inland lakes, ponds, marshes, hardwood and coniferous forests, and numerous birds and animals comprise this scenic area on Lake Superior. This is the first national lakeshore, authorized for addition to the National Park System on Oct. 15, 1966.

VISITOR ACTIVITIES: Besides accessibility at the rock promontory called Miner's Castle, the cliffs are visible from the Lakeshore Trail or by boat. Commercially operated scenic cruises are conducted daily in the summer from the city dock in Munising. Visitor activities include sightseeing, picnicking, scuba diving, camping, sunbathing, hiking, and photography. The water temperature of Lake Superior is normally too cold for all but the most hardy swimmers. Common throughout the area are inland lakes, ponds, streams, waterfalls and bogs, providing educational and recreational potential in the form of boating, fishing, hunting, and swimming. Winter activities include many miles of snowmobile trails and over seventeen miles of well groomed and maintained cross-country ski trails in the Munising and Grand Marais areas. Snowshoeing and winter camping are also enjoyed in this winter wonderland. **Permits:** backcountry camping permits required, available from visitor centers, Park Headquarters or any Ranger; **Fees:** Yes, there is a fee for privately operated scenic boat cruises on Lake Superior; **Visitor facilities:** nature walks and campfire programs in summer; see schedule at camping areas and Ranger Stations; **Any limitations on vehicle usage:** Vehicles and snowmobiles are restricted to designated roadways; **Hiking trails:** Yes, a 43 miles (63 km) lakeshore trail plus day use trails; **Backcountry camping:** Yes, permitted at backcountry campgrounds; **Camping:** Yes, camping areas accessible by auto at Hurricane River, Little Beaver Lake and Twelvemile Beach. Handicapped accessible campsites are available at the three campgrounds. They are held for use by handicapped persons until 6 p.m each day. Additional campgrounds are in nearby Lake Superior State Forest and Hiawatha National Forest; **Other overnight accommodations on site:** No; **Meals served in the park:** No; **Food and supplies obtainable in the park:** No; **Food and supplies obtainable nearby:** Yes, Munising and Grand Marais, MI; **Overnight accommodations:** Munising, County Road H-58; Grand Marais, State Highway M-77; **First Aid available in park:** Yes; **Nearest Hospital:** Munising, at west end of the park; **Days/Hours:** Open 24 hours a day, year-round; **Holiday Closings:** None; **Visitor attractions closed for seasons:** None; **Weather:** Over 200 inches of snow falls in winter. Summer is usually pleasant and warm. Pets not permitted in backcountry; must be on leash in other areas.

GENERAL INFORMATION: *For Your Safety*—Hikers should be especially cautious when near the steep cliffs of the Pictured Rocks. Boaters should note that Lake Superior is always cold, and frequently rough. Only boaters with proper equipment should venture on this lake. Summer visitors should be prepared for occasional cold, rainy weather and troublesome insects.

TRAVEL ACCESS: **Air:** American Airlines provides service into Marquette, MI and Escanaba, MI.

Sleeping Bear Dunes National Lakeshore
Empire, Michigan   **SEE CLIMATABLE NO. 81**

MAILING ADDRESS: Superintendent, Sleeping Bear Dunes National Lakeshore. P.O. Box 277, Empire, MI 49630 **Telephone:** 616-326-5134

DIRECTIONS: The Visitor Center and Headquarters are located in a combined facility in Empire, Michigan. The facility is open daily except for Christmas. It is accessible by Hwy M-22 from Leland and Frankfort, MI, and M-72 from Traverse City, MI.

Beaches, massive sand dunes, forests and inland lakes are outstanding characteristics of the major mainland portion and the 2 offshore Manitou Islands. Authorized for addition to the National Park System on Oct. 21, 1970.

VISITOR ACTIVITIES: bird- and wildlife-watching, fishing, camping, primitive camping, hiking, interpretive programs, canoeing, swimming, horseback riding, cross-country skiing; **Permits:** Michigan fishing and hunting license required; available at local outlets. Free backcountry camping permits required; available from local rangers; **Fees:** $6 per night campground fee at Platte River and D.H. Day Campgrounds; **Visitor facilities:** Maritime museum, campgrounds, interpretive programs, canoe rentals, bathhouse, beaches, trails, boat ramp and rentals; **Any limitations on vehicle usage:** All vehicles must remain on designated roads. Snowmobiles are restricted to county roads; **Hiking trails:** Yes, trails lead through forests and dune areas; **Backcountry:** Yes; **Camping:** Yes, no reservations are available for campsites; **Other overnight accommodations on site:** No; **Meals served in the park:** Yes, snacks at Dune Climb season; **Food and supplies obtainable in the park:** Yes; **Food and supplies obtainable nearby:** Yes, just outside the park and in Empire, Glen Arbor and Platte River campground area; **Overnight accommodations:** Glen Arbor, MI 22, 1 mile (1.6 km); Empire, MI 22; Honor, US 31, 6 miles (9.7 km); Frankfort, MI 22, 12 miles (19.3 km); **First Aid available in park:** Yes; **Nearest Hospital:** Traverse City, MI 72, 30 miles (48 km); **Days/Hours:** Lakeshore open all year. Visitor Center open from 9 a.m. to 5 p.m. daily; **Holiday Closings:** Christmas Day & Thanksgiving; **Visitor attractions closed for seasons:** Maritime museum closed Nov.-Apr. Campgrounds are open year around with limited winter facilities (no water). **Weather:** is tempered by Lake Michigan.

GENERAL INFORMATION: *A Safety Note:* High Lake Michigan water levels have created unstable shoreline conditions. Steep lakeshore bluffs are hazardous to climb and descend due to landslides and slumpage. On Lake Michigan, weather conditions can change drastically in a short time. If you are boating, be aware of the weather forecast and carry appropriate safety equipment. Avalanche conditions exist on steep, exposed slopes after heavy snows and/or strong winds. Hikers and cross country skiers take caution.

TRAVEL ACCESS: **Air:** Simmons, Northwest Airlines, and Midstates Airlines service Traverse City.

Minnesota

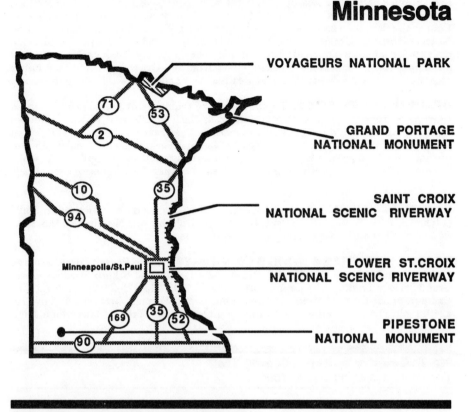

VOYAGEURS NATIONAL PARK

GRAND PORTAGE NATIONAL MONUMENT

SAINT CROIX NATIONAL SCENIC RIVERWAY

LOWER ST.CROIX NATIONAL SCENIC RIVERWAY

PIPESTONE NATIONAL MONUMENT

Minneapolis/St.Paul

Grand Portage National Monument
Grand Portage, Minnesota   **SEE CLIMATABLE NO. 84**

MAILING ADDRESS: Superintendent, Grand Portage National Monument, P.O. Box 666, Grand Marais, Minnesota 55604 **Telephone:** 218-387-2788

DIRECTIONS: The monument is located off US Highway 61, 36 miles (58 km) northeast of Grand Marais, MN, 145 miles (232 km) from Duluth, MN, and 45 miles (72 km) southwest of the Canadian city of Thunder Bay, Ontario. The Grand Portage bisects the reservation of the Grand Portage Band of the Minnesota Chippewa Tribe.

This 8.5 mile (13.6 km) portage was a rendezvous for traders and trappers on a principal route of Indians, explorers, missionaries, and fur traders into the Northwest. The fur trade depot and summer headquarters of the North West Company has been reconstructed here. Designated Sept. 15, 1951.

VISITOR ACTIVITIES: reconstruction of historic buildings; guided tours, exhibits, demonstrations, audio-visual programs, hiking, cross-country skiing, primitive camping, picnicking; **Permits:** for backcountry, can be obtained at the Monument; **Fees:** Yes; **Visitor facilities:** Cultural Center, parking, picnic area, hiking/cross-country ski trail; **Any limitations on vehicle usage:** No; **Hiking trails:** Yes, Mount Rose Trail is ½ mile (.8 km) long. The Grand Portage leads to the Site of Fort Charlotte, 8.5 miles (13.6 km) away; **Backcountry:** Yes, information can be obtained at the Monument or at Headquarters; **Camping:** No, nearby **Other overnight accommodations on site:** No; **Meals served in the park:** No, nearby; **Food and supplies obtainable in the park:** No; **Food**

and supplies obtainable nearby: Yes, Grand Portage, Grand Marais, Thunder Bay; **Overnight accommodations:** Nearby lodge, and motels along Lake Superior shore. Contact the Park for a list of nearby accommodations; **First Aid available in park:** Yes; **Nearest Hospital:** Grand Marais, MN, US 61, 36 miles (58 km); **Days/Hours:** Open daily from 8 a.m. to 5 p.m., mid-May to Mid-October; **Holiday Closings:** None; **Visitor attractions closed for seasons:** Stockade closed from mid-Oct. through mid-May. Other areas open all year; **Weather:** Summer weather can be cool and windy along the shore.

GENERAL INFORMATION: The portage hike requires sturdy hiking shoes and a willingness to endure the discomforts of the trail, which include mud, rocks, mosquitoes and flies. Hikers should remember that emergency assistance is a long way off. A boat leaves daily from the dock for Isle Royale National Park, located 22 miles (35 km) offshore (see listing in this book). Beware of uneven ground and irregular steps while visiting Grand Portage. Watch your children near the water; Lake Superior is extremely cold.

TRAVEL ACCESS: Bus: Triangle Transportation provides daily service within 1 mile (1.6 km) of Park; **Rail:** No (Nearest U.S. service in Duluth); **Air:** No (Nearest U.S. service in Duluth); **Other:** Bicycle, hiking, boat and canoe.

NEARBY FACILITIES & POINTS OF INTEREST: Hotel/Motel: Grand Portage Lodge, Grand Portage, MN 55605, 218-475-2401, 1 mile (1.6 km); **Food/Supplies:** Grand Portage Trading Post, Grand Portage, MN 55605, 218-475-2282, .2 mile (.3 km); **Campgrounds:** Grand Portage Campground, Grand Portage, MN 55605, 218-475-2249, 1 mile (1.6 km); **Parks, other points of interest:** Witch Tree, Mt. Josephine, High Falls.

North Country National Scenic Trail
For details see listing in New York

Pipestone National Monument
Pipestone, Minnesota   **SEE CLIMATABLE NO. 91**

MAILING ADDRESS: Superintendent, Pipestone National Monument, P.O. Box 727, Pipestone, Minnesota 56154 **Telephone:** 507-825-5464

DIRECTIONS: The 283-acre park is adjacent to the north side of the city of Pipestone, in southwest Minnesota, near Sioux Falls, South Dakota. Pipestone can be reached by US 75, and MN 23 and 30. A State Information Center is at Beaver Creek, directly off Interstate 90.

For at least three centuries Indians have obtained materials at this guarry for making ceremonial peace pipes. Established by act of Congress on August 25, 1937.

VISITOR ACTIVITIES: Besides the interestisng geology, history, archaeology, and the pipestone crafts, the park offers an opportunity to observe and appreciate the natural environment. Picnicking is available; **Permits:** No; **Fees:** Entrance Fee $1.00 per person; **Visitor facilities:** interpretive exhibits, audiovisual program, Indian Cultural Center, souvenir sales; **Any limitations on vehicle usage:** No; **Hiking trails:** Yes, a ¾ mile (1.2 km) self-guiding trail leads past the quarries and other points of interest; **Backcountry:** No; **Camping:** No; **Other overnight accommodations on site:** No, overnight camping and recreational facilities are available nearby at Split Rock Creek State Park, Route 2, Jasper, MN 56144, phone 507-348-7908, located on MN 23, south of Pipestone; and at Blue Mounds State Park, Route 1, Luverne, MN 56144, phone 507-283-4892, located on US 75, south of Pipestone. No reservations are available for campsites, contact the Parks for further information. Check with Park Rangers at Pipestone for locations of private campgrounds and other overnight facilities; **Meals served in the park:** No; **Food and supplies obtainable in the park:** No; **Food and supplies obtainable nearby:** Yes, at Pipestone; **Overnight accommodations:** Pipestone, 1 mile (1.6 km); **First Aid available in park:** Yes; **Nearest Hospital:** Pipestone, 1 mile (1.6 km); **Days/Hours:** Visitor and Cultural Center are open from 8 a.m. to 6 p.m. Mon.-Thur.: 8 a.m.-8 p.m. Fri-Sun. Memorial Day to Labor Day and from 8 a.m. to 5 p.m. the rest of the year; **Holiday Closings:** Dec. 25 and Jan. 1; **Weather:** Summer is hot and humid; Spring and Fall are cool and pleasant; Winter brings severe cold, strong winds and possible blizzards.

GENERAL INFORMATION: Visitors should see Winnewisa Falls, one of the stops on the scenic trail.

TRAVEL ACCESS: Rail: No; **Air:** Western, Ozark, United, NWA and Frontier provide daily service to Sioux Falls, S.D.

Lower St. Croix National Scenic Riverway
For details see listing in Wisconsin

Saint Croix National Scenic Riverway
For details see listing in Wisconsin

Voyageurs National Park
International Falls, Minnesota   **SEE CLIMATABLE NO. 94**

MAILING ADDRESS: Superintendent, Voyageurs National Park, P.O. Box 50, International Falls, Minnesota 56649 **Telephone:** 218-283-9821

DIRECTIONS: The periphery of the Park is easily approached by surfaced roads from four points along US 53 when travelling from Duluth. County Rte. 23-24 from Orr leads to Crane Lake at the eastern end of the Park; County Rte. 129, or Ash River Trail, provides access to Namakan Lake; County Rte. 122, south of International Falls, provides access to the South shore of Lake Kabetogama; MN 11, from International Falls, approaches the Park area at Black Bay. There are no roads beyond the edge of the Park; access is by power-boat, canoe, or float plane, hiking in summer; and snowmobiling and cross-country skiing in winter.

Once the route of French-Canadian voyageurs, scenic northern lakes are surrounded by forest in this historic and geologically important area. Authorized for addition to the National Park System on January 8, 1971; established on April 8, 1975.

VISITOR ACTIVITIES: fishing, power boating, canoeing, camping, hiking, swimming, cross-country skiing, snowmobiling; **Permits:** No; **Fees:** No; **Visitor facilities:** Visitor centers, naturalist-guided boat, canoe and hiking tours, campsites, boat ramps, boat and canoe rentals, lodging, food and supplies; **Any limitations on vehicle usage:** Yes, there are only 3 miles (4.8 km) of road in the Park. Access in the Summer is by watercraft, float plane or hiking; in the Winter, by ice road, snowmobile, ski plane, skiing, or snowshoeing; **Hiking trails:** Yes, there are about 25 miles (40 km) of trails which must be reached by watercraft or floatplane; **Backcountry:** Yes, contact Headquarters for details; **Camping:** Yes, 100 primitive campsites (accessible only by boat or floatplane) are scattered throughout the Park, mostly on the major lakes; **Other overnight accommodations on site:** Yes, Kettle Falls Hotel; **Meals served in the park:** Yes, Kettle Falls Hotel; **Food and supplies obtainable in the park:** No; **Food and supplies obtainable nearby:** Yes, in International Falls, Rainy Lake, Kabetogama, Ash River, Orr and Crane Lake; **Overnight accommodations:** International Falls, Rainy Lake, Kabetogama, Crane Lake, Ash River, Orr; **First Aid available in park:** Yes, Park Rangers on duty; **Nearest Hospital:** International Falls, Littlefork, Cook; **Days/Hours:** Park open year-round. Access is limited during lake freeze-up and ice-out periods, contact Headquarters for Visitor Center hours; **Holiday Closings:** No; **Weather:** Summer temperatures range from 50° to 90°F; Winter, − 30° to 30°F.

GENERAL INFORMATION: Some of the land is privately owned, and there are many private cottages. Please respect the rights of these property holders. Boaters not familiar with the waters should obtain the services of a guide or use charts, both of which are available locally. The large lakes can suddenly become very rough. Keep informed about weather conditions. Users of small boats and canoes should be particularly cautious and should be prepared to wait out rough water. State boating regulations apply.

TRAVEL ACCESS: Bus: Triangle Transportation Company provides daily service to International Falls, Orr; **Rail:** Amtrak offers service to Duluth, MN; **Air:** Norwest Airlines offers daily service to International Falls, MN; **Other:** Many resorts provide taxi service from bus or airline to their resort near the Park. Floatplanes provide access to the park from International Falls.

Mississippi

Brices Cross Roads National Battlefield Site
Baldwyn, Mississippi   **SEE CLIMATABLE NO. 83**

MAILING ADDRESS: Superintendent, Natchez Trace Parkway, R.R. 1, NT-143, Tupelo, Mississippi 38801 **Telephone:** 601-842-1572

DIRECTIONS: The Site is about 6 miles (10 km) west of Baldwyn on MS 370.
    The Confederate cavalry, under Gen. Nathan Bedford Forrest, was employed with extraordinary skill here during the battle of June 10, 1864. Established by act of Congress on Feb. 21, 1929.

VISITOR ACTIVITIES: The Park consists of one acre of land, but much of the scene of action is within view. Monuments and markers provide interpretation; **Permits:** No; **Fees:** No; **Visitor facilities:** None; **Any limitations on vehicle usage:** No; **Hiking trails:** No; **Meals served in the park:** No; **Food and supplies obtainable in the park:** No; **Food and supplies obtainable nearby:** Yes, in Tupelo; **Overnight accommodations:** Tupelo, US 45, 25 miles (40 km); Booneville, US 45, 13 miles (21 km); **First Aid available in park:** No, but nearby in Baldwyn, US 45; **Nearest Hospital:** Tupelo, South Gloster Street, 25 miles (40 km); **Days/Hours:** Open year-round; **Holiday Closings:** None.

Gulf Island National Seashore
For details see listing in Florida

Natchez Trace Parkway
Tupelo, Mississippi
(Also in Alabama and Tennessee)   **SEE CLIMATABLE MAP**

MAILING ADDRESS: Superintendent, Natchez Trace Parkway, R.R. 1, NT-143, Tupelo, Mississippi 38801 **Telephone:** 601-842-1572

DIRECTIONS: The Tupelo Visitor Center is 5 miles (8 km) north of Tupelo at the intersection of Natchez Trace Parkway and Bus. US 45 North.
    This historic route generally follows the old Indian trace, or trail, between Nashville, TN and Natchez, MS. 398 miles (637 km) of the planned 445 miles (712 km) are completed. Established by act of Congress on May 18, 1938.

VISITOR ACTIVITIES: hiking, walking, auto tours, camping, swimming, boating, horseback riding, exhibits, biking, interpretive film, fishing, running and jogging, ranger talks, crafts festival in fall; **Permits:** No; **Fees:** No; **Visitor facilities:** Visitor Center, interpretive film, hiking trails, campgrounds, picnic areas, boat ramp; **Any limitations on vehicle usage:** Hauling and commercial trucking are not permitted. Tent and trailer camping are permitted only at authorized campgrounds; **Hiking trails:** Yes, nature and hiking trails up to 4.6 miles (7.4 km) long; **Backcountry:** No; **Camping:** Yes, campgrounds are at Rocky Springs, Jeff Busby and Meriwether Lewis. Campsites cannot be reserved; stays are limited to 15 days during periods of heavy visitation. You should bring insect netting and repellent. Contact the Park for detailed information on facilities at each camping area; **Other overnight accommodations on site:** No; **Meals served in the park:** No; **Food and supplies obtainable in the park:** No; **Food and supplies obtainable nearby:** Yes, at Natchez, Port Gibson, Jackson, Tupelo, Cherokee, and many other towns along the parkway; **Overnight accommodations:** Same as where food and supplies are available; **First Aid available in park:** Yes; **Nearest Hospital:** Natchez, Jackson, Kosciusko, Tupelo, Columbia, Florence; **Days/Hours:** Park open year-round,

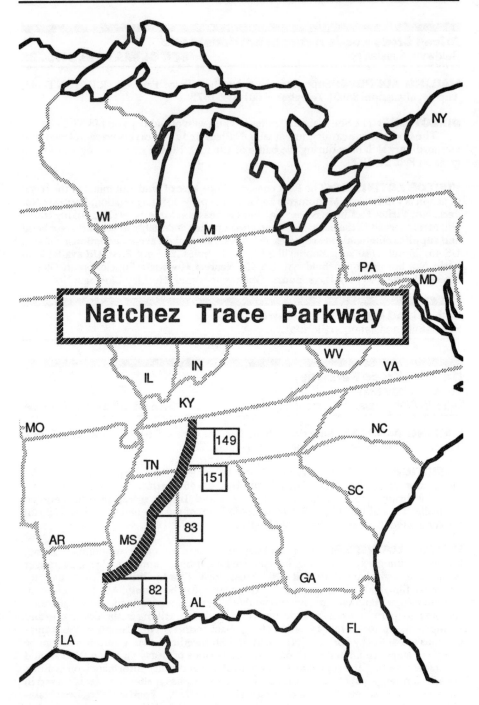

24 hours a day. Tupelo Visitor Center open from 8 a.m. to 5 p.m. 364 days; **Holiday Closings:** Tupelo Visitor Center closed Dec. 25; **Visitor attractions closed for seasons:** None; **Weather:** Summer weather is generally hot and humid. Winter is usually cold and damp with occasional warm periods. Spring and Autumn are mild and warm.

GENERAL INFORMATION: The only service station is at Jeff Busby. You can make the most of your visit by obtaining a brochure on Natchez Trace which is available by mail or at the Visitor Center. It provides detailed information of points of interest and facilities in different areas of the Parkway.

Tupelo National Battlefield
Tupelo, Mississippi   **SEE CLIMATABLE NO. 83**

MAILING ADDRESS: Superintendent, Natchez Trace Parkway, R.R. 1, NT-143, Tupelo, Mississippi 38801 **Telephone:** 601-842-1572

DIRECTIONS: The Park is within the city limits of Tupelo, MS, on MS 6 about 1 mile (1.6 km) west of its intersection with US 45. It is 1.2 miles (1.9 km) east of the Natchez Trace Parkway.
　　Here, on July 13-14, 1864, Gen. Nathan Bedford Forrest's cavalry battled a Union force of 14,000 sent to keep Forrest from cutting the railroad supplying Major Gen. William T. Sherman's march on Atlanta. Created by Presidential Proclamation on Feb. 21, 1929.

VISITOR ACTIVITIES: Signs and markers provide interpretation. Information about the area is available at the Tupelo Visitor Center of the Natchez Trace Parkway; **Permits:** No; **Fees:** No; **Visitor facilities:** None; **Any limitations on vehicle usage:** No; **Hiking trails:** No; **Backcountry:** No; **Camping:** No; **Other overnight accommodations on site:** No; **Meals served in the park:** No; **Food and supplies obtainable in the park:** No; **Food and supplies obtainable nearby:** Yes, at Tupelo; **Overnight accommodations:** Tupelo; **First Aid available in park:** No; **Nearest Hospital:** Tupelo, South Gloster Street, 2 miles (3.2 km); **Days/Hours:** Park is always open.

Vicksburg National Military Park
Vicksburg, Mississippi   **SEE CLIMATABLE NO. 82**

MAILING ADDRESS: Superintendent, Vicksburg National Military Park, 3201 Clay Street, Vicksburg, Mississippi 39180 **Telephone:** 601-636-0583

DIRECTIONS: The Park is just inside of Vicksburg on historic US 80 within 1 mile of Interstate 20.
　　Reconstructed fortifications of the 47-day siege of Vicksburg, which ended July 4, 1863, and 1,200 markers and monuments highlight a 16-mile tour route. Victory gave the North control of the Mississippi River and cut the Confederacy in two. Vicksburg National Cemetery, containing about 17,000 Union graves, is within the Park. Confederate dead lie in the city cemetery. The restored ironclad gunboat, *U.S.S. Cairo* and the *Cairo* Museum, which features artifacts recovered from the boat, are located near the National Cemetery. Established by act of Congress on Feb. 21, 1899.

VISITOR ACTIVITIES: interpretive audiovisual programs and exhibits, auto tours, guided and auto-tape tours; **Permits:** No; **Fees:** Yes; **Visitor facilities:** parking and restrooms at Visitor Center; **Any limitations on vehicle usage:** No; **Hiking trails:** No; **Backcountry:** No; **Camping:** No; **Other overnight accommodations on site:** No; **Meals**

served in the park: No; **Food and supplies obtainable in the park:** No; **Food and supplies obtainable nearby:** Yes, at Vicksburg; **Overnight accommodations:** Vicksburg, from one block to 5 miles (8 km); **First Aid available in park:** Yes; **Nearest Hospital:** Vicksburg, less than 1 mile (1.6 km) from the Visitor Center; **Days/Hours:** Open daily all year from 8 a.m. to 5 p.m. (June-Aug., 8 a.m. to 6 p.m.); **Holiday Closings:** Dec. 25.

GENERAL INFORMATION: *For your safety*—Drive carefully on winding roads. Beware of poisonous plants, insects, and reptiles.

TRAVEL ACCESS: Bus: Trailways, Greyhound provide daily service to Vicksburg; **Rail:** No.

NEARBY FACILITIES & POINTS OF INTEREST: Campgrounds: Battlefield Campground, I-20 Frontage Rd., 601-636-9946; **Parks, other points of interest:** The Old Court House Museum in Vicksburg features an exhibit of relics from the siege; The *U.S.S. Cairo* restored ironclad gunboat, and the *Cairo* Museum, feature artifacts recovered from the boat, are located near the National Cemetery.

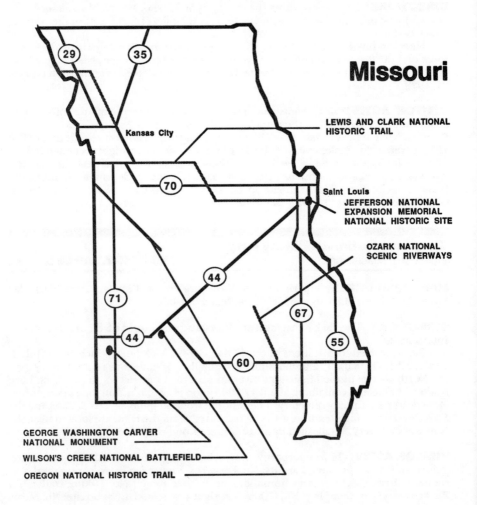

Missouri

Kansas City

LEWIS AND CLARK NATIONAL
HISTORIC TRAIL

Saint Louis
JEFFERSON NATIONAL
EXPANSION MEMORIAL
NATIONAL HISTORIC SITE

OZARK NATIONAL
SCENIC RIVERWAYS

GEORGE WASHINGTON CARVER
NATIONAL MONUMENT

WILSON'S CREEK NATIONAL BATTLEFIELD

OREGON NATIONAL HISTORIC TRAIL

George Washington Carver National Monument
Diamond, Missouri   **SEE CLIMATABLE NO. 95**

MAILING ADDRESS: Superintendent, George Washington Carver National Monument, P.O. Box 38, Diamond, Missouri 64840 **Telephone:** 417-325-4151

DIRECTIONS: From either Neosho or Carthage take US 71 Alternate to the town of Diamond. Go west 2 miles (3 km) on State Highway V and then south about 1 mile (1.6 km).

Authorized by Congress in 1943, George Washington Carver National Monument is both the Nation's first memorial to the achievements of a black man, and the first such honor to an individual other than a President. It preserves the birthplace Site and the natural environment which was instrumental in shaping the personality and ambitions of George Washington Carver, a man who played an important role in the social and agricultural history of 20th century America. Included within the Park is a museum detailing the life and achievements of Carver, and a Nature Trail which goes by some of the natural and historic points within the Park.

VISITOR ACTIVITIES: interpretive exhibits and film, guided tours, nature walks, picnicking; **Permits:** Yes; **Fees:** Yes; **Visitor facilities:** Visitor Center, parking and picnic areas; **Any limitations on vehicle usage:** No; **Hiking trails:** Yes, a ¾ mile (1.2 km) nature trail; **Backcountry:** No; **Camping:** No; **Other overnight accommodations on site:** No; **Meals served in the park:** No; **Food and supplies obtainable in the park:** No; **Food and supplies obtainable nearby:** Yes, in Diamond; **Overnight accommodations:** Neosho, US 71 A, 10 miles (16 km) & Joplin, 14 miles (22.5 km) northwest on Interstate 44; **First Aid available in park:** Yes; **Nearest Hospital:** Joplin, 14 miles (22.5 km), Interstate 44; Neosho, US 71 A, 10 miles (16 km); **Days/Hours:** Open daily from 8:30 a.m. to 5 p.m. Memorial Day—Labor Day 8:30-6:00. Grounds open until dark; **Holiday Closings:** Dec. 25; **Visitor attractions closed for seasons:** None; **Weather:** Summer, hot with occasional thunderstorms; Spring/Fall cool, mostly dry.

GENERAL INFORMATION: Learn to identify and avoid poison ivy found along nature trail. Prairie restoration project in progress.

TRAVEL ACCESS: Bus: No, there are no regular bus routes to the Park, although a number of bus "tours" do stop by the Park; **Rail:** No; **Air:** The nearest airport is approximately 30 miles west of the Park in the city of Joplin.

NEARBY FACILITIES & POINTS OF INTEREST: Parks, other points of interest: Within a one to two hour drive from Carver National Monument is Fort Scott NHS, Wilson's Creek NB, and Pea Ridge NB.

Harry S Truman National Historic Site
Independence, Missouri   **SEE CLIMATABLE NO. 213**

MAILING ADDRESS: 223 North Main Street, Independence, Missouri 64050 **Telephone:** (816) 254-7199

DIRECTIONS: East on Truman Road from I-435; or North on Noland Road from I-70. West on Truman Road from Noland Road.

Established December 8, 1982, the site interprets the home of President Harry S Truman.

VISITOR ACTIVITIES: Tickets for guided tours available *only* at Truman Home Ticket and Informtion Center at the corner of Truman Road and Main Street, adjacent to Independence Square; first-come, first-served ticket distribution; everyone must be present to pick up tickets; no advanced reservations; no special group accommodations; Walking tours of the Truman Neighborhood during summer season; **Permits:** No; **Fees:** Entrance fee is $1 per person. Golden Access, Golden Age, Golden Eagle, and Park Passports are accepted and available. Fee waived for visitors under 13 years of age; **Visitor facilities:** Information desk, audio-visual program, exhibits, restrooms at the ticket center; **Any limitations on vehicle usage:** limited parking at the site; please use shuttle from ticket center; **Hiking trails:** No; **Backcountry:** No; **Camping:** No; **Other overnight accommodations on site:** No; **Meals served in the park:** No; **Food and supplies obtainable in the park:** No; **Food and supplies obtainable nearby:** Yes, in Independence; **Overnight accommodations:** Independence, Missouri on U.S. Highway 24 and I-70 and Noland Road junction; **First Aid available in park:** Yes; also hospital one mile West; **Days/Hours:** Ticket Center, 8:30 a.m. to 5:00 p.m.; guided tours from 9:00 a.m. to 4:45 p.m.; **Holiday Closings:** January 1, Thanksgiving, and December 25; **Visitor attractions closed for seasons:** No guided tours on Mondays after Labor Day until Memorial Day; ticket center open for audio-visual program; **Weather:** Hot humid summers, mild springs and falls, cold winters with snow and ice.

GENERAL INFORMATION: In the summer, tour tickets frequently are all distributed by 12:30 p.m.; come early in the day to avoid disappointment.

TRAVEL ACCESS: Bus: Greyhound, 6 miles (10 km) south of ticket center; **Rail:** Amtrak, 1/2 mile (.8 km) southwest of site, morning/evening service; on shuttle bus route; **Air:** TWA, American, Eastern 25 miles northwest of site; **Shuttle:** The City of Independence operates a shuttle bus between the ticket center, Harry S. Truman Library, and the Truman Home; parking available at the ticket center and the Harry S. Truman Library.

NEARBY FACILITIES & POINTS OF INTEREST: Hotel/Motel: Independence (5 miles); **Food/Supplies:** Independence (1 mile); **Campgrounds:** Lake Jacomo County Park (11 miles); **Parks, other points of interest:** Harry S. Truman Library; Jackson County Courthouse (30-minute audio-visual program about Truman); Truman Railroad Station; Vaile Mansion; Bingham-Waggoner Estate; 1859 Marshal's Home and Jail Museum in Independence; Harry S. Truman Farm Home, Grandview, Missouri (19 miles south of site).

Jefferson National Expansion Memorial National Historic Site
St. Louis, Missouri   **SEE CLIMATABLE NO. 85**

MAILING ADDRESS: Superintendent, Jefferson National Expansion Memorial, 11 North Fourth Street, St. Louis, Missouri 63102 **Telephone:** 314-425-4465

DIRECTIONS: The Park is within easy walking distance of downtown St. Louis. The Old Courthouse, with a varied program of exhibits and activities is open daily, as are the Gateway Arch and Museum of Westward Expansion.

The Park, located on the Mississippi riverfront in St. Louis, memorializes Thomas Jefferson and others who directed the territorial expansion of the United States. Eero Saarinen's prize-winning, stainless steel Gateway Arch commemorates westward pioneers. Visitors may ascend the 630-foot high arch by elevator. In the nearby courthouse Dred Scott sued for freedom in the historic slavery case. Designated Dec. 20, 1935.

VISITOR ACTIVITIES: interpretive exhibits, walking, photography, ascending the arch; **Permits:** No; **Fees:** The fee for the elevator ride to the top of the arch is $2.50 for adults and 50¢ for children under 13; **Visitor facilities:** museum, parking lot with fee, restrooms; **Any limitations on vehicle usage:** No; **Meals served in the park:** No; **Food and supplies obtainable in the park:** No; **Food and supplies obtainable nearby:** Yes, in St. Louis, within 1 block of the Site; **Overnight accommodations:** in St. Louis, within walking distance; **First Aid available in park:** Yes; **Nearest Hospital:** St. Louis, within 8 miles (12 km); **Days/Hours:** Open daily from 9 a.m. to 6 p.m., 8 a.m. to 10 p.m. from Memorial Day through Labor Day; **Holiday Closings:** Thanksgiving, Dec. 25 & Jan. 1; **Weather:** Winters are cold and snowy.

GENERAL INFORMATION: Use caution on walkways, stairways, and step-down wells. Be extra careful in the Old Courthouse, which has many steps and varying floor levels.

Oregon National Historic Trail
Missouri (also in Kansas, Nebraska, Wyoming, Idaho,
Oregon, and Washington)   **SEE CLIMATABLE NO. MAP**

MAILING ADDRESS: Pacific Northwest Regional Office, National Park Service, 83 South King St., Seattle, Washington 98104 **Telephone:** 206-442-4720

DIRECTIONS: A comprehensive management and use plan for the 2000-mile long Oregon Trail has been prepared and is being implemented. This plan identifies the primary route and 125 historic sites and seven cross-country segments, and makes recommendations for management, protection and marking. Many of the sites and segments are on public lands and open to visitation, others, however, are located on private lands. Check with Landowners prior to entry. The Oregon Trail is not a recreational trail and crosses many arid areas. Check with local Chambers of Commerce to determine local conditions prior to embarking. Brochure is available from Pacific Northwest Regional Office.

Ozark National Scenic Riverways
Van Buren, Missouri   **SEE CLIMATABLE NO. 95**

MAILING ADDRESS: Superintendent, Ozark National Scenic Riverways, P.O. Box 490, Van Buren, Missouri 63965 **Telephone:** 314-323-4236

DIRECTIONS: The Riverways is in Missouri, an easy day's drive from two large metropolitan centers-175 miles (282 km) south of St. Louis, and 250 miles (402 km) southeast of Kansas City, MO.

The Current and Jacks Fork Rivers flow for about 140 miles (225 km) through a quiet world of nature. Notable features include numerous caves, huge freshwater springs, and tall bluffs. Authorized for addition to the National Park System on Aug. 27, 1964.

VISITOR ACTIVITIES: canoeing, camping, fishing, picnicking, float trips, boating, craft demonstrations, interpretive talks, cave tours, hunting, hiking, canoe demonstrations, swimming; **Permits:** No; **Fees:** Yes, for campsites, $6 per night per Site, collected at Big Spring, Round Spring, Alley Spring, Akers, Pulltite, and Powder Mill campgrounds year-round; **Visitor facilities:** picnic and camping areas, restrooms, stores, canoe and John Boat rentals, bathhouse, boat ramps and rentals, lodging; picnic shelters at some areas may be reserved April through Oct $5 non-refundable fee. **Any limitations on vehicle usage:** All vehicles are restricted to designated roadways; **Hiking**

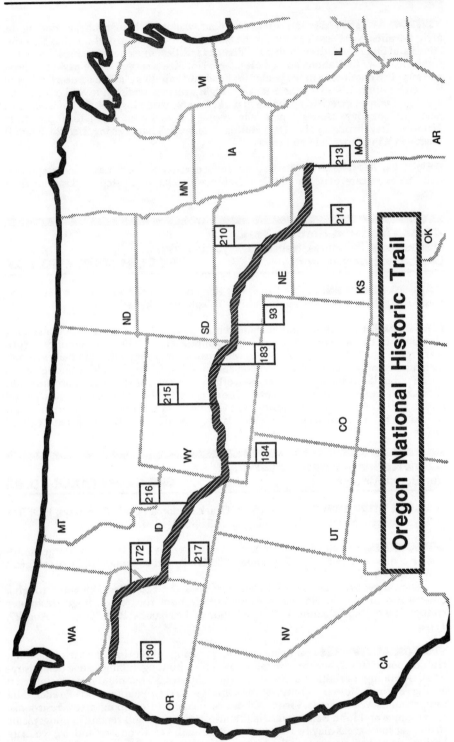

Oregon National Historic Trail

trails: Yes, many miles of old logging roads available for hiking. Nine miles of the Ozark Trail lies within the Riverways. This trail is being built in cooperation with other federal, state, and private conservation groups. When completed, the trail will extend the length of the Current River drainage to the Arkansas border; **Backcountry:** Yes, contact Superintendent for more details. No reservations or permits are required; **Camping:** Yes, no reservations for campsites, except for group sites, which are reserved by writing the Park; **Other overnight accommodations on site:** Yes, rustic housekeeping cabins available at the Big Spring Unit. Reservations can be made by contacting: Big Spring Concessioner, P.O. Box 602, Van Buren, MO 63965, phone 314-323-4423; **Meals served in the park:** Yes, Big Spring Concessioner; **Food and supplies obtainable in the park:** Yes, at Akers, Pulltite, Round, Two Rivers and Alley Springs; **Food and supplies obtainable nearby:** Yes, in adjacent towns: Eminence, Van Buren, Salem, Ellington, Mountain View, Winona, & Birch Tree, MO; **Overnight accommodations:** Eminence, Van Buren, Salem, Ellington, Mountain View, Winona, & Birch Tree; **First Aid available in park:** Yes, small medical clinics also located in Van Buren and Winona, MO; **Nearest Hospital:** Ellington, MO, 21 miles (34 km) from Riverways headquarters in Van Buren via MO State Highway "D" & 21; **Days/Hours:** Open 24 hours a day; modern camping facilities open Mar. 15-Oct. 30 when freezing is not a threat; **Holiday Closings:** None; **Visitor attractions closed for seasons:** Mild winters allow almost year round use of the Riverways. The upper stretches of the rivers are often more fun to float during the Winter and Spring because in Summer's low water, portages have to be made around exposed gravel bars and fallen trees.

GENERAL INFORMATION: Visitors should write for a pamphlet on the Riverways. Float trips can be hazardous for the unskilled.

For Your Safety: Lifejackets or boat cushions should be carried for each person in the boat or canoe. Non-swimmers and weak swimmers should wear lifejackets at all times. Pick campsites well above river level. Flash flood warnings will be issued when possible. Extinguish campfires before leaving; fire is a great peril here. Know what to expect before launching. Talk to a Park Ranger about river conditions and hazards. Carry first-aid kits, matches, billfolds and other valuables in waterproof containers. Stay out of caves until you check with a Park Ranger. The darkness may conceal mud pools, dropoffs and harmful fungi.

Wilson's Creek National Battlefield
Republic, Missouri   **SEE CLIMATABLE NO. 95**

MAILING ADDRESS: Superintendent, Wilson's Creek National Battlefield, P.O. Drawer C, Republic, Missouri 65738 **Telephone:** 417-732-2662

DIRECTIONS: The Site is 3 miles (4.8 km) east of Republic, MO and 10 miles (16 km) southwest of Springfield, MO. Take Int. 44 to MM Highway (Exit 70). Go south approx. 6.75 miles to Highway 60. Go straight on M Highway .7 miles to State Highway ZZ. Go south on ZZ 2 miles to the visitor center. Highway signs are present to show the route.

VISITOR ACTIVITIES: Self-guided auto tour, interpretive exhibits at Information Station, living history programs on Summer weekends; **Permits:** No; **Fees:** Adults $1 (up to $3/veh.), Children under 12 and senior citizens over 62 are free; **Visitor facilities:** Visitor Center, 5 mile tour road, trails, historic Ray House, picnic area, restrooms; **Any limitations on vehicle usage:** Vehicles are restricted to designated roadways; **Hiking trails:** Yes; **Backcountry:** No; **Camping:** No; **Other overnight accommodations on site:** No; **Meals served in the park:** No; **Food and supplies obtainable in the park:** No; **Food and supplies obtainable nearby:** Yes, at Republic; **Overnight accommodations:** Springfield, MO, 10 miles (16 km); **First Aid available in park:** Yes; **Nearest Hospital:** Springfield, 10 miles (16 km); **Days/Hours:** Summer-8 a.m. to 8 p.m. Winter-8 a.m. to 5 p.m. Closing hours vary spring and fall. **Holiday Closings:** Dec. 25, Jan. 1; **Visitor attractions closed for seasons:** No; **Weather:** Hot, humid Summer, cold with snow and ice in Winter.

GENERAL INFORMATION: The visitor center offers a 13-minute film, a 6-minute fiber optic map display, museum area, and sales and display area. A picnic area is located next to the visitor center. The historic Ray House has been restored to its 1861 appearance. Historic Wire Road has been stabilized. New 5 mile tour road with exhibits, and biking/jogging lane.

TRAVEL ACCESS: Bus: No (except by charter in Springfield); **Rail:** No; **Air:** Eastern, TWA, Northwest and American service Springfield Regional Airport.

NEARBY FACILITIES & POINTS OF INTEREST: Campgrounds: KOA, Route 7, Box 215A, Springfield, MO (417) 831-3645; **Parks, other points of interest:** George Washington Carver NM, Fort Scott NHS, Ozark National Scenic Riverways, Pea Ridge NMP, Buffalo National River.

Montana

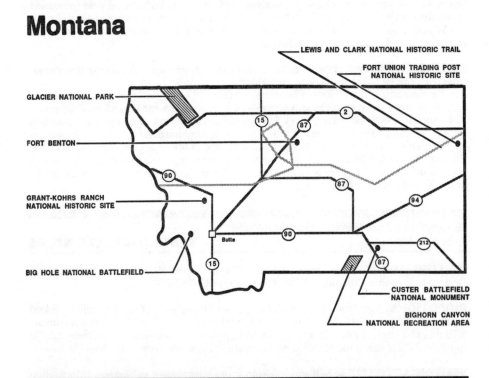

LEWIS AND CLARK NATIONAL HISTORIC TRAIL

FORT UNION TRADING POST NATIONAL HISTORIC SITE

GLACIER NATIONAL PARK

FORT BENTON

GRANT-KOHRS RANCH NATIONAL HISTORIC SITE

BIG HOLE NATIONAL BATTLEFIELD

Butte

CUSTER BATTLEFIELD NATIONAL MONUMENT

BIGHORN CANYON NATIONAL RECREATION AREA

Big Hole National Battlefield
Wisdom, Montana   **SEE CLIMATABLE NO. 87**

MAILING ADDRESS: Superintendent, Big Hole National Battlefield, P.O. Box 237, Wisdom, Montana 59761 **Telephone:** 406-689-3155

DIRECTIONS: The Battlefield is 10 miles (16 km) west of Wisdom, MT on MT 43. From Butte, take Interstate 15 southwest to Divide, then to Wisdom on MT 43; from the west, MT 43 intersects US 93 at the State line, between Salmon, Idaho and Hamilton, MT. Stop first at the Visitor Center.

Nez Perce Indians and U.S. Army troops fought here in 1877-a dramatic episode in the long struggle to confine the Nez Perce, and other Indians, to reservations. Established by Presidential Proclamation on June 23, 1910.

VISITOR ACTIVITIES: audiovisual and interpretive exhibits, self-guiding tours, picnicking, fishing; **Permits:** Montana fishing license can be obtained from local sporting goods dealers; **Fees:** Entrance fees May-Sept.-$1 per person or $3 per carload; **Visitor facilities:** restrooms, parking, and museum at Visitor Center, picnic tables; **Any limitations on vehicle usage:** No; **Hiking trails:** Yes, Big Hole Battlefield Trail follows the route of the Nez Perce War for 22.5 miles (36 km). It is a 2-day hiking and backpacking trail; **Backcountry:** Yes, obtain information from Headquarters; **Camping:** No; **Other overnight accommodations on site:** No, several non-reserved campsites are nearby. Check at Headquarters; **Meals served in the park:** No; **Food and supplies obtainable in the park:** No; **Food and supplies obtainable nearby:** Yes, in Wisdom (limited), Butte & Hamilton, MT, Salmon, ID; **Overnight accommodations:** Wisdom, MT 43, 10 miles (19.2 km) west. Other accommodations are in Butte, MT to the northeast, and Hamilton, MT or Salmon, ID to the West; **First Aid available in park:** Yes; **Nearest Hospital:** Hamilton, MT 93, 67 miles (108 km); **Days/Hours:** Open daily 8 a.m. to 5 p.m., until 8 p.m. from June 1 through Labor Day; **Visitor attractions closed for seasons:** Snow closes hiking trails; **Weather:** Winters are snowy, windy and cold.

GENERAL INFORMATION: *For Your Protection*—animals native to the Park are dangerous when startled or approached too closely. Always keep a safe distance. Pets must be under physical control at all times.

NEARBY FACILITIES & POINTS OF INTEREST: Hotel/Motel: Nez Perce Lodge, Wisdom, MT., (406) 689-3254, 10 miles from Park; **Food/Supplies:** Wisdom Grocery, Wisdom, MT., (406) 689-3271, 10 miles from Park; **Campgrounds:** May Creek, US Forest Service area, (406) 689-3243, 7 miles from Park.

Bighorn Canyon National Recreation Area
Fort Smith, Montana and Lovell, Wyoming   **SEE CLIMATABLE NO. 86**

MAILING ADDRESS: Superintendent, Bighorn Canyon National Recreation Area, P.O. Box 458, Fort Smith, Montana 59035 **Telephone:** 406-666-2412 (MT) or 307-548-2251 (WY)

DIRECTIONS: North end accessible via MT 313 from Hardin, MT, 43 miles (69 km); south end via WY 14A, Wyoming State Road 37, from Lovell, WY, 13 miles (21 km).

Bighorn Lake, formed by Yellowtail Dam on the Bighorn River, extends 71 miles (114 km)), including a large section through scenic Bighorn Canyon. Much of the area borders on the Crow Indian Reservation. Established by act of Congress in 1966.

VISITOR ACTIVITIES: year-round water activities (including Winter ice fishing) and recreational activities, sightseeing, weekend visitor programs in Summer; **Permits:** No; **Fees:** Yes, $3 per vehicle per night camping fee at Horseshoe Bend Campground; **Visitor facilities:** campgrounds, boat ramps, Visitor Centers, concessioner services at Horseshoe Bend; **Any limitations on vehicle usage:** All wheeled vehicles must stay on established roads; **Hiking trails:** Yes, short nature trails at both ends of the area; **Backcountry:** Yes, for information in Montana call 406-666-2412, in Wyoming, 307-548-2251; **Camping:** Yes, no reservations available for campsites; **Other overnight accommodations on site:** No; **Meals served in the park:** Yes, fast foods at Horseshoe Bend;

Food and supplies obtainable in the park: No; **Food and supplies obtainable nearby:** Yes, in Fort Smith, MT & Lovell, WY; **Overnight accommodations:** Hardin, MT, Hwy 313, 43 miles (69 km); Lovell, WY, Highway 14A, 13 miles (21 km); **First Aid available in park:** Yes; **Nearest Hospital:** Lovell, WY, Highway 14A, 13 miles (21 km); Hardin, MT 313, 43 miles (69 km); **Days/Hours:** Open year-round; **Holiday Closings:** Visitor Centers closed. Thanksgiving, Christmas, New Years; **Weather:** Average Summer temperature is in the 80's F; sub-zero temperatures with frequent snow in Winter.

Custer Battlefield National Monument
Crow Agency, Montana   **SEE CLIMATABLE NO. 86**

MAILING ADDRESS: Superintendent, Custer Battlefield National Monument, P.O. Box 39, Crow Agency, Montana 59022 **Telephone:** 406-638-2621

DIRECTIONS: The Monument lies within the Crow Indian Reservation in southeastern Montana. US 87 (I-90) passes 1 mile (1.6 km) to the west; US 212 connects the Monument with the Black Hills and Yellowstone National Park. The Crow Agency is 2 miles (3.2 km) north, and Hardin, MT is 18 miles (29 km) north. The nearest cities are Billings, MT, 65 miles (105 km) northwest, and Sheridan, WY, 70 miles (113 km) south.

The famous Battle of the Little Big Horn between 12 companies of the 7th U.S. Cavalry and the Sioux and Northern Cheyenne Indians was fought here on June 25-26, 1876. Lt. Col. George A. Custer and about 268 of his force were killed. Established as a national cemetery on Jan. 29, 1879; changed to Custer Battlefield National Monument by act of Congress on March 22, 1946.

VISITOR ACTIVITIES: interpretive talks and exhibits at Visitor Center, guided bus tours, hiking; **Permits:** No; **Fees:** $3.00 per vehicle, 62 or older free; **Visitor facilities:** parking and restrooms at Visitor Center, interpretive markers; **Any limitations on vehicle usage:** All vehicles are restricted to designated roadways; **Hiking trails:** Yes, self-guiding walking trails; **Backcountry:** No; **Camping:** No; **Other overnight accommodations on site:** No; **Meals served in the park:** No; **Food and supplies obtainable in the park:** No; **Food and supplies obtainable nearby:** Yes, in Hardin, Crow Agency; **Overnight accommodations:** Hardin, MT, 15 miles (25 km) north on I-90; **First Aid available in park:** Yes; **Nearest Hospital:** Hardin, MT, 15 miles (25 km) north on I-90; **Days/Hours:** Grounds open from 8 a.m. to sunset year-round. Visitor Center open from 8 a.m. to 7:45 p.m. from Memorial Day through Labor Day; from 8 a.m. to 4:30 p.m. from Labor Day to Memorial Day; until 6 p.m. during Daylight Savings Time; **Holiday Closings:** Thanksgiving, Dec. 25 & Jan. 1; **Visitor attractions closed for seasons:** No; **Weather:** Hot Summers, mild Spring and Fall, cold Winter.

GENERAL INFORMATION: *For Your Safety*—Beware of rattlesnakes. Stay on the pathways while walking on the battlefield.

TRAVEL ACCESS: Bus: Trailways provides daily service to Crow Agency 2 km from Park; **Rail:** No; **Air:** Big Sky, Delta, Continental, Northwest and United, Billings, MT. Aspen Air, Continental, (Sheridan, WY).

Fort Benton
Fort Benton, Montana   **SEE CLIMATABLE NO. 90**

MAILING ADDRESS: Fort Benton Museum, Box 69, Fort Benton, Montana 59442 **Telephone:** None.

DIRECTIONS: Federal facilities are not yet open to the public. In Summer, the community operates a museum, which is located in Old Fort Park. Telephone local newspaper for information 406-622-3311.

Founded in 1846, this American Fur Trading Company trading post was an important river port from 1859 through the Montana gold rush of 1862-1869 until rail service surpassed river cargo transport. Authorized for addition to the National Park System on Oct. 16, 1976. The National Park Service will manage the Visitor Center at Fort Benton when construction is completed.

TRAVEL ACCESS: Bus: Rimrock buses service to Riverview Greenhouse ½ block from park.

NEARBY FACILITIES & POINTS OF INTEREST: Parks, other points of interest: Old Fort Park, Montana Memorial to Lewis & Clark.

Fort Union Trading Post
For details see listing in North Dakota

Glacier National Park
West Glacier, Montana   SEE CLIMATABLE NO. 97

MAILING ADDRESS: Superintendent, Glacier National Park, West Glacier, Montana 59936 **Telephone:** 406-888-5441

DIRECTIONS: The Park is on US 2 and 89 and near US 90 and 93. St. Mary Visitor Center is open mid-May to mid-October; Apgar Information Center from mid-May through mid-December; and Logan Pass Visitor Center from mid-June to first of September. Opening and closing dates vary from year to year. For recorded telephone information on the Park, phone 406-888-5551.

This ruggedly beautiful land includes nearly 50 glaciers, many lakes and streams, and a variety of wildflowers and wildlife. Established May 11, 1910.

VISITOR ACTIVITIES: biking, horseback riding and tours, excursion boat cruises, non-fee fishing, cross-country skiing, snowshoeing, camping, hiking, auto, boat tours, picnicking, interpretive exhibits and programs; **Permits:** required for overnight stays in the backcountry, can be obtained from Apgar Information Center, St. Mary Visitor Center, and most Ranger Stations; **Fees:** $5 per vehicle entrance fee, $2.00 per person for those entering by means other than private non-commercial vehicles. Persons under 16 years and 62 years or older are not charged. Golden Eagle and Golden Age Passports accepted and available. Campsites are $5.00 or $7.00 per night, depending on facilities. Group campsites are $1.00 per night per person, backcountry campsites are free with permit; **Visitor facilities:** Visitor Center, boat rentals, hiking trails, campgrounds, picnic areas, hotels, lodges, cabins, telephones, food service, saddle horse, lake cruises and tour buses; **Any limitations on vehicle usage:** Vehicle units-July 1st to Sept. 1st. Not to exceed 30 feet in length. Before July or after Sept. length limit 35 feet, total width, including mirrors - 8 feet. Vehicles, including bicycles, are not allowed on trails or off the roads. Bicycles not allowed on portions of Going-to-the-Sun Road during peak travel hours; **Hiking trails:** Yes, there are more than 750 miles (1200 km) of wilderness trails. Check at Visitor Centers for further information; **Backcountry:** Yes, 65 backcountry campsites, permit required for backcountry, check at any Ranger Station or Information Center; **Camping:** No reservations available for campsites; arrive early for best choice; **Other overnight accommodations on site:** Yes. Accommodations in the Park are available from Glacier Park, Inc.: May 15-Sept. 15 write East Glacier Park, MT. 59434, phone 406-226-5551; Sept. 15-May 15 write Greyhound Tower, Station 5185 Phoenix, AZ 85077, phone 602-248-6000; Reservations are advised; deposits are required. Reservations for Granite Park and Sperry Chalets, accessible only by backcountry trails, are available from Belton Chalets, Inc., Box 188, West Glacier, MT 59936, phone 406-888-5511. Privately owned campgrounds are nearby; **Meals served in the park:** Yes, at Apgar, Swiftcurrent, Rising Sun. Many Glacier and Lake McDonald Hotels; **Food and supplies obtainable in the park:** Yes, Apgar, Lake McDonald, Swiftcurrent, Rising Sun & Two Medicine have campers' stores; **Food and supplies obtainable nearby:** Yes, St. Mary, West Glacier, East Glacier; **Overnight accommodations:** St. Mary, West Glacier, East Glacier (adjacent to park entrances); **First Aid available in park:** Yes; **Nearest Hospital:** Cardston, Alberta, Canada, 35 miles (56 km) north of St. Mary on US 89 and in Whitefish, MT, 24 miles (38 km) west of West Glacier on US 93; **Days/Hours:** Park open 24 hours a day, 7 days a week, Park Offices M-F 8:00 a.m. to 4:30 p.m.; **Holiday Closings:** None; **Visitor attractions closed for seasons:** Most roads are closed in Winter, except the one between Park Headquarters and Lake McDonald Lodge. Write the Park for detailed information on Winter activities; **Weather:** Severe storms come quickly, even in Summer, with attendant exposure to low temperatures, rain, snow, sleet and lightning.

GENERAL INFORMATION: *For Your Safety*—Never climb alone. Register before and after the climb. Avoid steep snowfields. Keep your distance from all animals, and never try to approach or feed wildlife.

TRAVEL ACCESS: Rail: Amtrak provides service from major cities to Terminals in Belton (West Glacier), and East Glacier; **Air:** Glacier International Airport (32 miles W. in Kalispell)—Delta & Horizon Airlines, Great Falls International Airport (Gt. Falls)—Western, NW Orient. Rental cars available in Kalispell, Cut Bank, East Glacier & Great Falls. Bus service to Great Falls & Kalispell on Intermountain Transportation.

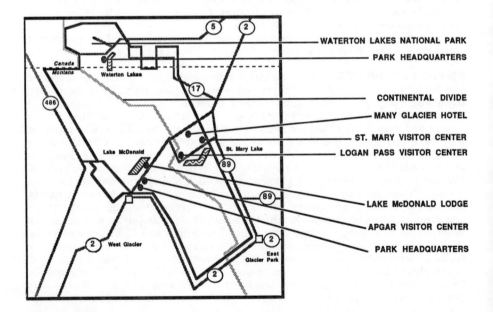

Grant-Kohrs Ranch National Historic Site
Deer Lodge, Montana   **SEE CLIMATABLE NO. 88**

MAILING ADDRESS: Superintendent, Grant-Kohrs Ranch National Historic Site, P.O. Box 790, Deer Lodge, Montana 59722 **Telephone:** 406-846-2070

DIRECTIONS: The ranch is located midway between Yellowstone and Glacier National Parks, ½ mile (.8 km) off Interstate 90 at Deer Lodge.

This was the headquarters of one of the largest and best known 19th-century range ranches in the country. Today the ranchhouse, bunkhouse, and outbuildings are much as they were in the 1800's. Authorized for addition to the National Park System on Aug. 25, 1972.

VISITOR ACTIVITIES: guided tours of the house, self-guiding walks, and exhibits; **Permits:** No; **Fees:** $1 per person over age of 12. Maximum charge $3 per carload. Educational groups free; **Visitor facilities:** Visitor Center, restrooms, self-guiding trail, seasonal demonstrations of ranch activities; **Any limitations on vehicle usage:** Vehicles are left at the Visitor Center. The ranch is ¼ mile (.4 km) away by paved trail; **Hiking trails:** No; **Backcountry:** No; **Camping:** No; **Other overnight accommodations on site:** No; **Meals served in the park:** No; **Food and supplies obtainable in the park:** No; **Food and supplies obtainable nearby:** Yes, at Deer Lodge; **Overnight accommodations:** Deer Lodge, Int. 90, ¼ mile (.4 km); **First Aid available in park:** Yes; on emergency basis; **Nearest Hospital:** Deer Lodge, Int. 90, ¼ mile (.4 km); **Days/Hours:** Open daily from 9 a.m. to 4:30 p.m.; until 7:30 p.m. in Summer; **Holiday Closings:** Thanksgiving, Dec. 25, Jan. 1; **Visitor attractions closed for seasons:** No; **Weather:** Spring is short; Summer, warm; Fall, brisk; Winter, cold.

GENERAL INFORMATION: Smoking is prohibited on the ranch site. Keep your distance from the animals. Pets are not allowed beyond the parking area.

Lewis and Clark Trail
For details see listing in Illinois

Nebraska

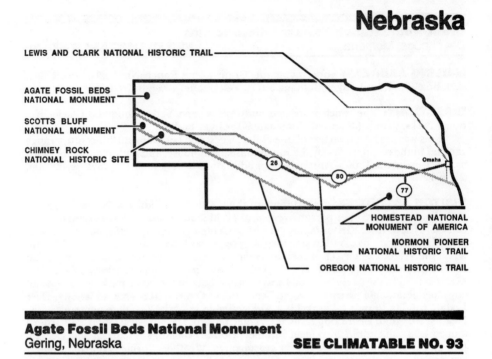

LEWIS AND CLARK NATIONAL HISTORIC TRAIL

AGATE FOSSIL BEDS
NATIONAL MONUMENT

SCOTTS BLUFF
NATIONAL MONUMENT

CHIMNEY ROCK
NATIONAL HISTORIC SITE

Omaha

HOMESTEAD NATIONAL
MONUMENT OF AMERICA

MORMON PIONEER
NATIONAL HISTORIC TRAIL

OREGON NATIONAL HISTORIC TRAIL

Agate Fossil Beds National Monument
Gering, Nebraska   **SEE CLIMATABLE NO. 93**

MAILING ADDRESS: Superintendent, Scotts Bluff National Monument, P.O. Box 427, Gering, Nebraska 69341 **Telephone:** 308-436-4340

DIRECTIONS: The Site is 34 miles (54.7 km) north of Mitchell on NE 29 and 3 miles (4.8 km) east on County Road; 22 miles (35 km) south of Harrison via NE 29 and 3 miles (4.8 km) east on County Road.
　　The Monument consists of 2,700 acres, including a 60-acre detached quarry Site. The quarries contain numerous concentrated, well-preserved Miocene mammal fossils, representing an important chapter in the evolution of mammals. Established by act of Congress on June 5, 1965.

VISITOR ACTIVITIES: interpretive exhibits, self-guiding hikes; **Permits:** No; **Fees:** No; **Visitor facilities:** Visitor Centr exhibits and nearby comfort stations, slide program, fishing, picnic tables and benches on trails; **Any limitations on vehicle usage:** Vehicles must stay on established roadways; **Hiking trails:** Yes, a 1 mile (1.6 km) paved trail leads to the fossil beds; **Backcountry:** No; **Camping:** No; **Other overnight accommodations on site:** No; **Meals served in the park:** No; **Food and supplies obtainable in the park:** No; **Food and supplies obtainable nearby:** Yes, in Harrison, NE, 25 miles (40 km) north; **Overnight accommodations:** Scottsbluff, Route 26, 45 miles (72 km), Harrison, NE 29, 25 miles (37 km) north, Mitchell, NE 29, 37 miles (56 km); **First Aid available in park:** Yes; **Nearest Hospital:** Scottsbluff, 45 miles (72 km); **Days/Hours:** Open daily from 8:30 a.m. to 5:30 p.m.; **Holiday Closings:** None; **Visitor attractions closed for seasons:** Visitor Center open weekends only, 8:00 a.m.-5:00 p.m., November-April.

GENERAL INFORMATION: *For Your Safety*—Watch for rattlesnakes while viewing the fossil areas or walking anywhere in the Park.

TRAVEL ACCESS: Bus: No; **Rail:** No; **Air:** Continental Express and G.P. Express Airlines daily service Scotts Bluff County Airport, Scotts Bluff, Nebraska; **Other:** Hertz and National Car Rentals are available at the Scotts Bluff County Airport; **Parks, other points of interest:** Badlands, Devils Tower, Fort Laramie, Jewel Cave, Mount Rushmore, Scotts Bluff, Wind Cave.

Chimney Rock National Historic Site
Bayard, Nebraska   **SEE CLIMATABLE NO. 93**

MAILING ADDRESS: Curator Branch Museums, Chimney Rock National Historic Site, Nebraska State Historical Society, Box 82554, Lincoln, Nebraska 68501 **Telephone:** 402-471-4755 (Lincoln)

DIRECTIONS: The Site is 3½ miles (5.6 km) southwest of Bayard, on the south side of the North Platte River. From Bayard, US 26 intersects NE 92 at a point about 1½ miles (2.4 km) from the Site. Gravel roads lead from NE 92 to within ½ mile (.8 km) of the Site. Travel from there is by foot only, on unimproved path.

Pioneers camped near this famous landmark as they travelled west. It stands 500 feet above the Platte River along the Oregon Trail. Designated a National Historic Site on Aug. 9, 1956. Jointly administered by National Park Service, City of Bayard and the Nebraska State Historical Society.

VISITOR ACTIVITIES: walking tours, picnicking, photography; **Permits:** No; **Fees:** No; **Visitor facilities:** information trailer, picnic area, pit toilets; **Any limitations on vehicle usage:** Vehicles are restricted to designated roadways; **Hiking trails:** Yes; **Backcountry:** No; **Camping:** No; **Other overnight accommodations on site:** No; **Meals served in the park:** No; **Food and supplies obtainable in the park:** No; **Food and supplies obtainable nearby:** Yes, Bayard; **Overnight accommodations:** Bayard, 4 miles (6.4 km); Bridgeport, 12 miles (19.3 km) east; **First Aid available in park:** No; **Nearest Hospital:** Scottsbluff, NE 92, approx. 25 miles (34 km); **Days/Hours:** Open during daylight hours, 365 days a year; **Visitor attractions closed for seasons:** Trailer #4 at the rest area on Neb. 92 operates from 9 a.m.-6 p.m. from Memorial Day through Labor Day; **Weather:** Expect violent storms in Summer.

GENERAL INFORMATION: *For Your Safety*—Watch out for rattlesnakes, rough terrain, and yucca plants. Boots and hiking clothes are essential.

TRAVEL ACCESS: Air: Scottsbluff is nearest terminal.

NEARBY FACILITIES & POINTS OF INTEREST: Parks, other points of interest: Wild Cat Hills, and Scotts Bluff National Monument.

Homestead National Monument of America
Beatrice, Nebraska   **SEE CLIMATABLE NO. 92**

MAILING ADDRESS: Superintendent, Homestead National Monument of America, Rt. 3 Box 47, Beatrice, Nebraska 68310 **Telephone:** 402-223-3514

DIRECTIONS: The Monument is located in southeastern Nebraska, about 4.5 miles (7 km) northwest of Beatrice and about 40 miles (65 km) south of Lincoln. Take NE 4 from Beatrice to the Monument.

One of the first claims under the Homestead Act of 1862 was filed for this land. Authorized for addition to the National Park System on Mar. 19, 1936.

VISITOR ACTIVITIES: audiovisual and interpretive exhibits, walking tours, living history demonstrations during special events in Summer, hiking, cross-country skiing;

Permits: No; **Fees:** No; **Visitor facilities:** parking and restrooms at Visitor Center, handicapped accessible, parking available for larger vehicles/trailers, picnic area. **Any limitations on vehicle usage:** Motorcycles, bicycles, and snowmobiles are not allowed on the trail or grounds; **Hiking trails:** Yes, a self-guiding trail around the Site; **Backcountry:** No; **Camping:** No; **Other overnight accommodations on site:** No, city-operated campsites are available in Beatrice. No reservations are accepted, but there is usually enough space to accommodate all campers. For further information, write Beatrice Park and Recreation Department, City Auditorium, Beatrice, NE 68310, or phone 402-228-3649; **Meals served in the park:** No; **Food and supplies obtainable in the park:** No; **Food and supplies obtainable nearby:** Yes, in Beatrice; **Overnight accommodations:** Beatrice, NE 4, 5 miles (8 km); **First Aid available in park:** Yes; **Nearest Hospital:** Beatrice, NE 4, 5 miles (8 km); **Days/Hours:** Open 7 days a week: 8 a.m. to 6 p.m., Memorial Day-Labor Day; 8:30 a.m.-5 p.m. the rest of the year; **Holiday Closings:** Dec. 25; **Visitor attractions closed for seasons:** Freeman School open regularly only in Summer; **Weather:** Summer is frequently hot with moderate humidity and the possibility of thundershowers. Winter is cold with occasional snow.

GENERAL INFORMATION: *For Your Safety*—Check carefully for ticks, which are most active from May through August. Do not smoke on the trail.
"Homestead Days" held in last week of June.

TRAVEL ACCESS: Bus: None; **Rail:** Amtrak provides daily service into Lincoln; **Air:** United Airlines, Continental Airline service to Lincoln.

Lewis and Clark Trail
For details see listing in Illinois

Missouri National Recreational River
Omaha, NE   **SEE CLIMATABLE NO. 218**

MAILING ADDRESS: Midwest Region, National Park Service, 1709 Jackson Street, Omaha, NE 68102 **Telephone:** 402-221-4856

DIRECTIONS: If you are driving north of Omaha, Nebraska, on I-29, exit west on South Dakota's Route U.S. 50 to Yankton. If you are driving south from Sioux Falls on I-29, exit west on South Dakota's Route U.S. 50 to Yankton.

VISITOR ACTIVITIES: No Federal landownership or development. State and local parks provide facilities and access to the 58-mile (92.8 km) river stretch. **Permits:** No permits required; **Fees:** Both the State of Nebraska and the State of South Dakota have entrance fees to use their facilities. **Visitor facilities:** None developed by the Federal Government; must use State and local access facilities; **Any limitations on vehicle usage:** No; **Hiking trails:** No; **Backcountry:** No; **Camping:** State and local parks in the area; **Other overnight accommodations on site:** Local motels; **Meals served in the park:** No; **Food and supplies obtainable in the park:** No; **Food and supplies obtainable nearby:** At local communities along this stretch of river; **Overnight accommodations:** Motels at Yankton, South Dakota, and Sioux City, Iowa; **First Aid available in park:** No; **Nearest Hospital:** Yankton, South Dakota, and Sioux City, Iowa; **Days/Hours:** None; **Holiday Closings:** No; **Visitor attractions closed for seasons:** State parks in area; **Weather:** Cool mornings and warm days in spring and fall. July and August daytime temperatures in mid to high 90's.

GENERAL INFORMATION: River is wide and current fast and carries a heavy silt load.

TRAVEL ACCESS: Bus: Yankton, SD, and Sioux City, IA; **Rail:** Yankton, SD, and Sioux City, IA; **Air:** Yankton, SD, and Sioux City, IA.

Mormon Pioneer Trail
For details see listing in Illinois

Oregon National Scenic Trail
For details see listing in Missouri

Scotts Bluff National Monument
Gering, Nebraska   **SEE CLIMATABLE NO. 93**

MAILING ADDRESS: Superintendent, Scotts Bluff National Monument, P.O. Box 427, Gering, Nebraska 69341 **Telephone:** 308-436-4340

DIRECTIONS: The Monument adjoins the south bank of the North Platte River 3 miles (4.8 km) west of Gering via NE 92, which bisects the area from east to west. From U.S. 26, travelers should connect with NE 71 south for 5 miles (8 km) to NE 92. From I-80, it is 45 miles (72 km) to the Monument via NE 71 and 92.

Rising 800 feet above the valley floor, this massive promontory was a landmark on the Oregon Trail, associated with the mass migration across the Great Plains between 1843 and 1869. Created by Presidential Proclamation on Dec. 12, 1919.

VISITOR ACTIVITIES: museum, interpretive talks, nature walks, hiking, biking, living history programs; **Permits:** No; **Fees:** $3 per car Summit Road entrance fee; Golden Eagle, Golden Access and Golden Age Passports accepted and available; **Visitor facilities:** museum, nature, hiking, and bicycle trails; **Any limitations on vehicle usage:** Vehicles must stay on established roads; trailers are not allowed to go to the top of the Summit Road; **Hiking trails:** Yes, 1.6 mile (2.8 km) Summit Trail from which visitors can view bluff formations, wildlife species, and view of the valley. On the Summit, trails lead to overlooks from which visitors may look down on historic Mitchell Pass and the North Platte River Valley. From the Museum, a 250 m (200 yd) paved trail leads to the west of the parking lot and takes one to the Oregon Trail, at this location, a trough, ground down by the passage of thousands of emigrants; **Backcountry:** No; **Camping:** No; **Other overnight accommodations on site:** No; **Meals served in the park:** No; **Food and supplies obtainable in the park:** No; **Food and supplies obtainable nearby:** Yes, in Gering, 3 miles (4.8 km) east of Park Headquarters; **Overnight accommodations:** In Gering, NE 92, 4.5 miles (7.2 km) and Scottsbluff, NE 92 and 71, 7 miles (11.2 km); **First Aid available in park:** Yes; **Nearest Hospital:** Scottsbluff, 10 miles (16 km); **Days/ Hours:** Open from 8 a.m. to 5:00 p.m. in Winter, extended hours in Summer; Winter visitor activities include the museum, hiking trails and on request walks and talks; The road to the top is closed intermittently by snow in Winter; **Weather:** Winter is snowy and windy.

GENERAL INFORMATION: *For Your Safety*—Remain on the Park Trail; do not venture toward the cliff's edge.

NEARBY FACILITIES & POINTS OF INTEREST: Parks, other points of interest: Chimney Rock (23 miles east); Fort Laramie NHS (55 miles west); Agate Fossil Beds National Monument (52 miles north).

Nevada

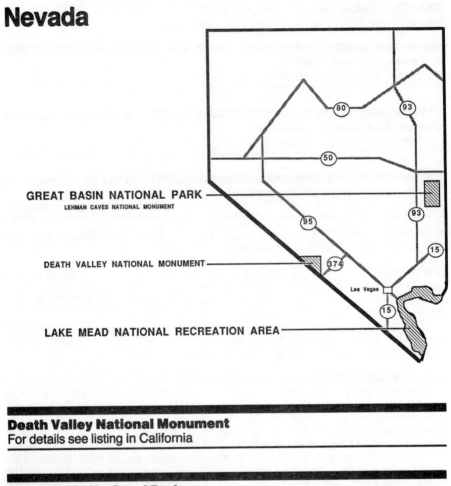

GREAT BASIN NATIONAL PARK
LEHMAN CAVES NATIONAL MONUMENT

DEATH VALLEY NATIONAL MONUMENT

Las Vegas

LAKE MEAD NATIONAL RECREATION AREA

Death Valley National Monument
For details see listing in California

Great Basin National Park
Baker, Nevada   **SEE CLIMATABLE NO. 98**

MAILING ADDRESS: Superintendent, Great Basin National Park, Baker, NV 89311
Telephone: 702-234-7331

DIRECTIONS: (from N, S, E, W) Park headquarters is located 10 miles (16 km) from
U.S. 6-50, near the Nevada-Utah boundary, and is reached via Nevada highways 487
and 488. From Salt Lake City the park is 230 miles (370 km) via Interstate 15 and U.S.
6-50. From Las Vegas the park is 286 miles (460 km) via Interstate 15, U.S. 93 and U.S.
6-50. From Reno the park is 385 miles (620 km) via Interstate 80 and U.S. 50.
    Great Basin National Park preserves 120 square miles (310 hectares) of the high
Snake Range, a prime example of the flora and fauna of the Great Basin Region. The
park's diverse environments range from high desert to alpine tundra and include stands
of bristlecone pines that are among the oldest known living things. The park also includes Lehman Caves, known widely for its delicate dripstone formations. Created by
Act of Congress on October 27, 1986. The former Lehman Caves National Monument
was created on January 24, 1922—the monument was absorbed into the new national
park.

VISITOR ACTIVITIES: Interpretive walks and talks, scenic drive, hiking, camping, exhibits, audiovisual programs, picknicking, wildlife and bird watching, cave tours, photography, cross-country skiing, fishing, climbing, spelunking. Ranger led tours of Lehman Caves are conducted daily on a 1/2 mile (1 km) paved trail with stairways. About 1 1/2 hours are required for the tour. The cave temperature averages a chilly 50°F (10°C), warm clothing is suggested. Tours are limited to a maximum of 30 people. Children under 16 must be accompanied by an adult. Ranger-led spelunking tours available through another cave in the park by reservation (from Memorial Day to Labor Day weekends only). This is a 3 hour tour and restrictions apply. Write ahead for reservation forms; **Permits:** Required for cave tours, available at visitor center. Spelunking Permit required for entry into any wild caves in the park. Voluntary registration for backcountry camping at visitor center. Nevada State fishing license and trout stamp required to fish the park streams; **Fees:** For Ranger-led cave tours: $3 for adults, $2 for children ages 6-15, $1.50 for Golden Age and Access Passport Holders, free for children under 6 years of age. For Ranger-led Spelunking Tours, $6 all participants. Dump station fee: $1. Camping fees $5 per night, $2.50 per night for Golden Age and Access Passport Holders; **Visitor facilities:** Visitor Center, exhibits, campgrounds, hiking trails, cafe and gift shop, picnic area, public telephone, trailer dump station; **Any limitations on vehicle usage:** Wheeled vehicles are restricted to designated roadways, prohibited on hiking trails; **Hiking trails:** Yes, a nature trail at the visitor center and a system of trails on Wheeler Peak. Ask at visitor center for information on the many trails; **Backcountry:** Yes, extensive high elevation areas from 9,000 to 11,000 feet (2,700 to 3,300 m) accessible chiefly from May to October. Backcountry campers are asked to register at the visitor center upon their arrival in the park. Knowledge of cross-country hiking skills recommended; **Camping:** Yes, 4 campgrounds. Available on a first-come, first-served basis only; **Other overnight accommodations on site:** No; **Meals served in the park:** Yes, Easter weekend and Memorial Day weekend to the end of October in a cafe adjacent to the Visitor Center; **Food and supplies obtainable in the park:** No; **Food and supplies obtainable nearby:** Yes, at Baker, NV 5 miles (8 km) east of Visitor Center; and Ely, NV 70 miles (112 km) west. Visitors travelling from the east should be aware that Delta, UT, 100 miles (160 km) east is the last stop for gas and supplies before reaching the vicinity of the park; **Overnight accommodations:** Limited accomodations available in the Baker area, 5 miles (8 km). Additional accomodations available in Ely, NV 70 miles (112 km), or Delta, UT 100 miles (160 km). **First Aid available in park:** Yes; **Nearest Hospital:** Ely, NV 70 miles (112 km) via U.S. 6-50; **Days/Hours:** Park always open. Visitor Center open year round from 8 a.m. to 5 p.m. Cave tours scheduled at least hourly in the summer; from October to May tours at 9:00, 11:00, 2:00, and 4:00. Evening programs and guided walks on a varying schedule in the summer; **Holiday Closings:** Thanksgiving, Dec. 25, and Jan. 1; **Visitor attractions closed for seasons:** Cafe and Gift Shop closed November through March. Wheeler Peak scenic drive inaccessible due to snow from approximately October to May, above the 7500 foot (2200 m) level; **Weather:** Winters are cold with highs 30°F (-1°C) to 0°F (-18°C). Summer temperatures reach 85° to 90°F (30° to 33°C) during the daytime.

GENERAL INFORMATION: Visitors to the area should remain aware of the high elevation—7,000 to 13,000 feet (2,100 to 3,900 m)—those with a heart condition or difficulty breathing should adjust their activity accordingly. On the cave tours beware of low ceilings and slippery conditions; use the handrails and stay with your group at all times.

A **Special Note:** Great Basin National Park is America's newest National Park, created by Act of Congress on October 27, 1986. Currently a major planning effort is underway to determine levels of visitor use and development in the new park. As a result, facilities, permit requirements, and length of use limits may evolve over time. We suggest that you stop at the visitor center for up-to-the-minute information due to the changing situation at the park, or contact the park by phone or mail in advance of your visit.

Lake Mead National Recreation Area
Boulder City, Nevada   **SEE CLIMATABLE NO. 99**

MAILING ADDRESS: Superintendent, Lake Mead National Recreation Area, 601 Nevada Highway, Boulder City, Nevada 89005 **Telephone:** 702-293-8906

DIRECTIONS: The Alan Bible Visitor Center is near the west end of Lake Mead, on US Highway 93, 4 miles (6.5 km) east of Boulder City.

Lake Mead in Nevada, formed by Hoover Dam, and Lake Mohave in Arizona, formed by Davis Dam, both on the Colorado River, dominate this first national recreation area. Established by Congress on Oct. 8, 1964.

VISITOR ACTIVITIES: swimming, fishing, boating, water skiing, dam tours, horseback riding, cruising, diving, backcountry hiking, hunting (in season only), camping; **Permits:** for fishing, an Arizona or Nevada fishing license, available at most marinas, is required; **Fees:** $6 per night for developed campsites; **Visitor facilities:** Visitor Center, botanical garden, interpretive programs, camping and trailer Sites, commercial boat trip, boat-mooring and marine supply rentals, many facilities are handicapped accessible, includes handicapped fishing pier at Lake Mead Marina only; **Any limitations on vehicle usage:** Off-road vehicle travel is prohibited; **Hiking trails:** No, most hiking is cross-country; ask a Ranger about good routes, write for maps of approved roads. Carry plenty of water with you. In Summer, the canyons heat up like furnaces. Hikers should have two or more quarts of water per person. There are no creeks or springs that have water suitable for drinking. Never enter abandoned mines or tunnels; shafts are deep and supporting timbers are old and rotten; **Backcountry:** Yes, check at the Visitor Center, see a Park Ranger; **Camping:** No reservations available for campsites. Nearly all developed areas have campgrounds equipped with individual campsites, fire grates, tables, water, restrooms, and sanitary disposal stations. Only at concessioner trailer courts are there utility hookups. To protect your gear, lock it when you leave camp and notify a Ranger if your campsite is left unattended for more than 24 hours. *Be alert for flash floods in stormy weather. Avoid wash bottoms, and never camp on low ground*; **Other overnight accommodations on site:** Yes, concession facilities are listed in a pamphlet available by mail from the Superintendent or at the Visitor Center; **Meals served in the park:** Yes, fast food available at each of the nine developed areas; **Food and supplies obtainable in the park:** Yes, at concession facilities; **Food and supplies obtainable nearby:** Yes, in Boulder City, Searchlight, Bullhead City, Overton, Henderson; **Overnight accommodations:** Boulder City, 4 miles (6.5 km); Bullhead City, 6 miles (9.7 km); Henderson, 15 miles (24 km); Las Vegas, 25 miles (40 km); **First Aid available in park:** Yes; **Nearest Hospital:** Boulder City, 4 miles (6.5 km); **Days/Hours:** Park never closes; **Visitor attractions closed for seasons:** No; **Weather:** From late September through late May, the weather is delightful. Even in July and August, when daytime temperatures may rise above 40°C (100°F), many visitors do not find the heat oppressive because of the low humidity. Summer nights are usually comfortable with low temperatures averaging 20°C (70°F). Be prepared for low temperatures on winter mornings and evenings. Bring warm clothing.

GENERAL INFORMATION: Safety Notes: For protection against brilliant sunshine, wear a hat and tinted glasses. When swimming, distances to the islands, buoys, and across coves are easily underestimated, Caution-air mattresses and blow-up toys, any inflatables, can blow away even on gentle wind, leaving you stranded far from shore. Never swim alone or from an unanchored boat. Remember, muscles tire quickly in cold water.

Always check the weather forecast and look for storm warning flags before going out boating or water skiing. If bad weather catches you on the water, put on your life jacket, head for the nearest sheltered cove, and wait it out. Call 702-736-3854 for a current forecast from the National Weather Service. Water skiers must wear a lifesaving device, and an observer must accompany the boat operator. Waters below Hoover Dam averge in the low 50°s F; unsafe for swimming in Black Canyon. Beware oleander bushes found in all campgrounds, they are poisonous. Do not let pets drink from the irrigation ditches. Do not use any part of this plant for firewood, or use their branches to roast marshmallows. Poison control phone 702-732-4989.

New Hampshire

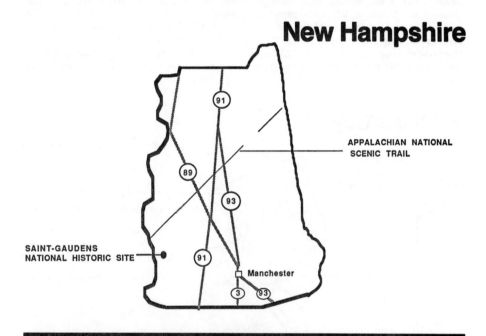

Appalachian National Scenic Trail
For details see listing in Maine

Saint-Gaudens National Historic Site
Cornish, New Hampshire   **SEE CLIMATABLE NO. 96**

MAILING ADDRESS: Superintendent, Saint-Gaudens National Historic Site, R.R. 2, Box 73, Cornish, New Hampshire 03745 **Telephone:** 603-675-2175

DIRECTIONS: The Site is located off of NH 12A in Cornish, NH, 9 miles (12.5 km) north of Claremont, NH, and 2 miles (3 km) from Windsor, VT. Visitors travelling via Int. 91 should use the Ascutney or Hartland, VT exits; via 89, they should use the West Lebanon, NH exit. Bridge to Windsor, VT may be closed through 1989.
     A Memorial to the great American sculptor Augustus Saint-Gaudens (1848-1907) contains his home, "Aspet" and his studios, gardens and artwork. Authorized for addition to the National Park System on Aug. 31, 1964. Established in 1977.

VISITOR ACTIVITIES: guided tours, exhibits, lectures, nature programs, picnicking, fishing, concerts and art exhibitions in Summer, snowshoe and cross-country skiing available on the grounds in Winter; **Permits:** No; **Fees:** Entrance fee is $1.00 per person, 12 and under free of charge (price is subject to change without notice; please call for current fee). Golden Eagle, Golden Age, and Golden Access Passports accepted and available; **Visitor facilities:** parking, restrooms, limited picnic facilities, museums, garden and grounds; **Any limitations on vehicle usage:** No snowmobiles or other off-road vehicles are allowed; **Hiking trails:** 1/4 mile and 2-1/2 mile nature trails; **Backcountry:** No; **Camping:** No; **Other overnight accommodations on site:** No; **Meals served in the park:** No; **Food and supplies obtainable in the park:** No; **Food and supplies obtainable nearby:** Yes, at Claremont, W. Lebanon & Plainfield, NH and Ascutney, Windsor, and White River Junction, VT; **Overnight accommodations:** Claremont, W. Lebanon NH, and Ascutney, Windsor, and White River Junction, VT; **First Aid available in park:** No; **Nearest Hospital:** Claremont, NH 12 miles (18 km); **Days/Hours:** Open Memorial Day weekend through October from 8:30 a.m. to 4:30 p.m. daily; **Holiday Closings:** None (in season); **Visitor attractions closed for seasons:** House and studios are closed from Nov. to Memorial Day weekend; **Weather:** Temperatures range from 65-80°F in Summer.

New Jersey

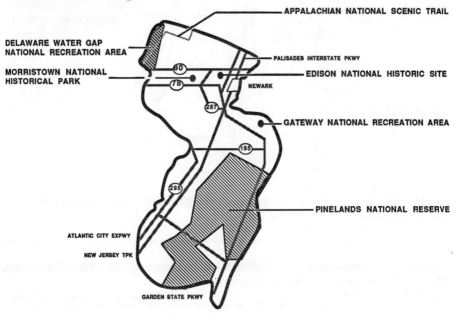

Appalachian National Scenic Trail
For details see listing in Maine

Delaware Water Gap National Recreation Area
For details see listing in Pennsylvania

Edison National Historic Site
West Orange, New Jersey **SEE CLIMATABLE NO. 100**

MAILING ADDRESS: Park Superintendent, Edison National Historic Site, Main Street at Lakeside Avenue, West Orange, New Jersey 07052 **Telephone:** 201-736-5050

DIRECTIONS: Site headquarters, on Main Street at Lakeside Avenue in West Orange, is 2 miles (3 km) west of Garden State Parkway and 1/2 mile (.8 km) north of Interstate 280.

Buildings and equipment used by Thomas A. Edison for many of his experiments are here, as are his library, papers, and models of some of his inventions. The Site also includes Glenmont, Edison's 23-room home, with original furnishings. Designated Dec. 6, 1955.

VISITOR ACTIVITIES: walking tours, interpretive exhibits and talks, reservations required for groups exceeding 10 persons; **Permits:** No; **Fees:** $2 per person entrance fee, except for those under 12 or over 62. Golden Age and Golden Eagle Passports accepted and available; **Visitor facilities:** restrooms and parking; **Any limitations on vehicle usage:** No strollers allowed on tour; no buses allowed at Glenmont; **Hiking trails:** No; **Meals served in the park:** No; **Food and supplies obtainable in the park:** No; **Food and supplies obtainable nearby:** Yes, shops within walking distance; **Overnight accommodations:** in the immediate area of West Orange, 1½ to 5 miles (2.5-8 km); **First Aid available in park:** Yes; **Nearest Hospital:** Orange, 2 miles (3 km); **Days/Hours:** Museum Lobby is open daily from 9:00 a.m. to 5:00 p.m. Guided tours of the laboratory are conducted Wednesday through Sunday, beginning at 9:30 a.m., with the last tour starting at 3:30 p.m. Glenmont open for tours on weekends throughout the year, with extended hours in summer months. Contact the park for days and hours of operation; **Holiday Closings:** Thanksgiving, Dec. 25, & Jan. 1; **Weather:** The Site is open year-round, and since tours go between buildings, inclement weather must be tolerated.

Gateway National Recreation Area
For details see listing in New York

Morristown National Historical Park
Morristown, New Jersey **SEE CLIMATABLE NO. 100**

MAILING ADDRESS: Superintendent, Morristown National Historical Park, Washington Place, Morristown, New Jersey 07960 **Telephone:** 201-539-2016

DIRECTIONS: The Park is most easily accessible by Int. 287. Southbond, use exit 32 for Washington's Headquarters and the Museum. Use exit 26B for the Jockey Hollow Area. Northbound, use exit 32A for the Headquarters and Museum, or for the Jockey Hollow Area use the exit for N. Maple Ave./Rte 202. Follow the brown directional signs. Morristown is also easily reached via US 202 or by NJ 24.

For two Winters during the Revolution—1777 and 1779-80—the Continental Army established winter quarters here. The Park is divided into two main areas. The Jockey Hollow Area includes the Visitor Center, the Wick House, reconstructed soldier huts, hiking trails, and a tour loop road: Washington's Headquarters includes both the Museum and the Ford Mansion. Authorized for addition to the National Park System on Mar. 2, 1933.

VISITOR ACTIVITIES: movies, exhibits, soldier life demonstrations, arts and crafts demonstrations, hiking, special events on weekends, wayside exhibits; **Permits:** No;

Fees: Entrance fee is $1 for adults, under 13 and over 62 are free. Golden Eagle and Golden Age Passports accepted and available; **Visitor facilities:** hiking trails, restrooms and sales areas throughout the Park; **Any limitations on vehicle usage:** Park in designated areas only. Park roads are open from 9 a.m. to sunset; **Hiking trails:** Yes, Jockey Hollow has an extensive woodland trail system. Obtain maps at Visitor Center; **Backcountry:** No; **Camping:** No; **Other overnight accommodations on site:** No, within 30-40 miles (48-64 km) there are six State-run parks or forests which have camping facilities. In addition, there are several privately-run campsites closer to Morristown. Contact the Park for further information; **Meals served in the park:** No, but picnic and eating facilities are available in the Lewis Morris County Park which is adjacent to the Jockey Hollow Area; **Food and supplies obtainable in the park:** No; **Food and supplies obtainable nearby:** Yes, in Morristown, Bernardsvile, Mendham; **Overnight accommodations:** About 5 miles (8 km) north of Morristown, near the intersection of Highways 10 and 202 East and West. Contact the Park for further information on nearby accommodations; **First Aid available in park:** Yes; **Nearest Hospital:** Morristown, Madison Avenue 1 mile (1.6 km) from HQ-5 miles from Jockey Hollow area; **Days/Hours:** Park buildings open 9 a.m.-5 p.m.; Park roads open 9 a.m.-sunset, 7 days a week year-round; **Holiday Closings:** All Park buildings closed Thanksgiving, Dec. 25 & Jan. 1; **Visitor attractions closed for seasons:** Park is occasionally closed by snow or hazardous driving conditions. Some buildings closed during Winter due to staff reductions.

GENERAL INFORMATION: Nearby points of interest include Edison National Historic Site (see listing in this book) and Great Swamp National Wildlife Refuge.

Pinelands National Reserve
New Jersey   **SEE CLIMATABLE NO. 101**

DIRECTIONS: ONLY STATE PARK AREAS HAVE BEEN DEVELOPED AS YET. For further information, contact: State of New Jersey Department of Environmental Protection, Division of Parks and Forestry, State Park Service, CN 404, Trenton, NJ 08625, phone 609-292-2797.

Local, State, and Federal governments and the private sector combine in a new "reserve" policy to protect diversely owned lands from encroachment. This largest undeveloped tract on the Eastern seaboard has the equivalent of a 2000 square-mile lake beneath the dwarfed pines and oaks of its shrubby, porous surface. Designated by Congress in 1978 as the country's first National Reserve.

New Mexico

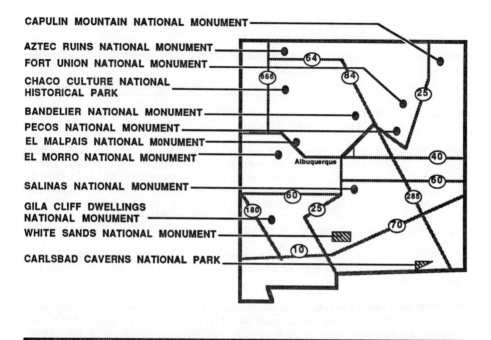

CAPULIN MOUNTAIN NATIONAL MONUMENT

AZTEC RUINS NATIONAL MONUMENT

FORT UNION NATIONAL MONUMENT

CHACO CULTURE NATIONAL HISTORICAL PARK

BANDELIER NATIONAL MONUMENT

PECOS NATIONAL MONUMENT

EL MALPAIS NATIONAL MONUMENT

EL MORRO NATIONAL MONUMENT

Albuquerque

SALINAS NATIONAL MONUMENT

GILA CLIFF DWELLINGS NATIONAL MONUMENT

WHITE SANDS NATIONAL MONUMENT

CARLSBAD CAVERNS NATIONAL PARK

Aztec Ruins National Monument
Aztec, New Mexico   **SEE CLIMATABLE NO. 102**

MAILING ADDRESS: Superintendent, Aztec Ruins National Monument, P.O. Box 640, Aztec, New Mexico 87410 **Telephone:** 505-334-6174

DIRECTIONS: The Monument is north of the city of Aztec, near the junction of US 550 and NM 44. You should stop first at the Visitor Center.

Ruins of this large Pueblo Indian community of 12th-century masonry and timber buildings have been largely excavated and stabilized. The ruins, misnamed by early settlers, are unrelated to the Aztecs of Mexico. Created by Presidential Proclamation on Jan. 24, 1923.

VISITOR ACTIVITIES: interpretive exhibits, picnicking, walking tours; **Permits:** No, (subject to change); **Fees:** $1 per person entrance fee. Golden Age, Golden Eagle and Golden Access Passports accepted and available; **Visitor facilities:** parking, restrooms and exhibits at Visitor Center, picnic area; **Any limitations on vehicle usage:** No, (subject to change); **Hiking trails:** Yes, a self-guiding trail leads through the west pueblo, its great Kiva, and the nearby Hubbard Ruin, a tri-walled structure; **Backcountry:** No; **Camping:** No; **Other overnight accommodations on site:** No; **Meals served in the park:** No; **Food and supplies obtainable in the park:** No; **Food and supplies obtainable nearby:** Yes, in Aztec; **Overnight accommodations:** Aztec, a short distance south on US 550 and NM 44; **First Aid available in park:** Yes, or nearby in Aztec; **Nearest Hospital:** Farmington, Maple Street, 15 miles (24 km); **Days/Hours:** Open daily from 8 a.m. to 5 p.m., longer hours from Memorial Day through Labor Day; **Holiday Closings:** Dec. 25

and Jan. 1; **Visitor attractions closed for seasons:** No; **Weather:** Summer: highs in the 90°'s, lows 40°s-50°s, thunderstorms late in the season. Fall & Spring: highs 40°s to 80°s, lows often below 32°, Spring is very windy. Winter: highs 20°s to 40°s, lows well below 32° with some snow.

GENERAL INFORMATION: The 800-year-old walls of those prehistoric Indian ruins are held together with mud: they crumble easily if disturbed.

Bandelier National Monument
Los Alamos, New Mexico   **SEE CLIMATABLE NO. 103**

MAILING ADDRESS: Superintendent, Bandelier National Monument, Los Alamos, New Mexico 87544 **Telephone:** 505-672-3861

DIRECTIONS: The Monument is 46 miles (74 km) west of Santa Fe, NM, and is reached from Santa Fe north on US 285 to Pojoaque, then west on NM 4. Approach may also be made through the scenic Jemez country from Albuquerque via NM 44 and NM 4. Inquiry should be made during bad weather before attempting the latter trip. The Visitor Center, 3 miles (4.8 km) inside the Monument, is 10 miles (16 km) southwest of White Rock and 13 miles (21 km) south of Los Alamos, both on NM 4 (loop). The detached Tsankawi section of the Monument is 11 miles (18 km) north of Frijoles Canyon on NM 4.

Ruins of many cliff houses of 15th-century Pueblo Indians lie on the canyon-slashed slopes of the Pajarito Plateau. Created by Presidential Proclamation on Feb. 11, 1916.

VISITOR ACTIVITIES: hiking, camping, interpretive and audiovisual exhibits, self-guiding walking tours, picnicking, horseback riding, campfire programs nightly in Summer; **Permits:** required for backcountry travel, can be obtained from the Visitor Center; **Fees:** $5.00 per car entrance fee; $2.00 per person for individuals on buses, on foot, or travelling by other means. Golden Age, Golden Access, and Golden Eagle Passports accepted and available. $5.00 per night per site camping fee, 1/2 price for Golden Age Passport holders; **Visitor facilities:** parking, restrooms, and exhibits at Visitor Center, campgrounds, picnic area, snack bar & curio shop in Summer; **Any limitations on vehicle usage:** Vehicles are restricted to paved roads. Trail bikes are not allowed in the Monument; Trailers not allowed in canyon during summer; parking on Mesa; **Hiking trails:** Yes, a 1 mile (1.6 km) round-trip trail from near the Visitor Center to the main ruin, and over 70 miles (97 km) of maintained backcountry trails; **Backcountry:** Yes, get information from a Park Ranger or by telephoning the Visitor Center; **Camping:** Yes, no reservations available for individual campsites. Group sites are reserved through the Superintendent's office; **Other overnight accommodations on site:** No; **Meals served in the park:** Yes, at Frijoles Canyon snack bar; **Food and supplies obtainable in the park:** Yes; **Food and supplies obtainable nearby:** Yes, at White Rock, Los Alamos, Santa Fe; **Overnight accommodations:** White Rock, NM 4, 10 miles (16 km); Los Alamos, NM 4, 13 miles (21 km); Santa Fe, NM 4 to Pojoaque, thence US 285 to Pojoaque, 46 miles (74 km); **First Aid available in park:** Yes; **Nearest Hospital:** Los Alamos, NM 4, 13 miles (21 km); **Days/Hours:** Open daily 8 a.m-5 p.m.; until 6 p.m. from Memorial Day-Labor Day; **Holiday Closings:** Dec. 25; **Visitor attractions closed for seasons:** Trails are not cleared of snow in Winter; **Weather:** From May-Sept., temperatures range from the low 50°sF at night to the high 80°sF in the daytime. The relative humidity is generally low. Thunderstorms, usually of short duration, are frequent in July and August.

GENERAL INFORMATION: Energy and endurance are required for longer hiking trips. You must be in good physical condition since trails lead into and out of deep, steep-walled canyons of the rough and broken country, and the altitude (about 7000 feet) places an additional burden on the heart and lungs.

TRAVEL ACCESS: Bus: Greyhound and Trailways provide daily service to Santa Fe; **Rail:** Amtrak serves Lamy (near Santa Fe); **Air:** Major airlines serves Albuquerque. Ross Airlines provides daily service to Los Alamos; **Other:** taxi, charter tours available from Santa Fe, about 45 miles away.

NEARBY FACILITIES & POINTS OF INTEREST: Campgrounds: Camel Rock Campground—north of Santa Fe on US 84-285; **Parks, other points of interest:** Pecos NM, Chaco Culture N.P.

Capulin Mountain National Monument
Capulin, New Mexico   **SEE CLIMATABLE NO. 104**

MAILING ADDRESS: Superintendent, Capulin Mountain National Monument, Capulin, New Mexico 88414 **Telephone:** 505-278-2201

DIRECTIONS: The Monument is in the northeast corner of New Mexico. The entrance is on NM 325, 3 miles (4.8 km) north of the town of Capulin. From Clayton, Capulin is 54 miles (87 km) west on US 64/87; from Raton, 30 miles (48 km) east. The Visitor Center is 1/2 mile (.8 km) past the entrance.
  This symmetrical cinder cone is an interesting example of a geologically recent volcano. Created by Presidential Proclamation on Aug. 9, 1916.

VISITOR ACTIVITIES: self-guiding trails; interpretive and audiovisual programs; picnicking; photography; flower-, bird-, and wildlife-watching; **Permits:** Yes, obtained at Visitor Center; **Fees:** $3 entrance fee per carload, 50¢ per person on commercial bus. Persons under 16 years of age or over 62 are admitted free. Golden Age, Golden Eagle, and Golden Access Passports accepted and available; **Visitor facilities:** parking, restrooms and water in the picnic area at the western base of the mountain; **Any limitations on vehicle usage:** Vehicles are restricted to designated roadways; **Hiking trails:** Yes, trails lead around the rim and into the crater; **Backcountry:** No; **Camping:** No; **Other overnight accommodations on site:** No; **Meals served in the park:** No; **Food and supplies obtainable in the park:** No; **Food and supplies obtainable nearby:** Yes, in Capulin or Raton; **Overnight accommodations:** Raton, 30 miles (48 km) west on US 64-87, to Int. 25; **First Aid available in park:** Yes; **Nearest Hospital:** Raton, 30 miles (48 km) west on US 64-87, to Int. 25; **Days/Hours:** Park open all year. Visitor Center is open from 8 a.m.-4:30 p.m. (Labor Day-Memorial Day); 7:30 a.m.-6:30 p.m. (Memorial Day to Labor Day); Crater Rim Road closed at Sunset; **Holiday Closings:** Dec. 25 & Jan. 1; **Visitor attractions closed for seasons:** The Monument is accessible throughout the year.

GENERAL INFORMATION: *For Your Safety*—The trails at Capulin Mountain are well-maintained but loose cinders on them can be hazardous. You should wear rubber-soled shoes on the hiking trails. Be on the lookout for rattlesnakes, which inhabit the area. **Handicap access:** Restroom and nature trail at Park Visitor Center.

TRAVEL ACCESS: Bus: Greyhound provides service to Raton, NM 30 miles west of Park; **Rail:** Amtrak provides service to Raton, NM, 30 miles west of Park; **Air:** Nearest air connections, Frontier flights to Pueblo, CO, 138 miles northwest of Park; **Other:** Rental cars available in Raton.

NEARBY FACILITIES & POINTS OF INTEREST: Campgrounds: Capulin Camp, Capulin, NM 505-278-2921, 3 miles from Park. Sugarite State Park located in Raton.

Carlsbad Caverns National Park
Carlsbad, New Mexico   **SEE CLIMATABLE NO. 158**

MAILING ADDRESS: Superintendent, Carlsbad Caverns National Park, 3225 National Parks Highway, Carlsbad, New Mexico 88220 **Telephone:** 505-885-8884 (Administration) Visitor Information No.: 505-785-2232

DIRECTIONS: The Park is on US 62-180, 20 miles (32 km) southwest of Carlsbad, NM, and 150 miles (242 km) east of El Paso, TX. The visitor center is near the cavern entrance, which is 7 miles (11 km) west of Highway 62-180.

This series of connected caverns, one of the largest underground chambers yet discovered, has countless magnificent and unusual formations. Created by Presidential Proclamation on Oct. 25, 1923. Redesignated a national park May 14, 1930.

VISITOR ACTIVITIES: picnicking, photography, cave tours, nature walks, exhibits, bat flight programs nightly in Summer, primitive lantern trips into New Cave; **Permits:** No; **Fees:** New Cave-$5.00 for Adults, $3.00 for 15 and under; Carlsbad Cavern-$4.00 for Adults, $2.00 for age 6 thru 15. Under 6 free; Golden Age and Access Passport holders 50% discount. **Visitor facilities:** visitor center, picnic areas, nature trails, restaurant, gift shop, nursery, kennel; **Any limitations on vehicle usage:** No, but be alert for deer and other animals bounding across the roadway; **Hiking trails:** Yes, hiking and backpacking opportunities in large, rugged backcountry but poorly marked trails. An adequate supply of water, good boots, and maps are essential; **Backcountry:** Yes, for safety, check with a park ranger before going into the backcountry; **Camping:** No; **Other overnight accommodations on site:** No; **Meals served in the park:** Yes, a restaurant is next to visitor center. Lunches and refreshments are also available underground; **Food and supplies obtainable in the park:** No; **Food and supplies obtainable nearby:** Yes, in Carlsbad and Whites City; **Overnight accommodations:** Carlsbad, 27 miles (43 km) and Whites City, 7 miles (11 km); **First Aid available in park:** Yes; **Nearest Hospital:** Carlsbad, 27 miles (43 km); **Days/Hours:** The Park and visitor center are open all year; **Holiday Closings:** December 25; **Visitor attractions closed for seasons:** No; **Weather:** Summers are usually hot and winters mild. However, extreme changes can come at any time of the year. In spring, winds can be strong. In summer, thunderstorms accompanied by brief, but often heavy downpours, may bring flash floods to the canyon bottoms. In winter the normally mild weather may be broken by a short-lived snowstorm or a bone-chilling cold front sweeping through on gale force winds. In the caverns, the temperature remains a constant 13°C (56°F) year round.

GENERAL INFORMATION: *Precautions:* A light sweater or jacket recommended and comfortable walking shoes with rubber soles and heels are a must for cavern trip. Stay on cavern trails and do not run. If electrical power fails while you are underground, stop and remain quiet until emergency lights come on. Watch for rattlesnakes when hiking on the surface. Beware of the cactus and other desert plants; their spines can inflict painful injury.

Chaco Culture National Historical Park
Bloomfield, New Mexico   **SEE CLIMATABLE NO. 102**

MAILING ADDRESS: Superintendent, Chaco Culture National Historical Park, Star Route 4, Box 6500, Bloomfield, New Mexico 87413 **Telephone:** 505-988-6727

DIRECTIONS: The Park is in northwestern New Mexico. From the north, turn off NM 44 at Blanco Trading Post or Nageezi Trading Post (7 miles-11.3 km south of Blanco), and follow NM 57 for 29 miles to park headquarters. This road is unpaved. From the south, turn north on NM 57 from I-40 at Thoreau and proceed 60 miles (96 km) to Chaco Canyon. A marked turnoff begins a 20 mile (32 km) stretch of unpaved NM Hwy 57, leading to the south entrance. The Visitor Center is just ahead. Because NM 57 is not paved into the Park, you should inquire locally regarding travel over this route in stormy weather.

The canyon, with hundreds of smaller ruins, contains 13 major Indian ruins unsurpassed in the United States, representing the highest point of Pueblo pre-Columbian civilization. Created by Presidential Proclamation on Mar. 11, 1907.

VISITOR ACTIVITIES: guided tours & campfire talks in summer; exhibits, walking tours, picnicking, day hiking; **Permits:** required for day hiking in the backcountry. Obtain permission at the visitor center. No overnight backpacking; **Fees:** An entrance fee is charged; **Visitor facilities:** restrooms, campgrounds with firegrates, drinking water at visitor center, exhibits, interpretive programs; **Any limitations on vehicle usage:** The Park's unpaved entrance roads are frequently rough, dusty and narrow; they are very slippery when wet. Do not drive off the graded roadway. Narrow bridge in park, weight limit, 9 tons. Housetrailers longer than 30 feet in length are not allowed in the campground; **Hiking trails:** Yes, 5 self-guiding trails take you through several ruin complexes. Walking time for each is about 1 hour. There are four longer hikes as well. Inquire at Visitor Center; **Backcountry:** Day use only, by permit; **Camping:** Yes, no reservations accepted for the campsites, which are 1 mile (1.6 km) from the Visitor Center. Write to Chaco for group campsite reservations; **Other overnight accommodations on site:** No; **Meals served in the park:** No; **Food and supplies obtainable in the park:** No; **Food and supplies obtainable nearby:** At Blanco and Nageezi Trading Posts and in Crownpoint; **Overnight accommodations:** Thoreau, 60 miles (96 km); Bloomfield, 60 miles (96 km); Farmington, 80 miles (129 km); **First Aid available in park:** Yes; **Nearest Hospital:** Farmington, 80 miles (129 km); **Days/Hours:** 7 days a week from 8 a.m. to 5 p.m.; **Holiday Closings:** Visitor Center is closed on Dec. 25 and Jan. 1; **Weather:** Although the climate is semi-arid, there is snow in Winter, and thunderstorms are possible from June through September. Summers are usually Hot and dry.

GENERAL INFORMATION: *For Your Safety*—Do not climb on the walls of the ruins, which are weak and dangerous. Other points of interest in the vicinity are Mesa Verde National Park, 157 miles (251.8 km) north by road, El Morro National Monument, 96 miles (155 km) south and Aztec Ruins National Monument 58 miles (93 km) (see listings in this book).

El Malpais National Monument
Grants, New Mexico

MAILING ADDRESS: Office of Public Affairs, Southwest Regional Office, National Park Service, Post Office Box 728, Sante Fe, New Mexico 87501 **Telephone:** 505-988-6375

DIRECTIONS: NOT YET OPEN TO PUBLIC. NO VISITOR FACILITIES. Site set aside to protect unique lava formations and ecosystem by Act of Congress, December 23, 1987.

El Morro National Monument
Ramah, New Mexico   **SEE CLIMATABLE NO. 102**

MAILING ADDRESS: Superintendent, El Morro National Monument, Ramah, New Mexico 87321 **Telephone:** 505-783-4226

DIRECTIONS: The Monument is 56 miles (90 km) southeast of Gallup via NM 32 and NM 53, and 42 miles (67.6 km) west of Grants via NM 53.

"Inscription Rock" is a soft sandstone monolith on which hundreds of inscriptions are carved, including those of 17th Century Spanish explorers and 19th Century American emigrants and settlers. Pre-Columbian petroglyphs are also here. Created by Presidential Proclamation in 1906.

VISITOR ACTIVITIES: hiking, camping, picnicking, campfire programs in Summer; **Permits:** No; **Fees:** Yes, $1 per person, $3 per carload entrance fee, no camping or picnicking fees. No charge for educational groups. Golden Age, Golden Eagle and Golden Access Passports accepted and available; **Visitor facilities:** self-guiding walk, campground and picnic area; **Any limitations on vehicle usage:** No off-road vehicles are allowed; vehicles are restricted to park roads; **Hiking trails:** Yes, 2 miles (3 km) of hiking trails (surfaced, with minimum inclines on the lower Inscription Rock Trail, suitable for a guided wheelchair), Mesa Top Trail rises 200 feet via switchbacks, a natural trail over the mesa top; **Backcountry:** No; **Camping:** Yes, no reservations accepted for campsites; **Other overnight accommodations on site:** No; **Meals served in the park:** No; **Food and supplies obtainable in the park:** No; **Food and supplies obtainable nearby:** Yes, limited supplies at Ramah, more extensive supplies at Grants and Gallup; **Overnight accommodations:** Grants, Int. 40, 42 miles (67.6 km); Gallup, Int. 40, 56 miles (90 km); **First Aid available in park:** Yes; **Nearest Hospital:** Grants, NM 53, 42 miles (67.6 km); Gallup, NM 53 & 32 56 miles (90 km); **Days/Hours:** Open daily from 8 a.m to 5 p.m. year-round; until 8 p.m in Summer, from approximately Memorial Day to Labor Day; **Holiday Closings:** Dec. 25; **Visitor attractions closed for seasons:** Mesa Top Trail closed during heavy snow accumulation; **Weather:** Warm sun (daytime) averaging 70's and 80's in Summer; averaging 40's and 50's in Winter; night-time average is 10's and 20's in Winter with some -0 readings, and 30's and 40's in Summer. Usually a nice breeze in Summer, average 16 to 18 inches of rain a year, and 4 to 12 inches of snow per storm.

GENERAL INFORMATION: Be cautious of soft terrain and high cliffs in this natural area. Dogs must be kept on a leash; hiking shoes or shoes with traction are recommended for the trails; children must be accompanied by an adult as the Mesa Top Trail is a natural trail climbing 200 feet. The Park has a wheelchair for use and a portion of the inscription trail has been modified for wheelchair use. Groups are welcome, advance notification is recommended to better accommodate the group.

Fort Union National Monument
Watrous, New Mexico   **SEE CLIMATABLE NO. 103**

MAILING ADDRESS: Superintendent, Fort Union National Monument, Watrous, New Mexico 87753 **Telephone:** 505-425-8025

DIRECTIONS: The Monument is 8 miles (13 km) north of I-25, at the end of NM 477. Watrous, NM is 1/2 mile (1 km) south of the intersection of these two highways.

Three successive U.S. Army forts were built on this site—a key defensive point on the Santa Fe Trail—and were occupied successively from 1851 to 1891. Ruins of the last fort, which was the largest military post in the Southwest, have been stabilized. Established by act of Congress on Apr. 5, 1956.

VISITOR ACTIVITIES: Interpretive exhibits, living history, walking tours, picnicking; **Permits:** No; **Fees:** No; **Visitor facilities:** restrooms and parking at Visitor Center, picnic area, interpretive trail; **Any limitations on vehicle usage:** All vehicles must park at the Visitor Center. No vehicles are allowed on the historic trail; **Hiking trails:** Yes, a 1½ mile (2.5 km) self-guiding trail; **Backcountry:** No; **Camping:** No; **Other overnight**

accommodations on site: No; **Meals served in the park:** No; **Food and supplies obtainable in the park:** No; **Food and supplies obtainable nearby:** Yes, in Las Vegas, NM; **Overnight accommodations:** Las Vegas, NM, I-25, 28 miles (42 km) southwest; **First Aid available in park:** Yes; **Nearest Hospital:** Las Vegas, I-25, 28 miles (42 km) southwest; **Days/Hours:** Open daily from 8 a.m. to 4:30 p.m., longer hours in Summer; **Holiday Closings:** Dec. 25 and Jan. 1; **Visitor attractions closed for seasons:** No; **Weather:** Summer is warm and windy with afternoon thundershowers. Winter is cold and windy; with infrequent but sometimes heavy snowfalls.

GENERAL INFORMATION: *For Your Safety*—Do not climb on the walls or foundations of the ruins. Stay on the trail, because rattlesnakes can be found in the high grass. The third fort arsenal site is closed to the public.

Gila Cliff Dwellings National Monument
Silver City, New Mexico   **SEE CLIMATABLE NO. 105**

MAILING ADDRESS: Gila Cliff Dwellings National Monument, Route 11, Box 100, Silver City, New Mexico 88061 **Telephone:** 505-536-9461

DIRECTIONS: The Monument is 44 miles (71 km) north of Silver City at the end of NM 15, a steep and winding two-lane blacktop highway. The trip to the Dwellings through the mountains takes about 2 hours each way. Silver City is located on US 180, about 120 air miles (193 km) northwest of El Paso, TX. Due to road conditions, trailers over 20 feet are advised to use NM 35 through the scenic Mimbres Valley and by Lake Roberts, instead of NM 15. This is reached from NM 61, north from San Lorenzo which is 19 miles (30.6 km) east of Silver City on Route 90.

These well-preserved cliff dwellings in natural alcoves on the face of a cliff were inhabited from about 1280 to the early 1300s. A.D. Created by Presidential Proclamation on Nov. 16, 1907.

VISITOR ACTIVITIES: picnicking, fishing, exhibits, photography, walking; **Permits:** No; **Fees:** No; **Visitor facilities:** self-guiding interpretive trail to the dwellings; **Any limitations on vehicle usage:** Restricted to pavement at Scorpion camping area; **Hiking trails:** Yes, a steep, 1 mile (1.6 km) trail leads to and through the Dwellings, situated about 180 feet above the canyon bottom. Plan about 1 hour for your visit; **Backcountry:** Yes, the Monument is surrounded by the Gila Wilderness; the trails are well-marked. Information at Gila Visitor Center. Wilderness permits are not required; **Camping:** No, but sites are available in Forest Service campgrounds nearby; **Other overnight accommodations on site:** No; **Meals served in the park:** No; **Food and supplies obtainable in the park:** No; **Food and supplies obtainable nearby:** Yes, Gila Hot Springs, about 3 miles (4.8 km) south of the Visitor Center; **Overnight accommodations:** limited accommodations at Gila Hot Springs, NM 15 3 miles (4.8 km); more extensive facilities at Silver City, NM 15, 44 miles (71 km); **First Aid available in park:** Yes; **Nearest Hospital:** Silver City, NM 15, 44 miles (71 km); **Days/Hours:** Open daily from 8 a.m. to 6 p.m., Memorial Day through Labor Day; 9 a.m. to 4 p.m. the rest of the year. Visitor Center open daily from 8 a.m.-5 p.m.; **Holiday Closings:** Dec. 25 & Jan. 1; **Weather:** Summer daytime temperatures vary between 80 and 100°F; at night, from 45 to 55°F. Temperatures drop lower in the higher elevations. Spring and Fall daytime temperatures range from 60 to 80°F, but nighttime temperatures require a selection of warm clothing. Warm bedding is a necessity, even in Summer.

GENERAL INFORMATION: *For Your Safety*—watch your step on the steep trails.

TRAVEL ACCESS: Bus: No; **Rail:** No; **Air:** No.

NEARBY FACILITIES & POINTS OF INTEREST: Camping, Hookups at Campbell's Vacation Center; **Food/Supplies:** Route 11 Box 80; **Campgrounds:** Silver City, NM 88061, (505) 534-9551, 3 miles from Park.

Pecos National Monument
Pecos, New Mexico   **SEE CLIMATABLE NO. 103**

MAILING ADDRESS: Superintendent, Pecos National Monument, Post Office Drawer 11, Pecos, New Mexico 87552 **Telephone:** 505-757-6414 or 757-6032

DIRECTIONS: The park is 25 miles (40 km) southeast of Santa Fe by way of Int. 25, and may be reached from the interchanges at Glorieta, 8 miles (13 km) west of the park via the town of Pecos, and Rowe, 3 miles (4.8 km) south.
    Foundations of a 17th-century Spanish mission church, ruins of an 18th-century Spanish church, and the ruins of the ancient pueblo of Pecos, comprise the Park. The site was once a landmark on the Santa Fe Trail, ruts of which are still in existence. Authorized for addition to the National Park System on June 28, 1965.

VISITOR ACTIVITIES: walking tours, picnicking; **Permits:** No; **Fees:** $1/person— $3/car—May 1-Oct. 31; **Visitor facilities:** Visitor Center, picnic area, self-guiding interpretive trails; **Any limitations on vehicle usage:** Vehicles are restricted to designated roadways; **Hiking trails:** Yes, a walking trail leads to the ruins; **Backcountry:** No; **Camping:** No; **Other overnight accommodations on site:** No, camping is available in the Santa Fe National Forest north of the village of Pecos, on State 63, and in other nearby areas. For further information, contact the Forest Supervisor, Santa Fe National Forest, P.O. Box 1689, Santa Fe, NM 98501, phone 505-988-6313; **Meals served in the park:** No, but in Pecos, NM, 2 miles (3 km) north of the Monument; **Food and supplies obtainable in the park:** No; **Food and supplies obtainable nearby:** Yes, in Pecos, 2 miles (3 km) north; **Overnight accommodations:** Pecos, adjacent to the Park; Santa Fe, 25 miles (40 km) northwest; Las Vegas, NM, 35 miles (56 km) east; **First Aid available in park:** Yes; **Nearest Hospital:** A small clinic is located in Pecos, NM, 2 miles (3 km) north of the Monument. A hospital is in Santa Fe, via I-25, 28 miles (45 km) distant; **Days/ Hours:** Open daily from 8 a.m. to 5 p.m., until 6 p.m. in Summer; **Holiday Closings:** Dec. 25 and Jan. 1; **Weather:** The elevation is 7000 feet. Summer daytime temperatures average in the 80's and 90's, with cool evenings. July and August are rainy. Winter temperatures are variable, ranging from 0° to the mid 40's, snowfall is heavy at times.

GENERAL INFORMATION: Visitors should use caution due to a few trail irregularities, an occasional prairie rattlesnake, and when using ladders into the restored kivas. Do not climb or stand on the fragile ruins.

Salinas National Monument
Mountainair, New Mexico   **SEE CLIMATABLE NO. 106**

MAILING ADDRESS: Superintendent, Salinas National Monument, P.O. Box 496 Mountainair, New Mexico 87036 **Telephone:** 505-847-2585

DIRECTIONS: Mountainair can be reached by taking I-25 south to Belen to NM 6 to U.S. 60 east 21 miles (32 km) to Mountainair. To travel the scenic route from the north, take I-40 east from Albuquerque to NM 14 turn south and drive 54 miles (88 km) to Mountainair. From U.S. 380 turn north at Carrizozo and drive 18 miles (29 km) via U.S. 54 to NM 14. Take NM 14 northwest and drive 61 miles (98 km) to U.S. 60. Area information is available at Salinas National Monument headquarters in Mountainair. Ruins of 17th century Spanish missions and associated Indian pueblos comprise Abo', Quarai, and Gran Quivira units of Salinas National Monument. Established Dec. 19, 1980.

The Gran Quivira Unit is 26 miles (42 km) south on NM 14 from Mountainair; the Quarai Unit is 8 miles (13 km) north on NM 14, Abo' is 9 miles (16 km) west on U.S. 60 from Salinas headquarters.

VISITOR ACTIVITIES: interpretive exhibits, a 30-minute self-guiding walking tour at Abo', Quarai and Gran Quivira Ruins, picnicking at Abo', Gran Quivira, and Quarai Ruins; **Permits:** No; **Fees:** May-Sept. $1.00 per person, maximum $3.00 per carload; **Visitor facilities:** Visitor Center, parking, restrooms, picnic areas at Gran Quivira and Quarai Ruins, parking, restrooms, and picnic area at Abo' Ruins; **Any limitations on vehicle usage:** No; **Hiking trails:** Yes; 1/4 mile (.4 km) trails around ruins at Abo', Quarai, and Gran Quivira Ruins; **Backcountry:** No; **Camping:** No; **Other overnight accommodations on site:** No; **Meals served in the park:** No; **Food and supplies obtainable in the park:** No; **Food and supplies obtainable nearby:** Yes, in Mountainair; **Overnight accommodations:** Mountainair; **First Aid available in park:** Yes, at Abo', Quarai and Gran Quivira Ruins of Mountainair; **Nearest Hospital:** Belen, I-25, 75 miles (120 km); **Days/Hours:** 8:00 a.m.-5:00 p.m. MST last Sunday in Oct. to last Sunday in April; 9:00 a.m.-6:00 p.m. MDT last Sunday in April to last Sunday in October; **Holiday Closings:** Christmas Day; **Visitor attractions closed for seasons:** No; **Weather:** Summer is warm with thundershowers likely, Winter daytime temperatures range from 40° to 60°F.

NEARBY FACILITIES & POINTS OF INTEREST: Hotel/Motel: El Rancho Motel, and Trails End Motel, Mountainair, New Mexico (505) 847-2577, and (505) 847-2544, 10 miles from Park; **Parks, other points of interest:** White Sands, Carlsbad Caverns, Pecos, Bandelier National Monument; **New information:** Gran Quivira National Monument became Salinas National Monument in Dec. 19, 1980. It also incorporates the former Abo' and Quarai State Monuments (Oct. 2, 1981) which are now units of Salinas National Monument. A headquarters with visitor reception and exhibits is located in the historic Shaffer Hotel in Mountainair, 1 block south of US 60-NM 14 junction.

White Sands National Monument
Alamogordo, New Mexico   **SEE CLIMATABLE NO. 107**

MAILING ADDRESS: Superintendent, White Sands National Monument, Box 458, Alamogordo, New Mexico 88311-0458 **Telephone:** 505-437-1058

DIRECTIONS: The Visitor Center is 15 miles (24.15 km)) southwest of Alamogordo on US Highway 70-82.

Dunes of sparkling white gypsum sands, 3.05 to 13.71 m (10 to 45 feet) high, are home to small, light-colored animals that have adapted to this harsh environment. Created by Presidential Proclamation on Jan. 18, 1933.

VISITOR ACTIVITIES: guided walks, illustrated evening programs, and star programs in Summer; hiking; picnicking; backcountry; **Permits:** None; **Fees:** $3 per car entrance fee. Golden Eagle and Golden Age Passports accepted and available; **Visitor facilities:** museum, gift shop, picnic areas, grills, comfort facilities, drinking water only at the Visitor Center; **Any limitations on vehicle usage:** Vehicles are restricted to roads and parking areas; **Hiking trails:** Yes, self-guiding nature trails; **Backcountry:** No; **Camping:** No campgrounds, but primitive backcountry camping is available requiring registration and clearance at Headquarters. The nearest public camping facilities are in Lincoln National Forest, 35 miles (56 km) to the east and a Aguirre Springs, 30 miles (48 km) to the west. Information on National Forest camping can be obtained from the

Forest Supervisor, Lincoln National Forest, Alamogordo, NM 88310. For information on Aguirre Springs, write the District Manager, Bureau of Land Management, P.O. Box 1420, Las Cruces, NM 88001. Several commercial campgrounds are open year-round in Alamogordo and Las Cruces, Oliver Lee Memorial State Park, 13 miles south of Alamogordo, off Highway 54, has 44 sites, some with full hook ups. Write Superintendent, Oliver Lee Memorial State Park, P.O. Box 1845, Alamogordo, NM 88310; **Meals served in the park:** No; **Food and supplies obtainable in the park:** No; **Food and supplies obtainable nearby:** Yes, at Alamogordo; **Overnight accommodations:** Alamogordo, Highway 70-82, 15 miles (24 km) northeast; **First Aid available in park:** Yes; **Nearest Hospital:** Alamogordo, Highway 70-82, 15 miles (24 km) northeast; **Days/ Hours:** Visitor Center: Summers 8 a.m. to 7 p.m. Remainder of year 8:30 a.m. to 5 p.m. Dunes Drive: Summer 8 a.m. to 10 p.m.; Rest of year 8:30 a.m. to ½ hour after sunset; **Holiday Closings:** Dec. 25; **Weather:** Hot, dry Summers, mild Winters.

TRAVEL ACCESS: Bus: New Mexico Transportation provides regular transportation to Alamogordo, NM and park area; **Rail:** Amtrak provides daily service to El Paso, TX, and Albuquerque, NM; **Air:** Airways of New Mexico provides service to Alamogordo, NM.

NEARBY FACILITIES & POINTS OF INTEREST: Hotel/Motel: Holiday Inn, Highway 54-70, 505-437-7100; Desert Aire Motor Hotel, Highway 54-70, 505-437-2110; **Campgrounds:** KOA campground, 412 24th St., Alamogordo, Breezy Point, Highway 82, 505-437-1761; **Parks, other points of interest:** New Tombaugh Omni Space Theater, International Space Hall of Fame in Alamogordo.

New York

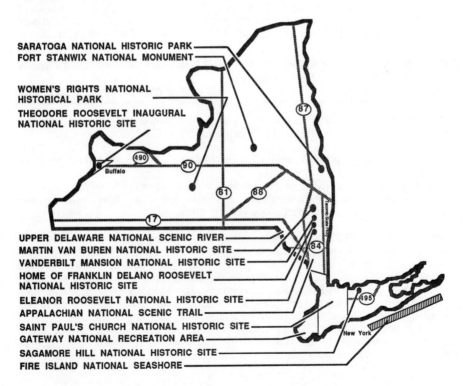

SARATOGA NATIONAL HISTORIC PARK
FORT STANWIX NATIONAL MONUMENT

WOMEN'S RIGHTS NATIONAL
HISTORICAL PARK
THEODORE ROOSEVELT INAUGURAL
NATIONAL HISTORIC SITE

Buffalo

UPPER DELAWARE NATIONAL SCENIC RIVER
MARTIN VAN BUREN NATIONAL HISTORIC SITE
VANDERBILT MANSION NATIONAL HISTORIC SITE
HOME OF FRANKLIN DELANO ROOSEVELT
NATIONAL HISTORIC SITE
ELEANOR ROOSEVELT NATIONAL HISTORIC SITE
APPALACHIAN NATIONAL SCENIC TRAIL
SAINT PAUL'S CHURCH NATIONAL HISTORIC SITE
GATEWAY NATIONAL RECREATION AREA
SAGAMORE HILL NATIONAL HISTORIC SITE
FIRE ISLAND NATIONAL SEASHORE

New York

Appalachian National Scenic Trail
For details see listing in Maine

Castle Clinton National Monument
New York, New York   **SEE CLIMATABLE NO. 109**

MAILING ADDRESS: Superintendent, Castle Clinton National Monument, National Park Service, Manhattan Sites, 26 Wall Street, New York, New York 10005 **Telephone:** (212) 344-7220

DIRECTIONS: The Monument is located in Battery Park at the southern tip of Manhattan. Public transportation is recommended.

Built in 1807-11, this structure served successively as a defense for New York harbor, an entertainment center and opera house 1824-1855, an immigration depot 1855-1890, and the New York City Aquarium 1896-1941. The structure today resembles its original appearance as a fort during the War of 1812 period. Castle Clinton also serves as the N.P.S. Visitor Center for the New York area and ticket sales area for the ferry to Statue of Liberty and (Ellis Island scheduled to begin in 1989). Authorized for addition to the National Park System, August 12, 1946.

VISITOR ACTIVITIES: Interpretive exhibits, tours, school programs; **Permits:** for special uses, commercial photography, public gatherings; **Fees:** For round-trip ferry to Statue of Liberty $3.25 for Adults and $1.50 for children under 12. Admission to Castle Clinton Museum is free; **Visitor facilities:** Museum, restrooms available; **Any limitations on vehicle usage:** no vehicles are allowed in the park; **Meals served in the park:** No; **Food and supplies obtainable in the park:** No; **Food and supplies obtainable nearby:** Yes; **Overnight accommodations:** in New York City; **First Aid available in park:** Yes; **Nearest Hospital:** Beekman Downtown Hospital 1/2 mile (.8 km); **Visitor attractions closed for seasons:** Monument open 7 days a week; **Days/Hours:** 7:30 a.m. to 7:30 p.m. (Winter months 8:30 a.m. to 5:00 p.m.) schedule subject to change dependent on ferry departures. Call Circle Cline at (212) 563-3590 for current ferry schedules; **Holiday Closings:** Christmas Day; **Weather:** windy and cold in winter, hot and humid in summer.

GENERAL INFORMATION: Castle Clinton is located in the Northwest corner of Battery Park. Accessible to wheelchairs. Food and pets are prohibited inside the Monument.

TRAVEL ACCESS: Bus: New York City buses M1, M6, or M15 to South Ferry, Battery Park; **Other:** Subway: Lexington Avenue IRT express (#4,5) to Bowling Green; RR BMT to Whitehall Street; 7th Avenue IRT local (#1) to South Ferry.

NEARBY FACILITIES & POINTS OF INTEREST: Federal Hall NM, Statue of Liberty NM, Ellis Island NM (see listings in this book), Battery Park, Fraunces Tavern, South Street Seaport, Staten Island Ferry, Governors Island, New York, Stock Exchange and World Trade Center.

Eleanor Roosevelt National Historic Site
Hyde Park, New York   **SEE CLIMATABLE NO. 108**

MAILING ADDRESS: Roosevelt-Vanderbilt National Historical Sites, 249 Albany Post Rd., Hyde Park, New York 12538 **Telephone:** 914-229- 9115

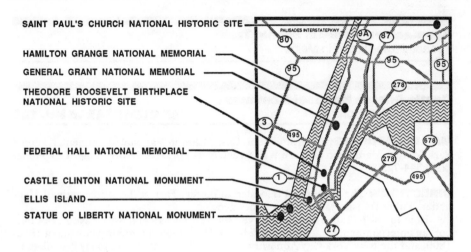

SAINT PAUL'S CHURCH NATIONAL HISTORIC SITE

HAMILTON GRANGE NATIONAL MEMORIAL

GENERAL GRANT NATIONAL MEMORIAL

THEODORE ROOSEVELT BIRTHPLACE
NATIONAL HISTORIC SITE

FEDERAL HALL NATIONAL MEMORIAL

CASTLE CLINTON NATIONAL MONUMENT

ELLIS ISLAND

STATUE OF LIBERTY NATIONAL MONUMENT

DIRECTIONS: Mrs. Roosevelt's home, known as Val-Kill, was authorized as a National Historic Site in 1977 "to commemorate for the education, inspiration, and benefit of present and future generations the life and work of an outstanding woman in American history." The site comprises several modest buildings in a setting of fields, woods, and wetlands.

VISITOR ACTIVITIES: guided tours; **Permits:** No; **Fees:** There is a fee for transportation to site by shuttle bus which leaves Franklin D. Roosevelt parking lot on a fixed schedule; **Visitor facilities:** Guided tour of Mrs. Roosevelt's home; **Hiking trails:** Yes, rough terrain, hiking boots needed; **Backcountry:** No; **Camping:** No; **Other overnight accommodations on site:** No; **Food and supplies obtainable in the park:** No; **Food and supplies obtainable nearby:** Yes, Town of Hyde Park; **Overnight accommodations:** in Town of Hyde Park; **First Aid available in park:** Yes; **Days/Hours:** Open seven days a week April-October 9:30 a.m.-5:00 p.m. Open Saturdays and Sundays in Nov., Dec., and March from 10:00-4:00, access by private vehicle. Groups of 10 or more may make reservations all year except on Tuesdays and Wednesdays, Nov- March; **Holiday Closings:** Thanksgiving Day, Dec. 25, Jan. 1; **Visitor attractions closed for seasons:** No.

NEARBY FACILITIES & POINTS OF INTEREST: Hotel/Motels: Several in area; **Food/Supplies:** Several in area; **Campgrounds:** Norrie State Park, Staatsburg, phone 889-4100; **Parks, other points of interest:** Home of Franklin D. Roosevelt, Vanderbilt Mansion.

Ellis Island
New York, New York   **SEE CLIMATABLE NO. 109**

MAILING ADDRESS: Superintendent, Statue of Liberty National Monument, Liberty Island, New York, NY 10004 **Telephone:** 212-363-3200

IMPORTANT INFORMATION: Due to restoration activities honoring the upcoming centennial in 1992 for the Immigration Station, Ellis Island is closed and will re-open to the public in 1989. Please call 212-363-3200 for information.

DIRECTIONS: Ellis Island is accessible only by ferry. Circle Line Ferries leave Battery Park in lower Manhattan and Liberty State Park in New Jersey. For schedule and group-rate information, call 212-269-5755.

More than half of the immigrants entering the United States between 1892 and 1924 passed through the gates of Ellis Island. Added by Presidential Proclamation to the Statue of Liberty National Monument on May 11, 1965.

VISITOR ACTIVITIES: Visitors can take advantage of guided tours, photographic tours, museum exhibits, library and movie theaters; **Permits:** Yes; **Fees:** $3.25 charge for adults and $1.50 for children under 12 for the round-trip ferry boat ride. No fees charged for the tour; **Visitor facilities:** restrooms, public telephones, refreshments, souvenirs and books relating to Immigration are available; **Any limitations on vehicle usage:** No docking is permitted for private boats; **Hiking trails:** No; **Camping:** No; **Other overnight accommodations on site:** No; **Meals served in the park:** yes, snacks available at refreshment stand; **Overnight accommodations:** New York City and nearby New Jersey; **First Aid available in park:** Yes; **Nearest Hospital:** New York-takes about 1 hour to reach **Days/Hours:** Open daily year-round from 9 a.m.-5 p.m., with extended hours in season; **Holiday Closings:** Dec. 25.

GENERAL INFORMATION: School groups should contact the school coordinator for pre-visit materials. Large groups should make reservations with the Circle Line Ferry, 212-269-5755.

TRAVEL ACCESS: Bus: Greyhound, Shortline and other long distance lines provide regular service to Port Authority Terminal; **Rail:** Amtrak, Conrail (Metropolitan Transit Authority intraregional lines) service both Pennsylvania Station and Grand Central Station; **Air:** Major and regional airlines provide regular service to Newark, La Guardia, and John F. Kennedy airports; **Other:** Metropolitan Transit Authority buses run frequently to South Ferry from Journal Square; Central Bus runs service morning and afternoon to Liberty State Park, Jersey City; Metropolitan Transit Authority provides subway service to South Ferry.

NEARBY FACILITIES & POINTS OF INTEREST: Parks, other points of interest: Liberty State Park, Jersey City, New Jersey.

Federal Hall National Memorial
New York, New York   **SEE CLIMATABLE NO. 109**

MAILING ADDRESS: Superintendent, Federal Hall National Memorial, Manhattan Sites, 26 Wall Street, New York, NY 10005 **Telephone:** (212) 264-8711

DIRECTIONS: The Memorial is located at the corner of Wall and Nassau Streets, 1 block east of Broadway. Public transportation is recommended. The building is on the site of the original City Hall where the trial of John Peter Zenger, involving freedom of the press was held in 1735 and the Stamp Act Congress met in 1765. City Hall was re-modeled into Federal Hall, the first capitol of the United States under the Constitution in 1788. George Washington was inaugurated and the Bill of Rights was written in Federal Hall in 1789. The present building was completed in 1842 as the U.S. Customs House. It also served as a Sub-Treasury, 1862-1920. Designated Federal Hall Memorial National Historic Site May 26, 1939, changed to Federal Hall National Memorial August 11, 1955.

VISITOR ACTIVITIES: Interpretive exhibits, audiovisual programs, films, school programs, tours, colonial folk music, Wednesday noontime classical concerts; **Permits:**

for special uses, commercial photography, public gatherings; **Fees:** No; **Visitor facilities:** museum, information center, restrooms, bookstore; **Any limitations on vehicle usage:** on-street parking extremely limited; **Hiking trails:** No; **Meals served in the park:** No, but available nearby; **Food and supplies obtainable in the park:** No; **Food and supplies obtainable nearby:** Yes; **Overnight accommodations:** in New York City; **First Aid available in park:** Yes; **Nearest Hospital:** Beekman Downtown Hospital, 1/4 mile (.4 km); **Days/Hours:** Open 9 a.m. to 5 p.m. Monday through Friday, year-round; **Holiday Closings:** Closed all major holidays except Washington's Birthday and July 4th; **Visitor attractions closed for seasons:** No; **Weather:** windy and cold in winter, hot and humid in summer.

GENERAL INFORMATION: Special interpretive programs for George Washington's Birthday, the Anniversary of Washington's Inauguration April 30, and July 4th. The information desk has brochures and information on National Park Service sites and sites in New York City. Golden Age, Eagle and Access Passports are available. Federal Hall is disabled accessible, enter at 15 Pine Street. Smoking, food and drink are prohibited in the building.

TRAVEL ACCESS: **Bus:** New York City, buses M1 and M6 to Wall Street and Broadway, M15 to Wall and Water Streets; **Other:** Subway: Lexington Avenue IRT express (#4,5) to Wall Street; "RR" BMT to Rector Street; J,M BMT to Borad Street; 7th Avenue IRT express (#2,3) to Wall Street; 8th Avenue IND ("A") to Fulton Street.

NEARBY FACILITIES & POINTS OF INTEREST: Castle Clinton NM, Statue of Liberty NM, Ellis Island NM (see listings in this book), New York Stock Exchange, Trinity Church, Fraunces Tavern, South Street Seaport, Federal Reserve Bank, World Trade Center.

Fire Island National Seashore
Patchogue, New York   **SEE CLIMATABLE NO. 111**

MAILING ADDRESS: Superintendent, Fire Island National Seashore, 120 Laurel Street, Patchogue, New York 11772 **Telephone:** 516-289- 4810

DIRECTIONS: By automobile you can reach the island via bridges at the state and county parks. Except for these two points, Fire Island is roadless. Several mainland ferryboat lines, operating from Bayshore, Sayville, and Patchogue, dock on the island. Sailors Haven and the Sunken Forest are served by the ferry terminal in Sayville; Watch Hill by the ferry terminal at Patchogue. All three mainland villages are serviced by the Long Island Railroad. Public ferries run from May 15 to Oct. 15.

This barrier island off the south shore of Long Island possesses opportunities for beach-oriented recreation and ecological observations. Authorized for addition to the National Park System on Sept. 11, 1964. Contains the only national wilderness area in New York state.

VISITOR ACTIVITIES: fishing, clamming, swimming, walking, picnicking, guided nature walks and talks in summer, wildlife- and bird-watching, camping, interpretive exhibits, hiking, boating, hunting, special boardwalk nature trail for the handicapped at Smith Point. The William Floyd Estate is a detached area of the National Seashore, located on Washington Ave. in Mastic Beach on Long Island. This 612-acre estate is the home of a Signer of the Declaration of Independence. Free guided tour of house daily, April 1-October 31, 10 a.m.-4:30 p.m. Self-guided grounds tour. Groups by appointment. No pets please. For street directions call 516-399-2030; **Permits:** for off-road vehicle travel, available at Smith Point only; **Fees:** No; **Visitor facilities:** campground, marinas, guarded swimming beaches, snack bars, Visitor Center with exhibits, picnic areas, nature trails, restrooms, bathhouse, telephones, grocery stores; **Any limitations on vehicle usage:** Vehicle usage is regulated; **Hiking trails:** Yes, nature trails are at Smith Point West, Watch Hill, and Sailors Haven; **Backcountry:** There is a 7 mile sand trail from Smith Point to Watch Hill in the National wilderness; **Camping:** Yes, reservations are required for the 25-site primitive campground at Watch Hill. Phone the number above; **Other overnight accommodations on site:** Yes, contact the park for further information on accommodations on the island; **Meals served in the park:** Yes, snacks are available at Watch Hill and Sailors Haven; **Food and supplies obtainable in the park:** Yes, Watch Hill and Sailors Haven; **Food and supplies obtainable nearby:** Yes, on mainland at Sayville, Patchogue and Bay Shore; **Overnight accommodations:** Motels are in most major communities on Long Island; **First Aid available in park:** Yes, **Nearest Hospital:** On mainland at Patchogue, Bay Shore; **Days/Hours:** Open 24 hours a day everyday; **Holiday Closings:** None; **Visitor attractions closed for seasons:** Marinas, visitor centers, and restrooms closed in Winter.

GENERAL INFORMATION: *For Your Safety*—Swim at protected beaches. Wear footgear on all boardwalks. Splinters are a common first aid problem. Watch for poison ivy, which abounds on the island. Do not walk on the dunes; their fragile vegetation is easily destroyed by human feet. Ticks are common in grass and underbrush, and may carry disease.

Fort Stanwix National Monument
Rome, New York   **SEE CLIMATABLE NO. 112**

MAILING ADDRESS: Superintendent, Fort Stanwix National Monument, 112 East Park Street, Rome, New York 13440 **Telephone:** 315-336-2090

DIRECTIONS: The Monument is in downtown Rome, NY, which may be reached by car, bus, train, or plane. State Routes 26, 46, 49, 69, and 365 pass within sight of the Fort. If you are traveling on the NY Thruway, take exits 32 or 33. A city parking garage is on North James Street, within 1/2 block of the Monument's entrance.

The American stand here in August, 1777 was a major factor in repulsing the British invasion from Canada. This was also the site of the Treaty of Fort Stanwix, negotiated with the Iroquois on Nov. 5, 1768. Also the site of the last treaty of the American Revolution, October 22, 1784 between the Iroquois Nation and the new United States. Authorized for addition to the National Park System on Aug. 21, 1935.

VISITOR ACTIVITIES: interpretive films and exhibits, guided tours, living history program from May-Sept. includes drill and occasional weapons- firing demonstrations; **Permits:** No; **Fees:** Yes, $1.00 per person, 12 years old and up; **Visitor facilities:** Restrooms inside the Fort; **Any limitations on vehicle usage:** No direct vehicle access to the park; **Hiking trails:** No; **Backcountry:** No; **Camping:** No; **Other overnight accommodations on site:** No; **Meals served in the park:** No; **Food and supplies obtainable in the park:** No; **Food and supplies obtainable nearby:** Yes, in Rome; **Overnight accommodations:** in and around Rome; **First Aid available in park:** Yes; **Nearest Hospital:** Rome Memorial, NY 49, 69, 365, 3 miles (4.8 km); **Days/Hours:** Open daily from 9 a.m. to 5 p.m.; **Holiday Closings:** Thanksgiving Day, Dec. 25; **Visitor attractions closed for seasons:** Closed from January through March; **Weather:** Summers are generally cool.

GENERAL INFORMATION: *For Your Safety*—Follow the staff's instructions during weapon demonstrations. Do not smoke inside wooden buildings.

Gateway National Recreation Area
New York & New Jersey   **SEE CLIMATABLE NO. 113**

MAILING ADDRESS: Superintendent, Gateway National Recreation Area, Floyd Bennett Field, Brooklyn, New York 11234 **Telephone:** (718) 338-3575

DIRECTIONS: Gateway National Recreation Area consists of four units. Three are in New York: Jamaica Bay Unit, in Brooklyn; Breezy Point Unit, located on the Rockaway Peninsula in Queens; and the Staten Island Unit, located on the Raritan Bay in Staten Island. The fourth area is the Sandy Hook Unit, situated on a peninsula in the northeast corner of New Jersey. Detailed mass transit and auto directions are available from Headquarters.

The Park contains beaches, marshes, islands, and adjacent waters in the New York harbor area, and is one of the first major urban parks in the National Park System. Established by act of Congress on Oct. 27, 1972.

VISITOR ACTIVITIES: swimming, picnicking, sunbathing, sports, interpretive programs, biking, fishing, boating, bird-watching, crabbing, horseback riding; **Permits:** A fishing permit is required at some locations. Permits are also required for baseball, softball, tennis, soccer, archery, football, and basketball facilities at Miller Field in the Staten Island Unit. Information and permits can be obtained by calling (718) 351-8700 or by writing the Unit Manager, P.O. Box 37, Staten Island, NY 10306; **Fees:** for boat launching and mooring facilities at Great Kills Park in the Staten Island Unit, mooring facilities at Barren Island Marina, and a parking fee at the Riis Park parking lot, Breezy Point Unit; and summer beach parking at Sandy Hook, N.J. Unit. **Visitor facilities:** marina, boathouse, beaches, sports facilities, restrooms, parking areas, wildlife refuge, bicycle trail, picnic areas; **Any limitations on vehicle usage:** Off-road vehicles are not permitted on beaches; **Hiking trails:** Yes, nature trails, ocean and waterfront areas; **Backcountry:** No; **Camping:** Yes, primitive campsites are available for use by organized youth groups on a reservation basis. These reservations must be made through the Unit Manager's office at Sandy Hook Unit, P.O. Box 437, Highlands, NJ 07732 or by calling 201-872-0115; **Other overnight accommodations on site:** No; **Meals served in the park:** Yes, fast food available in Summer at all four units; **Food and supplies obtainable in the park:** No; **Food and supplies obtainable nearby:** Yes, at Sandy Hook, Red Bank, Highlands, Staten Island, Jamaica Bay, Boroughs of Brooklyn and Queens, Breezy Point; **Overnight accommodations:** Snady Hook, Red Bank, Highlands, Staten Island, Jamaica Bay, Brooklyn and Queens, Breezy Point; **First Aid available in park:** Yes, in all 4 units during the Summer; **Nearest Hospital:** Sandy Hook: Patterson Army Hospital, River View Hospital; Staten Island: Staten Island Hospital; Jamacia Bay: Coney Island Hospital, Brookdale Hospital, Peninsula Hospital; Breezy Point, Peninsula Hospital; **Days/Hours:** Open 7 days a week, 52 weeks a year. Full services are provided from Memorial Day through Sept. 30 from 9 a.m.-8:30 p.m.; **Holiday Closings:** Jamaica Bay Wildlife Refuge is closed Dec. 25 and Jan. 1; **Visitor attractions closed for seasons:** Beach closed for season; **Weather:** Excellent beach weather, with temperatures in the 90's in June, July and August.

GENERAL INFORMATION: *For Your Safety*—Swim only where lifeguards are on duty. The ocean can be dangerous. Be alert for riptides. Do not take glass containers, rafts, rubber tubs, snorkels, and masks to any beach. Beware of sunburn. Some of the areas have large patches of poison ivy. Consult park personnel for locations of poison ivy. Write to Park Public Affairs Office, Floyd Bennett Field, Brooklyn, NY 11234 for free copy of "Seven Steps To Water Safety."

TRAVEL ACCESS: Bus: NY, Keansburg & Long Branch Bus from Port Auth. Terminal, NYC to Sandy Hook, NJ weekends on the hour. N.Y.C. Transit-Authority and Green Bus Lines to Riis Beach (Summers), Jamaica Bay and Breezy Point units and TA bus to Staten Island Unit.

General Grant National Memorial
New York, New York   **SEE CLIMATABLE NO. 109**

MAILING ADDRESS: Superintendent, General Grant National Memorial, Riverside Drive & 122nd Street, New York, New York 10027 **Telephone:** 212-666-1640

DIRECTIONS: The Memorial is located in Riverside Park near the Intersection of Riverside Drive and West 122nd Street. You can reach the vicinity of the memorial by IRT #1 subway to 116th or 125th Street, or 125th Street crosstown bus. Riverside Drive is also accessible from the Henry Hudson Parkway at several points. Parking is permitted near the Memorial.
  This Memorial to Ulysses S. Grant, the Union commander who brought the Civil War to an end, includes the sarcophagi of General and Mrs. Grant. As President of the United States (1869-1877), Grant signed the act establishing the first National Park, Yellowstone, on Mar. 1, 1872. Memorial dedicated on April 27, 1897.

VISITOR ACTIVITIES: interpretive talks and exhibits; **Permits:** No; **Fees:** No; **Visitor facilities:** exhibit rooms; **Any limitations on vehicle usage:** No; **Meals served in the park:** No; **Food and supplies obtainable in the park:** No; **Food and supplies obtainable nearby:** Yes, several blocks, in Manhattan; **Overnight accommodations:** New York City; **First Aid available in park:** Yes; **Nearest Hospital:** St. Luke's Amsterdam Ave., about 10 blocks; **Days/Hours:** Open Wednesday through Sunday 9:00 a.m. to 5:00 p.m.; **Holiday Closings:** Thanksgiving, Dec. 25 & Jan. 1; **Visitor attractions closed for seasons:** No; **Weather:** Cold Winters with occasional snow; hot humid Summers.

GENERAL INFORMATION: Please call to verify days and hours.

Hamilton Grange National Memorial
New York, New York   **SEE CLIMATABLE NO. 109**

MAILING ADDRESS: Superintendent, Hamilton Grange National Memorial, 287 Convent Avenue, New York, New York 10031 **Telephone:** 212-283-5154

DIRECTIONS: The Memorial is at Convent Ave. and West 141st Street. Access by public transportation is recommended. Take the 8th Avenue IND express subway to West 145th Street. You can also catch the Broadway Bus #4 to West 145th St. and Convent Avenue, or Convent Ave. bus #3 to 142nd Street.
  "The Grange," named after his grandfather's estate in Scotland, was the home of Alexander Hamilton, American Statesman and first Secretary of the U.S. Treasury. Authorized for addition to the National Park System on Apr. 27, 1962.

VISITOR ACTIVITIES: exhibits, guided tours, audio-visual program; **Permits:** No; **Fees:** No; **Visitor facilities:** restrooms available; **Any limitations on vehicle usage:** No vehicle usage in the Park; **Hiking trails:** No; **Meals served in the park:** No; **Food and supplies obtainable in the park:** No; **Food and supplies obtainable nearby:** Yes, in New York City; **Overnight accommodations:** New York; **First Aid available in park:** Yes; **Nearest Hospital:** New York City; **Days/Hours:** Open Wed.-Sun. from 9 a.m. to 5 p.m.; **Holiday Closings:** Thanksgiving, Dec. 25 and Jan. 1; **Visitor attractions closed for sea-**

sons: No; **Weather:** Cold Winters with snow; hot humid Summers. Pleasantly mild Spring and Fall.

GENERAL INFORMATION: Be careful walking up and down stairs; they are quite slippery when wet.

Home of Franklin D. Roosevelt National Historic Site
Hyde Park, New York   **SEE CLIMATABLE NO. 108**

MAILING ADDRESS: Superintendent, Roosevelt-Vanderbilt National Historic Sites, 249 Albany Post Rd., Hyde Park, New York 12538 **Telephone:** 914-229-9115

DIRECTIONS: The Home is on Route 9 in Hyde Park, just north of Poughkeepsie.
    This was the birthplace, lifetime residence, and "Summer White House" of the 32nd President, who entertained many distinguished visitors here. The gravesites of President and Mrs. Roosevelt are in the Rose Garden. Accepted by the Secretary of the Interior Nov. 21, 1945.

VISITOR ACTIVITIES: house tours, exhibits in the Franklin D. Roosevelt Library; **Permits:** No; **Fees:** $3.50 entrance fee permits access to Roosevelt Home and Library. Persons 12 & under and 62 & over are admitted free. Golden Eagle and Golden Age Passports accepted; **Visitor facilities:** bookstore, Tourist Information Center, parking, restrooms, library; **Any limitations on vehicle usage:** No; **Hiking trails:** No; **Meals served in the park:** No; **Food and supplies obtainable in the park:** No; **Food and supplies obtainable nearby:** Yes, in town of Hyde Park; **Overnight accommodations:** Hyde Park and vicinity; **First Aid available in park:** Yes; **Nearest Hospital:** Poughkeepsie, US 9, (6 miles); **Days/Hours:** Open daily from 9 a.m. to 5 p.m. Closed Tuesday & Wednesday November thru March; **Holiday Closings:** Dec. 25 & Jan. 1. Also closed on Thanksgiving Day.

GENERAL INFORMATION: For bus tour or large group reservations please write to Roosevelt-Vanderbilt National Historic Sites, 249 Albany Post Rd., Hyde Park, NY 12538 in advance.

TRAVEL ACCESS: Bus: Dutchess County Transportation, and Mountainview Coach Lines provide flag stop service daily to Poughkeepsie; **Rail:** Metro North service to Poughkeepsie, NY; **Air:** Command/Colegan/Air North provide service into Wappinger Falls, NY; **Other:** Rental cars are available at Dutchess County Airport in Wappinger Falls, NY.

NEARBY FACILITIES & POINTS OF INTEREST: Parks, other points of interest: F.D.R. Library Museum, Vanderbilt Mansion, Eleanor Roosevelt National Historic Site.

Martin Van Buren National Historic Site
Kinderhook, New York   **SEE CLIMATABLE NO. 108**

MAILING ADDRESS: Superintendent, Martin Van Buren National Historic Site, P.O. Box 545, Kinderhook, New York 12106 **Telephone:** 518-758-9689

DIRECTIONS: The Site is on route 9H in Kinderhook Township, 25 miles (40 km) south of Albany.
    Lindenwald estate, south of Albany, was the home of the eighth President for 21 years until his death in 1862. Authorized for addition to the National Park System on Oct. 26, 1974.

VISITOR ACTIVITIES: guided tours, special events—interpretive A-V program and exhibits, off-site programs (slide shows) for community and professional organizations; **Permits:** No; **Fees:** Entrance fee is $1.00 for adults. No charge for persons under 12 or 62 and over. Golden Eagle and Golden Age Passports accepted and available; **Visitor facilities:** Limited parking and restroom facilities; **Any limitations on vehicle usage:** Vehicles restricted to roadways; **Hiking trails:** No; **Backcountry:** No; **Camping:** No; **Other overnight accommodations on site:** No; **Meals served in the park:** No; **Food and supplies obtainable in the park:** No; **Food and supplies obtainable nearby:** Yes, in Kinderhook, 1½ miles (2.4 km) north; **Overnight accommodations:** Kinderhook; **First Aid available in park:** Yes; **Nearest Hospital:** Hudson, NY, 12 miles (19 km) south; **Days/Hours:** Open daily 9 a.m. to 5 p.m. (May-Oct.); open Wed-Sun 9 a.m. to 5 p.m. April and November. Grounds open throughout the year; **Holiday Closings:** Thanksgiving; **Visitor attractions closed for seasons:** Mansion closed Dec. 6 through late March; **Weather:** Summer is warm, humid, and breezy. The average temperature is in the high 70's or low 80's.

GENERAL INFORMATION: Group tours are requested to make reservations; Parking for handicapped people is available adjacent to Mansion.

TRAVEL ACCESS: Bus: Mt. View bus provides service Hudson-Albany, NY, 3 times daily; **Rail:** Amtrak provides service into Hudson; **Air:** U.S. Air, Delta, Eastern, Piedmont, American provide service to Albany, NY.

NEARBY FACILITIES & POINTS OF INTEREST: Hotel/Motel: Blue Spruce Motel, Rt. 9H, 518-758-9711, 5 miles from Site; **Food/Supplies:** Grand Union, Valatie, NY, 3 miles; **Campgrounds:** Lake Taghkanic State Park, Ancram, NY 518-851-3631, 30 miles; **Parks, other points of interest:** Columbia County Historic Society Museum, Kinderhook, NY 518-758-9265, 2 miles; The Shaker Museum, (Old) Chatham, NY; 518-794-9100, 11 miles; Olana State Historic Site, Hudson, NY; 518-828-0135, 12 miles.

North Country National Scenic Trail
New York, Pennsylvania, Ohio, Michigan, Wisconsin, Minnesota, North Dakota   **SEE CLIMATABLE MAP**

MAILING ADDRESS: c/o Midwest Regional Office, National Park Service, 1709 Jackson Street, Omaha, NE 68102 **Telephone:** 402-221-3481

DIRECTIONS: When completed, the Scenic Trail will extend approximately 3,200 miles from the vicinity of Crown Point, New York, to Lake Sakakawea State Park on the Missouri River in North Dakota, the route of the Lewis and Clark National Historic Trail. Approximately 1,000 miles are presently available for public use. Established by an act of Congress on March 5, 1980.

VISITOR ACTIVITIES: hiking, backpacking, camping, nature study. Some trail segments are open to horseback riding, bicycling, cross-country skiing; **Permits:** Yes; for a few trail segments; **Fees:** Yes, for some developed campgrounds within the National Forests, State Parks and similar areas along the trail; **Visitor facilities:** Various, as provided by the managing authority for a particular segment; **Any limitations on vehicle usage:** Use of motorized vehicles by the public is prohibited along the trail; **Hiking trails:** Yes; **Backcountry:** Yes, for information, write to the above address; **Camping:** As permitted; **Other overnight accommodations on site:** No; **Meals served in the park:** No; **Food and supplies obtainable in the park:** Yes, in some parks along the trail; **Food and supplies obtainable nearby:** Yes, in many communities along the trail; **Overnight**

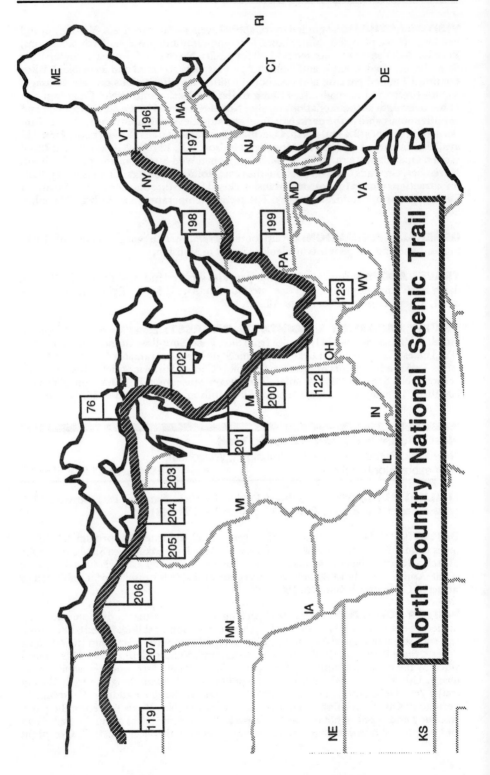

accommodations: In many communities along/near the trail; **First Aid available in park:** No; **Days/Hours:** Open at all times, except as limited by regulations governing individual parks/forests through which the trail passes.

TRAVEL ACCESS: Many points on or near the trail are accessible by bus, rail, or air.

NEARBY FACILITIES & POINTS OF INTEREST: Scenic, historic, natural, and cultural interests are located along the trail. **Campsites:** Reservation system in use for some public and private campgrounds.

Theodore Roosevelt Birthplace National Historic Site
New York, New York   **SEE CLIMATABLE NO. 109**

MAILING ADDRESS: Site Supervisor, Theodore Roosevelt Birthplace National Historic Site, 28 East 20th Street, New York, New York 10003 **Telephone:** 212-260-1616

DIRECTIONS: The Site can be reached from the 23rd Street or 14th Street stops of the IRT (Lexington Ave.) or BMT Subway. Parking space in the vicinity is scarce.
    The 26th President of the United States was born in the original house on this site on Oct. 27, 1858. Authorized for addition to the National Park System on July 25, 1962.

VISITOR ACTIVITIES: guided tours of Victorian-period rooms, museums, films and Sat. afternoon concerts; **Permits:** No; **Fees:** $1.00 per adult, Seniors and children under 12 FREE; **Visitor facilities:** restrooms; **Any limitations on vehicle usage:** No; **Meals served in the park:** No; **Food and supplies obtainable in the park:** No; **Food and supplies obtainable nearby:** Yes, in the neighborhood; **Overnight accommodations:** None; **First Aid available in park:** Yes; **Nearest Hospital:** Cabrini, Med. Center; **Days/Hours:** Open Wed.-Sun. 9 a.m.-5 p.m.; **Holiday Closings:** Closed on federal holidays; **Visitor attractions closed for seasons:** No.

NEARBY FACILITIES & POINTS OF INTEREST: Hotel/Motel: Gramercy Park, 2 Lexington Ave., 212-475-4320.

Theodore Roosevelt Inaugural National Historic Site
Buffalo, New York   **SEE CLIMATABLE NO. 114**

MAILING ADDRESS: Superintendent, Theodore Roosevelt Inaugural National Historic Site, 641 Delaware Ave., Buffalo, New York 14202 **Telephone:** 716-884-0095

DIRECTIONS: The entrance to the house is on Delaware Ave. near North St. Parking at the rear of the house is accessible from Franklin Street, a one-way street leading north from downtown Buffalo. Buses from downtown Buffalo stop in front of the Site.
    Here in the Ansley Wilcox House, Theodore Roosevelt took the oath of office as President of the United States on Sept. 14, 1901, shortly after the assassination of President William McKinley. Authorized for addition to the National Park System on Nov. 2, 1966. Site is operated by the Theodore Roosevelt Inaugural Site Foundation.

VISITOR ACTIVITIES: guided tours, quilt show, Victorian Christmas display, art shows, walking tours; **Permits:** No; **Fees:** $1.00 adults, 50¢ children, maximum family $2.50 entrance fee; **Visitor facilities:** parking, restrooms, art gallery; **Any limitations on vehicle usage:** No; **Meals served in the park:** No; **Food and supplies obtainable in the park:** No; **Food and supplies obtainable nearby:** Yes, Buffalo, across the street; **Overnight accommodations:** Buffalo; **First Aid available in park:** Yes; **Nearest Hospi-**

tal: Buffalo, ½ mile (.8 km) from the site; **Days/Hours:** Open Mon.-Fri: 10 a.m.-5 p.m.; Sat.-Sun: Noon-5 p.m.; **Holiday Closings:** Closed on federal holidays and closed Saturday Jan.-March; **Visitor attractions closed for seasons:** No.

NEARBY FACILITIES & POINTS OF INTEREST: Hotel/Motel: Site is in a preservation district; noteworthy architecture. Allentown area has many antique shops, boutiques, restaurants.

Sagamore Hill National Historic Site
Oyster Bay, New York   **SEE CLIMATABLE NO. 111**

MAILING ADDRESS: Superintendent, Sagamore Hill National Historic Site, 20 Sagamore Hill Road, Oyster Bay, New York 11771-1899 **Telephone:** 516-922-4447

DIRECTIONS: Sagamore Hill is on Cove Neck Road, 3 miles east of Oyster Bay, New York. It can be reached by the Long Island Railroad from New York City's Pennsylvania Station at 7th Avenue and 33rd Street. Taxis meet all trains. If travelling by car, take either Exit 41N from the Long Island Expressway or Exit 35 North from the Northern State Parkway to Route 106 Northbound. Follow Route 106 to the Village of Oyster Bay. Turn right at the third traffic light in Oyster Bay onto East Main Street. Follow the green and white signs marked "Sagamore Hill."
　　This estate was the home of Theodore Roosevelt, the 26th President of the United States, from 1885 until his death in 1919. Authorized for addition to the National Park System on July 25, 1962.

VISITOR ACTIVITIES: Visitors can tour the Roosevelt home, the pet cemetery, and the Old Orchard Home, containing exhibits relating to Theodore Roosevelt's political career, family life at Sagamore Hill, and the lives of his six children; **Permits:** No; **Fees:** $1.00 between 16 and 62 of age. Golden Eagle and Golden Age Passports are accepted and available; **Visitor facilities:** souvenir and book sales, parking; **Any limitations on vehicle usage:** Vehicles are limited to the entrance road and visitor parking area; **Hiking trails:** No; **Meals served in the park:** Snack shop open during summer season; **Food and supplies obtainable in the park:** No; **Food and supplies obtainable nearby:** Yes, in Oyster Bay, 3 miles (4.8 km) west; **Overnight accommodations:** East Norwich and Oyster Bay, South Street, Rt. 25A, 5 miles (8 km); **First Aid available in park:** Yes, in all buildings; **Nearest Hospital:** Glen Cove, St. Andrews Lane, 11.3 km (7 miles); **Days/Hours:** Open every day 9:30 a.m. to 5 p.m. **Holiday Closings:** Thanksgiving, Dec. 25 & Jan. 1; **Visitor attractions closed for seasons:** No; **Weather:** Temperatures range from 65-90° in Summer and 0-40° in Winter.

GENERAL INFORMATION: Poison ivy is common in the area; please keep to the established paths and walkways. Pets must be leashed or carried. Heat exhaustion is common in the Summer, so judge your limits. Park fences are historic and unsafe for climbing.

Saint Paul's National Historic Site with the Bill of Rights Museum
Mount Vernon, New York   **SEE CLIMATABLE NO. 109**

MAILING ADDRESS: Saint Paul's National Historic Site, 897 S. Columbus Ave., Mount Vernon, New York 10550 **Telephone:** 914-667-4116

DIRECTIONS: Take New England Thruway North (Rte. 95) to Conner Street Exit. Make a left, go up one light and make another left. Go straight and that road becomes

Rte. 22 (a.k.a. S. Columbus Ave.). Follow to St. Paul's #897. Or get off Hutchinson River Parkway North at US-1 Boston Post Road in Pelham Manor, NY. Turn left and go to Pelham Parkway. Make a right, follow to S. Columbus Ave. and make a left.

This 18th-century church is important because of its connection with the events leading to the John Peter Zenger trail involving freedom of the press, and because of its place in American history, and the Revolution. It is a significant example of American Colonial Architecture. This affiliated area of the National Park System was designated on July 5, 1943. Lands were donated to National Park Service on November 1, 1980 and July 4, 1981. Bill of Rights Museum opened October 28, 1984.

VISITOR ACTIVITIES: walking tours of the church, museum, and cemetery; Museum Shop available; **Permits:** No; **Fees:** No; **Visitor facilities:** parking and restrooms; **Any limitations on vehicle usage:** No; **Meals served in the park:** No; **Food and supplies obtainable in the park:** No; **Food and supplies obtainable nearby:** Yes, at Mount Vernon, in the immediate area; **Overnight accommodations:** Mount Vernon, Bronx, New Rochelle, or anywhere in metropolitan New York City; **First Aid available in park:** No; **Nearest Hospital:** Mount Vernon, N. 7th Ave., 2 miles (3 km); **Days/Hours:** Tuesday-Friday from 9 a.m.-5 p.m. by appointment. Saturday from 12 p.m.-4 p.m. without appointment. Groups over 5 are asked to call in advance for Saturday tours. Visitors services and Museum Shop available. **Visitor attractions closed for seasons:** Sundays, Mondays, and Saturdays prior to Federal holidays that fall on Mondays. Also Thanksgiving, Christmas and New Year's Day; **Weather:** Typical New York weather, with seasonal snow or rain.

Saratoga National Historical Park
Stillwater, New York   **SEE CLIMATABLE NO. 110**

MAILING ADDRESS: Superintendent, Saratoga National Historical Park, R.D. #2, Box 33 Stillwater, New York 12170 **Telephone:** 518-664-9821

DIRECTIONS: The Park entrance lies 30 miles (48 km) north of Albany, NY on US 4 and NY 32. Taxi service is available from Saratoga Springs and Mechanicville.

The American victory here over the British in 1777 was the turning point of the Revolution and one of the decisive battles in world history. Major General Philip Schuyler's country home and the Saratoga Monument both in Schuylerville are open during the summer months. Authorized for addition to the National Park System on June 1, 1938. Established by act of Congress on June 22, 1948.

VISITOR ACTIVITIES: Visual program, talks, and exhibits are available at the Visitor Center which is open from 9:00 a.m. to 5:00 p.m. Craft and weapon demonstrations are given in Summer. The Park is open all year for hiking and skiing; **Permits:** No; **Fees:** Yes; **Visitor facilities:** An interpretive tour starts at the Visitor Center; **Any limitations on vehicle usage:** snowmobiles are prohibited; **Hiking trails:** Yes, the historic 1777 road system is gradually being turned into hiking trails; includes Wm. Wilkinson National Historic Trail; **Backcountry:** No; **Camping:** No; **Other overnight accommodations on site:** No; **Meals served in the park:** No; **Food and supplies obtainable in the park:** No; **Food and supplies obtainable nearby:** Yes, in Stillwater and Schuylerville; **Overnight accommodations:** Schuylerville, 8 miles (13 km); **First Aid available in park:** Yes; **Nearest Hospital:** Saratoga Springs, Rte. 32 to 423 to 9P, 17 miles (27 km); **Days/Hours:** Park open from 9 a.m. to 5 p.m. daily. Park roads are open from about April 15 to Nov. 30 as weather permits; **Holiday Closings:** Visitor Center is closed Thanksgiving, Dec. 25 & Jan. 1.

Statue of Liberty National Monument
New York, New York   **SEE CLIMATABLE NO. 109**

MAILING ADDRESS: Superintendent, Statue of Liberty National Monument, Liberty Island, New York, NY 10004 **Telephone:** 212-363-3200

DIRECTIONS: Liberty Island is accessible only by ferry. Circle Line Ferries leave Battery Park in Lower Manhattan and Liberty State Park in New Jersey. For schedule and group-rate information, call 212-269-5755.
   The famous 152-foot copper statue bearing the torch of freedom was a gift of the French people in 1886 to commemorate the alliance of the two nations during the American Revolution. The Monument includes The American Museum of Immigration, in the base of the statue. Created by Presidential Proclamation on Oct. 15, 1924.

VISITOR ACTIVITIES: Visitors can reach the top of the pedestal by elevator or stairs. The public is not permitted access to the torch itself. You can climb stairs to the statue's crown; **Permits:** No; **Fees:** No. Round-trip concession boat fee is $3.25 for adults; children under 12 years-$1.50; **Visitor facilities:** restrooms, public telephones, refreshments, souvenirs and books relating to the Statue and to Immigration are available; **Any limitations on vehicle usage:** No vehicle access available; vehicle access available to Liberty State Park; **Hiking trails:** No; **Backcountry:** No; **Camping:** No; **Other overnight accommodations on site:** No; **Meals served in the park:** yes, snacks available at refreshment stand; **Food and supplies obtainable in the park:** No; **Food and supplies obtainable nearby:** No; **Overnight accommodations:** New York City; **First Aid available in the park:** Yes; **Nearest Hospital:** New York-takes about 1 hour to reach; **Days/Hours:** Open daily year-round from 9 a.m.-5 p.m., with extended hours in season; **Holiday Closings:** Dec. 25.

GENERAL INFORMATION: Ascent to the Statue's crown from the top of the pedestal is by spiral staircase only. The climb is equivalent to 12 stories and those with physical difficulties are urged not to attempt it.

TRAVEL ACCESS: Bus: Greyhound, Shortline and other long distance lines provide regular service to Port Authority Terminal; **Rail:** Amtrak, Conrail (Metropolitan Transit Authority intraregional lines) service both Pennsylvania Station and Grand Central Station; **Air:** Major and regional airlines provide regular service to Newark, La Guardia, and John F. Kennedy airports; **Other:** Metropolitan Transit Authority buses run frequently to South Ferry from Journal Square; Central Bus runs service morning and afternoon to Liberty State Park, Jersey City; Metropolitan Transit Authority provides subway service to South Ferry.

NEARBY FACILITIES & POINTS OF INTEREST: Parks, other points of interest: Liberty State Park, Jersey City, New Jersey.

Upper Delaware Scenic & Recreational River
New York (also in Pennsylvania)   **SEE CLIMATABLE NO. 115**

MAILING ADDRESS: Upper Delaware Scenic & Recreational River, P.O. Box C, Narrowsburg, NY 12764 **Telephone:** 717-729-8251

DIRECTIONS: The area is undeveloped at this time.
   Nearly 73 miles (120 km) of this free-flowing fishing stream are protected from Hancock, NY to the vicinity of Sparrow Bush, NY. Authorized for addition to the National Park System on Nov. 10, 1978.

VISITOR ACTIVITIES: Canoeing, kayaking, rafting, tubing and fishing; **Permits:** New York or Penn. fishing license required when fishing the Upper Delaware River; **Fees:** No; **Visitor facilities:** Information Center & 5 kiosks staffed during summer months for dispensing information. Boat rentals and campgrounds are available in the vicinity.

TRAVEL ACCESS: Bus: Short Line provides summer service to Narrowsburg, NY; **Rail:** N.J. Transit offers regular service to Port Jervis, NY.

NEARBY FACILITIES & POINTS OF INTEREST: Campgrounds: Contact area for directory of campgrounds; **Other points of interest:** Minisink Battleground Park, Fort Delaware, Zane Grey Museum; **Reservation system in use for campsites, other facilities:** Canoe rentals available at various locations along the Upper Delaware River, contact area for more information.

Vanderbilt Mansion National Historic Site
Hyde Park, New York **SEE CLIMATABLE NO. 108**

MAILING ADDRESS: Superintendent, Roosevelt-Vanderbilt National Historic Sites, 249 Albany Post Rd., Hyde Park, New York 12538 **Telephone:** 914-229-9115

DIRECTIONS: The Site is on US 9 about 8 miles (12.8 km) north of Poughkeepsie, NY. Entrance to the grounds is by the main gate on US 9 north in the village of Hyde Park. The Visitor Center is in the Pavilion near the mansion.
This palatial mansion is a fine example of homes built by 19th century financiers. Designated Dec. 18, 1940.

VISITOR ACTIVITIES: visit by tour only—beginning at Visitor Center, interpretive exhibits and audiovisual program; **Permits:** No; **Fees:** Entrance fee is $2.00. Golden Eagle and Golden Age Passports accepted and available; **Visitor facilities:** parking, restrooms; **Any limitations on vehicle usage:** No; **Hiking trails:** No; **Backcountry:** No; **Camping:** No; **Other overnight accommodations on site:** No; **Meals served in the park:** No; **Food and supplies obtainable in the park:** No; **Food and supplies obtainable nearby:** Yes, Town of Hyde Park; **Overnight accommodations:** Hyde Park and vicinity; **First Aid available in park:** Yes; **Nearest Hospital:** Poughkeepsie, US 9, 6 miles; **Days/ Hours:** Open Thursday thru Monday from 9 a.m. to 5 p.m. November-March. Open daily from 10 a.m. to 6:00 p.m. April-October; **Holiday Closings:** Dec. 25, Jan. 1 and Thanksgiving Day.

TRAVEL ACCESS: Bus: Dutchess County Transportation provides service to Poughkeepsie (7 miles); **Rail:** Conrail provides service to Poughkeepsie from New York City; **Air:** Command/Colegan/Air North operates into Wappingon Falls, NY.

NEARBY FACILITIES & POINTS OF INTEREST: Parks, other points of interest: F.D.R. Library Museum; Home of Franklin D. Roosevelt and Eleanor Roosevelt National Historic Site. **Reservation systems:** For groups or bus tour reservations please write to Roosevelt-Vanderbilt National Historic Sites, 249 Albany Post Rd., Hyde Park, NY 12538.

Women's Rights National Historical Park
Seneca Falls & Waterloo New York **SEE CLIMATABLE NO. 116**

MAILING ADDRESS: Women's Rights National Historical Park, P.O. Box 70, Seneca Falls, New York 13148

DIRECTIONS: New York Thruway Exit 41 onto State Route 414 South, 4 miles (6.4 km), then east on State Routes 5 & 20, 3 miles (4.8 km). Established in December 1980. Visitor Center is at 116 Fall Street, downtown Seneca Falls.

VISITOR ACTIVITIES: Permits: No; **Fees:** No; **Visitor facilities:** Visitor Center located on Rtes. 5 and 20 in downtown Seneca Falls; exhibits, audio-visual programs, special events. Elizabeth Cady Stanton home restored and open to public. Remaining principal sites not open to public: Wesleyan Chapel, Hunt and McClintock houses. Self-guided walking tours available. Guided interpretive tours available May through September; **Any limitations on vehicle usage:** No; **Hiking trails:** No; **Backcountry:** No; **Camping:** No; **Other overnight accommodations on site:** No; **Meals served in the park:** No; **Food and supplies obtainable in the park:** No; **Food and supplies obtainable nearby:** Yes; **Overnight accommodations:** Cayuga Lake State Park, Private Motels; **First Aid available in park:** Yes; **Holiday Closings:** Yes, closed all fall and winter holidays; **Visitor attractions closed for seasons:** Limited winter programs; (see below) **Weather:** 80° in Summer, 65° Spring and Fall, 30° in Winter.

GENERAL INFORMATION: Park Visitor Center open year round Monday thru Friday, 9 a.m. to 5 p.m. Open Saturday 9 a.m. to 5 p.m., May through October, Open Sunday 9 a.m. to 5 p.m., May through October. Call 315-568-2991 for more information or write for brochure.

TRAVEL ACCESS: Bus: Onondaga Coach in Seneca Falls; **Rail:** Amtrak in Syracuse; **Air:** USAir, Empire, Peoples Express in Syracuse, Rochester.

NEARBY FACILITIES & POINTS OF INTEREST: Hotel/Motel: Write Chamber of Commerce for listing; **Campgrounds:** Cayuga Lake State Park, Sampson State Park; **Parks, other points of interest:** National Women's Hall of Fame; Seneca Falls Historical Society, Montezuma National Wildlife Refuge 5 miles; **Reservation Systems in Use for Campsites, other facilities:** Write State Park Office and/or Chamber of Commerce; **New information, New Park Programs:** Stanton House now open (as of June 29, 1985).

North Carolina

CAPE HATTERAS NATIONAL SEASHORE

CAPE LOOKOUT NATIONAL SEASHORE

GUILFORD COURTHOUSE NATIONAL MILITARY PARK

APPALACHIAN NATIONAL SCENIC TRAIL

FORT RALEIGH NATIONAL HISTORIC SITE

WRIGHT BROTHERS NATIONAL MEMORIAL

52   85

77   Raleigh

40   85   17

1

Charlotte   70

95

GREAT SMOKY MOUNTAINS NATIONAL PARK

CARL SANDBURG HOME NATIONAL HISTORIC SITE

BLUE RIDGE PARKWAY

MOORES CREEK NATIONAL BATTLEFIELD

Appalachian National Scenic Trail
For details see listing in Maine

Blue Ridge Parkway
North Carolina and Virginia   **SEE CLIMATABLE MAP**

MAILING ADDRESS: Superintendent, Blue Ridge Parkway, 700 Northwestern Bank Building, Asheville, North Carolina 28801 **Telephone:** 704-259-0717

DIRECTIONS: The Parkway intersects many US and State highways, including Interstates 64, 77, 40 & 26. Obtain by mail or in person at any Visitor Center a copy of Blue Ridge Parkway Directory which provides detailed maps and information.

The first national parkway follows the crest of the Blue Ridge and other mountain ranges and includes several large recreation areas. The Parkway is 470 miles (752 km) long and links Shenandoah National Park in Virginia with Great Smoky Mountains National Park in North Carolina. Established by act of Congress on June 30, 1936.

VISITOR ACTIVITIES: auto tours, wildlife- and wildflower-watching, camping, exhibits, picnicking, hiking, fishing, interpretive walks and talks, craft sales and demonstrations; **Permits:** No; **Fees:** campground fee charged at developed areas; **Visitor facilities:** food service, gas, lodging, campgrounds, picnic areas, hiking trails, drinking water, restrooms; **Any limitations on vehicle usage:** Vehicles being used commercially are not allowed on the parkway unless they secure a special permit; **Hiking trails:** Yes, trails vary in length and difficulty; **Backcountry:** No, The Appalachian Trail roughly parallels the parkway from Mile 0 at Rockfish Gap to Mile 103 where the trail takes a more westerly route toward the Great Smoky Mountains and Georgia. Shelters, usually 1 day's hike apart, are available on a first-come, first-serve basis all along the trail. Information about the trail may be obtained from the Appalachian Trail Conference, P.O. Box 236, Harpers Ferry, WV 25425, phone 304-535-6331; **Camping:** Yes, the nine parkway campgrounds are open from May through Oct. only, but limited camping facilities are available in winter at Otter Creek, Roanoke Mountain, Price Park, and Linville Falls. Sites in each campground are designated for trailer use, but none are equipped for utility connections. Sanitary dumping facilities for trailers are provided at all campgrounds. Camping is limited to 14 days and campsites may not be reserved; **Other overnight accommodations on site:** Yes, Peaks of Otter Lodge, open all year, is operated by Virginia Peaks of Otter Co., Box 489, Bedford, VA 24523, phone 703-586-1081. To reserve at Rocky Knob Cabins, open June through Labor Day, write National Park Concessions, Inc., Meadows of Dan, VA 24120, phone 703-593-3503. For Bluffs Lodge (in Doughton Park), open May 1-Oct. 31, write National Park Concessions, Inc., Laurel Springs, NC 28644, phone 919-372-4499. For Pisgah Inn, open May 1-Oct. 31, contact Pisgah Inn, Inc., Route 2, Box 441, Canton, NC 28716, phone 704-235-8228; **Meals served in the park:** Yes, at Whetstone Ridge, Otter Creek, Peaks of Otter, Mabry Mill, Doughton Park, Crabtree Meadows, Mount Pisgah; **Food and supplies obtainable in the park:** Yes, limited food and supplies at some Parkway gas stations and at campground stores;
Food and supplies obtainable nearby: Yes, within a few miles of the Parkway in most of the larger communities; **Overnight accommodations:** at most nearby communities as well as Peaks of Otter, Rocky Knob, Doughton Park and Mount Pisgah on the parkway. For further information, obtain a copy of the pamphlet: Blue Ridge Parkway Directory from any Visitor Center or by mail from the Superintendent; **First Aid available in park:** Yes, from Park Rangers; **Nearest Hospital:** Roanoke, Ashville, and many other cities near the Parkway; **Days/Hours:** Open all year. Some sections of the Parkway may be closed in winter due to snow and ice; **Holiday Closings:** No; **Visitor attractions**

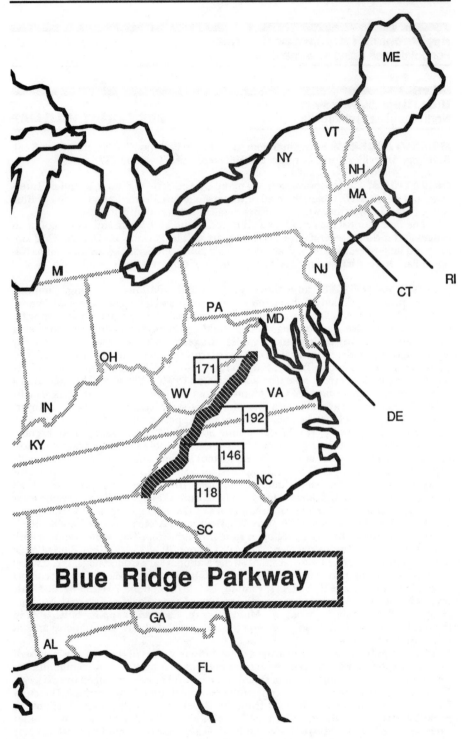

closed for seasons: Minerals Museum near Spruce Pine, NC and The Folk Art Center near Asheville, NC are open all year except Thanksgiving, Christmas and New Year's Day; Campgrounds, picnic areas, and other visitor accommodations are open May 1 through Oct. Limited camping facilities are available in Winter; **Weather:** Because of its length and range in elevation, the entire parkway seldom experiences the same weather at the same time. Most visitors come in Summer but Spring and Fall are pleasant, with fewer crowds. Winter brings snow and ice which may cause temporary closing of sections of the parkway.

GENERAL INFORMATION: See listings in this book for Great Smoky Mountains National Park at the southern end of Blue Ridge Parkway, and Shenandoah National Park, to the North.

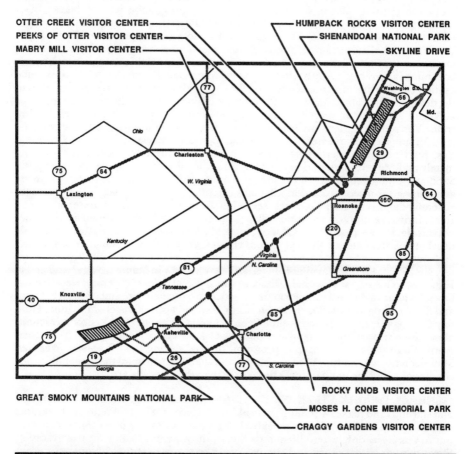

OTTER CREEK VISITOR CENTER
PEEKS OF OTTER VISITOR CENTER
MABRY MILL VISITOR CENTER
HUMPBACK ROCKS VISITOR CENTER
SHENANDOAH NATIONAL PARK
SKYLINE DRIVE
GREAT SMOKY MOUNTAINS NATIONAL PARK
ROCKY KNOB VISITOR CENTER
MOSES H. CONE MEMORIAL PARK
CRAGGY GARDENS VISITOR CENTER

Cape Hatteras National Seashore
Manteo, North Carolina   **SEE CLIMATABLE NO. 117**

MAILING ADDRESS: Superintendent, Cape Hatteras National Seashore, Route 1, Box 675, Manteo, North Carolina 27954 **Telephone:** 919-473-2111/919-995-5209

DIRECTIONS: The Whalebone Junction Information Center, at the park entrance, is at the intersection of US 158 and NC 12 and US 64-264 at the town of Nags Head, southeast of Manteo. Information is also available at Hatteras Island Visitor Center in Buxton; and at the Bodie Island Visitor Center (Nags Head) and Ocracoke Island Visitor Center (Ocracoke) late spring, summer, and early fall. Toll ferryboats operate between Ocracoke and Cedar Island (2¼ hours) connecting the park with the mainland. Visitors should check ferry schedules well in advance. Reservations are required. Call Ocracoke 919-928-3841; Cedar Island 919-225-3551.

Beaches, migratory waterfowl, fishing, and points of historical interest, including the Cape Hatteras Lighthouse overlooking the "graveyard of the Atlantic," are special features of the first national seashore. Authorized for addition to the National Park System on Aug. 17, 1937.

VISITOR ACTIVITIES: interpretive exhibits, picnicking, swimming, fishing, guided walks and evening talks in Summer, camping, exploring ships wrecks, biking, birdwatching, boating, hunting, surfing; **Permits:** No; **Fees:** only for campsites—$8.00 per night per site plus reservation fee of $2.00 during summer, maximum of 6 people per site; **Visitor facilities:** campgrounds, fishing piers, lifeguarded beaches in Summer, marina, nature trails, showers, restrooms, ferry service, wildlife refuge, picnic areas, boat ramps and rentals; **Any limitations on vehicle usage:** Bicyclists should use extreme caution because there are no established bike trails within the park. Park your car only in the designated parking areas to avoid getting stuck in soft sands. Check with Rangers or at Visitor Centers for special regulations governing off-road vehicle travel; **Hiking trails:** Yes, self-guiding nature trail near Cape Hatteras Lighthouse, and near Bodie Island Visitor Center and near Ocracoke Campground; **Backcountry:** No; **Camping:** Yes, reservations for certain campgrounds available through "Ticketron," approximately mid-May through mid-September. Educational group camping special request. Sand and wind conditions require longer than normal tent stakes. Awnings for shade and netting for insect protection will make camping more enjoyable; **Other overnight accommodations on site:** No; **Meals served in the park:** Yes, Lunch counter at Oregon Inlet Marina; restaurants in various villages adjacent to the seashore; **Food and supplies obtainable in the park:** Yes, Oregon Inlet Marina; **Food and supplies obtainable nearby:** Yes, in Hatteras, NC and various villages; **Overnight accommodations:** Hotels and motels in nearby communities. For a list, write Dare County Tourist Bureau, Manteo, NC 27954; **First Aid available in park:** Yes, or nearby in Manteo, Nags Head and in Hatteras, NC; **Nearest Hospital:** Elizabeth City, NC, 80 miles (128.7 km); **Days/Hours:** Open 24 hours a day. All campgrounds closed approximately November-March, Frisco and Salvo campgrounds close between Labor Day and approximately Mid-June; **Holiday Closings:** Hatteras Island Visitor Center closed Christmas Day; **Visitor attractions closed for seasons:** Bodie Island and Ocracoke Island Visitor Center closed November-April. No organized interpretive programs offered during the off season; **Weather:** Summer is hot and humid; Winter is humid and cold. Keep in mind that generally windy conditions make the temperatures feel cooler than they actually are.

GENERAL INFORMATION: *For Your Safety*—Strong littoral currents, rip currents, and shifting sand make swimming particularly dangerous. Tidal currents are hazardous near inlets. Offshore winds can quickly blow air mattresses and other flotation devices out to sea. *Swim* only where lifeguards are on duty. *Sunburn* can ruin your vacation. Short periods of exposure and the use of protective waterproof lotions are recommended. *Hurricanes* are not common but might occur in Aug. or Sept., and winter storms, called Northeasters, should not be taken lightly. Efforts will be made to warn you in time to leave low-lying areas should any of these storms occur. Be sure to walk—never drive—across the *barrier dune* to the sand beaches. *Mosquitoes* and other *insect pests* can make your trip an ordeal if you don't come prepared with repellent and suitable mosquito netting for camping. Lightweight *clothing* in Summer should be adequate to protect you from the sun and keep you comfortable in the cool evenings. You should wear shoes when walking to the beach. *Pets must be under physical restraint at all times.*

TRAVEL ACCESS: Bus: Virginia Dare Transportation Co. (Trailways) operates into Manteo, NC (15 miles), three trips daily to and from Elizabeth City, NC, and Norfolk, VA; **Rail:** Nearest passenger service Newsport News, VA (75 miles) and Rocky Mount, NC, (158 miles); **Air:** Dare County Regional Airport, Manteo, NC., commercial service at Norfolk, VA (80 miles).

NEARBY FACILITIES & POINTS OF INTEREST: Hotel/Motel: For hotels and campgrounds contact Dare County Tourist Bureau, Manteo, NC; **Parks, other points of interest:** Fort Raleigh NHS, Wright Brothers National Memorial (see listings in this book); **Reservation system in use for campsites:** Ticketron Reservation System.

Cape Lookout National Seashore
Beaufort, North Carolina   **SEE CLIMATABLE NO. 117**

MAILING ADDRESS: Superintendent, Cape Lookout National Seashore, P.O. Box 690, Beaufort, North Carolina 28516 **Telephone:** 919-728- 2121

DIRECTIONS: Park Headquarters is located on Front Street in Beaufort, NC. A District Office is located on Harkers Island, 20 miles (30 km) east of Beaufort. Ferry access to the Park is provided from Harkers Island, Davis, Atlantic and Ocracoke. Ferry from Harkers Island and Ocracoke transports passengers only. Others transport passengers and 4 wheel drive vehicles.

The Seashore embraces a series of barrier islands including 58 miles (93 km) of ocean beach, historic Portsmouth Village, and Cape Lookout lighthouse. Authorized for addition to the National Park System on March 10, 1966.

VISITOR ACTIVITIES: fishing, swimming, boating, shell collecting, photography, primitive camping, bird-watching; **Permits:** Yes, free permit required to drive on islands, obtainable from Park Headquarters, Ferry Operators or the Harkers Island District Office; **Fees:** Yes, for Concession and Charter Ferry; **Visitor facilities:** Interpretive programs offered in season. This is a developing park, and visitor facilities are limited; **Any limitations on vehicle usage:** No roads or bridges, four wheel drive vehicles only; **Hiking trails:** No; **Backcountry:** Yes, information from Park Headquarters; **Camping:** Yes, there are no developed campsites; **Other overnight accommodations on site:** Yes, concession operated rustic cabins; **Meals served in the park:** No; **Food and supplies obtainable in the park:** No; **Food and supplies obtainable nearby:** Yes, at Harkers Island and Beaufort; **Overnight accommodations:** Harkers Island and Beaufort; **First Aid available in park:** No; physicians are in Harkers Island and Beaufort; **Nearest Hospital:** Morehead City and Sea Level; **Days/Hours:** Open 24 hours a day; **Holiday Closings:** None; **Visitor attractions closed for seasons:** Interpretive programs offered only in Summer; **Weather:** Hot and humid in Summer.

GENERAL INFORMATION: This is a developing park, and visitor facilities are limited. Be prepared to carry with you everything you need, particularly food and water. Don't go out without a shirt and a hat, because there is little shade or shelter on the islands. Make sure your tent is strong and able to withstand wind. It should have a mosquito netting. Be prepared with repellent to combat many biting insects.

TRAVEL ACCESS: Bus: Trailways, Seashore Line, service Morehead City, N.C.; **Rail:** No; **Air:** No;

NEARBY FACILITIES & POINTS OF INTEREST: Hotel/Motel: several in the area; **Parks, other points of interest:** North Carolina Maritime Museum, Beaufort, NC; North Carolina Aquarium, Pine Knoll Shores, NC.

Carl Sandburg Home National Historic Site
Flat Rock, North Carolina   **SEE CLIMATABLE NO. 120**

MAILING ADDRESS: Superintendent, Carl Sandburg Home National Historic Site, 1928 Little River Road, Flat Rock, North Carolina 28731 **Telephone:** 704-693-4178

DIRECTIONS: The Site is 3 miles (4.8 km) south of Hendersonville. Turn off US 25 onto Little River Road at the Flat Rock Playhouse. The Park is 26 miles (42 km) south of Asheville via Int. 26.
    "Connemara" was the home of the noted poet-author Carl Sandburg for the last 22 years of his life. Authorized for addition to the National Park System on Oct. 17, 1968.

VISITOR ACTIVITIES: Self-guiding tour, guided house tours, exhibits; **Permits:** No; **Fees:** $1.00; **Visitor facilities:** restrooms at Information Center, parking; **Any limitations on vehicle usage:** Visitors must park in the designated area, and walk to the home, shuttle van available for handicapped access; **Hiking trails:** Yes, self-guiding paths and trails lead around the Site; **Backcountry:** No; **Camping:** No; **Other overnight accommodations on site:** No; **Meals served in the park:** No; **Food and supplies obtainable in the park:** No; **Food and supplies obtainable nearby:** Yes, Hendersonville; **Overnight accommodations:** Hendersonville, 3 miles (4.8 km) north on US 25; **First Aid available in park:** Yes; **Nearest Hospital:** Hendersonville, 4 miles (6.4 km); **Days/Hours:** Open daily 9 a.m. to 5 p.m. **Holiday Closings:** Dec. 25; **Weather:** Moderate Summers, cool Spring and Fall, cold Winters.

GENERAL INFORMATION: *For Your Safety*—Be cautious on trails, around ponds and lakes and while standing on the rock face atop Big Glassy Mountain. Be wary of farm animals that can bite or kick. Stay on established walks and paths, do not climb fences, and be alert for snakes and poison ivy.

TRAVEL ACCESS: Bus: Trailway and Greyhound provides service to Hendersonville, NC; **Rail:** Southern Railway provides service to Spartanburg and Greenville, SC; **Air:** Piedmont, Wheeler, Atlantic Southeast, Sunbird, and Metro Airlines provide service to Asheville.

Fort Raleigh National Historic Site
Manteo, North Carolina   **SEE CLIMATABLE NO. 117**

MAILING ADDRESS: Superintendent, Cape Hatteras National Seashore, Route 1, Box 675, Manteo, North Carolina 27954 **Telephone:** 919- 473-5772

DIRECTIONS: The site is on US 64-264, 3 miles (4.8 km) north of Manteo, NC, 92 miles (148 km) southeast of Norfolk, VA, and 67 miles (108 km) southeast of Elizabeth City, NC.
    The first English settlement was attempted here from 1585-87. The fate of Sir Walter Raleigh's "Lost Colony" remains a mystery. Designated Apr. 5, 1941.

VISITOR ACTIVITIES: interpretive exhibits and film, walking tours. In summer, "Lost Colony," a symphonic-drama, is produced in the Waterside Theater; **Permits:** No; **Fees:** only to see "Lost Colony"; **Visitor facilities:** parking, restrooms, picnic area; **Any limitations on vehicle usage:** No; **Hiking trails:** Yes, nature trails around the Site; **Backcountry:** No; **Camping:** No; **Other overnight accommodations on site:** No; **Meals served in the park:** No; **Food and supplies obtainable in the park:** No; **Food and supplies obtainable nearby:** Yes, at Manteo; **Overnight accommodations:** Manteo, 4 miles (6.4 km) or on the Outer Banks, 14-18 miles (22.5-29 km); **First Aid available in park:** Yes, or nearby in Manteo and Nags Head; **Nearest Hospital:** Elizabeth City, NC, US 158, 80 miles (128.7 km); **Days/Hours:** Open 9 a.m. to 8 p.m. in season, 9 a.m. to 6 p.m. on Sundays, 9 a.m. to 5 p.m. remainder of year; **Holiday Closings:** Dec. 25.

GENERAL INFORMATION: Adjacent to the Historic Site is the Elizabethan Garden, maintained by the Garden Club of North Carolina, Inc. The admission fee is set by that organization.

TRAVEL ACCESS: Bus: Virginia Dare Trans. Co. (Trailways) provides daily service into Manteo, NC from Elizabeth City, NC and Norfolk, VA; **Rail:** No, nearest passenger service is Rocky Mount, NC (140 miles) and Newport News, VA, (93 miles); **Air:** Charter flights may be arranged from airport at Manteo; nearest commercial service at Norfolk, VA (88 miles).

NEARBY FACILITIES & POINTS OF INTEREST: Campgrounds: NPS campgrounds on Cape Hatteras NS nearest at Oregon Inlet (17 miles); **Parks, other points of interest:** Cape Hatteras NS, Wright Brothers National Memorial.

Great Smoky Mountains National Park
For details see listing in Tennessee

Guilford Courthouse National Military Park
Greensboro, North Carolina   **SEE CLIMATABLE NO. 121**

MAILING ADDRESS: Superintendent, Guilford Courthouse National Military Park, P.O. Box 9806, Greensboro, North Carolina 27429-0806 **Telephone:** 919-288-1776

DIRECTIONS: The Visitor Center is near the intersection of Old Battleground Road and New Garden Road, just north of Greensboro.
   The battle fought here on March 15, 1781 opened the campaign that led to Yorktown and the end of the Revolution. Established by act of Congress on Mar. 2, 1917.

VISITOR ACTIVITIES: interpretive film and exhibits; auto, bicycle and walking tours, interpretive talks; **Permits:** No; **Fees:** No; **Visitor facilities:** parking and rest-rooms at Visitor Center; bicycle and foot trails; **Any limitations on vehicle usage:** One hour parking limits in most parking lots; **Hiking trails:** Yes, self-guiding foot trails; **Backcountry:** No; **Camping:** No; **Other overnight accommodations on site:** No; **Meals served in the park:** No; **Food and supplies obtainable in the park:** No; **Food and supplies obtainable nearby:** Yes, in Greensboro; **Overnight accommodations:** Greensboro, 2-10 miles (3-16 km); **First Aid available in park:** Yes; **Nearest Hospital:** Greensboro, 3 miles (5.8 km); **Days/Hours:** Open daily from 8:30 a.m. to 5 p.m. Jan. 2-Late May; 8:30-6:00 Late May-Sept. 1; 8:30-5:00 Sept-Dec. 31; **Holiday Closings:** Dec. 25 & Jan. 1; **Visitor attractions closed for seasons:** No; **Weather:** Hot, humid summer; cold moderate winter.

GENERAL INFORMATION: Watch out for traffic on New Garden Road and Old Battleground Road. Park has 28 monuments, including the Nathanael Greene Monument and the Signers Monument, where two of North Carolina's three signers of the Declaration of Independence are buried.

Moores Creek National Battlefield
Currie, North Carolina　　　　　　　　　**SEE CLIMATABLE NO. 124**

MAILING ADDRESS: Superintendent, Moores Creek National Battlefield, P.O. Box 69, Currie, North Carolina 28435 **Telephone:** 919-283-5591

DIRECTIONS: The park is about 20 miles (30 km) northwest of Wilmington, NC, and can be reached via US 421 and NC 210.

The brief, violent battle on Feb. 27, 1776 between North Carolina Patriots and Loyalists is commemorated here. The Patriot victory notably advanced the revolutionary cause in the South, ending Royal authority in the colony. This helped forestall a British invasion of the South and encouraged North Carolina to instruct its delegation to the Continental Congress, on April 12, 1776, to support total independence—the first colony to so act. Established June 2, 1926.

VISITOR ACTIVITIES: exhibits, walking tours, picnicking, wildflower-watching in season; **Permits:** No; **Fees:** No; **Visitor facilities:** restrooms, museum and trailside exhibits, picnic areas; **Any limitations on vehicle usage:** No; **Hiking trails:** Yes, a .7 mile (1.2 km) loop history trail and a .3 mile (.5 km) Tarheel Trail depicting the local Naval Stores Industry during the Revolution; **Backcountry:** No; **Camping:** No; **Other overnight accommodations on site:** No; **Meals served in the park:** No; **Food and supplies obtainable in the park:** No; **Food and supplies obtainable nearby:** Yes, at Currie, Atkinson, Burgaw, or Wilmington; **Overnight accommodations:** Wilmington, 20 miles (32 km) southeast of Moores Creek; **First Aid available in park:** Usually or nearby in Atkinson or at Hospital in Burgaw; **Nearest Hospital:** Pender Memorial Hospital in Burgaw, 14 miles (22 km) northeast of Moores Creek; **Days/Hours:** Open daily from 8 a.m. to 5 p.m.; 8 a.m. to 6 p.m. on weekends only during June, July and August; **Holiday Closings:** Dec. 25 & Jan. 1; **Visitor attractions closed for seasons:** No; **Weather:** Spring—sunny and mild; Summer—hot and humid; Fall—sunny and mild; Winter—mild with infrequent subfreezing weather.

GENERAL INFORMATION: When near the creek, be sure to watch your children. Visitors should be aware of several species of poisonous snakes that live in the Park.

TRAVEL ACCESS: Bus: Greyhound provides regular service to Wilmington, NC; **Rail:** None; **Air:** Piedmont Airlines provides daily service to Wilmington, NC; no commercial transportation between park and Wilmington except by taxi.

Wright Brothers National Memorial
(near) Manteo, North Carolina　　　　　　**SEE CLIMATABLE NO. 117**

MAILING ADDRESS: Superintendent, Wright Brothers National Memorial, c/o Cape Hatteras National Seashore, Rt. 1, Box 675, Manteo, North Carolina 27954 **Telephone:** 919-441-7430

DIRECTIONS: The Memorial is located on the Outer Banks of North Carolina in the town of Kill Devil Hills. The Visitor Center is 15 miles (24 km) northeast of Manteo on US 158.

The first sustained flight in a heavier-than-air machine was made here by Wilbur and Orville Wright on Dec. 17, 1903. Authorized March 2, 1927.

VISITOR ACTIVITIES: interpretive exhibits, including reproductions of the Wright Brothers' 1902 glider and 1903 flyer; walking tours, orientation talks year-round; **Per-**

mits: No; **Fees:** Yes, $1.00 per person or $3.00 per car; **Visitor facilities:** reconstruction of an airplane hangar and the Wright Brothers' workshop and residence, granite monuments mark the sites of glider experiments and the spot where the first plane left the ground; **Any limitations on vehicle usage:** No; **Hiking trails:** No; **Backcountry:** No; **Camping:** No; **Other overnight accommodations on site:** No; **Meals served in the park:** No; **Food and supplies obtainable in the park:** No; **Food and supplies obtainable nearby:** Yes, at Kitty Hawk, Kill Devil Hills and Nags Head; **Overnight accommodations:** Kitty Hawk, Kill Devil Hills and Nags Head, within a 14 mile (22.5 km) radius; **First Aid available in park:** Yes, or nearby in Nags Head, NC; **Nearest Hospital:** Elizabeth City, NC, 66 miles (106 km); **Days/Hours:** Open daily from 9:00 a.m. to 5:00 p.m.; 9:00 a.m. to 7:00 p.m. in Summer; **Holiday Closings:** Dec. 25; **Visitor attractions closed for seasons:** Reduced organized interpretive programs during off-season; **Weather:** Weather is generally moderate and windy.

GENERAL INFORMATION: *For Your Safety*—Keep in mind that the generally windy conditions make the temperatures feel cooler than they actually are. Even in relatively warm temperatures high winds can make hypothermia, the loss of body heat, a serious threat. From Spring through early Fall protect against sunburn, especially from 10 a.m. to 3 p.m.

Nearby points of interest include Cape Hatteras National Seashore, which is 10 miles (16 km) south of the Memorial; and Fort Raleigh National Historic Site, located on Roanoke Island about 18 miles (28 km) southwest of the Memorial (see listing in this book). This is the Site of what is known as the Lost Colony, England's unsuccessful first attempt to colonize the North American continent. It can be reached via U.S. 64-264.

TRAVEL ACCESS: **Bus:** Virginia Dare Transportation Co. (Trailways) operates into Manteo, NC (15 miles), three trips daily to and from Elizabeth City, NC, and Norfolk, VA; **Rail:** Nearest passenger service Newport News, VA (75 miles) and Rocky Mount, NC, (158 miles); **Air:** Yes, via private and charter flights to the Park's First Flight Airstrip. Nearest commercial service at Norfolk, VA (70 miles). Charter flight may be arranged from Dare County Regional Airport.

NEARBY FACILITIES & POINTS OF INTEREST: **Campgrounds:** NPS Campgrounds on Cape Hatteras, NS; **Parks, other points of interest:** Cape Hatteras National Seashore, Fort Raleigh NHS.

North Dakota

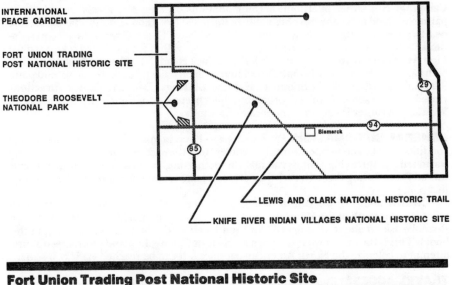

INTERNATIONAL
PEACE GARDEN

FORT UNION TRADING
POST NATIONAL HISTORIC SITE

THEODORE ROOSEVELT
NATIONAL PARK

Bismarck

LEWIS AND CLARK NATIONAL HISTORIC TRAIL

KNIFE RIVER INDIAN VILLAGES NATIONAL HISTORIC SITE

Fort Union Trading Post National Historic Site
North Dakota and Montana   **SEE CLIMATABLE NO. 89**

MAILING ADDRESS: Superintendent, Fort Union Trading Post National Historic Site, Buford Route, Williston, North Dakota 58801 **Telephone:** 701-572-9083

DIRECTIONS: The Site is on the border of North Dakota and Montana, and can be reached via US 2 and N.D. 1804 West from Williston, ND, which is 25 miles (40 km) to the northeast, or from Sidney, MT, 21 miles (34 km) south via ND58.
The trading post that stood here was the principal fur-trading depot in the Upper Missouri River region from 1829 to 1867. The National Park Service is partially reconstructing the fort and work will be finished in 1989. Authorized for addition to the National Park System on June 20, 1966.

VISITOR ACTIVITIES: interpretive exhibits, living history programs, walking tours; **Permits:** No; **Fees:** No; **Visitor facilities:** A Visitor Center is located in the reconstructed 1851 Bourgeois House at the site. Guided tours of the fort site and a teepee display are provided; **Any limitations on vehicle usage:** Vehicles are limited to established roadways; **Hiking trails:** No; **Backcountry:** No; **Camping:** No; **Other overnight accommodations on site:** No; **Meals served in the park:** No; **Food and supplies obtainable in the park:** No; **Food and supplies obtainable nearby:** Yes, at Williston or Sidney, MT; **Overnight accommodations:** Williston, Sidney; **First Aid available in park:** Yes; **Nearest Hospital:** Williston, 25 miles (40 km); **Days/Hours:** Open daily from 9 a.m. to 5:30 p.m.; 8 a.m. until 8 p.m. in Summer; **Holiday Closings:** Dec. 25 & Jan. 1; **Visitor attractions closed for seasons:** Living history programs offered only from mid-May through mid-October; **Weather:** Winters are cold with temperatures often below zero, Summers are warm and dry. Wet, cool Springs and dry, cool Falls are normal. Windy conditions may be expected during any season.

International Peace Garden
Dunseith, North Dakota   SEE CLIMATABLE NO. 125

MAILING ADDRESS: Superintendent, International Peace Garden, P.O. Box 116, Dunseith, North Dakota 58329 **Telephone:** 701-263-4390

DIRECTIONS: The Garden is 13 miles (20 km) north of Dunseith on US 281.

Peaceful relations between Canada and the United States are commemorated here. The Garden contains 2,339 acres (888 in North Dakota, 1,451 in Manitoba), which are administered by the International Peace Garden, Inc. The National Park Service has assisted in the master plan. This affiliated area of the National Park System was dedicated on July 14, 1932.

VISITOR ACTIVITIES: walking, picnicking, camping, guided tours, snowshoeing; **Permits:** No; **Fees:** Yes, $4 per vehicle per day or $5 per vehicle per season; **Visitor facilities:** landscaped gardens, amphitheatre, exhibits, picnic areas, campgrounds, food service, souvenir shops, chapel, bell tower, arboretum, International Music Camp, Canadian Legion Sports Camp, Masonic Auditorium, Peace Tower; **Any limitations on vehicle usage:** Vehicles are restricted to designated roadways; **Backcountry:** No; **Camping:** Yes, no reservations available for campsites; fee is $4 per night or $6 per night with electrical hookups. $8.00 per night for water & electrical hookups. Write or call the Garden for further information on camping facilities; **Other overnight accommodations on site:** No; **Meals served in the park:** Yes, at both American and Canadian concessions; **Food and supplies obtainable in the park:** Yes, at both American and Canadian concessions; **Food and supplies obtainable nearby:** Yes, in Dunseith and Boissevain; **Overnight accommodations:** Boissevain, Manitoba, 16 miles (25 km) north on Hwy 10; Dunseith, ND, 13 miles (21 km) south on Hwy 281; **First Aid available in park:** No; **Nearest Hospital:** Boissevain, Manitoba, Hwy 10, 16 miles (25 km); Bottineau, ND, US 281 to ND 5, 30 miles (48 km); **Days/Hours:** Open 24 hours a day year-round; **Holiday Closings:** None; **Visitor attractions closed for seasons:** Activities are curtailed in Winter; **Weather:** Occasional rain and wind with dry, cool evenings. Temperatures range from 60-95°F.

NEARBY FACILITIES & POINTS OF INTEREST: Parks, other points of interest: Turtle Mountain Provincial Parks (5 miles north), Lake Metigoshi State Park (25 miles west)—both have camping facilities.

Knife River Indian Villages National Historic Site
Stanton, North Dakota   SEE CLIMATABLE NO. 119

MAILING ADDRESS: Superintendent, Knife River Indian Villages National Historic Site, R.R. 1, Box 168, Stanton, North Dakota 58571 **Telephone:** 701-745-3300

DIRECTIONS: From I-94 at Bismarck, north on US 83 to ND 200 at Washburn, 40 miles (64 km); west on ND 200A to ND 31, 22 miles (35 km); north on ND 31 to Stanton, 2 miles (3.2 km). The visitor center is 3.5 miles north of Stanton.

Remnants of three Mandan, Hidatsa and Arikira villages are an archaeological treasure of the Plains Indians. Visitors to the area include Lewis and Clark, George Catlin, Karl Bodmer, Prince Maximilian and John James Audubon. Authorized for addition to the National Park System on Oct. 16, 1974.

VISITOR ACTIVITIES: Summer programs begin in mid-May. They include guided tours, museum exhibits, slide shows, Indian art and cultural programs and guest speakers. Daily programs continue until Labor Day. Special tours and programs are arranged upon request. Open daily all year. Summer hours 8:00 a.m. - 6:00 p.m. MDT, Winter hours 8:00 a.m. - 4:30 p.m. MDT.

NEARBY FACILITIES & POINTS OF INTEREST: Hotel/Motel: Yes, Stanton, ND; 3-1/2 miles south of Park; **Food/Supplies:** Yes, 3-1/2 miles south of Park; **Parks, other points of interest:** Fort Clark State Historic Site, 9 miles south; Garrison Dam and Sakakawea State Park, 16 miles north.

Lewis and Clark Trail
For details see listing in Illinois

North Country National Scenic Trail
For details see listing in New York

Theodore Roosevelt National Park
Medora, North Dakota   **SEE CLIMATABLE NO. 126**

MAILING ADDRESS: Superintendent, Theodore Roosevelt National Park, Medora, North Dakota 58645 **Telephone:** 701-623-4466

DIRECTIONS: The North Unit is 15 miles (24 km) south of Watford City and 55 miles (88.5 km) north of Belfield, on Highway 85. A stop at the Ranger Station will help you plan and enjoy your visit. The South Unit Visitor Center is at Medora, 17 miles (27 km) west of Belfield and 63 miles (101 km) east of Glendive, off Highway I-94. A rough, poorly maintained dirt road of about 20 miles (32 km) leads from the South Unit to the site of Theodore Roosevelt's second ranch, the Elkhorn. Almost nothing of this ranch exists today. Inquiry should be made before attempting this trip.

The Park contains scenic badlands along the Little Missouri River, the cabin from Roosevelt's Maltese Cross Ranch, and the site of Roosevelt's Elkhorn Ranch, as well as bison and some of the original prairie.

VISITOR ACTIVITIES: interpretive exhibits, guided walks, campfire programs, auto tours, hiking, camping, snowmobiling, photography, backcountry, horseback riding, picnicking, bird-watching, float trips, cross-country skiing; **Permits:** For backcountry, free permits available at Visitor Center; **Fees:** Yes, entrance fee is $3, camping is $6, group camping is $1 per person (subject to change). Golden Eagle and Golden Age Passports accepted and available; **Visitor facilities:** Visitor Centers, museum slide program, movie, campgrounds, scenic overlooks, picnic areas, guided trail rides, hiking trails, restrooms, parking, snowmobiling routes; **Any limitations on vehicle usage:** Off-road and cross-country vehicular travel are prohibited; **Hiking trails:** Yes, information on the many trails is available at the Visitor Center; **Backcountry:** Yes, backcountry use is regulated; for a backcountry camping permit and further information, check at Visitor Center; **Camping:** Yes, no reservations available for individual campsites, but group camping requires a written reservation from the Park Superintendent. Other Federal and state-maintained campsites are nearby; **Other overnight accommodations on site:** No; **Meals served in the park:** No; **Food and supplies obtainable in the park:** No; **Food and supplies obtainable nearby:** Yes, near the South Unit, Medora, in summer; Belfield, year-round. Near the North Unit, Watford City, 15 miles (24 km) north of the park entrance; **Overnight accommodations:** Medora and Watford City; **First Aid available in**

park: Yes; **Nearest Hospital:** Watford City and Dickinson; **Days/Hours:** The Park is open all year. Peak season is from May through October; **Holiday Closings:** Visitor Center closed Thanksgiving, Dec. 25 & Jan. 1; **Visitor attractions closed for seasons:** Portions of the park road may be closed during the Winter months, depending on snow conditions; trail ride concession closed from late Sept. to early May. Painted Canyon Visitor Contact Center closed from October through April, North Unit Visitor Contact Center closed from Labor Day to Memorial Day, and most attractions in Medora also closed for the same period; **Weather:** Generally mild, warm to hot days, cool nights. Expect thunderstorms in Summer.

GENERAL INFORMATION: *WARNING: Wildlife is dangerous*—So keep your distance. *Drinking water* should be obtained from approved water sources. Most backcountry water is not fit for human use. The *weather* in the badlands is very harsh with extremes in temperature and sudden violent storms. Prepare yourself for a variety of conditions.

Visitors to the area should also see the Chateau de Mores State Historic Site, a 27-room chateau across the river from Medora. The chateau is open to visitors from May through early October.

No firewood available in campground and picnic area; gathering of wood is prohibited.

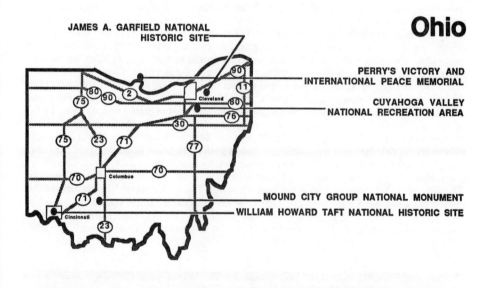

JAMES A. GARFIELD NATIONAL HISTORIC SITE

Ohio

PERRY'S VICTORY AND INTERNATIONAL PEACE MEMORIAL

CUYAHOGA VALLEY NATIONAL RECREATION AREA

MOUND CITY GROUP NATIONAL MONUMENT

WILLIAM HOWARD TAFT NATIONAL HISTORIC SITE

Cuyahoga Valley National Recreation Area
Brecksville, Ohio   **SEE CLIMATABLE NO. 127**

MAILING ADDRESS: Superintendent, Cuyahoga Valley National Recreation Area, 15610 Vaughn Road, Brecksville, Ohio 44141 **Telephone:** 216-650-4636

DIRECTIONS: Park Headquarters is at 15610 Vaughn Road Brecksville, Ohio, south of OH 82 on Riverview Road and east of OH 21 on Snowville Road. Happy Days Visitor Center (serving the south end of the park) is on OH 303 one mile west of OH 8 and two miles east of Peninsula. Canal Visitor Center (serving the north end of the park) is on Canal Road a mile south of Rockside Road in the Cleveland suburb of Valley View.

This recreation area links the urban centers of Cleveland and Akron and preserves the rural character of the Cuyahoga River Valley and the 150 year-old Ohio and Erie Canal system. Authorized for addition to the National Park System on Dec. 27, 1974.

VISITOR ACTIVITIES: hiking, biking, picnicking, auto tours, interpretive programs and exhibits, special events, environmental education, horseback riding, fishing, xc-skiing, ice skating, sledding, tobogganning, etc. Cooperating organizations within the park also provide: Blossom Music Center (summer home of the Cleveland Orchestra) - classical, pop, country and western concerts and ballet; Porthouse Theater (summer stock theater of Kent State University) - plays, musicals, operetta, both classical and popular/contemporary; Boston Mills Ski Resort - downhill skiing in winter/art classes and festivals in summer; Brandywine Ski Center and Dover Lake Park - downhill skiing in winter/camping, swimming, water slides in summer; Brandywine, Astorhust, Sleepy Hollow, and Shawnee Hills Golf Courses - golf; Cuyahoga Valley Line - historic steam train excursions through the park in summer (June-October) on weekends; Hale Farm and Village - historic village recreation with living history interpretation and traditional craft demonstrations of blacksmithing, glassblowing, pottery making, spinning and weaving, fireplace cooking, etc.; **Permits:** No; **Fees:** NPS facilities: $30.00 fee for reserving picnic shelters - No other NPS fee. Most Non-NPS facilities, Yes in varying amounts; **Visitor facilities:** trails, picnic areas, reservable picnic shelters, ponds, open playfields, warming shelters, contact stations, two visitor centers, scenic overlooks, restrooms, historic sites (Indians, Ohio and Erie Canal, Western Reserve settlement and life, etc.), cultural attractions (Blossom Music Center, Porthouse Theater, etc.), commercial downhill ski areas, commercial golf courses, Boy and Girl Scout camps, environmental education center, scenic roads, commercial camping and swimming area, commercial steam train excursion, sledding hills; **Any limitations on vehicle usage:** No; **Hiking trails:** Yes, there are many foot trails throughout the Park; **Backcountry:** No; **Camping:** commercial at Dover Lake Park; **Other overnight accommodations on site:** Stanford Farm Hostel operated by American Youth Hostels, Inc.; **Meals served in the park:** No; **Food and supplies obtainable in the park:** No; **Food and supplies obtainable nearby:** Yes, in any of the numerous communities surrounding the Park; **Overnight accommodations:** Motels on OH 8, in Brecksville on OH 21, and in Cleveland and Akron; **First Aid available in park:** Yes; **Nearest Hospital:** Cuyahoga Falls, OH, State Road, approx. 5 miles (8 km). Northern areas of the Park have some nearby hospitals in suburbs of Cleveland; **Days/Hours:** 7 days a week 8 a.m.-11 p.m., some areas closed at dusk; **Holiday Closings:** Thanksgiving, Christmas, and New Years Day for Visitor Centers; **Visitor attractions closed for seasons:** Blossom Music Center open in Summer only: Hale Farm and Village open May-Oct. and in Dec.; Porthouse Theatre open in summer only; Cuyahoga Valley Line runs June-Oct.; Golf course open summer only; ski areas (downhill) winter only.

James A. Garfield National Historic Site
Mentor, Ohio   **SEE CLIMATABLE NO. 127**

MAILING ADDRESS: Superintendent, James A. Garfield National Historic Site, Lawnfield, 8095 Mentor Avenue, Mentor, Ohio 44060

DIRECTIONS: This site preserves Lawnfield, home of 20th President James A. Garfield, in Mentor. This includes outbuildings; Carriage House, Pump House and Campaign Office. The Site, added to the National Park System on December 28, 1980, is operated by the Western Reserve Historical Society.

Mound City Group National Monument
Chillicothe, Ohio   **SEE CLIMATABLE NO. 123**

MAILING ADDRESS: Superintendent, Mound City Group National Monument, 16062 State Route 104, Chillicothe, Ohio 45601 **Telephone:** 614-774-1125

DIRECTIONS: Mound City is on the west bank of the Scioto River, on OH 104, 2 miles (3.2 km) north of the US 35 intersection and 3 miles (4.8 km) north of Chillicothe, OH.

Two thousand years ago (200 B.C.-500 A.D.), the Ohio River Valley was the focal point of the Hopewell Indian culture. The Hopewell Indians created some of the finest prehistoric art in North America, built vast geometrical earthworks and constructed burial mounds. The largest known concentration of these mounds is preserved at this Monument. The burial mounds yield copper breastplates, tools, obsidian blades, shells, ornaments of grizzly bear teeth and stone pipes carved as birds and animals. Authorized for addition to the National Park System on Mar. 2, 1923.

VISITOR ACTIVITIES: interpretive exhibits, walking, picnicking, organized groups may receive special services, advance arrangements should be made with the Superintendent; **Permits:** No; **Fees:** Yes, at entrance; **Visitor facilities:** Visitor Center, restrooms, picnic area, interpretive trails; **Any limitations on vehicle usage:** Vehicles are restricted to designated roadways; **Hiking trails:** Yes, self-guiding interpretive trail; **Backcountry:** No; **Camping:** No, camping is available in Chillicothe and in nearby state parks. Contact the Monument for further information; **Other overnight accommodations on site:** No; **Meals served in the park:** No; **Food and supplies obtainable in the park:** No; **Food and supplies obtainable nearby:** Yes, in Chillicothe; **Overnight accommodations:** Chillicothe, 3 miles (4.8 km) south on OH 104; **First Aid available in park:** Yes; **Nearest Hospital:** Medical Center Hospital, US 23, 6 miles (9.7 km) north; **Days/Hours:** From Labor Day until mid-June the Visitor Center is open from 8 a.m. to 5 p.m.; extended hours from mid-June to Labor Day. The Park is always open during daylight hours; **Holiday Closings:** Thanksgiving, Dec. 25 & Jan. 1. Handicap parking is available; most facilities are accessible to handicapped visitors.

GENERAL INFORMATION: *For Your Safety*—Watch for ground squirrel holes and uneven ground; be extra cautious along the Scioto River trail as it can be very slippery. Keep children under control near the water's edge. Southern Ohio is very rich in prehistoric Indian sites. Among those set aside as State memorials under the custody of the Ohio Historical Society are Fort Ancient, Fort Hill, Miamisburg Mound, Newark Earthworks, Seip Mound and Serpent Mound. You can see historical and archaeological exhibits in the Ross County Historical Society Museum in Chillicothe and at the Ohio Historical Center in Columbus.

The outdoor drama "Tecumseh!" depicts the story of the Shawnee leader. It is held at 8:00 p.m. on Monday through Saturday from mid-June through Labor Day at Sugarloaf Mountain Amphitheatre, which is 5 miles (8 km) from Chillicothe. For further information, write The Scioto Society, Inc., P.O. Box 73, Chillicothe, Ohio 45601. Call 614-775-0700 after Mar. 1.

TRAVEL ACCESS: Bus: Greyhound provides daily service to Chillicothe, Ohio (4 miles south); **Rail:** None.

NEARBY FACILITIES & POINTS OF INTEREST: Parks, other points of interest: Adena State Memorial; Several Ross County museums; Outdoor Drama-"Tecumseh!"; Four state parks nearby. Ross-Chillicothe Convention and Visitors Bureau provides information on entire area—write P.O. Box 73, Chillicothe, OH 45601 or phone (614) 775-4100.

North Country National Scenic Trail
For details see listing in New York

Perry's Victory and International Peace Memorial
Put-in-Bay, Ohio   **SEE CLIMATABLE NO. 128**

MAILING ADDRESS: Superintendent, Perry's Victory and International Peace Memorial, P.O. Box 549, Put-in-Bay, Ohio 43456 **Telephone:** 419-285-2184

DIRECTIONS: The Memorial is on South Bass Island in the village of Put-in-Bay. The island is about 4 miles (6.44 km) from Catawba, Ohio and 14 miles (22.5 km) from Port Clinton, Ohio. Ferry boats from both Catawba and Port Clinton to Put-in-Bay operate from mid-April to mid-Nov. Airplanes provide passenger service year-round.
    Commodore Oliver H. Perry won the greatest naval battle of the War of 1812 on Lake Erie. The Memorial (the World's most massive Doric Column) was constructed in 1912-15 "to inculcate the lessons of international peace by arbitration and disarmament." Established by Act of Congress on June 2, 1936.

VISITOR ACTIVITIES: A Visitor Center Information Station is near the entrance to the park. An elevator carries visitors to the top of the Memorial. Interpretive programs are presented several times each day during the Summer. Special arrangements may be made for interpretive talks at other times by writing or calling the Superintendent. Fishing is available; **Permits:** No; **Fees:** Elevator fee is $1.00 for persons over 12 years of age. No charge for educational or special groups upon request from administrative office. Golden Eagle and Golden Age Passports accepted; **Camping:** No, for further information on nearby camping facilities, contact South Bass Island State Park, Put-in-Bay, OH 43456, phone 419-285-2112; **Other overnight accommodations on site:** No; **Meals served in the park:** No; **Food and supplies obtainable in the park:** No; **Food and supplies obtainable nearby:** Yes, grocery store in village of Put-in-Bay or on mainland in Catawba or Port Clinton; **Overnight accommodations:** within several blocks of the Memorial. Reservations are advised, Contact the Put-in-Bay Chamber of Commerce for further information; **First Aid available in park:** Yes; **Nearest Hospital:** Port Clinton, OH 14 miles (22.5 km); **Days/Hours:** Mon.-Fri.: 10 a.m. to 5 p.m.; Sat. & Sun. upon request during early Spring and late Fall; 9:00 a.m. to 6:00 p.m., 7 days a week from June through Labor Day; **Holiday Closings:** None, during operating season; **Visitor attractions closed for seasons:** The Memorial is closed from the end of Oct. through mid-April.

TRAVEL ACCESS: Bus: No; **Air:** Island Airlines, 10 flights daily May 15-Labor Day 8:15 a.m.-7:30 p.m., more limited schedule during Fall, Winter and early Spring from Port Clinton, OH; **Other:** Miller Boat Line from Catawba, Ohio to island, 18 minute trip (Docks 2 miles from village of Put-in-Bay); Parker Boat Line from Port Clinton, Ohio to island, 1-1/2 hour trip (Docks downtown Village of Put-in-Bay); Bicycle rentals available near both boat lines; Golf cart rental near Miller Boat dock; Tour train near boat dock or downtown terminal.

NEARBY FACILITIES & POINTS OF INTEREST: Campgrounds: South Bass Island State Park, Put-in-Bay, Ohio, 419-285-2184, 125 Class B campsites; **Parks, other points of interest:** Winery, caves, gift shops; For a complete listing of facilities available write Put-in-Bay Chamber of Commerce, P.O. Box 76, Put-in-Bay, Ohio 43456.

William Howard Taft National Historic Site
Cincinnati, Ohio   **SEE CLIMATABLE NO. 122**

MAILING ADDRESS: Superintendent, William Howard Taft National Historic Site, 2038 Auburn Ave., Cincinnati, Ohio 45219 **Telephone:** 513-684-3262

DIRECTIONS: The Site is at 2038 Auburn Ave. near the intersection of Auburn and Dorchester Avenues.

This house was the birthplace and boyhood home of William Howard Taft, the only person to serve as President (1909-13) and Chief Justice of the United States (1921-30). Authorized for addition to the National Park System on Dec. 2, 1969.

VISITOR ACTIVITIES: Historic house undergoing restoration and refurnishing; expected to re-open, summer 1988; walking tours, interpretive exhibits, advance reservations are requested for groups of 25 or more; **Permits:** No; **Fees:** No; **Visitor facilities:** exhibits and walking tours; **Any limitations on vehicle usage:** On-street parking is available; **Meals served in the park:** No; **Food and supplies obtainable in the park:** No; **Food and supplies obtainable nearby:** Yes, within several blocks; **Overnight accommodations:** Cincinnati and vicinity; **First Aid available in park:** Yes; **Nearest Hospital:** The Christ Hospital, 2 blocks north of Site; **Days/Hours:** Open Monday through Friday from 8 a.m. to 4:30 p.m. Closed weekends. Expected to be open daily, 10 a.m. to 4 p.m., when restoration completed, mid-1988. **Holiday Closings:** Closed on all Federal holidays; **Visitor attractions closed for seasons:** None; **Weather:** Hot, humid Summers; cold, snowy or icy Winters; moderate Spring and Fall.

GENERAL INFORMATION: Visitors may also want to see the Taft Museum at 316 Pike Street in Cincinnati.

TRAVEL ACCESS: Bus: Queen City Metro; **Rail:** Amtrak to Cincinnati; **Air:** American, Delta, TWA, US Air, Conair, Piedmont, Republic.

Oklahoma

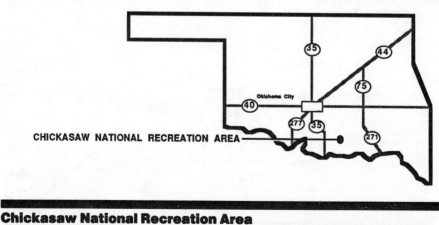

CHICKASAW NATIONAL RECREATION AREA

Chickasaw National Recreation Area
Sulphur, Oklahoma   **SEE CLIMATABLE NO. 129**

MAILING ADDRESS: Superintendent, Chickasaw National Recreation Area, P.O. Box 201, Sulphur, Oklahoma 73086 **Telephone:** 405-622-3161

DIRECTIONS: Chickasaw lies near Sulphur, Oklahoma on Routes US 177 & OK 7, accessible from Oklahoma City and Dallas-Fort Worth via Int. 35.

The man-made lake of the Arbuckles provides water recreation for extensive Midwest area, and numerous cold mineral and freshwater springs, including bromide waters, surface here. Established June 26, 1906.

VISITOR ACTIVITIES: interpretive exhibits, camping, picnicking, swimming, water skiing, fishing, boating, biking, walking, guided nature walks, hiking, hunting, campfire programs, and nature film; **Permits:** for camping—obtained from on duty Park Ranger; **Fees:** $5 nightly camping fee, Group camping $1 per person per night, minimum charge is $10 per night per site; **Visitor facilities:** campgrounds, picnic areas, beach, boat launches, trailer dump station, nature center; **Any limitations on vehicle usage:** Bicycles are not allowed on trails east of the Nature Center, and are not recommended on Bromide Hill trails; **Hiking trails:** Yes, self-guiding trails; **Backcountry:** No; **Camping:** Yes, reservations are not accepted for individual campsites, all are on a first come first serve basis. Reservations are accepted for group camping on a year round basis by calling 405-622-6121 or writing the Superintendent at the above address; **Other overnight accommodations on site:** No; **Meals served in the park:** No; **Food and supplies obtainable in the park:** No; **Food and supplies obtainable nearby:** Yes, in Sulphur; **Overnight accommodations:** Sulphur; **First Aid available in park:** Yes, West on State Highway 7; **Nearest Hospital:** Sulphur, 2 miles (3 km) west of the main entrance; **Days/Hours:** Park never closes; **Holiday Closings:** Travertine Nature Center closes on Christmas and New Years Day; **Weather:** Summers are hot and humid, with severe thunderstorms common in May and June. Tornadoes and thunderstorms are a threat in April through June. Temperatures above 37°C (100°F) occur and humidity frequently exceeds 50%. Winters are generally mild and rarely subject to prolonged freezing temperatures.

GENERAL INFORMATION: Be cautious of poisonous snakes and poison ivy.

TRAVEL ACCESS: Bus: Trailways provides daily service to Davis, OK, 10 miles from Park; **Rail:** No; **Air:** Nearest regular service is Oklahoma City, 92 miles from Parks.

NEARBY FACILITIES & POINTS OF INTEREST: Hotel/Motel: Chickasaw Motel, Sulphur, outside north entrance to Park, Super 8 Motel, West edge of Sulphur; **Campgrounds:** Murray State Park, 30 miles south and Turner Falls, 15 miles west.

Oregon

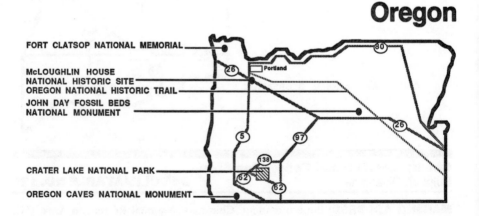

FORT CLATSOP NATIONAL MEMORIAL

McLOUGHLIN HOUSE
NATIONAL HISTORIC SITE
OREGON NATIONAL HISTORIC TRAIL
JOHN DAY FOSSIL BEDS
NATIONAL MONUMENT

CRATER LAKE NATIONAL PARK

OREGON CAVES NATIONAL MONUMENT

Crater Lake National Park
Crater Lake, Oregon   **SEE CLIMATABLE NO. 132**

MAILING ADDRESS: Superintendent, Crater Lake National Park, P.O. Box 7, Crater Lake, Oregon **Telephone:** 503-594-2211

DIRECTIONS: The south and west entrances on OR 62 are open all year. The north entrance off Hwy 138 and Rim Drive are open from mid-June to mid-October, weather permitting.

The Park's deep blue lake, formed by accumulated water from rain and snow, reaches 1,932 feet in depth. It lies in the heart of Mount Mazama, an ancient volcanic peak that collapsed centuries ago. Park established by act of Congress on May 22, 1902.

VISITOR ACTIVITIES: summer (mid-June through mid-Sept.) Ranger programs at Mazama Campground and in Rim Village, daily Ranger talks, interpretive walks, concession bus and boat tours around Crater Lake, wildlife-watching, auto tours, fishing, hiking, swimming, picnicking, and camping. Movie shown throughout the day at Headquarters upon request, snowmobile access to the Rim on the north side of the Park, cross-country skiing, snowshoeing, and other types of winter recreational activities; **Permits:** Backcountry permits obtained in Summer from Headquarters, Visitor Center or from a Park Ranger; in Winter, from Headquarters or a Park Ranger; **Fees:** $5 entrance fee; $6.50 camping fee. Fees are collected from mid-June through mid-Sept., or later if weather permits. Golden Eagle and Golden Age Passports accepted and available; **Visitor facilities:** picnic areas, restrooms, post office, are available throughout the summer. Campgrounds, lodging, food and tour services, curio shop, groceries, gasoline service- all from mid-June through mid-Sept. Hot meals and souvenirs at the cafeteria in rim Village during Winter. There are no overnight accommodations at Crater Lake during the winter months. Snowmobile and ski trails are available; **Any limitations on vehicle usage:** All vehicles are restricted to designated roadways; chains or snow tires may be required in Winter; **Hiking trails:** Yes, numerous scenic trails are described in the Park brochure available on request; **Backcountry:** Backcountry use permits are required for overnight stays in the backcountry. Yes, information can be obtained by writing Park Headquarters or stopping at any Visitor Information point in Summer; **Camping:** Yes, campsites are open from mid-June through Sept. No reservations accepted for campsites; **Other overnight accommodations on site:** Yes, reservations for Crater Lake Lodge, open during the Summer, can be made by contacting Crater Lake Lodge, Inc., Crater Lake, OR 97604, phone 503-594-2511; **Meals served in the park:** Yes, at Crater Lake Lodge and Rim Village cafeteria; **Food and supplies obtainable in the park:** Yes, some groceries available at Rim Village; **Food and supplies obtainable nearby:** Yes, at Fort Klamath, Union Creek; **Overnight accommodations:** Medford, 80 miles (128 km) from the west entrance on OR 62; of Klamath Falls, 54 miles (87 km) from the south entrance on OR 62 and US 97. Union Creek and Fort Klamath on OR 62; **First Aid available in park:** Yes, as well as ambulance service in Chiloquin, OR, OR 62; **Nearest Hospital:** Medford, OR 62, 80 miles (128 km); or Klamath Falls, OR 62 and 97, 54 miles (87 km); **Days/Hours:** 24 hours a day everyday in Summer. In Winter, the south and west road on OR 62 to Park Headquarters is open 24 hours. The road from Park Headquarters to Rim Village is open from 8 a.m to sunset; **Holiday Closings:** None; **Visitor attractions closed for seasons:** The north entrance road and Rim Drive are closed from approximately mid-Oct. to early July, depending on snow conditions. The Park averages 50 feet of snowfall annually. In Winter, overnight accommodations are available near the Park. Carry towrope, shovel, and tire chains, which may be necessary at any time.

GENERAL INFORMATION: *For Your Safety*—Stay on trails - especially along the caldera rim. Footing can be treacherous on this volcanic rock and soil. Descent to the lake is permitted only on the Cleetwood Trail.

Keep your distance from wildlife. Remember these animals are wild, and can be dangerous. Do *not* feed any wildlife.

Fort Clatsop National Memorial
Astoria, Oregon   **SEE CLIMATABLE NO. 131**

MAILING ADDRESS: Superintendent, Fort Clatsop National Memorial, Route 3, Box 604-FC, Astoria. Oregon 97103 **Telephone:** 503-861-2471

DIRECTIONS: The Visitor Center is 6 miles (10 km) southwest of Astoria on US 101.

The Lewis and Clark Expedition camped here in the winter of 1805-6. Authorized for addition to the National Park System on May 29, 1958.

VISITOR ACTIVITIES: interpretive exhibits, film and slide program, living history demonstrations in summer, walking, picnicking; **Permits:** No; **Fees:** April-September $1 ages 13-61, families $3 maximum, all others free; **Visitor facilities:** parking and restrooms at Visitor Center, picnic area; **Any limitations on vehicle usage:** No; **Hiking trails:** Yes, walking trails around the fort; **Backcountry:** No; **Camping:** No; **Other overnight accommodations on site:** No, camping facilities are at Fort Stevens State Park, 5 miles (8 km) away. Reserve space by writing to Fort Stevens State Park, Hammond, OR 97121; **Meals served in the park:** No; No food, bookstore in visitor center; **Food and supplies obtainable nearby:** Yes, at Astoria, Warrenton and Seaside; **Overnight accommodations:** Astoria, US 101, 6 miles (10 km); Seaside, US 101, 13 miles (21 km); **First Aid available in park:** Yes; **Nearest Hospital:** Astoria, US 101, 6 miles (10 km); **Days/Hours:** Open daily from 8 a.m. to 5 p.m.; until 6 p.m. in summer; **Holiday Closings:** Dec. 25; **Visitor attractions closed for seasons:** Living history program mid-June to Labor Day; **Weather:** There is frequent rainfall.

GENERAL INFORMATION: Be cautious when visiting the canoe landing, because the banks of the river and slough are often slippery and unstable. Within 25 miles (40 km) of Fort Clatsop are several sites described in the Lewis and Clark journals. These include the Salt Works at Seaside, the trail over Tillamook Head to Cannon Beach, and in the State of Washington, the camp and trail sites at McGowan, Cape Disappointment, and Long Beach.

John Day Fossil Beds National Monument
John Day, Oregon   **SEE CLIMATABLE NO. 133**

MAILING ADDRESS: Superintendent, John Day Fossil Beds National Monument, 420 West Main Street, John Day, Oregon 97845 **Telephone:** 503-575-0721

DIRECTIONS: The Monument Headquarters and one Visitor Center are in John Day. The Monument comprises three separate units: Sheep Rock Unit, 8 miles (13 km) north of Dayville; Painted Hills Unit, 10 miles (16 km) northwest of Mitchell; Clarno Unit, 20 miles (32 km) west of Fossil.

Plant and animal fossils show five epochs, from Eocene to the end of Pleistocene, at this site in north central Oregon. Authorized for addition to the National Park System on Oct. 26, 1974.

VISITOR ACTIVITIES: exhibits, interpretive talks, picnicking, wildlife- and wildflower-watching, hiking, fishing; **Permits:** No; **Fees:** No; **Visitor facilities:** Visitor Center, restrooms, picnic areas, hiking trails, drinking water; **Any limitations on vehicle usage:** Off road vehicles are prohibited; **Hiking trails:** Yes, three, (two self-guiding) at Painted Hills Unit; two, (one with exhibits) at Blue Basin in Sheep Rock Unit; two, (one self-guiding) at Clarno Unit; **Backcountry:** No; **Camping:** No; **Other overnight accommodations on site:** No, Federal and State-operated and private campgrounds are in the area. Camping information is posted in each unit; **Meals served in the park:** No; **Food and supplies obtainable in the park:** No; **Food and supplies obtainable nearby:** Yes, at John Day, Fossil, Dayville & Mitchell; **Overnight accommodations:** John Day, Hwy 26, US 395 intersection; Mount Vernon, also 26-395; Fossil, Hwy 218-19; Mitchell, Hwy 26-207; **First Aid available in park:** Yes, or at clinic in Fossil; **Nearest Hospital:** John Day, Madras, and Prineville; **Days/Hours:** You can visit the formations year-round. Headquarters in John Day are open weekdays all year; **Visitor attractions closed for seasons:** Visitor Center at Sheep Rock Unit is open from 9 a.m. to 6 p.m. from April 1 through October 30 and most weekdays November through March. **Weather:** Spring, wet and cool; Summer, dry and hot; Fall, warm and sunny.

GENERAL INFORMATION: *For Your Safety and protection of the fragile fossil resource—* Do not climb on the geologic formations. Be on the lookout for rattlesnakes. Beware of deer unexpectedly crossing roads at night.

TRAVEL ACCESS: Bus: Trailways provides daily service into Burns, Oregon; **Rail:** No; **Air:** Air Oregon, Republic provide daily service into Redmond, Oregon.

Lewis and Clark Trail
For details see listing in Illinois

McLoughlin House National Historic Site
Oregon City, Oregon   **SEE CLIMATABLE NO. 130**

MAILING ADDRESS: Superintendent, McLoughlin House National Historic Site, 713 Center Street, Oregon City, Oregon 97045 **Telephone:** 503-656-5146

DIRECTIONS: The McLoughlin House is in McLoughlin Park between 7th and 8th Streets, less than 4 blocks east of Pacific Hwy (US 99). Bus service is available from Portland, 13 miles (20 km) away.
 The house is one of the few remaining pioneer dwellings in the area once known as the "Oregon Country." Dr. John McLoughlin, often called the "Father of Oregon," who was prominent in the development of the Pacific Northwest as Superintendent of Fort Vancouver, built the house and lived here from 1846 to 1857. This affiliated area of the National Park System is owned and operated by the McLoughlin Memorial Association and was established by act of Congress in 1941.

VISITOR ACTIVITIES: guided house tours; **Permits:** No; **Fees:** Adults $2.50, Seniors $2, Students 6-17 $1, under 6 free if with parents—group rates for 12 or more; **Visitor facilities:** house tours; **Any limitations on vehicle usage:** No; **Meals served in the park:** No; **Food and supplies obtainable in the park:** No; **Food and supplies obtainable nearby:** Yes, at Oregon City; **Overnight accommodations:** Portland, I-5 and/or Pacific Hwy (99 E), 13 miles (20 km); Oregon City, McLoughlin Blvd., .6 mile (1 km); **First Aid available in park:** No; **Nearest Hospital:** Oregon City, Division Street, 2.5 miles (2.4 km); **Days/Hours:** The house is open every Sunday, 1 p.m. to 4 p.m. weekday hours

(Tuesday through Saturday) are 10 a.m. to 5 p.m. during Summer, 10 a.m. to 4 p.m. in winter. The Site is closed in January and holidays; **Weather:** The winters are fairly mild. The Summer hot 105°-107° (unusual) Rainy periods—Four seasons but usually not extreme.

GENERAL INFORMATION: The Park is more like the grounds of a private home 1/2 city block and no facilities. 7-11 store one block away, several small restaurants within a few blocks.

NEARBY FACILITIES & POINTS OF INTEREST: Hotel/Motel: International Dunes Edgewater, 1900 Clackwater Dr., 503-655-7141, 1 mile roughly (99E); Lewis Motel, 18710 S. Hwy. 99E, 503-656-7052 2 miles; Poolside Motel, 19224 McLoughlin Bus. (99E), 503-656-1955, 3 miles; **Parks, other points of interest:** Viewpoint falls of the Willamette River within walking distance Promenade along Cliff above original town. Clackamas County History Museum 2 blks away, open Thurs. and Sun. 1-4 p.m.; "End of the Oregon Trail" Interpretive Center 3 blocks from McLoughlin House, open: Wed.-Sat. 10-4 Sun. 1-4; Salmon Fishing seasonally in the Willamette River. Swimming in the Clackamas River where it runs into Willamette at Clackamette Park. Museum at Rose farm, built in 1847. The oldest American home in Oregon City and Oregon's first Territorial Governor was inaugurated on the balcony of the house in 1849.

Oregon Caves National Monument
Cave Junction, Oregon   **SEE CLIMATABLE NO. 134**

MAILING ADDRESS: Superintendent, Oregon Caves National Monument, 19000 Caves Highway, Cave Junction, Oregon 97523 **Telephone:** 503-592-2100

DIRECTIONS: The Monument is 20 miles (32 km) southeast of Cave Junction on Oregon 46, and can be reached by travelling either 50 miles (80 km) south of Grants Pass or 76 miles (122 km) north from Crescent City, on US 199. The last 8 miles (13 km) of Oregon 46 are quite narrow and winding. Information is available on OR 46 just as you exit OR 199.

Ground water dissolving marble bedrock formed these cave passages and intricate flowstone formations. Created by Presidential Proclamation on July 12, 1909.

VISITOR ACTIVITIES: cave tours, hiking, wildlife- and bird-watching, evening programs in summer; **Permits:** No; **Fees:** All visitors wishing to see the cave must do so on a guided tour provided by the Oregon Caves Company, a private concessioner, for a fee regulated by the U.S. Department of the Interior. Current fees are adults $5.25 children 6-11 $3. Daily tours are frequent and hours vary with season. Check for tour schedule at the time of your visit; **Visitor facilities:** parking, lodge, hiking trails, restrooms; **Any limitations on vehicle usage:** Towing trailers is not recommended due to narrow roads, infrequent turnarounds, and lack of parking space; **Hiking trails:** Yes, a maintained and marked system of trails provides access to the park for day hikers. Connecting trails lead into the adjacent Siskiyou National Forest. Snowshoes are usually required in Winter and Spring; check trail conditions with Park Rangers before setting out; **Backcountry:** No; **Camping:** No, but the U.S. Forest Service operates two campgrounds in the adjacent Siskiyou National Forest from approximately mid-June through the first week of Sept. Cave Creek campground is 4 miles (6.5 km) from the park on OR 46. No trailers are permitted. Grayback campground is 8 miles (13 km) down OR 46. Trailers are permitted in the campground. Although the campgrounds are rarely filled, campsites are assigned on a first-come, first-served basis. There are no showers and no utility connections. For further information, call 503-592-2166; **Other overnight accommodations on site:** Yes, the Oregon Caves company operates a lodge from approximately mid-June to the first week in Sept. For reservations and information, write to Oregon Caves Co., Oregon Caves, OR 97523, Telephone 503-592-3400; **Meals served in the park:** Yes, at the Chateau; **Food and supplies obtainable in the park:** No; **Food and supplies obtainable nearby:** Yes, at Cave Junction, 20 miles (32 km); **Overnight accommodations:** Motel on OR 46, about 12 miles (19.3 km) from the park. Several motels available on OR 199 in and around Cave Junction; **First Aid available in park:** Yes, there is also a doctor and clinic in Cave Junction, OR 46; **Nearest Hospital:** Grants Pass, 50 miles (80 km); **Holiday Closings:** Dec. 25; **Visitor attractions closed for seasons:** Campfire and interpretive programs during the Summer season only, excluding cave tours.

GENERAL INFORMATION: Because parking is quite limited, you should arrive at the park during the morning hours if you visit the park in Summer. Parking for trailers is extremely limited. If you are hiking, stay on the marked trails. *For Your Safety*—wear proper clothing, including a jacket and walking shoes. The cave temperature varies from 3° to 7°C (38 to 45°F). Cave passageways may be slippery. The cave tour is not recommended for anyone with heart, breathing, or walking difficulty. Stay with your guide. There is an emergency exit one-third of the way through the cave for those who do not wish to continue the tour. Do not touch any of the cave walls or formations. Canes, crutches, tripods, and sticks are not permitted within the cave. Children under 6 are not allowed in the cave. A childcare service is available at the concession for $3.

Oregon National Scenic Trail
For details see listing in Missouri

Pennsylvania

JOHNSTOWN FLOOD NATIONAL MEMORIAL
ALLEGHENY PORTAGE RAILROAD NATIONAL HISTORIC SITE
APPALACHIAN NATIONAL SCENIC TRAIL
DELAWARE WATER GAP NATIONAL RECREATION AREA
MIDDLE DELAWARE NATIONAL SCENIC RIVER
INDEPENDENCE NATIONAL HISTORICAL PARK
THADDEUS KOSCIUSZKO NATIONAL MEMORIAL
BENJAMIN FRANKLIN NATIONAL MEMORIAL
EDGAR ALLAN POE NATIONAL HISTORIC SITE
GLORIA DEI CHURCH NATIONAL HISTORIC SITE
VALLEY FORGE NATIONAL HISTORICAL PARK
HOPEWELL VILLAGE NATIONAL HISTORIC SITE
GETTYSBURG NATIONAL MILITARY PARK
EISENHOWER NATIONAL HISTORIC SITE

FRIENDSHIP HILL NATIONAL HISTORIC SITE
FORT NECESSITY NATIONAL BATTLEFIELD

Allegheny Portage Railroad National Historic Site
Cresson, Pennsylvania   **SEE CLIMATABLE NO. 135**

MAILING ADDRESS: Superintendent, Allegheny Portage Railroad National Historic Site, P.O. Box 247, Cresson, Pennsylvania 16630 **Telephone:** 814-886-8176

DIRECTIONS: The Site is on Old Route 22 off the Summit Exit of present Rt 22 between Duncansville and Cresson, PA. The Visitor Center is at Lemon House, built in 1931-32 near the summit of Allegheny Mountain as a rest stop and tavern.

The Site preserves structures and tracks of the 36-mile incline railroad built between 1831-34 to carry passengers and freight over the Allegheny Mountains between canal basins at Hollidaysburg and Johnstown. Established by act of Congress on August 31, 1964.

VISITOR ACTIVITIES: interpretive talks and costumed demonstrations near Visitor Center, interpretive exhibits and trails, hiking, picnicking; **Permits:** No; **Fees:** No; **Visitor facilities:** Visitor Center with restrooms, walking trails through quiet spots with benches, picnic facilities including water, tables, restrooms and grills; **Any limitations on vehicle usage:** Vehicles are restricted to the parking lot of the Visitor Center, park roads, and parking lot of the picnic areas; **Hiking trails:** Yes, dirt trails through site; **Backcountry:** No; **Camping:** No; **Other overnight accommodations on site:** No; **Meals served in the park:** No; **Food and supplies obtainable in the park:** No; **Food and supplies obtainable nearby:** Yes, in Cresson and Duncansville; **Overnight accommodations:** Altoona, US 220, 10 miles (16 km); Ebensburg, US 22, 10 miles (16 km); **First Aid available in park:** Yes, or nearby in Cresson and Duncansville, US 22; **Nearest Hospital:** Altoona, US 220, 10 miles (16 km); **Days/Hours:** Open 8:30 a.m. to 5 p.m. in Summer; **Holiday Closings:** Thanksgiving, Dec. 25 & Jan. 1; **Visitor attractions closed for seasons:** No tours or demonstrations in Winter; **Weather:** Warm days and cool nights in Summer; cold, windy and snowy in Winter.

GENERAL INFORMATION: Visitors to the area can also see the nearby Johnstown Flood National Memorial (see listing in this book), located along US 219 and PA 869 near St. Michael, PA.

TRAVEL ACCESS: Bus: Greyhound Bus stops at Cresson, Pa. twice daily; once in the morning; once in afternoon; **Rail:** Amtrak daily service to Altoona, Pa.; **Air:** Allegheny Airlines daily service to Martinsburg, Pa.; **Other:** Rental Car available in Altoona and at airport in Martinsburg; Park accessible by bicycle; however, it is atop Allegheny Mountain 2,290 feet.

NEARBY FACILITIES & POINTS OF INTEREST: Hotel/Motel: Lodging in nearby Altoona, 12 miles east and Ebensburg, 10 miles west; **Campgrounds:** Prince Gallitizin State Park (30 miles), Blue Knob State Park (20 miles), Lakemont Campground (14 miles) (814) 946-3330, Laurelwood (3 miles west), Woodland Park (12 miles west); **Reservation systems in use for campsites, other facilities:** State Parks do not accept reservations; first come, first served.

Appalachian National Scenic Trail
For details see listing in Maine

Benjamin Franklin National Memorial
Philadelphia, Pennsylvania   **SEE CLIMATABLE NO. 138**

MAILING ADDRESS: Public Relations Coordinator, Benjamin Franklin National Memorial, 20th Street & Benjamin Franklin Parkway, Philadelphia, Pennsylvania 19103 **Telephone:** 215-448-1200

DIRECTIONS: The Memorial is in the Franklin Institute Science Museum at 20th Street and Benjamin Franklin Parkway in Philadelphia.
James Earle Fraser's monumental statue of Franklin honors the inventor-statesman. This affiliated area of the National Park System, owned and administered by The Franklin Institute, was designated on Oct. 25, 1972.

VISITOR ACTIVITIES: exhibits of Franklin artifacts; **Permits:** No; **Fees:** admission to the Memorial is free. There is a separate admission fee for the adjacent Science Museum; **Visitor facilities:** parking, restrooms, snack bar in Science Museum; **Any limitations on vehicle usage:** No; **Hiking trails:** No; **Backcountry:** No; **Camping:** No; **Other overnight accommodations on site:** No; **Meals served in the park:** No, but available at snack bar in the Science Museum; **Food and supplies obtainable in the park:** No; **Food and supplies obtainable nearby:** Yes, in Philadelphia; **Overnight accommodations:** within walking distance in Philadelphia; **First Aid available in park:** No, but through local hospitals and doctors in Philadelphia area; **Nearest Hospital:** Hannemann Hospital, 314 North Broad St., about 3 blocks from the Memorial; **Days/Hours:** Open 10 a.m. to 5 p.m. Mon.-Sat.; 12 noon to 5 p.m. on Sunday; **Holiday Closings:** Dec. 24 and 25, Jan. 1, July 4, Thanksgiving.

Delaware Water Gap National Recreation Area
Bushkill, Pennsylvania also in New Jersey   **SEE CLIMATABLE NO. 137**

MAILING ADDRESS: Superintendent, Delaware Water Gap National Recreation Area, Bushkill, Pennsylvania 18324 **Telephone:** 717-588-6637

DIRECTIONS: The Area extends from the Delaware Water Gap for 35 miles (56 km) to Milford, PA. Int. 80 crosses the Gap. On the Pennsylvania side follow US 209. The best place to begin your visit is at the Kittatinny Point Visitor Center, open year-round, located on Int. 80 in NJ. Dingmans Falls Visitor Center, open May through Oct., is off U.S. 209, in PA.
This scenic area preserves relatively unspoiled land on both the New Jersey and Pennsylvania sides of the Delaware River. Authorized for addition to the National Park System on Sept. 1, 1965.

VISITOR ACTIVITIES: fishing, swimming, canoeing, hiking, hunting, auto tours, cross country skiing, ice fishing, snowmobiling, picnicking, craft demonstrations, conducted walks, interpretive exhibits, wildlife-watching, rock climbing; **Permits:** State licenses are required for hunting & fishing. Obtain them at nearby sporting goods stores. License fees vary in length of validity & cost; **Fees:** No; **Visitor facilities:** Parking and restrooms at Visitor Center, picnic areas, interpretive and hiking trails, launching ramps, environmental study areas, canoe rentals outside of the Park, lifeguarded swimming areas; **Any limitations on vehicle usage:** No; **Hiking trails:** Yes, approx. 26 miles (42 km) of the Appalachian Trail run through the area. Shorter nature trails are available. Check at the Visitor Center or write the Superintendent for further information;

Backcountry: Yes, information is available from the Visitor Center or the Superintendent; **Camping:** canoe camping in designated areas, two group campgrounds and one concession-operated family campground; **Other overnight accommodations on site:** No; **Meals served in the park:** No; **Food and supplies obtainable in the park:** No; **Food and supplies obtainable nearby:** Yes, Bushkill, Stroudsburg, Milford, Portland, and Delaware Water Gap, PA; Newton, Blairstown, and Branchville, NJ, Port Jervis, NY; **Overnight accommodations:** Bushkill, Stroudsburg, Milford, Portland, and Delaware Water Gap, PA; Newton, Blairstown, and Branchville, NJ, Port Jervis, NY; **First Aid available in park:** Yes; **Nearest Hospital:** East Stroudsburg, PA, Int. 80; Newton, NJ, NJ 206; Port Jervis, NY, US 209; **Days/Hours:** The Park is always open. Kittatinny Point Visitor Center is open daily from 9:00 a.m. to 5:00 p.m. April thru October, and 9:00 a.m. to 4:30 p.m. Friday thru Sunday November thru March; **Holiday Closings:** Dec. 25 and Jan. 1; **Visitor attractions closed for seasons:** Some facilities are closed during Winter, but the Park remains open for x-c skiing, ice fishing, and snowmobiling in designated areas. A park newspaper, available on request, is published three times a year and lists current activities.

GENERAL INFORMATION: Swim only at designated beaches. Climbers must register before climb and check out after completing with the Kittatinny Point Visitor Center.

TRAVEL ACCESS: Bus: Martz Trailways provides daily service to Stroudsburg which stops in the Park, Greyhound services the Stroudsburg Terminal.

Edgar Allan Poe National Historic Site
Philadelphia, Pennsylvania   **SEE CLIMATABLE NO. 138**

MAILING ADDRESS: Superintendent, Independence National Historical Park, 313 Walnut Street, Philadelphia, Pennsylvania 19123 **Telephone:** 215-597-8780

DIRECTIONS: The Site is located at 7th and Spring Garden Streets, Philadelphia, Pa. 19123.

Edgar Allan Poe, poet, writer, editor and critic lived with his wife and mother-in-law in this small brick house in the 1840s. Authorized for addition to the National Park System on Nov. 10, 1978.

VISITOR ACTIVITIES: Interpretive exhibits, school sessions, special events, children's programs, house tours and audiovisual programs; **Permits:** No; **Fees:** No; **Visitor facilities:** rest rooms; **Any limitations on vehicle usage:** No; **Meals served in the park:** No; **Food and supplies obtainable in the park:** No; **Food and supplies obtainable nearby:** Yes, in Philadelphia; **Overnight accommodations:** Philadelphia; **First Aid available in park:** No; **Nearest Hospital:** Philadelphia, within 4 blocks; **Days/Hours:** open daily from 9 a.m. to 5 p.m.; **Holiday Closings:** Dec. 25 & Jan. 1; **Visitor attractions closed for seasons:** None; **Weather:** Summers are hot and humid; some snow and sleet in winter.

TRAVEL ACCESS: Bus: Greyhound and Trailways provide regular service within 8 Blocks of Park; **Rail:** Amtrak serves Philadelphia; **Air:** Major Airlines service Philadelphia International Airport about 5 miles from Park.

Eisenhower National Historic Site
Gettysburg, Pennsylvania   **SEE CLIMATABLE NO. 139**

MAILING ADDRESS: Superintendent, Eisenhower National Historic Site, Gettysburg, Pennsylvania 17325 **Telephone:** 717-334-1124

DIRECTIONS: This was the home and farm of President and Mrs. Dwight D. Eisenhower. Designated Nov. 27, 1967. Opened to the public June, 1980. You should begin your tour at the Eisenhower Tour Information Center, in the lower end of the Gettysburg National Military Park Visitor Center, located on PA 134 (Taneytown Road) near its intersection with Business US 15 (Emmitsburg Road).

VISITOR ACTIVITIES: self-guided tours of house and grounds, ranger conducted programs; **Permits:** No; **Fees:** Yes, for shuttle bus transportation to the farm and entrance fee, $2.25 for adults and $.70 for children 6 to 12. Fees subject to change; **Visitor facilities:** Visitors Center, limited restroom facilities; **Any limitations on vehicle usage:** All visits to the farm are via shuttle bus from the Tour Information Center. No private vehicle access except to handicapped parking area; **Hiking trails:** No; **Backcountry:** No; **Camping:** No; **Other overnight accommodations on site:** No; **Meals served in the park:** No, in the town of Gettysburg; **Food and supplies obtainable in the park:** No; **Food and supplies obtainable nearby:** Yes, in Gettysburg, 1 mile (1.6 km); **Overnight accommodations:** numerous motels are adjacent to the Park; **First Aid available in park:** Yes; **Nearest Hospital:** Gettysburg, 1/2 mile (.8 km) from Tour Information Center, 2 miles (3.2 km) from farm; **Days/Hours:** Open daily April-Oct., Weds.-Sun. Nov.-April; First and last shuttle bus runs 9:00 a.m. and 4:00 p.m.; **Visitor attractions closed for seasons:** Park may be closed in January; **Holiday Closings:** Thanksgiving, Dec. 25, Jan. 1; **Weather:** Summers are hot, 60°-90°F, Winters are cold, 10°-50°F.

Fort Necessity National Battlefield
Farmington, Pennsylvania   **SEE CLIMATABLE NO. 136**

MAILING ADDRESS: Superintendent, Fort Necessity National Battlefield, The National Pike, RD 2-Box 528, Farmington, Pennsylvania 15437 **Telephone:** 412-329-5512

DIRECTIONS: The Battlefield is 11 miles east of Uniontown on US 40.
    Colonial troops commanded by Lt. Col George Washington, then 22 years old, were defeated here in the opening battle of the French and Indian War on July 3, 1754. The Park also includes Jumonville Glen, site of the first skirmish of the French and Indian War, Braddock's grave, and Mount Washington Tavern, an early 19th-century stage coach inn. Established by act of Congress on Mar. 4, 1931.

VISITOR ACTIVITIES: interpretive exhibits and slide presentation, hiking, cross-country skiing, picnicking; **Permits:** No; **Fees:** $1 per person over 12 and under 62, $3 maximum per family; **Visitor facilities:** parking, restrooms, picnic area (all wheelchair accessible); **Any limitations on vehicle usage:** Established roadway and parking lots only; **Hiking trails:** Yes, trails lead through the forest and meadow around the Battlefield; **Backcountry:** No; **Camping:** Primitive group campground available with prior reservation; short service project required; **Other overnight accommodations on site:** No, private and public campgrounds are located nearby; **Meals served in the park:** No; **Food and supplies obtainable in the park:** No; **Food and supplies obtainable nearby:** Yes, at Uniontown; **Overnight accommodations:** Uniontown, PA 40, (11 miles) west of the park; **First Aid available in park:** Yes; **Nearest Hospital:** Uniontown, PA, US 40, (11 miles) west of the Park; **Days/Hours:** Fort area and Braddock's Grave open daylight hours year around; Visitor Center core hours daily 10:30 a.m. to 5:00 p.m. year around; Tavern core hours daily 10:30 a.m. to 5:00 p.m. from mid-March through late October, weekends only other times; **Holiday Closings:** Thanksgiving, Dec. 25 & Jan. 1; **Visitor attractions closed for seasons:** Picnic area & Jumorville Glen Unit closed from Nov. 1-April 15.

Friendship Hill National Historic Site
Point Marion, Pennsylvania   **SEE CLIMATABLE NO. 136**

MAILING ADDRESS: c/o Fort Necessity National Battlefield, The National Pike, RD2, Box 528, Farmington, Pennsylvania 15437 **Telephone:** 412-329-5512 Park Office 412-725-9190

DIRECTIONS: 3 miles north of Point Marion along state route 166. Open to public on limited basis.
      Albert Gallatin (1761-1849), a Swiss immigrant prominent in American affairs throughout the nation's first seven decades, lived in this stone and brick house, built on a bluff above the Monongahela River. Authorized for addition to the National Park System on November 10, 1978.

VISITOR ACTIVITIES: Guided tours of unrestored Gallatin House, self guided tour of house grounds, interim contact station with display, slide program & ENP & MA sales outlet, hiking, cross-country skiing on 5 miles of foot trail, limited picnic facilities, fishing in the Monongahela River, state license required. Trail guide available, FestiFall, held annually on first Sunday in October. **Permits:** No; **Fees:** No; **Visitor facilities:** interim facilities only, contact station & chemical toilets accessible; **Any limitations on vehicle usage:** established roadway and parking lots only; **Hiking trails:** 5 miles of trails pass through woods and fields and along the Monongahela; **Backcountry:** No; **Camping:** No; **Meals served in the park:** No; **Food and supplies obtainable in the park:** No; **Food and supplies obtainable nearby:** Point Marion 3 miles south; **First Aid available in park:** Yes; **Nearest Hospital:** Morgantown, WV 12 miles south of park; **Days/Hours:** Memorial Day to Labor Day—7 days/week, 9:30 a.m. to 5:00 p.m. Labor Day to following Memorial Day—Sat. & Sun. only 9:30 a.m. to 5:00 p.m.; **Holiday Closings:** Weekends only (Fall, Winter and Spring); **Visitor attractions closed for seasons:** All or parts of Gallatin House may be closed due to restoration activities.

Gettysburg National Military Park
Gettysburg, Pennsylvania   **SEE CLIMATABLE NO. 139**

MAILING ADDRESS: Superintendent, Gettysburg National Military Park, Gettysburg, Pennsylvania 17325 **Telephone:** 717-334-1124

DIRECTIONS: You should start your tour of Gettysburg at the Visitor Center, which is located on PA 134 (Taneytown Road) near its intersection with US 15 (Emmitsburg Road).
      The decisive Civil War battle fought here July 1-3, 1863 repulsed the second Confederate invasion of the North. Gettysburg National Cemetery adjoins the Park. President Lincoln delivered his Gettysburg Address here in dedicating the cemetery on Nov. 19, 1863. The Park was established by act of Congress Feb. 11, 1895.

VISITOR ACTIVITIES: auto tours, ranger-conducted walks and talks, living history and campfire programs, hiking, biking, jogging, cross-country skiing, picnicking, Gettysburg Address is on loan from the Library of Congress and displayed during the summer months; **Permits:** No; **Fees:** Yes, for special programs, Electric map is $2.00 adults, children under 16 free. Senior Citizens (over 62) $1.50. Cyclorama is $1.00 for those 16 and older. Battlefield guide, $14 for a 2-hour tour per car; recreational vehicles, higher; **Visitor facilities:** Visitor Centers, restrooms, licensed battlefield guides; **Any limitations on vehicle usage:** Park only in designated areas or on the avenues but not on the grass; **Hiking trails:** Yes, trails vary in length and difficulty; **Backcountry:** No, an information brochure on the trails is available by mail or at the Visitor Center; **Camping:** Yes, but only for organized youth groups, Group sites available from mid-Apr. to mid-Oct. (no charge). Groups may wish to make advance reservations for bus tours with a licensed battlefield guide included ($25). Inquiry for both services should be made to the Park at the above address; **Other overnight accommodations on site:** No; **Meals served in the park:** No, in the town of Gettysburg; **Food and supplies obtainable in the park:** No; **Food and supplies obtainable nearby:** Yes, in Gettysburg, 1 mile (1.6 km); **Overnight accommodations:** Numerous motels are adjacent to the Park; **First Aid available in park:** Yes; **Nearest Hospital:** Gettysburg, 1/2 mile (.8 km) from the Visitor Center; **Days/Hours:** Cyclorama Center open 9:00 a.m. to 5 p.m.; Visitor Center 8:00 a.m. to 6 p.m. from mid-June to Labor Day; 8 a.m. to 5 p.m. the rest of the year; **Holiday Closings:** Visitor Center and Cyclorama closed Thanksgiving, Dec. 25 & Jan. 1; **Weather:** Summers are hot, 60°-90°F; Winters are cold, 10°-50°F.

GENERAL INFORMATION: *For Your Safety*—Do not climb on cannons and monuments. Running and climbing youngsters frequently fall and injure themselves, so parents are urged to closely supervise their children. Please use extreme caution driving the Park roads, especially when they intersect with heavily travelled highways. Bicycle riders are here in ever-increasing numbers; be cautious on blind curves and on one-way roads. Bikers should keep to the right with the flow of auto traffic.

Gloria Dei (Old Swedes') Church National Historic Site
Philadelphia, Pennsylvania   **SEE CLIMATABLE NO. 138**

MAILING ADDRESS: Superintendent, Gloria Dei Church National Historic Site, Delaware Ave. and Christian St., Philadelphia, Pennsylvania 19147 **Telephone:** 215-389-1513

DIRECTIONS: Located on the Delaware River, on Delaware Avenue between Christian Street and Washington Avenue; the site is north of the Walt Whitman Bridge and south of the Ben Franklin Bridge, and is next to I-95 on the Delaware River (east) side of I-95.
     This fine example of early Swedish religious architecture was erected about 1700 by a Swedish Lutheran congregation which was founded in 1677 and in 1845 became part of the Episcopal Church. This affiliated area of the National Park System was designated on Nov. 17, 1942. Church site owned and administered by Corporation of Gloria Dei (Old Swedes') Church.

VISITOR ACTIVITIES: The church and grounds are open to the public; arrangements should be made in advance if a guided tour for a group is desired; **Permits:** No; **Fees:** No; **Visitor facilities:** restrooms, church and grounds; **Any limitations on vehicle usage:** Vehicles not permitted on the church grounds; **Hiking trails:** No; **Backcountry:** No; **Camping:** No; **Other overnight accommodations on site:** No; **Meals served in the park:** No; **Food and supplies obtainable in the park:** No; **Food and supplies obtainable nearby:** Yes, in Philadelphia; **Overnight accommodations:** Philadelphia, 2 miles (3 km); **First Aid available in park:** No; **Nearest Hospital:** Philadelphia, 1-1/2 miles (2.4 km); **Days/Hours:** Open daily from 9 a.m. to 5 p.m.; **Holiday Closings:** No; **Visitor attractions closed for seasons:** No.

Hopewell Furnace National Historic Site
Elverson, Pennsylvania   **SEE CLIMATABLE NO. 140**

MAILING ADDRESS: Superintendent, Hopewell Furnace National Historic Site, R.D. 1, Box 345, Elverson, Pennsylvania 19520 **Telephone:** 215-582-8773

DIRECTIONS: The Site is 5 miles (9.7 km) south of Birdsboro on PA 345. It is 10 miles (16 km) from the Morgantown interchange on the PA Turnpike, via PA 23 East, and 345 North.

This is the finest example of a rural American 19th-century ironmaking community restored to the 1820-1840 period. The buildings include the blast furnace and its auxiliary structures. Designated Aug. 3, 1938.

VISITOR ACTIVITIES: interpretive programs and exhibits at Visitor Center, living history programs in Summer, hiking, self-guiding walking tours; **Permits:** No; **Fees:** Yes, $1.00/person, maximum of $3.00/family, 12 and under, 62 and over are free; **Visitor facilities:** parking and restrooms at Visitor Center, National Environmental Study Area; **Any limitations on vehicle usage:** No; **Hiking trails:** Yes, a nature trail, and a number of other trails through the park; **Backcountry:** No; **Camping:** No; **Other overnight accommodations on site:** No, swimming, picnicking, and unreserved camping facilities are available in the adjacent French Creek State Park; **Meals served in the park:** No; **Food and supplies obtainable in the park:** No; **Food and supplies obtainable nearby:** Yes, 5 miles away in Birdsboro and Elverson; **Overnight accommodations:** Morgantown, PA Turnpike, 10 miles (16 km); Pottstown, Rte 100, then 724 or 422, 13 miles (21 km); Reading, Rte 422, 15 miles (24 km); **First Aid available in park:** Yes, or at Birdsboro, PA 345 North; **Nearest Hospital:** Reading, 15 miles (24 km); **Days/Hours:** Open daily from 9 a.m. to 5 p.m.; Summer hours 9 a.m. to 6 p.m., mid June through Labor Day; **Holiday Closings:** Dec. 25 and Jan. 1; **Visitor attractions closed for seasons:** No; **Weather:** Hot, humid Summers and cold, icy Winters. Moderate Spring and Fall.

GENERAL INFORMATION: *For Your Safety*—Stay on established tour routes and do not climb on the unstable anthracite furnace ruins, fences, and other historic structures. The sharp slag can cause severe, jagged cuts. Do not enter fenced areas or feed or handle livestock. Those allergic to bee and wasp stings should be especially cautious.

Independence National Historical Park
Philadelphia, Pennsylvania   **SEE CLIMATABLE NO. 138**

MAILING ADDRESS: Superintendent, Independence National Historical Park, 313 Walnut Street, Philadelphia, Pennsylvania 19106 **Telephone:** Recorded information—215-627-1776 Visitor Center—215-597-8974 Telecommunications Device for the Deaf (TDD) (215) 597-8974.

DIRECTIONS: The best place to begin your visit is at the Visitor Center, located at Third and Chestnut Streets. The Park includes structures and properties in old Philadelphia associated with the American Revolution and the founding and growth of the United States, including: Independence Hall, the Second Bank of the United States, Franklin Court, the Liberty Bell Pavilion and many other sites. Authorized for addition to the National Park System on June 28, 1948.

The Deshler-Morris House, a unit of Independence National Historical Park, is located at 5442 Germantown Avenue, Philadelphia, PA. It is about 7 miles (11 km) from Independence National Historical Park. The site can be reached either by automobile (metered parking) or by public transportation. Trolley No. 23 from the center city or from the Park.

VISITOR ACTIVITIES: talks and tours in historic buildings, self-guiding outdoor walking tours; **Permits:** No; **Fees:** No; **Visitor facilities:** Visitor Center, audiovisual exhibits, films, interpretive displays, post office, various tours; **Any limitations on vehicle usage:** Avoid driving in downtown Philadelphia. Try to walk or use public transportation; **Hiking trails:** No; **Meals served in the park:** Yes, at City Tavern, 2nd and

Walnut (concessioner); **Food and supplies obtainable in the park:** No; **Food and supplies obtainable nearby:** Yes, in Philadelphia; **Overnight accommodations:** Philadelphia; **First Aid available in the park:** Yes; **Nearest Hospital:** within 4 blocks; **Days/ Hours:** Open 7 days a week, 9 a.m. to 5 p.m., with extended hours in Summer. Call the Park for detailed information on hours of various sites; **Holiday Closings:** All buildings except Independence Hall and the Liberty Bell Pavilion are closed on Dec. 25 & Jan. 1; **Visitor attractions closed for seasons:** None; **Weather:** Summers are hot and humid; some snow and sleet in Winter.

GENERAL INFORMATION: The 18th-century brick sidewalks are sometimes rough and uneven. Walk with caution. Try to avoid the midday crowds in Summer by arriving between 9 and 10 a.m. or after 2 p.m. Thursday and Friday in the Spring are also particularly busy because of school visitation.

TRAVEL ACCESS: Bus: Greyhound and Trailways provide service within 8 blocks of Park; **Rail:** Amtrak provides regular service to Philadelphia—24 blocks from Park; **Air:** Major Airlines provide service to Philadelphia International Airport; **Other:** Airport rail line stops at Market East station, 5 blocks from the Park. Philadelphia mass transit system (SEPTA) also provides access through buses, subway trains and trolleys. New Municipal Parking Garage on 2nd Street between Chestnut and Walnut.
NEW INFORMATION: New Municipal Parking Garage on 2nd Street between Chestnut and Walnut.

Johnstown Flood National Memorial
St. Michael, Pennsylvania   **SEE CLIMATABLE NO. 135**

MAILING ADDRESS: Superintendent, Johnstown Flood National Memorial, c/o Allegheny Portage National Historic Site, P.O. Box 247, Cresson, Pennsylvania 16630 **Telephone:** 814-886-8176

DIRECTIONS: The area is located along US 219 and PA 869 at the South Fork Dam Site, 10 miles (16 km) northeast of Johnstown near St. Michael, PA.
　　Remnants of the earthen South Fork Dam on the Little Conemaugh River, which burst on May 31, 1889, causing the devastating flood of Johnstown and nearby communities, are preserved here. Authorized for addition to the National Park System on Aug. 31, 1964.

VISITOR ACTIVITIES: picnicking, hiking, interpretive exhibits at Visitor Center; **Permits:** No; **Fees:** No; **Visitor facilities:** picnic area, interpretive trails, comfort stations, small Visitor Center at the dam site; **Any limitations on vehicle usage:** No; **Hiking trails:** Yes; **Backcountry:** No; **Camping:** No; **Other overnight accommodations on site:** No; **Meals served in the park:** No; **Food and supplies obtainable in the park:** No; **Food and supplies obtainable nearby:** Yes, at St. Michael (limited), Johnstown; **Overnight accommodations:** Johnstown US 219 & PA 56 10 miles (16 km); **First Aid available in park:** Yes, or nearby in St. Michael, Sidman PA 869; **Nearest Hospital:** Johnstown, US 219 and PA 56, 10 miles (16 km); **Days/Hours:** Open 8:30 a.m. to 5:00 p.m.; **Holiday Closings:** Thanksgiving, Dec. 25 & Jan. 1; **Visitor attractions closed for seasons:** None; **Weather:** Warm days and cool nights in Summer; cold, windy Winter with snow.

GENERAL INFORMATION: A short distance from the remains of the South Fork Dam is the Allegheny Portage Railroad National Historic Site.

TRAVEL ACCESS: Bus: Greyhound Bus, provides daily service to Johnstown, Pa.;

Rail: Amtrak provides daily service to Johnstown, Pa.; **Air:** Allegheny Airlines provides daily service to Johnstown, Pa.

NEARBY FACILITIES & POINTS OF INTEREST: Hotel/Motel: Quality Inn, 1540 Scalp Avenue, Johnstown, Pa. (814) 266-5851 8 miles from Memorial; **Food/Supplies:** Food Stores and Restaurants at Richland Mall area (8 miles) Johnstown (10 miles); **Campgrounds:** Blue Knob State Park (26 miles), does not accept reservations, first come first served; **Parks, other points of interest:** Allegheny Portage Railroad National Historic Site, Johnstown Flood Museum, Inclined Plane.

Middle Delaware National Scenic River
Pennsylvania (also in New Jersey)   **SEE CLIMATABLE NO. 137**

MAILING ADDRESS: c/o Delaware Water Gap National Recreation Area, Bushkill, Pennsylvania 18324 **Telephone:** 717-588-6637

DIRECTIONS: See listing for Delaware Water Gap National Recreation Area.
The portion of the river that passes through the Delaware Water Gap National Recreation area is designated the Middle Delaware National Scenic and Recreational River. Authorized for addition to the National Park System on Nov. 10, 1978.

North Country National Scenic Trail
For details see listing in New York

Steamtown National Historic Site
Scranton, Pennsylvania

MAILING ADDRESS: Superintendent, National Park Service, Federal Building, P.O. Box 1280, Scranton, Pennsylvania 18501-1280 **Telephone:** 717-343-0760

DIRECTIONS: Facilities under planning and development; not yet open to the public.
Established by Act of Congress in 1986 to commemorate the Nation's historic and working railroad industry.

Thaddeus Kosciuszko National Memorial
Philadelphia, Pennsylvania   **SEE CLIMATABLE NO. 138**

MAILING ADDRESS: Superintendent, Thaddeus Kosciuszko National Memorial, c/o Independence National Historical Park, 313 Walnut Street, Philadelphia, Pennsylvania 19106 **Telephone:** 215-597-8974

DIRECTIONS: The Memorial is located at 301 Pine Street, Philadelphia.
This small house, built in 1775, commemorates the life and work of General Thaddeus Kosciuszko, Polish-born patriot and hero of the American Revolution. Created by Presidential Proclamation on Oct. 21, 1972.

VISITOR ACTIVITIES: interpretive exhibits and audiovisual programs; **Permits:** No; **Fees:** No; **Visitor facilities:** restrooms; **Any limitations on vehicle usage:** Avoid driving in downtown Philadelphia. Try to walk or use public transportation; **Meals**

served in the park: No; **Food and supplies obtainable in the park:** No; **Food and supplies obtainable nearby:** Yes, in Philadelphia; **Overnight accommodations:** Philadelphia; **First Aid available in park:** Yes; **Nearest Hospital:** Philadelphia, within 6 blocks; **Days/Hours:** Open daily from 9 a.m. to 5 p.m.; **Holiday Closings:** Dec. 25 & Jan. 1; **Visitor attractions closed for seasons:** None; **Weather:** Summers are hot and humid; some snow and sleet in Winter.

TRAVEL ACCESS: Bus: Greyhound, Trailways provide regular service to nearby terminal; **Rail:** Amtrak; **Air:** Major airlines service Philadelphia International Airport; **Other:** Philadelphia mass transit system (SEPTA) also provides access through buses, subway trains and trolleys.

NEW INFORMATION: New Municipal Parking Garage on 2nd Street between Chestnut and Walnut.

Valley Forge National Historical Park
Valley Forge, Pennsylvania   **SEE CLIMATABLE NO. 140**

MAILING ADDRESS: Superintendent, Valley Forge National Historical Park, Valley Forge, Pennsylvania 19481 **Telephone:** 215-783-7700

DIRECTIONS: This park is about 20 miles (32 km) west of Philadelphia. Entrances to the Park from the major highways are well-marked. Travelling eastbound or westbound via the Pennsylvania Turnpike, take Exit 24 (Valley Forge). Stay in the right lane for the toll booth and immediately take the next right onto North Gulf Road. This will take you to the Visitor Center located at the intersection of Valley Forge Road and 23. Begin your tour here.

Westbound travellers on the Schuykill Expressway (Interstate 76) should use Goddard Blvd. exit, make a right at the traffic light onto Goddard Blvd. Then make a right at the first traffic light onto N. Gulph Road. This will bring you to the Park. Travellers on US 202 must take the Valley Forge-Betzwood Bridge exit (truck route US 202 North) and proceed 2 miles (3 km) to the Valley Forge exit (PA 23 West), turn right at the exit and follow PA 23 to entrance and Visitor Center.

This is the site of General Washington's Continental Army encampment in the Winter of 1777-78 during the Revolutionary War. A scenic drive through the Park leads to many historical features including Washington's Headquarters and earthern fortifications. Transferred to National Park Service administration on March 31, 1977.

VISITOR ACTIVITIES: 15 minute film and exhibits, self-guiding auto tour, picnicking, hiking, horseback riding, boating, fishing, biking, auto tape tour Apr.-Oct., interpretation of historic homes, soldier life demonstrations, guided walks; **Permits:** No; **Fees:** Presently, there is a fee for the Historic Buildings. The fee is $1 for adults ages 12-61; **Visitor facilities:** parking, hiking and bike trails, bus tours, picnic areas, boat ramp, snack bar; **Any limitations on vehicle usage:** All vehicles must stay on the Park roads, which are narrow; **Hiking trails:** Yes, paved and unpaved trails lead to nearly all of the Park's historical features; **Backcountry:** No; **Camping:** No; **Other overnight accommodations on site:** No; **Meals served in the park:** Yes, sandwiches are available on Route 23 near Washington's Headquarters; **Food and supplies obtainable in the park:** No; **Food and supplies obtainable nearby:** Yes, in King of Prussia; **Overnight accommodations:** All major hotels are within 5 miles (8 km); **First Aid available in park:** Yes; **Nearest Hospital:** Phoenixville, 6 miles (9.7 km); **Days/Hours:** Open daily from 8:30 a.m. to 5 p.m. Memorial Day through Labor Day 8:30 a.m.-6 p.m. throughout the rest of the year; **Holiday Closings:** Dec. 25; **Visitor attractions closed for seasons:** None; **Weather:** cold Winters, pleasantly mild Spring, Summer and Fall.

TRAVEL ACCESS: Bus: SEPTA Route #45, public transportation from Center City Philadelphia to Valley Forge Area, stops at all King of Prussia hotels, and return. Regular schedule Monday through Friday. Not available Saturday and Sunday. For schedule times, call: 215-734-1300 or 574-7800; **Air:** Nearest major airports are: Philadelphia International and Northeast Philadelphia Airport; **Other:** (a) Shuttle service from airport to hotel nearby Park is available. (b) Taxi service from King of Prussia, PA and other nearby communities. (c) Bicycle rentals available daily June through Labor Day. And on weekends Labor Day to the end of October from Valley Forge Park Interpretive Association during Summer months.

NEARBY FACILITIES & POINTS OF INTEREST: Parks, other points of interest: Independence National Historical Park and Hopewell Village National Historic Site.

Rhode Island

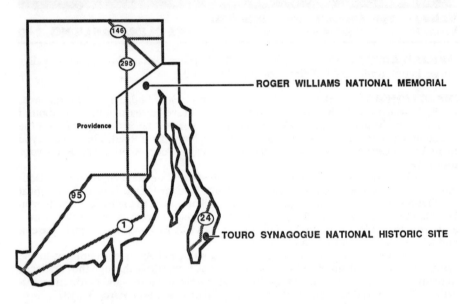

ROGER WILLIAMS NATIONAL MEMORIAL

TOURO SYNAGOGUE NATIONAL HISTORIC SITE

Roger Williams National Memorial
Providence, Rhode Island   **SEE CLIMATABLE NO. 141**

MAILING ADDRESS: Superintendent, Roger Williams National Memorial, P.O. Box 367, Annex Station, Providence, Rhode Island 02901 **Telephone:** 401-528-5385

DIRECTIONS: The Memorial is between Canal and North Main Streets, at the corner of Smith Street, in Providence.
    This Memorial is in honor of the founder of the Rhode Island Colony and a pioneer in religious freedom. Authorized for addition to the National Park System on Oct. 22, 1965.

VISITOR ACTIVITIES: interpretive exhibits; **Permits:** No; **Fees:** No; **Visitor facilities:** Park includes Visitor Center and over 4 acres of landscaped grounds; **Any limita-**

tions on vehicle usage: No; Hiking trails: No; Backcountry: No; Camping: No; Other overnight accommodations on site: No; Meals served in the park: No; Food and supplies obtainable in the park: No; Food and supplies obtainable nearby: Yes, Providence; Overnight accommodations: Providence; First Aid available in park: Yes; Nearest Hospital: within a 2 mile (3 km) radius; Days/Hours: Open 9:00 a.m. to 5:00 p.m. daily in summer, weekdays only in winter; Holiday Closings: Thanksgiving and Dec. 25, Jan. 1;Weather: Summers are hot and humid.

GENERAL INFORMATION: Stop at the Visitor Center for a list of nearby points of interest in historic Providence.

TRAVEL ACCESS: Bus: Rhode Island Public Transit provides local bus service; **Rail:** Amtrak; **Air:** USAir, American, TWA, Eastern, National, Piedmont, United provides access into Providence.

Touro Synagogue National Historic Site
Newport, Rhode Island   **SEE CLIMATABLE NO. 141**

MAILING ADDRESS: Touro Synagogue National Historic Site, 85 Touro Street, Newport, Rhode Island 02840 **Telephone:** 401-847-4794

DIRECTIONS: Touro Synagogue is on Touro Street in downtown Newport, Rhode Island, about 1-1/2 blocks east of the Old Colony on Washington Square.

Touro Synagogue is one of the most significant buildings in Newport and the oldest existing synagogue in the United States. This affiliated area was authorized for addition to the National Park System on Mar. 5, 1946.

VISITOR ACTIVITIES: guided tours offered from the last week of June until Labor Day; **Permits:** No; **Fees:** No; **Visitor facilities:** souvenir stand; **Any limitations on vehicle usage:** No; **Hiking trails:** No; **Backcountry:** No; **Camping:** No; **Other overnight accommodations on site:** No; **Meals served in the park:** No; **Food and supplies obtainable in the park:** No; **Food and supplies obtainable nearby:** Yes, in Newport; **Overnight accommodations:** In the city of Newport, Rhode Island; **First Aid available in park:** No; **Nearest Hospital:** Newport Hospital is about 1 mile (1.6 km) from the Synagogue; **Days/Hours:** Hours during regular tourist season are now Sunday through Friday from 10 a.m. to 5 p.m. The rest of the year from 2 p.m. to 4 p.m. on Sundays. Services are held on Fridays during the Summer at 7:30 p.m. and during the rest of the year at sunset. Saturday services are at 9 a.m.

TRAVEL ACCESS: Bus: via Bonanza and Greyhound; **Rail:** via Amtrak; **Air:** via Providence, R.I.

South Carolina

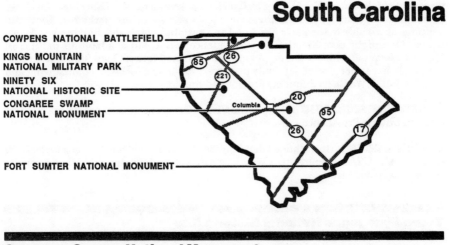

COWPENS NATIONAL BATTLEFIELD

KINGS MOUNTAIN
NATIONAL MILITARY PARK

NINETY SIX
NATIONAL HISTORIC SITE

CONGAREE SWAMP
NATIONAL MONUMENT

FORT SUMTER NATIONAL MONUMENT

Congaree Swamp National Monument
Columbia, South Carolina   **SEE CLIMATABLE NO. 142**

MAILING ADDRESS: Superintendent, Congaree Swamp National Monument, Suite 607, Strom Thurmond Federal Building, 1835 Assembly Street, Columbia, South Carolina 29201 **Telephone:** 803-765-5571 or 803-776-4396

DIRECTIONS: Adjacent to State Route 48, S.E. from Columbia, SC (currently marked by signs).
Located on an alluvial flood plain 20 miles (32 km) southeast of Columbia, the Monument contains the last significant tract of mature southern bottomland hardwoods in the southeastern United States. Located in the Monument are several national record-sized trees and many State record-sized trees. This new Park area was authorized by an Act of Congress on Oct. 18, 1976.

VISITOR ACTIVITIES: Hiking trails, canoeing, fishing; Guided tours are available by reservation only; **Permits:** No; **Fees:** No; **Visitor facilities:** Ranger Contact Station, 3/4 mile Boardwalk Trail and Environmental Education Center; **Any limitations on vehicle usage:** No; **Hiking trails:** Yes, 22 miles of marked trails; **Backcountry:** No; **Camping:** Yes, primitive with permit; **Other overnight accommodations on site:** No; **Meals served in the park:** No; **Food and supplies obtainable in the park:** No; **Food and supplies obtainable nearby:** Yes, in Columbia, S.C.; **Overnight accommodations:** Columbia, SC 48, 20 miles (32 km); **First Aid available in park:** Yes; **Nearest Hospital:** Baptist Hospital, Columbia, SC.

Cowpens National Battlefield
Chesnee, South Carolina   **SEE CLIMATABLE NO. 143**

MAILING ADDRESS: Cowpens National Battlefield, Superintendent, P.O. Box 308, Chesnee, SC 29323 **Telephone:** 803-461-2828

DIRECTIONS: The Battlefield is 11 miles (17.7 km) west of I-85 and Gaffney, S.C. and about 2 miles (3 km) east of US 221 and Chesnee, S.C.
Brig. Gen. Daniel Morgan won a decisive Revolutionary War Victory here over British Lt. Col. Banastre Tarleton on Jan. 17, 1781. Established on Mar. 4, 1929. Additional lands acquired in 1972.

VISITOR ACTIVITIES: Ranger-conducted walking tours, exhibits and audiovisual programs at the Visitor Center, auto tours; **Permits:** No; **Fees:** May-October $1 per person (under 13 free); **Visitor facilities:** restored 1830 log cabin, historic monuments, parking, tour road, walking trails, picnic area, information and exhibits; **Any limitations on vehicle usage:** Recreational vehicles are permitted; commercial vehicles are prohibited; **Hiking trails:** Yes, 1 mile (1.6 km) walking trail; **Backcountry:** No; **Camping:** No; **Other overnight accommodations on site:** No; **Meals served in the park:** No; **Food and supplies obtainable in the park:** No; **Food and supplies obtainable nearby:** Yes, in Chesnee, 2 miles (3 km). Limited food and gas stations within 3 miles (4.8 km) of the Park; **Overnight accommodations:** Gaffney, SC 11 and I-85, 11 miles (17.7 km) from the Park; **First Aid available in park:** Yes; **Nearest Hospital:** Gaffney, SC 11, 10 miles (16 km); **Days/Hours:** Open 7 days a week, 9 a.m. to 5 p.m.; **Holiday Closings:** Dec. 25; **Visitor attractions closed for seasons:** Weather conditions may limit access on roads and trails; **Weather:** Summers are hot and humid, Winters are mild with occasional snow.

TRAVEL ACCESS: Bus: Trailways and Greyhound provide daily service to Spartanburg; **Rail:** Southern Railway provides daily service to Spartanburg; **Air:** Eastern & Republic via Greenville/Spartanburg, SC.

NEARBY FACILITIES & POINTS OF INTEREST: Hotel/Motel: overnight lodging available in Gaffney and Spartanburg; **Campgrounds:** several private and state camping facilities within 30 miles; **Parks, other points of interest:** Kings Mountain National Military Park—32 miles North of Park, Walnut Grove Plantation—30 miles south of Park.

Fort Sumter National Monument
Sullivan's Island, South Carolina   **SEE CLIMATABLE NO. 144**

MAILING ADDRESS: Superintendent, Fort Sumter National Monument, 1214 Middle Street, Sullivan's Island, South Carolina 29482 **Telephone:** 803-883-3123

DIRECTIONS: Fort Sumter is in Charleston Harbor and can only be reached by boat. Tour boats leave from the city boat marina on Lockwood Drive, just south of US 17 in Charleston. For boat schedules, phone Fort Sumter Tours, 803-722-1691, or write 17 Lockwood Dr., Charleston, SC 29401. Fort Moultrie, administered together with Fort Sumter, is on west Middle Street on Sullivan's Island. From US 17, take SC 703 to Middle Street. The Visitor Center is at Fort Moultrie.
   The first engagement of the Civil War took place here on April 12, 1861. The Park also includes Fort Moultrie, scene of the patriot victory of June 28, 1776, one of the early defeats of the British in the Revolutionary War. Fort Sumter was authorized for addition to the National Park System on April 28, 1948. Fort Moultrie was added in 1960.

VISITOR ACTIVITIES: interpretive exhibits, film program, walking tours; **Permits:** No; **Fees:** Yes, tour boat to Fort Sumter is $7.00 for adults, $3.50 for children under 12. There is no admission fee at Fort Moultrie; **Visitor facilities:** restrooms at both forts, observation deck at Visitor Center; **Any limitations on vehicle usage:** No; **Hiking trails:** No; **Backcountry:** No; **Camping:** No; **Other overnight accommodations on site:** No; **Meals served in the park:** No; **Food and supplies obtainable in the park:** No; **Food and supplies obtainable nearby:** Yes, in Charleston & vicinity; **Overnight accommodations:** hotels in Charleston and Mount Pleasant; **First Aid available in park:** Yes; **Nearest Hospital:** Mt. Pleasant, Hwy. 17 North, 12 miles (19.2 km); **Days/Hours:** Open daily from 9 a.m. to 5 p.m.; until 6 p.m. in Summer; **Holiday Closings:** Dec. 25; **Visitor**

attractions closed for seasons: No; **Weather:** Summers are hot and humid; Winters are moderately cool with occasional days of extreme cold.

GENERAL INFORMATION: *For Your Safety*—Be especially careful on uneven surfaces, stairways, and near the chain barriers.

TRAVEL ACCESS: Bus: Greyhound, Continental provide daily service to Charleston; **Rail:** Amtrak provides regular service to Charleston; **Air:** Delta, Eastern, Piedmont and other airlines service Charleston.

NEARBY FACILITIES & POINTS OF INTEREST: Parks, other points of interest: Palmetto Islands State Park.

Kings Mountain National Military Park
Kings Mountain, South Carolina   **SEE CLIMATABLE NO. 143**

MAILING ADDRESS: Superintendent, Kings Mountain National Military Park, P.O.Box 40, Kings Mountain, North Carolina 28086 **Telephone:** 803-936-7921

DIRECTIONS: The park is easily reached from Charlotte, NC by Int. 85; from Spartanburg, SC by Int 85; and from York, SC by SC 161. Kings Mountain is on SC Hwy 216, off I-85, about 10 miles (16 km) from Kings Mountain, NC, and about 15 miles (24 km) southwest of Gastonia, NC, and northeast of Gaffney, SC.

American frontiersmen defeated the British here on Oct. 7, 1780, at a critical point during the struggle for independence and the battle was considered by Thomas Jefferson to be the turning point of the American Revolution.

VISITOR ACTIVITIES: interpretive exhibits and programs, walking tours, photography, horseback riding; **Permits:** No; **Fees:** No; **Visitor facilities:** Visitor Center, hiking trail, horseback riding trail; **Any limitations on vehicle usage:** Commercial vehicles are prohibited; drivers should be alert for pedestrians and hikers; **Hiking trails:** Yes, a foot trail leads from the Visitor Center to the chief features of the battlefield; **Backcountry:** Yes, information and brochure available at Visitor Center; **Camping:** Primitive campsite to accommodate backpackers; **Other overnight accommodations on site:** No, general camping is permitted only in Kings Mountain State Park, which adjoins the National Military Park on the east. You can also swim (in season) and picnic in the State Park; **Meals served in the park:** No; **Food and supplies obtainable in the park:** No; **Food and supplies obtainable nearby:** Yes, Kings Mountain, NC, Blacksburg, SC; York, SC; **Overnight accommodations:** Kings Mountain, NC, northeast of the park; **First Aid available in park:** Yes; **Nearest Hospital:** Kings Mountain, NC, 10 miles (16 km), SC-NC Hwy 216 to US 74 west; **Days/Hours:** Open daily from 9 a.m. to 5 p.m; until 6 p.m. in Summer; **Holiday Closings:** Thanksgiving Day, Dec. 25, Jan. 1; **Visitor attractions closed for seasons:** No; **Weather:** Summer is warm and humid. Spring and Fall are pleasantly mild. Winter is cold, but snow and ice are infrequent.

TRAVEL ACCESS: Bus: Trailways provides daily service to Kings Mountain; **Rail:** Amtrak provides daily service to Gastonia, NC; **Air:** Eastern, Delta, Piedmont provides daily service to Charlotte, NC.

NEARBY FACILITIES & POINTS OF INTEREST: Hotel/Motel: Holiday Inn, I-85 & NC 161, 704-739-2544, 8 miles from Park; **Camping:** Kings Mountain State Park (adjacent to Kings Mountain National Park); **Parks, other points of interest:** Cowpens National Battlefield, 30 miles southwest.

Ninety Six National Historic Site
Ninety Six, South Carolina   **SEE CLIMATABLE NO. 145**

MAILING ADDRESS: Superintendent, Ninety Six National Historic Site, P.O. Box 496, Ninety Six, South Carolina 29666 **Telephone:** 803-543-4068

DIRECTIONS: The Visitor Center is 2 miles (3 km) south of Ninety Six, S.C., off US 248 in Greenwood County.
   This colonial trading village dates from the 1730's and became an important government seat after 1768. Held by the British during the Revolutionary War, this Site contains earthwork embankments of a 1780 fortification. Authorized for addition to the National Park System on August 19, 1976.

VISITOR ACTIVITIES: interpretive exhibits, walking, hiking, fishing; **Permits:** No; **Fees:** No; **Visitor facilities:** parking and restrooms at Visitor Center, interpretive trail; **Any limitations on vehicle usage:** No vehicular traffic is allowed in the Park; **Hiking trails:** Yes, a 1 mile (1.6 km) interpretive trail; **Backcountry:** Yes; **Camping:** No; **Other overnight accommodations on site:** No; **Meals served in the park:** No; **Food and supplies obtainable in the park:** No; **Food and supplies obtainable nearby:** Yes, Ninety Six, 2 miles (3 km) north; **Overnight accommodations:** Greenwood, SC 34, 10 miles (16 km) west; **First Aid available in park:** Yes; **Nearest Hospital:** Greenwood, SC 34, 9 miles (14.5 km); **Days/Hours:** Open daily from 8 a.m. to 5 p.m.; **Holiday Closings:** Dec. 25 and Jan. 1; **Visitor attractions closed for seasons:** No; **Weather:** Summer is hot and humid, Winter is mild.

NEARBY FACILITIES & POINTS OF INTEREST: **Hotel/Motel:** Holiday Inn, Highway 25 in Greenwood 15 miles; **Campgrounds:** Greenwood State Park, Highway 702 in Greenwood; **Parks, other points of interest:** Greenwood Museum, Railway Museum in Greenwood, State Historical Markers nearby.

South Dakota

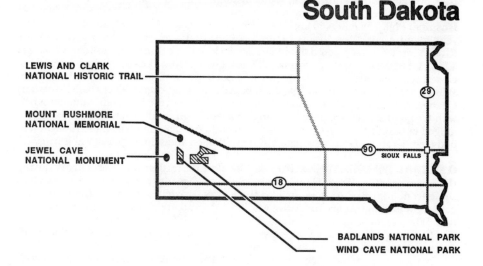

LEWIS AND CLARK
NATIONAL HISTORIC TRAIL

MOUNT RUSHMORE
NATIONAL MEMORIAL

JEWEL CAVE
NATIONAL MONUMENT

SIOUX FALLS

BADLANDS NATIONAL PARK
WIND CAVE NATIONAL PARK

Badlands National Park
Interior, South Dakota   **SEE CLIMATABLE NO. 148**

MAILING ADDRESS: Superintendent, Badlands National Park, P.O. Box 6, Interior, South Dakota 57750 **Telephone:** 605-433-5361

DIRECTIONS: The Cedar Pass Visitor Center, 2½ miles (4.3 km) northeast of Interior on Route SH240, 28 miles (45 km) southwest of Kadoka and 29 miles (47 km) southeast of Wall—both on I-90.

This Park, carved by erosion, contains animal fossils from 37-23 million years ago. Prairie grasslands support bison, bighorn sheep, deer, antelope, and prairie dogs. Proclaimed a national monument on January 25, 1939 it was redesignated a National Park by Congress on November 10, 1978.

VISITOR ACTIVITIES: Ranger conducted activities including nature walks, canyon climbs, evening programs, fossil preparation demonstrations in summer; camping, hiking, scenic drives, wildlife observation. **Permits:** No; **Fees:** $3 per vehicle entrance fee, $1 per person on commercial buses, $7 per campsite per night. Golden Eagle, Golden Age, and Golden Access Passports accepted and available; **Visitor facilities:** campgrounds, nature trails, two visitor centers, picnic areas, lodging, restaurant, souvenirs; **Any limitations on vehicle usage:** No offroad driving. Be on the lookout for wild animals, especially at night; **Hiking trails:** Yes, self-guiding trails of varying degrees of difficulty lead from the Park road; **Backcountry:** Yes, write ahead for complete backcountry and/or trail information. Otherwise, check at Cedar Pass or White River Visitor Centers; **Camping:** Yes, camping available year-round; no campsite reservations except for groups. Commercial campgrounds available at or near Interior, Cactus Flat, Wall, or Kadoka; **Other overnight accommodations on site:** Yes, reservations for lodging should be made with Cedar Pass Lodge (open early May-early Oct.) phone 605-433-5460; **Meals served in the park:** Yes, at Cedar Pass Lodge, from early May-early Oct.; **Food and supplies obtainable in the park:** Yes, at Cedar Pass Lodge; **Food and supplies obtainable nearby:** Yes, in Interior, Wall & Kadoka; **Overnight accommodations:** Wall, I-90, 30 miles (48 km) northwest, Kadoka, 28 miles (45 km) northeast; **First Aid available in park:** Yes, at ranger stations; doctors in Wall, Kadoka & Rapid City; **Nearest Hospital:** Philip 35 miles (56 km) NE of Cedar Pass; **Days/Hours:** Open 24 hours a day, year-round. Cedar Pass Visitor Center open every day except winter holidays; White River Visitor Center open daily in summer, closed in off-season; **Holiday Closings:** Visitors facilities closed Christmas, Thanksgiving, New Years; **Visitor attractions closed for seasons:** The most popular seasons are Spring, Summer, and Autumn. Winter visits can also be rewarding but blizzards may temporarily block roads; **Weather:** Changes in the weather can be sudden and quite drastic in the Badlands. Summer is hot, with frequent storms bringing lightning, hail, and high winds. Even on mild days, prolonged exposure to a shower can lead to hypothermia, a potentially fatal reduction in body temperature. Dress adequately and avoid open areas during electrical storms.

GENERAL INFORMATION: *Warning!* Be alert for rattlesnakes, particularly during the warm months. Water should be carried on longer hikes. Drinking water should come from approved sources, such as those at designated campgrounds. Other backcountry water sources are for native wildlife only, and are not fit for human consumption. When afoot, keep a safe distance from buffalo, 100 yards or more.

Climbing is discouraged on the steep, barren slopes where slippery clays and soft sediments may suddenly yield under foot.

No open fires are allowed anywhere in the Park. Cooking stoves and charcoal grills are permitted in campgrounds.

Other points of interest in the Black Hills include Jewel Cave, Wind Cave, and Mount Rushmore (see listings in this book).

Jewel Cave National Monument
Custer, South Dakota   **SEE CLIMATABLE NO. 150**

MAILING ADDRESS: Unit Manager, Jewel Cave National Monument, RR 1, Box 60AA, Custer, South Dakota, 57730 **Telephone:** 605-673-2288

DIRECTIONS: The area is accessible by US 16, which crosses the northern part of the Park between Custer, SD, and Newcastle, WY. The Visitor Center is on US 16, 13 miles (21 km) west of Custer.

Limestone formation caverns consist of a series of chambers connected by narrow passages, with many side galleries and fine calcite crystal encrustations. Created by Presidential Proclamation on Feb. 7, 1908.

VISITOR ACTIVITIES: interpretive exhibits, cave tours, picnicking; **Permits:** No; **Fees:** There is a guide fee for tours: ages 5 and under, free; 6 to 15, $1.00; 16 and over, $3.00; holders of Golden Age Passports, $1.50; Spelunking tours are $5; **Visitor facilities:** exhibits, information, sales counter, picnic area, drinking water, restrooms; **Any limitations on vehicle usage:** Vehicles must stay on the roads or in the parking area; **Hiking trails:** Yes, a short trail leads from the parking area to the historic cave entrance; **Backcountry:** No; **Camping:** No; **Other overnight accommodations on site:** No, several campgrounds are near Newcastle, WY and Custer, SD. Contact the monument for further information; **Meals served in the park:** No; **Food and supplies obtainable in the park:** No; **Food and supplies obtainable nearby:** Yes, in Newcastle, WY or Custer, SD; **Overnight accommodations:** Yes, in Newcastle 25 miles (40 km) west of the Monument on US 16, or Custer, 13 miles (21 km) east on US 16; **First Aid available in park:** Yes; **Nearest Hospital:** Custer, 13 miles (21 km) east on US 16, or Newcastle 25 miles (40 km) west on US 16; **Days/Hours:** the Visitor Center is open daily year-round. Portions of the cave are open to the public, and interpretive tours are offered daily from May through September. Tour schedules, if any, during the rest of the year are irregular and subject to change without notice; **Holiday Closings:** Thanksgiving, Dec. 25 and Jan. 1; **Weather:** Days are warm and sunny, temperatures at night are moderate. There are occasional afternoon thundershowers.

GENERAL INFORMATION: Wear low-heeled walking shoes with non-slip soles while touring the cave. Do not wear sandals or shoes with leather or hard composition soles or with high heels. A light sweater or jacket is desirable—the cave temperature is about 47°F (8.3°C) all year. Cave trails include numerous stairs. The tours are not recommended for individuals who have heart trouble or respiratory ailments, or for those who are recovering from a recent operation or hospitalization. Consider each tour description carefully before making a choice. Never leave a child or pet in a locked car. Due to the popularity of the scenic tour, lengthy waits of up to two hours may be encountered during mid-day.

TRAVEL ACCESS: Bus: Continental Trailways provides service into Custer, South Dakota; **Rail:** Amtrak provides service into Cheyenne, Wyoming; **Air:** Continental, Northwest and United provide service to Rapid City, South Dakota.

NEARBY FACILITIES & POINTS OF INTEREST: Campgrounds: Nearest public campground is USFS Comanche Park Campground, 7 miles east on US 16; **Parks, other points of interest:** Wind Cave National Park, 35 miles Southeast, Mt. Rushmore National Monument, 35 miles Northeast, Custer State Park, 15 miles east, Badlands National Park, 133 miles east, Devils Tower National Monument, 96 miles northwest (see listings).

Lewis and Clark Trail
For details see listing in Illinois

Mount Rushmore National Memorial
Keystone, South Dakota   **SEE CLIMATABLE NO. 150**

MAILING ADDRESS: Superintendent, Mount Rushmore National Memorial, P.O. Box 268, Keystone, South Dakota 57751 **Telephone:** 605-574-2523

DIRECTIONS: The Visitor Center is 3 miles (4.8 km) southwest of Keystone on SD 244 and 25 miles (40 km) south of Rapid City on US 16.
Monumental heads of Presidents George Washington, Thomas Jefferson, Abraham Lincoln, and Theodore Roosevelt were sculpted by Gutzon Borglum on the face of a granite mountain. Authorized for addition to the National Park System on Mar. 3, 1925.

VISITOR ACTIVITIES: evening programs in Summer, interpretive exhibits, audiovisual programs, wildlife- and bird-watching; **Permits:** Commercial film permits required; **Fees:** No; **Visitor facilities:** Visitor Center, restrooms, parking lot, feature-length film, floodlighted memorial, dining room, gift shop all year; **Any limitations on vehicle usage:** No commercial vehicles allowed through the park. Leave your vehicle in gear and set your handbrake when parking; **Hiking trails:** Yes, short trails provide varied views of the sculpture; **Backcountry:** No; **Camping:** No; **Picniking;** No; **Other overnight accommodations on site:** No, many commercial, state park, and U.S. Forest Service campgrounds exist in the surrounding Black Hills National Forest, Custer State Park and nearby towns of Rapid City, Rockerville, Keystone, Custer, Hill City, and Hot Springs, South Dakota. Most of these campgrounds can accommodate tents, trailers, and recreational vehicles. Contact: U.S. Forest Service, Black Hills National Forest, P.O. Box 792, Custer, SD 57730, phone 605-673-2251; Custer State Park, Hermosa, SD 57744, phone 605-255-4515; South Dakota Division of Tourism, Pierre, SD 57501, phone 605-773-3301; **Meals served in the park:** Yes, complete dining service is available at the concession area during the summer season. Limited food service available during most of the rest of the year; **Food and supplies obtainable in the park:** No; **Food and supplies obtainable nearby:** Yes, at Keystone and Hill City; **Overnight accommodations:** Keystone, 3 miles (4.8 km) northeast; Hill City, 15 miles (24 km) southwest; For further information on accommodations in the vicinity contact the Chamber of Commerce, P.O. Box 747, Rapid City, South Dakota 57701, phone 605-343-1744; **First Aid available in park:** Yes; **Nearest Hospital:** Rapid City, 25 miles (40 km) north on US 16; **Days/Hours:** Visitor Center open from 8 a.m. to 10 p.m. from mid-May through mid-Sept; from 8 a.m. to 5 p.m. the remainder of the year. Inquire locally to verify hours, which are subject to change; **Holiday Closings:** None; **Visitor attractions closed for seasons:** None; **Weather:** Summer daytime temperatures range from 70-90°F, cool evenings; Winter temperatures range from 40°F to -20°F.

GENERAL INFORMATION: Climbing of Mount Rushmore is prohibited. Stay on trails and stairways. Do not run. Visitors who have heart problems or who have trouble breathing should be aware of the high elevation (5,250 feet). For information on tourist attractions in the Black Hills area, contact the South Dakota Division of Tourism, Pierre, SD 57501, phone 605-773-3301.

TRAVEL ACCESS: Bus: Gray Line of the Black Hills (605) 342-4461, Stagecoach West (605) 343-3113, Jack Rabbit Bus Lines (605) 348-3300, provide charter service for park tours; **Rail:** No; **Air:** Western Airlines, United Airlines and Republic Airlines provide service to Rapid City Regional Airport.

NEARBY FACILITIES & POINTS OF INTEREST: Parks, other points of interest: Custer State Park, Wind Cave National Park, Jewel Cave National Monument, private attractions in Black Hills Region. **New park programs:** Programs for physically disadvantaged, hearing impaired, at Visitor Center.

Wind Cave National Park
Hot Springs, South Dakota   **SEE CLIMATABLE NO. 150**

MAILING ADDRESS: Superintendent, Wind Cave National Park, Hot Springs, South Dakota 57747 **Telephone:** 605-745-4600

DIRECTIONS: The Visitor Center is 11 miles (17.7 km) from the town of Hot Springs on US 385.
   This limestone cavern in the scenic Black Hills contains boxwork and calcite crystal formations. Elk, deer, prairie dogs, and bison live in the park. Established by act of Congress on Jan. 9, 1903.

VISITOR ACTIVITIES: guided cave tour, candlelight and spelunking tours, evening campfire programs, interpretive exhibits, picnicking, camping, cross-country hiking; **Permits:** No; **Fees:** Yes, for camping and cave tours. Camping is $7 per night per site. Cave tours: Regular (1/2 mile) tour is $3, Long (1 mile) and Candlelight tours are $4 each $1 for those 6-15 years old; under 6 free, 1/2 price for those holding Golden Age Passports. Spelunking tour, $5 (only 14 and over allowed); **Visitor facilities:** parking and restrooms at Visitor Center, picnic area, food service from May-Sept.; **Any limitations on vehicle usage:** Drive only on the roadways. Park at parking areas only; **Hiking trails:** Yes, 2 self-guiding nature trails; daytime cross-country hikes; **Backcountry:** Yes, an experimental backcountry camping plan went into effect in 1986. Check at the Visitor Center for permits and restrictions; **Camping:** Yes, no reservations accepted for campsites, which are open from about May 15 through Sept. Winter camping available, no water, no fee. There are many private campgrounds in the Black Hills. For further information, contact the South Dakota Division of Tourism, Pierre, SD 57501, phone 605-773-3301; **Other overnight accommodations on site:** No; **Meals served in the park:** Yes, complete lunch service at Visitor Center in Summer; **Food and supplies obtainable in the park:** No; **Food and supplies obtainable nearby:** Yes, at Hot Springs and Custer; **Overnight accommodations:** Hot Springs, 11 miles (17.7 km) south on Hwy 385; **First Aid available in park:** Only for major injuries; **Nearest Hospital:** Southern General Hills Hospital, Hot Springs, Hwy 385, 11 miles (17.7 km); **Days/Hours:** Park always open, Cave tours offered daily, with a very limited schedule in winter; **Holiday Closings:** Cave closed Thanksgiving, Dec. 25 & Jan. 1; **Visitor attractions closed for seasons:** Many of the Black Hills attractions are open only from Memorial Day through Labor Day. Cave tours are not given as often in winter; **Weather:** Fall is generally warm and pleasant, Spring can be blustery and is occasionally marred by heavy snowfalls. Winter is moderately severe, but icy roads, lack of accommodations, and closed tourist attractions discourage visitors.

GENERAL INFORMATION: The cave trail is dimly lit, and the surface is paved but uneven. Be sure to wear low-heeled walking shoes with non-slip soles, not sandals or high heels. A light sweater or jacket is desirable, since the cave temperature is about 53°F all year. Beware of bison, which may attack if disturbed or annoyed. Prairie dogs can bite, and their burrows may harbor rattlesnakes. Poison ivy abounds in the park and elsewhere in the Black Hills. Learn to recognize and avoid it. If you wish to avoid crowds, plan your visit for Spring or Fall.

TRAVEL ACCESS: Bus: Trailways Bus operates service into Hot Springs, South Dakota; **Rail:** Nearest Amtrak service into Cheyenne, Wyoming, 380 miles south of Park; **Air:** Major Airlines offer service into Rapid City, South Dakota, (60 miles, North).

NEARBY FACILITIES & POINTS OF INTEREST: Campgrounds: Elk Mountain Campground; **Parks, other points of interest:** Mt. Rushmore, 50 miles North; Custer State Park, 10 miles North; Jewel Cave National Monument, 35 miles Northwest.

Tennessee

BIG SOUTH FORK NATIONAL RIVER AND RECREATION AREA

CUMBERLAND GAP NATIONAL HISTORICAL PARK

OBED WILD AND SCENIC RIVER

STONES RIVER NATIONAL BATTLEFIELD AND CEMETERY

FORT DONELSON NATIONAL MILITARY PARK

APPALACHIAN NATIONAL SCENIC TRAIL

ANDREW JOHNSON NATIONAL HISTORIC SITE

GREAT SMOKY MOUNTAINS NATIONAL PARK

SHILOH NATIONAL MILITARY PARK

NATCHEZ TRACE PARKWAY

CHICKAMAUGA AND CHATTANOOGA NATIONAL MILITARY PARK

Andrew Johnson National Historic Site
Greeneville, Tennessee   **SEE CLIMATABLE NO. 146**

MAILING ADDRESS: Superintendent, Andrew Johnson National Historic Site, P.O. Box 1088, Greeneville, Tennessee 37744-1088 **Telephone:** 615-638-3551/1326

DIRECTIONS: From I-81 follow 11E North if traveling north or TN 172 if traveling south. Follow directional signs to the Visitor Center, located at the corner of College and Depot Streets. Rangers will direct visitors to the Homestead and National Cemetery.

This 16-acre Site was established by Presidential Proclamation on April 27, 1942, and preserves two homes, the tailor shop and cemetery where President Andrew Johnson lived, worked, and is buried.

VISITOR ACTIVITIES: interpretive exhibits and historic building tour, auto tours; **Permits:** No; **Fees:** Entrance fee at Homestead only for those 13 years or older, year-round. Golden Age, Golden Access, and Golden Eagle Passports accepted and available; **Visitor facilities:** Parking at the Visitor Center, Homestead, and National Cemetery. Restrooms at the Visitor Center; **Any limitations on vehicle usage:** Vehicles are restricted to tour roads and parking areas; **Hiking trails:** No; **Backcountry:** No; **Camping:** No; **Other overnight accommodations on site:** No; **Meals served in the park:** No; **Food and supplies obtainable in the park:** No; **Food and supplies obtainable nearby:**

Yes, Greeneville; **Overnight accommodations:** Several motels in Greeneville; **First Aid available in park:** Yes; **Nearest Hospital:** Laughlin Memorial and Takoma Adventist Hospitals, both in Greeneville; **Days/Hours:** Open daily from 9 a.m. to 5 p.m.; **Holiday Closings:** Dec. 25; **Visitor attractions closed for seasons:** No.

GENERAL INFORMATION: Three parts of the Historic Site are open to visitors. A museum and Andrew Johnson's tailor shop are located within the Visitor Center. The Andrew Johnson Homestead, last home of the 17th President, has been completely restored. President Johnson is buried in the Andrew Johnson National Cemetery.

TRAVEL ACCESS: Bus: Continental Trailways provides service to Greeneville; **Rail:** None; **Air:** Tri-City Airport 45 miles northeast of Greeneville. Knoxville's McGhee Tyson Airport 75 miles southwest.

NEARBY FACILITIES & POINTS OF INTEREST: Historic Jonesborough, oldest town in Tennessee, is 25 miles northeast on US 11E/321. Davy Crockett Birthplace State Historic Area is 15 miles northeast via US 11E/321. Camping at Forest Service campgrounds, Davy Crockett Birthplace State Historic Area, and Kinser Park.

Appalachian National Scenic Trail
For details see listing in Maine

Big South Fork National River and Recreation Area
Tennessee and Kentucky   **SEE CLIMATABLE NO. 152**

MAILING ADDRESS: Superintendent, Big South Fork National River and Recreation Area, P.O. Drawer 630, Oneida, Tennessee 37841 **Telephone:** 615-879-4890

DIRECTIONS: I-75 and I-40 are the major access routes to the Recreation Area. From I-75 proceed west via KY 80, 90, or 92, or TN 63 to US 27, and thence via US 27 to Oneida, TN. The Visitor Center is located 12 miles west off TN 297 in the Bandy Creek Campground. From I-40 proceed north via US 127 through Jamestown and then north on US 154 to TN 297. The Visitor Center is located 12 miles east of US 154 off TN 297 in the Bandy Creek Campground.
    The free-flowing Big South Fork of the Cumberland River and its tributaries pass through scenic gorges and valleys containing a wide range of natural and historic features. Authorized for addition to the National Park System in 1974.

VISITOR ACTIVITIES: Canoeing, raft trips, hiking, horseback riding, camping, interpretive walks, fishing, hunting, swimming picnicking; **Permits:** No; **Fees:** No; **Visitor facilities:** restrooms, parking, exhibits at Visitor Center, interpretive trails, Bandy Creek Campground, Blue Heron Campground and Alum Ford Campground, interpretive program, hiking and horse trails; **Any limitations on vehicle usage:** vehicles restricted from river gorge and limited to established roads; **Hiking trails:** Yes, over 140 miles completed; **Horse trails:** Yes, over 120 miles completed; **Backcountry:** Yes; ask at Visitor Center for details; **Camping:** Yes, Bandy Creek Campground, Blue Heron and Alum Ford Campgrounds; Lodging at Charit Creek Hostel; **Other overnight accommodations on site:** Yes, camping at Charit Creek and backcountry camping allowed; **Meals served in the park:** No; **Food and supplies obtainable in the park:** No; **Food and supplies obtainable nearby:** Yes, at Oneida or Jamestown, TN, or Whitley City, KY; **Overnight accommodations:** Oneida or Jamestown, TN or Whitley City, KY; **First Aid available in park:** Yes; **Nearest Hospital:** Oneida or Jamestown, TN.

GENERAL INFORMATION: The U.S. Army Corps of Engineers is responsible for planning, acquisition, and development. The National Park Service is responsible for management of the area. For your safety, paddling can be a dangerous sport on certain sections of the Big South Fork's rivers. Select a stream that matches your experience and abilities. Coast Guard approved life jackets must be carried, and should be worn, by all persons on the river.

Stay on designated hiking trails. Many trails pass close to high ledges and cliffs. Serious or fatal falls are possible. Carry a first aid kit at all times.

Steep grades (13%) and sharp hair pin turns will be encountered on highway 297 as it passes through the river gorge. Cars with trailers and large RV's are advised to use caution.

Chickamauga and Chattanooga National Military Park
For details see listing in Georgia

Cumberland Gap National Historic Park
For details see listing in Kentucky

Fort Donelson National Battlefield Park
Dover, Tennessee   **SEE CLIMATABLE NO. 149**

MAILING ADDRESS: Superintendent, Fort Donelson National Battlefield, P.O. Box 434, Dover, Tennessee 37058 **Telephone:** Office 615-232-5348; Visitor Center, 615-232-5706

DIRECTIONS: The Park is 1 mile (1.6 km) west of Dover town square and 3 miles (4.8 km) east of Land Between the Lakes National Recreation Area on US 79.

The first major victory for the Union Army in the Civil War occurred here in February 1862 under the leadership of Ulysses S. Grant. The Park was established by act of Congress on March 26, 1928. Fort Donelson National Cemetery (estab. 1867) adjoins the Park.

VISITOR ACTIVITIES: interpretive and audiovisual programs at Visitor Center, museum and wayside exhibits, auto tour, fishing, picnicking, hiking; **Permits:** Tennessee fishing license available from local stores. Licenses vary in length of validity and cost; **Fees:** There is a $1.00 fee per individual (children under 12 are free). Annual passes are available for $10.00. Golden Age, Golden Eagle, and Golden Access Passports are also available; **Visitor facilities:** Visitor Centers, restrooms, picnic area, hiking trails; **Any limitations on vehicle usage:** Park only in pull-offs. Bikers should ride single-file in the direction of the traffic; **Hiking trails:** Yes, self-guiding walking tours of natural and historical areas; **Backcountry:** No; **Camping:** primitive camping for organized youth groups only, group leader should contact the park; **Other overnight accommodations on site:** No; **Meals served in the park:** No; **Food and supplies obtainable in the park:** No; **Food and supplies obtainable nearby:** Yes, Dover; **Overnight accommodations:** Dover, Paris Landing State Park, 16 miles (25 km) southeast on US 79; Clarksville and Paris, TN both on US 79, 30 miles (48 km) in opposite directions; Murry, KY 30 miles (48 km) on KY 121; **First Aid available in park:** Yes, nearby or in Dover; **Nearest Hospital:** Erin, TN 49, 20 miles (32 km); **Days/Hours:** Open daily 8 a.m. to 4:30 p.m.; **Holiday Closings:** Dec. 25; **Visitor attractions closed for seasons:** Living history program offered only in Summer; **Weather:** Average Summer high 95°F; average Winter low 20°F; average rainfall 48"; average snowfall 5.6".

GENERAL INFORMATION: *For Your Safety*—Be cautious near the Cumberland River; it is swift and deep. Watch for poison ivy and poisonous snakes. Hikers should walk facing traffic along Park roads.

NEARBY FACILITIES & POINTS OF INTEREST: Campgrounds: TVA Land Between the Lakes, Golden Pond, Kentucky 42231; Paris Landing State Park, Buchanan, Tennessee.

Great Smoky Mountains National Park
Gatlinburg, Tennessee (also in North Carolina) **SEE CLIMATABLE NO. 118**

MAILING ADDRESS: Superintendent, Great Smoky Mountains National Park, Gatlinburg, Tennessee 37738 **Telephone:** 615-436-1200

DIRECTIONS: The Park Headquarters and Sugarlands Visitor Center are on US 441, 2 miles (3.2 km) south of Gatlinburg, TN. The Oconaluftee Visitor Center is 2 miles north of Cherokee, NC. There is also a visitor center in Cades Cove. Obtain a copy of the "Smokies Guide," a newspaper containing up-to-date information on activities, facilities, and medical services.

The loftiest range east of the Black Hills, and one of the oldest uplands on earth, the Smokies have a diversified and luxuriant plantlife, with specimens often of extraordinary size. Authorized for full development as part of the National Park System on June 15, 1934.

VISITOR ACTIVITIES: hiking, camping (available year-round), interpretive programs, nature walks, fishing, auto tours, horseback riding, wildflower- and bird-watching, picnicking; **Permits:** Backcountry camping permits available at any Ranger Station or Visitor Center. A TN or NC fishing permit, available locally, is required; **Fees:** $7 per night for developed campsites; $9 for reservation campgrounds (May 15-Oct 31); No fee for backcountry campsites; **Visitor facilities:** restrooms, developed campgrounds, picnic areas, trail shelters, horses for hire, lookout tower, nature and foot trails, limited lodging and supplies; **Any limitations on vehicle usage:** Motorists should be alert for hazards caused by changing natural conditions. Some secondary roads closed to buses and recreational vehicles; **Hiking trails:** Yes, short, self-guiding nature trails, and more than 900 miles (1286 km) of foot and horse trails. Trails are open all year; **Backcountry:** Yes, backcountry permit is required; available at Ranger Stations and Visitor Centers. Pick up a Trail Map and Guide when you obtain your permit; Because of overcrowding, it is necessary to ration several backcountry sites. Check the Trail Map and Guide for specifics; **Camping:** Yes, you must bring your own tent and other camping equipment. Backcountry shelters are located at 13 points along the Appalachian Trail and at Mt. LeConte, Laurel Gap, Kephart Prong, Scott Gap, and Rich Mountain. There are no showers or hookups for trailers. Three developed campgrounds are on the Ticketron reservation system from May 15 to Oct. 31; write Park Superintendent for information. Six other campgrounds are on a first-come, first-served basis. **Other overnight accommodations on site:** Yes, LeConte Lodge is accessible only by trail, and offers accommodations within the park from late March to early November. Allow 1/2 day to hike up a mountain trail to this secluded retreat. Reservations are necessary; call or write LeConte Lodge, Gatlinburg, TN 37738, 615-436-4473; Wonderland Club Hotel is accessible by car and offers accommodations from late May through October. For rates call or write Wonderland Club Hotel, Route 2, Gatlinburg, TN 37738, 615-436-5490. **Meals served in the park:** Yes, at Wonderland Hotel; **Food and supplies obtainable in the park:** Yes, at Cades Cove Campground; **Food and supplies obtainable nearby:** Yes, at Gatlinburg, Cosby and Townsend, TN and Cherokee, and Bryson City, NC; **First Aid available in park:** Yes; **Nearest Hospital:** The Park is served by numerous clinics, medical centers,

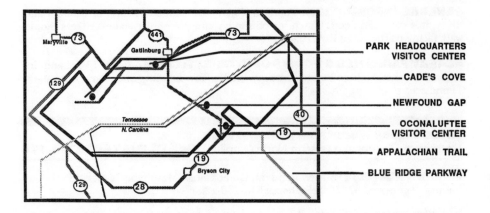

and hospitals; **Days/Hours:** Open daily year-round; **Holiday Closings:** Visitor Centers closed Dec. 25; **Visitor attractions closed for seasons:** Some picnic areas, campgrounds, roads and other facilities close in Winter. See "Smokies Guide" for further information; **Weather:** Wildflowers and migrating birds attract many visitors in late April and early May. If you intend to hike or camp in the Spring, bring warm clothing and be prepared for a variety of weather conditions including frequent rainstorms. Summer days are warm, and nights are usually cool. At higher elevations, temperatures may range from 15-20 degrees lower than those in the valleys. During June and July, the blooming of rhododendrons and azaleas is the outstanding natural event. July and August usually bring the heaviest rainfall, and thunderstorms sometimes come without warning. For greatest comfort on summer hikes, carry a raincoat and insect repellent. Autumn days are cool and clear—ideal for hiking. Winter is the most unpredictable season; yet you shouldn't discount it as a time to visit the Smokies. A quiet peace pervades the park. Be prepared, however, for sudden snowstorms and icy road conditions.

GENERAL INFORMATION: Hikers must be prepared to meet nature on its own terms. *For Your Safety*—don't travel alone, let someone know your schedule, have proper clothes and equipment, boil all drinking water, and observe park regulations. Stay on the trails, keep off waterfalls and cliff faces, and closely watch and control children. From Nov. through March, winter gear and clothing suitable for survival in deep snow and -20°F temperatures is necessary. *Bears* may appear tame, but they are dangerous wild animals and should not be approached closely or fed.

TRAVEL ACCESS: Air: Several major airlines provide service to Knoxville, TN, and Asheville, NC.

Obed Wild and Scenic River
Wartburg, Tennessee   **SEE CLIMATABLE NO. 152**

MAILING ADDRESS: Unit Manager, Obed Wild and Scenic River, P.O. Box 429, Wartburg, TN 37887 **Telephone:** 615-346-6294

DIRECTIONS: U.S. 27 or State Rt. 62 to Wartburg, TN.
Several tracts of land, totaling 1,234 acres have been purchased.
The Obed Wild and Scenic River consists of a portion of the Emory River, the Obed River, and their two main tributaries, Clear Creek and Daddy's Creek. These fast flowing rivers have cut into the Cumberland Plateau of East Tennessee, providing some of

the most rugged scenery and outstanding whitewater in the Southeast. Authorized for addition to the National Park System on October 12, 1976.

TRAVEL ACCESS: Bus: No; **Rail:** No; **Air:** closest commercial terminal is Knoxville/ Maryville.

NEARBY FACILITIES & POINTS OF INTEREST: Hotel/Motel: Hub Motel, Wartburg, TN, 615-346-3213, 10 miles; White Oak Lodge, Sunbright, TN, 615-628-2259, 22 miles; **Campgrounds:** Primitive Campground, Frozen Head State Park, Wartburg, TN, 615-346-3318.

Shiloh National Military Park
Shiloh, Tennessee   **SEE CLIMATABLE NO. 151**

MAILING ADDRESS: Superintendent, Shiloh National Military Park, Shiloh, Tennessee 38376 **Telephone:** 901-689-5275

DIRECTIONS: The Park is about 10 miles (16 km) south of Savannah and Adamsville, TN, via US 64 and State Route 22 and 23 miles (37 km) north of Corinth, MS, via MS 2 and TN 22.

The fierce battle fought here April 6-7, 1862 prepared the way for Major Gen. U.S. Grant's successful siege of Vicksburg. Well-preserved prehistoric Indian mounds overlook the river. Established by act of Congress on Dec. 27, 1894.

VISITOR ACTIVITIES: interpretive film and exhibits at Visitor Center, auto tours, hiking, biking, picnicking; **Permits:** No; **Fees:** Yes, $1; **Visitor facilities:** The Visitor Center is 12 miles (19 km) south of Savannah, via TN 22 and US 64; **Any limitations on vehicle usage:** Vehicles must stay on designated roadways; **Hiking trails:** Yes, interpretive military trail and environmental trail; **Backcountry:** No; **Camping:** No; **Other overnight accommodations on site:** No; **Meals served in the park:** No; **Food and supplies obtainable in the park:** No; **Food and supplies obtainable nearby:** Yes, in Shiloh, TN, TN 22; Adamsville and Savannah, TN, US 64; **Overnight accommodations:** Adamsville, TN, 10 miles (16 km) Savannah, TN, 12 miles (19 km); Selmer, TN, 15 miles (22 km), Pickwick Landing, TN, 15 miles (22 km), Corinth, MS, 22 miles (32 km); **First Aid available in park:** Yes; **Nearest Hospital:** Savannah, TN, US 64, 12 miles (19 km); **Days/ Hours:** The Visitor Center is open every day from 8 a.m. to 5 p.m.; **Holiday Closings:** Dec. 25; **Visitor attractions closed for seasons:** None.

GENERAL INFORMATION: You will be sharing the park roads with others. All motorists, hikers, and cyclists should use caution. Be extra careful near the river banks.

TRAVEL ACCESS: Bus: No; **Rail:** ICG, Southern offer service into Memphis, TN; **Air:** Atlantic Southeast provides daily service to Muscle Shoals, Ala.

NEARBY FACILITIES & POINTS OF INTEREST: Hotel/Motel: Pickwick Inn, Pickwick Landing State Park, 901-689-3135, 15 miles; **Campgrounds:** Battlefield Campground, Shiloh, TN, 3 miles; **Parks, other points of interest:** Pickwick Landing State Park.

Stones River National Battlefield and Cemetery
Murfreesboro, Tennessee   **SEE CLIMATABLE NO. 149**

MAILING ADDRESS: Superintendent, Stones River National Battlefield and Cemetery, Route 10, Box 495, Old Nashville Highway, Murfreesboro, Tennessee 37130 **Telephone:** 615-893-9501

DIRECTIONS: The Park is in the northwest corner of Murfreesboro, 27 miles (43 km) southeast of Nashville on US 41/70S. The Visitor Center should be your first stop, since orientation is necessary.

A fierce midwinter Civil War battle which began the Federal offensive to trisect the Confederacy took place here between Dec. 31, 1862 & Jan. 2, 1863. National Cemetery established June 26, 1865 and National Military Park established March 3, 1927.

VISITOR ACTIVITIES: slide program, museum, reference library, publication sales, auto tape tours and Visitor Center, self-guiding auto tours, living history weapon demonstrations from mid-June to Aug., biking; **Permits:** No; **Fees:** $1 per person ages 12-62, maximum $3 per vehicle; **Visitor facilities:** parking, restrooms, picnic area at Visitor Center, hiking trails, interpretive trails; **Any limitations on vehicle usage:** All motorized vehicles must use existing paved roads and parking areas only; **Hiking trails:** Yes, 2 and 5 mile (3 and 8 km) hiking trails, shorter interpretive trails along auto tour; **Backcountry:** No; **Camping:** No; **Other overnight accommodations on site:** No, public campgrounds and motels abound within a 10 mile (16 km) radius of the park; **Meals served in the park:** No, within 2 miles (3 km) of the park in Murfreesboro; **Food and supplies obtainable in the park:** No; **Food and supplies obtainable nearby:** Yes, in Murfreesboro; **Overnight accommodations:** Murfreesboro, US 41/70S, TN 96, US 231, and 124. Motels are within 5 miles (8 km) of the park; **First Aid available in park:** Yes; **Nearest Hospital:** In the center of Murfreesboro; **Days/Hours:** Park, Cemetery, and Visitor Center open daily 8 a.m. to 5 p.m.; **Holiday Closings:** Park closed Dec. 25, Jan. 1; **Visitor attractions closed for seasons:** Living history programs only offered mid-June-August; **Weather:** Temperatures range from 80°-95°F and dry June-Aug.; 45°-75°F, occasional rain (mostly pleasant) Sept.-Nov. and Mar.-May; 20°-40°F, frequent rain, some snow Dec.-Feb.

GENERAL INFORMATION: The oldest Civil War memorial, The Hazen Brigade Monument, is at tour stop 8.

Texas

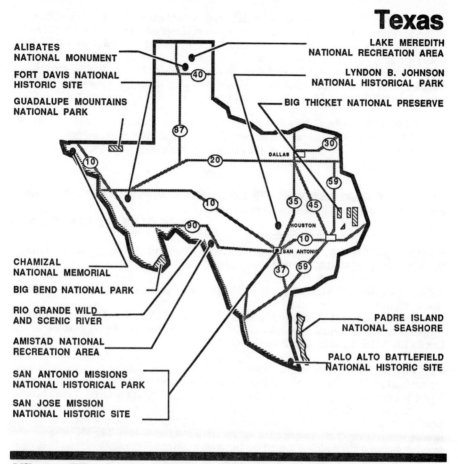

ALIBATES
NATIONAL MONUMENT

FORT DAVIS NATIONAL
HISTORIC SITE

GUADALUPE MOUNTAINS
NATIONAL PARK

LAKE MEREDITH
NATIONAL RECREATION AREA

LYNDON B. JOHNSON
NATIONAL HISTORICAL PARK

BIG THICKET NATIONAL PRESERVE

CHAMIZAL
NATIONAL MEMORIAL

BIG BEND NATIONAL PARK

RIO GRANDE WILD
AND SCENIC RIVER

AMISTAD NATIONAL
RECREATION AREA

SAN ANTONIO MISSIONS
NATIONAL HISTORICAL PARK

SAN JOSE MISSION
NATIONAL HISTORIC SITE

PADRE ISLAND
NATIONAL SEASHORE

PALO ALTO BATTLEFIELD
NATIONAL HISTORIC SITE

Alibates Flint Quarries National Monument
Fritch, Texas   **SEE CLIMATABLE NO. 153**

MAILING ADDRESS: Superintendent, Lake Meredith National Recreation Area, P.O. Box 1438, Fritch, Texas 79036 **Telephone:** 806-857-3151

DIRECTIONS: On Rte. 136, 6 miles (9.7 km) south of Fritch, take Alibates Road 5 miles (8 km) to Bates Canyon Information Station at Lake Meredith. Access to Alibates Flint quarries is available only by ranger-guided tours from Bates Canyon Information Station.

Undeveloped area authorized for addition to the National Park System on Aug. 31, 1965, preserves site where for more than 10,000 years pre-Columbian Indians dug agatized dolomite at these quarries to make projectile points, knives, scrapers and other tools.

VISITOR ACTIVITIES: Ranger-guided tours given twice daily from Bates Canyon Information Station at Lake Meredith National Recreation Area, exhibits; **Permits:** No; **Fees:** No; **Visitor facilities:** None; **Any limitations on vehicle usage:** No vehicles permitted; **Hiking trails:** Yes, for Ranger-guided tours only; **Backcountry:** No; **Camping:** No; **Other overnight accommodations on site:** No; **Meals served in the park:** No; **Food and supplies obtainable in the park:** No; **Food and supplies obtainable nearby:** Yes, in

Fritch, Borger, Dumas, Amarillo; **Overnight accommodations:** Fritch, Borger, Dumas, Amarillo; **First Aid available in park:** No; **Nearest Hospital:** Borger, TX 136, 21 miles (33.6 km); **Days/Hours:** Open 9:30 - 4:30 from Memorial Day through Labor Day. Tours are generally given at 10 a.m. and 2 p.m.; more frequently if need be. Off-season tours are by appointment only; **Holiday Closings:** None in season; **Visitor attractions closed for seasons:** From Labor Day to Memorial Day, except by appointment; **Weather:** Hot in Summer, cold in Winter, with winds especially high in Spring.

GENERAL INFORMATION: The Panhandle Plains Historical Museum, on the campus of West Texas State University, has several exhibits of archaeological material from this region and a model of what a Plains Village structure might look like. The Museum is in Canyon, TX, 16 miles (26 km) south of Amarillo.

Amistad National Recreation Area
Del Rio, Texas   **SEE CLIMATABLE NO. 154**

MAILING ADDRESS: Superintendent, Amistad Recreation Area, P.O. Box 420367, Del Rio, Texas 78842-0367 **Telephone:** 512-775-7491

DIRECTIONS: Park Headquarters and Visitor Reception are located in Del Rio on Route 90, west of San Antonio.
   The National Park Service manages the 85 miles (137 km) of Lake Amistad under a cooperative international agreement. The lake is formed by the confluence of the Devil's River, Rio Grande, and Pecos River.

VISITOR ACTIVITIES: boating, water skiing, swimming, fishing, hunting and camping on land and from boats, picnicking, hiking; **Permits:** for fishing—If you fish only in United States waters, a Texas State fishing license is all that is required. Texas licenses are sold at any hardware or bait shop in Del Rio, TX. If you cross from the United States portion of the lake to the Mexican portion to fish you must have a Mexican fishing license which costs $3.50 American money and is good for 90 days. The Mexican licenses may be obtained at a building just across the road from the Mexican Customs checkpoint at the end of the International bridge in the city of Acuna across from Del Rio, Texas; **Fees:** No; **Visitor facilities:** Ten major boat ramps, designated swim beaches, primitive camping facilities, boat rentals, rental slips, fuel, bait, ice, snacks, and beverages. Gasoline and store facilities are available in nearby towns; **Any limitations on vehicle usage:** Designated areas for driving to the waters' edge and boat launching from vehicles permitted only at those sites; **Hiking trails:** No; **Backcountry:** Yes; **Camping:** Yes, 4 campgrounds: 277 North and South, San Pedro Flats, and Governor's Landing. Picnic tables, firegrills, ramadas and chemical toilets. No water or electric; **Other overnight accommodations on site:** No; **Meals served in the park:** No; **Food and supplies obtainable in the park:** Yes; **Food and supplies obtainable nearby:** Yes, some supplies at Diablo East and Rough Canyon marinas; **Overnight accommodations:** Commercial campsites are available near Diablo East, Rough Canyon and Pecos. Motels, travel trailer parks, hotels, restaurant, service stations are in Del Rio and along US 90; **First Aid available in park:** Yes; **Nearest Hospital:** Del Rio, 7 miles (11.3 km); **Days/Hours:** Open daily from 8 a.m. - 5 p.m.; **Holiday Closings:** Thanksgiving, Dec. 25 & Jan. 1; **Visitor attractions closed for seasons:** No; **Weather:** Weather is suitable for swimming and water sports for 9 months of the year. December, January, and February will occasionally have low temperatures near 0°C (in the low 30°sF).

GENERAL INFORMATION: *For Your Safety*—Strong winds can make boating extremely hazardous—and in a very short time. Boaters should be familiar with safety precautions listed in a pamphlet available at Park Headquarters. Be sure to use the registration boxes which are provided at each launch ramp.

NEARBY FACILITIES & POINTS OF INTEREST: Hotel/Motel: Amistad Lodge Highway 90 West 512/775-8591 on the Lake (Boat Ramp Approximately 1 mile); Anglers Lodge, Highway 90 West, 512/775-1586, on the Lake (Boat Ramp Approximately 2 miles); **Food/Supplies:** Fina Service Station, Highwy 90 West, 512/775-8156, 1 mile to Diablo East Boat Ramp & Marina; **Campgrounds:** Amistad American, Highway 90 West, 512/775-6484, 3 miles to Diablo East Boat Ramp & Marina; Amistad Park Campground, Highway 90 West, 512/775-6491, 3 miles to Diablo East Boat Ramp & Marina; Holiday Trav-L-Park, Highway 90 West; 512/775-7784, 3 miles to Diablo East Boat Ramp & Marina; **Parks, other points of interest:** Seminole Canyon State Historical Park, Box 806, Comstock, TX 512/292-4464; **Reservation systems in use for campsites, other facilities:** None.

Big Bend National Park
Big Bend National Park, Texas   **SEE CLIMATABLE NO. 155**

MAILING ADDRESS: Superintendent, Big Bend National Park, Big Bend National Park, Texas 79834 **Telephone:** 915-477-2251

DIRECTIONS: From San Antonio, it is 410 miles (660 km) to Park headquarters at Panther Junction via US 90 to Marathon and south via US 385. From El Paso, it is 323 miles (520 km) to Panther Junction via Int. 10 to Van Horn, US 90 to Alpine, and south via TX 118; and it is 353 miles (568 km) via US 67 to Presidio and Texas Ranch Road 170-the "Camino del Rio". The Headquarters building is 27 miles (43.5 km) off Hwy 385, 70 miles (113 km) south of Marathon.

Mountain scenery contrasts with Chihuahuan Desert in this great bend of the Rio Grande, where a variety of unusual geological structures are found. Authorized for addition to the National Park System on June 20, 1935.

VISITOR ACTIVITIES: interpretive programs, camping, hiking, horseback riding, picnicking, fishing, walking and auto tours, boating, biking, bird-watching; **Permits:** for backcountry camping and boating on the Rio Grande available from Headquarters; **Fees:** Yes, entrance fee, and fees are charged for camping at developed campsites and concessioner-operated trailer sites; **Visitor facilities:** campgrounds, hiking trails, evening talks, lodge, food service, trailer parks, picnic tables, showers, stores, service stations, public telephones, post office, rental saddle horses and pack animals, laundry, restrooms; **Any limitations on vehicle usage:** No off-road travel permitted; take the numerous road dips slowly, trailers over 20 feet are not advised to try to enter the Basin, 5 miles continuous grade out of Castolon; **Hiking trails:** Yes, check at Headquarters for information on the many trails; **Backcountry:** Yes, information can be obtained from Headquarters; **Camping:** Yes, no reservations available for individual campsites; **Other overnight accommodations on site:** Yes, trailer parks and lodge. For reservations at Chisos Mountain Lodge, write to National Park Concessions, Inc., Big Bend National Park, TX 79834, phone 915-477-2291; **Meals served in the park:** Yes, at Chisos Mountain Lodge; **Food and supplies obtainable in the park:** Yes, limited supplies available at the Basin, Rio Grande Village, Castolon, and Panther Junction; **Food and supplies obtainable nearby:** Yes, at Alpine and Study Butte; **Overnight accommodations:** Terlingua, TX 118, 23 miles (37 km), Lajitas, TX 118 & TX Ranch Road 170, 39 miles (63 km) from Headquarters; **First Aid available in park:** Yes; **Nearest Hospital:** Alpine, 108 miles (183 km) from Headquarters; **Days/Hours:** Park is always open. Information desk open from 8 a.m. to 6 p.m.; with extended hours during busy periods; **Holiday Closings:** None; **Visitor attractions closed for seasons:** None; **Weather:** Winter is nippy in the mountains and comfortably warm during the day in the lowlands. Once or twice a year snow falls in the mountains. Spring weather arrives early. Midsummer temperatures in desert and river valley are likely to hover above 100° during the day. This is the best time to go to the mountains. In the Basin (5400-foot elevation), daytime temperatures average a comfortable 85°F, and nights are cool. Autumn is usually warm.

GENERAL INFORMATION: Be sure to obtain a pamphlet describing regulations and precautions, available at Headquarters. Carry your own first-aid supplies, including tweezers to extract cactus spines. Carry drinking water on the trail and in the desert. Check with a Park Ranger before travelling on any of the primitive roads. Wear stout shoes and tough clothing while you are hiking. Stay on the trails.

Big Thicket National Preserve
Beaumont, Texas   **SEE CLIMATABLE NO. 156**

MAILING ADDRESS: Superintendent, Big Thicket National Preserve, 3785 Milam, Beaumont, Texas 77701 **Telephone:** 409-839-2689

DIRECTIONS: The Preserve is located in southeastern Texas. The twelve separate units are bounded by US 96 on the East, US 90 on the South, US 59 on the West and US 190 on the North. Write or call in advance for a map of the area and information on facilities and activities in each area. The Preserve's temporary headquarters is at 3785 Milam, Beaumont. A small Visitor Station is in the southern end of the Turkey Creek Unit, on FM 420, 2½ miles (4 km) off the Hwy 69.
   The Preserve contains 84,550 acres composed of 12 units of various sizes spread over 50 miles square. It is an area of great plant diversity caused by the convergence of several major plant communities from the North, South, and West. The area has potential for a variety of recreational activities. Established by act of Congress on Oct. 11, 1974.

VISITOR ACTIVITIES: Development of the Preserve will be minimal, with only a few visitor facilities existing within the Preserve. There are six hiking trails; three in the Turkey Creek unit of the Preserve, and one each in the Beech Creek, Hickory Creek Savannah, and Big Sandy Creek Units. Kirby Nature Trail, in the Southern portion of the Turkey Creek unit contains insect, flower and fungi specimens and takes about 1½ hours to walk. The Turkey Creek trail extends 9.2 miles (15 km) south from road FM 1943 to the unnumbered road that transects the unit. Bring plenty of your own water if you hike this trail. There is also river access for boats and canoes at several points along the Pine Island Bayou and Neches River. A variety of facilities are outside the Preserve. Martin Dies Jr. State Recreation Park located on the B.A. Steinhagen Reservoir includes 3 separate units and provides for boating, camping, fishing, swimming, hiking, and nature study. John K. Kirby State Forest has picnic grounds, a self-guiding nature trail, varied shrubs and many wildflowers. The Roy E. Larson Sandyland Sanctuary protects some of the best examples of Arid Sandylands found throughout the Thicket region. A hiking trail is open to the public, and special tours may be arranged by contacting Caretaker, Roy E. Larson Sandyland Sanctuary, P.O. Box 909, Silsbee, TX 77656. Big Thicket Museum in Saratoga has a slide show and exhibits on the natural and cultural history of the area (closed Mondays). Chain-o-Lakes Campground is a private resort campground near Romayor, and has both primitive and developed campsites. The East Texas Indian Reservation has tours, a campground, and a visitor complex where demonstrations of Indian skills are performed (open seasonally). Woodville has museums and gardens. B.A. Steinhagen Lake area is managed by the Corps of Engineers and has boating, swimming, fishing, and improved campgrounds. **Permits:** a Texas fishing license, available locally, is required; **Fees:** No; **Visitor facilities:** A Visitor Information Station is located in the Turkey Creek Unit on FM420. Hiking trails are available; **Any limitations on vehicle usage:** Vehicles must stay on public roads; **Hiking trails:** Yes, Turkey Creek Trail 9 miles (14.5 km); Woodland Trail (6 miles); Kirby Nature Trail, 2½ miles (4 km), Sundew Trail, 1 mile (1.6 km). Beech Woods Trail 1 mile (1.6 km), Pitcher Plant Trail (¼ mile); **Backcountry:** Yes, write the Superintendent for information; **Camping:** No; **Other overnight accommodations on site:** No; **Meals served in the park:** No; **Food and supplies obtainable in the park:** No; **Food and supplies obtainable nearby:** Yes, at Beaumont, Kountze, Woodville, Silsbee; **Overnight accommodations:** Beaumont, Woodville, Kountze, Silsbee; **First Aid available in park:** Yes; **Nearest Hospital:** Beaumont, Woodville, Silsbee; **Days/Hours:** 24 hours a day, 364 days a year; **Holiday Closings:** Dec. 25; **Visitor attractions closed for seasons:** No; **Weather:** Summers are hot and humid; Winters are cold and wet.

GENERAL INFORMATION: Additional facilities will be made available as time and money permit. One can expect changes soon. **For Your Safety**—Wear clothing suitable for weather extremes if you hike. To avoid becoming disoriented in the woods, especially on cloudy days, carry a good compass, a map, and stay on the established trails. If you canoe or boat, wear a life jacket, take a partner and a first aid kit, let someone know where you are going and don't overload the boat. Always leave wildlife alone. Beware of snakes. Watch out for poison ivy, bees, wasps, hornets, chiggers, mosquitoes, and fire ants, which are all prevalent. Use plenty of repellent and watch where you sit or stand.

Pets must be on a leash or otherwise restrained at all times. Pets are not allowed on trails. Plants and animals must not be disturbed. All of the lands adjoining the Preserve units are in private ownership. If in doubt, don't trespass.

Chamizal National Memorial
El Paso, Texas **SEE CLIMATABLE NO. 157**

MAILING ADDRESS: Superintendent, Chamizal National Memorial, 700 E. San Antonio, Suite D 301, El Paso, Texas 79901 **Telephone:** 915-534-6277

DIRECTIONS: The Memorial is in south-central metropolitan El Paso immediately adjacent to the international boundary. Entrances to the park are from San Marcial Street and Delta Drive.

The peaceful settlement of a 100-year boundary dispute and the good will between the United States and Mexico is commemorated here. The Chamizal Treaty ending the dispute was signed in 1963. An amphitheater and 502-seat auditorium are used by theatrical groups from both nations. Authorized for addition to the National Park System on June 30, 1966.

VISITOR ACTIVITIES: picnicking, interpretive exhibits, Arts and Crafts presentations and film, guided tours, theatrical performances, Border Folk Festival the first weekend in October, Arts festival the week of July 4, Classic Spanish Drama Festival in March; Border Jazz Festival Memorial Day Weekend; Zarzuela Festival July-August; Ballet Forklorico Festival end of August; **Permits:** No; **Fees:** No entrance fee is charged, but tickets are sold for some special theatrical performances; **Visitor facilities:** parking and picnic areas, auditorium, restrooms; **Any limitations on vehicle usage:** No; **Hiking trails:** No; **Backcountry:** No; **Camping:** No; **Other overnight accommodations on site:** No; **Meals served in the park:** No; **Food and supplies obtainable in the park:** No; **Food and supplies obtainable nearby:** Yes, downtown El Paso, west of the park; **Overnight accommodations:** El Paso; **First Aid available in park:** Yes; **Nearest Hospital:** El Paso, North Stanton, 3 miles (4.8 km); **Days/Hours:** 8 a.m. to 5 p.m. (to 11 p.m. on evenings of cultural events) year-round; **Holiday Closings:** None; **Visitor attractions closed for seasons:** No.

GENERAL INFORMATION: Directly across the Rio Grande, the Republic of the United Mexican States has established a companion park on a portion of Mexico's Chamizal land. You are encouraged to visit the park, which includes formal gardens, outstanding architectural structures, a museum of art and history, an outdoor archeological museum, and statuary.

TRAVEL ACCESS: Bus: Local bus transportation to Park entrance hourly; **Rail:** Amtrak provides service to El Paso; **Air:** American, Eastern/Continental, America West, Delta, United, Southwest and other carriers service El Paso.

NEARBY FACILITIES & POINTS OF INTEREST: Campgrounds: KOA, commercial camps, 6-8 miles from Memorial; **Parks, other points of interest:** Chamizal Park of Mexico, 19 museums, 3 State Parks; **Information:** Call: 915-534-6668 or 6277 for information on programs (about 225 different programs per year, multi-lingual and multi-cultural, in the fine arts and folk arts, of Chamizal).

Fort Davis National Historic Site
Fort Davis, Texas   **SEE CLIMATABLE NO. 155**

MAILING ADDRESS: Superintendent, Fort Davis National Historic Site, P.O. Box 1456, Fort Davis, Texas 79734 **Telephone:** 915-426-3225

DIRECTIONS: The Site is on the northern edge of the town of Fort Davis, TX. It can be reached from Interstate 10 on the north and U.S. 90 on the south by Texas 17 and 118, and US 90 on the east by Texas 505, 166, and 17. Marfa is 21 miles (33.8 km) to the southeast.
   A key post in the West Texas defensive system, the fort guarded emigrants on the San Antonio-El Paso road from 1854 to 1891. Authorized for addition to the National Park System on Sept. 8, 1961.

VISITOR ACTIVITIES: self-guiding tours of buildings and grounds. During June, July and August refurnished Commanding Officer's Quarters, Enlisted Men's barracks, Officer's Kitchen and Servant's Quarters and Post Commissary open to public with interpreters dressed in styles of the 1880s; picnicking, interpretive exhibits, audiovisual programs, hiking; **Permits:** Yes, obtainable at the Visitor Center; **Fees:** Entrance fee is $1.00 per carload or 50¢ per person. Golden Age, Golden Access, and Golden Eagle Passports are accepted and available. No charge for groups from educational institutions; **Visitor facilities:** parking, restrooms at Visitor Center, hiking trails; **Any limitations on vehicle usage:** No driving tours in the park. Electric golf cart is available for handicapped persons only; **Hiking trails:** yes, 3 miles (4.8 km) of moderately strenuous hiking trails; **Backcountry:** No; **Camping:** No; **Other overnight accommodations on site:** No; **Meals served in the park:** No, but there are several restaurants in the Fort Davis area; **Food and supplies obtainable in the park:** No; **Food and supplies obtainable nearby:** Yes, in the Fort Davis area and at "Indian Lodge" in the Davis Mountain State Park, 4 miles (6.4 km) west on TX 118; **Overnight accommodations:** In Fort Davis and at nearby Davis Mountain State Park. The telephone number for reservations is 915-426-3254; **First Aid available in park:** Yes, and at firehouse (rescue squad); **Nearest Hospital:** Alpine, TX 26 miles (41 km); **Days/Hours:** Open daily from 8 a.m. to 5 p.m., until 6 p.m. in Summer; **Holiday Closings:** Dec. 25, Jan. 1; **Visitor attractions closed for seasons:** Living history programs offered in Summer; **Weather:** Average annual temperature is 63°, Summer 60°-90°, Winter, 20°-60°.

GENERAL INFORMATION: The Fort is a good stopover while traveling to Carlsbad Caverns National Park from Big Bend National Park (see listings in this book).

TRAVEL ACCESS: Bus: Trailways Bus System, provides service to Marfa, 21 miles from Park; **Rail:** Southern Pacific/Amtrak provide service to Alpine 26 miles from Park; **Air:** Nearest commercial air terminals in El Paso (200 miles) or Midland-Odessa (170 miles).

NEARBY FACILITIES & POINTS OF INTEREST: Hotel/Motel: In Fort Davis: Limpia Hotel and Stone Village Motel, in Davis Mountain State Park: Indian Lodge; **Parks, other points of interest:** McDonald Observatory, 17 miles northwest of Park.

Guadalupe Mountains National Park
Texas   **SEE CLIMATABLE NO. 158**

MAILING ADDRESS: Superintendent, Guadalupe Mountains National Park, HC 60, Box 400, Salt Flat, TX 79847-9400 **Telephone:** 915-828-3251 (Visitor Information) and 505-885-8884 (Administration)

DIRECTIONS: The Park is in western Texas, on Hwy 62-180 55 miles (88.5 km) southwest of Carlsbad, NM, and 110 miles (177 km) east of El Paso, TX. Van Horn, TX, is 65 miles (105 km) south on Hwy 54. Stop first at Frijole Visitor Center, on Hwy 62-180.

Rising abruptly from the desert, this mountain mass exposes portions of one of the world's most extensive and significant Permian limestone fossil reefs. Also noted for a tremendous earth fault, lofty peaks, rugged canyons, unusual flora and fauna. Authorized for addition to the National Park System on Oct. 15, 1966, established September 30, 1972.

VISITOR ACTIVITIES: Mainly hiking and backpacking. Two drive-in campgrounds, horseback riding (bring your own horse), guided tours, and evening programs in Summer; **Permits:** for overnight backcountry trips; obtained at Frijole Visitor Center; **Fees:** $5 per site camping fee at Pine Springs Campground; no fee at Dog Canyon Campground; **Visitor facilities:** Frijole Visitor Center provides literature for sale, information, Orientation Program, restrooms, and water. Pine Springs Campground, vehicle campground, offers flush toilets, picnic tables; located 1-1/2 mile west of Frijole Visitor Center. Limited road access to areas of park. Picnic area at McKittrick Canyon; **Any limitations on vehicle usage:** Existing roads are limited: approx. 4 miles (6.4 km) of Hwy 62-180 travels through the park, an 5 miles (8 km) paved road provides access from Hwy 62-180 to the mouth of McKittrick Canyon, and a 7 miles (13 km) 4-wheel drive road to Williams Ranch Historic Site requires permission to travel and a key to a locked gate (obtained at Visitor Center). No off-road vehicle use, no vehicles allowed on foot trails. NM State 137 and County Road 414 lead to Dog Canyon (northern side of the Park) all but 1 mile paved; **Hiking trails:** Yes, over 80 miles of hiking trails, in rugged mountainous terrain. **Backcountry:** Yes, contact Visitor Center. Hikers must sign in and out at trail registers and obtain free permits before starting overnight hikes. Hikers must carry all water. Topographic maps are for sale at Visitor Center; **Camping:** Yes, vehicle campgrounds at Pine Springs and Dog Canyon, also designated backcountry campsites, all on a first-come, first-served basis. No overnight lodging available in or near the park; **Other overnight accommodations on site:** No; **Meals served in the park:** No; **Food and supplies obtainable in the park:** No; **Food and supplies obtainable nearby:** Yes, Nearest food service: Carlsbad, NM and El Paso, Van Horn, and Dell City, TX; **Overnight accommodations:** Carlsbad, NM US 62-180 55 miles (88.5 km); Van Horn, TX, 65 miles (105 km) and El Paso, TX, US 62-180 110 miles (177 km); **First Aid available in park:** limited; **Nearest Hospital:** Carlsbad, NM, US 62-180 55 miles (88.5 km); **Days/ Hours:** Frijole Visitor Center open daily (including holidays and weekends, except Christmas Day) 8 a.m to 4:30 p.m., later in summer, Campground open daily. McKittrick Canyon hiking area open only during daylight hours, gate closes at night; **Holiday**

Closings: Visitor Center closed Christmas Day; **Visitor attractions closed for seasons:** Visitor use areas open all year except during occasional emergency situations caused by bad weather conditions; **Weather:** Anticipate storms and sudden weather changes. Thunderstorms are common in Summer; freezing rain and occasional snowstorms in Winter. Violent winds in Spring and Winter. Summer temperatures are extreme and winter temperatures usually mild but can suddenly drop to lows below freezing. Potential backpackers can call Frijole Visitor Center, 915-828-3251, for current weather conditions and forecasts.

GENERAL INFORMATION: *Safety Precautions:* Check with park ranger before hiking. Do not climb cliffs; rocks are unstable and considered unsuitable for technical climbing. Beware of cactus and spiny plants. Watch for and respect rattlesnakes during warmer months of the year. If planning a hike or backpack trip, come prepared; sturdy broken-in boots, a tent, tough clothing, cold weather gear in winter, water repellent clothing for winter and summer and capability to carry all your own water (one gallon per person per day is recommended).

Important regulations: Before bringing your pet, remember pets are not allowed on hiking trails and high summer and low winter temperatures make leaving your pet in a vehicle uncomfortable and potentially dangerous for the animal. The display or use of firearms is prohibited.

Lake Meredith National Recreation Area
Fritch, Texas   **SEE CLIMATABLE NO. 153**

MAILING ADDRESS: Superintendent, Lake Meredith National Recreation Area, P.O. Box 1438, Fritch, Texas 79036 **Telephone:** 806-857-3151

DIRECTIONS: The Park Headquarters building is on Hwy 136 in Fritch. Information about facilities at the various recreation sites is available here.

Man-made Lake Meredith on the Canadian River is a popular water-activity center in the Southwest. On the south side of the lake, Alibates Flint Quarries National Monument can be seen by free guided tours in Summer and by prior appointment at other times of the year. See Alibates listing in this book. Lake Meredith established by act of Congress on Mar. 15, 1965.

VISITOR ACTIVITIES: boating, water skiing, canoeing, fishing, picnicking, swimming, camping, hunting, scuba diving, sailing, motorcycling, interpretive exhibits; **Permits:** Texas hunting and fishing licenses available from Texas Parks and Wildlife Department or at local sporting goods stores; **Fees:** No entrance or camping fees; **Visitor facilities:** marinas, restrooms, drinking water, beaches, launching ramps, picnic and camping areas, snack bar; **Any limitations on vehicle usage:** Boats are subject to Federal and State regulations; **Hiking trails:** No; **Backcountry:** Yes, topographic maps and information available from park Headquarters; **Camping:** Yes, no reservations available for campsites. Campers may stay up to 14 days. No camping is allowed in the launching areas or parking lots. Private campgrounds with hookups are located in nearby towns; **Other overnight accommodations on site:** No; **Meals served in the park:** Yes, snacks available at Sanford-Yake marina; **Food and supplies obtainable in the park:** Yes, limited picnic supplies at Sanford-Yake marina; **Food and supplies obtainable nearby:** Yes, in Fritch, Sanford, Borger, Amarillo, Dumas; **Overnight accommodations:** Fritch, Borger, Amarillo, Dumas; **First Aid available in park:** No; **Nearest Hospital:** Borger, Hwy 136, 15 miles (24 km); Dumas, Hwy 13-19 to 19-13 to 152, 20 miles (32 km); Amarillo, Hwy 136, 25-45 miles (40-72 km); **Days/Hours:** Park never closes; **Holiday Closings:** None; **Visitor attractions closed for seasons:** Activities are curtailed and many areas closed due to inclement weather in Winter; **Weather:** Summers are hot, with temperatures above 100°F on some days. Winters are cold; high winds in Spring.

GENERAL INFORMATION: Boaters should be familiar with Federal and State boating regulations, which can be obtained from Park Rangers or from Lake Meredith headquarters. Listen for storm warnings! A sudden storm wind can reach 80 mph (130 km per hour) so fast that boats may have trouble getting off the lake. Get your boat to shore in a sheltered area and wait out the storm if ramps cannot be reached safely.

Lyndon B. Johnson National Historical Park
Johnson City, and Stonewall, Texas   **SEE CLIMATABLE NO. 159**

MAILING ADDRESS: Superintendent, Lyndon B. Johnson National Historical Park, P.O. Box 329, Johnson City, Texas 78636 **Telephone:** 512-868-7128

DIRECTIONS: There are two units to the park, one in Johnson City and one near Stonewall. Johnson City and Stonewall are about 50 miles (80 km) west of Austin and 60 miles (97 km) north of San Antonio. Both are located on US 290, an east-west highway connecting Austin and Fredericksburg. North-South US 281 connects San Antonio and Wichita Falls. In Johnson City, stop first at the Visitor Center in the center of town. Near Stonewall, begin your visit at the Visitor Center of the LBJ State Historical Park.

The Park includes the birthplace, boyhood home, grandfather's settlement, ranch and gravesite of the 36th President of the United States. Authorized for addition to the National Park System on Dec. 2, 1969.

VISITOR ACTIVITIES: Johnson City has guided tours of the boyhood home and the pioneer settlement of his grandparents. Stonewall: free tour buses to Johnson's school, birthplace, family cemetery, gravesite, and the LBJ Ranch. All bus tours are about 90 minutes long; **Permits:** No; **Fees:** No; **Visitor facilities:** Handicapped accessible, restrooms, interpretive activities. A full range of facilities is available in the surrounding area; **Any limitations on vehicle usage:** Access to the LBJ Ranch is by tour bus only. Access to the Johnson Settlement is by 1/4 mile walking trail; **Hiking trails:** No; **Backcountry:** No; **Camping:** No, but camping is available in Lady Bird Johnson Municipal Park in Fredericksburg, Pedernales Falls State Park, and Blanco State Park. There are a number of other state and commercial facilities in the immediate area. Contact the Park for further information; **Other overnight accommodations on site:** No; **Meals served in the park:** No; **Food and supplies obtainable in the park:** No; **Food and supplies obtainable nearby:** Yes, in Johnson City and Stonewall, TX; **Overnight accommodations:** Johnson City, Stonewall, Blanco, and Fredericksburg; **First Aid available in park:** Yes; **Nearest Hospital:** Fredericksburg, 30 miles (48 km) west of Johnson City and 17 miles (27.4 km) west of LBJ Ranch; **Days/Hours:** Johnson City: 9 a.m. to 5 p.m. every day; Stonewall: By tour bus only, 10 a.m. to 4:00 p.m. daily; **Holiday Closings:** Dec. 25 LBJ Ranch, and Dec. 25 and Jan. 1 at Boyhood Home and Settlement; **Visitor attractions closed for seasons:** No; **Weather:** Moderate weather. Summer temperatures are in the mid to upper 90°'sF but there is usually a light breeze. Winters average about 40°F with occasional showers. It rarely snows; rain occasionally freezes on the roads. Summer tours may be shortened when temperature and humidity criteria exceed predetermined comfort levels.

GENERAL INFORMATION: Advance reservations are required for assured group tours. Groups arriving without reservations may experience long delays prior to being accommodated. Arrangements may be made by calling 512-644-2241 or 512-868-7128.

Padre Island National Seashore
Corpus Christi, Texas   **SEE CLIMATABLE NO. 160**

MAILING ADDRESS: Superintendent, Padre Island National Seashore, 9405 S. Padre Island Dr., Corpus Christi, Texas 78418-5597 **Telephone:** 512-937-2621

DIRECTIONS: The only motor vehicle access to the National Seashore is from the North end. There are two approaches: The first leads over a causeway from Corpus Christi to North Padre Island (Park Road 22), the other leads from Port Aransas down Mustang Island via Park Road 53. The Visitor Center is approximately 10 miles (16 km) south of the junction of Park Roads 53 and 22.

Noted for its wide sand beaches, excellent fishing, and abundant bird and marine life, this barrier island stretches along the Gulf Coast for 66 miles (106 km). Authorized for addition to the National Park System on Sept. 28, 1962.

VISITOR ACTIVITIES: beach driving, fishing, swimming, surfing, bird- and wildlife-watching, hiking, shelling, water-skiing, interpretive exhibits and programs, charter bay fishing trips; **Permits:** Texas State fishing license required for those between 17 and 65 years of age; **Fees:** $1 per person entrance fee, $3 per 7 day stay, $4 camping fee ($2 with Golden Age Passports) at Malaquite Beach Campground; **Visitor facilities:** Presently closed for replacement, will re-open in 1989; nature trails; **Any limitations on vehicle usage:** Vehicles must remain on the roads and the beach. Driving on the beach in front of the campground is prohibited; **Hiking trails:** Yes, self-guiding nature trail. You are free to hike over the entire island except on dunes; **Backcountry:** No; **Camping:** Yes, no reservations available for campsites; open camping permitted on 7-1/2 miles of beach accessible by all 2 wheel drive vehicles. Open camping on 50 miles of beach accessible by 4 wheel drive vehicles. **Other overnight accommodations on site:** No, a paved campground with 40 sites, located south of the Ranger Station on the beach, can be used by trailers and recreational vehicles. Hookups are not provided. These facilities are available at the trailer park in Nueces County Park north of the National Seashore boundary and at the trailer park maintained in the Cameron County Park on South Padre Island near Port Isabel. For information on camping rates and facilities, write: Nueces County Parks, 10901 South Padre Island Dr., Box 3G, Corpus Christi, TX 78418 or Cameron County Parks, Box 666, Port Isabel, TX 78578; **Meals served in the park:** Closed for replacement, will re-open in 1989; **Food and supplies obtainable in the park:** Closed for replacement, will re-open in 1989; **Food and supplies obtainable nearby:** Full service at Port Isabel and Corpus Christi, about 16 miles (25 km) north of the seashore boundary, on the Park Road 22; **Overnight accommodations:** Port Isabel, Corpus Christi and South Padre Island; **First Aid available in park:** Yes, year-round at Gulf District Ranger Station; **Nearest Hospital:** Take crosstown freeway to Morgan Exit-Memorial Medical Center has emergency services; **Days/Hours:** Park always open; **Holiday Closings:** None; **Visitor attractions closed for seasons:** Closed for replacement, will re-open in 1989; **Weather:** Summer is usually quite humid, hot and windy. Late Fall is temperate and mild. Late Winter has many northers; cold and rainy Spring.

GENERAL INFORMATION: *Beware of the following hazards*—overexposure to the sun, swimming alone, rattlesnakes, Portuguese man-of-war jellyfish, small stingrays, fishing lines, broken glass and boards with nails, getting your car stuck in the sand, vehicle traffic on the beach, toxic waste in mislabeled or unmarked drums washed up on beach. Always wear shoes when hiking. Phone 512-949-8175 for a recorded informational message on park activities. Visitor Center open at Malaquite Beach (512) 949-8068.

TRAVEL ACCESS: Air: American, Southwest, Eastern, Continental and others service Corpus Christi, TX.

NEARBY FACILITIES & POINTS OF INTEREST: Hotel/Motel: For full information, contact: Corpus Christi Chamber of Commerce, (512) 882-6161, 1201 N. Shoreline, Corpus Christi, TX 78401.

Palo Alto Battlefield National Historic Site
Brownsville, Texas   **SEE CLIMATABLE NO. 160**

MAILING ADDRESS: Palo Alto Battlefield National Historic Site, c/o Padre Island National Seashore, 9405 South Padre Island Dr., Corpus Christi, TX 78418 **Telephone:** 512-937-2621

DIRECTIONS: NOT YET OPEN TO PUBLIC. NO VISITOR FACILITIES.
This area commemorates the site of one of two Mexican war battles fought on U.S. soil. Authorized for addition to the National Park Service on Nov. 10, 1978.

Rio Grande Wild and Scenic River
Texas   **SEE CLIMATABLE NO. 154**

MAILING ADDRESS: c/o Superintendent, Big Bend National Park, TX 79834 **Telephone:** (915) 477-2251 or for River Information (915) 477-2393

DIRECTIONS: This is an undeveloped area administered by Big Bend National Park. It extends from Mariscal Canyon in Big Bend National Park to the Terrell/Val Verde County line. See Big Bend National Park for directions.
Authorized for addition to the National Park System on November 10, 1978 to preserve a 191 mile (307 km) segment of the Rio Grande from above Mariscal Canyon in Big Bend National Park to Terrell/Val Verde County line in Texas.

VISITOR ACTIVITIES: Canoeing and rafting year round; **Permits:** required for floating. May be obtained at Persimmon Gap Visitor Center at the North Entrance of Big Bend National Park and any Ranger Station in the park; **Fees:** entrance fee applicable; **Visitor facilities:** Visitor Centers at Persimmon Gap and Rio Grande Village. Developed campground, store, trailer village, amphitheater at Rio Grande Village. No visitor facilities in the Lower Canyons outside of Big Bend National Park; **Any limitations on vehicle usage:** All vehicles must stay on developed roads. Little or no access to the Lower Canyons; **Hiking trails:** Only in Big Bend National Park; **Backcountry:** Primitive roadside camping in Big Bend National Park; **Camping:** backcounty camping in Lower Canyons, developed campgrounds in Big Bend; **Other overnight accommodations on site:** None near the Lower Canyons. See Big Bend National Park; **Meals served in the park:** see Big Bend; **Food and supplies obtainable in the park:** see Big Bend; **Food and supplies obtainable nearby:** see Big Bend; **First Aid available in park:** at any Ranger Station; **Nearest Hospital:** Alpine Texas, 100 miles from park headquarters; **Days/Hours:** N/A; **Holiday Closings:** None; **Visitor attractions closed for seasons:** Rio Grande Village Visitor Center closed June to October; **Weather:** Summer is hot. Mild the rest of the year.

GENERAL INFORMATION: Floating the Lower Canyons requires approximately seven days. There are no take-out points between La Linda Mexico and Dryden Crossing (83 miles). In an emergency parties should be prepared to evacuate themselves, rescue is difficult and patrols infrequent. Within the park there are two canyons (Mariscal and Boquillas) that are relatively easy and numerous put-in points. Write to park for equipment requirements.

TRAVEL ACCESS: See Big Bend National Park.

San Antonio Missions National Historical Park
San Antonio, Texas   **SEE CLIMATABLE NO. 161**

MAILING ADDRESS: 2202 Roosevelt Avenue, San Antonio, Texas 78210-4919 **Telephone:** 512-229-5701

DIRECTIONS: The park preserves Missions Concepcion; San Jose, San Juan, and Espada which represent, along with the Alamo, the country's greatest concentration of 18th Century Spanish Colonial missions. The Alamo (Mission San Antonio de Valero) is not included in the park. The park also preserves Mission Espada's irrigation system which consists of a stone dam and aqueduct and about five miles of irrigation ditch (acequia). It is the country's only functioning Spanish Colonial irrigation system. This affiliated area was authorized for addition to the National Park System on November 10, 1978, and began operation on April 1, 1983.

VISITOR ACTIVITIES: walking tours; **Permits:** No; **Fees:** No; **Visitor facilities:** Parking and restrooms; **Any limitations on vehicle usage:** None; **Hiking trails:** No; **Backcountry:** No; **Camping:** No; **Other overnight accommodations on site:** No; **Meals served in the park:** No; **Food and supplies obtainable in the park:** No; **Food and supplies obtainable nearby:** Yes, in San Antonio; **Overnight accommodations:** San Antonio; **First Aid available in park:** Yes; **Nearest Hospital:** San Antonio; **Days/Hours:** Open daily from 9 a.m. to 6 p.m., during daylight savings time and 8 a.m. to 5 p.m., during standard time; **Holiday Closings:** Dec. 25, Jan. 1; **Visitor attractions closed for seasons:** None.

Utah

GOLDEN SPIKE HISTORIC SITE

MORMON PIONEER
NATIONAL HISTORIC TRAIL

DINOSAUR NATIONAL MONUMENT

TIMPANOGOS CAVE NATIONAL MONUMENT

ARCHES NATIONAL PARK

CANYONLANDS NATIONAL PARK

CAPITOL REEF NATIONAL PARK

NATURAL BRIDGES NATIONAL MONUMENT

HOVENWEEP NATIONAL MONUMENT

RAINBOW BRIDGE NATIONAL MONUMENT

GLEN CANYON NATIONAL RECREATION AREA

SALT LAKE CITY

ZION
NATIONAL PARK

CEDAR BREAKS
NATIONAL MONUMENT

BRYCE CANYON NATIONAL PARK

Arches National Park
Moab, Utah   **SEE CLIMATABLE NO. 162**

MAILING ADDRESS: Superintendent, Arches National Park, P.O. Box 907, Moab, Utah 84532 **Telephone:** 801-259-8161

DIRECTIONS: The Visitor Center is 5 miles (8 km) northwest of Moab on US 191.

Extraordinary products of erosion in the form of giant arches, windows, pinnacles, and pedestals change color constantly in the sunlight. Arches National Monument created by Presidential Proclamation on Apr. 12, 1929, designated Arches National Park in 1971.

VISITOR ACTIVITIES: interpretive exhibits, walks and talks, auto tours, wildlife-watching, picnicking, backcountry, camping; **Permits:** required for overnight back-country use. They can be obtained from the Visitor Center; **Fees:** $3.00/vehicle, $10.00/annual/reciprocal at CANY, $1.00 walking or commercial, $5.00/camping per night, $5 camping fee (March through October). Golden Age and Golden Eagle Passports accepted and available; **Visitor facilities:** parking and restrooms at Visitor Center, foot trails, campground (no water-pit toilets in winter), picnic area, self-guiding trails; **Any limitations on vehicle usage:** All vehicles must stay on established roads; **Hiking trails:** Yes, obtain brochures describing self-guiding walking tours at the Visitor Center; **Back-country:** Yes, backcountry hikers must obtain backcountry permits at the Visitor Center; **Camping:** Yes; individual campsites cannot be reserved, but group sites are on a reservation system. Write the park for reservations. Campground will be closed for 2-3 weeks in June, 1988 for road repairs; **Other overnight accommodations on site:** No; **Meals served in the park:** No; **Food and supplies obtainable in the park:** No; **Food and**

supplies obtainable nearby: Yes, in Moab; **Overnight accommodations:** Moab, US 191, 5 miles (8 km); **First Aid available in park:** Yes; **Nearest Hospital:** Moab, US 191, 5 miles (8 km); **Days/Hours:** Open 24 hours a day, 7 days a week year-round; **Holiday Closings:** Visitor Center closes Dec. 25 and January 1 and Thanksgiving Day; Park remains open; **Visitor attractions closed for seasons:** No; **Weather:** Spring and Fall are the best times to visit Arches. Winters are mild and Summers are warm, with temperatures frequently above 100°.

GENERAL INFORMATION: *For Your Safety*—You should carry plenty of water, because daytime temperatures here can reach 110°F. Always hike or climb in the company of others. Don't leave your car with children or pets locked inside—the heat of the direct sun can harm them. When hiking, stay on trails, climbing on sandstone can be hazardous. Pets not allowed on any trails. Mountain bikes are considered wheeled vehicles and must stay on maintained roads. They are *not* allowed on any trails. Water available year round at Visitor Center.

Bryce Canyon National Park
Bryce Canyon, Utah   **SEE CLIMATABLE NO. 163**

MAILING ADDRESS: Superintendent, Bryce Canyon National Park, Bryce Canyon, Utah 84717 **Telephone:** 801-834-5322

DIRECTIONS: The Park is in southwestern Utah within a 5 hour drive of 10 other units of the National Park System. Take Utah 12 east from US 89. The park entrance is 4 miles off Route 12 on Utah 63. Utah 12 continues through Boulder to Capitol Reef National Park.

Pinnacles, walls and spires form amphitheaters whose colors are everchanging with light and weather. High altitude overlooks, spectacular scenery and clean air combine in some of the world's finest views. Set aside by Presidential Proclamation June 8, 1923.

VISITOR ACTIVITIES: Information, slide program, exhibits and sales publications at the Visitor Center. Sightseeing, photography, wildlife watching, hiking and camping year round. Guided walks, horse back rides, van tours and evening campfire programs during the summer. Cross country skiing and snow-shoeing in winter; **Permits:** Free permits are required for overnight backpack camping. Snowshoes are available for loan with security. Both are available at the Visitor Center; **Fees:** $5 per private vehicle; $2 per person on bus or non-motor vehicle; Golden Eagle, Golden Age and Golden Access available and accepted; $5 campsite fee (first come, first served); **Visitor facilities:** parking, restrooms at Visitor Center and Sunset Point year round (other areas seasonally); campgrounds; overlooks for viewing and photography; trails; picnic areas; conducted activities in summer; **Any limitations on vehicle usage:** Trailers not allowed beyond Sunset Campground—can be left at Visitor Center parking. All vehicles restricted to paved roads and designated overlooks. Speed limits vary with conditions, and are established for scenic viewing. Be prepared to stop for wildlife and other visitors; **Hiking trails:** Most trails descend into the canyons and are moderate to steep. High elevation requires extra exertion. Wear good shoes and watch your footing. You may want to carry water; **Backcountry:** Required permits, information and maps available at the Visitor Center; **Camping:** 200+ campsites, first come, first served. Arrive early. Only one loop open for winter camping; **Other overnight accommodations on site:** Bryce Canyon Lodge-motel units and historical cabins; open Mid-May through September. Reservations available from TW Recreation Services, 451 Main, P.O. Box 400, Cedar City, UT 84720, Telephone 801-586-7686; **Meals served in the park:** Bryce Canyon Lodge Dining Room; **Food and supplies obtainable nearby:** At stores and shops along routes into park and in nearby communities; **Overnight accommodations nearby:** At motels and campgrounds along routes into park and in nearby communities—seasonal and year round; **First Aid available in park:** At park Visitor Center year round. Also at Lodge in summer; **Nearest Hospital:** Panguitch (Utah Route 63 and Route 12 to US 89, then north to Panguitch—26 miles); **Days/Hours:** Park always open. Visitor Center open 8 a.m. to 4:30 p.m. with longer spring, summer and fall hours; **Holiday Closings:** Visitor Center closed December 25; **Visitor attractions closed for seasons:** Main park road open all year. Some spurs closed in winter to permit cross country ski access. Road and overlooks plowed when weather permits after winter snows; **Weather:** Pleasant days and cool nights from May through October; July and August thundershowers common. Snow from November through March at higher elevations. Bright, crisp winter days afford best views of year.

GENERAL INFORMATION: *For Your Safety*—Be aware of the extra needs at high altitude where there is less oxygen. Know your physical limits. Summer storms are accompanied by lightning strikes in open areas and along the rim—seek shelter in your car. Animals are wild and should not be fed or handled for your sake as well as theirs.

TRAVEL ACCESS: Bus: Color Country Tours provides service from Cedar City, Utah; **Rail:** None; **Air:** Closest commercial airport is in Cedar City. Private planes are permitted at the Bryce Canyon Airport, 4 miles from the park. Rental cars are available in Cedar City.

NEARBY FACILITIES & POINTS OF INTEREST: Campgrounds: US Forest Service, State and private campgrounds are located throughout southern Utah. Scenic Utah 12 offers local, state and Federal lands for a variety of recreational experiences. Contact the Scenic 12 Chamber of Commerce, P.O. Box 157, Tropic, UT 84776 for information.

Canyonlands National Park
Moab, Utah **SEE CLIMATABLE NO. 162**

MAILING ADDRESS: Superintendent, Canyonlands National Park, 125 W. 2nd South, Moab, Utah 84532 **Telephone:** 801-259-7164

DIRECTIONS: The Park is 35 miles (56 km) southwest of Moab. The Needles district is on UT 211, 35 miles (56 km) west of US 191. Island in the Sky is on UT 313, 30 miles (48 km) southwest of US 191. Maze district is 45 miles (72 km) east of UT 24 via dirt road.

The geological area includes rocks, spires, and mesas that rise more than 2377 m (7800 feet) & petroglyphs left by Indians 700-1200 years ago. Established by act of Congress on Sept. 12, 1964.

VISITOR ACTIVITIES: picnicking, camping, boating, rafting, backcountry, auto and guided tours, interpretive exhibits, hiking, horseback riding, fishing, bird-watching. Concession-operated jeep tours and jeep rentals available nearby; **Permits:** for backcountry issued at districts; boating permits are issued by the superintendent; **Fees:** Golden Age and Golden Eagle Passports available and accepted. Campground fee for The Needles district is $5 per night (collected only in Summer); **Visitor facilities:** restrooms, picnic areas, campgrounds, hiking trails. Limited concession facilities available at Needles Outpost in Needles district. Gas, small store, rentals (see pamphlet). Be certain you have ample gas, water, tools, emergency supplies, etc. **Any limitations on vehicle usage:** All vehicles must stay on established roads and four-wheel-drive routes. Trail bikes must be licensed, muffled, and operated by a licensed driver; **Hiking trails:** Yes, check with a Ranger for information on the many miles of hiking trails; **Backcountry:** Yes, information can be obtained from a Park Ranger. You must provide your own water for backcountry trips; **Camping:** Yes, no reservations for individual campsites.

Campers should bring their own fuel. For group site reservations, telephone 801-259-7164; **Other overnight accommodations on site:** No; **Meals served in the park:** No; **Food and supplies obtainable in the park:** No; **Food and supplies obtainable nearby:** Yes, in Monticello, Moab, Green River, Hanksville; **Overnight accommodations:** Monticello, US 191, 50 miles; Moab, US 191, 35 miles (56 km); Green River, I-70 to 191, 60 miles (96.6 km); **First Aid available in park:** Yes; **Nearest Hospital:** Moab, Hwy 191, 35 miles (56 km); **Days/Hours:** Park Headquarters (in Moab) and information station (Monticello) is open from 8 a.m. to 4:30 p.m. weekdays. The park is open year-round; **Visitor attractions closed for seasons:** No; **Weather:** This is desert country. Winter is usually short, with little snow. Spring and Autumn are long and pleasant, except for the high winds, sometimes accompanied by sand or dust storms in Spring.

GENERAL INFORMATION: Piped water is available near Squaw Flat Campground in The Needles area, but nowhere else in the park. Information also available at contact stations in the districts and at Arches NP visitor center daily.

Capitol Reef National Park
Torrey, Utah   SEE CLIMATABLE NO. 162

MAILING ADDRESS: Superintendent, Capitol Reef National Park, Torrey, Utah 84775 **Telephone:** 801-425-3791

DIRECTIONS: The Visitor Center is 11 miles (19 km) east of Torrey on UT 24.
Narrow high-walled gorges cut through 75 miles of the Waterpocket Fold uplift of colorful sedimentary formations. Dome-shaped white sandstone formations along the Fremont River accounts for the name. Created by Act of Congress 1971.

VISITOR ACTIVITIES: auto tours, interpretive exhibits, camping, picnicking, interpretive programs, hiking, backcountry; **Permits:** for backcountry available at Visitor Center; **Fees:** Entrance fee, $3, $5 camping fee per vehicle per night, except at Cedar Mesa and Cathedral Valley campgrounds, where there is no charge for camping; **Visitor facilities:** scenic drive, campgrounds, picnic areas, hiking trails, drinking water; **Any limitations on vehicle usage:** Vehicles and mountain bikes are restricted to established roads; **Hiking trails:** Yes, trails vary in length and difficulty; **Backcountry:** Yes, information is available from Visitor Center or by contacting the Superintendent; **Camping:** Yes, no reservations available for individual campsites. Group sites can be reserved in advance by writing the Superintendent. A complete list of nearby accommodations and services is available at the Visitor Center; **Other overnight accommodations on site:** No; **Meals served in the park:** No; **Food and supplies obtainable in the park:** No; **Food and supplies obtainable nearby:** Yes, Torrey, Bicknell, Loa, Hanksville; **Overnight accommodations:** in communities west of the park and at Hanksville to the east; **First Aid available in park:** Yes; **Nearest Hospital:** Richfield; Utah 24 to 119 to 89, 72 miles (116 km); **Days/Hours:** Park open 24 hours a day year-round; Visitor Center hours vary with the seasons; **Holiday Closings:** closed federal holidays, November through April; **Visitor attractions closed for seasons:** Weather conditions occasionally prohibit access to areas served by dirt and gravel roads; **Weather:** The elevation and desert climate make the area prone to temperature extremes. July and August are the hottest months, with midday temperatures in the upper 30°sC (90°sF) common. Summer evenings cool to the 10°-15°C (50°-60°F) range. Thunderstorms can bring flash floods from July through Sept. Spring and Fall are mild, with warm days and cool nights. Winter daytime temperatures average below 10°C (50°F), dropping below freezing at night. Bitter cold comes occasionally during the Winter, but snowfall is usually light. The average annual precipitation is about 18 cm (7 inches) with low relative humidity.

GENERAL INFORMATION: *For Your Safety*—Be sure to carry water with you even on short hikes. Most water in Capitol Reef is contaminated with minerals or by animals. Keep pets under physical restraint.

NEARBY FACILITIES & POINTS OF INTEREST: Hotel/Motel: Rim Rock Motel & Restaurant, U-24, 8 miles West, 801-425-3843, Capitol Reef Motel, 801-425-3271, (Torrey, 11 miles West of Visitor Center), Sunglow Motel & Cafe, 801-425-3821 and Aquarius Inn, 801-425-3835 (both in Bicknell, about 20 miles West of Visitor Center); **Campgrounds:** U.S. Forest Service Campgrounds in Sunglow (22 miles, off U-24), Singletree (22 miles, off U-12), Pleasant Creek (27 miles, off U-12), and Oak Creek (28 miles, off U-12), also private camping at Rim Rock Motel & Restaurant, 8 miles, 801-425-3843, and Chuck Wagon in Torrey, 11 miles West, 801-425-3288.

Cedar Breaks National Monument
Cedar City, Utah   **SEE CLIMATABLE NO. 163**

MAILING ADDRESS: Superintendent, Cedar Breaks National Monument, P.O. Box 749 Cedar City, Utah 84720; **Telephone:** 801-586-9451

DIRECTIONS: The Monument is reached via UT 14, 27 miles (43.5 km) from US 89 at Long Valley Junction, and 23 miles (37 km) from Int. 15 at Cedar City via UT 14. It can also be reached via UT 143, 14 miles (22.5 km) from Parowan. The Visitor Center is on the rim 1 mile (1.6 km) from the south entrance.

A huge natural amphitheater has eroded into the variegated Pink Cliffs (Wasatch Formation), which are 607 m (2000 feet) thick at this point. Created by Presidential Proclamation on Aug. 23, 1933.

VISITOR ACTIVITIES: camping, picnicking, interpretive talks, snowmobiling, wildflower-watching; **Permits:** No; **Fees:** Entrance fee $3 per vehicle, Campground fee is $4 per night; **Visitor facilities:** restrooms at Visitor Center, campground; **Any limitations on vehicle usage:** Drive only on established roads. Do not drive on meadows; **Hiking trails:** Yes, trails vary in length and difficulty. Amphitheater is largely inaccessible; **Backcountry:** No; **Camping:** Yes, no reservations available for campgrounds; **Other overnight accommodations on site:** No; **Meals served in the park:** No; **Food and supplies obtainable in the park:** No; **Food and supplies obtainable nearby:** Yes, in Cedar City, Parowan, Panguitch; **Overnight accommodations:** Cedar City, Parowan, Panguitch, or Brian Head 8 miles from Visitor Center; **First Aid available in park:** Yes; **Nearest Hospital:** Cedar City via UT 143-UT 14, 23 miles (37 km); **Days/Hours:** Visitor Center is open 8 a.m. to 6 p.m. from Memorial Day through late Sept.; road open June through October depending on the weather; **Holiday Closings:** None in season; **Visitor attractions closed for seasons:** The travel season extends from early June to late October, depending on the weather. At other times, check road conditions before driving to the Monument; **Weather:** usually permits comfortable camping from late June to Labor Day; at other times, freezing temperatures are common at night.

GENERAL INFORMATION: Nearby points of interest include Zion National Park, 79 miles (127 km) away via Cedar City and Int. 15, or 73 miles (117.5 km) via Long Valley Junction and US 89; Bryce Canyon National Park, 65 miles (105 km) away (see listings in this book).

TRAVEL ACCESS: Bus: Greyhound provides daily service to Cedar City about 23 miles from park; **Rail:** Amtrak provides regular service to Milford, UT; **Air:** Skywest Airlines provides daily service to Cedar City; **Other:** Color Country Touring Vans provide access directly to park from Cedar City.

NEARBY FACILITIES & POINTS OF INTEREST: Campgrounds: KOA Campground Main Street, Cedar City, Utah, several U.S. Forest Service campgrounds nearby; **Parks, other points of interest:** Bryce Canyon National Park, Zion National Park, Navajo Lake (USFS), Duck Creek (USFS).

Dinosaur National Monument
For details see listing in Colorado

Glen Canyon National Recreation Area
For details see listing in Arizona

Golden Spike National Historic Site
Brigham City, Utah   **SEE CLIMATABLE NO. 165**

MAILING ADDRESS: Superintendent, Golden Spike National Historic Site, P.O. Box W, Brigham City, Utah 84302 **Telephone:** 801-471-2209

DIRECTIONS: The Site is about 30 miles (48 km) west of Brigham City. To reach the Site, drive 23 miles (37 km) westward on UT 83 to the Promontory Junctions; turn left and go 2 miles (3.2 km) to the next junction; then turn right and go 8 km (5 miles). Roads are well-marked.

Completion of the first transcontinental railroad in the United States was celebrated here when the Central Pacific and Union Pacific Railroads met in 1869. Authorized July 30, 1965.

VISITOR ACTIVITIES: interpretive exhibits, audio-visual programs, picnicking, history programs in Summer, working replica steam locomotives exhibited May through Sept.; **Permits:** No; **Fees:** $3 per vehicle, $1 per bus passenger; **Visitor facilities:** Visitor Center, parking, restrooms, picnic area; **Any limitations on vehicle usage:** Drive only on established roads; **Hiking trails:** Yes, trails follow the historic railroads; **Backcountry:** No; **Camping:** No; **Other overnight accommodations on site:** No; **Meals served in the park:** No; **Food and supplies obtainable in the park:** Soda pop and snack vending machines, film at Visitor Center; **Food and supplies obtainable nearby:** Yes, Brigham City or Tremonton, UT; **Overnight accommodations:** Brigham City, 30 miles (48 km) east on UT 83, or Tremonton, 30 miles (48 km) northeast on UT 83 and 102; **First Aid available in park:** Yes; **Nearest Hospital:** Brigham City, 30 miles (48 km) east; **Days/ Hours:** Open daily from 8 a.m. to 4:30 p.m.; until 6 p.m. in Summer; **Holiday Closings:** Dec. 25 and Thanksgiving Day; **Visitor attractions closed for seasons:** Self-guided auto tours are not available in Winter.

TRAVEL ACCESS: Bus: Service into Brigham City, Utah; **Rail:** service into Salt Lake City, Utah; **Air:** service into Salt Lake City, Utah.

Hovenweep National Monument
For details see listing in Colorado

Mormon Pioneer Trail
For details see listing in Illinois

Natural Bridges National Monument
(near) Blanding, Utah   **SEE CLIMATABLE NO. 162**

MAILING ADDRESS: Superintendent, Natural Bridges National Monument, Box 1, Lake Powell, Utah 84533 **Telephone:** 801-259-5174

DIRECTIONS: The Visitor Center is 120 miles (193 km) south of Moab on US 191 and State 95, and 42 miles west of Blanding on State 95. It is 26 miles (41 km) east of Fry Canyon on Utah 95 and 44 miles (71 km) north of Mexican Hat on Route 261.
  Three natural bridges carved out of sandstone are protected here. The highest is 67 m (220 feet) above the streambed, with a span of 268 feet. Created by Presidential Proclamation on April 16, 1908, the first NPS area in Utah.

VISITOR ACTIVITIES: interpretive exhibits, camping, picnicking, auto tours, hiking; **Permits:** No; **Fees:** $3 per vehicle entrance fee, Golden Eagle and Golden Age Passports accepted and available; **Visitor facilities:** Visitor Center, campground, picnic area, parking lot, loop road; **Any limitations on vehicle usage:** Camping limited to 21 foot vehicles; **Hiking trails:** Yes, dirt trails lead to the three bridges. Short paved trails go to viewpoints at each bridge; **Backcountry:** No; **Camping:** Yes, no reservations available for the 13 campsites; **Other overnight accommodations on site:** No; **Meals served in the park:** No; **Food and supplies obtainable in the park:** No; **Food and supplies obtainable nearby:** Yes, Fry Canyon and Blanding; **Overnight accommodations:** Yes, Blanding, US 191 and State 95, 42 miles (67.6 km); Mexican Hat, Route 261, 44 miles (71 km); **First Aid available in park:** Yes, or nearby in Blanding, US 191; **Nearest Hospital:** Monticello, US 191, 64 miles (103 km) from the park; **Days/Hours:** Visitor Center is open 8 a.m. to 4:30 p.m.; **Holiday Closings:** Thanksgiving, Dec. 25 & Jan. 1; **Visitor attractions closed for seasons:** Hiking trails into the canyons may be closed in Winter due to snow and ice; **Weather:** best from late April through October.

GENERAL INFORMATION: Visitors can see other points of interest in the area. They include Canyonlands and Arches National Park (see listings in this book), Lake Powell and Monument Valley. *Warning:* there is hazardous terrain throughout the area; lightning may strike overlooks and viewpoints during storms. Do not enter any ruins you may come across. If these or artifacts are disturbed in any way, a priceless archaeological story could be destroyed forever. The nearest source of gasoline is Fry Canyon, 26 miles (41 km) away.

Rainbow Bridge National Monument
Utah   **SEE CLIMATABLE NO. 162**

MAILING ADDRESS: Superintendent, c/o Glen Canyon National Recreation Area, P.O. Box 1507, Page, Arizona 86040 **Telephone:** 602-645-2471

DIRECTIONS: You can reach Rainbow Bridge on foot or on horseback (contact 602-672-3852) on the trail from Navajo Mountain Trading Post 15 miles (24 km) or on a trail that begins at the abandoned Rainbow Lodge on foot 13 miles (20 km). But the most commonly used approach is by boat on Lake Powell. Many visitors now take the water route of 50 miles (80 km) from Wahweap, Bullfrog, or Halls Crossing to the landing at Bridge Canyon and then walk about ¼ mile (.5 km) up the Canyon to the bridge.

Greatest of the world's known natural bridges, this symmetrical arch of salmon-pink sandstone rises 290 feet above the floor of Bridge Canyon. Created by Presidential Proclamation on May 30, 1910.

VISITOR ACTIVITIES: hiking, walking trails; **Permits:** Yes, obtain through the Navajo Tribe, Window Rock, AZ; **Fees:** No; **Visitor facilities:** For people who bring their own boats, there are launching ramps at Wahweap, Halls Crossing, Bullfrog, and Hite. Concessioners at these places sell boating and camping supplies, and they will provide guided boat tours from Wahweap and Bullfrog. Closest marina facilities are at Dangling Rope Marina, 7 miles west (accessible by boat only); **Any limitations on vehicle usage:** No road access to Monument; **Hiking trails:** Yes; **Backcountry:** No; **Camping:** No; **Other overnight accommodations on site:** No; **Meals served in the park:** No; **Food and supplies obtainable in the park:** No; **Food and supplies obtainable nearby:** No; **Overnight accommodations:** Page, AZ, on US 89, near Glen Canyon Dam, 50 miles (80 km) Wahweap and Bullfrog, also 50 miles (80 km) away by water; **First Aid available in park:** Yes, at Dangling Rope Marina, 7 miles west, (accessible only by boat); **Days/Hours:** Park never closes; **Holiday Closings:** No; **Visitor attractions closed for seasons:** No; **Weather:** Extremely hot, sunny Summers.

GENERAL INFORMATION: Before beginning a trail trip, be sure to call Navajo Mountain Trading Post, Tuba City, AZ 602-672-2852, about the following: the condition of the trails, whether or not trading posts are open, and places at which water and supplies are available. Summer visitors should wear cool clothing and thick-soled shoes. Bring a hat, sunglasses, and protective lotion. Hikers should carry 1 gallon of water per person per day in summer. Many hikers arrange for one-way transportation by boat after hiking from Navajo Mountain.

NEARBY FACILITIES & POINTS OF INTEREST: Parks, other points of interest: Lake Powell, Glen Canyon National Recreation Area, Navajo National Monument, Grand Canyon National Park.

Timpanogos Cave National Monument
American Fork, Utah   **SEE CLIMATABLE NO. 164**

MAILING ADDRESS: Superintendent, Timpanogos Cave National Monument, Rural Route 3, Box 200, American Fork, Utah 84003 **Telephone:** 801-756-5238

DIRECTIONS: If you are driving south from Salt Lake City on I-15, turn east at UT 92, the Alpine exit #285. If you are driving north from Provo, turn east at Pleasant Grove exit #273 or American Fork exit #277. Timpanogos Cave is 7 miles (11 km) from either town via UT 146 or UT 92.
This series of three limestone caverns on the side of Mt. Timpanogos is noted for its colorful water-created formations and geological history. The first cave was discovered in 1887 and the Monument was created by Presidential Proclamation on Oct. 14, 1922.

VISITOR ACTIVITIES: Visitors follow a 1.5 mile (2.4 km) trail from the Visitor Center up to the cave entrance rising 1,065 feet in elevation. Picnicking, hiking, fishing, and nature walks are available; **Permits:** No; **Fees:** Purchase tickets for cave tours at the Visitor Center. A user fee of $3.00 is charged for persons 16 and over, $2.00 for 6 to 16, under 6 is free. Golden Age Passport holders are admitted for 1/2 price; **Visitor facilities:** picnic area, snacks, and souvenirs in Summer; **Any limitations on vehicle usage:** Vehicles confined to UT 92 and authorized parking areas; **Hiking trails:** Yes, two short trails on site; other hiking trails and backcountry available nearby at Uinta National Forest; **Backcountry:** Information on backcountry available at Visitor Center or by contacting: Supervisor, Uinta National Forest, U.S. Forest Service, 88 West 100 North, Provo, UT 84601, phone 801-377-5780; **Camping:** No; **Other overnight accommodations on site:** No, reserved and non-reserved campsites are available nearby at Uinta National Forest. Contact the forest for reservations and further information; **Meals served in the park:** Yes, snacks at the concession stand from mid-May to mid-Sept.; **Food and supplies obtainable in the park:** No; **Food and supplies obtainable nearby:** Yes, in Highland, American Fork, and Pleasant Grove; **Overnight accommodations:** Minimal accommodations at American Fork, 7 miles (11 km) west of the cave on UT 92 and Pleasant Grove 10 miles (16 km) southeast of the cave on US 89 or I-15; **First Aid available in park:** Yes; **Nearest Hospital:** American Fork, UT 92, 7 miles (11 km); **Days/Hours:** The cave is open daily from about mid-May through Sept. 30 depending on weather. Visitor Center is open year-round; **Holiday Closings:** Thanksgiving, Dec. 25 and Jan. 1; **Visitor attractions closed for seasons:** Snow and ice make the trail to the cave impassable from late Oct.-Apr.; **Weather:** Cool mornings and warm days in Spring and Fall. July and August day time temperatures in mid to high 90°sF. Occasional summer rains close the cave trail temporarily. Winter months are cold with considerable snow accumulation.

GENERAL INFORMATION: About 3 hours are required for the hike and tour of the cave. Because tour sizes are limited, frequently it is not possible to accommodate all visitors who wish to tour the cave. It is advisable to call for current conditions before coming, (801) 756-5238. Temperature within the caves is a damp, chilly 6°C (43°F). A warm jacket or sweater and comfortable walking shoes with gripping soles are advised.

Zion National Park
Springdale, Utah   **SEE CLIMATABLE NO. 167**

MAILING ADDRESS: Superintendent, Zion National Park, Springdale, Utah 84767 **Telephone:** 801-772-3256

DIRECTIONS: New Visitor Center at Kolob Canyons exit 40 from I-15. I-15 passes west of Zion and connects with UT 9 and 17 to the park. US 89 passes east and connects with UT 9 to the Park. The Visitor Center is a short distance from the Park's South Entrance.

Colorful canyon and mesa scenery includes erosion and rockfault patterns and evidence of former volcanic activity. Established by Act of Congress on Nov. 19, 1919.

VISITOR ACTIVITIES: interpretive films, exhibits, & programs (schedules posted throughout the park), driving, walking and hiking, mountain climbing, wading, camping, biking, horseback trips (make arrangements at Zion Lodge), 1-1/2 hour tram tour of major points of interest leaves from Zion Lodge in Summer, wildlife- and bird-watching; **Permits:** Required for backcountry, available at Visitor Centers; **Fees:** $5 per vehicle or $2 per person on commercial vehicles is the entrance fee for persons 12 and over. Camping fee is $6 per night per site. Golden Eagle and Golden Age Passports are accepted and available; **Visitor facilities:** Visitor Center, campgrounds, tap water, fire grates, tables, sanitary disposal station, telephones, picnic sites, religious services (May-Sept.), lodging and food service April through October; **Any limitations on vehicle usage:** Do not park on curves. Watch for deer. Your car's lights must be in good working order; they are essential when travelling through the tunnel on East Entrance Road; **Hiking trails:** Yes, a wide variety of trails is available; **Backcountry:** Backcountry permits are required for overnight trips and use of the Narrows; **Camping:** Yes, camping is permitted only in designated campsites and is limited to 14 days. Campgrounds are run on a first-come, first-served basis; **Other overnight accommodations on site:** Zion Lodge is operated by the Utah Parks Division of TWRS (451 North Main Street, Cedar City, Utah 84720). Zion Lodge has cabin and motel accommodations within the Park

(Apr. thru Oct.). Reservations are advisable. Call 801-586-7686. Communities in the vicinity offer year-round accommodations; **Meals served in the park:** Yes, Zion Lodge has a dining room and a soda fountain; **Food and supplies obtainable in the park:** No; **Food and supplies obtainable nearby:** Yes, at Springdale; **Overnight accommodations:** Springdale and other nearby communities; **First Aid available in park:** Yes, at the Visitor Center year-round. Physician's assistant in Springdale in summer - A physician is in Hurricane, 24 miles (39 km) west of the Park; **Nearest Hospital:** St. George, 45 miles (72 km) west of the Park, Cedar City, 60 miles (97 km) north, and Kanab, 42 miles (68 km) east; **Days/Hours:** Open 24 hours a day year-round; **Holiday Closings:** None; **Visitor attractions closed for seasons:** Higher hiking trails are closed by snow in Winter. The Virgin River Narrows hike is closed typically from mid to late Oct. through June (closed due to cold water and air temperatures and high river levels). During the open season, trips thru the Narrows are permitted. The danger of flash floods exists during thunderstorms (July, Aug. and early Sept.). Best times for the trip are late June, late Sept. and early Oct. Then, go only after thorough preparation. Permits are required for all through Virgin River Narrows hikes (short trips from the bottom no longer require a permit); **Weather:** Snow may fall intermittently from Dec. to March; average winter maximum and minimum temperatures are 12°C (53°F) & -1°C (30°F). May to Oct. daytime temps. range from 22°C (72°F) to 39°C (103°F); nighttime, from 7°C (45°F) to 23°C (73°F).

GENERAL INFORMATION: *For Your Safety*—All hikers should take precautions. Obtain detailed information from a Park Ranger before attempting backcountry trails; tell someone where you plan to go and when you plan to return. Do not hike alone. Stay on established trails; taking shortcuts may endanger yourself and others. Stay out of drainage areas during thunderstorms as dry washes can become raging torrents in minutes. Watch your step if taking pictures near cliffs. Be alert for rockfalls and landslides.

The town of Springdale is situated within easy commuting distance of Bryce Canyon, the North Rim of the Grand Canyon and other well-known attractions. Many campers use the campground as a base of operations from which to explore the area. Other nearby attractions include "Ghost Towns" in Washington County and the Shakespearean Festival in Cedar City, which runs from mid-July to mid-August.

TRAVEL ACCESS: Bus: Greyhound provides service to Hurricane, Utah and Trailways serves Kanab, Utah; **Rail:** No; **Air:** Sky West Airlines provides service to St. George, and Cedar City, Utah; **Other:** Color Country Tours operate from Cedar City, Utah, and St. George, Tuesday, Thursday & Saturday in season. Utah Toll-free 1-800-634-3905.

NEARBY FACILITIES & POINTS OF INTEREST: Campgrounds: Zion Canyon Campground, Springdale, Utah 84767 801-772-3237; **Parks, other points of interest:** Bryce-2 hour drive, Pipe Spring-1-1/2 hour drive, Cedar Breaks-1-1/2 hour drive; **New Park Programs:** Zion Nature Center for children 6 thru 12, June-early August.

Virginia

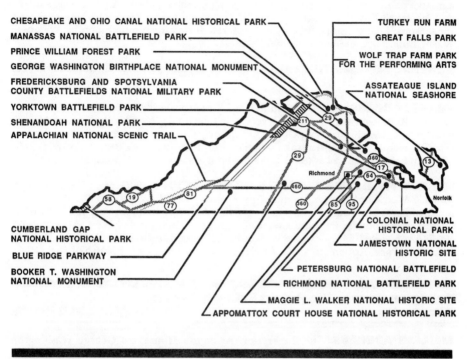

CHESAPEAKE AND OHIO CANAL NATIONAL HISTORICAL PARK
MANASSAS NATIONAL BATTLEFIELD PARK
PRINCE WILLIAM FOREST PARK
GEORGE WASHINGTON BIRTHPLACE NATIONAL MONUMENT
FREDERICKSBURG AND SPOTSYLVANIA
COUNTY BATTLEFIELDS NATIONAL MILITARY PARK
YORKTOWN BATTLEFIELD PARK
SHENANDOAH NATIONAL PARK
APPALACHIAN NATIONAL SCENIC TRAIL

TURKEY RUN FARM
GREAT FALLS PARK
WOLF TRAP FARM PARK
FOR THE PERFORMING ARTS
ASSATEAGUE ISLAND
NATIONAL SEASHORE

Richmond

Norfolk

CUMBERLAND GAP
NATIONAL HISTORICAL PARK
BLUE RIDGE PARKWAY
BOOKER T. WASHINGTON
NATIONAL MONUMENT

COLONIAL NATIONAL
HISTORICAL PARK
JAMESTOWN NATIONAL
HISTORIC SITE
PETERSBURG NATIONAL BATTLEFIELD
RICHMOND NATIONAL BATTLEFIELD PARK
MAGGIE L. WALKER NATIONAL HISTORIC SITE
APPOMATTOX COURT HOUSE NATIONAL HISTORICAL PARK

Appalachian National Scenic Trail
For details see listing in Maine

Appomattox Court House National Historical Park
Appomattox, Virginia   **SEE CLIMATABLE NO. 170**

MAILING ADDRESS: Superintendent, Appomattox Court House National Historical Park, P.O. Box 218, Appomattox, Virginia 24522 **Telephone:** 804-352-8987

DIRECTIONS: The Visitor Center is in the reconstructed Courthouse on VA 24, 3 miles (4.8 km) northeast of the town of Appomattox, VA.
General Robert E. Lee surrendered the Confederacy's largest field army to Lt. Gen. Ulysses S. Grant here on Apr. 9, 1865. The village has been restored. Authorized for addition to the National Park System on June 18, 1930.

VISITOR ACTIVITIES: walking tours (pamphlet available at the Visitor Center), living history talks in Summer, interpretive exhibits; **Permits:** No; **Fees:** $1 per person, ages 13-61, entrance fee is charged year round; **Visitor facilities:** parking areas and restrooms, interpretive exhibits, furnished historic buildings; **Any limitations on vehicle usage:** No vehicles are permitted in the village area; **Hiking trails:** Yes, self-guiding trails throughout the Park; **Backcountry:** No; **Camping:** No, but picnic areas and camping facilities are nearby; **Other overnight accommodations on site:** No; **Meals served in the park:** No; **Food and supplies obtainable in the park:** No; **Food and supplies obtainable nearby:** Yes, town of Appomattox; **Overnight accommodations:** Appomattox, VA

24, 3 miles (4.8 km); **First Aid available in park:** Yes, Rescue squad in Appomattox, VA; **Nearest Hospital:** Lynchburg, US 460, 25 miles (40 km); **Days/Hours:** Open daily 9:00 a.m. to 5 p.m.; **Holiday Closings:** Washington's Birthday, Martin Luther King's Birthday, Veteran's Day, Thanksgiving, Dec. 25, New Year's Day; **Visitor attractions closed for seasons:** Living history talks are only offered during the summer months; **Weather:** Warm, humid Summers; cool, humid Winters.

GENERAL INFORMATION: All pets must be kept on a leash while in the Park. Pets not allowed in public buildings.

TRAVEL ACCESS: Bus: Greyhound Bus Lines provides daily service into Appomattox, Va.; **Rail:** Amtrak provides daily service to Lynchburg, Va.; **Air:** Lynchburg Municipal Airport, Lynchburg, Va.; **Other:** Lynchburg Taxi Cab Service available at Lynchburg Municipal Airport, Amtrak Station or Bus Terminal, Avis Rent-a-car (804) 239-3622, and Hertz Rent-a-car (804) 239-3251 both at Lynchburg Municipal Airport.

NEARBY FACILITIES & POINTS OF INTEREST: Hotel/Motel: Traveler's Inn Motel, 7 West Confederate Avenue, Appomattox, Va. 24552, (804) 352-7451, 2 miles South of Park; Lee-Grant Motel—Hwy. 460 (5 miles), Appomattox, Va. 24522, 804-352-5234; **Campgrounds:** Paradise Lake Campground, Highway 460 West, Appomattox, Va. 24522 804-993-3332—9 miles West of Park; **Parks, other points of interest:** Holiday Lake State Park, Appomattox, Va. 24522, 804-248-6308, 10 miles North of Park.

Arlington House, The Robert E. Lee Memorial
Arlington, Virginia   **SEE CLIMATABLE NO. 38**

MAILING ADDRESS: Site Supervisor, Arlington House, c/o George Washington Memorial Parkway, Turkey Run Park, McLean, Virginia 22101 **Telephone:** 703-557-0613

DIRECTIONS: Access from Washington is via the Memorial Bridge. Parking available at the Arlington Cemetery Visitor Center. No vehicles allowed in cemetery. House is a ten minute walk from Visitors Center. Tourmobile available.

This was the home of Robert E. Lee, which he left to take command of the military forces of Virginia during the Civil War. It is located in Arlington Cemetery, overlooking the Potomac River and the city of Washington. Established by Act of Congress on Mar. 4, 1925.

VISITOR ACTIVITIES: interpretive exhibits, guided and self-guiding tours of the house; **Permits:** No; **Fees:** No; **Visitor facilities:** parking at Visitors Center, restrooms and bookstore on site; **Any limitations on vehicle usage:** No vehicles are allowed on House grounds; **Hiking trails:** No; **Backcountry:** No; **Camping:** No; **Other overnight accommodations on site:** No; **Meals served in the park:** No; **Food and supplies obtainable in the park:** No; **Food and supplies obtainable nearby:** Yes, Arlington, VA or Washington, D.C.; **Overnight accommodations:** in Washington metropolitan area; **First Aid available in park:** Yes; **Nearest Hospital:** Arlington, VA and Washington, D.C.; **Days/Hours:** Open daily from 9:30 a.m. to 4:30 p.m. Oct.-Mar.; until 6 p.m. Apr.-Sept.; **Holiday Closings:** Dec. 25, Jan. 1; **Visitor attractions closed for seasons:** No.

Blue Ridge Parkway
For details see listing in North Carolina

Booker T. Washington National Monument
Hardy, Virginia   **SEE CLIMATABLE NO. 170**

MAILING ADDRESS: Superintendent, Booker T. Washington National Monument, Route 3, Box 310, Hardy, Virginia 24101 **Telephone:** 703-721-2094

DIRECTIONS: The Monument is 16 miles (25.7 km) northeast of Rocky Mount, VA, via VA 122N, and 20 miles (32 km) southeast of Roanoke, VA, via VA 116S and 122N 21 miles (34 km) south of Bedford, VA via Rt 122.

This was the birthplace and early childhood home of the famous black leader and educator. Authorized for addition to the National Park System on Apr. 2, 1956.

VISITOR ACTIVITIES: audiovisual programs, conducted tours, craft demonstrations from mid-June through Labor Day, picnicking, photography; **Permits:** No; **Fees:** No; **Visitor facilities:** Visitor Center and Environmental Education and Cultural Center, picnic area, parking, sales area, restrooms; **Any limitations on vehicle usage:** No; **Hiking trails:** Yes, walking and nature trails; **Backcountry:** No; **Camping:** No; **Other overnight accommodations on site:** No; **Meals served in the park:** No; **Food and supplies obtainable in the park:** No; **Food and supplies obtainable nearby:** Yes, within a 10 mile (16 km) radius; more extensive facilities are at Roanoke, Rocky Mount and Bedford; **Overnight accommodations:** Roanoke, VA, 122S and 116N, 20 miles (32 km); Rocky Mount, VA, 122S, 16 miles (25.7 km); Beford, VA, VA 122N, 21 miles (34 km); **First Aid available in park:** Yes; **Nearest Hospital:** Roanoke, VA 122S and 116N, 20 miles (32 km); Rocky Mount, VA 122S, 16 miles (25.7 km); **Days/Hours:** The grounds are open during daylight hours. Visitor Center open 8:30 a.m. to 5 p.m. daily; **Holiday Closings:** Thanksgiving, Dec. 25 & Jan. 1; **Visitor attractions closed for seasons:** No; **Weather:** Spring is warm and mild; Summer, is warm to hot; Fall is mild, cool & pleasant; Winter is generally mild with a few light snowfalls.

GENERAL INFORMATION: *For Your Safety*—Keep your distance from the animals. Do not enter the pastures or pens.

NEARBY FACILITIES & POINTS OF INTEREST: For Hotel and campground information please telephone (703) 721-2094 or write to the Park; **Parks, other points of interest:** Blue Ridge Parkway, Fairy Stone State Park, and Smith Mountain Lake.

Chesapeake and Ohio Canal National Historical Park
For details see listing in Maryland

Colonial National Historical Park
Yorktown, Virginia   **SEE CLIMATABLE NO. 166**

MAILING ADDRESS: Superintendent, Colonial National Historical Park, P.O. Box 210, Yorktown, Virginia 23690 **Telephone:** 804-898-3400

DIRECTIONS: Both Jamestown and Yorktown are located off major highways: Rte. 17 and I-64. Both sites are accessible via the Colonial Parkway which joins Jamestown, Williamsburg and Yorktown. The Park encompasses most of Jamestown Island, site of the first permanent English settlement in America in 1607; Yorktown, scene of the culminating battle of the American Revolution in 1781; the 23 miles (37 km) Colonial Parkway connecting these and other colonial sites including Williamsburg; and Cape Henry

Memorial which marks the approximate site of the first landing of Jamestown's colonists in 1607. Authorized for addition to the National Park System on July 3, 1930.

VISITOR ACTIVITIES: self-guided auto and walking tours, guided walking tours, interpretive exhibits, living history and children's programs; **Permits:** Yes, a $3 bus permit is required for Colonial Parkway. Available at Jamestown Entrance Station and Yorktown Visitor Center; **Fees:** Yes, Jamestown Entrance Station fee is $5 per vehicle, or $2.00 per person for those 16 and over who arrive by bus or bicycle. Educational groups and holders of Golden Age and Golden Eagle Passports are admitted free; **Visitor facilities:** Souvenirs, exhibits, and audiovisual programs are offered at Jamestown and Yorktown (see listings in this book); **Any limitations on vehicle usage:** Park only in designated areas. There are no service stations, and the road is closed to commercial traffic except buses, for which permits are required; **Hiking trails:** No; **Backcountry:** No; **Camping:** No; **Other overnight accommodations on site:** No, City- and privately-operated campgrounds are nearby. Contact the Park for further information on directions and facilities; **Meals served in the park:** No, there are picnic areas along the Colonial parkway and at Yorktown Beach; **Food and supplies obtainable in the park:** No; **Food and supplies obtainable nearby:** Yes, at Yorktown and Williamsburg; **Overnight accommodations:** Restaurant and Motel Facilities are available in Yorktown and nearby along Rte. 17, and in Williamsburg; **First Aid available in park:** Yes; **Nearest Hospital:** Mary Immaculate Hospital, Newport News, 5 miles from Yorktown; Williamsburg Community Hosp. is 9½ miles (15.3 km) from Jamestown; **Days/Hours:** Jamestown Entrance Station open daily from 8:30 a.m. to 4:30 p.m. with extended hours from April through Oct.; Yorktown Visitor Center open daily from 8:30 a.m. to 5 p.m. with extended hours from Apr.-Oct.; **Holiday Closings:** Dec. 25; **Visitor attractions closed for seasons:** Moore House, Nelson House and picnic areas are closed in Winter.

NEARBY FACILITIES & POINTS OF INTEREST: Campgrounds: Newport News City Park is the closest campground to Yorktown, but there are many others nearby. There are also many campgrounds along Route 31 near Jamestown Island.

Cumberland Gap National Historical Park
For details see listing in Kentucky

Fredericksburg and Spotsylvania County Battlefields Memorial National Military Park
Fredericksburg, Virginia   **SEE CLIMATABLE NO. 168**

MAILING ADDRESS: Superintendent, Fredericksburg and Spotsylvania County Battlefields Memorial National Military Park, P.O. Box 679, Fredericksburg, Virginia 22404 **Telephone:** 703-373-4461

DIRECTIONS: The Visitor Center is in Fredericksburg on US 1 at the foot of Marye's Heights. Another Visitor Center is on the Chancellorsville Battlefield 10 miles (16 km) west of Fredericksburg on VA 3.
   Portions of four major Civil War Battlefields-Fredericksburg, Chancellorsville, the Wilderness, Spotsylvania Court House and several smaller historic sites comprise the Park. The battles occurred during 1862, 1863, and 1864. Established by act of Congress on Feb. 14, 1927.

VISITOR ACTIVITIES: museums, interpretive exhibits, living history demonstrations in Summer, biking, auto tours, hiking, fishing, picnicking; **Permits:** No; **Fees:** No;

Visitor facilities: museums, historic houses, trails, picnic sites; **Any limitations on vehicle usage:** All motorized vehicles must stay on established roadways that are open to the public; **Hiking trails:** Yes, along historic traces and to historic sites; **Backcountry:** No; **Camping:** No; **Other overnight accommodations on site:** No, camping is available at Prince William Forest Park (see listings in this book), 20 miles (32 km) north on Int. 95; **Meals served in the park:** No; **Food and supplies obtainable in the park:** No; **Food and supplies obtainable nearby:** Yes, in Fredericksburg; **Overnight accommodations:** Fredericksburg; **First Aid available in park:** Yes; **Nearest Hospital:** Fredericksburg, Jefferson Davis Hwy (Rte. 1 bypass); **Days/Hours:** Park roads open during daylight hours; Visitor Centers open daily, 9 a.m. to 5 p.m. generally until 6 p.m. in Summer; **Holiday Closings:** Dec. 25 and Jan. 1.

GENERAL INFORMATION: *For Your Safety*—Auto tours require turning onto and off of heavily travelled roadways. Beware of poisonous insects, plants and reptiles which may be encountered during your visit. Watch your footing while on the trails. Physically handicapped visitors are encouraged to start their visits at the Chancellorsville Visitor Center, which is best equipped for access needs.

TRAVEL ACCESS: Bus: Greyhound & Trailways Bus Systems provide daily service to Washington, Richmond and other cities; **Rail:** Amtrak provides service to Washington and Richmond within 1 mile of Park; **Air:** Byrd Airport in Richmond, 60 miles; Washington's Dulles Airport, 55 miles; Washington's National Airport, 45 miles; **Other:** Groome transportation runs shuttle buses and limousines between Byrd and National Airports with an intermediate stop in Fredericksburg. It is even possible to rent a bicycle at several downtown locations.

NEARBY FACILITIES & POINTS OF INTEREST: Hotel/Motel: Sheraton, Interstate 95 off Route 3, 703-786-8321, 4 miles from Park.

George Washington Birthplace National Monument
Washington's Birthplace, Virginia   **SEE CLIMATABLE NO. 168**

MAILING ADDRESS: Superintendent, George Washington Birthplace National Monument, RR 1, Box 717, Washington's Birthplace, VA 22575 **Telephone:** 804-224-1732

DIRECTIONS: The Monument is on the Potomac River, 38 miles (61 km) east of Fredericksburg, VA, and is accessible over VA 3 and VA 204.
   Birthplace of the first U.S. President, the park includes a Visitor Center, memorial mansion, colonial farm, gardens, and a family burial ground containing memorial tablets of his father, grandfather, and great-grandfather. Established by act of Congress on Jan. 23, 1930.

VISITOR ACTIVITIES: picnicking, interpretive exhibits and film, guided tours of memorial house, self-guided nature walks; **Permits:** No; **Fees:** No; **Visitor facilities:** restrooms and parking area, Visitor Center, historic mansion, colonial farm, burial ground, hiking and nature trails, picnic areas; **Any limitations on vehicle usage:** No; **Hiking trails:** Yes, nature trail; **Backcountry:** No; **Camping:** No; **Other overnight accommodations on site:** No; **Meals served in the park:** No; **Food and supplies obtainable in the park:** No; **Food and supplies obtainable nearby:** Yes, in Montross and Colonial Beach; **Overnight accommodations:** Fredericksburg, 38 miles (61 km); Montross, 12 miles (19 km); Colonial Beach, 10 miles (16 km); **First Aid available in park:** Yes; **Nearest Hospital:** Fredericksburg, 38 miles (61 km); **Days/Hours:** Open daily from 9 a.m. to 5 p.m.; **Holiday Closings:** Dec. 25 and Jan. 1.

GENERAL INFORMATION: Visitors to the area can also see the birthplace of Robert E. Lee, Stratford Hall, which is several miles south of Washington's Birthplace. *For Your Safety*—Do not feed or tease the animals or enter the pastures or pens. Poisonous plants are common in the area.

George Washington Memorial Parkway
McLean, Virginia   **SEE CLIMATABLE NO. 38**

MAILING ADDRESS: Superintendent, George Washington Memorial Parkway, Turkey Run Park, McLean, Virginia 22101 **Telephone:** 703-285-2598

DIRECTIONS: Access to the Parkway is from Exit 14 of the Capital Beltway (Int. 495) from Chain Bridge on Rte. 123; or from Washington, the 14th Street, Memorial or Theodore Roosevelt Bridges.

The Parkway is a landscape scenic road which parallels the Potomac River for much of its route. There are several places for recreation along the Parkway. Established by act of Congress on May 29, 1930.

VISITOR ACTIVITIES: Areas assigned to the Parkway's administration such as Arlington House, Great Falls Park, Clara Barton NHS, Glen Echo Park and Theodore Roosevelt Island offer opportunities for interpretive talks, exhibits, picnicking, hiking, climbing, biking, & fishing; **Permits:** Yes, picnic permit. Ft. Hunt Park, Thurs.-Sun., Apr.-Oct.; **Fees:** No; **Visitor facilities:** picnic tables, restrooms, parking, boat ramp, bike trail; **Any limitations on vehicle usage:** All vehicles are restricted to paved roads; **Hiking trails:** Yes, trails vary in slope and difficulty; **Backcountry:** No; **Camping:** No; **Other overnight accommodations on site:** No; **Meals served in the park:** Yes, in Great Falls Park, VA; Mount Vernon; Dangerfield Island; Lady Bird Johnson Park; **Food and supplies obtainable in the park:** No;**Food and supplies obtainable nearby:** Yes, in all local towns; **Overnight accommodations:** in the Washington, D.C. metropolitan area; **First Aid available in park:** Yes; **Nearest Hospital:** Virginia suburbs; **Days/Hours:** Open during daylight hours, the parks close at dark; **Holiday Closings:** Dec. 25; Theodore Roosevelt Island remains open; **Visitor attractions closed for seasons:** Glen Echo Carousel - Oct.-Apr.; **Weather:** Hot and humid in Summer, very pleasant and mild Spring and Fall. Moderate Winters.

GENERAL INFORMATION: Visitor use areas managed by the Parkway also include U.S. Navy Marine Memorial, Mount Vernon Bike Trail, Riverside Park, Fort Hunt Park, Fort Marcy and Dyke Marsh.

Great Falls Park
Great Falls, Virginia   **SEE CLIMATABLE NO. 169**

MAILING ADDRESS: Site Manager, Great Falls Park, P.O. Box 66, Great Falls, Virginia 22066 **Telephone:** 703-285-2966

DIRECTIONS: The Park is about 15 miles (24 km) from Washington, D.C. at the intersection of VA 193 (Georgetown Pike) and VA 738 (Old Dominion Drive) in Great Falls, Virginia. Beltway exit #13.

The Park provides a fine view of the Great Falls of the Potomac from the Virginia side of the river. Authorized for addition to the National Park System in 1968.

VISITOR ACTIVITIES: tours, hiking, fishing, picnicking, horseback riding, rock climbing (registration at Visitor Center is required) cross-country skiing in Winter; **Per-**

mits: a VA or MD fishing license is required; available at local sporting goods stores; Fees: $3.00 per vehicle, $10.00 annual park pass, $25.00 Golden Eagle, 62 and over free; Visitor facilities: interpretive tours and hikes, picnic tables and limited number of grills (charcoal and artificial fuels only), horse trails, snack bar; Any limitations on vehicle usage: Motor vehicles are not allowed on trails or in the picnic area. Park only in designated areas; Hiking trails: Yes, novice and expert hikers will find suitably enjoyable trails within the Park; Backcountry: No; Camping: No; Other overnight accommodations on site: No, information on campgrounds in the Washington area is available at the Visitor Center or on request to the Superintendent; Meals served in the park: Yes, snacks are available at the Visitor Center; Food and supplies obtainable in the park: No; Food and supplies obtainable nearby: Yes, in Great Falls, 2 miles; Overnight accommodations: In Virginia or the Washington, D.C. metropolitan area; First Aid available in park: Yes, or nearby in Great Falls & McLean, VA; Nearest Hospital: Reston, VA 7 miles; Days/Hours: Visitor Center open 9 a.m. to 5 p.m. Park open sunrise to dark; Holiday Closings: Dec. 25; Visitor attractions closed for seasons: None; Weather: Summers are hot & humid, temperatures range from 65-95°; Winters are mild to cold, 25-45°.

GENERAL INFORMATION: These warnings must be heeded for a safe visit: Strong currents are extremely hazardous at *all* places along the banks of the Potomac River in the park. Fish from the shoreline only. NO SWIMMING OR WADING; no alcoholic beverages permitted. This prohibition is strictly enforced. STAY OFF ROCKS AT WATER'S EDGE. Check in with Ranger Station before boating the Potomac.

Jamestown National Historic Site
Jamestown, Virginia   SEE CLIMATABLE NO. 166

MAILING ADDRESS: Superintendent, Colonial National Historical Park, P.O. Box 210, Yorktown, Virginia 23690 **Telephone:** 804-898-3400

DIRECTIONS: Follow I-64 to Hwy 199 West and take the Colonial Parkway to Jamestown Island.
Part of the site of the first permanent English settlement in North America (1607) is on the upper end of Jamestown Island, scene of the first representative government on this continent, July 30, 1619. Designated Dec. 18, 1940. A portion of the Site is administered by the Association for the Preservation of Virginia Antiquities.

VISITOR ACTIVITIES: auto and foot tours, 15-minute orientation film, exhibits of artifacts, foundations of 17th century structures, glassmaking demonstrations at the Jamestown Glasshouse; **Permits:** $3 bus permit is required for Colonial Parkway. Available at Jamestown Entrance Station and Yorktown Visitor Center; **Fees:** Jamestown Entrance Station fee is $5 per vehicle, or $2.00 per person for those 16 and over who arrive by bus or bicycle. Educational groups and holders of Golden Age and Golden Eagle Passports are admitted free; **Visitor facilities:** post office, gift shop, interpretive signs, recorded messages, loop drive, glasshouse, wayside exhibits; **Any limitations on vehicle usage:** Park only in designated areas; **Hiking trails:** No; **Backcountry:** No; **Camping:** No, campgrounds are located nearby in Williamsburg, Newport News, and James City County. Contact the park for further information on directions and facilities; **Other overnight accommodations on site:** No; **Meals served in the park:** No; **Food and supplies obtainable in the park:** No; **Food and supplies obtainable nearby:** Yes, at Yorktown and Williamsburg; **Overnight accommodations:** Motel facilities available in Yorktown and nearby along Rt. 17, and in Williamsburg; **First Aid available in park:** Yes; **Nearest Hospital:** Williamsburg, 9½ miles (15.3 km); **Days/Hours:** Jamestown Entrance Station open daily from 8:30 a.m. to 4:30 p.m. with extended hours from April through October; **Holiday Closings:** Dec. 25; **Visitor attractions closed for seasons:** None; **Weather:** Weather is temperate.

GENERAL INFORMATION: *For Your Safety*—Keep on the paths and watch your children. Stay off the ruins and away from the river, which is deep here.

TRAVEL ACCESS: Jamestown does not receive direct airline, bus or rail service. Transportation to either site is limited to taxi or limousine service from Williamsburg, Fort Eustis, Patrick Henry International Airport in Newport News, Norfolk International Airport and Byrd International Airport in Richmond. **Bus:** Daily direct service by Greyhound to Williamsburg and Fort Eustis; Trailways to Richmond and Norfolk; **Rail:** Direct service by Amtrak to Williamsburg, Lee Hall and Newport News from New York, Philadelphia, Baltimore and Washington once a day. **Air:** Approximately 15 miles from Patrick Henry International Airport in Newport News and 45 miles from Norfolk International Airport and Byrd International Airport in Richmond. **Other:** The Virginia Division of Tourism, under the Department of Conservation and Economic Development of the Commonwealth of Virginia, in New York, Washington and Richmond can provide further information and reservations. The Colonial Williamsburg Foundation can also be called toll free from anywhere in the Continental United States by dialing 1-800-446-8956 (1-800-446-8976).

Maggie L. Walker National Historic Site
Richmond, Virginia   **SEE CLIMATABLE NO. 173**

MAILING ADDRESS: c/o Richmond National Battlefield Park, 3215 East Broad Street, Richmond, Virginia 23223 **Telephone:** 804-780-1380

DIRECTIONS: Maggie L. Walker, black leader, became the first American woman to establish a bank, the St. Luke Penny Savings Bank in her native Richmond in 1903, presently known as the Consolidated Bank and Trust Co. Later she lived here in this large house of Victorian-Italianate Style with a Colonial Revival porch located at 110½ East Leigh Street. Authorized for addition to the National Park System on Nov. 10, 1978.

VISITOR ACTIVITIES: Guided tours; **Fees:** No; **Visitor facilities:** restrooms; **Food and supplies obtainable nearby:** Yes, in downtown Richmond; **Days/Hours:** Open only during daylight hours. Maggie Walker house open 9:00 a.m. to 5:00 p.m. Thursday through Sunday; **Holiday Closing:** Jan. 1 and Dec. 25; **Weather:** Hot and humid Summers, mild Spring and Fall, and moderate Winters.

TRAVEL ACCESS: Bus: Greyhound, Trailways provide access to Richmond, Greater Richmond Transit services Site; **Rail:** Amtrak provides service to Richmond; **Air:** Eastern, Piedmont, United, American, USAir provide service to Richmond's Byrd International Airport.

Manassas National Battlefield Park
Manassas, Virginia   **SEE CLIMATABLE NO. 169**

MAILING ADDRESS: Superintendent, Manassas National Battlefield Park, P.O. Box 1830, Manassas, Virginia 22110 **Telephone:** 703-754-7107

DIRECTIONS: The Park is 26 miles (42 km) southwest of Washington, D.C., near the intersection of Int. 66 and VA 234. The Visitor Center is on VA 234, ¾ mile (1.2 km) north of the intersection of I-66 and VA 234.

Gen. Thomas J. ("Stonewall") Jackson figured prominently in two Confederate victories here. Also called "Bull Run" the First Battle of Manassas, July 21, 1861, ended any illusion of a short war. The Second Battle of Manassas, August 28-30, 1862, brought Southern forces to the height of their military power. Designated May 10, 1940.

VISITOR ACTIVITIES: interpretive exhibits, slide programs, conducted tours in season, auto tours, hiking, horseback riding, picnicking, Living history programs in Summer; **Permits:** for certain group activities, inquire of superintendent at Visitor Center; **Fees:** Yes, $1 for adults; **Visitor facilities:** parking, hiking and bridle trails, sales, picnic area; **Any limitations on vehicle usage:** Parking is not allowed on the road shoulders. All motorized vehicles must stay on established roadways and may not stop on grassy areas or trails; **Hiking trails:** Yes, there are self-guiding walking tours of Henry Hill and unfinished railroad; **Backcountry:** No; **Camping:** No; **Other overnight accommodations on site:** No; **Meals served in the park:** No; **Food and supplies obtainable in the park:** No; **Food and supplies obtainable nearby:** Yes, Manassas, south on VA 234; **Overnight accommodations:** Manassas, south on VA 234; **First Aid available in park:** Yes; **Nearest Hospital:** Manassas, VA 234, 4 miles; **Days/Hours:** Park open daily from sunrise to sunset. Visitor Center open daily from 8:30 a.m to 5:00 p.m. and until 6 p.m. in Summer; **Holiday Closings:** Park and Visitor Center closed Dec. 25; **Visitor attractions closed for seasons:** Stone House is closed in Winter; **Weather:** Winters are mild to moderate; Summers are moderate.

GENERAL INFORMATION: *CAUTION:* Two heavily travelled roadways divide the Park. Use extreme caution while driving across or turning onto and off of these highways.

Petersburg National Battlefield
Petersburg, Virginia **SEE CLIMATABLE NO. 173**

MAILING ADDRESS: Superintendent, Petersburg National Battlefield, P.O. Box 549, Petersburg, Virginia 23804 **Telephone:** 804-732-3531

DIRECTIONS: The Main Park Visitor Center is 2½ miles (4 km) east of the center of Petersburg on State Route 36.
The Union Army waged a 10-month campaign here in 1864-65 to seize Petersburg, center of the railroads supplying Richmond and the Confederate Army of Northern Virginia. Established by act of Congress on July 3, 1926.
The City Point Unit in the City of Hopewell, at the corner of Pecan Avenue and Cedar Lane, was the location of Grant's Headquarters throughout the Siege. Here also the Union army organized the largest supply base and supply operation of the Civil War. Appomattox Manor, ancestral home of the Eppes family, is on the grounds and open to the public. U.S. Grant's Headquarters cabin is on the grounds.

VISITOR ACTIVITIES: A 17-minute map presentation is offered hourly at the Visitor Center. In Summer, demonstrations of mortar, and cannon, with actual firings, and soldier life may be seen. Biking, picnicking, hiking, self-guiding auto tours; **Permits:** No; **Fees:** Yes; **Visitor facilities:** bike trails, parking, restrooms, picnic area; **Any limitations on vehicle usage:** The Park tour roads are often congested, so drive slowly and carefully; **Hiking trails:** Yes; **Backcountry:** No; **Camping:** No; **Other overnight accommodations on site:** No, reservations for campsites can be made at Holiday Inn Travel Park which is 7 miles (11.3 km) from the Battlefield. Contact the Park at Route 4, Box 500, Petersburg, VA 23803, phone 804-861-2616; **Meals served in the park:** No; **Food and supplies obtainable in the park:** No; **Food and supplies obtainable nearby:** Yes, ½ mile west on Route 36; **Overnight accommodations:** Petersburg, VA, via Route 36, 2½ miles west; **First Aid available in park:** Yes; **Nearest Hospital:** Petersburg, VA, Rte. 36

to Washington St. to Sycamore St., 3½ miles; **Days/Hours:** Battlefield open 8 a.m. to dark year-round; Visitor Center open from 8 a.m. to 5 p.m., until 7 p.m. in Summer; **Holiday Closings:** Dec. 25 & Jan. 1; **Visitor attractions closed for seasons:** Living history program operates only from mid-June through late August; **Weather:** Spring and Fall are generally mild. Summers are very hot and humid. Winters are moderately cold and humid.

GENERAL INFORMATION: Visitors to the area can also see the nearby Poplar Grove National Cemetery, which contains the graves of more than 6,000 soldiers. It is on Va 675, three miles south of Petersburg.

TRAVEL ACCESS: Bus: Greyhound, Trailways provide regular service to Petersburg; **Rail:** Amtrak serves Richmond, VA; **Air:** Piedmont, Eastern, United provide service to Byrd International, 30 miles North.

NEARBY FACILITIES & POINTS OF INTEREST: Hotel/Motel: Petersburg, Virginia. **Points of Interest:** Old town in Petersburg and Quartermaster Museum in nearby Fort Lee, Virginia. Hopewell and Vicinity: Weston Manor and numerous historic James River Plantations nearby.

Prince William Forest Park
Triangle, Virginia   **SEE CLIMATABLE NO. 168**

MAILING ADDRESS: Superintendent, Prince William Forest Park, P.O. Box 209, Triangle, Virginia 22172 **Telephone:** 703-221-7181 (Travel Trailer Village 703-221-2474.)

DIRECTIONS: The Park is about 32 miles (52 km) south of Washington, D.C. The main entrance is west on VA 619, just off I-95 near the Quantico Marine Base. The main Information Center is less than 1 mile (1.5 km) from the main entrance. If you are arriving in a travel trailer and desire hookups, take the VA 234 west exit from I-95. Follow signs to Travel Trailer Village.

The park's 18,000 acres are an example of a mature eastern deciduous Piedmont forest on the fall line. Authorized for addition to the National Park System in 1932.

VISITOR ACTIVITIES: biking, camping, fishing, wildlife-watching, interpretive exhibits, nature walks, picnicking, backcountry, backcountry camping, cross-country skiing; **Permits:** State of Virginia fishing license required; **Fees:** family camping fee is $5 per night per site; **Visitor facilities:** Park information at Headquarters, exhibits at Nature Center, nature trails, picnic areas, concessioner trailer village, backcountry campsites, individual family, and group campgrounds, group cabins by reservation only, cross country skiing; **Any limitations on vehicle usage:** All vehicles are restricted to designated roadways and parking areas. No off-road use; **Hiking trails:** Yes, the Park has approx. 35 miles (56 km) of trails and fire roads; **Backcountry:** Yes. Backcountry permits are required, free of charge, and available in person or by writing to Park Headquarters; **Camping:** Yes. No reservations are available for family tent camping, only for group tent camping and cabin camping. Backcountry permits are available in advance. Contact the park for further information; **Other overnight accommodations on site:** No; **Meals served in the park:** No; **Food and supplies obtainable in the park:** No; **Food and supplies obtainable nearby:** Yes, Triangle or Dumfries; **Overnight accommodations:** Triangle or Dumfries, Rte. 234 and I-95, within a 1 to 5 mile (1.6 to 8 km) radius; **First Aid available in park:** Yes; **Nearest Hospital:** Potomac Hospital, Woodbridge, 9 miles (14.5 km) from the park; **Days/Hours:** Park open during daylight hours; campgrounds always open; **Holiday Closings:** None; **Visitor attractions closed for seasons:** No.

TRAVEL ACCESS: Bus: Greyhound provides service to Triangle, VA; **Rail:** Amtrak provides service to Quantico, VA, call 800-523-5720; **Air:** Access through Washington, D.C. airports; **Other:** Radio Cab Co. Greyhound Bus Terminal, Triangle, VA 703-221-3993; Quantico Yellow Cab Co., Amtrak Station Quantico, VA, 703-640-6464; Airport Limo Inc., Triangle, VA, 703-243-5466.

NEARBY FACILITIES & POINTS OF INTEREST: Hotel/Motel: Econo Travel 17005 Dumfries Road, Dumfries, VA 703-221-4172, 1-3/4 miles; Holiday Inn, Dumfries Road, Dumfries, VA, 703-221-1141, 1-1/2 miles; Quality Inn, 4204 Inn Road, Triangle, VA, 800-228-5151, 1 mile; **Parks, other points of interest:** Manassas National Battlefield, Fredericksburg National Battlefield, Historic Fredericksburg, Washington, D.C.; **Reservation systems in use for campsites, other facilities:** Required for group cabins and tenting areas. Permits available for backcountry camping. Contact Park Headquarters at 703-221-7181; P.O. Box 209, Triangle, VA 22172.

Richmond National Battlefield Park
Richmond, Virginia   **SEE CLIMATABLE NO. 173**

MAILING ADDRESS: Superintendent, Richmond National Battlefield Park, 3215 East Broad St., Richmond, Virginia 23223 **Telephone:** 804-226-1981

DIRECTIONS: You should begin your tour at Chimborazo Visitor Center, 3215 East Broad Street, Richmond. Small Visitor Centers with exhibits are available at Cold Harbor and Fort Harrison.

The Park commemorates several battles to capture Richmond, which was the Confederate Capital during the Civil War. Chimborazo Visitors Center occupies the site of one of the Confederacy's largest hospitals. Extensive remains of Union and Confederate earthworks are preserved in several park areas.

VISITOR ACTIVITIES: interpretive exhibits and audiovisual programs, self-guided auto tours, picnicking, environmental program, living history programs in season; **Permits:** No; **Fees:** No; **Visitor facilities:** parking, restrooms, sales desk, picnic facilities, information desk, small museum, interpretive trails with exhibits, historic houses; **Any limitations on vehicle usage:** Park only in designated areas; **Hiking trails:** Trails at four battle sites totaling 3.5 miles; **Backcountry:** No; **Camping:** No; **Other overnight accommodations on site:** No; **Meals served in the park:** No; **Food and supplies obtainable in the park:** No; **Food and supplies obtainable nearby:** Yes, along the tour route and in Richmond; **Overnight accommodations:** along the tour route and in Richmond; **First Aid available in park:** Yes; **Nearest Hospital:** Medical College of VA, Broad Street, 12 blocks west of Chimborazo Visitor Center; **Days/Hours:** Open only during daylight hours. Chimborazo Visitor Center is open 9 a.m to 5 p.m. daily year-round; **Holiday Closings:** Jan. 1 and Dec. 25; **Visitor attractions closed for seasons:** Fort Harrison Visitor Center is open daily June through August from 9:30 a.m. to 5:30 p.m.; **Weather:** Hot and humid Summers, mild Spring and Fall, moderate Winters.

GENERAL INFORMATION: Whenever possible, spend some time walking in each area; it is the best way to gain a real understanding of its significance.

Shenandoah National Park
Luray, Virginia   **SEE CLIMATABLE NO. 171**

MAILING ADDRESS: Superintendent, Shenandoah National Park, Rt. 4, Box 348, Luray, Virginia 22835 **Telephone:** 703-999-2243

DIRECTIONS: The Headquarters of Shenandoah National Park is 4 miles (6.4 km) west of Thornton Gap and 4 miles (6.4 km) east of Luray on US 211. Visitor Centers are at Dickey Ridge and Big Meadows. Skyline Drive winds through hardwood forest along the crest of the Blue Ridge Mountains. Authorized for addition to the National Park System on May 26, 1926; fully established Dec. 26, 1935.

VISITOR ACTIVITIES: Driving, horseback riding, picnicking, camping, field trips, campfire programs, nature walks. Pick up a Park newspaper from any Visitor Center, entrance station, or concession lodge; **Visitor facilities:** Food service, gift shops, service stations, grocery and camping supply stores, showers and laundry buildings, ice and wood sales, 2 lodges, riding stables, self-guiding nature trails; **Any limitations on vehicle usage:** Vehicles must stay on public roads. Commercial trucking is restricted to park business only. Bicycles and other vehicles are prohibited on trails. Chains and snow tires may be required in Winter; **Hiking trails:** Yes, about 500 miles of trails including self-guiding nature trails can be enjoyed year-round; **Backcountry:** Yes, information available at Visitors Centers and Park Headquarters, or by mail from the Superintendent; **Camping:** Yes, advance reservations are accepted for organized groups at Dundo campground. For camping at Big Meadows contact Ticketron Reservations Office, P.O. Box 2715, San Francisco, CA 94126. Other campgrounds are on a first-come, first-served basis; **Other overnight accommodations on site:** Yes, for lodging information and reservations, contact ARA-Virginia Sky-Line Company, Box 727, Luray, Virginia 22835, Telephone: 703-743-5108; **Meals served in the park:** Yes, at Skyland, Big Meadows, Loft Mountain, Panorama, Elkwallow; **Food and supplies obtainable in the park:** Yes, Big Meadows, Loft Mountain, Panorama and Elkwallow; **Food and supplies obtainable nearby:** Yes, in towns along Highways 340, 211, 33. Some of these are within 10 miles (16 km); **First Aid available in park:** Yes; **Nearest Hospital:** Front Royal, Highway 340, 6 miles (9.7 km); Luray, Highway 211, 10 miles (16 km); Harrisonburg, Highway 33; Waynesboro, 250; **Days/Hours:** Park always open. Sections of the drive may be closed due to weather or for resource management; **Holiday Closings:** None; **Visitor attractions closed for seasons:** All facilities are operated in Summer; some are available in Spring and Autumn; **Weather:** Weather is temperate.

GENERAL INFORMATION: *For Your Safety*—wear proper footwear when walking on trails. Most visitor injuries are caused by falls. Do your sightseeing from overlooks and trails, not while driving. Do not feed or approach park animals. Bears roam the park, so safeguard all food to protect yourself and your property. Know where your children are at all times. Always plan where to meet if you become separated. Stay on trails.

TRAVEL ACCESS: Bus: Trailways provides regular service to Waynesboro, VA; **Rail:** No; **Air:** No.

The Claude Moore Colonial Farm at Turkey Run
McLean, Virginia   **SEE CLIMATABLE NO. 169**

MAILING ADDRESS: The Claude Moore Colonial Farm at Turkey Run, 6310 Georgetown Pike, McLean, Virginia 22101 **Telephone:** 703-442-7557

DIRECTIONS: From the Capital Beltway (Int. 495), take Exit 13, Route 193 south toward Langley; drive 2.3 miles (3.7 km); and turn left at Claude Moore Colonial Farm sign onto access road, the parking lot is ½ mile on the left. From Washington, D.C., take the George Washington Memorial Parkway north to the exit for Route 123 toward McLean (Note: Do not take exit for Turkey Run Picnic Area located nearby); drive almost 1 mile (1.6 km) and bear right on Route 193; make the first right at Claude Moore Colonial Farm sign and follow access road ½ mile to parking lot on the left.

The day-to-day operations of a small-scale, low income colonial farm of the 18th century are re-enacted in this wooded setting. Established by act of Congress in 1973.

The Farm is operated by "Friends of The Claude Moore Colonial Farm at Turkey Run, Inc." a private, non-profit organization in cooperation with the National Park Service.

VISITOR ACTIVITIES: Living history demonstrations, self-guided walks, picnicking; **Permits:** No; **Fees:** $1.00 adults; 50¢ children; members free; **Visitor facilities:** Parking, restrooms, picnic tables; **Any limitations on vehicle usage:** No vehicles, visitors must walk from the parking lot; **Hiking trails:** No; **Backcountry:** No; **Camping:** No; **Other overnight accommodations on site:** No; **Meals served in the park:** No; **Food and supplies obtainable in the park:** No; **Food and supplies obtainable nearby:** Yes, McLean, VA; **Overnight accommodations:** McLean, VA or metropolitan Washington, DC; **First Aid available in park:** Yes; **Nearest Hospital:** Fairfax Hospital, Falls Church, VA; **Days/Hours:** April-Dec.: Wed.-Sun. 10 a.m.-4:30 p.m.; **Holiday Closings:** Thanksgiving and Christmas; **Visitor attractions closed for seasons:** Closed: Jan.-Mar.; **Weather:** The farm is an outdoor experience. Remember to dress for the weather. The Farm is closed on rainy days.

GENERAL INFORMATION: The need to preserve the 18th century atmosphere of the site precludes the use of guided tours by park staff. Visitors are invited to observe the "farm family's" activities and ask questions.

U.S. Marine Corps War Memorial and Netherlands Carillon
Arlington, Virginia   **SEE CLIMATABLE NO. 38**

MAILING ADDRESS: Superintendent, George Washington Memorial Parkway, Turkey Run Park, McLean, Virginia 22101 **Telephone:** 703-285-2598

DIRECTIONS: The Memorial and Carillon are located in Arlington, VA, off US 50, and can be reached from Washington, D.C. via Memorial Bridge or Key Bridge.

Also known as the Iwo Jima Memorial, this monumental sculpture is dedicated to all Marines who have died for their country. Authorized for addition to the National Park System on Nov. 10, 1954. The 49-bell Netherlands Carillon symbolizes the gratitude of the Dutch people for U.S. aid given during and after World War II. Carillon dedicated on May 5, 1960.

VISITOR ACTIVITIES: Sunset parades by the U.S. Marine Drum and Bugle Corps and the Silent Drill Team are held at the Memorial on Tues. evenings, June, July, Aug.; Carillon concerts Saturday afternoons, Apr, May, Sept. June through August 6:30-8:30 pm; **Permits:** No; **Fees:** No; **Visitor facilities:** Parking area; **Any limitations on vehicle usage:** Vehicles are restricted to paved roads; **Hiking trails:** No; **Backcountry:** No; **Camping:** No; **Other overnight accommodations on site:** No; **Meals served in the park:** No; **Food and supplies obtainable in the park:** No; **Food and supplies obtainable nearby:** Yes, Arlington, VA or Washington, DC; **Overnight accommodations:** Arlington, VA or metropolitan Washington, DC; **First Aid available in park:** No; **Nearest Hospital:** Arlington, VA; **Days/Hours:** Memorial never closes; **Holiday Closings:** None; **Visitor attractions closed for seasons:** No; **Weather:** Hot, humid Summers; cold, snowy Winters.

Wolf Trap Farm Park for the Performing Arts
Vienna, Virginia   **SEE CLIMATABLE NO. 169**

MAILING ADDRESS: Director, Wolf Trap Farm Park, 1551 Trap Road, Vienna, Virginia 22180 **Telephone:** 703-255-1800

DIRECTIONS: From downtown Washington, D.C.: Take the George Washington Memorial Parkway to Capital Beltway (I-495) heading south into Virginia. Exit I-495 at Exit 11-S (Tyson's Corner—VA Rte. 123). Follow Rte. 123 briefly to U.S. Route 7 (Leesburg Pike) and turn right. Travel west on Route 7 to Towlston Road. Turn left on Towlston Road at Wolf Trap Farm Park sign. The Park entrance is 1 mile (1.6 km) from this turn and is well marked. Driving time from downtown Washington D.C. is 30 minutes in nonrush hour traffic, where you will find free parking. Cars may also enter from the Dulles Toll Road up to two hours before performance time ONLY. Take exit 12B (from I-495) or exit 20 (from Rte. 66) and follow to the Wolf Trap exit.
   Established by an Act of Congress on October 15, 1966, as the Nation's only Park for the performing arts, the Filene Center can accommodate an audience of 6,786 including 3,000 on the sloping lawn in a setting of rolling hills and woods.

VISITOR ACTIVITIES: attending performance ranging from ballet to pop; free pre-performance previews; free children's programs; picnicking; walking tours of the Filene Center; interpretive programs; **Permits:** Yes; **Fees:** Yes, tickets are required for most performances. See local newspaper or call the box office at 703-255-1860 for information on events; **Visitor facilities:** refreshment bar, food service during Filene Center performances; parking; restrooms; picnic areas; **Any limitations on vehicle usage:** Park only in designated areas; **Hiking trails:** No; **Backcountry:** No; **Camping:** No; **Other overnight accommodations on site:** No; **Meals served in the park:** Yes, during June, July and August. The dining pavilion adjacent to the Filene Center offers a choice of meal services beginning two hours before each performance. A buffet dinner is available, or a variety of picnic box suppers may be orderd in advance. Reservations are required by 1 p.m. on the day of the performance. Telephone 703-281-4256. Snack bars serve sandwiches, soft drinks and assorted snacks prior to each performance and at intermission; **Food and supplies obtainable in the park:** No; **Food and supplies obtainable nearby:** Yes, Vienna, VA and Tyson's Corner, where you can prepare your own picnic; **Overnight accommodations:** In suburban Virginia or Washington, D.C.; **First Aid available in park:** Yes, physician in attendance at most performances; **Nearest Hospital:** Reston Hospital Center, Reston, Virginia; **Days/Hours:** Park open year-round from 8:30 a.m. to 5 p.m.; until the completion of the performance season, Labor Day Weekend. The Filene Center is open for performances from June through Labor Day; **Holiday Closings:** None; **Visitor attractions closed for seasons:** The Filene Center, the free children's programs and nature walks are in operation only in summer.

GENERAL INFORMATION: Special arangements for the handicapped can be made in advance by calling 703-255-1800. The park will also furnish wheelchairs upon request.
   Free transportation from the parking lots to the Filene Center is available by Ranger-operated carts for those who need it.

Yorktown Battlefield
Yorktown, Virginia   **SEE CLIMATABLE NO. 166**

MAILING ADDRESS: Superintendent, Colonial National Historical Park, P.O. Box 210, Yorktown, Virginia 23690 **Telephone:** 804-898-3400

DIRECTIONS: Follow I-64 to Hwy 199 East, then Colonial Parkway to Yorktown.

Yorktown was the scene of the culminating battle of the American Revolution when Washington triumphed over Cornwallis in 1781. Authorized for addition to the National Park System on July 3, 1930.

VISITOR ACTIVITIES: interpretive exhibits, artifact displays, 12-minute film, rooftop overlook, self-guiding auto tour, bookstore, tape player rentals for tours. Theatrical presentation on Thomas Nelson, Jr., a signer of the Declaration of Independence and the commander of the Virginia militia at the Siege of Yorktown, is offered at the Nelson House; **Permits:** $3 bus permit is required for Colonial Parkway available at Jamestown Entrance Station and Yorktown Visitor Center; **Fees:** No; **Visitor facilities:** interpretive exhibits, Visitor Center, orientation map, film, overlook, bookstore, encampment and battlefield drives, theatrical presentations at Moore House and Nelson House, picnic area at Yorktown Beach; **Any limitations on vehicle usage:** Park only in designated areas; **Hiking trails:** No; **Backcountry:** No; **Camping:** No; **Other overnight accommodations on site:** No, campgrounds are located nearby in Williamsburg, Newport News, and James City County. Contact the park for further information on directions and facilities; **Meals served in the park:** No; **Food and supplies obtainable in the park:** No; **Food and supplies obtainable nearby:** Yes, Yorktown and Williamsburg; **Overnight accommodations:** Along Rte 17 in Yorktown and vicinity and in Williamsburg; **First Aid available in park:** Yes; **Nearest Hospital:** Mary Immaculate Hospital, five miles; **Days/Hours:** Daily from 8:30 a.m. to 5:00 p.m., with extended hours from Apr.-Oct.; **Holiday Closings:** Dec. 25; **Visitor attractions closed for seasons:** Moore House, Nelson House and picnic areas closed in winter.

TRAVEL ACCESS: Yorktown does not receive direct airline, bus or rail service. Transportation to either site is limited to taxi or limousine service from Williamsburg, Fort Eustis, Patrick Henry International Airport in Newport News, Norfolk International Airport and Byrd International Airport in Richmond. **Bus:** Daily direct service by Greyhound to Williamsburg and Fort Eustis; Trailways to Richmond and Norfolk; **Rail:** Direct service by Amtrak to Williamsburg, Lee Hall and Newport News from New York, Philadelphia, Baltimore and Washington once a day. **Air:** Approximately 5 miles from Patrick Henry International Airport in Newport News and 45 miles from Norfolk International Airport and Byrd International Airport in Richmond. **Other:** The Virginia Division of Tourism, under the Department of Conservation and Economic Development of the Commonwealth of Virginia, in New York, Washington and Richmond can provide further information and reservations. The Colonial Williamsburg Foundation can also be called toll free from anywhere in the Continental United Stated by dialing 1-800-446-8956 (1-800-446-8976).

Washington

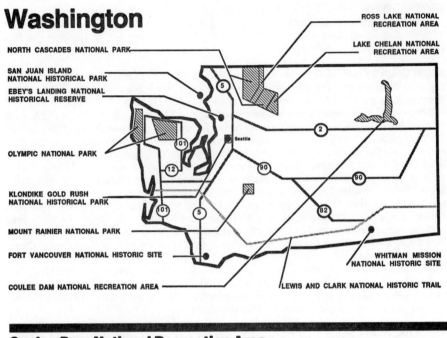

ROSS LAKE NATIONAL
RECREATION AREA

LAKE CHELAN NATIONAL
RECREATION AREA

NORTH CASCADES NATIONAL PARK

SAN JUAN ISLAND
NATIONAL HISTORICAL PARK

EBEY'S LANDING NATIONAL
HISTORICAL RESERVE

OLYMPIC NATIONAL PARK

KLONDIKE GOLD RUSH
NATIONAL HISTORICAL PARK

MOUNT RAINIER NATIONAL PARK

FORT VANCOUVER NATIONAL HISTORIC SITE

WHITMAN MISSION
NATIONAL HISTORIC SITE

COULEE DAM NATIONAL RECREATION AREA

LEWIS AND CLARK NATIONAL HISTORIC TRAIL

Seattle

Coulee Dam National Recreation Area
Coulee Dam, Washington   **SEE CLIMATABLE NO. 174**

MAILING ADDRESS: Superintendent, Coulee Dam National Recreation Area, P.O. Box 37, Coulee Dam, Washington 99116 **Telephone:** 509-633-9441

DIRECTIONS: Information about access to the entire area is available from the National Recreation Area Headquarters in Coulee Dam. There is a Visitor Center at Fort Spokane and Kettle Falls.

Formed by the Grand Coulee Dam (part of the Columbia River Basin project), the 241 km (150 mile) long Franklin D. Roosevelt Lake is the principal recreation feature here. Admitted to the National Park System on Dec. 18, 1946.

VISITOR ACTIVITIES: water skiing, boating, swimming, camping, bird-watching, picnicking, audiovisual programs, interpretive talks and exhibits, fishing, hunting; **Permits:** for fishing and hunting available at local sporting goods stores, licenses vary in length of validity and cost; **Fees:** $6 camping fee at the following sites: Kettle Falls, Evans, Ft. Spokane, Spring Canyon, Keller Ferry, Hunters Gifford, Porcupine Bay; **Visitor facilities:** picnic areas, boat ramps, guarded beaches, individual and group campsites, boat and trailer dump stations, drinking water, bathhouse, ferry service; **Any limitations on vehicle usage:** Off-road vehicle use is prohibited; **Hiking trails:** Yes, four short, 1 mile (1.6 km) nature trails; **Backcountry:** No; **Rental boats:** Houseboats, runabouts & skiff rentals at Keller Ferry concessioner. **Camping:** Yes, no reservations available for campsites; **Other overnight accommodations on site:** No, for further information on lodging in the vicinity, contact: Chamber of Commerce, Grand Coulee, WA 99133, phone 509-633-0361; **Meals served in the park:** Yes, during summer at Spring Canyon Campground; **Food and supplies obtainable in the park:** Yes, at various marinas; **Food and supplies obtainable nearby:** Yes, in Grand Coulee, Coulee Dam, Colville, Kettle Falls, Northport; **Overnight accommodations:** Grand Coulee, Coulee Dam, Colville, Kettle Falls, Northport; **First Aid available in park:** Yes; **Nearest Hospi-**

tal: Grand Coulee, 5 miles (8 km) from Spring Canyon campground; Davenport, 25 miles (40 km) from Fort Spokane campground; and Colville, 10 miles (16 km) from Kettle Falls campground; **Days/Hours:** Park always open. Visitor Centers are open daily from 8 a.m. to 4:30 p.m., with extended hours in season; **Holiday Closings:** Visitor Center closed Thanksgiving, Christmas, New Year's Day; **Visitor attractions closed for seasons:** The recreation season is May through Oct.; **Weather:** The west arm of the lake is usually quite warm and sunny, while the north arm, influenced by the mountains, tends to be cooler and have more clouds and precipitation. Summer temperatures range from 75°-100°F during the day and between 50° and 60° at night. It is somewhat cooler in Spring and Autumn. Bring a light jacket for chilly evenings. Occasional foggy and cloudy days occur in Winter and Spring.

GENERAL INFORMATION: *For Your Safety*—Be alert to avoid floating logs and debris. Approach log rafts with caution-cables extend between the rafts and tugboats. Be sure to drown your campfires.

TRAVEL ACCESS: Bus: Empire Lines provides twice daily service to Coulee Dam; **Rail:** No; **Air:** No.

Ebey's Landing National Historical Reserve
Whidbey Island, Washington   **SEE CLIMATABLE NO. 175**

MAILING ADDRESS: Post Office Box 774, Coupeville, Washington 98239 **Telephone:** 206-678-6084

DIRECTIONS: THERE ARE NO DEVELOPED NPS FACILITIES. ALL COMMUNITY SERVICES ARE NEARBY.
   The area preserves and protects a rural community which provides an unbroken historical record from the 19th century exploration and settlement to the present. It commemorates Captain George Vancouver's 1792 exploration of Puget Sound; settlement of Whidbey Island by Colonel Isaac Ebey, killed by Indians in 1857; the Early Settlement of the Island during the Donation Land Claim (1850-55) and thereafter; and the growth of the historic town of Coupeville since 1883. Established by act of Congress on Nov. 10, 1978.

GENERAL INFORMATION: Ebey's Landing NHR is excellent for sightseeing by car or bike. An informal 8 mile coastal trail connecting Fort Casey and Fort Ebey State Parks exists. The NPS will be developing interpretive facilities in the next few years.

TRAVEL ACCESS: Bus: Evergreen Trailways provides service to Coupeville (Prairie Center); **Rail:** None; **Air:** Harbor Airlines has daily service (Sea-Tac to Oak Harbor 206-675-6666); **Other:** Washington State Ferry System from Port Townsend to Keystone. Keystone is adjacent to Fort Casey State Park.

NEARBY FACILITIES & POINTS OF INTEREST: Campgrounds: Fort Casey and Fort Ebey State Parks (within the 17,400 Ac. Reserve).

Fort Vancouver National Historic Site
Vancouver, Washington   **SEE CLIMATABLE NO. 130**

MAILING ADDRESS: Superintendent, Fort Vancouver National Historic Site, 612 E. Reserve St., Vancouver, Washington 98661 **Telephone:** 206-696-7655

DIRECTIONS: To reach the site, turn east off I-5 at the Mill Plain Boulevard interchange and then follow signs to the Visitor Center on East Evergreen Boulevard.

Fort Vancouver was a fur-trade depot for the Hudson's Bay Company from 1825 to 1860. From the fort, John McLoughlin, chief factor from 1825 to 1845, administered the company's fur operations in what is now British Columbia, Washington, Oregon, Idaho, and western Montana.

In 1849, the U.S. Army established a post near Fort Vancouver. The site of the Hudson's Bay company fort was purchased by the Army in the late 1860's. A portion of Vancouver Barracks still remains active today. The site of the historic trading post was authorized for addition to the National Park Service on June 19, 1948.

VISITOR ACTIVITIES: interpretive exhibits and tours of reconstructed buildings at the fort site; **Permits:** No; **Fees:** Yes, entrance fee at fort site, $1 adults, $3 family, 12 and under free; **Visitor facilities:** parking and restrooms at the Visitor Center and at the Fort Site, information and sales desk; **Any limitations on vehicle usage:** No; **Hiking trails:** No; **Backcountry:** No; **Camping:** No; **Other overnight accommodations on site:** No; **Meals served in the park:** No; **Food and supplies obtainable in the park:** No; **Food and supplies obtainable nearby:** Yes, in Vancouver; **Overnight accommodations:** Vancouver; **First Aid available in park:** Yes; **Nearest Hospital:** Vancouver Memorial Hospital, 2 miles (3 km); **Days/Hours:** Open daily from 9:00 a.m.-5:00 p.m. with shortened hours during the Winter; **Holiday Closings:** M. L. King, Jr.'s Birthday, Washington's Birthday, Columbus Day, Veteran's Day, Thanksgiving, Dec. 25 & Jan. 1; **Visitor attractions closed for seasons:** Living history demonstrations are not offered from October through May; **Weather:** Rain is common from October through May; cold weather from November through February. Summers are warm.

GENERAL INFORMATION: *For Your Safety*—Watch your step at the fort because ground is uneven.

TRAVEL ACCESS: Bus: Local transportation via Vancouver Transit runs regularly within one block of site, Greyhound provides inter-city service to terminal 1-1/2 miles away; **Rail:** Amtrak (Burlington Northern) provides regular service to terminal 2 miles away; **Air:** major airlines access through Portland International Airport, 6 miles away.

NEARBY FACILITIES & POINTS OF INTEREST: Parks, other points of interest: McLoughlin House National Historical Site, Oregon City, Oregon.

Klondike Gold Rush National Historical Park
For details see listing in Alaska

Lewis and Clark Trail
For details see listing in Illinois

Lake Chelan National Recreation Area
Chelan, Washington   **SEE CLIMATABLE NO. 176**

MAILING ADDRESS: District Manager, Lake Chelan National Recreation Area, P.O. Box 7, Stehekin, Washington 98852 **Telephone:** 509-682-2549

DIRECTIONS: Access to the North Cascades area from Burlington on the west and Twisp on the east follows WA 20. The main access to Stehekin in LCNRA is by boat or float plane from the town of Chelan on Hwy 97. There is no road access into Stehekin. Service is provided by Lake Chelan Boat Co., Chelan, WA 98816, phone 509-682-2224. Daily boat service from Stehekin to Chelan is maintained from May 15 to Oct. 15. From Oct. 16 to May 14 the boats go on Sunday, Monday, Wednesday, and Friday. There is no Sunday boat from Jan. 1-Feb. 14. Air service is available for charter year round, weather permitting, from Chelan Airways, Chelan, WA 98816, phone 509-682-5555.

Here the scenic Stehekin Valley, with a portion of Fjordlike Lake Chelan, adjoins the southern unit of North Cascades National Park. Established by act of Congress Oct. 2, 1968.

VISITOR ACTIVITIES: interpretive exhibits, guided and self-guiding tours, picnicking, camping, hiking, mountain climbing, horseback riding, boating, fishing, hunting, commercial river rafting; **Permits:** required for backcountry, are available at Ranger Stations at Stehekin, Chelan, and Marblemount; **Fees:** No; **Visitor facilities:** Picnic area, campground, backcountry, boat and bicycle rentals, restaurant, lodging, supplies, post office, shuttle bus; **Any limitations on vehicle usage:** The Area is inaccessible to vehicles; **Hiking trails:** Yes, a variety from low land day hikes to elevation gains of 6,000 feet; **Backcountry:** Yes; **Camping:** Yes, no permits are required for boat camps. First come first served basis only for campsites. Backcountry, crosscountry and trail camps require a permit. Group camp-grounds are available by mail reservation; **Other overnight accommodations on site:** Yes, Lodge rooms and housekeeping facilities available year round. Write or call North Cascades Lodge, Stehekin, WA 98852, 509-682-4711. Various private cabins for rent also; **Meals served in the park:** Yes, at North Cascades Lodge and other facilities; **Food and supplies obtainable in the park:** Yes, at North Cascades Lodge; **Food and supplies obtainable nearby:** Yes, Chelan; **Overnight accommodations:** Chelan, 50 miles (80 km); **First Aid available in park:** Yes, at ranger station; **Nearest Hospital:** Chelan, 50 miles (80 km); **Days/Hours:** Open 24 hours a day everyday; **Holiday Closings:** None; **Visitor attractions closed for seasons:** guided walks and programs from late June to early Sept. Shuttle bus from May 15 to Oct. 15; **Weather:** Outdoor recreation can be enjoyed year-round. The lower levels of the valley are snow free from early Apr. to mid-Nov.

GENERAL INFORMATION: See listing in this book for North Cascades National Park and Ross Lake National Recreation Area, the two other areas of the North Cascades National Park Service Complex. For your safety in the backcountry: hang all food out of the reach of bears. Stream crossings can be hazardous during periods of high water. Check conditions with a Park Ranger before starting out. Snow may linger in higher places. Crossing snowfields may require special equipment. Visitors on horseback should carry adequate feed for their trip, since forage is scarce in most of the Area. A camping permit is required for livestock use.

Mount Rainier National Park
Ashford, Washington   **SEE CLIMATABLE NO. 177**

MAILING ADDRESS: Superintendent, Mount Rainier National Park, Tahoma Woods, Star Route, Ashford, Washington 98304 **Telephone:** 206-569-2211

DIRECTIONS: The Paradise Visitor Center is 74 miles (113 km) southeast of Tacoma on Route 7 to Elbe, then Route 706 to Longmire. It is 98 miles (153 km) southeast of Seattle, and 87 miles (139 km) west of Yakima.

This greatest single-peak glacial system in the contiguous U.S. radiates from the summit and slopes of an ancient dormant volcano, with dense forests and sub-alpine flowered meadows below. Established by act of Congress on Mar. 2, 1899.

VISITOR ACTIVITIES: backcountry hiking and mountain climbing, snowshoeing, camping, crosscountry skiing, picnicking, winter sports, interpretive programs, wildlife-watching; **Permits:** required for backcountry camping from June 15 to end of Sept., available at Ranger Stations and Visitor Centers; **Fees:** $5.00, Golden Age and Golden Eagle Passports are accepted and available; **Visitor facilities:** exhibits at Visitor Centers, restrooms, lodging, hiking trails, picnic areas, cross-country ski lessons and rentals, mountain climbing equipment rentals, food service, nature trails; **Any limitations on vehicle usage:** Vehicles must stay on public automobile roads, no commercial vehicles (other than buses); **Hiking trails:** Yes, self-guiding nature trails in different areas of the Park; **Backcountry:** Yes, permit required, inquire at Ranger Stations or Visitor Centers; **Camping:** Yes, no reservations available for campsites; **Other overnight accommodations on site:** Yes, accommodations are available at National Park Inn at Longmire (may be closed for renovation during the 1988 season, otherwise open year round) and at Paradise Inn (early June thru early Oct.). For information on schedule and rates, write or call Mount Rainier Guest Service, Star Route, Ashford, WA 98304, phone 206-569-2275; **Meals served in the park:** Yes, Longmire, Paradise Inn, Paradise Visitor Center and Sunrise; **Food and supplies obtainable in the park:** Yes, at Longmire and Sunrise; **Food and supplies obtainable nearby:** Yes, at Ashford, Elbe, Packwood, Enumclaw; **Overnight accommodations:** Ashford, Hwy 706, Alder & Elbe, Hwy 7 immediately adjacent to the Park; **First Aid available in park:** Yes; **Nearest Hospital:** Enumclaw, Hwy 410, 45 miles (64 km); Morton, Hwy 12, 40 miles (74.2 km); **Days/Hours:** Open 24 hours a day year-round; **Holiday Closings:** None; **Visitor attractions closed for seasons:** Snow closes roads for short periods. Chains may be required for winter driving. Except for the roads from Nisqually Entrance to Paradise (WA 706), many park roads are usually closed from late Nov. through June or July.

GENERAL INFORMATION: *For Your Safety*—In the backcountry, hike only in the company of others; remember your limitations. Be prepared for sudden and extreme weather changes. Bring your own shelter. Conducted climbs are given by Rainier Mountaineering Inc. 201 St. Helens, Tacoma, WA 98042, 206-627-6242. From June to Sept. Paradise, WA 98398, 206-569-2227.

North Cascades National Park
Sedro Woolley, Washington   **SEE CLIMATABLE NO. 176**

MAILING ADDRESS: Superintendent, North Cascades National Park, 2105 Highway 20, Sedro Woolley, Washington 98284 **Telephone:** 206-856-5700

DIRECTIONS: Access to the North Cascades area from Burlington on the west and Twisp on the East follows WA 20 with branch routes to Baker River and Cascade River. Hiking access and roadside views of the northwest corner are available from WA 542 east from Bellingham. Access to Stehekin Valley is by boat, float-plane or trail. Vehicle access to Ross Lake is by unimproved road from Canada.

High jagged peaks intercept moisture-laden winds, producing glaciers, icefalls, waterfalls, and other water phenomena in this wild alpine region, with varied plant and animal communities in the valleys. Established by act of Congress on Oct. 2, 1968.

VISITOR ACTIVITIES: camping, backcountry, viewing scenery, hiking, mountain climbing, horseback riding, fishing, auto tours, boating, wildlife- and bird-watching; **Permits:** for backcountry, available without charge at Park Offices or Ranger Stations. A Washington State fishing license, available locally, is required; **Fees:** Yes, fees are charged in the developed road access campgrounds in Ross Lake NRA; **Visitor facilities:** campgrounds, launching ramps, resorts, hiking trails, horse and mule rentals nearby, professional guide and packtrain services; **Any limitations on vehicle usage:**

Vehicles are restricted to maintained roads; **Hiking trails:** Yes, about 360 miles (576 km) of hiking and horse trails throughout the four North Cascades units; **Backcountry:** Yes, information can be obtained from Park Offices or Ranger Stations; **Camping:** Yes, no reservations available for campsites; **Other overnight accommodations on site:** Yes, for information on lodging, contact North Cascades Lodge, Stehekin, WA 98852, Diablo Lake Resort, P.O. Box 176 Rockport, WA 98283, Ross Lake Resort, Rockport, WA 98283; **Meals served in the park:** Yes, North Cascades Lodge at Stehekin and Diablo Lake Resort; **Food and supplies obtainable in the park:** Yes, Stehekin and Diablo Lake Resort; **Food and supplies obtainable nearby:** Yes, Marblemount and Newhalem; **Overnight accommodations:** The larger cities and towns near the North Cascades group have the usual tourist accommodations, but are 2-to-3 hour drives from park boundaries. Small communities within or adjacent to the areas have limited guest accommodations. The chambers of commerce for each of of the counties and towns surrounding the North Cascades group have information on accommodations, packers, guides, and other outdoor services; **First Aid available in park:** Yes, at Ranger Stations; **Nearest Hospital:** Sedro Woolley; **Days/Hours:** Park open all year, but snow conditions prevent access during the winter; **Holiday Closings:** None; **Visitor attractions closed for seasons:** restricted access to most areas in Winter; **Weather:** Outdoor recreation can be enjoyed year-round. The lower elevations and the big lakes are accessible from early April to mid-October, but at higher elevations the season is from mid-July to mid-Sept. The western side of the North Cascades gets more rain, has more lakes and streams, and more abundant vegetation. Consequently, it has less sunshine and cooler days than the eastern side of the mountains, where more sunshine, warm rock surfaces, and sparse vegetation afford warm days and cool nights typical of a dry climate.

GENERAL INFORMATION: See listings in this book for two other units of the North Cascades Group: Lake Chelan and Ross Lake National Recreation Areas. *For Your Safety in the backcountry*: hang all food out of the reach of bears. Stream crossings can be hazardous during periods of high water. Check conditions with a Park Ranger before starting out. Snow may linger in higher places. Crossing snowfields may require special equipment. Horsemen should carry adequate feed for their trip. Forage is scarce in most of the park. Grazing not permitted in the Park. A special permit is required for livestock use.

Olympic National Park
Port Angeles, Washington   **SEE CLIMATABLE NO. 178**

MAILING ADDRESS: Superintendent, Olympic National Park, 600 East Park Avenue, Port Angeles, Washington 98362 **Telephone:** 206-452-4501, extension 230

DIRECTIONS: Visitor Centers at Port Angeles and Hoh Rain Forest are open year-around. Kalaloch and Storm King Visitor Centers are open only in the summer.

This mountain wilderness contains the finest remnant of Pacific Northwest rain forest (the only temperate zone rain forest in North America), active glaciers, rare Roosevelt elk and 57 miles of wild, scenic ocean shore. Proclaimed a national monument on March 2, 1909; established as a national park on June 29, 1938. Olympic is a World Heritage Park and Biosphere Reserve.

VISITOR ACTIVITIES: Interpretive and audiovisual programs, camping, auto tours, bird- and wildlife-watching, picnicking, nature walks, hiking, horseback riding, mountain climbing, fishing, backcountry, swimming, skiing, snowshoeing; **Permits:** for backcountry, available at Ranger Stations; **Fees:** Entrance fees (good for 7 days) will be collected at Heart O' the Hills/Hurricane Ridge, Hoh and Soleduck entrance stations from Memorial Day through Labor Day or later. Year round for camping in developed "class

A" campgrounds; **Visitor facilities:** nature trails, parking, restrooms, campgrounds, fireplaces, picnic area, beaches, bathhouse, ski and snowshoe trails, lodging; **Any limitations on vehicle usage:** Vehicles are restricted to designated roadways; **Hiking trails:** Yes, trails vary from those requiring a day or less to wilderness pathways taking up to a week or more. Trails open year-round with higher elevations accessible normally between July 15-October 1. Trail condition reports are available at Visitor Centers and Ranger Stations; **Backcountry:** Yes, information available at Ranger Stations and Visitor Centers; **Camping:** Yes, reservations for groups only at Kalaloch, Mora, or Ozette Ranger Stations; **Other overnight accommodations on site:** Yes, reserve lodging by the lodging facility; Kalaloch Lodge, Inc., HC-80, Box 1100, Forks, WA 98331, phone 206-962-2271; Log Cabin Resort, 6540 E. Beach Road, Port Angeles, WA 98362, phone 206-928-3245; Lake Crescent Lodge, HC-62, Box 11, Port Angeles, WA 98362, phone 206-928-3211; Sol Duc Hot Springs Resort, P.O. Box 1355, Port Angeles, WA 98362, phone 206-327-3583; **Meals served in the park:** Yes, at Hurricane Ridge, Sol Duc, Fairholm, Kalaloch, Lake Crescent; **Food and supplies obtainable in the park:** Yes, at small grocery at some lodges; **Food and supplies obtainable nearby:** Yes, at supermarkets at Sequim, Port Angeles, Forks, Shelton, and Aberdeen; **Overnight accommodations:** Port Angeles, Aberdeen, Forks, Sequim and Shelton. For information on facilities near the park, write the Olympic Peninsula Resort and Hotel Association, Coleman Ferry Terminal, Seattle, WA 98104; **First Aid available in park:** Yes, at most Ranger Stations; **Nearest Hospital:** Port Angeles, Forks, Shelton, Aberdeen-Hoquiam; **Days/Hours:** Park open year-round. Only Visitor Centers and Ranger Stations have closing hours. Most Ranger Stations open 8 a.m.-5 p.m. Hoh Visitor Center: 9 a.m.-6 p.m. Port Angeles Visitor Center: 8 a.m.-4 p.m.; **Holiday Closings:** Buildings closed December 25 & January 1; **Visitor attractions closed for seasons:** Some lodges are open only in summer. All roads in high elevations are usually open June 1-October 1; high elevation trails normally open July 15-October 1.

GENERAL INFORMATION: *For your safety*—Stay on trails. Backcountry campers should include a tent and a backpacker's stove in their equipment. Keep your distance from animals. When hiking on the beach, round the headlands only on the outgoing tide to avoid being trapped against the headland cliffs by the incoming tide. The tide and cliffs permit no escape.

Ross Lake National Recreation Area
Sedro Woolley, Washington   **SEE CLIMATABLE NO. 176**

MAILING ADDRESS: Superintendent, Ross Lake National Recreation Area, c/o North Cascades National Park, 2105 Highway 20, Sedro Woolley, Washington 98284 **Telephone:** 206-873-4590 or 206-856-5700

DIRECTIONS: Access to the Park is via WA 20 from Burlington on the West and Winthrop on the East.
Ringed by mountains, this recreation area in the Skagit River drainage separates the north and south units of North Cascades National Park. Established by act of Congress on Oct. 2, 1968.

VISITOR ACTIVITIES: hiking, boating, canoeing, viewing scenery, rock climbing, camping, wildlife- and bird-watching, auto tours, backcountry, horseback riding; **Permits:** required for backcountry, can be obtained at all Ranger Stations; **Fees:** Camping fee is $5 per night per site at Colonial Creek and Newhalem Creek Campgrounds; $3 per night at Goodell Creek Campground (camping fees subject to change for 1988 season); **Visitor facilities:** boat rentals, campgrounds, lodging, boat launching ramps, wayside exhibits; **Any limitations on vehicle usage:** Only one vehicle is allowed at each campsite. Vehicles are restricted to maintained roads; **Hiking trails:** Yes, seven major trails lead outward from Ross Lake into the backcountry; **Backcountry:** Yes, information can be obtained by writing the Superintendent or visiting park offices in Sedro Woolley, Chelan, or Marblemount; **Camping:** Yes, no reservations available for campsites; **Other overnight accommodations on site:** Yes, for information on lodging, contact: Diablo Lake Resort, Rockport, Washington 98283, phone 206 Operator, Newhalem 5578, Ross Lake Resort, Rockport, WA 98283, phone 206 Operator, Newhalem 7735; **Meals served in the park:** Yes, Diablo Lake Resort; **Food and supplies obtainable in the park:** Yes, at Diablo Lake Resort and Newhalem, WA; **Food and supplies obtainable nearby:** Yes, at Marblemount, WA and Concrete, WA; **Overnight accommodations:** Marblemount, WA, 8 miles (13 km); Concrete, WA, 28 miles (45 km); **First Aid available in park:** Yes, or nearby in Diablo and Newhalem, WA; **Nearest Hospital:** Sedro Woolley, WA 20, 45 miles (74.2 km); **Days/Hours:** Park open year-round; **Holiday Closings:** Office closed Dec. 25 and Jan. 1; **Visitor attractions closed for seasons:** Hwy 20 and all campgrounds except Goodell Creek are closed in Winter; **Weather:** Summer is warm and sometimes quite hot with temperatures frequently in the high 90°sF. Fall has warm days and cool nights. Hazardous strong winds and whitecaps on lake waters occur frequently and without warning.

GENERAL INFORMATION: See listings in this book for other units of the North Cascades Group: Lake Chelan National Recreation Area and North Cascades National Park. *For Your Safety in the backcountry:* hang all food out of the reach of bears. Stream crossings can be hazardous during periods of high water. Check conditions with the Park Ranger before starting out. Snow may linger in higher places. Crossing snowfields may require special equipment. Horsemen should carry adequate feed for their trip. Forage is scarce in most of the park. Grazing not permitted in the park. A special permit is required for livestock use.

San Juan Island National Historical Park
Friday Harbor, Washington   **SEE CLIMATABLE NO. 175**

MAILING ADDRESS: Superintendent, San Juan Island National Historical Park, Box 429, Friday Harbor, Washington 98250 **Telephone:** 206-378-2240

DIRECTIONS: San Juan Island is reached by Washington State Ferries from Anacortes, WA, 83 miles (133.6 km) north of Seattle; or from Sidney, British Columbia, 15 miles (24 km) north of Victoria. The island is also accessible by private boats. There are good docking facilities at Friday and Roche Harbors. Commercial air flights are scheduled regularly from Bellingham and Seattle, WA, to Friday Harbor. Private one- and two-engine planes can land at airstrips at Friday and Roche Harbors.

The park commemorates the peaceful relations maintained by the United States, Great Britain and Canada since the 1859 boundary dispute here. British and American military campsites are included. Authorized for addition to the National Park System on Sept. 9, 1966.

VISITOR ACTIVITIES: picnicking, hiking, interpretive exhibits—no camping is allowed at either American or English Camps; **Permits:** No; **Fees:** No; **Visitor facilities:** Park headquarters and informtion center is located in Friday Harbor at 125 Spring Street. It is open 8 a.m. to 4:30 p.m. Mon. thru Fri. in fall, winter and spring and 8 a.m. to 6 p.m. daily in summer. Visitor facilities: Rangers are on duty during the summer to answer questions and explain points of interest. Picnic areas are available at both camps. Drinking water is available at English Camp. Water is available at American Camp. Facilities for small fires are provided at American Camp; **Any limitations on vehicle usage:** Off-road vehicle travel is not allowed within the park; **Hiking trails:** Yes, American and English Camps have historic trails; **Backcountry:** No; **Camping:** No; **Other overnight**

accommodations on site: No; **Meals served in the park:** No, but, nearby at Friday and Roche Harbors; **Food and supplies obtainable in the park:** No; **Food and supplies obtainable nearby:** Yes, Friday Harbor (year-round); **Overnight accommodations:** Friday Harbor, 6 miles (9.7 km) from American Camp, and 11 miles (17.7 km) from English Camp; **First Aid available in park:** Yes; **Nearest Hospital:** Friday Harbor, 6 miles (9.7 km) from American Camp, and 11 miles (17.7 km) from English Camp; **Days/Hours:** The roads through the park are open year-round. The buildings are open about 9 a.m. to 6 p.m. daily during the summer and on weekends during spring and fall; **Holiday Closings:** Thanksgiving, Dec. 25 and Jan. 1; **Visitor attractions closed for seasons:** Buildings and exhibits at English Camp are closed for the winter; **Weather:** winters can be cold, windy and rainy; summers are warm, but never hot.

GENERAL INFORMATION: Safety Notes: *Watch your Step*, especially in the vicinity of the American Camp. The San Juan rabbit digs many holes that can cause sprained ankles and broken bones. *Swimming is discouraged* because the water temperature remains below 50° all year. Try beachcombing instead. *Tree climbing is dangerous* for you and harmful to the trees. *Look out for insecure footing* on the primitive trails and watch for overhanging branches and downed limbs.

Whitman Mission National Historic Site
Walla Walla, Washington   **SEE CLIMATABLE NO. 172**

MAILING ADDRESS: Superintendent, Whitman Mission National Historic Site, Route 2, Box 247, Walla Walla, Washington 99362 **Telephone:** 509-522-6360

DIRECTIONS: The Visitor Center is 7 miles (13 km) west of Walla Walla on US 12. It is 3 miles (6 km) west of College Place.
    Dr. and Mrs. Marcus Whitman ministered to spiritual and physical needs of the Indians here until slain by a few of them in 1847. The Mission was a landmark on the Oregon Trail. Authorized for addition to the National Park System on June 29, 1936.

VISITOR ACTIVITIES: interpretive exhibits, picnicking, cultural demonstrations; **Permits:** No; **Fees:** Yes, $1.00 per adult, $3.00 maximum per family; **Visitor facilities:** self-guiding foot trails, wayside exhibits, museum with audiovisual program, picnic area; **Any limitations on vehicle usage:** No; **Hiking trails:** No, there are 9/10 mile (1.4 km) of foot trails; **Backcountry:** No; **Camping:** No; **Other overnight accommodations on site:** No; **Meals served in the park:** No; **Food and supplies obtainable in the park:** No; **Food and supplies obtainable nearby:** Yes, College Place and Walla Walla; **Overnight accommodations:** Walla Walla and College Place, 6-8 miles (9.7-13 km) east of the park; **First Aid available in park:** Yes, in the Visitor Center; **Nearest Hospital:** Walla Walla, 8 miles (13 km) east of the park; **Days/Hours:** Open daily from 8 a.m. to 4:30 p.m., with extended hours in Summer; **Holiday Closings:** Thanksgiving, Dec. 25 and Jan 1; **Visitor attractions closed for seasons:** Cultural demonstrations are only offered in Summer; **Weather:** Summer is hot and dry; Winter is cold and dry.

West Virginia

HARPERS FERRY
NATIONAL HISTORICAL PARK

APPALACHIAN NATIONAL
SCENIC TRAIL

NEW RIVER GORGE NATIONAL RIVER

Appalachian National Scenic Trail
For details see listing in Maine

Harpers Ferry National Historical Park
Harpers Ferry, West Virginia   **SEE CLIMATABLE NO. 68**

MAILING ADDRESS: Superintendent, Harpers Ferry National Historical Park, P.O. Box 65, Harpers Ferry, West Virginia 25425 **Telephone:** 304-535-6371 extension 6222

DIRECTIONS: The Park is 20 miles (32 km) northwest of Frederick, MD, via US 340. It is 6 miles (9.7 km) north of Charles Town. The Visitor Center is less than 1 mile (1.6 km) off US 340, after a right turn beyond the bridge over the Shenandoah River.
    A Federal Armory was established at Harpers Ferry in the late 1700's. John Brown's raid took place here in 1859. Because of its strategic location at the confluence of the Shenandoah and Potomac Rivers, the town changed hands many times during the Civil War. Authorized for addition to the National Park System on June 20, 1944.

VISITOR ACTIVITIES: interpretive audiovisual progam, walking tours, mountain climbing, hiking, fishing, living history demonstrations, wildflower-watching, Christmas festival on the first weekend in December; **Permits:** Yes, permit for climbing, must be obtained at Park Ranger's office; **Fees:** Yes; **Visitor facilities:** Parking, restrooms, restored sites. Picnic areas and campgrounds are in the immediate area, but there are none in the park itself; **Any limitations on vehicle usage:** Drive carefully; automobile traffic on the narrow streets is often quite heavy; **Hiking trails:** Yes, variety of hiking trails are located nearby; **Backcountry:** No; **Camping:** No; **Other overnight accommodations on site:** No, but several campgrounds are nearby. KOA Campground is within 1 mile (1.6 km) of the park. For further information and reservations, contact KOA at Harpers Ferry, WV 25425, phone 304-535-6895; **Meals served in the park:** No; **Food and supplies obtainable in the park:** No; **Food and supplies obtainable nearby:** Yes, in the towns of Harpers Ferry, Boliver, Charles Town, and other nearby communities; **Over-**

night accommodations: Harpers Ferry, Charles Town, on US 340, 7 miles (11.3 km); **First Aid available in park:** Yes, at the Ranger Office; **Nearest Hospital:** Charles Town, US 340, 7 miles (11.3 km); **Days/Hours:** The Visitor Center and National Park Service sites are open daily all year, from 8 a.m. to 5 p.m.; **Holiday Closings:** Dec. 25; **Visitor attractions closed for seasons:** Most of the activities in the park are centered around the spring and summer months. In the Fall and Spring, park activities are usually restricted to weekends, but the Visitor Center and several of the historic buildings do remain open. Wildflowers abound in late Spring, and fall colors are striking.

GENERAL INFORMATION: Brick and natural stone walkways and steps are sometimes uneven or slippery. Pedestrians, especially children, should be cautious, as automobile traffic is often quite heavy. Mountain climbers must register at the Ranger Station before climbing the cliffs on Maryland Heights. Beware of the rivers. At low water they appear calm and peaceful. This is deceptive, however, as deep holes and swift undercurrents make them treacherous at any time of the year. There are no frequent checks on pollutants. Swimming is not advised. Fishermen and boaters should wear life jackets.

TRAVEL ACCESS: Bus: No; **Rail:** Baltimore, & Ohio (Chessie System), Amtrak provides daily service between Washington, D.C. and Harpers Ferry; **Air:** No.

NEARBY FACILITIES & POINTS OF INTEREST: Hotel/Motel: Hilltop House Hotel, Harpers Ferry West VA 25425, 304-535-6321, ½ mile from park; Cliffisde Motor Inn, Harpers Ferry West VA 25425, 304-725-2066, 1 mile from park; **Food/Supplies:** Coffee Mill on Potomac Street in Harpers Ferry; **Campgrounds:** KOA 1 mile from Park on #340 - Canal Campgrounds 4 miles away; **Parks, other points of interest:** Antietam National Battlefield (16 miles), Gettysburg (60 miles).

New River Gorge National River
West Virginia   **SEE CLIMATABLE NO. 180**

MAILING ADDRESS: New River Gorge National River, P.O. Box 1189, WV 25901 **Telephone:** 304-465-0508

DIRECTIONS: Two visitor centers are open to serve the public. The Canyon Rim Visitor Center is on U.S. Route 19 near Fayetteville at the north end of the New River Gorge Bridge. This Center is open year-round. The Hinton Visitor Center is beside the New River at State Route 3 By-Pass in Hinton. It is open seasonally. Both Centers offer a variety of services to the visiting public. Special interpretive programs are scheduled through the year.

Eastern National Park and Monument Association provides sales literature for more in-depth information about the Park.

The area preserves 52 miles of the New River, from Hinton to Fayetteville as a free-flowing stream abundant in natural, scenic, historic, and recreational values. Authorized for addition to the National Park System on Nov. 10, 1978.

TRAVEL ACCESS: Bus: Greyhound provides service to Beckley, and Hinton, WV; **Rail:** Amtrak service at Prince and Hinton, WV with Thurmond, WV as a flagstop; **Air:** Service to Charleston (1 hour drive away) and Beckley. Private airports are located closer to the river. **Other:** Taxicab service available from Oak Hill, Beckley and Hinton. Contact the National River or the West Virginia Department of Natural Resources for outfitters who provide whitewater rafting.

NEARBY FACILITIES & POINTS OF INTEREST: **Hotel/Motel:** Towns close to the river provide lodging. Chain motels include the Holiday Inn, Ramada Inn, Best Western, Beckley, WV., a Holiday Inn and Comfort Inn located at Oak Hill and Fayetteville, respectively; **Campgrounds:** Babcock State Park is located within the National River boundary; Private campgrounds and other state park campgrounds are located throughout the national river vicinity; **Parks, other points of interest:** Nearby state parks offer a variety of recreational attractions including two outdoor dramas at Grandview State Park. An exhibition coal mine is at Beckley. The largest single arch bridge in the world is located at Fayetteville.

Wisconsin

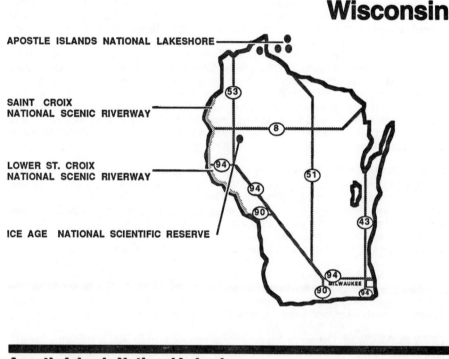

APOSTLE ISLANDS NATIONAL LAKESHORE

SAINT CROIX
NATIONAL SCENIC RIVERWAY

LOWER ST. CROIX
NATIONAL SCENIC RIVERWAY

ICE AGE NATIONAL SCIENTIFIC RESERVE

Apostle Islands National Lakeshore
Bayfield, Wisconsin   **SEE CLIMATABLE NO. 182**

MAILING ADDRESS: Superintendent, Apostle Islands National Lakeshore, Route 1, Box 4, Bayfield, Wisconsin 54814 **Telephone:** 715-779-3397

DIRECTIONS: East of Duluth from US 2, WI 13 leads north up the east shore of Bayfield Peninsula to Bayfield, site of the Park Headquarters and Visitor Center.
    The Lakeshore comprises twenty-one picturesque wooded islands and a 11 mile (17.7 km) strip of adjacent Bayfield Peninsula in the southwestern portion of Lake Superior characterized by sand beaches, high clay banks and sandstone cliffs. Established by act of Congress on Sept. 26, 1970.

VISITOR ACTIVITIES: Island camping, hiking, picnicking, swimming, boating, excursion boats, chartered fishing trips, rental sail boats and outstanding sport fishing are available; **Permits:** Yes, Wisconsin State fishing license is available locally. Free backcountry permits available at Visitor Center; **Fees:** No; **Visitor facilities:** Interpretive exhibits and audio-visual programs at Visitor Center and in Summer, evening programs and nature walks are presented at various mainland and island locations. Tours of lighthouse conducted during summer months. Campgrounds in numerous designated areas, concessioners provide shuttle trips between islands and excursion trips. Sailboat rental, charter fishing trips, marina, launch ramps, parking and showers also available; **Any limitations on vehicle usage:** No motor vehicles permitted on islands within the park; **Hiking trails:** Yes, wide range from maintained trails to old logging and railroad trails overgrown with underbrush or rocky trails which may be slippery or loose; **Backcountry:** Yes, on islands; **Camping:** Yes; **Other overnight accommodations on site:** No; **Meals served in the park:** No; **Food and supplies obtainable in the park:** No; **Food and supplies obtainable nearby:** Yes, at Bayfield, Cornucopia, Ashland, Washburn, and Madeline Island; **Overnight accommodations:** Bayfield, Washburn, Ashland, Cornucopia, and the nearby Chequamegon National Forest; **First Aid available in park:** Yes; **Nearest Hospital:** Ashland, Hwy 13, 23 miles (37 km); **Days/Hours:** 8 a.m. to 6 p.m. Memorial Day through Labor Day; daily 8:00 a.m. to 4:30 p.m. Labor Day through the last weekend in October, and Monday through Friday, 8 a.m. to 4:30 p.m. the remainder of the year; **Holiday Closings:** Thanksgiving, Christmas and New Years; **Visitor attractions closed for seasons:** None; **Weather:** Winter temperatures of -35°C (-30°F) and wind chill factors of -50°C (-60°F) are not uncommon. Nearly 250 cm (100 inches) of snow falls each year. Winter ice conditions vary with temperature, snowfall, and wind. Extreme caution is required for travelling across ice, as shifting winds may cause cracks and floes. Summer temperatures average 80°F during the day and 55°F at night. Thundershowers are common.

GENERAL INFORMATION: Biting insects are common from early May to mid-Aug. When hiking or camping, be prepared. Insect repellents are useful, but clothing that covers exposed skin is the best protection. Black bears can be found on several of the islands. To keep bears out of a campsite, keep it clean and store food in plastic bags suspended at least 10 ft. off the ground between two trees. Hiking near cliffs can be dangerous! Wet rocks are slippery and loose rocks may cause falls. Beware of dangerous waters. Even in Summer, Lake Superior's waters are dangerously cold, and sudden storms may break its surface. The temperature of the water a meter or so from shore may be 10°C (50°F) or less-cold enough to cause a strong swimmer to drown in 15 minutes.

About 3 miles (5 km) north of Bayfield is the Red Cliff Indian Reservation, the home of approximately 600 Chippewa Indians. The Red Cliff Cultural Center, (open seasonally) contains exhibits and artifacts. Hand-crafted items are offered for sale.

TRAVEL ACCESS: Other: Park accessible by private boat (power & sail), and through the Apostle Islands Cruise Service and the Apostle Islands Water-Taxi, Inc.

Ice Age National Scientific Reserve
Wisconsin   **SEE CLIMATABLES NO. 79, 179, 181, 185**

MAILING ADDRESS: Wisconsin Department of Natural Resources, P.O. Box 7921, Madison, Wisconsin 53707 **Telephone:** 608-266-2181

DIRECTIONS: Devils Lake and Mill Bluff are accessible from Int. 90-94. Kettle Moraine is accessible from WI 67, which runs through the unit. Access to Interstate Unit is from US 8 and WI 35.

This first national scientific reserve contains significant features of continental glaciation. There are nine separate units located across the State from Lake Michigan on the east to the St. Croix River on the Minnesota-Wisconsin border. Five of the nine units are operational; The Kettle Moraine State Forest, and Devils Lake, Mill Bluff, and Interstate Parks and the Horicon Marsh Wildlife Area. Authorized for addition to the National Park System on Oct. 13, 1964.

VISITOR ACTIVITIES: interpretive exhibits, auto tours, camping, hiking, fishing, swimming, picnicking, naturalist services, cross-country skiing; **Permits:** Wisconsin fishing licenses, available from local sporting goods stores or from the Department of Natural Resources, are required; **Fees:** Vehicle use fees are $3.50 per day or $14.00 annually for residents of Wisconsin; $6.00 per day or $30.00 annually for non-residents. Camping fees vary from $4.00 to $10.00 per site, depending on facilities. Golden Eagle, Golden Age and Golden Access Passports accepted for admission and available; **Visitor facilities:** scenic drives, hiking trails, beaches, campgrounds, picnic areas, restrooms, ski trails; Visitor Centers at Kettle Moraine and Interstate; Nature Center at Devils Lake; **Any limitations on vehicle usage:** Motor vehicles should be operated only where permitted; **Hiking trails:** Yes, trails vary from nature walks to a 30 mile (48 km) hiking trail at Kettle Moraine, which offers reserved shelters; **Backcountry:** Yes, by contacting Kettle Moraine, phone 414-626-2116; **Camping:** Yes, information by contacting the following units: Devils Lake, phone 608-356-8301; Northern Kettle Moraine, phone 414-626-2116; Interstate, phone 715-483-3747, Mill Bluff, phone 608-427-6692; **Other overnight accommodations on site:** No; **Meals served in the park:** No; **Food and supplies obtainable in the park:** Yes, at Kettle Moraine and Devils Lake; **Food and supplies obtainable nearby:** Yes, Baraboo, Campbellsport, St. Croix Falls, Horicon and other nearby towns; **Overnight accommodations:** Baraboo, Campbellsport, St. Croix Falls and other towns near the Ice Age Units; **First Aid available in park:** Yes; **Nearest Hospital:** Fond du Lac, Baraboo, Campbellsport, St. Croix Falls and other nearby communities; **Days/Hours:** Most parks open from 6 a.m. to 11 p.m.; **Holiday Closings:** None; **Visitor attractions closed for seasons:** Naturalist activities are curtailed at most units during the off-season, but are offered year-round at Kettle Moraine, Devils Lake and Interstate.

GENERAL INFORMATION: *For Your Safety*—When hiking, stay on designated trails. Swim only in authorized areas when lifeguards are on duty.

Ice Age National Scenic Trail
Wisconsin   **SEE CLIMATABLE MAP**

MAILING ADDRESS: National Park Service, 6417 Normandy Lane, Madison, Wisconsin 53719 **Telephone:** 608-276-3847

DIRECTIONS: When completed, this scenic Trail will meander approximately 1000 miles across Wisconsin following a chain of glacial landscape features-moraines, eskers, kames, kettles, erractics, etc. Six of the nine units of the Scientific Reserve are linked together by the trail. Four hundred miles of the trail are presently available for public use and will be marked with official Ice Age National Scenic Trail marker by 1988.
Designated by an act of Congress on October 3, 1980.

VISITOR ACTIVITIES: hiking, backpacking, camping, nature study. Some trail segments are open to horseback riding, bicycling, cross-country skiing, and limited snowmobiling; **Permits:** Yes, for a few trail segments; **Fees:** Yes, for some developed campgrounds within the National Forest, and State Parks along the trail; **Visitor facilities:** various, as provided by the managing authority for a particular segment; **Any limitations on vehicle usage:** Except for certain segments open to snowmobiling, use of motorized vehicles by the public is prohibited along the trail; **Hiking trails:** Yes; **Backcountry:** Yes, for information, write to the above address; **Camping:** As permitted; **Other overnight accommodations on site:** No; **Meals served in the park:** No; **Food and supplies obtainable in the park:** Yes, in some parks along the trail; **Food and supplies obtainable nearby:** Yes, in many communities along the trail; **Overnight accommodations:** In many communities along/near the trail; **First Aid available in park:** No; **Days/**

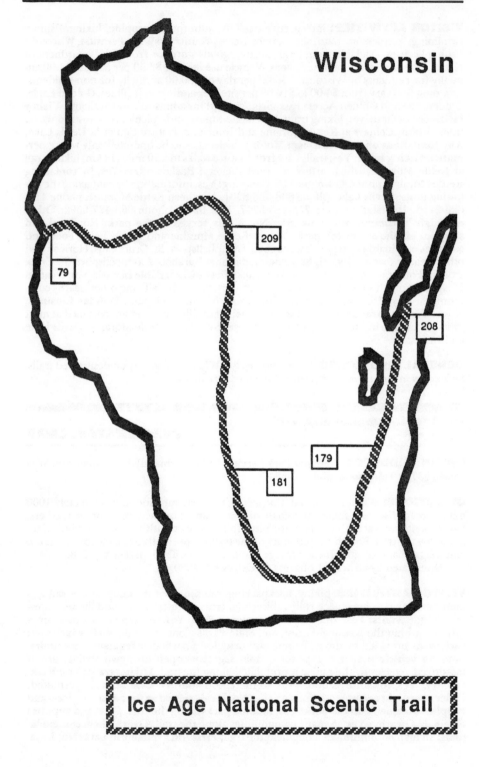

Wisconsin

209

79

208

179

181

Ice Age National Scenic Trail

Hours: Open at all times, except as limited by regulations governing individual parks/ forests or private lands through which the trail passes.

TRAVEL ACCESS: Many points on or near the trail are accessible by bus, rail, or air.

NEARBY FACILITIES & POINTS OF INTEREST: Scenic, historic, natural, and cultural interests are located along the trail. The main theme of the trail is Wisconsin's glacial features. **Campsites:** Reservation systems in use for some public and private campgrounds.

Lower St. Croix National Scenic Riverway
Wisconsin (also in Minnesota)   **SEE CLIMATABLE NO. 79**

MAILING ADDRESS: Superintendent, Lower Saint Croix River, c/o Saint Croix National Scenic River, P.O. Box 708, St. Croix Falls, Wisconsin 54024 **Telephone:** 715-483-3284

DIRECTIONS: Park Headquarters located at the corner of Hamilton and Massachusetts Streets in St. Croix Falls, WI.

Recreational opportunities for much of the upper Midwest are provided here along this 52 miles (84 km) segment of the St. Croix River, a component of the Wild and Scenic River System. Authorized for addition to the National Park System on Oct. 25, 1972. 27 miles (43.5 km) of this segment is administered by the National Park Service with the remaining 25 miles (40 km) administered by the states of Wisconsin and Minnesota.

VISITOR ACTIVITIES: boating, fishing, camping, interpretive exhibits, swimming, hunting, and hiking within state parks located along the Riverway, commercial boat trips; **Permits:** No; **Fees:** No; **Visitor facilities:** campgrounds, boat ramps, canoe rentals, commercial guided boat trip available on the river at Taylor's Falls and Stillwater, MN; **Any limitations on vehicle usage:** Recreational vehicle use discouraged at designated canoe landings with road access; **Hiking trails:** No, but hiking trails are within state parks located along Riverway; **Backcountry:** No; **Camping:** Yes, no reservations for campsites on Federal lands. For information and reservations in state parks write the Departments of Natural Resources in either St. Paul, MN 55155, phone 612-296-6157 or Madison, WI 53702, phone 608-266-2621; **Other overnight accommodations on site:** No; **Meals served in the park:** No; **Food and supplies obtainable in the park:** No; **Food and supplies obtainable nearby:** Yes, Marine on St. Croix, Osceola, Stillwater; **Overnight accommodations:** Hudson, Stillwater and other towns along the riverway; **First Aid available in park:** Yes, at Park Headquarters or State Park Ranger Stations; **Nearest Hospital:** Osceola, Hudson, and St. Croix Falls, WI and Stillwater, MN; **Days/ Hours:** Riverway open year-round but normal season is from Memorial Day through Labor Day with most activities available from about April through Oct.; **Holiday Closings:** Park Headquarters closed Thanksgiving, Dec. 25 & Jan. 1; **Visitor attractions closed for seasons:** Seasonal Visitor Center closed in winter months. Commercial boat trips closed in Winter.

GENERAL INFORMATION: Before setting out for canoeing, make sure you have a life preserver for each person, an extra paddle, insect repellent, a small gasoline stove, and drinking water. Firewood is very scarce in the vicinity of the campsites, and the cutting of trees or brush is prohibited. Drinking water is available at only a few places along the river.

TRAVEL ACCESS: **Bus:** Greyhound Lines provides daily service to Hudson, WI; **Rail:** Rail Service to Minneapolis/St. Paul; **Air:** Major airlines to Minneapolis/St. Paul

Airport; **Other:** People arriving by bus, rail, or air need to make special transportation arrangements to visit most of the Riverway.

Saint Croix National Scenic Riverway
Wisconsin (also in Minnesota)   **SEE CLIMATABLE NO. 79**

MAILING ADDRESS: Superintendent, Saint Croix National Scenic Riverway, P.O. Box 708, Saint Croix Falls, Wisconsin 54024 **Telephone:** 715-483-3284

DIRECTIONS: Park Headquarters is at the corner of Hamilton and Massachusetts Streets in St. Croix Falls. Interpretive pamphlets and maps are available here.
   Over 200 miles (321 km) of the scenic St. Croix River and it Namekagon tributary make up this area, an initial component of the National Wild and Scenic River System. Authorized for addition to the National Park System on Oct. 2, 1968.

VISITOR ACTIVITIES: fishing, canoeing, wildlife- and bird-watching, swimming, boating, interpretive exhibits, camping, hiking in nearby state forests and parks, hunting, commercial launch trips at Hayward Lake near Hayward, WI; **Permits:** No; **Fees:** No; **Visitor facilities:** campsites, boat launching sites, light outfitting services, and canoe rentals. There are limited Federal facilities along the riverway; **Any limitations on vehicle usage:** Recreational vehicle use is discouraged at designated canoe landings with road access; **Hiking trails:** No, hiking trails available in nearby state forests and parks; **Backcountry:** No; **Camping:** Type B campsites and state campgrounds are available nearby. For information, contact: State Departments of Natural Resources, St. Paul, MN 55155, phone 612-296-6157 and Madison, WI 53702, phone 608-266-2621; **Meals served in the park:** No; **Food and supplies obtainable in the park:** No; **Food and supplies obtainable nearby:** Yes, at Cable, Hayward, Trego, Grantsberg, Saint Croix Falls, Taylor's Falls, Stillwater; **Overnight accommodations:** Hayward, Trego, Saint Croix Falls, Taylor's Falls, and other communities near the riverway; **First Aid available in park:** Yes, at Ranger Stations on the Riverway; **Nearest Hospital:** Hayward, Spooner, Grantsburg, and St. Croix Falls, WI, all of which are within 10 miles (16 km) of the Riverway; **Days/Hours:** Riverway open year-round but normal season is from Memorial Day to Labor Day with most activities available from about April through Oct. Information Stations closed in Winter; **Holiday Closings:** Park Headquarters closed on Thanksgiving, Dec. 25 and Jan. 1; **Visitor attractions closed for seasons:** Seasonal Visitor Information Stations closed in winter months, as are commercial launch trips on Lake Hayward. The uppermost sections of the St. Croix and Namekagon may become too shallow for canoeing during periods of low water, usually in late Summer and Autumn.

GENERAL INFORMATION: Before setting out for canoeing, make sure you have a life preserver for each person, an extra paddle, insect repellent, a small gasoline stove, and drinking water. Firewood is very scarce in the vicinity of the campsites, and the cutting of trees or brush is prohibited. Drinking water is available at only a few places along the River.

TRAVEL ACCESS: Rail: None; **Other:** People arriving by air or bus must arrange for shuttle to other areas on Riverway by private canoe outfitters located along or near the Riverway.

North Country National Scenic Trail
For details see listing in New York

Wyoming

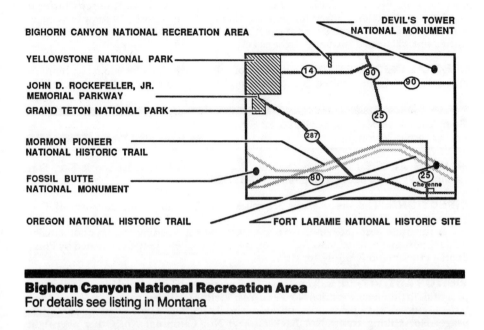

BIGHORN CANYON NATIONAL RECREATION AREA

DEVIL'S TOWER
NATIONAL MONUMENT

YELLOWSTONE NATIONAL PARK

JOHN D. ROCKEFELLER, JR.
MEMORIAL PARKWAY

GRAND TETON NATIONAL PARK

MORMON PIONEER
NATIONAL HISTORIC TRAIL

FOSSIL BUTTE
NATIONAL MONUMENT

OREGON NATIONAL HISTORIC TRAIL

FORT LARAMIE NATIONAL HISTORIC SITE

Bighorn Canyon National Recreation Area
For details see listing in Montana

Devils Tower National Monument
Devils Tower, Wyoming   **SEE CLIMATABLE NO. 186**

MAILING ADDRESS: Superintendent, Devils Tower National Monument, Devils Tower, Wyoming 82714 **Telephone:** 307-467-5370

DIRECTIONS: The monument entrance, off WY 24, is 7 miles (11 km) north of US 14; 28 miles (47 km) northwest of Sundance, WY; 33 miles (53 km) northeast of Moorcroft, WY; and 52 miles (84 km) southwest of Belle Fourche, SD. The Visitor Center is about 3 miles (5 km) from the Monument's east entrance and close to the Tower.

This 865-foot (264 m) tower of columnar rock, the remains of a volcanic eruption, is the Nation's first national monument. Created by Presidential Proclamation on Sept. 24, 1906.

VISITOR ACTIVITIES: interpretive exhibits, photography, walking, camping, hiking, mountain climbing, picnicking, fishing, bird- and wildlife-watching; **Permits:** No; **Fees:** Entrance fee is $3 per vehicle, $1 for each bus passenger, $1 for individual (biker, hiker, etc.), those under 13 or 62 and over-U.S. citizens are admitted free. Golden Eagle and Golden Age Passports accepted and available; **Visitor facilities:** parking and restrooms at the Visitor Center, picnic area, Administration office, campground; **Any limitations on vehicle usage:** Vehicles are restricted to designated roadways; **Hiking trails:** Yes, self-guiding nature trails of varying lengths; **Backcountry:** No; **Camping:** Yes, no reservations accepted for campsites. Fee is $6 per site per night (camping), with a 14 day limit during Summer; **Other overnight accommodations on site:** No; **Meals served in the park:** No; **Food and supplies obtainable in the park:** No; **Food and supplies obtainable nearby:** Yes, within 2 miles (3 km) of the campground; **Overnight accommoda-**

tions: Sundance, WY & US 14, 28 miles (45 km); Hulett, 11 miles (17.7 km) east; Moorcroft, WY 24 & US 14, 34 miles (54.7 km); **First Aid available in park:** Yes; **Nearest Hospital:** Sundance, via WY 24 & US 14, 28 miles (45 km); **Days/Hours:** The Monument is open all year. Visitor Center is open from mid-May through Oct.; **Holiday Closings:** No; **Visitor attractions closed for seasons:** Campground is closed by snow in Winter; **Weather:** In Summer, the days are generally sunny, but when the sun sets or during storms you will need a sweater or light jacket.

GENERAL INFORMATION: Be cautious of rattlesnakes, which seldom bite humans unless disturbed or mistreated. Stay clear of prairie dogs, which carry fleas and can bite.

Fort Laramie National Historic Site
Fort Laramie, Wyoming   **SEE CLIMATABLE NO. 183**

MAILING ADDRESS: Superintendent, Fort Laramie National Historic Site, Fort Laramie, Wyoming 82212 **Telephone:** 307-837-2221

DIRECTIONS: The site is about 3.1 miles (5 km) southwest of the town of Fort Laramie, WY, off US 26.
    A fur-trade post once stood here, but the surviving buildings are those of a major military post that guarded covered-wagon trails to the West, 1849-90. Created by Presidential Proclamation on July 16, 1938.

VISITOR ACTIVITIES: walking tours, interpretive exhibits, picnicking, living history programs in Summer; **Permits:** No; **Fees:** Yes; **Visitor facilities:** parking at Visitor Center, self-guided tours, picnic area and audio-visual program; **Any limitations on vehicle usage:** No; **Hiking trails:** No; **Backcountry:** No; **Camping:** No; **Other overnight accommodations on site:** No; **Meals served in the park:** No; **Food and supplies obtainable in the park:** No; **Food and supplies obtainable nearby:** Yes, in towns of Fort Laramie, Guernsey, Lingle or Torrington; **Overnight accommodations:** Lingle, 10 miles east on U.S. 26, Fort Laramie 3.1 miles northeast on Hwy 160, Guernsey, 13 miles (21 km) northwest of Fort Laramie or in Torrington, 20 miles (32 km) southeast of Fort Laramie; both on US 26; **First Aid available in park:** Yes; **Nearest Hospital:** Torrington 20 miles (32 km) southeast of Fort Laramie by US 26; **Days/Hours:** From mid-June through Labor Day, 8 a.m. to 7 p.m.; 8 a.m. to 4:30 p m. the remainder of the year; **Holiday Closings:** Thanksgiving day, Dec. 25, and Jan. 1; **Visitor attractions closed for seasons:** No living history programs are offered between Labor Day and Memorial Day; **Weather:** Winters can be severe. Summer temperatures can reach 100°F with low humidity. Summer night are usually cool.

Fossil Butte National Monument
Kemmerer, Wyoming   **SEE CLIMATABLE NO. 184**

MAILING ADDRESS: Superintendent, Fossil Butte National Monument, P.O. Box 527, Kemmerer, Wyoming 83101 **Telephone:** 307-877-3450

DIRECTIONS: The Monument is in southwest Wyoming, about 11 miles (17.7 km) west of Kemmerer. The Butte is located just north of US 30 N and the Union Pacific Railroad, both of which traverse the valley.
    An abundance of rare fish fossils, 48-52 million years old, is evidence of former habitation of this now semiarid region. Established by act of Congress on Oct. 23, 1972.

VISITOR ACTIVITIES: picnicking, fossil displays, auto tours, wildlife- and bird-watching, hiking; **Permits:** No; **Fees:** No; **Visitor facilities:** interpretive exhibits, restrooms. The site is largely unimproved; **Any limitations on vehicle usage:** Rain or snow may make travel difficult or impossible. Check with Administrative offices on Hwy 189 in Kemmerer. Monday-Friday, 8:30 to 4:30; **Hiking trails:** Yes, 1½ mile (2.4 km) interpretive trail; **Backcountry:** No; **Camping:** No; **Other overnight accommodations on site:** No; **Meals served in the park:** No; **Food and supplies obtainable in the park:** No; **Food and supplies obtainable nearby:** Yes, Kemmerer and Cokeville; **Overnight accommodations:** Kemmerer, 11 miles (17.1 km) east on US 30 N, and Cokeville, 33 miles (53 km) west on US 30 N; **First Aid available in park:** Yes, when employees are available. The park is routinely patrolled; **Nearest Hospital:** Kemmerer; **Days/Hours:** The Visitor Contact Station is staffed from 8:30 a.m. to 5:30 p.m. 7 days a week from June 1 through Labor Day, and as weather permits during May and October; **Holiday Closings:** None; **Visitor attractions closed for seasons:** Park is usually closed by snow from Nov.-early May; **Weather:** The climate is semiarid and cool-temperate.

GENERAL INFORMATION: Reservations for accommodations in the area should be made well in advance of the visit. Contact the Monument for further information on local lodging.

Grand Teton National Park
Moose, Wyoming   **SEE CLIMATABLE NO. 187**

MAILING ADDRESS: Superintendent, Grand Teton National Park, P.O. Drawer 170, Moose, Wyoming 83012 **Telephone:** 307-733-2880

DIRECTIONS: Park Headquarters and a Visitor Center are at Moose, 13 miles (21 km) north of Jackson on US 26, 89, and 191.
　　This scenic area of mountain peaks, alpine lakes, and sagebrush flats is filled with moose, elk, trumpeter swans and other wildlife. It offers a great variety of recreational opportunities to the visitor. Much of the Teton Range was protected as a National Park on Feb. 26, 1929 and expanded in 1950 to include most of the valley called Jackson Hole.

VISITOR ACTIVITIES: exhibits, ranger-led activities, picnicking, camping, backcountry hiking, mountain climbing, horseback riding, boating, fishing, biking, snowmobiling, cross-country skiing, animal and bird watching; **Permits:** required for fishing (State license), backcountry camping, boating and oversnow travel; **Fees:** $10 for motorboats, $5 for non-motorized boats and snowmobiles. $5 entrance fee good for 1 week in both Yellowstone & Grand Teton National Parks. Golden Eagle, Golden Age, and Golden Access Passports accepted and available; **Visitor facilities:** Visitor centers, campgrounds, trails, picnic areas, boat rentals and ramps, snowmobile route, cross-country ski trails, lodging, meals, gas, groceries, post office, religious services, restrooms, telephones; **Any limitations on vehicle usage:** Drive only on established roadways. Keep motor vehicles off bikelanes; **Hiking trails:** Yes, over 200 miles (320 km) of maintained park trails; **Backcountry:** Yes, information can be obtained at Visitor Centers or Jenny Lake Ranger Station; **Camping:** Yes, no reservations available for individual campsites. Reservations for the trailer village with all hookups at Colter Bay can be made by contacting the Grand Teton Lodge Company, P.O. Box 240, Moran, WY 83013, phone 307-543-2855. Group campsites are reserved in advance by writing the Chief Ranger between January 1 and June 1. More than a dozen Forest Service and commercial campgrounds are located near the park; **Other overnight accommodations on site:** Yes, for information and reservations at other accommodations, contact the Grand Teton Lodge Company, Reservations Dept., P.O. Box 240, Moran, WY 83013, phone 307-543-2855, or Signal Mountain Lodge, Moran, WY 83013, phone 307-543-2831;

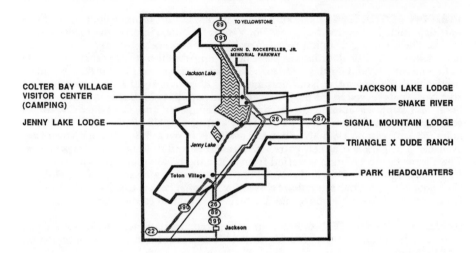

Meals served in the park: Yes, at Dornans, Colter Bay, Jackson Lake, Jenny Lake, and Signal Mountain Lodges; **Food and supplies obtainable in the park:** Yes, at Colter Bay Village, Jackson Lake Lodge, Jenny Lake, Signal Mountain, Moose, & Kelly; **Food and supplies obtainable nearby:** Yes, at Jackson; **Overnight accommodations:** Jackson, 4 miles (6 km) south; **First Aid available in park:** at Visitor Centers, Ranger Stations, and Jackson Lake Lodge; **Nearest Hospital:** St. John's Hospital in Jackson, south of Park; **Days/Hours:** The Park is open year-round, 24 hours a day; **Holiday Closings:** Moose Visitor Center closed Dec. 25; **Visitor attractions closed for seasons:** Most facilities are closed during the winter (Oct. through May); Colter Bay Visitor Center closed Oct. 1 through mid-May; **Weather:** Latitude and elevation are the main factors producing cool summers and cold winters. Despite frequent rains and cool temperatures, spring visitors may enjoy wildflowers, moose, elk and migrating birds. Be prepared for a variety of weather conditions. It snows even in May and June. Raingear and warm clothing (layers work best) are essential. Spring temperatures can range from below zero to 20°C (70°F).

Summer days during July and Aug. are generally warm and occasionally hot. Afternoon thundershowers are possible. Daytime temperatures average near 30°C (80°F), dropping to 4°C (40°F) at night. Summer visitation exceeds two million. Most campgrounds usually fill by early afternoon. The Cascade Canyon Trail is often crowded.

Autumn color is best about the first week of Oct. Days are generally cool & clear during Sept. and Oct.—to many visitors this is the best time to visit. Most park facilities are open in Sept. when it's easy to find space in lodges and campgrounds. During late October and November, elk migrate through the Park to their winter range. Expect frosty nights warming to 15-20°C (about 65°F) during the day in early Autumn.

Winter lasts from Nov. through Apr. with an average 5 meters (16 feet) of snowfall. Blizzards may last for several days, making travel hazardous. Carry tire chains.

GENERAL INFORMATION: A recorded information service is available on a 24-hour basis all year. Phone 307-733-2220. To talk with park personnel, call 307-733-2880. For State of Wyoming travel information, contact the Wyoming Travel Commission, Cheyenne, WY 82001; 307-777-7777.

For Your Safety—Register at Jenny Lake Ranger Station in Summer and at Park Headquarters during other seasons before starting any off-trail hike or climb. Do not feed or touch any park animal. Lightning-caused fires are allowed to burn in some parts of the Park. If one is in progress, check with a Ranger before planning a trip to the burn area.

Dogs are prohibited on all hiking trails and in the backcountry. Bicycles are not allowed on any trail.

John D. Rockefeller, Jr. Memorial Parkway
Wyoming   **SEE CLIMATABLE NO. 187**

MAILING ADDRESS: Superintendent, Grand Teton National Park, P.O. Drawer 170, Moose, Wyoming 83012 **Telephone:** 307-733-2880

DIRECTIONS: The Parkway Ranger Station is located just north of Flagg Ranch Village on US 89. Information on the parkway is available through Dial-A-Park in Grand Teton: 307-733-2220.

This 7 mile (11 km) long area linking Yellowstone and Grand Teton National Parks commemorates Mr. Rockefeller's role in aiding the establishment of many parks, including Grand Teton. Authorized for addition to the National Park System on Aug. 25, 1972.

VISITOR ACTIVITIES: Information and self-guiding trails are provided through the Parkway. River float trips, horseback riding, snowmobiling, and cross-country skiing are available; **Permits:** Required for snowmobiling, boating, backcountry camping and fishing (State license). Available (except fishing) from Moose Visitor Center in Grand Teton National Park; **Fees:** $10 for motorboat, $5 for non-motorized boat and snowmobile permits; **Visitor facilities:** At Flagg Ranch Village, gasoline is available during the summer and winter seasons. From May 15-Sept. 30: lodging, food store, float trips, horseback riding, trailer park with and without full hookups. From Dec. 15-Mar. 15: lodging, food store, snowmobile and cross-country ski rentals and snowcoach rides. **Any limitations on vehicle usage:** Drive only on established roadways; **Hiking trails:** Yes, 3 miles (4.8 km); **Backcountry:** Yes, information available at Ranger Station on Parkway or Visitor Centers or Ranger Station in Grand Teton National Park; **Camping:** Yes, Flagg Ranch Village and Snake River Campground; **Other overnight accommodations on site:** Yes, Flagg Ranch Village, Moran, WY 83103 phone 307-543-2861. Both camping and lodge are open in season; inquire about exact dates of operation; **Meals served in the park:** Yes, at Flagg Ranch Village; **Food and supplies obtainable in the park:** Yes, at Flagg Ranch Village in season; **Food and supplies obtainable nearby:** Yes, during the summer at Colter Bay Village 18 miles (29 km) south and Grant Village in Yellowstone; **Overnight accommodations:** Jackson, 55 miles (88 km) south, Colter Bay Village, 18 miles (29 km) south, Jackson Lake Lodge, 23 miles (37 km) south, Signal Mountain Lodge, 27 miles (43 km) south, Jenny Lake Lodge, 35 miles (56 km) south, or Yellowstone to the north; **First Aid available in park:** Yes, emergency first aid at Ranger Station, Medical Clinic at Jackson Lake Lodge 23 miles (37 km) south during summer; **Nearest Hospital:** St. John's Hospital, Jackson, WY, 55 miles (88 km) south; **Days/Hours:** Park is open year-round, 24 hours a day; **Holiday Closings:** None; **Visitor attractions closed for seasons:** Normal seasonal closings affect appropriate activities.

GENERAL INFORMATION: Visitors to the area can also see Yellowstone and Grand Teton National Parks (See listings in this book).

Mormon Pioneer Trail
For details see listing in Illinois

Oregon National Scenic Trail
For details see listing in Missouri

Yellowstone National Park
Yellowstone National Park, Wyoming   **SEE CLIMATABLE NO. 187**

MAILING ADDRESS: National Park Service, P.O. Box 168, Yellowstone National Park, Wyoming 82190 **Telephone:** 307-344-7381

DIRECTIONS: The Park can be reached from many directions: from the North US 89; from the Northeast, US 212; from the east through Cody, US 20, 14, and 16, merged; from the South, via the John D. Rockefeller, Jr. Memorial Parkway, US 89 and US 26 and from the West via West Yellowstone, US 191 & 20.

This is the world's greatest geyser area, with Old Faithful and some 10,000 other geysers and hot springs. Here, too are lakes, waterfalls, high mountains, and the Grand Canyon of the Yellowstone—all set apart in 1872 as the world's first national park. Yellowstone is the largest Park in the lower 48 states. Established Mar. 1, 1872.

VISITOR ACTIVITIES: fishing, camping, boating, driving, hiking, horseback riding, bird- and wildlife-watching, biking, stagecoach rides, boat and bus tours, snowmobiling, skiing, snowshoeing, interpretive and campfire programs; **Permits:** required for fishing, boating, and backcountry camping and can be obtained at any Visitor Center or Ranger Station; **Fees:** Yes, fees for campsites vary from free backcountry sites to $5-6 for well-developed campsites. A $5 fee is charged for all non-motorized boating permits and a $10 fee is required for all motorized boating permits for recreational use within the park. Fees are also charged for horseback riding, stagecoach rides, boat and bus tours, and trailer park with utilities. There is a combination entrance fee to both Yellowstone and Grand Teton National Parks—$5 per vehicle, including motorcycles, which is valid for 7 days. Persons entering on foot, bicycle, or by bus will be charged $2 per visit. Golden Eagle, Golden Access, and Golden Age passports are accepted and available; **Visitor facilities:** roadside radio interpretation, interpretive display boards, hotels, cabins, amphitheatres, boat rentals, campgrounds, church services, food service, gasoline stations, horse rental, laundries, photo shops, post offices, sewage dump stations, showers, tour buses, fee trailer park with utilities, Visitor Centers, marina, bike trails; **Any limitations on vehicle usage:** Motor vehicles are restricted to designated roads. Bicycles are restricted to roads and designated bicycle trails. Visitors may encounter snow and hazardous driving conditions during Spring and Fall, with temporary road closures. Oversnow vehicles are subject to park rules and regulations; **Hiking trails:** Yes, about 1000 miles (1600 km) of trails lead to remote sections of the Park. Some offer easy part-day trips over gentle terrain, others require strength and endurance because of their elevation, length and ruggedness. Good topographic maps, which can be purchased at any Visitor Center, are highly recommended. Always check trail conditions with a Ranger before setting out on an overnight or long hike; **Backcountry:** Yes, permits are required and are available at any Ranger Station or Visitor Center on a first-come, first-served basis; **Camping:** Yes, campgrounds are filled on a first-come, first-served basis; **Other overnight accommodations on site:** Yes, reservations for hotels, lodges, cabins, and a trailer park, all open from mid-June through Labor Day, can be made by writing the TW Services, Inc., Yellowstone National Park, WY 82190, phone 307-344-7311. Reservations are advised, especially during July and August. Those visitors already in Yellowstone may make advance room reservations at any hotel or lodge anywhere in the Park; **Meals served in the park:** Yes, Lake, Canyon, Tower-Roosevelt, Mammoth Hot Springs, Old Faithful, Grant Village; **Food and supplies obtainable in the park:** Yes, at Lake, Fishing Bridge, Canyon, Tower-Roosevelt, Tower Falls, West Thumb, Mammoth Hot Springs, Grant Village, Old Faithful; **Food and supplies obtainable nearby:** Yes, at each community near the 5 park entrances: Livingston, Bozeman, Gardiner, MT, West Yellowstone, Red Lodge, Cooke City/Silver Gate, MT; Cody & Jackson, WY; **Overnight accommodations:** Gardiner, Cooke City/Silver Gate, Livingston, Bozeman, West Yellowstone, and Red Lodge, MT; Cody and Jackson, WY;

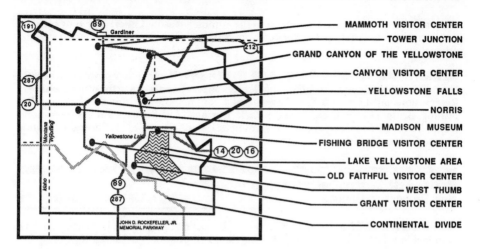

First Aid available in park: Yes; **Nearest Hospital:** Lake Hospital, Mammoth Clinic, Old Faithful Clinic hours vary; **Days/Hours:** Open 24 hours a day, every day; **Holiday Closings:** None; **Visitor attractions closed for seasons:** Park roads and entrances, except the North Entrance to Cooke City, MT, are ordinarily closed by snow to auto traffic between Oct. 31 and May 1. Most park campgrounds do not open before June, except at Mammoth, where camping is available all year.

Wintertime activities abound. In recent years, thousands of visitors have entered the Park by oversnow vehicle. Heated snow coaches are operated by concessioners from West Yellowstone, Mammoth Hot Springs and South Entrance. Private snowmobiles may also use the unplowed roads, but no cross-country vehicle use is permitted. Ski and snowshoe touring are also on the increase. The Albright Visitor Center and Museum in Mammoth is open year-round, with interpretive activities scheduled. The Old Faithful Visitor Center is open during the Winter from about mid-Dec. to mid-Mar., providing information, evening programs and Winter walks. Meals and overnight lodging are available through the winter at Old Faithful. Mammoth Hot Springs Hotel offers overnight lodging, as well as snowmobile and cross-country ski rental, restaurant and gift shop. The only roads open for auto traffic are Gardiner to Mammoth and from there to the Northeast Entrance and Cooke City. This drive offers an excellent opportunity to see wildlife. Special information on winter activities and services may be obtained by writing to the Park. Reservations for winter facilities may be made by writing to the TW Services, Inc., Yellowstone National Park, WY 82190. Reservations may also be made by telephoning (307) 344-7311, and are advised, especially during the holidays.

GENERAL INFORMATION: Assistance for any emergency in the park can be obtained anytime by calling Park Headquarters at 307-344-7381. 911 is available for emergency assistance. Write the above address for informative pamphlets and a map. Five national forests providing recreational opportunites border on Yellowstone. To the south lies Grand Teton National Park, with many concessioner and Federal facilities (see listing in this book).

TRAVEL ACCESS: Bus: Greyhound serves Billings, Bozeman, Livingston, and West Yellowstone, in Montana; Idaho Falls in Idaho. TW Services, Inc., the park concessioner, has a connecting bus service into the Park from Bozeman, Livingston, and West Yellowstone, in the summer season; **Rail:** There is no easy or convenient train service to Yellowstone. Amtrak provides service to Shelby, Whitefish and Havre, Montana. Both routes are far to the north of the Park; **Air:** Airline service is available to Billings, Bozeman, West Yellowstone, in Montana; and Jackson Hole and Cody, Wyoming. The airports at West Yellowstone are limited to the summer season. **Other:** The only in-park public transportation is via TW Services, Inc. tour buses. There is no shuttle-bus system, other than TW.

NEARBY FACILITIES & POINTS OF INTEREST: Parks, other points of interest: Grand Teton National Park, Wyoming; **Reservation systems in use for other facilities:** Reservations must be made for all overnight accommodations within the Park, and for Fishing Bridge Recreational Vehicle Park, through TW Services Inc., Reservations Dept., Yellowstone National Park, Wyoming 82190, (307) 344-7311. Campsites cannot be reserved in advance.

Roosevelt Campobello International Park
New Brunswick, Canada   **SEE CLIMATABLE NO. 71**

MAILING ADDRESS: Executive Secretary, Roosevelt Campobello International Park Commission, P.O. Box 97, Lubec, Maine 04652 **Telephone:** 506-752-2922

DIRECTIONS: Follow Maine Route 1 to 189. Cross Roosevelt Memorial Bridge at Lubec, Maine to New Brunswick Route 774. The Park is about 1½ miles (2.4 km) from Canadian Customs.

At the age of 39, President Franklin D. Roosevelt was striken by poliomyelitis here at his summer home. The Park has scenic vistas in a 2800-acre natural area. This is the first international park to be administered by a joint commission. Established by act of Congress in 1964.

VISITOR ACTIVITIES: tours of the Roosevelt Cottage, orientation film, visual aid displays, picnicking, beach activities; **Permits:** No; **Fees:** No; **Visitor facilities:** parking and restrooms at the Reception Center, exhibits; **Any limitations on vehicle usage:** Cars must be parked at the Reception Center in the cottage area; **Hiking trails:** Yes, trails are located in the natural area. Obtain maps at the Reception Center; **Backcountry:** No; **Camping:** No; **Other overnight accommodations on site:** No, tourist facilities are at Welshpool and Wilson's Beach, just north of the park. The Province of New Brunswick maintains a Park with tent and trailer sites and picnic areas at the northern end of Herring Cove. There are also tourist facilities in and near Lubec. The State of Maine has two parks in the area, with tenting and trailer facilities at Cobscook Bay Park in the Moosehorn Game Refuge at Whiting and picnic areas at Quoddy Head State Park; **Meals served in the park:** No; **Food and supplies obtainable in the park:** No; **Food and supplies obtainable nearby:** Yes, Wilson's Beach, NB and Lubec, ME; **Overnight accommodations:** On the Island, within 5 miles (8 km); **First Aid available in park:** No, nearby at Welshpool Health Center, 2 miles (3 km); **Nearest Hospital:** Machias, ME, US Rt. 1, 30 miles (48 km); **Days/Hours:** Open 7 days per week, 9 a.m. to 5 p.m., from late May through mid-October; **Holiday Closings:** No; **Visitor attractions closed for seasons:** Park is closed from mid-October through May; **Weather:** July and August are warm months. September has warm days and cool nights.

Northern Mariana Islands

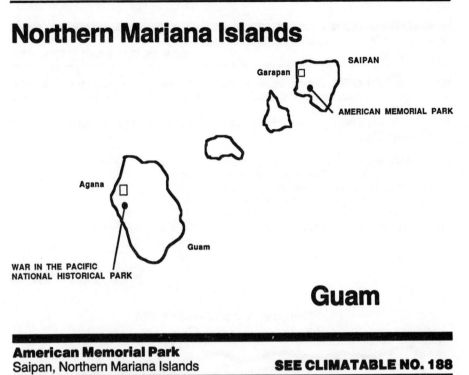

Guam

American Memorial Park
Saipan, Northern Mariana Islands   **SEE CLIMATABLE NO. 188**

MAILING ADDRESS: P.O. Box 198 CHRB, Saipan, CM 96950

DIRECTIONS: The Park lies just north of Garapan Village. 133 acres of partially developed memorial and recreation facilities. Established on August 18, 1978.

VISITOR ACTIVITIES: swimming, picnicking, boating, other recreation; **Permits:** No; **Fees:** No; **Visitor facilities:** picnic facilities, monument, tour boats, launching ramp, jogging path, and sports fields. Excellent beach. **Any limitations on vehicle usage:** Not allowed on beach; **Hiking trails:** No; **Backcountry:** No; **Camping:** No; **Other overnight accommodations on site:** No; **Meals served in the park:** No; **Food and supplies obtainable in the park:** No; **Food and supplies obtainable nearby:** Yes, in Garapan; **Overnight accommodations:** several hotels within 1 mile of park; **First Aid available in park:** Yes; **Nearest Hospital:** adjacent to park; **Days/Hours:** Park open year-round; **Holiday Closings:** None; **Visitor attractions closed for seasons:** None; **Weather:** Humid tropical climate year round. Rainy season June-November. Subject to typhoons.

GENERAL INFORMATION: Park is dedicated as a memorial to those who died in the Marianas Campaign of World War II.

TRAVEL ACCESS: Bus: No; **Rail:** No; **Air: Continental** Air Micronesia. **Other:** Direct flights to Saipan from Guam and Japan.

NEARBY FACILITIES & POINTS OF INTEREST: Hotel/Motel: Hyatt Regency, Intercontinental, Hafa Dai, Saipan Grand; **Food/Supplies:** Several stores and restaurants near park; **Parks, other points of interest:** Invasion Beaches, Mt. Takpochao, Suicide Cliff, Bonzai Cliff, Grotto, Bird Island, Kalabera Cave, Command Post, Managaha Island, and Sugar King.

War in the Pacific National Historical Park
Agana, Guam   **SEE CLIMATABLE NO. 189**

MAILING ADDRESS: Superintendent, War in the Pacific National Historical Park, Marine Dr. Asan P.O. Box FA, Agana, Guam 96910 **Telephone:** Guam: 671-477-9362 or 472-7240*
*Guam is fourteen hours ahead of Eastern Standard Time. Guam does not observe Daylight Savings Time.

DIRECTIONS: Portions of the Park are open, including a Visitor Information Center with museum and an audiovisual program in English and Japanese.
    As a memorial to those participating in the Pacific Theater, this scenic and historic Park offers public enjoyment of natural and World War II historic features. Authorized for addition to the National Park System on Aug. 18, 1978. There are several sites of underwater WW II wreckage that are open to qualified SCUBA divers.

Puerto Rico

San Juan National Historic Site

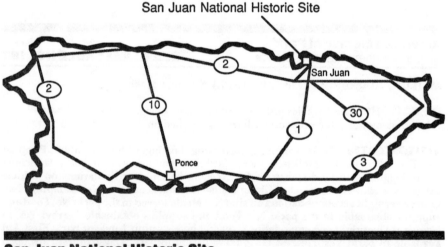

San Juan National Historic Site
Old San Juan, Puerto Rico   **SEE CLIMATABLE NO. 147**

MAILING ADDRESS: Superintendent, San Juan National Historic Site, P.O. Box 712, Old San Juan, Puerto Rico 00902 **Telephone:** 809-724-1974

DIRECTIONS: The Site's information desk and other visitor facilities are on the entry plaza levels of forts El Morro and San Cristobal. The site includes the Spanish-built forts of El Morro, San Cristobal, El Cañuelo, and the city walls.
    These massive masonry fortifications, the oldest in the territorial limits of the United States, were begun by the Spanish in the 16th Century to protect a strategic harbor guarding the sea lanes to the New World. Designated Feb. 14, 1949.

VISITOR ACTIVITIES: exhibits; **Permits:** No; **Fees:** $1 for adults; **Visitor facilities:** restrooms, drinking fountains, museums; **Any limitations on vehicle usage:** Limited parking available at Fort San Cristobal; ample parking at El Morro; **Hiking trails:** No; **Backcountry:** No; **Camping:** No; **Other overnight accommodations on site:** No; **Meals served in the park:** No; **Food and supplies obtainable in the park:** No; **Food and supplies obtainable nearby:** Yes, the city of San Juan; **Overnight accommodations:** San Juan, within walking distance; **First Aid available in park:** Yes; **Nearest Hospital:** San Juan, within 5 miles (8 km); **Days/Hours:** Open 7 days a week from 8 a.m. to 6 p.m.; **Holiday Closings:** None; **Visitor attractions closed for seasons:** No; **Weather:** Warm to hot all year with no change of seasons.

GENERAL INFORMATION: Walking shoes with rubber soles and low heels are recommended.

TRAVEL ACCESS: Bus: Metro Bus Authority provides regular service to Plaza Colon; **Rail:** No; **Air:** Eastern, Delta, American, Avianca, BWIA provide service to San Juan. City of San Juan mini-bus stops near El Morro Grounds main gate.

NEARBY FACILITIES & POINTS OF INTEREST: Hotel/Motel: Caribe Hilton, Muñoz Rivera Ave., San Juan, PR, (809) 721-0303, 2-1/2 miles from Site, El Convento & Rest. Hotel, 100 Cristo St., San Juan, P.R., 723-9621; **Food/Supplies:** La Mallorca Rest., La Mallorquina Rest., Siglo Veinte Rest, Pueblo Supermarket (all in old San Juna) within walking distance; **Parks, other points of interest:** San Jose church, San Juan Cathedral, La Fortaleza, Cristo Chapel.

Virgin Islands

Buck Island Reef National Monument
Saint Croix, Virgin Islands						**SEE CLIMATABLE NO. 190**

MAILING ADDRESS: Superintendent, Christiansted National Historic Site, P.O. Box 160, Christiansted, Saint Croix, Virgin Islands 00820 **Telephone:** 809-773-1460

DIRECTIONS: Access to the Monument is by NPS Concessioners or private boat. Concession boats are available at Christainsted Wharf. The Monument is a 5½ mile (8.9 km) sail from Christiansted.

Coral, grottoes, sea fans, gorgonias, and tropical fishes-along an underwater trail-make this one of the finest marine gardens in the Caribbean. The Island is a rookery for frigate birds and pelicans and the habitat of green turtles. Created by Presidential Proclamation on Dec. 28, 1961.

VISITOR ACTIVITIES: swimming, snorkeling, boat trips, hiking, bird-watching, picnicking; **Permits:** No; **Fees:** concession boat fees; **Visitor facilities:** picnic tables, charcoal grilles, changing house (no showers), a sheltered picnic pavilion, restrooms, nature trail; **Any limitations on vehicle usage:** Boats should be maneuvered slowly through park waters. Water skiing, speeding, and reckless boating are prohibited; **Hiking trails:** Yes, nature trail; **Backcountry:** No; **Camping:** No, but you may camp on your boat; **Other overnight accommodations on site:** No; **Meals served in the park:** No; **Food and supplies obtainable in the park:** No; **Food and supplies obtainable nearby:** No; **Overnight accommodations:** St. Croix; **First Aid available in park:** Yes; **Nearest Hospital:** 6½ miles (10.4 km) from downtown Christiansted; **Days/Hours:** 24 hrs.; **Holiday Closings:** None; **Visitor attractions closed for seasons:** No; **Weather:** Temperatures range from 75° in Winter to 90° in Summer.

GENERAL INFORMATION: *For Your Safety*—Avoid sunburn. Short periods in the sun and the use of protective waterproof lotions are recommended. Use Caution in the water. Cuts from coral can inflict painful wounds that may be slow to heal. The common spiny sea urchins are a particularly sharp hazard. Jellyfish, the Portuguese man-of-war, and fire corals can sting and burn, some severely. Treat all underwater creatures with respect. If you haven't snorkelled before, be sure to practice in shallow water before daring the reef. Make sure your face mask fits snugly.

Christiansted National Historic Site
Christiansted, Virgin Islands   **SEE CLIMATABLE NO. 190**

MAILING ADDRESS: Superintendent, Christiansted National Historic Site, P.O. Box 160, Christiansted, Virgin Islands 00820 **Telephone:** 809-773-1460

DIRECTIONS: National Park Service Headquarters is in The Old Customs House in downtown Christiansted. Begin your tour at the Fort.
  Christiansted is one of the most picturesque towns in the West Indies because of its harbor setting and the dignity and charm of its 18th and 19th century architecture which developed during the years it was the capital of the Danish West Indies. Christiansted National Historic Site allows you to step back two centuries as you visit the old Danish Fort, the Scale House, the Customs House, and the Steeple Building Museum. The Danish West Indies were purchased from Denmark in 1917. Designated on 4 March 1952.

VISITOR ACTIVITIES: self-guided walking tours, interpretive exhibits; **Permits:** No; **Fees:** Yes, $1.00 entrance fee for persons between 12-62, for Fort and Steeple Building Museum; **Visitor facilities:** restrooms, museum (open 8 a.m. to 5 p.m., Monday through Friday, and 9 a.m. to 5 p.m. on Saturday and Sunday); **Any limitations on vehicle usage:** No; **Hiking trails:** No; **Backcountry:** No; **Camping:** No; **Other overnight accommodations on site:** No; **Meals served in the park:** No; **Food and supplies obtainable in the park:** No; **Food and supplies obtainable nearby:** Yes, Christiansted; **Overnight accommodations:** Christiansted; **First Aid available in park:** Yes; **Nearest Hospital:** St. Croix, 6 miles (10 km) from the downtown area; **Days/Hours:** 8 a.m. to 5:00 p.m.; **Holiday Closings:** None; **Visitor attractions closed for seasons:** No; **Weather:** Average temperatures are 75° in Winter and 90° in Summer.

GENERAL INFORMATION: Beware of uneven walkways and stairs.

Virgin Islands National Park
St. John, Virgin Islands   **SEE CLIMATABLE NO. 191**

MAILING ADDRESS: Superintendent, Virgin Islands National Park, P.O. Box 7789, Charlotte Amalie, St. Thomas, Virgin Islands 00801 **Telephone:** Cruz Bay Visitor Center: 809-776-6201 or Headquarters: 809-775-6238

DIRECTIONS: Park headquarters and Visitor Center are in Red Hook at the National Park Service Dock on St. Thomas. A Visitor Center is at Cruz Bay on St. John. You can fly directly to Charlotte Amalie, St. Thomas, or via San Juan, or travel by ship. Taxis and buses run between Charlotte Amalie and Red Hook. A ferry operates hourly 7 a.m. to 11 p.m. across Pillsbury Sound from Red Hook to Cruz Bay. Water taxi service is available after hours. A special boat for guests at Caneel Bay Plantation runs between the Red Hook Visitor Station and Caneel Bay. Very popular with those who can stay only a day are the package vehicle tours and scenic boat charters that leave from St. Thomas with all transportation arranged. See a travel agent or make arrangements in advance. Taxi service is available on St. John.

The Park covers about two-thirds of St. John and includes quiet coves, blue-green waters, and white sandy beaches fringed by lush green hills. The remains of Danish colonial sugar plantations are found in the Park, several of which have been restored. Authorized for addition to the National Park System on Aug. 2, 1956.

VISITOR ACTIVITIES: interpretive talks and exhibits, hiking, camping, guided snorkel trips, cultural demonstrations, picnicking, swimming, snorkeling, fishing, auto tours; **Permits:** Persons returning to the US mainland from the Virgin Islands must go through Customs and Immigration at San Juan, Puerto Rico, St. Thomas or other US ports of entry. A special permit from the Department of Agriculture is required to exit with fruits, vegetables, plant cuttings, and seeds; **Fees:** No; **Visitor facilities:** Self-guiding walking and underwater trails, picnic areas, beaches, campgrounds, boat rentals, rental vehicles (make reservations in Cruz Bay well in advance); **Any limitations on vehicle usage:** Speed limit is 20 miles (32 km) per hour. Remember to drive on the left. Sound your horn at blind curves; **Hiking trails:** Yes, trails range from easy walks to difficult climbs. Bring tennis or hiking shoes and cool clothing. Small knapsacks and belt canteens are also handy. Water is not available along hikings trails; **Backcountry:** No; **Camping:** Yes; **Other overnight accommodations on site:** yes, cottage and tent site reservations must be made well in advance, but not more than eight months prior to the visit. Primitive, unequipped campsites can also be reserved. Contact the Concessioner, Cinnamon Bay Campground, P.O. Box 720, St. John, V.I. 00830, phone 809-776-6330, or see a travel agent; **Meals served in the park:** Yes, at Cruz Bay, Trunk Bay, Cinnamon Bay; **Food and supplies obtainable in the park:** Yes, at Cruz Bay; **Food and supplies obtainable nearby:** Yes, at St. Thomas; **Overnight accommodations:** St. Thomas, 4 miles (6.4 km) by water; **First Aid available in park:** Yes; **Nearest Hospital:** The clinic at Cruz Bay is open Monday-Friday from 7 a.m. to 11 p.m.; Saturday and Sunday, 8 a.m. to 11 p.m., telephone 809-776-6400. A nurse and doctor are on 24-hour call daily; you can reach them by phoning the Dept. of Public Safety, 809-776-6471; **Days/Hours:** The Park is open every day. Park Headquarters and Visitor Center in Red Hook open from 8:30 a.m. to 5 p.m.; Cruz Bay Visitor Center open from 8 a.m. to 4:30 p.m.; **Holiday Closings:** None; **Visitor attractions closed for seasons:** None; **Weather:** The yearly temperature averages 26°C (79°F) and varies little between Winter and Summer. Temperatures rarely exceed 37°C (98°F) or fall below 18°C (65°F). Rainfall averages approximately 100 cm (40 inches) per year, coming mostly in brief night showers.

GENERAL INFORMATION: *For Your Safety*—Insect repellent may be useful because of mosquitoes and sand flies. While snorkeling and swimming, use lifeguard-posted beaches and avoid touching or standing on corals which are fragile and can cause nasty cuts and scrapes. Protect yourself from sunburn. Avoid heavy surf and never go out alone. While hiking, avoid long and strenuous hikes in the heat of the day (10 a.m. to 3 p.m.). Bring drinking water. Avoid eating unidentified plants. Stay on the trails-do not shortcut. Do not climb around or over ruins. Wear sturdy hiking shoes or boots. Tell someone of your plans and *do not hike alone.*

Climatables

CLIMATABLE NO. 1

Horseshoe Bend NMP, Tuskegee Institute NHS

WEATHER PARAMETERS	J	F	M	A	M	J	J	A	S	O	N	D
TEMPERATURE												
Normal Daily Maximum	58	61	68	76	83	89	90	90	86	77	67	58
Normal Daily Minimum	37	38	44	52	59	66	68	68	64	53	42	38
Extreme High	81	85	89	94	98	107	108	106	108	99	90	84
Extreme Low	-2	-5	8	27	37	42	53	50	37	25	9	-1
Days Above 90°	0	0	0	0	0	6	19	19	10	1	0	0
Days Below 32°	15	11	5	0	0	0	0	0	0	1	6	12
PRECIPITATION												
Normal	4.5	5.0	6.0	4.8	3.8	3.7	5.1	4.0	4.0	2.5	3.3	5.0
Maximum	12.1	19.1	17.5	16.4	10.3	11.5	21.1	11.0	11.2	11.7	17.8	13.9
Maximum 24 Hour Precipitation	5.6	5.8	5.1	7.4	4.5	5.2	7.0	3.7	7.1	4.0	7.0	4.9
Maximum Snowfall	3	2	2	0	0	0	0	0	0	0	0	2
Days With Measurable Precip.	10	10	10	8	8	10	12	10	8	6	7	10
Average No. Thunderstorms	2	3	7	7	9	12	16	12	5	2	2	2
SUNSHINE/CLOUDINESS												
No. of Clear Days	8	8	8	10	9	8	6	8	10	14	11	9
No. Partly Cloudy Days	6	6	8	8	10	12	14	14	9	7	6	6
No. Cloudy Days	17	14	15	12	12	10	11	9	11	10	13	16
% Possible Sunshine	50	54	59	65	69	64	62	64	62	65	55	50

etc.

- From late June to middle of August, nearly all precipitation is from local afternoon thunderstorms.
- Some heavy rains from August through October are associated with tropical disturbances moving in from the Gulf of Mexico.
- Severe cold weather is rare; below-zero temperatures are unusual.

TEMPERATURE NORMALS AND EXTREMES

% OF SUNNY/PTLY CLOUDY/CLOUDY DAYS

☐ Clear   ▥ Ptlycldy   ■ Cloudy

CLIMATABLE NO. 2

Russell Cave, NM

TEMPERATURE NORMALS AND EXTREMES

WEATHER PARAMETERS	J	F	M	A	M	J	J	A	S	O	N	D
TEMPERATURE												
Normal Daily Maximum	49	53	61	73	80	87	89	89	84	73	61	52
Normal Daily Minimum	29	31	39	48	55	63	67	66	61	47	37	31
Extreme High	78	80	87	93	99	105	107	105	105	96	85	80
Extreme Low	-10	-8	8	24	32	39	49	48	29	20	4	-2
Days Above 90°	0	0	0	0	3	10	18	16	6	0	0	0
Days Below 32°	20	16	10	1	0	0	0	0	0	2	11	18
PRECIPITATION												
Normal	5.4	4.9	6.8	4.7	4.2	3.5	4.7	3.3	4.5	2.9	4.2	5.3
Maximum	12.3	11.0	16.5	11.9	9.2	9.4	11.8	9.0	14.2	9.9	13.6	13.7
Maximum 24 Hr. Precipitation	4.4	4.0	6.5	3.7	3.5	4.8	5.8	3.7	6.6	4.0	4.6	5.8
Maximum Snowfall	8	10	10	1	0	0	0	0	0	0	2	9
Days With Measurable Precip.	12	10	12	10	10	10	11	10	8	7	9	11
Average No.Thunderstorms	2	3	6	7	10	13	15	11	6	2	2	1
SUNSHINE/CLOUDINESS												
No. Clear Days	7	7	8	9	9	8	7	8	10	13	10	8
No. Partly Cloudy Days	7	6	8	8	10	12	13	13	10	8	7	6
No. Cloudy Days	17	15	15	13	12	10	11	10	10	10	13	17
% Possible Sunshine	43	49	52	61	65	65	61	62	64	62	52	44

% OF SUNNY/PTLY CLOUDY/CLOUDY DAYS

☐ Clear   ▦ Ptly Cloudy   ■ Cloudy

etc.

• Snow falls on the average of twice each winter.

• Zero-degree temperatures occur an average of once every 7 years, but temperatures as low as 10 degrees occur an average of twice each winter.

CLIMATABLE NO. 3

Katmai NP, Lake Clark NP, Alagnak Wild River

WEATHER PARAMETERS

WEATHER PARAMETERS	J	F	M	A	M	J	J	A	S	O	N	D
TEMPERATURE												
Normal Daily Maximum	24	26	31	41	55	63	67	64	57	41	32	22
Normal Daily Minimum	3	4	8	22	32	40	45	45	38	25	15	5
Extreme High	54	54	56	63	78	86	90	88	75	66	53	53
Extreme Low	−42	−50	−50	−11	13	24	25	22	11	−5	−20	−48
Days Above 70°	0	0	0	0	1	4	10	4	0	0	0	0
Days Below 32°	29	26	29	25	16	3	2	2	5	24	27	28
PRECIPITATION												
Normal	2.1	1.4	1.9	2.4	1.5	1.8	2.2	4.2	3.5	3.1	2.4	2.5
Maximum	3.0	3.0	2.4	3.0	3.0	3.9	4.9	11.2	6.6	6.4	3.4	3.6
Maximum 24 Hr. Precipitation	1.0	0.8	0.8	1.0	0.6	1.3	1.3	3.5	1.9	2.4	1.1	1.2
Maximum Snowfall	21	24	36	30	10	1	0	0	1	15	28	17
Days With Measurable Precip.	10	8	10	10	11	12	14	16	15	13	11	11
Average No. Thunderstorms	0	0	0	0	0	0	0	0	0	0	0	0
SUNSHINE/CLOUDINESS												
No. Clear Days	8	8	7	4	3	1	1	1	2	4	6	7
No. Partly Cloudy Days	5	6	6	6	5	5	5	6	6	7	5	6
No. Cloudy Days	18	15	18	20	22	24	25	22	20	19	18	18
% Possible Sunshine	NA	NA	NA	NA	NA	NA	NA	NA	NA	NA	NA	NA

etc.

- Wide variations in weather are experienced in the Parks due to differences in terrain and exposure to prevailing wind.
- Precipitation is highest on the windward or eastern slopes and sharply decreases on the leeward sides.
- In the area of the glaciers, total annual precipitation is 100 to 200".

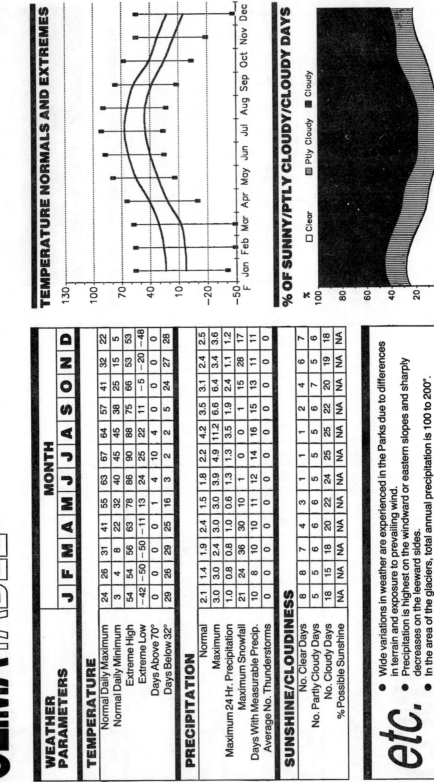

TEMPERATURE NORMALS AND EXTREMES

% OF SUNNY/PTLY CLOUDY/CLOUDY DAYS

☐ Clear   ▦ Ptly Cloudy   ■ Cloudy

CLIMATABLE NO. 4

Wrangell-St. Elias NP, Aniakchak NM, Kenai Fjords NP

WEATHER PARAMETERS	J	F	M	A	M	J	J	A	S	O	N	D
TEMPERATURE												
Normal Daily Maximum	29	31	35	42	49	57	61	60	54	44	35	30
Normal Daily Minimum	14	19	21	28	34	42	46	45	41	33	24	17
Extreme High	58	55	59	67	82	84	86	86	72	64	58	54
Extreme Low	-30	-21	-24	-9	6	29	32	30	20	-1	-8	-23
Days Above 70°	0	0	0	0	0	1	1	1	0	0	0	0
Days Below 32°	28	24	28	22	10	1	0	0	3	16	23	27
PRECIPITATION												
Normal	6.1	6.8	5.4	5.7	5.8	4.7	6.2	6.8	13.1	14.5	10.4	9.5
Maximum	15.8	19.0	12.4	12.2	13.6	13.2	17.8	18.3	27.7	26.6	30.6	19.8
Maximum 24 Hr. Precipitation	3.2	4.1	2.4	4.4	3.6	3.0	4.6	4.4	4.7	5.0	4.6	4.5
Maximum Snowfall	46	80	89	61	16	0	0	0	T	15	48	71
Days With Measurable Precip.	17	16	16	15	16	15	15	14	15	16	17	17
Average No. Thunderstorms	0	0	0	0	0	0	0	0	0	0	0	0
SUNSHINE/CLOUDINESS												
No. Clear Days	5	6	7	5	5	3	3	4	5	7	6	6
No. Partly Cloudy Days	4	4	5	5	6	6	6	6	6	5	5	4
No. Cloudy Days	22	18	19	20	22	21	22	21	19	19	19	21
% Possible Sunshine	NA	NA	NA	NA	NA	NA	NA	NA	NA	NA	NA	NA

TEMPERATURE NORMALS AND EXTREMES

% OF SUNNY/PTLY CLOUDY/CLOUDY DAYS

□ Clear   ▥ Ptly Cloudy   ▨ Cloudy

etc.
- As evidenced by the glaciers, precipitation is greater at higher elevations.
- Record annual precipitation for Alaska of 332.29" was recorded on Montague Island in 1976.
- At Thompson Pass just north of Valdez, a seasonal snowfall of 974.5" was recorded in 1952-53.

CLIMATABLE NO.5

**Bering Land Bridge NP, Kobuk Valley NP, Noatak NP
Gates of the Arctic NP, Cape Krusenstern NM**

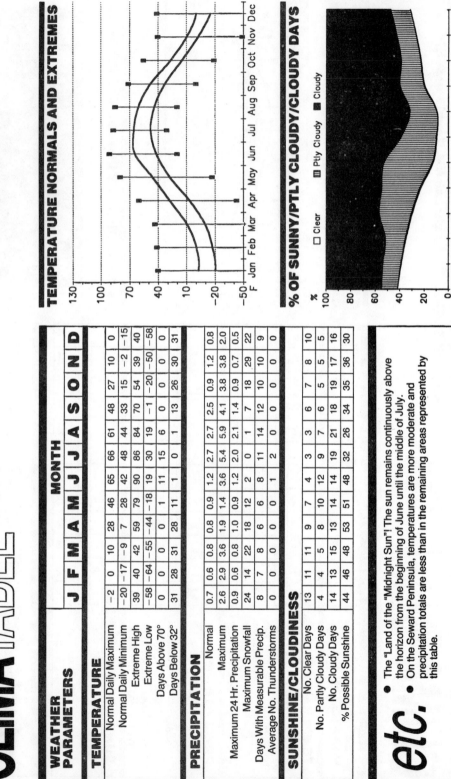

TEMPERATURE NORMALS AND EXTREMES

% OF SUNNY/PTLY CLOUDY/CLOUDY DAYS

☐ Clear   ▦ Ptly Cloudy   ■ Cloudy

WEATHER PARAMETERS	MONTH											
	J	F	M	A	M	J	J	A	S	O	N	D
TEMPERATURE												
Normal Daily Maximum	-2	0	10	28	46	65	66	61	48	27	10	0
Normal Daily Minimum	-20	-17	-9	7	28	42	48	44	33	15	-2	-15
Extreme High	39	40	42	59	79	90	86	84	70	54	39	40
Extreme Low	-58	-64	-55	-44	-18	19	30	19	-1	-20	-50	-58
Days Above 70°	0	0	0	0	1	11	15	6	0	0	0	0
Days Below 32°	31	28	31	28	11	1	0	1	13	26	30	31
PRECIPITATION												
Normal	0.7	0.6	0.8	0.8	0.9	1.2	2.7	2.7	2.5	0.9	1.2	0.8
Maximum	2.6	2.9	3.6	1.9	1.4	3.6	5.4	5.9	4.1	3.8	3.8	2.0
Maximum 24 Hr. Precipitation	0.9	0.6	0.8	1.0	0.9	1.2	2.0	2.1	1.4	0.9	0.7	0.5
Maximum Snowfall	24	14	22	18	12	2	0	1	7	18	29	22
Days With Measurable Precip.	8	7	8	6	6	8	11	14	12	10	10	9
Average No. Thunderstorms	0	0	0	0	0	1	2	0	0	0	0	0
SUNSHINE/CLOUDINESS												
No. Clear Days	13	11	11	9	7	4	3	3	6	7	8	10
No. Partly Cloudy Days	4	4	5	8	10	12	9	7	6	5	5	5
No. Cloudy Days	14	13	15	13	14	14	19	21	18	19	17	16
% Possible Sunshine	44	46	48	53	51	48	32	26	34	35	36	30

etc.

- The "Land of the "Midnight Sun"! The sun remains continuously above the horizon from the beginning of June until the middle of July.
- On the Seward Peninsula, temperatures are more moderate and precipitation totals are less than in the remaining areas represented by this table.

CLIMATABLE NO. 6

Denali NP, Yukon-Charley NP

TEMPERATURE NORMALS AND EXTREMES

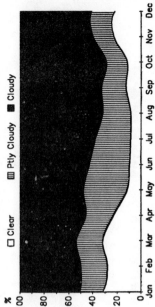

WEATHER PARAMETERS — MONTH

TEMPERATURE

	J	F	M	A	M	J	J	A	S	O	N	D
Normal Daily Maximum	-2	8	20	37	55	68	70	63	51	30	11	0
Normal Daily Minimum	-20	-12	-6	14	30	42	46	41	32	15	-5	-15
Extreme High	51	51	53	65	90	93	94	86	78	63	52	45
Extreme Low	-60	-50	-47	-32	-8	2	23	19	3	-27	-51	-60
Days Above 70°	0	0	0	0	2	14	15	8	1	0	0	0
Days Below 32°	31	28	31	29	20	2	1	5	16	30	30	31

PRECIPITATION

	J	F	M	A	M	J	J	A	S	O	N	D
Normal	0.6	0.5	0.5	0.4	0.8	2.0	2.2	2.0	1.3	0.9	0.6	0.5
Maximum	1.9	2.2	3.1	1.8	3.8	5.8	7.7	6.8	4.4	2.0	5.3	3.0
Maximum 24 Hr. Precipitation	1.0	1.2	1.9	1.6	2.7	2.1	3.3	2.6	1.8	0.9	1.6	1.3
Maximum Snowfall	30	40	41	21	14	3	0	4	16	35	69	36
Days With Measurable Precip.	6	5	5	5	7	10	13	13	10	9	7	7
Average No. Thunderstorms	0	0	0	0	0	2	2	1	0	0	0	0

SUNSHINE/CLOUDINESS

	J	F	M	A	M	J	J	A	S	O	N	D
No. Clear Days	10	8	10	7	4	3	3	3	4	4	7	7
No. Partly Cloudy Days	6	6	7	7	11	10	9	7	6	5	5	6
No. Cloudy Days	15	14	14	16	16	17	19	21	20	22	18	18
% Possible Sunshine	34	50	61	58	55	53	45	35	31	28	28	29

% OF SUNNY/PTLY CLOUDY/CLOUDY DAYS

☐ Clear   ▤ Ptly Cloudy   ■ Cloudy

etc.

- In June, length of day ranges from 19 to 23 hours; in December, duration of daylight is 3 to 5 hours.
- Yukon-Charley NP has colder winters and warmer summers than Denali NP, but weather is more variable in Denali NP.
- Alaska's record high temperature of 100 degrees was recorded at Fort Yukon in June, 1915.

CLIMATABLE NO. 7

Sitka NHP, Glacier Bay NP, Klondike Gold Rush NHP

WEATHER PARAMETERS	J	F	M	A	M	J	J	A	S	O	N	D
TEMPERATURE												
Normal Daily Maximum	32	38	41	48	55	62	63	62	57	48	41	35
Normal Daily Minimum	23	28	29	34	39	44	48	48	44	38	32	27
Extreme High	60	63	65	76	85	85	88	86	82	70	65	64
Extreme Low	-8	-4	-5	6	26	30	34	30	28	16	-1	-6
Days Above 70°	0	0	0	0	1	2	2	2	1	0	0	0
Days Below 32°	26	21	22	13	2	0	0	0	0	5	15	22
PRECIPITATION												
Normal	5.1	5.8	5.0	4.4	4.4	2.9	4.9	7.7	11.7	12.8	9.4	7.2
Maximum	17.7	18.8	13.6	13.4	10.4	9.8	12.0	21.0	25.5	26.6	25.8	18.2
Maximum 24 Hr. Precipitation	3.8	2.7	3.2	2.2	3.1	2.0	2.1	4.2	6.4	4.9	4.3	3.2
Maximum Snowfall	44	24	32	12	1	0	0	T	19	26	40	
Days With Measurable Precip.	17	18	17	17	16	13	17	18	22	25	23	21
Average No. Thunderstorms	0	0	0	0	0	0	0	0	0	0	0	0
SUNSHINE/CLOUDINESS												
No. Clear Days	6	4	4	3	3	3	3	4	3	2	4	3
No. Partly Cloudy Days	3	3	4	4	4	4	5	4	3	2	2	2
No. Cloudy Days	22	21	24	23	23	23	23	23	24	27	24	26
% Possible Sunshine	32	32	37	39	39	34	31	32	26	19	23	20

TEMPERATURE NORMALS AND EXTREMES

130 · 100 · 70 · 40 · 10 · -20 · -50

F Jan Feb Mar Apr May Jun Jul Aug Sep Oct Nov Dec

% OF SUNNY/PTLY CLOUDY/CLOUDY DAYS

□ Clear   ▨ Ptly Cloudy   ▦ Cloudy

% 100 · 80 · 60 · 40 · 20 · 0

etc.

- Climate moderated by warm Alaska current flowing northward along the coast.
- In higher elevation areas, temperatures are lower and precipitation is greater than shown in the table.
- Wind speeds greater than 50 mph are often experienced in winter; watch the wind chill temperature!

CLIMATABLE NO. 8

Hubbell Trading Post NHS, Canyon de Chelly NM, Navajo NM

TEMPERATURE NORMALS AND EXTREMES

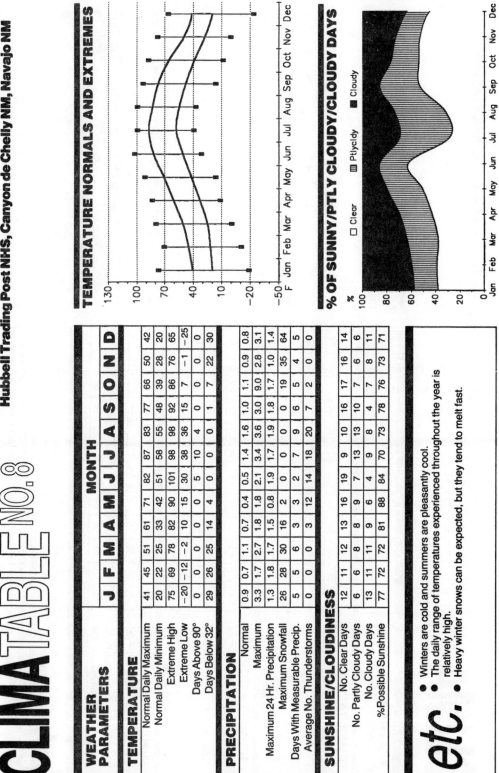

WEATHER PARAMETERS	J	F	M	A	M	J	J	A	S	O	N	D
TEMPERATURE												
Normal Daily Maximum	41	45	51	61	71	82	87	83	77	66	50	42
Normal Daily Minimum	20	22	25	33	42	51	58	55	48	39	28	20
Extreme High	75	69	78	82	90	101	98	98	92	86	76	65
Extreme Low	−20	−12	−2	10	15	30	38	36	15	7	−1	−25
Days Above 90°	0	0	0	0	0	5	10	4	0	0	0	0
Days Below 32°	29	26	25	14	4	0	0	0	1	7	22	30
PRECIPITATION												
Normal	0.9	0.7	1.1	0.7	0.4	0.5	1.4	1.6	1.0	1.1	0.9	0.8
Maximum	3.3	1.7	2.7	1.8	1.8	2.1	3.4	3.6	3.0	9.0	2.8	3.1
Maximum 24 Hr. Precipitation	1.3	1.8	1.7	1.5	0.8	1.9	1.7	1.9	1.8	1.7	1.0	1.4
Maximum Snowfall	26	28	30	16	2	0	0	0	0	19	35	64
Days With Measurable Precip.	5	5	6	3	3	2	7	9	6	5	4	5
Average No. Thunderstorms	0	0	0	3	12	14	18	20	7	2	0	0
SUNSHINE/CLOUDINESS												
No. Clear Days	12	11	12	13	16	19	9	10	16	17	16	14
No. Partly Cloudy Days	6	6	8	8	9	7	13	13	10	7	6	6
No. Cloudy Days	13	11	11	9	6	4	9	8	4	7	8	11
%Possible Sunshine	77	72	72	81	88	84	70	73	78	76	73	71

% OF SUNNY/PTLY CLOUDY/CLOUDY DAYS

☐ Clear   ▦ Ptlycldy   ▨ Cloudy

etc. :
- Winters are cold and summers are pleasantly cool.
- The daily range of temperatures experienced throughout the year is relatively high.
- Heavy winter snows can be expected, but they tend to melt fast.

CLIMATABLE NO. 9

Casa Grande Ruins NM, Hohokam Pima NM, Tonto NM

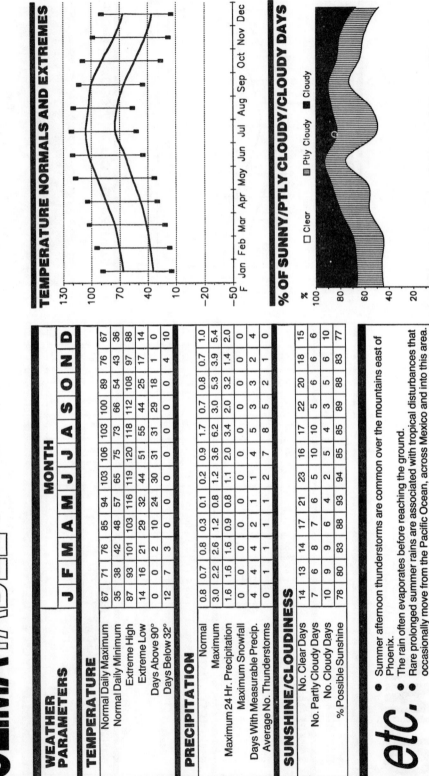

TEMPERATURE NORMALS AND EXTREMES

% OF SUNNY/PTLY CLOUDY/CLOUDY DAYS

☐ Clear   ⬛ Ptly Cloudy   ■ Cloudy

WEATHER PARAMETERS	J	F	M	A	M	J	J	A	S	O	N	D
TEMPERATURE												
Normal Daily Maximum	67	71	76	85	94	103	106	103	100	89	76	67
Normal Daily Minimum	35	38	42	48	57	65	75	73	66	54	43	36
Extreme High	87	93	101	103	116	119	120	118	112	108	97	88
Extreme Low	14	16	21	29	32	44	51	55	44	25	17	14
Days Above 90°	0	0	2	10	24	30	31	31	29	18	1	0
Days Below 32°	12	7	3	0	0	0	0	0	0	0	4	10
PRECIPITATION												
Normal	0.8	0.7	0.8	0.3	0.1	0.2	0.9	1.7	0.7	0.8	0.7	1.0
Maximum	3.0	2.2	2.6	1.2	0.8	1.2	3.6	6.2	3.0	5.3	3.9	5.4
Maximum 24 Hr. Precipitation	1.6	1.6	1.6	0.9	0.8	1.1	2.0	3.4	2.0	3.2	1.4	2.0
Maximum Snowfall	0	0	0	0	0	0	0	0	0	0	0	0
Days With Measurable Precip.	4	4	4	2	1	1	4	5	3	3	2	4
Average No. Thunderstorms	0	1	1	1	1	2	7	8	5	2	1	0
SUNSHINE/CLOUDINESS												
No. Clear Days	14	13	14	17	21	23	16	17	22	20	18	15
No. Partly Cloudy Days	7	6	8	7	6	5	10	10	5	6	6	6
No. Cloudy Days	10	9	9	6	4	2	5	4	3	5	6	10
% Possible Sunshine	78	80	83	88	93	94	85	85	89	88	83	77

etc.

- Summer afternoon thunderstorms are common over the mountains east of Phoenix.
- The rain often evaporates before reaching the ground.
- Rare prolonged summer rains are associated with tropical disturbances that occasionally move from the Pacific Ocean, across Mexico and into this area.

CLIMATABLE NO. 10

Fort Bowie NHS, Chiricahua NM, Coronado NM

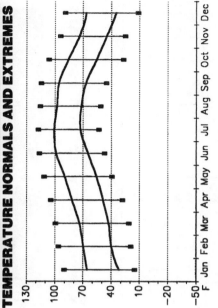

TEMPERATURE NORMALS AND EXTREMES

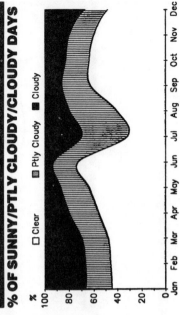

% OF SUNNY/PTLY CLOUDY/CLOUDY DAYS

☐ Clear   ▥ Ptly Cloudy   ■ Cloudy

WEATHER PARAMETERS	J	F	M	A	M	J	J	A	S	O	N	D
TEMPERATURE												
Normal Daily Maximum	66	70	74	82	90	99	101	98	96	86	74	67
Normal Daily Minimum	32	40	43	49	56	65	73	72	67	56	45	35
Extreme High	89	95	98	103	110	115	116	114	113	105	93	88
Extreme Low	14	18	20	27	38	46	52	50	44	26	24	10
Days Above 90°	0	0	0	0	6	18	27	30	25	12	1	0
Days Below 32°	7	4	1	0	0	0	0	0	0	0	1	6
PRECIPITATION												
Normal	0.8	0.6	0.7	0.2	0.1	0.1	1.9	1.9	1.2	0.8	0.6	1.0
Maximum	2.9	2.5	2.3	1.7	0.7	1.5	6.2	7.9	5.1	5.0	1.9	5.0
Maximum 24 Hr. Precipitation	1.2	1.3	1.1	0.7	1.1	1.2	2.5	3.0	3.0	2.5	1.7	1.6
Maximum Snowfall	4	4	6	2	0	0	T	T	0		6	7
Days With Measurable Precip.	4	4	4	2	1	2	11	9	5	3	3	4
Average No. Thunderstorms	0	0	0	1	1	3	20	17	7	2	0	0
SUNSHINE/CLOUDINESS												
No. Clear Days	14	13	15	17	20	22	10	13	19	20	18	15
No. Partly Cloudy Days	7	6	7	7	7	6	12	12	7	6	6	6
No. Cloudy Days	10	9	9	6	4	2	9	6	4	5	6	10
% Possible Sunshine	83	86	88	92	94	96	84	86	90	88	86	81

etc.

- The period from April through June is very dry...a period of drought.
- Flash floods from summer thunderstorms do, on occasion, cause considerable local damage.
- Mean annual lake evaporation is about 80".
- This area borders on the sunniest region of the United States.

CLIMATABLE NO. 11

Glen Canyon NRA, Grand Canyon NP

TEMPERATURE NORMALS AND EXTREMES

% OF SUNNY/PTLY CLOUDY/CLOUDY DAYS

□ Clear   ▦ Ptlycldy   ■ Cloudy

WEATHER PARAMETERS	MONTH											
	J	F	M	A	M	J	J	A	S	O	N	D
TEMPERATURE												
Normal Daily Maximum	42	48	59	69	79	88	94	91	85	68	54	44
Normal Daily Minimum	21	26	31	37	49	58	65	63	57	42	31	23
Extreme High	72	75	84	90	98	109	107	106	104	94	80	73
Extreme Low	-16	-14	-3	9	13	28	31	30	25	3	-1	-13
Days Above 90°	0	0	0	0	4	17	28	24	9	0	0	0
Days Below 32°	26	18	13	4	1	0	0	0	0	1	11	26
PRECIPITATION												
Normal	1.2	1.1	1.3	0.9	0.5	0.5	1.4	2.1	1.0	0.9	0.8	1.4
Maximum	NA	NA	NA	NA	NA	NA	NA	NA	NA	NA	NA	NA
Maximum 24 Hr. Precipitation	1.7	1.8	4.0	1.1	1.2	2.2	2.6	2.2	2.7	1.8	1.3	2.2
Maximum Snowfall	60	33	44	46	19	0	0	0	0	12	22	32
Days With Measurable Precip.	6	6	7	5	4	4	7	9	5	5	5	6
Average No. Thunderstorms	0	0	0	1	4	5	13	14	7	2	0	0
SUNSHINE/CLOUDINESS												
No. Clear Days	12	11	12	13	16	19	9	10	16	17	16	14
No. Partly Cloudy Days	6	6	8	8	9	7	13	13	10	7	6	6
No. Cloudy Days	13	11	11	9	6	4	9	8	4	7	8	11
% Possible Sunshine	77	72	72	81	88	84	70	73	78	76	73	71

etc.

- There is a strong temperature contrast between the floor and the rim of the Grand Canyon. The summer climate of the Canyon floor is torrid! Temperatures can become dangerously high. The Canyon floor is considerably drier than the rim.
- The Glen Canyon area is even drier than the Grand Canyon.

CLIMATABLE NO. 12

Tuzigoot NM, Montezuma Castle NM

TEMPERATURE NORMALS AND EXTREMES

% OF SUNNY/PTLY CLOUDY/CLOUDY DAYS

☐ Clear   ▨ Ptly Cloudy   ■ Cloudy

WEATHER PARAMETERS	J	F	M	A	M	J	J	A	S	O	N	D
TEMPERATURE												
Normal Daily Maximum	58	64	69	78	84	96	100	97	93	83	70	60
Normal Daily Minimum	27	30	34	41	47	56	64	63	56	45	33	28
Extreme High	82	87	94	99	107	117	114	111	111	100	89	78
Extreme Low	−1	7	12	16	24	36	45	39	35	20	8	7
Days Above 90°	0	0	0	3	13	25	30	28	22	8	0	0
Days Below 32°	23	16	13	4	0	0	0	0	0	2	10	24
PRECIPITATION												
Normal	0.9	0.9	1.4	0.6	0.4	0.4	1.7	2.2	1.1	0.8	0.7	1.1
Maximum	7.6	6.6	5.3	4.0	1.3	2.5	7.5	10.5	5.2	7.8	6.0	7.0
Maximum 24 Hr. Precipitation	1.5	1.9	1.6	1.7	1.8	3.0	2.2	3.0	3.3	2.3	1.1	2.0
Maximum Snowfall	17	4	4	6	0	0	0	0	0	0	11	46
Days With Measurable Precip.	6	6	7	5	3	2	11	10	6	4	4	5
Average No. Thunderstorms	0	0	1	1	4	5	21	21	11	4	1	0
SUNSHINE/CLOUDINESS												
No. Clear Days	12	11	12	13	16	19	10	16	17	16	14	14
No. Partly Cloudy Days	6	6	8	8	9	7	13	10	7	7	6	6
No. Cloudy Days	13	11	11	9	6	4	9	8	4	7	8	11
% Possible Sunshine	77	72	72	81	88	84	70	73	78	76	73	71

etc. :

- Low relative humidity minimizes the discomfort felt from excessively high daytime temperatures in summer.
- Summer thunderstorms rarely last more than 30 minutes.
- From the spring to the early fall, day/night temperature variations of 40 degrees or more are common.

CLIMATABLE NO. 13

Tumacacori NM, Saguaro NM, Organ Pipe Cactus NM

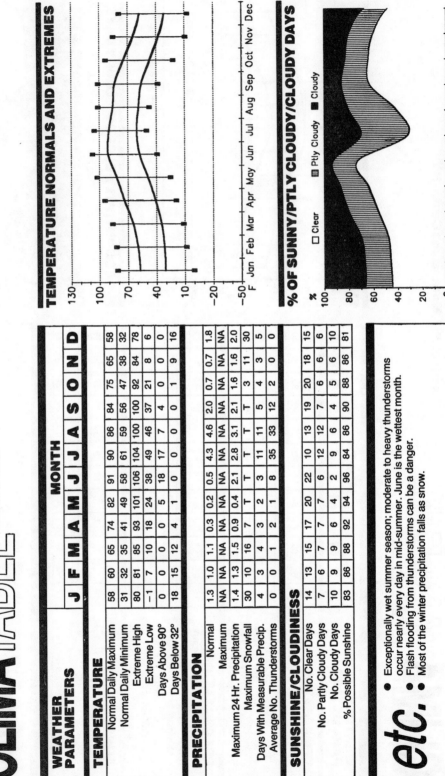

TEMPERATURE NORMALS AND EXTREMES

% OF SUNNY/PTLY CLOUDY/CLOUDY DAYS

☐ Clear   ▨ Ptly Cloudy   ■ Cloudy

WEATHER PARAMETERS	MONTH											
	J	F	M	A	M	J	J	A	S	O	N	D
TEMPERATURE												
Normal Daily Maximum	58	60	65	74	82	91	90	86	84	75	65	58
Normal Daily Minimum	31	32	35	41	49	58	61	59	56	47	38	32
Extreme High	80	81	85	93	101	106	104	100	100	92	84	78
Extreme Low	-1	7	10	18	24	38	49	46	37	21	8	6
Days Above 90°	0	0	0	0	5	18	17	7	4	0	0	0
Days Below 32°	18	15	12	4	1	0	0	0	0	1	9	16
PRECIPITATION												
Normal	1.3	1.0	1.1	0.3	0.2	0.5	4.3	4.6	2.0	0.7	0.7	1.8
Maximum	NA	NA	NA	NA	NA	NA	NA	NA	NA	NA	NA	NA
Maximum 24 Hr. Precipitation	1.4	1.3	1.5	0.9	0.4	2.1	2.8	3.1	2.1	1.6	1.6	2.0
Maximum Snowfall	30	10	16	7	T	T	T	T	3	11	11	30
Days With Measurable Precip.	4	3	4	3	2	3	11	11	5	4	3	5
Average No. Thunderstorms	0	0	1	2	1	8	35	33	12	2	0	0
SUNSHINE/CLOUDINESS												
No. Clear Days	14	13	15	17	20	22	10	13	19	20	18	15
No. Partly Cloudy Days	7	6	7	7	7	6	12	12	7	6	6	6
No. Cloudy Days	10	9	9	6	4	2	9	6	4	5	6	10
% Possible Sunshine	83	86	88	92	94	96	84	86	90	88	86	81

etc.
- Exceptionally wet summer season; moderate to heavy thunderstorms occur nearly every day in mid-summer. June is the wettest month.
- Flash flooding from thunderstorms can be a danger.
- Most of the winter precipitation falls as snow.

CLIMATABLE No. 14

Petrified Forest NP, Walnut Canyon NM, Sunset Crater NM, Wupatki NM

TEMPERATURE NORMALS AND EXTREMES

% OF SUNNY/PTLY CLOUDY/CLOUDY DAYS

□ Clear   ▦ Ptly Cloudy   ■ Cloudy

WEATHER PARAMETERS	J	F	M	A	M	J	J	A	S	O	N	D
TEMPERATURE												
Normal Daily Maximum	47	54	60	70	78	88	94	91	86	73	58	48
Normal Daily Minimum	21	24	28	34	44	52	61	59	52	40	29	21
Extreme High	76	81	85	92	100	107	108	109	106	93	81	75
Extreme Low	-27	-19	-2	-1	13	23	34	31	15	2	-10	-18
Days Above 90°	0	0	0	0	2	18	26	18	8	0	0	0
Days Below 32°	28	24	23	11	2	0	0	0	0	4	21	28
PRECIPITATION												
Normal	0.4	0.4	0.5	0.3	0.4	0.4	1.2	1.7	0.9	1.0	0.5	0.5
Maximum	1.7	2.7	2.9	1.8	1.9	3.0	4.7	4.7	3.2	7.8	2.3	2.6
Maximum 24 Hr. Precipitation	0.6	1.0	1.3	1.0	1.4	2.0	2.5	1.8	2.4	2.0	0.7	0.9
Maximum Snowfall	10	16	40	7	0	0	0	0	0	11	18	32
Days With Measurable Precip.	4	4	5	3	3	2	7	9	5	4	3	4
Average No. Thunderstorms	0	0	0	1	3	5	15	16	8	2	0	0
SUNSHINE/CLOUDINESS												
No. Clear Days	12	11	13	15	17	20	11	12	18	16	16	14
No. Partly Cloudy Days	7	7	9	9	9	7	12	13	8	7	6	7
No. Cloudy Days	12	10	9	6	5	3	8	6	4	6	8	10
% Possible Sunshine	77	72	72	81	88	84	70	73	78	76	73	71

etc.

- Summers are very pleasant! The higher elevation areas have even cooler summer temperatures.
- Thunderstorms tend to be gentle and of short duration; there is very little destructive weather of any kind.
- Some areas in this region experience very heavy winter snowfalls that can exceed 200".

CLIMATABLE NO. 15

Pipe Spring NM

TEMPERATURE NORMALS AND EXTREMES

% OF SUNNY/PTLY CLOUDY/CLOUDY DAYS

☐ Clear   ▦ Ptlycldy   ■ Cloudy

WEATHER PARAMETERS	J	F	M	A	M	J	J	A	S	O	N	D
TEMPERATURE												
Normal Daily Maximum	53	56	61	68	81	89	96	94	87	76	62	52
Normal Daily Minimum	28	30	36	40	52	60	69	69	60	48	37	28
Extreme High	79	76	82	89	97	118	108	105	100	96	82	69
Extreme Low	–9	8	4	17	20	34	41	38	29	10	9	–7
Days Above 90°	0	0	0	0	4	13	28	27	9	1	0	0
Days Below 32°	25	21	15	11	3	0	0	0	0	3	12	25
PRECIPITATION												
Normal	0.6	0.9	0.9	0.9	0.5	0.4	0.9	1.6	0.7	0.4	1.1	1.0
Maximum	3.3	3.1	4.2	4.0	0.9	1.5	2.4	4.0	3.0	2.6	3.1	3.6
Maximum 24 Hr. Precipitation	1.1	1.0	0.7	0.8	1.5	1.4	0.9	1.4	1.1	0.9	1.8	1.0
Maximum Snowfall	6	8	10	7	0	0	0	0	0	0	8	10
Days With Measurable Precip.	2	3	4	3	2	2	3	4	3	2	4	4
Average No. Thunderstorms	0	0	0	1	3	4	12	16	7	2	0	0
SUNSHINE/CLOUDINESS												
No. Clear Days	14	12	14	16	18	22	18	15	23	21	16	14
No. Partly Cloudy Days	6	7	9	8	8	5	10	13	5	6	7	7
No. Cloudy Days	11	9	8	6	5	3	3	3	2	4	7	10
% Possible Sunshine	77	81	83	87	88	93	78	85	91	87	80	77

etc.

- Discomfort from extremely hot summer days is mitigated by the low humidity . . . see Heat Index Chart. Summer nights are pleasantly cool.
- Winters are quite chilly; occasional incursions of cold air masses from Canada result in bitterly cold temperatures . . . watch the Wind Chill temperatures.

CLIMATABLE NO. 16

Arkansas Post NM

TEMPERATURE NORMALS AND EXTREMES

% OF SUNNY/PTLY CLOUDY/CLOUDY DAYS

WEATHER PARAMETERS	J	F	M	A	M	J	J	A	S	O	N	D
TEMPERATURE												
Normal Daily Maximum	52	58	66	76	84	91	94	93	87	77	65	56
Normal Daily Minimum	33	36	43	52	60	68	71	69	63	51	42	35
Extreme High	83	84	93	92	101	105	110	110	106	96	90	82
Extreme Low	−5	0	16	29	40	48	54	53	36	26	14	−2
Days Above 90°	0	0	0	0	6	19	25	23	12	2	0	0
Days Below 32°	17	11	5	0	0	0	0	0	0	0	6	13
PRECIPITATION												
Normal	4.6	4.3	5.6	5.3	5.2	3.2	4.6	3.1	3.7	2.8	4.3	4.3
Maximum	10.2	12.0	14.8	12.8	14.5	8.4	10.9	8.1	11.0	8.4	10.7	11.0
Maximum 24 Hr. Precipitation	4.8	4.6	4.0	5.2	4.9	4.3	6.4	7.8	5.4	3.9	4.8	3.4
Maximum Snowfall	14	8	12	0	0	0	0	0	0	0	1	11
Days With Measurable Precip.	9	9	11	10	9	8	9	7	8	7	9	9
Average No. Thunderstorms	3	4	8	8	9	10	12	8	6	3	4	3
SUNSHINE/CLOUDINESS												
No. Clear Days	8	8	8	9	8	10	10	12	12	14	10	9
No. Partly Cloudy Days	6	6	7	7	10	11	12	11	8	7	6	6
No. Cloudy Days	17	14	16	14	13	9	9	8	10	10	14	16
% Possible Sunshine	50	54	56	64	69	74	74	75	69	70	58	50

etc. : The late summer and early fall tend to be dry and sunny. Summer precipitation is predominantly in the form of showers. The chance of a tornado occurring in this area is greatest from March through May, though the chance of a tornado impacting any specific location is never large.

CLIMATABLE NO. 17

Pea Ridge NMP, Buffalo National River

WEATHER PARAMETERS	J	F	M	A	M	J	J	A	S	O	N	D
TEMPERATURE												
Normal Daily Maximum	45	50	58	70	77	85	90	90	82	72	58	49
Normal Daily Minimum	23	27	35	46	54	62	66	64	57	46	35	28
Extreme High	76	83	89	90	93	103	114	107	104	96	82	78
Extreme Low	-15	-15	2	16	27	41	45	44	31	17	4	-14
Days Above 90°	0	0	0	0	1	6	17	16	6	1	0	0
Days Below 32°	25	20	14	4	0	0	0	0	0	3	13	23
PRECIPITATION												
Normal	1.9	2.6	3.6	4.3	5.6	5.2	3.6	3.2	4.1	3.5	3.3	2.5
Maximum	4.7	8.5	10.4	11.5	19.4	10.6	12.0	9.4	11.2	9.6	9.6	6.9
Maximum 24 Hr. Precipitation	3.9	3.6	3.8	4.8	5.8	4.7	5.9	3.8	3.6	3.7	4.8	3.1
Maximum Snowfall	18	15	16	2	0	0	0	0	0	0	8	9
Days With Measurable Precip.	8	8	9	10	10	8	8	7	8	7	7	7
Average No. Thunderstorms	2	2	5	9	10	10	8	8	6	3	3	2
SUNSHINE/CLOUDINESS												
No. Clear Days	9	9	9	9	8	10	12	12	13	11	9	10
No. Partly Cloudy Days	6	6	7	7	10	10	11	11	7	6	7	7
No. Cloudy Days	16	13	15	14	13	10	8	8	10	11	13	14
% Possible Sunshine	51	55	57	59	62	69	73	72	66	64	55	51

MONTH

TEMPERATURE NORMALS AND EXTREMES

130
100
70
40
10
-20
-50
F

Jan Feb Mar Apr May Jun Jul Aug Sep Oct Nov Dec

% OF SUNNY/PTLY CLOUDY/CLOUDY DAYS

☐ Clear   ▦ Ptlycldy   ■ Cloudy

%
100
80
60
40
20
0

Jan Feb Mar Apr May Jun Jul Aug Sep Oct Nov Dec

etc.

- The wettest time of the year is late spring and early summer. Heavy local thunderstorms are common in the spring.
- Summer night temperatures are quite pleasant.
- The late fall is usually a time of sunny, pleasant weather.
- Sleet and ice storms provide the worst winter weather.

CLIMATABLE NO. 18   Fort Smith NHS

TEMPERATURE NORMALS AND EXTREMES

% OF SUNNY/PTLY CLOUDY/CLOUDY DAYS

Legend: ☐ Clear   ▦ Ptlcldy   ■ Cloudy

WEATHER PARAMETERS	J	F	M	A	M	J	J	A	S	O	N	D
TEMPERATURE												
Normal Daily Maximum	49	54	62	74	81	88	94	93	86	76	62	52
Normal Daily Minimum	27	31	38	49	58	66	70	69	62	49	38	30
Extreme High	81	86	94	93	98	105	111	110	106	96	86	82
Extreme Low	-10	-9	7	22	35	47	50	51	33	22	8	-1
Days Above 90°	0	0	0	0	1	12	23	21	10	2	0	0
Days Below 32°	24	18	8	1	0	0	0	0	0	1	9	20
PRECIPITATION												
Normal	1.9	2.5	3.9	4.2	4.8	3.7	3.2	3.0	3.2	3.2	3.5	2.9
Maximum	11.3	7.9	8.5	10.3	12.1	10.4	10.4	6.6	9.0	12.0	14.0	10.1
Maximum 24 Hr. Precipitation	5.4	4.4	3.6	5.1	5.6	3.5	7.1	5.1	4.0	5.9	6.9	5.8
Maximum Snowfall	13	12	5	T	0	0	0	0	0	0	5	7
Days With Measurable Precip.	8	8	9	10	10	8	8	7	8	7	7	7
Average No. Thunderstorms	1	3	6	8	11	11	10	8	6	4	3	2
SUNSHINE/CLOUDINESS												
No. Clear Days	9	9	9	9	8	10	12	12	12	13	11	10
No. Partly Cloudy Days	6	6	7	7	10	10	11	11	8	7	6	7
No. Cloudy Days	16	13	15	14	13	10	8	8	10	11	13	14
% Possible Sunshine	51	55	57	59	62	69	73	72	66	64	55	51

etc.

- The humidity can be uncomfortably high in the summer . . . see Heat Index chart.
- Springtime tends to be wet.
- Winters tend to be relatively dry, though the seasonal snowfall total does vary widely from year to year. Ice storms can be more frequent than snow.

CLIMATABLE NO. 19   Hot Springs NP

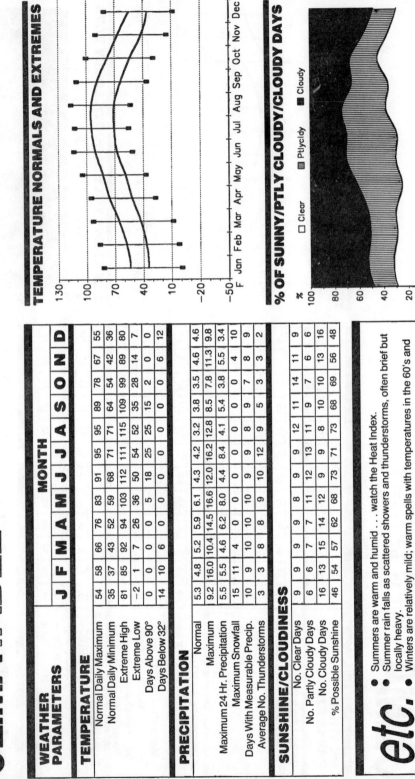

TEMPERATURE NORMALS AND EXTREMES

% OF SUNNY/PTLY CLOUDY/CLOUDY DAYS

☐ Clear   ▥ Ptlycldy   ■ Cloudy

WEATHER PARAMETERS	J	F	M	A	M	J	J	A	S	O	N	D
TEMPERATURE												
Normal Daily Maximum	54	58	66	76	83	91	95	95	89	78	67	55
Normal Daily Minimum	35	37	43	52	59	68	71	71	64	54	42	36
Extreme High	81	85	92	94	103	112	111	115	109	99	89	80
Extreme Low	-2	1	7	26	36	50	54	52	35	28	14	7
Days Above 90°	0	0	0	0	0	5	18	25	25	15	2	0	0
Days Below 32°	14	10	6	0	0	0	0	0	0	0	6	12
PRECIPITATION												
Normal	5.3	4.8	5.2	5.9	6.1	4.3	4.2	3.2	3.8	3.5	4.6	4.6
Maximum	9.2	16.0	10.4	14.5	16.6	12.0	16.2	12.8	8.5	7.8	11.3	9.8
Maximum 24 Hr. Precipitation	5.5	5.5	4.6	6.2	8.0	4.4	8.4	4.1	5.4	3.8	5.5	3.4
Maximum Snowfall	15	11	4	0	0	0	0	0	0	0	4	10
Days With Measurable Precip.	10	9	10	10	10	9	9	8	9	7	8	9
Average No. Thunderstorms	3	3	8	8	9	10	12	9	5	3	3	2
SUNSHINE/CLOUDINESS												
No. Clear Days	9	9	9	9	8	9	9	12	11	14	11	9
No. Partly Cloudy Days	6	6	7	7	11	12	13	11	9	7	6	6
No. Cloudy Days	16	13	15	14	12	9	9	8	10	10	13	16
% Possible Sunshine	46	54	57	62	68	73	71	73	68	69	56	48

etc. :
- Summers are warm and humid . . . watch the Heat Index.
- Summer rain falls as scattered showers and thunderstorms, often brief but locally heavy.
- Winters are relatively mild; warm spells with temperatures in the 60's and 70's are not uncommon.

CLIMATABLE NO. 20

Cabrillo NM, Channel Islands NP, Santa Monica Mts. NRA

TEMPERATURE NORMALS AND EXTREMES

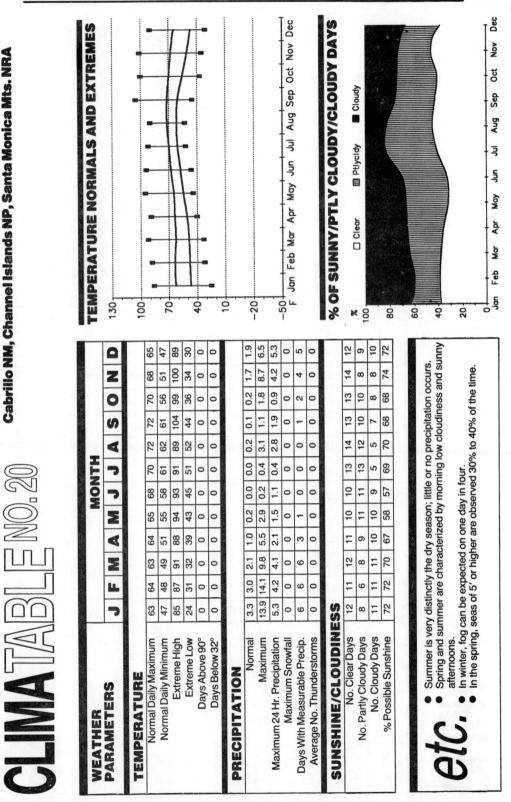

WEATHER PARAMETERS	MONTH											
	J	F	M	A	M	J	J	A	S	O	N	D
TEMPERATURE												
Normal Daily Maximum	63	64	63	64	65	68	70	72	72	70	68	65
Normal Daily Minimum	47	48	49	51	55	58	61	62	61	56	51	47
Extreme High	85	87	91	88	94	93	91	89	104	99	100	89
Extreme Low	24	31	32	39	43	45	51	52	44	36	34	30
Days Above 90°	0	0	0	0	0	0	0	0	0	0	0	0
Days Below 32°	0	0	0	0	0	0	0	0	0	0	0	0
PRECIPITATION												
Normal	3.3	3.0	2.1	1.0	0.2	0.0	0.0	0.2	0.1	0.2	1.7	1.9
Maximum	13.9	14.1	9.8	5.5	2.9	0.2	0.4	3.1	1.1	1.8	8.7	6.5
Maximum 24 Hr. Precipitation	5.3	4.2	4.1	2.1	1.5	1.1	0.4	2.8	1.9	0.9	4.2	5.3
Maximum Snowfall	0	0	0	0	0	0	0	0	0	0	0	0
Days With Measurable Precip.	6	6	6	3	1	0	0	0	1	0	2	4	5
Average No. Thunderstorms	0	0	0	0	0	0	0	0	0	0	0	0
SUNSHINE/CLOUDINESS												
No. Clear Days	12	11	12	11	10	13	13	14	13	13	14	12
No. Partly Cloudy Days	8	6	8	9	11	11	13	12	10	10	8	9
No. Cloudy Days	11	11	11	10	10	9	5	5	7	8	8	10
% Possible Sunshine	72	72	70	67	58	57	69	70	68	68	74	72

% OF SUNNY/PTLY CLOUDY/CLOUDY DAYS

☐ Clear   ▥ Ptlycldy   ■ Cloudy

etc. :
- Summer is very distinctly the dry season; little or no precipitation occurs.
- Spring and summer are characterized by morning low cloudiness and sunny afternoons.
- In winter, fog can be expected on one day in four.
- In the spring, seas of 5' or higher are observed 30% to 40% of the time.

CLIMATABLE NO. 21

Death Valley NM

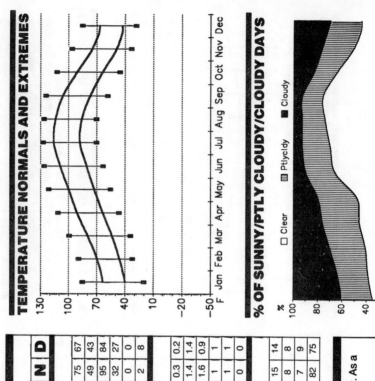

TEMPERATURE NORMALS AND EXTREMES

WEATHER PARAMETERS	MONTH											
	J	F	M	A	M	J	J	A	S	O	N	D
TEMPERATURE												
Normal Daily Maximum	64	70	80	91	100	109	116	114	106	91	75	67
Normal Daily Minimum	40	46	54	64	73	81	88	86	77	64	49	43
Extreme High	84	88	98	110	120	125	126	125	123	111	95	84
Extreme Low	19	31	33	45	54	62	69	69	57	44	32	27
Days Above 90°	0	0	0	2	7	19	30	29	19	4	0	0
Days Below 32°	10	6	0	0	0	0	0	0	0	0	2	8
PRECIPITATION												
Normal	0.4	0.5	0.3	0.4	0.1	0.1	0.2	0.4	0.2	0.2	0.3	0.2
Maximum	0.9	1.5	0.7	0.8	0.4	0.4	0.6	0.7	1.5	0.8	1.4	1.4
Maximum 24 Hr. Precipitation	0.7	1.6	1.0	0.9	0.5	0.7	0.8	0.7	1.1	0.8	1.6	0.9
Maximum Snowfall	13	5	4	0	0	0	0	0	0	0	1	1
Days With Measurable Precip.	1	1	1	1	1	1	1	2	2	2	1	1
Average No. Thunderstorms	0	0	0	0	0	1	1	1	1	1	0	0
SUNSHINE/CLOUDINESS												
No. Clear Days	11	11	13	14	15	20	22	23	23	20	15	14
No. Partly Cloudy Days	8	7	9	9	10	7	7	6	5	6	8	8
No. Cloudy Days	12	10	9	7	6	3	2	2	5	7	9	9
% Possible Sunshine	75	80	80	82	90	90	90	92	92	90	82	75

% OF SUNNY/PTLY CLOUDY/CLOUDY DAYS

☐ Clear   ▦ Ptlycldy   ■ Cloudy

etc.

- Summer daytime temperatures are quite hot, but humidities are low. As a result, summer evenings are cool.
- Winters are generally mild, but some very cold temperatures are experienced.
- The highest temperature ever recorded in the Western Hemisphere, 134 degrees, was recorded in Death Valley.

CLIMATABLE NO. 22   Yosemite NP, Devil's Postpile NM

TEMPERATURE NORMALS AND EXTREMES

% OF SUNNY/PTLY CLOUDY/CLOUDY DAYS

Legend: □ Clear   ▦ Ptlycldy   ■ Cloudy

WEATHER PARAMETERS	J	F	M	A	M	J	J	A	S	O	N	D
TEMPERATURE												
Normal Daily Maximum	47	55	59	66	73	82	90	90	85	74	58	46
Normal Daily Minimum	26	29	31	35	42	48	53	52	47	39	31	26
Extreme High	69	79	89	90	91	102	104	104	102	98	86	65
Extreme Low	7	10	10	20	26	30	38	32	28	21	16	-1
Days Above 90°	0	0	0	0	1	6	18	18	9	1	0	0
Days Below 32°	27	22	21	11	2	0	0	0	0	5	21	27
PRECIPITATION												
Normal	6.6	5.0	4.6	3.5	1.5	0.6	0.4	0.3	0.7	1.4	4.7	6.9
Maximum	22.3	17.2	11.5	12.1	4.8	1.6	1.6	1.3	5.2	4.6	13.0	29.8
Maximum 24 Hr. Precipitation	5.8	4.6	2.9	2.9	1.9	1.0	1.0	0.7	3.2	2.3	3.4	6.9
Maximum Snowfall	49	89	67	81	7	0	0	0	0	T	21	51
Days With Measurable Precip.	12	10	11	9	6	3	1	1	2	5	9	11
Average No. Thunderstorms	0	0	1	2	3	4	5	3	2	0	0	0
SUNSHINE/CLOUDINESS												
No. Clear Days	9	8	9	10	12	19	26	25	23	16	10	9
No. Partly Cloudy Days	5	5	5	7	8	5	3	4	4	6	5	5
No. Cloudy Days	17	15	17	13	11	6	2	2	3	9	15	17
% Possible Sunshine	60	60	70	75	70	80	90	90	90	80	70	60

etc.

- Temperature and precipitation, especially snowfall, vary considerably with elevation, the higher elevation areas being cooler and wetter.
- Summer evenings can be quite chilly.

CLIMATABLE NO. 23

John Muir NHS, Eugene O'Neill NHS, Fort Point NHS

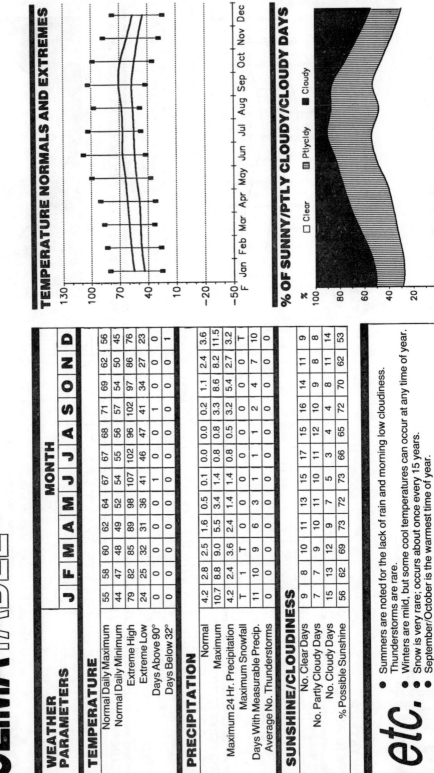

TEMPERATURE NORMALS AND EXTREMES

% OF SUNNY/PTLY CLOUDY/CLOUDY DAYS

☐ Clear   ▤ Ptlycldy   ▥ Cloudy

WEATHER PARAMETERS	MONTH											
	J	F	M	A	M	J	J	A	S	O	N	D
TEMPERATURE												
Normal Daily Maximum	55	58	60	62	64	67	67	68	71	69	62	56
Normal Daily Minimum	44	47	48	49	52	54	55	56	57	54	50	45
Extreme High	79	82	85	89	98	107	102	96	102	97	86	76
Extreme Low	24	25	32	31	36	41	46	47	41	34	27	23
Days Above 90°	0	0	0	0	0	1	0	0	1	0	0	0
Days Below 32°	0	0	0	0	0	0	0	0	0	0	0	1
PRECIPITATION												
Normal	4.2	2.8	2.5	1.6	0.5	0.1	0.0	0.0	0.2	1.1	2.4	3.6
Maximum	10.7	8.8	9.0	5.5	3.4	1.4	0.8	0.8	3.3	8.6	8.2	11.5
Maximum 24 Hr. Precipitation	4.2	2.4	3.6	2.4	1.4	1.4	0.8	0.5	3.2	5.4	2.7	3.2
Maximum Snowfall	T	1	T	0	0	0	0	0	0	0	0	T
Days With Measurable Precip.	11	10	9	6	3	1	1	1	2	4	7	10
Average No. Thunderstorms	0	0	0	0	0	0	0	0	0	0	0	0
SUNSHINE/CLOUDINESS												
No. Clear Days	9	8	10	11	13	15	17	15	16	14	11	9
No. Partly Cloudy Days	7	7	9	10	11	10	11	12	10	9	8	8
No. Cloudy Days	15	13	12	9	7	5	3	4	4	8	11	14
% Possible Sunshine	56	62	69	73	72	73	66	65	72	70	62	53

- Summers are noted for the lack of rain and morning low cloudiness.
- Thunderstorms are rare.
- Winters are mild, but some cool temperatures can occur at any time of year.
- Snow is very rare; occurs about once every 15 years.
- September/October is the warmest time of year.

CLIMATABLE NO. 24

Muir Woods NM, Golden Gate NRA

TEMPERATURE NORMALS AND EXTREMES

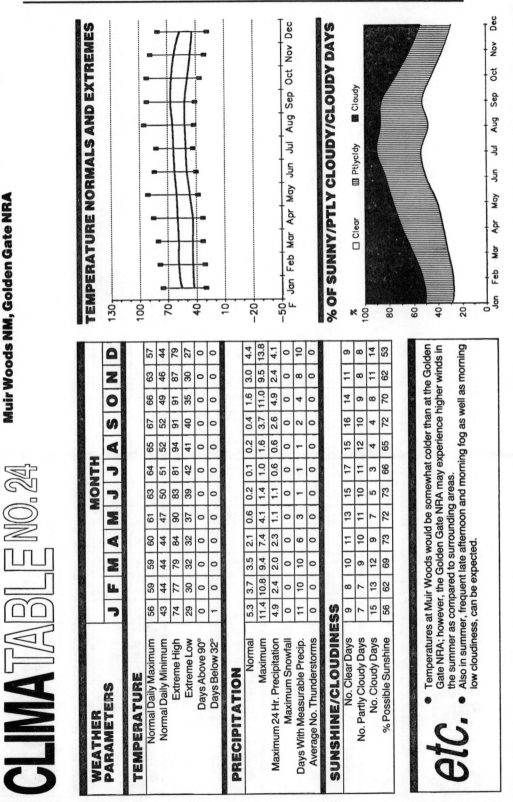

WEATHER PARAMETERS	MONTH											
	J	F	M	A	M	J	J	A	S	O	N	D
TEMPERATURE												
Normal Daily Maximum	56	59	59	60	61	63	64	65	67	66	63	57
Normal Daily Minimum	43	44	44	44	47	50	51	52	52	49	46	44
Extreme High	74	77	79	84	90	83	81	94	91	91	87	79
Extreme Low	29	30	32	32	37	39	42	41	40	35	30	27
Days Above 90°	0	0	0	0	0	0	0	0	0	0	0	0
Days Below 32°	1	0	0	0	0	0	0	0	0	0	0	0
PRECIPITATION												
Normal	5.3	3.7	3.5	2.1	0.6	0.2	0.1	0.2	0.4	1.6	3.0	4.4
Maximum	11.4	10.8	9.4	7.4	4.1	1.4	1.0	1.6	3.7	11.0	9.5	13.8
Maximum 24 Hr. Precipitation	4.9	2.4	2.0	2.3	1.1	1.1	0.6	0.6	2.6	4.9	2.4	4.1
Maximum Snowfall	0	0	0	0	0	0	0	0	0	0	0	0
Days With Measurable Precip.	11	10	10	6	3	1	1	1	2	4	8	10
Average No. Thunderstorms	0	0	0	0	0	0	0	0	0	0	0	0
SUNSHINE/CLOUDINESS												
No. Clear Days	9	8	10	11	13	15	17	16	14	14	11	9
No. Partly Cloudy Days	7	7	9	10	11	10	11	12	10	9	8	8
No. Cloudy Days	15	13	12	9	7	5	3	4	8	8	11	14
% Possible Sunshine	56	62	69	73	72	73	66	65	72	70	62	53

% OF SUNNY/PTLY CLOUDY/CLOUDY DAYS

□ Clear   ▦ Ptlycldy   ▦ Cloudy

etc.

- Temperatures at Muir Woods would be somewhat colder than at the Golden Gate NRA; however, the Golden Gate NRA may experience higher winds in the summer as compared to surrounding areas.
- Also in summer, frequent late afternoon and morning fog as well as morning low cloudiness, can be expected.

CLIMATABLE NO. 25

Joshua Tree NM

TEMPERATURE NORMALS AND EXTREMES

% OF SUNNY/PTLY CLOUDY/CLOUDY DAYS

□ Clear   ▦ Ptlycldy   ▨ Cloudy

WEATHER PARAMETERS		J	F	M	A	M	J	J	A	S	O	N	D
TEMPERATURE													
Normal Daily Maximum		64	69	74	81	89	99	104	103	98	87	73	65
Normal Daily Minimum		37	41	44	51	58	66	75	74	65	54	44	38
Extreme High		86	89	94	102	110	118	118	115	115	104	92	86
Extreme Low		13	18	23	24	35	43	54	43	38	24	21	15
Days Above 90°		0	0	1	6	18	27	31	31	26	14	1	0
Days Below 32°		10	4	2	0	0	0	0	0	0	0	2	8
PRECIPITATION													
Normal		0.4	0.2	0.2	0.1	0.0	0.0	0.2	0.4	0.2	0.3	0.3	0.4
Maximum		1.8	0.9	1.0	0.8	0.9	0.5	2.6	3.0	1.7	2.7	1.4	2.6
Maximum 24 Hr. Precipitation		1.3	0.7	0.8	0.5	0.3	0.5	2.4	2.2	1.4	2.6	1.1	1.4
Maximum Snowfall		10	1	0	0	0	0	0	0	0	T	2	10
Days With Measurable Precip.		3	3	3	2	1	1	3	3	2	2	2	2
Average No. Thunderstorms		0	0	0	0	0	0	1	3	1	0	0	0
SUNSHINE/CLOUDINESS													
No. Clear Days		14	12	14	16	18	22	20	21	23	21	16	14
No. Partly Cloudy Days		6	7	9	8	8	5	8	7	5	6	7	7
No. Cloudy Days		11	9	8	6	5	3	3	3	2	4	7	10
% Possible Sunshine		77	81	83	87	88	93	87	88	91	87	80	77

etc.
- Summer heat is accompanied by very low humidity.
- Scattered, locally heavy showers do occasionally occur during the summer dry season.
- Wintertime temperatures can be moderate to cold.

CLIMATABLE NO. 26

Whiskeytown-Shasta-Trinity NRA, Lassen Volcanic NP

TEMPERATURE NORMALS AND EXTREMES

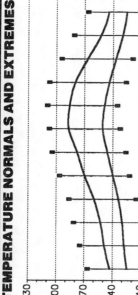

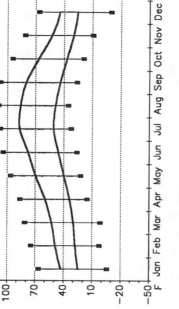

% OF SUNNY/PTLY CLOUDY/CLOUDY DAYS

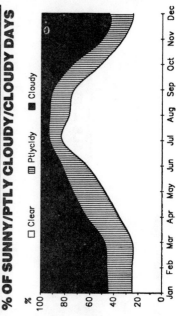

Legend: □ Clear ▦ Ptlycldy ■ Cloudy

WEATHER PARAMETERS	J	F	M	A	M	J	J	A	S	O	N	D
TEMPERATURE												
Normal Daily Maximum	43	49	53	60	70	78	87	86	80	67	53	45
Normal Daily Minimum	25	28	30	34	40	46	51	49	44	37	30	26
Extreme High	65	73	80	85	95	103	106	108	106	93	80	65
Extreme Low	-7	1	0	14	21	25	31	34	25	18	8	-11
Days Above 90°	0	0	0	0	1	7	19	17	7	1	0	0
Days Below 32°	26	22	21	12	4	1	0	0	2	7	19	26
PRECIPITATION												
Normal	3.7	2.2	1.8	0.9	0.8	0.8	0.4	0.6	0.6	1.2	2.3	3.8
Maximum	8.0	6.8	6.2	3.4	3.2	3.4	2.0	3.2	3.2	8.0	6.7	13.7
Maximum 24 Hr. Precipitation	3.0	2.1	2.1	1.1	1.1	1.1	1.2	1.3	1.4	2.8	2.6	4.6
Maximum Snowfall	48	23	22	10	2	0	0	3	1		33	28
Days With Measurable Precip.	11	9	10	7	4	2	1	1	2	5	9	10
Average No. Thunderstorms	0	1	1	1	1	2	2	1	1	1	0	0
SUNSHINE/CLOUDINESS												
No. Clear Days	8	7	8	11	15	19	26	24	22	16	10	8
No. Partly Cloudy Days	6	6	7	8	8	6	3	5	5	7	5	6
No. Cloudy Days	17	15	16	11	8	5	2	2	3	8	15	17
% Possible Sunshine	54	64	70	81	86	89	96	94	92	81	61	53

etc.
- Precipitation is a maximum in winter; heavy, persistent rains over periods of 7-10 days may be experienced.
- Near Mt. Shasta, North America's record snowfall of 189" for a single snowstorm, occurred.
- Precipitation amounts are markedly less on the eastern slopes of the mountains.

CLIMATABLE NO. 27 — Redwood NP, Lava Beds NM

WEATHER PARAMETERS	J	F	M	A	M	J	J	A	S	O	N	D
TEMPERATURE												
Normal Daily Maximum	53	55	57	60	62	64	64	65	65	62	58	54
Normal Daily Minimum	41	42	42	43	47	50	51	52	51	48	45	42
Extreme High	78	85	80	92	94	99	96	96	103	96	81	79
Extreme Low	21	26	29	32	32	39	39	42	39	32	29	18
Days Above 90°	0	0	0	0	0	0	0	0	1	0	0	0
Days Below 32°	2	1	1	0	0	0	0	0	0	0	0	2
PRECIPITATION												
Normal	12.0	9.0	8.0	4.0	3.0	1.0	0.3	0.8	2.0	4.0	9.0	12.0
Maximum	20.0	16.0	15.0	11.5	8.0	4.0	2.5	6.0	7.0	13.0	18.0	19.0
Maximum 24 Hr. Precipitation	5.5	4.7	4.5	2.8	4.2	2.5	1.0	2.5	3.0	5.8	5.0	6.9
Maximum Snowfall	5	1	1	0	0	0	0	0	0	0	T	2
Days With Measurable Precip.	18	15	15	12	8	5	2	2	4	9	14	16
Average No. Thunderstorms	1	1	1	0	0	0	0	0	0	0	1	1
SUNSHINE/CLOUDINESS												
No. Clear Days	6	6	7	7	7	6	6	5	9	8	6	6
No. Partly Cloudy Days	6	7	8	10	10	11	11	11	9	8	7	6
No. Cloudy Days	19	17	18	15	14	13	14	15	12	15	17	19
% Possible Sunshine	42	45	52	57	57	58	54	49	54	49	43	40

TEMPERATURE NORMALS AND EXTREMES

% OF SUNNY/PTLY CLOUDY/CLOUDY DAYS

☐ Clear ▦ Ptlycldy ▤ Cloudy ■ Cloudy

- Usually over 90% of the annual precipitation falls in the period October through April; the total wintertime precipitation increases with distance north of Eureka.
- With extended periods of heavy winter precipitation, some flooding can be expected along the Klamath River.

CLIMATABLE NO. 28   Pinnacles NM

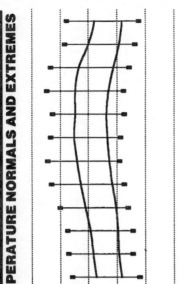
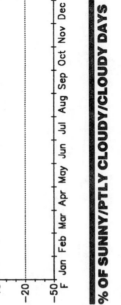

TEMPERATURE NORMALS AND EXTREMES

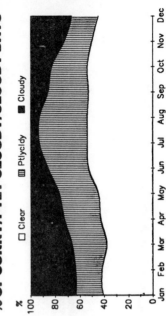

% OF SUNNY/PTLY CLOUDY/CLOUDY DAYS

☐ Clear   ▦ Ptlycldy   ■ Cloudy

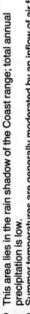

WEATHER PARAMETERS	MONTH											
	J	F	M	A	M	J	J	A	S	O	N	D
TEMPERATURE												
Normal Daily Maximum	62	65	68	73	78	82	85	84	84	80	70	64
Normal Daily Minimum	35	38	39	41	45	48	50	51	49	44	38	35
Extreme High	86	90	91	99	108	112	109	107	113	109	94	92
Extreme Low	15	22	22	27	31	36	35	31	32	26	20	16
Days Above 90°	0	0	0	1	3	5	6	5	7	5	0	0
Days Below 32°	13	8	6	2	0	0	0	0	0	1	7	14
PRECIPITATION												
Normal	2.4	2.3	1.7	1.0	0.2	0.0	0.0	0.0	0.1	0.3	1.1	2.0
Maximum	6.8	6.5	5.4	4.1	1.2	0.6	0.2	1.1	2.6	2.1	5.3	7.7
Maximum 24 Hr. Precipitation	3.3	2.0	1.7	1.5	1.7	0.6	0.2	0.9	2.6	1.6	1.7	2.4
Maximum Snowfall	5	0	0	0	0	0	0	0	0	0	0	0
Days With Measurable Precip.	5	5	3	2	1	0	0	0	1	2	3	4
Average No. Thunderstorms	0	0	0	0	0	0	0	0	0	0	0	0
SUNSHINE/CLOUDINESS												
No. Clear Days	13	12	13	14	16	17	17	16	17	15	14	14
No. Partly Cloudy Days	7	6	9	9	10	10	12	12	9	9	7	7
No. Cloudy Days	11	10	10	8	7	4	2	2	4	5	8	10
% Possible Sunshine	55	63	70	70	75	80	75	75	78	75	65	52

etc.

- This area lies in the rain shadow of the Coast range; total annual precipitation is low.
- Summer temperatures are generally moderated by an inflow of air from Monterey Bay. September tends to be the hottest month.
- Morning low cloudiness is common in the summer.

CLIMATABLE NO. 29 Point Reyes National Seashore

WEATHER PARAMETERS	J	F	M	A	M	J	J	A	S	O	N	D
TEMPERATURE												
Normal Daily Maximum	57	59	59	60	61	63	64	65	67	66	63	58
Normal Daily Minimum	38	40	41	43	45	50	51	51	51	47	41	38
Extreme High	74	77	79	84	90	83	81	94	91	91	87	79
Extreme Low	29	30	32	32	37	39	42	41	40	35	30	27
Days Above 90°	0	0	0	0	0	0	0	0	0	0	0	0
Days Below 32°	1	0	0	0	0	0	0	0	0	0	0	1
PRECIPITATION												
Normal	5.3	4.5	3.5	2.1	0.6	0.2	0.1	0.2	0.4	1.6	3.0	4.9
Maximum	11.4	10.8	9.4	7.4	4.1	1.4	1.0	1.6	3.7	11.0	9.5	13.8
Maximum 24 Hr. Precipitation	4.9	2.8	2.7	2.4	1.1	1.1	0.6	0.6	2.6	4.9	2.4	4.1
Maximum Snowfall	0	0	0	0	0	0	0	0	0	0	0	0
Days With Measurable Precip.	11	10	10	6	3	1	1	1	2	4	8	10
Average No. Thunderstorms	0	0	0	0	0	0	0	0	0	0	0	0
SUNSHINE/CLOUDINESS												
No. Clear Days	9	8	10	11	13	17	15	15	16	14	11	9
No. Partly Cloudy Days	7	7	9	10	11	11	11	12	10	9	8	8
No. Cloudy Days	15	13	12	9	7	5	3	4	4	8	11	14
% Possible Sunshine	55	60	65	70	72	73	66	65	72	70	60	50

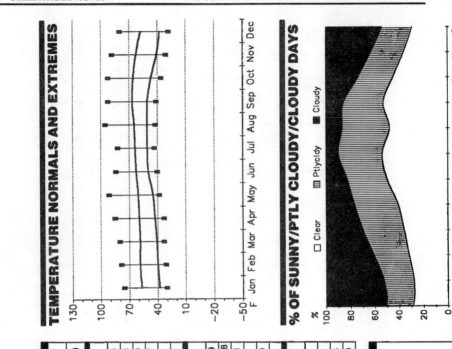

TEMPERATURE NORMALS AND EXTREMES

etc.

- Somewhat higher winds are experienced along the seashore as compared to surrounding areas. The water is cold and the surf is good!
- Summers are dry! Only 5% of the total annual precipitation falls in the period from May through September.

% OF SUNNY/PTLY CLOUDY/CLOUDY DAYS

□ Clear   ▥ Ptlycldy   ■ Cloudy

CLIMATABLE NO.30

Sequoia & Kings Canyon NP's

TEMPERATURE NORMALS AND EXTREMES

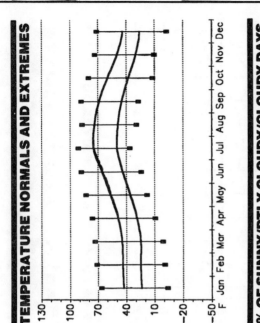

% OF SUNNY/PTLY CLOUDY/CLOUDY DAYS

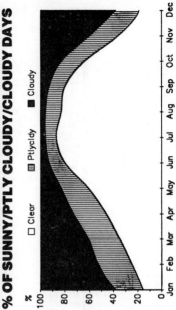

☐ Clear   ▥ Ptlycldy   ■ Cloudy

WEATHER PARAMETERS	MONTH											
	J	F	M	A	M	J	J	A	S	O	N	D
TEMPERATURE												
Normal Daily Maximum	43	44	45	49	57	66	75	74	69	60	50	44
Normal Daily Minimum	24	25	25	29	36	44	50	49	45	38	30	26
Extreme High	65	70	72	75	82	87	90	86	87	79	72	70
Extreme Low	-5	-2	0	8	17	23	35	28	26	11	9	-4
Days Above 90°	0	0	0	0	0	0	0	0	0	0	0	0
Days Below 32°	28	24	26	20	10	1	0	0	1	7	20	26
PRECIPITATION												
Normal	8.8	6.4	6.0	4.5	1.5	0.5	0.1	0.1	0.6	1.3	4.9	7.8
Maximum	38.2	23.6	16.5	14.9	8.3	2.2	0.6	0.5	2.2	3.4	14.0	28.3
Maximum 24 Hr. Precipitation	7.5	6.8	4.6	4.0	5.1	1.2	0.4	0.4	1.4	2.7	3.9	10.1
Maximum Snowfall	101	154	168	143	31	8	0	0	4	11	57	80
Days With Measurable Precip.	10	9	10	8	5	2	1	1	2	3	7	10
Average No. Thunderstorms	0	0	0	2	2	2	1	1	2	0	0	0
SUNSHINE/CLOUDINESS												
No. Clear Days	5	7	11	14	19	24	27	26	24	20	11	6
No. Partly Cloudy Days	7	8	8	7	4	3	4	4	5	6	7	6
No. Cloudy Days	19	13	12	8	5	2	1	1	2	5	12	19
% Possible Sunshine	47	65	77	85	90	94	96	96	93	88	65	45

etc.

- The distinct summer dry season is typical of California.
- Winter precipitation and snowfall can be extremely heavy along the western slopes of the Sierra Nevada mountains.

CLIMATABLE NO. 31 — Bent's Old Fort NHS

TEMPERATURE NORMALS AND EXTREMES

% OF SUNNY/PTLY CLOUDY/CLOUDY DAYS

□ Clear · ▦ Pttlycldy · ▨ Ptlycldy · ■ Cloudy

WEATHER PARAMETERS	MONTH											
	J	F	M	A	M	J	J	A	S	O	N	D
TEMPERATURE												
Normal Daily Maximum	44	51	57	69	79	90	95	92	84	73	56	48
Normal Daily Minimum	14	20	26	37	47	57	63	60	51	39	25	17
Extreme High	78	83	90	92	101	109	109	107	103	96	85	81
Extreme Low	−25	−23	−21	5	22	29	42	43	28	14	−13	−22
Days Above 90°	0	0	0	0	5	18	25	22	10	1	0	0
Days Below 32°	30	26	24	8	0	0	0	0	0	7	25	30
PRECIPITATION												
Normal	0.3	0.3	0.6	1.1	1.9	1.3	2.2	1.8	0.8	0.7	0.5	0.3
Maximum	1.4	1.8	3.4	4.4	4.8	5.7	6.2	4.2	4.3	2.8	1.7	1.1
Maximum 24 Hr. Precipitation	1.0	0.6	1.3	1.8	2.0	1.9	3.6	2.7	2.1	2.0	1.1	0.6
Maximum Snowfall	16	28	23	12	4	0	0	0	0	8	18	17
Days With Measurable Precip.	4	4	6	6	8	7	7	8	5	4	4	4
Average No. Thunderstorms	0	0	0	2	7	9	11	8	3	1	0	0
SUNSHINE/CLOUDINESS												
No. Clear Days	12	9	10	9	8	13	11	12	16	15	12	12
No. Partly Cloudy Days	9	8	9	10	12	11	15	13	8	8	9	9
No. Cloudy Days	10	11	12	11	11	6	5	6	6	9	9	10
% Possible Sunshine	75	74	74	75	74	79	78	78	80	78	73	72

etc.

- Summer days are hot, but the low humidity keeps them from being oppressive.
- Between 70% and 80% of the annual precipitation falls from April through September.
- Strong northerly winds and rapid drops in temperature can be experienced in winter.

CLIMATABLE NO. 32

Curecanti NRA, Black Canyon of the Gunnison NM, Colorado NM

TEMPERATURE NORMALS AND EXTREMES

WEATHER PARAMETERS	J	F	M	A	M	J	J	A	S	O	N	D
TEMPERATURE												
Normal Daily Maximum	38	44	52	62	73	84	90	87	78	67	50	40
Normal Daily Minimum	15	20	26	34	43	52	58	56	47	37	26	18
Extreme High	63	72	77	85	93	103	102	102	100	89	73	65
Extreme Low	-23	-21	2	9	21	33	35	37	26	14	-8	-15
Days Above 90°	0	0	0	0	0	9	23	12	2	0	0	0
Days Below 32°	30	27	26	14	3	0	0	0	1	11	26	30
PRECIPITATION												
Normal	0.6	0.7	0.7	0.8	0.7	0.6	0.8	1.7	1.0	1.0	0.7	0.7
Maximum	3.5	2.5	3.3	2.1	2.1	2.5	3.8	3.6	3.6	4.1	1.9	2.9
Maximum 24 Hr. Precipitation	1.4	0.8	0.8	1.4	0.8	1.6	0.9	2.6	1.5	1.7	0.8	1.6
Maximum Snowfall	62	19	17	9	6	0	0	0	5	7	18	31
Days With Measurable Precip.	7	6	7	7	6	5	5	6	7	7	7	6
Average No. Thunderstorms	0	0	1	3	7	10	14	14	8	3	0	0
SUNSHINE/CLOUDINESS												
No. Clear Days	9	8	8	8	10	14	12	11	16	15	11	9
No. Partly Cloudy Days	7	7	8	9	11	10	14	14	8	8	7	8
No. Cloudy Days	15	13	15	13	10	6	5	6	8	8	12	14
% Possible Sunshine	60	64	64	69	72	80	78	76	78	73	63	60

% OF SUNNY/PTLY CLOUDY/CLOUDY DAYS

☐ Clear   ▦ Ptlycldy   ■ Cloudy

etc.
- Hot summers and cold winters!
- In the spring, the combination of thunderstorms and melting snow at times produces some local flash flooding.
- Precipitation is generally well distributed over the entire year.

CLIMATABLE NO.33

Dinosaur NM

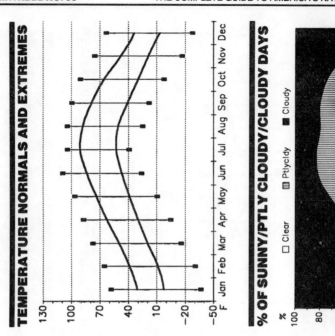

TEMPERATURE NORMALS AND EXTREMES

% OF SUNNY/PTLY CLOUDY/CLOUDY DAYS

☐ Clear ▦ Ptlycldy ■ Cloudy

WEATHER PARAMETERS	J	F	M	A	M	J	J	A	S	O	N	D
TEMPERATURE												
Normal Daily Maximum	31	39	50	63	74	84	91	88	79	66	48	34
Normal Daily Minimum	3	9	20	30	39	47	53	51	41	30	19	7
Extreme High	57	64	76	86	95	108	103	103	98	89	74	62
Extreme Low	-38	-32	-17	-6	8	25	38	24	17	1	-18	-29
Days Above 90°	0	0	0	0	1	11	23	16	3	0	0	0
Days Below 32°	31	28	29	18	4	1	0	0	4	21	29	31
PRECIPITATION												
Normal	0.6	0.5	0.7	0.8	0.9	0.6	0.6	0.9	0.8	0.6	0.6	0.6
Maximum	1.9	2.6	3.2	2.2	2.8	2.9	2.2	3.2	4.4	2.4	2.0	2.1
Maximum 24 Hr. Precipitation	1.0	1.0	1.5	1.0	0.9	2.0	1.4	1.4	1.1	1.2	1.0	0.9
Maximum Snowfall	22	19	29	16	3	0	0	0	13	10	22	29
Days With Measurable Precip.	7	6	8	6	6	4	5	6	6	6	6	6
Average No. Thunderstorms	0	0	0	1	2	4	6	7	3	1	0	0
SUNSHINE/CLOUDINESS												
No. Clear Days	9	8	8	8	10	15	14	14	16	15	11	9
No. Partly Cloudy Days	7	7	8	9	11	9	12	11	8	8	7	8
No. Cloudy Days	15	13	15	13	10	6	5	6	6	8	12	14
% Possible Sunshine	60	64	64	69	72	80	78	76	78	73	63	60

etc.

- Precipitation is fairly evenly distributed through the year in this semi-arid region.
- Winters are very cold and summers are hot; the low humidity keeps the summer temperatures from being oppressive.

CLIMATABLE NO. 34

Florissant Fossil Beds NM

TEMPERATURE NORMALS AND EXTREMES

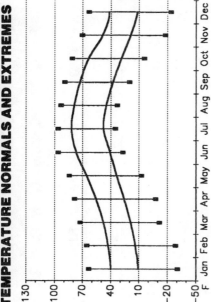

% OF SUNNY/PTLY CLOUDY/CLOUDY DAYS

☐ Clear   ▦ Ptlycldy   ■ Cloudy

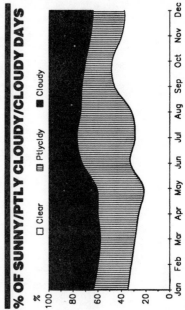

WEATHER PARAMETERS	J	F	M	A	M	J	J	A	S	O	N	D
TEMPERATURE												
Normal Daily Maximum	40	43	48	56	66	77	82	79	73	64	49	42
Normal Daily Minimum	11	14	19	26	34	41	48	45	38	29	19	12
Extreme High	62	64	71	77	83	95	95	92	88	80	69	62
Extreme Low	-32	-30	-13	-9	6	26	34	32	19	3	-19	-25
Days Above 90°	0	0	0	0	0	0	1	0	0	0	0	0
Days Below 32°	31	28	30	26	12	1	0	0	5	21	28	31
PRECIPITATION												
Normal	0.4	0.4	0.7	0.9	1.0	0.6	1.6	1.9	0.9	0.8	0.7	0.5
Maximum	2.0	2.3	1.8	3.2	4.2	2.6	4.7	6.9	2.9	2.9	2.4	2.0
Maximum 24 Hr. Precipitation	1.5	0.6	1.1	1.5	1.3	1.0	1.3	1.8	1.8	1.4	1.2	0.6
Maximum Snowfall	25	26	24	38	15	8	0	0	21	31	46	22
Days With Measurable Precip.	5	5	8	7	10	9	13	12	6	5	4	4
Average No. Thunderstorms	0	0	0	3	13	18	26	19	7	1	0	0
SUNSHINE/CLOUDINESS												
No. Clear Days	11	9	9	8	7	10	9	10	14	15	12	12
No. Partly Cloudy Days	9	8	9	10	12	12	15	13	8	7	8	8
No. Cloudy Days	11	11	13	12	12	8	7	8	8	9	10	11
% Possible Sunshine	55	60	60	60	60	70	70	70	70	70	60	60

etc.

- This area of Colorado experiences quite large variations in climate over short distances because of the mountainous terrain.
- Summers in the mountains can be cool and refreshing; bright sunshine keeps summer days comfortable.

CLIMATABLE NO. 35

Great Sand Dunes NM

WEATHER PARAMETERS	MONTH											
	J	F	M	A	M	J	J	A	S	O	N	D
TEMPERATURE												
Normal Daily Maximum	35	39	46	56	66	76	81	78	72	61	45	36
Normal Daily Minimum	10	15	19	28	37	45	49	48	42	31	20	12
Extreme High	54	61	67	77	91	91	90	89	87	81	65	61
Extreme Low	-25	-10	-7	0	15	25	31	33	22	7	-12	-19
Days Above 90°	0	0	0	0	0	1	0	0	0	0	0	0
Days Below 32°	31	28	30	23	8	1	0	0	1	18	29	31
PRECIPITATION												
Normal	0.4	0.3	0.5	0.7	1.2	0.9	1.0	2.2	1.1	0.8	0.3	0.3
Maximum	0.8	1.1	1.1	2.0	3.8	4.3	5.0	4.2	3.9	2.2	0.7	0.7
Maximum 24 Hr. Precipitation	0.4	0.3	0.7	1.1	2.0	1.1	1.8	1.4	1.2	1.1	0.5	0.4
Maximum Snowfall	18	16	18	20	5	T	T	T	T	28	13	13
Days With Measurable Precip.	4	4	5	5	6	5	10	10	6	5	4	4
Average No. Thunderstorms	0	0	0	2	7	9	16	14	5	1	0	0
SUNSHINE/CLOUDINESS												
No. Clear Days	13	11	10	9	14	14	9	11	15	17	14	14
No. Partly Cloudy Days	10	10	12	14	8	12	17	14	10	8	9	10
No. Cloudy Days	8	7	9	8	8	4	5	6	5	6	7	7
% Possible Sunshine	60	60	60	60	70	70	70	70	70	70	60	55

etc. • An arid region with cold winters, moderate summers, and much sunshine.
• Occasional blowing dust can be expected in the spring and summer.
• Summer precipitation is in the form of scattered light showers and thunderstorms with some hail.

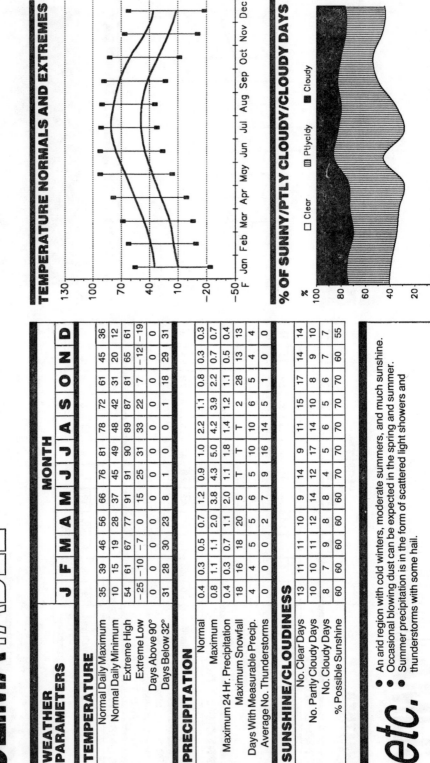

TEMPERATURE NORMALS AND EXTREMES

% OF SUNNY/PTLY CLOUDY/CLOUDY DAYS

□ Clear   ▦ Ptlycldy   ■ Cloudy

CLIMATABLE NO. 36

Hovenweep NM, Yucca House NM, Mesa Verde NP

WEATHER PARAMETERS — MONTH

WEATHER PARAMETERS	J	F	M	A	M	J	J	A	S	O	N	D
TEMPERATURE												
Normal Daily Maximum	40	45	51	61	71	83	88	85	78	67	51	41
Normal Daily Minimum	16	20	25	32	41	50	57	55	48	37	26	18
Extreme High	62	66	76	80	91	100	101	99	100	85	72	67
Extreme Low	-27	-20	-3	8	17	28	40	36	24	11	-7	-22
Days Above 90°	0	0	0	0	0	6	14	7	1	0	0	0
Days Below 32°	30	26	26	16	4	0	0	0	1	9	24	30
PRECIPITATION												
Normal	1.6	1.3	1.4	1.3	1.0	0.7	1.9	2.2	1.2	1.9	1.3	1.9
Maximum	5.5	4.3	3.8	3.7	3.4	2.1	5.9	4.8	4.3	7.4	2.5	5.0
Maximum 24 Hr. Precipitation	1.1	1.3	1.3	1.3	1.2	1.4	1.9	1.5	1.7	1.5	1.4	1.5
Maximum Snowfall	56	39	46	22	5	0	0	0	2	15	22	52
Days With Measurable Precip.	8	7	7	6	5	5	5	6	6	7	6	8
Average No. Thunderstorms	0	0	0	2	4	6	9	12	5	2	0	0
SUNSHINE/CLOUDINESS												
No. Clear Days	9	8	8	8	10	15	14	16	15	11		9
No. Partly Cloudy Days	7	7	8	9	11	9	12	8	8	7		8
No. Cloudy Days	15	13	15	13	10	6	5	6	8	12		14
% Possible Sunshine	60	64	64	69	72	80	78	76	78	73	63	60

TEMPERATURE NORMALS AND EXTREMES

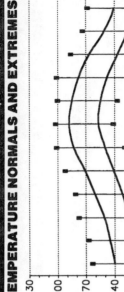
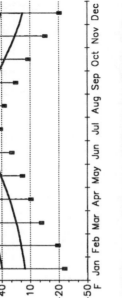

% OF SUNNY/PTLY CLOUDY/CLOUDY DAYS

☐ Clear   ▦ Ptlycldy   ▨ Cloudy

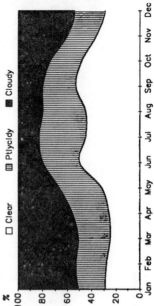

etc.

- Precipitation is fairly evenly distributed throughout the year. There is a slight maximum of precipitation in winter while June tends to be the driest month.

CLIMATABLE NO. 37 — Rocky Mountain NP

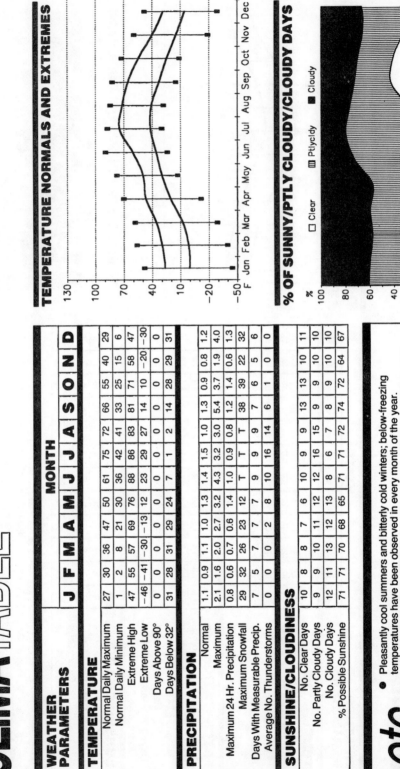

TEMPERATURE NORMALS AND EXTREMES

% OF SUNNY/PTLY CLOUDY/CLOUDY DAYS

□ Clear   ▥ Ptlycldy   ■ Cloudy

WEATHER PARAMETERS	MONTH											
	J	F	M	A	M	J	J	A	S	O	N	D
TEMPERATURE												
Normal Daily Maximum	27	30	36	47	50	61	75	72	66	55	40	29
Normal Daily Minimum	1	2	8	21	30	36	42	41	33	25	15	6
Extreme High	47	55	57	69	76	88	86	83	81	71	58	47
Extreme Low	−46	−41	−30	−13	12	23	29	27	14	10	−20	−30
Days Above 90°	0	0	0	0	0	0	0	0	0	0	0	0
Days Below 32°	31	28	31	29	24	7	1	2	14	28	29	31
PRECIPITATION												
Normal	1.1	0.9	1.1	1.0	1.3	1.4	1.5	1.0	1.3	0.9	0.8	1.2
Maximum	2.1	1.6	2.0	2.7	3.2	4.3	3.2	3.0	5.4	3.7	1.9	4.0
Maximum 24 Hr. Precipitation	0.8	0.6	0.7	0.6	1.4	1.0	0.9	0.8	1.2	1.4	0.6	1.3
Maximum Snowfall	29	32	26	23	12	T	T	T	38	39	22	32
Days With Measurable Precip.	7	5	7	7	7	9	9	9	7	6	5	6
Average No. Thunderstorms	0	0	0	2	8	10	16	14	6	1	0	0
SUNSHINE/CLOUDINESS												
No. Clear Days	10	8	8	7	6	10	9	9	13	13	10	11
No. Partly Cloudy Days	9	9	10	11	12	12	15	9	9	9	10	10
No. Cloudy Days	12	11	13	12	13	8	6	7	8	9	10	10
% Possible Sunshine	71	71	70	68	65	71	71	72	74	72	64	67

etc.

- Pleasantly cool summers and bitterly cold winters; below-freezing temperatures have been observed in every month of the year.
- Snow has fallen in every month of the year; near the National Park, a 24-hour snowfall of 76", the record for North America, was recorded.

CLIMATABLE NO. 38

All District of Columbia sites, Arlington House, Robert E. Lee Memorial, George Washington Memorial Parkway, U.S. Marine Corps War Memorial and Netherlands Carillon

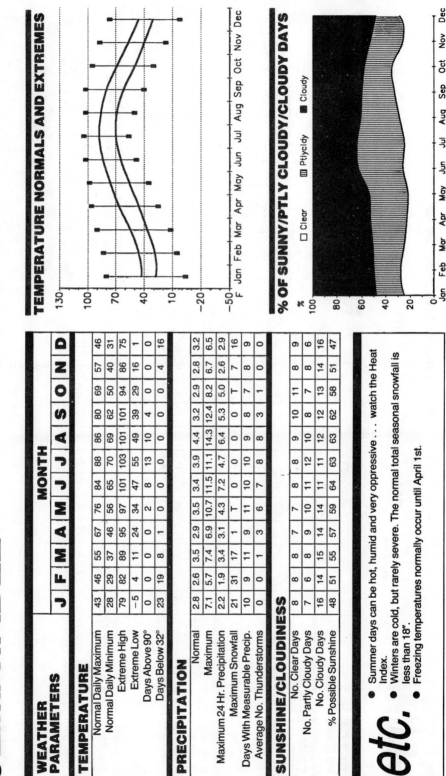

TEMPERATURE NORMALS AND EXTREMES

WEATHER PARAMETERS	MONTH											
	J	F	M	A	M	J	J	A	S	O	N	D
TEMPERATURE												
Normal Daily Maximum	43	46	55	67	76	84	88	86	80	69	57	46
Normal Daily Minimum	28	29	37	46	56	65	70	69	62	50	40	31
Extreme High	79	82	89	95	97	101	103	101	101	94	86	75
Extreme Low	−5	4	11	24	34	47	55	49	39	29	16	1
Days Above 90°	0	0	0	0	2	8	13	10	4	0	0	0
Days Below 32°	23	19	8	1	0	0	0	0	0	0	4	16
PRECIPITATION												
Normal	2.8	2.6	3.5	2.9	3.5	3.4	3.9	4.4	3.2	2.9	2.8	3.2
Maximum	7.1	5.7	7.4	6.9	10.7	11.5	11.1	14.3	12.4	8.2	6.7	6.5
Maximum 24 Hr. Precipitation	2.2	1.9	3.4	3.1	4.3	7.2	4.7	6.4	5.3	5.0	2.6	2.9
Maximum Snowfall	21	31	17	1	T	0	0	0	T	T	7	16
Days With Measurable Precip.	10	9	11	9	11	10	10	9	8	7	8	9
Average No. Thunderstorms	0	0	1	3	6	7	8	8	3	1	0	0
SUNSHINE/CLOUDINESS												
No. Clear Days	8	8	8	7	7	8	8	9	10	11	8	9
No. Partly Cloudy Days	7	6	8	9	10	11	12	10	8	7	8	6
No. Cloudy Days	16	14	15	14	14	11	11	12	12	13	14	16
% Possible Sunshine	48	51	55	57	59	64	63	63	62	58	51	47

% OF SUNNY/PTLY CLOUDY/CLOUDY DAYS

etc.
- Summer days can be hot, humid and very oppressive . . . watch the Heat Index.
- Winters are cold, but rarely severe. The normal total seasonal snowfall is less than 18″.
- Freezing temperatures normally occur until April 1st.

CLIMATABLE NO. 39

Big Cypress NP, Everglades NP

WEATHER PARAMETERS	MONTH											
	J	F	M	A	M	J	J	A	S	O	N	D
TEMPERATURE												
Normal Daily Maximum	76	76	80	83	86	88	90	90	89	85	81	77
Normal Daily Minimum	56	57	61	65	69	73	75	75	74	70	63	58
Extreme High	88	89	92	96	98	98	99	98	99	95	90	88
Extreme Low	28	30	32	43	53	60	65	64	65	49	33	29
Days Above 90°	0	0	0	1	9	15	22	24	20	6	0	0
Days Below 32°	0	0	0	0	0	0	0	0	0	0	0	0
PRECIPITATION												
Normal	2.1	2.0	1.9	3.1	6.5	9.2	6.0	7.0	8.1	7.1	2.7	1.9
Maximum	6.8	8.1	10.6	17.3	18.5	23.5	17.4	16.9	24.4	21.1	13.2	6.4
Maximum 24 Hr. Precipitation	2.7	6.0	7.1	16.2	11.6	10.1	4.6	6.9	7.6	10.0	7.9	4.4
Maximum Snowfall	0	0	0	0	0	0	0	0	0	0	0	0
Days With Measurable Precip.	6	6	6	6	10	15	16	17	17	14	8	7
Average No. Thunderstorms	1	1	2	4	11	19	22	24	16	6	1	1
SUNSHINE/CLOUDINESS												
No. Clear Days	10	9	9	8	6	3	3	2	2	6	8	9
No. Partly Cloudy Days	13	12	14	15	15	14	17	18	15	14	14	13
No. Cloudy Days	8	7	8	7	10	13	11	11	13	11	8	9
% Possible Sunshine	69	68	77	78	71	74	76	75	72	72	67	65

etc.

- Summers are hot and humid; frequent daytime thunderstorms are often accompanied by rapid drops in temperature that persist for the remainder of the day.
- Summer showers are typically short; rainfall generally extends over less than 10% of the day.

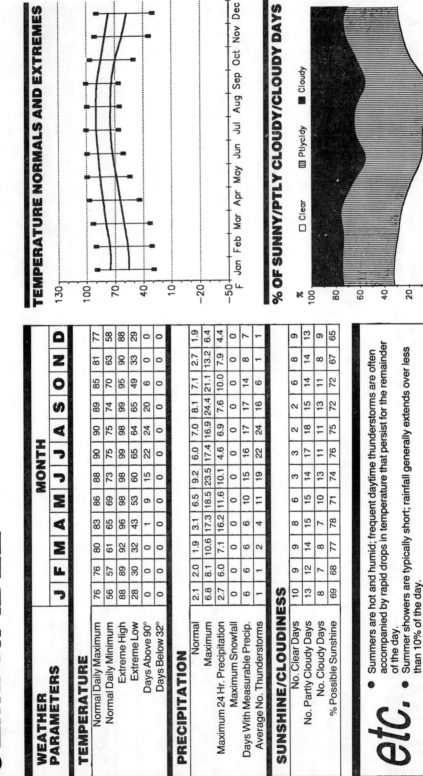

TEMPERATURE NORMALS AND EXTREMES

130
100
70
40
10
-20
-50
F   Jan Feb Mar Apr May Jun Jul Aug Sep Oct Nov Dec

% OF SUNNY/PTLY CLOUDY/CLOUDY DAYS

☐ Clear   ▤ Ptlycldy   ■ Cloudy

%
100
80
60
40
20
0

CLIMATABLE NO. 40

Biscayne NP

WEATHER PARAMETERS

TEMPERATURE

	MONTH											
	J	F	M	A	M	J	J	A	S	O	N	D
Normal Daily Maximum	74	77	80	83	86	87	88	86	83	79	75
Normal Daily Minimum	63	66	71	74	76	78	78	77	74	69	64
Extreme High	86	88	91	94	95	97	98	98	96	93	90	85
Extreme Low	34	38	41	48	61	65	68	68	68	55	39	35
Days Above 90°	0	0	0	1	1	2	3	5	2	0	0	0
Days Below 32°	0	0	0	0	0	0	0	0	0	0	0	0

PRECIPITATION

Normal	2.0	2.1	1.6	2.4	4.3	7.0	4.4	4.3	7.1	6.1	2.5	1.7
Maximum	6.3	7.3	4.3	10.4	11.7	18.9	8.0	14.0	16.0	18.0	10.9	7.8
Maximum 24 Hr. Precipitation	3.1	2.5	1.6	6.9	5.9	6.3	4.9	5.8	8.4	5.3	6.7	3.2
Maximum Snowfall	0	0	0	0	0	0	0	0	0	0	0	0
Days With Measurable Precip.	6	6	6	6	9	12	11	11	12	12	7	6
Average No. Thunderstorms	1	1	2	4	9	17	20	22	14	6	1	1

SUNSHINE/CLOUDINESS

No. Clear Days	10	9	9	8	6	3	3	2	2	6	8	9
No. Partly Cloudy Days	13	12	14	15	15	14	17	18	15	14	14	13
No. Cloudy Days	8	7	8	7	10	13	11	11	13	11	8	9
% Possible Sunshine	69	68	77	78	71	74	76	75	72	72	67	65

etc.
- The intensity of the sunshine in summer can be distressing!
- Daily summer showers are most frequent in the morning; in nearby inland areas, they are more frequent in the afternoon. Total annual rainfall is significantly less along the coast.
- No freezing temperatures have ever been recorded.

TEMPERATURE NORMALS AND EXTREMES

% OF SUNNY/PTLY CLOUDY/CLOUDY DAYS

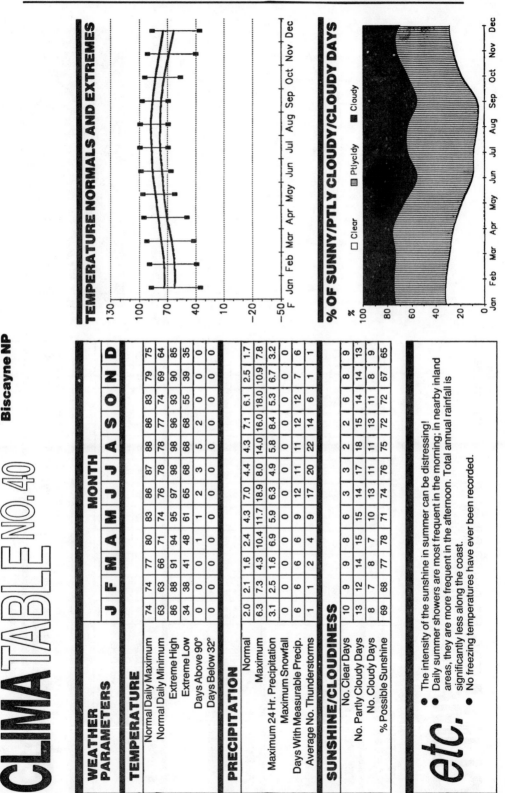

CLIMATABLE NO. 41   Canaveral NS

WEATHER PARAMETERS	MONTH											
	J	F	M	A	M	J	J	A	S	O	N	D
TEMPERATURE												
Normal Daily Maximum	68	69	75	80	85	88	90	89	87	81	75	70
Normal Daily Minimum	47	48	54	59	65	70	72	73	72	65	56	49
Extreme High	86	89	91	96	100	102	102	99	95	89	89	86
Extreme Low	15	24	26	35	44	52	60	55	52	41	27	19
Days Above 90°	0	0	0	2	5	11	16	14	6	1	0	0
Days Below 32°	2	1	0	0	0	0	0	0	0	0	0	2
PRECIPITATION												
Normal	2.4	3.1	3.0	2.2	3.4	6.4	5.5	6.3	6.7	4.6	2.6	2.2
Maximum	7.2	9.1	7.8	7.1	12.3	15.2	14.6	19.9	15.2	13.0	11.0	12.0
Maximum 24 Hr. Precipitation	4.4	4.4	5.7	4.0	4.2	6.3	4.2	4.8	6.3	9.3	5.8	5.2
Maximum Snowfall	0	0	0	0	0	0	0	0	0	0	0	0
Days With Measurable Precip.	7	8	8	6	8	12	14	13	11	11	7	8
Average No. Thunderstorms	1	1	3	4	9	16	19	17	11	4	1	1
SUNSHINE/CLOUDINESS												
No. Clear Days	10	9	10	11	10	6	4	5	5	9	10	9
No. Partly Cloudy Days	9	8	10	11	11	13	15	13	13	11	10	9
No. Cloudy Days	12	11	11	8	10	11	12	11	12	10	10	13
% Possible Sunshine	62	65	68	72	70	68	63	63	58	59	62	60

etc.

- The climate is tempered by the effects of land and sea breezes in this area. Afternoon sea breezes and local thunderstorms limit the occurrences of 90 degree temperatures.
- Tropical storms and hurricanes have not been a great threat to this segment of the Florida coast.

TEMPERATURE NORMALS AND EXTREMES

% OF SUNNY/PTLY CLOUDY/CLOUDY DAYS

☐ Clear   ▦ Ptlycldy   ■ Cloudy

CLIMATABLE NO. 42

Fort Caroline NM, Castillo de San Marcos NM, Fort Matanzas NM

TEMPERATURE NORMALS AND EXTREMES

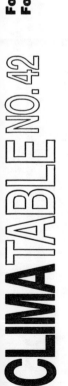

WEATHER PARAMETERS	MONTH											
	J	F	M	A	M	J	J	A	S	O	N	D
TEMPERATURE												
Normal Daily Maximum	66	68	74	80	85	88	90	90	87	80	73	68
Normal Daily Minimum	44	45	51	57	63	69	72	72	70	61	51	45
Extreme High	86	90	91	96	100	103	105	102	100	96	88	85
Extreme Low	7	19	23	33	43	47	60	63	48	36	21	11
Days Above 90°	0	0	0	2	8	14	21	20	9	1	0	0
Days Below 32°	5	3	1	0	0	0	0	0	0	0	1	3
PRECIPITATION												
Normal	3.0	4.0	3.8	2.9	4.3	5.4	6.4	6.8	7.8	4.6	2.4	2.6
Maximum	8.6	10.7	11.0	11.6	10.4	12.9	16.2	19.2	21.8	13.4	10.4	7.1
Maximum 24 Hr. Precipitation	3.0	6.2	7.1	8.2	5.4	5.9	10.1	7.9	10.2	6.7	5.4	3.8
Maximum Snowfall	T	2	T	0	0	0	0	0	0	0	0	T
Days With Measurable Precip.	8	8	8	6	8	12	15	14	13	9	6	8
Average No. Thunderstorms	1	2	5	5	11	16	23	18	10	2	1	1
SUNSHINE/CLOUDINESS												
No. Clear Days	9	9	10	10	9	6	5	5	5	10	11	9
No. Partly Cloudy Days	8	7	9	10	12	13	14	15	12	9	8	8
No. Cloudy Days	14	12	13	10	10	11	12	11	13	12	11	14
% Possible Sunshine	58	62	68	72	70	63	62	60	56	58	60	56

% OF SUNNY/PTLY CLOUDY/CLOUDY DAYS

☐ Clear   ▨ Ptlycldy   ▥ Cloudy   ■ Cloudy

etc.
- Winters are mild, though periodic invasions of cool to cold air are experienced.
- Though temperatures do occasionally fall below freezing in the winter, on most of those days, afternoon temperatures will reach comfortable levels.
- Summers are long, warm and humid.

CLIMATABLE NO. 43

De Soto NM

TEMPERATURE NORMALS AND EXTREMES

% OF SUNNY/PTLY CLOUDY/CLOUDY DAYS

□ Clear   ▦ Ptlycldy   ▨ Cloudy

WEATHER PARAMETERS	MONTH											
	J	F	M	A	M	J	J	A	S	O	N	D
TEMPERATURE												
Normal Daily Maximum	72	74	78	82	87	90	90	90	89	86	78	73
Normal Daily Minimum	51	51	55	59	64	69	71	69	71	65	56	52
Extreme High	91	90	92	93	97	100	99	98	98	96	90	90
Extreme Low	20	21	26	37	44	55	61	62	56	39	27	19
Days Above 90°	0	0	0	1	9	21	22	24	16	1	0	0
Days Below 32°	0	0	0	0	0	0	0	0	0	0	0	0
PRECIPITATION												
Normal	2.5	2.8	2.7	2.3	2.8	7.1	9.6	9.3	7.7	3.3	1.7	2.1
Maximum	7.8	7.3	8.6	9.8	9.7	25.6	24.5	19.7	17.3	12.0	6.8	7.2
Maximum 24 Hr. Precipitation	3.5	4.7	4.7	5.5	4.0	10.8	8.3	8.6	8.0	6.2	4.7	3.0
Maximum Snowfall	0	0	0	0	0	0	0	0	0	0	0	0
Days With Measurable Precip.	5	5	5	4	5	12	15	15	12	6	4	5
Average No. Thunderstorms	1	2	4	4	8	20	31	30	15	3	1	1
SUNSHINE/CLOUDINESS												
No. Clear Days	10	9	11	11	10	5	2	3	4	11	12	10
No. Partly Cloudy Days	10	9	10	11	12	14	16	16	14	11	9	10
No. Cloudy Days	11	10	10	8	9	11	13	12	12	9	9	11
% Possible Sunshine	64	66	72	75	75	67	61	60	61	64	65	61

etc.

- Thunderstorms can be expected everyday in July and August; the duration of the rainfall is short.
- Hurricanes have tended to impact the west coast of Florida late in the season, generally in September or October. However, tropical storms have reached this area anywhere from June to November.

CLIMATABLE NO. 44   Fort Jefferson NM

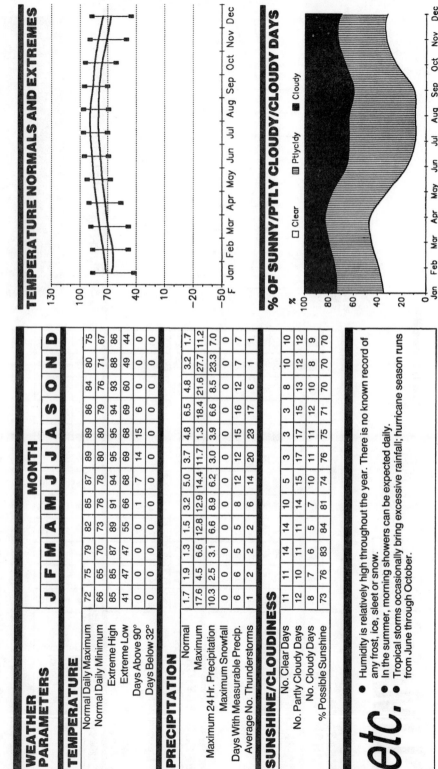

TEMPERATURE NORMALS AND EXTREMES

% OF SUNNY/PTLY CLOUDY/CLOUDY DAYS

WEATHER PARAMETERS	J	F	M	A	M	J	J	A	S	O	N	D
TEMPERATURE												
Normal Daily Maximum	72	75	79	82	85	87	89	89	86	84	80	75
Normal Daily Minimum	66	65	70	73	76	78	80	80	79	76	71	67
Extreme High	85	85	87	89	91	94	95	95	94	93	88	86
Extreme Low	41	47	47	55	66	68	69	68	69	60	49	44
Days Above 90°	0	0	0	0	0	1	7	14	15	6	0	0
Days Below 32°	0	0	0	0	0	0	0	0	0	0	0	0
PRECIPITATION												
Normal	1.7	1.9	1.3	1.5	3.2	5.0	3.7	4.8	6.5	4.8	3.2	1.7
Maximum	17.6	4.5	6.6	12.8	12.9	14.4	11.7	1.3	18.4	21.6	27.7	11.2
Maximum 24 Hr. Precipitation	10.3	2.5	3.1	6.6	8.9	6.2	3.0	3.9	6.6	8.5	23.3	7.0
Maximum Snowfall	0	0	0	0	0	0	0	0	0	0	0	0
Days With Measurable Precip.	6	6	5	5	8	12	12	15	16	12	7	7
Average No. Thunderstorms	1	2	2	2	6	14	20	23	17	6	1	1
SUNSHINE/CLOUDINESS												
No. Clear Days	11	11	14	14	10	5	3	3	3	8	10	10
No. Partly Cloudy Days	12	10	11	11	14	15	17	17	15	13	12	12
No. Cloudy Days	8	7	6	5	7	10	11	11	12	10	8	9
% Possible Sunshine	73	76	83	84	81	74	76	75	71	70	70	70

etc.:
- Humidity is relatively high throughout the year. There is no known record of any frost, ice, sleet or snow.
- In the summer, morning showers can be expected daily.
- Tropical storms occasionally bring excessive rainfall; hurricane season runs from June through October.

CLIMATABLE NO. 45

Gulf Islands NS

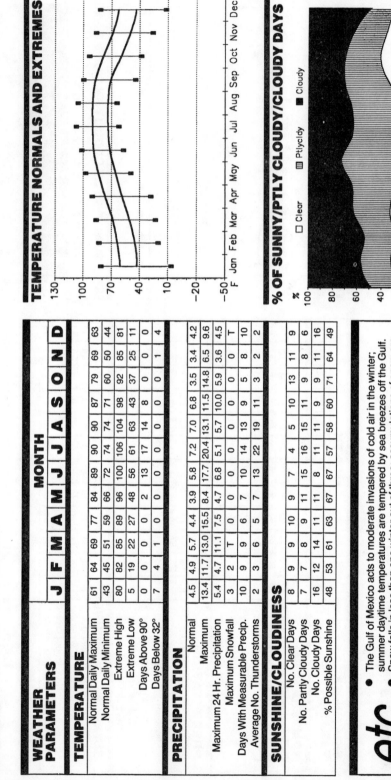

TEMPERATURE NORMALS AND EXTREMES

% OF SUNNY/PTLY CLOUDY/CLOUDY DAYS

☐ Clear   ▦ Ptlycldy   ■ Cloudy

WEATHER PARAMETERS	J	F	M	A	M	J	J	A	S	O	N	D
TEMPERATURE												
Normal Daily Maximum	61	64	69	77	84	89	90	90	87	79	69	63
Normal Daily Minimum	43	45	51	59	66	72	74	74	71	60	50	44
Extreme High	80	82	85	89	96	100	106	104	98	92	85	81
Extreme Low	5	19	22	27	48	56	61	63	43	37	25	11
Days Above 90°	0	0	0	0	2	13	17	14	8	0	0	0
Days Below 32°	7	4	1	0	0	0	0	0	0	0	1	4
PRECIPITATION												
Normal	4.5	4.9	5.7	4.4	3.9	5.8	7.2	7.0	6.8	3.5	3.4	4.2
Maximum	13.4	11.7	13.0	15.5	8.4	17.7	20.4	13.1	11.5	14.8	6.5	9.6
Maximum 24 Hr. Precipitation	5.4	4.7	11.1	7.5	4.7	6.8	5.1	5.7	10.0	5.9	3.6	4.5
Maximum Snowfall	3	2	T	0	0	0	0	0	0	0	0	T
Days With Measurable Precip.	10	9	9	6	7	10	14	13	9	5	8	10
Average No. Thunderstorms	2	3	6	5	7	13	22	19	11	3	2	2
SUNSHINE/CLOUDINESS												
No. Clear Days	8	9	9	10	9	7	4	5	10	13	11	9
No. Partly Cloudy Days	7	7	8	9	11	15	16	15	11	9	8	6
No. Cloudy Days	16	12	14	11	11	8	11	11	9	9	11	16
% Possible Sunshine	48	53	61	63	67	67	57	58	60	71	64	49

etc.

- The Gulf of Mexico acts to moderate invasions of cold air in the winter; summer daytime temperatures are tempered by sea breezes off the Gulf. Snow falls in less than one winter out of three; accumulations of snow are even more rare.
- Heavy fog is experienced on about 35 days/year.

CLIMATABLE NO. 46

Ocmulgee NM, Andersonville NHS

TEMPERATURE NORMALS AND EXTREMES

WEATHER PARAMETERS	J	F	M	A	M	J	J	A	S	O	N	D
MONTH												
TEMPERATURE												
Normal Daily Maximum	58	62	69	79	85	90	91	91	87	78	69	61
Normal Daily Minimum	37	38	45	53	61	67	70	69	65	53	43	38
Extreme High	84	85	95	96	100	106	108	105	102	100	90	82
Extreme Low	−6	9	14	31	40	46	54	55	35	26	10	2
Days Above 90°	0	0	0	1	6	18	22	21	12	1	0	0
Days Below 32°	15	11	4	0	0	0	0	0	0	0	5	11
PRECIPITATION												
Normal	4.5	4.7	5.1	3.7	3.8	4.1	4.9	3.9	3.6	2.0	2.5	4.1
Maximum	13.7	9.3	11.9	8.4	11.8	9.1	13.6	11.2	11.5	9.4	9.4	12.3
Maximum 24 Hr. Precipitation	4.9	5.2	4.2	3.6	5.4	5.0	5.3	3.5	5.2	5.4	3.5	4.7
Maximum Snowfall	4	2	0	0	0	0	0	0	0	0	T	T
Days With Measurable Precip.	10	10	11	7	9	10	13	10	8	6	7	9
Average No. Thunderstorms	2	3	4	6	9	13	18	13	4	1	1	1
SUNSHINE/CLOUDINESS												
No. Clear Days	9	8	9	11	9	8	5	9	9	14	12	10
No. Partly Cloudy Days	7	7	8	8	11	11	13	12	10	7	6	7
No. Cloudy Days	15	13	14	11	11	13	13	10	11	10	12	14
% Possible Sunshine	55	60	64	70	71	70	65	70	65	69	63	57

% OF SUNNY/PTLY CLOUDY/CLOUDY DAYS

☐ Clear   ▥ Ptlycldy   ▦ Cloudy

etc.
- Autumn is characterized by long periods of mild, sunny weather; October is the driest month.
- Snowfalls are generally light and of little significance.
- Daytime temperatures in winter almost always move above freezing.

CLIMATABLE NO. 47

Chattahoochee River NRA, Kennesaw Mountain NBP, Martin Luther King NHS

WEATHER PARAMETERS	J	F	M	A	M	J	J	A	S	O	N	D
TEMPERATURE												
Normal Daily Maximum	51	55	63	73	80	86	88	88	82	73	63	54
Normal Daily Minimum	33	34	42	50	59	66	69	69	64	51	41	35
Extreme High	79	79	85	93	95	101	105	102	98	95	84	77
Extreme Low	-8	5	10	26	37	46	53	55	36	28	0	0
Days Above 90°	0	0	0	0	0	1	7	8	3	0	0	0
Days Below 32°	18	14	6	0	0	0	0	0	0	0	5	14
PRECIPITATION												
Normal	4.9	4.4	5.9	4.4	4.0	3.4	4.7	3.4	3.2	2.5	3.4	4.2
Maximum	10.8	12.8	11.7	11.9	8.4	7.5	11.3	8.7	7.5	7.5	15.7	9.9
Maximum 24 Hr. Precipitation	3.9	5.7	5.1	5.6	5.1	3.4	5.4	5.1	5.5	3.9	4.1	3.8
Maximum Snowfall	8	4	8	T	0	0	0	0	0	0	1	2
Days With Measurable Precip.	11	10	11	9	9	10	12	10	8	6	8	10
Average No. Thunderstorms	2	2	5	5	8	11	14	9	3	1	1	1
SUNSHINE/CLOUDINESS												
No. Clear Days	9	8	9	10	9	8	6	7	10	14	12	9
No. Partly Cloudy Days	6	6	7	8	10	12	13	13	10	7	6	7
No. Cloudy Days	16	14	15	12	12	10	12	11	10	10	12	15
% Possible Sunshine	49	54	58	66	68	67	63	64	67	59	51	

etc.

- Summers are rather warm though prolonged periods of hot weather are unusual; temperatures of 100 degrees are rare.
- Winters are mild; cold spells are short-lived.
- Ice storms can be expected to occur in two out of every three winters. When snow falls and accumulates, it melts very quickly.

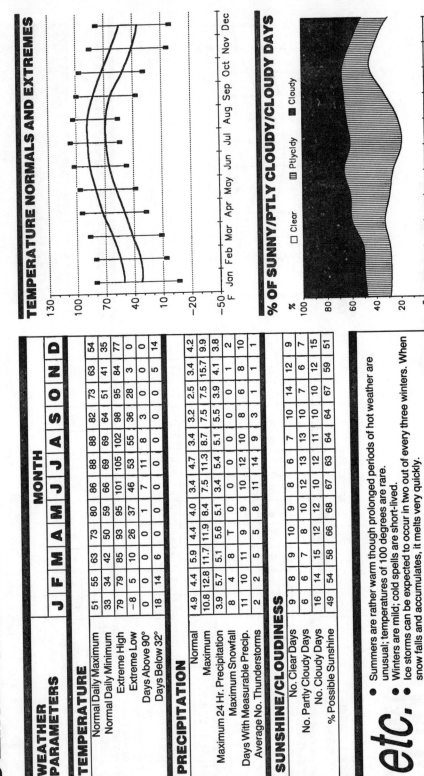

TEMPERATURE NORMALS AND EXTREMES

(130, 100, 70, 40, 10, −20, −50 — Jan Feb Mar Apr May Jun Jul Aug Sep Oct Nov Dec)

% OF SUNNY/PTLY CLOUDY/CLOUDY DAYS

☐ Clear ▨ Ptlycldy ■ Cloudy

(%: 100, 80, 60, 40, 20, 0 — Jan Feb Mar Apr May Jun Jul Aug Sep Oct Nov Dec)

CLIMATABLE NO. 48

Chickamauga & Chattanooga NMP

TEMPERATURE NORMALS AND EXTREMES

% OF SUNNY/PTLY CLOUDY/CLOUDY DAYS

□ Clear   ▦ Ptlycldy   ▩ Cloudy

WEATHER PARAMETERS	J	F	M	A	M	J	J	A	S	O	N	D
TEMPERATURE												
Normal Daily Maximum	48	53	61	73	80	86	89	89	83	72	60	51
Normal Daily Minimum	29	31	39	48	56	64	68	67	62	48	38	32
Extreme High	78	82	87	93	99	104	106	105	104	95	84	81
Extreme Low	−12	−6	8	22	29	37	47	47	29	19	4	−2
Days Above 90°	0	0	0	0	3	10	16	14	5	0	0	0
Days Below 32°	20	16	9	1	0	0	0	0	0	1	10	18
PRECIPITATION												
Normal	5.2	4.7	6.3	4.6	4.0	3.3	4.6	3.4	4.3	2.9	4.2	5.1
Maximum	12.3	11.0	16.3	11.9	9.2	9.4	11.8	7.5	14.2	9.9	13.6	13.7
Maximum 24 Hr. Precipitation	4.4	3.9	6.5	3.4	3.5	4.8	5.8	3.7	6.6	4.0	4.6	5.2
Maximum Snowfall	8	10	10	1	T	0	0	0	0	T	3	9
Days With Measurable Precip.	12	10	12	10	10	10	12	10	8	7	9	11
Average No. Thunderstorms	2	3	6	7	10	13	15	12	5	2	2	1
SUNSHINE/CLOUDINESS												
No. Clear Days	7	7	8	9	9	8	7	8	10	13	10	8
No. Partly Cloudy Days	7	6	8	8	10	12	13	13	10	8	7	6
No. Cloudy Days	17	15	15	13	12	10	11	10	10	10	13	17
% Possible Sunshine	43	49	52	61	65	65	61	62	64	62	52	44

etc.

- Winters are quite cold, but many days are warm enough for outdoor activities.
- Freezing rain or ice storms are not uncommon in the winter.
- Some heavy snowfalls have occurred, but accumulations rarely remain on the ground for more than a few days.
- The sunniest time of the year is the fall.

CLIMATABLE NO. 49

Fort Pulaski NM, Fort Frederica NM, Cumberland Is. NS

TEMPERATURE NORMALS AND EXTREMES

% OF SUNNY/PTLY CLOUDY/CLOUDY DAYS

☐ Clear   ▦ Ptlycldy   ■ Cloudy

WEATHER PARAMETERS	J	F	M	A	M	J	J	A	S	O	N	D
TEMPERATURE												
Normal Daily Maximum	62	64	69	76	83	88	89	89	85	77	70	62
Normal Daily Minimum	43	45	50	58	66	72	74	74	71	61	51	43
Extreme High	81	85	89	94	100	102	100	100	97	94	89	80
Extreme Low	20	18	26	36	46	58	64	62	50	37	21	14
Days Above 90°	0	0	0	0	4	10	15	15	4	1	0	0
Days Below 32°	5	3	1	0	0	0	0	0	0	0	1	5
PRECIPITATION												
Normal	2.5	3.1	3.8	3.4	3.1	5.6	5.9	5.3	10.3	4.8	2.2	2.5
Maximum	8.1	6.9	9.3	7.2	7.3	12.4	12.4	17.3	21.2	11.7	7.4	5.7
Maximum 24 Hr. Precipitation	2.8	2.4	2.9	4.4	3.3	4.5	4.8	3.8	9.8	4.9	5.9	2.0
Maximum Snowfall	2	4	0	0	0	0	0	0	0	0	0	T
Days With Measurable Precip.	8	8	9	7	8	11	13	11	12	7	7	8
Average No. Thunderstorms	1	1	4	5	11	14	21	17	8	2	1	1
SUNSHINE/CLOUDINESS												
No. Clear Days	10	9	9	11	9	7	5	6	6	12	11	9
No. Partly Cloudy Days	6	6	9	8	10	11	14	13	11	8	7	7
No. Cloudy Days	15	13	13	11	12	12	12	13	13	11	12	15
% Possible Sunshine	55	58	62	70	67	65	62	62	58	63	61	55

etc. :
- Outdoor recreational activities can usually be enjoyed throughout the winter; on 90% of winter days, the temperature rises above 50 degrees.
- November is the driest month.
- Historically, the full force of hurricanes and tropical storms has seldom been felt; main effect has been heavy rain.

CLIMATABLE NO. 50   Haleakala NP

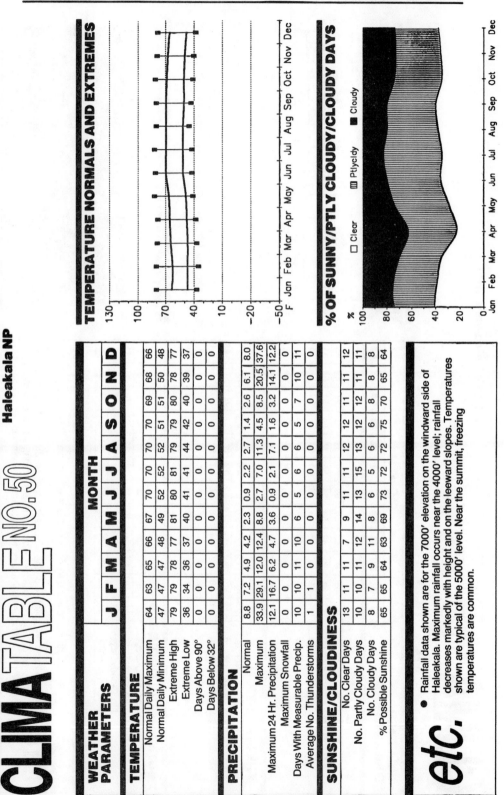

TEMPERATURE NORMALS AND EXTREMES

% OF SUNNY/PTLY CLOUDY/CLOUDY DAYS

☐ Clear   ▦ Pttlycldy   ▪ Cloudy

WEATHER PARAMETERS	J	F	M	A	M	J	J	A	S	O	N	D
TEMPERATURE												
Normal Daily Maximum	64	63	65	66	67	70	70	70	70	69	68	66
Normal Daily Minimum	47	47	47	48	49	52	52	52	51	51	50	48
Extreme High	79	79	78	77	81	80	81	79	79	80	78	77
Extreme Low	36	34	36	37	40	41	41	44	42	40	39	37
Days Above 90°	0	0	0	0	0	0	0	0	0	0	0	0
Days Below 32°	0	0	0	0	0	0	0	0	0	0	0	0
PRECIPITATION												
Normal	8.8	7.2	4.9	4.2	2.3	0.9	2.2	2.7	1.4	2.6	6.1	8.0
Maximum	33.9	29.1	12.0	12.4	8.8	2.7	7.0	11.3	4.5	8.5	20.5	37.6
Maximum 24 Hr. Precipitation	12.1	16.7	6.2	4.7	3.6	0.9	2.1	7.1	1.6	3.2	14.1	12.2
Maximum Snowfall	0	0	0	0	0	0	0	0	0	0	0	0
Days With Measurable Precip.	10	10	11	10	6	5	6	6	5	7	10	11
Average No. Thunderstorms	1	1	0	0	0	0	0	0	0	0	0	0
SUNSHINE/CLOUDINESS												
No. Clear Days	13	11	11	7	9	11	11	12	11	11	11	12
No. Partly Cloudy Days	10	10	11	12	14	13	15	13	12	12	11	11
No. Cloudy Days	8	7	9	11	8	6	5	6	8	8	8	8
% Possible Sunshine	65	65	64	63	69	73	72	72	75	70	65	64

etc.

- Rainfall data shown are for the 7000' elevation on the windward side of Haleakala. Maximum rainfall occurs near the 4000' level; rainfall decreases markedly with height and on the leeward slopes. Temperatures shown are typical of the 5000' level. Near the summit, freezing temperatures are common.

CLIMATABLE NO. 51

Hawaii Volcanoes NP

WEATHER PARAMETERS	MONTH											
	J	F	M	A	M	J	J	A	S	O	N	D
TEMPERATURE												
Normal Daily Maximum	66	65	66	66	68	69	70	71	71	71	68	66
Normal Daily Minimum	50	50	50	52	53	54	55	55	54	54	53	51
Extreme High	77	81	77	76	83	83	85	81	85	80	79	75
Extreme Low	39	37	38	42	44	46	48	44	45	45	44	40
Days Above 90°	0	0	0	0	0	0	0	0	0	0	0	0
Days Below 32°	0	0	0	0	0	0	0	0	0	0	0	0
PRECIPITATION												
Normal	12.1	10.3	11.9	10.9	8.0	4.2	4.9	7.2	4.5	6.5	12.9	12.3
Maximum	34.6	28.4	28.4	33.8	23.4	8.7	9.4	17.2	7.5	24.2	26.1	34.3
Maximum 24 Hr. Precipitation	10.5	4.8	5.2	7.4	4.8	3.6	3.7	11.0	4.2	10.0	11.7	9.4
Maximum Snowfall	0	0	0	0	0	0	0	0	0	0	0	0
Days With Measurable Precip.	17	18	24	25	25	24	27	26	23	24	23	21
Average No. Thunderstorms	1	1	2	1	1	0	0	0	0	1	1	1
SUNSHINE/CLOUDINESS												
No. Clear Days	7	5	3	1	1	2	1	1	3	3	3	5
No. Partly Cloudy Days	11	10	10	8	10	11	12	12	12	12	11	11
No. Cloudy Days	13	13	18	21	20	17	18	18	15	16	16	15
% Possible Sunshine	47	45	40	35	37	43	42	42	44	39	35	38

etc.

- Precipitation amounts are very sensitive to elevation and exposure to the trade winds.
- Maximum precipitation on the windward slopes occurs at elevations between 2000 and 4000 feet. Near the peaks, rainfall is scarce, humidity is very low, and below-freezing temperatures are common.

TEMPERATURE NORMALS AND EXTREMES

F Jan Feb Mar Apr May Jun Jul Aug Sep Oct Nov Dec

% OF SUNNY/PTLY CLOUDY/CLOUDY DAYS

☐ Clear   ▦ Ptlycldy   ■ Cloudy

CLIMATABLE NO. 52

Kalaupapa NHS

WEATHER PARAMETERS

	J	F	M	A	M	J	J	A	S	O	N	D
TEMPERATURE												
Normal Daily Maximum	80	80	81	82	84	86	86	87	88	86	84	81
Normal Daily Minimum	63	63	65	66	67	69	70	71	70	69	68	65
Extreme High	89	88	90	91	92	93	94	96	95	96	93	90
Extreme Low	48	50	55	54	57	58	58	61	60	58	55	52
Days Above 90°	0	0	0	0	1	2	4	7	8	5	1	0
Days Below 32°	0	0	0	0	0	0	0	0	0	0	0	0
PRECIPITATION												
Normal	4.2	3.3	3.0	1.2	0.7	0.3	0.4	0.5	0.4	0.9	2.3	2.8
Maximum	14.5	8.3	10.9	4.0	2.7	2.5	1.1	1.5	1.2	5.7	9.3	9.5
Maximum 24 Hr. Precipitation	7.0	5.0	5.4	2.2	2.0	2.4	0.8	1.2	1.2	4.8	5.5	5.8
Maximum Snowfall	0	0	0	0	0	0	0	0	0	0	0	0
Days With Measurable Precip.	10	10	11	10	6	5	6	6	5	7	10	11
Average No. Thunderstorms	1	1	0	0	0	0	0	0	0	0	0	0
SUNSHINE/CLOUDINESS												
No. Clear Days	13	11	11	7	9	11	11	12	12	11	11	12
No. Partly Cloudy Days	10	10	11	12	14	13	15	13	12	12	11	11
No. Cloudy Days	8	7	9	11	8	6	5	6	6	8	8	8
% Possible Sunshine	65	65	64	63	69	73	72	72	75	70	65	64

etc.

- This area is subject to frequent trade wind showers in the summer. It is not unusual to experience 8 to 10 brief showers in a day, none of which would produce more than 0.01" of rain.

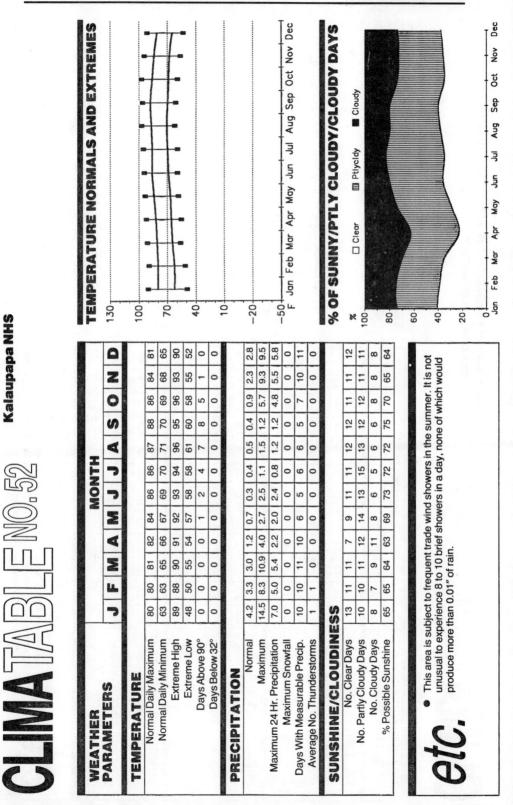

TEMPERATURE NORMALS AND EXTREMES

% OF SUNNY/PTLY CLOUDY/CLOUDY DAYS

☐ Clear   ▦ Ptlycldy   ■ Cloudy

CLIMATABLE NO. 53

Puukohola Heiau NHS, Kaloko-Honokohau NHP
Pu'uhonua o Honaunau NHP

WEATHER PARAMETERS	MONTH											
	J	F	M	A	M	J	J	A	S	O	N	D
TEMPERATURE												
Normal Daily Maximum	76	77	77	77	77	79	79	80	80	80	79	77
Normal Daily Minimum	63	63	64	66	67	67	68	68	68	67	66	64
Extreme High	83	88	85	88	86	88	89	91	91	91	88	86
Extreme Low	49	48	52	53	54	57	58	58	58	58	56	50
Days Above 90°	0	0	0	0	0	0	0	0	0	0	0	0
Days Below 32°	0	0	0	0	0	0	0	0	0	0	0	0
PRECIPITATION												
Normal	5.3	3.0	4.7	5.6	6.7	6.4	8.0	7.4	7.2	5.3	4.0	3.5
Maximum	19.0	9.5	14.5	12.1	11.5	13.3	14.0	13.1	15.4	10.5	11.4	8.3
Maximum 24 Hr. Precipitation	6.0	2.9	5.2	3.8	2.4	2.5	3.4	5.0	5.0	4.4	3.1	2.7
Maximum Snowfall	0	0	0	0	0	0	0	0	0	0	0	0
Days With Measurable Precip.	10	9	11	14	17	17	18	17	18	13	10	9
Average No. Thunderstorms	NA	NA	NA	NA	NA	NA	NA	NA	NA	NA	NA	NA
SUNSHINE/CLOUDINESS												
No. Clear Days	NA	NA	NA	NA	NA	NA	NA	NA	NA	NA	NA	NA
No. Partly Cloudy Days	NA	NA	NA	NA	NA	NA	NA	NA	NA	NA	NA	NA
No. Cloudy Days	NA	NA	NA	NA	NA	NA	NA	NA	NA	NA	NA	NA
% Possible Sunshine	NA	NA	NA	NA	NA	NA	NA	NA	NA	NA	NA	NA

TEMPERATURE NORMALS AND EXTREMES

etc.

- The Kona coast of Hawaii is unique in the islands in that the summer is the rainy season.
- Daytime skies are likely clear 60% of the time in the winter and 30% of the time in the summer. However, there are no cloudiness/sunshine summaries available that properly represent the Kona coast.

CLIMATABLE NO. 54

Nez Perce NHP, Lewis and Clark NHT

TEMPERATURE NORMALS AND EXTREMES

% OF SUNNY/PTLY CLOUDY/CLOUDY DAYS

□ Clear ▦ Ptlycldy ■ Cloudy

WEATHER PARAMETERS	MONTH											
	J	F	M	A	M	J	J	A	S	O	N	D
TEMPERATURE												
Normal Daily Maximum	38	47	54	64	74	81	92	91	80	64	47	39
Normal Daily Minimum	24	28	30	36	43	49	52	51	44	37	31	27
Extreme High	67	69	82	97	101	105	112	116	107	92	71	62
Extreme Low	-20	-8	-1	20	24	30	36	34	25	9	-10	-16
Days Above 90°	0	0	0	0	2	6	21	19	6	0	0	0
Days Below 32°	26	21	19	8	2	0	0	0	2	9	17	25
PRECIPITATION												
Normal	2.2	1.6	2.2	2.9	3.0	2.8	0.7	1.1	1.7	2.5	2.2	2.1
Maximum	4.8	3.5	4.3	5.3	6.1	5.5	2.2	3.2	5.0	5.2	3.9	4.6
Maximum 24 Hr. Precipitation	1.0	1.0	1.2	1.5	1.7	1.7	1.2	2.0	1.3	1.8	1.1	1.2
Maximum Snowfall	32	20	11	4	0	0	0	0	0	3	20	22
Days With Measurable Precip.	12	10	10	10	9	8	4	4	6	8	10	12
Average No. Thunderstorms	0	0	0	0	3	5	5	5	2	0	0	0
SUNSHINE/CLOUDINESS												
No. Clear Days	3	3	4	4	6	9	19	16	13	9	3	3
No. Partly Cloudy Days	4	4	6	7	9	9	7	8	7	7	5	4
No. Cloudy Days	24	21	21	19	16	13	5	7	10	15	22	24
% Possible Sunshine	28	35	50	60	63	70	82	81	75	60	35	20

etc.

- This area shows a very distinct wintertime maximum of precipitation and a summer dry season.
- Periods of extreme heat or extreme cold extending beyond a week are quite rare.
- Area is susceptible to flash flooding from heavy downpours asssociated with thunderstorms.

CLIMATABLE NO. 55

USS Arizona Memorial

WEATHER PARAMETERS	J	F	M	A	M	J	J	A	S	O	N	D
TEMPERATURE												
Normal Daily Maximum	80	80	81	83	85	86	87	88	88	87	84	81
Normal Daily Minimum	65	65	67	69	70	72	73	74	73	72	69	66
Extreme High	87	88	88	89	90	91	92	93	94	94	93	89
Extreme Low	53	53	55	57	60	65	67	67	66	64	58	54
Days Above 90°	0	0	0	0	0	1	3	8	8	4	0	0
Days Below 32°	0	0	0	0	0	0	0	0	0	0	0	0
PRECIPITATION												
Normal	3.8	2.7	3.5	1.5	1.2	0.5	0.5	0.6	0.6	1.9	3.2	3.4
Maximum	14.7	13.7	20.8	8.9	7.2	2.5	2.0	2.7	3.1	11.2	14.7	12.1
Maximum 24 Hr. Precipitation	6.7	6.9	17.1	4.2	3.4	2.3	1.4	1.4	2.4	7.6	9.2	8.1
Maximum Snowfall	0	0	0	0	0	0	0	0	0	0	0	0
Days With Measurable Precip.	10	9	9	9	7	6	8	6	7	9	9	10
Average No. Thunderstorms	1	1	1	1	0	0	0	0	0	1	1	1
SUNSHINE/CLOUDINESS												
No. Clear Days	9	7	7	5	6	6	8	8	8	8	7	9
No. Partly Cloudy Days	13	13	14	14	15	17	18	17	16	15	14	13
No. Cloudy Days	9	8	10	11	10	7	5	6	6	8	9	9
% Possible Sunshine	62	64	68	67	69	70	73	75	75	68	61	59

TEMPERATURE NORMALS AND EXTREMES

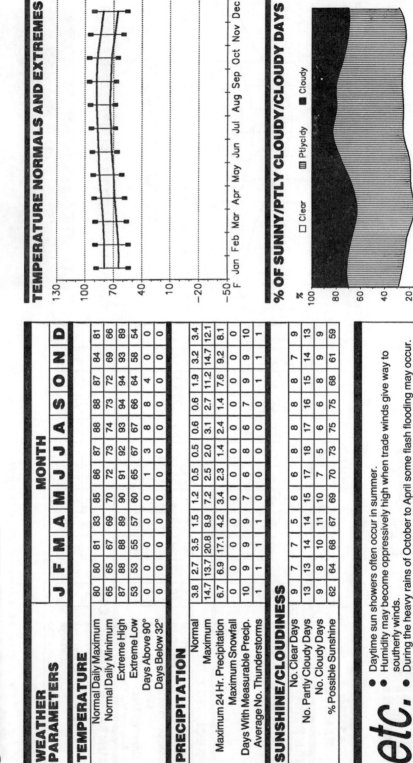

% OF SUNNY/PTLY CLOUDY/CLOUDY DAYS

☐ Clear ▦ Ptlycldy ■ Cloudy

etc.

- Daytime sun showers often occur in summer.
- Humidity may become oppressively high when trade winds give way to southerly winds.
- During the heavy rains of October to April some flash flooding may occur. Honolulu has the highest average winter temperature, 73 degrees, in the United States.

CLIMATABLE NO. 56

Craters of the Moon NM

TEMPERATURE NORMALS AND EXTREMES

% OF SUNNY/PTLY CLOUDY/CLOUDY DAYS

☐ Clear   ▥ Ptlycldy   ■ Cloudy

WEATHER PARAMETERS	MONTH											
	J	F	M	A	M	J	J	A	S	O	N	D
TEMPERATURE												
Normal Daily Maximum	28	35	42	56	67	76	85	83	74	62	43	32
Normal Daily Minimum	3	9	17	27	36	43	48	45	37	28	18	7
Extreme High	52	58	71	82	90	95	102	100	94	82	69	59
Extreme Low	−31	−27	−19	5	11	21	30	26	16	8	−21	−37
Days Above 90°	0	0	0	0	0	2	8	5	0	0	0	0
Days Below 32°	31	28	30	24	8	2	0	1	7	22	29	31
PRECIPITATION												
Normal	1.0	0.8	0.6	0.7	1.2	1.3	0.6	0.8	0.7	0.4	0.7	1.1
Maximum	4.8	2.3	2.2	2.4	4.2	4.1	1.4	3.9	2.3	1.8	1.6	4.3
Maximum 24 Hr. Precipitation	1.0	0.8	1.2	0.7	1.9	2.2	1.0	1.6	1.3	0.9	0.9	1.0
Maximum Snowfall	40	22	17	5	6	0	0	0	T	6	17	35
Days With Measurable Precip.	12	10	10	8	9	7	4	5	5	5	9	11
Average No. Thunderstorms	0	0	0	1	5	6	7	7	3	1	0	0
SUNSHINE/CLOUDINESS												
No. Clear Days	3	4	5	6	8	12	18	15	15	12	5	3
No. Partly Cloudy Days	6	6	8	8	10	9	9	11	8	8	7	7
No. Cloudy Days	22	18	18	16	13	9	4	5	7	11	18	21
% Possible Sunshine	39	52	61	65	67	74	82	80	78	70	47	39

etc.

- Daytime temperatures above 90 degrees are common in July and August; discomfort is tempered by the low humidity.
- Winter temperatures can be bitterly cold with dangerous wind chill temperatures.
- This area borders on the driest region of Idaho.

CLIMATABLE NO. 57   Chicago Portage NHS

TEMPERATURE NORMALS AND EXTREMES

% OF SUNNY/PTLY CLOUDY/CLOUDY DAYS

□ Clear   ▦ Ptlycldy   ■ Cloudy

WEATHER PARAMETERS	MONTH											
	J	F	M	A	M	J	J	A	S	O	N	D
TEMPERATURE												
Normal Daily Maximum	32	35	45	59	70	81	84	83	76	65	48	35
Normal Daily Minimum	17	20	29	40	50	60	65	64	56	46	33	22
Extreme High	67	75	83	88	95	104	103	101	101	94	81	71
Extreme Low	−19	−15	−7	16	29	35	46	43	34	20	−2	−14
Days Above 90°	0	0	0	0	1	5	8	5	2	0	0	0
Days Below 32°	25	28	20	5	1	0	0	0	0	2	14	25
PRECIPITATION												
Normal	1.8	1.6	2.7	3.8	3.4	4.0	4.1	3.1	3.0	2.6	2.2	2.1
Maximum	4.1	3.4	5.4	8.3	7.6	8.9	9.0	9.7	14.2	12.1	5.0	6.7
Maximum 24 Hr. Precipitation	2.9	1.5	2.5	4.1	3.6	4.6	6.2	3.8	4.2	5.6	2.9	2.8
Maximum Snowfall	32	22	22	11	T	0	0	0	0	4	14	33
Days With Measurable Precip.	11	10	13	13	12	10	9	8	9	8	10	11
Average No. Thunderstorms	0	1	4	7	7	11	11	9	7	6	2	1
SUNSHINE/CLOUDINESS												
No. Clear Days	7	7	5	6	8	8	10	10	11		6	6
No. Partly Cloudy Days	6	5	9	9	9	10	12	10	8		7	6
No. Cloudy Days	18	16	17	15	14	12	9	9	10	12	17	19
% Possible Sunshine	44	47	51	54	61	67	70	68	63	61	41	38

etc.

- Summer temperatures are often modified by a lake breeze, especially early in the season when the lake waters are relatively cold; night temperatures are warmer near the lake.
- Winter "lake effect" snow squalls can be locally heavy.
- The nickname "windy city" is a misnomer for Chicago though some channeling of the wind through downtown "canyons" does occur.

CLIMATABLE NO. 58

Lincoln Home NHS

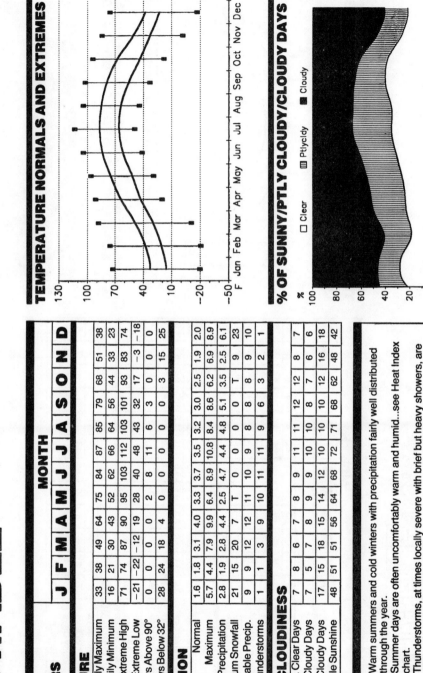

TEMPERATURE NORMALS AND EXTREMES

% OF SUNNY/PTLY CLOUDY/CLOUDY DAYS

□ Clear · ▨ Ptlycldy · ▪ Cloudy

WEATHER PARAMETERS	J	F	M	A	M	J	J	A	S	O	N	D
TEMPERATURE												
Normal Daily Maximum	33	38	49	64	75	84	87	85	79	68	51	38
Normal Daily Minimum	16	21	30	43	52	62	66	64	56	44	33	23
Extreme High	71	74	87	90	95	103	112	103	101	93	83	74
Extreme Low	-21	-22	-12	19	28	40	48	43	32	17	-3	-18
Days Above 90°	0	0	0	0	2	8	11	6	3	0	0	0
Days Below 32°	28	24	18	4	0	0	0	0	0	3	15	25
PRECIPITATION												
Normal	1.6	1.8	3.1	4.0	3.3	3.7	3.5	3.2	3.0	2.5	1.9	2.0
Maximum	5.7	4.4	7.9	9.9	6.4	8.9	10.8	8.4	8.6	6.2	6.9	8.9
Maximum 24 Hr. Precipitation	2.8	1.9	2.8	4.4	2.5	4.7	4.4	4.8	5.1	3.5	2.5	6.1
Maximum Snowfall	21	15	20	7	T	0	0	0	0	T	9	23
Days With Measurable Precip.	9	9	12	12	11	10	9	8	8	8	9	10
Average No. Thunderstorms	1	1	3	9	10	11	11	9	6	3	2	1
SUNSHINE/CLOUDINESS												
No. Clear Days	7	8	6	7	7	8	9	11	12	12	8	7
No. Partly Cloudy Days	7	5	7	8	8	9	10	10	8	7	6	6
No. Cloudy Days	17	15	18	15	14	12	10	10	10	12	16	18
% Possible Sunshine	48	51	51	56	64	68	72	71	68	62	48	42

etc.

- Warm summers and cold winters with precipitation fairly well distributed through the year.
- Summer days are often uncomfortably warm and humid...see Heat Index chart.
- Thunderstorms, at times locally severe with brief but heavy showers, are common during hot weather.

CLIMATABLE NO. 59

Herbert Hoover NHS, Mormon Pioneer NHT

TEMPERATURE NORMALS AND EXTREMES

% OF SUNNY/PTLY CLOUDY/CLOUDY DAYS

Clear □   Ptlycldy ▦   Cloudy ■

WEATHER PARAMETERS	MONTH											
	J	F	M	A	M	J	J	A	S	O	N	D
TEMPERATURE												
Normal Daily Maximum	29	35	46	63	74	83	87	85	78	67	49	35
Normal Daily Minimum	10	16	26	39	50	60	64	62	53	42	29	18
Extreme High	60	68	82	93	94	99	101	99	99	93	76	66
Extreme Low	-24	-17	-17	16	27	38	45	40	31	12	-6	-20
Days Above 90°	0	0	0	0	1	6	10	7	2	0	0	0
Days Below 32°	30	27	23	7	0	0	0	0	0	5	19	28
PRECIPITATION												
Normal	1.1	1.0	2.4	3.8	3.9	4.3	4.9	3.9	3.5	2.6	1.8	1.4
Maximum	3.6	3.1	5.0	8.3	9.5	8.5	12.0	11.3	10.6	5.6	5.8	4.5
Maximum 24 Hr. Precipitation	2.1	1.4	2.3	4.1	2.2	5.1	6.9	3.5	4.4	2.7	4.7	2.9
Maximum Snowfall	20	17	21	14	0	0	0	0	0	4	12	20
Days With Measurable Precip.	7	7	10	11	12	10	8	8	9	8	7	8
Average No. Thunderstorms	0	1	3	7	9	11	11	9	6	3	1	1
SUNSHINE/CLOUDINESS												
No. Clear Days	8	8	6	7	7	7	10	11	12	8	8	7
No. Partly Cloudy Days	7	6	8	8	10	11	13	11	9	8	7	6
No. Cloudy Days	16	14	17	15	14	12	8	9	10	11	15	18
% Possible Sunshine	53	55	55	60	64	71	77	77	72	71	56	51

etc.

- Winters tend to be mild with infrequent heavy snowfalls. When they do occur, the heaviest snows are most likely in late winter.
- Thunderstorms are frequent in June and July and are occasionally accompanied by hail, high winds, heavy rains or even a tornado.

CLIMATABLE NO. 60

Lincoln Boyhood NM, George Rogers Clark NHP

TEMPERATURE NORMALS AND EXTREMES

% OF SUNNY/PTLY CLOUDY/CLOUDY DAYS

□ Clear   ▤ Ptlycldy   ▨ Cloudy

WEATHER PARAMETERS	J	F	M	A	M	J	J	A	S	O	N	D
TEMPERATURE												
Normal Daily Maximum	39	44	53	66	76	85	88	88	82	70	55	44
Normal Daily Minimum	21	24	33	44	52	62	66	64	57	44	34	26
Extreme High	74	77	82	89	97	105	107	104	106	96	83	72
Extreme Low	-18	-19	-10	18	30	41	46	44	34	19	2	-12
Days Above 90°	0	0	0	0	0	2	9	12	5	1	0	0
Days Below 32°	26	22	17	4	0	0	0	0	0	3	14	23
PRECIPITATION												
Normal	3.2	2.9	4.5	4.4	4.4	4.2	4.3	3.8	3.0	2.5	3.8	3.4
Maximum	8.1	8.1	16.2	14.1	12.1	7.6	13.3	12.4	6.8	6.9	10.0	7.4
Maximum 24 Hr. Precipitation	2.5	2.8	4.0	6.0	5.2	4.0	3.9	4.2	3.6	2.6	3.6	2.7
Maximum Snowfall	27	18	20	4	0	0	0	0	0	0	10	12
Days With Measurable Precip.	10	9	12	12	11	10	9	8	7	7	10	10
Average No. Thunderstorms	2	2	5	7	9	10	10	6	4	3	2	1
SUNSHINE/CLOUDINESS												
No. Clear Days	7	7	7	7	8	8	9	11	12	8	8	7
No. Partly Cloudy Days	5	6	8	8	9	11	12	11	9	8	7	6
No. Cloudy Days	19	15	16	15	14	11	10	9	10	11	15	18
% Possible Sunshine	43	48	55	59	65	72	74	75	70	65	48	41

etc.

- Area experiences large year to year variations in temperature, rainfall and snowfall.
- Located along a frequent path of low pressure centers moving eastward to the Ohio Valley; small variations in storm tracks often result in major differences in the type and amount of winter precipitation.

CLIMATABLE NO. 61

Indiana Dunes NLS

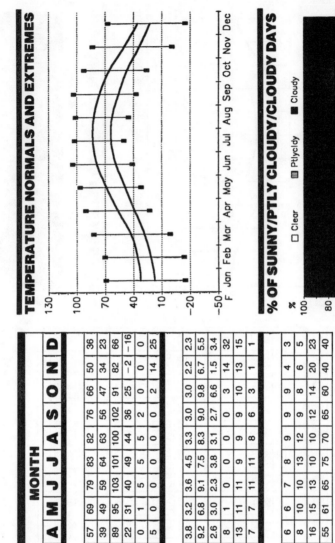

TEMPERATURE NORMALS AND EXTREMES

% OF SUNNY/PTLY CLOUDY/CLOUDY DAYS

☐ Clear   ▤ Ptlycldy   ■ Cloudy

WEATHER PARAMETERS	J	F	M	A	M	J	J	A	S	O	N	D
TEMPERATURE												
Normal Daily Maximum	33	36	43	57	69	79	83	82	76	66	50	36
Normal Daily Minimum	18	22	29	39	49	59	64	63	56	47	34	23
Extreme High	68	69	81	89	95	103	101	100	102	91	82	66
Extreme Low	-16	-15	0	22	31	40	49	44	36	25	-2	-16
Days Above 90°	0	0	0	0	1	5	5	5	2	0	0	0
Days Below 32°	28	25	22	5	0	0	0	0	0	2	14	25
PRECIPITATION												
Normal	2.1	2.1	2.9	3.8	3.2	3.6	4.5	3.3	3.0	3.0	2.2	2.3
Maximum	5.3	5.2	8.0	9.2	6.8	9.1	7.5	8.3	9.0	9.8	6.7	5.5
Maximum 24 Hr. Precipitation	2.2	2.0	1.6	2.6	3.0	2.3	3.8	3.1	2.7	6.6	1.5	3.4
Maximum Snowfall	29	20	20	8	1	0	0	0	0	3	14	32
Days With Measurable Precip.	16	13	14	13	11	11	9	9	9	10	13	15
Average No. Thunderstorms	1	1	3	7	7	11	11	8	6	3	1	1
SUNSHINE/CLOUDINESS												
No. Clear Days	3	4	5	6	6	7	8	9	9	9	4	3
No. Partly Cloudy Days	6	5	7	8	10	10	13	12	9	8	6	5
No. Cloudy Days	22	19	19	16	15	13	10	10	12	14	20	23
% Possible Sunshine	40	45	55	55	61	65	75	70	65	60	40	40

etc.

- Climate is moderated by Lake Michigan, especially in the spring and fall. In the spring, lake breezes keep the temperatures cool; in the fall, the onset of freezing temperatures is delayed.
- The snowfall here is much less than occurs in the area just to the east of the lake shore.

CLIMATABLE NO. 62

Effigy Mounds NM

TEMPERATURE NORMALS AND EXTREMES

% OF SUNNY/PTLY CLOUDY/CLOUDY DAYS

☐ Clear ▦ Pt'ly cldy ■ Cloudy

WEATHER PARAMETERS	J	F	M	A	M	J	J	A	S	O	N	D
TEMPERATURE												
Normal Daily Maximum	27	33	44	61	73	82	86	84	76	64	47	33
Normal Daily Minimum	7	12	23	37	48	58	62	60	52	41	28	16
Extreme High	55	62	80	96	94	100	105	102	99	93	75	62
Extreme Low	-37	-30	-33	0	25	37	43	38	27	16	-17	-25
Days Above 90°	0	0	0	0	1	5	9	6	2	0	0	0
Days Below 32°	30	27	25	11	1	0	0	0	0	6	20	29
PRECIPITATION												
Normal	1.0	1.0	2.1	3.3	3.7	3.8	4.0	4.1	2.9	2.2	1.7	1.2
Maximum	2.8	3.3	5.6	5.6	6.5	8.9	9.5	10.2	7.8	4.7	4.3	2.9
Maximum 24 Hr. Precipitation	0.9	1.3	1.5	2.2	2.6	3.7	3.0	3.5	3.0	1.9	2.2	1.2
Maximum Snowfall	39	24	29	18	0	0	0	0	0	1	14	28
Days With Measurable Precip.	9	8	11	11	12	11	10	9	9	9	8	10
Average No. Thunderstorms	0	1	3	7	9	11	11	9	6	3	1	0
SUNSHINE/CLOUDINESS												
No. Clear Days	7	7	6	6	7	6	8	9	10	10	7	7
No. Partly Cloudy Days	7	6	8	8	8	11	12	11	8	8	6	6
No. Cloudy Days	17	15	17	16	16	13	11	11	12	13	17	18
% Possible Sunshine	48	53	55	57	61	63	72	68	64	62	45	42

etc.

- This area experiences marked seasonal changes in weather with hot summers and cold winters.
- Autumn is relatively mild and dry, with lots of sunshine.
- Flooding is most frequent from March to June, resulting from a combination of the frozen ground, snow melt and thunderstorms.

CLIMATABLE NO. 63

Fort Larned NHS

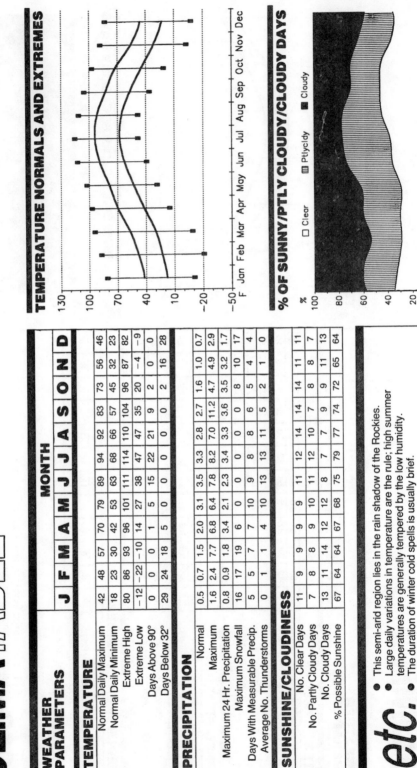

TEMPERATURE NORMALS AND EXTREMES

% OF SUNNY/PTLY CLOUDY/CLOUDY DAYS

☐ Clear ▥ Ptlycldy ■ Cloudy

WEATHER PARAMETERS	MONTH											
	J	F	M	A	M	J	J	A	S	O	N	D
TEMPERATURE												
Normal Daily Maximum	42	48	57	70	79	89	94	92	83	73	56	46
Normal Daily Minimum	18	23	30	42	53	63	68	66	57	45	32	23
Extreme High	80	86	93	96	101	111	114	110	104	96	87	82
Extreme Low	-12	-22	-10	14	27	38	47	47	35	20	-4	-9
Days Above 90°	0	0	0	1	5	15	22	21	9	2	0	0
Days Below 32°	29	24	18	5	0	0	0	0	0	2	16	28
PRECIPITATION												
Normal	0.5	0.7	1.5	2.0	3.1	3.5	3.3	2.8	2.7	1.6	1.0	0.7
Maximum	1.6	2.4	7.7	6.8	6.4	7.8	8.2	7.0	11.2	4.7	4.9	2.9
Maximum 24 Hr. Precipitation	0.8	0.9	1.8	3.4	2.1	2.3	3.4	3.3	3.6	3.5	3.2	1.7
Maximum Snowfall	16	17	19	6	0	0	0	0	0	8	10	17
Days With Measurable Precip.	5	5	7	7	10	9	8	8	6	5	4	4
Average No. Thunderstorms	0	1	1	4	10	13	13	11	5	2	1	0
SUNSHINE/CLOUDINESS												
No. Clear Days	11	9	9	9	9	11	12	14	14	14	11	11
No. Partly Cloudy Days	7	8	8	9	10	11	12	10	7	8	8	7
No. Cloudy Days	13	11	14	12	12	8	7	7	9	9	11	13
% Possible Sunshine	67	64	64	67	68	75	79	77	74	72	65	64

etc.

- This semi-arid region lies in the rain shadow of the Rockies.
- Large daily variations in temperature are the rule; high summer temperatures are generally tempered by the low humidity.
- The duration of winter cold spells is usually brief.

CLIMATABLE NO. 64   Fort Scott NHS

TEMPERATURE NORMALS AND EXTREMES

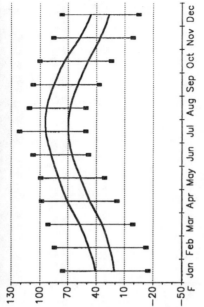

WEATHER PARAMETERS					MONTH								
	J	F	M	A	M	J	J	A	S	O	N	D
TEMPERATURE												
Normal Daily Maximum	41	48	58	71	80	88	94	93	85	74	58	46
Normal Daily Minimum	21	26	34	47	57	66	70	68	60	49	36	27
Extreme High	74	83	90	97	98	106	120	110	106	99	84	75
Extreme Low	−16	−14	0	17	30	47	50	50	36	23	0	−6
Days Above 90°	0	0	0	0	2	13	24	23	10	2	0	0
Days Below 32°	26	20	14	3	0	0	0	0	0	2	12	23
PRECIPITATION												
Normal	1.6	1.6	3.0	3.5	4.7	5.4	3.9	3.5	4.6	3.4	2.4	1.8
Maximum	4.1	4.3	11.9	7.4	11.4	14.6	12.8	9.2	14.0	8.0	6.4	5.1
Maximum 24 Hr. Precipitation	2.0	1.7	2.9	3.3	3.9	3.7	5.2	5.1	4.6	3.6	4.5	3.0
Maximum Snowfall	20	17	13	4	0	0	0	0	0	T	14	26
Days With Measurable Precip.	8	8	10	11	11	10	8	8	8	8	8	9
Average No. Thunderstorms	1	2	5	9	13	14	11	10	8	4	2	2
SUNSHINE/CLOUDINESS												
No. Clear Days	8	7	7	8	7	9	12	12	12	13	10	8
No. Partly Cloudy Days	7	6	8	8	10	10	10	11	8	7	7	7
No. Cloudy Days	16	15	16	14	14	11	9	8	10	11	13	16
% Possible Sunshine	51	53	56	60	62	66	72	72	68	64	53	48

% OF SUNNY/PTLY CLOUDY/CLOUDY DAYS

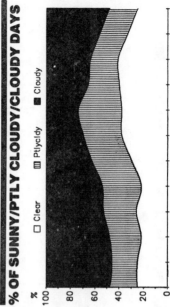

☐ Clear   ▥ Ptlycldy   ■ Cloudy

etc.

- Characterized by an extremely large annual range of temperature.
- The driest season is the winter. The wettest time of year is late spring and early summer when damaging flash floods may occur in conjunction with heavy thunderstorms.

CLIMATABLE NO. 65

Abraham Lincoln Birthplace NHS, Mammoth Cave NP

WEATHER PARAMETERS	J	F	M	A	M	J	J	A	S	O	N	D
TEMPERATURE												
Normal Daily Maximum	45	49	58	70	78	86	88	88	82	72	58	48
Normal Daily Minimum	25	26	35	45	52	60	64	62	56	44	36	28
Extreme High	76	82	86	90	94	105	108	102	106	97	85	80
Extreme Low	−20	−21	−8	21	27	37	44	43	31	19	1	−11
Days Above 90°	0	0	0	0	2	7	12	12	5	0	0	0
Days Below 32°	22	20	15	4	1	0	0	0	0	4	13	20
PRECIPITATION												
Normal	4.2	3.8	5.1	4.4	4.5	4.6	4.7	3.4	3.6	2.6	4.0	4.5
Maximum	10.7	10.3	13.8	13.3	10.5	9.0	10.2	8.5	12.2	5.6	13.1	11.7
Maximum 24 Hr. Precipitation	3.9	3.2	4.3	5.0	4.2	3.6	4.0	3.7	4.8	3.2	6.7	3.1
Maximum Snowfall	22	15	24	2	0	0	0	0	0	0	15	11
Days With Measurable Precip.	11	11	13	12	12	10	10	9	8	8	10	11
Average No. Thunderstorms	2	2	6	8	10	12	15	10	5	3	2	1
SUNSHINE/CLOUDINESS												
No. Clear Days	6	6	6	6	8	8	10	10	11	7	6	6
No. Partly Cloudy Days	6	6	8	9	9	11	12	9	8	6	6	6
No. Cloudy Days	19	16	17	15	14	11	10	9	11	12	17	19
% Possible Sunshine	42	47	50	55	61	66	66	67	65	61	46	40

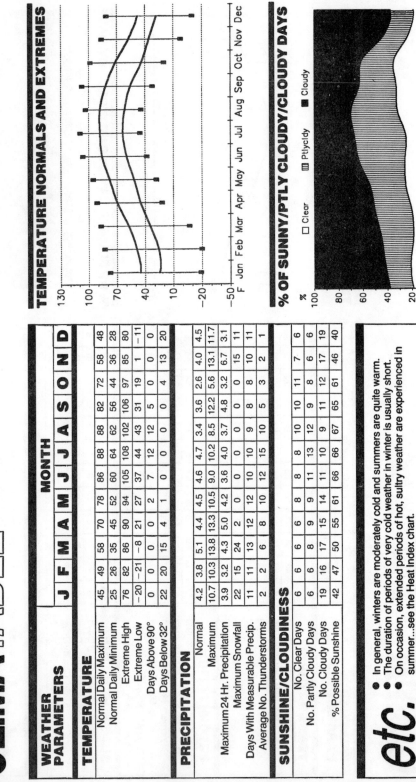

TEMPERATURE NORMALS AND EXTREMES

% OF SUNNY/PTLY CLOUDY/CLOUDY DAYS

☐ Clear   ▦ Ptlycldy   ■ Cloudy

etc.

- In general, winters are moderately cold and summers are quite warm.
- The duration of periods of very cold weather in winter is usually short.
- On occasion, extended periods of hot, sultry weather are experienced in summer...see the Heat Index chart.
- Autumn is the driest season.

CLIMATABLE NO. 66 Cumberland Gap NHP

TEMPERATURE NORMALS AND EXTREMES

% OF SUNNY/PTLY CLOUDY/CLOUDY DAYS

□ Clear   ▥ Ptlycldy   ■ Cloudy

WEATHER PARAMETERS	MONTH											
	J	F	M	A	M	J	J	A	S	O	N	D
TEMPERATURE												
Normal Daily Maximum	46	50	59	70	78	84	87	86	81	70	58	49
Normal Daily Minimum	25	26	33	42	50	58	63	62	56	43	33	27
Extreme High	77	79	86	89	94	100	100	100	104	94	82	72
Extreme Low	-15	-14	-4	0	26	34	42	40	32	16	7	-11
Days Above 90°	0	0	0	0	1	5	10	8	3	0	0	0
Days Below 32°	23	20	16	6	1	0	0	0	0	6	16	22
PRECIPITATION												
Normal	5.0	4.2	5.8	4.3	4.4	4.6	4.8	3.8	3.0	3.0	4.3	5.1
Maximum	10.3	9.4	12.3	9.6	9.8	8.3	13.3	7.4	7.5	6.2	11.0	10.0
Maximum 24 Hr. Precipitation	3.2	2.9	4.2	4.0	3.7	2.7	8.4	3.9	2.5	3.2	5.0	3.4
Maximum Snowfall	24	21	22	T	0	0	0	0	0	0	7	9
Days With Measurable Precip.	12	11	13	11	11	10	12	10	8	8	10	11
Average No. Thunderstorms	0	1	3	5	10	12	13	10	4	1	1	0
SUNSHINE/CLOUDINESS												
No. Clear Days	8	8	8	10	10	10	9	10	10	13	9	8
No. Partly Cloudy Days	6	5	7	6	8	10	11	11	8	7	7	6
No. Cloudy Days	17	15	16	14	13	10	12	10	12	11	14	17
% Possible Sunshine	38	42	49	52	60	60	60	60	58	58	45	38

etc.

- The mountains to the west retard the influx of cold polar air from the north and west and act to moderate the winter climate.
- Summer days are quite warm but evenings are usually comfortable.
- Extreme heat is relatively infrequent.
- Normal seasonal snowfall is just over 10".

CLIMATABLE NO. 67

Thomas Stone NHS, Piscataway Park, Fort Washington Park, Oxon Hill Farm, Greenbelt Park, Clara Barton NHS, Potomac Heritage NST, Glen Echo Park

TEMPERATURE NORMALS AND EXTREMES

WEATHER PARAMETERS	MONTH											
	J	F	M	A	M	J	J	A	S	O	N	D
TEMPERATURE												
Normal Daily Maximum	43	47	56	68	76	84	87	86	80	70	58	47
Normal Daily Minimum	24	26	32	42	52	60	64	64	56	44	36	28
Extreme High	75	80	88	96	97	102	105	102	102	96	86	77
Extreme Low	-9	-12	-1	18	28	35	38	39	28	19	9	-3
Days Above 90°	0	0	0	1	1	6	11	8	3	0	0	0
Days Below 32°	25	22	15	5	1	0	0	0	0	4	13	23
PRECIPITATION												
Normal	3.1	2.9	3.7	3.3	3.6	3.8	4.0	5.0	3.5	3.2	3.2	3.4
Maximum	9.1	6.8	7.1	7.6	8.5	14.7	12.4	14.7	13.8	8.0	7.8	7.7
Maximum 24 Hr. Precipitation	2.4	1.7	3.4	2.5	2.5	7.9	4.3	9.8	6.3	5.4	2.8	2.4
Maximum Snowfall	23	31	24	2	0	0	0	0	0	3	10	20
Days With Measurable Precip.	10	9	11	9	11	10	10	9	8	7	8	9
Average No. Thunderstorms	0	0	1	3	6	7	8	8	3	1	0	0
SUNSHINE/CLOUDINESS												
No. Clear Days	8	8	8	7	7	8	8	9	10	11	8	9
No. Partly Cloudy Days	7	6	8	9	10	11	12	10	8	7	8	6
No. Cloudy Days	16	14	15	14	14	11	11	12	12	13	14	16
% Possible Sunshine	48	51	55	57	59	64	63	63	62	58	51	47

% OF SUNNY/PTLY CLOUDY/CLOUDY DAYS

☐ Clear   ▥ Ptlycldy   ■ Cloudy

etc.
* Summer is characteristically quite warm with several hot, humid periods; winter is cold, but not severe.
* Late season snowfalls in March and April can be significant.
* During some winters, the Potomac becomes blocked with ice; when augmented with spring thunderstorms, flooding can result.

CLIMATABLE NO. 68

Monocacy NB, Harper's Ferry NHP, Antietam NB, C&O Canal NHP

TEMPERATURE NORMALS AND EXTREMES

% OF SUNNY/PTLY CLOUDY/CLOUDY DAYS

WEATHER PARAMETERS	MONTH											
	J	F	M	A	M	J	J	A	S	O	N	D
TEMPERATURE												
Normal Daily Maximum	40	42	52	65	74	83	87	86	79	67	54	43
Normal Daily Minimum	21	23	31	41	50	58	63	62	54	42	34	25
Extreme High	76	78	86	95	96	100	104	103	102	93	86	78
Extreme Low	−17	−9	−1	18	26	36	42	43	29	17	6	−11
Days Above 90°	0	0	0	0	1	6	11	9	4	0	0	0
Days Below 32°	27	23	19	5	1	0	0	0	0	5	15	24
PRECIPITATION												
Normal	2.4	2.3	3.3	3.2	3.6	3.5	3.3	3.6	2.9	3.0	2.6	2.7
Maximum	6.0	4.3	5.5	8.2	8.6	8.0	8.5	9.7	9.4	9.1	6.2	6.4
Maximum 24 Hr. Precipitation	1.7	1.7	2.0	2.2	3.6	3.5	2.3	3.1	3.6	3.6	2.2	3.8
Maximum Snowfall	27	39	27	4	0	0	0	0	0	1	15	22
Days With Measurable Precip.	8	8	9	10	11	9	10	9	8	7	7	7
Average No. Thunderstorms	0	0	1	4	7	8	8	7	3	1	0	0
SUNSHINE/CLOUDINESS												
No. Clear Days	7	7	7	6	6	7	7	8	9	10	6	6
No. Partly Cloudy Days	7	7	8	9	10	11	12	11	9	8	8	8
No. Cloudy Days	17	14	16	15	15	12	12	12	12	13	16	17
% Possible Sunshine	49	54	57	59	60	65	69	68	62	57	46	45

etc.

- Warm summer days are usually followed by comfortable evening temperatures. Normally, one or two periods of hot, uncomfortable weather can be expected each summer.
- In this area, the world's record 1-minute rainfall of 1.23" was recorded on July 4, 1956.

CLIMATABLE NO. 69

Catoctin Mountain Park, Appalachian NST

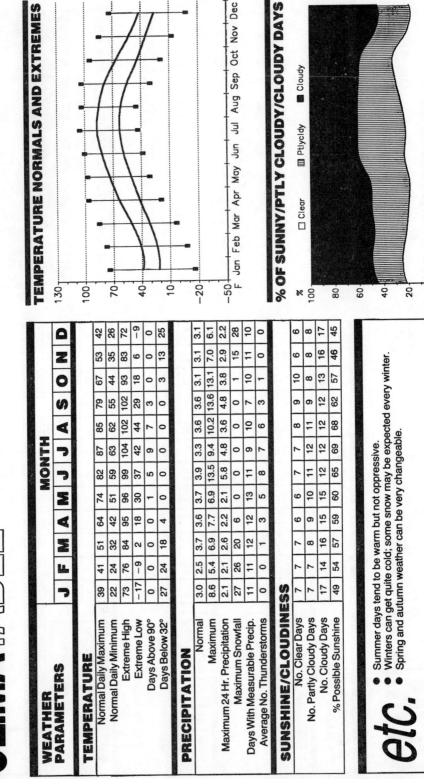

TEMPERATURE NORMALS AND EXTREMES

% OF SUNNY/PTLY CLOUDY/CLOUDY DAYS

☐ Clear   ▥ Ptlycldy   ■ Cloudy

WEATHER PARAMETERS	J	F	M	A	M	J	J	A	S	O	N	D
TEMPERATURE												
Normal Daily Maximum	39	41	51	64	74	82	87	85	79	67	53	42
Normal Daily Minimum	22	24	32	42	51	59	63	62	55	44	35	26
Extreme High	73	76	84	95	96	99	104	102	102	93	83	72
Extreme Low	-17	-9	2	18	30	37	42	44	29	18	6	-9
Days Above 90°	0	0	0	0	1	5	9	7	3	0	0	0
Days Below 32°	27	24	18	4	0	0	0	0	0	3	13	25
PRECIPITATION												
Normal	3.0	2.5	3.7	3.6	3.7	3.9	3.3	3.6	3.6	3.1	3.1	3.1
Maximum	8.6	5.4	6.9	7.7	6.9	13.5	9.4	10.2	13.6	13.1	7.0	6.1
Maximum 24 Hr. Precipitation	2.1	2.1	2.6	2.2	2.1	5.8	4.8	3.6	4.8	3.8	2.9	2.2
Maximum Snowfall	27	26	20	6	0	0	0	0	0	1	15	28
Days With Measurable Precip.	11	11	12	12	13	11	9	10	7	10	11	10
Average No. Thunderstorms	0	0	1	3	5	8	7	6	3	1	0	0
SUNSHINE/CLOUDINESS												
No. Clear Days	7	7	7	6	6	7	7	8	9	10	6	6
No. Partly Cloudy Days	7	7	8	9	10	11	12	11	9	8	8	8
No. Cloudy Days	17	14	16	15	15	12	12	12	12	13	16	17
% Possible Sunshine	49	54	57	59	60	65	69	68	62	57	46	45

etc.

- Summer days tend to be warm but not oppressive.
- Winters can get quite cold; some snow may be expected every winter.
- Spring and autumn weather can be very changeable.

CLIMATABLE NO. 70

Jean Lafitte NHP, Chalmette NHP

TEMPERATURE NORMALS AND EXTREMES

% OF SUNNY/PTLY CLOUDY/CLOUDY DAYS

Legend: ☐ Clear   ▦ Ptlycldy   ■ Cloudy

WEATHER PARAMETERS	J	F	M	A	M	J	J	A	S	O	N	D
TEMPERATURE												
Normal Daily Maximum	62	65	71	79	84	90	91	90	87	79	70	64
Normal Daily Minimum	43	45	52	59	65	71	74	73	70	59	50	45
Extreme High	83	85	89	91	96	100	101	102	101	92	87	84
Extreme Low	14	19	25	32	41	50	60	60	42	35	24	14
Days Above 90°	0	0	0	0	3	16	20	20	9	1	0	0
Days Below 32°	5	3	1	0	0	0	0	0	0	0	1	4
PRECIPITATION												
Normal	5.0	5.2	4.7	4.5	5.1	4.6	6.7	6.0	5.9	2.7	4.1	5.3
Maximum	13.6	12.6	19.1	16.1	14.3	12.3	13.1	16.1	16.7	13.2	14.6	10.8
Maximum 24 Hr. Precipitation	6.1	5.6	7.9	8.0	9.9	4.2	4.3	4.8	6.5	4.5	8.7	5.7
Maximum Snowfall	T	2	T	0	0	0	0	0	0	0	T	3
Days With Measurable Precip.	10	9	9	7	8	10	15	13	10	6	7	10
Average No. Thunderstorms	2	4	6	6	8	13	20	17	9	2	2	3
SUNSHINE/CLOUDINESS												
No. Clear Days	7	8	8	10	9	5	7	10	14	10	8	8
No. Partly Cloudy Days	7	6	8	11	11	14	14	14	10	8	8	8
No. Cloudy Days	17	14	15	11	10	9	12	10	9	12	15	15
% Possible Sunshine	48	52	59	64	62	67	62	61	64	66	53	52

etc.

- A very humid climate moderated by the proximity of the Gulf. Frequent and sometimes heavy rain is typical. Persistent river fogs can be expected in the winter and spring.
- In winter, subject to occasional large and sudden drops in temperature; these cold spells are not prolonged.

CLIMATABLE NO. 71

Acadia NP, Roosevelt Campobello International Park, Saint Croix Island NM

TEMPERATURE NORMALS AND EXTREMES

% OF SUNNY/PTLY CLOUDY/CLOUDY DAYS

☐ Clear ▦ Ptlycldy ■ Cloudy

WEATHER PARAMETERS	MONTH											
	J	F	M	A	M	J	J	A	S	O	N	D
TEMPERATURE												
Normal Daily Maximum	31	32	39	50	61	70	76	74	66	57	46	35
Normal Daily Minimum	15	16	24	34	42	50	54	54	49	42	33	20
Extreme High	57	54	63	82	88	93	96	94	92	81	71	61
Extreme Low	-16	-16	-3	10	25	35	41	35	30	21	6	-11
Days Above 90°	0	0	0	0	0	0	1	0	0	0	0	0
Days Below 32°	29	27	26	14	2	0	0	0	0	4	16	26
PRECIPITATION												
Normal	4.4	4.1	3.8	3.8	3.9	2.9	3.0	3.0	3.8	4.2	5.5	5.2
Maximum	12.0	9.9	10.7	8.1	11.0	8.2	7.2	6.1	6.0	9.2	9.6	10.3
Maximum 24 Hr. Precipitation	3.5	2.8	3.3	2.8	6.3	2.6	2.9	3.4	3.8	3.5	3.5	4.5
Maximum Snowfall	54	43	44	18	6	0	0	0	0	3	16	53
Days With Measurable Precip.	11	10	11	12	13	11	10	10	8	9	12	12
Average No. Thunderstorms	0	0	1	1	2	5	6	5	2	1	0	0
SUNSHINE/CLOUDINESS												
No. Clear Days	10	9	9	8	6	7	8	9	10	10	8	9
No. Partly Cloudy Days	7	7	7	7	10	10	11	11	8	8	7	7
No. Cloudy Days	14	12	15	15	15	13	12	11	12	13	15	15
% Possible Sunshine	56	59	56	55	55	59	64	63	62	58	48	52

etc.

- In winter, "northeasters" bring considerable rain, freezing rain, wet snow and high tides to these coastal areas; inland precipitation is mostly snow.
- Lies in the foggiest area of the U.S. east coast; heavy fog occurs on the average of 60 days/year. Over 1500 hours per year are foggy.

CLIMATABLE NO. 72   Assateague Island NS

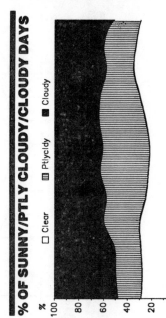

TEMPERATURE NORMALS AND EXTREMES

% OF SUNNY/PTLY CLOUDY/CLOUDY DAYS

☐ Clear   ▥ Ptlycldy   ■ Cloudy

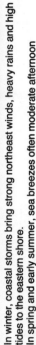

WEATHER PARAMETERS	J	F	M	A	M	J	J	A	S	O	N	D
TEMPERATURE												
Normal Daily Maximum	46	48	56	67	74	80	84	83	80	70	60	50
Normal Daily Minimum	28	29	36	44	55	64	68	67	59	48	38	30
Extreme High	75	77	83	95	97	101	102	99	98	89	88	76
Extreme Low	-7	0	7	18	26	36	40	40	33	22	14	-5
Days Above 90°	0	0	0	0	1	3	6	5	1	0	0	0
Days Below 32°	20	17	10	2	0	0	0	0	0	2	7	17
PRECIPITATION												
Normal	3.7	3.3	3.9	2.9	3.8	3.4	5.2	5.3	4.4	3.4	2.9	3.2
Maximum	6.5	6.2	7.8	7.2	7.4	11.1	12.2	13.7	8.4	11.3	7.0	6.1
Maximum 24 Hr. Precipitation	2.8	2.7	2.6	3.6	3.4	4.4	5.5	7.4	5.1	5.6	3.0	2.8
Maximum Snowfall	20	21	16	0	0	0	0	0	0	0	2	13
Days With Measurable Precip.	10	10	11	10	10	9	11	10	8	8	8	9
Average No. Thunderstorms	0	0	2	3	6	6	10	8	3	1	1	0
SUNSHINE/CLOUDINESS												
No. Clear Days	9	8	9	8	7	7	8	9	11	10	9	9
No. Partly Cloudy Days	6	6	7	9	10	12	12	10	7	8	7	7
No. Cloudy Days	15	14	15	12	13	11	12	11	13	12	15	15
% Possible Sunshine	56	58	63	65	65	67	64	65	64	59	57	57

etc.

- In winter, coastal storms bring strong northeast winds, heavy rains and high tides to the eastern shore.
- In spring and early summer, sea breezes often bring moderate afternoon temperatures.
- Late summer can bring some hot and humid days.

CLIMATABLE NO. 73

Fort McHenry NHS, Hampton NHS

TEMPERATURE NORMALS AND EXTREMES

% OF SUNNY/PTLY CLOUDY/CLOUDY DAYS

☐ Clear   ▥ Ptlycldy   ■ Cloudy

WEATHER PARAMETERS	J	F	M	A	M	J	J	A	S	O	N	D
TEMPERATURE												
Normal Daily Maximum	44	45	53	65	75	83	87	85	79	68	56	46
Normal Daily Minimum	30	30	36	47	57	66	71	69	62	52	41	32
Extreme High	79	83	90	95	98	105	107	105	101	97	87	77
Extreme Low	−7	−7	5	15	32	40	51	45	35	25	12	−3
Days Above 90°	0	0	0	0	1	6	10	6	2	0	0	0
Days Below 32°	20	18	10	1	0	0	0	0	0	0	5	17
PRECIPITATION												
Normal	3.4	3.0	3.9	3.7	4.2	3.9	4.4	4.6	3.6	3.2	3.1	3.2
Maximum	6.8	7.1	7.9	8.7	7.3	9.4	11.5	17.7	12.4	7.8	6.9	7.1
Maximum 24 Hr. Precipitation	3.7	3.5	4.1	4.0	3.9	4.5	4.1	7.8	6.1	5.3	4.2	3.2
Maximum Snowfall	31	34	26	9	T	0	0	0	0	2	10	17
Days With Measurable Precip.	11	10	12	11	11	10	11	11	8	8	9	10
Average No. Thunderstorms	0	0	1	3	5	7	8	7	3	1	0	0
SUNSHINE/CLOUDINESS												
No. Clear Days	9	9	10	9	10	9	10	11	12	13	10	9
No. Partly Cloudy Days	9	9	10	10	11	13	12	11	9	9	10	10
No. Cloudy Days	13	10	11	11	10	8	9	9	9	9	10	12
% Possible Sunshine	48	56	59	59	61	64	65	63	64	63	55	49

etc.

- Hot and muggy periods of weather do occur in the summer...see the Heat Index. Some relief is frequently realized from afternoon thunderstorms.
- The mountains to the west and the proximity of Chesapeake Bay and the Ocean to the east keep the climate fairly temperate.

CLIMATABLE NO. 74

Frederick Law Olmsted NHS, Adams NHS, JFK NHS, Minute Man NHP, Salem NHS, Longfellow NHS, Saugus Iron Works NHS, and all Boston Sites

WEATHER PARAMETERS

MONTH

WEATHER PARAMETERS	J	F	M	A	M	J	J	A	S	O	N	D
TEMPERATURE												
Normal Daily Maximum	36	38	46	58	68	78	83	81	73	63	52	40
Normal Daily Minimum	20	21	30	39	48	58	64	62	54	44	36	24
Extreme High	65	70	85	96	96	100	102	104	101	91	77	73
Extreme Low	-16	-12	-2	14	21	39	45	38	29	21	10	-9
Days Above 90°	0	0	0	0	1	4	6	4	1	0	0	0
Days Below 32°	28	25	20	6	0	0	0	0	0	4	12	25
PRECIPITATION												
Normal	4.0	3.6	4.1	3.7	3.4	3.0	3.1	3.8	3.6	3.5	4.3	4.4
Maximum	13.0	7.8	11.0	7.8	13.4	13.2	8.1	17.1	13.6	8.7	8.9	9.7
Maximum 24 Hr. Precipitation	3.1	2.7	4.1	2.3	5.7	4.2	4.2	8.4	6.4	4.3	3.3	4.2
Maximum Snowfall	38	50	45	13	5	0	0	0	0	1	10	28
Days With Measurable Precip.	12	11	12	11	12	11	9	10	8	9	11	12
Average No. Thunderstorms	0	0	1	1	3	5	5	5	2	1	0	0
SUNSHINE/CLOUDINESS												
No. Clear Days	9	8	8	7	6	7	7	9	10	11	8	9
No. Partly Cloudy Days	7	7	8	8	10	10	12	11	8	8	7	7
No. Cloudy Days	15	13	15	15	15	13	12	11	12	12	15	15
% Possible Sunshine	53	56	57	56	58	63	66	65	64	60	50	52

etc.

- Hot summer afternoons in the city are often made quite pleasant by a cooling sea breeze; this cooling effect rarely reaches the western suburbs.
- New England weather is notable for being so changeable!
- Precipitation is well distributed throughout the year.

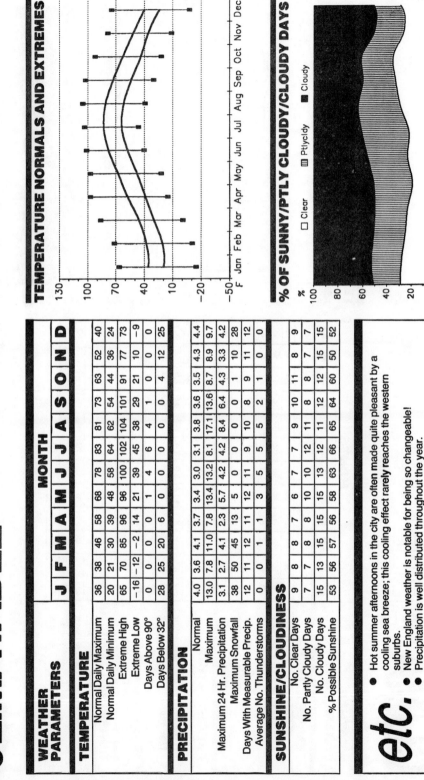

TEMPERATURE NORMALS AND EXTREMES

% OF SUNNY/PTLY CLOUDY/CLOUDY DAYS

☐ Clear   ▦ Ptlycldy   ■ Cloudy

CLIMATABLE NO. 75   Cape Cod NHS

TEMPERATURE NORMALS AND EXTREMES

% OF SUNNY/PTLY CLOUDY/CLOUDY DAYS

☐ Clear   ▦ Ptlycldy   ■ Cloudy

WEATHER PARAMETERS	J	F	M	A	M	J	J	A	S	O	N	D
TEMPERATURE												
Normal Daily Maximum	39	38	44	54	65	74	80	78	72	63	52	42
Normal Daily Minimum	26	25	30	38	46	56	62	62	56	47	39	29
Extreme High	58	60	76	83	86	98	97	94	93	82	71	65
Extreme Low	-4	-3	10	19	28	41	44	42	30	25	16	-6
Days Above 90°	0	0	0	0	0	0	0	1	0	0	0	0
Days Below 32°	24	23	19	4	0	0	0	0	0	1	7	20
PRECIPITATION												
Normal	4.0	3.4	3.9	3.7	2.5	3.0	2.3	3.3	4.3	3.8	3.7	3.4
Maximum	8.2	8.1	8.9	8.4	10.4	5.0	7.4	6.7	9.5	7.5	7.8	9.5
Maximum 24 Hr. Precipitation	2.8	2.0	3.1	1.8	2.6	2.6	2.0	2.5	9.9	4.2	3.4	2.2
Maximum Snowfall	36	18	19	T	T	0	0	0	0	0	4	18
Days With Measurable Precip.	12	11	12	11	12	11	9	10	8	9	11	12
Average No. Thunderstorms	0	0	1	1	3	5	5	5	2	1	0	0
SUNSHINE/CLOUDINESS												
No. Clear Days	9	8	8	7	6	7	7	9	10	11	8	9
No. Partly Cloudy Days	7	7	8	8	10	10	12	11	8	8	7	7
No. Cloudy Days	15	13	15	15	15	13	12	11	12	12	15	15
% Possible Sunshine	53	56	57	56	58	63	66	65	64	60	50	52

etc.

- Characterized by moderate temperatures with ample but not excessively frequent precipitation. Daily temperature ranges are much less than are experienced in the interior of New England.
- Summer sea breezes keep daytime temperatures cool; very hot weather is uncommon.

CLIMATABLE NO. 76

Pictured Rocks National Lakeshore, Father Marquette NM, North Country NST

TEMPERATURE NORMALS AND EXTREMES

% OF SUNNY/PTLY CLOUDY/CLOUDY DAYS

□ Clear   ▥ Ptlycldy   ■ Cloudy

WEATHER PARAMETERS	J	F	M	A	M	J	J	A	S	O	N	D
TEMPERATURE												
Normal Daily Maximum	26	27	35	48	61	71	76	76	66	57	41	30
Normal Daily Minimum	10	9	16	28	37	46	52	53	46	38	27	17
Extreme High	50	55	80	85	95	96	103	103	98	84	70	60
Extreme Low	-27	-31	-26	-4	15	24	31	28	21	15	-10	-18
Days Above 90°	0	0	0	0	0	0	1	1	0	0	0	0
Days Below 32°	31	28	30	22	11	2	0	0	2	9	22	30
PRECIPITATION												
Normal	2.2	1.6	1.7	2.2	2.9	3.0	2.8	3.4	3.7	3.0	3.0	2.6
Maximum	3.6	2.8	3.7	6.0	7.4	4.3	6.4	5.8	6.0	6.9	5.1	3.6
Maximum 24 Hr. Precipitation	1.8	2.7	2.8	2.4	2.0	2.2	2.2	2.2	2.6	2.6	1.6	1.5
Maximum Snowfall	76	61	37	14	10	0	0	0	0	6	30	61
Days With Measurable Precip.	19	16	12	11	13	12	9	11	15	13	16	19
Average No. Thunderstorms	0	0	1	2	4	8	7	7	4	2	0	0
SUNSHINE/CLOUDINESS												
No. Clear Days	3	5	6	7	7	6	8	9	6	5	3	2
No. Partly Cloudy Days	7	6	7	7	10	12	13	10	10	8	5	6
No. Cloudy Days	21	17	18	16	14	12	10	12	14	18	22	23
% Possible Sunshine	31	40	49	54	55	59	66	60	52	46	26	27

etc.
* Springtime is marked by sharp and rapid changes in daily maximum temperature.
* Lake-effect snow squalls are frequent in the winter; an inch or more of snow falls on the average of 12 days each winter month.
* The average annual snowfall on this lake shore is 120"-140".

CLIMATABLE NO. 77   Lowell NHP

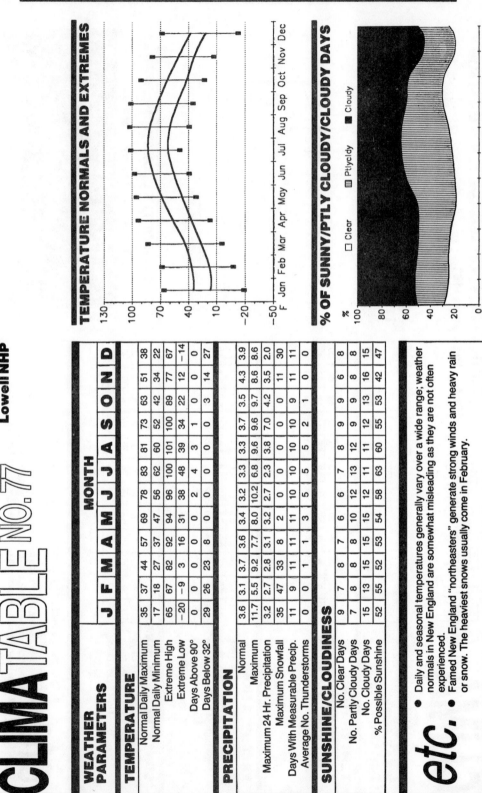

WEATHER PARAMETERS

	J	F	M	A	M	J	J	A	S	O	N	D
TEMPERATURE												
Normal Daily Maximum	35	37	44	57	69	78	83	81	73	63	51	38
Normal Daily Minimum	17	18	27	37	47	56	62	60	52	42	34	22
Extreme High	65	67	82	92	94	96	100	101	100	89	77	67
Extreme Low	-20	-9	3	16	31	38	48	39	34	22	12	-14
Days Above 90°	0	0	0	0	0	2	4	3	1	0	0	0
Days Below 32°	29	26	23	8	0	0	0	0	0	3	14	27
PRECIPITATION												
Normal	3.6	3.1	3.7	3.6	3.4	3.2	3.3	3.3	3.7	3.5	4.3	3.9
Maximum	11.7	5.5	9.2	7.7	8.0	10.2	6.8	9.6	9.6	9.7	8.6	8.6
Maximum 24 Hr. Precipitation	3.2	2.7	2.8	3.1	3.2	2.7	2.3	3.8	7.0	4.2	3.5	2.0
Maximum Snowfall	35	47	33	8	2	0	0	0	0	0	11	30
Days With Measurable Precip.	11	9	11	11	11	10	10	10	10	9	11	11
Average No. Thunderstorms	0	0	1	1	3	5	5	5	2	1	0	0
SUNSHINE/CLOUDINESS												
No. Clear Days	9	7	8	7	6	6	7	8	9	9	6	8
No. Partly Cloudy Days	7	8	8	8	10	12	13	12	9	9	8	8
No. Cloudy Days	15	13	15	15	15	12	11	11	12	13	16	15
% Possible Sunshine	52	55	52	53	54	58	63	60	55	53	42	47

TEMPERATURE NORMALS AND EXTREMES

% OF SUNNY/PTLY CLOUDY/CLOUDY DAYS

☐ Clear   ▥ Ptlycldy   ■ Cloudy

etc.

- Daily and seasonal temperatures generally vary over a wide range; weather normals in New England are somewhat misleading as they are not often experienced.
- Famed New England "northeasters" generate strong winds and heavy rain or snow. The heaviest snows usually come in February.

CLIMATABLE NO. 78 Springfield Armory NHS

TEMPERATURE NORMALS AND EXTREMES

% OF SUNNY/PTLY CLOUDY/CLOUDY DAYS

□ Clear ▦ Ptlycldy ■ Cloudy

WEATHER PARAMETERS	J	F	M	A	M	J	J	A	S	O	N	D
TEMPERATURE												
Normal Daily Maximum	35	37	46	60	71	80	85	83	75	64	51	38
Normal Daily Minimum	18	20	28	38	48	57	62	61	53	43	34	22
Extreme High	64	67	84	94	94	98	99	101	102	89	78	65
Extreme Low	-15	-10	1	10	28	33	44	39	27	23	13	-13
Days Above 90°	0	0	0	0	1	3	7	4	1	0	0	0
Days Below 32°	29	25	22	7	0	0	0	0	0	3	14	26
PRECIPITATION												
Normal	3.3	2.9	4.0	4.1	3.6	3.9	3.6	4.0	3.9	3.5	4.0	4.2
Maximum	10.0	5.5	9.6	7.1	6.6	8.9	9.1	22.4	8.7	10.2	7.7	9.0
Maximum 24 Hr. Precipitation	2.1	2.3	2.2	3.3	2.4	2.4	4.0	11.5	3.4	3.7	2.4	3.6
Maximum Snowfall	29	26	51	6	5	0	0	0	0	0	10	31
Days With Measurable Precip.	12	11	12	11	12	11	10	10	9	9	12	13
Average No. Thunderstorms	0	0	1	1	3	6	7	5	2	1	0	0
SUNSHINE/CLOUDINESS												
No. Clear Days	9	7	7	7	6	6	6	8	9	10	7	7
No. Partly Cloudy Days	8	7	8	9	10	12	12	11	9	8	8	8
No. Cloudy Days	14	14	16	14	15	13	13	12	12	13	15	16
% Possible Sunshine	57	57	56	56	58	60	64	62	59	58	47	49

etc.

- Frequent changes from fair to stormy conditions; there are often abrupt changes in temperature, moisture, sunshine and wind, irregularly interrupted by periods during which the same weather persists for several days.
- Summers are pleasant and winters are cold.

CLIMATABLE NO. 79

Saint Croix NSR, Ice Age NSR (Interstate State Park, WI)
Lower Saint Croix NSR, Ice Age NST

TEMPERATURE NORMALS AND EXTREMES

% OF SUNNY/PTLY CLOUDY/CLOUDY DAYS

□ Clear   ▥ Ptlycldy   ▦ Cloudy

WEATHER PARAMETERS	J	F	M	A	M	J	J	A	S	O	N	D
TEMPERATURE												
Normal Daily Maximum	20	26	38	56	68	78	82	80	70	59	40	26
Normal Daily Minimum	-3	2	15	32	43	53	58	56	46	36	22	7
Extreme High	50	57	77	95	95	99	102	101	98	88	74	62
Extreme Low	-44	-39	-39	-2	15	29	36	32	21	7	-24	-40
Days Above 90°	0	0	0	0	0	2	4	2	1	0	0	0
Days Below 32°	31	28	29	17	4	0	0	0	2	13	26	31
PRECIPITATION												
Normal	1.0	0.8	1.6	2.4	3.5	4.7	4.1	4.8	3.4	2.2	1.4	1.0
Maximum	3.4	2.2	4.2	6.9	8.4	11.9	9.2	10.6	8.3	7.3	5.1	4.2
Maximum 24 Hr. Precipitation	1.6	1.0	1.6	3.7	3.5	4.4	3.4	5.6	5.8	2.7	1.8	1.7
Maximum Snowfall	28	24	33	8	4	0	0	0	0	5	14	34
Days With Measurable Precip.	9	8	10	10	11	12	10	10	10	8	8	9
Average No. Thunderstorms	0	0	1	4	7	10	10	8	5	2	0	0
SUNSHINE/CLOUDINESS												
No. Clear Days	9	8	7	7	7	8	10	10	10	10	5	6
No. Partly Cloudy Days	7	6	8	8	9	10	12	11	8	7	7	7
No. Cloudy Days	15	14	16	15	15	12	9	10	12	14	18	18
% Possible Sunshine	52	57	56	57	61	65	72	68	61	55	39	41

etc.

- Winters are very cold with an average snowfall of 48". Heavy snowfalls with blizzard conditions can be expected about twice each winter.
- Summer is the "wet" season, with precipitation mostly in the form of showers and thunderstorms.

CLIMATABLE NO. 80   Isle Royale NP

WEATHER PARAMETERS	MONTH											
	J	F	M	A	M	J	J	A	S	O	N	D
TEMPERATURE												
Normal Daily Maximum	11	20	32	45	54	62	68	69	60	52	33	18
Normal Daily Minimum	–11	–5	9	25	36	43	50	54	47	39	17	–1
Extreme High	48	53	66	70	79	87	89	86	82	72	65	57
Extreme Low	–46	–44	–38	–5	19	32	37	34	29	12	–32	–41
Days Above 90°	0	0	0	0	0	0	0	0	0	0	0	0
Days Below 32°	31	28	30	22	8	0	0	0	1	6	28	31
PRECIPITATION												
Normal	1.2	0.9	1.8	2.2	2.5	3.1	2.5	3.2	3.4	2.1	1.7	1.3
Maximum	4.7	2.4	5.1	5.8	7.7	8.0	8.5	10.3	6.6	7.5	5.0	3.7
Maximum 24 Hr. Precipitation	1.7	1.4	2.4	2.3	2.6	2.5	2.3	1.8	4.5	1.8	2.6	2.1
Maximum Snowfall	47	32	46	32	8	0	0	0	4	9	38	44
Days With Measurable Precip.	12	10	11	11	12	13	11	11	12	10	11	12
Average No. Thunderstorms	0	0	0	0	1	2	2	2	2	1	0	0
SUNSHINE/CLOUDINESS												
No. Clear Days	7	7	7	6	6	5	7	7	6	6	4	6
No. Partly Cloudy Days	7	6	7	8	9	11	13	12	9	8	6	6
No. Cloudy Days	17	15	17	16	16	14	11	12	15	17	20	19
% Possible Sunshine	49	52	55	55	56	58	65	60	51	46	35	40

etc. • Summers are cool and winters are very cold; periods of warm summer temperatures rarely exceed 2 to 3 days in length.
• Day to day temperature changes are strongly moderated by the surrounding waters of Lake Superior, the coldest of the Great Lakes.

TEMPERATURE NORMALS AND EXTREMES

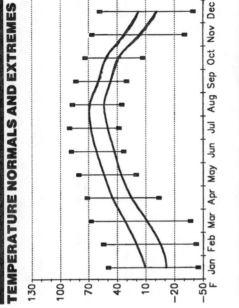

% OF SUNNY/PTLY CLOUDY/CLOUDY DAYS

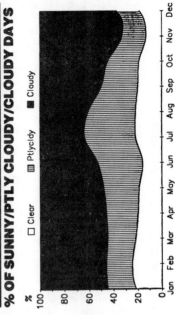

CLIMATABLE NO. 81

Sleeping Bear Dunes National Lakeshore

TEMPERATURE NORMALS AND EXTREMES

% OF SUNNY/PTLY CLOUDY/CLOUDY DAYS

☐ Clear   ▦ Ptlycldy   ■ Cloudy

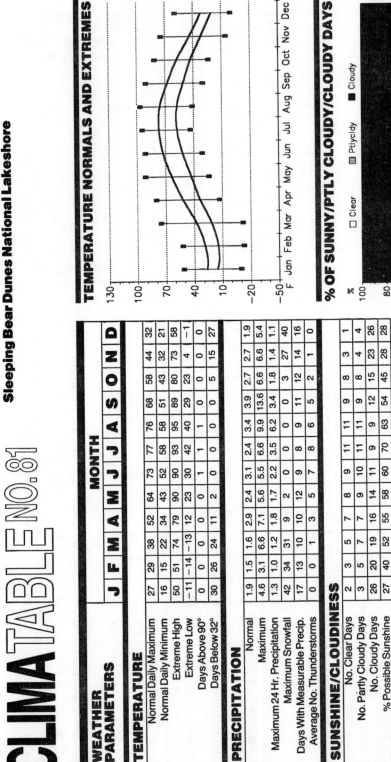

WEATHER PARAMETERS	MONTH											
	J	F	M	A	M	J	J	A	S	O	N	D
TEMPERATURE												
Normal Daily Maximum	27	29	38	52	64	73	77	76	68	58	44	32
Normal Daily Minimum	16	15	22	34	43	52	58	58	51	43	32	21
Extreme High	50	51	74	79	90	90	93	95	89	80	73	58
Extreme Low	−11	−14	−13	12	23	30	42	40	29	23	4	−1
Days Above 90°	0	0	0	0	0	1	1	1	0	0	0	0
Days Below 32°	30	26	24	11	2	0	0	0	0	5	15	27
PRECIPITATION												
Normal	1.9	1.5	1.6	2.9	2.4	3.1	2.4	3.4	3.9	2.7	2.7	1.9
Maximum	4.6	3.1	6.6	7.1	5.6	5.5	6.6	9.9	13.6	6.6	6.6	5.4
Maximum 24 Hr. Precipitation	1.3	1.0	1.2	1.8	1.7	2.2	3.5	6.2	3.4	1.8	1.4	1.1
Maximum Snowfall	42	34	31	9	2	0	0	0	0	3	27	40
Days With Measurable Precip.	17	13	10	10	12	9	8	9	11	12	14	16
Average No. Thunderstorms	0	0	1	3	5	7	8	6	5	2	1	0
SUNSHINE/CLOUDINESS												
No. Clear Days	2	3	5	7	8	9	11	11	9	8	3	1
No. Partly Cloudy Days	3	5	7	7	9	10	11	11	9	8	4	4
No. Cloudy Days	26	20	19	16	14	11	9	9	12	15	23	26
% Possible Sunshine	27	40	52	55	58	60	70	63	54	45	28	28

etc.

- Summer days are often kept pleasantly cool by lake breezes. There are some hot days associated with strong, southerly winds.
- Winter temperatures are also strongly moderated by Lake Michigan. Many lake-effect snow squalls occur in early winter; even greater snowfall is encountered inland.

CLIMATABLE NO. 82

Vicksburg NMP, Natchez Trace Parkway

TEMPERATURE NORMALS AND EXTREMES

% OF SUNNY/PTLY CLOUDY/CLOUDY DAYS

☐ Clear   ▥ Ptlycldy   ■ Cloudy

WEATHER PARAMETERS	J	F	M	A	M	J	J	A	S	O	N	D
TEMPERATURE												
Normal Daily Maximum	56	60	68	77	83	89	91	91	86	78	67	60
Normal Daily Minimum	37	39	46	55	62	69	72	71	66	55	45	40
Extreme High	81	86	86	90	97	102	101	100	100	93	89	85
Extreme Low	2	6	15	31	43	52	57	55	41	31	17	9
Days Above 90°	0	0	0	0	3	16	23	21	10	1	0	0
Days Below 32°	11	8	2	0	0	0	0	0	0	0	3	8
PRECIPITATION												
Normal	5.5	4.9	6.0	5.8	4.8	3.2	3.4	3.1	3.2	2.8	3.9	6.0
Maximum	18.2	13.7	15.4	12.7	12.0	8.1	9.0	16.6	9.9	12.8	9.0	14.3
Maximum 24 Hr. Precipitation	3.6	4.9	8.1	8.8	3.9	3.2	2.7	6.2	3.7	7.5	2.7	4.1
Maximum Snowfall	5	10	8	0	0	0	0	0	0	0	0	2
Days With Measurable Precip.	11	9	10	9	9	8	10	10	8	6	8	10
Average No. Thunderstorms	3	4	9	10	11	11	16	13	6	2	2	3
SUNSHINE/CLOUDINESS												
No. Clear Days	8	8	9	9	8	10	8	9	10	14	10	9
No. Partly Cloudy Days	6	6	7	7	11	11	13	13	9	7	7	6
No. Cloudy Days	17	14	15	14	12	9	10	9	11	10	13	16
% Possible Sunshine	48	55	60	64	63	70	65	65	61	65	54	48

etc.

- Summers are long, warm and humid though extended periods of very hot weather are rare.
- Overall, winters are short and mild.
- Thunderstorms occur on about 1 out of every 3 summer days.
- Snowfall averages less than 2" a season; 2 out of every 3 years, there is essentially no snow at all.

CLIMATABLE NO. 83

Brices Cross Roads NBS, Tupelo NB, Natchez Trace Parkway

TEMPERATURE NORMALS AND EXTREMES

% OF SUNNY/PTLY CLOUDY/CLOUDY DAYS

☐ Clear   ▥ Ptlycldy   ■ Cloudy

WEATHER PARAMETERS	MONTH											
	J	F	M	A	M	J	J	A	S	O	N	D
TEMPERATURE												
Normal Daily Maximum	51	56	65	75	83	90	92	92	86	76	63	55
Normal Daily Minimum	31	34	41	50	58	66	69	68	62	48	39	33
Extreme High	80	83	88	90	98	104	106	105	104	95	85	81
Extreme Low	−12	−1	7	23	30	41	50	50	32	24	11	−1
Days Above 90°	0	0	0	0	6	16	24	22	10	1	0	0
Days Below 32°	18	14	8	1	0	0	0	0	0	2	9	15
PRECIPITATION												
Normal	5.6	4.6	6.9	5.7	5.2	3.7	4.6	2.8	3.6	3.0	4.6	5.6
Maximum	14.8	9.3	17.2	11.3	18.0	9.5	11.5	10.3	10.0	9.0	14.9	11.3
Maximum 24 Hr. Precipitation	4.2	3.7	9.4	7.3	5.3	3.2	5.0	7.1	3.6	4.4	3.7	4.1
Maximum Snowfall	13	4	11	0	0	0	0	0	0	0	1	6
Days With Measurable Precip.	7	10	8	9	11	9	6	8	6	9	10	10
Average No. Thunderstorms	3	4	8	10	9	10	11	9	4	2	3	3
SUNSHINE/CLOUDINESS												
No. Clear Days	8	8	8	9	8	10	10	12	12	14	10	9
No. Partly Cloudy Days	6	6	7	7	10	11	12	11	8	7	6	6
No. Cloudy Days	17	14	16	14	13	9	9	8	10	10	14	16
% Possible Sunshine	50	54	56	64	69	74	74	75	69	70	58	50

etc.

- Snow is not infrequent in the winter, though the seasonal average is less than 2.5".
- Tornadoes, though quite rare, have occurred in this area. They are most probable in the period February to April, though they have been observed in Mississippi in all months.

CLIMATABLE NO. 84   Grand Portage NM

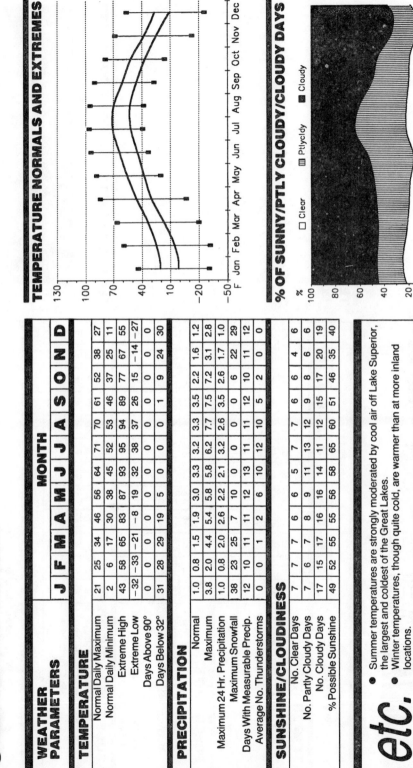

TEMPERATURE NORMALS AND EXTREMES

% OF SUNNY/PTLY CLOUDY/CLOUDY DAYS

□ Clear   ▓ Ptlycldy   ■ Cloudy

WEATHER PARAMETERS	MONTH											
	J	F	M	A	M	J	J	A	S	O	N	D
TEMPERATURE												
Normal Daily Maximum	21	25	34	46	56	64	71	70	61	52	38	27
Normal Daily Minimum	2	6	17	30	38	45	52	53	46	37	25	11
Extreme High	43	58	65	83	87	93	95	94	89	77	67	55
Extreme Low	−32	−33	−21	−8	19	32	38	37	26	15	−14	−27
Days Above 90°	0	0	0	0	0	0	0	0	0	0	0	0
Days Below 32°	31	28	29	19	5	0	0	0	1	9	24	30
PRECIPITATION												
Normal	1.0	0.8	1.5	1.9	3.0	3.3	3.2	3.3	3.5	2.2	1.6	1.2
Maximum	3.8	2.0	4.4	5.4	5.8	5.8	6.2	7.7	7.5	7.2	3.1	2.8
Maximum 24 Hr. Precipitation	1.0	0.8	2.0	2.6	2.2	2.1	3.2	2.6	3.5	2.6	1.7	1.0
Maximum Snowfall	38	23	25	7	10	0	0	0	0	6	22	29
Days With Measurable Precip.	12	10	11	11	12	13	11	11	12	10	11	12
Average No. Thunderstorms	0	0	1	2	6	10	12	10	5	2	0	0
SUNSHINE/CLOUDINESS												
No. Clear Days	7	7	7	6	6	5	7	7	6	6	4	6
No. Partly Cloudy Days	7	6	7	8	9	11	13	12	9	8	6	6
No. Cloudy Days	17	15	17	16	16	14	11	12	15	17	20	19
% Possible Sunshine	49	52	55	55	56	58	65	60	51	46	35	40

etc.

- Summer temperatures are strongly moderated by cool air off Lake Superior, the largest and coldest of the Great Lakes.
- Winter temperatures, though quite cold, are warmer than at more inland locations.
- The cold lake water tends to inhibit the development of thunderstorms here in summer.

CLIMATABLE NO. 85

Jefferson National Expansion Memorial NHS, Lewis and Clark NHT

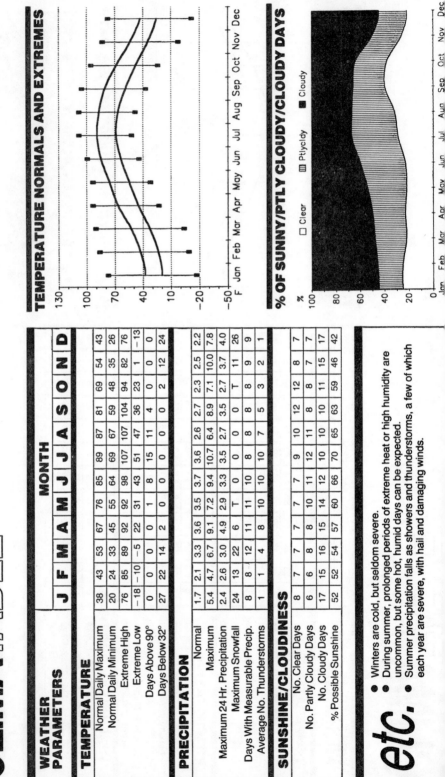

TEMPERATURE NORMALS AND EXTREMES

% OF SUNNY/PTLY CLOUDY/CLOUDY DAYS

☐ Clear   ▦ Ptlycldy   ■ Cloudy

WEATHER PARAMETERS	MONTH											
	J	F	M	A	M	J	J	A	S	O	N	D
TEMPERATURE												
Normal Daily Maximum	38	43	53	67	76	85	89	87	81	69	54	43
Normal Daily Minimum	20	24	33	45	55	64	69	67	59	48	35	26
Extreme High	76	85	89	92	92	98	107	107	104	94	82	76
Extreme Low	-18	-10	-5	22	31	43	51	47	36	23	1	-13
Days Above 90°	0	0	0	0	1	8	15	11	4	0	0	0
Days Below 32°	27	22	14	2	0	0	0	0	0	2	12	24
PRECIPITATION												
Normal	1.7	2.1	3.3	3.6	3.5	3.7	3.6	2.6	2.7	2.3	2.5	2.2
Maximum	5.4	4.7	6.7	9.1	7.2	9.4	10.7	6.4	8.9	7.1	10.0	7.8
Maximum 24 Hr. Precipitation	2.4	2.6	3.0	4.9	2.9	3.3	3.5	2.7	3.5	2.7	3.7	4.0
Maximum Snowfall	24	13	22	6	T	0	0	0	0	T	11	26
Days With Measurable Precip.	8	8	12	11	11	10	8	8	8	8	9	9
Average No. Thunderstorms	1	1	4	8	10	10	10	7	5	3	2	1
SUNSHINE/CLOUDINESS												
No. Clear Days	8	7	7	7	7	9	10	12	12	8	8	7
No. Partly Cloudy Days	6	6	8	8	10	11	11	11	8	8	7	7
No. Cloudy Days	17	15	16	15	14	12	10	10	10	11	15	17
% Possible Sunshine	52	52	54	57	60	66	70	65	63	59	46	42

etc.

- Winters are cold, but seldom severe.
- During summer, prolonged periods of extreme heat or high humidity are uncommon, but some hot, humid days can be expected.
- Summer precipitation falls as showers and thunderstorms, a few of which each year are severe, with hail and damaging winds.

CLIMATABLE NO. 86

Custer Battlefield NM, Bighorn Canyon NRA, Lewis and Clark NHT

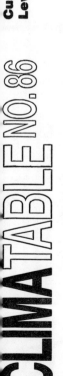

WEATHER PARAMETERS

MONTH

WEATHER PARAMETERS	J	F	M	A	M	J	J	A	S	O	N	D
TEMPERATURE												
Normal Daily Maximum	31	38	44	56	66	76	86	84	72	62	44	36
Normal Daily Minimum	10	17	22	31	42	50	56	54	44	35	23	15
Extreme High	70	76	79	92	96	105	106	106	103	91	78	72
Extreme Low	-35	-38	-23	-5	13	27	35	34	6	1	-25	-37
Days Above 90°	0	0	0	0	0	2	12	11	2	0	0	0
Days Below 32°	30	27	28	19	6	0	0	0	4	16	28	30
PRECIPITATION												
Normal	0.9	0.8	1.0	1.9	2.4	2.2	0.8	1.0	1.2	1.2	0.8	0.8
Maximum	2.4	2.7	3.3	4.8	7.7	9.5	3.8	3.5	5.0	3.8	2.3	2.0
Maximum 24 Hr. Precipitation	1.4	1.1	2.2	3.8	2.8	3.4	2.3	2.5	2.2	1.9	1.4	1.0
Maximum Snowfall	28	35	37	42	16	4	0	0	21	23	26	29
Days With Measurable Precip.	8	8	10	10	11	11	7	6	8	7	7	8
Average No. Thunderstorms	0	0	0	1	5	10	8	8	2	0	0	0
SUNSHINE/CLOUDINESS												
No. Clear Days	5	4	4	4	5	7	14	14	10	10	6	6
No. Partly Cloudy Days	8	8	9	9	11	12	12	11	9	9	8	8
No. Cloudy Days	18	16	18	17	15	11	5	6	12	12	16	17
% Possible Sunshine	48	53	61	60	61	64	76	75	67	61	46	45

etc.

- Bitterly cold winters with below-zero temperatures, strong winds and blowing snow...see the Wind Chill chart.
- Summer days are usually warm enough for light, summer clothing; but some rather cool days should be expected. Summer nights are invariably cool and pleasant.

TEMPERATURE NORMALS AND EXTREMES

% OF SUNNY/PTLY CLOUDY/CLOUDY DAYS

☐ Clear   ▓ Ptlycldy   ■ Cloudy

CLIMATABLE NO. 87

Big Hole NB, Lewis and Clark NHT

WEATHER PARAMETERS

						MONTH						
	J	F	M	A	M	J	J	A	S	O	N	D
TEMPERATURE												
Normal Daily Maximum	31	37	42	53	65	73	84	82	70	58	43	33
Normal Daily Minimum	10	15	18	28	37	44	50	48	39	31	20	13
Extreme High	57	63	71	80	90	94	101	101	92	83	71	58
Extreme Low	-33	-25	-22	4	14	25	33	30	14	-2	-29	-33
Days Above 90°	0	0	0	0	0	1	8	7	0	0	0	0
Days Below 32°	30	27	29	23	8	1	0	0	6	17	27	30
PRECIPITATION												
Normal	0.3	0.2	0.5	0.9	1.6	2.1	0.8	0.9	0.8	0.5	0.4	0.3
Maximum	0.6	0.8	1.4	2.0	3.2	5.1	2.4	2.4	2.4	1.5	1.2	1.3
Maximum 24 Hr. Precipitation	0.5	0.4	0.7	1.0	0.9	2.0	1.0	0.9	0.9	0.8	0.8	0.8
Maximum Snowfall	16	16	17	12	1	0	0	0	7	16	12	12
Days With Measurable Precip.	12	10	10	8	9	7	4	5	5	9	11	11
Average No. Thunderstorms	0	0	0	1	6	14	16	12	4	1	0	0
SUNSHINE/CLOUDINESS												
No. Clear Days	3	4	5	6	7	12	18	15	12	5	5	3
No. Partly Cloudy Days	6	6	8	8	10	9	9	11	8	8	7	7
No. Cloudy Days	22	18	18	16	14	9	4	5	7	11	18	21
% Possible Sunshine	39	52	61	65	67	74	82	80	78	70	47	39

etc.

- Periods of hot weather in the summertime are infrequent and of short duration; even then, nights are cool.
- Winter is a time of extensive cloudiness.
- Severe thunderstorms are rare; precipitation from showers is often light.
- The weather in autumn is exceptionally nice.

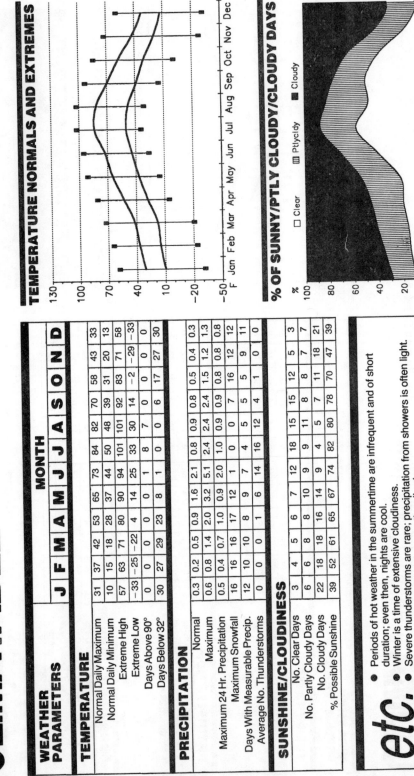

TEMPERATURE NORMALS AND EXTREMES

130
100
70
40
10
-20
-50
°F Jan Feb Mar Apr May Jun Jul Aug Sep Oct Nov Dec

% OF SUNNY/PTLY CLOUDY/CLOUDY DAYS

☐ Clear   ▦ Pttycldy   ■ Cloudy

%
100
80
60
40
20
0

CLIMATABLE NO. 88

Grant-Kohrs Ranch NHS, Lewis and Clark NHT

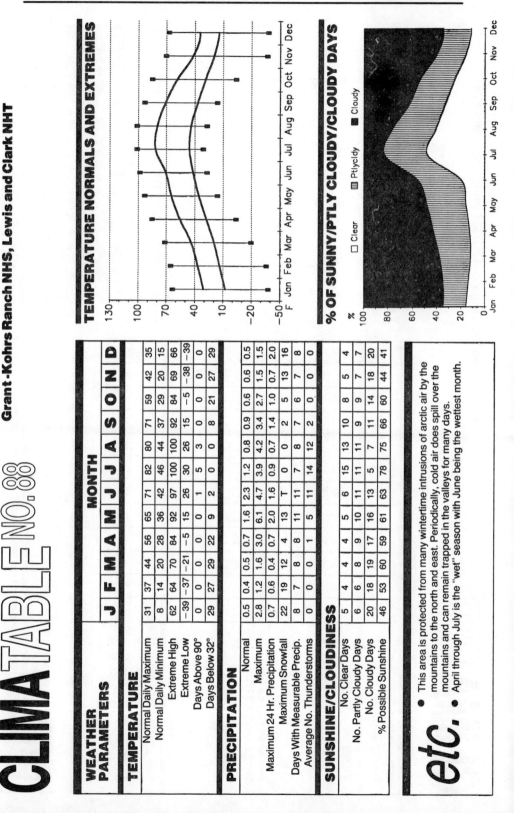

TEMPERATURE NORMALS AND EXTREMES

% OF SUNNY/PTLY CLOUDY/CLOUDY DAYS

☐ Clear   ▥ Ptlycldy   ▦ Cloudy

WEATHER PARAMETERS	J	F	M	A	M	J	J	A	S	O	N	D
TEMPERATURE												
Normal Daily Maximum	31	37	44	56	65	71	82	80	71	59	42	35
Normal Daily Minimum	8	14	20	28	36	42	46	44	37	29	20	15
Extreme High	62	64	70	84	92	97	100	100	92	84	69	66
Extreme Low	-39	-37	-21	-5	15	26	30	26	15	-5	-38	-39
Days Above 90°	0	0	0	0	0	1	5	3	0	0	0	0
Days Below 32°	29	27	29	22	9	2	0	0	8	21	27	29
PRECIPITATION												
Normal	0.5	0.4	0.5	0.7	1.6	2.3	1.2	0.8	0.9	0.6	0.6	0.5
Maximum	2.8	1.2	1.6	3.0	6.1	4.7	3.9	4.2	3.4	2.7	1.5	1.5
Maximum 24 Hr. Precipitation	0.7	0.6	0.4	0.7	2.0	1.6	0.9	0.7	1.4	1.0	0.7	2.0
Maximum Snowfall	22	19	12	4	13	T	0	0	2	5	13	16
Days With Measurable Precip.	8	7	8	8	11	11	7	8	7	6	7	8
Average No. Thunderstorms	0	0	0	1	5	11	14	12	2	0	0	0
SUNSHINE/CLOUDINESS												
No. Clear Days	5	4	4	4	5	6	15	13	10	8	5	4
No. Partly Cloudy Days	6	6	8	9	10	11	11	11	9	9	7	7
No. Cloudy Days	20	18	19	17	16	13	5	7	11	14	18	20
% Possible Sunshine	46	53	60	59	61	63	78	75	66	60	44	41

etc.

• This area is protected from many wintertime intrusions of arctic air by the mountains to the north and east. Periodically, cold air does spill over the mountains and can remain trapped in the valleys for many days.

• April through July is the "wet" season with June being the wettest month.

CLIMATABLE NO. 89

Fort Union Trading Post NHS, Lewis and Clark NHT

WEATHER PARAMETERS	J	F	M	A	M	J	J	A	S	O	N	D
TEMPERATURE												
Normal Daily Maximum	21	29	39	56	69	77	84	83	71	60	40	28
Normal Daily Minimum	-2	6	16	29	41	50	54	52	42	32	18	7
Extreme High	58	67	80	95	102	102	102	102	100	92	70	68
Extreme Low	-42	-42	-29	-17	17	33	35	34	15	1	-22	-37
Days Above 90°	0	0	0	0	1	2	8	7	1	0	0	0
Days Below 32°	31	28	29	19	4	0	0	0	3	16	28	31
PRECIPITATION												
Normal	0.4	0.4	0.5	1.2	2.1	2.8	1.8	1.6	1.3	0.8	0.5	0.4
Maximum	1.4	1.1	1.6	3.2	6.1	6.1	6.3	4.2	3.9	3.8	1.5	0.9
Maximum 24 Hr. Precipitation	0.4	0.6	0.8	1.6	1.9	3.0	1.9	2.4	2.5	1.6	0.4	0.6
Maximum Snowfall	19	20	23	19	6	0	0	0	3	7	20	18
Days With Measurable Precip.	8	7	8	8	10	10	9	7	7	5	6	8
Average No. Thunderstorms	0	0	0	1	5	12	12	9	3	0	0	0
SUNSHINE/CLOUDINESS												
No. Clear Days	5	5	7	6	6	7	11	12	9	9	7	6
No. Partly Cloudy Days	9	7	8	9	11	12	13	11	8	8	7	8
No. Cloudy Days	17	16	16	15	14	11	7	8	13	14	16	17
% Possible Sunshine	52	57	61	61	63	67	76	75	64	59	43	49

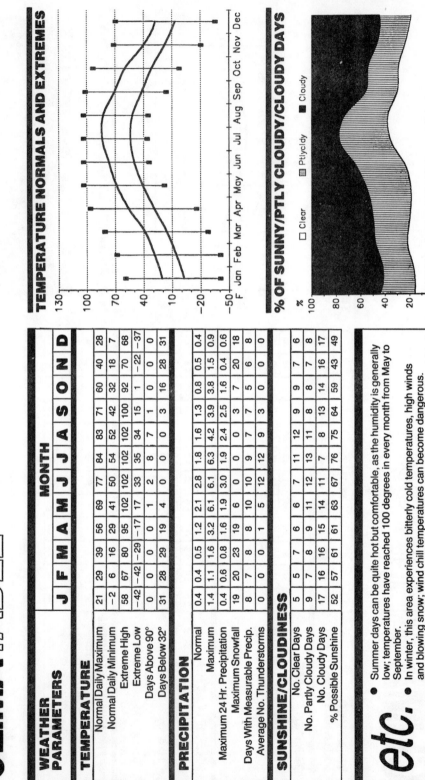

TEMPERATURE NORMALS AND EXTREMES

% OF SUNNY/PTLY CLOUDY/CLOUDY DAYS

□ Clear ▦ Ptlycldy ■ Cloudy

etc.

- Summer days can be quite hot but comfortable, as the humidity is generally low; temperatures have reached 100 degrees in every month from May to September.
- In winter, this area experiences bitterly cold temperatures, high winds and blowing snow; wind chill temperatures can become dangerous.

CLIMATABLE NO.90

Fort Benton, Lewis and Clark NHT

TEMPERATURE NORMALS AND EXTREMES

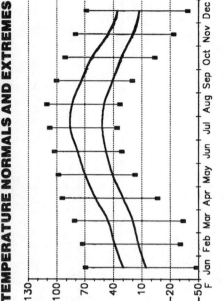

% OF SUNNY/PTLY CLOUDY/CLOUDY DAYS

□ Clear   ▥ Ptlycldy   ■ Cloudy

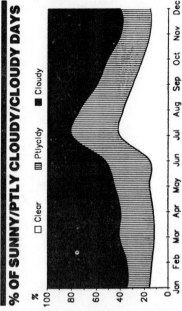

WEATHER PARAMETERS	J	F	M	A	M	J	J	A	S	O	N	D
TEMPERATURE												
Normal Daily Maximum	30	39	46	59	70	78	86	84	74	63	46	36
Normal Daily Minimum	6	14	20	30	41	48	52	50	41	32	20	13
Extreme High	68	71	80	93	97	101	106	109	99	90	79	67
Extreme Low	−49	−32	−35	−8	16	30	35	32	19	−5	−25	−40
Days Above 90°	0	0	0	0	1	3	11	9	2	0	0	0
Days Below 32°	29	26	27	18	4	0	0	0	5	16	25	28
PRECIPITATION												
Normal	0.8	0.6	0.7	1.3	2.5	3.0	1.2	1.2	1.0	0.8	0.6	0.7
Maximum	2.4	1.8	2.0	3.2	6.8	7.1	4.1	3.7	3.5	2.5	2.2	1.9
Maximum 24 Hr. Precipitation	0.8	0.7	1.7	1.8	2.6	2.8	2.0	1.9	1.6	1.2	0.8	0.7
Maximum Snowfall	49	36	27	30	3	2	0	0	8	8	27	37
Days With Measurable Precip.	9	8	9	9	11	12	7	8	7	6	7	8
Average No. Thunderstorms	0	0	0	1	4	8	9	7	2	0	0	0
SUNSHINE/CLOUDINESS												
No. Clear Days	5	4	4	4	5	13	12	12	9	7	5	5
No. Partly Cloudy Days	6	6	9	8	9	11	12	11	9	9	7	8
No. Cloudy Days	20	18	18	18	17	14	6	8	12	15	18	18
% Possible Sunshine	49	55	65	61	62	64	79	76	67	60	46	44

- Chinook winds, a downslope flow of air off the Continental Divide to the west, often produce sharp rises (40 degrees in 24 hours) in winter temperatures. Another result of the chinook winds, nicknamed "snow eaters", is that snow seldom remains on the ground for more than a few days.

CLIMATABLE NO. 91

Pipestone NM

WEATHER PARAMETERS	MONTH											
	J	F	M	A	M	J	J	A	S	O	N	D
TEMPERATURE												
Normal Daily Maximum	20	26	38	56	70	79	84	83	73	61	42	27
Normal Daily Minimum	-1	5	17	32	43	54	58	56	46	34	20	8
Extreme High	55	67	82	93	99	100	104	105	102	89	75	60
Extreme Low	-36	-33	-26	-2	15	31	32	35	19	6	-20	-33
Days Above 90°	0	0	0	0	1	3	8	6	2	0	0	0
Days Below 32°	31	28	28	17	4	0	0	0	2	14	27	31
PRECIPITATION												
Normal	0.5	0.8	1.3	2.2	3.4	4.1	3.0	3.4	2.8	1.8	0.9	0.7
Maximum	1.8	2.6	4.1	5.0	9.0	9.7	7.5	8.3	6.1	5.2	2.8	2.1
Maximum 24 Hr. Precipitation	0.6	1.2	1.5	1.9	4.2	6.2	2.6	3.7	2.5	3.1	1.3	0.9
Maximum Snowfall	20	24	27	14	1	0	0	0	0	5	14	25
Days With Measurable Precip.	6	6	9	9	10	11	9	9	8	6	6	6
Average No. Thunderstorms	0	0	1	4	8	12	11	10	7	2	0	0
SUNSHINE/CLOUDINESS												
No. Clear Days	8	7	6	7	7	9	12	12	12	11	7	7
No. Partly Cloudy Days	8	7	8	8	10	11	12	10	8	8	7	7
No. Cloudy Days	15	14	17	15	14	10	7	9	10	12	16	17
% Possible Sunshine	55	58	58	60	62	62	73	71	66	63	50	48

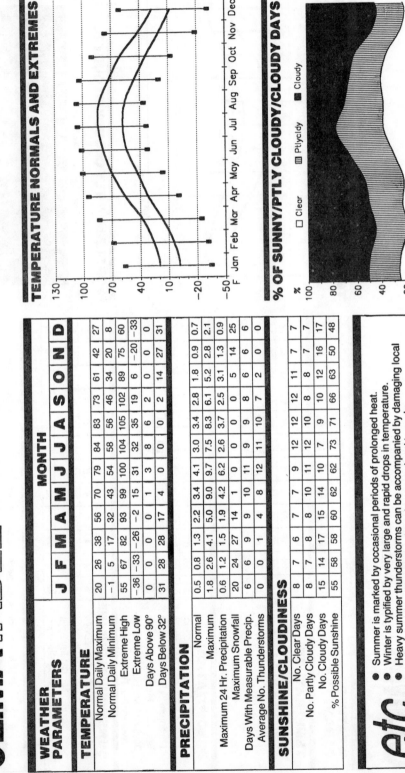

TEMPERATURE NORMALS AND EXTREMES

% OF SUNNY/PTLY CLOUDY/CLOUDY DAYS

☐ Clear   ▥ Ptlycldy   ■ Cloudy

etc.

- Summer is marked by occasional periods of prolonged heat.
- Winter is typified by very large and rapid drops in temperature.
- Heavy summer thunderstorms can be accompanied by damaging local winds, hail (4 to 5 times/year), and an occasional tornado.

CLIMATABLE NO. 92

Homestead NM, Lewis and Clark NHT, Mormon Pioneer NHT

TEMPERATURE NORMALS AND EXTREMES

WEATHER PARAMETERS	MONTH											
	J	F	M	A	M	J	J	A	S	O	N	D
TEMPERATURE												
Normal Daily Maximum	34	41	51	66	76	85	91	89	80	69	52	40
Normal Daily Minimum	13	19	28	41	52	61	67	64	55	43	30	20
Extreme High	66	83	88	91	99	104	114	107	103	95	80	77
Extreme Low	-21	-17	-12	9	28	41	44	44	28	15	-5	-13
Days Above 90°	0	0	0	0	0	2	9	17	6	1	0	0
Days Below 32°	30	26	21	6	0	0	0	0	0	5	19	29
PRECIPITATION												
Normal	0.7	0.9	2.0	2.6	4.0	4.3	4.0	3.9	3.6	2.4	1.2	0.7
Maximum	2.1	2.4	6.7	6.0	7.1	11.4	10.9	15.4	11.9	6.3	3.7	2.0
Maximum 24 Hr. Precipitation	0.9	1.9	2.0	1.8	2.9	4.1	3.4	3.2	5.2	3.3	1.8	1.6
Maximum Snowfall	18	27	19	8	0	0	0	T	0	4	11	16
Days With Measurable Precip.	6	6	9	10	11	8	8	9	8	7	6	5
Average No. Thunderstorms		0	1	2	5	11	12	11	7	3	1	0
SUNSHINE/CLOUDINESS												
No. Clear Days	9	8	8	8	8	10	12	12	11	8	8	8
No. Partly Cloudy Days	6	6	7	8	10	10	10	7	7	7	7	7
No. Cloudy Days	16	14	16	13	13	10	9	11	13	15	16	16
% Possible Sunshine	58	56	57	59	62	70	73	71	66	63	54	52

% OF SUNNY/PTLY CLOUDY/CLOUDY DAYS

☐ Clear ▦ Ptlycldy ■ Cloudy

etc.

- Some summer days can be very hot and uncomfortably humid...see the Heat Index.
- Chinooks, or downslope winds, off the Rocky Mountains often produce large and rapid rises in winter temperatures.
- Some severely cold winter weather has occasionally persisted for more than a week.

CLIMATABLE NO. 93

Chimney Rock NHS, Scotts Bluff NM, Agate Fossil Beds NM, Oregon NHT, Mormon Pioneer NHT

TEMPERATURE NORMALS AND EXTREMES

% OF SUNNY/PTLY CLOUDY/CLOUDY DAYS

☐ Clear　▥ Ptlycldy　■ Cloudy

WEATHER PARAMETERS	J	F	M	A	M	J	J	A	S	O	N	D
TEMPERATURE												
Normal Daily Maximum	38	44	50	62	72	83	90	88	79	68	51	42
Normal Daily Minimum	11	16	22	32	44	53	58	56	46	34	22	14
Extreme High	74	80	87	90	95	106	110	106	102	92	81	77
Extreme Low	−35	−29	−27	−11	15	28	34	36	19	9	−13	−27
Days Above 90°	0	0	0	0	2	8	18	15	5	0	0	0
Days Below 32°	31	28	27	14	2	0	0	0	2	14	27	30
PRECIPITATION												
Normal	0.4	0.4	0.9	1.4	2.8	2.9	2.2	1.2	1.2	0.8	0.4	0.4
Maximum	1.5	1.9	2.6	3.9	6.6	9.3	5.0	5.1	5.8	3.0	1.8	1.5
Maximum 24 Hr. Precipitation	1.0	0.8	1.7	1.5	3.2	3.8	2.5	2.0	3.3	1.3	1.2	0.9
Maximum Snowfall	24	20	24	18	9	1	0	0	5	22	18	18
Days With Measurable Precip.	6	5	7	9	11	11	9	7	7	5	5	5
Average No. Thunderstorms	0	0	0	2	9	16	13	9	5	1	0	0
SUNSHINE/CLOUDINESS												
No. Clear Days	8	7	7	6	10	13	14	14	13	9	9	9
No. Partly Cloudy Days	8	8	9	11	11	12	11	8	8	8	8	8
No. Cloudy Days	15	13	15	14	9	6	6	8	10	13	14	14
% Possible Sunshine	61	65	65	61	60	68	72	65	70	68	60	60

etc.
- Severe blizzards of extended duration are relatively rare, but severe cold waves can be expected about 5 times each winter season.
- Rapid wintertime warmings and melting of snow often results from downslope winds or "chinooks" off the mountains to the west.

CLIMATABLE NO. 94

Voyageurs NP

TEMPERATURE NORMALS AND EXTREMES

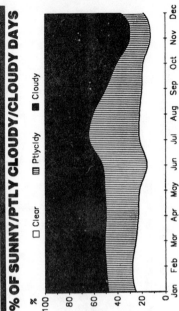

% OF SUNNY/PTLY CLOUDY/CLOUDY DAYS

☐ Clear   ▦ Ptlycldy   ■ Cloudy

WEATHER PARAMETERS	J	F	M	A	M	J	J	A	S	O	N	D
TEMPERATURE												
Normal Daily Maximum	11	20	32	49	64	73	78	75	64	53	33	18
Normal Daily Minimum	-11	-5	9	27	39	49	54	51	42	33	17	-1
Extreme High	48	53	76	93	95	98	98	95	95	88	73	57
Extreme Low	-46	-44	-38	-14	11	23	35	30	20	7	-32	-41
Days Above 90°	0	0	0	0	0	1	2	1	0	0	0	0
Days Below 32°	31	28	30	22	8	0	0	0	5	15	28	31
PRECIPITATION												
Normal	0.9	0.7	1.1	1.6	2.4	3.7	3.8	3.0	3.2	1.8	1.3	0.9
Maximum	3.0	1.8	3.1	3.3	6.7	8.2	9.5	11.3	7.4	4.8	3.5	1.7
Maximum 24 Hr. Precipitation	1.5	1.1	1.8	1.6	2.5	3.8	4.9	4.8	3.4	2.6	1.6	1.2
Maximum Snowfall	43	26	32	23	13	T	0	T	2	8	30	23
Days With Measurable Precip.	12	9	10	9	11	13	11	12	12	10	11	12
Average No. Thunderstorms	0	0	0	1	5	10	12	9	4	1	0	0
SUNSHINE/CLOUDINESS												
No. Clear Days	8	8	8	7	7	7	7	7	6	6	4	6
No. Partly Cloudy Days	7	6	8	8	9	11	13	12	9	7	5	6
No. Cloudy Days	16	14	15	15	15	14	11	12	15	18	21	19
% Possible Sunshine	NA	NA	NA	NA	NA	NA	NA	NA	NA	NA	NA	NA

etc.

- From December through February, the temperature falls below zero on most days and occasionally remains below zero for a week or more.
- Winter can bring some heavy snowfalls with blizzard conditions and severely drifting snow.

CLIMATABLE NO. 95

Wilson's Creek NB, George Washington Carver NM, Ozark National Scenic Riverways

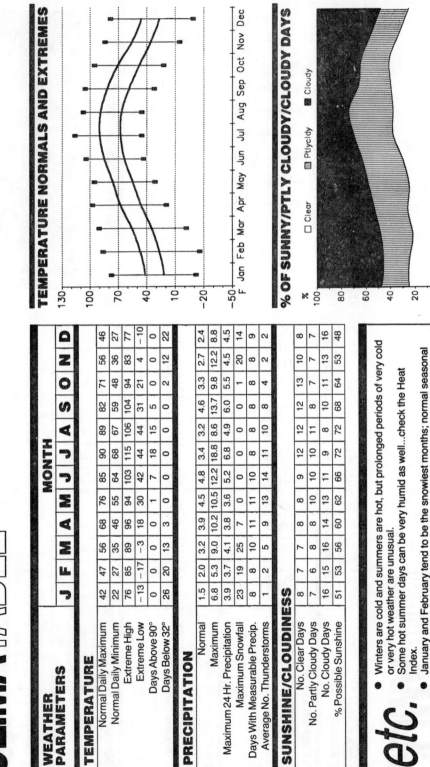

TEMPERATURE NORMALS AND EXTREMES

% OF SUNNY/PTLY CLOUDY/CLOUDY DAYS

☐ Clear   ▥ Ptlycldy   ▦ Cloudy

WEATHER PARAMETERS	J	F	M	A	M	J	J	A	S	O	N	D
TEMPERATURE												
Normal Daily Maximum	42	47	56	68	76	85	90	89	82	71	56	46
Normal Daily Minimum	22	27	35	46	55	64	68	67	59	48	36	27
Extreme High	76	85	89	96	94	103	115	106	104	94	83	77
Extreme Low	-13	-17	-3	18	30	1	44	44	31	21	4	-10
Days Above 90°	0	0	0	0	0	1	18	15	5	0	0	0
Days Below 32°	26	20	13	3	0	0	0	0	0	2	12	22
PRECIPITATION												
Normal	1.5	2.0	3.2	3.9	4.5	4.8	3.4	3.2	4.6	3.3	2.7	2.4
Maximum	6.8	5.3	9.0	10.2	10.5	12.2	18.8	8.6	13.7	9.8	12.2	8.8
Maximum 24 Hr. Precipitation	3.9	3.7	4.1	3.8	3.6	5.2	6.8	4.9	6.0	5.5	4.5	4.5
Maximum Snowfall	23	19	25	7	0	0	0	0	0	1	20	14
Days With Measurable Precip.	8	8	10	11	11	10	8	8	8	8	8	9
Average No. Thunderstorms	1	2	5	9	13	14	11	10	8	4	2	2
SUNSHINE/CLOUDINESS												
No. Clear Days	8	7	7	8	8	9	12	12	12	13	10	8
No. Partly Cloudy Days	7	6	8	8	10	10	10	11	8	7	7	7
No. Cloudy Days	16	15	16	14	13	11	9	8	10	11	13	16
% Possible Sunshine	51	53	56	60	62	66	72	72	68	64	53	48

etc.

- Winters are cold and summers are hot, but prolonged periods of very cold or very hot weather are unusual.
- Some hot summer days can be very humid as well...check the Heat Index.
- January and February tend to be the snowiest months; normal seasonal snowfall is 17".

CLIMATABLE NO. 96

Saint-Gaudens NHS, Appalachian NST

WEATHER PARAMETERS	J	F	M	A	M	J	J	A	S	O	N	D
TEMPERATURE												
Normal Daily Maximum	28	32	41	54	68	76	81	79	70	59	45	32
Normal Daily Minimum	6	8	20	31	41	51	56	54	46	36	27	13
Extreme High	60	64	81	91	94	99	98	97	95	87	74	62
Extreme Low	-34	-30	-18	3	20	30	38	30	20	13	-10	-27
Days Above 90°	0	0	0	0	0	2	3	2	0	0	0	0
Days Below 32°	30	28	28	18	6	0	0	0	2	12	22	29
PRECIPITATION												
Normal	2.6	2.2	2.5	2.9	3.3	2.8	3.0	3.2	3.2	2.9	3.2	3.0
Maximum	6.5	3.9	5.1	4.4	7.3	5.7	7.1	9.0	6.3	7.0	6.2	7.1
Maximum 24 Hr. Precipitation	1.5	1.9	1.5	1.9	2.2	3.1	3.8	2.9	3.5	2.8	2.1	2.2
Maximum Snowfall	37	47	38	12	4	0	0	0	0	3	23	41
Days With Measurable Precip.	11	10	11	12	12	11	10	10	9	9	11	11
Average No. Thunderstorms	0	0	0	1	3	6	8	5	2	1	0	0
SUNSHINE/CLOUDINESS												
No. Clear Days	9	7	8	7	6	6	7	8	9	9	6	8
No. Partly Cloudy Days	7	8	8	8	10	12	12	12	9	9	8	8
No. Cloudy Days	15	13	15	15	15	12	12	11	12	13	16	15
% Possible Sunshine	52	55	52	53	54	58	63	60	55	53	42	47

TEMPERATURE NORMALS AND EXTREMES

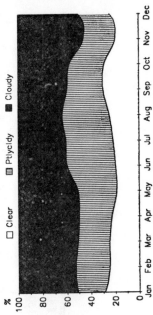

% OF SUNNY/PTLY CLOUDY/CLOUDY DAYS

☐ Clear   ▦ Ptlycldy   ■ Cloudy

etc.

- This area is characterized by quite large year to year variations in temperature, precipitation and snowfall.
- Weather is very changeable and marked by abrupt changes in temperature, moisture, sunshine and wind; to experience "normal" weather is the exception and not the rule.

CLIMATABLE NO. 97

Glacier NP

WEATHER PARAMETERS

WEATHER PARAMETERS	\multicolumn{12}{c}{MONTH}												
	J	F	M	A	M	J	J	A	S	O	N	D
TEMPERATURE												
Normal Daily Maximum	27	33	39	52	63	69	79	77	66	55	39	32
Normal Daily Minimum	11	15	20	28	36	44	47	46	39	32	22	17
Extreme High	58	60	66	80	91	93	101	96	91	83	72	61
Extreme Low	−44	−40	−38	−12	1	24	30	30	11	−9	−33	−37
Days Above 90°	0	0	0	0	0	0	2	1	0	0	0	0
Days Below 32°	30	27	28	22	8	1	0	0	6	16	25	29
PRECIPITATION												
Normal	2.7	1.9	1.6	1.6	1.7	2.2	1.2	1.3	1.3	1.9	2.3	2.8
Maximum	4.7	2.5	3.4	4.5	5.3	9.2	5.7	4.9	3.2	2.3	2.9	3.0
Maximum 24 Hr. Precipitation	3.0	2.1	1.4	2.0	2.0	5.9	2.6	2.1	1.6	1.8	1.8	1.4
Maximum Snowfall	123	81	73	87	28	16	T	T	17	61	77	94
Days With Measurable Precip.	10	7	6	6	7	8	4	3	5	7	8	10
Average No. Thunderstorms	0	0	0	0	5	8	10	8	3	0	0	0
SUNSHINE/CLOUDINESS												
No. Clear Days	2	2	4	4	5	7	15	13	10	6	2	2
No. Partly Cloudy Days	4	4	6	6	9	9	9	9	7	7	5	3
No. Cloudy Days	25	22	21	20	17	14	7	9	13	18	23	26
% Possible Sunshine	30	40	40	45	50	50	70	70	60	40	30	20

TEMPERATURE NORMALS AND EXTREMES

% OF SUNNY/PTLY CLOUDY/CLOUDY DAYS

etc.

- Annual precipitation varies within the Park from 20″ to nearly 200″ at the higher elevations of the windward slopes. The seasonal snowfall may exceed 1000″ in some areas. Near the eastern border of the Park, the record 24-hour drop in temperature for the U.S. of 100 degrees was recorded.

CLIMATABLE NO. 98

Great Basin NP

TEMPERATURE NORMALS AND EXTREMES

% OF SUNNY/PTLY CLOUDY/CLOUDY DAYS

☐ Clear   ▥ Ptlycldy   ■ Cloudy

WEATHER PARAMETERS	J	F	M	A	M	J	J	A	S	O	N	D
TEMPERATURE												
Normal Daily Maximum	41	44	48	56	66	76	86	83	75	62	49	42
Normal Daily Minimum	18	21	24	31	40	48	57	56	47	37	26	20
Extreme High	67	65	70	77	88	97	100	95	92	80	70	64
Extreme Low	-20	-12	0	10	13	25	39	32	21	6	-6	-13
Days Above 90°	0	0	0	0	0	1	7	3	0	0	0	0
Days Below 32°	29	25	26	18	7	1	0	0	2	10	23	29
PRECIPITATION												
Normal	0.9	1.0	1.4	1.3	1.1	0.9	0.9	1.1	0.9	1.0	1.2	1.2
Maximum	3.2	3.6	5.0	3.0	4.7	3.4	2.1	3.7	2.7	3.0	3.4	3.4
Maximum 24 Hr. Precipitation	2.2	1.6	1.5	1.6	1.6	1.4	1.1	0.8	2.4	1.1	1.5	1.6
Maximum Snowfall	34	39	52	35	23	8	0	0	2	42	48	46
Days With Measurable Precip.	7	7	8	8	7	5	6	5	4	5	5	6
Average No. Thunderstorms	0	0	0	1	5	7	12	12	4	1	0	0
SUNSHINE/CLOUDINESS												
No. Clear Days	9	7	8	8	8	13	15	15	17	15	10	9
No. Partly Cloudy Days	7	7	8	9	11	10	11	12	8	8	8	8
No. Cloudy Days	15	14	15	13	12	7	5	4	5	8	12	14
% Possible Sunshine	67	67	70	69	72	80	80	81	82	75	66	65

etc.
- This is a fairly arid area with a slight maximum of precipitation in the spring.
- Thunderstorms are relatively infrequent and, for the most part, are not severe.
- Local mountain and valley winds noticeably influence temperatures throughout the year.

CLIMATABLE NO. 99

Lake Mead NRA

TEMPERATURE NORMALS AND EXTREMES

WEATHER PARAMETERS	J	F	M	A	M	J	J	A	S	O	N	D
TEMPERATURE												
Normal Daily Maximum	54	60	67	76	85	96	102	99	93	80	65	56
Normal Daily Minimum	38	43	46	52	61	70	76	74	68	58	46	39
Extreme High	74	86	91	95	106	114	117	111	106	99	83	78
Extreme Low	14	22	25	31	37	41	62	59	46	30	28	21
Days Above 90°	0	0	0	1	12	24	31	30	21	4	0	0
Days Below 32°	6	2	1	0	0	0	0	0	0	0	1	4
PRECIPITATION												
Normal	0.6	0.5	0.7	0.4	0.2	0.1	0.5	0.8	0.5	0.4	0.5	0.4
Maximum	2.4	2.4	3.6	3.0	1.4	0.7	2.1	3.1	3.8	2.2	2.7	1.8
Maximum 24 Hr. Precipitation	0.7	1.0	1.7	1.0	1.1	0.7	1.0	1.9	2.6	1.2	1.9	0.8
Maximum Snowfall	4	2	0	0	0	0	0	0	0	0	3	2
Days With Measurable Precip.	3	3	3	2	1	1	3	3	2	2	2	2
Average No. Thunderstorms	0	0	0	1	1	2	6	6	2	1	0	0
SUNSHINE/CLOUDINESS												
No. Clear Days	14	12	14	16	18	22	20	23	21	21	16	14
No. Partly Cloudy Days	6	7	9	8	8	5	8	5	6	6	7	7
No. Cloudy Days	11	9	8	6	5	3	3	3	4	4	7	10
% Possible Sunshine	77	81	83	87	88	93	87	88	91	87	80	77

% OF SUNNY/PTLY CLOUDY/CLOUDY DAYS

☐ Clear   ▦ Ptlycldy   ■ Cloudy

etc.

- Wide daily ranges in temperature can be expected; after the hottest days, the nights are generally quite cool.
- The summers are long; the winters are short and mild.
- Thunderstorms are infrequent; there is lots of summer sunshine.

CLIMATABLE NO. 100   Edison NHS, Morristown NHP

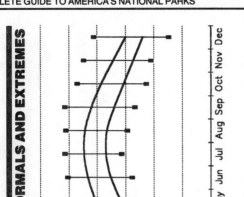

TEMPERATURE NORMALS AND EXTREMES

WEATHER PARAMETERS	MONTH											
	J	F	M	A	M	J	J	A	S	O	N	D
TEMPERATURE												
Normal Daily Maximum	36	39	48	61	72	80	84	83	76	66	53	40
Normal Daily Minimum	18	20	28	38	46	56	61	60	52	42	32	22
Extreme High	67	73	84	94	98	100	103	102	103	90	83	72
Extreme Low	−14	−10	−4	0	26	32	43	37	29	17	12	−7
Days Above 90°	0	0	0	0	1	3	6	3	2	0	0	0
Days Below 32°	29	26	23	8	0	0	0	0	0	6	16	27
PRECIPITATION												
Normal	3.6	3.2	4.5	4.3	4.1	3.9	4.4	4.8	4.4	3.8	4.3	4.1
Maximum	13.2	5.7	9.4	9.1	9.5	14.7	12.7	14.9	11.8	9.0	10.6	10.7
Maximum 24 Hr. Precipitation	4.2	2.5	4.0	2.7	6.3	5.9	4.3	9.1	5.2	5.2	5.2	3.1
Maximum Snowfall	30	29	32	9	0	0	0	0	0	1	5	27
Days With Measurable Precip.	11	10	11	11	12	10	10	9	8	8	10	11
Average No. Thunderstorms	0	0	1	2	4	6	8	6	3	1	0	0
SUNSHINE/CLOUDINESS												
No. Clear Days	8	7	8	7	6	7	7	8	10	11	8	8
No. Partly Cloudy Days	8	8	9	9	11	11	12	11	9	8	8	8
No. Cloudy Days	15	13	14	14	14	12	12	12	11	12	14	15
% Possible Sunshine	50	50	53	55	60	62	62	62	60	60	50	48

% OF SUNNY/PTLY CLOUDY/CLOUDY DAYS

☐ Clear   ▦ Ptlycldy   ▪ Cloudy

etc.

- Some extended periods of hot, humid weather can be expected in the summer...check the Heat Index.
- Winters can be quite cold, with some blustery weather immediately following outbreaks of cold, polar air...see the Wind Chill chart.

CLIMATABLE NO. 101   Pinelands National Reserve

WEATHER PARAMETERS	J	F	M	A	M	J	J	A	S	O	N	D
TEMPERATURE												
Normal Daily Maximum	41	43	52	64	74	83	86	86	80	68	57	45
Normal Daily Minimum	22	23	31	40	49	58	63	62	54	44	35	26
Extreme High	75	76	83	95	98	103	105	104	100	92	84	77
Extreme Low	-16	-12	3	15	23	35	42	37	27	17	10	-5
Days above 90°	0	0	0	0	1	6	10	9	3	0	0	0
Days Below 32°	27	24	19	8	1	0	0	0	0	4	14	24
PRECIPITATION												
Normal	3.4	3.1	4.1	3.6	3.5	3.6	4.6	4.8	3.7	3.3	3.7	4.0
Maximum	9.4	6.8	7.4	7.3	7.9	8.4	14.0	12.6	12.0	6.6	9.2	9.2
Maximum 24 Hr. Precipitation	3.1	2.2	2.8	5.2	3.3	3.4	4.7	7.2	5.1	3.5	3.0	3.0
Maximum Snowfall	17	21	19	2	0	0	0	0	0	1	9	17
Days With Measurable Precip.	11	10	11	11	10	9	9	9	8	7	9	10
Average No. Thunderstorms	0	0	1	3	6	8	10	9	4	1	1	0
SUNSHINE/CLOUDINESS												
No. Clear Days	8	7	8	7	6	7	7	8	10	10	7	8
No. Partly Cloudy Days	8	7	8	10	11	11	11	11	8	9	9	8
No. Cloudy Days	15	14	15	13	14	12	13	12	12	12	14	15
% Possible Sunshine	49	51	54	55	55	58	60	63	60	56	48	44

TEMPERATURE NORMALS AND EXTREMES

% OF SUNNY/PTLY CLOUDY/CLOUDY DAYS

☐ Clear   ▥ Ptlycldy   ■ Cloudy

etc.
- In winter, most precipitation results from storms moving northeastward along the coast.
- This area tends to be somewhat cooler in winter and warmer in summer than the adjoining seashore areas, though summer evenings are usually comfortable.
- Summer precipitation falls mostly as thunderstorms.

CLIMATABLE NO. 102

El Morro NM, Chaco Culture NHP, Aztec Ruins NM

WEATHER PARAMETERS

	J	F	M	A	M	J	J	A	S	O	N	D
TEMPERATURE												
Normal Daily Maximum	42	48	56	67	77	87	92	89	82	70	54	43
Normal Daily Minimum	14	18	24	30	39	48	56	54	44	34	22	14
Extreme High	68	70	79	90	96	104	102	103	99	92	77	65
Extreme Low	−37	−18	−17	7	10	25	33	28	19	8	−12	−38
Days Above 90°	0	0	0	0	1	12	22	14	4	0	0	0
Days Below 32°	30	27	28	17	6	0	0	0	2	14	27	31
PRECIPITATION												
Normal	0.4	0.5	0.5	0.4	0.4	1.0	1.3	1.0	1.2	1.2	0.5	0.6
Maximum	0.7	1.2	1.9	1.6	1.4	1.5	3.2	2.8	2.7	5.9	1.6	3.9
Maximum 24 Hr. Precipitation	0.6	0.5	0.7	0.8	1.0	0.8	1.6	1.6	1.2	1.8	0.8	0.8
Maximum Snowfall	15	14	17	4	2	0	0	0	0	10	15	18
Days With Measurable Precip.	4	4	5	3	4	4	9	9	6	5	4	4
Average No. Thunderstorms	0	0	1	1	3	4	8	8	4	3	1	0
SUNSHINE/CLOUDINESS												
No. Clear Days	13	11	13	13	15	18	12	14	17	17	15	14
No. Partly Cloudy Days	8	8	9	9	10	8	14	12	8	8	8	8
No. Cloudy Days	10	10	8	8	6	4	5	5	5	6	7	9
% Possible Sunshine	73	73	73	77	80	83	76	76	79	79	76	72

TEMPERATURE NORMALS AND EXTREMES

(chart, °F scale: 130, 100, 70, 40, 10, −20, −50; months F J F M A M J J A S O N D)

% OF SUNNY/PTLY CLOUDY/CLOUDY DAYS

□ Clear   ▥ Ptlycldy   ■ Cloudy

(chart, % scale: 100, 80, 60, 40, 20, 0; months Jan Feb Mar Apr May Jun Jul Aug Sep Oct Nov Dec)

etc.

- The climate is mild and dry with low humidity and abundant sunshine.
- Half the annual precipitation falls as brief summer afternoon thundershowers; prolonged rainy spells are rare.
- Winter snows usually melt within hours. Subzero temperatures can be expected to occur about 6 times a season.

CLIMATABLE NO. 103   Pecos NM, Bandelier, NM, Fort Union NM

TEMPERATURE NORMALS AND EXTREMES

% OF SUNNY/PTLY CLOUDY/CLOUDY DAYS

□ Clear   ▦ Ptlycldy   ■ Cloudy

WEATHER PARAMETERS	J	F	M	A	M	J	J	A	S	O	N	D
TEMPERATURE												
Normal Daily Maximum	45	48	54	62	72	81	85	82	77	66	54	47
Normal Daily Minimum	16	20	24	32	41	50	54	53	46	36	24	18
Extreme High	74	76	77	84	91	98	99	96	93	88	80	77
Extreme Low	-28	-30	-19	-3	21	31	39	40	25	10	-13	-14
Days Above 90°	0	0	0	0	0	3	5	2	1	0	0	0
Days Below 32°	30	27	27	16	3	0	0	0	1	11	26	30
PRECIPITATION												
Normal	0.5	0.4	0.7	0.8	1.5	1.5	2.6	2.8	1.6	1.2	0.6	0.6
Maximum	1.5	1.5	1.7	2.8	2.3	3.1	6.1	4.7	2.7	3.2	2.1	2.0
Maximum 24 Hr. Precipitation	1.2	0.7	2.2	1.3	3.2	2.3	3.7	2.2	4.7	2.0	1.6	1.0
Maximum Snowfall	22	24	30	20	4	0	0	0	3	7	18	32
Days With Measurable Precip.	4	5	6	5	7	5	11	11	6	4	3	3
Average No. Thunderstorms	0	0	1	2	5	8	15	14	6	2	1	0
SUNSHINE/CLOUDINESS												
No. Clear Days	13	11	11	13	15	18	12	14	17	17	15	14
No. Partly Cloudy Days	8	8	10	9	10	8	14	12	8	8	8	8
No. Cloudy Days	10	9	10	8	6	4	5	5	6	6	7	9
% Possible Sunshine	73	73	73	77	80	83	76	76	79	79	76	72

etc.

- Summers are pleasant with warm days and cool nights.
- Winters are clear, crisp and dry. On only a few days each winter will the temperature fail to rise above freezing.
- The elevation and low humidity lead to a fairly large daily range of temperatures in all seasons.

CLIMATABLE NO. 104

Capulin Mountain NM

TEMPERATURE NORMALS AND EXTREMES

% OF SUNNY/PTLY CLOUDY/CLOUDY DAYS

□ Clear   ▦ Pttlycldy   ■ Cloudy

WEATHER PARAMETERS	J	F	M	A	M	J	J	A	S	O	N	D
TEMPERATURE												
Normal Daily Maximum	46	48	53	62	72	81	84	82	76	67	54	47
Normal Daily Minimum	16	18	22	32	42	51	56	54	47	36	24	18
Extreme High	69	74	81	85	91	96	99	95	93	89	76	75
Extreme Low	−27	−21	−9	3	19	31	38	40	24	10	−12	−16
Days Above 90°	0	0	0	0	0	3	5	3	1	0	0	0
Days Below 32°	29	27	27	17	4	0	0	0	1	11	25	30
PRECIPITATION												
Normal	0.3	0.4	0.8	0.9	2.3	1.7	3.8	2.8	1.7	1.2	0.5	0.4
Maximum	1.3	1.0	2.6	3.0	7.2	4.3	7.6	6.4	4.6	3.8	1.8	1.4
Maximum 24 Hr. Precipitation	0.8	0.5	0.8	1.2	3.1	1.6	2.4	1.8	2.6	2.6	1.3	0.5
Maximum Snowfall	13	16	24	12	5	0	0	0	7	14	19	12
Days With Measurable Precip.	3	3	5	5	8	8	11	10	6	4	3	3
Average No. Thunderstorms	0	0	1	3	10	14	17	17	6	2	0	0
SUNSHINE/CLOUDINESS												
No. Clear Days	12	11	11	12	12	14	12	15	17	18	15	14
No. Partly Cloudy Days	7	7	9	9	9	10	12	10	6	6	6	7
No. Cloudy Days	12	10	11	9	10	6	7	6	7	7	9	10
% Possible Sunshine	72	72	71	69	69	78	75	75	73	72	72	70

etc.
- Summer daytime temperatures are quite warm, but very hot temperatures normally occur only about once a season.
- Winters are cold, but below-freezing temperatures are normally experienced only about 3 times each winter.
- Some heavy snow with high winds do occur from time to time.

CLIMATABLE NO. 105 Gila Cliff Dwellings NM

TEMPERATURE NORMALS AND EXTREMES

% OF SUNNY/PTLY CLOUDY/CLOUDY DAYS

☐ Clear   ▥ Ptlycldy   ■ Cloudy

WEATHER PARAMETERS	J	F	M	A	M	J	J	A	S	O	N	D
TEMPERATURE												
Normal Daily Maximum	52	55	60	69	77	86	87	84	80	71	60	52
Normal Daily Minimum	24	25	30	36	43	52	58	56	50	40	30	25
Extreme High	73	77	80	91	95	105	104	102	97	90	81	70
Extreme Low	−6	1	7	15	23	30	44	43	33	18	4	−3
Days Above 90°	0	0	0	0	1	10	10	4	2	0	0	0
Days Below 32°	27	23	20	9	1	0	0	0	0	4	18	27
PRECIPITATION												
Normal	0.7	0.5	0.6	0.2	0.3	0.8	3.3	3.3	1.9	1.3	0.5	0.9
Maximum	2.1	1.6	2.9	0.9	1.4	3.6	6.2	6.1	4.9	6.0	1.8	3.2
Maximum 24 Hr. Precipitation	0.8	0.7	0.7	0.7	1.0	2.5	2.0	2.4	2.5	2.4	0.8	1.3
Maximum Snowfall	13	17	24	2	0	0	0	0	0	0	7	20
Days With Measurable Precip.	5	5	5	4	4	6	12	11	7	5	3	6
Average No. Thunderstorms	0	0	1	2	3	6	15	15	6	3	0	0
SUNSHINE/CLOUDINESS												
No. Clear Days	14	13	15	17	20	22	10	13	19	20	18	15
No. Partly Cloudy Days	7	6	7	7	7	6	12	12	7	6	6	6
No. Cloudy Days	10	9	9	6	4	2	9	6	4	5	6	10
% Possible Sunshine	81	84	86	91	94	93	78	81	87	88	85	80

etc.

- Summer temperatures are moderated by elevation; the warmest days most often occur in June before the peak of the thunderstorm season.
- Winters are cold; subzero temperatures, though not a frequent occurrence, should be expected.
- Normally about half of the winter precipitation falls as snow.

CLIMATABLE NO. 106　Salinas NM

TEMPERATURE NORMALS AND EXTREMES

% OF SUNNY/PTLY CLOUDY/CLOUDY DAYS

☐ Clear　▦ Ptlycldy　■ Cloudy

WEATHER PARAMETERS	J	F	M	A	M	J	J	A	S	O	N	D
TEMPERATURE												
Normal Daily Maximum	46	50	57	66	75	86	88	84	79	70	56	47
Normal Daily Minimum	19	22	26	32	41	50	55	53	47	36	25	20
Extreme High	67	71	77	87	92	98	100	98	93	84	75	67
Extreme Low	-25	-24	0	10	20	28	39	35	24	11	-10	-14
Days Above 90°	0	0	0	0	0	9	12	5	1	0	0	0
Days Below 32°	30	26	25	16	4	0	0	0	1	10	25	29
PRECIPITATION												
Normal	0.6	0.8	0.6	0.6	0.6	0.8	2.6	2.3	1.7	1.2	0.6	0.8
Maximum	1.4	3.2	2.1	2.3	2.4	3.4	7.9	5.0	5.0	6.1	1.9	2.2
Maximum 24 Hr. Precipitation	0.8	2.0	1.2	1.2	1.4	1.7	4.0	2.8	1.7	1.9	0.8	1.4
Maximum Snowfall	17	35	19	16	11	0	0	0	0	6	18	22
Days With Measurable Precip.	5	5	5	5	4	4	9	9	8	5	4	5
Average No. Thunderstorms	0	0	1	2	5	6	13	13	6	3	1	0
SUNSHINE/CLOUDINESS												
No. Clear Days	13	11	13	15	18	12	14	17	17	15	14	14
No. Partly Cloudy Days	8	8	9	10	8	14	12	8	8	8	8	8
No. Cloudy Days	10	9	10	8	6	4	5	5	6	7	9	9
% Possible Sunshine	73	73	77	80	83	76	76	79	79	76	72	72

etc.

- The climate here is arid. Summer days are hot with low humidity; summer nights are cool.
- Much of the wintertime precipitation falls as snow. Some very cold temperatures are apt to be encountered in winter, but daytime temperatures are usually moderate.

CLIMATABLE NO. 107   White Sands NM

TEMPERATURE NORMALS AND EXTREMES

WEATHER PARAMETERS	MONTH											
	J	F	M	A	M	J	J	A	S	O	N	D
TEMPERATURE												
Normal Daily Maximum	57	61	68	78	86	96	95	93	87	78	66	58
Normal Daily Minimum	28	31	37	44	52	62	65	64	58	46	34	28
Extreme High	76	80	89	97	104	109	110	106	102	94	84	75
Extreme Low	−14	5	12	24	33	41	51	51	39	25	0	−1
Days Above 90°	0	0	0	1	11	27	26	23	14	1	0	0
Days Below 32°	22	17	8	1	0	0	0	0	0	1	12	23
PRECIPITATION												
Normal	0.6	0.5	0.5	0.2	0.4	0.8	2.2	2.2	1.6	1.1	0.4	0.6
Maximum	1.4	1.4	3.0	1.1	2.4	2.4	6.4	6.7	6.2	5.7	2.9	1.8
Maximum 24 Hr. Precipitation	0.7	0.9	1.2	0.8	0.8	2.0	1.8	2.5	2.0	1.4	1.0	0.6
Maximum Snowfall	10	6	6	0	0	0	0	0	0	0	6	10
Days With Measurable Precip.	5	3	3	3	4	5	9	8	7	5	3	4
Average No. Thunderstorms	0	0	1	2	4	8	17	14	6	3	0	0
SUNSHINE/CLOUDINESS												
No. Clear Days	11	12	14	14	13	17	11	13	13	18	16	15
No. Partly Cloudy Days	9	8	9	9	12	10	15	12	8	6	7	9
No. Cloudy Days	11	8	8	7	6	3	5	6	9	7	7	7
% Possible Sunshine	60	68	75	77	80	83	77	73	72	77	73	71

% OF SUNNY/PTLY CLOUDY/CLOUDY DAYS

☐ Clear   ▦ Ptlycldy   ■ Cloudy

etc.

- Summer rain falls from brief but frequently intense thunderstorms. More than half the annual rainfall falls from July to September.
- Evaporation usually exceeds the normal annual precipitation.
- Warm days, quite cool nights and reduced precipitation makes autumn a very attractive season here.

CLIMATABLE NO. 108

Eleanor Roosevelt NHS, Home of FDR NHS, Vanderbilt Mansion NHS, Martin Van Buren NHS, Appalachian NST

TEMPERATURE NORMALS AND EXTREMES

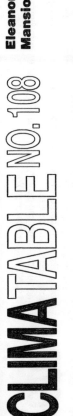

% OF SUNNY/PTLY CLOUDY/CLOUDY DAYS

☐ Clear   ▦ Pt'ycldy   ■ Cloudy

WEATHER PARAMETERS	J	F	M	A	M	J	J	A	S	O	N	D
TEMPERATURE												
Normal Daily Maximum	34	37	46	60	70	79	84	82	74	63	51	38
Normal Daily Minimum	15	17	26	36	46	56	60	59	51	40	31	20
Extreme High	63	72	84	94	96	99	103	100	101	88	78	66
Extreme Low	-30	-23	-13	13	27	36	43	38	26	18	11	-13
Days Above 90°	0	0	0	0	1	3	6	4	1	0	0	0
Days Below 32°	29	26	24	11	2	0	0	0	1	8	18	27
PRECIPITATION												
Normal	2.8	2.4	3.3	3.7	3.6	3.4	3.5	3.8	3.7	3.3	3.6	3.2
Maximum	8.7	5.2	6.6	7.4	7.7	8.0	13.6	12.7	7.9	10.4	8.1	8.6
Maximum 24 Hr. Precipitation	2.0	1.5	2.2	2.5	2.8	2.8	4.7	4.0	3.8	4.5	2.2	2.4
Maximum Snowfall	31	31	35	20	4	0	0	0	0	1	8	31
Days With Measurable Precip.	12	11	12	12	12	11	10	10	10	9	11	12
Average No. Thunderstorms	0	0	1	2	4	7	8	6	2	1	0	0
SUNSHINE/CLOUDINESS												
No. Clear Days	6	5	6	6	5	5	6	7	8	8	4	5
No. Partly Cloudy Days	8	7	8	8	9	11	13	11	10	9	8	7
No. Cloudy Days	17	16	17	16	17	14	12	13	12	14	18	19
% Possible Sunshine	46	51	53	54	55	59	63	60	57	51	36	38

etc.

- This region does experience rather warm summers with frequent periods of elevated and uncomfortable humidity...see Heat Index.
- Snowfall is significant though somewhat less in this region than in most other areas of the state. Very heavy snows can be deposited by coastal storms.

CLIMATABLE NO. 109

Ellis Island, Statue of Liberty NM and all New York City sites, St. Paul's NHS, Theodore Roosevelt Birthplace NHS

TEMPERATURE NORMALS AND EXTREMES

% OF SUNNY/PTLY CLOUDY/CLOUDY DAYS

☐ Clear   ▦ Ptlycldy   ■ Cloudy

WEATHER PARAMETERS	MONTH											
	J	F	M	A	M	J	J	A	S	O	N	D
TEMPERATURE												
Normal Daily Maximum	38	40	49	61	72	80	85	84	76	66	54	42
Normal Daily Minimum	26	27	34	44	53	63	68	67	60	50	41	30
Extreme High	72	75	86	96	99	101	106	104	102	94	84	72
Extreme Low	-6	-15	3	12	32	44	52	50	39	28	5	-13
Days Above 90°	0	0	0	0	1	3	7	4	2	0	0	0
Days Below 32°	23	20	12	2	0	0	0	0	0	0	5	18
PRECIPITATION												
Normal	3.2	3.1	4.2	3.8	3.8	3.2	3.8	4.0	3.7	3.4	4.2	3.8
Maximum	10.5	6.9	10.4	8.8	9.7	9.8	11.9	10.9	16.8	13.3	12.4	10.0
Maximum 24 Hr. Precipitation	3.9	3.0	4.2	4.2	4.9	4.7	3.6	5.8	8.3	11.2	8.1	3.2
Maximum Snowfall	27	28	30	14	T	0	0	0	0	1	19	30
Days With Measurable Precip.	11	10	12	11	11	10	11	10	8	8	9	10
Average No. Thunderstorms	0	0	1	2	4	6	7	7	3	1	1	0
SUNSHINE/CLOUDINESS												
No. Clear Days	8	8	8	8	8	8	9	9	11	12	9	9
No. Partly Cloudy Days	9	9	10	10	12	12	13	10	10	10	9	9
No. Cloudy Days	14	11	12	12	11	10	10	12	9	9	12	13
% Possible Sunshine	50	55	56	59	61	64	65	64	62	61	52	49

etc.

- City exhibits a very definite "heat island" effect; overnight temperatures are often distinctly warmer in both winter and summer as compared to surrounding suburban areas.
- Some summer days can be very hot and humid; however, both warm and cold spells tend not to be prolonged.

CLIMATABLE NO. 110

Saratoga, NHP, Appalachian NST

TEMPERATURE NORMALS AND EXTREMES

% OF SUNNY/PTLY CLOUDY/CLOUDY DAYS

□ Clear   ▥ Ptlycldy   ■ Cloudy

WEATHER PARAMETERS	MONTH											
	J	F	M	A	M	J	J	A	S	O	N	D
TEMPERATURE												
Normal Daily Maximum	29	32	42	57	69	77	82	80	72	60	47	34
Normal Daily Minimum	10	12	24	35	44	54	59	57	49	38	30	17
Extreme High	62	67	86	92	94	99	100	99	100	89	82	71
Extreme Low	-33	-29	-21	9	22	32	40	34	24	15	-1	-29
Days Above 90°	0	0	0	0	0	1	4	2	0	0	0	0
Days Below 32°	30	27	27	14	3	0	0	0	1	10	19	29
PRECIPITATION												
Normal	2.4	2.4	3.0	3.0	3.2	3.2	3.0	3.2	3.1	2.9	3.0	3.0
Maximum	6.4	5.0	6.4	8.0	9.0	7.4	7.2	7.3	7.9	8.8	8.1	7.6
Maximum 24 Hr. Precipitation	1.9	1.9	2.5	2.7	2.2	3.5	2.7	4.5	3.7	3.6	2.0	4.0
Maximum Snowfall	42	44	35	18	2	0	0	0	0	3	25	58
Days With Measurable Precip.	12	11	12	12	13	11	10	10	10	9	12	12
Average No. Thunderstorms	0	0	1	1	5	7	9	6	3	1	0	0
SUNSHINE/CLOUDINESS												
No. Clear Days	6	5	6	6	5	5	6	7	8	8	4	5
No. Partly Cloudy Days	8	7	8	8	9	11	13	11	10	9	8	7
No. Cloudy Days	17	16	17	16	17	14	12	13	12	14	18	19
% Possible Sunshine	46	51	53	54	55	59	63	60	57	51	36	38

etc.

- Moderately cold winters with wide variations in temperature.
- Summer days are warm; an occasional influx of warm, humid air makes the days less comfortable. Summer evenings are almost always cool.
- One or two periods of "indian summer" weather can be expected each fall.

CLIMATABLE NO. 111

Fire Island NS, Sagamore Hill NHS

WEATHER PARAMETERS	MONTH											
	J	F	M	A	M	J	J	A	S	O	N	D
TEMPERATURE												
Normal Daily Maximum	38	40	47	58	68	76	82	81	75	65	54	43
Normal Daily Minimum	21	22	29	37	47	57	63	62	55	44	35	26
Extreme High	67	65	71	90	94	99	98	102	95	85	75	67
Extreme Low	-12	-6	-7	12	28	34	46	40	33	17	12	0
Days Above 90°	0	0	0	0	0	1	3	2	1	0	0	0
Days Below 32°	27	24	21	8	1	0	0	0	0	3	13	24
PRECIPITATION												
Normal	3.8	3.6	4.3	4.0	3.7	2.9	3.3	4.5	3.4	3.9	4.0	4.4
Maximum	12.4	6.0	8.3	7.9	8.3	7.5	8.2	11.0	7.8	12.9	6.9	8.1
Maximum 24 Hr. Precipitation	3.4	2.0	2.9	2.8	1.8	2.4	4.2	5.5	5.7	4.9	3.5	3.8
Maximum Snowfall	25	29	29	2	0	0	0	0	0	0	4	21
Days With Measurable Precip.	11	10	10	11	10	12	9	8	7	7	12	11
Average No. Thunderstorms	0	0	1	2	4	6	7	7	3	1	1	0
SUNSHINE/CLOUDINESS												
No. Clear Days	8	8	8	8	7	7	8	7	10	11	8	8
No. Partly Cloudy Days	9	7	9	9	12	11	12	13	9	9	8	8
No. Cloudy Days	14	13	14	13	12	12	11	11	11	11	14	15
% Possible Sunshine	50	55	55	55	60	62	62	62	61	60	50	50

TEMPERATURE NORMALS AND EXTREMES

% OF SUNNY/PTLY CLOUDY/CLOUDY DAYS

☐ Clear   ▦ Ptlycldy   ■ Cloudy

etc.

- Summer sea breezes often greatly moderate afternoon temperatures, but temperatures will exceed 90 degrees an average of 7 times each summer.
- Winters are relatively mild; the principal source of heavy precipitation are the coastal storms or "northeasters" bound for New England.

CLIMATABLE NO. 112   Fort Stanwix NM

TEMPERATURE NORMALS AND EXTREMES

% OF SUNNY/PTLY CLOUDY/CLOUDY DAYS

□ Clear   ▥ Ptlycldy   ■ Cloudy

WEATHER PARAMETERS	J	F	M	A	M	J	J	A	S	O	N	D
TEMPERATURE												
Normal Daily Maximum	29	31	40	54	67	77	81	79	72	62	46	33
Normal Daily Minimum	13	14	23	34	45	54	59	57	50	40	31	17
Extreme High	65	61	82	87	92	99	99	96	100	87	79	64
Extreme Low	−30	−26	−27	0	26	32	41	40	26	21	4	−26
Days Above 90°	0	0	0	0	0	2	3	2	1	0	0	0
Days Below 32°	29	26	25	11	3	0	0	0	1	6	14	25
PRECIPITATION												
Normal	4.2	3.8	3.2	3.8	3.8	3.4	3.9	3.4	3.4	3.1	4.0	4.0
Maximum	6.8	8.8	6.0	6.4	6.3	10.5	8.7	7.6	8.4	10.1	7.5	8.3
Maximum 24 Hr. Precipitation	2.1	2.1	2.9	1.3	2.0	2.8	3.9	2.6	2.5	3.0	3.0	3.0
Maximum Snowfall	63	46	41	9	1	0	0	0	T	1	16	43
Days With Measurable Precip.	19	16	17	14	13	11	11	11	11	12	16	19
Average No. Thunderstorms	0	0	1	3	6	10	11	10	5	1	1	0
SUNSHINE/CLOUDINESS												
No. Clear Days	3	3	4	6	6	8	8	7	7	6	2	2
No. Partly Cloudy Days	6	6	7	7	10	10	12	11	10	8	6	5
No. Cloudy Days	22	19	20	17	15	12	11	13	13	17	22	24
% Possible Sunshine	34	39	45	51	55	59	64	59	53	44	26	25

etc.

- Winters are long and cold with abundant snowfall; the seasonal snowfall ranges between 90" and 130", much of it from lake-effect snow squalls.
- Summers are pleasant and warm with lots of sunshine; thunderstorms occur on about 1 out of every 3 summer days.

CLIMATABLE NO. 113 Gateway NRA

TEMPERATURE NORMALS AND EXTREMES

% OF SUNNY/PTLY CLOUDY/CLOUDY DAYS

☐ Clear ▦ Ptlycldy ■ Cloudy

WEATHER PARAMETERS	MONTH											
	J	F	M	A	M	J	J	A	S	O	N	D
TEMPERATURE												
Normal Daily Maximum	39	41	48	59	68	78	83	82	75	65	54	44
Normal Daily Minimum	24	25	32	41	50	60	65	64	58	47	38	28
Extreme High	70	73	79	90	94	99	102	99	96	89	81	73
Extreme Low	−3	−3	6	22	29	40	46	43	35	25	15	−2
Days Above 90°	0	0	0	0	1	2	5	3	1	0	0	0
Days Below 32°	25	22	15	4	0	0	0	0	0	2	9	21
PRECIPITATION												
Normal	3.6	3.6	4.6	3.8	3.8	3.1	3.9	5.1	3.9	3.6	3.9	4.2
Maximum	9.0	6.7	7.7	7.9	9.4	7.2	9.1	11.0	9.7	7.3	9.9	10.5
Maximum 24 Hr. Precipitation	2.8	3.4	2.2	2.3	2.9	2.7	5.5	4.5	4.7	3.6	3.7	6.6
Maximum Snowfall	26	26	23	4	0	0	0	0	0	0	3	16
Days With Measurable Precip.	11	10	11	11	12	10	10	9	8	8	10	11
Average No. Thunderstorms	0	0	1	2	4	6	8	6	3	1	0	0
SUNSHINE/CLOUDINESS												
No. Clear Days	8	7	8	7	6	7	7	8	10	11	8	8
No. Partly Cloudy Days	8	8	9	9	11	11	12	11	9	9	8	8
No. Cloudy Days	15	13	14	14	14	12	12	12	11	12	14	15
% Possible Sunshine	50	55	56	59	61	64	65	64	62	61	52	49

etc.
- Major winter snows are associated with coastal storms moving northeastward along the coast, the same storms that become New England's "northeasters".
- On occasion, tropical storms bring heavy rain, some wind and high tides to the area, usually in the late summer or early fall.

CLIMATABLE NO. 114   Theodore Roosevelt Inaugural NHS

TEMPERATURE NORMALS AND EXTREMES

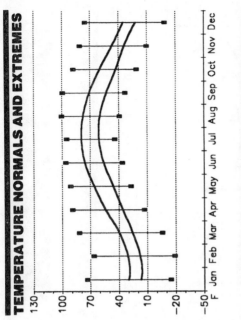

% OF SUNNY/PTLY CLOUDY/CLOUDY DAYS

☐ Clear   ▤ Ptlycldy   ■ Cloudy

WEATHER PARAMETERS	\multicolumn{12}{c}{MONTH}
	J	F	M	A	M	J	J	A	S	O	N	D
TEMPERATURE												
Normal Daily Maximum	30	31	40	54	66	76	80	78	71	60	47	35
Normal Daily Minimum	17	18	26	36	46	56	61	60	53	43	34	22
Extreme High	72	65	81	88	90	95	94	98	98	87	80	74
Extreme Low	-16	-20	-7	12	26	35	43	38	32	20	9	-10
Days Above 90°	0	0	0	0	0	0	1	0	0	0	0	0
Days Below 32°	29	26	24	11	1	0	0	0	0	4	14	26
PRECIPITATION												
Normal	3.0	2.4	3.0	3.1	2.9	2.7	3.0	4.2	3.4	2.9	3.6	3.4
Maximum	6.9	5.8	5.6	5.9	6.4	6.9	6.4	10.7	9.0	9.1	9.8	8.0
Maximum 24 Hr. Precipitation	2.6	2.3	2.1	1.7	3.5	3.0	3.4	3.9	4.9	3.5	2.5	2.2
Maximum Snowfall	68	54	29	15	2	T	0	0	0	3	31	68
Days With Measurable Precip.	20	17	16	14	12	10	10	11	11	11	16	20
Average No. Thunderstorms	0	0	2	4	4	7	8	9	4	2	2	1
SUNSHINE/CLOUDINESS												
No. Clear Days	1	2	4	5	5	6	7	6	7	7	2	1
No. Partly Cloudy Days	6	5	7	8	10	12	13	12	10	8	5	6
No. Cloudy Days	24	21	20	17	16	12	11	14	12	16	23	24
% Possible Sunshine	32	38	45	52	58	65	68	64	58	50	29	26

etc.

- Famous for the locally heavy lake-effect snow squalls of late autumn and early winter.
- Winters are quite cold, though cold air masses are often drastically moderated by the Great Lakes.
- The cold lake waters usually delay the onset of typical spring temperatures until late May or June.

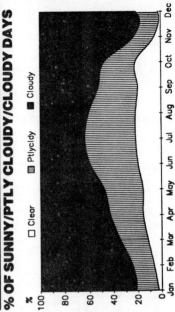

CLIMATABLE NO. 115   Upper Delaware NSR

WEATHER PARAMETERS	J	F	M	A	M	J	J	A	S	O	N	D
TEMPERATURE												
Normal Daily Maximum	35	38	48	62	73	81	85	83	74	63	50	38
Normal Daily Minimum	16	18	26	36	46	55	59	58	51	40	32	21
Extreme High	65	75	87	96	98	99	104	102	103	89	79	64
Extreme Low	-20	-14	-9	13	21	35	36	35	25	18	10	-10
Days Above 90°	0	0	0	0	1	4	7	3	1	0	0	0
Days Below 32°	30	26	25	11	2	0	0	0	0	7	17	27
PRECIPITATION												
Normal	3.2	2.7	3.8	3.8	3.6	3.6	4.1	4.1	3.5	3.4	3.8	3.5
Maximum	8.9	5.3	8.6	9.1	6.8	9.5	7.3	18.0	6.8	9.2	9.5	9.0
Maximum 24 Hr. Precipitation	1.9	1.8	2.6	2.4	3.1	3.0	3.0	5.8	3.6	4.3	4.8	3.1
Maximum Snowfall	37	26	38	10	0	0	0	0	0	T	17	37
Days With Measurable Precip.	17	15	16	14	13	12	10	11	10	12	15	18
Average No. Thunderstorms	0	0	1	3	5	9	10	8	3	1	0	0
SUNSHINE/CLOUDINESS												
No. Clear Days	2	2	4	5	5	5	5	6	6	6	3	2
No. Partly Cloudy Days	7	6	7	7	9	11	13	12	10	8	6	6
No. Cloudy Days	22	20	20	18	17	14	13	14	14	17	21	23
% Possible Sunshine	37	41	44	51	56	61	64	60	56	48	31	27

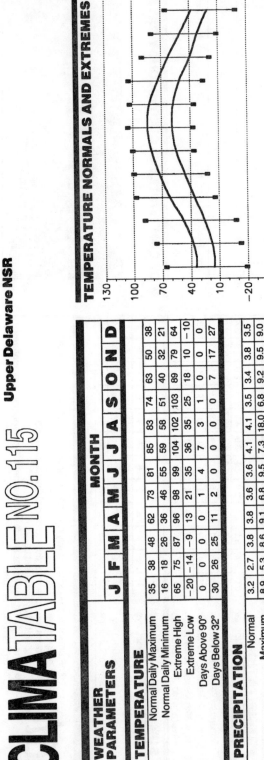

TEMPERATURE NORMALS AND EXTREMES

% OF SUNNY/PTLY CLOUDY/CLOUDY DAYS

☐ Clear   ▥ Ptlycldy   ■ Cloudy

etc.

- Warm summer days are usually free of oppressive humidity; summer nights tend to be cool and pleasant.
- Winters are cold with occasional periods of severe cold.
- The weather in the spring and fall tends to be very variable.

CLIMATABLE NO. 116   Women's Rights NHP

TEMPERATURE NORMALS AND EXTREMES

% OF SUNNY/PTLY CLOUDY/CLOUDY DAYS

☐ Clear   ▦ Ptlycldy   ■ Cloudy

WEATHER PARAMETERS	MONTH											
	J	F	M	A	M	J	J	A	S	O	N	D
TEMPERATURE												
Normal Daily Maximum	31	32	41	55	66	76	81	80	72	61	48	35
Normal Daily Minimum	15	16	25	36	45	55	60	58	51	41	32	21
Extreme High	71	69	83	89	91	99	99	99	100	89	75	64
Extreme Low	-25	-20	-3	10	26	35	43	40	28	21	6	-12
Days Above 90°	0	0	0	0	0	2	4	2	1	0	0	0
Days Below 32°	30	27	25	11	2	0	0	0	0	5	16	27
PRECIPITATION												
Normal	2.0	2.0	2.6	2.8	2.8	3.5	2.9	3.1	2.9	3.0	2.7	2.5
Maximum	4.9	4.7	4.8	5.3	5.3	10.6	6.0	8.1	7.3	11.8	6.2	4.6
Maximum 24 Hr. Precipitation	1.2	2.7	2.0	2.0	1.9	3.4	1.8	2.5	3.9	2.8	2.2	1.7
Maximum Snowfall	54	35	27	18	3	0	0	0	0	10	15	40
Days With Measurable Precip.	19	16	17	14	13	11	11	11	11	12	16	19
Average No. Thunderstorms	0	0	1	2	4	8	10	8	4	1	1	0
SUNSHINE/CLOUDINESS												
No. Clear Days	3	3	4	6	6	8	8	7	7	6	2	2
No. Partly Cloudy Days	6	6	7	7	10	10	12	11	10	8	6	5
No. Cloudy Days	22	19	20	17	15	12	11	13	13	17	22	24
% Possible Sunshine	34	39	45	51	55	59	64	59	53	44	26	25

etc.
- Summer days are moderately warm, but evenings are generally cool and comfortable.
- Winters are cold and at times severe. Nearby Lake Ontario induces much cloudiness in the late autumn and winter as well as many snow squalls. The typical seasonal snowfall is over 60".

CLIMATABLE NO. 117

Wright Brothers NM Fort Raleigh NHS, Cape Hatteras NS, Cape Lookout NS

WEATHER PARAMETERS	MONTH											
	J	F	M	A	M	J	J	A	S	O	N	D
TEMPERATURE												
Normal Daily Maximum	53	54	59	67	74	81	84	84	81	72	64	57
Normal Daily Minimum	38	38	43	51	60	68	72	72	68	58	48	41
Extreme High	75	76	79	89	88	95	95	94	92	89	81	77
Extreme Low	6	14	19	26	39	44	54	56	45	32	22	12
Days Above 90°	0	0	0	0	0	1	2	2	0	0	0	0
Days Below 32°	11	10	4	0	0	0	0	0	0	0	1	6
PRECIPITATION												
Normal	4.7	4.1	4.0	3.2	4.1	4.2	5.4	6.1	5.8	4.8	4.8	4.5
Maximum	9.7	8.4	9.3	7.1	11.4	10.8	10.0	16.1	12.8	15.0	16.2	8.6
Maximum 24 Hr. Precipitation	5.0	2.9	2.9	5.6	3.6	6.6	5.5	8.1	5.5	7.7	7.7	3.6
Maximum Snowfall	4	8	0	0	0	0	0	0	0	0	T	2
Days With Measurable Precip.	11	10	10	8	10	9	12	10	9	9	9	10
Average No. Thunderstorms	1	2	2	4	8	8	13	12	4	3	2	1
SUNSHINE/CLOUDINESS												
No. Clear Days	9	9	10	10	8	6	6	8	10	10	10	10
No. Partly Cloudy Days	7	5	7	9	10	11	10	10	9	8	8	7
No. Cloudy Days	15	14	14	11	13	12	15	13	11	12	12	14
% Possible Sunshine	49	52	61	67	63	62	63	63	63	58	55	48

TEMPERATURE NORMALS AND EXTREMES

% OF SUNNY/PTLY CLOUDY/CLOUDY DAYS

etc.

- Summers are cooler and winters warmer than on the mainland.
- This is the breeding ground for the fall and winter coastal storms of the northeastern U.S.
- Tropical storms and hurricanes occasionally threaten the region in late summer and autumn, bringing high winds, heavy rains and high tides.

CLIMATABLE NO. 118

Great Smoky Mountains NP, Blue Ridge Parkway, Appalachian NST

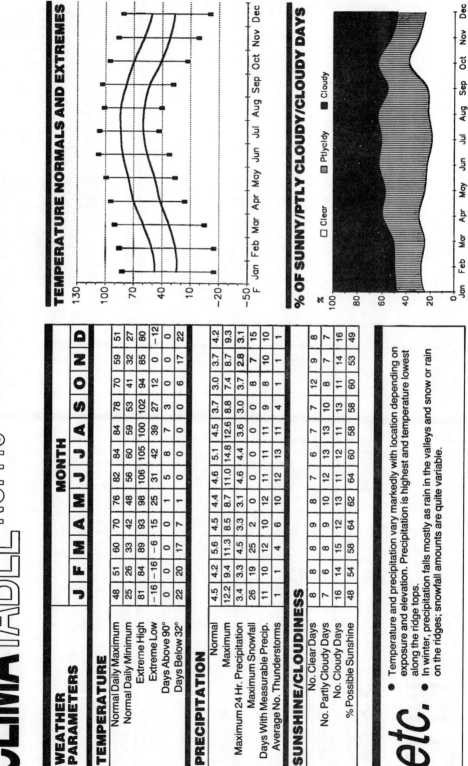

TEMPERATURE NORMALS AND EXTREMES

% OF SUNNY/PTLY CLOUDY/CLOUDY DAYS

☐ Clear　▦ Pt'ycldy　■ Cloudy

WEATHER PARAMETERS		J	F	M	A	M	J	J	A	S	O	N	D
TEMPERATURE													
Normal Daily Maximum		48	51	60	70	76	82	84	84	78	70	59	51
Normal Daily Minimum		25	26	33	42	48	56	60	59	53	41	32	27
Extreme High		81	84	89	93	98	106	105	100	102	94	85	80
Extreme Low		-16	-16	-6	15	25	31	42	39	27	12	0	-12
Days Above 90°		0	0	0	0	1	5	8	7	3	0	0	0
Days Below 32°		22	20	17	7	1	0	0	0	0	6	17	22
PRECIPITATION													
Normal		4.5	4.2	5.6	4.5	4.4	4.6	5.1	4.5	3.7	3.0	3.7	4.2
Maximum		12.2	9.4	11.3	8.5	8.7	11.0	14.8	12.6	8.8	7.4	8.7	9.3
Maximum 24 Hr. Precipitation		3.4	3.3	4.5	3.3	3.1	4.6	4.4	3.6	3.0	3.7	2.8	3.1
Maximum Snowfall		26	19	25	2	0	0	0	0	0	8	7	15
Days With Measurable Precip.		11	10	12	10	12	11	11	11	9	8	10	10
Average No. Thunderstorms		1	1	4	6	10	12	13	11	4	1	1	1
SUNSHINE/CLOUDINESS													
No. Clear Days		8	8	8	9	8	7	6	7	7	12	9	8
No. Partly Cloudy Days		7	6	8	9	10	12	13	13	10	8	7	7
No. Cloudy Days		16	14	15	12	13	11	12	11	13	11	14	16
% Possible Sunshine		48	54	58	64	62	64	60	58	58	60	53	49

etc.

- Temperature and precipitation vary markedly with location depending on exposure and elevation. Precipitation is highest and temperature lowest along the ridge tops.
- In winter, precipitation falls mostly as rain in the valleys and snow or rain on the ridges; snowfall amounts are quite variable.

CLIMATABLE NO. 119

Knife River Indian Villages NHS, Lewis and Clark NHT, North Country NST

TEMPERATURE NORMALS AND EXTREMES

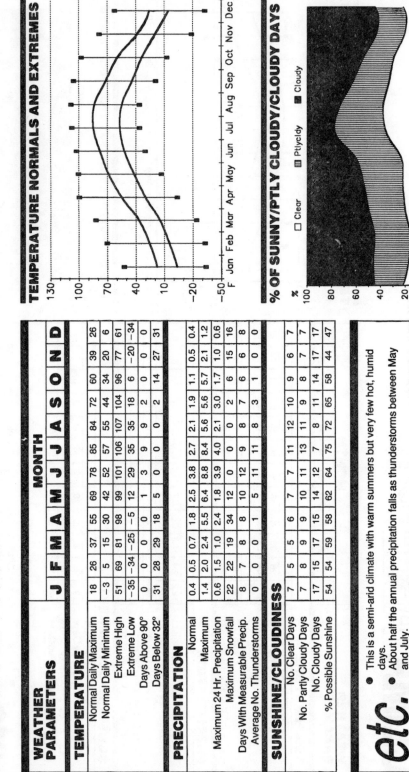

WEATHER PARAMETERS	J	F	M	A	M	J	J	A	S	O	N	D
TEMPERATURE												
Normal Daily Maximum	18	26	37	55	69	78	85	84	72	60	39	26
Normal Daily Minimum	−3	5	15	30	42	52	57	55	44	34	20	6
Extreme High	51	69	81	98	99	101	106	107	104	96	77	61
Extreme Low	−35	−34	−25	−5	12	29	35	35	18	6	−20	−34
Days Above 90°	0	0	0	0	1	3	9	9	2	0	0	0
Days Below 32°	31	28	29	18	5	0	0	0	2	14	27	31
PRECIPITATION												
Normal	0.4	0.5	0.7	1.8	2.5	3.8	2.7	2.1	1.9	1.1	0.5	0.4
Maximum	1.4	2.0	2.4	5.5	6.4	8.8	8.4	5.6	5.6	5.7	2.1	1.2
Maximum 24 Hr. Precipitation	0.6	1.5	1.0	2.4	1.8	3.9	4.0	2.1	3.0	1.7	1.0	0.6
Maximum Snowfall	22	22	19	34	12	0	0	0	2	6	15	16
Days With Measurable Precip.	8	7	8	8	10	12	9	8	7	6	6	8
Average No. Thunderstorms	0	0	0	1	5	11	11	8	3	1	0	0
SUNSHINE/CLOUDINESS												
No. Clear Days	7	5	5	6	7	7	11	12	10	9	6	7
No. Partly Cloudy Days	7	8	9	9	10	11	13	11	9	8	7	7
No. Cloudy Days	17	15	17	15	14	12	7	8	11	14	17	17
% Possible Sunshine	54	54	59	58	62	64	75	72	65	58	44	47

% OF SUNNY/PTLY CLOUDY/CLOUDY DAYS

☐ Clear   ▥ Pticldy   ▨ Cloudy

etc.
- This is a semi-arid climate with warm summers but very few hot, humid days.
- About half the annual precipitation falls as thunderstorms between May and July.
- Winter snows are often accompanied by strong winds...watch the Wind Chill temperature! Drifting and blowing snow can be a problem.

CLIMATABLE NO. 120 Carl Sandburg Home NHS

TEMPERATURE NORMALS AND EXTREMES

WEATHER PARAMETERS	J	F	M	A	M	J	J	A	S	O	N	D
TEMPERATURE												
Normal Daily Maximum	48	51	59	70	76	82	84	84	78	68	58	50
Normal Daily Minimum	26	27	34	42	50	57	61	60	54	42	33	27
Extreme High	76	81	83	89	92	97	100	97	97	91	81	75
Extreme Low	−8	−2	4	21	24	35	45	40	30	17	4	−3
Days Above 90°	0	0	0	0	0	3	4	3	1	0	0	0
Days Below 32°	23	21	15	5	1	0	0	0	0	6	16	22
PRECIPITATION												
Normal	4.2	4.3	6.1	4.5	4.7	5.0	4.6	5.8	4.5	4.2	3.9	4.4
Maximum	9.2	9.2	11.7	8.6	11.2	11.1	9.6	18.1	10.2	10.7	8.4	10.6
Maximum 24 Hr. Precipitation	2.6	5.0	4.4	3.2	4.9	3.6	4.4	9.2	4.9	3.2	3.7	3.8
Maximum Snowfall	3	4	3	0	0	0	0	0	0	0	1	1
Days With Measurable Precip.	10	11	11	10	12	11	12	12	9	8	10	10
Average No. Thunderstorms	1	1	3	4	10	12	14	13	4	1	1	0
SUNSHINE/CLOUDINESS												
No. Clear Days	10	9	9	10	8	6	5	5	7	12	10	10
No. Partly Cloudy Days	7	6	9	9	9	12	13	14	10	8	7	7
No. Cloudy Days	14	13	13	11	14	12	13	12	13	11	13	14
% Possible Sunshine	56	61	62	66	61	64	59	54	55	60	57	57

% OF SUNNY/PTLY CLOUDY/CLOUDY DAYS

☐ Clear   ▦ Ptlycldy   ■ Cloudy

etc.
- This area is shielded from some winter outbreaks of cold polar air by the mountains to the west. When cold air does cross the Appalachians, it is often warmed by its downslope flow.
- Snowfall here is not significant; some sleet and freezing rain is experienced in winter.

CLIMATABLE NO. 121   Guilford Court House NMP

WEATHER PARAMETERS	J	F	M	A	M	J	J	A	S	O	N	D
TEMPERATURE												
Normal Daily Maximum	48	51	59	71	78	84	87	86	80	70	60	50
Normal Daily Minimum	27	29	36	46	55	63	67	66	59	47	37	30
Extreme High	78	81	90	94	98	102	102	101	100	95	85	78
Extreme Low	−8	−4	5	21	32	42	48	45	35	20	10	0
Days Above 90°	0	0	0	0	1	6	11	8	2	0	0	0
Days Below 32°	23	20	10	2	0	0	0	0	0	2	10	18
PRECIPITATION												
Normal	3.5	3.4	3.9	3.2	3.4	3.9	4.3	4.2	3.6	3.2	2.6	3.4
Maximum	8.2	7.0	8.8	6.2	8.4	8.0	12.7	12.5	13.3	9.6	8.3	6.4
Maximum 24 Hr. Precipitation	3.1	3.0	3.1	2.7	3.1	4.9	4.4	4.5	7.5	6.2	3.3	3.6
Maximum Snowfall	23	16	21	T	0	0	0	0	0	0	6	14
Days With Measurable Precip.	10	10	11	9	10	10	12	11	8	7	8	9
Average No. Thunderstorms	0	1	2	4	9	10	13	11	4	2	0	0
SUNSHINE/CLOUDINESS												
No. Clear Days	9	9	9	9	8	7	6	7	10	14	11	10
No. Partly Cloudy Days	7	6	8	9	11	13	13	13	9	7	7	6
No. Cloudy Days	15	13	14	12	12	10	12	11	11	10	12	15
% Possible Sunshine	53	57	60	64	65	66	63	63	63	65	58	55

TEMPERATURE NORMALS AND EXTREMES

% OF SUNNY/PTLY CLOUDY/CLOUDY DAYS

☐ Clear   ▦ Ptlycldy   ■ Cloudy

etc. :

• Winter temperatures and rainfall are somewhat modified by the mountains to the west.

• Summer temperatures are generally mild.

• Seasonal snowfall totals vary greatly from year to year. In any case, the snow sledom remains on the ground for more than a few days

CLIMATABLE NO. 122
William Howard Taft NHS, North Country NST

TEMPERATURE NORMALS AND EXTREMES

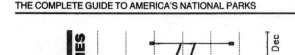

% OF SUNNY/PTLY CLOUDY/CLOUDY DAYS

☐ Clear   ▦ Ptlycldy   ■ Cloudy

WEATHER PARAMETERS	J	F	M	A	M	J	J	A	S	O	N	D
TEMPERATURE												
Normal Daily Maximum	40	43	52	66	75	84	87	86	80	69	53	42
Normal Daily Minimum	24	26	34	45	54	62	66	64	57	47	36	27
Extreme High	77	77	88	90	95	102	109	103	101	92	83	71
Extreme Low	-17	-9	3	18	28	40	48	43	32	20	1	-13
Days Above 90°	0	0	0	0	1	5	10	8	4	0	0	0
Days Below 32°	24	21	16	3	0	0	0	0	0	2	11	22
PRECIPITATION												
Normal	3.4	3.0	4.1	3.8	4.0	3.9	4.0	3.0	2.7	2.2	3.1	2.9
Maximum	13.7	6.2	11.5	8.6	10.2	9.1	10.0	6.5	8.7	9.5	6.5	6.9
Maximum 24 Hr. Precipitation	4.5	2.4	4.6	3.4	4.8	3.5	4.1	3.5	3.7	2.4	3.0	3.3
Maximum Snowfall	20	15	13	5	T	0	0	0	0	5	10	16
Days With Measurable Precip.	12	11	13	12	12	12	10	9	9	10	10	11
Average No. Thunderstorms	1	1	4	6	8	10	10	8	5	2	1	0
SUNSHINE/CLOUDINESS												
No. Clear Days	5	5	5	6	6	7	8	8	10	10	6	5
No. Partly Cloudy Days	6	6	7	7	9	10	11	12	9	9	6	6
No. Cloudy Days	20	17	19	17	16	13	12	11	11	13	18	20
% Possible Sunshine	41	45	50	55	60	67	68	66	66	59	44	38

etc.
- Summers are warm and humid, at times uncomfortable, with many showers and thunderstorms.
- Winters are moderately cold with frequent periods of extensive cloudiness.
- Autumn is quite pleasant with a minimum of rainfall, lots of sunshine and comfortable temperatures.

CLIMATABLE NO. 123

Mound City Group NM, North Country NST

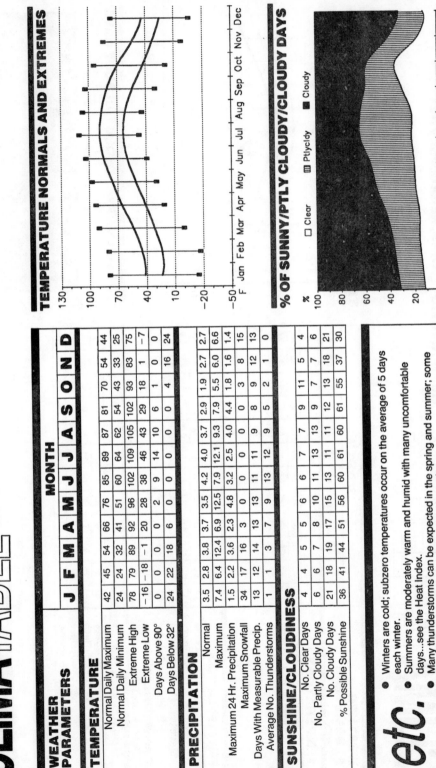

TEMPERATURE NORMALS AND EXTREMES

% OF SUNNY/PTLY CLOUDY/CLOUDY DAYS

☐ Clear   ▦ Ptlycldy   ■ Cloudy

WEATHER PARAMETERS	MONTH											
	J	F	M	A	M	J	J	A	S	O	N	D
TEMPERATURE												
Normal Daily Maximum	42	45	54	66	76	85	89	87	81	70	54	44
Normal Daily Minimum	24	24	32	41	51	60	64	62	54	43	33	25
Extreme High	78	79	89	92	96	102	109	105	102	93	83	75
Extreme Low	−16	−18	−1	20	28	38	46	43	29	18	1	−7
Days Above 90°	0	0	0	0	2	9	14	10	6	1	0	0
Days Below 32°	24	22	18	6	0	0	0	0	0	4	16	24
PRECIPITATION												
Normal	3.5	2.8	3.8	3.7	3.5	4.2	4.0	3.7	2.9	1.9	2.7	2.7
Maximum	7.4	6.4	12.4	6.9	12.5	7.9	12.1	9.3	7.9	5.5	6.0	6.6
Maximum 24 Hr. Precipitation	1.5	2.2	3.6	2.3	4.8	3.2	2.5	4.0	4.4	1.8	1.6	1.4
Maximum Snowfall	34	17	16	3	0	0	0	0	0	3	8	15
Days With Measurable Precip.	13	12	14	13	13	11	11	9	8	9	12	13
Average No. Thunderstorms	1	1	3	7	9	12	13	12	9	5	2	0
SUNSHINE/CLOUDINESS												
No. Clear Days	4	4	5	5	6	6	7	7	9	11	5	4
No. Partly Cloudy Days	6	6	7	8	10	11	13	13	9	7	7	6
No. Cloudy Days	21	18	19	17	15	13	11	11	12	13	18	21
% Possible Sunshine	36	41	44	51	56	60	61	61	60	55	37	30

etc.

- Winters are cold; subzero temperatures occur on the average of 5 days each winter.
- Summers are moderately warm and humid with many uncomfortable days...see the Heat Index.
- Many thunderstorms can be expected in the spring and summer; some can become severe or even spawn a tornado.

CLIMATABLE NO. 124   Moores Creek NB

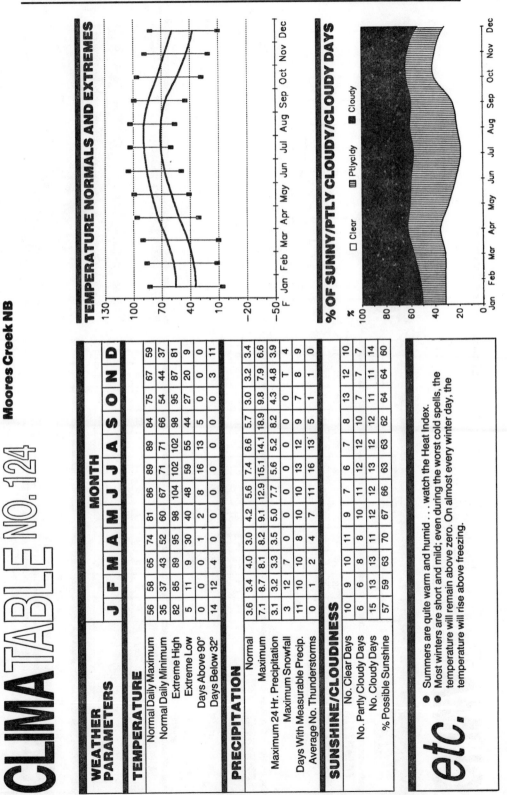

TEMPERATURE NORMALS AND EXTREMES

% OF SUNNY/PTLY CLOUDY/CLOUDY DAYS

☐ Clear   ▦ Ptlycldy   ▨ Cloudy

WEATHER PARAMETERS	J	F	M	A	M	J	J	A	S	O	N	D
TEMPERATURE												
Normal Daily Maximum	56	58	65	74	81	86	89	89	84	75	67	59
Normal Daily Minimum	35	37	43	52	60	67	71	71	66	54	44	37
Extreme High	82	85	89	95	98	104	102	102	98	95	87	81
Extreme Low	5	11	9	30	40	48	59	55	44	27	20	9
Days Above 90°	0	0	0	1	2	8	16	13	5	0	0	0
Days Below 32°	14	12	4	0	0	0	0	0	0	0	3	11
PRECIPITATION												
Normal	3.6	3.4	4.0	3.0	4.2	5.6	7.4	6.6	5.7	3.0	3.2	3.4
Maximum	7.1	8.7	8.1	8.2	9.1	12.9	15.1	14.1	18.9	9.8	7.9	6.6
Maximum 24 Hr. Precipitation	3.1	3.2	3.3	3.5	5.0	7.7	5.6	5.2	8.2	4.3	4.8	3.9
Maximum Snowfall	3	12	7	0	0	0	0	0	0	0	T	4
Days With Measurable Precip.	11	10	10	8	10	10	13	12	9	7	8	9
Average No. Thunderstorms	0	1	2	4	7	11	16	13	5	1	1	0
SUNSHINE/CLOUDINESS												
No. Clear Days	10	9	10	11	9	7	6	7	8	13	12	10
No. Partly Cloudy Days	6	6	8	8	10	11	12	12	10	7	7	7
No. Cloudy Days	15	13	13	11	12	12	13	12	12	11	11	14
% Possible Sunshine	57	59	63	70	67	66	63	63	62	64	64	60

etc.

- Summers are quite warm and humid . . . watch the Heat Index.
- Most winters are short and mild; even during the worst cold spells, the temperature will remain above zero. On almost every winter day, the temperature will rise above freezing.

CLIMATABLE NO. 125 International Peace Garden

TEMPERATURE NORMALS AND EXTREMES

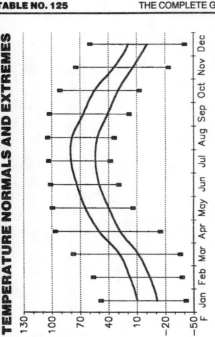

% OF SUNNY/PTLY CLOUDY/CLOUDY DAYS

☐ Clear   ▦ Ptlycldy   ■ Cloudy

WEATHER PARAMETERS	MONTH											
	J	F	M	A	M	J	J	A	S	O	N	D
TEMPERATURE												
Normal Daily Maximum	10	18	29	50	65	74	80	79	67	55	34	19
Normal Daily Minimum	-11	-3	9	28	40	50	54	52	41	30	14	-1
Extreme High	47	55	76	95	98	100	102	103	101	90	73	58
Extreme Low	-43	-39	-37	-16	13	28	37	33	17	6	-25	-42
Days Above 90°	0	0	0	0	0	1	4	4	1	0	0	0
Days Below 32°	31	28	30	21	7	0	0	0	5	19	29	31
PRECIPITATION												
Normal	0.5	0.4	0.6	1.3	2.2	3.3	2.8	2.9	2.0	1.0	0.5	0.5
Maximum	1.1	2.3	1.8	7.3	4.9	10.4	6.3	10.5	8.3	4.6	1.2	1.4
Maximum 24 Hr. Precipitation	0.4	0.6	0.8	2.8	2.4	2.5	3.4	4.0	5.0	1.6	0.7	1.0
Maximum Snowfall	20	24	20	14	3	0	0	0	2	19	12	14
Days With Measurable Precip.	8	7	8	8	10	12	11	10	7	6	6	8
Average No. Thunderstorms	0	0	0	1	5	11	11	8	3	1	0	0
SUNSHINE/CLOUDINESS												
No. Clear Days	7	5	5	6	7	7	11	12	10	9	6	7
No. Partly Cloudy Days	7	8	9	9	10	11	13	11	9	8	7	7
No. Cloudy Days	17	15	17	15	14	12	7	8	11	14	17	17
% Possible Sunshine	54	59	58	58	62	64	75	72	65	58	44	47

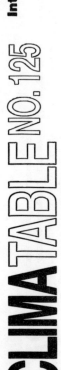

etc.

- Winters are long and bitterly cold, but summers can be hot. The annual range of temperature is extremely large.
- Three-quarters of the annual precipitation falls between May and September, mostly as showers and thunderstorms.
- The normal seasonal snowfall is about 34".

CLIMATABLE NO. 126   Theodore Roosevelt NP

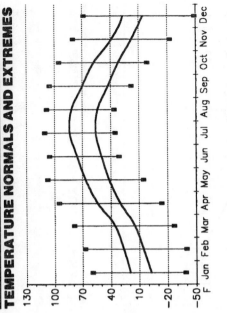

TEMPERATURE NORMALS AND EXTREMES

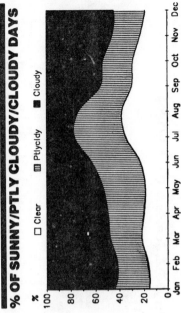

% OF SUNNY/PTLY CLOUDY/CLOUDY DAYS

□ Clear   ▥ Pt'ycldy   ■ Cloudy

WEATHER PARAMETERS	MONTH											
	J	F	M	A	M	J	J	A	S	O	N	D
TEMPERATURE												
Normal Daily Maximum	20	27	36	54	67	76	84	82	70	58	39	27
Normal Daily Minimum	−2	6	15	30	42	50	56	54	43	32	18	6
Extreme High	58	66	78	94	106	104	109	107	104	94	79	67
Extreme Low	−40	−41	−28	−15	4	30	34	35	17	0	−24	−50
Days Above 90°	0	0	0	0	1	2	8	9	2	0	0	0
Days Below 32°	31	28	29	18	4	0	0	0	3	15	28	31
PRECIPITATION												
Normal	0.5	0.5	0.6	1.5	2.1	3.0	2.0	1.5	1.4	0.8	0.5	0.5
Maximum	1.4	1.5	2.5	4.8	7.4	7.7	6.2	5.6	6.2	3.6	1.6	1.4
Maximum 24 Hr. Precipitation	0.5	1.0	1.0	2.0	2.7	3.1	5.0	2.8	2.2	2.2	0.8	0.9
Maximum Snowfall	24	16	31	22	16	4	0	0	4	14	17	16
Days With Measurable Precip.	8	7	8	8	10	10	9	7	7	5	6	8
Average No. Thunderstorms	0	0	0	1	5	12	12	9	3	0	0	0
SUNSHINE/CLOUDINESS												
No. Clear Days	5	5	7	6	6	7	11	12	9	9	7	6
No. Partly Cloudy Days	9	7	8	9	11	12	13	11	8	8	7	8
No. Cloudy Days	17	16	16	15	14	11	7	8	13	14	16	17
% Possible Sunshine	52	57	61	61	63	67	76	75	64	59	43	49

etc.

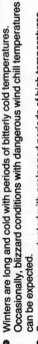

- Winters are long and cold with periods of bitterly cold temperatures. Occasionally, blizzard conditions with dangerous wind chill temperatures can be expected.
- Summers are punctuated with prolonged periods of high temperatures, though low humidity minimizes discomfort; nights are usually cool.

CLIMATABLE NO. 127

Cuyahoga Valley NRA, James A. Garfield NHS

TEMPERATURE NORMALS AND EXTREMES

% OF SUNNY/PTLY CLOUDY/CLOUDY DAYS

□ Clear   ▥ Ptlycldy   ■ Cloudy

WEATHER PARAMETERS	J	F	M	A	M	J	J	A	S	O	N	D
TEMPERATURE												
Normal Daily Maximum	33	36	46	59	70	79	82	81	74	63	49	38
Normal Daily Minimum	17	19	28	38	48	57	61	60	53	42	33	23
Extreme High	73	69	83	88	92	101	103	102	101	90	82	77
Extreme Low	-24	-15	-5	10	24	31	41	38	32	20	-1	-15
Days Above 90°	0	0	0	0	0	2	4	2	1	0	0	0
Days Below 32°	28	24	21	9	1	0	0	0	0	3	14	24
PRECIPITATION												
Normal	2.6	2.2	3.4	3.3	3.6	3.3	4.0	3.3	3.0	2.2	2.5	2.6
Maximum	8.7	5.2	8.8	6.6	9.6	9.1	11.4	9.0	7.8	9.5	9.4	5.6
Maximum 24 Hr. Precipitation	3.0	2.6	3.3	2.2	3.7	4.0	4.2	3.1	6.3	3.4	2.7	2.1
Maximum Snowfall	43	27	26	16	3	0	0	0	T	8	22	30
Days With Measurable Precip.	16	15	16	14	13	11	11	10	9	10	14	16
Average No. Thunderstorms	0	0	3	6	9	11	12	9	5	2	1	0
SUNSHINE/CLOUDINESS												
No. Clear Days	3	3	4	5	6	7	7	8	9	9	4	3
No. Partly Cloudy Days	6	6	7	8	9	11	13	12	9	8	6	5
No. Cloudy Days	22	19	20	17	16	12	11	11	12	14	20	23
% Possible Sunshine	31	37	44	53	58	65	67	63	60	53	31	26

etc.

- Winter temperatures are tempered by nearby Lake Erie. This area is subject to some brief but heavy lake-effect snow squalls in the fall and early winter.
- The normal seasonal snowfall decreases with distance from the lakeshore.

CLIMATABLE NO. 128

Perry's Victory and International Peace Memorial

TEMPERATURE NORMALS AND EXTREMES

% OF SUNNY/PTLY CLOUDY/CLOUDY DAYS

WEATHER PARAMETERS	J	F	M	A	M	J	J	A	S	O	N	D
TEMPERATURE												
Normal Daily Maximum	33	35	43	55	67	78	82	81	75	64	49	36
Normal Daily Minimum	20	21	28	39	51	62	67	66	60	49	36	25
Extreme High	66	71	75	87	92	99	104	101	99	93	78	64
Extreme Low	−15	−7	0	20	30	43	51	50	41	29	10	−8
Days Above 90°	0	0	0	0	0	2	3	3	1	0	0	0
Days Below 32°	28	25	21	5	0	0	0	0	0	0	8	24
PRECIPITATION												
Normal	2.0	1.9	2.4	3.0	3.0	3.1	3.0	3.1	2.1	2.1	1.8	1.7
Maximum	5.8	3.6	4.5	6.3	6.9	6.9	6.3	6.3	5.5	4.5	3.6	4.1
Maximum 24 Hr. Precipitation	1.9	2.2	2.0	2.2	3.5	2.2	2.5	2.4	2.9	2.0	1.6	1.4
Maximum Snowfall	12	19	21	8	0	0	0	0	0	0	7	20
Days With Measurable Precip.	9	8	9	10	10	9	7	7	7	6	8	8
Average No. Thunderstorms	0	1	3	6	8	11	11	8	5	2	1	0
SUNSHINE/CLOUDINESS												
No. Clear Days	4	4	5	6	6	7	8	8	9	8	4	3
No. Partly Cloudy Days	7	7	7	8	11	12	13	12	9	9	7	6
No. Cloudy Days	20	17	19	16	14	11	10	11	12	14	19	22
% Possible Sunshine	42	47	50	53	60	64	67	63	61	55	38	33

etc.

- Experiences moderately warm and humid summers and reasonably cold and cloudy winters.
- Winter temperatures are somewhat tempered by Lake Erie.
- This is the driest area of Ohio; the cool lake water inhibits the formation of afternoon thunderstorms in the spring and early summer.

CLIMATABLE NO. 129   Chickasaw NRA

TEMPERATURE NORMALS AND EXTREMES

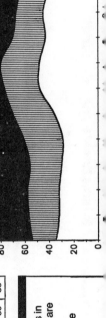

WEATHER PARAMETERS	MONTH											
	J	F	M	A	M	J	J	A	S	O	N	D
TEMPERATURE												
Normal Daily Maximum	53	58	65	76	82	89	95	96	88	78	65	56
Normal Daily Minimum	28	32	39	51	59	67	71	70	62	51	39	31
Extreme High	85	89	92	96	97	107	110	111	108	99	89	87
Extreme Low	–10	–4	1	25	33	41	50	48	31	22	11	–1
Days Above 90°	0	0	0	1	3	16	26	27	14	3	0	0
Days Below 32°	21	15	10	2	0	0	0	0	0	2	10	18
PRECIPITATION												
Normal	1.7	2.0	2.8	4.1	5.5	4.1	2.9	2.6	3.8	3.8	2.2	2.0
Maximum	5.0	4.0	7.2	13.6	11.6	9.4	6.3	11.7	10.5	8.0	6.4	5.5
Maximum 24 Hr. Precipitation	2.8	4.8	3.0	4.7	6.5	4.9	4.0	4.3	6.3	11.6	3.1	7.4
Maximum Snowfall	10	8	14	0	0	0	0	0	0	0	1	6
Days With Measurable Precip.	6	6	7	8	10	8	6	6	7	6	6	6
Average No. Thunderstorms	1	2	4	7	13	10	9	8	6	3	2	1
SUNSHINE/CLOUDINESS												
No. Clear Days	11	9	10	9	9	11	15	15	13	14	12	12
No. Partly Cloudy Days	6	7	8	8	10	10	9	10	8	7	7	6
No. Cloudy Days	14	12	13	13	12	9	7	6	9	10	11	13
% Possible Sunshine	60	60	64	66	67	74	79	80	73	69	60	59

% OF SUNNY/PTLY CLOUDY/CLOUDY DAYS

☐ Clear   ▦ Ptlycldy   ■ Cloudy

etc.

• About 70% of the annual precipitation is derived from thunderstorms in the period from April to October. On occasion, these thunderstorms are accompanied by large hail and destructive winds.

• Winters are cold, but generally not extreme; on most winter days, the temperature rises above freezing.

CLIMATABLE NO. 130

McLoughlin House NHS, Fort Vancouver NHS, Lewis and Clark NHT, Oregon NHT

TEMPERATURE NORMALS AND EXTREMES

% OF SUNNY/PTLY CLOUDY/CLOUDY DAYS

Clear   Ptlycldy   Cloudy

WEATHER PARAMETERS	J	F	M	A	M	J	J	A	S	O	N	D
TEMPERATURE												
Normal Daily Maximum	45	51	55	61	68	74	80	80	75	64	54	47
Normal Daily Minimum	33	36	37	40	46	50	54	54	50	44	38	35
Extreme High	64	73	80	91	100	100	107	107	101	94	73	66
Extreme Low	-2	-3	19	24	29	34	38	35	28	21	9	-2
Days Above 90°	0	0	0	0	0	1	4	4	2	0	0	0
Days Below 32°	13	8	7	2	0	0	0	0	0	2	6	10
PRECIPITATION												
Normal	6.7	4.3	3.8	2.6	2.2	1.6	0.6	1.2	1.9	3.5	5.6	7.0
Maximum	12.8	9.2	7.8	4.6	4.2	3.5	2.9	5.1	4.8	7.2	12.9	11.5
Maximum 24 Hr. Precipitation	2.2	1.8	1.4	1.4	1.2	1.8	1.8	1.6	1.5	2.3	3.0	2.3
Maximum Snowfall	42	6	6	0	0	0	0	0	0	0	4	9
Days With Measurable Precip.	18	16	17	14	12	9	4	5	8	13	18	19
Average No. Thunderstorms	0	0	1	1	2	1	1	1	1	0	0	0
SUNSHINE/CLOUDINESS												
No. Clear Days	3	3	3	4	5	6	13	11	10	6	3	2
No. Partly Cloudy Days	3	3	5	6	7	8	9	10	8	7	4	3
No. Cloudy Days	25	22	23	20	19	16	9	10	12	18	23	26
% Possible Sunshine	27	37	47	52	57	56	70	66	61	43	29	23

etc.

- Winters are mild with extensive cloudiness and frequent gentle rains; heavy downpours are uncommon.
- Summers are pleasantly mild and sunny; very hot temperatures are rare.
- Through the spring and summer, thunderstorms occur about once a month.

CLIMATABLE NO. 131

Fort Clatsop, Lewis and Clark NHT

TEMPERATURE NORMALS AND EXTREMES

% OF SUNNY/PTLY CLOUDY/CLOUDY DAYS

□ Clear   ▥ Ptlycldy   ■ Cloudy

WEATHER PARAMETERS	MONTH											
	J	F	M	A	M	J	J	A	S	O	N	D
TEMPERATURE												
Normal Daily Maximum	47	51	52	56	60	64	68	69	68	61	54	49
Normal Daily Minimum	35	37	37	40	44	49	52	53	49	44	40	37
Extreme High	67	72	73	83	87	93	100	96	95	85	71	64
Extreme Low	11	19	22	29	30	37	39	39	33	26	15	6
Days Above 90°	0	0	0	0	0	0	0	0	0	0	0	0
Days Below 32°	10	6	6	2	0	0	0	0	0	0	5	8
PRECIPITATION												
Normal	11.3	7.8	7.3	4.6	2.8	2.4	1.0	1.6	3.1	6.2	9.9	11.6
Maximum	18.9	21.9	13.5	8.0	6.6	5.5	4.4	5.2	6.9	12.6	16.8	16.6
Maximum 24 Hr. Precipitation	5.1	3.3	2.7	2.3	1.8	2.4	2.0	1.6	2.6	3.7	4.2	3.6
Maximum Snowfall	26	4	7	1	0	0	0	0	T	T	5	19
Days With Measurable Precip.	22	20	20	18	15	13	7	8	11	16	20	23
Average No. Thunderstorms	1	0	1	1	0	0	0	0	1	2	1	2
SUNSHINE/CLOUDINESS												
No. Clear Days	3	3	3	3	3	3	6	6	8	5	3	3
No. Partly Cloudy Days	4	3	5	6	9	8	10	10	7	7	5	4
No. Cloudy Days	24	22	23	21	19	19	15	15	15	19	22	24
% Possible Sunshine	25	35	40	48	49	49	50	50	48	40	25	20

etc.
- Winter is known for heavy cloudiness, frequent high winds and abundant rain; seasonal snowfall is 5". Winds of hurricane force can occur several times a year.
- This is the foggiest area along the west coast of the United States. On the average, there are over 2500 hours a year of fog.

CLIMATABLE NO. 132 Crater Lake NP

TEMPERATURE NORMALS AND EXTREMES

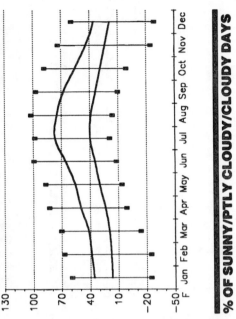

% OF SUNNY/PTLY CLOUDY/CLOUDY DAYS

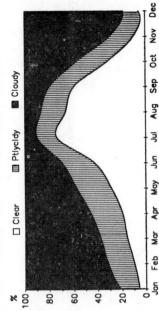

☐ Clear ▦ Ptlycldy ■ Cloudy

WEATHER PARAMETERS	MONTH											
	J	F	M	A	M	J	J	A	S	O	N	D
TEMPERATURE												
Normal Daily Maximum	36	39	42	50	56	66	77	75	68	56	44	36
Normal Daily Minimum	17	18	20	24	30	35	40	39	34	29	24	19
Extreme High	58	66	69	82	86	98	97	101	96	87	72	58
Extreme Low	−26	−26	−15	0	5	0	18	15	9	0	−26	−30
Days Above 90°	0	0	0	0	0	0	1	1	0	0	0	0
Days Below 32°	31	28	30	27	20	11	5	6	13	22	26	30
PRECIPITATION												
Normal	10.8	8.7	8.2	4.3	3.3	2.5	0.6	0.6	2.0	6.4	8.0	11.7
Maximum	20.9	19.7	15.2	11.6	8.7	9.2	2.9	5.3	6.9	19.1	17.2	38.5
Maximum 24 Hr. Precipitation	3.8	3.5	2.3	4.2	1.9	2.0	1.5	1.1	2.6	3.2	2.6	5.1
Maximum Snowfall	313	248	194	144	103	14	T	5	20	88	128	196
Days With Measurable Precip.	17	15	16	12	10	7	3	3	5	10	13	16
Average No. Thunderstorms	0	0	0	1	2	3	2	2	1	0	0	0
SUNSHINE/CLOUDINESS												
No. Clear Days	2	3	5	6	9	13	23	21	18	10	3	2
No. Partly Cloudy Days	5	6	7	8	9	8	5	6	6	8	6	4
No. Cloudy Days	24	19	19	16	13	9	3	4	6	13	21	25
% Possible Sunshine	30	40	50	60	60	70	90	80	80	60	35	30

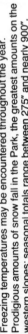

etc.

- Freezing temperatures may be encountered throughout the year.
- Prodigious amounts of snow fall in the Park, the greatest amounts on the western slopes; seasonal totals range between 275" and nearly 900". Snow depths can reach 20'.
- Summers are sunny with only brief, infrequent showers.

CLIMATABLE NO. 133   John Day Fossil Beds NM

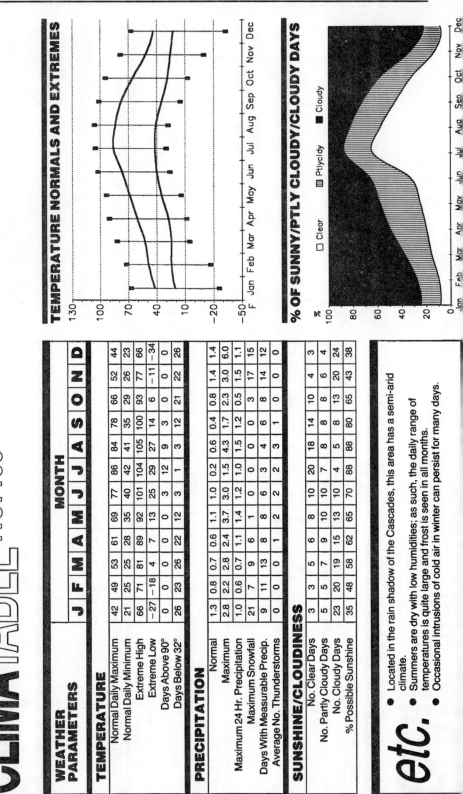

WEATHER PARAMETERS	\ MONTH \											
	J	F	M	A	M	J	J	A	S	O	N	D
TEMPERATURE												
Normal Daily Maximum	42	49	53	61	69	77	86	84	78	66	52	44
Normal Daily Minimum	21	25	25	28	35	40	42	41	35	29	26	23
Extreme High	66	71	81	89	92	101	104	105	100	93	77	66
Extreme Low	-27	-18	4	7	13	25	29	27	14	6	-11	-34
Days Above 90°	0	0	0	0	0	3	12	9	3	0	0	0
Days Below 32°	26	23	26	22	12	3	1	3	12	21	22	26
PRECIPITATION												
Normal	1.3	0.8	0.7	0.6	1.1	1.0	0.2	0.6	0.4	0.8	1.4	1.4
Maximum	2.8	2.2	2.8	2.4	3.7	3.0	1.5	4.3	1.7	2.3	3.0	6.0
Maximum 24 Hr. Precipitation	1.0	0.6	0.7	1.1	1.4	1.2	1.0	1.5	1.2	0.5	1.5	1.1
Maximum Snowfall	21	7	9	6	1	0	0	0	0	3	17	15
Days With Measurable Precip.	9	11	13	8	8	6	3	4	6	8	14	12
Average No. Thunderstorms	0	0	0	1	2	2	2	3	1	0	0	0
SUNSHINE/CLOUDINESS												
No. Clear Days	3	3	5	6	8	10	20	18	14	10	4	3
No. Partly Cloudy Days	5	5	7	9	10	10	7	8	8	8	6	4
No. Cloudy Days	23	20	19	15	13	10	4	5	8	13	20	24
% Possible Sunshine	35	48	58	62	65	70	88	88	80	65	43	38

TEMPERATURE NORMALS AND EXTREMES

% OF SUNNY/PTLY CLOUDY/CLOUDY DAYS

□ Clear   ▦ Ptlycldy   ■ Cloudy

etc.

- Located in the rain shadow of the Cascades, this area has a semi-arid climate.
- Summers are dry with low humidities; as such, the daily range of temperatures is quite large and frost is seen in all months.
- Occasional intrusions of cold air in winter can persist for many days.

CLIMATABLE NO. 134   Oregon Caves NM

WEATHER PARAMETERS	J	F	M	A	M	J	J	A	S	O	N	D
TEMPERATURE												
Normal Daily Maximum	40	43	44	51	59	67	76	74	70	59	47	42
Normal Daily Minimum	30	32	31	33	39	45	52	52	50	43	36	32
Extreme High	66	67	74	82	91	95	100	97	97	87	77	66
Extreme Low	-2	9	15	19	22	27	36	36	26	20	11	2
Days Above 90°	0	0	0	0	0	0	1	1	0	0	0	0
Days Below 32°	18	16	20	16	7	0	0	0	0	3	11	18
PRECIPITATION												
Normal	7.0	4.4	4.0	2.1	1.9	1.0	0.3	0.7	1.3	3.2	6.0	6.4
Maximum	19.0	10.3	9.0	7.5	7.3	4.7	3.8	4.2	4.3	13.9	24.1	20.0
Maximum 24 Hr. Precipitation	6.0	4.0	2.6	2.0	3.1	2.2	2.2	1.7	2.3	5.2	4.7	4.4
Maximum Snowfall	106	58	45	44	13	2	0	T	3	17	43	80
Days With Measurable Precip.	16	15	17	12	9	6	2	3	6	10	15	17
Average No. Thunderstorms	0	0	0	0	1	1	1	1	1	0	0	0
SUNSHINE/CLOUDINESS												
No. Clear Days	5	5	5	6	9	13	23	21	17	11	6	5
No. Partly Cloudy Days	5	4	5	7	7	7	5	6	6	6	5	4
No. Cloudy Days	21	19	21	17	15	10	3	4	7	14	19	22
% Possible Sunshine	30	40	50	50	50	60	70	70	60	50	38	29

etc.

- Winter is a time of extensive cloudiness and frequent precipitation which falls as rain in the valleys and as snow at the higher elevations.
- Except on the highest peaks, accumulations of snow are rare.
- Summer weather is fair with lots of sunshine.

TEMPERATURE NORMALS AND EXTREMES

% OF SUNNY/PTLY CLOUDY/CLOUDY DAYS

□ Clear   ▦ Ptlycldy   ■ Cloudy

CLIMATABLE NO. 135

Allegheny Portage Railroad NHS, Johnstown Flood NM

TEMPERATURE NORMALS AND EXTREMES

% OF SUNNY/PTLY CLOUDY/CLOUDY DAYS

☐ Clear   ▦ Ptlycldy   ■ Cloudy

WEATHER PARAMETERS	J	F	M	A	M	J	J	A	S	O	N	D
TEMPERATURE												
Normal Daily Maximum	36	38	47	61	72	80	84	82	76	64	50	39
Normal Daily Minimum	20	20	28	38	48	56	60	58	52	41	32	24
Extreme High	78	75	84	95	94	100	100	100	104	94	82	76
Extreme Low	-20	-20	-4	8	25	32	40	36	25	18	4	-12
Days Above 90°	0	0	0	0	1	5	9	6	3	0	0	0
Days Below 32°	28	25	22	9	2	0	0	0	0	6	17	26
PRECIPITATION												
Normal	3.5	3.0	4.1	4.2	4.3	4.5	4.8	3.8	3.2	3.1	3.2	3.2
Maximum	9.8	7.6	8.2	7.2	7.2	9.4	14.0	10.1	9.0	8.2	6.5	5.6
Maximum 24 Hr. Precipitation	1.6	1.5	4.1	2.2	4.2	3.1	8.8	3.2	2.4	3.6	3.9	2.7
Maximum Snowfall	46	37	34	7	1	0	0	0	0	2	20	32
Days With Measurable Precip.	16	14	16	14	12	12	11	10	9	11	13	16
Average No. Thunderstorms	0	0	1	4	6	9	10	7	4	1	1	0
SUNSHINE/CLOUDINESS												
No. Clear Days	5	5	6	6	6	6	6	6	7	7	4	4
No. Partly Cloudy Days	8	7	8	8	10	12	13	13	11	9	7	7
No. Cloudy Days	18	16	17	16	15	12	12	12	13	15	19	20
% Possible Sunshine	30	40	48	48	51	57	58	56	58	50	37	29

etc.

- Winter nights are often colder in the valleys than on the surrounding ridges. Precipitation and snowfall are greater along the ridge tops.
- Summers are generally pleasant; uncomfortable heat and humidity are rare.
- Deep fog collects in the valleys on many mornings, especially in the fall.

CLIMATABLE NO. 136

Friendship Hill NHS, Fort Necessity NB, Chesapeake and Ohio Canal NHP

TEMPERATURE NORMALS AND EXTREMES

% OF SUNNY/PTLY CLOUDY/CLOUDY DAYS

☐ Clear   ▦ Ptlycldy   ■ Cloudy

WEATHER PARAMETERS	J	F	M	A	M	J	J	A	S	O	N	D
TEMPERATURE												
Normal Daily Maximum	39	41	52	64	73	81	84	83	77	66	54	43
Normal Daily Minimum	21	22	30	40	49	58	62	61	54	42	34	26
Extreme High	73	75	85	92	91	96	99	99	99	92	84	76
Extreme Low	-17	-16	-3	16	23	33	40	39	31	18	1	-4
Days Above 90°	0	0	0	0	0	3	4	3	1	0	0	0
Days Below 32°	26	22	19	8	2	0	0	0	0	6	15	23
PRECIPITATION												
Normal	2.9	2.5	3.6	3.7	4.1	4.0	4.1	3.9	3.2	2.6	2.7	2.9
Maximum	5.2	5.7	8.6	6.1	6.9	10.9	9.2	9.0	6.0	8.2	4.6	6.0
Maximum 24 Hr. Precipitation	1.6	1.4	3.2	1.9	2.4	4.3	3.8	3.4	2.6	4.6	1.7	2.3
Maximum Snowfall	34	29	20	3	2	0	0	0	0	2	10	17
Days With Measurable Precip.	16	14	16	14	12	12	11	10	9	11	13	16
Average No. Thunderstorms	1	1	3	6	8	10	12	10	4	1	1	0
SUNSHINE/CLOUDINESS												
No. Clear Days	3	3	4	5	5	5	5	6	8	8	4	2
No. Partly Cloudy Days	6	6	7	8	9	12	13	12	10	8	6	6
No. Cloudy Days	22	19	20	17	17	13	13	13	12	15	20	23
% Possible Sunshine	33	37	44	48	51	57	58	58	52	37		29

etc.
- Summers are generally pleasant, though some intrusions of warm, humid air can be expected.
- Early morning fog frequently forms in the river valleys; in the fall and winter, the fog can be persistent.
- Some precipitation can be expected on one winter day out of every two.

CLIMATABLE NO. 137

Delaware Water Gap NRA, Middle Delaware NSR, Appalachian NST

TEMPERATURE NORMALS AND EXTREMES

% OF SUNNY/PTLY CLOUDY/CLOUDY DAYS

☐ Clear ▥ Ptlycldy ▦ Cloudy

WEATHER PARAMETERS	J	F	M	A	M	J	J	A	S	O	N	D
TEMPERATURE												
Normal Daily Maximum	35	38	48	62	73	81	86	83	75	64	50	38
Normal Daily Minimum	16	18	26	36	46	54	58	58	50	40	32	21
Extreme High	65	75	87	96	98	100	104	103	106	92	80	66
Extreme Low	−25	−16	−11	10	21	32	36	32	20	16	5	−14
Days Above 90°	0	0	0	0	1	3	8	5	2	0	0	0
Days Below 32°	30	26	25	12	2	0	0	0	1	8	18	27
PRECIPITATION												
Normal	3.4	3.0	4.0	4.0	3.8	3.7	4.0	4.2	4.0	3.6	4.0	3.9
Maximum	10.4	5.5	8.6	10.8	8.0	9.5	8.1	18.0	9.0	9.5	10.5	10.1
Maximum 24 Hr. Precipitation	2.8	1.9	2.6	3.0	3.1	4.7	3.6	5.8	4.2	4.3	4.8	5.3
Maximum Snowfall	37	42	47	10	0	0	0	0	0	4	17	37
Days With Measurable Precip.	12	11	13	12	12	11	11	11	10	10	12	13
Average No. Thunderstorms	0	0	1	3	5	8	11	8	4	1	0	0
SUNSHINE/CLOUDINESS												
No. Clear Days	4	4	6	7	6	7	6	7	7	8	4	4
No. Partly Cloudy Days	7	7	7	7	10	11	13	12	10	9	6	6
No. Cloudy Days	20	17	18	16	15	12	12	12	13	14	20	21
% Possible Sunshine	43	47	49	53	56	60	62	60	55	51	35	34

etc.

- Summers are pleasant with warm days and cool nights. Shower and thunderstorm activity peak in July.
- Summer evenings tend to be very damp along the river with light fog present on many mornings.
- Winters are cold, but generally not severe. From time to time, some heavy snow does fall.

CLIMATABLE NO. 138

Independence National Historical Park, Thaddeus Kosciuszko NM, Ben Franklin NM, Edgar Allen Poe NHS, Gloria Dei Church NHS

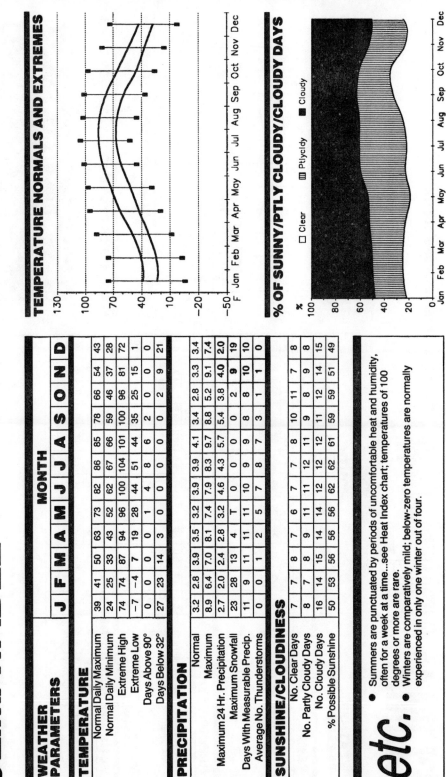

TEMPERATURE NORMALS AND EXTREMES

% OF SUNNY/PTLY CLOUDY/CLOUDY DAYS

□ Clear   ▨ Ptlycldy   ■ Cloudy

WEATHER PARAMETERS	J	F	M	A	M	J	J	A	S	O	N	D
TEMPERATURE												
Normal Daily Maximum	39	41	50	63	73	82	86	85	78	66	54	43
Normal Daily Minimum	24	25	33	43	52	62	67	66	59	46	37	28
Extreme High	74	74	87	94	96	100	104	101	100	96	81	72
Extreme Low	-7	-4	7	19	28	44	51	44	35	25	15	1
Days Above 90°	0	0	0	0	1	4	8	6	2	0	0	0
Days Below 32°	27	23	14	3	0	0	0	0	0	2	9	21
PRECIPITATION												
Normal	3.2	2.8	3.9	3.5	3.2	3.9	3.9	4.1	3.4	2.8	3.3	3.4
Maximum	8.9	6.4	7.0	8.1	7.4	7.9	8.3	9.7	8.8	5.2	9.1	7.4
Maximum 24 Hr. Precipitation	2.7	2.0	2.4	2.8	3.2	4.6	4.3	5.7	5.4	3.8	4.0	2.0
Maximum Snowfall	23	28	13	4	T	0	0	0	0	2	9	19
Days With Measurable Precip.	11	9	11	11	11	10	9	9	8	8	10	10
Average No. Thunderstorms	0	0	1	2	5	7	8	7	3	1	1	0
SUNSHINE/CLOUDINESS												
No. Clear Days	7	7	8	7	6	7	7	8	10	11	7	8
No. Partly Cloudy Days	8	7	8	9	11	11	12	11	9	8	9	8
No. Cloudy Days	16	14	15	14	14	12	12	12	11	12	14	15
% Possible Sunshine	50	53	56	56	56	62	62	61	59	59	51	49

etc.

- Summers are punctuated by periods of uncomfortable heat and humidity, often for a week at a time...see Heat Index chart; temperatures of 100 degrees or more are rare.
- Winters are comparatively mild; below-zero temperatures are normally experienced in only one winter out of four.

CLIMATABLE NO. 139

Gettysburg NMP, Eisenhower NHS

TEMPERATURE NORMALS AND EXTREMES

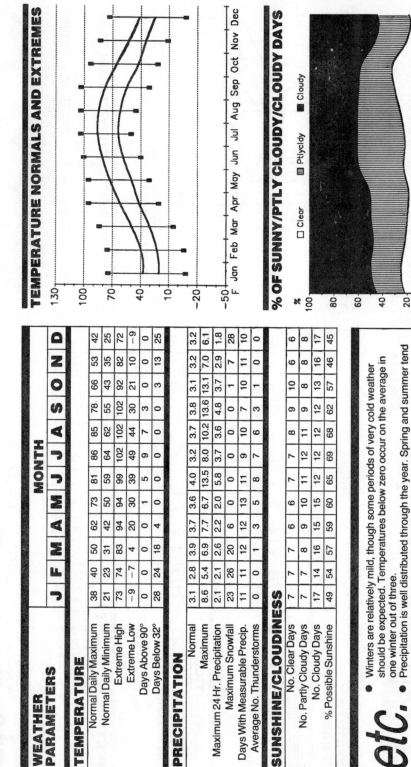

WEATHER PARAMETERS	J	F	M	A	M	J	J	A	S	O	N	D
MONTH												
TEMPERATURE												
Normal Daily Maximum	38	40	50	62	73	81	86	85	78·	66	53	42
Normal Daily Minimum	21	23	31	42	50	59	64	62	55	43	35	25
Extreme High	73	74	83	94	94	99	102	102	102	92	82	72
Extreme Low	−9	−7	4	20	30	39	49	44	30	21	10	−9
Days Above 90°	0	0	0	0	1	5	9	7	3	0	0	0
Days Below 32°	28	24	18	4	0	0	0	0	0	3	13	25
PRECIPITATION												
Normal	3.1	2.8	3.9	3.7	3.6	4.0	3.2	3.7	3.8	3.1	3.2	3.2
Maximum	8.6	5.4	6.9	7.7	6.7	13.5	8.0	10.2	13.6	13.1	7.0	6.1
Maximum 24 Hr. Precipitation	2.1	2.1	2.6	2.2	2.0	5.8	3.7	3.6	4.8	3.7	2.9	1.8
Maximum Snowfall	23	26	20	6	0	0	0	0	0	1	7	28
Days With Measurable Precip.	11	11	12	12	13	11	9	10	7	10	11	10
Average No. Thunderstorms	0	0	1	3	5	8	7	6	3	1	0	0
SUNSHINE/CLOUDINESS												
No. Clear Days	7	7	7	6	6	7	7	8	9	10	6	6
No. Partly Cloudy Days	7	7	8	9	10	11	12	11	9	8	8	8
No. Cloudy Days	17	14	16	15	15	12	12	12	12	13	16	17
% Possible Sunshine	49	54	57	59	60	65	69	68	62	57	46	45

% OF SUNNY/PTLY CLOUDY/CLOUDY DAYS

☐ Clear   ▥ Ptlycldy   ■ Cloudy

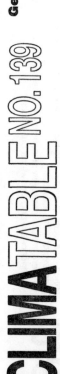

etc.

- Winters are relatively mild, though some periods of very cold weather should be expected. Temperatures below zero occur on the average in one winter out of three.
- Precipitation is well distributed through the year. Spring and summer tend to be the wettest seasons; February is the driest month.

CLIMATABLE NO. 140

Valley Forge NHP, Hopewell Village NHS

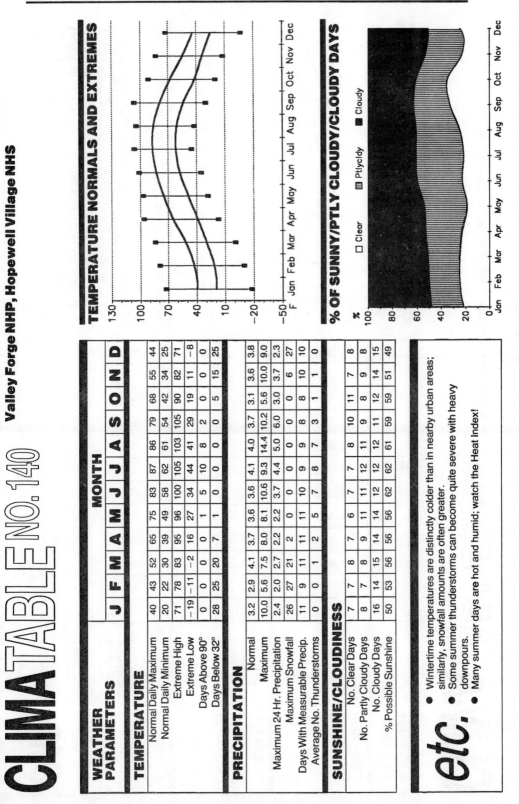

WEATHER PARAMETERS

	J	F	M	A	M	J	J	A	S	O	N	D
TEMPERATURE												
Normal Daily Maximum	40	43	52	65	75	83	87	86	79	68	55	44
Normal Daily Minimum	20	22	30	39	49	58	62	61	54	42	34	25
Extreme High	71	78	83	95	96	100	105	103	105	90	82	71
Extreme Low	−19	−11	−2	16	27	34	44	41	29	19	11	−8
Days Above 90°	0	0	0	0	1	5	10	8	2	0	0	0
Days Below 32°	28	25	20	7	1	0	0	0	0	5	15	25
PRECIPITATION												
Normal	3.2	2.9	4.1	3.7	3.6	3.6	4.1	4.0	3.7	3.1	3.6	3.8
Maximum	10.0	5.6	7.5	8.0	8.1	10.6	9.3	14.4	10.2	5.6	10.0	9.0
Maximum 24 Hr. Precipitation	2.4	2.0	2.7	2.2	2.2	3.7	4.4	5.0	6.0	3.0	3.7	2.3
Maximum Snowfall	26	27	21	2	0	0	0	0	0	0	6	27
Days With Measurable Precip.	11	9	11	11	10	9	9	8	8	8	10	10
Average No. Thunderstorms	0	0	1	2	5	7	8	7	3	1	1	0
SUNSHINE/CLOUDINESS												
No. Clear Days	7	7	8	7	6	7	7	8	10	11	7	8
No. Partly Cloudy Days	8	7	8	9	11	11	12	11	9	8	9	8
No. Cloudy Days	16	14	15	14	14	12	12	12	11	12	14	15
% Possible Sunshine	50	53	56	56	56	62	62	61	59	59	51	49

TEMPERATURE NORMALS AND EXTREMES

% OF SUNNY/PTLY CLOUDY/CLOUDY DAYS

☐ Clear   ▦ Ptlycldy   ■ Cloudy

etc.

- Wintertime temperatures are distinctly colder than in nearby urban areas; similarly, snowfall amounts are often greater.
- Some summer thunderstorms can become quite severe with heavy downpours.
- Many summer days are hot and humid; watch the Heat Index!

CLIMATABLE NO. 141

Touro Synagogue NHS, Roger Williams NM

TEMPERATURE NORMALS AND EXTREMES

% OF SUNNY/PTLY CLOUDY/CLOUDY DAYS

□ Clear   ▥ Ptlycldy   ■ Cloudy

WEATHER PARAMETERS	J	F	M	A	M	J	J	A	S	O	N	D
TEMPERATURE												
Normal Daily Maximum	37	38	46	58	68	76	82	80	73	64	52	41
Normal Daily Minimum	20	21	28	37	46	56	62	60	52	42	34	24
Extreme High	66	72	78	98	94	96	100	104	100	86	78	70
Extreme Low	−18	−18	−10	9	25	33	40	33	25	15	10	−16
Days Above 90°	0	0	0	0	1	2	4	2	1	0	0	0
Days Below 32°	28	25	23	11	2	0	0	0	1	8	16	25
PRECIPITATION												
Normal	4.2	3.7	4.4	4.0	3.8	3.0	3.0	4.2	3.8	3.9	4.4	4.5
Maximum	12.4	7.6	10.1	12.7	9.6	11.1	8.1	13.6	10.6	11.9	11.0	10.8
Maximum 24 Hr. Precipitation	3.9	3.3	4.5	4.4	5.2	5.0	4.8	6.7	6.5	6.6	4.2	3.8
Maximum Snowfall	34	31	34	8	7	0	0	0	0	2	4	22
Days With Measurable Precip.	11	10	12	11	11	11	9	10	8	8	11	12
Average No. Thunderstorms	0	0	1	1	3	5	6	5	2	1	1	0
SUNSHINE/CLOUDINESS												
No. Clear Days	10	8	8	8	7	7	7	8	10	11	8	8
No. Partly Cloudy Days	7	7	8	8	10	10	12	11	8	8	7	8
No. Cloudy Days	14	13	15	14	14	13	12	12	12	12	15	15
% Possible Sunshine	57	57	57	56	58	60	63	60	61	60	50	53

etc.

- Summers are warm with relatively few 90 degree days. Sea breezes keep coastal areas especially cool.
- Coastal storms or "northeasters" often bring strong winds, heavy rains and sometimes heavy snow.
- Snowfall averages 20" to 30" per winter with most of it falling in January and February.

CLIMATABLE NO. 142   Congaree SW...

TEMPERATURE NORMALS AND EXTREMES

WEATHER PARAMETERS	J	F	M	A	M	J	J	A	S	O	N	D
TEMPERATURE												
Normal Daily Maximum	56	60	67	77	84	88	92	90	86	76	68	59
Normal Daily Minimum	33	35	42	50	59	66	70	69	64	50	42	35
Extreme High	84	84	91	96	101	107	107	107	102	101	91	83
Extreme Low	-1	5	4	26	34	44	54	53	40	23	12	4
Days Above 90°	0	0	0	2	6	14	21	19	9	1	0	0
Days Below 32°	18	14	6	1	0	0	0	0	0	1	8	15
PRECIPITATION												
Normal	4.2	4.0	4.9	3.4	4.0	4.5	5.5	5.4	4.2	2.5	2.4	3.4
Maximum	9.3	8.7	10.9	10.7	9.8	14.8	13.9	16.7	12.0	12.1	7.5	8.5
Maximum 24 Hr. Precipitation	2.8	3.7	3.6	3.7	5.6	5.4	5.8	7.7	6.6	5.5	3.0	3.2
Maximum Snowfall	4	17	5	0	0	0	0	0	0	0	0	9
Days With Measurable Precip.	10	10	10	8	9	9	12	11	7	6	7	9
Average No. Thunderstorms	1	2	4	5	9	14	19	14	5	1	1	1
SUNSHINE/CLOUDINESS												
No. Clear Days	10	9	9	12	10	8	6	8	10	14	12	11
No. Partly Cloudy Days	6	6	8	7	10	12	13	13	9	7	6	6
No. Cloudy Days	15	13	14	11	11	10	12	10	11	10	12	14
% Possible Sunshine	57	60	65	70	68	68	67	67	66	66	63	60

% OF SUNNY/PTLY CLOUDY/CLOUDY DAYS

Legend: ☐ Clear   ▥ Ptlycldy   ■ Cloudy

etc.
- Summers are long, hot and humid; watch the Heat Index!
- The Appalachian mountains to the west often prevent the intrusion of very cold polar air; as a result, winters are generally mild.
- Most pleasant season is autumn; driest period is October and November when "Indian summer" prevails.

CLIMATABLE NO. 143   Cowpens NB, Kings Mountain NMP

TEMPERATURE NORMALS AND EXTREMES

WEATHER PARAMETERS	MONTH											
	J	F	M	A	M	J	J	A	S	O	N	D
TEMPERATURE												
Normal Daily Maximum	52	56	64	74	81	87	90	89	83	73	63	54
Normal Daily Minimum	31	32	39	48	57	64	68	67	61	49	39	33
Extreme High	79	80	87	92	97	107	106	102	101	95	85	79
Extreme Low	2	4	-1	25	31	40	54	49	34	25	11	4
Days Above 90°	0	0	0	1	4	10	16	15	5	0	0	0
Days Below 32°	18	16	8	1	0	0	0	0	0	1	8	17
PRECIPITATION												
Normal	4.2	4.1	5.2	3.6	4.1	4.1	4.2	4.4	3.9	2.8	2.9	3.7
Maximum	8.0	9.8	10.3	9.4	12.6	9.6	9.9	14.0	8.0	9.5	8.4	6.8
Maximum 24 Hr. Precipitation	2.4	3.0	4.1	3.1	4.6	2.8	3.3	4.9	3.3	4.0	2.9	4.3
Maximum Snowfall	12	17	17	0	0	0	0	0	0	0	0	6
Days With Measurable Precip.	10	10	11	9	10	10	11	10	7	7	8	10
Average No. Thunderstorms	1	1	3	4	8	9	12	9	3	1	1	1
SUNSHINE/CLOUDINESS												
No. Clear Days	9	9	9	10	8	7	7	8	9	13	12	10
No. Partly Cloudy Days	7	6	8	9	10	11	11	12	10	8	6	6
No. Cloudy Days	15	13	14	11	13	12	13	11	11	10	12	15
% Possible Sunshine	56	59	63	69	68	70	67	68	66	67	59	57

% OF SUNNY/PTLY CLOUDY/CLOUDY DAYS

☐ Clear   ▦ Ptlycldy   ▨ Cloudy

etc.

- Summers are long and hot with afternoon temperatures often in the 90's.
- Winters are pleasant; daytime temperatures remain below freezing on relatively few days. Extreme cold is rare, but does occur from time to time. Snow is infrequent and rarely remains on the ground for more than 2 days.

CLIMATABLE NO. 144   Fort Sumter

TEMPERATURE NORMALS AND EXTREMES

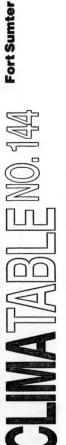

% OF SUNNY/PTLY CLOUDY/CLOUDY DAYS

☐ Clear   ▦ Ptlycldy   ■ Cloudy

WEATHER PARAMETERS	MONTH											
	J	F	M	A	M	J	J	A	S	O	N	D
TEMPERATURE												
Normal Daily Maximum	57	59	65	73	81	86	88	88	84	77	68	60
Normal Daily Minimum	40	41	48	56	64	70	74	74	69	58	49	42
Extreme High	78	81	90	89	99	105	100	102	97	93	84	78
Extreme Low	12	12	21	32	37	52	59	60	48	33	22	12
Days Above 90°	0	0	0	0	2	6	12	12	3	0	0	0
Days Below 32°	7	5	1	0	0	0	0	0	0	0	1	5
PRECIPITATION												
Normal	3.3	3.4	4.2	2.2	3.7	4.9	5.6	6.0	4.7	3.2	2.4	3.2
Maximum	7.0	7.7	9.5	4.8	14.3	17.9	17.9	20.6	11.2	12.5	10.2	6.4
Maximum 24 Hr. Precipitation	3.0	3.1	3.2	2.6	6.5	3.4	6.0	4.8	4.5	7.2	7.6	3.9
Maximum Snowfall	1	7	2	0	0	0	0	0	0	0	0	4
Days With Measurable Precip.	10	9	10	7	9	11	14	12	9	6	7	8
Average No. Thunderstorms	1	1	3	4	9	13	16	15	5	2	1	1
SUNSHINE/CLOUDINESS												
No. Clear Days	9	9	9	11	8	6	5	6	7	12	12	10
No. Partly Cloudy Days	7	6	8	8	11	11	12	13	11	8	6	7
No. Cloudy Days	15	13	14	11	12	13	14	12	12	11	12	14
% Possible Sunshine	58	61	67	71	70	68	68	65	63	65	62	58

etc.

- Temperatures in both summer and winter are greatly moderated by the coastal waters.
- Summer sea breezes shift many thunderstorms inland of this location, significantly reducing summer precipitation as compared to nearby inland areas.
- Some snow does fall; significant amounts are uncommon.

CLIMATABLE NO. 145   Ninety-Six NHS

WEATHER PARAMETERS	J	F	M	A	M	J	J	A	S	O	N	D
MONTH												
TEMPERATURE												
Normal Daily Maximum	53	56	64	74	82	88	90	90	84	74	64	55
Normal Daily Minimum	31	31	38	47	56	63	67	67	61	48	38	32
Extreme High	79	80	89	92	97	105	106	107	104	100	89	78
Extreme Low	2	2	3	27	34	42	55	50	35	25	13	1
Days Above 90°	0	0	0	0	4	12	19	18	7	0	0	0
Days Below 32°	19	17	10	1	0	0	0	0	0	2	9	18
PRECIPITATION												
Normal	4.7	4.0	5.5	3.9	4.0	3.5	4.2	3.6	4.1	2.9	2.9	3.6
Maximum	7.7	9.2	11.1	8.5	8.8	8.4	9.4	10.6	9.4	11.5	7.5	8.0
Maximum 24 Hr. Precipitation	3.4	2.9	4.2	3.6	3.4	3.8	4.1	7.1	3.5	8.0	4.1	2.0
Maximum Snowfall	5	9	10	0	0	0	0	0	0	0	0	5
Days With Measurable Precip.	10	10	10	8	9	9	12	11	7	6	7	9
Average No. Thunderstorms	1	2	4	5	9	14	19	14	5	1	1	1
SUNSHINE/CLOUDINESS												
No. Clear Days	10	9	9	12	10	8	6	8	10	14	12	11
No. Partly Cloudy Days	6	6	8	7	11	12	13	13	9	7	6	6
No. Cloudy Days	15	13	14	11	10	10	12	10	11	10	12	14
% Possible Sunshine	57	60	65	70	68	68	67	66	66	63	60	60

TEMPERATURE NORMALS AND EXTREMES

% OF SUNNY/PTLY CLOUDY/CLOUDY DAYS

□ Clear   ▦ Ptlycldy   ■ Cloudy

etc.

- Summers are long with quite hot and humid days; see the Heat Index chart.
- Spring is the season of most changeable weather, varying between cold snaps and warm, pleasant weather.
- Autumn is relatively dry and pleasant; first freezing temperatures normally do not occur until early November.

CLIMATABLE NO. 146

Andrew Johnson NHS, Blue Ridge Parkway, Appalachian NST

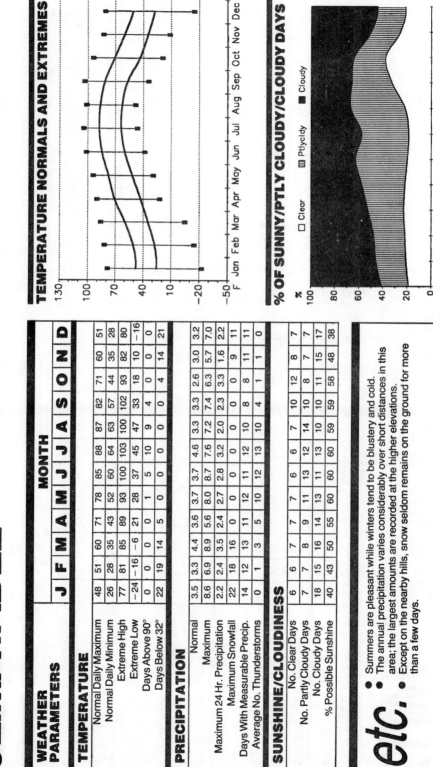

TEMPERATURE NORMALS AND EXTREMES

% OF SUNNY/PTLY CLOUDY/CLOUDY DAYS

WEATHER PARAMETERS	J	F	M	A	M	J	J	A	S	O	N	D
TEMPERATURE												
Normal Daily Maximum	48	51	60	71	78	85	88	87	82	71	60	51
Normal Daily Minimum	26	28	35	43	52	60	64	63	57	44	35	28
Extreme High	77	81	85	89	93	100	103	100	102	93	82	80
Extreme Low	−24	−16	−6	21	28	37	45	47	33	18	10	−16
Days Above 90°	0	0	0	0	1	5	10	9	4	0	0	0
Days Below 32°	22	19	14	5	0	0	0	0	0	4	14	21
PRECIPITATION												
Normal	3.5	3.3	4.4	3.6	3.7	3.7	4.6	3.3	3.3	2.6	3.0	3.2
Maximum	8.6	6.9	8.9	5.6	8.0	8.7	7.6	7.2	7.4	6.3	5.7	7.0
Maximum 24 Hr. Precipitation	2.2	2.4	3.5	2.4	2.7	2.8	3.2	2.0	2.3	3.3	1.6	2.2
Maximum Snowfall	22	18	16	0	0	0	0	0	0	0	9	11
Days With Measurable Precip.	14	12	13	11	12	11	12	10	8	8	11	11
Average No. Thunderstorms	0	1	3	5	10	12	13	10	4	1	1	0
SUNSHINE/CLOUDINESS												
No. Clear Days	6	6	7	7	7	6	6	7	10	12	8	7
No. Partly Cloudy Days	7	7	8	9	11	12	13	14	10	8	7	7
No. Cloudy Days	18	15	16	14	13	13	12	10	11	11	15	17
% Possible Sunshine	40	43	50	55	60	60	60	59	59	58	48	38

etc.

- Summers are pleasant while winters tend to be blustery and cold.
- The annual precipitation varies considerably over short distances in this area; the largest amounts are recorded at the higher elevations.
- Except on the nearby hills, snow seldom remains on the ground for more than a few days.

CLIMATABLE NO. 147   San Juan NHS

WEATHER PARAMETERS	J	F	M	A	M	J	J	A	S	O	N	D
TEMPERATURE												
Normal Daily Maximum	83	83	84	85	87	88	88	88	88	88	86	84
Normal Daily Minimum	70	70	71	72	74	75	76	76	76	75	73	72
Extreme High	92	96	96	97	96	97	95	97	97	98	96	91
Extreme Low	61	62	60	64	66	69	69	70	69	67	66	63
Days Above 90°	0	1	2	3	5	9	8	9	10	8	2	0
Days Below 32°	0	0	0	0	0	0	0	0	0	0	0	0
PRECIPITATION												
Normal	3.0	2.0	2.3	3.6	5.6	4.7	4.9	5.9	6.0	5.9	5.6	4.5
Maximum	7.6	6.7	5.4	8.9	15.0	11.0	9.4	11.8	11.4	15.1	16.0	16.8
Maximum 24 Hr. Precipitation	5.1	2.7	3.9	6.4	4.7	3.6	2.3	5.1	4.2	5.0	7.1	8.4
Maximum Snowfall	0	0	0	0	0	0	0	0	0	0	0	0
Days With Measurable Precip.	16	13	12	13	17	16	19	18	17	17	18	19
Average No. Thunderstorms	0	0	0	1	5	5	5	6	8	7	3	1
SUNSHINE/CLOUDINESS												
No. Clear Days	8	7	9	7	3	4	4	4	3	4	5	5
No. Partly Cloudy Days	19	17	18	17	16	16	18	18	17	17	18	19
No. Cloudy Days	4	4	4	6	12	10	9	9	10	10	7	7
% Possible Sunshine	67	70	74	69	61	62	67	67	61	61	59	60

TEMPERATURE NORMALS AND EXTREMES

% OF SUNNY/PTLY CLOUDY/CLOUDY DAYS

☐ Clear   ▦ Ptlycldy   ◼ Cloudy

etc.

- Temperatures are very uniform throughout the year.
- From November to April, the trailing edge of cold fronts sweeping out of the U.S. will occasionally bring heavy and continuous rainfall that may last for several days.
- The more normal rain showers occur in the afternoon and evening.

CLIMATABLE NO. 148   Badlands NP

WEATHER PARAMETERS

	MONTH											
	J	F	M	A	M	J	J	A	S	O	N	D
TEMPERATURE												
Normal Daily Maximum	32	36	46	61	71	81	91	89	78	66	48	36
Normal Daily Minimum	6	9	19	32	42	53	59	56	46	33	20	10
Extreme High	75	74	88	92	105	114	116	113	108	98	81	77
Extreme Low	−42	−41	−28	−12	13	31	36	27	10	−7	−29	−41
Days Above 90°	0	0	0	0	1	6	17	16	5	0	0	0
Days Below 32°	30	27	27	16	4	0	0	0	2	14	27	30
PRECIPITATION												
Normal	0.4	0.4	0.8	1.8	2.8	3.0	1.8	1.6	1.1	0.9	0.4	0.4
Maximum	3.1	1.8	2.7	5.5	6.9	9.5	6.5	7.8	3.9	4.0	2.7	1.8
Maximum 24 Hr. Precipitation	2.3	1.0	1.7	2.0	4.0	3.0	2.5	5.2	3.3	2.4	1.4	0.8
Maximum Snowfall	19	16	24	28	8	0	0	0	T	12	21	17
Days With Measurable Precip.	3	3	4	7	9	10	7	6	5	4	2	3
Average No. Thunderstorms	0	0	0	2	7	15	15	11	4	0	0	0
SUNSHINE/CLOUDINESS												
No. Clear Days	7	6	6	6	7	9	13	14	13	12	8	8
No. Partly Cloudy Days	8	8	9	9	11	11	13	12	9	8	8	8
No. Cloudy Days	16	14	16	15	13	10	5	5	8	11	14	15
% Possible Sunshine	55	59	61	60	58	63	72	73	68	65	54	54

etc.

- Summer days are quite hot, but low humidity keeps the heat from feeling oppressive.
- Rainfall from late summer thunderstorms often evaporates before reaching the ground.
- Winters are bitterly cold; temperatures of 20 degrees below zero can be expected several times each winter.

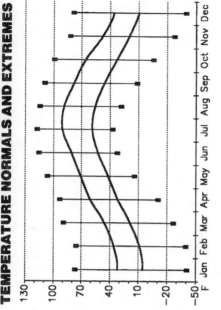

TEMPERATURE NORMALS AND EXTREMES

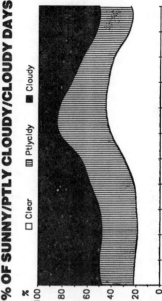

% OF SUNNY/PTLY CLOUDY/CLOUDY DAYS

☐ Clear   ▥ Ptlycldy   ■ Cloudy

CLIMATABLE NO. 149
Stones River NB, Fort Donelson NMP, Natchez Trace Parkway

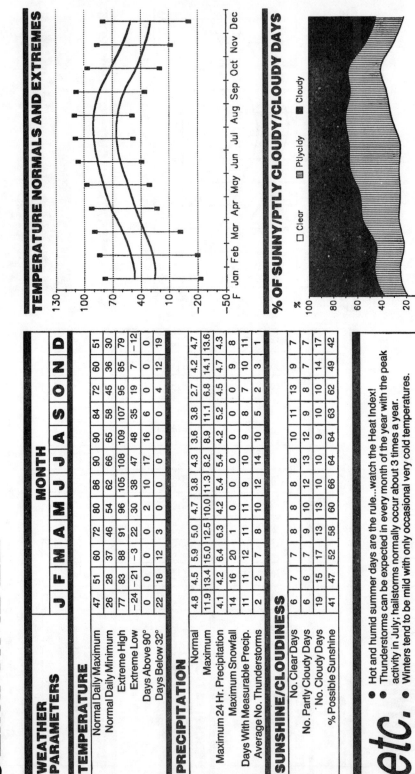

TEMPERATURE NORMALS AND EXTREMES

% OF SUNNY/PTLY CLOUDY/CLOUDY DAYS

☐ Clear ▤ Ptlycldy ■ Cloudy

WEATHER PARAMETERS	J	F	M	A	M	J	J	A	S	O	N	D
TEMPERATURE												
Normal Daily Maximum	47	51	60	72	80	86	90	90	84	72	60	51
Normal Daily Minimum	26	28	37	46	54	62	66	65	58	45	36	30
Extreme High	77	83	88	91	96	105	108	109	107	95	85	79
Extreme Low	-24	-21	-3	22	30	38	47	48	35	19	7	-12
Days Above 90°	0	0	0	0	2	10	17	16	6	0	0	0
Days Below 32°	22	18	12	3	0	0	0	0	0	4	12	19
PRECIPITATION												
Normal	4.8	4.5	5.9	5.0	4.7	3.8	4.3	3.6	3.8	2.7	4.2	4.7
Maximum	11.9	13.4	15.0	12.5	10.0	11.3	8.2	8.9	11.1	6.8	14.1	13.6
Maximum 24 Hr. Precipitation	4.1	4.2	6.4	6.3	4.2	5.4	5.4	4.2	5.2	4.5	4.7	4.3
Maximum Snowfall	14	16	20	1	0	0	0	0	0	0	9	8
Days With Measurable Precip.	11	11	12	11	11	9	10	9	8	7	10	11
Average No. Thunderstorms	2	2	7	8	10	12	14	10	5	2	3	1
SUNSHINE/CLOUDINESS												
No. Clear Days	6	7	7	8	8	8	8	10	11	13	9	7
No. Partly Cloudy Days	6	6	7	9	10	12	13	12	9	8	7	7
No. Cloudy Days	19	15	17	13	13	10	10	9	10	10	14	17
% Possible Sunshine	41	47	52	58	60	66	64	64	63	62	49	42

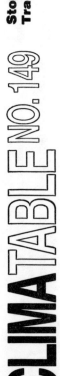

etc.

- Hot and humid summer days are the rule...watch the Heat Index!
- Thunderstorms can be expected in every month of the year with the peak activity in July; hailstorms normally occur about 3 times a year.
- Winters tend to be mild with only occasional very cold temperatures.

CLIMATABLE NO. 150

Mount Rushmore NM, Jewel Cave NM, Wind Cave NP

TEMPERATURE NORMALS AND EXTREMES

% OF SUNNY/PTLY CLOUDY/CLOUDY DAYS

☐ Clear   ▦ Ptlycldy   ■ Cloudy

WEATHER PARAMETERS	J	F	M	A	M	J	J	A	S	O	N	D
TEMPERATURE												
Normal Daily Maximum	34	39	42	51	62	72	80	79	70	60	45	38
Normal Daily Minimum	6	10	15	25	34	43	49	46	37	27	16	10
Extreme High	64	68	70	80	90	97	100	96	97	85	76	68
Extreme Low	-43	-34	-30	-15	5	19	30	22	8	4	-25	-37
Days Above 90°	0	0	0	0	0	1	3	2	1	0	0	0
Days Below 32°	31	28	30	26	13	2	0	1	10	24	29	30
PRECIPITATION												
Normal	0.4	0.5	0.9	1.9	3.1	3.5	3.0	2.0	1.2	0.7	0.5	0.5
Maximum	1.0	1.8	2.1	3.9	8.8	6.4	7.6	4.1	3.5	2.4	1.5	1.6
Maximum 24 Hr. Precipitation	0.5	0.6	1.0	2.0	4.0	3.4	2.0	2.4	1.3	1.6	0.4	0.6
Maximum Snowfall	26	29	38	49	26	13	0	0	15	22	27	46
Days With Measurable Precip.	7	7	9	9	12	12	9	8	7	5	6	6
Average No. Thunderstorms	0	0	0	2	7	15	15	11	4	0	0	0
SUNSHINE/CLOUDINESS												
No. Clear Days	7	6	6	6	7	9	13	14	13	12	8	8
No. Partly Cloudy Days	8	8	9	9	11	11	13	12	9	8	8	8
No. Cloudy Days	16	14	16	15	13	10	5	5	8	11	14	15
% Possible Sunshine	55	59	61	60	58	63	72	73	68	65	54	54

etc.

• Summer days range from warm to hot; nights are cool and comfortable.
• Sunny skies, the frequent occurrence of a warm, downslope wind or "chinook", and the tendency for cold, arctic air masses to stay east of the Black Hills, makes this region the warmest part of South Dakota in winter.

CLIMATABLE NO. 151

Shiloh NMP, Natchez Trace Parkway

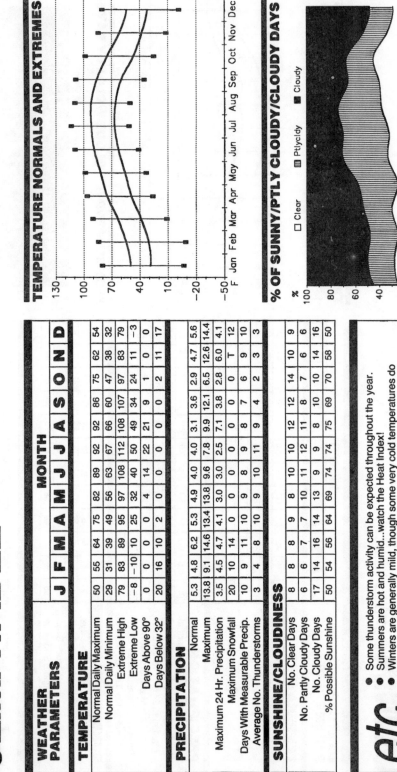

TEMPERATURE NORMALS AND EXTREMES

% OF SUNNY/PTLY CLOUDY/CLOUDY DAYS

☐ Clear   ▥ Ptlycldy   ■ Cloudy

WEATHER PARAMETERS	MONTH											
	J	F	M	A	M	J	J	A	S	O	N	D
TEMPERATURE												
Normal Daily Maximum	50	55	64	75	82	89	92	92	86	75	62	54
Normal Daily Minimum	29	31	39	49	56	63	67	66	60	47	38	32
Extreme High	79	83	89	95	97	108	112	108	107	97	83	79
Extreme Low	−8	−10	10	25	32	40	50	49	34	24	11	−3
Days Above 90°	0	0	0	0	4	14	22	21	9	1	0	0
Days Below 32°	20	16	10	2	0	0	0	0	0	2	11	17
PRECIPITATION												
Normal	5.3	4.8	6.2	5.3	4.9	4.0	4.0	3.1	3.6	2.9	4.7	5.6
Maximum	13.8	9.1	14.6	13.4	13.8	9.6	7.8	9.9	12.1	6.5	12.6	14.4
Maximum 24 Hr. Precipitation	3.5	4.5	4.7	4.1	3.0	3.0	2.5	7.1	3.8	2.8	6.0	4.1
Maximum Snowfall	20	10	14	0	0	0	0	0	0	0	T	12
Days With Measurable Precip.	10	9	11	10	9	8	9	8	7	6	9	10
Average No. Thunderstorms	3	4	8	10	9	10	11	9	4	2	3	3
SUNSHINE/CLOUDINESS												
No. Clear Days	8	8	8	9	8	10	10	12	12	14	10	9
No. Partly Cloudy Days	6	6	7	7	10	11	12	11	8	7	6	6
No. Cloudy Days	17	14	16	14	13	9	9	8	10	10	14	16
% Possible Sunshine	50	54	56	64	69	74	75	69	70	58	50

etc.

- Some thunderstorm activity can be expected throughout the year.
- Summers are hot and humid...watch the Heat Index!
- Winters are generally mild, though some very cold temperatures do occur.
- The average date of the first frost is in early November; the last frost

CLIMATABLE NO. 152

Big South Fork NRRA, Obed Wild & Scenic River

TEMPERATURE NORMALS AND EXTREMES

% OF SUNNY/PTLY CLOUDY/CLOUDY DAYS

☐ Clear   ▦ Ptlycldy   ■ Cloudy

WEATHER PARAMETERS	MONTH											
	J	F	M	A	M	J	J	A	S	O	N	D
TEMPERATURE												
Normal Daily Maximum	44	48	57	68	76	82	86	86	80	70	58	48
Normal Daily Minimum	24	25	34	43	52	59	63	62	56	43	34	27
Extreme High	77	82	88	91	99	100	105	102	101	96	83	75
Extreme Low	-17	-11	-6	19	28	34	44	44	31	16	4	-17
Days Above 90°	0	0	0	0	1	4	8	7	3	0	0	0
Days Below 32°	25	21	16	5	1	0	0	0	0	5	15	22
PRECIPITATION												
Normal	5.7	5.0	6.8	5.2	5.0	4.6	5.1	3.4	4.2	3.2	4.6	5.8
Maximum	12.0	10.9	16.5	11.0	15.0	9.0	13.2	8.3	8.9	6.4	9.8	11.6
Maximum 24 Hr. Precipitation	3.8	2.9	5.3	2.6	7.1	4.3	3.6	3.3	3.8	4.1	3.8	3.6
Maximum Snowfall	18	24	20	4	0	0	0	0	0	0	9	13
Days With Measurable Precip.	11	11	12	11	11	9	10	9	8	7	10	11
Average No. Thunderstorms	2	2	6	9	12	13	17	12	7	2	2	1
SUNSHINE/CLOUDINESS												
No. Clear Days	6	7	7	8	8	8	8	10	11	13	9	7
No. Partly Cloudy Days	6	6	7	9	10	12	13	12	9	8	7	7
No. Cloudy Days	19	15	17	13	13	10	10	9	10	10	14	17
% Possible Sunshine	41	47	52	58	60	66	64	64	63	62	49	42

etc.

- The wettest times of year are the winter and early spring with a secondary maximum of precipitation in mid-summer resulting from thunderstorm activity.
- Damaging ice storms occur every 5 or 6 years, but snowfall is generally light. Blizzard conditions are essentially unknown here.

CLIMATABLE NO. 153

Alibates NM, Lake Meredith NRA

TEMPERATURE NORMALS AND EXTREMES

% OF SUNNY/PTLY CLOUDY/CLOUDY DAYS

□ Clear   ▥ Ptlycldy   ■ Cloudy

WEATHER PARAMETERS						MONTH						
	J	F	M	A	M	J	J	A	S	O	N	D
TEMPERATURE												
Normal Daily Maximum	51	56	64	74	81	90	93	92	85	75	61	54
Normal Daily Minimum	24	28	34	44	53	62	67	65	58	47	34	27
Extreme High	80	89	95	99	102	107	106	106	101	96	88	82
Extreme Low	-11	-12	1	20	29	44	54	50	36	22	2	-2
Days Above 90°	0	0	0	1	6	17	24	21	10	2	0	0
Days Below 32°	25	18	14	3	0	0	0	0	0	1	13	24
PRECIPITATION												
Normal	0.5	0.8	1.0	1.3	3.2	2.9	3.1	2.5	1.6	1.3	0.7	0.5
Maximum	1.4	2.9	4.2	4.8	7.4	8.4	9.7	6.2	4.8	4.1	2.3	4.8
Maximum 24 Hr. Precipitation	0.7	1.6	1.9	2.4	3.8	2.2	3.1	2.4	3.0	2.5	1.1	2.0
Maximum Snowfall	13	26	20	6	3	0	0	0	0	8	18	11
Days With Measurable Precip.	4	4	5	5	8	8	8	8	6	5	3	4
Average No. Thunderstorms	0	1	2	4	12	12	12	11	5	3	1	0
SUNSHINE/CLOUDINESS												
No. Clear Days	13	10	11	11	11	13	13	15	15	16	14	13
No. Partly Cloudy Days	7	8	9	10	10	11	12	10	7	7	7	8
No. Cloudy Days	11	10	11	10	10	6	6	6	8	8	9	10
% Possible Sunshine	69	69	71	73	72	77	78	77	73	74	71	67

etc.

- Winters are generally mild, but cold fronts sweeping down from the north can produce large and rapid drops in temperature; drops of 50 to 60 degrees in 12 hours are common. Temperature drops of 40 degrees within a few minutes have been recorded.
- Numerous thunderstorms occur through the year.

CLIMATABLE NO. 154

Rio Grande Scenic River, Amistad NRA

TEMPERATURE NORMALS AND EXTREMES

% OF SUNNY/PTLY CLOUDY/CLOUDY DAYS

☐ Clear   ▥ Ptlycldy   ■ Cloudy

WEATHER PARAMETERS	J	F	M	A	M	J	J	A	S	O	N	D
TEMPERATURE												
Normal Daily Maximum	64	69	77	85	90	96	98	98	92	83	72	66
Normal Daily Minimum	38	42	50	60	66	72	74	74	69	59	48	40
Extreme High	89	99	105	106	108	112	110	112	109	106	95	94
Extreme Low	10	10	21	33	45	55	64	61	48	33	22	13
Days Above 90°	0	0	3	8	16	26	29	29	21	6	0	0
Days Below 32°	8	4	1	0	0	0	0	0	0	0	2	6
PRECIPITATION												
Normal	0.6	0.8	0.6	1.8	2.6	2.1	1.8	2.0	2.8	2.4	0.8	0.6
Maximum	3.0	2.8	3.1	11.7	7.2	14.7	13.2	8.7	15.8	11.3	4.0	3.5
Maximum 24 Hr. Precipitation	1.3	1.7	2.4	4.6	4.0	4.9	6.3	6.4	5.5	7.6	2.9	2.4
Maximum Snowfall	10	3	3	0	0	0	0	0	0	0	1	T
Days With Measurable Precip.	5	5	5	5	7	5	4	4	7	5	4	5
Average No. Thunderstorms	0	1	2	7	10	5	5	5	5	3	1	0
SUNSHINE/CLOUDINESS												
No. Clear Days	10	10	11	8	6	8	12	11	9	12	12	11
No. Partly Cloudy Days	7	7	7	8	9	13	11	12	11	9	7	6
No. Cloudy Days	14	11	13	14	16	9	8	8	10	10	11	14
% Possible Sunshine	55	59	60	63	60	69	75	80	70	69	60	58

etc.

- The climate is semi-arid, but summer thunderstorms can produce heavy downpours that result in local flash flooding.
- Winter is the dry season with only 20% of the annual rainfall falling from October through March.
- Summers are hot, but the low humidity minimizes discomfort.

CLIMATABLE NO. 155

Big Bend NP, Fort Davis NHS

TEMPERATURE NORMALS AND EXTREMES

% OF SUNNY/PTLY CLOUDY/CLOUDY DAYS

□ Clear   ▦ Ptlycldy   ■ Cloudy

WEATHER PARAMETERS	J	F	M	A	M	J	J	A	S	O	N	D
TEMPERATURE												
Normal Daily Maximum	59	64	70	78	85	90	88	87	83	76	67	61
Normal Daily Minimum	36	38	43	50	58	64	64	63	58	52	42	37
Extreme High	82	85	91	97	101	105	104	103	99	93	89	81
Extreme Low	–3	3	10	21	32	38	53	49	36	26	8	1
Days Above 90°	0	0	0	1	8	15	14	11	5	0	0	0
Days Below 32°	14	10	6	1	0	0	0	0	0	1	4	12
PRECIPITATION												
Normal	0.8	0.4	0.3	0.6	1.5	2.3	2.9	2.4	1.9	1.4	0.4	0.6
Maximum	1.9	3.1	1.7	2.8	3.0	5.4	7.6	7.4	11.1	4.8	3.2	2.3
Maximum 24 Hr. Precipitation	1.3	1.3	0.8	1.2	1.7	2.6	3.3	2.9	2.4	4.3	1.4	1.1
Maximum Snowfall	26	7	2	2	0	0	0	0	0	.T	4	9
Days With Measurable Precip.	4	3	2	2	2	3	8	8	5	4	3	4
Average No. Thunderstorms	0	0	1	1	3	5	13	11	4	2	0	0
SUNSHINE/CLOUDINESS												
No. Clear Days	14	14	15	16	19	20	12	14	18	19	17	15
No. Partly Cloudy Days	7	7	8	8	8	7	13	12	7	7	6	7
No. Cloudy Days	10	7	8	6	4	3	6	5	5	5	7	9
% Possible Sunshine	77	82	85	87	89	89	80	81	82	83	82	78

etc.

- Marked variations in weather are experienced over short distances due to changes in elevation and exposure.
- Summer is the "rainy" season with showers and thunderstorms. Even more precipitation occurs on the high mountains, especially on the windward slopes.

CLIMATABLE NO. 156

Big Thicket National Preserve

TEMPERATURE NORMALS AND EXTREMES

% OF SUNNY/PTLY CLOUDY/CLOUDY DAYS

WEATHER PARAMETERS	J	F	M	A	M	J	J	A	S	O	N	D
TEMPERATURE												
Normal Daily Maximum	62	66	73	80	86	91	94	94	89	81	72	64
Normal Daily Minimum	37	41	46	56	61	66	68	68	64	53	46	40
Extreme High	86	90	92	94	99	104	111	111	103	100	90	88
Extreme Low	5	4	18	29	38	49	51	50	34	27	17	13
Days Above 90°	0	0	0	0	5	20	27	26	15	2	0	0
Days Below 32°	12	7	5	0	0	0	0	0	0	1	4	10
PRECIPITATION												
Normal	4.4	4.0	3.5	4.6	5.0	3.9	4.7	3.5	5.0	3.8	4.5	5.2
Maximum	14.2	8.5	10.9	10.3	13.2	11.9	10.5	11.1	14.5	13.6	9.5	13.4
Maximum 24 Hr. Precipitation	3.1	4.0	4.1	6.6	4.3	3.8	6.4	9.8	8.6	6.2	4.2	4.1
Maximum Snowfall	4	12	0	0	0	0	0	0	0	0	0	T
Days With Measurable Precip.	10	8	8	7	7	8	11	12	10	6	8	9
Average No. Thunderstorms	3	4	5	7	8	10	19	17	.9	3	3	3
SUNSHINE/CLOUDINESS												
No. Clear Days	7	8	7	6	7	9	6	7	9	12	10	9
No. Partly Cloudy Days	6	6	8	8	12	14	16	15	12	10	7	6
No. Cloudy Days	18	14	16	16	12	7	9	9	9	9	13	16
% Possible Sunshine	42	52	52	52	64	69	65	63	62	67	57	47

etc. •
- Rainfall, usually as thunderstorms, is normally abundant and well distributed throughout the year. However, there is a considerable variation in total annual rainfall from year to year.
- Winters tend to be mild; cold spells rarely last more than one or two days.

CLIMATABLE NO. 157   Chamizal NM

TEMPERATURE NORMALS AND EXTREMES

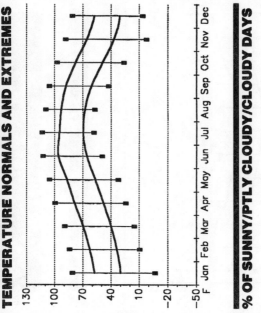

% OF SUNNY/PTLY CLOUDY/CLOUDY DAYS

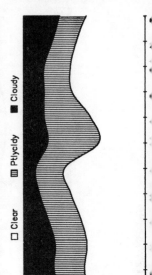

☐ Clear   ▥ Ptlycldy   ■ Cloudy

WEATHER PARAMETERS							MONTH						
		J	F	M	A	M	J	J	A	S	O	N	D
TEMPERATURE													
Normal Daily Maximum		58	63	70	79	87	96	95	93	88	78	66	58
Normal Daily Minimum		30	34	40	48	57	66	70	68	61	49	37	31
Extreme High		80	83	88	98	104	111	112	108	104	96	87	80
Extreme Low		–8	8	14	23	31	48	57	56	41	25	1	5
Days Above 90°		0	0	0	2	13	26	27	24	12	2	0	0
Days Below 32°		19	12	5	1	0	0	0	0	0	0	7	19
PRECIPITATION													
Normal		0.4	0.4	0.3	0.2	0.2	0.6	1.6	1.2	1.4	0.7	0.3	0.4
Maximum		1.8	1.7	2.3	1.4	1.9	3.2	5.5	5.6	6.7	4.3	1.6	2.6
Maximum 24 Hr. Precipitation		0.6	0.9	1.7	1.1	1.2	1.6	2.6	2.3	2.5	1.8	1.2	1.0
Maximum Snowfall		8	9	7	16	0	0	0	0	0	0	13	18
Days With Measurable Precip.		4	3	2	2	2	3	8	8	5	4	3	4
Average No. Thunderstorms		0	0	1	1	3	5	13	11	4	2	0	0
SUNSHINE/CLOUDINESS													
No. Clear Days		14	14	15	16	19	20	12	14	18	19	17	15
No. Partly Cloudy Days		7	7	8	8	8	7	13	12	7	7	6	7
No. Cloudy Days		10	7	8	6	4	3	6	5	5	5	7	9
% Possible Sunshine		77	82	85	87	89	89	80	81	82	83	82	78

etc.

* Sandstorms are the most unpleasant weather, most frequently in March and April. With dry, loose soils and sparse vegetation, even moderate winds raise dust.
* Rainfall is light; over half the annual total falls in July to September. There is some snow each winter; rarely as much as an inch.

CLIMATABLE NO. 158

Guadalupe Mountains NP, Carlsbad Caverns NP

WEATHER PARAMETERS

						MONTH						
	J	F	M	A	M	J	J	A	S	O	N	D
TEMPERATURE												
Normal Daily Maximum	57	60	68	78	86	93	92	91	86	77	66	58
Normal Daily Minimum	30	33	38	48	56	64	68	66	60	50	39	33
Extreme High	81	84	90	96	103	108	106	105	101	94	88	88
Extreme Low	-13	-10	9	21	30	47	50	50	33	23	14	3
Days Above 90°	0	0	0	2	10	23	24	22	11	1	0	0
Days Below 32°	18	15	8	1	0	0	0	0	0	1	6	16
PRECIPITATION												
Normal	0.4	0.3	0.4	0.6	0.9	1.3	1.8	2.0	1.9	1.3	0.4	0.5
Maximum	2.4	2.0	3.6	5.8	10.9	4.0	6.0	5.7	12.3	5.1	1.6	2.6
Maximum 24 Hr. Precipitation	1.1	1.0	1.2	4.6	3.0	2.5	3.1	2.7	3.9	3.6	1.1	0.8
Maximum Snowfall	13	10	8	T	0	0	0	0	0	T	18	18
Days With Measurable Precip.	4	3	2	2	4	4	8	8	6	4	3	4
Average No. Thunderstorms	0	0	1	2	5	7	13	11	4	2	0	0
SUNSHINE/CLOUDINESS												
No. Clear Days	14	12	14	14	16	18	13	16	16	16	14	14
No. Partly Cloudy Days	6	8	8	8	9	8	12	8	8	6	6	7
No. Cloudy Days	11	8	9	8	6	4	6	6	6	8	8	10
% Possible Sunshine	73	76	79	82	84	83	84	79	80	74	77	71

etc.

- Spring is a comfortable season with mild sunny days and cool nights; an occasional dust storm can be expected.
- Summer days are hot and nights are pleasantly cool.
- In the high mountain areas, temperatures are 10 to 20 degrees colder and the precipitation is double that shown in the table.

TEMPERATURE NORMALS AND EXTREMES

% OF SUNNY/PTLY CLOUDY/CLOUDY DAYS

□ Clear   ▨ Ptlycldy   ■ Cloudy

CLIMATABLE NO. 159 Lyndon B. Johnson NHS

TEMPERATURE NORMALS AND EXTREMES

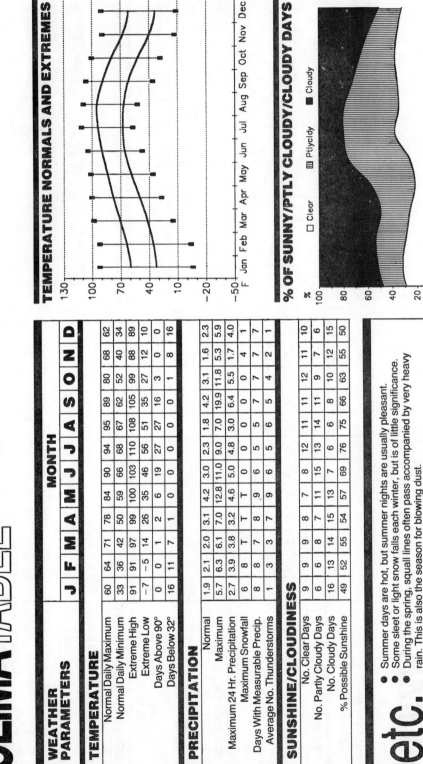

% OF SUNNY/PTLY CLOUDY/CLOUDY DAYS

☐ Clear ▦ Pt'lycldy ■ Cloudy

WEATHER PARAMETERS	J	F	M	A	M	J	J	A	S	O	N	D
TEMPERATURE												
Normal Daily Maximum	60	64	71	78	84	90	94	95	89	80	68	62
Normal Daily Minimum	33	36	42	50	59	66	68	67	62	52	40	34
Extreme High	91	91	97	99	100	103	110	108	105	99	88	89
Extreme Low	−7	−5	14	26	35	46	56	51	35	27	12	10
Days Above 90°	0	0	1	2	6	19	27	27	16	3	0	0
Days Below 32°	16	11	7	1	0	0	0	0	0	1	8	16
PRECIPITATION												
Normal	1.9	2.1	2.0	3.1	4.2	3.0	2.3	1.8	4.2	3.1	1.6	2.3
Maximum	5.7	6.3	6.1	7.0	12.8	11.0	9.0	7.0	19.9	11.8	5.3	5.9
Maximum 24 Hr. Precipitation	2.7	3.9	3.8	3.2	4.6	5.0	4.8	3.0	6.4	5.5	1.7	4.0
Maximum Snowfall	6	8	T	T	T	0	0	0	0	0	4	1
Days With Measurable Precip.	8	8	7	8	9	6	5	7	7	7	7	7
Average No. Thunderstorms	1	3	3	7	9	6	5	6	5	4	2	1
SUNSHINE/CLOUDINESS												
No. Clear Days	9	9	9	8	7	8	12	11	11	12	11	10
No. Partly Cloudy Days	6	6	8	7	11	15	13	14	11	9	7	6
No. Cloudy Days	16	13	14	15	13	7	6	6	8	10	12	15
% Possible Sunshine	49	52	55	54	57	69	76	75	66	63	55	50

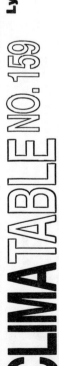

etc.

- Summer days are hot, but summer nights are usually pleasant.
- Some sleet or light snow falls each winter, but is of little significance.
- During the spring, squall lines often pass accompanied by very heavy rain. This is also the season for blowing dust.

CLIMATABLE NO. 160

Padre Island NS, Palo Alto Battlefield NHS

TEMPERATURE NORMALS AND EXTREMES

% OF SUNNY/PTLY CLOUDY/CLOUDY DAYS

☐ Clear　▦ Ptlycldy　■ Cloudy

WEATHER PARAMETERS	J	F	M	A	M	J	J	A	S	O	N	D
TEMPERATURE												
Normal Daily Maximum	67	71	77	82	87	91	94	94	90	84	76	70
Normal Daily Minimum	48	50	57	65	70	74	76	76	73	65	56	50
Extreme High	93	98	106	102	103	101	103	104	98	98	95	94
Extreme Low	14	18	24	33	47	58	64	63	50	40	29	14
Days Above 90°	0	0	1	2	6	20	27	27	17	5	0	0
Days Below 32°	2	1	0	0	0	0	0	0	0	0	0	1
PRECIPITATION												
Normal	1.6	1.6	0.8	2.0	3.0	3.4	2.0	3.5	6.2	3.2	1.6	1.4
Maximum	10.8	8.1	4.8	8.0	9.4	13.4	11.9	14.8	20.3	11.0	8.5	7.8
Maximum 24 Hr. Precipitation	6.4	4.8	2.7	7.2	4.6	5.6	4.6	8.9	8.8	7.2	3.4	3.9
Maximum Snowfall	1	1	T	0	0	0	0	0	0	0	T	T
Days With Measurable Precip.	8	7	6	5	6	6	5	6	9	7	6	7
Average No. Thunderstorms	2	1	1	4	6	4	3	5	7	3	1	1
SUNSHINE/CLOUDINESS												
No. Clear Days	7	7	7	6	6	9	11	10	12	9	9	8
No. Partly Cloudy Days	7	6	8	9	12	15	14	13	12	10	9	6
No. Cloudy Days	17	15	16	15	13	6	6	7	8	9	12	17
% Possible Sunshine	46	51	55	57	61	73	82	77	68	68	56	46

etc.

- Winters are mild. Some winters pass with no freezing temperatures. On occasion, damaging cold rides in on "northers", surges of arctic air plunging southward out of Canada.
- About once a decade, a tropical storm can bring torrential rains and high winds to the area in late summer or early fall.

CLIMATABLE NO. 161 — San Antonio Missions NHP, San Jose Mission NHS

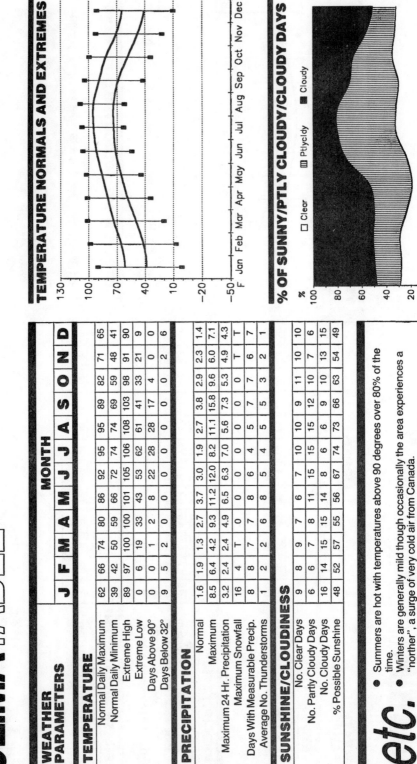

WEATHER PARAMETERS	MONTH											
	J	F	M	A	M	J	J	A	S	O	N	D
TEMPERATURE												
Normal Daily Maximum	62	66	74	80	86	92	95	95	89	82	71	65
Normal Daily Minimum	39	42	50	59	66	72	74	74	69	59	48	41
Extreme High	89	97	100	100	101	105	106	108	103	98	91	90
Extreme Low	0	6	19	33	43	53	62	61	41	33	21	9
Days Above 90°	0	0	1	2	8	22	28	28	17	4	0	0
Days Below 32°	9	5	2	0	0	0	0	0	0	0	2	6
PRECIPITATION												
Normal	1.6	1.9	1.3	2.7	3.7	3.0	1.9	2.7	3.8	2.9	2.3	1.4
Maximum	8.5	6.4	4.2	9.3	11.2	12.0	8.2	11.1	15.8	9.6	6.0	7.1
Maximum 24 Hr. Precipitation	3.2	2.4	2.4	4.9	6.5	6.3	7.0	5.6	7.3	5.3	4.9	4.3
Maximum Snowfall	16	4	T	0	0	0	0	0	0	0	T	T
Days With Measurable Precip.	8	8	7	7	8	6	4	5	7	7	6	7
Average No. Thunderstorms	1	2	2	6	8	5	4	5	5	3	2	1
SUNSHINE/CLOUDINESS												
No. Clear Days	9	8	9	7	6	7	10	10	9	11	10	10
No. Partly Cloudy Days	6	6	7	8	11	15	15	15	12	10	7	6
No. Cloudy Days	16	14	15	15	14	8	6	6	9	10	13	15
% Possible Sunshine	48	52	57	55	56	67	74	73	66	63	54	49

- Summers are hot with temperatures above 90 degrees over 80% of the time.
- Winters are generally mild though occasionally the area experiences a "norther", a surge of very cold air from Canada.
- Measureable snow falls only about once in every 3 to 4 years.

CLIMATABLE NO. 162

Rainbow Bridge NM, Natural Bridges NM, Canyonlands NP, Capitol Reef NP, Arches NP

WEATHER PARAMETERS

						MONTH						
	J	F	M	A	M	J	J	A	S	O	N	D
TEMPERATURE												
Normal Daily Maximum	42	50	59	69	84	95	98	95	86	73	55	43
Normal Daily Minimum	17	24	31	40	49	58	65	64	54	42	29	20
Extreme High	67	75	85	91	101	109	111	108	108	94	80	68
Extreme Low	-28	-21	7	16	23	32	38	36	28	-6	-8	-15
Days Above 90°	0	0	0	0	6	20	30	26	12	0	0	0
Days Below 32°	30	22	17	6	0	0	0	0	0	5	20	29
PRECIPITATION												
Normal	0.3	0.3	0.5	0.4	0.3	0.4	0.9	0.6	0.7	0.4	0.4	0.5
Maximum	2.2	1.8	3.2	2.7	2.1	2.2	3.0	2.4	3.8	1.9	1.9	2.1
Maximum 24 Hr. Precipitation	0.6	0.8	1.2	2.1	1.5	0.9	2.0	1.3	1.9	0.8	0.8	0.9
Maximum Snowfall	20	15	8	2	0	0	0	0	0	7	8	17
Days With Measurable Precip.	7	7	8	6	3	5	6	4	4	4	5	6
Average No. Thunderstorms	0	0	1	1	4	4	9	11	5	2	0	0
SUNSHINE/CLOUDINESS												
No. Clear Days	9	7	9	10	12	17	16	18	17	11	11	10
No. Partly Cloudy Days	8	8	8	9	10	8	10	8	7	7	8	8
No. Cloudy Days	14	13	14	11	9	5	5	5	7	11	11	13
% Possible Sunshine	56	64	60	68	74	83	77	79	80	75	63	60

TEMPERATURE NORMALS AND EXTREMES

% OF SUNNY/PTLY CLOUDY/CLOUDY DAYS

□ Clear   ▦ Ptlcldy   ▪ Cloudy

etc.

- This is a fairly arid region, lying in the rain shadow of the mountains to the west.
- Winters are quite cold, though below-zero temperatures are not common. On clear, still nights, cold air drainage keeps the valley bottoms significantly colder than the adjoining high elevation areas.

CLIMATABLE NO. 163   Bryce Canyon NP, Cedar Breaks NM

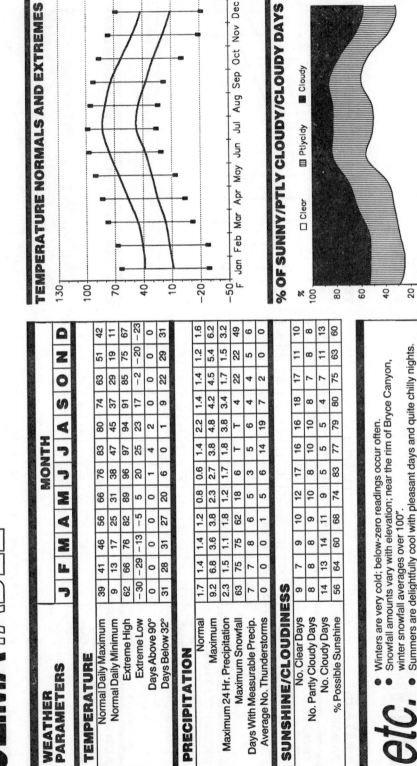

TEMPERATURE NORMALS AND EXTREMES

WEATHER PARAMETERS	J	F	M	A	M	J	J	A	S	O	N	D
TEMPERATURE												
Normal Daily Maximum	39	41	46	56	66	76	83	80	74	63	51	42
Normal Daily Minimum	9	13	17	25	31	38	47	45	37	29	19	11
Extreme High	62	66	76	82	89	96	97	94	91	85	75	67
Extreme Low	−30	−29	−13	−5	5	20	25	23	17	−2	−20	−23
Days Above 90°	0	0	0	0	0	1	4	2	0	0	0	0
Days Below 32°	31	28	31	27	20	6	0	1	9	22	29	31
PRECIPITATION												
Normal	1.7	1.4	1.4	1.2	0.8	0.6	1.4	2.2	1.4	1.4	1.2	1.6
Maximum	9.2	6.8	3.6	3.8	2.3	2.7	3.8	4.8	4.2	4.5	5.4	6.2
Maximum 24 Hr. Precipitation	2.3	1.5	1.1	1.8	1.2	1.7	1.8	3.8	3.4	1.7	1.5	3.2
Maximum Snowfall	63	75	75	62	18	6	T	T	4	22	22	49
Days With Measurable Precip.	7	7	8	6	5	3	5	6	4	4	5	6
Average No. Thunderstorms	0	0	0	1	5	6	14	19	7	2	0	0
SUNSHINE/CLOUDINESS												
No. Clear Days	9	7	9	10	12	17	16	16	18	17	11	10
No. Partly Cloudy Days	8	8	8	9	10	8	10	10	8	7	8	8
No. Cloudy Days	14	13	14	11	9	5	5	5	4	7	11	13
% Possible Sunshine	56	64	60	68	74	83	77	79	80	75	63	60

% OF SUNNY/PTLY CLOUDY/CLOUDY DAYS

☐ Clear   ▦ Ptlycldy   ■ Cloudy

etc.

- Winters are very cold; below-zero readings occur often.
- Snowfall amounts vary with elevation; near the rim of Bryce Canyon, winter snowfall averages over 100".
- Summers are delightfully cool with pleasant days and quite chilly nights. Temperatures reach 90 degrees on just a few days a year.

CLIMATABLE NO. 164   Timpanogos Cave NM, Mormon Pioneer NHT

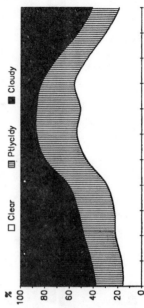

TEMPERATURE NORMALS AND EXTREMES

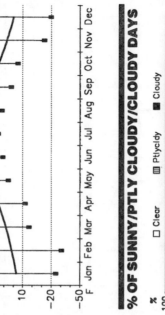

WEATHER PARAMETERS	MONTH											
	J	F	M	A	M	J	J	A	S	O	N	D
TEMPERATURE												
Normal Daily Maximum	38	44	52	62	72	83	92	90	80	68	51	40
Normal Daily Minimum	17	22	28	36	42	50	58	56	46	36	27	20
Extreme High	63	70	80	89	96	104	108	105	100	90	78	68
Extreme Low	−26	−32	2	6	24	30	35	31	21	14	−14	−21
Days Above 90°	0	0	0	0	1	9	24	19	4	0	0	0
Days Below 32°	30	26	24	12	4	0	0	0	2	13	25	29
PRECIPITATION												
Normal	1.4	1.3	1.3	1.2	1.2	0.8	0.7	1.0	0.7	1.4	1.2	1.3
Maximum	2.9	3.2	3.1	4.0	2.9	2.3	2.0	3.0	2.0	5.4	2.3	4.1
Maximum 24 Hr. Precipitation	1.1	1.3	1.6	1.5	1.4	1.2	1.2	1.6	1.0	1.8	1.7	1.0
Maximum Snowfall	28	20	28	4	4	0	0	0	0	4	14	34
Days With Measurable Precip.	10	9	10	10	8	6	5	6	5	6	8	9
Average No. Thunderstorms	0	1	1	2	6	9	9	10	6	2	0	0
SUNSHINE/CLOUDINESS												
No. Clear Days	5	5	7	7	9	14	17	16	17	14	9	6
No. Partly Cloudy Days	7	7	8	9	10	10	10	11	8	8	7	7
No. Cloudy Days	19	16	16	14	12	6	4	4	5	9	14	18
% Possible Sunshine	45	54	63	67	72	79	83	83	82	72	53	42

% OF SUNNY/PTLY CLOUDY/CLOUDY DAYS

□ Clear   ▥ Ptlycldy   ■ Cloudy

etc.

- Precipitation here increases significantly toward the east as the elevation increases.
- Winter precipitation is fairly uniformly distributed; summer thunderstorm activity is somewhat more erratic.
- Winters tend to be moderately cold; some extremely cold weather can be expected each year.

CLIMATABLE NO. 165

Golden Spike NHS

WEATHER PARAMETERS	MONTH											
	J	F	M	A	M	J	J	A	S	O	N	D
TEMPERATURE												
Normal Daily Maximum	36	42	50	61	72	82	92	89	80	66	48	37
Normal Daily Minimum	15	20	28	37	46	54	60	57	48	38	28	20
Extreme High	53	66	74	84	93	101	104	100	97	90	70	60
Extreme Low	−21	−19	−7	19	26	35	41	33	30	18	−3	−12
Days Above 90°	0	0	0	0	0	7	23	17	3	0	0	0
Days Below 32°	30	26	22	8	1	0	0	0	0	6	22	29
PRECIPITATION												
Normal	1.2	1.0	0.9	1.4	1.3	1.2	0.4	0.6	0.9	1.0	1.0	1.0
Maximum	3.3	2.4	3.1	3.0	3.8	3.7	1.6	2.4	3.0	2.7	2.8	2.7
Maximum 24 Hr. Precipitation	1.0	1.1	1.0	1.4	1.5	2.2	0.9	1.4	2.3	1.4	1.1	1.1
Maximum Snowfall	28	19	12	7	T	0	0	0	0	5	10	22
Days With Measurable Precip.	10	9	10	10	8	6	5	6	5	6	8	9
Average No. Thunderstorms	0	1	1	2	6	9	9	10	6	2	0	0
SUNSHINE/CLOUDINESS												
No. Clear Days	5	5	7	7	9	14	17	16	17	14	9	6
No. Partly Cloudy Days	7	7	8	9	10	10	10	11	8	8	7	7
No. Cloudy Days	19	16	16	14	12	6	4	4	5	9	14	18
% Possible Sunshine	45	54	63	67	72	79	83	83	82	72	53	42

TEMPERATURE NORMALS AND EXTREMES

% OF SUNNY/PTLY CLOUDY/CLOUDY DAYS

☐ Clear ▦ Ptlycldy ■ Cloudy

etc.

- This is a semi-arid region on the eastern edge of the Great Salt Lake Desert.
- In late fall and winter, a high pressure area can stagnate over the Great Basin for several weeks. This results in accumulations of smoke and haze, a persistent fog, and much reduced visibilities.

CLIMATABLE NO. 166

Yorktown Battlefield, Colonial National Historical Park, Jamestown NHS, Potomac Heritage NST

TEMPERATURE NORMALS AND EXTREMES

% OF SUNNY/PTLY CLOUDY/CLOUDY DAYS

WEATHER PARAMETERS	MONTH											
	J	F	M	A	M	J	J	A	S	O	N	D
TEMPERATURE												
Normal Daily Maximum	49	51	60	71	78	85	88	87	82	71	62	52
Normal Daily Minimum	28	29	36	45	54	62	67	66	60	48	39	31
Extreme High	80	81	87	96	97	104	100	102	103	96	85	80
Extreme Low	0	3	13	25	31	37	51	44	40	21	15	3
Days Above 90°	0	0	0	1	2	7	12	11	4	0	0	0
Days Below 32°	22	19	12	3	0	0	0	0	0	2	9	18
PRECIPITATION												
Normal	3.7	3.5	4.2	3.0	4.4	4.2	5.2	4.7	4.4	3.6	3.2	3.4
Maximum	6.7	6.0	8.0	5.4	9.4	10.0	10.4	10.8	18.4	10.0	8.0	6.5
Maximum 24 Hr. Precipitation	2.5	2.2	2.2	1.8	2.6	4.2	3.8	6.2	10.0	3.9	3.5	3.0
Maximum Snowfall	22	14	13	0	0	0	0	0	0	0	0	10
Days With Measurable Precip.	10	10	11	10	10	9	11	10	8	8	8	9
Average No. Thunderstorms	0	0	2	3	6	6	10	8	3	1	1	0
SUNSHINE/CLOUDINESS												
No. Clear Days	9	8	9	9	8	7	7	8	9	11	10	9
No. Partly Cloudy Days	6	6	7	9	10	12	12	12	10	7	8	7
No. Cloudy Days	15	14	15	12	13	12	12	11	11	13	12	15
% Possible Sunshine	56	58	63	65	65	67	64	65	64	59	57	57

etc.

- Summers are warm and humid with several hot periods each year; the heat and humidity is often oppressive . . . see the Heat Index.
- Winters are generally mild; some winters pass with no snow. In about one winter in four, a heavier snowfall can be expected; most snowfall is light and melts in a day.

CLIMATABLE NO. 167　Zion NP

WEATHER PARAMETERS	J	F	M	A	M	J	J	A	S	O	N	D
TEMPERATURE												
Normal Daily Maximum	52	57	63	73	83	93	100	97	91	78	63	53
Normal Daily Minimum	29	31	36	43	52	60	68	66	60	49	37	30
Extreme High	71	78	86	94	102	114	115	111	110	97	83	71
Extreme Low	-2	4	12	23	22	40	51	50	33	23	13	6
Days Above 90°	0	0	0	1	8	21	30	28	18	3	0	0
Days Below 32°	19	14	10	3	0	0	0	0	0	1	9	18
PRECIPITATION												
Normal	1.6	1.7	1.3	0.7	0.6	0.8	0.8	1.6	0.8	1.0	1.2	1.5
Maximum	4.9	5.0	4.4	2.8	3.6	3.6	4.8	6.7	3.3	3.3	3.2	4.3
Maximum 24 Hr. Precipitation	1.6	0.9	1.2	1.8	2.2	1.1	0	1.6	1.4	1.3	1.3	2.0
Maximum Snowfall	26	18	14	3	T	0	0	T		1	5	21
Days With Measurable Precip.	7	7	8	6	5	3	5	6	4	4	5	6
Average No. Thunderstorms	0	0	0	1	4	5	14	15	5	2	0	0
SUNSHINE/CLOUDINESS												
No. Clear Days	9	7	9	10	12	17	16	16	18	17	11	10
No. Partly Cloudy Days	8	8	8	9	10	8	10	10	8	7	8	8
No. Cloudy Days	14	13	14	11	9	5	5	4	4	7	11	13
% Possible Sunshine	56	64	60	68	74	83	77	79	80	75	63	60

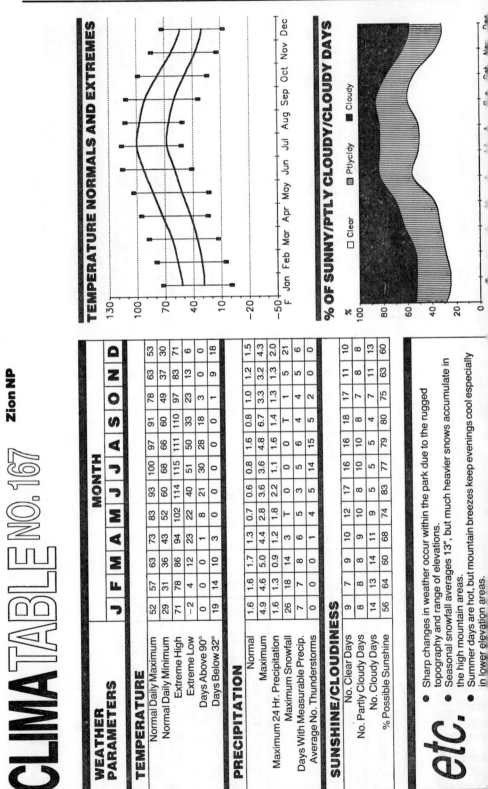

TEMPERATURE NORMALS AND EXTREMES

% OF SUNNY/PTLY CLOUDY/CLOUDY DAYS

□ Clear　▥ Pttlycldy　■ Cloudy

etc.

- Sharp changes in weather occur within the park due to the rugged topography and range of elevations.
- Seasonal snowfall averages 13", but much heavier snows accumulate in the high mountain areas.
- Summer days are hot, but mountain breezes keep evenings cool especially in lower elevation areas.

CLIMATABLE NO. 168

Fredericksburg & Spotsylvania NMP, George Washington Birthplace NM, Prince William Forest Park, Potomac Heritage NST

MONTH

WEATHER PARAMETERS	J	F	M	A	M	J	J	A	S	O	N	D
TEMPERATURE												
Normal Daily Maximum	45	47	56	68	77	85	88	87	80	70	58	48
Normal Daily Minimum	25	26	34	44	53	62	66	65	58	46	36	28
Extreme High	78	79	88	97	97	102	105	104	106	86	89	79
Extreme Low	-7	-10	7	20	28	40	45	44	30	21	4	1
Days Above 90°	0	0	0	1	2	8	15	12	5	0	0	0
Days Below 32°	24	21	15	4	0	0	0	0	0	3	13	22
PRECIPITATION												
Normal	2.9	2.9	3.6	3.1	3.3	3.3	3.6	4.5	3.1	2.9	3.0	3.3
Maximum	7.5	6.4	6.9	5.7	9.2	10.8	10.5	13.7	10.9	7.9	7.0	7.8
Maximum 24 Hr. Precipitation	1.8	1.9	2.7	1.9	2.3	5.7	5.0	5.2	4.0	3.4	4.4	3.1
Maximum Snowfall	29	23	25	4	0	0	0	0	0	T	17	18
Days With Measurable Precip.	10	9	10	10	12	10	10	10	8	8	9	10
Average No. Thunderstorms	0	0	2	3	5	7	9	7	3	1	0	0
SUNSHINE/CLOUDINESS												
No. Clear Days	8	8	7	7	7	8	8	9	10	7	8	8
No. Partly Cloudy Days	7	6	8	9	10	11	11	11	9	8	8	6
No. Cloudy Days	16	14	16	14	14	12	12	12	13	15	17	17
% Possible Sunshine	54	57	61	65	65	67	66	64	61	57	53	53

etc.

- Winters are generally mild, but some snow can be expected. On the average, snowfalls of 4" or more will occur twice each winter.
- Freezing temperatures can be expected until late April.
- Summers are warm and humid; some summer days can be most uncomfortable.

TEMPERATURE NORMALS AND EXTREMES

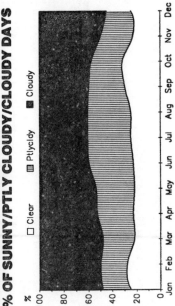

(Vertical axis: 130, 100, 70, 40, 10, -20, -50 °F; horizontal axis: Jan Feb Mar Apr May Jun Jul Aug Sep Oct Nov Dec)

% OF SUNNY/PTLY CLOUDY/CLOUDY DAYS

Legend: ☐ Clear   ▦ Ptlycldy   ■ Cloudy

(Vertical axis: 100, 80, 60, 40, 20, 0 %; horizontal axis: Jan Feb Mar Apr May Jun Jul Aug Sep Oct Nov Dec)

CLIMATABLE NO. 169

Great Falls Park, Manassas NBP, Turkey Run Farm, Wolf Trap Farm Park, Potomac Heritage NST

TEMPERATURE NORMALS AND EXTREMES

% OF SUNNY/PTLY CLOUDY/CLOUDY DAYS

□ Clear   ▦ Ptlycldy   ■ Cloudy

WEATHER PARAMETERS	J	F	M	A	M	J	J	A	S	O	N	D
TEMPERATURE												
Normal Daily Maximum	44	47	56	68	76	84	88	86	80	70	58	46
Normal Daily Minimum	24	26	32	43	52	60	64	63	56	45	36	26
Extreme High	77	87	87	94	97	100	105	106	102	93	85	78
Extreme Low	−8	−4	−5	19	29	37	48	45	32	20	9	−5
Days Above 90°	0	0	0	0	2	8	13	10	4	0	0	0
Days Below 32°	25	22	17	4	0	0	0	0	0	3	12	23
PRECIPITATION												
Normal	2.6	2.5	3.2	3.2	4.0	3.8	4.1	4.4	3.4	2.8	3.0	3.3
Maximum	4.8	4.8	6.4	10.2	11.5	15.1	12.2	14.6	12.5	10.8	7.2	6.5
Maximum 24 Hr. Precipitation	2.1	1.7	4.5	2.1	3.2	8.3	4.6	3.8	6.0	3.8	2.9	2.0
Maximum Snowfall	39	25	30	5	0	0	0	0	0	1	12	16
Days With Measurable Precip.	9	8	9	10	11	9	10	10	7	7	8	8
Average No. Thunderstorms	0	0	1	3	6	7	8	8	3	1	0	0
SUNSHINE/CLOUDINESS												
No. Clear Days	8	8	7	7	7	7	8	8	9	10	7	8
No. Partly Cloudy Days	7	6	8	9	10	11	11	11	9	8	8	6
No. Cloudy Days	16	14	16	14	14	12	12	12	12	13	15	17
% Possible Sunshine	42	51	53	60	62	65	65	62	61	61	52	45

etc.

- Winters are mild, though some rather cold days can be expected. Snowfall varies greatly from year to year; a winter with no snow is extremely unusual.
- Summer heat and humidity can become very uncomfortable.
- Precipitation is fairly uniform through the year though it tends to peak in August.

CLIMATABLE NO. 170

Appomattox Court House NHP, Booker T. Washington NM

TEMPERATURE NORMALS AND EXTREMES

% OF SUNNY/PTLY CLOUDY/CLOUDY DAYS

☐ Clear   ▦ Ptlycldy   ■ Cloudy

WEATHER PARAMETERS	MONTH											
	J	F	M	A	M	J	J	A	S	O	N	D
TEMPERATURE												
Normal Daily Maximum	46	48	57	68	76	83	86	85	80	70	58	48
Normal Daily Minimum	26	27	34	44	51	60	64	62	56	45	35	28
Extreme High	80	79	87	92	101	100	103	102	101	98	83	78
Extreme Low	-10	-1	0	20	28	36	44	42	30	21	7	-4
Days Above 90°	0	0	0	0	1	6	10	8	3	0	0	0
Days Below 32°	24	21	14	4	0	0	0	0	0	3	13	21
PRECIPITATION												
Normal	3.0	3.0	3.7	3.0	3.7	3.6	4.3	3.8	3.8	3.3	2.8	3.2
Maximum	7.8	6.3	9.2	6.7	9.1	8.6	10.3	11.4	12.7	11.4	8.8	7.2
Maximum 24 Hr. Precipitation	3.4	2.9	2.5	3.7	3.5	6.3	4.8	5.6	4.8	5.0	3.8	6.1
Maximum Snowfall	34	19	25	5	0	0	0	0	0	2	13	18
Days With Measurable Precip.	11	10	11	10	11	10	11	10	8	8	9	10
Average No. Thunderstorms	0	0	1	3	7	8	11	9	4	1	1	0
SUNSHINE/CLOUDINESS												
No. Clear Days	9	8	9	9	8	8	8	9	10	13	11	10
No. Partly Cloudy Days	7	7	9	9	10	12	11	11	9	7	7	7
No. Cloudy Days	15	13	13	12	13	10	12	11	11	11	12	14
% Possible Sunshine	52	56	59	61	63	66	62	62	61	55	55	53

etc.

- The summer heat and humidity can become very uncomfortable . . . see the Heat Index. Temperatures exceeding 100 degrees are very rare.
- Winters are relatively mild but can produce some very cold temperatures. The seasonal snowfall averages 17", but is highly variable from year to year.

CLIMATABLE NO. 171

Shenandoah NP, Blue Ridge Parkway, Appalachian NST

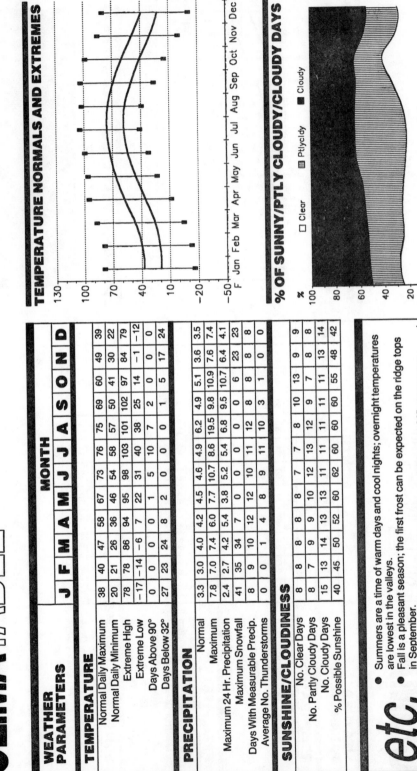

TEMPERATURE NORMALS AND EXTREMES

% OF SUNNY/PTLY CLOUDY/CLOUDY DAYS

☐ Clear   ▥ Ptlycldy   ■ Cloudy

WEATHER PARAMETERS	J	F	M	A	M	J	J	A	S	O	N	D
TEMPERATURE												
Normal Daily Maximum	38	40	47	58	67	73	76	75	69	60	49	39
Normal Daily Minimum	20	21	26	36	46	54	58	57	50	41	30	22
Extreme High	78	78	86	94	95	98	103	101	102	97	84	79
Extreme Low	-17	-14	-6	7	22	31	40	38	25	14	-1	-12
Days Above 90°	0	0	0	0	1	5	10	7	2	0	0	0
Days Below 32°	27	23	24	8	2	0	0	0	1	5	17	24
PRECIPITATION												
Normal	3.3	3.0	4.0	4.2	4.5	4.6	4.9	6.2	4.9	5.1	3.6	3.5
Maximum	7.8	7.0	7.4	6.0	7.7	10.7	8.6	19.5	9.8	10.9	7.6	7.4
Maximum 24 Hr. Precipitation	2.4	2.7	4.2	5.4	3.8	5.2	5.4	6.8	9.5	10.7	6.4	4.1
Maximum Snowfall	41	35	34	7	0	0	0	0	0	6	23	23
Days With Measurable Precip.	8	9	10	12	12	10	11	12	8	8	8	8
Average No. Thunderstorms	0	0	1	4	8	9	11	10	3	1	0	0
SUNSHINE/CLOUDINESS												
No. Clear Days	8	8	8	8	8	7	7	8	10	13	9	9
No. Partly Cloudy Days	8	7	9	9	10	12	13	12	9	7	8	8
No. Cloudy Days	15	13	14	13	13	11	11	11	11	11	13	14
% Possible Sunshine	40	45	50	52	60	62	60	60	60	55	48	42

etc.

- Summers are a time of warm days and cool nights; overnight temperatures are lowest in the valleys.
- Fall is a pleasant season; the first frost can be expected on the ridge tops in September.
- Winters are cold. Typically, seasonal snowfall is near 36"; even more snow falls on the ridge tops.

CLIMATABLE NO. 172

Whitman Mission NHS, Lewis and Clark NHT, Oregon NHT,

TEMPERATURE NORMALS AND EXTREMES

% OF SUNNY/PTLY CLOUDY/CLOUDY DAYS

□ Clear   ▦ Ptlycldy   ■ Cloudy

WEATHER PARAMETERS	J	F	M	A	M	J	J	A	S	O	N	D
TEMPERATURE												
Normal Daily Maximum	40	47	54	62	71	79	89	86	77	64	49	43
Normal Daily Minimum	28	34	37	42	49	56	62	61	54	44	36	31
Extreme High	71	77	79	93	101	106	112	113	103	90	80	73
Extreme Low	−16	−14	13	19	28	41	46	45	26	15	−5	−14
Days Above 90°	0	0	0	0	1	5	15	13	3	0	0	0
Days Below 32°	19	12	5	0	0	0	0	0	0	1	9	18
PRECIPITATION												
Normal	2.1	1.4	1.4	1.4	0.9	0.4	0.7	0.8	1.4	1.4	1.9	2.2
Maximum	5.9	4.0	4.2	3.7	4.2	3.0	1.8	2.9	4.5	4.2	4.2	4.3
Maximum 24 Hr. Precipitation	1.4	1.4	1.4	1.6	1.9	2.0	1.2	1.6	1.4	3.1	1.4	1.4
Maximum Snowfall	31	33	6	4	T	0	0	0	0	4	20	22
Days With Measurable Precip.	13	12	12	9	8	7	3	3	6	8	12	14
Average No. Thunderstorms	0	0	0	0	2	2	2	2	1	0	0	0
SUNSHINE/CLOUDINESS												
No. Clear Days	2	3	6	7	9	12	21	20	15	11	4	2
No. Partly Cloudy Days	5	6	8	10	11	10	7	7	8	7	6	4
No. Cloudy Days	24	19	17	13	11	8	3	4	7	13	20	25
% Possible Sunshine	22	33	50	60	65	71	84	82	72	59	30	18

etc.

- This semi-arid area is under a prevailing flow of Pacific air from which most of the moisture is removed in its ascent over the Cascades.
- Occasional outbreaks of cold polar air result in winter cold spells; some relief comes from the downslope or "chinook" winds off the mountains to the west.

CLIMATABLE NO. 173

Petersburg NB, Richmond NB Park, Maggie L. Walker NHS

TEMPERATURE NORMALS AND EXTREMES

% OF SUNNY/PTLY CLOUDY/CLOUDY DAYS

□ Clear   ▥ Ptlycldy   ■ Cloudy

WEATHER PARAMETERS	J	F	M	A	M	J	J	A	S	O	N	D
TEMPERATURE												
Normal Daily Maximum	48	52	60	72	79	86	89	88	82	72	62	52
Normal Daily Minimum	28	30	37	46	55	63	68	67	60	48	38	31
Extreme High	80	83	93	96	100	104	105	102	103	99	87	81
Extreme Low	-12	-10	11	23	30	40	51	46	35	21	10	-1
Days Above 90°	0	0	0	0	1	10	16	13	6	0	0	0
Days Below 32°	21	18	10	2	0	0	0	0	0	2	9	19
PRECIPITATION												
Normal	3.2	3.2	3.6	2.9	3.6	3.6	5.1	5.0	3.5	3.7	3.3	3.4
Maximum	8.0	6.0	8.6	5.9	8.9	9.2	18.9	14.1	11.0	9.4	7.6	7.1
Maximum 24 Hr. Precipitation	3.3	2.7	2.5	2.6	3.1	4.6	5.7	8.8	4.0	6.5	4.1	3.2
Maximum Snowfall	38	21	20	2	0	0	0	0	0	0	7	12
Days With Measurable Precip.	10	9	11	9	11	10	11	10	8	7	8	9
Average No. Thunderstorms	0	0	2	3	7	9	11	8	4	1	1	0
SUNSHINE/CLOUDINESS												
No. Clear Days	8	8	8	8	7	7	7	7	9	9	10	10
No. Partly Cloudy Days	7	6	8	9	10	12	11	12	9	7	7	6
No. Cloudy Days	16	14	15	13	14	11	13	12	13	13	13	15
% Possible Sunshine	54	57	61	65	65	69	67	66	64	61	57	53

etc.

- Summers are hot and humid; temperatues above 100 degrees are not uncommon but do not necessarily occur every summer.
- Winters are generally mild, though some subzero temperatures are experienced.
- The normal annual snowfall is about 14"; snow does not usually remain on the ground for long.

CLIMATABLE NO. 174   Coulee Dam NRA

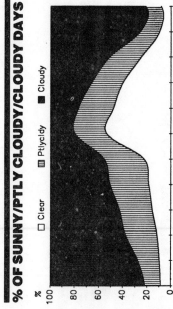

TEMPERATURE NORMALS AND EXTREMES

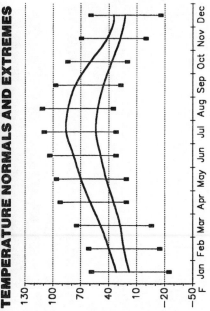

% OF SUNNY/PTLY CLOUDY/CLOUDY DAYS

☐ Clear   ▤ Ptlycldy   ■ Cloudy

WEATHER PARAMETERS	MONTH											
	J	F	M	A	M	J	J	A	S	O	N	D
TEMPERATURE												
Normal Daily Maximum	32	40	49	60	70	78	86	84	76	60	42	35
Normal Daily Minimum	18	24	28	35	43	49	54	52	46	37	28	23
Extreme High	57	60	73	91	95	102	108	110	96	83	68	58
Extreme Low	-26	-16	-7	20	20	31	31	34	26	19	-1	-17
Days Above 90°	0	0	0	0	1	3	11	9	2	0	0	0
Days Below 32°	29	25	23	11	3	0	0	0	3	9	20	27
PRECIPITATION												
Normal	2.2	1.4	1.2	1.0	1.6	1.5	0.8	1.2	0.9	1.2	2.0	2.5
Maximum	3.9	3.3	2.1	2.4	3.4	3.0	2.6	3.7	1.9	2.9	6.4	4.7
Maximum 24 Hr. Precipitation	1.4	2.0	1.0	1.2	1.2	1.0	1.0	1.0	0.9	0.8	1.8	1.0
Maximum Snowfall	43	21	15	5	0	0	0	0	0	3	24	34
Days With Measurable Precip.	14	12	11	9	9	8	4	5	6	8	13	15
Average No. Thunderstorms	0	0	0	1	2	4	3	3	1	0	0	0
SUNSHINE/CLOUDINESS												
No. Clear Days	3	3	4	5	6	7	17	15	12	8	3	3
No. Partly Cloudy Days	4	5	8	8	10	10	8	9	8	8	5	4
No. Cloudy Days	24	20	19	17	15	13	6	7	10	15	22	24
% Possible Sunshine	27	38	53	60	63	66	80	77	70	53	28	21

etc.

• Summers are warm, dry and sunny.

• Winters are cold and cloudy with considerable fog. Numerous cold snaps, though of short duration, occur each winter.

• Most winter precipitation falls as snow; the ground remains snow covered from mid-December to mid-March, the higher mountains even longer.

CLIMATABLE NO. 175   Ebey's Landing NHS, San Juan Island NHP

WEATHER PARAMETERS	J	F	M	A	M	J	J	A	S	O	N	D
TEMPERATURE												
Normal Daily Maximum	44	48	51	57	63	68	71	71	67	58	50	46
Normal Daily Minimum	33	35	36	40	44	47	50	50	47	43	38	36
Extreme High	65	66	68	79	85	92	95	98	91	79	66	62
Extreme Low	−8	5	14	26	28	35	40	38	29	20	8	3
Days Above 90°	0	0	0	0	0	0	0	0	0	0	0	0
Days Below 32°	12	10	7	2	0	0	0	0	0	1	6	8
PRECIPITATION												
Normal	3.7	2.5	2.1	1.7	1.3	1.2	1.0	1.0	1.4	2.4	3.2	4.0
Maximum	8.1	4.6	3.5	3.0	2.2	2.9	3.0	2.6	3.1	5.7	5.5	7.4
Maximum 24 Hr. Precipitation	1.7	1.2	1.0	0.8	1.3	1.0	1.4	1.6	1.0	1.0	1.7	2.4
Maximum Snowfall	26	14	18	2	0	0	0	T	T	10	6	9
Days With Measurable Precip.	16	14	14	11	9	7	5	6	9	10	15	18
Average No. Thunderstorms	0	0	1	1	1	1	1	1	1	0	0	0
SUNSHINE/CLOUDINESS												
No. Clear Days	3	3	4	5	7	7	12	10	9	5	3	3
No. Partly Cloudy Days	5	6	8	9	10	8	10	10	8	8	6	5
No. Cloudy Days	23	19	19	16	14	15	9	11	13	18	21	23
% Possible Sunshine	28	34	42	47	52	49	63	56	53	37	28	23

etc.

- These islands are shielded by the Olympic Mountains, Vancouver Island and the Cascades. This region lies within the driest area of western Washington.
- Summers are cool and dry; winters are rather mild though cloudy.
- In late summer & early fall, considerable fog can be expected to occur.

TEMPERATURE NORMALS AND EXTREMES

% OF SUNNY/PTLY CLOUDY/CLOUDY DAYS

☐ Clear   ▦ Pt'ly cldy   ■ Cloudy

CLIMATABLE NO. 176

North Cascades NP, Ross Lake NRA, Lake Chelan NRA

TEMPERATURE NORMALS AND EXTREMES

% OF SUNNY/PTLY CLOUDY/CLOUDY DAYS

□ Clear   ▦ Ptlycldy   ■ Cloudy

WEATHER PARAMETERS	MONTH											
	J	F	M	A	M	J	J	A	S	O	N	D
TEMPERATURE												
Normal Daily Maximum	37	42	48	57	66	70	78	77	70	58	45	40
Normal Daily Minimum	26	29	32	37	43	48	52	52	48	41	34	31
Extreme High	62	60	73	85	94	99	106	100	83	65	65	57
Extreme Low	−8	−10	3	24	29	35	38	37	35	21	5	8
Days Above 90°	0	0	0	0	0	1	3	3	1	0	0	0
Days Below 32°	23	19	16	4	0	0	0	0	0	1	11	19
PRECIPITATION												
Normal	10.3	8.6	6.8	4.4	2.5	2.1	1.2	1.3	3.5	8.0	10.5	12.3
Maximum	26.5	20.4	12.8	14.0	5.1	5.3	2.5	3.8	10.8	18.0	19.5	18.6
Maximum 24 Hr. Precipitation	4.1	6.2	3.0	3.3	1.6	1.4	1.8	1.9	2.5	6.5	4.0	3.8
Maximum Snowfall	81	69	34	10	0	0	0	0	0	1	25	78
Days With Measurable Precip.	19	17	18	15	12	10	8	9	12	16	20	21
Average No. Thunderstorms	0	0	0	0	1	2	1	2	1	0	0	0
SUNSHINE/CLOUDINESS												
No. Clear Days	3	2	3	3	4	6	13	12	10	6	3	2
No. Partly Cloudy Days	2	3	4	5	6	5	7	8	6	5	3	2
No. Cloudy Days	26	23	24	22	21	19	11	11	14	20	24	27
% Possible Sunshine	28	35	42	50	52	55	65	65	55	45	30	20

etc.

• The table typifies the lower western slopes of the North Cascades.
• Temperatures are considerably colder and precipitation considerably greater in the high mountain areas to the east. In these areas, winter season snowfall ranges from 400" to 600"; snow depths can exceed 20'.

CLIMATABLE NO. 177 Mount Rainier NP

WEATHER PARAMETERS

TEMPERATURE

	J	F	M	A	M	J	J	A	S	O	N	D
Normal Daily Maximum	34	38	43	51	59	64	74	75	68	57	42	34
Normal Daily Minimum	12	15	19	25	32	37	42	41	35	29	22	19
Extreme High	55	60	73	80	88	93	101	97	94	85	65	61
Extreme Low	−38	−35	−18	−3	13	22	27	24	18	−5	−12	−16
Days Above 90°	0	0	0	0	0	0	2	2	1	0	0	0
Days Below 32°	30	28	30	27	17	5	1	1	9	21	28	30

PRECIPITATION

	J	F	M	A	M	J	J	A	S	O	N	D
Normal	14.6	10.2	8.9	6.3	4.0	3.8	1.6	2.9	4.6	7.7	12.1	15.9
Maximum	30.4	20.8	19.5	12.5	9.1	8.0	6.0	7.2	15.2	23.6	25.4	29.1
Maximum 24 Hr. Precipitation	5.7	4.8	3.3	5.4	2.2	2.8	2.3	2.5	4.5	5.3	7.9	7.9
Maximum Snowfall	193	182	155	107	46	9	6	T	27	65	138	164
Days With Measurable Precip.	22	20	21	19	16	15	9	11	13	16	20	23
Average No. Thunderstorms	0	0	0	0	1	2	1	2	1	0	0	0

SUNSHINE/CLOUDINESS

	J	F	M	A	M	J	J	A	S	O	N	D
No. Clear Days	3	2	3	3	4	6	13	12	10	6	3	2
No. Partly Cloudy Days	2	3	4	5	6	5	7	8	6	5	3	2
No. Cloudy Days	26	23	24	22	21	19	11	11	14	20	24	27
% Possible Sunshine	28	35	42	50	52	55	65	55	55	45	30	20

etc.

- The temperature data shown typify the moderate elevation areas; the precipitation data typify the higher elevations.
- Winter season snowfall along the summit of the Cascades is 300'-500'; snow depths range from 10' to 25'. The record single season snowfall for North America of 1122" was set here.

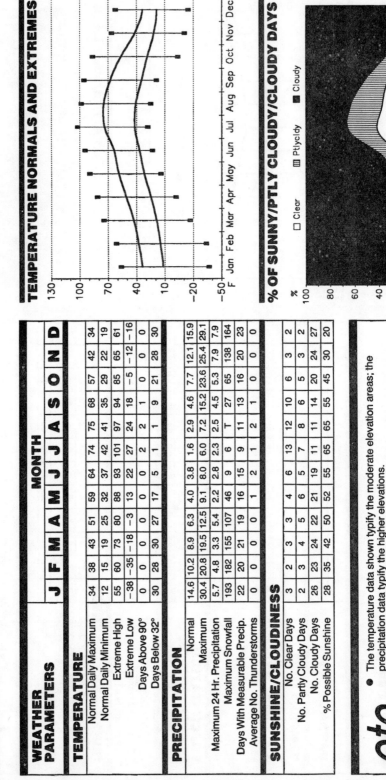

TEMPERATURE NORMALS AND EXTREMES

% OF SUNNY/PTLY CLOUDY/CLOUDY DAYS

Clear   Ptlycldy   Cloudy

CLIMATABLE NO. 178   Olympic NP

TEMPERATURE NORMALS AND EXTREMES

WEATHER PARAMETERS	J	F	M	A	M	J	J	A	S	O	N	D
TEMPERATURE												
Normal Daily Maximum	45	48	50	55	60	64	69	69	67	59	51	46
Normal Daily Minimum	33	35	34	37	42	46	49	50	47	42	37	35
Extreme High	65	72	70	79	90	96	95	99	92	81	69	64
Extreme Low	7	15	19	24	29	33	38	36	28	24	5	7
Days Above 90°	0	0	0	0	0	0	0	0	0	0	0	0
Days Below 32°	14	10	11	6	1	0	0	0	0	4	8	13
PRECIPITATION												
Normal	15.1	12.1	11.3	7.1	4.7	3.1	2.3	2.8	5.3	10.5	13.9	16.3
Maximum	23.3	20.6	21.9	13.9	12.4	8.5	11.0	10.1	10.9	27.2	29.1	27.8
Maximum 24 Hr. Precipitation	8.3	5.1	4.2	2.8	3.5	2.0	6.4	3.1	4.1	5.5	5.4	6.8
Maximum Snowfall	40	13	10	3	T	T	0	0	T	T	16	12
Days With Measurable Precip.	22	20	21	20	16	14	12	11	13	18	22	23
Average No. Thunderstorms	0	0	1	0	0	0	0	0	1	1	1	1
SUNSHINE/CLOUDINESS												
No. Clear Days	3	3	3	3	3	6	6	7	7	5	3	4
No. Partly Cloudy Days	3	3	6	6	8	7	8	9	8	7	5	4
No. Cloudy Days	25	22	22	21	20	17	16	15	19	22	23	23
% Possible Sunshine	21	27	31	35	36	42	43	43	43	33	21	18

% OF SUNNY/PTLY CLOUDY/CLOUDY DAYS

☐ Clear   ▥ Ptlycldy   ■ Cloudy

etc.

- The data shown are for the Pacific shore segment of the Park. In the high mountain areas of the Olympic Peninsula, temperatures are lower and total precipitation exceeds 200".
- Winter is the rainy season; it rains often and moderately hard. Both gale force winds and fog are not unusual here.

CLIMATABLE NO. 179

Ice Age NSR (Kettle Moraine SP, Horicon Marsh),
Ice Age NST

WEATHER PARAMETERS	J	F	M	A	M	J	J	A	S	O	N	D
TEMPERATURE												
Normal Daily Maximum	26	32	41	58	70	79	84	82	74	62	46	32
Normal Daily Minimum	10	14	23	35	45	55	60	58	50	41	28	16
Extreme High	59	66	79	90	93	100	100	101	100	89	75	62
Extreme Low	-37	-26	-20	8	17	32	39	37	26	16	-10	-17
Days Above 90°	0	0	0	0	1	3	5	4	1	0	0	0
Days Below 32°	30	28	26	12	2	0	0	0	0	6	20	29
PRECIPITATION												
Normal	1.2	1.2	2.2	3.2	3.2	3.7	4.0	3.7	3.6	2.6	2.1	1.8
Maximum	3.8	4.2	6.0	6.5	8.0	8.8	12.2	7.9	10.9	8.9	4.3	5.0
Maximum 24 Hr. Precipitation	1.2	1.4	1.8	2.8	3.1	3.1	6.6	3.9	3.8	4.0	2.0	1.9
Maximum Snowfall	40	40	29	16	2	0	0	0	0	3	20	33
Days With Measurable Precip.	11	10	12	12	12	11	10	9	9	9	10	11
Average No. Thunderstorms	0	1	2	5	6	9	8	7	5	2	1	0
SUNSHINE/CLOUDINESS												
No. Clear Days	7	6	6	6	7	8	10	10	9	9	6	6
No. Partly Cloudy Days	6	6	8	8	10	10	11	9	9	9	6	6
No. Cloudy Days	18	16	17	16	14	12	10	11	13	13	18	19
% Possible Sunshine	44	47	50	53	59	64	70	66	59	54	40	37

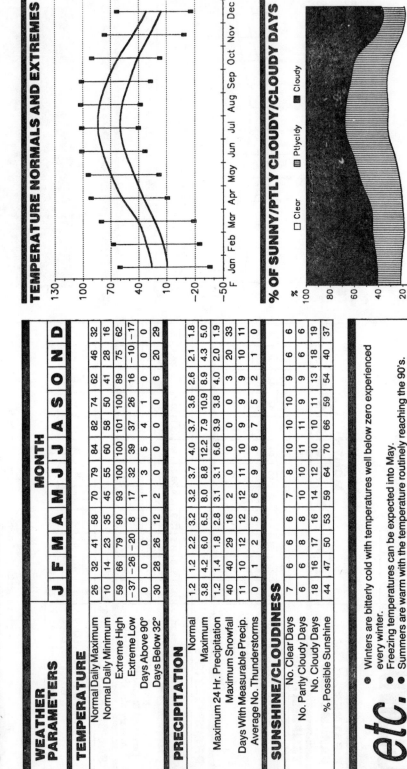

TEMPERATURE NORMALS AND EXTREMES

% OF SUNNY/PTLY CLOUDY/CLOUDY DAYS

□ Clear   ▦ Ptlycldy   ▤ Cloudy

etc.

- Winters are bitterly cold with temperatures well below zero experienced every winter.
- Freezing temperatures can be expected into May.
- Summers are warm with the temperature routinely reaching the 90's. Temperatures of 100 degrees are rare.

CLIMATABLE NO. 180   New River Gorge NR

TEMPERATURE NORMALS AND EXTREMES

WEATHER PARAMETERS	J	F	M	A	M	J	J	A	S	O	N	D
TEMPERATURE												
Normal Daily Maximum	40	43	52	64	73	80	83	82	77	66	54	44
Normal Daily Minimum	20	21	29	39	47	54	59	58	52	40	31	24
Extreme High	73	76	86	89	89	95	99	97	98	93	80	76
Extreme Low	-17	-8	-2	14	24	34	41	39	28	13	1	-8
Days Above 90°	0	0	0	0	0	2	3	2	1	0	0	0
Days Below 32°	27	24	20	9	2	0	0	0	0	7	18	25
PRECIPITATION												
Normal	3.6	3.1	4.2	3.7	4.1	3.9	5.2	4.3	3.6	3.0	3.1	3.3
Maximum	6.8	6.3	9.6	7.2	8.8	6.9	10.1	7.2	7.4	8.0	5.8	6.9
Maximum 24 Hr. Precipitation	2.1	1.5	2.4	2.0	1.7	2.6	3.4	2.8	4.0	3.9	1.5	1.6
Maximum Snowfall	41	30	30	4	0	0	0	0	0	6	11	24
Days With Measurable Precip.	16	15	15	14	14	12	14	12	11	10	13	15
Average No. Thunderstorms	0	0	2	5	8	7	9	8	3	1	0	0
SUNSHINE/CLOUDINESS												
No. Clear Days	5	4	5	5	5	4	3	4	7	9	5	5
No. Partly Cloudy Days	5	6	6	7	9	10	12	11	9	7	7	6
No. Cloudy Days	21	18	20	18	17	16	16	16	14	15	18	20
% Possible Sunshine	35	39	40	48	58	60	60	59	58	52	40	37

% OF SUNNY/PTLY CLOUDY/CLOUDY DAYS

□ Clear   ▦ Ptlycldy   ■ Cloudy

etc.

- The climate here is characterized by sharp seasonal temperature contrasts and large day to day temperature variations. Winters have seen both subzero temperatures and temperatures in the 70's.
- Cold waves can be expected 2 or 3 times a winter; the severe cold will usually last only 2 or 3 days.

CLIMATABLE NO. 181

Ice Age NSR (Devil's Lake SP), Ice Age NST

WEATHER PARAMETERS	MONTH											
	J	F	M	A	M	J	J	A	S	O	N	D
TEMPERATURE												
Normal Daily Maximum	25	30	40	57	69	78	82	80	72	61	44	31
Normal Daily Minimum	4	8	20	34	44	54	58	56	47	37	25	12
Extreme High	56	57	79	92	91	98	101	99	99	99	76	64
Extreme Low	−45	−35	−34	5	22	34	39	35	23	12	−17	−28
Days Above 90°	0	0	0	0	0	2	4	3	1	0	0	0
Days Below 32°	31	28	27	14	3	0	0	0	2	11	23	30
PRECIPITATION												
Normal	1.0	1.0	2.1	3.3	3.3	3.6	3.8	3.9	3.5	2.2	1.9	1.3
Maximum	2.2	3.1	4.8	7.1	6.4	8.4	9.5	11.7	11.3	6.0	4.8	3.4
Maximum 24 Hr. Precipitation	1.1	1.3	1.6	2.4	3.4	4.1	5.2	4.2	3.4	2.0	2.2	1.2
Maximum Snowfall	27	27	27	12	T	0	0	0	0	2	11	24
Days With Measurable Precip.	10	8	11	11	8	11	10	9	9	9	9	10
Average No. Thunderstorms	0	0	2	5	8	11	10	9	6	3	1	0
SUNSHINE/CLOUDINESS												
No. Clear Days	8	7	6	6	7	7	9	9	10	9	6	6
No. Partly Cloudy Days	6	6	8	8	9	10	11	11	8	8	6	6
No. Cloudy Days	17	15	17	16	15	13	11	11	12	14	18	19
% Possible Sunshine	48	51	53	52	58	64	68	66	60	54	40	39

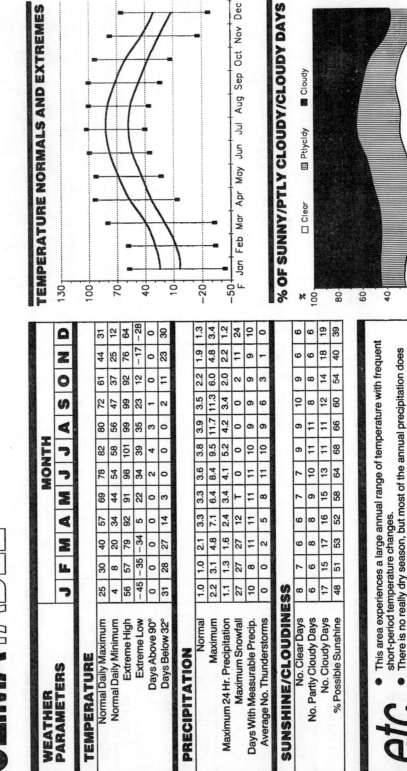

TEMPERATURE NORMALS AND EXTREMES

% OF SUNNY/PTLY CLOUDY/CLOUDY DAYS

☐ Clear   ▥ Ptlycldy   ■ Cloudy

etc.

- This area experiences a large annual range of temperature with frequent short-period temperature changes.
- There is no really dry season, but most of the annual precipitation does fall during the growing season.
- The ground can be expected to be covered with snow through much of the winter.

CLIMATABLE NO. 182

Apostle Islands NL

TEMPERATURE NORMALS AND EXTREMES

% OF SUNNY/PTLY CLOUDY/CLOUDY DAYS

□ Clear   ▦ Ptlycldy   ■ Cloudy

WEATHER PARAMETERS	J	F	M	A	M	J	J	A	S	O	N	D
TEMPERATURE												
Normal Daily Maximum	21	27	36	51	64	74	80	78	68	58	40	27
Normal Daily Minimum	0	2	14	28	38	48	54	53	45	36	23	8
Extreme High	52	58	71	90	93	97	99	97	100	87	74	59
Extreme Low	-35	-40	-30	-2	16	28	33	30	23	11	-16	-28
Days Above 90°	0	0	0	0	0	0	1	1	0	0	0	0
Days Below 32°	31	28	29	21	8	1	0	0	3	12	25	31
PRECIPITATION												
Normal	1.0	0.8	1.6	2.5	3.7	3.6	4.1	4.6	3.5	2.2	2.0	1.3
Maximum	3.2	2.3	5.9	8.1	8.1	8.6	9.1	8.8	5.8	6.0	8.4	4.6
Maximum 24 Hr. Precipitation	0.8	0.8	2.4	3.6	2.6	3.2	3.5	4.9	3.0	2.4	2.4	1.8
Maximum Snowfall	33	22	26	11	12	0	0	0	0	6	26	42
Days With Measurable Precip.	12	10	11	11	12	13	11	11	12	10	11	12
Average No. Thunderstorms	0	0	0	1	3	7	8	7	2	0	0	0
SUNSHINE/CLOUDINESS												
No. Clear Days	7	7	7	6	6	7	7	6	6	4	6	6
No. Partly Cloudy Days	7	6	7	8	9	11	13	12	9	8	6	6
No. Cloudy Days	17	15	17	16	16	14	11	12	15	17	20	19
% Possible Sunshine	49	52	55	55	56	58	65	60	51	46	35	40

etc.

- Winters are quite cold; temperatures down to −30 degrees can be expected each winter.
- Summers are cool with the temperature seldom reaching the 90's. Development of afternoon thunderstorms is inhibited by the cold lake waters.
- Snowfall on the Islands is generally less than on inland areas.

CLIMATABLE NO. 183   Fort Laramie NHS, Oregon NHT, Mormon Pioneer NHT

WEATHER PARAMETERS	J	F	M	A	M	J	J	A	S	O	N	D
TEMPERATURE												
Normal Daily Maximum	40	46	52	62	72	83	90	88	79	68	52	44
Normal Daily Minimum	11	16	21	31	41	50	55	52	42	30	20	14
Extreme High	70	75	81	89	99	105	111	105	101	91	79	70
Extreme Low	−36	−32	−19	−17	21	29	39	32	21	5	−21	−27
Days Above 90°	0	0	0	0	1	8	18	15	4	0	0	0
Days Below 32°	30	27	28	18	4	0	0	0	4	19	28	29
PRECIPITATION												
Normal	0.3	0.3	0.7	1.6	2.5	2.5	1.7	1.0	1.0	0.8	0.4	0.4
Maximum	0.9	1.0	1.7	3.4	6.1	8.1	4.4	2.6	4.7	2.4	1.1	1.0
Maximum 24 Hr. Precipitation	0.5	0.9	1.1	1.5	2.5	5.4	1.6	1.2	2.7	1.7	0.6	0.6
Maximum Snowfall	20	13	31	29	6	0	0	0	0	9	15	18
Days With Measurable Precip.	6	6	9	10	12	11	11	10	7	6	6	5
Average No. Thunderstorms	0	0	0	2	11	16	18	13	6	1	0	0
SUNSHINE/CLOUDINESS												
No. Clear Days	9	7	7	6	5	8	10	10	13	10	9	9
No. Partly Cloudy Days	9	9	10	10	12	13	15	13	9	9	9	9
No. Cloudy Days	13	12	14	14	14	9	6	8	9	11	11	13
% Possible Sunshine	63	66	66	61	60	65	68	68	70	69	61	60

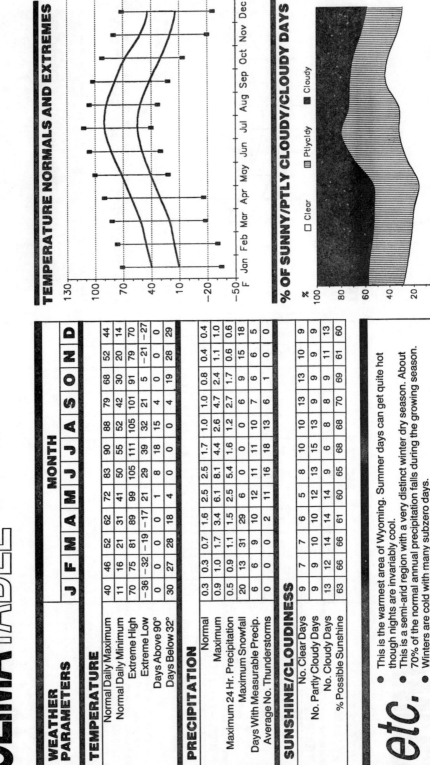

TEMPERATURE NORMALS AND EXTREMES

% OF SUNNY/PTLY CLOUDY/CLOUDY DAYS

☐ Clear   ▤ Ptlycldy   ▥ Cloudy

etc.

- This is the warmest area of Wyoming. Summer days can get quite hot though nights are invariably cool.
- This is a semi-arid region with a very distinct winter dry season. About 70% of the normal annual precipitation falls during the growing season.
- Winters are cold with many subzero days.

CLIMATABLE NO. 184   Fossil Butte NM, Mormon Pioneer NHT

WEATHER PARAMETERS

						MONTH						
	J	F	M	A	M	J	J	A	S	O	N	D
TEMPERATURE												
Normal Daily Maximum	32	35	40	51	63	73	83	80	72	60	43	34
Normal Daily Minimum	6	8	14	23	32	38	44	42	34	25	15	8
Extreme High	52	59	68	75	83	92	95	94	89	80	69	57
Extreme Low	-35	-33	-22	-1	9	19	28	23	10	-8	-22	-34
Days Above 90°	0	0	0	0	0	0	2	1	0	0	0	0
Days Below 32°	31	28	31	28	17	5	1	2	12	26	29	31
PRECIPITATION												
Normal	0.8	0.6	0.8	1.2	1.2	1.0	0.7	0.9	0.9	1.0	0.8	0.8
Maximum	2.8	1.6	1.5	2.8	4.5	2.9	2.8	3.6	3.2	2.6	1.9	2.8
Maximum 24 Hr. Precipitation	0.8	0.4	0.9	1.0	1.4	1.0	1.9	1.2	1.0	1.2	1.3	0.8
Maximum Snowfall	28	17	31	19	7	0	0	0	5	14	15	19
Days With Measurable Precip.	12	10	10	8	9	7	4	5	5	5	9	11
Average No. Thunderstorms	0	0	0	1	5	6	7	7	3	1	0	0
SUNSHINE/CLOUDINESS												
No. Clear Days	3	4	5	6	8	12	18	15	15	12	5	3
No. Partly Cloudy Days	6	6	8	8	10	9	9	11	8	8	7	7
No. Cloudy Days	22	18	18	16	13	9	4	5	7	11	18	21
% Possible Sunshine	39	52	61	65	67	74	82	80	78	70	47	39

etc.

- Summer days are quite warm but dry and comfortable; nights are generally cool, even cold in the valleys.
- The winters are very cold but punctuated with warm spells brought on by the chinooks, the warm, downslope winds off the mountains.
- The first freeze normally occurs in late summer.

TEMPERATURE NORMALS AND EXTREMES

(graph with temperature axis from -50 to 130, months Jan–Dec)

% OF SUNNY/PTLY CLOUDY/CLOUDY DAYS

Legend: □ Clear   ▥ Pttycldy   ▦ Cloudy

(graph with % axis from 0 to 100, months Jan–Dec)

CLIMATABLE NO. 185

Ice Age NSR (Mill Bluff SP)

WEATHER PARAMETERS	J	F	M	A	M	J	J	A	S	O	N	D
TEMPERATURE												
Normal Daily Maximum	27	31	41	59	71	79	84	83	74	63	44	32
Normal Daily Minimum	6	9	21	35	46	56	60	59	50	39	26	14
Extreme High	57	59	79	92	92	96	109	100	99	88	78	64
Extreme Low	-48	-40	-19	13	25	30	41	34	22	12	-16	-35
Days Above 90°	0	0	0	0	0	2	6	6	2	0	0	0
Days Below 32°	31	28	27	13	2	0	0	0	2	9	23	30
PRECIPITATION												
Normal	0.9	0.9	1.5	2.6	3.4	4.6	3.2	3.2	3.3	1.9	1.6	1.0
Maximum	2.9	2.6	3.8	7.3	8.8	9.5	9.2	9.8	10.5	5.1	3.7	2.6
Maximum 24 Hr. Precipitation	1.0	1.2	1.1	1.5	2.3	5.1	2.2	3.0	4.0	2.4	2.0	0.8
Maximum Snowfall	23	22	32	9	T	T	0	0	T	1	13	21
Days With Measurable Precip.	8	7	10	11	11	11	10	10	10	8	8	9
Average No. Thunderstorms	0	0	2	4	8	11	11	10	8	5	1	0
SUNSHINE/CLOUDINESS												
No. Clear Days	7	8	7	7	7	7	7	9	9	11	6	7
No. Partly Cloudy Days	7	7	7	9	11	11	11	9	7	7	6	6
No. Cloudy Days	17	13	17	16	15	12	10	11	12	13	18	18
% Possible Sunshine	45	51	55	57	60	64	71	67	64	60	45	40

etc.

- Summers are warm and, at times, hot and humid . . . watch the Heat Index. Periods of heat and humidity can last up to a week.
- Winters are relatively long, cold and snowy.
- Two-thirds of the annual precipitation falls from May through September, mostly in the form of showers and thunderstorms.

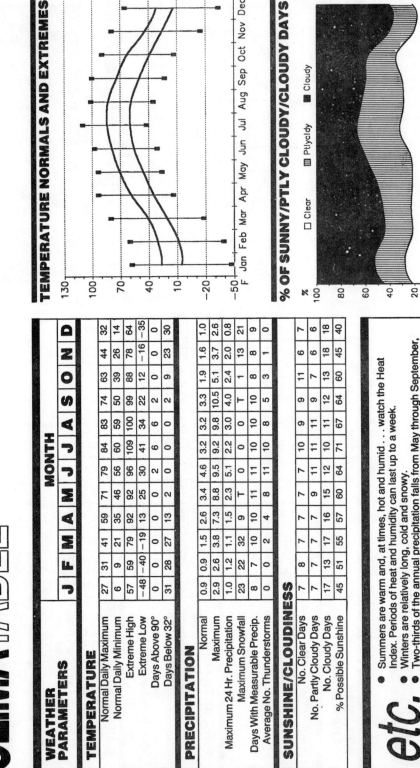

TEMPERATURE NORMALS AND EXTREMES

% OF SUNNY/PTLY CLOUDY/CLOUDY DAYS

☐ Clear   ▦ Ptlycldy   ■ Cloudy

CLIMATABLE NO. 186   Devil's Tower NM

TEMPERATURE NORMALS AND EXTREMES

WEATHER PARAMETERS	MONTH											
	J	F	M	A	M	J	J	A	S	O	N	D
TEMPERATURE												
Normal Daily Maximum	30	36	42	54	64	74	83	82	72	60	42	33
Normal Daily Minimum	8	13	19	29	39	48	55	53	43	34	21	14
Extreme High	58	61	72	82	92	100	102	101	96	86	74	62
Extreme Low	-32	-23	-21	-2	9	27	34	31	20	5	-23	-36
Days Above 90°	0	0	0	0	1	5	34	5	1	0	0	0
Days Below 32°	31	28	28	20	6	1	0	0	4	13	26	30
PRECIPITATION												
Normal	0.6	0.7	0.8	1.8	2.8	3.5	1.7	1.6	1.3	0.9	0.7	0.6
Maximum	1.6	1.8	1.6	3.9	9.8	8.2	3.4	6.0	3.6	2.8	1.4	1.2
Maximum 24 Hr. Precipitation	0.4	0.6	1.2	1.4	2.0	2.6	2.3	2.8	1.3	1.0	0.7	0.4
Maximum Snowfall	27	34	23	30	19	8	0	0	16	21	24	28
Days With Measurable Precip.	9	9	11	11	12	11	7	6	8	7	8	9
Average No. Thunderstorms	0	0	0	1	6	13	13	10	3	1	0	0
SUNSHINE/CLOUDINESS												
No. Clear Days	6	5	5	5	6	8	14	14	12	10	6	6
No. Partly Cloudy Days	8	8	9	9	10	12	12	11	9	9	8	8
No. Cloudy Days	17	15	17	16	15	10	5	6	9	12	16	17
% Possible Sunshine	55	59	61	59	59	64	75	74	67	62	53	53

% OF SUNNY/PTLY CLOUDY/CLOUDY DAYS

☐ Clear   ▥ Ptlycldy   ■ Cloudy

etc.

- Summer days can be hot, though the low humidity keeps summer weather quite pleasant. Summer nights are cool, often down to the 50's.
- Wintertime characteristically has rapid and frequent changes between mild and cold spells; usually experience as many as 10 cold waves each winter.

CLIMATABLE NO. 187

Yellowstone NP, Grand Teton NP, John D. Rockefeller Jr. Memorial Parkway

TEMPERATURE NORMALS AND EXTREMES

% OF SUNNY/PTLY CLOUDY/CLOUDY DAYS

Legend: □ Clear ▥ Ptlycldy ■ Cloudy

WEATHER PARAMETERS	MONTH											
	J	F	M	A	M	J	J	A	S	O	N	D
TEMPERATURE												
Normal Daily Maximum	26	32	38	48	60	70	80	78	68	56	38	28
Normal Daily Minimum	5	8	10	24	31	38	42	41	34	26	16	7
Extreme High	55	60	64	75	85	98	95	96	93	84	65	58
Extreme Low	−60	−63	−43	−28	0	18	24	18	7	−20	−36	−52
Days Above 90°	0	0	0	0	0	0	2	1	0	0	0	0
Days Below 32°	31	27	30	26	19	6	2	4	14	26	28	31
PRECIPITATION												
Normal	1.4	0.8	1.1	1.3	1.9	2.2	1.2	1.4	1.3	1.0	1.1	1.2
Maximum	3.8	1.8	3.0	2.8	2.9	4.0	2.2	3.9	3.7	2.6	2.5	4.1
Maximum 24 Hr. Precipitation	0.9	0.7	1.2	0.9	1.2	0.9	0.9	0.9	1.5	0.7	0.9	1.7
Maximum Snowfall	42	30	32	24	14		6	2	8	18	23	31
Days With Measurable Precip.	14	12	12	10	10	10	7	8	8	9	10	13
Average No. Thunderstorms	0	0	0	1	5	11	14	12	2	0	0	0
SUNSHINE/CLOUDINESS												
No. Clear Days	13	11	12	11	12	15	19	18	16	15	13	13
No. Partly Cloudy Days	7	7	9	9	9	8	8	8	7	7	6	6
No. Cloudy Days	11	10	10	10	10	8	4	5	9	9	11	12
% Possible Sunshine	46	53	60	59	61	63	78	75	66	60	44	41

etc.

- The table characterizes the lower elevation areas of the Parks. Most of the park area is at higher elevations and, as such, temperatures will average at least 5 degrees colder. Precipitation will be much greater; the precipitation on the high windward slopes can be expected to be twice that shown here.

CLIMATABLE NO. 188

American Memorial Park, Saipan

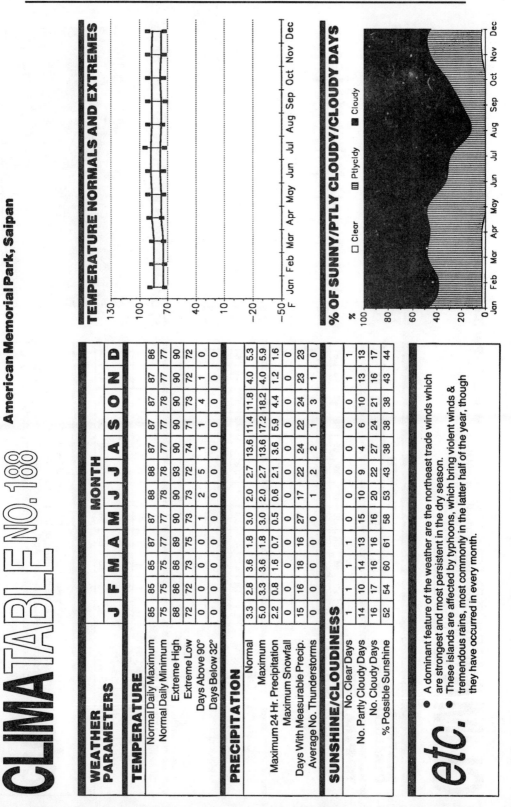

WEATHER PARAMETERS — MONTH

WEATHER PARAMETERS	J	F	M	A	M	J	J	A	S	O	N	D
TEMPERATURE												
Normal Daily Maximum	85	85	86	87	87	88	88	87	87	87	87	86
Normal Daily Minimum	75	75	75	77	77	78	78	77	78	78	77	77
Extreme High	88	86	86	89	90	90	93	90	90	90	90	90
Extreme Low	72	72	73	75	73	73	72	74	71	73	72	72
Days Above 90°	0	0	0	0	1	2	5	1	1	4	1	0
Days Below 32°	0	0	0	0	0	0	0	0	0	0	0	0
PRECIPITATION												
Normal	3.3	2.8	3.6	1.8	3.0	2.0	2.7	13.6	11.4	11.8	4.0	5.3
Maximum	5.0	3.3	3.6	1.8	3.0	2.0	2.7	13.6	17.2	18.2	4.0	5.9
Maximum 24 Hr. Precipitation	2.2	0.8	1.6	0.7	0.5	0.6	2.1	3.6	5.9	4.4	1.2	1.6
Maximum Snowfall	0	0	0	0	0	0	0	0	0	0	0	0
Days With Measurable Precip.	15	16	18	16	27	17	22	24	22	24	23	23
Average No. Thunderstorms	0	0	0	0	0	1	2	2	1	3	1	0
SUNSHINE/CLOUDINESS												
No. Clear Days	1	1	1	1	0	0	0	0	0	0	1	1
No. Partly Cloudy Days	14	10	14	13	15	10	9	4	6	10	13	13
No. Cloudy Days	16	17	16	16	16	20	22	27	24	21	16	17
% Possible Sunshine	52	54	60	61	58	53	43	38	38	38	43	44

TEMPERATURE NORMALS AND EXTREMES

% OF SUNNY/PTLY CLOUDY/CLOUDY DAYS

☐ Clear   ▦ Ptlycldy   ■ Cloudy

etc.

- A dominant feature of the weather are the northeast trade winds which are strongest and most persistent in the dry season.
- These islands are affected by typhoons, which bring violent winds & tremendous rains, most commonly in the latter half of the year, though they have occurred in every month.

CLIMATABLE NO. 189   War in the Pacific NHP, Guam

TEMPERATURE NORMALS AND EXTREMES

% OF SUNNY/PTLY CLOUDY/CLOUDY DAYS

☐ Clear   ▦ Ptlycldy   ■ Cloudy

WEATHER PARAMETERS	J	F	M	A	M	J	J	A	S	O	N	D
TEMPERATURE												
Normal Daily Maximum	83	84	86	87	86	86	86	86	86	86	83	84
Normal Daily Minimum	71	71	72	73	73	72	72	72	72	72	73	73
Extreme High	87	88	89	90	91	92	94	91	95	91	89	89
Extreme Low	56	59	59	54	59	62	63	64	61	64	62	61
Days Above 90°	0	0	0	0	1	2	1	0	0	0	0	0
Days Below 32°	0	0	0	0	0	0	0	0	0	0	0	0
PRECIPITATION												
Normal	5.4	4.8	4.2	4.1	6.4	5.5	10.3	13.9	14.2	13.9	9.0	6.1
Maximum	20.4	14.8	16.9	19.6	40.1	14.6	20.0	25.7	27.1	26.0	18.1	16.2
Maximum 24 Hr. Precipitation	6.3	9.2	3.6	6.4	27.0	4.6	7.9	8.3	7.5	12.1	7.3	6.1
Maximum Snowfall	0	0	0	0	0	0	0	0	0	0	0	0
Days With Measurable Precip.	20	18	19	20	20	24	26	25	26	26	25	23
Average No. Thunderstorms	1	0	0	0	1	2	4	6	7	4	2	0
SUNSHINE/CLOUDINESS												
No. Clear Days	1	1	1	1	0	0	0	0	0	0	1	1
No. Partly Cloudy Days	14	10	14	13	15	10	9	4	6	10	13	13
No. Cloudy Days	16	17	16	16	16	20	22	27	24	21	16	17
% Possible Sunshine	52	54	60	61	58	53	43	38	38	38	43	44

etc.

- Weather is uniformly warm and humid throughout the year.
- The seasons are actually defined by the precipitation. The "dry" season extends from January through April. The "rainy" season runs from mid-July to mid-November. The remaining months are transition periods that vary from year to year.

CLIMATABLE NO. 190

Christiansted NHS, Buck Island Reef NM

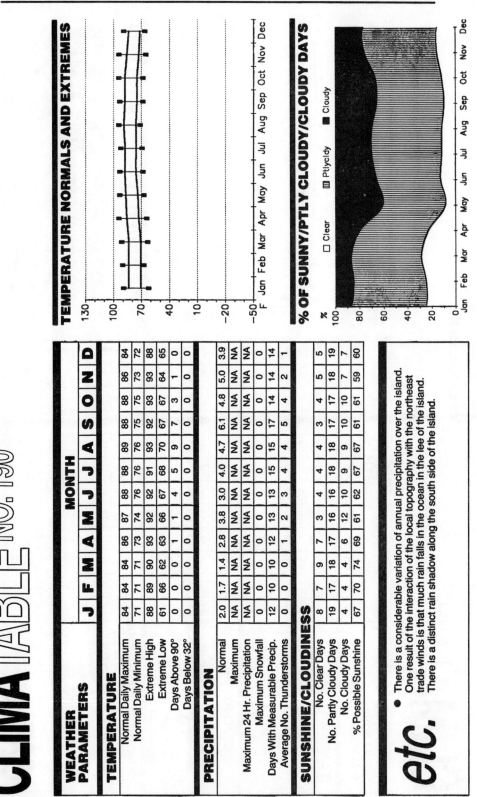

TEMPERATURE NORMALS AND EXTREMES

% OF SUNNY/PTLY CLOUDY/CLOUDY DAYS

☐ Clear   ▦ Ptlycldy   ■ Cloudy

WEATHER PARAMETERS	MONTH											
	J	F	M	A	M	J	J	A	S	O	N	D
TEMPERATURE												
Normal Daily Maximum	84	84	84	86	87	88	88	89	88	88	86	84
Normal Daily Minimum	71	71	71	73	74	76	76	76	75	75	73	72
Extreme High	88	89	90	93	92	92	91	93	92	93	93	88
Extreme Low	61	66	62	63	66	67	68	70	67	67	64	65
Days Above 90°	0	0	0	1	1	4	5	9	7	3	1	0
Days Below 32°	0	0	0	0	0	0	0	0	0	0	0	0
PRECIPITATION												
Normal	2.0	1.7	1.4	2.8	3.8	3.0	4.0	4.7	6.1	4.8	5.0	3.9
Maximum	NA	NA	NA	NA	NA	NA	NA	NA	NA	NA	NA	NA
Maximum 24 Hr. Precipitation	NA	NA	NA	NA	NA	NA	NA	NA	NA	NA	NA	NA
Maximum Snowfall	0	0	0	0	0	0	0	0	0	0	0	0
Days With Measurable Precip.	12	10	10	12	13	13	15	15	17	14	14	14
Average No. Thunderstorms	0	0	0	1	2	3	4	4	5	4	2	1
SUNSHINE/CLOUDINESS												
No. Clear Days	8	7	9	7	7	4	4	4	3	4	5	5
No. Partly Cloudy Days	19	17	18	17	16	16	18	18	17	17	18	19
No. Cloudy Days	4	4	4	6	12	10	9	9	10	10	7	7
% Possible Sunshine	67	70	74	69	61	62	67	67	61	61	59	60

etc.

- There is a considerable variation of annual precipitation over the island. One result of the interaction of the local topography with the northeast trade winds is that much rain falls in the ocean in the lee of the island. There is a distinct rain shadow along the south side of the island.

CLIMATABLE NO. 191   Virgin Islands NP

TEMPERATURE NORMALS AND EXTREMES

WEATHER PARAMETERS	MONTH											
	J	**F**	**M**	**A**	**M**	**J**	**J**	**A**	**S**	**O**	**N**	**D**
TEMPERATURE												
Normal Daily Maximum	82	83	84	85	86	87	88	88	88	87	86	84
Normal Daily Minimum	71	71	72	74	75	77	77	77	76	76	74	73
Extreme High	86	87	88	90	90	91	92	92	92	91	90	88
Extreme Low	63	65	66	65	69	69	71	67	71	68	67	64
Days Above 90°	0	0	0	0	0	2	6	8	4	1	0	0
Days Below 32°	0	0	0	0	0	0	0	0	0	0	0	0
PRECIPITATION												
Normal	2.4	1.9	1.7	2.2	4.6	3.2	3.3	4.1	6.9	5.6	3.9	3.9
Maximum	NA	NA	NA	NA	NA	NA	NA	NA	NA	NA	NA	NA
Maximum 24 Hr. Precipitation	NA	NA	NA	NA	NA	NA	NA	NA	NA	NA	NA	NA
Maximum Snowfall	0	0	0	0	0	0	0	0	0	0	0	0
Days With Measurable Precip.	13	11	10	12	13	13	14	14	15	14	14	13
Average No. Thunderstorms	0	0	0	0	1	2	2	2	2	2	1	0
SUNSHINE/CLOUDINESS												
No. Clear Days	8	7	9	7	3	4	4	3	4	5	5	5
No. Partly Cloudy Days	19	17	18	17	16	16	18	18	17	17	18	19
No. Cloudy Days	4	4	4	6	12	10	9	9	10	10	7	7
% Possible Sunshine	67	70	74	69	61	62	67	67	61	61	59	60

% OF SUNNY/PTLY CLOUDY/CLOUDY DAYS

☐ Clear   ▥ Ptycldy   ▨ Cloudy

etc.

- The dominant weather features are the consistent temperatures, the steady northeast trade winds, the daytime sea breezes and the afternoon showers.
- Tropical storms and disturbances can bring high winds and heavy rains, most commonly in the summer or fall.

CLIMATABLE NO. 192

Appalachian NST, Blue Ridge Parkway

TEMPERATURE NORMALS AND EXTREMES

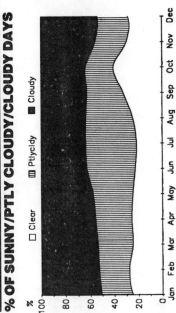

% OF SUNNY/PTLY CLOUDY/CLOUDY DAYS

☐ Clear   ▦ Ptlycldy   ▨ Cloudy

WEATHER PARAMETERS	J	F	M	A	M	J	J	A	S	O	N	D
TEMPERATURE												
Normal Daily Maximum	45	48	57	68	76	83	87	86	79	69	57	48
Normal Daily Minimum	26	28	35	44	53	60	65	64	57	45	36	29
Extreme High	78	80	87	95	96	100	104	105	101	93	83	76
Extreme Low	-11	1	10	20	31	39	48	42	34	22	9	-4
Days Above 90°	0	0	0	0	1	5	10	7	2	0	0	0
Days Below 32°	24	20	13	2	0	0	0	0	0	2	10	20
PRECIPITATION												
Normal	2.8	3.2	3.7	3.1	3.5	3.3	3.4	3.9	3.1	3.5	2.6	2.9
Maximum	6.1	7.2	7.8	8.0	8.4	7.6	7.8	9.5	9.2	9.7	12.4	7.1
Maximum 24 Hr. Precipitation	2.7	2.6	3.0	5.6	4.0	4.0	2.7	5.2	3.8	6.4	6.6	3.4
Maximum Snowfall	41	28	30	7	T	0	0	0	T	1	14	23
Days With Measurable Precip.	10	10	11	10	12	10	12	11	8	8	9	9
Average No. Thunderstorms	0	0	1	4	8	9	11	10	3	1	0	0
SUNSHINE/CLOUDINESS												
No. Clear Days	8	8	8	8	8	7	7	8	10	13	9	9
No. Partly Cloudy Days	8	7	9	9	10	12	13	12	9	7	8	8
No. Cloudy Days	15	13	14	13	13	11	11	11	11	11	13	14
% Possible Sunshine	52	56	59	61	63	66	62	62	61	61	55	53

etc.
- This area exhibits a generally mild climate with relatively few occurrences of severe weather.
- Surrounding mountains provide a barrier to some intrusions of cold polar air.
- Summers are warm with pleasantly cool nights.
- Some snow can be expected each winter; seasonal total averages 24".

CLIMATABLE NO. 193 Appalachian NST

TEMPERATURE NORMALS AND EXTREMES

% OF SUNNY/PTLY CLOUDY/CLOUDY DAYS

☐ Clear   ▦ Ptlycldy   ■ Cloudy

WEATHER PARAMETERS	J	F	M	A	M	J	J	A	S	O	N	D
MONTH												
TEMPERATURE												
Normal Daily Maximum	49	52	60	71	78	84	86	86	80	70	60	52
Normal Daily Minimum	29	31	37	46	54	61	65	64	59	47	38	31
Extreme High	76	76	84	89	94	100	103	98	100	92	81	73
Extreme Low	-6	-1	6	25	30	43	53	52	32	23	12	-3
Days Above 90°	0	0	0	0	1	5	9	7	2	0	0	0
Days Below 32°	19	17	10	2	0	0	0	0	0	2	9	18
PRECIPITATION												
Normal	6.3	5.7	7.9	5.7	5.2	4.1	5.7	5.0	4.6	3.5	4.8	5.9
Maximum	10.3	12.2	19.7	13.6	14.6	10.5	12.3	18.2	9.6	10.4	10.2	15.5
Maximum 24 Hr. Precipitation	4.3	4.6	6.3	3.5	5.5	3.6	3.7	3.9	4.0	4.2	2.6	5.9
Maximum Snowfall	4	5	8	0	0	0	0	0	0	0	T	3
Days With Measurable Precip.	11	11	12	10	10	10	12	10	9	8	10	11
Average No. Thunderstorms	1	2	6	6	9	12	17	11	5	1	2	1
SUNSHINE/CLOUDINESS												
No. Clear Days	7	7	8	8	9	8	7	8	10	13	10	8
No. Partly Cloudy Days	7	6	8	8	10	12	13	13	10	8	7	6
No. Cloudy Days	17	15	15	13	12	10	11	10	10	10	13	17
% Possible Sunshine	43	49	52	61	65	65	61	62	64	62	52	44

etc.

- Winters are colder than elsewhere in Georgia, but still are not severe.
- Autumns are characterized by long periods of mild, sunny weather.
- Rainfall is abundant throughout the year with the heaviest rains coming in winter.
- The average winter snowfall is about 2".

CLIMATABLE NO. 194 Appalachian NST

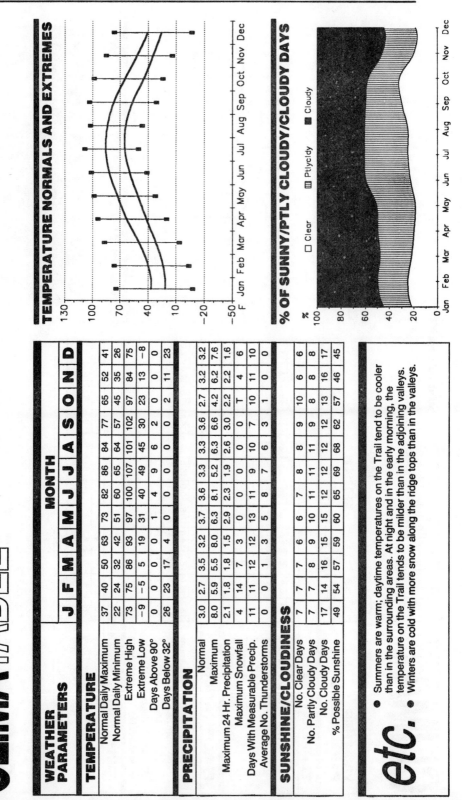

TEMPERATURE NORMALS AND EXTREMES

% OF SUNNY/PTLY CLOUDY/CLOUDY DAYS

☐ Clear ▥ Ptlycldy ■ Cloudy

WEATHER PARAMETERS	MONTH											
	J	F	M	A	M	J	J	A	S	O	N	D
TEMPERATURE												
Normal Daily Maximum	37	40	50	63	73	82	86	84	77	65	52	41
Normal Daily Minimum	22	24	32	42	51	60	65	64	57	45	35	26
Extreme High	73	75	86	93	97	100	107	101	102	97	84	75
Extreme Low	-9	-5	5	19	31	40	49	45	30	23	13	-8
Days Above 90°	0	0	0	0	1	4	9	6	2	0	0	0
Days Below 32°	26	23	17	4	0	0	0	0	0	2	11	23
PRECIPITATION												
Normal	3.0	2.7	3.5	3.2	3.7	3.6	3.3	3.3	3.6	2.7	3.2	3.2
Maximum	8.0	5.9	5.5	8.0	6.3	8.1	5.2	6.3	6.6	4.2	6.2	7.6
Maximum 24 Hr. Precipitation	2.1	1.8	1.8	1.5	2.9	2.3	1.9	2.6	3.0	2.2	2.2	1.6
Maximum Snowfall	4	14	7	3	0	0	0	0	0	T	4	6
Days With Measurable Precip.	11	11	12	12	13	11	9	10	7	10	11	10
Average No. Thunderstorms	0	0	1	3	5	8	7	6	3	1	0	0
SUNSHINE/CLOUDINESS												
No. Clear Days	7	7	7	6	6	7	8	8	9	10	6	6
No. Partly Cloudy Days	7	7	8	9	10	11	11	11	9	8	8	8
No. Cloudy Days	17	14	16	15	15	12	12	12	12	13	16	17
% Possible Sunshine	49	54	57	59	60	65	69	68	62	57	46	45

etc.
- Summers are warm; daytime temperatures on the Trail tend to be cooler than in the surrounding areas. At night and in the early morning, the temperature on the Trail tends to be milder than in the adjoining valleys.
- Winters are cold with more snow along the ridge tops than in the valleys.

CLIMATABLE NO. 195 Appalachian NST

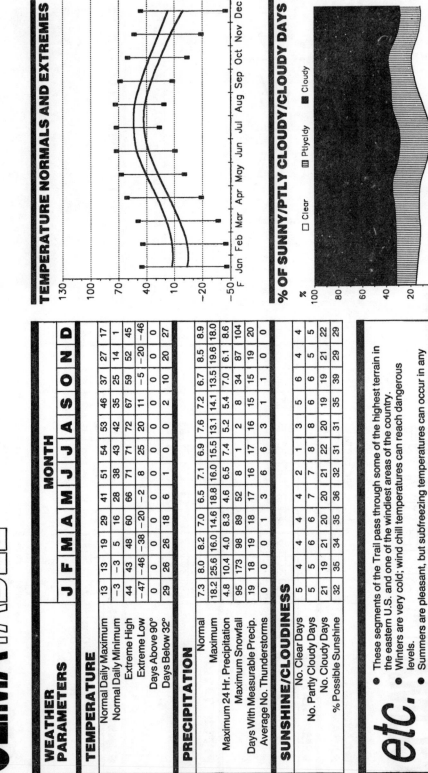

TEMPERATURE NORMALS AND EXTREMES

% OF SUNNY/PTLY CLOUDY/CLOUDY DAYS

☐ Clear   ▦ Ptlycldy   ■ Cloudy

WEATHER PARAMETERS	J	F	M	A	M	J	J	A	S	O	N	D
TEMPERATURE												
Normal Daily Maximum	13	13	19	29	41	51	54	53	46	37	27	17
Normal Daily Minimum	-3	-3	5	16	28	38	43	42	35	25	14	1
Extreme High	44	43	48	60	66	71	71	72	67	59	52	45
Extreme Low	-47	-46	-38	-20	-2	8	25	20	11	-5	-20	-46
Days Above 90°	0	0	0	0	0	0	0	0	0	0	0	0
Days Below 32°	29	26	26	18	6	1	0	0	2	10	20	27
PRECIPITATION												
Normal	7.3	8.0	8.2	7.0	6.5	7.1	6.9	7.6	7.2	6.7	8.5	8.9
Maximum	18.2	25.6	16.0	14.6	18.8	16.0	15.5	13.1	14.1	13.5	19.6	18.0
Maximum 24 Hr. Precipitation	4.8	10.4	4.0	8.3	4.6	6.5	7.4	5.2	5.4	7.0	6.1	8.6
Maximum Snowfall	95	173	98	89	52	1	2	2	8	34	87	104
Days With Measurable Precip.	19	18	19	18	17	16	17	16	15	15	19	20
Average No. Thunderstorms	0	0	0	1	3	6	6	3	1	1	0	0
SUNSHINE/CLOUDINESS												
No. Clear Days	5	4	4	4	2	1	3	5	6	4	4	4
No. Partly Cloudy Days	5	5	6	6	7	7	8	8	6	6	5	5
No. Cloudy Days	21	19	21	20	20	21	22	20	19	19	21	22
% Possible Sunshine	32	35	34	35	36	32	31	31	35	39	29	29

etc.

- These segments of the Trail pass through some of the highest terrain in the eastern U.S. and one of the windiest areas of the country.
- Winters are very cold; wind chill temperatures can reach dangerous levels.
- Summers are pleasant, but subfreezing temperatures can occur in any month.

CLIMATABLE NO. 196

North Country NST

TEMPERATURE NORMALS AND EXTREMES

% OF SUNNY/PTLY CLOUDY/CLOUDY DAYS

☐ Clear   ▦ Ptlycldy   ■ Cloudy

WEATHER PARAMETERS	MONTH											
	J	F	M	A	M	J	J	A	S	O	N	D
TEMPERATURE												
Normal Daily Maximum	26	28	38	52	66	75	80	77	69	58	43	30
Normal Daily Minimum	8	10	20	32	44	53	58	56	49	39	28	14
Extreme High	55	60	77	86	90	94	98	97	95	83	72	61
Extreme Low	-31	-25	-14	1	20	32	42	35	25	15	-3	-28
Days Above 90°	0	0	0	0	0	0	1	2	1	0	0	0
Days Below 32°	31	28	28	15	3	0	0	0	1	8	21	29
PRECIPITATION												
Normal	1.8	2.0	2.1	2.5	2.9	3.4	3.4	3.6	3.1	3.1	2.6	2.6
Maximum	4.8	4.8	3.6	4.2	7.6	6.8	6.7	6.8	8.8	6.9	5.3	5.2
Maximum 24 Hr. Precipitation	1.5	2.3	1.6	1.6	2.2	1.7	3.4	2.4	2.2	2.8	1.6	1.8
Maximum Snowfall	45	40	48	28	3	0	0	0	4	29	65
Days With Measurable Precip.	14	12	13	12	14	12	12	12	12	12	14	15
Average No. Thunderstorms	0	0	0	1	3	8	10	8	3	1	1	0
SUNSHINE/CLOUDINESS												
No. Clear Days	4	4	6	5	5	5	5	6	6	6	2	3
No. Partly Cloudy Days	7	6	7	8	9	11	13	12	10	8	5	6
No. Cloudy Days	20	18	18	17	17	14	13	13	14	17	22	22
% Possible Sunshine	41	47	50	49	54	58	64	59	53	47	30	32

etc.
- Winters are long and cold; subzero temperatures can be expected to be encountered on over 40 days each winter. Some severe wind chill temperatures are experienced.
- Summers are generally cool; temperatures above 90 degrees are relatively uncommon.

CLIMATABLE NO. 197   North Country NST

TEMPERATURE NORMALS AND EXTREMES

% OF SUNNY/PTLY CLOUDY/CLOUDY DAYS

☐ Clear   ▦ Ptlycldy   ■ Cloudy

WEATHER PARAMETERS	MONTH											
	J	F	M	A	M	J	J	A	S	O	N	D
TEMPERATURE												
Normal Daily Maximum	28	29	39	54	66	75	80	78	70	58	45	32
Normal Daily Minimum	13	14	24	35	45	55	60	58	51	40	32	19
Extreme High	61	64	83	87	92	98	100	95	98	86	76	70
Extreme Low	-28	-21	-12	7	23	35	42	38	27	17	3	-23
Days Above 90°	0	0	0	0	0	1	2	1	0	0	0	0
Days Below 32°	30	27	26	12	2	0	0	0	0	5	16	28
PRECIPITATION												
Normal	3.4	3.0	3.4	3.5	3.6	3.8	4.2	3.6	3.8	3.4	3.9	4.0
Maximum	6.8	8.8	6.0	6.4	6.3	10.5	8.7	7.6	8.4	10.1	7.5	8.3
Maximum 24 Hr. Precipitation	1.8	2.4	2.0	2.0	1.7	3.3	6.1	3.0	3.1	3.1	2.0	2.2
Maximum Snowfall	50	41	46	18	2	0	0	0	0	2	25	56
Days With Measurable Precip.	19	16	17	14	13	11	11	11	11	12	16	19
Average No. Thunderstorms	0	0	1	2	4	8	9	7	3	1	0	0
SUNSHINE/CLOUDINESS												
No. Clear Days	3	3	4	6	6	8	8	7	7	6	2	2
No. Partly Cloudy Days	6	6	7	7	10	10	12	11	10	8	6	5
No. Cloudy Days	22	19	20	17	15	12	11	13	13	17	22	24
% Possible Sunshine	34	39	45	51	55	59	64	59	53	44	26	25

etc.
- This area is impacted by "lake effect" snowstorms in winter. The average seasonal snowfall exceeds 90".
- Pleasantly warm summers are the rule with occasional periods of hot, humid weather.
- Summer precipitation falls mostly as thunderstorms.

CLIMATABLE NO. 198   North Country NST

TEMPERATURE NORMALS AND EXTREMES

% OF SUNNY/PTLY CLOUDY/CLOUDY DAYS

☐ Clear   ▦ Ptlycldy   ■ Cloudy

WEATHER PARAMETERS	J	F	M	A	M	J	J	A	S	O	N	D
TEMPERATURE												
Normal Daily Maximum	33	36	45	59	70	79	82	80	73	62	48	37
Normal Daily Minimum	16	16	24	34	44	53	57	57	50	39	32	22
Extreme High	64	68	81	92	92	97	97	97	100	89	77	64
Extreme Low	−19	−34	−18	10	22	29	37	38	26	14	3	−12
Days Above 90°	0	0	0	0	0	2	3	2	1	0	0	0
Days Below 32°	29	26	24	14	4	0	0	0	1	7	18	27
PRECIPITATION												
Normal	2.8	2.4	3.3	3.6	3.9	4.5	4.1	4.1	3.9	3.4	3.6	3.3
Maximum	5.2	4.4	5.3	7.3	8.1	9.3	7.9	9.8	8.3	8.4	6.1	5.6
Maximum 24 Hr. Precipitation	1.4	1.3	1.6	1.6	2.4	3.5	3.7	3.3	2.8	4.7	1.8	1.6
Maximum Snowfall	47	36	24	18	2	0	0	0	0	9	21	44
Days With Measurable Precip.	18	15	15	14	12	10	10	11	11	13	16	19
Average No. Thunderstorms	0	1	3	5	7	8	9	9	5	3	2	1
SUNSHINE/CLOUDINESS												
No. Clear Days	2	2	4	6	7	8	9	9	7	6	3	1
No. Partly Cloudy Days	4	6	7	8	10	11	12	11	9	8	4	3
No. Cloudy Days	25	20	19	16	14	11	10	11	14	17	23	27
% Possible Sunshine	33	37	44	48	51	57	58	56	58	52	37	29

etc.

- Weather conditions are very changeable. Precipitation tends to occur very frequently in smaller amounts. Total annual precipitation is not excessive.
- Winters can be quite cold, even severe at times. With the influence of "lake effect" snowstorms, the normal annual snowfall reaches 75" to 80".

CLIMATABLE NO. 199   North Country NST

WEATHER PARAMETERS

	J	F	M	A	M	J	J	A	S	O	N	D
TEMPERATURE												
Normal Daily Maximum	34	37	48	61	71	79	83	81	75	63	50	38
Normal Daily Minimum	19	21	29	39	48	57	61	60	53	42	33	24
Extreme High	69	69	82	88	91	96	99	97	97	87	82	74
Extreme Low	-18	-12	-1	14	26	34	42	39	31	16	-1	-12
Days Above 90°	0	0	0	0	0	1	3	1	1	0	0	0
Days Below 32°	28	24	20	8	1	0	0	0	0	4	14	25
PRECIPITATION												
Normal	2.9	2.4	3.6	3.3	3.5	3.3	3.8	3.3	2.8	2.5	2.3	2.6
Maximum	6.2	6.0	6.1	7.6	6.4	8.2	7.4	7.6	5.4	8.2	11.0	5.2
Maximum 24 Hr. Precipitation	1.7	2.3	2.0	2.2	2.4	2.8	3.0	3.1	2.2	3.6	2.0	1.8
Maximum Snowfall	40	24	21	7	3	0	0	0	0	2	11	21
Days With Measurable Precip.	16	14	16	14	12	12	11	10	9	11	13	16
Average No. Thunderstorms	0	0	3	5	8	10	11	11	8	4	2	0
SUNSHINE/CLOUDINESS												
No. Clear Days	3	3	4	5	5	5	6	8	8	8	4	2
No. Partly Cloudy Days	6	6	7	8	9	12	13	12	10	8	6	6
No. Cloudy Days	22	19	20	17	17	13	13	12	12	15	20	23
% Possible Sunshine	33	37	44	48	51	57	58	56	58	52	37	29

TEMPERATURE NORMALS AND EXTREMES

% OF SUNNY/PTLY CLOUDY/CLOUDY DAYS

□ Clear   ▦ Ptlycldy   ■ Cloudy

etc.

- Summers are warm with frequent intrusions of humid air; watch the Heat Index.
- In the late fall and early winter, northwest winds bring periods of cloudy, showery weather.
- In the colder months, early morning fogs can be quite persistent in the river valleys.

CLIMATABLE NO. 200

North Country NST

TEMPERATURE NORMALS AND EXTREMES

% OF SUNNY/PTLY CLOUDY/CLOUDY DAYS

☐ Clear   ▦ Ptlycldy   ■ Cloudy

WEATHER PARAMETERS	J	F	M	A	M	J	J	A	S	O	N	D
TEMPERATURE												
Normal Daily Maximum	33	36	47	62	73	82	86	84	78	66	50	38
Normal Daily Minimum	17	19	28	39	49	58	62	60	54	42	33	22
Extreme High	65	70	78	90	94	105	103	106	105	94	77	67
Extreme Low	-17	-17	-5	13	25	39	48	39	30	19	2	-14
Days Above 90°	0	0	0	0	1	5	8	5	2	0	0	0
Days Below 32°	29	26	23	9	1	0	0	0	0	4	16	26
PRECIPITATION												
Normal	2.2	1.9	2.9	3.5	3.4	3.4	4.1	3.3	2.5	2.2	2.6	2.5
Maximum	4.8	4.2	4.8	7.1	7.6	6.4	12.3	11.6	6.0	6.0	6.6	6.9
Maximum 24 Hr. Precipitation	1.8	1.6	2.2	3.2	2.6	2.2	2.7	4.5	2.1	2.4	2.8	3.7
Maximum Snowfall	32	22	14	12	0	0	0	0	0	1	13	24
Days With Measurable Precip.	14	11	14	13	12	10	9	9	10	9	12	14
Average No. Thunderstorms	0	1	3	6	8	11	11	8	5	2	1	0
SUNSHINE/CLOUDINESS												
No. Clear Days	4	4	5	6	6	7	8	8	9	8	4	3
No. Partly Cloudy Days	7	7	7	8	11	12	13	12	9	9	7	6
No. Cloudy Days	20	17	19	16	14	11	10	11	12	14	19	22
% Possible Sunshine	42	47	50	53	60	64	67	63	61	55	38	33

etc.

- Summers can be quite hot with temperatures occasionally exceeding 100 degrees.
- Winters are very cold with frequent subfreezing temperatures.
- This area is subject to some severe thunderstorms in summer.
- The first freezing temperatures can be expected in mid-October.

CLIMATABLE NO. 201

North Country NST

TEMPERATURE NORMALS AND EXTREMES

% OF SUNNY/PTLY CLOUDY/CLOUDY DAYS

□ Clear   ▥ Ptlycldy   ▨ Cloudy

WEATHER PARAMETERS — MONTH

PARAMETER	J	F	M	A	M	J	J	A	S	O	N	D
TEMPERATURE												
Normal Daily Maximum	29	32	42	57	69	79	83	81	73	61	46	32
Normal Daily Minimum	15	16	24	36	46	55	60	58	51	40	31	21
Extreme High	62	67	78	88	92	96	97	100	93	87	77	67
Extreme Low	-21	-19	-8	3	22	33	41	39	28	18	5	-18
Days Above 90°	0	0	0	0	0	2	5	2	0	0	0	0
Days Below 32°	30	26	24	12	2	0	0	0	0	6	18	28
PRECIPITATION												
Normal	1.9	1.5	2.5	3.6	3.0	3.9	3.0	3.4	3.1	2.9	2.9	2.6
Maximum	4.4	3.3	5.1	6.1	8.3	8.2	6.4	7.4	11.8	6.3	7.8	6.6
Maximum 24 Hr. Precipitation	1.8	1.5	1.8	2.1	5.5	3.3	2.5	2.4	4.6	2.0	2.7	2.8
Maximum Snowfall	46	21	36	12	T	0	0	T	T	8	17	35
Days With Measurable Precip.	16	12	13	13	11	10	9	9	10	11	13	17
Average No. Thunderstorms	0	0	3	5	9	9	9	8	6	2	2	1
SUNSHINE/CLOUDINESS												
No. Clear Days	2	3	4	6	7	7	9	8	7	6	3	2
No. Partly Cloudy Days	5	6	7	7	9	11	12	11	9	8	5	4
No. Cloudy Days	24	19	20	17	15	12	10	12	14	17	22	25
% Possible Sunshine	30	39	44	51	54	61	64	61	54	43	28	21

etc.

- The onset of warmer temperatures in the spring and colder temperatures in the fall is delayed by the moderating effects of Lake Michigan.
- The prevailing flow of air across the Lake in winter results in excessive cloudiness and frequent snow flurries.
- November tends to be a windy month.

CLIMATABLE NO. 202   North Country NST

TEMPERATURE NORMALS AND EXTREMES

% OF SUNNY/PTLY CLOUDY/CLOUDY DAYS

☐ Clear   ⬚ Ptlycldy   ■ Cloudy

WEATHER PARAMETERS	J	F	M	A	M	J	J	A	S	O	N	D
TEMPERATURE												
Normal Daily Maximum	25	28	37	53	66	75	79	76	68	57	42	30
Normal Daily Minimum	9	8	18	31	42	51	55	54	46	38	28	16
Extreme High	53	59	71	86	89	93	96	92	92	85	70	63
Extreme Low	-26	-34	-23	3	21	29	33	29	24	16	0	-21
Days Above 90°	0	0	0	0	0	0	1	0	0	0	0	0
Days Below 32°	31	28	28	18	5	0	0	0	2	10	22	30
PRECIPITATION												
Normal	1.5	1.3	1.9	2.6	2.6	3.1	2.9	3.0	2.8	2.3	2.3	1.9
Maximum	3.1	3.4	5.7	4.6	6.0	6.7	5.0	7.2	9.5	5.4	4.8	4.5
Maximum 24 Hr. Precipitation	1.4	1.4	2.2	1.3	1.9	2.6	3.8	3.1	2.6	1.6	1.8	1.7
Maximum Snowfall	38	24	29	12	2	0	T	0	T	4	19	30
Days With Measurable Precip.	15	12	13	12	11	11	9	10	12	12	13	16
Average No. Thunderstorms	0	0	1	2	4	8	7	7	4	2	0	0
SUNSHINE/CLOUDINESS												
No. Clear Days	3	5	6	7	7	6	8	9	6	5	3	2
No. Partly Cloudy Days	7	6	7	10	12	12	13	10	10	8	5	5
No. Cloudy Days	21	17	18	16	14	12	10	12	14	18	22	24
% Possible Sunshine	38	44	52	54	59	63	67	60	51	44	30	27

etc.

- Summers are warm, though extremely hot weather is uncommon. Temperatures reach 100 degrees in only one summer out of ten.
- Snowfall averages about 80" a year; but total snowfall varies considerably from year to year.
- The late fall and early winter are cloudy times of year.

CLIMATABLE NO. 203   North Country NST

TEMPERATURE NORMALS AND EXTREMES

% OF SUNNY/PTLY CLOUDY/CLOUDY DAYS

☐ Clear ▦ Ptlycldy ■ Cloudy

WEATHER PARAMETERS	J	F	M	A	M	J	J	A	S	O	N	D
TEMPERATURE												
Normal Daily Maximum	20	25	36	52	66	74	79	76	66	56	38	25
Normal Daily Minimum	1	3	13	29	40	50	55	53	45	36	23	8
Extreme High	50	62	67	88	91	97	97	94	95	86	74	55
Extreme Low	-40	-41	-33	-8	16	26	35	30	22	9	-18	-35
Days Above 90°	0	0	0	0	0	1	1	0	0	0	0	0
Days Below 32°	31	28	29	20	7	1	0	0	3	12	25	31
PRECIPITATION												
Normal	1.8	1.3	1.9	2.3	3.7	4.2	4.0	4.5	3.5	2.8	2.9	2.0
Maximum	4.2	3.2	4.5	7.9	6.9	8.0	8.4	7.2	6.2	5.9	5.7	5.1
Maximum 24 Hr. Precipitation	1.0	1.1	1.5	3.0	2.0	3.1	2.0	4.3	1.7	2.0	1.7	1.2
Maximum Snowfall	86	54	50	33	17	0	0	0	T	27	52	89
Days With Measurable Precip.	12	10	11	11	12	13	11	11	12	10	11	12
Average No. Thunderstorms	0	0	1	2	6	10	12	10	5	2	0	0
SUNSHINE/CLOUDINESS												
No. Clear Days	7	7	6	6	6	5	7	7	6	6	4	6
No. Partly Cloudy Days	7	6	7	8	9	11	13	12	9	8	6	6
No. Cloudy Days	17	15	17	16	16	14	11	12	15	17	20	19
% Possible Sunshine	49	52	55	55	56	58	65	60	51	46	35	40

etc.

- This area is typified by cold, snowy winters and pleasantly warm summers.
- Subfreezing temperatures are experienced on almost every winter day. Summer temperatures occasionally exceed 100 degrees; however near-freezing temperatures have been observed in every summer month.

CLIMATABLE NO. 204 North Country NST

TEMPERATURE NORMALS AND EXTREMES

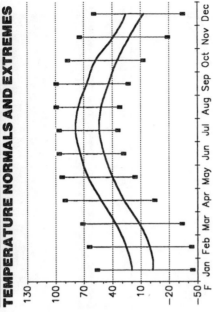
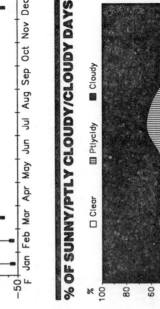

WEATHER PARAMETERS	MONTH											
	J	F	M	A	M	J	J	A	S	O	N	D
TEMPERATURE												
Normal Daily Maximum	20	26	37	52	66	74	79	76	67	58	39	26
Normal Daily Minimum	-2	1	12	28	40	49	54	52	44	35	22	7
Extreme High	55	63	70	89	92	95	95	98	98	86	73	58
Extreme Low	-46	-45	-35	-6	15	27	33	31	22	6	-20	-36
Days Above 90°	0	0	0	0	0	1	2	1	0	0	0	0
Days Below 32°	31	28	29	21	8	1	0	0	3	13	25	31
PRECIPITATION												
Normal	1.3	0.9	1.8	2.6	3.9	4.0	4.4	4.8	3.6	2.5	2.5	1.5
Maximum	3.4	2.2	4.7	8.3	7.4	7.8	8.3	8.7	7.2	4.7	7.4	4.7
Maximum 24 Hr. Precipitation	1.0	0.8	1.2	3.3	3.1	2.6	3.0	3.8	3.4	1.7	3.2	1.4
Maximum Snowfall	47	31	40	19	15	0	0	0	T	10	42	58
Days With Measurable Precip.	12	10	11	11	12	13	11	11	12	10	11	12
Average No. Thunderstorms	0	0	1	4	7	10	10	8	6	2	1	0
SUNSHINE/CLOUDINESS												
No. Clear Days	7	7	7	6	6	5	7	7	6	6	4	6
No. Partly Cloudy Days	7	6	7	8	9	11	13	12	9	8	6	6
No. Cloudy Days	17	15	17	16	16	14	11	12	15	17	20	19
% Possible Sunshine	49	52	55	55	56	58	65	60	51	46	35	40

% OF SUNNY/PTLY CLOUDY/CLOUDY DAYS

☐ Clear   ☐ Ptlycldy   ▨ Cloudy

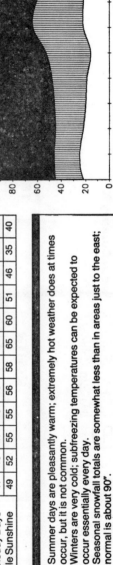

etc.
- Summer days are pleasantly warm; extremely hot weather does at times occur, but it is not common.
- Winters are very cold; subfreezing temperatures can be expected to occur essentially every day.
- Seasonal snowfall totals are somewhat less than in areas just to the east; normal is about 90".

CLIMATABLE NO. 205   North Country NST

WEATHER PARAMETERS

	J	F	M	A	M	J	J	A	S	O	N	D
TEMPERATURE												
Normal Daily Maximum	16	22	32	48	61	70	76	74	64	53	35	22
Normal Daily Minimum	-3	2	14	29	39	48	54	53	44	35	21	6
Extreme High	52	55	78	88	90	93	97	97	95	86	70	55
Extreme Low	-39	-32	-28	-5	17	27	36	32	22	8	-23	-34
Days Above 90°	0	0	0	0	0	0	1	1	0	0	0	0
Days Below 32°	31	28	29	20	5	0	0	0	3	11	25	31
PRECIPITATION												
Normal	1.2	0.9	1.8	2.2	3.2	4.0	4.0	4.1	3.3	2.2	1.7	1.3
Maximum	4.7	2.4	5.1	5.8	7.7	8.0	8.5	10.3	6.6	7.5	5.0	3.7
Maximum 24 Hr. Precipitation	1.7	1.4	2.4	2.3	3.2	4.0	3.4	5.8	3.8	2.9	2.6	2.1
Maximum Snowfall	47	32	46	32	8	T	0	T	1	8	38	44
Days With Measurable Precip.	12	10	11	11	12	13	11	11	12	10	11	12
Average No. Thunderstorms	0	0	1	2	6	10	12	10	5	2	0	0
SUNSHINE/CLOUDINESS												
No. Clear Days	7	7	7	6	6	5	7	7	6	6	4	6
No. Partly Cloudy Days	7	6	7	8	9	11	13	12	9	8	6	6
No. Cloudy Days	17	15	17	16	16	14	11	12	15	17	20	19
% Possible Sunshine	49	52	55	55	56	58	65	60	51	46	35	40

etc.

- Summers are generally mild; winters are bitterly cold.
- Summer temperatures are kept cooler and winter temperatures warmer by easterly winds from Lake Superior.
- Another influence of the nearby Lake, is the relatively low frequency of severe weather such as thunderstorms, hail & tornadoes.

TEMPERATURE NORMALS AND EXTREMES

% OF SUNNY/PTLY CLOUDY/CLOUDY DAYS
□ Clear   ▦ Ptlycldy   ■ Cloudy

CLIMATABLE NO. 206 — North Country NST

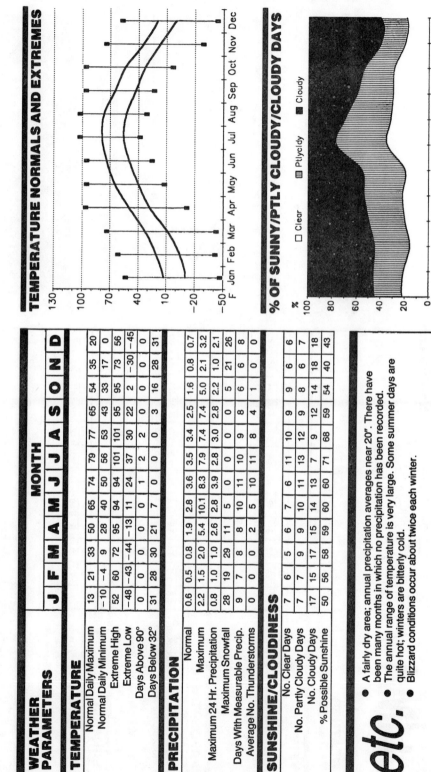

TEMPERATURE NORMALS AND EXTREMES

% OF SUNNY/PTLY CLOUDY/CLOUDY DAYS

☐ Clear   ▥ Ptycldy   ■ Cloudy

WEATHER PARAMETERS	J	F	M	A	M	J	J	A	S	O	N	D
TEMPERATURE												
Normal Daily Maximum	13	21	33	50	65	74	79	77	65	54	35	20
Normal Daily Minimum	-10	-4	9	28	40	50	56	53	43	33	17	0
Extreme High	52	60	72	95	94	101	101	95	95	73	56	
Extreme Low	-48	-43	-44	-13	11	24	37	30	22	2	-30	-45
Days Above 90°	0	0	0	0	0	1	2	2	0	0	0	0
Days Below 32°	31	28	30	21	7	0	0	0	3	16	28	31
PRECIPITATION												
Normal	0.6	0.5	0.8	1.9	2.8	3.6	3.4	2.5	1.6	0.8	0.7	
Maximum	2.2	1.5	2.0	5.4	10.1	8.3	7.9	7.4	7.4	5.0	2.1	3.2
Maximum 24 Hr. Precipitation	0.8	1.0	1.0	2.6	2.8	3.9	3.0	2.8	2.2	2.2	1.0	2.1
Maximum Snowfall	28	19	29	11	5	0	0	0	0	5	21	26
Days With Measurable Precip.	9	7	8	8	10	11	10	9	8	6	6	8
Average No. Thunderstorms	0	0	0	2	5	10	11	8	4	1	0	0
SUNSHINE/CLOUDINESS												
No. Clear Days	7	6	5	6	7	6	10	9	9	6	6	6
No. Partly Cloudy Days	7	7	9	9	10	11	13	12	9	8	6	7
No. Cloudy Days	17	15	17	15	14	13	9	10	12	14	18	18
% Possible Sunshine	50	56	58	59	60	71	68	59	54	40	43	

etc.

- A fairly dry area; annual precipitation averages near 20". There have been many months in which no precipitation has been recorded.
- The annual range of temperature is very large. Some summer days are quite hot; winters are bitterly cold.
- Blizzard conditions occur about twice each winter.

CLIMATABLE NO. 207   North Country NST

WEATHER PARAMETERS	J	F	M	A	M	J	J	A	S	O	N	D
TEMPERATURE												
Normal Daily Maximum	12	19	31	51	67	76	82	80	68	56	35	20
Normal Daily Minimum	-7	-1	13	31	42	52	56	54	44	34	18	2
Extreme High	47	65	80	100	101	100	100	103	101	87	75	54
Extreme Low	-36	-35	-29	-8	5	30	30	32	20	7	-23	-32
Days Above 90°	0	0	0	0	1	2	4	5	1	0	0	0
Days Below 32°	31	28	29	18	5	0	0	0	2	14	28	31
PRECIPITATION												
Normal	0.8	0.5	0.8	1.3	2.0	2.9	2.9	2.6	2.0	1.1	0.8	0.6
Maximum	1.8	1.5	3.1	3.6	4.9	7.9	7.3	7.9	5.6	3.1	2.9	1.6
Maximum 24 Hr. Precipitation	0.7	1.2	1.7	1.9	1.3	2.4	2.6	3.8	2.9	1.7	1.2	0.6
Maximum Snowfall	18	14	29	11	6	0	0	0	0	5	21	14
Days With Measurable Precip.	9	7	8	8	10	11	10	9	8	6	6	8
Average No. Thunderstorms	0	0	0	1	4	8	9	6	3	1	0	0
SUNSHINE/CLOUDINESS												
No. Clear Days	7	6	5	6	7	6	10	10	9	6	6	6
No. Partly Cloudy Days	7	7	9	9	10	11	13	12	8	6	6	7
No. Cloudy Days	17	15	17	15	14	13	7	9	12	14	18	18
% Possible Sunshine	50	56	58	59	60	60	71	68	59	54	40	43

MONTH

TEMPERATURE NORMALS AND EXTREMES

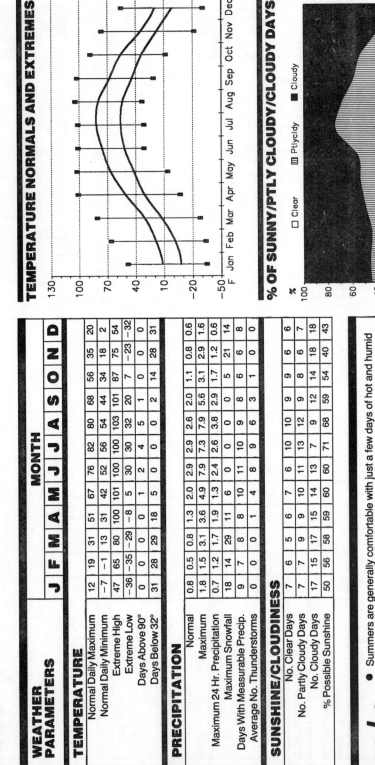

% OF SUNNY/PTLY CLOUDY/CLOUDY DAYS

☐ Clear   ▦ Ptlycldy   ■ Cloudy

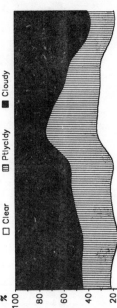

etc.

- Summers are generally comfortable with just a few days of hot and humid weather. Nights are pleasantly cool.
- Winters are very cold; temperatures rise above freezing on relatively few days.
- About 75% of the annual precipitation falls during the growing season, often as severe thunderstorms.

CLIMATABLE NO. 208   Ice Age NST

WEATHER PARAMETERS

WEATHER PARAMETERS	J	F	M	A	M	J	J	A	S	O	N	D
TEMPERATURE												
Normal Daily Maximum	25	28	38	52	64	74	79	78	69	58	43	31
Normal Daily Minimum	9	11	21	33	42	51	58	57	50	41	30	17
Extreme High	48	58	70	85	89	96	96	102	95	86	70	58
Extreme Low	-26	-23	-23	7	21	30	39	36	28	20	-1	-17
Days Above 90°	0	0	0	0	0	1	1	1	0	0	0	0
Days Below 32°	31	28	28	15	4	0	0	0	0	5	19	29
PRECIPITATION												
Normal	1.3	1.1	1.9	2.9	3.3	3.3	3.4	3.3	3.5	2.3	2.0	1.7
Maximum	3.2	3.3	5.8	5.7	8.9	7.9	6.3	6.0	10.4	5.4	3.6	5.0
Maximum 24 Hr. Precipitation	1.3	1.4	1.7	1.8	3.8	2.5	2.2	2.4	3.7	2.2	1.4	3.6
Maximum Snowfall	31	27	28	8	6	0	0	0	0	0	14	28
Days With Measurable Precip.	10	8	11	11	11	11	10	10	10	9	9	11
Average No. Thunderstorms	0	0	2	4	6	10	9	8	6	3	1	0
SUNSHINE/CLOUDINESS												
No. Clear Days	8	7	6	7	7	8	9	8	7	5	6	6
No. Partly Cloudy Days	6	6	8	8	9	11	12	10	8	7	7	6
No. Cloudy Days	17	15	16	15	15	12	11	12	16	18	19	19
% Possible Sunshine	48	52	53	52	60	64	66	63	55	48	38	39

TEMPERATURE NORMALS AND EXTREMES

% OF SUNNY/PTLY CLOUDY/CLOUDY DAYS

☐ Clear   ▦ Ptlycldy   ■ Cloudy

etc.

- Seasonal variations of temperatures are greatly reduced by the proximity to Lake Michigan and Green Bay. Summer temperatures only occasionally exceed 90 degrees; there are few occurrences of subzero temperatures in winter.
- Summer thunderstorms are often accompanied by high winds and heavy rain.

CLIMATABLE NO. 209   Ice Age NST

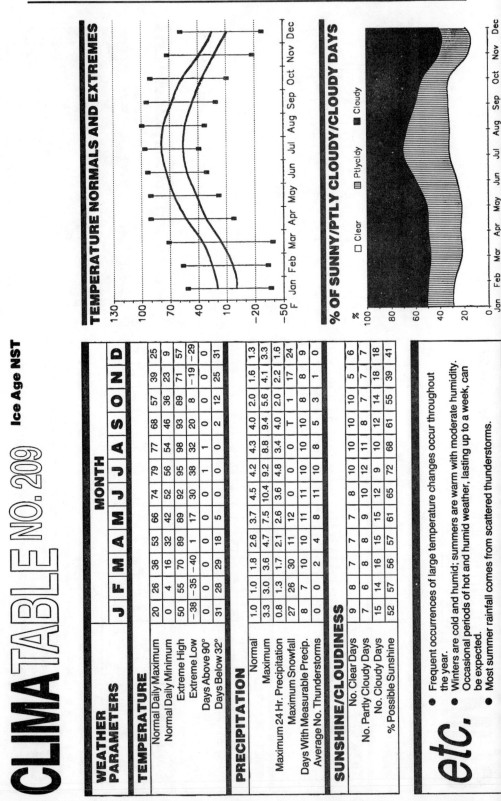

TEMPERATURE NORMALS AND EXTREMES

% OF SUNNY/PTLY CLOUDY/CLOUDY DAYS

☐ Clear   ▦ Ptlycldy   ■ Cloudy

WEATHER PARAMETERS	J	F	M	A	M	J	J	A	S	O	N	D
TEMPERATURE												
Normal Daily Maximum	20	26	36	53	66	74	79	77	68	57	39	25
Normal Daily Minimum	0	4	16	32	42	52	56	54	46	36	23	9
Extreme High	50	55	70	89	89	92	95	98	93	89	71	57
Extreme Low	-38	-35	-40	1	17	30	38	32	20	8	-19	-29
Days Above 90°	0	0	0	0	0	0	1	1	0	0	0	0
Days Below 32°	31	28	29	18	5	0	0	0	2	12	25	31
PRECIPITATION												
Normal	1.0	1.0	1.8	2.6	3.7	4.5	4.2	4.3	4.0	2.0	1.6	1.3
Maximum	3.3	3.0	3.6	4.7	7.5	10.4	9.2	8.8	9.4	5.6	4.1	3.3
Maximum 24 Hr. Precipitation	0.8	1.3	1.7	2.1	2.6	3.6	4.8	3.4	4.0	2.0	2.2	1.6
Maximum Snowfall	27	26	30	11	12	0	0	T	T	1	17	24
Days With Measurable Precip.	8	7	10	10	11	11	10	10	10	8	8	9
Average No. Thunderstorms	0	0	2	4	8	11	10	8	5	3	1	0
SUNSHINE/CLOUDINESS												
No. Clear Days	9	8	7	7	7	8	10	10	10	10	5	6
No. Partly Cloudy Days	7	6	8	8	9	10	12	11	8	7	7	7
No. Cloudy Days	15	14	16	15	15	12	9	10	12	14	18	18
% Possible Sunshine	52	57	56	57	61	65	72	68	61	55	39	41

etc.

- Frequent occurrences of large temperature changes occur throughout the year.
- Winters are cold and humid; summers are warm with moderate humidity. Occasional periods of hot and humid weather, lasting up to a week, can be expected.
- Most summer rainfall comes from scattered thunderstorms.

CLIMATABLE NO. 210

Mormon Pioneer NHT, Oregon NHT

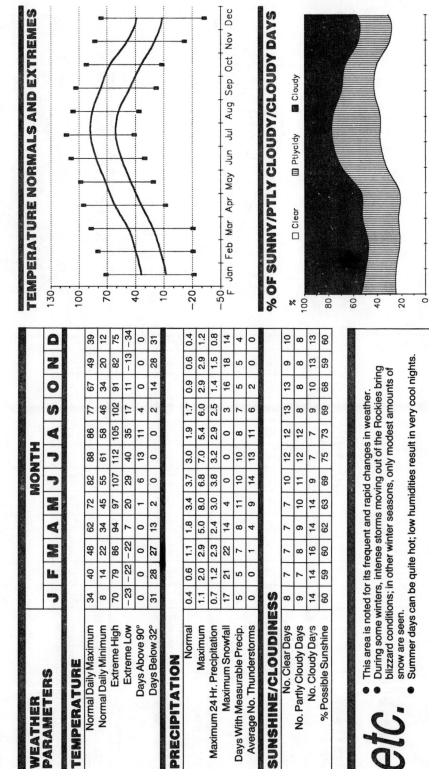

TEMPERATURE NORMALS AND EXTREMES

% OF SUNNY/PTLY CLOUDY/CLOUDY DAYS

☐ Clear   ▦ Ptlycldy   ▨ Cloudy

WEATHER PARAMETERS	J	F	M	A	M	J	J	A	S	O	N	D
TEMPERATURE												
Normal Daily Maximum	34	40	48	62	72	82	88	86	77	67	49	39
Normal Daily Minimum	8	14	22	34	45	55	61	58	46	34	20	12
Extreme High	70	79	86	94	97	107	112	105	102	91	82	75
Extreme Low	−23	−22	−22	7	20	29	40	35	17	11	−13	−34
Days Above 90°	0	0	0	0	1	6	13	11	4	0	0	0
Days Below 32°	31	28	27	13	2	0	0	0	2	14	28	31
PRECIPITATION												
Normal	0.4	0.6	1.1	1.8	3.4	3.7	3.0	1.9	1.7	0.9	0.6	0.4
Maximum	1.1	2.0	2.9	5.0	8.0	6.8	7.0	5.4	6.0	2.9	2.9	1.2
Maximum 24 Hr. Precipitation	0.7	1.2	2.3	2.4	3.0	3.8	3.2	2.9	2.5	1.4	1.5	0.8
Maximum Snowfall	17	21	22	14	4	0	0	0	3	16	18	14
Days With Measurable Precip.	5	5	7	8	11	10	10	8	7	5	5	4
Average No. Thunderstorms	0	0	1	4	9	14	13	11	6	2	0	0
SUNSHINE/CLOUDINESS												
No. Clear Days	8	7	7	7	7	10	12	12	13	13	9	10
No. Partly Cloudy Days	9	7	8	9	10	11	12	12	8	8	8	8
No. Cloudy Days	14	14	16	14	14	9	7	7	9	10	13	13
% Possible Sunshine	60	59	60	62	63	69	75	73	69	68	59	60

etc.

- This area is noted for its frequent and rapid changes in weather.
- During some winters, intense storms moving out of the Rockies bring blizzard conditions; in other winter seasons, only modest amounts of snow are seen.
- Summer days can be quite hot; low humidities result in very cool nights.

CLIMATABLE NO. 211   Mormon Pioneer NHT

TEMPERATURE NORMALS AND EXTREMES

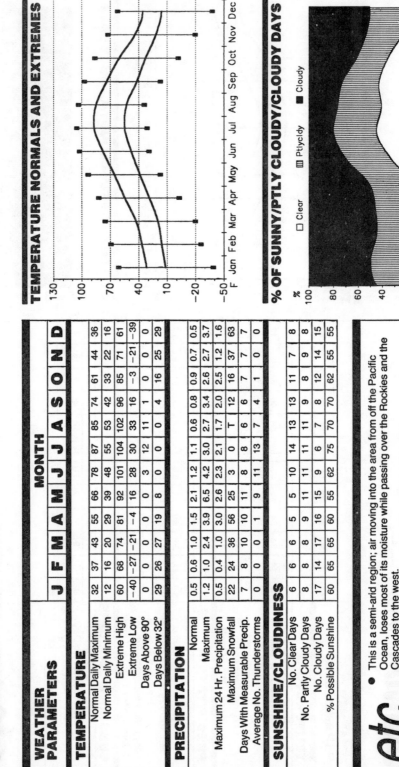

WEATHER PARAMETERS	MONTH											
	J	F	M	A	M	J	J	A	S	O	N	D
TEMPERATURE												
Normal Daily Maximum	32	37	43	55	66	78	87	85	74	61	44	36
Normal Daily Minimum	12	16	20	29	39	48	55	53	42	33	22	16
Extreme High	60	68	74	81	92	101	104	102	96	85	71	61
Extreme Low	-40	-27	-21	-4	16	28	30	33	16	-3	-21	-39
Days Above 90°	0	0	0	0	0	3	12	11	1	0	0	0
Days Below 32°	29	26	27	19	8	0	0	0	4	16	25	29
PRECIPITATION												
Normal	0.5	0.6	1.0	1.5	2.1	1.2	1.1	0.6	0.8	0.9	0.7	0.5
Maximum	1.2	1.0	2.4	3.9	6.5	4.2	3.0	2.7	3.4	2.6	2.7	3.7
Maximum 24 Hr. Precipitation	0.5	0.4	1.0	3.0	2.6	2.3	2.1	1.7	2.0	2.5	1.2	1.6
Maximum Snowfall	22	24	36	56	25	3	0	T	12	16	37	63
Days With Measurable Precip.	7	8	10	10	11	8	8	6	6	7	7	7
Average No. Thunderstorms	0	0	0	1	9	11	13	7	4	1	0	0
SUNSHINE/CLOUDINESS												
No. Clear Days	6	6	6	5	5	10	14	13	13	11	7	8
No. Partly Cloudy Days	8	8	8	9	11	11	11	11	9	8	9	8
No. Cloudy Days	17	14	17	16	15	9	6	7	8	12	14	15
% Possible Sunshine	60	65	65	60	55	62	75	70	70	62	55	55

% OF SUNNY/PTLY CLOUDY/CLOUDY DAYS

☐ Clear   ▦ Ptlycldy   ■ Cloudy

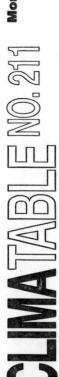

etc.
- This is a semi-arid region; air moving into the area from off the Pacific Ocean, loses most of its moisture while passing over the Rockies and the Cascades to the west.
- Characterized by very large daily and annual variations in temperature.
- Winter and spring are particularly windy seasons.

CLIMATABLE NO. 212 Mormon Pioneer NHT

TEMPERATURE NORMALS AND EXTREMES

% OF SUNNY/PTLY CLOUDY/CLOUDY DAYS

WEATHER PARAMETERS	MONTH											
	J	F	M	A	M	J	J	A	S	O	N	D
TEMPERATURE												
Normal Daily Maximum	31	38	44	55	66	76	86	84	73	60	43	35
Normal Daily Minimum	8	14	20	30	40	48	55	53	44	33	19	11
Extreme High	63	68	76	82	91	100	101	101	94	85	70	64
Extreme Low	-37	-28	-16	-2	18	25	39	35	10	0	-18	-37
Days Above 90°	0	0	0	0	0	2	10	7	1	0	0	0
Days Below 32°	30	28	28	19	5	0	0	0	3	14	28	31
PRECIPITATION												
Normal	0.5	0.6	1.1	2.2	2.7	1.4	0.7	0.5	0.9	1.2	0.8	0.5
Maximum	1.6	2.2	3.3	5.5	6.0	6.9	2.5	2.3	4.7	3.6	3.4	1.6
Maximum 24 Hr. Precipitation	0.8	0.9	1.3	2.2	2.8	3.6	2.1	1.1	2.2	1.7	1.4	1.2
Maximum Snowfall	26	44	52	66	34	18	0	0	33	40	49	28
Days With Measurable Precip.	4	5	7	8	9	6	6	5	5	5	5	5
Average No. Thunderstorms	0	0	0	1	5	10	13	8	4	0	0	0
SUNSHINE/CLOUDINESS												
No. Clear Days	8	7	7	6	6	10	14	13	14	12	8	9
No. Partly Cloudy Days	10	10	10	10	11	11	12	12	9	9	10	10
No. Cloudy Days	13	11	14	14	14	9	5	6	7	10	12	12
% Possible Sunshine	66	68	71	67	65	73	76	76	73	69	60	64

etc.
- Winter is noted for the frequent occurrence of moderating downslope winds or "chinooks."
- Summers are warm but not oppressive as the humidity is low. Temperatures rise above 90 degrees on many days, but nights are quite cool.
- Spring is a short season; snowfalls have occurred in June.

CLIMATABLE NO. 213 Oregon NHT, Lewis & Clark NHT, Harry S. Truman NHS

TEMPERATURE NORMALS AND EXTREMES

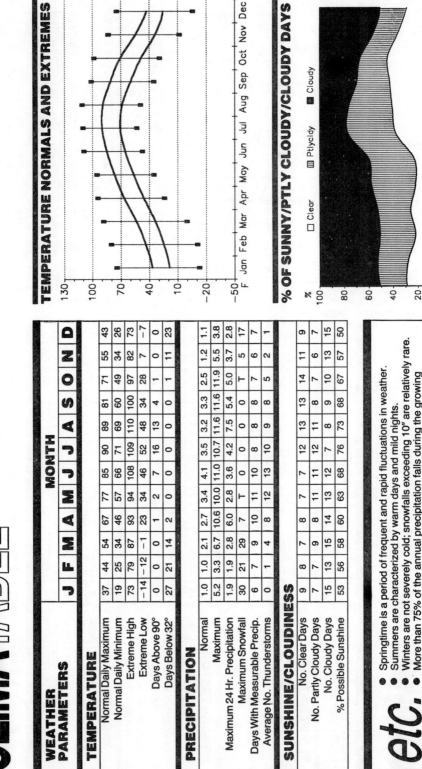

WEATHER PARAMETERS	MONTH											
	J	F	M	A	M	J	J	A	S	O	N	D
TEMPERATURE												
Normal Daily Maximum	37	44	54	67	77	85	90	89	81	71	55	43
Normal Daily Minimum	19	25	34	46	57	66	71	69	60	49	34	26
Extreme High	73	79	87	93	94	108	109	110	100	97	82	73
Extreme Low	−14	−12	−1	23	34	46	52	48	34	28	0	−7
Days Above 90°	0	0	0	1	2	7	16	13	4	1	0	0
Days Below 32°	27	21	14	2	0	0	0	0	0	1	11	23
PRECIPITATION												
Normal	1.0	2.1	2.7	3.4	4.1	3.5	3.2	3.3	3.3	2.5	1.2	1.1
Maximum	5.2	6.7	10.6	10.0	11.0	10.7	11.6	11.6	11.9	5.5	3.8
Maximum 24 Hr. Precipitation	1.9	2.8	6.0	2.8	3.6	4.2	7.5	5.4	5.0	3.7	2.8
Maximum Snowfall	30	29	7	7	0	0	0	0	0	T	5	17
Days With Measurable Precip.	6	7	9	10	11	10	8	8	8	7	6	7
Average No. Thunderstorms	0	1	4	8	12	13	10	9	8	5	2	1
SUNSHINE/CLOUDINESS												
No. Clear Days	9	8	7	8	7	7	12	13	13	14	11	9
No. Partly Cloudy Days	7	7	9	8	11	11	12	11	8	7	6	7
No. Cloudy Days	15	13	15	14	13	12	7	8	9	10	13	15
% Possible Sunshine	53	56	58	60	63	68	76	73	68	67	57	50

% OF SUNNY/PTLY CLOUDY/CLOUDY DAYS

☐ Clear ▦ Ptlycldy ▨ Cloudy

etc. • • • • Springtime is a period of frequent and rapid fluctuations in weather.
Summers are characterized by warm days and mild nights.
Winters are not severely cold; snowfalls exceeding 10" are relatively rare.
More than 75% of the annual precipitation falls during the growing season.

CLIMATABLE NO. 214   Oregon NHT

TEMPERATURE NORMALS AND EXTREMES

% OF SUNNY/PTLY CLOUDY/CLOUDY DAYS

☐ Clear   ▦ Ptlycldy   ▨ Cloudy

WEATHER PARAMETERS	J	F	M	A	M	J	J	A	S	O	N	D
TEMPERATURE												
Normal Daily Maximum	35	42	51	65	75	85	91	89	80	69	52	41
Normal Daily Minimum	15	20	28	41	52	62	67	65	56	44	30	21
Extreme High	71	86	88	92	99	109	109	108	104	96	84	82
Extreme Low	-17	-15	-7	14	26	41	48	45	29	17	-4	-16
Days Above 90°	0	0	0	0	1	8	19	14	5	1	0	0
Days Below 32°	29	24	19	5	0	0	0	0	0	3	18	29
PRECIPITATION												
Normal	0.6	0.8	1.9	2.3	4.0	4.2	3.4	3.4	3.0	1.8	1.0	0.7
Maximum	1.8	2.5	7.4	6.0	9.7	14.1	10.2	10.7	8.5	4.8	4.9	3.6
Maximum 24 Hr. Precipitation	0.8	1.2	2.0	2.1	5.2	5.5	3.9	4.6	3.2	4.2	3.2	2.6
Maximum Snowfall	14	21	9	6	T	0	0	0	T	5	10	17
Days With Measurable Precip.	6	5	8	10	10	10	9	9	8	6	5	5
Average No. Thunderstorms	0	1	2	6	10	11	10	8	6	3	1	0
SUNSHINE/CLOUDINESS												
No. Clear Days	11	9	9	9	10	14	13	13	13	10	10	10
No. Partly Cloudy Days	7	6	7	7	7	10	10	7	6	6	6	7
No. Cloudy Days	13	13	15	14	13	8	8	10	12	14	14	14
% Possible Sunshine	63	63	63	65	68	79	76	69	69	69	60	58

etc.

- Although heavy winter snowfalls are not uncommon, severe winter storms are rare.
- Sustained periods of hot, dry, windy weather frequently occur in July and August; maximum daily temperatures can exceed 100 degrees for a week or more at a time.
- October is a time of mild, dry "indian summer."

CLIMATABLE NO. 215

Oregon NHT

WEATHER PARAMETERS

	J	F	M	A	M	J	J	A	S	O	N	D
TEMPERATURE												
Normal Daily Maximum	33	37	42	54	66	76	84	81	72	61	44	36
Normal Daily Minimum	10	13	18	26	35	43	49	46	38	28	18	12
Extreme High	57	62	69	77	86	97	100	95	89	81	68	58
Extreme Low	-42	-34	-23	-12	14	23	30	25	17	-8	-16	-30
Days Above 90°	0	0	0	0	0	3	1	1	0	0	0	0
Days Below 32°	30	28	30	24	11	2	0	1	8	22	28	30
PRECIPITATION												
Normal	0.5	0.4	0.7	1.0	1.3	0.9	0.9	1.0	0.8	1.0	0.5	0.5
Maximum	2.0	1.0	2.0	3.2	3.6	2.3	3.1	2.1	2.9	3.7	1.5	1.5
Maximum 24 Hr. Precipitation	0.7	0.4	1.0	0.9	1.9	1.7	1.5	1.2	1.6	1.0	1.0	0.6
Maximum Snowfall	24	16	22	29	10	4	0	0	26	14	20	26
Days With Measurable Precip.	6	6	7	8	9	7	7	8	7	7	6	6
Average No. Thunderstorms	0	0	0	1	5	7	9	7	3	1	0	0
SUNSHINE/CLOUDINESS												
No. Clear Days	10	8	8	7	6	10	9	9	13	13	10	11
No. Partly Cloudy Days	9	9	10	11	12	12	16	15	9	9	10	10
No. Cloudy Days	12	11	13	12	13	8	6	7	8	9	10	10
% Possible Sunshine	71	71	70	68	65	71	71	72	74	72	64	67

TEMPERATURE NORMALS AND EXTREMES

% OF SUNNY/PTLY CLOUDY/CLOUDY DAYS

etc.

- During the summer, showers occur quite frequently but generally result in very little rain. On occasion a thunderstorm will produce a locally heavy downpour and the possibility of flash flooding.
- Daytime temperatures in the summer can be quite high, but the nights are invariably cool.

CLIMATABLE NO. 216   Oregon NHT

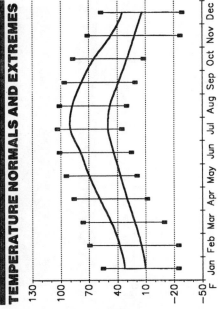

TEMPERATURE NORMALS AND EXTREMES

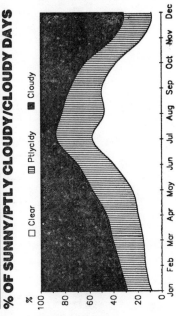

% OF SUNNY/PTLY CLOUDY/CLOUDY DAYS

□ Clear   ▥ Ptlycldy   ▦ Cloudy

WEATHER PARAMETERS	MONTH											
	J	F	M	A	M	J	J	A	S	O	N	D
TEMPERATURE												
Normal Daily Maximum	33	38	47	59	70	79	90	88	78	65	47	35
Normal Daily Minimum	11	15	22	30	37	44	50	48	39	30	22	14
Extreme High	54	68	75	85	93	100	102	100	95	86	70	56
Extreme Low	−26	−26	−11	7	18	24	34	29	20	11	−28	−30
Days Above 90°	0	0	0	0	0	4	19	14	2	0	0	0
Days Below 32°	30	27	28	20	7	1	0	0	6	21	27	30
PRECIPITATION												
Normal	1.3	1.0	1.0	1.1	1.5	1.4	0.8	0.9	0.8	0.9	1.0	1.1
Maximum	3.5	2.0	2.9	3.3	5.6	4.6	2.2	3.4	3.9	3.0	3.1	3.5
Maximum 24 Hr. Precipitation	0.7	0.8	0.8	0.9	1.6	1.3	2.1	1.1	2.0	1.2	1.4	0.7
Maximum Snowfall	21	20	17	10	2	0	0	0	1	2	16	27
Days With Measurable Precip.	12	10	10	8	7	7	4	5	5	5	9	11
Average No. Thunderstorms	0	0	0	1	6	7	9	10	4	1	0	0
SUNSHINE/CLOUDINESS												
No. Clear Days	3	4	5	6	8	12	18	15	15	12	5	3
No. Partly Cloudy Days	6	6	8	8	10	9	11	8	8	8	7	7
No. Cloudy Days	22	18	18	16	13	9	4	7	7	11	18	21
% Possible Sunshine	39	52	61	65	67	74	82	80	78	70	47	39

etc.

- Temperatures warm gradually through the spring; June afternoons can be mild, but night temperatures remain quite cold.
- Long summer periods of hot weather are quite uncommon.
- Winter weather varies between periods of southwest winds with mild temperatures and near zero-degree weather.

CLIMATABLE NO. 217   Oregon NHT

TEMPERATURE NORMALS AND EXTREMES

% OF SUNNY/PTLY CLOUDY/CLOUDY DAYS

WEATHER PARAMETERS	J	F	M	A	M	J	J	A	S	O	N	D
TEMPERATURE												
Normal Daily Maximum	37	44	52	61	71	80	91	87	78	65	49	39
Normal Daily Minimum	23	28	31	36	44	52	58	57	49	39	30	25
Extreme High	63	70	81	92	98	109	111	110	102	91	73	65
Extreme Low	-17	-12	6	19	22	31	35	37	23	11	-3	-23
Days Above 90°	0	0	0	0	1	5	18	15	3	0	0	0
Days Below 32°	26	21	18	8	2	0	0	0	0	6	18	25
PRECIPITATION												
Normal	1.6	1.1	1.0	1.2	1.2	1.0	0.3	0.4	0.6	0.8	1.3	1.3
Maximum	3.9	3.7	2.8	3.0	4.0	3.4	1.6	2.4	2.9	2.2	2.4	4.2
Maximum 24 Hr. Precipitation	1.5	1.0	1.6	1.3	1.5	2.2	0.9	1.6	1.7	0.8	0.9	1.2
Maximum Snowfall	21	25	12	8	4	T	0	0	0	3	19	26
Days With Measurable Precip.	12	10	10	8	8	6	2	3	4	6	10	12
Average No. Thunderstorms	0	0	1	1	3	3	2	2	1	1	0	0
SUNSHINE/CLOUDINESS												
No. Clear Days	4	4	6	7	9	12	21	18	17	12	6	5
No. Partly Cloudy Days	5	6	7	9	10	10	7	7	8	8	6	6
No. Cloudy Days	22	18	18	14	12	8	3	5	6	11	18	20
% Possible Sunshine	38	49	62	68	71	75	87	85	80	68	44	38

etc.

- Temperatures exceeding 100 degrees occur every summer, but such hot weather rarely lasts for more than a few days. Occasional but moderate dust storms are experienced at this time of year.
- Autumn is often a prolonged period of nearly ideal weather.

CLIMATABLE NO. 218   Lewis & Clark NHT, Missouri National Recreation River

TEMPERATURE NORMALS AND EXTREMES

% OF SUNNY/PTLY CLOUDY/CLOUDY DAYS

Legend: ☐ Clear   ▦ Ptlycldy   ■ Cloudy

WEATHER PARAMETERS

	J	F	M	A	M	J	J	A	S	O	N	D
TEMPERATURE												
Normal Daily Maximum	26	32	42	59	72	81	87	85	75	64	46	32
Normal Daily Minimum	4	10	20	35	46	57	62	59	49	37	23	12
Extreme High	62	69	90	95	95	104	108	107	102	94	79	67
Extreme Low	−29	−23	−25	2	24	33	41	41	25	14	−15	−21
Days Above 90°	0	0	0	0	2	6	12	10	3	0	0	0
Days Below 32°	31	28	27	13	2	0	0	0	1	10	25	31
PRECIPITATION												
Normal	0.3	0.6	1.4	2.2	3.5	3.9	3.2	3.1	2.3	1.4	0.9	0.5
Maximum	1.1	2.0	4.5	4.5	11.7	7.9	8.9	7.8	7.4	4.4	3.4	1.4
Maximum 24 Hr. Precipitation	0.5	1.6	2.2	1.4	3.7	4.2	3.7	3.7	3.0	2.0	2.4	1.2
Maximum Snowfall	16	32	21	6	0	0	0	0	0	4	18	28
Days With Measurable Precip.	6	6	9	9	10	11	9	9	8	6	6	6
Average No. Thunderstorms	0	0	1	4	8	12	11	10	7	2	0	0
SUNSHINE/CLOUDINESS												
No. Clear Days	8	7	6	7	7	9	12	12	12	11	7	7
No. Partly Cloudy Days	8	7	8	8	10	11	12	10	8	8	7	7
No. Cloudy Days	15	14	17	15	14	10	7	9	10	12	16	17
% Possible Sunshine	55	58	58	60	62	62	73	71	66	63	50	48

etc.

- Winter is characterized by sharp and rapid drops in temperature with strong and gusty winds. Drops in temperature of 20 to 30 degrees in 24 hours are common.
- Summer days may be hot, but summer nights are usually quite comfortable. Temperatures of 100 degrees occur in 1 out of every 3 summers.

CLIMATABLE NO. 219 Lewis & Clark NHT

WEATHER PARAMETERS	J	F	M	A	M	J	J	A	S	O	N	D
TEMPERATURE												
Normal Daily Maximum	22	29	39	57	70	79	87	86	75	62	42	29
Normal Daily Minimum	1	8	17	32	43	53	58	56	46	35	20	9
Extreme High	61	70	80	97	103	105	107	110	105	98	75	65
Extreme Low	−33	−26	−28	0	19	35	38	38	20	11	−17	−32
Days Above 90°	0	0	0	0	1	4	12	11	3	0	0	0
Days Below 32°	31	28	29	16	3	0	0	0	1	13	27	31
PRECIPITATION												
Normal	0.4	0.6	0.9	2.0	2.9	3.4	2.0	2.4	1.2	1.1	0.6	0.6
Maximum	1.1	2.1	4.2	4.8	6.3	7.6	4.3	5.7	3.7	3.6	3.8	1.5
Maximum 24 Hr. Precipitation	0.5	1.2	1.2	1.7	4.0	4.2	2.3	2.9	1.7	1.9	2.2	0.8
Maximum Snowfall	12	18	33	25	2	0	0	0	0	7	18	17
Days With Measurable Precip.	6	6	7	8	10	10	8	8	6	5	6	6
Average No. Thunderstorms	0	0	1	2	6	10	10	8	3	1	0	0
SUNSHINE/CLOUDINESS												
No. Clear Days	8	6	6	7	7	9	12	12	11	10	6	7
No. Partly Cloudy Days	7	6	8	7	10	10	13	11	8	8	7	7
No. Cloudy Days	16	16	17	16	14	11	6	8	11	13	17	17
% Possible Sunshine	58	60	59	60	65	69	77	74	68	63	52	50

etc. •
- Winter is characteristically cold and dry with storms of short duration. Subzero temperatures may occur as early as the end of November. Watch the Wind Chill temperatures!
- Summers are pleasant with lots of sunshine, warm days, low humidity and cool, comfortable nights.

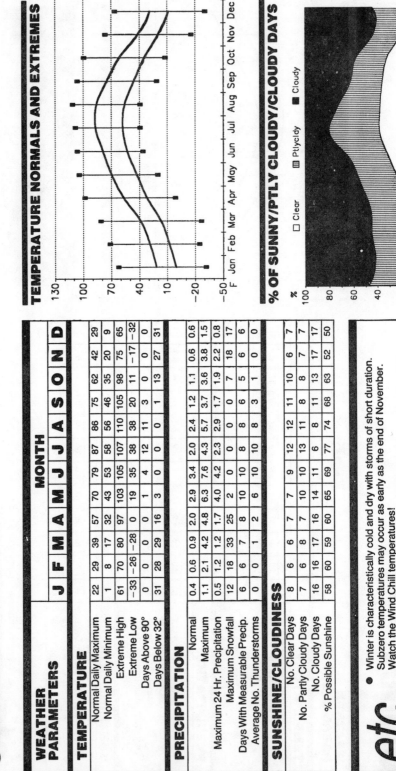

TEMPERATURE NORMALS AND EXTREMES

F Jan Feb Mar Apr May Jun Jul Aug Sep Oct Nov Dec

130 100 70 40 10 −20 −50

% OF SUNNY/PTLY CLOUDY/CLOUDY DAYS

□ Clear ▦ Ptlycldy ■ Cloudy

% 100 80 60 40 20

CLIMATABLE NO. 220   Lewis & Clark NHT

TEMPERATURE NORMALS AND EXTREMES

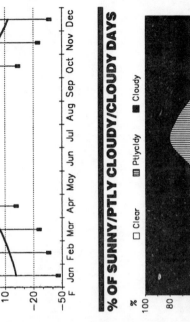

WEATHER PARAMETERS	MONTH											
	J	F	M	A	M	J	J	A	S	O	N	D
TEMPERATURE												
Normal Daily Maximum	18	26	37	54	67	76	84	83	70	59	40	26
Normal Daily Minimum	-1	6	16	31	42	51	57	55	44	34	19	7
Extreme High	55	62	77	91	99	100	104	108	103	88	75	59
Extreme Low	-47	-37	-27	-3	20	33	41	37	20	-5	-26	-38
Days Above 90°	0	0	0	0	1	2	9	9	2	0	0	0
Days Below 32°	31	28	28	16	3	0	0	0	2	12	27	31
PRECIPITATION												
Normal	0.5	0.4	0.4	0.9	1.8	2.5	1.6	1.4	0.9	0.6	0.3	0.4
Maximum	1.2	0.7	0.9	2.0	3.7	5.4	5.2	5.7	4.1	1.8	1.3	1.0
Maximum 24 Hr. Precipitation	0.4	0.3	0.4	1.2	2.1	2.4	4.0	5.0	2.0	1.2	0.4	0.4
Maximum Snowfall	24	16	15	14	11	0	0	0	2	7	17	14
Days With Measurable Precip.	9	7	7	7	10	10	8	7	7	5	6	8
Average No. Thunderstorms	0	0	0	1	5	8	11	7	2	0	0	0
SUNSHINE/CLOUDINESS												
No. Clear Days	6	5	5	5	6	7	13	12	9	8	6	5
No. Partly Cloudy Days	7	7	9	8	10	12	12	11	9	9	7	8
No. Cloudy Days	18	16	17	17	15	11	6	8	12	14	17	18
% Possible Sunshine	51	61	70	70	73	76	85	82	74	65	50	46

% OF SUNNY/PTLY CLOUDY/CLOUDY DAYS

☐ Clear   ▥ Ptlycldy   ■ Cloudy

etc.

- A large annual variation of temperature with little precipitation is typical of this area.
- Nearly 80% of the annual precipitation falls in the period from April through September.
- Nearly all winter precipitation falls as snow, but it seldom accumulates to any great depth.

CLIMATABLE NO. 221   Lewis & Clark NHT

WEATHER PARAMETERS	MONTH											
	J	F	M	A	M	J	J	A	S	O	N	D
TEMPERATURE												
Normal Daily Maximum	22	30	40	55	68	76	85	84	72	60	42	30
Normal Daily Minimum	0	9	17	30	41	49	54	52	42	32	18	8
Extreme High	63	68	75	91	98	105	106	111	101	90	78	65
Extreme Low	-52	-35	-28	-14	24	31	39	36	18	-16	-30	-50
Days Above 90°	0	0	0	0	0	4	10	10	2	0	0	0
Days Below 32°	30	27	27	17	3	0	0	0	4	16	27	30
PRECIPITATION												
Normal	0.6	0.4	0.5	1.1	1.6	2.1	1.2	1.2	0.9	0.6	0.4	0.5
Maximum	2.3	1.0	2.0	2.6	5.0	4.7	4.0	3.6	5.8	2.1	1.2	2.0
Maximum 24 Hr. Precipitation	0.5	0.4	1.8	1.6	2.1	2.2	2.6	2.3	2.4	1.3	0.4	0.8
Maximum Snowfall	41	19	30	33	31	T	0	0	6	10	19	25
Days With Measurable Precip.	9	6	8	8	10	10	8	7	8	5	6	8
Average No. Thunderstorms	0	0	0	0	2	5	7	7	1	0	0	0
SUNSHINE/CLOUDINESS												
No. Clear Days	4	4	5	4	6	7	14	13	9	7	5	5
No. Partly Cloudy Days	7	7	8	9	11	11	11	10	8	8	8	7
No. Cloudy Days	20	17	18	17	14	12	6	8	13	16	17	19
% Possible Sunshine	51	61	70	70	73	76	85	82	74	65	50	46

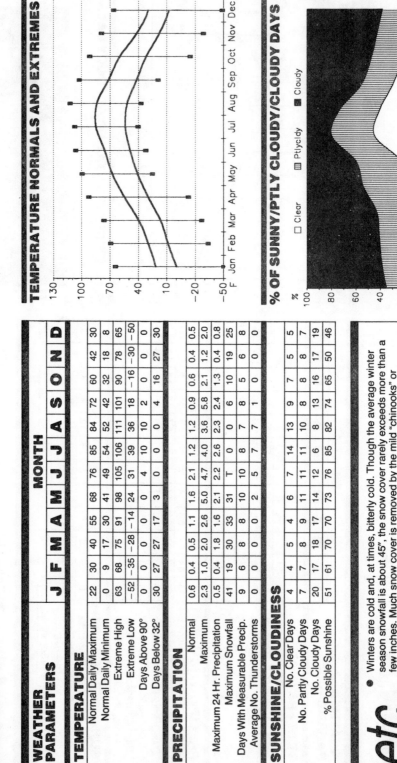

TEMPERATURE NORMALS AND EXTREMES

% OF SUNNY/PTLY CLOUDY/CLOUDY DAYS

☐ Clear   ▦ Ptlycldy   ■ Cloudy

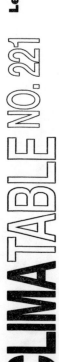

etc.

- Winters are cold and, at times, bitterly cold. Though the average winter season snowfall is about 45", the snow cover rarely exceeds more than a few inches. Much snow cover is removed by the mild "chinooks" or downslope winds off the mountains to the west. These winds are nicknamed "snoweaters."

CLIMATABLE NO. 222   Lewis & Clark NHT

TEMPERATURE NORMALS AND EXTREMES

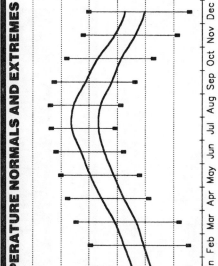

% OF SUNNY/PTLY CLOUDY/CLOUDY DAYS

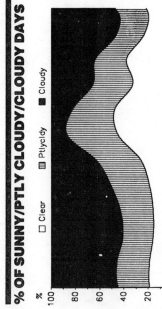

☐ Clear   ▥ Ptlycldy   ■ Cloudy

WEATHER PARAMETERS	MONTH											
	J	F	M	A	M	J	J	A	S	O	N	D
TEMPERATURE												
Normal Daily Maximum	24	33	43	57	69	79	89	87	74	61	43	32
Normal Daily Minimum	4	12	20	33	44	54	60	58	46	36	21	11
Extreme High	62	67	83	92	99	104	109	110	106	93	75	69
Extreme Low	-37	-37	-27	5	15	32	41	35	20	0	-25	-38
Days Above 90°	0	0	0	0	1	4	16	14	3	0	0	0
Days Below 32°	30	27	27	14	2	0	0	0	2	11	26	30
PRECIPITATION												
Normal	0.6	0.6	0.6	1.4	2.3	2.8	1.5	1.3	1.1	0.9	0.6	0.6
Maximum	1.8	1.3	1.8	4.2	6.8	9.8	4.6	4.0	4.7	6.3	2.2	1.8
Maximum 24 Hr. Precipitation	0.4	0.8	0.6	1.4	2.4	2.7	2.2	1.6	2.7	1.4	1.2	0.5
Maximum Snowfall	17	19	18	17	12	2	0	0	7	13	19	18
Days With Measurable Precip.	8	7	7	8	11	11	8	6	7	6	6	7
Average No. Thunderstorms	0	0	0	1	5	10	9	7	2	0	0	0
SUNSHINE/CLOUDINESS												
No. Clear Days	6	5	5	5	6	8	14	15	10	12	7	7
No. Partly Cloudy Days	8	8	8	8	10	11	13	11	10	8	7	8
No. Cloudy Days	17	15	18	17	15	11	4	5	10	11	16	16
% Possible Sunshine	55	59	61	59	59	64	75	74	67	62	53	53

etc.

- Frequent periods of subzero temperatures, usually lasting 2 to 4 days, are experienced every winter.
- Temperatures exceeding 90 degrees are common in the summer.
- Precipitation in the spring and summer is often in the form of thunderstorms, but periods of a more general rain can be expected.

CLIMATABLE NO. 223   Lewis & Clark NHT

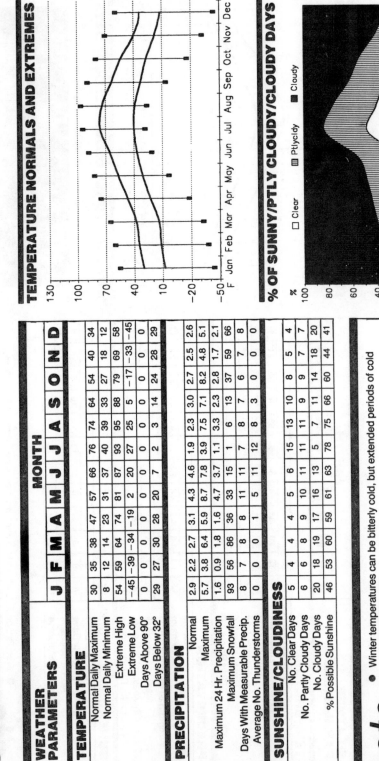

TEMPERATURE NORMALS AND EXTREMES

% OF SUNNY/PTLY CLOUDY/CLOUDY DAYS

□ Clear   ▨ Ptlycldy   ■ Cloudy

WEATHER PARAMETERS	J	F	M	A	M	J	J	A	S	O	N	D
TEMPERATURE												
Normal Daily Maximum	30	35	38	47	57	66	76	74	64	54	40	34
Normal Daily Minimum	8	12	14	23	31	37	40	39	33	27	18	12
Extreme High	54	59	64	74	81	87	93	95	88	79	69	58
Extreme Low	-45	-39	-34	-19	2	20	27	25	5	-17	-33	-45
Days Above 90°	0	0	0	0	0	0	0	0	0	0	0	0
Days Below 32°	29	27	30	28	20	7	2	3	14	24	28	29
PRECIPITATION												
Normal	2.9	2.2	2.7	3.1	4.3	4.6	1.9	2.3	3.0	2.7	2.5	2.6
Maximum	5.7	3.8	6.4	5.9	8.7	7.8	3.9	7.5	7.1	8.2	4.8	5.1
Maximum 24 Hr. Precipitation	1.6	0.9	1.8	1.6	4.7	3.7	1.1	3.3	2.3	2.8	1.7	2.1
Maximum Snowfall	93	56	86	36	33	15	1	6	13	37	59	66
Days With Measurable Precip.	8	7	8	8	11	11	7	8	7	6	7	8
Average No. Thunderstorms	0	0	0	1	5	11	12	8	3	0	0	0
SUNSHINE/CLOUDINESS												
No. Clear Days	5	4	4	4	5	6	15	13	10	8	5	4
No. Partly Cloudy Days	6	6	8	9	10	11	11	9	9	7	7	
No. Cloudy Days	20	18	19	17	16	13	5	7	11	14	18	20
% Possible Sunshine	46	53	60	59	61	63	78	75	66	60	44	41

etc.

- Winter temperatures can be bitterly cold, but extended periods of cold weather are rare.
- Winter snowfall is quite heavy, normally near 225". Heavy snowstorms occur as early as October and as late as April.
- Extremely hot weather is rare, but summer days are warm enough for light clothing.

WINDCHILL

The **wind chill temperature** is a measure of how cold a person is made to feel under the combined effects of temperature and wind. At temperatures below 50° F, increasing wind speeds result in a greater transfer of heat and a greater evaporation rate from the body. The result is an increased feeling of "cold." This chilling effect of the wind can be expressed as the temperature at which a person would feel equivalently cold in just a light breeze (actually, 4 mph is assumed).

To determine the **wind chill temperature** in the accompanying table, find the column corresponding to the air temperature in F and move down to the line corresponding to the wind speed. Along the left side of the chart, the wind speed is given in miles per hour; along the right side of the chart, you will find the wind speed in knots. For example, at a temperature of 16° F and a wind speed of 12 mph (10 knots), to the average person it would feel as if the temperature were −5 F.

WIND SPEED / M.P.H. (left) — **WIND SPEED / KNOTS** (right) — **TEMPERATURE °F**

M.P.H.	Knots	40	38	36	34	32	30	28	26	24	22	20	18	16	14	12	10	8	6	4	2	0	−2	−4	−6	−8	−10
4	3.5	40	38	36	34	32	30	28	26	24	22	20	18	16	14	12	10	8	6	4	2	0	−2	−4	−6	−8	−10
6	5	35	33	31	29	26	24	22	20	18	15	13	11	9	7	5	2	0	−2	−4	−6	−9	−11	−13	−15	−17	−20
8	7	31	29	27	24	22	20	17	15	13	10	8	6	3	1	−1	−4	−6	−8	−11	−13	−15	−18	−20	−22	−25	−27
10	9	28	26	23	21	18	16	13	11	9	6	4	1	−1	−4	−6	−9	−11	−14	−16	−18	−21	−23	−26	−28	−31	−33
12	10	26	23	21	18	15	13	10	8	5	3	0	−3	−5	−8	−10	−13	−15	−18	−20	−23	−26	−28	−31	−33	−36	−38
14	12	23	21	18	16	13	11	7	5	2	0	−3	−6	−8	−11	−14	−16	−19	−22	−24	−27	−30	−32	−35	−38	−40	−43
16	14	21	19	16	14	11	8	5	2	0	−3	−6	−9	−11	−14	−17	−19	−22	−25	−28	−30	−33	−36	−38	−41	−44	−47
18	16	20	18	14	13	10	7	3	0	−3	−6	−9	−11	−14	−17	−19	−22	−25	−28	−30	−33	−36	−39	−42	−44	−47	−50
20	17	18	15	13	11	9	6	2	−2	−5	−8	−12	−13	−16	−19	−22	−24	−27	−30	−33	−36	−39	−42	−44	−47	−50	−53
22	19	17	14	11	10	7	4	0	−3	−6	−9	−14	−15	−18	−21	−24	−27	−29	−32	−35	−38	−41	−44	−47	−50	−53	−56
24	21	16	13	10	8	5	2	−2	−5	−8	−11	−15	−17	−20	−23	−25	−28	−31	−34	−37	−40	−43	−46	−49	−52	−55	−58
26	23	15	12	9	7	4	1	−3	−6	−9	−12	−16	−18	−21	−24	−27	−30	−33	−36	−39	−42	−45	−48	−51	−54	−57	−60
28	24	14	11	8	6	3	0	−4	−7	−10	−13	−18	−19	−22	−25	−28	−31	−35	−38	−41	−44	−47	−50	−53	−56	−59	−62
30	26	13	10	7	5	2	−1	−5	−8	−11	−14	−19	−21	−24	−27	−30	−33	−36	−39	−42	−45	−48	−51	−54	−57	−60	−63
32	28	12	9	6	4	1	−2	−6	−9	−12	−15	−20	−22	−25	−28	−31	−34	−37	−40	−43	−46	−49	−52	−55	−59	−62	−65
34	30	12	9	6	3	0	−3	−7	−10	−13	−16	−21	−23	−26	−29	−32	−35	−38	−41	−44	−47	−50	−54	−57	−60	−63	−66
36	31	11	8	5	2	−1	−4	−8	−11	−14	−17	−22	−24	−27	−30	−33	−36	−39	−42	−45	−48	−51	−55	−58	−61	−64	−67
38	33	11	8	5	2	−1	−5	−8	−11	−15	−18	−23	−25	−28	−30	−33	−37	−40	−43	−46	−49	−52	−55	−59	−62	−65	−68
40	35	10	7	4	1	−2	−6	−9	−12	−15	−18	−21	−25	−28	−31	−34	−37	−40	−43	−47	−50	−53	−56	−59	−62	−66	−69

Severity categories (left to right): COOL — COLD — VERY COLD — BITTER — EXPOSED FLESH FREEZES

HEAT INDEX

The heat stress felt in hot weather is influenced by the air temperature, the humidity, the wind and exposure to direct sunshine. In direct sunlight, heat is added to the body and you feel warmer than in the shade. At temperatures higher than the normal temperature of the body (98.6°F), winds above 10 mph also add heat to the body. These factors aside, the air temperature and the humidity are the key elements affecting discomfort. The National Weather Service uses **heat index** to measure discomfort and the potential danger of sunstroke and heat exhaustion. The **heat index** is expressed as an "apparent temperature." It expresses what any combination of temperature and relative humidity feels like to a person standing in the shade with a light breeze.

To determine the **heat index** or "apparent temperature", find the column closest to the air temperature and move down that column to the line corresponding to the closest value of the relative humidity. For example, if the temperature were 90°F with a relative humidity of 60%, to a person standing in the shade, it would feel as if it were 100°F. **CAUTION:** In direct sunlight, it would feel 5 to 10 degrees **warmer!**

A Very warm; fatigue possible with prolonged exposure

B Hot; Sunstroke, Heat Cramps & Heat Exhaustion **possible** with prolonged exposure

C Very Hot; **Danger:** Sunstroke, Heat Cramps, or Heat Exhaustion **likely** with prolonged exposure

D **Extreme Danger:** Heat/Sunstroke **highly likely**

RELATIVE HUMIDITY % — AIR TEMPERATURE °F

> APPARENT TEMPERATURES CONTINUE TO RISE WITH INCREASING RELATIVE HUMIDITY

RH % \ Temp °F	70	72	74	76	78	80	82	84	86	88	90	92	94	96	98	100	102	104	106	108	110	112	114	116	118	120
0	64	66	68	70	72	73	75	77	78	80	83	84	86	88	90	91	93	95	96	98	99	101	103	105	106	107
5	64	66	68	71	72	74	76	77	79	81	84	86	87	89	91	93	95	97	98	100	102	104	106	108	110	111
10	65	67	69	71	73	75	77	79	81	82	85	86	88	91	93	95	97	99	101	104	105	107	109	112	115	117
15	65	68	70	72	74	76	78	80	82	83	86	87	90	92	95	97	99	102	105	107	108	110	115	117	120	123
20	66	68	71	73	75	77	79	81	83	85	87	89	92	95	97	99	102	105	107	110	112	115	120	124	127	130
25	67	69	72	74	76	78	80	82	85	87	88	91	94	96	98	101	105	108	110	114	117	121	125	130	135	139
30	67	70	72	75	77	79	81	83	86	88	90	93	95	98	101	104	107	110	115	120	124	129	134	139	143	148
35	68	70	73	75	77	79	82	84	86	89	91	95	97	100	104	107	111	116	120	126	130	135	139			
40	68	71	73	76	78	80	82	85	87	90	93	96	99	103	107	110	116	121	127	132	137					
45	69	72	74	76	79	81	84	86	88	91	95	98	101	106	110	115	121	127	132	138	143					
50	69	72	74	78	80	81	84	87	90	93	96	100	105	109	115	120	127	133	138							
55	70	72	75	79	81	82	85	87	91	95	98	103	107	114	120	126	133	138								
60	70	73	76	79	82	83	86	89	93	97	100	106	110	118	125	132	139									
65	70	73	77	80	82	84	88	91	95	99	103	109	115	124	131	138										
70	70	74	77	81	83	85	89	92	97	101	106	113	120	129	138	144										
75	70	74	77	81	84	86	90	93	99	105	110	118	125	132	140											
80	71	74	78	82	85	87	91	95	101	107	114	122	130	140												
85	71	75	78	83	85	88	91	96	103	111	117	127	137													
90	71	75	79	83	86	89	93	98	105	115	122	131														
95	72	75	80	83	86	90	95	100	110	118	125	135														
100	72	76	79	83	87	91	97	103	115	121	130	140														

Danger category markers (at boundaries): A, B, C, D

Peak Visitation

While a visit to one of our National Park areas is almost always enjoyable and enriching, the experience can be all the more relaxing if you can avoid making the visit during the heaviest visitor season. As the crowds disappear, your opportunities to explore more thoroughly, to ask questions, or simply to pause and reflect in an area of spectacular natural beauty or lasting historic significance, all increase. The frustrations of traffic, crowded facilities, and lodging or camping difficulties will be reduced.

The National Park Service does maintain records of peak visitation, indicating the relative peak times when more visitors are present. How significant these peak periods should be to you in planning your visit depend on many factors. You should not necessarily be discouraged from planning your visit, simply because you would be travelling during the particular park's peak visitation month. For example, some parks are not overcrowded, even during the peak visitation period. Conversely, for other parks, visitation may be constantly high, nearing the point of overcrowding for *several* months, so that while visitation is *heaviest* in one month, it may not be that much greater during the peak month than it is in one or more other months. From the visitor's standpoint, you may only be able to visit during the peak period. Your willingness to visit under less ideal climate conditions and the extent to which you are seeking solitude will influence your plans as well. Nonetheless, as a possible aid in your planning we are including a listing of the month in which each park area is the most crowded–the month of peak visitation.

Abraham Lincoln BPL NHS (*July*)
Acadia NP (*August*)
Adams NHS (*July*)
Agate Fossil Beds NM (*July*)
Alibates NM (*July*)
Allegheny Portage RR NHS (*July*)
Amistad NRA (*May*)
Andersonville NHS (*May*)
Andrew Johnson NHS (*May*)
Antietam NB (*September*)
Apostle Islands NL (*August*)

Appomattox Crt Hse NHP (*July*)
Arches NP (*August*)
Arkansas Post NMEM (*May*)
Arlington Hse RELee NMEM (*July*)
Assateague Island NS (*August*)
Aztec Ruins NM (*August*)

Badlands NM (*August*)
Bandelier NM (*July*)
Bent's Old Fort NHS (*July*)
Big Bend NP (*April*)
Big Cypress NPRES (*March*)
Big Hole NB (*July*)
Big Thicket NPRES (*May*)
Bighorn Canyon NRA (*July*)
Biscayne NM (*August*)
Black Canyon OTG NM (*August*)
Blue Ridge Parkway (*August*)
Booker T. Washington NM (*August*)
Boston NHP (*August*)
Brices Cross Roads NBS (*August*)
Bryce Canyon NP (*August*)
Buck Island Reef NM (*February*)
Buffalo NR (*June*)

C&O Canal NHP (*July*)
Cabrillo NM (*January*)
Canaveral NS (*July*)
Canyon de Chelly NM (*May*)
Canyonlands NP (*May*)
Cape Cod NS (*August*)
Cape Hatteras NS (*July*)
Cape Krusenstern NM (*September*)
Cape Lookout NS (*July*)
Capitol Reef NP (*May*)
Capulin Mountain NM (*July*)
Carl Sandburg Home NHS (*August*)
Carlsbad Caverns NP (*July*)
Casa Grande NM (*March*)
Castillo De San Marcos NM (*July*)
Castle Clinton NM (*August*)
Catoctin Mtn Park (*August*)
Cedar Breaks NM (*July*)
Chaco Culture NM (*August*)
Chamizal NMEM (*July*)
Channel Islands NP (*August*)
Chick Chatt NMP (*July*)
Chickasaw NRA (*June*)
Chiricahua NM (*May*)
Christiansted NHS (*January*)
Clara Barton NHS (*August*)
Colonial NHP (*July*)
Colorado NM (*August*)

Coronado NMEM (*April*)
Coulee Dam NRA (*August*)
Cowpens NM (*June*)
Crater Lake NP (*July*)
Craters of the Moon NM (*July*)
Cumberland Gap NHP (*July*)
Cumberland Islands NS (*April*)
Curecanti NRA (*July*)
Custer Battlefield NM (*July*)
Cuyahoga Valley NRA (*July*)

DeSoto NMEM (*March*)
Death Valley NM (*April*)
Delaware Water Gap NRA (*July*)
Denali NP (*August*)
Devils Postpile NM (*August*)
Devils Tower NM (*August*)
Dinosaur NM (*July*)

Edgar Allen Poe NHS (*August*)
Edison NHS (*August*)
Effigy Mounds NM (*July*)
Eisenhower NHS (*July*)
El Morro NM (*August*)
Everglades NP (*March*)

Federal Hall NMEM (*July*)
Fire Island NS (*August*)
Florissant Fossil Beds NM (*August*)
Ford's Theatre NHS (*May*)
Fort Bowie NHS (*March*)
Fort Caroline NMEM (*July*)
Fort Clatsop NMEM (*August*)
Fort Davis NHS (*March*)
Fort Donelson NMP (*February*)
Fort Frederica NM (*March*)
Fort Jefferson NM (*July*)
Fort Laramie NHS (*July*)
Fort Larned NHS (*August*)
Fort Matanzas NM (*July*)
Fort McHenry NM&HS (*June*)
Fort Necessity NB (*July*)
Fort Point NHS (*May*)
Fort Pulaski NM (*June*)
Fort Raleigh NHS (*August*)
Fort Scott NHS (*June*)
Fort Smith NHS (*July*)
Fort Stanwix NM (*July*)
Fort Sumter NM (*July*)
Fort Union NM (*July*)
Fort Union Trad Post NHS (*July*)
Fort Vancouver NHS (*July*)
Fort Washington Park (*May*)
Fossil Butte NM (*July*)
Fredericksburg & Spotsylvania NMP
   (*August*)
Fredrk Douglass Home NM (*February*)

Gates of the Arctic NP & PRES (*August*)

Gateway NRA (*July*)
General Grant NMEM (*May*)
Geo Wash Birthplace NM (*May*)
Geo Wash Carver NM (*July*)
Geo Wash Mem Pkwy (*July*)
George Rogers Clark NHP (*May*)
Gettysburg NMP (*July*)
Gila Cliff Dwellings NM (*August*)
Glacier Bay NP & PRES (*August*)
Glacier NP (*July*)
Glen Canyon NRA (*August*)
Golden Gate NRA (*August*)
Golden Spike NHS (*July*)
Grand Canyon NP (*August*)
Grand Portage NM (*August*)
Grand Teton NP (*July*)
Grant-Kohrs NHS (*July*)
Great Basin NP (*August*)
Great Sand Dunes NM (*July*)
Great Smoky Mtns NP (*July*)
Greenbelt Park (*May*)
Guadalupe Mountains NP (*May*)
Guilford Courthouse NMP (*March*)
Gulf Islands NS (*June*)

Haleakala NP (*July*)
Hamilton Grange NMEM (*August*)
Hampton NHS (*September*)
Harpers Ferry NHP (*May*)
Harry S Truman NHS (*July*)
Hawaii Volcanoes NP (*September*)
Herbert Hoover NHS (*July*)
Home of FDR NHS (*August*)
Homestead NM of America (*June*)
Hopewell Furnace NHS (*August*)
Horseshoe Bend NMP (*April*)
Hot Springs NP (*July*)
Hovenweep NM (*July*)
Hubbell Trad Post NHS (*May*)

Independence NHP (*July*)
Indiana Dunes NL (*June*)
Isle Royale NP (*August*)

Jean Lafitte NHP (*March*)
Jefferson NEM NHS (*August*)
Jewel Cave NM (*July*)
JFK Ctr Perf Arts (*April*)
John D. Rockefeller Pkwy (*July*)
John Day Fossil Beds NM (*July*)
John F. Kennedy NHS (*August*)
John Muir NHS (*April*)
Johnstown Flood NMEM (*July*)
Joshua Tree NM (*April*)

Katmai NM (*July*)
Kenai Fjords NP (*July*)
Kennesaw Mountain NBP (*April*)
Kings Canyon NP (*August*)

Kings Mountain NMP (*July*)
Klondike Gold Rush NHP (*July*)
Knife River NHS (*July*)
Kobuk Valley NP (*July*)

Lake Clark NP & Pres (*August*)
Lake Mead NRA (*June*)
Lake Meredith RA (*May*)
Lassen Volcanic NP (*September*)
Lava Beds NM (*August*)
Lincoln Boyhood NMEM (*August*)
Lincoln Home NHS (*July*)
Lincoln Memorial (*July*)
Longfellow NHS (*August*)
Lowell NHP (*July*)
Lyndon B. Johnson NHS (*March*)

Mammoth Cave NP (*July*)
Manassas NBP (*May*)
Martin L. King, Jr. NHS (*January*)
Mesa Verde NP (*July*)
Minute Man NHP (*July*)
Montezuma Castle NM (*April*)
Moores Creek NMP (*July*)
Morristown NHP (*August*)
Mound City Group NM (*August*)
Mount Rainier NP (*August*)
Mount Rushmore NMEM (*July*)
Muir Woods NM (*August*)

Natchez Trace Parkway (*July*)
National Capital Parks (*May*)
Natural Bridges NM (*June*)
Navajo NM (*August*)
New River Gorge NR(*July*)
Nez Perce NHP (*August*)
Noatah NPRES (*August*)
North Cascades NP (*August*)

Ocmulgee NM (*March*)
Olympic NP (*August*)
Oregon Caves NM (*August*)
Organ Pipe Cactus NM (*March*)
Ozark NSR (*July*)

Padre Island NS (*August*)
Pea Ridge NMP (*July*)
Pecos NM (*August*)
Perry's Victory & IPM (*July*)
Petersburg NB (*March*)
Petrified Forest NP (*July*)
Pictured Rocks NL (*August*)
Pinnacles NM (*April*)
Pipe Spring NM (*June*)
Pipestone NM (*July*)
Piscataway Park (*May*)
Point Reyes NS (*July*)
Prince William For Pk (*May*)
Pu'uhonua O Honaunau NHP (*July*)

Puukohola Heiau NHS (*August*)

Rainbow Bridge NM (*August*)
Redwood NP (*July*)
Richmond NBP (*July*)
Rock Creek Park (*August*)
Rocky Mountain NP (*August*)
Roger Williams NM (*August*)
Russel Cave NM (*July*)

Sagamore Hill NHS (*July*)
Saguaro NM (*February*)
Saint Croix NSR (*July*)
Saint-Gaudens NHS (*July*)
Salem Maritime NHS (*July*)
Salinas NM (*July*)
San Antonio Missions NHP (*May*)
San Juan Island NHP (*August*)
San Juan NHS (*March*)
Santa Monica Mtns. NRA (*May*)
Saratoga NHP (*August*)
Saugus Iron Works NHS (*August*)
Scott's Bluff NM (*June*)
Sequoia NP (*August*)
Shadow Mountain RA (*July*)
Shenandoah NP (*August*)
Shiloh NMP (*April*)
Sitka NHP (*August*)
Sleeping Bear Dunes NL (*August*)
Springfield Armory NHS (*August*)
Statue of Liberty NM (*August*)
Steamtown NHS (*not yet open to public*)
Stones River NB (*July*)
Sunset Crater NM (*July*)

Theo Roosevelt Inaug NHS (*June*)
Theo Roosevelt Bpl NHS (*May*)
Theo Roosevelt Is (*May*)
Theo Roosevelt NP (*June*)
Thomas Jefferson Memorial (*April*)
Timpanogos Cave NM (*July*)
Tonto NM (*March*)
Tumacacori NM (*March*)
Tupelo NM (*August*)
Tuskegee Institute NHS (*September*)
Tuzigoot NM (*April*)

U.S.S. Arizona MEM (*July*)
Upper Delaware NSR (*July*)

Valley Forge NHP (*May*)
Vanderbilt Mansions NHS (*July*)
Vicksburg NMP (*August*)
Virgin Islands NP (*April*)
Voyageurs NP (*June*)

Walnut Canyon NM (*August*)
Washington Monument (*May*)
Whiskeytown NRA (*August*)
White House (*April*)

White Sands NM (*July*)
Whitman Mission NHS (*June*)
William Howard Taft NHS (*May*)
Wilson's Creek NB (*June*)
Wind Cave NP (*August*)
Wolf Trap Farm Park (*July*)
Women's Rights NHP (*July*)
Wrangell-St. Elais NP & PRES (*August*)
Wright Brothers NMEM (*August*)
Wupatki NM (*July*)

Yellowstone NP (*July*)
Yosemite NP (*August*)
Yukon Charley Rivers NPRES (*September*)

Zion NP (*August*)

Index